W9-BFD-426

CONSUMER BEHAVIOR

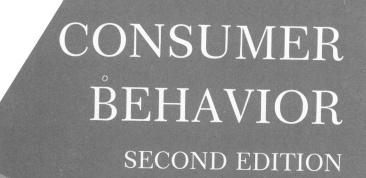

CONSUMER BEHAVIOR

SECOND EDITION

William L. Wilkie

University of Notre Dame

JOHN WILEY & SONS
NEW YORK   CHICHESTER   BRISBANE   TORONTO   SINGAPORE

Copyright © 1986, 1990, by John Wiley & Sons, Inc.

All rights reserved. Published simultaneously in Canada.

Reproduction or translation of any part of
this work beyond that permitted by Sections
107 and 108 of the 1976 United States Copyright
Act without the permission of the copyright
owner is unlawful. Requests for permission
or further information should be addressed to
the Permissions Department, John Wiley & Sons.

Library of Congress Cataloging in Publication Data:

Wilkie, William L.
  Consumer behavior / William L. Wilkie.
      p.   cm.
  Includes bibliographical references.
  ISBN 0-471-61352-5
  1. Consumer behavior.   I. Title.
HF5415.3.W536   1990   89-70773
658.8'342--dc20   CIP

Printed in the United States of America

10 9 8 7 6 5 4 3 2

Editor: John Woods
Design Supervised by Sheila Granda
Copy Editing Supervised by Gilda Stahl
Copy Editing by Sally Ann Bailey
Production Supervised by Nancy Prinz
Photo Research by Barbara Salz
Photo Research Supervised by Stella Kupferberg
Text Design: David L. Levy
Cover Design: Sheila Granda
Cover Painting: © 1990 ARS N.Y./SPADEM, courtesy
Giraudon/Art Resource, N.Y.
Cover Art: Hand marbleized paper by Katherine Radcliffe © 1985

Throughout the long days devoted to developing, then revising, this text, my family provided me with encouragement and much assistance in this effort. In so doing, they made room in their lives for me to work and gave up much of the time I might have shared with them. With much love and great appreciation I dedicate this book to Barbara, and to Billy, Alexandria, and James.

ABOUT THE AUTHOR

William L. Wilkie is the Aloysius and Eleanor Nathe Professor of Marketing Strategy at the University of Notre Dame. There he teaches popular undergraduate and graduate courses in consumer behavior and consults for business and government agencies on consumer behavior topics. Dr. Wilkie has served as President of the Association for Consumer Research, an international professional group with members in 26 nations around the world. He has also served as a member of the editorial boards of the *Journal of Consumer Research, Journal of Marketing, Journal of Marketing Research, Journal of Public Policy and Marketing,* and the *Journal of International Consumer Marketing.* Dr. Wilkie's research in marketing and consumer behavior has received a number of awards and recognitions. He is listed in *Who's Who in America.* He has been recognized as one of the most-cited authors in the field of marketing; one of his articles has been named a "Citation Classic in the Social Sciences" by the Institute for Scientific Information. He recently served as a member of the American Marketing Association's Task Force on the Development of Marketing Thought and as a member of the Academic Advisory Council of the Marketing Science Institute.

Dr. Wilkie holds a B.B.A. degree from the University of Notre Dame, where he majored in marketing and minored in management science. He holds M.B.A. and Ph.D. degrees from Stanford University, where he was also a fellow in the year-long Stanford-Sloan Executive Development Program. Prior to joining the University of Notre Dame, he served as an in-house consultant to the Federal Trade Commission in Washington, D.C., as a research professor at the Marketing Science Institute in Cambridge, Massachusetts, and as a faculty member at Purdue University, Harvard University, and the University of Florida. He now lives in South Bend with his wife, Barbara; three children, Billy, Allie, and Jimmy; and his dog, Blaze.

PREFACE

This book is governed by my belief that consumer behavior is a fascinating topic. It is about people and the way we live. It is about consumers buying and marketers selling. It is about many forms of influence, from the subtle shaping of our culture, through the social forces from our family, friends, and peers, to the persuasive attempts from advertising and salespersons. It is about what we know (and what we don't know), what we like (and what we avoid). It is about the detailed choices we make, and the ways in which we allocate our resources. It is about the benefits we seek through our purchases, and the satisfactions we obtain through our consumption of products and services.

For all these reasons, consumer behavior is important. It plays a significant role in our lives, from literally sustaining life itself (foods, medicines . . .), to providing comfort and convenience (electricity, clothing, cars . . .), to enriching our leisure and social lives (perfumes, education, entertainment . . .). Moreover, because it is an activity in which we all engage, consumer behavior has *huge* economic impacts in our society. When consumer purchasing is high, jobs are created and profits encourage more business investments. For any particular firm, customer patronage is the key determinant of success or failure.

In addition to being important, consumer behavior is also a most interesting phenomenon. Why are people attracted to some products but not to others? Why do some consumers never buy certain products while others consume them regularly? Why do some consumers spend frugally while others run up large debts? What role does the marketing system play in all of this behavior? Is influencing consumer behavior an easy task for a marketer, or is it actually quite difficult? What are some of the "rules of thumb" that marketers use when interacting with consumers? How does advertising really work? These questions can go on and on, of course, but they represent only a few dimensions of what is truly a fascinating field.

MY GOALS FOR THE BOOK

As a student, I came to appreciate those occasions when a book would capture my interest and stimulate me to think more about a particular idea or theory. I especially appreciated those books that were able to provide me with useful frameworks to help guide my further thinking—frameworks that would reveal how the basic elements related to one another, and what implications these basic relations might have. When I decided to write this textbook, my goal was to produce this type of book for others to read and enjoy. As a professor, however, I also wanted the book to contain the best and latest concepts, findings, and applications. And, to the extent possible, I wished to see the book make a useful contribution to knowledge in the field as well as to the knowledge of its individual readers.

In this book, therefore, you will find a number of interesting and useful frameworks. These frameworks tie concepts together and bring them to the level of the real world that we experience in our lives as marketers and/or consumers. In some chapters I was able to use frameworks that are already widely accepted within the field, whereas in other chapters new frameworks were developed especially for this text.

Another basic element of this text is its reliance on the importance of *perspective,* or the view we choose to take of a particular topic. Just as a person looks different from the back than from the front, and different still if viewed from the side, so too will a topic appear different depending on the perspective we use in analyzing it. Recognizing this, the book contains several chapters that directly discuss key perspectives on consumer behavior.

THE STYLE OF THIS BOOK

In accordance with my goals, the style of this book attempts to capture the innate excitement of consumer behavior while also delivering the best of theory and applications. It seeks to stimulate a personal interest in reading the material and thinking more about it, simply because the topics are interesting. It provides many examples of the real world of marketing and consumer behavior; in addition to adding interest, these examples indicate the differing ways in which concepts relate to reality. Occasionally it asks the reader to hazard a prediction of how a study turned out or to suggest another way to resolve a realistic marketing problem.

Also in accord with my goals, great attention was paid to effectively communicating the material to the reader. In the process of writing the first edition, several focus groups of readers were conducted for each individual chapter; following each session, the chapter was revised to clarify and streamline the discussion. Now the second edition has further benefitted from professors' and students' suggestions in actual coursework as well. At this point I am able to report that almost all of the consumer behavior students who have read this text are enthusiastic about it; they report that they find the book to be stimulating, to provide clear explanations, and to be a pleasure to read.

With respect to contents, in striving to present the best of theory and concepts, this text adopts the approach of stressing the basic issues in each area. Students and professors who wish to go beyond these basics in any given area will find that a strong foundation has been laid for this effort and that extensive reference notes have been provided. Students and professors who wish to move on to the next topic will find that they can do so without being diverted. In a sense, then, this book has been written for several levels of reader involvement and to support different forms of teaching orientations. The text is thus suitable for both undergraduate and graduate courses. Sufficient background on research approaches is provided that advanced readings can be assigned to extend text discussions. Sufficient marketing decision–orientation is included that cases can be assigned to extend the application of concepts to the reality of a marketing manager's role. Given the interesting nature of the topics, moreover, a class discussion format is easily supported, as are lectures to explain and extend topic coverage.

By far the majority of consumer behavior courses are presently taught within marketing departments of business schools. This book maintains this general orientation and has been designed to be successful in this setting. There is no reason, however, that students with other majors should not be able to enjoy and use it effectively as well (students without a basic background in marketing should pay careful attention to Chapter 2, however, to obtain the rudiments of this significant perspective).

IMPROVEMENTS IN THIS EDITION

Readers familiar with the first edition will notice several positive additions in the present book. Our topical coverage has been reorganized to reflect the order in which many professors prefer to teach this course. Also, coverage of the key concept of market segmentation has been expanded and now appears as a separate chapter near the beginning of the book. Coverage of organizational buying behavior has also been added and appears as Chapter 22 of the book. Photos and advertisements have been added and lend tone to our coverage. Many recent marketing applications have also been added to this edition. And, to better serve the interests of both those readers who will not consult the references and those who wish to spend much time with them, an expanded and up-to-date "Notes" section has been compiled at the back of the book rather than at the end of each chapter. Finally, of course, our coverage of the concepts and findings in consumer behavior has been updated to reflect the latest developments in this vibrant field.

ACKNOWLEDGMENTS

This project and its revision has taken a long time to complete, and over the years many people have helped in its development and refinement. For the first edition, graduate students at the University of Florida, especially Henry More-head, Melanie Albert, Alain D'Astous, Carolyn Simmons, Amardeep Assar, William Baker, Kunal Basu, Amitava Chattopadhyay, Alan Dick, Douglas Hausknecht, Howard Marmorstein, Darrell Miller, Prakash Nedungadi, Elizabeth Moore-Shay, and Jane Petty, all offered useful insights at various stages. My daily work activities at the University of Florida were much assisted by the pleasant personalities of Jody Imperi, Carrie Patterson, Astrid Barranco, Yvette Ellison, Connie Kaminski-Krueger, and Jackie Liszak-May. At the University of Notre Dame, this revision has depended on the help of my student assistants Megan Duffy, Brian Vogel, Kathy Fitzgerald, and Edward Balog. Donna Smith, then Dee Sequin have done fine work on much of this revision, and have earned my respect and gratitude.

At John Wiley, John Woods has been a fine and stimulating Editor, continually pushing this author to practice the marketing concept, and being interested in discussing ways to make this the best book possible. I have also enjoyed my (numerous) telephone interactions with the talented members of the editorial, design, photo, and production teams at Wiley, including Gilda Stahl, Barbara Heaney, Sally Ann Bailey, Sheila Granda, Stella Kupferberg, and Nancy Prinz.

The insightful reviews and suggestions I received from numerous faculty members have clearly helped to shape both editions of this book. For the first edition inputs I wish to again thank David Aaker (University of California, Berkeley), William O. Bearden (University of South Carolina), Tim Hartman (Ohio University), Harold Kassarjian (UCLA), Richard J. Lutz (University of Florida), George Prough (University of Akron), Mary Lou Roberts (Boston University), and Carol Scott (UCLA). For this revision, the reviews and suggestions by Raymond Burke (Wharton), Peter Dacin (Wisconsin), Richard Durand (Maryland), Jack Faricy (Florida), Ron Goldsmith (Florida State), Jeff Kasmer (California State, Long Beach), Debbie MacInnis (Arizona), Naresh Malhotra (Georgia Tech), Lee Meadow (Salisbury State), Jim Muncy (Clemson), Ivan Ross (Minnesota), Debra Stephens (Maryland), Jeff Stoltman (Wayne State), and Judy Vilmain (Kent State) were absolutely instrumental in improving this offering. As noted on the chapter itself, I wish to offer special thanks to Dr. Darrel Miller (University of South Florida), who contributed the organizational buying chapter to this book.

For their special contributions to the original and the revised editions, I wish to express my warmest appreciation to my friends and colleagues, Joel Cohen and John Lynch (University of Florida), and Rich George (Saint Joseph's University). They have offered me encouragement from the very start, while also providing useful critiques, feedback from course testing, and ideas for specific sections. Rich has also developed the Instructional Manual to accompany this text, and devoted many hours to ensuring that the companion publication will provide our readers with high quality comments, projects, and suggestions. Finally, I wish to express my deepest thanks to my wife, Barbara, for her support, encouragement, and insightful critiques of virtually every draft on every topic.

William L. Wilkie
South Bend, Indiana
November 1989

Contents in Brief

Contents

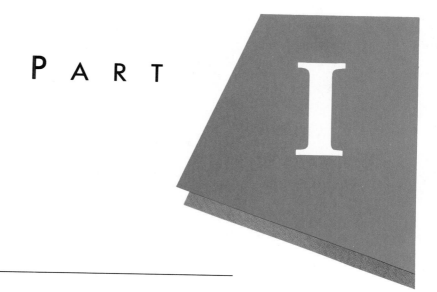

P A R T I

Introduction to the Field of Consumer Behavior

In this part of the book—Chapters 1–4—we examine the major perspectives from which one might view the fascinating field of consumer behavior. In Chapter 1, Consumer Behavior as a Body of Knowledge, we look at the academic aspects of the field, determining what is included in this area and how we study it. In Chapter 2, Marketers' and Consumers' Views of Consumer Behavior, we consider the special perspectives of marketers and consumers, the two major "players" in this field, reflecting on how marketers view consumer behavior and how consumers view their own behavior. In Chapter 3, Aggregate Perspectives of Consumer Behavior, we look at consumer behavior in terms of the huge and dynamic marketplace, examining both the size and the emerging trends. Finally, in Chapter 4, Market Segmentation, we consider how the larger market can be usefully divided into key target segments, learning the chief criteria that qualify segments and the major approaches for identifying segments.

As you'll see, there is much fascinating material in the pages ahead, so let's get started!

C H A P T E R 1

Consumer Behavior as a Body of Knowledge

Analyzing Consumer Behavior

Consumer behavior is important and interesting. As a marketer, you will want to understand as much as possible about it. For example consider these quotes (excerpted from the chapter) from two consumers:

I was so happy for Amanda when she married Jonathan! She's my best friend, and I know they'll be happy together. . . . The trip, hotel, and my outfit were expensive, and so was my gift—a vase from Gump's. But money was no object . . . I like the "finer things in life" for my friends and myself.

—*Jennifer Anderson, attorney*

I'd never use [detergent brand]! My daughter plays with a neighbor's child whose clothes have a yellowish tinge, which doesn't say much for her mother. She uses it. I'll only use Tide; it's the best one, in my opinion. I think it's one of the leading sellers, too.

—*Janet Rodgers, housewife*

In this chapter, we'll learn a few powerful concepts that will help us to understand more about what's going on in these cases (and in millions of others).

Welcome to the fascinating field of consumer behavior!

■ ■ ■

3

Consumer behavior is an exciting and challenging subject! It's about people—what we purchase and why we purchase the way we do. It's about marketing—how products and services are designed for, and sold to, consumers in the marketplace. And it's about the consumer marketplace itself, in which *billions* of individual purchases occur each year, in *millions* of marketing outlets.

In this introductory chapter, we'll focus on some essential characteristics found in the academic field of consumer behavior. The chapter is organized in three major sections. The first describes some of the basic characteristics of consumer behavior as it exists today, and how it has evolved to its present status. The second provides an overview of the major academic concepts in this field. The closing section summarizes "where we are going" in the remainder of the book and shows how the many interesting aspects of consumer behavior are related.

CHARACTERISTICS OF MODERN CONSUMER BEHAVIOR

Consumer Behavior Is . . .

All Around Us

We are all consumers: each of us undertakes many forms of consumer behavior every day of our lives. If we could step back and view this in the aggregate, we'd see a massive amount of consumer and marketing activity at work across the country and around the world. For example, the U.S. market alone consists of some 250 million persons, each consuming food, housing, furniture, clothing, transportation, and thousands of other products and services, day after day after day. The consumption system operates continuously and is devoted to the production, transfer, use, and disposal of billions of individual products and services.

A Major Contributor to Society

This staggering level of activity plays an important role in the economic and social fabric of our society. Consumer spending in the United States accounts for about two-thirds of the nation's gross national product (GNP) each year. As of the early 1990s the U.S. GNP is approximately $5 trillion, and *U.S. consumers are spending about $3.5 trillion per year!*[1]

Of course, $3.5 trillion is hard to imagine in the abstract. Exhibit 1-1, however, offers a graphic representation of how far $3.5 trillion would extend if the actual dollar bills were stretched end to end. The dollars spent by consumers in the United States each year would stretch all the way from the Earth to the sun, around the sun and back to the Earth (assuming no scorching factor!), and there would still be enough bills remaining for over 600 trips to the moon! Examined another way, $3.5 trillion is such a huge number that, if we were to try to count to it, at one dollar per second, it would take us over 100,000 years, or much longer than the history of civilization!

EXHIBIT 1-1 HOW FAR DOES THE CONSUMER'S DOLLAR STRETCH?

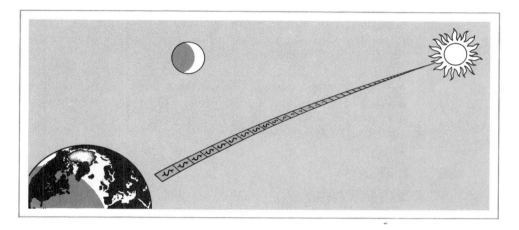

As of the 1990s, U.S. consumers are spending enough dollar bills to stretch from the Earth to the sun and back to the Earth, with enough remaining for over 600 lines to the moon!

Consumers' purchases actually form the ultimate basis for most of our economic system. They provide rewards for the design, production, and delivery of valued goods and services. They provide profits for firms and jobs and incomes for employees of the firms. *Changes* in consumer spending have important effects on the overall health of the economy, affecting a business's chance of success or failure, a worker's chance of being unemployed, prospects for economic growth or recession, the prices we pay, the interest rates we are charged, and so on.

Socially, consumer purchases help to provide the basis by which we function as a society. Consider, for example, how such consumer products as food, travel, and clothing all help us to live our daily lives in the fashions that we most desire. Even more broadly, telephones, television, and magazines not only serve as sources of entertainment, but also perform important communication functions within our society. These are, of course, supported with consumer dollars through both advertising revenues and direct purchases.

Further, consumer behavior involves more than physical goods. Consumers' use of *services*, such as medical care, auto repair, or hair styling, accounts for about one-half of all consumer spending, equal to product purchases. In addition, we engage in other types of consumer "purchases" as well—as voters, students, patients, worshippers, and so on. All these acts are also studied in the field of consumer behavior. In total, then, consumer behavior constitutes a broad and important set of activities in our society. It merits our careful study, partially because of its economic impacts and partially because it is such a good reflection of our social style of life.

Subtle and Interesting

In many ways consumer behavior is a subtle phenomenon. The reasons for our behavior are not always clear. Our actions as consumers are sometimes difficult to predict, and sometimes even hard to explain. As we examine this field, we'll be asking such interesting questions as

- Why do different consumers purchase different products?
- What is the best way for a consumer to go about buying a particular product?
- How does advertising work to influence consumer preferences?

In addressing them, we will encounter some of the subtle complexities of this field of study.

Relevant Personally and Professionally

A positive aspect of the study of consumer behavior is that each of us has spent a goodly portion of our lives observing others' consumer behavior, as well as participating in our own consumer decisions. This experience base can provide us with a strong "feel" for the subject matter—we can easily recognize the key issues and see why they are important.

However, we'll also see that, despite all this experience, most consumers do not possess a great deal of expertise regarding their own behaviors. As consumers, most of us are not highly aware of the external influences that guide us toward purchases nor of our own internal processes at work to bring the decisions to fruition. Increased understanding of consumer behavior as a field can thus translate to improving our personal consumer behaviors in our daily lives.

On a professional level, most readers of this text are involved in marketing, advertising, and related fields of endeavor. As we'll see, an understanding of consumer behavior is increasingly recognized as a key factor between success and failure in these fields. The careful study of the material in this text can lead to a professional advantage for those who are able to use it well in their careers.

Consumer Behavior as a Field of Study

The field of consumer behavior is comprised of a diverse set of persons interested in describing, understanding, or predicting behavior by consumers. Compared to most academic fields, it is *very* young. The first books with consumer behavior as a focus appeared in the mid-1950s. The first major textbook did not appear until 1968. Most colleges and universities didn't even offer this course until the 1970s!

In recent years, however, the field has grown rapidly. For example, a small professional group—the Association for Consumer Research (ACR)—was formed in 1970. By 1990, ACR has grown to over 1300 members, in 26 nations of the world. Many companies have hired persons with consumer behavior training in marketing positions. Government agencies have also begun to hire consumer behavior specialists. In addition, consulting firms and not-for-profit organizations (e.g., universities, hospitals, religious groups) also hired persons with consumer behavior knowledge.

Historical Forces

Although the formal field is young, consumer behavior itself has been of interest for a long time. Since early peoples began to barter and trade, they have had to decide what they wanted and what they were willing to give up to get it. As money economies began to develop, consumers faced new questions of saving versus immediate spending—and how to allocate their resources across purchase categories.

The impact of technology and the Industrial Revolution led to significant changes in consumer behavior and our marketing systems. For example, during the early years of the twentieth century, the telephone, radio, and moving pictures provided new ways of informing consumers about the products and services available to them. Automobiles not only opened new vistas for recreation; they also fueled the growth of a mass consumer market. The success of the auto industry provided jobs for hundreds of thousands of workers, in the auto plants themselves and also in support businesses (raw materials, components, dealerships, road construction, gas stations, repair shops, etc.). The new income available for these workers was, in turn, used for consumer purchases that provided jobs in the manufacturing and selling of consumer products. As the industrial wheel turned faster, the beginnings of a mass consumer market were apparent during the "Roaring Twenties." Much of this momentum was halted by the Great Depression in the 1930s, however.

Then, during World War II, millions of people were earning money in the military and in civilian jobs, but couldn't spend it freely. Manufacturing capacity was redirected toward military uses: civilian production (houses, cars, clothing, etc.) was restricted in support of the war effort. When the war ended, consumers had both the money and desire to purchase the items they had been denied during the years of sacrifice. This burst of consumer demand coincided with the "baby boom" of the late 1940s through the early 1960s. Demand for new homes, big enough for growing families, pushed out from city neighborhoods, and the suburbs were born.

Large chain stores, which had begun during the Great Depression of the 1930s, pushed to expand to the suburbs to meet the huge demand. The shopping center appeared in the 1950s and became a popular suburban gathering spot. A new

U.S. interstate highway system added to the momentum, as marketers could now efficiently distribute mass-produced goods by truck from centralized warehouses. Finally, a key element took hold in the 1950s—television. Every night, in every corner of the land, millions of families watched, listened, and learned from the same network program. From the marketing viewpoint, a single commercial offered instantaneous communication with millions. The era of the mass consumer market had been born.

Recent Forces for Growth in Consumer Research

The availability of a mass market meant huge profit opportunities for marketers who could successfully develop products that would satisfy consumers' desires. The **marketing concept** was introduced shortly after World War II by the General Electric Company. It was explicit recognition of the potentials in mass markets:

> *Rather than making what you've always made, then trying to sell it, find out what will sell, then try to make it.*

"Finding out what will sell" meant that marketers needed to solve two problems. First, they had to discover *what* was selling, what was not selling, *who* was buying, and who was not. This required **descriptive consumer research**. Second, the marketer had to discover *why* consumers were behaving the way they were, and *how* they would likely react to new types of products or services. This required **inferential consumer research** (as we'll discuss, consumers are typically unable to provide complete answers to these questions, so consumer researchers need to infer what the true answers are).

To solve these problems, researchers had to go out and gather evidence in the marketplace. In earlier years some economists had been studying how consumer spending patterns were influenced by economic factors. During the 1950s these economists were joined by a number of researchers in marketing, who were especially interested in how marketing factors worked to influence consumer behavior. Thus the field of consumer research began to grow slowly during the 1950s. Unfortunately, there was still no efficient way to handle the data that were obtained; arduous manual calculation was the order of the day for the commercial analysts who studied consumer markets.

Then came the computer and tremendous advances in analytical methods. The quantitative approach to research in marketing and advertising began to blossom during the 1960s. In 1964, for example, the *Journal of Marketing Research* was founded, and four years after the *Journal of Advertising Research*. Researchers were now able to gather information from large samples of consumers about their purchases, attitudes, and backgrounds. The computer's flexibility in data analysis allowed researchers to test various approaches. For example, the capability of trying out different ways of segmenting consumer markets served to advance dramatically the use of market segmentation within marketing.

By the late 1960s some of these researchers decided that they would like to focus on consumer behavior as a subject in its own right rather than simply as a subtopic within marketing research. During the 1970s they were joined by persons from home economics (who had been studying how to help consumers to buy more wisely for many years) and some psychologists and sociologists (who saw the consumer setting as an important context in which human behavior could be studied). People in business and government organizations also played key roles in identifying problems and supporting research efforts. Another new publication, the *Journal of Consumer Research,* was started in 1974, joining the *Journal of Consumer Affairs,* which had begun in 1967. The Association for Consumer Research began to publish the proceedings of its annual conference under the title *Advances in Consumer Research,* while the American Marketing Association continued to give consumer behavior a great deal of attention in its conferences and publications. Thus, by the mid-1970s the field of consumer behavior research had clearly arrived as a significant area for study. As of 1990, the field continues to flourish. Many persons who have studied consumer behavior are now gaining authoritative positions in businesses of all types as well as in universities, marketing research firms, and advertising agencies. Numerous journals and trade publications are now available, and marketers are continuously conducting consumer research to help make better marketing decisions. Kraft Foods, for example, recently reported that it had run over 5000 consumer research studies (costing over $100 million!) during the 1980s, when it was still an independent company.[2]

MAJOR CONCEPTS IN THE STUDY OF CONSUMER BEHAVIOR

The Nature of Consumer Behavior

In this section we'll begin our analysis of consumer behavior. To start, study the consumer quotes reported in Exhibit 1-2 (we'll be referring to these in our discussions that follow). While the vignettes are not a representative sample of all consumer behavior, they do portray the wide range of the consumer experience. Notice also how easily we can relate to the basic phenomena. This indicates that we already possess implicit or hidden theories about this field. For example, in reading the quotes most of us implicitly accept that there is an underlying system at work: that the behavior is not simply random. If we take any individual quote, for instance, we can usually pick out one or more consumer characteristics—sex, age, marital status, and so on—that we would expect to have a fairly reliable relationship to the consumer behavior being reported. Scott Campbell's quote isn't too surprising coming from him, for example, but what if Helen Mercanti

EXHIBIT 1-2   *QUOTES FROM CONSUMERS*

I was so happy for Amanda when she married Jonathan! She's my best friend, and I know they'll be happy together. . . . The trip, hotel, and my outfit were expensive, and so was my gift—a vase from Gump's. But money was no object . . . I like the "finer things in life" for my friends and myself.

—Jennifer Anderson, attorney

I just saw an ad for used tools at a garage sale, so I'll be there early in the morning. Deb and I are adding a room, and I don't have all the tools I need. Since my wallet's thin, I'm hoping to get them cheap.

—Anthony Grant, production manager

I was a little down, and I called home to talk to my mother. She tried to cheer me up; she suggested I buy something nice as a sort of reward for doing well in my classes. So I . . . just leisurely looked at clothes. Finally I saw just what I wanted. It was a beige satin blouse with puffed sleeves and pearl buttons. It made me look soft and curvy. The only problem was the price—it was almost $80! The saleslady showed me how it was well made and told me how nice it looked on me. I gulped and bought it!

—Jill Prado, student

[In store] I want Captain Crunch! Can I have Froot Loops? I want Cookie Crisp! Mom, look what comes in Sugar Crisp . . . may I have it, pleeease? (chorus) Cheerios? awwhh. . . . Can I get a cookie at the bakery? Me, too! Me, too!

—Billy, Allie, and Jimmy Wilkie, ages 9, 7, and 5

Why did I go to that hospital? That's where my doctor sent me. It cost a lot, I bet. It's a good thing we have Medicare and other insurance.

—Helen Mercanti, retired

My car decision was real easy . . . I knew just what I wanted. The Camaro was for me . . . long, low, powerful, dark and handsome. Alriggght!

—Scott Campbell, student

I'd never use [detergent brand]! My daughter plays with a neighbor's child whose clothes have a yellowish tinge, which doesn't say much for her mother. She uses it. I'll only use Tide; it's the best one. I think it's one of the leading sellers, too.

—Janet Rodgers, housewife

I had a very hard time deciding on a college. . . . I thought about location, costs, activities, academics, and a lot of other things. I sent for some catalogs and visited a couple of places. I also talked with my folks and relatives about it, and the school counselor, too. My older sister Kim was a big help—she's a junior at State. I didn't talk about it as much with my friends as I thought I would . . . we're starting to go different ways, and it was a little awkward. Mark came here, though, and I'm glad I knew somebody from home . . . (pause) I don't know, sometimes I think I made a bad decision, but most of the time it's okay.

—Michael Taylor, student

were making this statement? In each instance that we see as typical, we are reflecting our beliefs about the nature of an underlying system for consumer behavior.

While there is an underlying system at work within consumer behavior, though, it is also true that most of the relationships we'll examine are far from being perfect or straightforward. Throughout the remainder of this text we will be striving to (1) *deepen* our understanding of the causes of consumer behavior and (2) *broaden* our appreciation of how consumer behavior knowledge can be applied to solve problems.

Definition of Consumer Behavior

A formal definition helps to focus attention on key points and concepts. Consumer behavior is here defined as

> *The activities that people engage in when selecting, purchasing, and using products and services so as to satisfy needs and desires. Such activities involve mental and emotional processes, in addition to physical actions.*

While this definition is short, it is rich in basic implications about the topic. Understanding these implications is the key to knowing this field, as indicated in our following discussion of the "seven keys" to consumer behavior.

The "Seven Keys" to Consumer Behavior

In any field of study there are basic theories and assumptions that experts use to guide their approaches to the subject. Surprisingly, however, these guidelines often become so accepted by the experts that they aren't clearly identified when speaking about the subject matter. Here we will explain and examine seven of the most basic characteristics of consumer behavior as it is viewed by leading persons in this field. As individual points, each is basic and makes sense. When we put them together, moreover, they add up to a rich conceptual structure for the body of knowledge in the field.

The "Seven Keys" are outlined in Figure 1-1. Some students have successfully used the acronym MAP TRIP to help recall the keys and their exact ordering. Of far greater importance than recalling them, of course, is a strong understanding of the nature and implications of each characteristic. The following sections provide brief explanations of each of these key concepts in the field.

Key I: Consumer Behavior Is Motivated Behavior

Probably the most basic question we can ask is, "*Why* does consumer behavior occur . . . ?" Our definition for consumer behavior provided the most basic answer: ". . . so as to satisfy needs and desires." This means that, in general, consumer behavior is motivated behavior aimed at achieving particular goals. The behavior

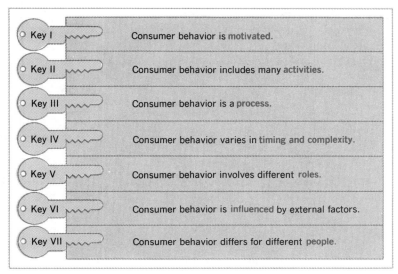

Key I	Consumer behavior is motivated.
Key II	Consumer behavior includes many activities.
Key III	Consumer behavior is a process.
Key IV	Consumer behavior varies in timing and complexity.
Key V	Consumer behavior involves different roles.
Key VI	Consumer behavior is influenced by external factors.
Key VII	Consumer behavior differs for different people.

FIGURE 1-1 **Seven Keys to Consumer Behavior**

itself is a *means to an end,* with the "end" being the satisfaction of needs and desires.

Note that the consumer quotes of Exhibit 1-2 provide numerous examples of "means-end" relationships. For example, Anthony Grant will buy tools in order to build his new room, while Jennifer Anderson's purchase of the vase was a means by which she could express her feelings of friendship for Amanda. In all the cases, products or services were desired to achieve goals held by the person. In addition, however, we should also note that the thoughts and motivations of consumers are usually hidden within them and are not observable by us. This means that theories are especially useful in helping us understand what may be going on, and research methods help us try to actually measure it.

Three Further Points We cannot delve deeply into the area of motivation in this introductory chapter, but it is useful to recognize three further points. First, some consumer behaviors can be primarily *functional* in nature (an example is Anthony's tool purchase), whereas others can be primarily means of *self-expression,* as with Jennifer's gift.

Second, most behaviors have more than one goal, so that a *mix of motivations* is present. Many of us think of detergents as a rather simple product, for example, but let us look again at what Janet Rodgers was saying. While she obviously uses detergents for the functional purpose of obtaining clean clothes, there are strong indications that Mrs. Rodgers also views this product as relating to such goals as being a good mother, having her daughter appear attractive, being seen by others as a worthwhile person, and so forth. Similarly, Scott Campbell's description of his car also suggests a mix of goals, including appearance, performance, and image of the owner.

The third additional point relates to the ease with which we can *identify* motivations. Some motivations are apparent to the consumer and to others, and purchases appear to be fairly straightforward. Anthony's need for tools might exemplify this instance. When decisions are complex or are tied in with heavy self-expression, however, some motivations can be quite difficult to identify. Consider how difficult it would be to identify exactly each motivation operating in Jennifer's case or in Michael Taylor's choice of a college.

Why Marketers Are Interested Notice that when multiple motives are present, a consumer is actually buying a "bundle of benefits" in a product or service purchase. If a marketer can identify the benefits consumers are seeking, he or she can design a product to deliver maximum satisfaction. Consumers' motivations are thus of central importance to marketers. All the foregoing points, together with marketing implications, will be discussed in our chapter on consumer motivation (Chapter 6). For now, however, it is important that the basic point be reiterated; consumer behavior consists of activities that are goal oriented—it is a *means to an end.*

Key II: Consumer Behavior Includes Many Activities

Our definition of consumer behavior focused on activity as a basic characteristic, and now it appears as a key to understanding the topic. Why is there such attention paid to this point? The answer is that *there are many important facets to consumer behavior.* As consumers, we have thoughts, feelings, plans, decisions, purchases, and the experiences that follow. An observer who looks only at the act of purchase will miss many of the relevant activities. Also, a narrow view of consumer behavior will tend to underrepresent its significance in our daily lives. Finally, this range of activities provides marketers with a rich set of possible ways by which to reach, appeal to, and satisfy consumers. Thus an understanding of consumer activities provides a useful basis for developing marketing strategies.

Figure 1-2 summarizes some of the types of activities that make up consumer behavior. Notice that nearly 30 separate activities are shown. Further, think about how many versions each activity on the list might have. "Viewing ads," for example, could include reading ads in magazines, in newspapers, or in the mail; watching them on television; listening to them on radio; or seeing billboards during car travel. Similarly, displays are prominent in supermarkets, in retail stores, and in store windows. Given the number of outlets for ads and displays, and the number of brands using them, imagine what a very large number of marketing stimuli a typical consumer must see over the course of a week, month, or year!

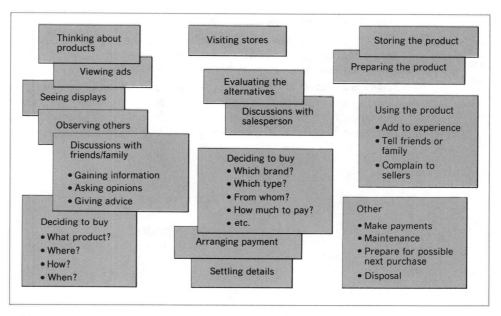

FIGURE 1-2 **Some Activities Involved in Consumer Behavior**

For the activities that are product specific, such as "Deciding to buy," think about how many products and services there are in our marketing economy. Even though you may not personally buy most of these, some consumers *are* thinking about buying and using every product and service that is available. In total, an enormous amount of time, energy, and money goes into these consumer activities.

As a final note, it is helpful to recognize a distinction between *deliberate* and *incidental* activities. Some of the activities on the list—particularly those near the center, such as "Discussions with salespersons" and "Deciding to buy"—are clearly **deliberate consumer behaviors** (that is, we choose to undertake these for a specific purpose involving purchase or consumption). **Incidental consumer behaviors**, on the other hand, usually occur as by-products of other, nonconsumer, activities. For example, few persons turn on the television or radio to catch their favorite commercial! When we stroll through stores, we may have certain products in mind, but we'll also encounter many other products for which we'd not been looking, and we'll often buy some of these. The deliberate/incidental distinction is an important one for marketers who are attempting to gain consumers' attention and interest.

Key III: Consumer Behavior Is a Process

The concept of a *process,* in which a series of related steps occur, has become a major feature of the field of consumer behavior in the last 20 years. Note that the definition not only explicitly mentioned "mental and emotional processes" but also referred to "selecting, purchasing, and using products." Implicit in these steps is the concept that a consumer's selection would precede purchase, which would in turn precede usage. Notice that Figure 1-2 also implicitly contains a process orientation: if we were to label the columns, therefore, we might show

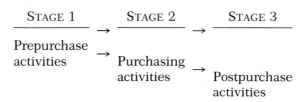

This stage relationship represents the **decision process approach** to consumer behavior. By stressing the fact that the actual purchase is only one step in a series of related steps, the decision process approach helps to analyze *why* a certain purchase will be made by a certain individual. It also helps to clarify what activities are likely to precede a purchase and what effects that purchase might have on later actions of the same consumer. Because of its importance and usefulness, this approach will be analyzed in greater detail at several points later in the text.

Key IV: Consumer Behavior Differs in Timing and Complexity

Timing refers to *when* the decision takes place and *how long* the entire process takes. *Complexity,* meanwhile, refers to the *number of activities* involved in a decision and the *difficulty* of the decision itself. Timing and complexity will typically be correlated. That is, all other factors being equal, the more complex a decision is, the more time will usually be spent on it.

The Inherent Complexity of Consumer Decisions   In the abstract, many consumer decisions are inherently rather complex and could involve nearly all the activities listed in Figure 1-2. If we consumers were to strive to make the absolutely correct choice, at just the right price, we would have to engage in many **prepurchase activities**. A few purchases are so important, and occur so seldom, that we do come close to doing all of this. Michael Taylor's decision on which college to attend was probably the most complex of our consumer vignettes. He considered a number of alternatives, weighed them on many dimensions, used a number of information sources, and took a long time. Even after enrolling, he is still "consuming" the educational service and making many other decisions related to it (such as which classes to take, which residence to rent, etc.). Finally, notice that his **postpurchase evaluation** is continuing to occur and is not entirely favorable at this time. Most consumers report similarly complex decisions with respect to housing choices, career options, and some major purchases.

Consumers Try to Simplify Given that each of us has other things to do with our time, and that complex consumer decisions require effort, there are incentives to find ways to simplify and speed up our decision processes. Some of the major **decision simplifiers** are

- Aiming for a "satisfactory" decision rather than the best one possible.
- Relying on other people's recommendations of what to buy.
- Becoming "brand loyal" for products that we repurchase fairly often.

However, unless we are willing to become habitual purchasers of the same brand every time we buy, some complexity will remain in every consumer decision.

This Leads to a Conflict This discussion leads us to recognize an especially interesting conflict that can occur between the forces for simplification and our desires to satisfy positive goals. Let's take the case of Janet Rodgers as an example. Notice that she can create a fast and easy decision process for herself by merely pulling Tide off the store shelf, regardless of circumstances. If she does this, however, she runs certain risks. For example, she could miss out on a new brand that might be better or miss out on a large price savings or a free gift (premium) from a competing brand that is as good as her favorite brand. In other words, she will not guarantee receiving the best value for her money by pursuing a strict brand-loyalty decision rule. As consumers, we have all experienced this type of conflict. Most of us resolve it by retaining some *flexibility* in our purchasing processes, so that we can take advantage when the situation allows.

This is a key point for marketing managers. Basically, the forces toward simplification can offer a given brand (e.g., Tide) profit opportunities through brand loyalty. Notice the challenge facing Tide's competitors trying to sell to Janet Rodgers, who likely is paying no attention to them! However, consumers' desires for the best overall set of benefits will offer competing brands (Wisk, Fresh Start, Cheer, etc.) opportunities through trial purchases and brand switching by even those consumers who favor Tide. In Janet Rodgers's case, the competitors need to somehow capture her attention and interest, then stimulate a trial purchase.

Key V: Consumer Behavior Involves Different Roles

There are at least three significantly different functions performed within the consumer behavior process. Each of these functions has a **consumer role** associated with it. In brief, a consumer can be an

- Influencer.
- Purchaser.
- User.

A consumer can play different combinations of these roles on any given occasion. Also, for any particular purchase, more than one person may be involved in one or more of the roles. Even though we often can overlook the influence of others, when more than one person is involved, the consumer decision process is affected.

Figure 1-3 outlines the various role combinations. First, a consumer can play all three roles during a purchase: this is particularly common when we are "on our own" and are purchasing for ourselves. Jill Prado's purchase of her blouse is a good example. Even here, however, other influencer roles were active in the process. Those mentioned by Jill were her mother, who suggested the purchase, and the saleslady, who provided reinforcement at the moment of decision.

The remaining combinations all have at least some incompleteness to them, in that one of the normal functions is missing. Jennifer's gift purchase, for example, will not involve personal usage on her part. Billy, Allie, and Jimmy's ages indicate that they will not often be purchasers although they already hold strong desires to influence particular purchases, and to consume the products. Kim Taylor, Michael's sister, was not really involved in either purchasing or using his college education, but did act as an influence on the decision. (This is a relatively common role.)

Helen Mercanti's hospital purchases were virtually dictated to her by her physician, thereby removing the "Influencer" role from her. This is relatively common for consumers of professional services, unless they are assertive. The consumer quotes do not provide direct evidence of either of the last two categories.

FIGURE 1-3 **Combinations of Roles a Consumer Can Play**

Topic	Example from Vignette
Influencer, purchaser and user	Jill Prado
Influencer and purchaser only	Jennifer Anderson
Influencer and user only	Billy, Allie, and Jimmy
Influencer only	Kim Taylor (Michael's sister)
Purchaser and user only	Helen Mercanti
Purchaser only	Mother of Billy, Allie, and Jimmy
User only	Daughter of Janet Rodgers

Billy, Allie, and Jimmy's mother might act as a "purchaser only" if she gives in to one of the requests and does not exert influence on the actual choice. Similarly, Janet Rodgers's daughter will be a consumer of the detergent's benefits but is not likely to exert direct influence on the purchase.

As we'll see in later chapters, this three-level system of roles can easily be expanded to offer further insights into consumer behavior. Even though simple, however, it has provided us with eight combinations of roles. Further, notice how crucial the exact roles can be in deciding what consumer behavior actually occurs. Jill, for example, could have acted quite differently had the influencers in her case been different: what if her mother had suggested she take in a movie, or splurge on sweets, or come home for a weekend? What if the salesperson had insulted her, or had simply suggested a sweater, or jewelry, or something else? There is thus a wide array of possibilities: the actual consumer behaviors we see stem from the interactions of roles during the process.

At a more abstract level, consumer roles arise because of social interactions. Think about how frequent and significant these social interactions are in consumer behavior: there are actually very few purchases we make that do not in any way involve anyone else acting in any of these roles. It is also important to note that the roles tend to change over a consumer's lifetime. Children do not purchase often. Young single persons, without the role of child, spouse, or parent to perform, can be more individualistic in their buying decisions. If and when marriage brings spouse and parental roles, however, these same persons will become heavily involved in using, purchasing for others and in being influenced by their wants and needs.

For marketers, the fact that *multiple persons* are involved in these roles poses problems and opportunities. For example, frequently there is a need to advertise to the influencers while selling to the purchaser. To do this well, marketers must be able to identify which types of people play which roles for particular purchases. This requires detailed understanding of the workings of social roles, household decision-making patterns, the operation of "buying centers" in organizational purchases, and other topics that we'll be examining later in this text.

Key VI: Consumer Behavior Is Influenced by External Factors

The concept of **influence** was already raised, but it deserves special focus because of its importance in understanding consumer behavior. Essentially, this reflects the fact that consumer behavior is *adaptive* in nature: consumers adapt to the situations that surround them. Being influenced, in turn, means that a consumer's decision process has somehow been affected by outside forces. As we'll see, some forms of influence occur over long time periods, while others work within brief episodes.

Influence is a natural occurrence in the consumer world: influence is not necessarily good or bad. Most people agree that some forms of influence such as manipulation or coercion, are bad. However, some forms of influence are recognized to be quite beneficial. In consumer behavior, for example, beneficial influence forms might include learning about new products and services, learning of price specials, adopting new decision criteria, receiving good purchase advice, and so forth.

Numerous Influence Sources Many external sources act to influence our consumer behaviors. Figure 1-4 lists the major types. **Culture** refers to the beliefs, values, and views we share as members of a society. It acts on us throughout our lives and has pervasive influence on all our behaviors. One role of culture is to identify boundaries for what we see as acceptable products, services, and consumer activities. **Subcultures** refers to groups of people, within an entire culture, who tend to share particular patterns of values and behaviors. A consumer can belong to several subcultures. Subcultures are defined on bases such as sex, race, nationality, age, and religion. Examples include the black subculture, the Hispanic subculture, the teenage subculture, the Mormon subculture, and so forth. **Social class,** meanwhile, incorporates variables such as occupation, income, and educational level. These variables combine to affect our **life-styles**, which in turn have great influence on our consumption patterns.

Family helps to develop its childrens' consumer "personalities" as shoppers and spenders. As adults, although our roles have changed, our family's past continues to exert strong influence on our lives through the values and habits we have internalized. **Reference groups** and friends influence consumer behavior by providing guidelines to appropriate behaviors for those people who identify with them. Fraternities, sororities, athletes, and career professionals are frequent reference group figures. In addition to explicit discussions with our **friends,** we are also frequently influenced simply by observing their behaviors and their reactions to our purchases.

External conditions refers to such factors as inflation, unemployment, credit availability, and so forth. They are often, but not always, economically oriented (another form of external condition, such as a long-term illness in the family, could also shift purchase plans). External conditions clearly affect many consumers' decisions on how much to spend and when to buy a given product. In the **marketing environment** we find numerous efforts by marketers to reach and influence our decisions. These efforts include attractively designing the products, advertising, displays, salespersons, prices, and the environment of the store itself. As we'll discuss in the next chapter, however, this does not mean that the marketer's task is a simple one. Finally, **situational effects** refer to temporary forces that stem from particular settings in which consumers find themselves for short periods of time. Usually, consumers will adapt to the situational context. For example, a gin and tonic may be fine for a cocktail party, but not for a breakfast meeting, while a hot dog is fine at a ball game but not as an entree for the boss at dinner.

Underlying Source Characteristics In addition to the list of influences, several points can be gained by considering Figure 1-4. First, the figure is or-

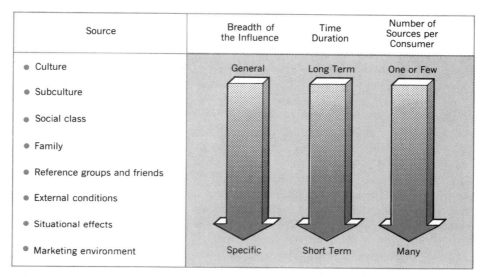

Source	Breadth of the Influence	Time Duration	Number of Sources per Consumer
• Culture	General	Long Term	One or Few
• Subculture			
• Social class			
• Family			
• Reference groups and friends			
• External conditions			
• Situational effects			
• Marketing environment	Specific	Short Term	Many

FIGURE 1-4 **Sources of External Influences on Consumer Behavior**

ganized in approximate order of *breadth* of influence—from the broadest and most general types of influence to those that are most purchase specific. Culture, for example, may not be a determining factor in our choice of one brand as opposed to another, but it probably has played an important role in the fact that the product itself is even available for sale. Second, a difference in *time dimension* is also reflected in the figure. The influence of culture and subculture extends over many years. Even in our adult years we are influenced by cultural factors we internalized as children. At the other extreme, the effect of marketing variables and situations might occur during a very short time period and have little lasting impact.

Third, the *number* of influences—for any particular consumer—increases as we go down the list. Most of us belong to only one culture, one social class, and one or two families. At the high-frequency extreme are marketing influences and situations. Finally—not reflected in the figure—we might notice that each source provides a consumer with an *internally consistent* set of guidelines. That is, the culture provides the same set of values for every member. This is also true for each subculture, social class, family, reference group, and marketer. The differential influences we see on consumer behavior thus arise from *multiple sources*. For example, different cultures and different families will provide some different sets of guidelines to their members. Similarly, different friends might recommend different cars, restaurants, and so on. Finally, our competitive system is *based on* different marketers recommending different brands. The net result is that a consumer *must develop ways to deal with different sources of influence*. Marketers, in turn, must take these consumer adaptations into account in developing successful marketing strategies. As we'll see, this point is of central importance to understanding consumer behavior in our modern world.

Key VII: Consumer Behavior Differs for Different People

It is obvious that each of us undertakes somewhat different consumer activities and makes somewhat different purchases in line with our somewhat different preferences. The reason that this topic—formally termed *individual differences*—is raised is that to understand consumer behavior, we must understand *why* people would engage in different behaviors. We need to accurately generalize about "types" of consumers. This problem is very real for marketing managers who must attempt to predict *who* will respond favorably to a certain program and *how many* of such persons there are in the consumer market.

Finally, individual differences make it difficult for us to summarize consumer behavior easily. This places a premium on our ability to understand the basic processes involved in that behavior. It also provides the rationale for **market segmentation**, the process by which we identify key target groups within the consumer marketplace.

Four "Pitfalls" in the Study of Consumer Behavior

Consumer behavior is a pulsating, interesting topic. At the same time, though, it *is* broad and complex. The Seven Keys will prove to be valuable guides, but there are pitfalls that can hinder the learning experience in this field. Four common pitfalls are listed in Figure 1-5. Each reflects an underlying issue regarding the development of knowledge.

Pitfall 1: The Unspecified Target

This issue concerns our *focus* when addressing a topic in consumer behavior and warns us to check that we are focusing correctly in light of the problem at hand. In scientific terms, the issue stresses the importance of specifying the *level of analysis* that we are using.

Most concepts we'll encounter can exist at various levels of specification. For example, it is often tempting to talk about "the consumer." When we use this term we sometimes mean the aggregate or total market, while at other times we're thinking of a subgroup. A common possibility is that we're really considering an individual consumer, but are viewing him or her as somehow representative of all people in the market. It is obviously helpful—both for our own thinking and for communicating with others—to specify at which level we are thinking at the time.

A similar problem is also typically found with terms such as "choice" or "purchase." Candidate levels of analysis for these terms include the product class, a particular item (or brand) within the product class, and, sometimes, the store at which the purchase occurs. For each level of analysis the relevant factors can differ. Jill Prado's purchase of a blouse provides a good example of this point.

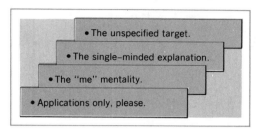

- The unspecified target.
- The single-minded explanation.
- The "me" mentality.
- Applications only, please.

FIGURE 1-5 **Four Common Pitfalls**

Even though the product, store, and item levels were all related within her purchase process, notice how different are the factors that we'd want to use to best explain: (1) Jill's decision to search for clothes in the first place, (2) her selection of the stores in which to shop, and (3) her choice of the particular blouse that she ended up taking home with her.

At a practical level, this issue assumes particular importance. Marketing managers cannot afford to focus only on the individual consumer level, even though they can gain important insights from it. They must also analyze market segments, as well as aggregate market sales statistics. With respect to purchases, marketers must also use different variables to predict store choice than to predict product purchase, then still different variables for brand choice. In general, specifying the target level of analysis will sharpen insights into consumer behavior.

Pitfall 2: The Single-Minded Explanation

Sometimes it is tempting to explain a behavior by pointing to a single factor and viewing it as if it alone "caused" the behavior. However, as was evident in the consumer vignettes, there are almost always a number of factors at work, and some of these are not apparent at the surface. A refusal to consider other explanations can thus lead us to miss important insights. For example, a "single-minded explainer" might assert that consumers buy toothpaste to clean their teeth or beer to quench thirst or that consumers purchase on a price basis. None of these explanations is entirely wrong, of course, but all are incomplete. In the case of toothpaste, for example, consumers are also interested in decay prevention, sweet breath, whitening and brightening power, and other important attributes. The recent successes of brands such as Aqua-fresh show the power of recognizing combinations of these attributes to appeal to multiple consumer motivations.

Pitfall 3: The "Me" Mentality

Much of the appeal of consumer behavior lies in the fact that each of us is a consumer. In learning this field we can use our personal experiences as a means of understanding important consumer concepts. In fact, Chapter 1 has encouraged the use of self-analysis (introspection) for exactly these reasons. What, then, is the problem?

The problem is that a *sole reliance* on our own experience can lead to a non-representative view of consumer behavior. Each of us has limited experience in some consumer behaviors and limited interests in many others. We will also have different values from some other consumers, act within different economic circumstances and social situations, and be subject to our personal set of perceptual biases. All these factors limit the power of introspection.

For example, many readers have not yet had much experience with the purchase concerns of senior citizens, or with buying houses. Many males might view Jill's blouse search as a mystery; some readers might also judge this purchase to have been "too extravagant." Many people lack the mechanical experience to handle Anthony Grant's tools in the way he plans to. More broadly, many consumers experience unemployment, mounting debts, and sharp curtailment of purchases, but many readers may not have had this happen to them. Thus, because the scope of consumer behavior is so vast, each of us needs to reach out far beyond our own experience base. This means reading and thinking about matters beyond our personal day-to-day interests. Within the business world, it means gathering as much information as possible about the consumer market and applying concepts and techniques as appropriate. Avoiding the "me" mentality, in fact, is the basic reason that marketers use consumer research.

Pitfall 4: Applications Only, Please

Many persons studying consumer behavior are interested in marketing-related careers. Given this career path, there is a natural tendency to look for helpful hints for marketing decisions. This translates into a healthy interest in marketing applications of consumer behavior. This healthy interest can turn into a pitfall, however, when a short-term stress on applications becomes a *dominating focus* and begins to drive out appreciation for basic concepts and research methods. This leads to two significant risks. First, the ability to adopt various perspectives is an important asset in a field such as consumer behavior, since these reveal new dimensions of the topic. In an academic sense, then, a stress on "applications only" will risk the loss of a significant degree of learning.

Second, this pitfall can turn around to shortchange even the most applications-oriented career in the longer run. This is due to the fact that *marketing applications are by their nature situation specific.* What worked for one firm in the past may not work for another firm in the future. If competitors institute changes, moreover, the marketing challenge is to search for new ideas, not past examples. The underlying *reasons* for consumer behavior continue across situations and are a valuable source of new marketing ideas. These reasons are embodied in the concepts and theories of the field. Thus, while marketing applications are quite relevant, they are not primary. Generalizations and concepts are the key elements of the body of knowledge in consumer behavior.

EXHIBIT 1-3   **A FRAMEWORK FOR THE STUDY OF CONSUMER BEHAVIOR**

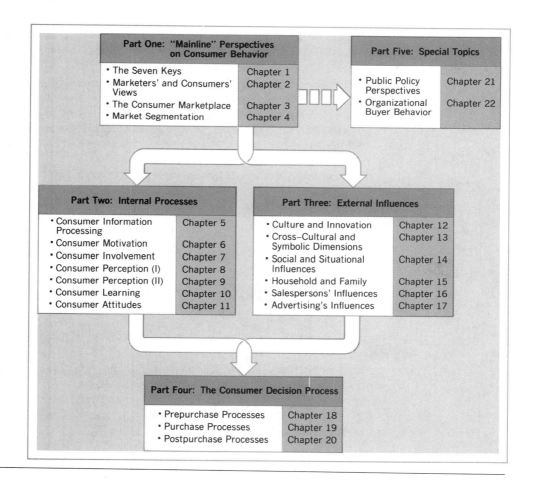

WHERE DO WE GO FROM HERE?

Our discussions in this chapter have provided a strong sense for the nature of the field of consumer behavior. Exhibit 1-3 indicates where we'll be going in the remainder of the text, as we broaden and deepen our appreciation of the concepts and applications of the seven keys. The book itself is organized into five parts, reflecting two fundamental positions regarding knowledge in this field:

- *Position 1: Perspective is important. Consumer behavior can be studied from several significantly different viewpoints. The perspective we choose will guide what we will discover. Learning is fostered by the ability to adopt different perspectives as appropriate to the problem at issue.* Part One of the book thus presents several "mainline" perspectives on consumer behavior. Here we can perceive new ideas and insights arising from special vantage points. Part Five presents additional perspectives of interest to some persons in the field.
- *Position 2: The primary forces that drive and direct all consumer behavior stem from some combination of the consumer's environment and the personal elements of that consumer.* Thus Part Two of the book covers **internal processes** of consumer behavior, while Part Three examines **external influences** on consumer behavior. Part Four then combines both elements in examining **consumer decision processes**.

Beyond this simple framework, of course, there are many interesting topics. Exhibit 1-3 provides a more detailed picture of how the topics relate to each other. In our next chapter, we'll examine how marketers and consumers have different views of consumer behavior, and what this means for the field.

 SUMMARY

Characteristics of Modern Consumer Behavior

We began this chapter by describing four of the basic characteristics of the field of consumer behavior: that it is widespread, that it has great economic and social significance, that it is subtle and interesting, and that it is both professionally and personally relevant to us. The forces that spurred the growth of the consumer behavior field were then identified. Among the most important of these were the availability of a mass consumer market, the marketing concept, and the development of computerized statistical methods for studying large samples of consumers.

Major Concepts in the Study of Consumer Behavior

Following a discussion of our definition of consumer behavior, the central academic concepts in this field were introduced in the Seven Keys to consumer behavior. The first key to understanding consumer behavior is to recognize that it is *motivated* by goals that consumers have. Motivations are, however, sometimes difficult to identify, and a single behavior can stem from a mix of motivations. The second key recognizes that consumer behavior includes many types of *activities* beyond the purchase of products. The third key highlights the view of consumer behavior as a *process*. This decision process approach emphasizes how analysis of prepurchase and postpurchase activities can give us insights into *why* an individual makes a particular purchase. The fourth key stresses how the *timing* and *complexity* of a decision process are important factors to consider. Consumers often face conflicts involving how much time and effort to spend on each decision to achieve the best results.

The fifth key points out the importance that *roles* play in consumer behavior. For example, on any given occasion, a consumer may be an influencer, purchaser, and/or user. These roles flow from social relationships, and shift over the course of the consumer's lifetime. The sixth key stresses how consumer behavior is *influenced* by several external factors. Further insights into consumer behavior are gained by understanding how consumers adapt to each of these sources of influence. Finally, the seventh key recognizes that consumer behavior *differs for different people*. This means that basic processes and market segmentation—the process by which we identify meaningful target groups within a larger consumer market—are extremely important.

Following the Seven Keys, our attention turned to a brief discussion of four "pitfalls" in the study of consumer behavior. Pitfall 1, the unspecified target, points out the need to be clear about what we mean when we use such terms as "the consumer," or "purchase." Pitfall 2, the single-minded explanation, refers to the fact that there usually are multiple factors at work in consumer behavior. The "me" mentality, pitfall 3, points out the dangers of relying too heavily on our own personal views as if they are representative of all consumers. Finally, pitfall 4, applications only, please, shows how consumer behavior concepts are important in providing marketers with a solid basis for strong decisions when confronting new challenges.

Where Do We Go From Here?

Our final brief section of the chapter provided an overview of how we will be addressing the study of consumer behavior in the remainder of this text. The two basic principles guiding our study are (1) perspective is important, and multiple perspectives give us multiple insights, and (2) consumer behavior is determined by the interplay of external influences and internal processes of each consumer. The book is thus organized by important perspectives (in Parts One and Five), and by internal processes, external influences, and the consumer decision process (in Parts Two, Three, and Four). Exhibit 1-3 provides a graphic illustration of this plan.

KEY TERMS

As a useful review of your mastery of the concepts in this chapter, you may wish to check your understanding of these key words and terms:

marketing concept	inferential consumer research
descriptive consumer research	deliberate consumer behavior

incidental consumer behavior   social class
decision process approach   life-style
prepurchase activities   family
postpurchase evaluation   reference group
decision simplifiers   friends
consumer role   external conditions
influence   marketing environment
culture   situational effects
subcultures   market segmentation

REVIEW QUESTIONS AND EXPERIENTIAL EXERCISES
[E = Application extension or experiential exercise]

1. In its discussion of the characteristics of consumer behavior, the chapter asserts that consumer behavior is "economically and socially significant."
   a. Describe three ways in which consumer behavior is of economic significance. Just how significant is consumer spending in the U.S. economy?
   b. What is the social significance of consumer behavior? In your personal life, in what ways does consumer behavior have social importance for you?

2. For each of the Seven Keys, select three of the consumer vignettes from Exhibit 1-2 and explain how that key is likely to apply to the situation described.

3. How do marketers determine what motivates consumer behavior?

4. How does the level of activities involved with consumer behavior differ by type of product or service? Provide examples.

5. Describe your decision process for purchasing the following:
   a. A soft drink.
   b. A vacation.
   c. A new automobile.
   d. A personal computer.
   e. A pair of designer jeans.

6. How do marketers attempt to deal with the issues of timing and complexity in consumer decision making?

7. Assume you are a consumer involved in all three roles in a purchase. In what activities do you engage to fulfill each role? Are these functions continuous during the process?

8. How do the various sources of external influence affect consumer decision making? How might these influences vary for different consumers? How might they vary for different product classes? Provide examples.

9. What are the two basic position statements that have guided the development of this book? How are they reflected in the organization of its chapters?

10. The chapter discusses four common "pitfalls" that some students report having encountered in studying consumer behavior. For each of the four, indicate whether you've observed its occurrence in any other classes. Which, if any, do you think is most likely to occur in this course?

[E] 11. Consider a recent large consumer purchase and relate each of the Seven Keys to that purchase.

[E] 12. Arrange to interview an acquaintance who is or was involved in marketing to consumers (e.g., store owner, salesperson, advertiser, brand manager). Discuss the Seven Keys with him or her. For each key, ask about marketing implications. Prepare a brief report on your findings.

CHAPTER 2

Marketers' and Consumers' Views of Consumer Behavior

It Wasn't All Gravy

Several years ago Standard Brands, a major marketer of margarine (Blue Bonnet is its leading brand), decided that one way to sell more margarine would be to use it as an ingredient in another product. Executives decided to concentrate on the prepared gravy market, which was valued at almost $100 million and which everyone agreed had enormous growth potential. The product development effort was then geared to producing a quality-tasting gravy that utilized the technical and production skills available in the firm.

The resulting product, named Smooth & Easy, was marketed as a refrigerated gravy bar that consumers could slice like margarine, then heat in the pan with water. Three flavors were offered: brown gravy, chicken gravy, and white sauce. It was priced about 69 cents per bar. One year after introduction—and after spending $6 million to market the new product and having converted a margarine plant to manufacture it—Standard Brands' executives decided to remove Smooth & Easy from the market because of its poor sales performance.[1]

■ ■ ■

MARKETING DECISIONS AND CONSUMER BEHAVIOR

As noted in Chapter 1, consumer behavior is a broad field that contains many interesting applied and theoretical issues. We will be examining these issues from various perspectives throughout this text. It is a good idea, therefore, to begin by clarifying exactly what the concept of perspective itself implies.

The Importance of Perspective

Perspective is a term derived from the original Latin word *prospectus*, meaning "a mental view of a scene." It is a good term for describing the standpoint from which we choose to analyze something. For example, a man looks different when seen from the back than from the front and different yet if viewed from the side. In general, viewing an object from only one perspective will *highlight* certain characteristics, but will *hide* other characteristics from our analysis. For this reason, to understand an important topic well, it is a good idea to adopt several perspectives on it.

Three important sets of persons active in dealing with consumer behavior are marketers, consumers, and public policymakers. *Marketers* and *consumers* are each active on a daily basis, each approaching the marketplace for the purpose of making *transactions*. Thus marketers and consumers share certain interests and goals. The transactions themselves, however, involve quite different tasks for the two parties—marketers must *sell,* and consumers must *buy.* These two tasks create quite different perspectives for the two parties, and these we shall examine in this chapter.

From the Source . . .
Although often overlooked in marketing textbooks, the fact that marketers and consumers bring different perspectives to the marketplace is a central issue for our market system to consider. In this regard, Adam Smith, the architect of the free market system, said:

> Consumption is the sole end and purpose of all production; and the interest of the producer ought to be attended to, only so far as it may be necessary for promoting that of the consumer. . . . But in the mercantile system the interest of the consumer is almost certainly sacrificed to that of the producer; and it seems to consider production, and not consumption, as the ultimate end and object of all industry and commerce.

—From *The Wealth of Nations,* 1776.[2]

Before moving to our analysis of marketers' and consumers' perspectives, we should also take note of the third set of persons with an important perspective on this field. *Public policymakers* are primarily concerned that the marketplace function well—that it operate in an efficient fashion and that it be fair for marketers and consumers alike. Their tools involve laws, regulations, and economic policies. Our detailed examination of interesting issues in this area appears in Chapter 21. Interested readers may wish to glance through it to gain a better idea of the kinds of issues that arise in public policy. At this point, however, let's turn our attention to examining how the marketing and consumer perspectives differ, and what this can tell us about the field of consumer behavior. We'll begin with the marketing perspective.

Controllable Marketing Decisions: The 4 P's

Much of the research in the field of consumer behavior has been undertaken by marketing professors and those working in marketing and advertising jobs in industry. The **marketing perspective** on consumer behavior is thus a dominant viewpoint in the field. Our discussion of the marketing perspective reflects the underlying purpose of the marketing concept—that every firm needs to match its products and services to meet the needs of the vast number of potential customers. Understanding consumer behavior is thus crucial for marketing success.

Within marketing, a set of management decisions culminates in what has come to be known as the **marketing mix**.[3] This is basically the entire *package* that a firm offers consumers in hopes of meeting their wants and needs while making a profit. E. Jerome McCarthy, a leading thinker in the marketing field, pointed out that these **controllable factors** fall into four basic categories, popularly known as the 4 Ps:[4]

- Product
- Price
- Place
- Promotion

Although you may already be familiar with the 4 P's, let's review each area briefly to focus on how consumer behavior relates to the decisions that marketers make in developing their marketing mixes.

Product Decisions

Product decisions refer to all aspects of the design, materials, and quality control that are built into a particular product or service offering. Most marketers offer a *product portfolio* that consists of a range of offerings aimed at different consumer preferences in the market. Also, new products are continually being developed, while old products are dropped when they lose consumers' favor. As just one example of the continuing pressures present in product decisions, let's consider the auto industry.

"Team Taurus" Brings It Home

Not too long ago, Ford Motor was in trouble. It had just lost $3.2 billion in 18 months, and, as company chairman Donald Petersen put it, "we had to make some very substantial changes." One change was the creation of "Team Taurus," a group of marketers, designers, engineers, and manufacturing personnel charged with developing a new car to rescue the firm. The team relied heavily on consumer interviews and chose 700 features for the new car from these discussions. The team also conducted consumer "focus group" sessions at 10 further stages in the process and modified the developing auto to reflect the feedback

from these potential buyers. In addition, the team bought models of competing cars that were most popular with consumers and then systematically tore them apart to analyze the best product features (over 400 features were reportedly "borrowed" in this process). Finally, since high production quality was absolutely essential, numerous suggestions were solicited from company personnel who would be responsible for quality production. The results from Team Taurus's efforts? One of the most popular cars ever produced, and a dramatic turnaround for Ford, whose corporate market share rose from 16 percent to 29 percent during the 1980s![5]

Price Decisions

In addition to designing the product or service itself, marketers must also decide on the best price to charge consumers. This determination involves many issues, including manufacturing costs and the structure of demand in the marketplace. Usually, however, pricing decisions are made with considerable uncertainty about what their actual outcomes will be.

How Much to Pay, for USA Today?

Marketers at the newspaper USA Today faced a dilemma shortly after the paper had been expensively launched as the nation's first daily newspaper. The paper itself had exceeded expectations of consumer acceptance: it was selling very well. Unfortunately, however, it was falling short in attracting advertisers. Thus total revenues were off target, and losses were mounting. Management pondered the possibility of raising the price to consumers to raise revenues and stem the losses. But what was at risk if a price increase were to fail? And what would be the best increase to try? Management first tried to move from 25 cents to 35 cents per copy. Some consumers reacted negatively—unit sales dropped by some 6 percent—but the higher prices increased total revenues by over $100,000 per day. When this trend was clear, management decided to raise the price again, this time to the present level of 50 cents per copy. The paper has now become even more popular, and advertisers have joined in. As of its fifth year, *USA Today* turned profitable.[6]

Place Decisions

Place decisions refer to the manner in which a product or service is made available to customers for purchase. In general, the distribution sector is well structured to meet the needs of consumers. Occasionally, however, a manufacturer has difficulty in making the right place decision, as described in the following tale:

Soloflex Needs More Strength

The recent physical fitness boom helped many firms to achieve success. Soloflex, a home exercise machine, has been one of the most successful. It wasn't always that way, however, recalls Jerry Wilson, president of the firm and developer of this device. At first, Mr. Wilson attempted to use sporting goods stores to sell the machine, but this approach didn't work:

> I couldn't get the clerks to demonstrate them right, reports Mr. Wilson. They got all sweaty and didn't understand how it worked.

Mr. Wilson then removed Soloflex from retail stores. Deciding that demonstration of the machine was absolutely necessary, Wilson came up with a creative solution—to use a video "brochure." This was a 20-minute video cassette that was closely scripted and designed to create a positive aura for the machine. More than $150,000 went into production of the film. Each cassette cost the firm $6.50 to produce and mail, but consumers who received the cassette bought at twice the rate as consumers who received only print brochures. As the product became established, the firm moved toward Cable TV showings of its brochure, and stayed with its direct selling channel to consumers.[7]

Promotion Decisions

The total effect of the product, place, and price decisions is physically to create the opportunity for a transaction to occur. The role for **promotion** is to inform potential customers about the mix and to encourage them persuasively to consider purchasing the firm's product. Promotion is, therefore, the chief communication link between the firm and its customers.

Dull, Boring, and Wimpy

These were the findings of consumer research commissioned by the California Raisin Advisory Board into the image of this fruit in consumers' minds. Bumper crops had doubled the supply over the demand for raisins, and consumer sales were sluggish. While consumers liked the taste of raisins, they didn't see them as a "hip" product to buy. Late in

the 1980s, a promotional campaign was launched to turn this image around. The Clay-mation technique was used to create appealing, hip raisin characters who would dance, sing, and generally dispense their cool into the consumer world. The choice of theme song was a natural: the classic "I Heard It Through the Grapevine." Results? A memorable campaign, characters licensed for other product tie-ins, and a reversal of the sales decline, with consumer purchases of raisins up![8]

Uncontrollable Factors: The 5 C's

Notice how important consumer behavior was in each of the 4 P areas. These, however, were all controllable decisions, and the real world of marketing also contains a number of important factors that a manager *does not* control. These **uncontrollable factors** can be quite significant in determining the success or failure of a marketing mix. The marketing manager must try to understand these factors as well as possible, then respond by *adapting* the marketing mix to account best for them. These factors can be summarized in a fashion similar to the controllable variables: the uncontrollable constraints will be termed here the **5 C's.**[9]

- Competitors
- Company
- Channels
- Conditions
- Customers

The Competitive Constraint

One severe complicating factor for most marketers is the fact that competitors are striving to make sales themselves and are also devising marketing mixes for this purpose. The search for consumer advantages for our brand thus becomes an important activity. It is also the case that the presence of competitors serves to reduce our realistic options in terms of the 4 P decisions we'll make. For example, we often can't price too much above the prices other firms are charging, nor can we easily drop prices without risking price retaliations (and perhaps a "price war") from the competition. Also, it can be dangerous to make our product or package too different or to offer our product through nontraditional retail channels (if consumers aren't used to looking there). Finally, efforts by competitors stimulate responses by consumers and frequently call for adaptations on the part of a marketer whose mix had been quite profitable up until this point. Thus a 4 P decision that may seem optimal by itself will need to be changed due to competitive actions.

Trouble Down the Road

"It's the end of the world," moaned an auto dealer recently. Driven by shifting consumer preferences, currency values, and import quotas, auto firms around the world have been busy creating new alliances, new plants, and new auto brands. Across the marketplace, competition is reaching red-hot levels. By 1992 we will see at least 225 distinct car models, up 34 percent since 1985. The luxury auto segment alone will have 55 competing models, up 67 percent in only seven years! Excess capacity is a serious problem; auto plant capacity is growing to be 50 percent higher than consumer demand. This heated competitive environment will force each marketer to search for new advantages through quality and design improvements, possible new forms of dealerships, and heavy price promotions. Given the intense competition, moreover, some firms and many dealers will almost certainly be forced to close or merge in the coming years, and adaptation to competitive developments will certainly be the order of the day![10]

The Company Constraint

The **company** constraint is one that is not often encountered in textbook discussions of marketing, but it is a real factor in the world of business. In brief, this constraint recognizes that *companies* are different: some marketing mixes are better for some firms than for others. If a firm does not have a strong financial base, for example, it may not be able to afford to invest in a new technology to produce an innovative food product. Similarly, if your company has a low risk-taking profile, as a marketing manager you may be precluded from attempting certain marketing strategies.

Among the most significant factors in the company constraint are the *strengths and weaknesses of the people* that the marketing manager must call on to help implement the marketing mix. For example, all salespersons don't work as hard as they possibly could. Some may be satisfied with their current income and work load and aren't willing to put forth further efforts just because you would like them to. Similarly, in some firms the product you develop might encounter quality control problems in the production process, or the design may be less than perfect, the advertising may not be the best ever done, and so forth. While it is usually possible to try to improve weaker areas, it is also realistic for marketers to plan on adapting their marketing mixes to feature the company's strengths and work around the areas of weakness. In summary, the company for which you work helps to determine what's best to do.

A Brand New Game

"My whole life was grease," mused the former brand manager for Crisco. Among his chief competitors was the brand manager for Puritan, who worked just down the hall at Procter & Gamble (P&G pioneered brand management in the 1930s to encourage dynamic marketing for all brands). The profile of a brand manager: young, talented, and powerful. Each brand manager runs his or her assigned brand as its own business, using R&D, the plant, and so on for support as needed. One former brand manager for Folgers coffee remembers the job as pressured and pivotal: "It's an up or out position . . . spend 12 or 18 months on a brand . . . get your stripes and bolt" to a more senior position. The job can bring great success (P&G's chairman was the brand manager who brought Crest to the top by gaining the endorsement of the American Dental Association) or problems (for years, brand managers assigned to poor-selling Pringle's were tagged as being "sent to Siberia").

Recently, however, P&G has been modifying its internal structure. "Brand management isn't dead—it just isn't enough today," reports one consultant. P&G has been experimenting with "teams," in which members from other functional areas (R&D, finance, manufacturing, etc.) join the brand manager in developing plans. These new members usually don't have the brand manager's short-term time horizon and sometimes want to focus on broader issues than just one brand within a category. Also, some brand managers have resented losing their former authority within the team environment. As a former brand manager for Tenderleaf put it, "With teams, it's difficult to . . . see how good you really are. I wanted the opportunity . . .".[11]

The Channel Constraint

The third "C" bears a close relationship to the place variable of the marketing mix. Here, however, we explicitly recognize the fact that the **channels** consist of *independent* wholesalers and retailers. While this fact itself is obvious, let's think a bit about its implications for how the marketing mix must be adapted to reflect the reality of channel members' desires. For example, even if a supermarket carries a wide variety of items, there will be many marketers fighting to get their products on its shelves. To deal with this situation, supermarket chains create buying committees that meet to consider which, if any, new items to carry. Presentations from a large number of manufacturers are considered. Decisions are not easy, as the present stores are already full. This means that each time a new item is added, a current item must either be dropped or have its shelf space reduced. The point is that channels will exercise their own best judgments in whether to carry a product and, if so, exactly how the product will be carried. In general, channels are independent businesspersons who can be expected to behave in their own self-interest. Marketers must adapt to the characteristics of their channel customers if they are to effectively reach the larger consumer market, as the following example attests.

Roasted Chicken Lays Egg

Holly Farms, excited about the prospects for its new roasted chicken product, spent $20 million to build a plant to produce it. The idea of a more convenient, time-saving alternative to raw chicken seemed on target. Indeed, consumer research in the Atlanta test market showed 22 percent of women tried it, with 90 percent indicating they would buy again. Based on this kind of feedback, Holly Farms began nationwide distribution. However, it soon became apparent that the product wasn't succeeding. The giant Safeway supermarket chain, for example, had dropped the product after only two weeks. What was the problem? It wasn't the product—one Safeway executive even described it as "outstanding." The problem was that Holly Farms had not devoted enough attention to the needs and desires of its retailers. The "shelf life" of the roasted chicken, for example, was conservatively labeled at 14 days in the plant. Unfortunately, it could then take 9 days to get from the plant to a store, which didn't leave grocers much time to sell the products. Afraid of being stuck with out-of-date stock, grocers reacted by waiting until they were out of stock before reordering. No Holly Farms roasted chicken would be sold to consumers until the next shipment was delivered.

What to do? Holly Farms began a three-pronged campaign to win over its channels: (1) develop a new nitrogen packing system to add 5–10 days to shelf life, (2) consider a new delivery system separate from raw chicken, and (3) shift substantial consumer advertising dollars to store promotions and incentives for meat department managers.[12]

The Conditions Constraint

The fourth "C" refers to a host of broader economic and social forces that can impact on the success or failure of marketing programs. These include *economic* **conditions** such as inflation, recession, monetary exchange rates, and so on. *Labor* unrest can mean delays in production, which can destroy careful product introduction plans. *Weather* conditions can impact as well. For example, when ski areas have a warm winter period, the sales of equipment, rooms, and so on all drop immediately. *Government* regulations are another source of external constraints on some marketing mixes. Increased product safety level requirements, for example, are likely to raise prices of many products.

What can the marketing manager do about these kinds of external conditions? In some cases, such as government regulations, a company can join in political efforts to change the government's programs. In most cases, however, the marketing manager must simply *adapt* the marketing mix to the external conditions as well as is possible. Sometimes clever new marketing strategies can be designed to overcome consumer problems with a certain external condition. Often, however, external conditions are extremely powerful and may swamp marketing efforts to adapt.

Motor Homes Crash

As we'd expect, motor home sales are very sensitive to such factors as prices, interest rates, credit availability, and gasoline. In 1980 these external conditions all went wrong at the same time—gasoline prices soared, interest rates rocketed, and credit was crunched. Put simply, many consumers didn't buy. What happened to the marketers in this industry, most of which had had quite successful marketing mixes up to this time? *Half* of the nation's 4000 motor home dealers went out of business in that single year! Those who survived had been able to adapt to the new conditions and weather the storm until better times returned.[13]

The Customer Constraint

The fifth constraint represents the actual level at which success or failure is determined. As we saw, each of the other "C's" involves **customer** behavior as a key factor. *Competitors* are trying to appeal to the same market of customers and to take the same sales dollars. *Channels* are set up to reach all customers and deliver them products and services. Every *company* wants to sell to a defined group of customers using the resources available. Finally, *conditions* are important because they influence consumers' readiness to purchase products. The key point is that a marketing manager must *understand* his or her customers and must be capable of developing a marketing mix that appeals to them. In past years many marketers did this in an intuitive fashion, which sometimes relied heavily on actual experience in the product class. Some were notable successes with this formula, but many more were not.

As the size of firms and markets has increased, the dollar stakes for both failure and success have risen. Consumer research is now used heavily by marketers, especially at the major consumer goods firms. For example, the president of Lever Brothers reports,

> *Understanding . . . consumer behavior is our key to planning and managing in the ever-changing environment.*

To learn more about consumer behavior, Lever Brothers' researchers talk to 4000 consumers *every week,* seeking their views of products, new ideas, and trends in their styles of living.[14]

Scans Make Fans

Universal Product Code scanning systems have revolutionized the world of consumer research. For operations, these computer systems offer stores easy price changes and strong inventory control. Beyond this, since the systems instantly record consumer purchases, they can provide incredibly valuable information for retailers. "Direct product profits" are now calculated to measure exactly how much each item in the store is contributing: results are used to drop products quickly, to shift shelf space (facings), and to demand higher "slotting fees" from manufacturers for the shelf space.

Further, both manufacturers and retailers face new research horizons with this information. It is now possible to quickly know how displays, coupons, and ads affect sales, how sale prices affect consumers, and so forth. Special research services such as Infoscan offer even further insights, by arranging to measure exactly which consumers are buying what. They do this by having a sample of households use special credit cards in cooperating stores, so that personal information about the purchaser can be combined with actual purchase patterns. As one example, this information was credited with saving Ocean Spray's Mauna Lai guava juice when it had initially sold poorly, since the firm discovered that the customers who were buying the product were a narrower segment than had been assumed. Similarly, as another rescued product's manager reports: "We expected some problems with trial, but not what we wound up getting. We would never have been able to react in time without scanning data . . . we live and die with household panel data."[15]

COMPARING MARKETERS' AND CONSUMERS' VIEWS

How Marketers View Consumer Behavior

The 4 P's and 5 C's provide a realistic look into ways in which consumer behavior is important to marketing managers. Continuing with this view, we'll now take a closer look at the nature of the marketing perspective on consumer behavior. This perspective has several key characteristics. These characteristics follow naturally from the tasks that a marketing manager is charged with undertaking. The five key characteristics are

- An *external* view of consumers.
- An *aggregate* or *market* point of view.
- A *product-specific* point of view.
- A *brand preference/purchase* point of view.
- A *behavioral influence* orientation.

The marketer's view is naturally an *external* one, for example, since marketers are necessarily selling to other persons (each consumer, conversely, will take an internal view of his or her own purchasing behaviors). And, because economics and volume are important, and the market itself is huge, the manager is virtually forced to adopt an *aggregate* view that stresses the *market* as an entity rather than focusing on each consumer as an individual.

The *product-specific* nature of the marketing perspective again is a natural phenomenon. For example, marketers of cosmetics will naturally be most interested in consumers' behavior toward cosmetics and related products, not in consumer behavior in general. They will therefore stress *some* different aspects of consumer behavior than would marketers of automobiles or sports equipment. Some types of questions will be the same, of course, but when we arrive at the day-to-day work level, the specific consumer behaviors, purchase data, and reasoning all have to be *customized* for the cosmetic product.

Similar reasoning applies to the *brand-specific* nature of the perspective. Marketing managers place great stress on the specific brand choices that consumers are making within the product category. Brand switches are not insignificant: a 1 percent change in the market share of Tide or Folgers is worth from $20 million to $30 million in large consumer product classes such as detergents and coffee.

A final key characteristic of the marketing perspective is that it stresses the process of *behavioral influence,* as marketers strive to increase sales. A good marketing manager recognizes that there are basically three types of consumers in the marketplace:

- Persons who now use his or her brand.
- Persons who now use other competing brands.
- Persons who do not use the product at all.

Strategically, then, the marketer can decide to focus the mix on

- Keeping current users of the brand, while increasing their usage level.
- Switching current users of other brands to his or her brand.
- Creating new users of the product *and* getting them to buy the right brand.

Regardless of which strategy is chosen (and it may not be easy to decide), it is obvious that the marketer is heavily involved in trying to *influence* consumers to behave in a particular way, that is, to purchase and use the right brand.

How Consumers View Consumer Behavior

At this point, we'll want to shift our mental gears consciously and begin to adopt the **consumer's perspective** on consumer behavior. This will allow us to *compare* the two perspectives and gain insights into this field of study. Let's begin by reviewing a few basic points.

First, as consumers, we approach the marketplace with purposes in mind and a willingness to trade money to accomplish our purposes. Marketers offer products that will help us to achieve our goals, with the hope of receiving our consumer dollars. When a positive *transaction* occurs between marketer and consumer, both sides are better off then they were before the purchase was made. Thus *there are clear points of common interest* for the marketer and the consumer. However, in terms of perspective, things look very different from the consumer's position. While the marketer is interested in *selling,* the consumer is interested in *buying.*

As technology has developed, the producer-consumer relationship has grown to be increasingly impersonal and distant. Only in the case of very small manufacturers or individual service providers (e.g., a photographer, a dentist, a mechanic) does the consumer actually come into contact on a person-to-person basis with the creator of the product or service. The point is that we, as typical consumers, often do not "know" the marketer very well, nor do we think very much about the marketer's goals or programs. As we'll see in the next section, this leads to several interesting conclusions.

Contrasts Between the Two Perspectives

What are the impacts of the differences between the consumer and marketer perspectives? These are summarized in Table 2-1, which contrasts the two views on exactly the same dimensions used to characterize the marketing perspective.

External Versus Internal Views

The distinction between **external versus internal views** relates to the degree to which consumer behavior is viewed from within, or outside of, the consumer decision maker. Although we may not normally think of our own behaviors in precisely this way, it is clear that, as consumers, most of our behaviors are *internally* focused and driven. That is, we tend to think silently, observe privately, and evaluate according to our own personal dictates. (There are, of course, many cases in which external factors—salesperson, friends, or family—can influence our behavior. Even here, however, we maintain an internal view of our own decision.)

Marketers, because they are different people playing a different role, must necessarily take an *external* view of consumers' behaviors. To get a better idea of what this means, think about the times that you have simply observed other

TABLE 2-1 COMPARING THE TWO PERSPECTIVES

Characteristic	*Marketer's Perspective*		*Consumer's Perspective*
A. Point of view	External ("buyers")	vs.	Internal ("me")
B. Level of interest	Aggregate ("market")	vs.	Individual ("myself")
C. Scope of interest	Product specific ("what I make")	vs.	Across products ("what I buy")
D. "Correct" choice	Brand specific ("my brand")	vs.	Best alternative ("best brand for me")
E. Role of influence	Influence behavior	vs.	Handle behavioral influence

consumers as they were shopping in a store. In these instances, you were taking an external view.

One important implication of the external view is that it doesn't allow much insight into the underlying reasons for consumer behavior. To gain such insight about others, we need to rely upon *concepts* of consumer behavior and *research* that somehow can obtain consumer's internal views from them. Even these assists can't fully tap the richness of each individual's internal perspectives, but they go a long way toward overcoming the inherent shortcomings of the external view. This is the major reason that marketers use consumer research.

Aggregate Versus Individual-Level Views

The contrast inherent in **aggregate versus individual-level views** is closely related to the previous distinction, in that our focus on our own internal needs, desires, and plans brings with it a necessary focus on ourselves as *individual* consumers. (For our purposes here, shared decisions within a household will be treated as individual-level decisions.)

As noted earlier, marketers don't have the luxury of being able to view their markets at the individual person or household level. There are *so many* consumers that they need to be viewed together somehow if a marketer is to have any chance of comprehending that market. This is why marketers view market segmentation to be so important (in contrast, most consumers have never even heard of this term!). Market segmentation attempts to find submarkets within the total market that are (1) large enough to be important but that also (2) buy differently and (3) have characteristics that make each segment in effect a separate market. There are many ways marketers can form segments: we'll be examining the topic of market segmentation in Chapter 4.

Turning to consumers again, notice that much of the time we really don't think in terms of a market at all, so individualized is our perspective. Even though our thoughts may sometimes include the popularity of a brand, rarely do they involve an analysis of how many persons in total are in the market, what prices they are paying, and so forth.

Product-Specific Versus Across-Product Views

Whereas the marketer will tend to *specialize* in only certain categories of products or services, the consumer cannot afford to do this. Consumers need to purchase items from *all* important product and service categories. Because of this characteristic, consumers deal with many different marketers for many types of products and services. In fact, if it were not the case that supermarkets and large retailers bring together offerings from numerous manufacturers, the enormous breadth of our consumer interactions with marketers would be even more apparent to us.

The key outcome from this **product-specific versus across-product orientation** is that, as consumers, we *cannot* afford to view our world in a product-specific manner. This has a very important implication—it means that we will not be very expert for many of our purchases. The time and effort it will take us to learn about them can be costly to us. This can also lead to consumers making mistakes such as buying the wrong quality levels, paying too much, or selecting products that don't suit their actual set of needs. Each marketer, on the other hand, *is* expert on his or her brand and product category, and in fact spends most of his or her professional time working on it. However, a product-specific focus can lead a marketer to overlook the purchase allocation needs of consumers.

Brand-Specific Versus "Best Alternative" Views

The **brand-specific versus "best alternative"** distinction makes an interesting point with major implications for marketers. From a marketer's point of view, the best brand for a particular consumer should be the brand that he or she is offering to the consumer. That is, the "right" behavior is the purchase of "my" brand, whatever that may be. A consumer, on the other hand, does not enter the purchase process with such a clear-cut answer as to the best choice. Our interest is usually in obtaining the best alternative for us, regardless of which brand it is, or who happens to make it. We are usually confronted with a number of competing brands, each of which is marketed as if it is the best choice for us. *The fact that we are going to choose only one brand from that set thus means that we will be making the "wrong" choice from the point of view of every marketer but one!* As marketers, therefore, we need to take care not to simply assume that our interest is the same as the consumer's interest: we need to work hard to ensure that there is a match.

While the basic interests of marketers and consumers thus do not always match at this level, there are some roles that brand names do play on behalf of both marketers and consumers. They serve as handy identification tags, allowing the consumer to understand what a particular alternative will be like (if the consumer has had previous experience with that brand). Knowing that a can of soft drink is Coca-Cola, for example, tells us a lot about what the product inside it will be, how it will appear when we open the can, how it will taste, and so on. If the quality control is good, moreover, an established brand name acts as a type of guarantee that we can count on the product performing or tasting exactly as we've learned to expect. Imagine, how shocked we'd be if a Coke came out tasting like root beer!

Thus branding allows consumers to save significant amounts of time and energy in making choices. We can rely on our past experience, as well as on things we may have heard about the brand from friends who have tried it. Over the longer run, we can develop easy decision rules as to whether or not we would even consider buying a brand. Marketers—knowing that there can be severe penalties to future brand sales following a bad consumer experience—work to develop a consistently positive offering before they place a brand name on it and take it to the market. In a broad sense, then, brand names help the quality and consistency of a product offering to consumers. Their prices in turn tend to reflect this.

Influencing Behavior Versus Handling Behavioral Influence

The last dimension—**influencing behavior versus handling behavioral influence**—is an especially interesting distinction that we'll examine at some length. As noted earlier, each marketing manager's role is to influence consumers to feel favorably toward and buy his or her brand on a regular basis. At any one time, then, we would see marketing managers for Budweiser, Burger King, Ford, Sears, *Newsweek,* and so forth, all attempting to influence consumer behaviors for their particular product classes.

Consumers' Handling of the Sheer Number of Influence Attempts   How do we, as consumers, react to this continuous array of persuasive stimuli from the marketing system? First let's consider the fact that *it takes some time and some effort for us to react at all.* That is, we usually have to make an effort to talk with a salesperson, read an ad, or attend to a TV commercial.

Marketers are, of course, aware of this, and try to design their stimuli to be interesting and to require as little extra effort on the consumer's part as is reasonable. Nonetheless, the enormous number of marketing stimuli that are competing for our attention means that we consumers *must adapt* somehow. We simply cannot afford the time and effort that would be needed to deal fully with each of the influence attempts of every marketer every time that one appears.

What do we do, then? Basically, *we simply ignore most marketing stimuli* most of the time. For confirmation, take this little test—go through today's or yesterday's newspaper and look carefully at each advertisement. How many did you notice when you read the paper the first time? Did you even read that section of the paper the first time? How long would it take you to read and consider carefully all the ads? For what percentage of the products being advertised do you even have an interest?

Sometimes, of course, it is difficult to ignore *entirely* a particular stimulus. Examples of these **intrusive stimuli** (so-called because they intrude upon our attention) include TV commercials, checkout displays in supermarkets, and so on. When our attention is captured in this way, however, we consumers have developed another means to retain control of our time and effort—we often *don't pay very much attention* to the stimulus. That is, we don't think much about it, and we don't watch it all the way to its conclusion.

Marketer's Reactions to Consumers' Low Level of Attention   Thus far our discussion has centered on the sheer quantity of marketing stimuli. Consumers cannot possibly devote their attention to all these stimuli because (1) we have other interests and activities that are more important in our day-to-day living, (2) we are not even interested in some of the products that are being offered to us, and (3) even if we wished to, it would take a high level of effort to process all of the marketing stimuli with which the system is confronting us. Thus consumers have *had* to adapt to deal with the high level of stimuli from the marketing system.

As might be expected, these consumer adjustments to the quantity of marketing stimuli cause *severe problems* for each marketing manager attempting to influence behavior. Thus marketers have had to refine their programs to overcome some of these problems. Examples of marketing mix refinements include

■ Targeting segments of consumers who are most interested.

■ Repeating ads so that consumers may "get the message" the third or fourth time they're exposed.

■ Creating stimuli that are intrinsically interesting for consumers, even though they may not provide a "hard-sell" message for the brand.

■ Ensuring that the stimuli are simple and easy for consumers to handle mentally.

The Marketing System's Recommendations

In addition to the basic issue of consumer attention, there is the equally serious question: "How *should* a consumer deal with influence attempts, assuming that he or she is interested and is willing to pay attention?" To address this issue, we need to consider what the marketing system is in fact telling consumers.

Figure 2-1 diagrams the essentials of this issue. Notice how clear and straightforward this situation appears on the left side, reflecting an individual marketer's (Budweiser's) perspective. We must recall, however, that the "system" really consists of millions of individual marketers, each providing his or her own influence attempts. This is depicted on the right side, reflecting an individual consumer's perspective. Since the marketers are competing for consumers' time, attention, and money, there is *much inherent conflict* within the marketing system, a point to which we'll return shortly. Even so, however, the system as a whole is consistently presenting the consumer with three *general types of recommendations:*

■ Consumers should buy and use products and services.

■ Consumers should buy often.

■ Consumers should buy brands (i.e., the specific alternative choice is important).

For this reason, we sometimes hear social philosophers—ranging from communists to clergymen—describing the Western nations as **consumerist economies**, in which the pursuit of material goods can become so strong that people may give up some personal and social virtues (sharing, family time, volunteering) in a drive for more income and more consumption (the appendix to Chapter 11 discusses this further).

In addition, though not fully depicted in Figure 2-1, the marketing system presents consumers with *brand-competitive influence attempts*. Although Budweiser is the only beer shown in the figure, it is clearly *not* the only beer that is striving for consumer influence—Miller, Molson, Pabst, Michelob, Stroh's, Coors,

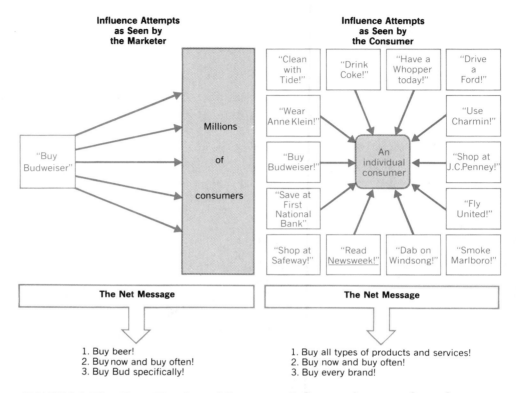

FIGURE 2-1 **The Huge Number of Consumer Influence Attempts from the Marketing System**

Olympia, Rolling Rock, Schmidt's, Iron City, Corona, St. Pauli Girl, and many others are all sending consumers numerous stimuli for their brand. Thus the myriad *brand-specific recommendations* add a multiplicative factor to the messages coming from the marketing system.

Conclusion 1: Consumers Cannot Follow the Marketing System's Consumption Allocation Recommendations

The beer example is a good one to illustrate our first basic conclusion in this discussion: consumers *cannot follow* the set of general recommendations from the marketing system. This is because the total set of recommendations from the marketing system simply *proposes too much consumption*.

Each of us has a limited income, as well as a limited (if large) set of desires and a limited time available to satisfy those desires. We are unable to purchase all the products that are recommended to us through the marketing system. As an example, imagine the person who would purchase and consume a bottle of beer each time that he or she came into contact with a marketing influence attempt. Moreover, since the system doesn't constrain itself to beer as the only appropriate liquid to consume—milk, soft drinks, bottled water, liquor, fruit juices, coffee, tea, and so on are also heavily promoted for purchase and consumption— it is clear that consumers *cannot depend on the marketing system to tell us how to allocate our spending.* As consumers, we *can* rely on the marketing system as a good source of ideas on what we might buy, and to provide us with useful information about positive aspects of the alternatives. We *cannot,* however, rely on it as a guide for what *not* to buy or for suggesting which overall mix of purchases would be best for us.

Conclusion 2: Consumers Cannot Follow All the Brand Recommendations Either

Beyond this, there is another—and perhaps even more serious—problem for consumers, one that arises from the brand-competitive nature of the marketing system. For this discussion we will need to work briefly with Figure 2-2.

Creating the Brand Environment for Toothpaste

All products and services can be described in terms of some number of characteristics (technically termed **attributes**) that they possess. Attributes deliver the benefits that we are seeking from the product. Important attributes of toothpaste, for example, might include cleaning ability, decay prevention, taste, breath freshening, whitening power, and value for the money. These attributes are shown in the table within Figure 2-2.

To complete the example, first fill in some familiar brand names across the top columns of the matrix. Now, adopt the perspective of a marketing manager for each brand in turn, beginning with Crest. As brand manager for Crest, your task is to fill in the cells of the

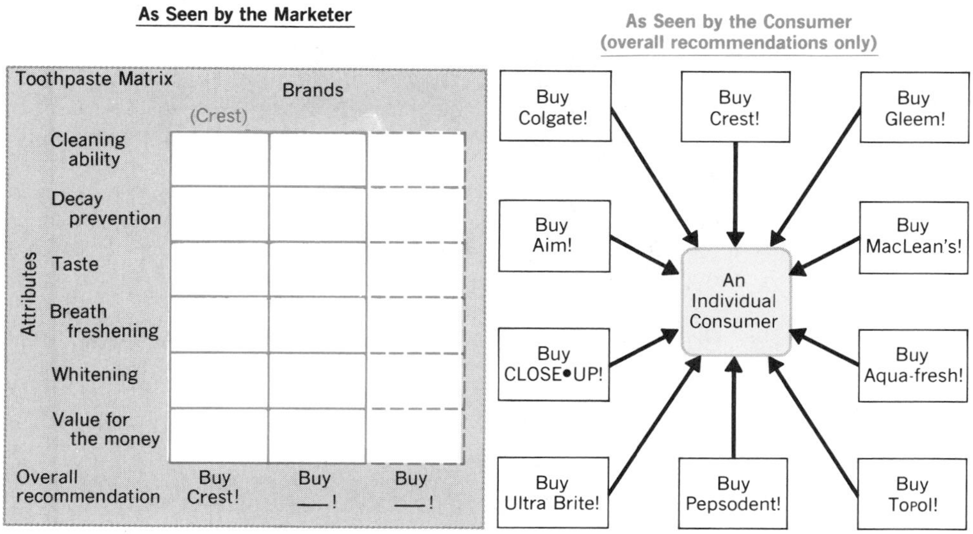

FIGURE 2-2 **The Nature of Marketing System Recommendations (Within a Product Category)**

table with the information about Crest that you would like to provide to consumers to maximize your sales and profits. You should enter a desired marketing rating for each attribute. A scale of "very bad," "mediocre," and "very good" can be used for this purpose. As the brand manager for Crest, what rating would you like to give on each of the attributes? Please enter them in the appropriate boxes.

Next, change your job and now assume that you are the brand manager for whichever brand you listed next in the table. As the marketing manger for this brand, what ratings would you like it to have for each attribute? Enter these ratings in the appropriate boxes. Next, change your job again and take over the management of the third toothpaste brand listed. Drawing on your extensive industry experience at this point, again enter the ratings you'd like to provide consumers so that they'll choose your brand.

When you have finished the entire table, go back and see if there are any scores that are unsatisfactory. If there are, what managerial actions should you take? Now assume that you are creating an ad for your brand. How likely would you be to feature any unsatisfactory score in your campaign? Would you even be likely to mention it? Most marketers naturally would not, but would concentrate their influence attempts on the strongest features of their brands. Notice, in fact, the natural impulse toward wanting to say only positive things about your brand, even when there may be some negative elements to it.

Consumers' Reactions to the Brand Stimuli

Completion of the brand table represents the development of our "marketing stimulus environment" aimed at consumers. Now let's switch roles and adopt the consumer's perspective. Assume that you're interested in buying toothpaste and you don't happen to know very much about the brands available. What would we learn from the marketing system's stimuli? Basically, that *every brand is good* (if we had allowed superlatives in our exercise, these would surely appear liberally).

Now let's assume that we need to make a choice—which one brand should we pick from all the brands available? Which is clearly the best brand for us? Notice that some of the information from the marketing stimuli will prove to be helpful to us, especially if the product class is differentiated enough that the brands are clearly distinguished in terms of features, price levels, and quality levels. Also, we'll learn about different product forms (gels, pastes, etc.), packages (pumps, tubes), and promotional prices and premiums that are available. Thus a consumer will be able to learn some things about the brand matrix as he or she gains experience in a product class.

Notice, however, that the matrix of marketing stimuli that we've developed does *not* itself provide us with the answer to our brand choice problem—each of the brands available is attempting to influence us to accept that brand as the best one for purchase. Since we cannot purchase all of them, we are going to have to make our choice on some other basis than the system's recommendations alone. In terms of the initial topic for this section, therefore, our second basic conclusion is: brand influence attempts from the marketing system are as a set *inherently inconsistent* with a consumer's need to choose one specific alternative for purchase.

Implications of Consumer's Reactions to Marketer Recommendations

Alert readers will recognize that the intent of the foregoing discussion was not to paint marketers as evil, or to suggest that their influence attempts are not often helpful sources of information to many consumers. Instead, our analysis explains why consumers exhibit different types of skepticism about marketing efforts. Such skepticism represents an entirely necessary *adaptation* on the part of the consumer. For individual marketers, therefore, *consumers' resistance to persuasion attempts makes success that much harder to achieve.* It heightens the importance of practicing the marketing concept and using consumer behavior knowledge in an intelligent way.

As we might expect, the realities of consumer reactions to the nature of the marketing system's recommendations are fairly complex and subtle. They range from the ways we gain information about products to strategies we develop to reduce our risks and minimize our time spent in shopping around. Future chapters will discuss these topics. It is also the case, however, that more research is needed. If you are interested, you may wish to turn to Appendix 2A, which presents a brief discussion of future research needs in this area.

At this point, however, we need to delve into a second, different implication that comes from the nature of our marketing system. This implication is that consumers need to do *more* than simply handle influence attempts well. Consumers also need to *develop their own abilities* to make good consumer decisions. In other words, consumers need to act, as well as react, in their own self-interests.

ON BEING A WISE CONSUMER

What does it take to be a wise consumer? What kinds of skills do we need to possess? What storehouse of knowledge should we have available in our heads, to draw upon when needed?

All of us have at least a rough idea of the types of knowledge and skills needed to be a "wise" consumer. As we'll see shortly, though, it is surprising to discover how many topics there are in this area. There is, in fact, so much material that we will be unable to cover it adequately within this book. In this section of the chapter, we'll strive to gain an overall sense for the scope of the issues.

How Skilled Are We?

What is involved in being a "good" consumer? "How good a consumer am I?" When we begin to think seriously about these questions, we can begin to see just how complex this area will become. Several years ago a team of professors of consumer economics administered a Test of Consumer Competency to over 4000 prospective teachers of consumer education courses at the grade school and high school level. There were 55 questions on the test. What was the average score of these prospective educators? Just over 32 items correct, or a percentage of under 60 percent! Which areas were strong and which were weak? These teachers knew relatively more about recreation, clothing, and household furnishings and appliances, which all had average scores over 68 percent. The worst areas were in savings and investment, food, and taxes, all with scores less than 50 percent.[16]

Why Are Skill Levels So Low?

Some good explanations are immediately available as to why most consumers reveal a low level of knowledge on tests of consumer skills. Part of the reason is simply that we *do not purchase* some product areas at all and purchase others only on a very infrequent basis. In these cases it may be much more efficient for us to *learn what we need to know at the time we need to know it* and not to worry about it before then. (We will be addressing this possibility in Chapter 18.)

In taking these tests, however, many consumers discover that there are a number of topics in which they seem to have *little interest* (as well as having little knowledge about them). This reaction might stem from different stages in one's life—many readers have yet to make some of the major consumer purchases personally (such as housing, large appliances, and insurance) or dealt much with investment planning or heavy taxes. Before too long, however, most readers will be active in these areas as well. **Life-cycle stages** are only a partial answer, however. It is also important that we admit the possibility that much of the material inherent in wise consumer behavior really just *isn't very interesting to most consumers!*

Economics Is Important

In part the surprisingly low interest level in wise consumership seems to be due to consumer behavior's clear economic underpinnings. Significant amounts of money are sometimes at stake, there are sometimes sizable risks associated with decisions that we make, and at times our funds might not stretch as far as we'd like them to. Therefore, there can be considerable *stress* associated with consumer behavior and a clear need for "rational" (as opposed to pleasurable) decision making.

Let's consider briefly the five areas that serve as *background* for most consumer behavior:

- Money management and budgeting.
- Consumer protection.
- Resource allocation and timing.
- Planning for the future.
- Financial decisions (credit, savings, investments, taxes).

Notice that none of the foregoing issues would be considered "fun" by most of us. It is also interesting to note that the marketing system doesn't attempt to help us in these areas (except in that financial services are available for consumers to purchase). Mastering any of the areas requires much work, and managing our affairs well is a never-ending task. Another factor is that no one (other than possibly family members) monitors our personal behaviors on these topics, and it is easy to let them slide. For all these reasons, it is not surprising that many consumers are not very expert, or even conscientious, in these aspects of their own consumer behaviors.

The Major Spending Categories

Beyond the background underpinnings just listed, consumers must make numerous decisions with respect to specific purchases. Almost all money spent by consumers falls into the categories shown in Table 2-2. Notice that the table compares the spending patterns of two extreme groups in our society: those 20 percent within the highest incomes and those 20 percent with the lowest incomes. As we'd expect, high-income households spend much more—almost four times as much as in total—than the low-income group. This is true across the board: in every category high-income consumers spend more dollars. As Table 2-2 shows, however, the *percentage* each group spends does differ somewhat. Low-income consumers spend over half of their dollars on food and shelter, for example, whereas those with higher incomes spend only 40 percent of their dollars for these goods, but substantially more on insurance and pension savings.

If we now shift our focus in Table 2-2 away from group differences we can also detect clear differences in the *nature* of the spending. Some of the categories (food, for example) are purchased and repurchased on a *frequent* basis. They tend to be consumed rather quickly and tend to have lower prices associated with them. Other categories are purchased quite infrequently and usually have higher

TABLE 2-2 HOW CONSUMERS SPEND, BY INCOME LEVEL (MID-1980s)

	Income Group		
	Lowest 20%	*Highest 20%*	*Direction of Percent Change as Income Increases*
Average yearly expenditures	$11,000	$42,000	—
Percentage of spending on			
Housing	34%	28%	Decreases
Transportation	17	20	Increases
Food	19	13	Decreases
Insurance and pensions	4	13	Increases
Clothing	5	6	About constant
Entertainment	4	6	Increases
Health care	7	3	Decreases
Other	11	12	About constant

Source: Adapted from *Sales & Marketing Management*, December 1987, p. 25.

prices associated with them. Once purchased, however, they are "consumed" on a *continuous* basis. Thus the consumer faces very different types of consumption decisions even within the most common list of purchases. This means that product-specific knowledge is a key toward making good consumer decisions. If you are interested in reading more about this, consumer economics texts provide a good starting point, as do publications such as *Consumer Reports* magazine.

SUMMARY

Marketing Decisions and Consumer Behavior

The chapter introduced the importance of *perspectives* used to view the field of consumer behavior. *Marketers* and *consumers* are the two major groups who engage in day-to-day activities in the marketplace. Each has a unique perspective on consumer behavior. A third important party is the *public policymaker,* who takes a broader view concerned with the marketplace and how it is operating.

Marketing decisions are summarized in the marketing mix. The 4 P's—product, price, place, and promotion—reflect the areas of controllable marketing decisions. The 5 C's reflect the largely uncontrollable constraints. *Competitors* will work to overcome our 4 P efforts. The strengths and weaknesses of the *company* create an important constraint on realistic marketing decisions. The *channels* constraint reflects that wholesalers and retailers are independent businesses, each looking out for their own best interests. Marketing programs are sometimes strongly affected by the *conditions* constraint, which reflects primarily economic events. Finally, the *customer* constraint represents the the persons who will ultimately decide whether or not to purchase the offerings of the firm. Examples of each factor were included in these discussions.

Comparing Marketers' and Consumers' Views

In this section of the chapter the consumer's perspective was contrasted to the marketer's perspective along five specific dimensions. The marketer's perspective is (1) *external,* (2) *aggregate,* and (3) *product specific,* whereas the consumer's perspective is (1) *internal,* (2) *individual,* and (3) *extends across many products.* Further, the marketer has a (4) *specific brand* to sell and (5) *exerts influence* to do so. The consumer, however, is looking to buy (4) the *best alternative,* and (5) must *handle influence* attempts to do so. Thus we saw how the overall marketing system advances three general recommendations to consumers:

- Consumers should buy and use products and services.
- Consumers should buy often.
- The alternative chosen is important.

In considering these issues further, we discussed why marketers' recommendations cannot simply be adopted and followed by consumers. Essentially, this is due to the fact that *consumers' needs and marketers' needs are often inconsistent.* It is this inconsistency that leads to much of the consumer resistance to persuasion that makes a marketer's job that much harder. This also means that *consumers need to develop their own abilities to be wise consumers* and to make good decisions in the marketplace.

On Being a Wise Consumer

In the closing section of the chapter we discussed the fact that even teachers of consumer education courses didn't score well on a test of consumer competencies (under 60 percent) and that in general consumers seem to have low skill levels. We then briefly examined the role of economics in consumer behavior and the major spending categories in which consumers buy (housing, transportation, and food lead the list). In addition to the chapter's coverage, you may wish to consider either the discussion of future research needs (Appendix 2A) or applying your marketing management skills to solving the "It Wasn't All Gravy" Case on the opening page of this chapter (our Review Questions and Experiential Exercises section contains some guidance for attacking this case).

KEY TERMS

perspective	channels
marketing perspective	conditions
marketing mix	customers
controllable factors	consumer's perspective
4 P's	external versus internal view
product	aggregate versus individual view
price	product-specific versus across-products view
promotion	brand-specific versus best alternative view
place	influencing versus handling influence view
uncontrollable factors	intrusive stimuli
5 C's	consumerist economies
competitors	attributes
company	life-cycle stages

REVIEW QUESTIONS AND EXPERIENTIAL EXERCISES

[E = Application extension or experiential exercise]

1. Briefly discuss why perspective is important in viewing any field of knowledge. How would this apply to consumer behavior?

2. Describe the purpose and dimensions of the 4 P and 5 C frameworks. Use an actual brand for examples of each dimension.

3. For each of the following examples from the chapter, indicate the 4P/5C dimension it represented, and whether success or failure was an issue.
   - a. Team Taurus
   - b. Holly Farms
   - c. Soloflex
   - d. California Raisins
   - e. *USA Today*
   - f. Motor home dealers
   - g. Procter & Gamble

4. Describe the nature of the trends associated with each of the following. Which 4P/5C dimension is represented?
   - a. Number of auto models
   - b. UPC scanner systems

5. How does the consumer's perspective of the marketplace differ from the marketer's perspective? Be specific.

[E] 6. Assume you are hired as marketing manager for Bud Light. What are some behavioral influence strategies you might consider using? Which ones do you think would be most effective? Why?

[E] 7. Write a brief report expressing your personal opinions on how marketers view consumers. If you have work experience in marketing, use this as your basis. If you don't have work experience in this field, do a short interview with a salesperson or marketer as your basis.

[E] 8. How do consumers handle the huge number of informational messages and influence attempts emanating from the marketing system? Observe your own consumer reactions to the marketing system as described in this chapter. On which strategies do you rely most often?

[E] 9. Choose a product or service for which you feel you have a special level of expertise or insight as a consumer (whether through your own experience or your hobbies and interests). Write a brief report covering:

   > Several common mistakes you feel many consumers make when buying this product or service.

   > Three tips that would help consumers buy this good more wisely.

[E] 10. What are the major categories for consumer spending? How does your household's (or personal) spending deviate from the averages shown in Table 2-2? Why do you feel these differences exist?

[E] **11.** Conduct one or two personal interviews with a real estate agent, concentrating on the common mistakes that consumers are likely to make when buying a home. Summarize your findings.

[E] **12.** Think about the consumer behavior patterns exhibited by one of your relatives and two of your close friends. In which areas do they seem to have high levels of expertise? In which areas do they appear to lack consumer strengths? Write a brief report summarizing your findings (an interesting follow-up to this exercise is to talk with them afterwards to gain their own impressions and ask whether or not they desire to change).

[E] **13.** Seek out one or more sources of consumer assistance, such as *Consumer Reports Magazine* or a consumer economics textbook in your library. Spend a half hour or more examining its design and contents. What seems to be the goal and target audience of this publication? How well do you believe it is achieving this goal?

[CASE] **14.** Read "It Wasn't All Gravy" again on the first page of this chapter. To gain experience in analyzing this live marketing case, prepare answers for each of the following questions:

a. Evaluate the 5 C's in this situation.
   (1.) Although not much information has been provided, which of the 5 C's do you think were likely to have been favorable for the success of this product? Which were likely to pose roadblocks?
   (2.) Concentrating on the "customer" constraint, what issues in consumer behavior would you suggest are most important for Standard Brands to consider? (You may wish to use the Seven Keys from Chapter 1 to help with this question.)

b. Consider the 4 P decisions that were reported. In each instance, discuss your estimates of consumers' reactions and, if you feel the decision could be improved, provide your suggested improvements:
   (1.) *Product form:* a refrigerated gravy bar.
   (2.) *Product form:* the flavors offered.
   (3.) *Product name:* Smooth & Easy. (Should the company have used its Blue Bonnet name to help this new product along?)
   (4.) *Price:* 69 cents per bar.
   (5.) *Place:* Dairy cases in supermarkets.

c. Assume now that you are a rising young marketing executive with Standard Brands. You are called in and are offered the option of taking over the brand management of Smooth & Easy. Assuming no pressure to accept (that is, your career will proceed normally if you decline this position), would you accept the job? Why or why not? If so, what marketing mix would you use to turn this brand around, and what arguments would you use to justify further marketing expenditures on this brand?

APPENDIX 2A   *RESEARCH IMPLICATIONS FOR THE FUTURE OF CONSUMER BEHAVIOR*

Our analysis of the consumer's perspective has raised a number of interesting issues. While some consumer researchers have recognized some of these elements as being significant, surprisingly little formal research has been directed toward many of the points we have been discussing in this chapter. As noted in Chapter 1, consumer research is a relatively young field, and researchers have largely employed the marketing perspective in their research to date. We saw within the present chapter, however, how adopting the consumer's perspective can be a useful way to gain insights to complement those arising from the marketing perspective. In the future, therefore, we might expect to see new research arising from this viewpoint. For example, the following topics all appear to be significant and to deserve further attention from researchers in consumer behavior:

- *The marketing system's impacts.* Here the interest would be on the nature of marketing stimuli as an *entire system* affecting consumer behavior. That is, research can also study how consumers are responding to the total set of stimuli they are receiving. For example, "How do consumers handle the conflicting purchase recommendations they receive from the marketing system as a whole?" "How should consumers be handling these stimuli?" Although the text suggested some answers, this topic has received surprisingly little formal research attention to date.
- *Low-involvement consumer behavior.* How does consumer behavior occur when consumers become used to ignoring stimuli and otherwise not investing a great deal of effort in many of their decisions? Does it become less "rational"? This topic has received a great deal of attention recently; we'll be looking more closely at it in several later chapters of this text. Even so, there are still many interesting issues that have yet to be studied in this field. For example, "Could low involvement lead to less price sensitivity?" "Could this in turn be partially responsible for price inflation in the consumer sector of the economy?"
- *Consumer "ignorance."* Here we would examine how the low levels of consumer expertise could have serious financial or health and safety consequences. For example, "How bad are the decisions that consumers make when they are not very informed about an important product or service?" "What are the real risks that people run in today's American marketplace?"
- *Consumer allocations of time, energy, and money.* For example, "How do consumers go about allocating money across the range of spending, saving, and debt?
- *"Normative" approaches.* That is, what is the "right" way for consumers to behave to maximize their own self-interests? Economists have offered some guidance in this area, but much more study could be undertaken. For example, "What is the best *time* to buy particular products?" "What is the *best price*

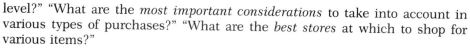

level?" "What are the *most important considerations* to take into account in various types of purchases?" "What are the *best stores* at which to shop for various items?"

- *Consumer education.* This topic is closely related to the normative issues just discussed. While many persons agree that consumer education is a good approach, we need to come to grips with such issues as the apparent low level of interest that many of us seem to hold for our own consumer knowledge and skill areas. For example, "Is this low level of interest in learning consumer knowledge and skills an accurate reflection of how consumers really feel?" "If so, is there much hope that consumer education can ever really succeed in this country?"

These are just a few of the basic kinds of questions raised by adopting the consumer perspective on consumer behavior. Although they are not directly concerned with how to market more effectively, it is clear that the answers to these questions will have important implications for the marketing community, as well as for consumers.

If you have an interest in pursuing further topics in this area, you may wish to consult an important recent book entitled *Research in the Consumer Interest: The Frontier* (Columbia, Mo: American Council on Consumer Interests, 1988), edited by E. Scott Maynes and the ACCI research committee. This book brings together academic, business, and government perspectives from around the world. It not only reviews major topics, but also provides rich commentaries and many suggestions.

CHAPTER

3

Aggregate Perspectives of Consumer Behavior: The Consumer Marketplace

---

The Facts Behind Pampers

Pampers disposable diapers are considered by many marketing experts to be the greatest new product success in recent marketing history. The idea for the disposable diaper was generated in the 1960s when a man was babysitting for his first grandchild: "There has to be a better way!" he thought, as he kept changing soggy and soiled cloth diapers. It happened that this man was an engineer at Procter & Gamble, a firm that had considerable experience producing absorbent paper products such as paper towels. He felt the possibility of disposable paper diapers would be of interest to the firm.

The idea did capture P & G's interest, but management first had to develop a preliminary estimate of potential market size. What were the major determinants of potential market size? Management decided that the number of U.S. diaper changes per year would be a good starting point. One way to estimate this would involve the following steps:

1. Take the number of babies in diaper-using age groups.
2. Multiply this by the number of days in a year (this yields a "total diaper-days" figure).
3. Multiply by the average number of diapers used per day.

Try this yourself (using rough estimates, such as 3.5 million births per year), and see what you calculate as an approximate market size. Does this look large enough to continue with a new product? (If you're interested in seeing what P & G's more sophisticated approach found, see Note 1, listed at the end of the book under Chapter 3.)

■ ■ ■

MARKET SIZE—A KEY ISSUE

As the Pampers' story illustrates, the *number of potential consumers* for a particular product or service is a basic piece of information. Learning about the consumer market represents a first step for a host of managerial decisions, ranging from investments in plants, to hiring workers, to planning advertising campaigns. Thus beyond an estimate of market size, we will also want to know about:

- Market composition (*who* buys and who doesn't?).
- Market location (*where* are the buyers?).
- Market trends (*what* will the future bring?).

The **aggregate perspective** on consumer behavior stresses the markets that exist for consumer purchases. In this chapter we'll examine some of the most basic dimensions of the consumer marketplace. Our focus is on **demographics**, or the statistical study of human populations. We begin by analyzing our consumer population, how it is growing, and what this growth means. We then assess several key trends that will have major impacts on consumer behavior in the future. At the close of the chapter, we examine how marketers use demographic data in their decision making.

Population Information: Sources

The primary source of U.S. population data is the national census, conducted every 10 years. The census attempts to count every person in the country and to gather a few vital pieces of information about them. When all these pieces are assembled, an overall picture of society emerges.

The first census was conducted in 1790, during George Washington's presidency. A total of 3.9 million persons was counted at that time. Today, the Bureau of the Census is part of the U.S. Department of Commerce—a strong indication of just how vital population information is for the business community of our nation. Within a typical business, moreover, the *marketing* function has been the primary beneficiary of this type of information. Almost all the information we will examine in this chapter is based on the census. To keep up with this area, it is useful to know about *American Demographics,* a magazine aimed at a general audience, with brief, interesting articles about current trends on the topics we'll be discussing in this chapter. Another useful source is the *Statistical Abstract*

of the United States, published by the federal government. The Notes at the end of the book also provide useful specific readings.

Patterns of Growth

Past Patterns of Growth

The current U.S. population is approximately 250 million people. This number has been increasing at a rate of less than 1 percent a year, so that it is expected to reach almost 270 million by the year 2000.

Table 3-1 presents some key years and numbers that show the pattern of population growth in our history. Note, for example, that shortly after the Civil War, the United States was home to 50 million persons. This number increased by *50 percent,* to 75 million, in the next 20 years alone—an explosive rate of increase that was fueled by waves of immigrants from Europe coming to the industrializing new country. After 1900, the *rate* of population growth slowed somewhat, but was still very high due to immigration. In the 20 years following the turn of the century population increased by 40 percent. When the Great Depression of the 1930s hit, however, growth slowed substantially, and U.S. population grew only 7 percent in the decade (less than 10 million people). This trend continued during World War II, when young men were away in the service and young women were working to support production in the war effort.

When these men and women returned home, however, the pattern of personal lives changed sharply toward work, consumption, and family life. Population again grew rapidly, increasing by almost 55 million people in the 20 years fol-

TABLE 3-1 U.S. POPULATION TRENDS IN SELECTED YEARS, 1790–2010

	1790	1880	1900	1915	1950	1968	1990	2010
Millions of people	4	50	76	100	150	200	250	280

	Periods of Growth					
	1880–1900	1900–1920	1930–1940	1945–1965	1970–1990	1990–2010
Population change	+25 million	+30 million	+10 million	+55 million	+45 million	+30 million
Percentage change[a]	+50%	+40%	+7%	+40%	+20%	+12%

[a]Note that the 1930–1940 period represents only 10 years.

Source: Author's calculations based on data in the U.S. Department of Commerce, Bureau of the Census, *Statistical Abstract of the United States, 1988* (Washington, D.C.: U.S. Government Printing Office, 1988), and "2010," *American Demographics,* February 1989, p. 20.

lowing World War II (representing another almost 40 percent increase in U.S. population). Unlike earlier periods, when immigration provided the impetus, this period of growth was driven by births of millions of children and came to be known as the "baby boom era" (we'll be discussing its impacts shortly).

For the past 20 years, the total population increase has been only 20 percent, or an average of about 1 percent per year. Even though we have seen a large increase in absolute numbers (up 45 million people), this is still 10 million *fewer* people than were added to the country in the 20-year period from 1945 to 1965. What lies ahead? Projections for the next 20 years show even further slowing, with a gain of only 12 percent.

The Population in the Future

The abrupt shifts in growth trends we've seen over the past 100 years provides a sharp reminder that projecting future population growth can be complex. Given that we are discussing *millions* of people, moreover, the impact of over- or under-estimations can be severe! For this reason, many businesses and government agencies work with a combination of "high," "low," and "moderate" estimated populations for the future, rather than a single estimate, as we used in Table 3-1's projection for 1990.

What are the major factors in population growth? There are three: births, deaths, and immigration. Let's examine each factor briefly.

Factors Determining Population Growth

Birth Rate: Fertility

The birth rate—technically termed **fertility**—has long been the most significant factor for U.S. population growth. As indicated in Table 3-2 there are currently about 3.9 million babies born in the United States each year. We can see how the pattern of births parallels the recent overall population trends we've discussed. Note, for example, that by 1960, over 2 million more babies were being born each year than in 1933! This number declined sharply during the late 1960s and early 1970s and then began a slow rise during the 1980s. Even now, though, the number of births is still several hundred thousand lower than in the baby boom years, when the population was much smaller (by 50 million people).

Given the fact that our base population has been growing over the years, experts have had to develop more complex measures to study fertility trends. Table 3-2 shows data for one of these. A **fertility rate** represents the yearly number of births per 1000 women of child-bearing age. By accounting for size, the fertility rate improves our ability to compare across time periods. Notice, for example, that the 1975 fertility rate was only about half that of the 1960 rate.

These numbers document the sweeping social changes in our society. As you may know, recent birth rates have been substantially below the levels required for a **replacement rate** of zero population growth. This requirement is that 2100

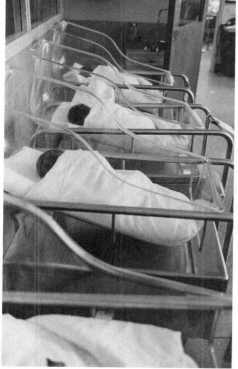

The major factors in U.S. population change: births, deaths, and immigration.

TABLE 3-2 U.S. FERTILITY TRENDS IN SELECTED YEARS, 1933–2000

	Births During Key Years of Each Period (millions)							
	Depression 1933	Prewar 1940	Baby Boom 1960	Vietnam 1968	The 1970s 1975	The 1980s 1980	1990 (est.)	2000 (est.)
Millions of births	2.1	2.6	4.3	3.5	3.1	3.6	3.9	3.5
Percentage difference[a]	—	+25%	+65%	−20%	−10%	+15%	+8%	−10%
Fertility rate[b]	75	80	120	85	65	70	65	60

[a]Percentage difference comparison is against previous listed year. For example, 1940's births were 25 percent greater than 1933's births.

[b]Number of births per year per thousand women who were of child-bearing ages (15 to 44 years old) that year.

Source: See Note 2.

children be born, on average, to every 1000 females of child-bearing age. Unless the birth rate increases above its levels of the past 10 years, there will be a long-term population *decrease* in this nation. Three factors underlying the lower fertility rates during the past 20 years are

- Increased access to birth control methods.
- Rising costs of raising a family.
- Changing roles of women.

These three key factors are also likely to determine population in the future. What will our population be in 2000, 2010, and so on? Notice that Table 3-2 predicts a decreasing number of births during the 1990s and an all-time low fertility rate by the year 2000. Can this be right?

Death Rate: Mortality

Mortality is the technical term referring to death. Mortality statistics for the United States show about 2 million deaths per year. This number has been fairly constant for some time and should tend toward only a slight increase in the foreseeable future. The constant total, however, has resulted from two offsetting trends that have tended to balance out each other's effects: the U.S. *death rate* has been *decreasing*, while the U.S. *population* has been *increasing*.

The decreasing death rate stems primarily from declining rates of heart disease and improvements in infant mortality rates. As you may know, we have seen sharp increases in **life expectancy** during recent years. Between 1970 and 1990, for example, the average American's life expectancy went up by six years, a remarkable jump! This trend is likely to continue during the 1990s, leading to a three-year increase by 2000, when the average American born that year should expect to live about 79 years. (However, there are differences hidden by this overall figure. For example, the 1990 life expectancy for men is about 72 years, whereas women expect to live *nine years longer,* on average.)[3]

Immigration

The third factor affecting total population growth is **net immigration**, which reflects people either moving into or out of a country. Although immigration was an extremely important factor in building America, it no longer plays as significant a role as do birth and death rates. The number of *legal* immigrants to America, for example, has been relatively stable since World War II, rising slightly in recent years (to 600,000 persons per year).[4]

In recent years, though, *illegal* immigration has been up sharply, reflecting in part political and economic problems in some other countries. This has had major impacts in the border communities of the West and Southwest, in the coastal areas of South Florida, and in some of the major cities of the nation. (In this regard, you may be familiar with the political disputes over allocations of federal funds based on official census statistics. When illegal aliens are not reflected in these counts, the local communities in which they live must bear additional costs for education, health, and welfare, but these communities are not compensated for such outlays and, thus, have to raise local taxes. As the rate of illegal immigrants has increased, these disputes have become increasingly open and heated.)

MAJOR TRENDS IN THE MARKETPLACE

An Aging America

Not only is the country growing, but its age structure is evolving as well. Some astute marketers have already begun to anticipate the shifts and are altering their strategies to position themselves well for the future. One statistic that's often used to represent the nation's age structure is *median age,* or that point at which half the population is younger and half is older. Table 3-3 reports some highlights over time. Note, for example, that currently the "average" American is about 33 years old. Due to the lower recent birth rates and to sharply increased life expectancies, this is the highest median age in the nation's history and will continue to increase in the future.

Implications of the Shifting Age Structure

Age Groups and Sizes Median age is only one summary statistic, and it cannot capture important elements for marketers and others interested in consumer behavior. Another, more useful, breakdown involves the study of separate

TABLE 3-3 THE AGE OF THE AMERICAN POPULATION IN SELECTED YEARS

Median Age Trends

1860	*1880*	*1950*	*1970*	*1980*	*2000*	*2050*
19	21	30	28	30	36	42

Shifting Age Distributions

Age Group	1990 (est.) No. of People (millions)	1990 (est.) % of Population	2000 (est.) No. of People (millions)	2000 (est.) % of Population	Change 1990–2000 (est.) No. of People (millions)	Change 1990–2000 (est.) Percentage Change
Under 18	64	26%	66	25%	+2	+3%[a]
18–24	26	10	25	9	−1	−4
25–34	44	18	37	14	−7	−16
35–44	38	15	44	16	+6	+16
45–54	25	10	37	14	+12	+48
55–64	21	8	24	9	+3	+14
65 plus	32	13	35	13	+3	+9

[a]To be read: "The number of persons aged less than 18 will be 3 percent higher in 2000 than in 1990."
Source: See Note 5.

age groups, as shown in the first column of Table 3-3. Since the years within each group are not equal, mental adjustments may need to be made to compare relative sizes in the tables. Note, for example, how very large the 25- to 34-year-old group is on a relative basis, while the 45- to 54- and 55- to 64-year-old groups are proportionately smaller.

Since age progresses in a very systematic manner, we are able to predict with considerable precision how the age structure will move in future years. The right side of Table 3-3 presents expected age structure changes. Note that by the year 2000, 45- to 54-year-olds will have increased dramatically, up 12 million people over 1990, for an almost 50 percent increase in this age group! However, the 25- to 34-year-olds will actually *decrease* in number by about 7 million people (down 16 percent from 1990).

Societal Impacts Table 3-4 summarizes some broad aspects that the shifting age structure is likely to have on our society.[6] Some are surprising, such as a *decrease in crime* in future years! Others pose *serious public policy dilemmas.* For example,

- *The military.* Given that the number of people turning 18 is decreasing, should the armed services maintain its current force size? Should the draft be reinstated to accomplish this? If so, should men only be drafted? Should anyone receive exemptions from service? Or should the force remain voluntary, with higher taxes provided to subsidize more attractive pay and benefit packages? Notice that issues of philosophy, fairness, and economics are all involved here.
- *The retirement system.* Social Security and Medicare have already run into funding problems, with outflows of funds larger than those available. As our population ages, more people will depend on these programs (and for more years, as life expectancy increases). What is a fair funding system for these programs? Should younger wage earners be taxed at higher rates to maintain

TABLE 3-4 SOME BROADER EFFECTS OF THE SHIFTING AGE STRUCTURE

Area	Nature of Effects
Education	*Recent past:* Declining enrollments in schools; empty buildings. Boom in higher education enrollments. *Short-term future:* Increases in elementary and secondary schools, but declining enrollments in colleges. *Long-term future:* Declining enrollments.
Labor force	*Recent past:* Large influx of new workers, likely contributing to lower productivity (inexperience) and higher unemployment rates. *Short-term future:* Decrease in number of new workers. Productivity increases, unemployment rate decreases. *Long-term future:* Possible labor shortages; job retraining needed.
Military	*Recent past:* Shift to all volunteer military in 1973; relatively successful by recruiting about 20 percent of men turning 18 each year. Problems increased as pool of 18-year-olds began to shrink. *Short-term future:* Problems to continue. Military must recruit a higher percentage of young males, turn more toward young females, or increase the retention rate. Strategy options include reintroducing the draft, substantial increases in pay and benefits, and universal military service. *Long-term future:* Possible shift in the nature of military service and preparedness strategy.
Crime	*Recent past:* Most violent crimes are committed by people aged 18 to 24. Two-thirds of all arrests are for persons aged 13 to 29. Crime rate increased as size of these groups increased. These groups peaked in 1980 and began to decline in size. *Short-term future:* Possible decrease in crime rate. *Long-term future:* Possible decrease in crime rate.

Source: See Note 6.

benefits? (You may not be aware that in recent years the average worker was paying more in Social Security tax than in income tax.) Should benefits be cut? Should the system be made voluntary for everyone, or is there some better alternative? The numbers are clear and startling: the ratio of workers to pensioners in the United States has dropped from 16 to 1 in 1950 to 3 to 1 presently. By 2025, about the time many of us might be retiring, it will be 2 to 1![7]

Marketing Opportunities Beyond these serious social impacts, there are many marketing opportunities and problems associated with the shifting age structure. For example, a continued increase in senior citizens offers great potential for products and services geared to this group. Prescription drug sales should grow strongly, especially if public support programs are maintained. Health-related products and services, ranging from pain remedies to nursing facilities, should also increase. Other aspects of seniors' consumptions, such as investment services, specialty housing, and leisure products, should grow as well.

Marketing Problems Not all age shifts will bring promise, however. Notice the number of 25- to 34-year-olds will drop sharply during this decade. Marketers of products and services appealing to this age group (e.g., certain night clubs, home builders, furniture stores) must adjust their marketing mixes to accommodate this trend. Already we are seeing some retailers shifting their product lines, decor, and hiring slightly older salespeople to stay with their large markets as they become slightly older.

A Special Case: The Baby Boom Tidal Wave

A *tidal wave* suggests a huge mass moving with inexorable speed and power. It is a good term to describe the baby boom age group as it moves through its lifetime. When the boom arrives at an age, there is an immediate swell of persons that age. When it leaves, there are fewer. While it is there, its effects on all of us—older and younger—are huge.

There were *19 years* of the **American baby boom**.[8] It began in 1946, the first year after the end of World War II. The reasons are not difficult to imagine; millions of young men returned home after having been away at war for several years or more! During 1946, and in every year thereafter until the boom ended in 1964, millions of babies were born into the American society. *Seventy-six million people*—or about one-third of our present population—were born during this time, for an average of 4 million people per year (this from a much smaller population base than we have today). The peak year, in which more babies were born than in any other year before or since, was 1957, with over 4.3 million births.

Many readers of this book may have been born in the years following the baby boom. If you were born between 1965 and 1976, you belong to what has been named the "Baby Bust Generation." There are 43 million "baby busters." Most demographers believe baby busters are an extremely fortunate group, as they face less competition for favored positions in society than did members of the crowded baby boom generation.[9]

Massive Social Impacts Figure 3-1 shows some of the social impacts as baby boomers age.[10] Beginning in 1952, baby boomers (age 6) began to arrive at grade schools. Thousands of new teachers, buses, and classrooms were needed, together with millions of pencils, lunches, and other supporting products. Classes became significantly more crowded. The rise in first graders continued until 1970, when the 1964 children began school. Following 1970, enrollments in elementary schools began to drop sharply; by 1980 there were about *1 million fewer* first graders than in 1970, a drop of 22 percent in demand. There was a huge decline in job openings for college graduates who had majored in education. As the tide moved on, closed and shuttered elementary school buildings stood as mute testimony to the tidal wave's effects. Baby busters, however, studied in smaller classes.

Effects were not only felt in terms of size, however. Perhaps in part due to overcrowding, for example, the SAT scores of high school seniors declined *every year* for 19 years, coinciding almost exactly with the passage of the baby boom through the public school system of the country. Similar events occurred with other public institutions as the boom generation arrived. Jails became over-crowded; large new middle and high schools were erected; bowling alleys and movie theaters captured huge crowds of young people, and then lost them to other leisure pursuits.

What Should Colleges Do?

Colleges provide a relevant current case. In 1964 the first members of the baby boom hit college age. Higher education began to grow at almost 10 percent per year and became, by 1970, an industry with more employees than such giants as steel or autos! Universities expanded to take on the huge demand: they added professors, class buildings, and dorms.

Then the boom generation moved on. As shown in Figure 3-1, this happened in 1982, with the last boom class of college freshmen: What does the passing of the boom generation mean for colleges? The number of 18- to 24-year-olds will be decreasing for the rest of this century. In 1994, for example, this age group will number about 7 million fewer than in 1980, a drop of 23 percent! Assuming the same proportion of college enrollments from this group, this would mean a decline of over 2.5 million college students nationwide. This is about 1 of every 4 students enrolled in 1980 and presents an appalling picture to college trustees. As the president of Boston University pointed out, this loss is the equiv-alent of the disappearance of 50 universities—one for each state—of 50,000 students each.

The picture is very different by state, however. Looking farther ahead, California and Florida, for example, are expecting 63 *percent increases* in the number of high school graduates by the year 2004, while most northeast and midwestern states expect decreases.

How should colleges react? Through the late 1980s, most were successfully fighting off this trend, and enrollments were holding steady. Three factors were contributing: (1) more women were pursuing college degrees and became a majority of college students; (2) older persons (age 25 and over) returned to school in large numbers; (3) many students pursued part-time studies while working, so that the average time devoted to achieving a degree moved well beyond four years. All of these factors were assisted by the fact that

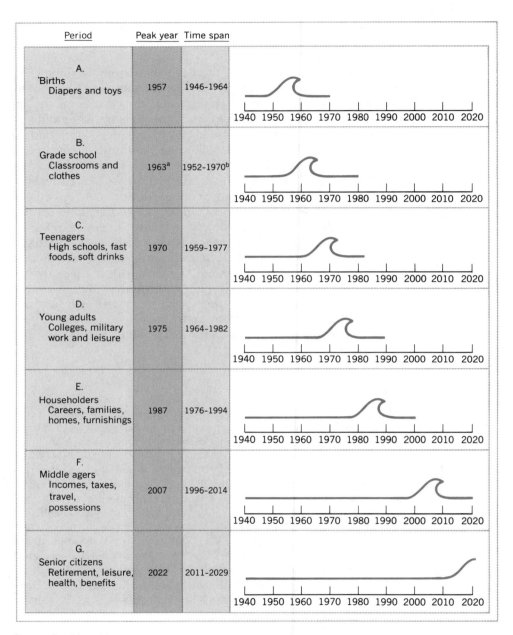

Period	Peak year	Time span	
A. Births — Diapers and toys	1957	1946-1964	
B. Grade school — Classrooms and clothes	1963[a]	1952-1970[b]	
C. Teenagers — High schools, fast foods, soft drinks	1970	1959-1977	
D. Young adults — Colleges, military work and leisure	1975	1964-1982	
E. Householders — Careers, families, homes, furnishings	1987	1976-1994	
F. Middle agers — Incomes, taxes, travel, possessions	2007	1996-2014	
G. Senior citizens — Retirement, leisure, health, benefits	2022	2011-2029	

Source: See Note 10.

[a]"Peak year" represents year at which the highest number of persons entered each stage; 1963 reflects year with the highest number of first graders.

[b]"Time span" represents years during which all baby boom persons *entered* the stage; first baby boomers entered grade school 1952; last baby boomers entered in 1970.

FIGURE 3-1 **The Baby Boom Tidal Wave Moves Through Life**

AUCTION

COLLEGE CAMPUS FOR SALE	VINTAGE SCHOOL BUILDING
ROBERT MORRIS COLLEGE	REHAB POTENTIAL
CARTHAGE CAMPUS	HOLY FAMILY ACADEMY
COLLEGE AVENUE, CARTHAGE, ILLINOIS	1444 W. DIVISION ST.; CHICAGO, IL

This currently operating private college campus consists of fifteen buildings, totalling approximately 160,000 square feet, on an approximately 20 acre landsite. There are seven residence halls accommodating 484 students, four classroom buildings, a dining hall, a 750-seat auditorium, a learning resource center and an approximately 16,940 sq. ft. recreational center. The town of Carthage is located approximately 210 miles southwest of Chicago, 130 miles north of St. Louis, 85 miles west of Peoria, 20 miles west of Macomb and just 15 miles from the Mississippi River and the Iowa/Missouri border. The campus can be purchased as a whole or in individual parcels and is ideal for a school, corporate training center or redevelopment.
Sugg. Opening Bid: $400,000.

Well located just 2 blocks west of the Kennedy Expressway, this 98,800 sq. ft. classic school building and adjacent 14,000 sq. ft. paved parking lot are in pristine condition. Features include 35 classrooms, 34 sleeping rooms, 4 laboratories, indoor swimming pool, gymnasium, auditorium, 2 classically designed chapels, large kitchen, 2 cafeterias and numerous other features. Ideal for user or rehabber.
Sugg. Opening Bid: $450,000.

AUCTION DATE AND LOCATION:
Sunday, April 9th - 11:30 a.m.
O'Hare Marriott Hotel
8535 W. Higgins, Chicago, IL

CERTIFIED OR CASHIER'S CHECK NEEDED TO BID ON EACH PROPERTY

For brochure, open house dates, terms of sale and additional information, call:
**(312) 630-0915 or
(312) 346-1500**

$75,000 CERTIFIED OR CASHIER'S CHECK NEEDED TO BID

AUCTION DATE AND LOCATION:
Thursday, May 18th - 1:00 p.m.
On Site (Earhart Student Center)

SHELDON GOOD & COMPANY
Commercial Real Estate Brokers • Auctioneers through its affiliate Real Estate Auctions, Inc.
333 W. Wacker Drive • Chicago, IL 60606
Chicago • Dallas • Denver • Ft. Lauderdale
Houston • Los Angeles • New York • San Antonio

Schools in the wake of the Baby Boom tidal wave.

colleges discovered *marketing* during this period and put it to work with a vengeance. As the president of Oberlin College relates, "The numbers gave us a good swift kick . . . [we] determined our competitive position in a very quantitative way. It was a fundamental change in the way we make decisions."

As we've seen, though, the numbers are huge, and demographic trends are relentless. It is not clear that colleges can continue to hold off enrollment declines. In 1989, for example, Harvard, Stanford, University of California-Berkeley, and many other prestigious schools reported 5 to 10 percent declines in applications. As the applicant pools for these schools are so large, the sizes of their enrollments are not threatened, but do these declines signal the start of the larger trend? You may wish to check at your own school to learn how enrollment is going, and what marketing efforts are underway.[11]

Settling Down and Settling In Returning to Figure 3-1, we'll use age 30 to represent the age at which men and women begin to settle into stable household units and purchase housing facilities. Using this age, we see that the nation should be nearing the end of a boom in housing construction. However, this stage is particularly susceptible to economic conditions. Because of the high interest rates during most years since 1976, and due to the recession that began in the early 1980s, the older baby boomers in the householder stage had *less than average* purchasing in the construction sector. How should we read this result? Do baby boomers want to own homes?

If so, it appears that a huge pent-up demand has been created in this sector, as millions of baby boomers await their chance to buy. When economic conditions are right, then (as they may have become by the time you read this) a major boom is likely in housing. Marketers of building supplies, appliances, real estate, and houses should have bright futures (at least until 1994). These are the kinds of statistics that create "bulls" on Wall Street. The baby boom market has arrived as adult consumers and promises a booming economy while it's here.

Plenty to Spend The next stage of Figure 3-1 uses age 50 to represent a period of settled middle age. Here we see a person's peak level of earnings, fewer demands on the family's money (as children have likely departed), and higher levels of discretionary consumer spending. Note that this era has yet to occur for baby boom members: it is due to begin in 1996, lasting until 2014.

Retirement Time—and Possible Trouble Then, beginning in the year 2011, the tidal wave will begin to hit age 65. On average, retirement brings a lower income, lower tax payments, and consumption that is partly funded from savings. What will happen when the baby boom hits retirement age? There are obvious marketing opportunities to consider (medications, specialty services, etc.) noted in Figure 3-1. Also, however, there is the difficult question of huge numbers of people moving out of "productive" activities in the economy. The consumer market might be strongly affected, since increased taxation reduces the discretionary income available (to those people who are taxed) for consumer spending on goods and services. This is an emotional and sensitive dilemma for our society. Forcing us to answer this question may ultimately become the most cruelly divisive impact that the baby boom tidal wave will leave in its historic wake.

The Educated Americans

Rising educational levels represent another important long-term trend in our society. At present, *3 out of every 10* Americans' primary activity is involved with education. Economically, this field accounts for about 8 percent of the nation's gross national product. Education is a major industry, and, as pointed out earlier, it is affected tremendously by changes in the birth rate in the nation.

"Educated Americans" celebrate a passage . . .

Educational Attainment: Rising Rapidly

Table 3-5 reveals some very interesting measures of the educational level of the society. The basis for the table is "all adults over 25 years old," reflecting the age at which formal education has probably been completed. Measures of educational attainment are presented over time, and the startling effects of our national policy of compulsory education are evident.

In 1940, for example, when our parents were young, three-fourths of all American adults had *not* graduated from high school. By 1986, however, this percentage had decreased to 25 percent. (In reading the table, notice that these numbers may be subtracted from 100 to represent higher levels of educational attainment. For example, three-fourths of U.S. adults now hold at least a high school degree.) Corresponding statistics for the black citizens of our nation show even stronger progress. In 1940, only 5 percent of black adults held a high school degree, while 60 percent of this group does today. Adults of Spanish origin have a slightly lower level of educational attainment, on average, but one that is climbing rapidly as well.

TABLE 3-5 EDUCATIONAL ATTAINMENT OF AMERICAN CONSUMERS IN
SELECTED YEARS, 1940–1980

All Adults over 25 Years Old in	Did Not Complete High School			Median Years of Schooling		
	Total All Races	Blacks Only	Spanish-Origin Only	Total All Races	Blacks Only	Spanish-Origin Only
1940	75%[a]	95%	NA	8.5 years[b]	6 years	NA
1950	65	90	NA	9.5	7	NA
1960	60	80	NA	11	8	NA
1970	50	70	60[c]	12	10	9.5[c]
1980	35	50	55	12.5	12	11
1986	25	40	50	12.6	12.3	11.7
Adults Aged 25–29 Only in						
1986	14[d]	17	41	12.9	12.7	12.3

Note: All data have been rounded: percentages to nearest 5 percent increment, years to nearest
half-year increment (except most recent).

[a]To be read: "Of all American adults in 1940, 75 percent had not completed their high school
education. Considering black adults only, 95 percent had not completed this level. Statistics for
adults of Spanish origin were not available for this time."

[b]To be read: "Half of all American adults in 1940 had completed less than 8.5 years of school,
while half had completed more than this level."

[c]Statistics shown for 1970 adults of Spanish origin reflect 1975 measures, the first year for which
such breakouts were available.

[d]To be read: "Considering only adults who were between 25 and 29 years old in 1986, 14 percent
had not completed high school. For black adults in this age group, the figure is 17 percent."

NA—Not available.

Source: U.S. Department of Commerce, Bureau of the Census, Statistical Abstract of the United
States, 1988 (Washington, D.C.: U.S. Government Printing Office, 1988), pp. 125–126.

The right-hand column of the table represents another way to describe educational attainment. Notice there that the median years of schooling has increased
from 8.6—that is, some ninth grade schooling—in 1940, to 12.6 years—that is,
some college—as of 1986. To isolate the most recent trends, the bottom row of
the table reports measures for adults between 25 and 29 years old. Notice that
about six out of seven of these younger adults hold high school degrees (but only
three in five of the Hispanic population of this age). In terms of grades completed,
the average young adult now has completed about one year of college. Finally,
though not shown in the table, you may be interested in how many persons have

completed college degrees. As of 1986, 19 percent of all adults held this distinction. Among younger adults, 25 to 29, about one in four had achieved this level.

Implications for Consumer Behavior

As we know, educational level is a means by which access to particular occupations is granted. This can impact strongly on a person's earnings and consumer spending potential. In addition, education works in more subtle ways. Education allows movement into other social classes (upward social mobility) and helps to determine our consumer life-styles. In turn, these reflect different orientations toward which stores to shop, how much to pay, and so on.

At a more basic level, educational statistics are indicative of the possession (or lack thereof) of skills necessary to be a "good consumer." Rising educational attainment has virtually wiped out illiteracy: less than 1 percent of adults in this nation are unable to read and write a simple message in some language. **Functional illiteracy**, however, remains a serious problem with a large segment of the American consumer population. According to recent estimates, at least 25 million adults—that's 1 in 5—lack the reading and writing abilities to handle the minimal demands of daily living in an effective manner.[12] Many of the most basic activities within consumer behavior require such skills. Consider, for example, the basic skills that are required to balance a checking account, calculate "good buys," figure out interest rates, fend off high-pressure sales presentations, analyze good and bad attributes of competitive products, and appreciate one's rights under a product warranty.

Another look at Table 3-5 indicates the size of the gap still remaining in terms of consumer skills. Even today, 25 percent of all adults have less than a high school degree; this translates to about 40 million people! Although many of these persons are quite capable of handling consumer responsibilities very well, a large number are not and are living less well than they could if they were more skilled as consumers.

Americans on the Move

Another dimension of importance to consumer behavior is *where* consumers are located and how long they'll stay in one place. **Mobility** is the technical term for change of residence. Mobility statistics for U.S. consumers are quite surprising. For example, what's your estimate of the answers to the following questions:

1. About how many people move each year in the United States (1 million, 10 million, 23 million, 45 million)? _____.
2. Is the average mobility rate increasing sharply, decreasing sharply, or generally remaining about the same? _____.
3. How likely is it that the average American consumer will move this year (1 chance in 50, 1 in 26, 1 in 13, 1 in 6)? _____.

4. Within the next five years, what proportion of consumers will move at least once (1 of 20, 1 of 10, 1 of 5, 1 of 2)? _____.

5. How many times can you, as an average consumer, expect to move in your lifetime? _____.

After completing the items, you may wish to turn to Note 13 for the answers (this is found at the back of this book, under Chapter 3's listings).[13]

What Does Mobility Mean for Consumption?

There are three major effects that mobility has on consumer behavior. First, it shifts market locations for retail purchases on local levels. Second, it creates regions of relative growth and regions of relative decline. Third, for consumers

Mobility has a strong impact on consumer behavior.

who move, it creates demand for certain purchases and for new patterns of patronage.

At an aggregate level, mobility means **shifting local markets**, as some areas grow and others decline. This is particularly important for retailers, as they must plan ahead to be where consumers are going to want to shop. *Most consumer behavior is "local" in nature:* consumers stay fairly close to home for most of their purchases. For this reason, shifts within local market areas are important marketing phenomena. Until the middle of this century, most localities' population growth was clustered in central urban centers and along railway lines offering easy access to those centers. Following World War II, autos became more available, housing demand boomed, and the suburbs became prime growth centers. The suburban shopping center emerged as a new concept in retailing. Today suburbs and the small towns outside them have 50 percent more consumers than do our nations' cities. In the Washington, D.C. area, for example, suburban consumers now account for 80 percent of the area's drugstore and car dealer sales, 75 percent of food store sales, and almost 90 percent of department store sales![14]

Growth Regions   In addition to shifts within local markets, we are all aware of larger trends toward certain regions of the country. Figure 3-2 shows how the Census Bureau defines the largest regions of the United States. Several key facts indicate how strong is the migration toward the Sunbelt. From 1990 to the year 2000, for example,

- The South will gain the most people (up 10 million).
- The West will have the highest percentage gain (up almost 14 percent).
- The South will stay the most populous region (over 90 million people).
- Just three states will account for over 50 percent of total growth in national population (California will gain over 4 million people, with Florida and Texas gaining another 2.5 million each). Together with fast-growing Georgia and North Carolina, these five states will be home to 85 million consumers by the year 2000, or about one-third of the entire national market![15]

Growth of such regions as the Sunbelt is having enormous social and economic consequences. There are business opportunities for new products and services, higher demand levels from the greater affluence in the area, and increased sales potentials due simply to the greater number of consumers living there.

Mobility Means New Purchases and Patronage   When a person changes his or her residence, needs for certain types of products and services arise. Housing must be purchased or leased, representing a major financial commitment. The move itself may also involve thousands of dollars, including possible purchases of moving company services, gasoline, food, and motels. Then, once at their new residence, many consumers discover needs for new furnishings, new

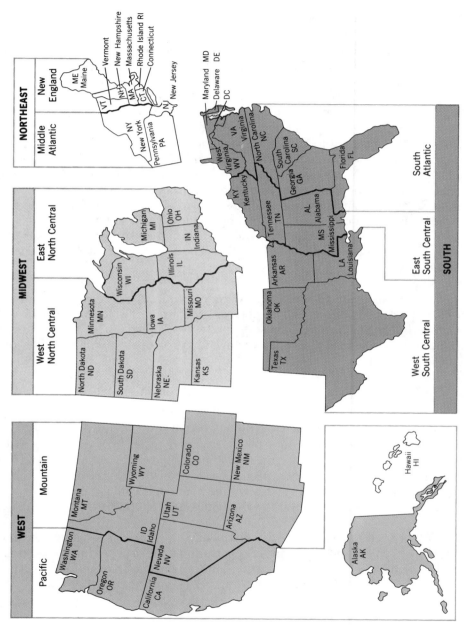

Source: U.S. Department of Commerce, Bureau of Census, in *Statistical Abstract of the United States, 1984* (Washington, D.C.: U.S. Government Printing Office, 1985).

FIGURE 3-2 **Map of the United States Showing Census Divisions and Regions**

appliances, and many other items associated with their new life-styles, such as new clothing and leisure products.

In addition to the purchases themselves, an interesting aspect of mobility involves consumers' needs to establish *new patterns of market patronage.* Hundreds of little decisions and questions are involved in this process of settling in. "Where shall I shop for groceries?" "Which doctor should I contact?" "Where should I set up a checking account?" are questions that millions of new arrivals are asking themselves. Notice that in some cases the initial choices made by a newly arrived consumer can be very significant since they are difficult to "try out" without making a commitment. Examples include services such as rental housing, insurance, bank, doctor, and dentist, and products such as furniture and appliances. *Word-of-mouth advice* from experienced residents is often a key factor in these decisions. National retail chains (Sears, K-mart, Penney, Safeway) provide familiar outlets for the mobile consumer. The local Yellow Pages are often consulted as well, as are retail ads. In addition, organizations such as the Welcome Wagon often contact the new resident to help direct him or her toward using specific marketers in the locality.

Exploding Households

"Shared" Consumption is Important

A substantial proportion of all consumption involves the *shared* use of products and services. Most houses and apartments are shared. In turn, so are many of the products and services consumed therein, such as food, appliances, utilities, and services. According to the U.S. Census Bureau, every occupied housing unit in the nation comprises one **household**. Thus, a large family, a husband and wife, a single person living alone, and an apartment with three roommates all count as individual households. Every American except those living within institutional quarters (such as prisons, dormitories, etc.) is viewed as living within one household. There are now about 95 million households, containing 98 percent of the total population.[16]

Trends in household statistics reflect other shifts in our society as well. For example, the number of households has exploded during the 1970s and 1980s. Two key factors were higher divorce rates and persons marrying for the first time at somewhat older ages. The fact that the rate of household formation has far surpassed the rate of population growth also means that the average *size* of household would be dropping. This happened as well—the 1970 average of 3.1 persons per household fell to a record low 2.6 as we enter the 1990s. Historically, this continues a long-term trend: our first census in 1790 revealed an average of six persons per household. At present, more than half of all households have only 1 or 2 people.

A major distinction in households is between *family* and *nonfamily* categories. Family households have at least two related people living together; the nonfamily category is reserved for persons either living alone (24 percent of all households) or with other people with whom they are not related by family ties (only 4 percent of all households). Thus, the family unit is still the dominant form of household.

Families Are Changing

One function that television is said to perform is reflecting the life experiences and aspirations of the average person in the society. It is no accident, then, that the portrayal of families has changed sharply since television's early days in the 1950s. Back then, the "typical" American family was seen to have a father who worked all day, a mother who kept the house clean and running smoothly, and two or three children under the age of 18. Such shows as "Leave It to Beaver," "Ozzie and Harriet," and "Father Knows Best" reflected the family life-styles aspired to in those times. Today, the "ideal" family of the 1950s has given way to various other forms of living: the husband/housewife/two children at home family now accounts for less than 10 percent of all husband-wife families and an even smaller proportion of all households! The average (median) family size is now only slightly larger than three persons.

Why are these numbers so low? There are a number of reasons. First, the portrait itself is age dependent: families whose children have left home would not be counted, nor would younger couples who had not yet had their children. Thus we should expect the actual incidence of "typical" families to be somewhat higher than the 7 percent figure. Nonetheless, significant societal changes have affected the portrait of a family strongly, including

■ Postponing the age of marriage.
■ Increasing divorce rates.
■ Increasing single parent families.

To Wed or Not to Wed, That Is the Question

Many young men and women are waiting longer before marrying. Of persons aged 25 to 29, for example, about one in three women and two in five men have not been married. For persons aged 20 to 24, the numbers are of course higher: three in five women and three in four man have yet to wed. To recognize the degree of change over time, let's contrast these data with those for your parents' generation (selecting 1960 as a base year when they might have been in this age range). At that time, only one in nine females and one in five males between 25 and 29 had not been married. For those aged 20 to 24, only one woman in four had not yet married (one-half of the men had yet to wed).[17] As one alternative to earlier marriages, many young couples have begun to live together outside of marriage. Approximately 5 percent of unmarried adults (2 million people) are now living together as male-female couples.

The Deluge of Divorce Approximately 2 million divorces occur each year. In almost all cases, new household arrangements have to be made. In statistical terms, this often creates both a "single-person, nonfamily" household, and a "single-parent family" unit as replacements for the previous husband-wife family unit. It is also typical for *both* households to move to new residences after a

A young family today.

An "award winning" family of the 1950s.

An atypical family for either generation!

divorce. Thus, in addition to the pain and unhappiness involved, the divorce process also stimulates additional consumption needs.

The *rate* of divorce now appears to be leveling off, and even declining slightly, after experiencing a rapid increase during the "divorce decade" of the 1970s. At present, about one out of each two couples marrying each year can expect to see that marriage end in a divorce. Remarriages are, however, increasingly common and now account for about half of all marriages. About three-fourths of divorced persons can expect to remarry within five years. Thus, despite the heavy divorce rate, marriage remains the institutional norm for American consumers, with many citizens moving in, out, and back into this state.[18]

Single-Parent Families: Alone Together One of the strongest areas of effects of recent social trends has been the internal family unit. The number of *two-parent families has actually been dropping*. In contrast, the number of *one-parent families has more than doubled* since 1970. Today, one in two American children can expect to spend part of his or her childhood in a single-parent family.

There are many sociological factors associated with **single-parent families**. About 90 percent are headed by a woman. As of 1986, three of five black families with children present were in this category, versus one in five white families. Both groups had seen sharp increases in recent years. Divorce accounts for about two in five single-parent families, while separation or abandonment accounts for

Single-parent families have increased substantially.

another one-fifth (other important factors are the death of a spouse and non-marriages).

As we might expect, then, *income* is a real problem for many of these households. Sharp family income drops occur at the end of a marriage (these average a 30 percent decrease for widows with children, a 40 percent decrease for divorced mothers, and an over 50 percent drop for separated mothers). Most of these women enter the work force, but still many of these families must also rely on other sources of support such as Social Security (widows), child support payments (divorces), and food stamps and other social welfare programs. Consumption is often limited to essential purchases and is constrained by the time limitations of a working mother.[19]

Rising Consumer Incomes

The Economic Setting

Basically, people who have more money also spend more money. The matter of consumer incomes is thus fundamental to consumer purchasing. Most income comes from employment. Employment, in turn, is highly sensitive to the economy's condition. The actual relationship between income and economic conditions is extremely complex, however. Not only do consumer incomes depend on economic activity, but economic activity depends on consumer spending, and consumer spending in turn depends on incomes. Thus there is a circular relationship that is very difficult to disentangle.

Numerous other factors also affect the relationship. *Price inflation,* for example, encourages consumers to spend sooner because their money is losing its purchasing power. *High interest rates* have the effect of raising prices for consumer products purchased on credit (During the early 1980s, for example, many young consumers were paying more in monthly payments for their cars than their older brothers and sisters were spending for monthly mortgage payments on their houses!) In addition, *taxes* remove money directly from taxpayers' wallets, thus holding down their consumption. (Often, however, the government spends the money to hire workers, purchase goods and services, or transfer incomes to needy citizens. Such spending can contribute to employment and to later consumer spending on the part of those employed.)

As you can recognize, this description is much too simplified to portray accurately the entire relationship, and it should certainly not be read as an economic policy prescription! There are, however, several very basic relationships that consumer incomes have been found to exhibit, and these should help us to appreciate better the aggregate view of consumer behavior.

Consumer Incomes Differ by Demographics

Looking only at total numbers can hide some major differences that are significant for consumer behavior. The roots of these differences stem from the fact that *consumers have a wide range of incomes.* From the consumer's perspective, then, we face very different situations in terms of our *capabilities* to undertake purchasing. From the marketer's perspective, different income segments exist in the consumer market and offer very different levels of **purchasing potentials**.

A Cautionary Note As we're all aware, income differences don't occur on a random basis. Instead, income differences are systematically related to personal characteristics, such as those measured by demographics. Figure 3-3 graphs five of these relationships, showing just how important they are.

Before briefly examining each one, though, we should also take into account the fact that demographics tend to be correlated with each other. For example, we have already discussed such relationships as age and education (younger people have on average completed considerably more schooling than older people did) and education and race (minority groups have on average completed less schooling than whites have). When we see the very strong effect that education seems to have on income (as we will in Figure 3-3), however, how can we separate out such other related factors as age and race?

This is an extremely sticky task that demonstrates the wisdom behind the adage that "Correlation does not imply causation!" In practice, this analysis would likely require highly sophisticated statistical techniques (such as those used in a branch of economics known as econometrics). Large marketers employ these techniques, as do government agencies. For our present purposes, however, we will briefly examine the variables one at a time, bearing the cautionary note in mind.

Age and Income The first graph in the figure shows a "curvilinear effect" of age on income—household income is low when the household is young, reaches the overall average between the ages of 25 and 34, continues to its highest level between 45 and 54, and then declines after the age of 65. Consumer spending, though not shown on the chart, *doesn't vary as much* (that is, it shows a flatter line over the years). On average, younger households (especially those under 25) and the older households (over 65) actually *spend more than they earn*. This is technically termed *consumer dissaving* and represents taking out loans and mortgages, buying on credit, and dipping into savings during retirement. In the middle years of one's life, when income is highest, the reverse is true, resulting in a buildup of savings.

Race and Income There is a large gap, shown in Figure 3-3, between the household incomes of blacks and those of whites. There are many possible explanations for this finding, including such issues as proportions of single-parent families, age differences, sex differences, and educational level differences, in addition to questions of job opportunities. At the individual level, the gap is even larger: the average black American's per capita income is 60 percent of that of the average white American (per capita income of Hispanics is barely lower, at 57 percent of that for whites).

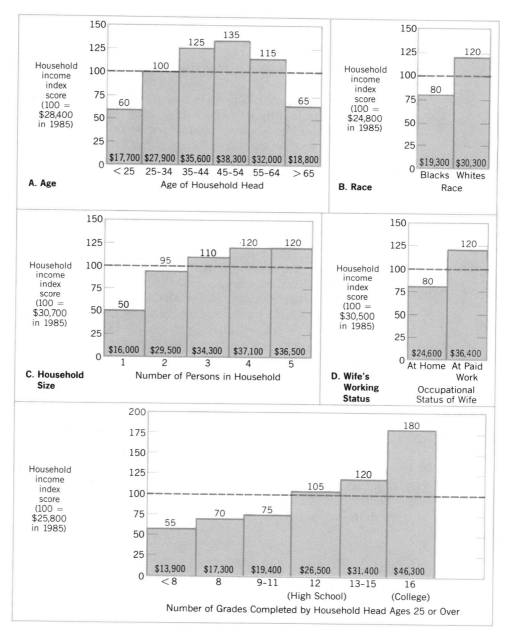

Source: These data have been developed by the author, based on data in the *Statistical Abstract of the United States: 1988, pp 424–429.* The author has created "income indices" to show relationships. Each index is based on the average income for the six categories shown, unweighted by their representation in the population. Thus the actual "average" income for the population is not shown on these charts, but the average income for each category **is** shown (at the bottom of each bar), as is its position relative to the other categories. The index numbers have been rounded to the nearest 5 percent level.

FIGURE 3-3 **How Demographics Affect Consumer Incomes**

Household Size and Income Figure 3-3 shows an increasing (*monotonic*) relationship between income and household size. Much of this is due to the number of persons contributing to the income flow as well as a likely effect of age levels. This finding has many interesting implications for marketers, such as which sizes of households would be the best prospects for purchasing certain types of products. Of course, marketers of products that are consumed by almost everyone would seem well advised to pay particular heed to the larger household units as a good way to increase the volume of sales.

Wife's Working Status and Income The graph for this relationship shows a definite increase in family income when both husband and wife are working. This is something that we might expect, of course. The dual-earner phenomenon holds strong implications for marketing managers. *Time* is a very important consideration in the consumer behavior of the dual-earning couple. And, if the wife is a professional or in a sales capacity, her *role* may demand more job-related purchases of certain products and services. Finally, the additional income means more money available for consumer spending. In sum, we might expect to see higher demand (and a willingness to pay) for products and services that offer convenience, home work reduction, child care, leisure, and a way to "get away" occasionally from the external demands of both work and home.

Education and Income The final graph demonstrates an extremely strong correlation between income and educational level. How is consumer behavior affected by educational level? At the start, more highly educated consumers have more money available to spend. College graduates account for less than 20 percent of all households but for almost 30 percent of all income. More broadly, we know that educational level is closely tied to occupation and to life-style. Since *consumption is a means toward living the types of lives we wish to live,* we can expect education to affect which types of products to buy, what kinds of stores to buy them in, and what prices to be willing to pay.

HOW MARKETERS USE DEMOGRAPHIC INFORMATION

Three age-old business sayings are

- "Know thy customer."
- "Be there before your competitor."
- "Information is power."

Astute marketers use demographics on a continuing basis. For example, over 4000 businesses employ the services of the Conference Board, Inc., at annual fees that range up to $100,000. Important elements of the Conference Board's services involve the interpretation of demographics as they relate to consumer behavior.[20]

Marketers use demographics in many ways. They must be alert to trends of the types we've discussed. In addition, they can improve decisions on site location, sales territories, and advertising by employing this type of information. Let's briefly examine some examples:

Homing in on Housing Trends

As the nature of the consumer market changes, an astute marketer must change the marketing mix to keep pace. For example, consider the following reports from persons in real estate:[12]

> In 1957 when I started in real estate, we were selling homes to families with four, five, and six children. Today you're talking about families with one or two children, being raised in day care centers because the mother and father both have careers.
>
> —Colorado Realtor

> We're selling to more singles than we did in previous years. Divorcees, widows, and widowers are making up a large segment of our market now too.
>
> —Minnesota Realtor

> We see a very precipitous drop in the demand (for rental housing).
>
> —Harvard Professor

Given strong regional and local differences, what implications do demographic trends have for home builders? How should their marketing mixes change, in terms of housing styles, prices, locations, and so on? Where are the marketing opportunities for the 1990s?

Out of Site, Out of Mind!

A favorite saying in retailing is

> A store's success depends on three factors: Location, location, and location!

This quotation explains why retailers invest heavily to research potential store sites. According to the research director of Federated Department Stores (which operated over 300 stores in 19 chains such as I. Magnin & Co., Filene, Bloomingdale's, and Abraham & Straus), a firm may spend up to $50,000 to analyze a potential location. In a typical study, demographic information on an area's local residents is first obtained, then combined with details of consumer **expenditure potentials** for different product lines. Once a store site has been targeted (and it has been determined that it is not already "overstored" by nearby competitors), the retailer will attempt to identify exactly which customers can be expected to shop there. Through such methods as consumer interviews (or even by monitoring license plates of cars passing by the location), researchers define the size and demographic profile of potential store customers. Since a department store can generate millions in sales per year, good consumer research can contribute substantially to profitability.[22]

Retailers know: it's location, location, location!

Zip Hits Target

Much of the "copy" and "creative" developed for advertising campaigns is based on the **demographic profile** of target consumers for the campaign. Beyond this, the same demographic profile guides media decisions on where to place the advertising. This is often done by a computer program that analyzes how well each magazine, television show, and so on reaches the particular consumer profile, and at what cost.

Another form of advertising—*direct mail*—takes advantage of the fact that our postal system reaches virtually all consumers with individual deliveries. Since people tend to live near others like themselves, there are natural demographic divisions by neighborhoods, and marketers can target advertising to specific demographic households. The U.S. Census Bureau assists business in this task. It maintains demographic data at several levels of aggregation, beginning with city blocks, then groups of blocks, then census tracts (neighborhoods), then towns or cities, then to metropolitan areas. Specialized firms take this data to create gigantic computer banks of consumers' addresses grouped by demographic characteristics. For example, a service called PRIZM (Potential Rating Index Zip Markets) rates over 35,000 zip code areas on 34 different demographic factors, then groups the areas by demographic similarity. Forty groups of neighborhoods have been identified, including the "blue blood estates," "money and brains," and the "hard scrabble." For each type of neighborhood, PRIZM offers information on over 1000 types of purchases and preferences that consumers in this type of neighborhood have. Marketers can then send their messages directly to those zip codes.[23]

Related developments have also been possible for magazines and newspapers, since these also are delivered to consumers' addresses. Thus the advertisements vary according to the audience. Recently, for example, *Time* was offering advertisers a choice from 1 national edition, 11 regional editions, 34 metropolitan editions, 50 state editions, and 7 demographic editions (aimed at special markets such as students, top managers, doctors, etc.).[24] We will continue our discussion of these segmentation options in the next chapter.

SUMMARY

Market Size—A Key Issue

An *aggregate perspective* stresses the examining of the whole of the market. In this chapter we stressed the huge size of the consumer market and the trends that are shaping the future of our society and marketplace. Our focus was on *demographics,* or the statistical study of human populations. We began with the issue of population and population growth. The present size of the U.S. population is about 250 million persons. It has grown in an erratic fashion. It is currently growing at less than one percent per year. The major factors affecting its growth are *fertility, mortality,* and *net immigration.*

Major Trends in the Marketplace

We then discussed the major demographic trends affecting the United States. First, the age structure of the population is shifting to become older. At present the median age for Americans is about 33 years old. This is the highest median age in the country's history, and promises to keep climbing in the future. The structure of different age groups is also shifting. 25- to 34-year-olds for example, are declining in numbers, while the 45- to 54-year olds are increasing dramatically in numbers. Senior citizens are also increasing in numbers. This shifting age structure holds many implications which we examined in this section. We particularly stressed the *baby boom tidal wave,* which is continuing to bring massive changes to our society. We also indicated some implications for the baby busters generation.

Next we examined the rapid increases in educational attainment of American consumers. Approximately 75 percent of American adults now hold high school degrees, for example, versus only 25 percent in 1940. We also saw that education is a major industry in the nation and that it is strongly affected by demographic trends. Among the direct implications of this sector we briefly considered *functional illiteracy* and the presence of minimum consumer skills in some segments of the consumer population. Our further coverage in the chapter considered consumer mobility, households, and incomes. We saw that mobility has strong effects on consumer behavior and on consumer markets. We also saw that the number of households is exploding, reflecting the changes in our life-styles. This trend has significant implications for consumer behavior as well. As a final major trend, we discussed rising consumer incomes, which bode well for marketers and consumers overall. In this section we noted the general relationships that income holds with other demographic factors.

How Marketers Use Demographic Information

In the final section of the chapter we noted how important demographic trends are for marketers, and investigated some ways marketers use *demographic information* in making decisions such as choosing retail site locations and choosing advertising media. Our next chapter of the book examines market segmentation, and continues our discussion of this area.

KEY TERMS

aggregate perspective	American baby boom
demographics	functional illiteracy
fertility	mobility
fertility rate	shifting local markets
replacement rate	household
mortality	single-parent families
life expectancy	purchasing potentials
net immigration	expenditure potentials

REVIEW QUESTIONS AND EXPERIENTIAL EXERCISES

[E = Application extension or experiential exercise]

1. Why should a marketer develop an aggregate perspective of consumer behavior? Is this of more, less, or equal importance to an individual-level perspective?

2. How could marketers of the following estimate their potential market sizes:
   a. Dry beer
   b. Carpeting
   c. Fast food restaurants
   d. Public transportation

3. What are some of the consumer behavior implications associated with marketing the following products to senior citizens:
   a. Grocery products
   b. Banking services
   c. Health care

4. Identify, providing rationale, three products whose purchase and consumption varies directly/inversely with an individual's education level.

5. Given the mobility pattern of Americans, describe direct implications for marketers as individuals seek new homes, new shopping, and new medical services.

6. Indicate, providing rationale, four products or services that would be most affected (positively or negatively) by the following societal changes:

   a. Postponing the age of marriage

   b. Increasing divorce rates

   c. Increasing single-parent families

7. The text discusses the relationship between income and five different demographic variables. Select any two of the five graphs in Figure 3-3, interpret them, and indicate their implications for marketers and for public policymakers.

8. Assume you are the marketing manager for the following products. How specifically could you employ consumer demographic information for any three of them?

   a. Kerosene products (kerosene heaters)   d. Revlon cosmetics

   b. IBM personal computers   e. K-mart

   c. American Airlines   f. Your university

[E]   9. Interview an official in the Admissions Department of your college about any changes that have been made in recruiting in response to the population shifts described in the chapter.

[E] 10. Visit your local or university library to obtain back issues of *American Demographics* magazine. Read through several issues of this publication. Write a brief report summarizing what you found that is important for marketing managers.

[E] 11. Visit your university library to employ the reference department's assistance in locating recent articles on demographic trends and implications for marketers. Choose one or more of the following topics and report on your findings.

   a. Households   d. Residential mobility

   b. Baby boom/baby bust   e. Age structure

   c. Consumer income   f. Regional and local markets

[E] 12. Visit your local Office for Economic Development (this may be in city or county government or affiliated with the Chamber of Commerce). Interview the chief officer there governing his or her use of demographic data and marketing efforts.

[E] **13.** Visit a supermarket with the following mission in mind: a. Walk through the store, noting brands, packaging devices, products, and so forth that reflect the changing age structure in society; b. Then consider what two of these products might be like in 10 years, as the age structure continues to evolve; c. As a strategic marketing planner for a grocery retailer, what would you recommend your firm plan to do in these areas? Write a brief report on your findings and thoughts.

Market Segmentation

GM Shifts Gears

Many consumers are not aware that the giant General Motors Corporation was founded in the 1920s on an elegant but simple segmentation scheme: each of the five GM brands would play a role in consumers' lives. Chevrolet would bring the first-time car buyer into the GM system with a price appeal. As that customer became more affluent, he or she would move up to Pontiac, then Oldsmobile, Buick, and finally, Cadillac. Using this scheme, the company prospered for decades. In the mid-1980s, however, this segmentation scheme was undone by organizational and styling changes: the brands came to look much more like each other, sales dropped dramatically, and archrival Ford's profits drove ahead of GM for the first time in history.

Now GM has reported a new segmentation strategy for the 1990s. It has identified 19 target segments, based on customer's preferences for body styles, size, image, and so on. Buick will now be presented as "the premium American motor car" with a contemporary classic look. Oldsmobile is positioned as a technological leader, while Pontiac will be marketed for sporty road performance. Chevrolet will continue to go after price-and-value-sensitive consumers, with a special effort to appeal to women. Cadillac, meanwhile, will strive to regain its exclusive image by no longer producing any middle-price market models.[1]

■ ■ ■

As we've seen in Chapter 3, the aggregate market is so huge that any single marketer needs to capture only a small portion of it to be very successful. Market segmentation offers an efficient way for marketers to plan for attaining their desired shares. As you probably already know, market segmentation is among the most popular and important concepts in the entire field of marketing. Professors teach it, students learn it, managers practice it, and researchers examine it—all with interest and enthusiasm. It has become so popular, in fact, that many persons are no longer entirely sure what a market segment really is! In our first section, therefore, we'll briefly examine this question.[2] We'll begin by recognizing that market segmentation is something more valuable than taking any possible group of consumers and just giving it a fancy label.

BACKGROUND ON SEGMENTATION

Market segmentation was introduced to the marketing field in a classic 1956 article by Wendell Smith in the *Journal of Marketing*.[3] Because market segmentation simultaneously addressed the roles of both marketers and customers, this concept quickly captured the attention of many innovative individuals in the field. Coincidently, the segmentation concept appeared shortly before the arrival of computers brought about a revolutionary burst of activity in marketing research. During this new era, it became possible to analyze efficiently and powerfully large numbers of variables obtained from large samples in the consumer population. Given its nature, market segmentation became one of the chief beneficiaries of this new technology, and quickly became a central topic for marketing researchers and strategists during the decades of the 1960s, 1970s, 1980s, and yet today as we move through the 1990s. It is truly a centerpiece of marketing.

A Basic Marketing View

In most companies, significant differences among customers are recognized and used as a basis for marketing planning. As George Day, an academic noted for his contributions to marketing strategy, has noted to industrial manufacturers:

> It is useful to think of [levels] of segments. . . . At the top are 'strategic' customer segments, where virtually no element of the marketing programme for one segment is transferable to another strategic segment. This is the reason that tire manufacturers approach auto [manufacturers] and replacement tire markets as entirely separate businesses, appliance manufacturers have different marketing strategies for retail buyers and contract buyers such as home builders, and food companies often have separate divisions for institutional markets. The need for different strategies leads to totally different cost and price structures. [However, beyond this very natural type of segmentation] within each "strategic" customer segment there will be further groups which . . . lead to opportunities for differentiation from competitors. Much of segmentation research has been directed at this type of segmentation.[4]

Thus the most basic advantage offered by market segmentation is that it pro-

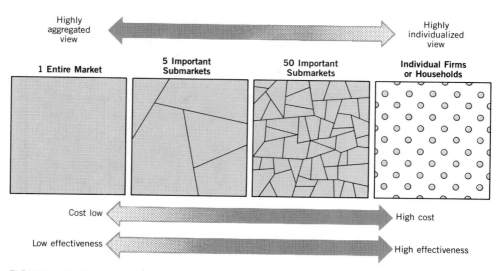

FIGURE 4-1 **Alternative Views of the Market**

vides us with a structured means of "viewing" the marketplace (which may consist of millions of consumers) confronting a firm. Consider the alternative views of the market depicted in Figure 4-1. At the left, with no segmentation, consumers are all grouped together and viewed as a single market. If there are significant differences within the market (as invariably there are) it becomes difficult to describe the market. As a consequence, an aggregate view of the market provides little guidance for strategy development.

At the other extreme (the right of Figure 4-1), each consumer is viewed individually. This offers considerable insight into a single customer's behavior and permits the marketer to develop an offering *specifically tailored* to meet the needs of that individual (or firm). The drawbacks, of course, are the feasibility and costs of viewing each customer individually. Thus we face a situation—shown in Figure 4-1—in which costs and effectiveness are likely to travel together in the same direction. Viewing the market as a single aggregate is low in cost, but also low in effectiveness. Viewing the market as thousands or millions of individuals, on the other hand, is high in effectiveness but very high in cost. There are so many individual consumers in most markets that they must somehow be grouped together if management is to have any chance of understanding, much less reaching, a sizable portion of the market.

The middle boxes of Figure 4-1 represent moves to segmented views of the market. Notice, however, how many possibilities there are, and how differently they will appear to a manager! Until a marketer can decide on the number and membership of target segments, he or she cannot undertake a clean segmentation program. This is usually not an extremely easy task. Thus it is helpful for us to appreciate some of the criteria and bases that are used to define market segments. This will be the major topic of our chapter.

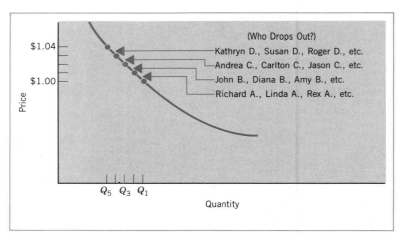

FIGURE 4-2 **An Inside Look at the Demand Curve (Or, Who Drops Out When the Price Rises?)**

A Theoretical Base in Economics

Although it is known as a popular marketing concept, segmentation has its theoretical basis in the microeconomic theory of **price discrimination**. This theory points out that a firm with monopoly power can increase its revenues by charging different customers different prices, reflecting the highest level that each is willing to pay. That is, charging a single price to everyone generally means that some customers will be paying less than they would have been willing to pay, while other potential customers will not buy because the single price charged is higher than the maximum they will pay. A quick look at Figure 4-2 shows this point. If the firm charges $1.01, Richard A., Linda A, Rex A., and all others in their group will not buy the product. All of the "D" group (Kathryn, Susan, Roger, etc.), however, will be very pleased at the $1.01 price, since they are actually willing to pay even more. Thus we can see that if the firm could somehow approach each consumer set separately, and have them pay the most they are willing to, it would maximize its revenues, and each of its customers would still regard his or her purchase as worthwhile (disregarding equity and legal considerations). In today's world of market segmentation, the theory's reliance on price has simply been broadened to now include any combination of the 4P's marketing mix.

A Formal Definition

We will define market segmentation as a managerial strategy that adapts a firm's marketing mix to best fit the various consumer demand curves existing in a market. It is an *adaptive* strategy that seeks to obtain competitive advantage by doing a better job of satisfying customer requirements. As Foote noted,

I. Definition:

"A managerial strategy that adapts a firm's marketing mix to best fit the various demand curves existing in a market."

II. The Three-Stage Process:

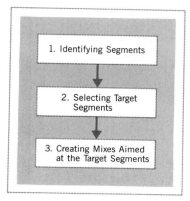

FIGURE 4-3 **The Essentials of Market Segmentation**

The very incentive for exploring market segmentation is to gain advantage—to seek some basis for customer preference—against the array of competitors and their offerings . . . [The marketer] must seek to identify those offerings which most appeal to some desirable segment of the total market. . . .[5]

Market Segmentation as a Process

In practice, a full application of market segmentation consists of three basic stages, as shown in Figure 4-3:

1. *Identifying segments.* This first stage involves dividing the consumer market into meaningful buyer groups who, by virtue of distinct characteristics such as needs, use patterns, demographics, and so on, represent "opportunities" for distinct marketing programs. Consumer research plays the primary role in this stage.

2. *Selecting particular segments to target.* The second stage will differ for each firm depending on a host of strategic and competitive considerations. Marketing management plays the primary role in this stage.

3. *Creating marketing mixes aimed at target segments.* This third stage involves the development and deployment of specific marketing mixes, specially designed for target segments. Marketing management also has the key role in this stage.

The first stage—identification of segments—is thus a crucial part of the process. Segmentation usually requires marketing research aimed at classifying customers and providing a detailed understanding of how they differ from each other.

Three Criteria for a "True Market Segment"

Although the process is flexible, a useful segment must satisfy several criteria. Many possible standards have been suggested, but they all reduce to a set of three basic criteria for market segmentation itself:

1. *Group identity.* The criterion of **group identity** simply represents our desire to ensure good groupings (since most segmentation will be conducted using research methods, statistical terms are often used). The first criterion refers to the fact that members of a segment must be *similar* to other consumers in that same segment (*homogeneity*) and that the members of one segment must be *different* from consumers who are in other segments (*heterogeneity*).
2. *Systematic behaviors.* The concept of **systematic behaviors** refers to consumer behavior itself—members of a segment should behave in a similar manner and be likely to react similarly to a particular marketing mix. Members of different segments should behave differently, and react differently to a marketing mix.
3. *Marketing mix efficiency potential.* This third criterion—**efficiency potential**—asks the practical question whether or not a marketing mix can be developed to reach efficiently and appeal differentially to the possible segment grouping.

In concept, the requirement for a true market segment should now be clear: the search is for a customer grouping that: (1) will behave differently from other groups; and (2) will be responsive to an efficient marketing mix aimed at it. Our following discussions will clarify what this means for marketing practice.

THE START OF A SEGMENTATION STUDY: CLASSIFYING CUSTOMERS

The marketing research director of Ford Motor Co. summarized both the opportunity and the problem in this area when he reported . . . If we want to, we can use 200 or 300 different measuring points to identify our customer.[6]

Stage I of the segmentation process—identifying market segments—requires us to pay careful attention to the issue of customer classification. The choices made at this initial stage not only guide the direction of later analyses, but categories omitted from this stage will not again be available for subsequent segmentation decisions. Thus, it is particularly important to appreciate the nature of the options here, and to choose intelligently among them.

The "Three Levels" of Consumer Classification

As the Ford manager pointed out, there are literally hundreds of ways in which a market researcher might choose to classify any customer. Fortunately, however, these reduce to three levels or types of classification:

- Personal characteristics of the consumer.
- Benefits sought by the consumer.
- Behavioral measures of the consumer.

Level 1: Personal Characteristics

As Figure 4-4 shows, a particularly useful aspect of this three-level approach is that the levels are themselves related in a systematic way. At the left are the

FIGURE 4-4 **The Three Levels of Consumer Classification**

LEVEL 1.

Personal Characteristics

Mary Winthrop is:
- a 36-year-old female
- unmarried
- an attorney
- a West Side homeowner
- black
- a $50,000-a-year earner
- a convenience-oriented shopper
- interested in obtaining "the better things in life"

Kevin Powers is:
- a 33-year-old male
- unmarried
- an advertising account executive
- a downtown renter
- white
- a $50,000-a-year earner
- an active consumer of travel and entertainment
- a subscriber to *Sports Illustrated*

LEVEL 2.

Benefits Sought

Mary Winthrop Seeks:
- high quality in clothing.
- a businesslike image at work.
- a stylishly feminine image at leisure.

Kevin Powers Seeks:
- style in his automobile
- power
- performance
- an image of success and achievement

LEVEL 3.

Behavioral Measures

Mary Winthrop:
- prefers status brands such as Anne Klein.
- buys fine clothing often.
- spends heavily.
- tends to be loyal to only a few stores.

Kevin Powers:
- buys a new car every year or two.
- favors Porsche and Jaguar, dislikes subcompacts.
- Is not loyal: has switched makes his last four purchases.

personal characteristics of the individual—those can be used to identify or describe particular individuals as people or as consumers. For example, as shown, a consumer named Mary Winthrop might be classified as a female, a 36-year-old, an attorney, an unmarried person, and so forth. These types of descriptions can all be helpful in gaining a general "picture" of this person, her stage and status in life, and her likely areas of interest. Simply put, these measures indicate who the consumers are, where they are, what they find interesting, and how they might be reached (Kevin Powers, for example, reads *Sports Illustrated*).

Thus level 1 has a broad orientation geared toward a person's overall life. These measures are relevant for many marketers, which offers cost efficiencies for research buyers. Level 1 applies to all products and brands. Notice that Mary Winthrop's descriptions here will not be affected by what any marketer might do.

Level 2: Benefits Sought

The second level moves to consider explicitly both the person and the product category rather than just the person alone. The title for this level of classification— **benefits sought**—represents an enormously popular approach that is being used by many consumer marketers. Here emphasis is placed on *the nature of consumer demand for various features* of a product or service offering. For example, an automobile maker might classify Mary Winthrop's benefits sought in such terms as importance of price, styling, gas economy, status, size, warranty, and so forth. As shown in Figure 4-4, however, a clothier would need to use a quite different set of benefits to describe Mary, as would other classes of marketers, each depending on the nature of the product or service offering.

In terms of the overall system, three basic assumptions are embedded in this level 2 classification. First, different people will in fact prefer different mixes of features, quality levels, and prices. Second, these preferences will be influenced by personal factors (e.g., age, location, income, type of residence) represented at our first level (personal characteristics). Third, people will *act upon* these different preferences—purchase behaviors will in fact differ depending on the exact mix of benefits a marketer chooses to offer.

Level 3: Behavioral Measures

In contrast to the first two levels, this level—**behavioral measures**—classifies each consumer on the basis of his or her *actual behavior* in the marketplace. Many options are available for the precise handling of these measures. Some popular options include

- Product ownership or use.
- Quantity purchased.
- Brand loyalty, supplier loyalty, store loyalty, and so on.

Marketing Implications from the Three Levels

The discussions to this point provide the basis for a key implication for marketing's treatment of the three levels of customer classification. Notice that Figure 4-5 has now added the position of the marketer in the three-levels system and that relationships are represented by the arrows shown. These arrows illustrate the following basic point: since the variables in the left side of the figure (level 1) are basically unchanging, a marketer cannot hope to influence consumers on these variables. Marketers cannot ignore this level, however: level 1 is important because it represents the external and internal influences that direct consumers' interests. Therefore, rather than either ignoring or trying to influence level 1, *the astute marketer will endeavor to adapt to these consumer characteristics*, to help locate target consumers and appeal to their general interests in life.

As we move to levels 2 and 3, however, notice that change in the consumer measure is more likely. Because level 2 (benefits sought) is a relatively stable level, it is typically not highly susceptible to marketers' change attempts, although these sometimes can be successful. This level thus presents the marketer with two options (represented by the two-way arrows in the figure). Usually a marketer will attempt an **adaptation strategy**—here measures are taken of the mix of benefits that consumers are seeking, then marketing mixes are developed that stress that same mix of benefits. Occasionally, however, a marketer attempts a **proactive strategy**, and attempts to change the desires of the target consumers. (Proactive strategies are used especially if it is felt that consumers might not be fully aware of the advantages of certain attributes in a new product or service offering).

At level 3, change and influence are the norms. Other than that group of consumers who are already behaving exactly in the preferred manner, the marketer will be trying to employ his or her tools to bring the remainder of the market toward new behaviors. Consumers who do not yet own heat pumps, those who

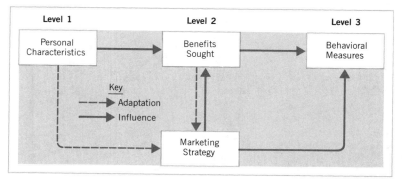

FIGURE 4-5 **Primary Influence Flows and the Marketer's Role**

have not yet tried our new brand of cereal, those who are shopping at our competitors' store, and so forth, will all be potential targets for marketing programs in these areas.

USING THE LEVELS FOR SEGMENTATION

A leading marketing consultant recently predicted,

The importance of strategy in marketing is going to become paramount. . . . Marketers need large-scale quantitative market studies that describe buying behavior, consumer beliefs and attitudes, and communications exposure. This is the only way marketers can pin down the narrow segments at which they're aiming.[7]

The large-scale studies mentioned by this consultant are likely to include measures from all three of our levels of classification. As a practical matter, therefore, we have three basic options in handing them in a segmentation study. Figure 4-6 illustrates these options. Notice that each option starts with one of our levels of classification and creates (defines) potential segment groups, then evaluates these groups using one or both of the other classification levels. The evaluation is done to see if the groups will meet our criteria as true segments (you may recall that these criteria require segments to have group identity, to exhibit systematic behaviors, and to offer efficiency for the marketing mix). For example, let's assume we started with the third option in Figure 4-6, and defined

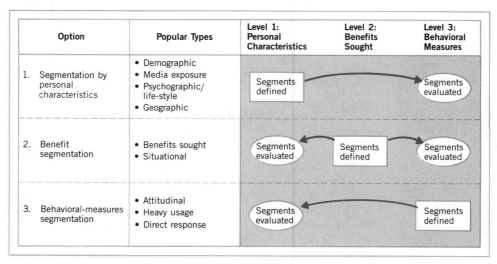

FIGURE 4-6 **The Three Primary Options for Segmentation Studies**

a possible segment as "heavy users of paper towels." This would provide a basis for group identity, and would score well on our systematic behavior criterion (since heavy usage *is* a behavior). However, we still need to evaluate this segment to discover what personal characteristics these heavy users have, so that we can locate them, understand their interests, and can create appeals for them.

As the Ford research manager noted earlier, the fact that 200–300 measures of a consumer might be gathered means that the actual segmentation process offers a wide range of possible approaches. Our discussion to this point has been abstract, but now we will turn to actual marketing practice. Now we shall examine a number of the more popular segmentation approaches used by marketers, noting examples of applications for each. As Figure 4-6 suggests, we'll organize our investigation in terms of the three basic options, starting with the case in which segments are formed on the basis of consumers' personal characteristics.

Segmentation by Personal Characteristics

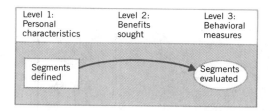

As indicated in the illustration, in this approach our tentative segments are first formed using consumers' personal characteristics, and they they are evaluated using the behavioral measures from level 3. Four basic approaches are highly popular in marketing today:

1. Demographic segmentation.
2. Media exposure segmentation.
3. Life-style/psychographic segmentation.
4. Geographic segmentation.

Each of these approaches contains numerous further possibilities, which makes for an interesting menu from which marketers may choose! In the discussions that follow, we'll briefly examine some prime alternatives.

Demographic Segmentation

As discussed in Chapter 3, demographics reflect the easily measurable vital statistics of a society. Within marketing, demographic and SES (socioeconomic status) variables are often used as bases for describing types of consumers. Differences in age, race or ethnic heritage, sex, education, occupation, and income are all commonly used, and are sometimes combined into specific indexes (such as "family life cycle" or "social class," which we will discuss in later chapters). The following examples illustrate applications of **demographic segmentation**.

Segmentation by Sex

As a basic illustration of our approach, the segments would first be created on the basis of a personal characteristic (here, male or female), then evaluated for potential differences in purchasing behavior. For many products, markets have long been clearly segmented either to females or males due to particular differences in personal needs and social roles. Notice that traditional sex segmentation has often included *both* systematic differences in purchasing behaviors (i.e., women bought some products while men bought others) *and* opportunities for marketing efficiency (e.g., some magazines, TV shows, stores, etc. geared to either sex, allowing them to be reached more efficiently). Moreover, in recent years, as women's roles have changed, new opportunities for segmentation have arisen.

For example, women now buy about 45 percent of all cars sold in the United States (this is a dramatic rise from 22 percent only 10 years ago: women now constitute the

fastest-growing segment of auto buyers). In terms of systematic purchasing behaviors, women also tend to concentrate on certain styles of cars. For example, women account for 65 percent of sales of the Nissan Pulsar NX model; overall they buy more subcompacts than do men, and about as many compacts and small sporty cars. At present, however, they buy only a third or fewer of the luxury and large car models (although influencing many more purchases in these categories when bought jointly with a spouse).

Given its growing significance, manufacturers are striving to develop segmented appeals for this huge market segment. Their efforts stretch to all areas of the marketing mix, including car design, credit programs, and special promotions and consumer education materials. One area receiving special attention is the dealers' salesroom. Because over 90 percent of salespersons currently are men, special "sales sensitivity" seminars are being run to improve the interactions salespersons have with the female market segment. Segmented advertising campaigns are also evident. Women's service and professional magazines carry many auto ads, for example, and the design and copy of the ads themselves often reflect research done on this segment (for example, Toyota discovered that women's ad recall scores are higher when a woman is shown driving a car; ads were developed accordingly).[8]

Ethnic and Race Segmentation

In this approach, consumers are first assigned to a potential segment based upon their ethnic or racial group membership; then these segments are evaluated on the marketing efficiency and systematic purchasing behavior criteria. Ethnic segmentation in marketing used to involve particularly local markets, in which different neighborhood retailers would cater to enclaves of immigrants from different nations of Europe, or to neighborhoods segregated by racial characteristics. Over time these forces have weakened, as social and physical mobility have worked to shift residential patterns, and second-, third-, and fourth-generation citizens of different ethnic and racial origins have become assimilated into the larger mosaic of U.S. society. Today, the nature of potential ethnic segments has changed, and there is considerable uncertainty in marketers' minds about when and how market segmentation might best be accomplished. Let's briefly consider the following:

- "Black people aren't dark-skinned white people, "states one advertising executive. "We have different preferences and customs, and we require a special effort."[9]
- A recent seminar on marketing to Hispanics revealed that in New York City alone, the Hispanic population has now surpassed 2.5 million, with a buying power about the same size as the gross national product of the nation of Chile ($19 billion)![10]
- California, the most populous U.S. state and with a population of trendsetters, is experiencing enormous changes in its ethnic makeup. Projections indicate that by the year 2010, that is, within the next 20 years, *every* ethnic group will be a minority in the state. Whites ("Anglos") will fall to 47 percent of the population, while Hispanics will grow to 33 percent and Asian Americans to 12.5 percent (one of eight residents), and blacks will remain at about 7.5 percent.[11]
- Hispanics are considered by many marketers to be brand loyal, and thus are courted heavily by some brands. Research in New York City, for example, found that Nestlé's Quik holds an 89 percent share of the Hispanic market, versus a 44 percent share in the non-Hispanic market (this gives it a 55 percent share overall). However, U.S. Hispanics are not homogeneous in terms of their own cultural backgrounds. Those in

California and the Southwest typically have come from Mexico, those in Florida from Cuba, while those in the Northeast have come primarily from Puerto Rico and the Dominican Republic. The backgrounds, incomes, and interests of these groups can differ significantly (many Cubans, for example, were doctors, lawyers, and business executives who emigrated to the United States 30 years ago when the communist government took over in Cuba, and have now become establishment figures in Florida). Marketers are thus wrestling with the question of how to most effectively appeal to Hispanics, while minimizing costs. One current marketing controversy, in fact, is whether English versus Spanish should be used in ads aimed at Hispanics![12]

■ Ethnic segmentation is a key factor in other markets around the world as well as in the United States. In Canada, for example, about 45 percent of the citizens are of British origin, about 30 percent are of French origin, and others are from a variety of other nations. Geographically and culturally, however, these ethnic backgrounds have not entirely assimilated into a single national marketplace. In Quebec, for example, over 80 percent of consumers are of French origin, with only some 10 percent of English origin. The daily languages differ, and a number of customs and preferences differ as well. This has led one Canadian researcher to conclude that "in Canada, cross-cultural studies are not a luxury but a necessity," especially due to government policies aimed at encouraging cultural diversity.[13]

The foregoing points all indicate that large groups of consumers are living daily lives that involve identification with distinct subcultures. In most cases there are marketing efficiencies available, such as specialized radio stations, magazines, and retailers. Also, in some cases there are systematic purchasing differences, such as in food preferences. Nonetheless, just as marketers need to guard against stereotyping all women as a single market segment, so do we need to guard against stereotyping any particular ethnic group. Detailed understanding of each potential ethnic market is needed before distinct segmentation is undertaken (if you would like to pursue further reading on issues of ethnic and race segmentation, you may wish to begin with the references in Note 14 at the back of the book, under Chapter 4's listings).

The application examples for sex and ethnic segmentation provide enough illustrations for us to recognize the basic types of segmentation opportunities for the other main demographic and SES variables. *Segmentation by age,* for example, has long been practiced by some marketers for the baby market, children, teens, young adults, senior citizens, and so on. As we discussed in Chapter 3, the shifting of the huge "baby boom" generation is currently focusing much marketing attention to understanding the 35- to 54-year-old segment for the 1990s! *Segmentation by income* is also frequently studied by marketers, since different consumer spending levels spring from this variable. For example, as a practicing marketer you will find many reports available on the preferences and spending habits of the "affluentials" (a term variously defined as households with incomes over $50,000, $75,000, or other high figures). Sometimes, *segmentation by marital status* or *segmentation by occupation* (e.g., accountants, interior designers) can be very helpful for targeting particular products or services to special interest groups.

In summary, demographic segmentation offers a multitude of possibilities for

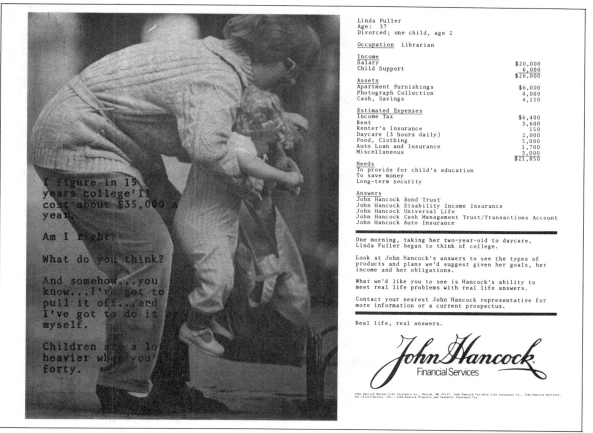

Financial Services aim toward a growing market segment.

classifying consumers according to easily identifiable personal characteristics. In each case, the demographic variable is intended to "stand for" certain special dimensions of these people in terms of how they live their daily lives, what they find to be of particular interest, and how they might behave differentially as consumers.

Media Exposure Segmentation

This approach—**media exposure segmentation**—is much more limited than demographic segmentation, since here the focus is only on choosing effective media (magazines, newspapers, radio and TV stations, etc.) by which to reach

For when your tastes grow up.
Now with a new look.

Canada Dry aims a soft drink at the growth segment of adult consumers.

A recent 7-Up addition to assist in attracting the younger segment.

desirable consumers with advertising messages. In terms of our segmentation framework, a potential segment here is first *defined* as consumers who are likely to be in the audience for a particular medium. These segments are then *evaluated* by advertisers in terms of their prospective purchasing behaviors.

To assist advertisers in this evaluation (and to help them decide to place advertising dollars with their firm), large media companies employ market research to develop "profiles" of their readers or audience members. These profiles concentrate on who these consumers are (often using demographics) and their purchasing behaviors for particular product types. The media then advertise to marketers, and compete for marketers' dollars on the basis of the "fit" of their audiences' consumer profiles and the prices they charge to reach the consumers in that media segment.

In summary, this is a somewhat narrow category of market segmentation. It is, however, frequently used in the daily world of advertising, and does offer marketing mix efficiency through better media decisions.

Segmentation by Life-styles and Psychographics

In contrast to the narrow focus of the media exposure approach, the **life-style/ psychographic segmentation** approach can be extremely broad. It was first

An ad aimed at advertisers, to assist media exposure segmentation.

used in marketing about 25 years ago: before then marketers had relied on general demographic and personality measures for segmentation. As we've seen for demographics (and will see in Chapter 7 for personality), however, these are general measures that extend to many aspects of a person's life beyond those of interest to marketers. Thus marketers were interested in creating *new forms of measures that would focus more on consumption and less on other aspects of a person.* The two forms of new measurements that emerged were termed "life-styles" and "psychographics." At the start of their development, then, life-styles and psychographics were conceptually *two distinct streams of work,* with life-styles deriving more from demographic bases and psychographics deriving more from personality bases.

Consumer Life-styles: "AIO Patterns"

The concept of "life-styles" has a long and honored place in the annals of social science, including the work of the great German sociologist, Max Weber, in his study of social classes in society (see Chapter 13). In general, **life-style** reflects people choosing activities that represent the ways they *wish* to live. Our life-styles don't just arise and exist in a vacuum. They are largely molded by three factors: (1) the ways in which we were raised, (2) our personal interests and values, and (3) the current demands of our daily lives (notice that this suggests that demographic variables such as age, education, and occupation will be associated strongly with different consumer life-styles). Moreover, different consumer life-styles should lead to differences in peoples' consumption behaviors, since many products and services act to support us in living our daily lives in the fashion we most desire.

Thus there was a strong conceptual reason to expect that consumer life-styles would be a useful segmentation approach. The earliest work in marketing then developed a large number of "AIO" questions asked of consumers: **AIO** stands for **activities, interests**, and **opinions**.[15] Questions range from work and social activities, through family, food, and media interests, to opinions about oneself, politics, social issues, and the future. Figure 4-7 presents some illustrative questions used in consumer life-style studies.

In conducting life-style segmentation, surveys of this type are given to large, national samples of consumers. Then the data are analyzed using multivariate statistical techniques to search for groups of people who report that they have similar activities, interests, and opinions. In one famous study by a leading advertising agency, for example, adult U.S. men and women were each classified into five life-style segments (the female segments were descriptively named "Eleanor," the elegant socialite, "Cathy," the contented housewife, "Thelma," the old-fashioned traditionalist, "Mildred," the militant mother, and "Candice," the chic suburbanite). These segments were then evaluated by comparing their patterns of consumption behaviors: as we might expect from their names, differences in product and store preferences were found, as were differences in media exposure.[16] Thus an insightful marketer using life-style segmentation can discern which types of consumers are strong prospects for his or her brand, what other things appeal to these prospects, and how they might best be reached through the media.

Consumer Psychographics

In an insightful review of this area, William Wells has defined **psychographics** as "quantitative research intended to place consumers on psychological—as distinguished from demographic—dimensions."[17] Thus the *intention* of psychographic research is quite clear.

FIGURE 4-7 **Illustrative Questions in a Life-Style Study**

A. Activities

*About how many times
in the last 12 months have you:*

	None	Once or Twice	3 to 5 Times	6 to 18 Times	19 to 35 Times	About Once a Week	Almost Daily
Gone to church							
Traveled out of state							
Used a credit card							
Attended a picnic							
Placed a bet							
Gone hunting							
Dialed information							

(and so forth; hundreds of questions are possible.)

B. Interests and Opinions

Please indicate the extent to which you agree or disagree with each statement below.
Use the following response scale to record a number next to each statement:

Definitely Disagree	−3	−2	−1	0	+1	+2	+3	Definitely Agree

_____ I live a well-planned life.
_____ My family is the most important thing in my life.
_____ I try to work out physically on a regular basis.
_____ The government should be cut back.
_____ I like parties.
(and so forth; hundreds of questions are possible.)

At the same time that life-style research was developing in marketing, there was a concern that pure demographics and pure life-style research would not capture what was going on in consumers' minds—marketers also strongly desired to have psychological information available. Until that time, two types of psychological information had been available: motivation research and personality research. As we will see in future chapters, however, both these research streams faced problems. Motivation research had been questioned on grounds of the representativeness of its very small samples and the validity of its conclusions, while personality research continued to be plagued with consistently low correlations with consumer behavior.

Was it possible, though, to *combine* the strengths of these approaches into a new consumer research approach? Could new measures be constructed that portrayed consumers' personal needs, fears, and desires (as motivation research did), but within large samples that could be quantitatively analyzed (as personality research did) and that could also reflect the different types of lives that these people were living (as demographics did)?

Several groups of researchers thought that this could be done, and set out to develop psychographics as an area of study.[18]

Since there is no single theory of psychographics, researchers in advertising have used a wide variety of approaches to this area. To illustrate, one study of the stomach remedy market divided consumers into four psychographic segments: (1) "severe sufferers" are anxious people who take ailments seriously and believe they suffer more severely than others; (2) "active medicators" are emotionally well adjusted, but lead demanding lives and use remedies to relieve every ache and pain; (3) "hypochondriacs" are afraid of new ingredients, extra potency, and possible side effects of remedies, but are deeply concerned over their health and seek medical guidance in treatment; and (4) "practicalists" are emotionally stable and little concerned over ailments or remedy dangers, but accept discomforts and use fewest remedies. When these segments were evaluated according to brands used, interesting differences emerged: brands A and B (names were disguised in the release of this study) drew most heavily from the severe sufferer segment, brand C relied on active medicators, brand D relied on hypochondriacs, whereas brand E drew most heavily from the practicalists![19]

Combining Psychographics and Life-styles Although the backgrounds of these two topics are quite distinct, their measures have typically been lumped together with many other segmentation-related measures (demographics, media exposure, and brand preferences and buying behaviors) in marketing studies. The primary interest of this research, moreover, was to try to solve managerial problems rather than to develop a rigorous theory of psychographics or life-styles. The end result, however, is that during the past 25 years, the field of marketing has come to view psychographics and life-style research as so intertwined that it is hard to separate the two.

This has led to some serious criticisms by professionals in advertising as to the validity of this approach. Everyone involved now agrees that psychographic/life-style research has moved away from a solid grounding in psychological theory. This means that its users must make special efforts to be careful in their measurements, statistical analyses, and interpretations of results if they are to uncover valid information on consumer behavior. This suggests that when you are in a position actually to use such research, recognize that special care is warranted in evaluating its quality before beginning to make marketing decisions. (If you would like to read more about these issues, you may wish to begin with Note 20 at the back of the book, under the listings for Chapter 4.) In the meantime, you may be interested in how one combination system, VALS, has been applied to marketing problems.

Why "A Breed Apart"? The VALS System

In response to concerns about the quality of research in this area, the VALS (Values and Life-Styles) program for segmenting the consumer market is an important development. VALS was created by SRI International, a management consulting firm in California, and has been used by many marketers and advertising agencies to plan their market segmentation efforts. The essence of the VALS program is a classification scheme that assigns each adult American to one VALS segment. The original VALS system had nine segments—

in each the people had similar patterns of values (beliefs, desires, prejudices, etc.) and life-style activities. The following application illustrates how the system was used by marketers:

There's an interesting VALS story behind the famous Merrill Lynch advertising campaign showing various scenes in which a lone bull stalks, highlighting the firm's theme, "A Breed Apart." An earlier Merrill Lynch campaign, which ran for a long period during the 1970s, had featured pictures of a herd of bulls galloping across the plains, with the theme "Merrill Lynch Is Bullish on America!" Besides its striking graphics and patriotic overtones, this campaign capitalized on the well-known Wall Street terminology for people who expect increasing stock prices (and therefore, profits for investors).

Several years ago, however, the firm changed ad agencies and shifted its campaign to the lone bull, "breed apart" theme. Why? Dr. Plummer, a leading life-style researcher, and an executive with the new ad agency, explained that the agency's VALS-based research discovered that the "bullish on American theme" was not appealing to Merrill Lynch's primary target segment—the Achievers segment, who have the money and the interest to be heavy stock investors. While it may have appealed well to "Belongers," the idea of a "herd instinct" is not appealing to someone who wants to think of himself or herself as a driving individualist or an entrepreneurial investor. Thus the shift to "A Breed Apart" and the picture of a lone but powerful bull. According to Dr. Plummer, "Our strategy shift was clearly emotionally on track with the Achiever target audience." The results were impressive: the percentage of consumers who noticed and remembered the firm's ads increased from 8 percent to 55 percent and its share of market increased as well.[21]

Thus the combination of psychographic and life-style segments can lead to useful marketing insights, even though it is controversial. The original VALS system has recently been modified into a new system, called VALS-2. If you would like to learn more about the development of VALS-2, exactly what its segments are (there are eight), and how they differ in their consumption behaviors, an overview appears in Appendix 4-A.

Geographic Segmentation

Although we often don't think of it this way, most consumer behavior is "local" in nature, as individual purchases occur in local retail outlets, and through local service providers. Thus the potentials for **geographic segmentation** are large. For local businesses, a basic form of geographic segmentation occurs each time the businessperson adapts to his or her local customers' preferences. For national marketers, moreover, two particular forms of geographic segmentation offer interesting possibilities—**regional segmentation** (in which distinct mixes are created for different regions) and **zip clustering** (sometimes called "geodemographic clustering," in which distinct mixes are created for similar types of neighborhoods stretched across the nation). In terms of our framework, in each approach segments are first formed based on a consumer's geographic location; then the segments are evaluated with regard to the marketing efficiency and systematic purchasing behavior criteria.

Melting Pot or Not? Regions Do Differ . . .

Historically, many forces have worked to develop regional differences in the United States and other countries. Differences in *climate, geography,* and *natural resources,* for example, led to regional differences in both work and leisure activities, while differences in *immigration patterns* created strong regional differences in cultures. In contrast, the more recent forces of *mobility* and *technology* have worked to reduce regional differences, as people move to new areas, travel widely, and receive a steady stream of communications from various centers around the nation and the world. However, marketers have discovered that a number of regional differences still remain. These have led companies such as Campbell Soup to create special product versions (e.g., spicy soup for the Southwest, more bland for the North) and special sales promotions for each region. Some examples of regional differences are the following:

Fifty percent of Southerners report that they "nearly always have meat at breakfast," against only 10 percent of Easterners. Easterners, on the other hand, eat an incredible number of doughnuts, and drink 66 percent more hot tea than the national average, and consume the most whisky. Southerners drink the least whisky and wine, but compensate with huge soft drink consumption to wash down all those potato chips they buy. Westerners tend toward a more healthful life-style: they compensate for their high consumption of wine by downing plenty of vitamins, cheese, and fresh fruits and vegetables. Midwesterners are about at the norm for most products, except that their "sweet tooths" for high levels of ice cream, candy, and snacks lead them to work off the calories with higher levels of bowling.[22]

As we'd expect, consumers also show a preference for TV life-styles that are familiar to them. A Nielsen ratings study several years ago, for example, showed that ratings in the Northeast were 46 percent higher for the show "Taxi" than were ratings in the South ("Hill Street Blues" was 35 percent higher). Conversely, shows with rural or frontier themes drew much better in the South: "Dallas" had 48 percent higher ratings in Dixie, with "Dukes of Hazzard" 45 percent higher than in the Northeast.[23]

As we move to local market areas we find even stronger instances of unique consumer preference patterns. In comparing Los Angeles with Philadelphia, for example, marketers know that cocktail mixes sell very well in Los Angeles (at a rate three times greater than the national average) but at only one-sixth this rate in Philadelphia. Why might this be true? In a reversal of this pattern, frozen meat is very popular in Philadelphia (selling at almost four times the national average), while it is almost absent in Los Angeles, selling at a rate only one-fourth of the national rate and only one-fifteenth of that in Philadelphia.[24] With data such as these, marketers can begin to probe why a product is selling well or not in a given city and can better assess prospects for new entries in related categories.

Zipping Straight to Neighborhood Targets

Zip clustering is a geodemographic segmentation approach that concentrates on finding similar types of consumer neighborhoods across the nation.[25] Claritas Corporation originated this concept some 15 years ago, and is one of the major suppliers of these data today. Essentially, Claritas's approach relies on market research data for huge samples of American consumers. These are combined with detailed data from the U.S. Census, organized by postal zip codes (in total, over 60 consumer measures are used to describe each of the 36,000 U.S. zip code areas). Cluster analysis—a sophisticated form of statistical analysis—is then used to find patterns of similarity among zip codes. These are then "clustered" together into particular segments, or groups of zip codes in which consumers tend to have similar life-styles and consumption behaviors. Claritas's **PRIZM system** offers 40 such segments: you may find it interesting to look at Exhibit 4-1, which illustrates six of these (if you would like to learn more about this approach, you may wish to consult the book cited at the bottom of the exhibit).

How do marketers use this information? Three primary ways are

1. *Direct marketing.* Direct-mail pieces can be crafted to appeal to a particular segment's consumers, then sent only to those zip codes either nationally or in a smaller geographic area. One Virginia savings bank, for example, boosted its response rate from 2 percent to 7 percent using this method.
2. *Site selection.* Decisions on where to locate stores, restaurants, and other outlets can be guided by these data. The U.S. Army, for example, found that its top recruits come from the zip cluster called "Shotguns & Pickups," so it opted to place its new recruiting centers in many neighborhoods in this cluster.
3. *Store layout and stocking.* Decisions such as what foods to feature or stock heavily in neighborhood supermarkets can also be guided by these data. Also, test promotions that work well in certain clusters can be considered for use in other stores belonging to the same cluster.

EXHIBIT 4–1   **PRIZM'S NEIGHBORHOOD CLUSTERS AS MARKET SEGMENTS**[a]

Blue Blood Estates

1.1% of U.S. households
Median household income: $70,307
Age group: 35–44
Wealthy, white, college-educated families; posh big-city townhouses
Characteristics: Buy: U.S. Treasury notes: Drive: Mercedes-Benzes; Read: *The New York Times, Gourmet,* Eat: natural cold cereal, skim milk; TV: *David Letterman,* Sample ZIPs: Beverly Hills, Calif. 90212; Potomac, Md. 20854; Scarsdale, N.Y. 10583; McLean, Va. 22101; Lake Forest, Ill. 60045

Bohemian Mix

1.1% of U.S. households
Median household income: $21,916
Age group: 18–34
White-collar college graduates; singles, racially mixed
Characteristics: Buy: wine by the case, common stock; Drive: Alfa Romeos, Peugeots; Read: *GQ, Harper's;* Eat: Whole-wheat bread, frozen waffles; TV: *Nightline.* Sample ZIPs: Greenwich Village, N.Y. 10014; Dupont Circle, Washington, D.C. 20036; Cambridge, Mass. 02139; Lincoln Park, Chicago 60614; Shadyside, Pittsburgh 15232; Haight-Ashbury, San Francisco 94117

[a]The "Characteristics" entry indicates products consumed at much higher rate than the average for all Americans.

EXHIBIT 4-1   PRIZM'S NEIGHBORHOOD CLUSTERS AS MARKET SEGMENTS CONTINUED

Levittown, USA

3.1% U.S. households
Median household income: $28,742
Age group: 55–plus
High-school-educated white couples
post-war tract subdivisions
Characteristics: Watch ice hockey, go
bowling; Read: *Stereo Review, Barron's;*
Eat: Instant iced tea, English muffins;
TV: *Newhart, Sale of the Century.*
Sample ZIPs: Norwood, Mass. 02062;
Cuyahoga Falls, Ohio 44221; Donolson,
Nashville, Tenn. 37214; Stratford, Conn.
06497; Cheswick, Pa. 15024

Middle America

3.2% of U.S. households
Median household income: $24,431
Age group: 45–64
High-school educated, white families;
middle-class suburbs
Characteristics: Use domestic air
charters, Christmas clubs; Drive:
Plymouth Sundances, Chevy Chevettes;
Read: *Saturday Evening Post,* Eat: Pizza
mixes, TV dinners; TV: *Family Ties,*
Sample ZIPs: Marshall, Mich. 49068;
Sandusky, Ohio 44870; Hagerstown, Md.
21740; Oshkosh, Wis. 54901;
Stroudsburg, Pa. 18360; Elkhart, Ind.
46514

Black Enterprise

0.8% of U.S. households
Median household income: $33,149
Age group: 35–54
Black achievers, intelligentsia
High educational levels
Characteristics: Use cigars, malt liquor;
Drive: Yugos; Read: *Ebony, Ms;* Eat:
frozen dessert pies; TV: *American
Bandstand, Nightline.* Sample ZIPs:
Capitol Heights, Md. 20743; Auburn
Park, Chicago 60620; Seven Oaks,
Detroit 48235; Mount Airy, Philadelphia
19119; South De Kalb, Atlanta 30034;
Cranwood, Cleveland 44128

Towns and Gowns

1.2% of U.S. households
Median household income: $17,862
Age group: 18–34
College-educated, white singles
Middle-class college towns
Characteristics: Use civic, country clubs;
Drive: Mercury Sables, Subaru DL4s;
Read: *Natural History, GQ;* Eat:
Mexican foods, canned stews; TV: *Good
Morning America.* Sample ZIPs: State
College, Pa. 16801; Bloomington, Ind.
47401; Ithaca, N.Y. 14850; Gainesville,
Fla. 32606; Corvallis, Ore. 97330;
College Station, Texas 77840

Source: Michael J. Weiss, *The Clustering of America* (New York: Harper & Row, 1988).

Segmentation by Benefits Sought

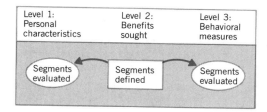

As illustrated, our second major segmentation option begins by creating segments on our second level of consumer classification—benefits sought from a product or service—and then evaluates these segments for differences on *both* personal characteristics and purchasing behavior (levels 1 and 3 of consumer classification). **Benefit segmentation** is an enormously popular approach marketers use to understand their markets better and to develop segmentation strategies for them. As Russell Haley, the developer of benefit segmentation, explained, "The benefits which people are seeking in consuming a given product are the basic reasons for the existence of true market segments."[26]

Table 4-1 illustrates Haley's classic summary of benefit segments in the toothpaste market. Notice that the four groups are first defined on the basis of the

TABLE 4-1 A BENEFIT SEGMENTATION ANALYSIS OF THE TOOTHPASTE MARKET

	"The Sensory Segment"	"The Sociables"	"The Worriers"	"The Independents"
Principal benefit sought	Flavor, product appearance	Brightness of teeth	Decay prevention	Price
Demographic strengths	Children	Teens, young people	Large families	Men
Special behavioral characteristics	Users of spearmint flavored toothpaste	Smokers	Heavy users	Heavy users
Brands disproportionately favored	Colgate, Stripe	Macleans, Plus White, Ultra Brite	Crest	Brands on sale
Personality characteristics	High self-involvement	High sociability	High hypochondriasis	High autonomy
Life-style characteristics	Hedonistic	Active	Conservative	Value oriented

Source: Russell I. Haley, "Benefit Segmentation: A Decision-Oriented Research Tool," *Journal of Marketing,* July 1968, Table 1, p. 33.

primary benefit they are seeking; then they are evaluated according to differences in some personal characteristics (suggesting potential efficiencies in reaching and appealing to them) and differences in purchase behavior potentials. Although not shown in the table, this type of information can then be used to suggest marketing mix strategies. For example, notice how particular product features, pricing strategies, advertising appeals, and media suggest themselves if we spend a few moments analyzing even the highly summarized information in this table. The types of more complete information usually gathered in a benefit segmentation study would allow us to see also how consumers in each segment regard competing brands, what further benefits they are seeking, and so forth. Benefit segmentation is thus a rich tool for marketing management.

The key to this approach lies in the term "benefits." For consumers, this refers to *positive consequences* they will experience from using a particular product. For marketers, this refers to the *mix of product characteristics* that needs to be designed into the product or service in order to deliver those positive consequences that consumers are seeking. Three key dimensions result from this view of benefits:

1. Specific benefits will differ widely from product to product; thus marketers need to do *customized research studies* for benefit segmentation. We cannot rely on the kinds of syndicated consumer data we have been discussing in the first set of segmentation approaches ("syndicated" refers to a single large study done by a research firm, then sold to marketers of many products for application to their own situations: census demographics, media exposure surveys, VALS, PRIZM, and so forth are all examples of this). In forthcoming chapters we will be learning more about how to study consumer benefits, so we need not be concerned about research details at this point.

2. By definition, benefits are desirable, so most consumers will want most benefits. Opportunities for segmentation arise from *trade-offs* consumers are willing to make among the benefits possible (and the prices paid to obtain them). *Only when different groups of consumers prefer different "packages" of benefits will we have an opportunity for benefit segmentation.* Fortunately, however, this is common in the consumer marketplace. Consider why such very different types of clothing stores are patronized, why such very different types of automobiles are purchased, and so forth. In fact, when we think about it, we can see this occurring in virtually all aspects of consumer behavior!

3. Because it focuses on product characteristics, *benefit segmentation is particularly suited for product, pricing, or service design decisions.* This in part accounts for its popularity, since it does in a real sense represent "the marketing concept in action"—finding out what consumers want and need, and then making it available to them. It is also appealing in a competitive sense, as it offers opportunities to distinguish one brand from its competitors by offering the set of benefits its target segment of consumers most desire. (If you would like to read more about benefit segmentation, you may wish to consult Note 27 at the back of the book, under Chapter 4's listings.)

Before leaving this topic, we should give special mention to *situational segmentation,* which is related to the traditional benefit segmentation approach, and which introduces some further interesting ideas about consumer behavior and marketing strategy. As pointed out by Peter Dickson, for many products and services, consumer demand actually occurs because of the situation in which a person finds himself or herself.[28] Shotgun shells, for example, are needed for hunting, special dress clothes are needed for formal social occasions, and so forth. Exposure to particular situations, moreover, does not occur randomly, but in a systematic fashion. This means that we should be able to predict which types of consumers are likely to be in which types of situations:

What Do I Want Most? It Depends . . .

For marketing strategy in certain product categories, it is important to recognize that the nature of the situation can strongly influence that exact pattern of benefits a consumer is seeking. In one national study of home appliances, for example, Dickson and Wilkie found that over three-fourths of all consumer purchases of refrigerators in the United States resulted from one of three circumstances (situations): (1) in 36 percent of the cases the existing refrigerator had broken down completely, (2) in 18 percent, buyers were involved in a residential move, and (3) in 24 percent, buyers had an old refrigerator that needed repair, though it was still working at some level. Notice that each of these situations introduces different strong forces into the types of benefits a consumer is seeking, and the ways in which a purchase will be made. For example, in which case is immediate delivery likely to be most important? As expected, this research found that the purchase process differed depending on which situation was governing the purchase. (We will study the broader topic of situational influences in Chapter 14).[29]

Behavioral-Measures Segmentation

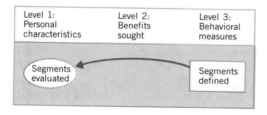

Segmentation by behavioral measures is emerging as the "hottest" option for segmentation developments in the 1990s! As illustrated, it begins at level 3 of the consumer classification system—the level that reflects brand-specific measures of consumers' beliefs, attitudes, and actual behaviors. In this option, we first create groups of consumers who behave similarly or who hold similar purchase predispositions. In terms of our overall segmentation framework, notice that this beginning guarantees that the "systematic behavior" criterion for a market segment is met: our only remaining question is whether the marketing mix efficiency criterion can also be met.

For example, let's assume that we begin by grouping together all those consumers in our sample who buy mascara at much higher than average rates: we'll call this the "heavy user" group. Notice that we *know* that this group systematically differs in its purchase behavior, but we don't yet know "who" these people are. Thus we need to evaluate the grouping to see which—if any—personal characteristics (demographics, life-styles, media exposure, etc.) actually distinguish heavy purchasers of mascara from the rest of the consumer market. After eyeing this information, we can use it to put the lid on an efficient segmented marketing program that will lash the competition! There are many detailed alternatives possible within behavioral-measures segmentation. Let's look more closely at three types.

Attitudinal Segmentation

Attitudinal segmentation is a special form of behavioral segmentation that groups together consumers who hold similar beliefs, attitudes, or preferences within a particular product category. These groups are then evaluated for differences that will distinguish them on personal characteristic measures. In addition, because attitudes do not necessarily reflect actual purchasing behaviors, marketers often attempt to also evaluate these segments in terms of additional measures of how they behave in the marketplace. The following study helps us see how this can be done:

Buying for Frying: Loyal Toward Oil?

In one recent study of cooking oil, three attitudinal segments were isolated: (1) the *single-brand group,* those consumers who believe that one single brand of cooking oil (regardless of which brand) is the best on the market; (2) the *multibrand group,* those consumers who believe that there is a set of very good brands that they like; and (3) a *parity group,* those consumers who believe that all brands are about the same.

A brief review of some of the study's findings demonstrates how these groups were further evaluated for marketing purposes. For example, the single-brand segment was found to be older and have a lower level of education; the multibrand segment was found to be younger, likely to have attended college, and to live in the Midwest or West; while the parity group seemed to draw from various sectors and had few strong identifying characteristics. In examining other behavioral measures, the multibrand segment was found to use coupons more heavily, and to recall advertising at a higher rate, whereas the parity segment bought more heavily on price specials. At the brand level, Wesson (the market leader) sold well to all three segments, while Mazola, the third-ranking brand, was strongest in the single-brand segment but weak in the parity segment. While this summary is not sufficient to indicate a clear strategic direction, detailed analyses of the entire set of findings would suggest different advertising, promotion, and pricing strategies for different brands in this market.[30]

Heavy-User Segmentation

You may already be aware that many marketers operate by using the "80–20 Rule"—that "80 percent of my business comes from only 20 percent of my customers!" While 80–20 is not always accurate, it is often true that the **heavy-**

users segment provides a surprisingly high percentage of total product sales, and marketers do search to discover exactly who these heavy users are. This can be done either for an entire product class or for customers of a particular brand or service, as indicated in the following examples.

Behind Your Banker's Smile . . .

Leader Federal Savings and Loan of Memphis, Tennessee, recently reported how it has successfully analyzed its own records in a segmentation study of its existing customers, based on their volume of usage of different product lines. Five segments emerged from the analysis:

1. "Givers," who comprise 20 percent of customers and account for over 60 percent of the firm's deposits and investments, but only 6 percent of the nonmortgage loans (not surprisingly, these are older persons).

2. "High rollers," who comprise less than 10 percent of all customers, but are quite active in financial matters, accounting for about 25 percent in each of the firm's various business categories (these were found to be dual-income households in their early middle-aged years).

3. "Takers," who comprise 15 percent of customers, account for only 4 percent of deposits, but who borrow over 50 percent of the firm's nonmortgage credit (these are younger families with house, auto, and child expenses).

4 and 5. Each of the preceding segments (1, 2, and 3) is a "heavy user" in at least one of the major product lines of this business, and is then targeted for special programs that fit its profile. However, the other two segments (4 and 5) reflect only light users of all product lines: they comprise about 50 percent of all customers, but account for only 10 percent of the firm's business. Although the firm is proud of its marketing sophistication, the names given to these two segments might suggest possible problems with a "customer-oriented marketing concept" in this business: the S&L's management labeled these groups as "marginal players" and "clutter!"[31]

Wheeling and Dealing

In addition to segmenting the present customers of a business, marketers are also often interested in segmenting the buyers of an entire product category. In the U.S. auto market, for example, one structural distinction occurs among domestic brands, Asian imports, and European imports. A survey of 25,000 purchasers revealed a number of interesting personal characteristic differences among the groups who bought each type. For example, buyers of domestic brands were 11–12 years older than were buyers of imports, and less likely to hold an executive or professional occupation. Some 60 percent of European-import buyers had college educations, compared to 50 percent of Asian-import buyers and 40 percent of domestic purchasers. At the brand level, Jaguar and Mercedes-Benz buyers have the highest household incomes, Saab owners are the most likely to be college graduates, Yugo and Volkswagen buyers are the youngest, and Peugeot, Volkswagen, and Volvos are the brands that women buy at the highest rates relative to men.[32]

Direct-Response Segmentation

Direct-response segmentation is especially concerned with targeting promotions to consumers who are most likely to react favorably. During its early years, the segmentation literature contained many studies of which types of consumers are most likely to buy on price deals, to use coupons, to switch brands, and so forth. As we move into the 1990s, however, new developments in "database management" are shifting this interest into new areas:

Getting to Know You . . .

As was the case for our savings and loan example, some marketers are fortunate enough to have natural records that identify their customers by name and record all the purchasing behavior that customer does with the firm. If this is representative of that customer's total activity within the product class, this can become an extremely valuable **consumer database** for segmentation purposes. Airlines, for example, have begun to use their "frequent flyer" program records to identify where and how often their prime customers are flying. Similarly, financial service firms are also developing their database profiles. Imagine, for example, how much Visa and American Express can discover about each cardholder's interests and buying habits if they choose to study the receipts they receive in the course of their business!

Beyond the natural records of transactions, of course, marketers and research firms have the option of requesting consumers' participation in the development of their databases, and are doing so at a dramatically increasing rate. One research firm, for example, is now offering marketers use of its Select & Save database consisting of 25 million households, with 1000 pieces of detailed information for each (including product usage, brand preferences, demographics, and psychographics). This database has been developed by sending out surveys seeking this information from consumers, in return for a gift, coupons, and the opportunity to receive future promotional offers from marketers who use the service. Each coupon, however, is encoded to identify precisely which household has received it! This means that a household's survey information can be used in conjunction with its behavioral responses to the promotions. Thus, over time, the database is updated to record exactly how prone each household is to redeem each coupon or to respond to each promotional offer. Since the survey also reports which competing brands that household uses, promotions can be targeted on this basis. For example, Folgers might decide to send a very-high-value coupon to heavy coffee-using households that currently use Maxwell House or Hills Brothers, but send a smaller refund offer to its current users of Folgers. As a measure of the value of this type of consumer information in the huge, competitive American market, we might note that fees for this service are steep: the basic charge to participate is $250,000, with another $50,000 to license the database and additional charges for further services such as tracking household responses to offers.[33]

A Database Battle Burns in Cigarettes

Outside of the research industry itself, two leaders in the development of database marketing are R. J. Reynolds and Philip Morris, the two cigarette giants that have been buying up giant food firms such as General Foods, Kraft, and Nabisco (each of which, interestingly, can also benefit mightily from developments of consumer databases). Within cigarettes alone, RJR reportedly spent $100 million to put together its own giant database of about half of the 55 million Americans who smoke. During the late 1980s Philip Morris reacted to RJR's successes in targeting heavy users of PM's brands and began to mount its own database. Its first effort, which was an insert card in *Time*, asked smokers to fill in some information about their current brands, then mail the card in return for two free packs of a mystery brand. Close to 2 million smokers returned these cards and were rewarded with two packs of Merits, together with a more detailed questionnaire that was entered into the database. RJR later responded with four-page print ads with exploding champagne corks, to call attention to its offer for a free Salem T-shirt: this attracted over 500,000 phone responses and more information for the ever-expanding consumer database. Much more activity than this has continued to go on in the years since, and is spreading rapidly to other product classes.[34] As consumers, we may not easily recognize the amount of activity since we are not likely to see it, unless we happen to belong to a specific "response prone" or "heavy-user" segment and a database marketer wishes to communicate directly with us!

Where Are We Headed?

At the start of our discussion of behavioral-measure segmentation, we mentioned that this was becoming the "hottest" area for development during the 1990s. Given our brief summary of the area, it should now be clear why this is the case! This approach is closely related to the explosion of spending on direct promotion in marketing and benefits from the increasing sophistication of computer technologies. It is virtually certain that this segmentation option will continue to develop and expand in the future.

Before ending this chapter, a brief comment may be in order. As we've seen, market segmentation is an extremely relevant and valuable concept. When we dig into it, we are actually trying to come to grips with the immensity and diversity of the entire consumer marketplace, and this is not fundamentally an easy task. However, the stakes for marketing decisions can be high, and it will pay marketing professionals to have insights about the segmentation options available to them.

As we leave this chapter, we bring the first section of the book to a close. We have now examined various perspectives, and can see how segmentation acts as a bridging concept between the aggregate consumer market and the individuals who comprise that market. In Part 2 of the book we delve more deeply into consumers as individuals, and examine why they behave in the ways they do.

SUMMARY

Background on Segmentation

In this chapter we examined *market segmentation*, which provides a structured means of viewing the marketplace. The theoretical basis for market segmentation is the economic theory of *price discrimination*, which explains how a monopolist firm can maximize revenues by adapting its price to each customer's willingness to pay. In modern marketing, the concept of segmentation expands this consideration to include any of the marketing mix elements in addition to price alone. Our formal definition of market segmentation is a managerial strategy that adapts a firm's marketing mix to best fit the various consumer demand curves existing in a market.

Segmentation is a three-stage process: (1) identifying segments, (2) selecting target segments, and (3) creating marketing mixes for each target segment. Consumer research plays an especially key role in the first stage, identifying segments. Here there are also three criteria that a true market segment must meet: (1) *group identity*, (2) *systematic behavior*, and (3) *efficiency potential* for the marketing mix. In other words, our search is for a customer grouping that will behave differently from other groups and that will be responsive to an efficient marketing mix aimed at it.

The Start of a Segmentation Study: Classifying Customers

Because an actual segmentation project can involve hundreds of possibilities, a basic framework is helpful for marketing managers and researchers. Our "three levels" framework in the chapter pointed out that every consumer can be classified in three basic ways: (1) according to his or her *personal characteristics*, (2) according to *benefits sought*, and (3) according to *behavioral measures* of actual purchasing. Any segmentation study can start by forming groups on one of the levels, and then evaluating them on one or both of the other levels.

Using the Levels for Segmentation

The remainder of the chapter examined the most popular segmentation approaches in marketing. Within *segmentation by personal characteristics*, we examined four popular approaches. *Demographic segmentation* defines segments on such bases as sex, ethnic group, age, income, and so on. *Media exposure segmentation* is a narrower approach: profiles of a medium's audience detail exactly which types of consumers can be reached by advertising in that medium. *Life-style/psychographic segmentation* is a much broader approach in which activities, interests, and opinions (*AIOs*) and various consumer psychological measures are used to produce distinct groupings. Our discussion examined the roots of this approach (also a detailed look at VALS 2, a major life-styles/psychographic system, is provided in Appendix 4-A). *Geographic segmentation* is the fourth popular type of segmentation by personal characteristics; we saw how this can be done either by *regions*, or through *zip clustering*, in which distinct marketing mixes are targeted to similar types of neighborhoods.

Our second major option is *segmentation by benefits sought*. Here the marketer begins by defining groups who are seeking similar mixes of benefits and then evaluates these groups to see if they differ on personal characteristics and purchase behaviors. A subset of this category involves situational segmentation, in which consumers desire different sets of benefits depending on their situations at the time. Our third major approach is termed *behavioral-measure segmentation*. Here the chapter examined *attitudinal segmentation*, segmenting by *heavy users* and *direct response*. In each of these cases, consumers are first grouped according to their similarity in attitudes, usage rates, or responsiveness to promotions; then the segments are evaluated according to what personal characteristics they may have in common. These approaches reflect recent developments in creating massive *consumer databases*, and using them for direct consumer promotions.

This chapter closes our first section of the book. Given the nature of segmentation, it acts as a natural bridge between the aggregate perspective (Chapter 3) and the individual level of consumer behavior. In Part Two, beginning with Chapter 5, we will be examining the interesting world of individual consumer behavior.

KEY TERMS

market segmentation
price discrimination
group identity
systematic behaviors
efficiency potential
personal characteristics
benefits sought
behavioral measures
adaptation strategy
proactive strategy
demographic segmentation
media exposure segmentation
life-style/psychographic segmentation

life-styles
AIOs
psychographics
geographic segmentation
regional segmentation
zip clustering
PRIZM system
benefit segmentation
behavioral-measures segmentation
attitudinal segmentation
heavy-user segmentation
direct-response segmentation
consumer database

APPENDIX 4 TERMS

VALS 2
resources
self-orientation
principle-oriented consumers
status-oriented consumers
action-oriented consumers
actualizers

fulfilleds
believers
achievers
strivers
experiencers
makers
strugglers

REVIEW QUESTIONS AND EXPERIENTIAL EXERCISES
[E = Application extension or experiential exercise]

1. What are the three criteria for a true market segment? Explain, using two different examples, why marketers would wish to have *both* the marketing

mix efficiency and systematic behavior criteria satisfied before targeting a particular segment.

2. For three of the products listed, provide descriptions of yourself using the chapter's levels of consumer classification (for each of the three levels, list at least three measures that accurately describe you).

    a. Automobiles   d. Soft drinks
    b. Cereal   e. Fast-food outlets
    c. Music   f. Stock brokerages

3. Choose two of the products or services listed below, and suggest three or four possible types of benefit segments or situations segments you would expect to find in the consumer market.

    a. Automobiles   d. Soft drinks
    b. Cereal   e. Fast-food outlets
    c. Music   f. Stock brokerages

[E] 4. Using the chapter notes located at the back of this book, read several classic articles to gain further understanding of market segmentation. Prepare a brief report on your findings. Good options include:

    a. Beginnings (Note 3)   c. Psychographics (Note 20)
    b. Life-styles (Note 15)   d. Benefit segmentation (Notes 26, 27)

[E] 5. The story at the opening of the chapter reported General Motor's new segmentation strategy. Gather several examples of print ads for each of the GM cars. Also, if possible, monitor television ads for these same cars. In each case, is this strategy evident? If so, how? Does it appear that the strategy is working?

[E] 6. The story at the opening of the chapter reported General Motor's new segmentation strategy. Use the business periodicals references of your library to locate recent articles on the GM brands. What is currently happening with them? Does this segmentation strategy seem viable?

[E] 7. Select two of the personal characteristics bases for market segmentation (age, ethnic background, sex, income, and so forth). Find magazines that are targeted to at least two different groups within each base (e.g., Blacks, Hispanics, teens, senior citizens). Analyze the ads appearing in each publication as to the products and services represented, and the appeals used. Select several ads as representative, and include them with a brief report on your findings.

[E] 8. Interview a sales representative or marketing manager for an advertising medium concerning the measures of consumers they use to sell their service. Write a brief report on your findings.

[E] 9. Interview a salesperson at an auto dealership regarding any differences seen between male and female car buyers. Probe for differences in (a) how the consumers buy, and (b) how the salespersons sell. Ask about any ads directed toward females. Does a male/female segmentation scheme make sense here, or is a more detailed breakdown necessary? Write a brief report on your findings.

[E] 10. Assume you are a marketing planner for Safeway, Kroger, or another large supermarket chain. Choose four of the "ZIP clusters" segments from Exhibit 4-1. For each, suggest three specific products that you would consider featuring in special promotions for testing in selected supermarkets in this cluster type. Explain your reasoning.

[E] 11. Read carefully the illustrated "ZIP cluster" segments in Exhibit 4-1, then consider the various types of neighborhoods in your town. Select two supermarkets from different ZIP codes that you believe are certain to represent distinct types of neighborhood clusters. Interview a store manager in each market concerning the special products, layouts, and policies they use to especially appeal to their customer segment. Write a brief report detailing your findings.

[E] 12. Read the book, *The Clustering of America,* by Michael Weiss (Harper & Row, 1988). Prepare a brief written report extending the text's coverage of the PRIZM system and how it is used by members. Be prepared to present this to the class as well.

[E] 13. Use your library's reference section to discover recent readings on consumer databases used for promotions and segmentation. Write a brief report on your findings.

[E] 14. Use your library's reference section to discover recent developments on segmentation approaches of interest to you based on the reports in this chapter. Write a brief report on your findings.

APPENDIX 4-A   VALS-2: A NEW SEGMENTATION APPROACH

In order to better understand some of the general dimensions of consumer segmentation in the United States market, we can take a look at one of the major general approaches—the VALS (Values and Life-Styles) program for segmenting the consumer market. VALS was created by SRI International, a management consulting firm in California, and has been used by many marketers and advertising agencies, sometimes with success and sometimes not. As we noted in the chapter, it has recently been updated and released in a new version called **VALS-2**.[35]

The essence of the VALS-2 program is a classification scheme that assigns each adult American to one of eight VALS-2 segments. These segments are determined by both the values and the life-styles of the people in them ("values" here refers to a wide array of an individual's beliefs, aspirations, prejudices, etc.). Thus VALS represents a linkage between the personality orientation of psychographics and the activities orientation of life-style research.

The Essentials of VALS-2

As the decade of the 1980s moved along, it became apparent to SRI management that the original VALS system for segmentation, launched in 1978, would need to be revised and updated. Not only were Americans' life-styles shifting, but marketing researchers were questioning some elements of both the usefulness and the validity of the original VALS system.[36] The planners of VALS-2 thus shifted their emphasis. Readers familiar with the original system will note that VALS-2 places somewhat less emphasis on values and more emphasis on the psychological underpinnings of behavior, influenced by consumer resources. They will also note that the segments are approximately equal in size (thus improving marketing mix efficiency potentials) and that they have been created to ensure that the consumer behaviors actually differ among the groups. In some sense, then, the new VALS-2 system is less theoretical and more pragmatic in nature. Two national surveys, each with over 2200 consumers, were used in developing the VALS-2 system.

The two key dimensions underlying VALS-2 are resources and self-orientation. **Resources**, according to VALS-2, refers to the full range of capacities (material, physical, psychological, etc.) consumers have to draw upon. It encompasses education, income, self-confidence, health, and so on, and can range from minimal to abundant. With respect to consumer behavior, we would expect that persons with more abundant resources would be able to undertake more purchasing behavior for most product classes. **Self-orientation**, meanwhile, refers to each person's social self-image, and the patterns of attitudes and activities that a person undertakes to help reinforce or act out that image. According to VALS, there are three major patterns of self-orientation: **principle-oriented consumers** are guided in their choices by their beliefs, rather than by feelings or desire for approval, **status-oriented consumers** are heavily influenced by the actions, approval, and opinions of others, and **action-oriented consumers** are guided by a desire for social or physical activity, variety, and risk taking. Given such differences in orientations, we would expect consumers in each grouping to be living different types of consumer life-styles.

VALS-2: Who Is Who?

Figure 4A-1 shows the network of eight segments defined by VALS-2. Notice that low resources are represented at the bottom, while high resources are at the top. Similarly, each of the three self-orientations occupies one column. Thus the network locations *do* have meaning: segments shown next to each other have some elements in common, and are "closer" than segments shown further apart. Brief descriptions of each of the segments follow (you may wish to look through Figure 4A-2 and Figure 4A-3 as you read these

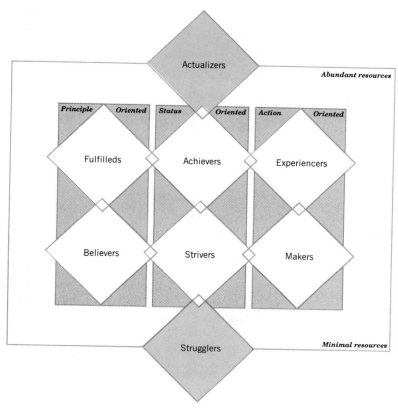

Source: From SRI International, Menlo Park, CA. Used by permission.

FIGURE 4A-1 **The Eight Consumer Segments of VALS-2**

FIGURE 4A-2 **Demographic and Life-Style Characteristics of the VALS 2 Segment**

Segment	Percent of Population	Sex (M)	Median Age	Median Income	Education (Some College)	Occupation (White Collar)	Married
Actualizer	8%	59%	43	$58,000	95%	68%	72%
Fulfilled	11	47	48	38,000	81	50	73
Believer	16	46	58	21,000	6	11	70
Achiever	13	39	36	50,000	77	43	73
Striver	13	41	34	25,000	23	19	60
Experiencer	12	53	26	19,000	41	21	34
Maker	13	61	30	23,000	24	19	65
Struggler	14	37	61	9,000	3	2	47

Continued

FIGURE 4A-2 **Demographic and Life-Style Characteristics of the VALS 2 Segment** *Continued*

Segment	Percent of Population	Sex (M)	Median Age	Median Income	Education (Some College)	Occupation (White Collar)	Married

Actualizers
Value personal growth
Wide intellectual interests
Varied leisure activities
Well informed; concerned
with social issues
Highly social
Politically active

Fullfilleds
Moderately active
in community and politics
Leisure centers on home
Value education and travel
Health conscious
Politically moderate
and tolerant

Achievers
Lives center on
career and family
Have formal social relations
Avoid excess change
or stimulation
May emphasize work at
expense of recreation
Politically
conservative

Experiencers
Like the new,
offbeat, and risky
Like exercise, socializing,
sports, and outdoors
Concerned about image
Unconforming, but admire
wealth, power, and fame
Politically
apathetic

Believers
Respect rules and
trust authority figures
Enjoy settled, comfortable,
predictable existence
Socialize within family and
established groups
Politically conservative
Reasonably well
informed

Strivers
Narrow interests
Easily bored
Somewhat isolated
Look to peer group for
motivation and approval
Unconcerned about health
or nutrition
Politically apathetic

Makers
Enjoy outdoors
Prefer "hands on" activities
Spend leisure with family
and close friends
Avoid joining organizations,
except unions
Distrust politicians,
foreigners, and
big business

Strugglers
Limited interests
and activities
Prime concerns are safety
and security
Burdened with health problems
Conservative and traditional
Rely on organized
religion

Source: From SRI International, Menlo Park, CA. Used by permission.

FIGURE 4A-3 **Psychological Characteristics of the VALS 2 Segments**

Actualizers
Optimistic
Self-confident
Involved
Outgoing
Growth oriented

Fulfilleds	**Achievers**	**Experiencers**
Mature	Moderate	Extraverted
Satisfied	Goal oriented	Unconventional
Reflective	Conventional	Active
Open-minded	Deliberate	Impetuous
Intrinsically	In control	Energetic
motivated		

Believers	**Strivers**	**Makers**
Traditional	Dissatisfied	Practical
Conforming	Unsure	Self-sufficient
Cautious	Alienated	Constructive
Moralistic	Impulsive	Committed
Settled	Approval seeking	Satisfied

Strugglers
Powerless
Narrowly focused
Risk averse
Burdened
Conservative

Source: From SRI International, Menlo Park, CA. Used by permission.

descriptions: they provide further details on the demographics, life-styles, and psychological characteristics of each of the segments):

Actualizers (8 percent of the population) are successful, sophisticated people with high self-esteem and abundant resources. Actualizers are among the established and emerging leaders in business and government. They have a wide range of interests, are concerned with social issues, and are open to change. Their possessions and recreation reflect a cultivated taste for the finer things in life.

Fulfilleds (11 percent of the population) are people with high levels of resources and who are "principle oriented" (that is, they seek to make their behavior consistent with their views of how the world should be). Fulfilleds are mature people who value order, knowledge, and responsibility. They are well informed about world events. Content with their station in life, their leisure activities tend to center around their homes. They are open-minded about new ideas and social change. Fulfilleds are practical consumers; they look for value and durability in the products they buy.

Believers (16 percent of the population) are the largest segment—one of every six adults belongs this group. Believers are also principle oriented, but have more modest levels of resources. They are conservative people who hold strong beliefs based on traditional codes. Among the oldest of the segments, they follow established routines, organized in large part around their homes, families, and the social or religious organizations to which they belong. As consumers, believers favor American products and established brand names.

Achievers (13 percent of the population) are the "status-oriented" consumers who have high levels of resources. Achievers are successful career people who feel in control of their lives. They value structure and stability over risk and self-discovery. Work provides them a sense of duty, material rewards, and prestige. Their social lives are structured around family, church, and business. Image is important to them. As consumers, they favor established products that demonstrate their success.

Strivers (13 percent of the population) are also status-oriented people, but with more modest levels of resources. They are striving to find a secure place in life and are deeply concerned about the opinions and approval of others. Money defines success for strivers, who don't have enough of it, and who sometimes feel that life has given them a raw deal. Strivers are easily bored and can be impulsive. As consumers, many strivers seek to be stylish, and emulate those who own impressive possessions.

Experiencers (12 percent of the population) are "action-oriented" people with high levels of resources. Experiencers are the youngest segment and are enthusiastic and impulsive. They seek variety and excitement and are still in the process of forming life values and patterns of behavior. They tend to be politically uncommitted. Experiencers are avid consumers and spend much of their income on clothing, fast food, music, movies, and videos.

Makers (13 percent of the population) are also action-oriented people, but with more modest levels of resources. Makers are practical people who value self-sufficiency. They live within a traditional context of family, practical work, and physical recreation: they have little interest in what lies outside this context. As consumers, makers are unimpressed by material possessions, but do value those which offer practical purposes to assist in daily family life, work, and recreation.

Strugglers (14 percent of the population) are people whose lives are dominated by their very low levels of resources. This is the oldest segment, with the lowest incomes, educations, and work skills. Often concerned about their health, and without strong social bonds, strugglers tend to be focused on meeting the needs of the present. Their chief concerns are for security and safety. As consumers, they are cautious. They represent a very modest market for most products and services but are loyal to favorite brands.

Do VALS-2 Segments Differ in Consumer Behavior?

The short answer to this question is, "Yes, very strongly!" Some illustrative differences are shown in Table 4A-1 and Figure 4A-4. You may find them to be interesting indications of the reality of consumer segmentation in the marketplace. Let's take a closer look at Table 4A-1. The numbers represent indexes, in which each segment is compared to the national average for all segments (thus 1.6 indicates 60 percent higher than average, while 0.9 indicates 10 percent lower than average). If we examine Table 4A-1 by each segment, we can see that the product ownership, activities, and media exposure seem to follow the descriptions

TABLE 4A-1 VALS-2 SEGMENTS AND CONSUMER BEHAVIOR (National Average Rate = 1.0)

Segment	Product Ownership				Activities			Media		
	Dish-washer	Fishing Rod & Reel	Color TV	Pickup Truck	Do Wood-working	Do Kids' Activities	Politics Active	Reader's Digest	Watch "Dallas"	Watch "Moonlighting"
Actualizers	1.6[a]	0.9	1.1	0.7	1.2	1.5	3.1	0.6	0.3	0.5
Fulfilleds	1.4	0.9	1.1	1.0	1.0	1.3	1.4	1.4	0.9	0.7
Achievers	1.4	0.9	1.1	1.0	0.6	1.4	0.8	0.9	1.0	1.1
Experiencers	0.5	1.1	0.9	0.9	1.0	0.9	0.8	0.6	0.5	1.4
Believers	1.2	1.1	1.1	1.1	1.1	0.6	1.1	1.5	1.5	0.8
Strivers	0.9	0.8	1.0	1.0	0.5	1.1	0.6	0.6	1.0	1.3
Makers	0.8	1.4	1.0	1.5	2.0	1.2	0.6	0.9	0.7	1.3
Strugglers	0.4	0.9	0.9	0.5	0.5	0.4	0.5	1.3	1.8	0.7

[a]To be read: "actualizers own dishwashers at a much higher rate than the national average (1.6, or 60% higher than the average). Fulfilleds (1.4), Achievers (1.4), and Believers (1.2) also have higher than average ownership of this appliance. Each of the other segments has a lower than average rate of ownership."

Source: SRI International, Menlo Park, CA. Used with permission.

FIGURE 4A-4 **Consumer Characteristics of the VALS 2 Segments**

Actualizers

Enjoy the "finer things"
Receptive to new products,
technologies, distribution
Skeptical of advertising
Frequent readers of a wide
variety of publications
Light TV viewers

Fulfilleds

Little interest in image
or prestige
Above-average consumers of
products for the home
Like educational and public
affairs programming
Read widely
and often

Achievers

Attracted to premium
products
Prime target for variety of
products
Average TV watchers
Read business, news,
and self-help
publications

Experiencers

Follow fashion and fads
Spend much of disposable
income on socializing
Buy on impulse
Attend to advertising
Listen to rock music

Believers

Buy American
Slow to change habits
Look for bargains
Watch TV more than average
Read retirement,
home and garden
and general interest
magazines

Strivers

Image conscious
Limited discretionary income,
but carry credit balances
Spend on clothing and
personal care products
Prefer TV
to reading

Makers

Shop for comfort,
durability, value
Unimpressed by luxuries
Buy the basics
Listen to radio
Read auto, home mechanics,
fishing, outdoors
magazines

Strugglers

Brand loyal
Use coupons and watch
for sales
Trust advertising
Watch TV often
Read tabloids and
women's
magazines

Source: From SRI International, Menlo Park, CA. Used by permission.

in our earlier figures and discussion. If we examine the table by columns, we can begin to get a picture of which segments present strong and weak prospects for marketing action. Notice that the dishwasher market appears highly segmented, for example. Fishing rods and pickup trucks, meanwhile, have some segmentation in them, with the makers segment appearing particularly strong. Color televisions, on the other hand, appear not to be very segmented, at least in terms of product ownership (for future purchases, however, further data concerning the number of sets owned, ages of current sets, and styles and price ranges would need to be consulted as well).

With respect to activities, this type of data can be helpful in deciding on useful appeals geared to different segments. For example, notice that actualizers tend to undertake wood working activities at higher than normal rates, while achievers are quite low on this activity. The data on media exposure, moreover, indicate directly how various segments might best be reached. Notice, for example, that *Reader's Digest* has specific appeals to certain groups, as did the television shows "Dallas" and "Moonlighting."

P A R T   II

Internal Processes of Consumer Behavior

In this part of the book—Chapters 5–11—we will examine the basic "building blocks" of consumer behavior, the internal processes that guide us in our actions as consumers. In Chapter 5, Consumers as Individuals, we consider some new and interesting ways to view consumers as individuals. In Chapters 6 and 7, Understanding Consumer Motivation and Consumer Personality, Values, and Involvement, we tackle the question of *why* consumers behave as they do. In Chapters 8 and 9, Consumer Perception (I) and (II), we'll learn about the fascinating area of consumer perception, or how the external world gets translated into the world as we see it. Chapter 10, Consumer Learning, then describes how our experiences shape our behaviors as consumers. In our final chapter of this part of the book, Chapter 11, Consumer Attitudes, we introduce the important roles that consumer attitudes play in guiding our behavior in the future.

As we'll see, each of these topics holds significant implications for us as marketing managers and as consumers. So, dig in and enjoy!

C H A P T E R 5

Consumers as Individuals

What Do We Find in the Mind?

This chapter begins our look at internal processes of consumer behavior. In it, we'll look at some insights as to how consumer's minds work. But why would we want to do this? Let's consider two quotes to help us see why:

A marketing tactic is a mental angle. It has to work in the mind....

—From Bottom-Up Marketing[1]

[Our memory] is the root of our individual personalities; it holds all the things that we've liked, disliked, enjoyed, and feared and all that we personally aspire to achieve ... mental content plays an extremely important role in ... our individual reactions to marketing strategies ... [Memory] is the most important sector for consumer information processing.

—Excerpted from this chapter.

■ ■ ■

This is an important chapter. In it, we examine the dominant academic perspective in the field: viewing the consumer as an individual. The material here is not only important in itself, but it also serves as a basis for discussions of many topics to come.

Why should anyone want to pursue the study of consumer behavior at the individual consumer level? There are at least two good ways to begin to answer this question. One is to point out that most consumer purchases are made by individuals: this means that the "market" would not exist were it not for these individual actions. Second, the only way that we can hope really to *understand* consumer behavior is to study it at the individual level. Knowledge of the people involved is crucial to our understanding of the processes themselves. At the individual consumer level, we can see where needs arise, how external influences work their effects, and how decisions are made. It is at this level that we will concentrate most of our attention in the text, for the purpose of better understanding why consumers behave the ways they do.

VIEWS OF THE INDIVIDUAL CONSUMER

There are a number of approaches that we can take in viewing the individual consumer. The simplest approach would select one very important factor, then deduce or draw logical conclusions about consumers' behavior in response to changes in this factor.[2]

For example, the **economic consumer** represents the consumer as seen in economic theory, which concentrates on such factors as incomes and prices, and how they affect consumer behavior. The theory views the consumer as an entirely rational person, who acts in his or her own self-interest to maximize total personal "utility" or satisfaction. Purchases are made only after a consumer in some fashion undertakes a calculation process that compares marginal utility to marginal costs. In contrast, the **organizational consumer** views consumers (or buyers) within a very different situational context. Here the buyer is operating within some form of organization (such as a firm or a family) and has adopted the role of purchaser on behalf of the organization. Most of the purchases will not be consumed personally, but will instead be used by others in the organization. Thus, to understand consumer behavior here, we need to consider *both* the organization's goals *and* the person's goals.

The **conditioned consumer** adopts yet a third perspective, stressing that behavior patterns are *learned* by the people and that such learning tends to be mechanical in nature. This view emphasizes the importance of stimuli in our external environment, and how we develop responses to those stimuli. The development of these responses is termed *conditioning*. Its overall stress is on how powerful external stimuli can be and how humans can be made to behave differently when stimuli are manipulated. The **psychoanalytic consumer** is a fourth approach that emphasizes the powerful influences of our inner drives on our behaviors. It is based upon the psychoanalytic theories of Sigmund Freud, that each of us enters the world with powerful instinctual needs. As we mature, we develop socially acceptable ways to control our inner urges. In adults' consumer behavior, this theory stresses the importance of *symbolic functions* that products serve for consumers. A fifth basic approach would deal with the **social consumer**. This stresses the fact that each of us is heavily influenced by other people. These social influences stem both from our past (so that they're now ingrained in our personalities) and from our present social milieu.

Notice how each of the five approaches contains an important perspective on what causes and influences our behavior as individuals. At the same time, however, no one of these approaches is sufficient by itself to explain all aspects of behavior. We will not, therefore, simply adopt one of them for the entire text, but will draw upon each of them to illuminate specific consumer topics.

At this point we'll turn to a more limited—but more specific—approach to the study of an individual's consumer behavior. Rather than providing a sweeping explanation for *why* behavior occurs, this second approach attempts to describe *how* it occurs. It is, therefore, a model of a behavioral process. The model we will feature—called the hierarchy of effects—was developed by marketers and has had a great impact on the field of consumer behavior.

THE HIERARCHY OF EFFECTS MODEL

In 1961, Robert Lavidge, a marketing consultant, and Gary Steiner, a behavioral sciences professor, published an article describing a new model of how consumers come to purchase a particular brand.[3] This model later came to be known as the **hierarchy of effects**, and has stimulated much discussion within marketing. The original purpose of the model was to assist advertising managers in their decisions. The thinking behind the model went something like this:

> While the ultimate purpose of advertising is to create sales, it is obvious that consumers rarely rush out to buy a brand immediately after seeing an ad. Instead, there seems to be a longer-term impact of advertising. However, for there to be a longer-term impact, there must be some kind of short-term effect going on. What kinds of short-term effects are there?

To answer this question, Lavidge and Steiner attempted to outline a logical process of how a consumer arrives at brand purchase. The viewpoint was that of a brand manager looking at the consumer market.

Nature of the Hierarchy

Hierarchy is a word that refers to any type of organized structure that has a clear beginning, followed by a series of steps in a particular order. Figure 5-1 diagrams the hierarchy of effects model. Note that it consists of seven stages, beginning

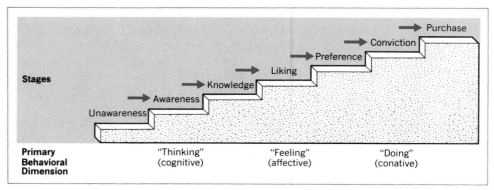

FIGURE 5-1 **Stages in the Hierarchy of Effects**

with "Unawareness" and culminating in "Purchase." With respect to a particular consumer, Jill Jones, and a particular brand, say, Allure mascara, the model would postulate the following:

> *Jill begins by being totally* unaware *that Allure is on the market. At some point she becomes* aware *of the brand name, but only at a very surface level. At some point later she gains* knowledge *about what Allure has to offer, including its patented "lash lengthener" formula. She then develops a* liking *for Allure, in the sense that she thinks it may be a candidate for purchase. At some later point Jill develops a* preference *for Allure over other brands. This preference then turns into a* conviction *that it will be wise to choose Allure the next time she buys mascara. When that time arrives, the brand* purchase *finally occurs.*

Important Characteristics of the Hierarchy

Because this is a relatively formal model, there are several underlying points that we should be sure to understand about it. First, the "hierarchical" nature of the model requires a *fixed order* to the seven stages; unawareness must come first, then awareness, then knowledge, then liking, and so on. This is a strong assumption, although it certainly seems reasonable for many cases. Second, the model allows for *individual differences* in that different people can be at different stages. Some consumers will remain unaware of some brands for their entire lives, while others are happily purchasing and using those same brands. Third, the model allows for *timing differences*. One consumer might, for example, move from unawareness all the way to purchase within a single day's shopping for a small appliance. In contrast, that same consumer might take three months to move from awareness to knowledge of a cosmetic brand, then in only two days move on through to purchase.

The "Think-Feel-Do" View

A fourth assumption embedded in the model is that consumer behavior consists of three major dimensions: cognitive, affective, and conative. This view is widely accepted in the behavioral sciences and in marketing (a popularized description is the "think-feel-do" view of consumer behavior). In brief, the **cognitive component** refers to rational elements involved with mental thought, the **affective component** refers to our emotional or feeling states, and the **conative component** involves the tendency to action or behavior on our part. In terms of fixed order, the model suggests that the cognitive operations come first, followed by affective, then conative.

Controversies and Extensions

Part of the contribution from the hierarchy of effects model comes from the further thinking that its strong assumptions have sparked in the field. Consider, for example, such questions as

- "Do consumers have to go through all the stages?"
- "Do the stages have to occur in the order shown?"
- "What about impulse purchases?"

The answers according to the strict model would have to be, "Yes (unless they don't reach purchase)," "Yes (but they can do so at different speeds)," and "Impulse purchases are those in which the timing is *very* compressed and the stages occur quickly."

Another way to answer these questions is to disagree with the model and respond that "The hierarchy has its limitations, and won't be able to reflect exactly how consumers will proceed in every situation." Professor Michael Ray, for example, has proposed an alternative "think-do-feel" ordering of effects for situations in which consumers have **low involvement** and aren't viewing a purchase to be very serious.[4] Nancy Ward, for example, may realize that she's running low on paper towels as she passes the display in the supermarket. She isn't very interested in this product and doesn't have a favorite brand. She does recall seeing some commercials for Brawny, though, and decides to give it a try. Thus Nancy's purchase really is a trial: not until she actually uses the brand will she have either a positive or negative feeling toward it.

Uses of the Hierarchy

As indicated earlier, the original purpose of the hierarchy of effects model was to assist marketers in decision making. One benefit to brand managers, for example, involves a new way to view the market for your brand. This can be done by estimating the proportion of consumers who have reached each of the steps in the hierarchy. Are there a significant number of potential buyers who are still unaware of your brand? Are most persons not very knowledgeable, or is the problem that most consumers are presently not at a level of liking or preference for your brand? Constructing this type of analysis for competing brands as well as for your own can provide useful insights. (This use of the hierarchy, in fact, has been the basis for highly sophisticated "mathematical models" that have recently become popular with marketing managers.)[5] Once you know where consumers stand, you can decide on which step to concentrate and can create programs geared to this stage. Many marketers prefer to try to move one step at a time. For example, special ad campaigns are often created to generate awareness of a new brand and then are replaced by other ads providing more information about the brand.

In addition to its value for business purposes, the hierarchy of effects has provided the field of consumer behavior with a useful basic framework. As we move through this text, we will encounter basic concepts—learning, change, attitudes, and so on—that are embedded in this model. For example, let's think briefly about how a consumer moves from one state to the next. When Jill was unaware of Allure mascara, what changes occurred when she became aware of the new brand? What processes went on in her mind when she later moved from liking to preference for the Allure brand? These kinds of questions represent basic issues for the topic of consumer information processing, the subject of our next section.

CONSUMER INFORMATION PROCESSING

As noted earlier, the **consumer information processing (CIP)** approach to studying consumer behavior is relatively new, but it has been enthusiastically received by many marketers. CIP is inherently interesting—it deals with our minds and how they work. Beyond this, CIP holds the potential to contribute new kinds of understanding of consumer behavior.

Benefits of the CIP Approach

As shown in Figure 5-2, the traditional approach to studying consumer behavior, called the **black box model**, concentrated on external inputs and the outputs that seemed to ensue from them. For example, dropping the price of Folger's coffee with a 40 cent coupon (external input) might be found to increase sales by 100,000 units (external output). At the individual consumer level, the 40 cent coupon might be found to lead to a purchase by Mark Moore, but not by Laura Jackson. The black box model would record these facts, but would offer no way to trace the internal processes that somehow led Mark to purchase and Laura not to purchase. As we have discussed in earlier chapters, for example, the checkout scanning systems in supermarkets now allow for enormous quantities of this type of black box model information for marketing planners to use.

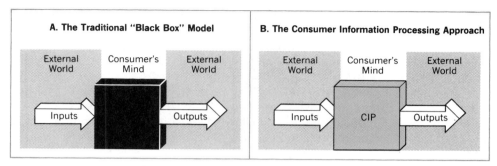

FIGURE 5-2 **How the CIP Approach Improves the "Black Box" Model**

In contrast, the **CIP approach** would concentrate on the thoughts and re-actions that the consumers were having when they received the Folger's coupon. The CIP approach concentrates on the middle of the input-output system. Its contributions lie in illuminating what is going on in consumers' minds. Because of this focus, it is not particularly strong in studying the inputs or the outputs by themselves. This means that CIP will never be a *substitute* for other ap-proaches; it will instead be an important *complement* or addition to our set of approaches to use in understanding consumer behavior.

The Nature of CIP

Consumer information processing involves sequences of mental activities that people use within consumption contexts. There are two primary systems involved in CIP: our *sensory system* and our *conceptual system.* The **sensory system** refers to the operations of our five senses—sight, touch, smell, hearing, and taste—the means that each of us uses to contact all aspects of our external world. The **conceptual system**, in turn, is our system for dealing with mental con-cepts—it is the means by which we think.

CIP relates to an amazingly wide range of consumer activities. CIP relates to our *learning* about and accepting important cultural values, as well as learning the name of a new bubble gum brand. CIP also relates to *evaluative* activities, such as our development of likes and dislikes for products. In addition, CIP relates to our *decision processes,* our *purchasing strategies,* our *usage* behaviors, our *satisfactions,* and any other thoughts we have about products, stores, and so on.

The Computer Analogy

The major force behind the development of information processing models was the invention and growth of computers after World War II. This allowed re-searchers to conduct studies of very-high-speed operations; such studies had simply been too unwieldy to undertake prior to this time. Because of this heritage, there has been a strong tendency to view CIP as being similar to the workings of a computer.[6]

For example, look back at Figure 5-2 for a moment and consider the following consumer behavior class lecture:

> One way to think of CIP is to view it as being similar to the workings of a computer, where you have input, a central processing unit, and output. The input would be some form of consumption-related stimulus, such as an ad. The information could come from a number of sources, such as TV or the radio, or it might even arise as you're walking through a shopping center and see someone wearing something you find to be attractive.
>
> The central processing unit is internal. Here your mind will take the input and deal with it in whatever ways you decide are appropriate. The processing might be very brief, or it might be long and involved.
>
> There are many types of outputs that can come from the processing, and these can be either retained privately in your head (for example, you simply decide to buy) or they can also be placed into the external world (for example, telling your girlfriend that you've decided to buy). In more technical language, outputs can consist of an addition of new facts into your memory, changes of a brand attitude, purchases of a new brand, and so on. There is one important shortcoming of the computer analogy, however, that should be kept in mind. The computer example always seems to start with external information and have the central processor react to those inputs from the outside. In consumer behavior, though, we know that a lot of CIP really begins with *internal* inputs, such as when we begin to think about a particular past purchase or begin to plan for a future one. The computer analogy is helpful, then, but we don't want to fall into the trap of viewing consumers in too mechanical a way. When we talk about consumers, remember that we are talking about ourselves!

General Findings About CIP

Before studying the details of CIP, it may be useful to consider some generalizations about what is involved when we consumers process information:[7]

- *CIP is adaptive.* The exact thinking we undertake is highly dependent on the particular situation we are in at the time. We will adapt our thoughts to be most relevant to the situation. Since the normal purpose of CIP is to help us deal effectively with our external world, CIP must be flexible and adaptive.
- *Consumers' memories are important.* Processing occurs in our minds and will be guided by our minds. While external influences can be quite important, we cannot forget the crucial role that our memory plays in guiding our thought processes.
- *Consumers have limited CIP capacity.* We are simply unable to process everything that could be processed at any one time. This means that we must pay

attention to some things and ignore others. We must selectively decide what to process, and how to allocate our processing resources at any one time.

■ *Consumers solve small problems.* Because of our limited CIP capacities, we find it difficult or impossible to reach a decision in one giant "optimal" step. Instead we tend to break larger problems into a series of smaller subproblems, which are more manageable. Taken together, however, these smaller decisions may be less than optimal in an overall sense (for example, was our actual spending pattern for last month as wise as it might have been had we carefully allocated our budget?).

Each of these four CIP generalizations has been receiving increased attention by consumer researchers. We will be examining their findings in later chapters.

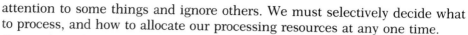

STRUCTURE OF THE CIP SYSTEM

[An Important Note] Scientists have made tremendous advances in understanding the biochemical and electrical characteristics of the human brain. Their work is not close to being complete, however, and is highly technical. Discussion of the physiology of the brain is beyond the scope of our discussion of consumer behavior and will not appear in this book. In this text we will stress a less technical approach to the mind— one that concentrates on how information processing seems to occur. We should be clear, however, that when the term "structure" is used, we are not talking about a physical model of the mind. Instead, we will be referring to a functional representation of the CIP system. In other words, our CIP structure is a good one for explaining how people process information. To get the most out of the following sections, then, try to use the book's discussion to help you think about how you personally process information as a consumer. If you are interested in more advanced models or issues, you should find the notes at the end of this and following chapters useful guides for further reading.

The System's Three Sectors

The **CIP system** is outlined in Figure 5-3. The first important aspect of the figure is that it shows the *outside world* on the left and the *inside world* of the mind on the right. Much of the emphasis of CIP research refers to how the realities of the external world are translated and handled in each person's inner mental world.

The second important aspect of the figure is that it shows the CIP system as being comprised of three sectors: the sensory register, short-term or working memory, and the long-term memory. (As we'd expect with something as complicated as the brain, our CIP system is one of many possible representations: if you would like to read more about this topic, you may wish to pursue the readings in Note 8.) In the sections that follow, we'll learn much more about each of the three primary sectors of our CIP system.

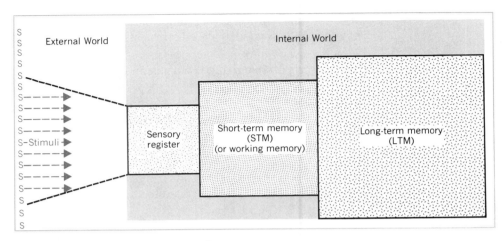

FIGURE 5-3 **A Hypothetical CIP System**

The External World's Many Stimuli

The funnel shown in Figure 5-3 is intended to indicate that CIP deals with relatively *few* of the stimuli present in the external world. For example, think about a fairly quiet classroom and the stimuli that could be attended to by someone in it. There are the sounds of the professor's voice, but other sounds as well— noises from outside, slight squeaking of chairs, turning papers, whispering voices, and so on. There are faint odors, and perhaps breezes or temperature changes hitting your skin. There are also an incredible number of visual stimuli available— even though the room has been designed to have as few distractions as possible. There are *colors* of clothing, hair, and walls; *shapes* of heads, bodies, and furniture; and *movement* in the bodies in the room and the world outside the windows.

Despite the large number of stimuli around us, *we do not pay attention to most of them,* especially if we're interested in the lecture (or in the person next to us). Our information processing systems are *choosing* not to deal with most stimuli, so that we can deal better with the stimuli upon which we want to concentrate.

The External World and the Sensory Register

The **sensory register** is the CIP sector in which external stimuli are gathered by each of our senses. Here they are "held" for a very brief time in the "front of our mind." Experts in the field of cognitive psychology have had difficulty in pinning down an exact time limit; in general, however, it appears that a sensory impression can be held for something less than 1 second—say, half a second— before it decays in strength and fades out of the sensory register.[9]

This time limit is not as seriously negative as it might first appear, however. Our CIP systems can work at incredibly fast speeds, so that half a second is a fairly long time. (For example, consider how long you focus on any one word while reading a newspaper—try timing yourself for a paragraph, then dividing through by the number of words in it.) In addition, we are often able to go back out and *reacquire a particular stimulus* if we desire to do so: we can reread a sentence, look back to a picture or a product label, and so forth. Finally, there are many stimuli that we don't *want* to process at a particular time, and the decay feature of the sensory register handily allows us to dispense with them easily.

Thus, the "holding" function of the sensory register is important because it allows us to provide some *order* and *control* to our CIP activities. By combining focused attention on only certain stimuli, and then being able to bring certain of these stimuli in our CIP system on a slightly delayed basis, we are able to insulate or *buffer* ourselves from what would otherwise be an extremely complicated and diverting external world. Thus, while it's still necessary for each of us to strike a good balance as to the amount of external stimulation we want to have, the sensory register's ability to hold sensory impressions is crucial to helping us with this task.

Short-Term Memory

You may have noticed that Figure 5-3 denotes the second sector of the system as **short-term memory (STM)** and also as **working memory**. This is because the primary feature of STM is that it is the work center of your CIP system. To appreciate this point more fully, let's listen in on an explanation given in a consumer behavior class:

> One important characteristic of our CIP systems is that they have to be so amazingly *flexible*. Each of us has to be able to deal with a wide range of situations and people. We can't go through the world with specialized approaches that we use regardless of circumstances. Our CIP systems have thus been geared to be highly flexible and able to respond to millions of kinds of external inputs and mental tasks. Such flexibility calls for a special kind of *work system* for our memories. One good analogy is that STM is like an empty production room and LTM is like a warehouse.
>
> To understand this distinction, let's assume that you decided to go into a customized manufacturing business, but—similar to our CIP needs for flexibility—you were unable to specialize in producing any one line of products. Instead, your production system would have to be able to produce many different kinds of products, in as efficient a way as possible.
>
> To design a good system for this business, let's think of some key characteristics. First, you would need to be able to receive an order from the market quickly and put your production facility to work. This would mean setting up exactly the right machinery and bringing in exactly the right plans, procedures, and raw materials. You would *not* want your workroom to be cluttered with machinery and materials from other tasks. One efficient way to design your production system would thus be to keep your workroom

as *empty* as possible between jobs, but to devise ways for rapid and efficient setup for each new job. Of course, this would also impact on the way you would design your warehouse, or storage center.

This analogy provides the basis for our structure of the CIP system. **Long-term memory (LTM)** is the storage center of the CIP system. It contains everything you need to process, except for some special raw materials that are imported from the outside world in the form of external stimuli (information). Short-term memory, conversely, is the work center of the CIP system. To perform its functions most efficiently, *nothing* is stored in STM unless it is related to current work-in-process. All contents of STM have either been imported from the external world or from LTM, or created during the work process itself, in STM.

Where do the outputs go? There are three logical routes: contents of STM can decay and fade out of the system, they can be sent to the external world as outputs, and/or they can be sent to LTM to be stored.

Now let's try a math example to demonstrate some of these ideas. First, try to "clear out" your STM to prepare for this little math problem that I'll put on the board:

$$4 + 9 \times 2 = ?$$

Notice how your CIP system works in solving this problem. First, you had to read the problem in, through your visual sensory register. The reading itself was quite a process, when we realize that what we've actually seen were some special arrangements of splotches on a surface. For each splotch, we had to bring in the sensory impression and try to give it meaning. For each number and word, this meant that signals had to be sent back to LTM asking, basically, "What is this . . . ?" An extremely rapid search of LTM ensued and likely resulted in a correct identification of each number and word. These were sent to STM, the work center of the system. Also, the process was likely assisted by the fact that I'd indicated that I wanted you to work on a *math* problem. Things should have gone faster because certain parts of your LTM (where you store your math knowledge) were "primed" to be used in STM and thus could be found and retrieved more quickly. That is, you were "ready" for this problem.

Next, notice that the key information you needed from LTM included the basic tables for addition and multiplication, together with specific arithmetic rules to tell yourself exactly what to do. Now, it turns out that this little problem tends to lead to *two different answers, depending on the particular rule* that people take from LTM and use in STM. I won't ask each of you to give your answer here, but my guess is that many of you came up with 22, while most others arrived at 26. The two different answers arise from a slight difference in your *processing* of the problem. The basic difference seems to be that the first group asks LTM if there is a specific math rule to govern the order in which the operations are performed. Their LTM says something like, "Yes, multiplication and division should be done before addition and subtraction, unless parentheses are included . . .". If you were in this group of students, you then had to shift the problem around in STM and attack it in a different order from how you had read it initially. It wouldn't be surprising, in fact, if you *took another look or two* at the board to help you reorder the numbers—in reality, you were using your sensory register to relieve some of the pressures on STM's having to remember the exact numbers! Your CIP problem solving then became something like 9 × 2 = . . . 18 . . . + 4 = . . . 22.

If you were in the "26" group, you arrived at a different answer because your *process* was different. Usually, this occurs because you either didn't ask your LTM if there is a special math rule that governs order or you asked about the rule, but it wasn't retrieved from LTM. Since *STM always needs to follow some kind of rule,* you probably just used the common cultural rule for English-speaking students. This says, "You should read from the left and take things in the order that they occur, moving from left to right." In this case, the problem becomes 4 + 9 = . . . 13 . . . × 2 = . . . 26.

Let me again stress this final point about how important it is that LTM provides *guidance* for our processing activities in STM. Not only does LTM provide interpretations of incoming stimulus patterns, but it also—by sending rules to guide STM—allows us to direct and control our own internal thought processes!

STM's Capacity Limitations

You may recall that one of our four general findings about CIP involved **capacity limitations**. We are all aware that we seem to be limited in the number of separate things we can watch, listen to, or think about at the same time. The CIP system's capacity limitations affect, not only how much information we can process at any time, but also how the processing itself occurs. It is important for us to recognize that most of the capacity constraints exist in STM. At the front end of the system, the sensory register is capable of detecting huge numbers of stimuli; as we discussed earlier, however, most of them decay rapidly and never enter STM, or working memory. At the other end of the system, long-term memory has a huge, perhaps infinite capacity for storing information. Many scientists, in fact, believe that we never lose anything that's been stored in LTM.[10] As we go through life we are constantly adding information to our LTM storage system.

There are two types of STM capacity constraints—time and size. With respect to *time* constraints, information being held in working memory will slowly decay and fade out as its energy is dissipated or lost. Just as with the sensory register, scientists have had difficulty estimating exactly how long STM's time decay might take, but it would clearly be measured in numbers of seconds (say, 10 to 30 seconds) versus the fractions of a second in the case of the sensory register.[11]

The more important STM capacity constraint involves the number of information items that can be processed at any one time. This translates to a *size* limitation of the working memory. As with all other estimates, scientists have had difficulty determining STM's exact size limits. A classic article by G. A. Miller proposed "The Magic Number Seven, Plus or Minus Two . . ." as the basic size limit.[12] This suggested that we are able to retain about seven items of information—the length of a telephone number—in STM. Miller pointed out, however, that this limit would vary somewhat (from five to nine pieces), depending on the person and the nature of the information. Since Miller's paper appeared some 30 years ago, other scholars have also worked on this problem. Their results tend to show a somewhat lower limit for STM, about three or four pieces of information.[13] Our CIP systems are powerful, however, so why is this important?

Why Are Capacity Limits Important?

Since information can come into STM from either the external world *or* from LTM, we usually have a highly active flow of information into STM. However, if there is only room for a limited amount of information, something must happen to the information that's already there. If the earlier information hasn't yet been processed, it probably will be lost from working memory so the valuable STM capacity can be used by more important information. If, on the other hand, the prior information is being processed with inputs from LTM, it is likely that it will be sent back to LTM and stored there for future reference. Also, if the processing is important and will take a bit longer, STM may simply not accept new inputs from the external environment during this time. A good example of this occurs when we try to *concentrate* and deliberately shut out other stimuli from interfering with our processing.

Although the inability to define an absolute size limitation is disturbing at first, we should understand that the practical importance of the size limit depends on how well we can *merge the flows between STM and LTM*. As we've already seen with regard to reading and interpreting the math example, our CIP systems can work at amazingly fast speeds. Thus, if we are able to arrange the appropriate transfers between STM and LTM (in a technical process called *rehearsal*), we can use LTM's *huge capacity* partially to overcome problems arising from STM's *limited capacity*. The more easily we can find a particular piece of information stored in LTM, the easier the strain on STM capacity.

Scientists have used the concept of **chunking** in relation to this process. Chunking refers to grouping together several pieces of information and treating them as a single unit. For example, let's assume that we've just met an interesting new person and want to remember her phone number. We could, for example, treat the telephone number as seven separate digits (9–2–4–1–8–6–3), as two groups of digits (581–2475), or as one group of digits (9876543). Notice that the more related the digits are, the easier it is to chunk them. Once into LTM, we can think of a chunk as a set of information elements in LTM that are strongly associated with each other. Therefore, once we have brought one of them into STM, it is relatively easy to find others in LTM, and bring them into STM in some series that does not overwhelm STM's capacity limits. When we think of

Ford, for example, many other pieces of LTM information are readily available to come into STM, and we are able to process a lot without hitting the capacity limits. Marketers strive to achieve this LTM structure for their brands, so that once the brand comes into STM, it is relatively easy for the consumer to go into LTM to come up with further thoughts about the brand and bring them rapidly into STM. Consider, for example, how your CIP flows work for such names as Budweiser, or Heinz, or BMW, or Geritol. To understand this process better, let's now focus on the nature of long-term memory.

Long-Term Memory

To obtain a broad sense for LTM, let's listen in again to the consumer behavior class lecture:

> If we step back and think about it a little, we can see that LTM is truly a remarkable center! What is stored in long-term memory very much determines and describes each of us as a person. Long term memory contains the surviving traces of all that each of us has ever experienced, all that we privately value and in which we believe, and all that we know and feel. LTM is the root of our individual personalities; it holds all the things what we've liked, disliked, enjoyed, and feared and all that we personally aspire to achieve. It is the center from which our personal thoughts and future behaviors will be created.
>
> As consumers, think about what your LTM contains. Here we find a vast number of facts, memories, and opinions about various products, stores, and consumer situations. This mental content plays an extremely important role in determining our future consumer behaviors and our individual reactions to marketing strategies. So, while we think of LTM as a storage center or warehouse, please don't misunderstand this to mean that it is in any way an uninteresting part of our CIP system. On the contrary, LTM is the most important sector for consumer information processing.

Episodic and Semantic Memories

One interesting characteristic of LTM is that it seems to include two distinct types of contents: episodic and semantic. **Episodic memories** reflect the way in which we remember events or episodes out of our personal life experiences. These are in picture form, something akin to snapshots from our past. We use episodic memories when we recall special moments in our lives, even though they may have occurred years ago. Also, of course, many episodic memories are less significant, such as browsing at the store yesterday. The other form of LTM contents is known as **semantic memories**. These reflect the facts and other information we refer to when we speak of having "learned something." Semantic memories provide our basis for being able to use language. The field of semantics is in fact the study of signs and word meanings. (One area of research that has received much recent attention in marketing involves this distinction: if you would like to read more about *imagery processing* you may wish to begin with the readings in Note 14.)

Networks, Nodes, and Linkages

Another important characteristic of LTM is that it appears to have something like a **network organization.** Figure 5-4 shows a much simplified portion of a network that a consumer might have for soft drinks. In technical terms, we see a set of **nodes** connected by **linkages** or arcs into a network of concepts. Each node is a center that represents a word, idea, or concept. Nodes are connected to other nodes as a function of whether or not a person *associates* one idea with the other. The stronger we see a relationship between nodes to be, the stronger the associative linkages will be (notice, for example, that in Figure 5-4, "Water" is not linked to "Sugar," whereas "Sweet" is).

When working memory (STM) calls for certain information to be drawn from LTM, the network organization comes into play. Since some nodes are more prominent than others, they will tend to be activated first (we can think of **activation** as a kind of energy flow into the areas that are activated). Once the first node is activated, all the other nodes that are connected with it become more available to STM, if the processing continues.[15] Let's assume that Tom Mason is a consumer with this particular LTM structure and that Tom becomes thirsty. Notice on the left side of Figure 5-4 that there are many possible nodes linked

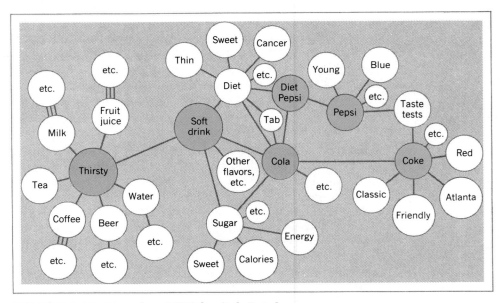

FIGURE 5-4 **Portion of an LTM for Soft Drinks**

to "Thirsty," since Tom has considerable past experience with this situation. His choice of a drink will in large part depend on which alternatives "come to mind"— that is, which LTM nodes are activated and brought into STM.

The "Soft drink" node may or may not be activated; this will in part depend on how strongly Tom feels about soft drinks as reasonable alternatives for satisfying thirst. If he does process "Soft drinks," his thoughts, and their order, will be heavily influenced by the organization of LTM—which nodes are strong and which connections have been developed in the past. For example, if Tom is concerned about his weight, he might pursue the "Diet" node first. If he is very brand loyal to Coke, conversely, he might go directly to that node.

Pursuing the example just a bit farther, consider what impacts marketing stimuli could have if they were to enter the sensory register just at the time that Tom is considered which LTM nodes to pursue. A big red "Coke" sign might well swing him into the Coca-Cola node system and keep him out of the non-Cola and Pepsi Cola systems. A Budweiser display might divert his CIP from soft drinks into beers, or a sale on lettuce could even divert his CIP into an entirely different node system. Given this type of reasoning, we can see why point-of-purchase (POP) materials in stores can so successfully stimulate sales. (We'll be reading more about this in Chapter 19.)

Marketing Implications of LTM's Organization

Creating Content in LTM With respect to advertising strategy, marketers face the problem of how to create and strengthen the brand's node in LTM and give it many positive associations with other nodes. The following example allows us to take a much closer look at this issue.

Who Knows What . . . Lurks in the Minds of Men? The LTM Nodes . . .

Sometimes marketers are successful in creating strong brand name nodes by creating a catchy phrase that consumers store in their LTMs, then using ad repetition to ingrain that phrase deeply. They often use musical "jingles" to help in this process. Listed below are some classic "Blasts from the Past." How many are still in your LTM? (Some may be too old . . . if so, it's fun to ask older relatives or friends and see how easy it is for them!)

1. "It's the heartbeat of America, it's today's _____!"
2. "In the valley of the Jolly (Ho, Ho, Ho) _____ _____!"
3. "Please don't squeeze the _____."
   (Bonus: Who said this? Mr. _____.)
4. "Hot dogs, _____ hot dogs . . . what kinds of kids love _____ hot dogs?"
5. "This is not your father's _____! This is the new generation of _____!"
6. Don't just ask for a light beer, ask for _____!"
7. "Where's the beef!?" _____
8. "You deserve a break today, so get out and get away, to _____."

9. "Nobody doesn't like _____ _____."
10. "Aren't you glad you use _____? Don't you wish everybody did?"

Grand Bonus Sing-Along
"My baloney has a first name, it's __ __ __ __ __, my baloney has a second name, it's __ __ __ __ __."

Total Score: _____   (Answers are listed in Note 16 for this chapter, at the back of the book, if you'd like to check any).

Beyond the enjoyment this kind of mental exercise brings to people, we are now in a position to also review some key CIP concepts we encountered while doing it. Let's again listen in on the consumer behavior class lecture, now at a point when they've just taken this same little quiz:

Let's think about what happened while we were doing the exercise. Most of you probably noticed that some of the brand names didn't make it into STM at all, others made it with a little difficulty, and some popped in very quickly. Let's look at these options. Why would some *not* make it? There really are two possibilities: either they weren't there at all, or they were there but we couldn't track them down in LTM. According to most CIP theory, the only way these phrases wouldn't be in your LTM is if you never processed them in the first place. If you ever did process these ads, though, their traces should still be in LTM. In this case, your problem in the exercise became one of **retrieval processes**, or locating the proper LTM nodes and bringing them into STM. So point 1 is "retrieval": what we often think is "forgetting," then, is actually our failure to accurately find and retrieve the proper node. Two important factors in our ability to retrieve a particular node are **interference** and **external retrieval cues**.[17] Interference refers to the process in which the presence of other, related information nodes in LTM seems to block (that is, to interfere with) recalling a particular node from LTM to STM. For example, Burke and Srull found that the advertising done by competing brands creates LTM nodes that interfere with a consumer's ability to recall an ad they have seen for a particular brand in the category.[18] While interference is generally negative for retrieval, however, external cues can be quite positive in helping to retrieve a particular node from LTM to STM. Keller, for example, has demonstrated increased recall of ads when consumers were later provided with cues such as the photo or headline from the ad (but without the brand name). He points out that Quaker Oats' putting a photo of "Mikey" on the boxes of LIFE cereal would serve to cue consumers in the supermarket to think of its classic advertising campaign featuring Mikey.[19]

Point 2 moves from later retrieval to the earlier process called **encoding**. This involves how we categorize a stimulus, then choose a storage location for it back in LTM. If we think a little more about this, we can see that our chances for good later retrieval of a node go up if we've taken care to store it wisely in LTM in the first place. (As an aside, this is why we professors stress that you should "understand" the material and not just memorize it for an exam—"understanding" the material actually means placing each piece of information within the right set of related LTM nodes. Memorization, on the other hand, does work at fixing it firmly back in LTM, but usually doesn't provide a rich network of other nodes to help us retrieve it later, especially after a few days!) The point is that a node's location is a lot easier to find when it is embedded in a cluster of other nodes that are going to be brought to STM either together, or one right after another. For example, notice how the first few words of one of the ad themes, taken together, helped you find the right storage area in LTM. As you went on, your confidence grew that this was the right set of nodes, and the brand name emerged easily into STM. Here you were experiencing the effects of *chunking* in action—the operations of strong linkages between particular nodes!

A third point—briefly—is that we should take notice of how incredibly helpful the musical jingles were! Our theory is still developing in this area, but it is clear that music not only helped us pay attention and learn the jingles in the first place, but that it also helps us locate the right LTM nodes, provides a rhythm for the retrieval process to STM, and somehow adds pleasure and emotion to our processing experience.

Point 4 involves *mistakes:* some of us thought we had the right name, but somehow got it wrong (and were surprised!). Why would this happen? One possibility is that we encoded wrong originally, and now have the wrong brand name actually stored with this theme back in LTM. As we'll see later in the course, marketers have discovered that this is reasonably common among consumers. Another possibility is that we didn't search LTM fully enough. This means that we focused on some part of the ad theme, searched LTM for a strong match on only part of it, then brought the brand name from that network into STM and announced that as our answer. One good example of this form of interference is the hot dog theme—some consumers are likely to first think of the processed meats category, then search back in LTM for nodes relating to branded processed meats, kids, jingles, and so on. Because Oscar Mayer was so successful with its long-running musical kids campaign, many of us will hit that node network quickly and, if we don't check critically, may confidently give that answer! Of course, if you didn't do this, you may say my explanation is "baloney"!

So it's time to finish our discussion with point 5, involving **ad repetition**. We should realize that it is rare that such strong node networks would be built up in only one or two CIP episodes. Instead, the linkages between nodes get progressively stronger as they are *practiced* over and over again. This is part of the reason that music sometimes works so well, since kids and adults sing or hum the jingles to themselves and thereby practice locating the node network in LTM, then retrieving it from LTM to STM. This is also the reason that ads are repeated so frequently: each time a consumer does pay attention to an ad, he or she is likely to practice locating the brand's node network in LTM, bringing it to STM, and then perhaps even adding new nodes and linkages to it back in its original storage area.

Creating Attention and Involvement One continuing problem marketers face is how to capture consumers' attention and maintain a sense of interest. We'll examine this topic in upcoming chapters. But here we can note one special strategy that "tricks" CIP into paying attention by taking advantage of LTM's organization.

Pedro the Punster on I-95

We can also detect the operation of STM and LTM by noticing how "puns" operate (a pun is a word or phrase used deliberately with a different meaning or spelling than the listener will expect). We realize we've been exposed to a pun when the contents of STM don't quite "match." We then need to go back and search LTM for the matching meanings and bring them to STM. The "groan" typical from a pun recipient is an acknowledgment that this process has occurred and that the CIP work required wasn't worth the effort! Some-

times puns can work for marketers, since they increase the chances a consumer will pay attention to the message as he or she tries to get it straight. On the other hand, this strategy can backfire if the recipient resents having to undertake the extra mental effort.

Travelers along I-95, the Maine to Miami interstate route, have long been entertained (frustrated?) by the puns presented on the billboards for South of the Border, a roadside stop located on the border between North Carolina and South Carolina. These are presented by "Pedro," they stretch for 400 miles along the route, and they have made "S.O.B." one of the most successful roadside attractions in the United States, with 6 million visitors annually. How do you react to the following billboard examples?[20]

"Pedro's Weather Report, Chili Today—Hot Tamale!"
"You never sausage a place! You're always a wiener at Pedro's!"
"Pedro's Fireworks! (Does Yours?)"

"Positioning" the Brand in Consumers' Minds   Marketers strive to have the right kinds of adjectives ("good value," "high quality," etc.) associated with their brands, but also face the challenge of having their brand's name be considered when the consumer is thinking about buying. In marketing terms, the goal is to have your brand be accepted into the consumer's evoked set. The **evoked set** consists of those brands that are likely to come to mind (enter STM) when a purchase is being considered. Research has shown that this is usually a small number of brands, ranging from one (in cases of brand loyalty) to only three or four under most conditions.[21] Thus there is a major payoff likely for marketers who can achieve this goal.

This Uncola Season Drink Un and Un and Un...

With Big Un, twist-off, resealable bottles of 7UP®.

Just twist off the cap, drink what you want, then twist it back on and save the rest for later.

Get several Big Un bottles this Uncola Season and give Un to others and others and others.

"7UP," "SEVEN-UP," "THE UNCOLA" AND "UN" ARE TRADEMARKS IDENTIFYING THE PRODUCT OF THE SEVEN-UP COMPANY.

The "UnCola" Campaign

This type of challenge confronted 7-Up brand managers some years ago, when the brand was still a minor factor in the soft drink market. Although consumers liked the product, it did not hold a large market share. The company then tried a new advertising slogan that positioned 7-Up as "The UnCola." Although the people involved had likely never heard of CIP, we can analyze this campaign in CIP terms to see why this was such a clever strategy.

To make sense of the slogan in an ad, a consumer had to search through LTM to locate the "Cola" node, then bring this information to STM. The "Cola" node, though, was already closely tied to "soft drinks," "Coke," and "Pepsi," making these also more likely to be brought to STM. Over time, with repeated exposures to this slogan, many consumers were likely to build linkages between 7-Up and these other nodes. In this way, 7-Up became more a part of the soft drink evoked set for many consumers, and sales responded accordingly.

The story has an interesting postcript. The UnCola campaign had been dropped in the mid-1970s, a new corporate owner took over the brand, and a new ad agency went to work on it. Then, in 1985, the company sponsored a consumer research study that discovered that a large percentage of consumers continued to describe 7-Up as "the UnCola," *even though the campaign had not been run for over 10 years!* In fact, only a current Coke campaign theme scores higher than "the UnCola" tag. According to 7-Up's president,

> *I don't care what the competition says . . . "The UnCola" is the strongest, most singular product identifier in the soft drink business.*[22]

This is an excellent example of the role of LTM and the power that it can display.

CIP and Consumer Research

Three "Thinking" Streams of Study

Within marketing and consumer behavior research, special attention has been given to three basic types of CIP research.[23] First, research on information acquisition is keyed to consumers' search for information in the marketplace. It reflects an *active* picture of the consumer, who is seeking to obtain desired inputs for CIP. There are many interesting topics related to **information acquisition**. Examples include why consumers do—and don't—search for information, how friends can influence the search process, the roles that salespersons play, and the types of information that can prove most helpful. All these topics, and others, will be covered in upcoming chapters.

The second CIP research area, **information integration**, focuses on what happens to information once it has entered working memory, whether from the external world, or from existing LTM. That is, how do pieces of information get integrated or intermingled with other information that already exists in LTM? As we would expect, the topics that have received most attention involve what is in LTM, how LTM influences treatment of new information, and how consumers combine pieces of information to make judgements and decisions. The most heavily researched topics are, therefore, consumers' attitudes toward brands and consumers' "rules" for making purchase decisions. Each topic has a long history of interest and research within marketing. We'll examine each topic in depth in Chapters 11, 18, and 19.

The third CIP research area has been particularly focused on how we consumers receive and process advertising. In contrast to the active view of information acquisition research, **initial information processing** research tends to view consumers in a more *reactive* light, as recipients of a persuasive message. The central concerns of this research zone involve *communication* and *persuasion,* usually from the viewpoint of the advertiser. There is far more published research on consumer reactions to advertising than any other topic within the fields of marketing and consumer behavior. We will delve into these in Chapter 17. If you are interested in learning more about the CIP issues that apply to advertising, however, you may wish to read the interesting material in Appendix A to the present chapter!

The Rise of Emotion

Before we complete our look at the basics of CIP research, we should insert a subtle note: The frameworks we have stressed in this chapter can be usefully supplemented by also learning more about the role that *emotions* play in consumer behavior. As we have already seen, marketing's view of the individual consumer has long included the area of emotion. The hierarchy of effects model, for example, clearly places its affective (feeling) stages at the center of the model. Also, virtually all advertising research has stressed the importance of affect. Finally, though we didn't specifically discuss it, the CIP approach provides for affect also—it includes LTM nodes that represent traces of past emotional experiences: These can then be called into STM so that consumers can again experience emotions during normal behaviors.[24] For example, notice how easy it is to recall how you feel when you are angry, or afraid, or extremely happy!

Even though our cognitive frameworks thus include emotional dimensions, most experts would likely agree that these frameworks do not handle the whole of the emotional range easily—that is, emotion itself is something more than a cognitive approach can entirely capture. This is due to the fact that emotion has strong physiological (bodily) elements in addition to psychological ones, and produces changes in the state of the person who is experiencing it.[25] For this reason, a number of consumer researchers have recently been examining useful ways to better understand the role of emotions in consumer behavior.

This research has covered a very broad set of topics, much of which we will cover in the chapters ahead. For example, Hirschman and Holbrook coined the term **hedonic consumption** to make the point that people experience many things beyond thoughts when they engage in consumer behavior: Hedonic consumption refers to the sensory, fantasy, and emotive aspects of a person's experiences with products.[26] Muncy has also recently pointed out the potential uses of **psychophysiological approaches** for consumer research: This refers to the use of physiological measures of the body (such as brainwaves, pulse, eye dilation, eye directions, skin response, and so forth) to better understand the emotional and thinking processes that consumers are experiencing.[27] Zajonc and Markus, meanwhile, have opened a controversial topic by asking whether it is possible to create positive effect (liking) for a brand simply by exposing consumers to it often enough that their familiarity with it will lead them to like it without any role for thinking in this affect development process![28]

Finally, perhaps most of the direct emotion-related research attention recently has been given to the topic of mood and its effects, particularly as it relates to advertising. As defined by Gardner, a **mood** is a feeling state that is subjectively perceived by the individual, and which lasts for a relatively short time period.[29] Moods are interesting in that they affect both how consumers act *and* how they react. For example, research attention has been given to how different moods affect consumers' receptivity to different kinds of advertising, but also to how different kinds of television programs and different kinds of ads affect consumers' moods. Because of the clear managerial implications for both advertising design and copy testing, recent research is developing and testing scales to measure consumers' moods and emotions, to measure characteristics of different ads in terms of their "warmth," "irritation," and so forth, and to measure consumers' affective, emotional reactions to advertising. (We will be examining some of this research in future chapters, but if you would like to pursue this issue in more depth at the present time, you may wish to begin with the readings in Note 30 for this chapter, located at the back of the book.)

SUMMARY

Five Views of the Individual Consumer

This important chapter provides us with a strong conceptual basis for understanding consumer behavior at the individual level. For example, the *economic consumer* is seen as an entirely rational person whose actions are aimed at the maximization of total personal utility. The *organizational consumer* stresses buyers operating in a context characterized by conflicting goals. Here the consumer's decisions are essentially compromises to achieve both sets of goals—the organization's and the individual's. The *conditioned consumer,* meanwhile, is driven by powerful external stimuli: this theory stresses that behavior patterns are actually learned responses that are highly mechanical in nature. In contrast, the *psychoanalytical consumer* emphasizes the extremely strong influences of our deepest inner drives on behavior. Finally, the *social consumer* ascribes great importance to our needs for acceptance, image, and our social ties as determinants of behavior. Since each theory presents such a strong single perspective on what causes behavior, none can simply be adopted as "best." Instead, we will draw upon each to illuminate specific areas to which they apply.

The Hierarchy of Effects Model

In the second section of the chapter, a key marketing model—the *hierarchy of effects*—was examined. Here we learned how consumers can move in fixed stages from unawareness to purchase of a brand. We also saw how marketers can use this framework to assist their planning and how the framework has some limitations when consumer decisions are characterized by low involvement.

Consumer Information Processing

In the third section of the chapter, we discussed the consumer information processing (CIP) approach to the study of an individual's consumer behavior. CIP deals with our mind and how it works. It concentrates on the thoughts and reactions we have as we operate as consumers in the marketplace.

Structure of the CIP System

In this section we examined the three centers of the CIP system—the *sensory register,* the *short-term memory* (STM), and *long-term memory* (LTM). We discussed the functions of the sensory register, the capacity constraints that operate on STM, and the key role that LTM plays within the CIP system. We examined the network model of LTM, noting how associations between concepts enable us to think rapidly and logically. We discussed several ways in which the CIP approach applies to consumer behavior, as in the 7-Up example. We also gained some appreciation for the issues that lie ahead, as we briefly examined three CIP research areas in consumer behavior: information acquisition, information integration, and initial information processing. Finally, we briefly noted the increasing attention to emotion-related issues in consumer research, and identified several interesting streams of research here as well. Then, in Appendix 5-A we discuss CIP issues pertaining to print versus television as media, and why they affect consumers differently. As we noted at the start, this is an especially important chapter because it presents a number of concepts that we'll continue to use in future chapters of this text.

KEY TERMS

economic consumer

organizational consumer

conditioned consumer

psychoanalytic consumer

social consumer

hierarchy of effects

cognitive component

affective component

conative component

low involvement

consumer information processing (CIP)

black box model

CIP approach

sensory system

conceptual system

CIP system

sensory register

short-term memory (STM)

working memory

long-term memory (LTM)

chunking

capacity limitations

episodic memories	encoding
semantic memories	ad repetition
network organization	evoked set
nodes	information acquisition
linkages	information integration
activation	initial information processing
retrieval process	hedonic consumption
interference	psychophysiological approaches
external retrieval cues	mood

APPENDIX 5-A TERMS

intrusive medium	low involvement
passive processing	

REVIEW QUESTIONS AND EXPERIENTIAL EXERCISES
[E = Application extension or experiential exercise]

1. Indicate at what stage of the hierarchy of effects model you are currently located for the following products/services. Provide rationale.
   a. Video games
   b. Ivory soap
   c. Sanka
   d. Taurus
   e. Club Med
   f. IRA
   g. Cellular telephones

2. Consider the market for Guess designer jeans.
   a. How would you analyze the market in terms of the hierarchy of effects model?
   b. What percentage of consumers are found at each stage?
   c. What are the relevant characteristics of these consumers?
   d. What are the marketing implications of such an analysis?

3. What the advantages to the marketing manager of employing a CIP approach versus a black box approach to study potential consumers? What are the advantages of the black box approach? Is it possible to apply both approaches?

4. Capacity limitations were discussed in the CIP section of the chapter:
   a. What exactly are these? To which system sectors do they apply?
   b. Think about your own consumer behavior. Have you ever run into capacity limitations? What were their effects?

[E] 5. From your LTM structure, map individual network organizations for two of the following:
   a. Recreation   d. Video
   b. Personal hygiene e. Budweiser
   c. Education

[E] 6. Leaf through several popular magazines, examining the ads as you go. Choose on example each of ads that appear to be aimed primarily at each stage of the hierarchy. Clip them out and attach brief explanations of your reasoning.

[E] 7. The 7-Up example demonstrates how marketers can try to use the LTM network to "associate" a brand name with some other concepts that consumers hold in their minds. Look for other good examples of this strategy in current advertisements. Find two ads that attempt this, briefly analyze how they go about it, and indicate whether you believe they are likely to be successful.

[E] 8. Using the relevant Notes for this chapter at the back of the book, or the reference section of your library, read in more depth about a CIP topic of interest to you. Write a brief report on your findings.

[E] 9. Using Notes 29 and 30 for this chapter (they are in the back of the book), locate further readings about mood and/or affect in advertising. Write a brief report on your findings.

[E] 10. Using Note 21 for this chapter, locate further readings on the concept of evoked set. Write a brief report on your findings.

[E] 11. Conduct the demonstration project suggested in Appendix 5-A's section "Applying CIP Concepts to Advertising." Write a brief report on your findings.

[E] 12. Try to observe CIP in action within the marketing-consumer environment. Go shopping with a friend or relative. Do not inform your shopping companion about the nature of your exercise, but do make a special effort to observe and monitor his or her CIP as you both move through the store setting. Encourage your companion to voice thoughts and reactions as you move along. What stimuli are being processed, and which ones are being missed? What seems to attract your companion's attention? How strong a role is LTM playing, versus external stimuli? Does CIP seem to be as rapid a process as the book claims? Write a brief report summarizing what you observed here.

[E] 13. The chapter and appendix mention that CIP is likely to change as consumers see repetitions of any particular advertisement. If you have access to a VCR, try taping an ad, then replaying it for a total of four to six repetitions (such as every half hour or each time other commercials appear during a regular TV program). Try to watch this ad as naturally as you normally would. Notice whether the relative roles of the ad itself and your LTM change over the receptions. Notice also whether your pace, timing, and reactions to the ad change or not. Write a brief report summarizing your findings.

APPENDIX A   APPLYING CIP CONCEPTS TO ADVERTISING

A Demonstration Project

There is mounting evidence that the broadcast media may have strangely different means of communicating, informing, and influencing people as compared to the printed media (newspapers, magazines, direct mail, etc.). You may wish to try a brief test on yourself to see if you can recognize some of the differences right off:

First, take a few unfamiliar magazine ads and read them through carefully and thoroughly. Now, turn on the television and watch a few unfamiliar commercials carefully and thoroughly. After finishing both tasks, sit down and think about the differences you experienced in your CIP activities. List them briefly in outline form. Also, list any differences you observed in the characteristics of the advertising stimuli in print versus broadcast. What are your findings?

The Dynamics of Television

The differences you have noticed in doing the demonstration project stem from differences between the print and broadcast media themselves. Figure 5A-1 lists five such media differences.

The first two are apparent when we consider the nature of the television stimulus. Television is *multisensory;* it impacts on both vision and hearing. Print media, on the other hand, impacts only on the visual sense register. Television also portrays *movement* to a much greater degree than does print; it is basically a series of many still pictures shown in rapid succession.

The remaining three differences are more apparent if we ask how CIP for television might differ from CIP for print stimuli. First, television is known as an **intrusive medium**—its stimuli force themselves, or intrude upon, our sensory register. While we can obviously find ways to avoid processing a TV ad, we do have to shift CIP to do so. In print media the consumer controls the *CIP timing:* here we are free to spend as much (or as little) time as we wish with each ad. Television's time-controlled property, however, has an upper limit (usually 30 seconds) to the time that we can give to processing a commercial while it's still in front of us. With television, even if we are very interested in a certain commercial, we *cannot* have it available to us for any longer CIP (we often choose to spend less time, of course, but do so knowing that we are missing some of the ad).

CIP's *pace* is related to the timing issue. With print ads we can control our own CIP pace, going faster when we wish, and slowing down at other points. TV

FIGURE 5A-1 **Special Properties of Television Advertising**

	Contrast: Print Versus TV		
Property	*Print Ad*		*TV Ad*
I. Sensory systems	Single sense (visual)	vs.	Multisensory (audio and visual)
II. Motion	Stationary	vs.	Movement
III. Attention	Nonintrusive	vs.	Intrusive
IV. CIP timing	Controlled by consumer	vs.	Controlled by ad
V. CIP pace	Controlled by consumer	vs.	Controlled by ad

ads, on the other hand, have a pace control built into them. Each commercial is scripted to proceed within the exact time limit. All the contents, *and* the pace or rate at which they appear, are entirely controlled by the advertiser and are fixed on the tape. The flow of stimuli to us, the consumers, has been determined before we are exposed to the stimulus at all. This will have powerful implications for the consumer's CIP during exposure to each type of ad.

CIP for Print Ads

Let's consider what happens when we read an interesting ad in a magazine. First, we can use as much time as we desire for our CIP. Second, we're able to look through the ad in whatever manner we decide is appropriate for us. This could mean, for example, glancing at a picture or two, skipping to the headline, then to the closing tag lines to identify the sponsor, and finally going back to begin to read the paragraphs from top to bottom. Within the process, we'll likely linger over parts of the ad and skim over other parts. Also, we're free to (and often do) look back at something we'd seen earlier, perhaps to check on a certain point. Although the alert advertiser will have designed the ad to help create a natural flow through it, each of us is free to set our own pathway and pace for processing it.

CIP for TV Ads

We don't have this freedom with a television commercial. Here we must follow the preset sequence, at the specified rate, or we risk missing some of the ad.

Notice the challenges to our limited CIP capacity. The TV commercial is sending out a constant stream of visual and sound stimuli, over a 30-second period. Our CIP system must maintain a constant interpretation process during each 30-second ad. Processing capacity must be used to decode what the light and sound waves from the TV set are in fact showing and saying. In addition, further STM capacity must be used for us to figure out how the sights and sounds tie together, and still further capacity must be used to decide what meaning the ad has for us personally.

Because we can't control the pace, however, we can't stop or slow down the process to think more deeply about something that has come up (unless, again, we are willing to miss some of the ad). Also, of course, we are totally unable to skip back, say 12 seconds, to recheck a scene or statement that occurred earlier in the commercial.

How Do Consumers Adapt?

How do we consumers adapt to this loss of control over our own CIP when we watch television (or listen to a lecture, for that matter)? One type of CIP adaptation involves developing a style we'll call **passive processing.** Here we'll tend to sit back and observe rather than sit up and participate. Although we may enjoy TV ads at one level, we'll not tend to get very involved in thinking about them and may find that our attention tends to wander. This type of consumer reaction has been called **low involvement** and has been charged to be a natural reaction to broadcast media.

Another type of adaptation involves what happens to CIP when TV ads are *repeated.* Each time that we see a familiar commercial, we are capable of exerting a little more control over our own CIP. Because we've already stored some information about the ad in our LTM, we can in effect "play it back" to ourselves at much faster speeds than on TV. Thus we can use this internal LTM to STM process to "hop ahead" easily to find the sponsor's brand name, the punch line, or some other salient aspect of the ad. In this way we can decide which parts of the commercial to watch carefully and which parts to ignore. After some point, however, ads seem to "wear out" and are not able to invoke further responses from the audience. Exhibit 5-A1 reports one student's recent experiences with ad repetition. Does it seem that he is close to "wear out" with this ad?

The topic of low involvement and ad repetition are just two of many interesting issues that can be studied in CIP research. Each will be discussed further in later sections of the book. If, however, you wish to pursue these topics further right now, you may wish to read the articles listed in Notes 31 and 32 at the back of this book, listed under this chapter.

EXHIBIT 5A-1 *AD REPETITION: GETTING THE 501 BLUES*

How does repetition work? Let's hear from one student who reports his experience:

"I picked a Levi's 501 Blues commercial. I don't know if you've seen one, but the commercial is bizarre . . . it starts out with a view of a young, extremely attractive woman shown with a rear view from the waist down. Of course, she is wearing 501 Blues. Along with this, there is what sounds like a barbershop quartet singing a very rhythmic tune. The ad continues with a barrage of scenes showing unusual characters wearing 501s . . . [they] seem to be having the time of their lives.

The first time I saw the commercial I thought it was very entertaining due to the pretty girls and music. However, I did not really feel an urge to rush out and buy a pair of 501s. The next time I saw the commercial, I did not really anticipate the next scenes, but I did remember them when they were flashed across the screen. I caught myself humming the tune, for the ad is full of energy and excitement. As the repetitions increased I began anticipating and expecting the next scene. I knew exactly when the really shapely girls were going to be flashed, and that was what I was waiting for! By now, I also knew most of the words to the jingle and I was singing along as if I was a player in the commercial. The faces and bodies became incredibly familiar. I can distinctly see and remember many of the details that I did not even notice the first couple of viewings. I also began looking forward to specific parts and began overlooking other parts in anticipation of some of the scenes. I knew exactly what was going to happen, but I still was enjoying it tremendously due mainly to the 501 tune being sung behind each scene.

I felt a yearning to become like the people in the ad. To do that I needed to buy a pair of 501 Blues. The ad gets better with each viewing. I felt a stronger and stronger desire to purchase a pair of those jeans . . .".

CHAPTER 6

Understanding Consumer Motivation

Why, Why, Why?

Perhaps the most basic question we can ask about consumer behavior is "Why do consumers do what they do?" As one marketing consultant explains,

If we believe our overall values drive our behavior, then we should be concentrating on [the important, underlying motives that drive consumers to make product or service choices] rather than simply product attributes.[1]

Burleigh Gardner, a leading consumer consultant, reports,

The thing to know is "Why." We want to know how to influence behavior, so we must dig below the surface.[2]

Dr. Ernest Dichter, the famous and controversial Freudian motivation researcher, relates what happened when the book, The Hidden Persuaders, charged that he was helping marketers learn how to manipulate consumers' minds:

It was a bombshell . . . and I was the big villain. So I got calls [from businesspeople] from foreign countries and all over the United States. And the people said, "What you're doing is terrible! How much does it cost?" [from the chapter]

■ ■ ■

172

TABLE 6-1 **KEY CHARACTERISTICS OF CONSUMER MOTIVATION**

(M) Consumer motivation has two *major components: energy* and *direction.*

(O) Consumers' motives are both *overt* and *hidden.*

(T) Consumers are driven by *tension reduction.*

(I) Consumers are motivated by both *internal* and *external forces.*

(V) Consumer motives have *valence*—they can be positive or negative.

(A) Consumers are motivated to *achieve goals.*

(T) Consumers have a *thirst for variety.*

(I) Consumers' motivations reflect *individual differences.*

(O) Consumers desire *order* in the world.

(N) Consumers are guided by the *need hierarchy.*

The marketing concept says that marketers should try to create products and services that best meet the wants and needs of consumers. As indicated in the opening quotes, this means that marketers must find out what needs consumers have, and what motivates them to buy. The field of **motivation** seeks to explain *why* behavior occurs. The term "motivation" itself is derived from the Latin verb *movere,* meaning "to move." Basically, then, motivation refers to *the processes that move a person to behave in certain ways.* Motivation deals with how behavior gets started, is energized, is sustained, is directed, and is stopped.[3] Motivation is the basis for all consumer activities.

In this chapter we will concentrate on a powerful summary framework consisting of 10 of the most significant concepts in the field of human motivation. Our framework is organized as a set of 10 statements in Table 6-1. Notice that a key word or phrase in each statement has been underlined—the beginning letters combine to form the acronym MOTIVATION. The separate points of the MOTIVATION framework offer different basic insights into consumer motivations. As consumer motivations tend to be specific to different products and situations, it is important for marketing managers to have a basic foundation of knowledge to draw from when faced with a new situation. Each element in the framework adds to our base of insight, and creates a basis for our forthcoming chapters.

KEY CHARACTERISTICS OF CONSUMER MOTIVATION

(M) Major Components of Consumer Motivation

There are two major components of motivation: *energy* and *direction.* Energy refers to the fact that *all* behavior—thinking, moving, looking, and so on—requires us to expend an internal supply of energy. Direction, on the other hand, is needed to channel our inner energies into productive, attractive behaviors and to allow us to behave efficiently. All consumer behaviors have both energy and direction as components.

Insights from the Energy Component

Researchers who study the energy dimension often use *physiological measures* of the body's arousal—consumers' pulse rates, blood pressures, brain waves, and skin chemistries can all offer clues to the energy dimension. Within consumer research, these measures are used to gauge consumers' reactions to advertising, brand names, and other marketing appeals.

With any consumer decision process, *intensity,* or the strength of the motivation itself, is an extremely important issue. As consumers, we must constantly deal with questions such as "How many stores should I shop before buying?" "Is it worth the effort to read the warranty, or the instructions?" and so forth. When intensity is low **consumer inertia** is present and leads to marketers facing problems in gaining attention for their products and promotions. This makes it difficult for a marketer to induce us to switch brands, even if he or she is offering a better value in the market. It also makes it increasingly difficult to stimulate consumers to act—even when the consumers themselves would agree that the action is in their best interests.

Why Don't Recalls Work?

The first million Ford Pintos sold in the United States were later discovered to have defective fuel systems that exposed their passengers to the risk that a rear-end collision could result in a fiery explosion that would kill driver and occupants. About the same time as this finding by the National Highway Traffic Safety·Administration, the same agency also found that over 7.5 million Firestone 500 tires were susceptible to blowouts and other failures that could result in deaths to riders in cars with these tires. Product recalls were ordered in both cases: Pinto owners could have their autos modified free of charge by taking them to a Ford dealer, and Firestone owners could obtain free replacement tires at their dealers. Two years later, despite extensive efforts at reaching and informing consumers with these products, 350,000 consumers continued to drive unmodified Pintos, and over 3.5 million potentially dangerous tires had yet to be returned.[4]

Emotion is also closely related to the energy dimension of motivation. An interesting aspect of emotion is that, although it is often sparked by our thoughts, *we experience it through special feelings* in addition to thoughts. Love, anger, fear, and pleasure are some common emotions we experience. Notice how these are primarily *felt* within us and how they have the power to make us *want to act* (that is, expend energy). If we are angry, for example, it is difficult to "restrain ourselves." Love, on the other hand, leads us to "reach out" to another person, whereas fear makes us want to "get away" from the danger. Because of their powerful effects, emotions occupy a special position for us as consumers. Marketers, realizing this, strive to evoke emotions in advertising campaigns and to offer emotional gratifications to customers. Because of the importance of emotions in consumer behavior, the term *affect* (meaning feelings) has become one of the most important concepts in all of marketing. We will be returning to this concept frequently. In the interim, though, let's consider briefly whether there might be limits to the extent that marketers use emotional appeals:

How Much Is Too Much?

Should advertising ever make people uncomfortable? The long-running debate over this question arose again recently when a division of American Health Corporation tried to place ads on TV networks. It seems that, of the 12 million diabetics in the United States, half don't know that they have the disease, and many others are ignoring some of its dangers. The company, which sells treatment services, discovered that its clients were reporting that they had spend years in "self-denial," refusing to come to grips with having the disease. Accordingly, the firm created a campaign aimed at "getting people off the fence" and into the treatment centers. In one TV spot, for example, a man is shown taking off his shoes, then his socks, then his leg prosthesis, as the announcer says, "If you give diabetes an inch, it'll take a foot." The networks reacted negatively to running this campaign, however: "We don't want to discuss the possible harmful effects of wrong treatment of diabetes . . . we consider this scare copy," said CBS. The ad agency and the company (which was experiencing both positive and negative reactions from local broadcast stations) indicate that their consumer research studies show the scare ad outdrawing an ad with a positive appeal ("You can learn to live with diabetes with a little help . . .") by a 3-to-1 margin. According to an executive from the advertising agency, "The positive campaign gave people a chance to deny the problems of their disease. The negative one didn't. It spurred them to action." About the networks' banning these ads: "We're going to see more health-care advertising everywhere, and these questions are going to keep coming up."[5]

The question is: *What goes on in consumers' minds when they see ads like this? If you were a broadcasting executive, would you allow "scare" ads?*

The Direction Component

The direction component refers to exactly *which* behavior is chosen from all those possible, and *why*. In general, motivation theory asserts that the direction taken in a behavior is in large part determined by the particular purposes we are trying to achieve with that behavior (this is technically termed **purposive behavior**). If consumer behavior is purposive, it should be possible to understand *why* a particular direction was chosen. For example, the concept of **primary motives** involves the purposes behind consumers' decisions to use or not to use entire classes of products. Why do some people drink alcoholic beverages, for example, while others do not? **Selective motives**, on the other hand, refer to consumers' decisions as to exactly which stores, brands, and model features will be used or purchased. Why would a patron order a Corona in the bar rather than a Miller?

The directional component thus underlies all consumer decisions to (1) purchase a product at all and (2) choose a particular alternative from that product class. These are, of course, the essential underpinnings of consumer demand in the marketplace and are of crucial importance to the marketing field. The better that marketers are able to understand the purposes being served through consumption, the better they are able to attract consumer patronage and serve consumers' interests well. As consumers, moreover, the better we are able to identify our own goals, the better we should be able to make consumer decisions in our own self-interest.

(O) Overt and Hidden Motives

Our framework's second statement maintains an emphasis on purposive behavior by turning our attention to **motives**. A *motive is a concept used by researchers to explain the reasons for behavior.* Researchers cannot observe a person's motives, only his or her behavior—from that behavior, they must try to *infer* the exact motives that caused it. One definition of a motive is "a strong and persistent internal stimulus around which behavior is organized."[6] The final statement of our framework, pertaining to the need hierarchy, will address the nature of motives in considerable detail. At this stage, we are only concerned with two basic points—that consumers have *multiple* motives and that some of these motives are **overt** (that is, as consumers we are well aware of these reasons behind our behavior) while others are **hidden** in the minds of consumers (that is, consumers are themselves not aware of what these motives are).

Multiple Motives, Multiple Acts

Each of us has many motives that guide our behaviors on a daily basis. Unfortunately, however, the study of motives is quite difficult. Part of this difficulty is due to the fact that *any particular motive can usually be satisfied by several different types of behaviors.* For example, let's assume that Bob Reston has been studying hard and is motivated to break from his work to relax and refresh himself. Notice that there are many options available for this purpose—he could go to a movie, play racquetball, read a novel, and so on. It is also true that *different motives might lead to the same behavior.* For example, suppose we see Bob in a restaurant. He might be there because of a hunger motive, but he might also be there because he wanted to take a break from his studies, he wanted to meet new people, and so forth. Also, of course, several of these motives might have been acting in combination in creating this behavior.

Simply observing consumer behavior, therefore, will not be sufficient to detect the motives that are at work. Marketers must try to measure the motives that are operating with respect to particular purchases. Notice how this was done in a study on shopping:

Why Do People Shop?

It is clear that we shop to make purchases. What else, though, is involved? One interesting study used in-depth interviews with consumers to identify some typical motivations.[7] Among the findings:

- *Role playing.* Shopping is sometimes important to a person's role (e.g., a "provider" feels that it is expected, important, and gratifying to shop for food for the household.)
- *Diversion.* Shopping can offer a break from routine and is a form of recreation.

- *Self-gratification.* Shopping can offer us a sense of companionship when bored or can allow us to buy something nice for ourselves when we are depressed.
- *Learning.* Shopping allows us to learn about new products and new trends.
- *Exercise.* For some consumers, browsing is a regular form of physical exercise.
- *Sensory stimulation.* Shopping presents us with lights, colors, movements, scents, sounds, and so forth, much of which can be pleasant.
- *Communication.* Shopping provides opportunities to communicate with friends or sales-persons, often about matters of personal interest.
- *Peer group attraction.* Shopping can involve affiliating with an important reference group, such as the "in group" at a bar, the music crowd at a record stores, and so on.
- *Status and authority.* Some shoppers appreciate the sense of power and attention that flows from being "waited on" by store personnel.
- *Pleasure from bargain hunting or negotiating.* Some shoppers enjoy a "competitive" dimension in their shopping, through searching for "best buys" or attempting to negotiate lower prices with salespersons.

Even with this partial list, we can see that the topic of consumer motivation will encompass a broad range of issues and that some of these will be subtle.

Hidden Motives and the Unconscious Mind

Until this point, we have assumed that all consumer behavior stems from conscious decisions. When attempting to understand motives, however, some researchers take the theories of Sigmund Freud into consideration. Freud's studies of patients with mental problems provided evidence that a person's actions are often determined by influences of which he or she is, at the time, completely unaware. His notion of **unconscious motivation** means that the person is *unable* to report at least some of the true motives for a particular behavior, since he or she is truly not conscious of them. To understand this point better, you may wish to review Exhibit 6-1. More recent research has expanded on this topic. For example, we now know that that consumers are **unaware** of many of their motivations, partially because their CIP processes work imperfectly and yet very rapidly. Thus these motives *are* hidden, but not because of Freud's unconscious. Other motives may be truly unconscious, however, such that consumers would not be aware of them even if their CIP processes were working perfectly. Let's look more directly into this now.

Hidden Motives and Marketing Research

Within marketing the idea of hidden motives has had a major impact, primarily through the work of "motivation researchers." Apart from controversies as to the research methods themselves (which we'll discuss after our examples), motivation research has made two key contributions to the field of consumer behavior:

1. Stressing the **symbolic nature** of products and advertising.
2. Stressing the value of **qualitative research** methods.

EXHIBIT 6-1   **FREUD'S PSYCHOANALYTIC THEORY**

Sigmund Freud worked in Vienna, Austria, during the late 1880s and early 1900s. His controversial theories were stimulated by questions such as, "What do dreams mean?" and "How does hypnosis work?" From these beginnings, Freud evolved a major theory of unconscious motivation. This theory is built around three basic systems: the id, the ego, and the superego.

Freud believed that the **id** is the most basic system, and is intimately related to a person's physiological system. The id is entirely unconscious, but very powerful. It is the source of our psychic energy behind all behavior. The psychic energy itself is termed **libido** and operates according to the **pleasure principle** (*libido* means "lust" in Latin). Based upon the instincts with which we are born, the id is *entirely geared toward achieving pleasure and avoiding pain.* It is very powerful and demands immediate gratification. Unlike our conscious processes, the id is nonrational, and not logical. It is totally internal and has no knowledge of objective reality. The behavior of a newborn baby indicates the id's workings, since the other systems have not yet developed.

The **ego** is the system that is in contact with the external world and that develops to take charge of the person's actual behavior. The ego is governed by the **reality principle**— it seeks to achieve the pleasurable demands of the id in as realistic a way as possible. Since many of the id's demands are quite unrealistic, the ego must develop ways to postpone them, deflect them, or substitute feasible gratifications to satisfy the id's cravings. Some of the ego's work goes on at the unconscious level (where it relates to the id) and some of the conscious level (where it relates to the reality of the world). As a child matures growth stages in the ego can be identified.

The *superego* is the last of the three structures to develop. It has two functions—to *reward* "good" behavior and to *punish* unacceptable actions by creating guilt. Thus the superego represents a person's "conscience" and works *against* the unacceptable impulses of the id (rather than seeking to manage them, as does the ego). The superego is also primarily unconscious: it represents ideal rather than real behavior and strives for perfection rather than pleasure.

Within Freud's theory, the ways these three systems develop in the child is crucial to the different "personalities" that people develop as they become adults. Basically, as the ego develops within each person, it creates systematic ways of dealing with the incredibly strong and conflicting demands coming from the id and the superego. These systematic behaviors form the bases for individual personality traits. Since Freud's emphasis was on the power of the sexual drive from the id, his personality theory reflects a decidedly sexual orientation (in much of his psychiatric work he was dealing with female patients with sexual disorders). Although his theories are controversial as to detail, much of the work in psychiatry and clinical psychology has developed directly from his original thinking.

Chapter 13 discusses symbolic consumer behavior, so we need not pursue it in depth here. The matter of qualitative research does merit some discussion, however.

Qualitative research uses unstructured research methods in which consumers are enticed to reveal what they can about their innermost thoughts, feelings, and reactions to stimuli. These approaches are controversial, since typically their validity and reliability are unknown. That is, they may not yield accurate answers. However, they are widely used in marketing.

One extremely popular research technique is called the *focus group study*. A typical **focus group** brings 8 to 12 consumers from the target market together, seats them in a conversational setting, and asks them to talk freely about the subject. A trained moderator moves the discussion along, ensuring that the client's (marketer's) questions of interest do get addressed, but also giving freedom to the group members to express their opinions during the 1- to 2-hour session. **In-depth personal interviews** are also commonly used in qualitative research in marketing.

Qualitative research usually employs some mix of *direct* and *indirect* questions. Direct questions ask for a consumer's thoughts or feelings in a direct manner, sometimes with answer categories suggested, but usually with some degree of freedom, or "open-endedness." For example, in the Open-ended Sentence Completion Task ("Lipsticks are . . ." "Women who wear pink lipstick are . . .") the consumer is asked to respond quickly with what first comes to mind. The Thematic Apperception Test, or TAT, is also often used—the consumer is asked to tell a story about a situation depicted in a picture, such as that of a young man standing in front of a ring display in a jewelry store. A TAT-related technique uses cartoons, with the consumer asked to fill in the blank balloons representing thoughts of the characters. Another common technique asks the consumer about *other* people or *most* consumers (e.g., "What kind of person likes to use hair coloring?").

The last three methods are termed **projective tests**. Because the situation is deliberately ambiguous or unfinished, it is clear that there are no right or wrong answers. Also, the consumer is not placed in the position of answering personally about himself or herself. The researchers' hope is that the consumers, given a lack of pressure for "acceptable" answers, but pressed for detailed answers, will draw upon the sources they know best—and *project* their own unconscious feelings into the answers.

Advertising agencies have increased use of projective tests in recent years. For example, one major agency gives consumers stacks of photos of peoples' faces, then asks them to sort out who might be typical users of various brands (each face has been chosen to represent a particular emotional reaction to the product). Another major agency asks consumers to draw shapes expressing their reactions to new product ideas—the twist is that every consumer has to use his or her *left hand* to do the drawing, since the researchers believe that the portion of the brain that controls feelings also controls the left hand. A third major agency, searching for consumers' true images of a brand, asks them to assume that a certain brand has "died" and to write a newspaper obituary for it (e.g., a young, virile brand that was the victim of an accident is presumed more healthy than a worn-out brand that finally has died of old age). This agency also favors the use of "stick-figure sketches," as related in the following example.[8]

Sticking It To Them!

One strange twist that marketing managers frequently encounter is that consumers will say one thing, but will do another. Recently, for example, a major ad agency faced the problem that its client's new brand of roach killer wasn't selling well with a key segment—low-income women in the South—where the infestation problem means that potential sales are very high. The puzzler: why weren't sales strong? The agency knew that the *earlier advertising had worked* with these consumers: they knew about the product—a plastic tray device—and they believed that it did offer the key benefits of effective eradication in a tidy hidden manner. Nonetheless, the women weren't buying, instead staying with the old bug sprays they had used for years. To gain better insight into the reasons, the agency asked some target consumers to draw rough pictures of roaches, then write little stories explaining their sketches. Exhibit 6-2 shows some of the results.

The researchers were surprised to notice that all the roaches pictured were males! According to the research director, many of the women viewed the roach as symbolizing men who had mistreated them in the past. "Killing the roaches with a bug spray and watching them squirm and die allowed the women to express their hostility toward men *and* have greater control over the roaches," she reported.

In summary, there is a broad range of research that falls under the "qualitative research" label. Many managers find that they like some techniques but not others. The area of projective tests is particularly controversial, and has gathered groups of supporters and critics. In the words of one supporter (the roach project director), "We're using a whole battery of psychological techniques—some new and some old—to understand the emotional bond between consumers and brands . . .". The director of advertising research at another major agency agrees: "Brands are not just commercial products we buy and use; they're our companions in life as well." However, the head of the consumer behavior group at a different major agency is critical of this type of research: "I'm really skeptical about these psychoanalysts . . .".

Much of the debate involves serious scientific research concerns. Since qualitative research can be expensive on a per consumer basis, sampling size and representativeness is often a problem (e.g., What percentage of women actually hold these symbolic views of roaches?). Much of the research is therefore treated as "exploratory" and is used as a source of ideas and insights (notice, however, that if the sample is not representative, these insights could be misleading). The subjective nature of the researcher's interpretations is also a difficulty from a scientific viewpoint—two motivation researchers might well reach different conclusions about what certain answers mean or what should be done about them. Finally, motivation research in marketing is inherently situation specific and not geared toward providing generalizations about all consumer behavior.

EXHIBIT 6-2   CONSUMER "PICTURE-STORIES" ABOUT ROACHES

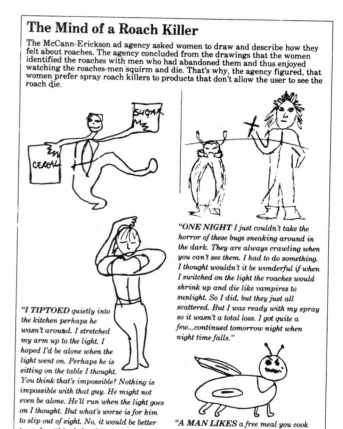

The Mind of a Roach Killer

The McCann-Erickson ad agency asked women to draw and describe how they felt about roaches. The agency concluded from the drawings that the women identified the roaches with men who had abandoned them and thus enjoyed watching the roaches-men squirm and die. That's why, the agency figured, that women prefer spray roach killers to products that don't allow the user to see the roach die.

"I TIPTOED quietly into the kitchen perhaps he wasn't around. I stretched my arm up to the light. I hoped I'd be alone when the light went on. Perhaps he is sitting on the table I thought. You think that's impossible? Nothing is impossible with that guy. He might not even be alone. He'll run when the light goes on I thought. But what's worse is for him to slip out of sight. No, it would be better to confront him before he takes control and 'invites a companion'."

"ONE NIGHT I just couldn't take the horror of these bugs sneaking around in the dark. They are always crawling when you can't see them. I had to do something. I thought wouldn't it be wonderful if when I switched on the light the roaches would shrink up and die like vampires to sunlight. So I did, but they just all scattered. But I was ready with my spray so it wasn't a total loss. I got quite a few...continued tomorrow night when night time falls."

"A MAN LIKES a free meal you cook for him, as long as there is food he will stay."

For these reasons, the academic field of marketing and consumer behavior has treated motivation research at some distance and has given little attention to this area in recent years. Within the world of marketing management, however, various aspects of the approach are used frequently. For example, until the 1980s (when he moved to smaller quarters after suffering a heart attack), the best known motivation researcher, Dr. Ernest Dichter maintained a thriving research and

Every time you sell a self-indulgent product,
you have to assuage the buyer's guilt feeling.

consulting practice at his castle overlooking the Hudson River. Dr. Dichter was trained in Vienna in the Freudian school of psychology, and offered colorful and opinionated explanations. The advertising and marketing managers who came seeking his insights about consumers' hidden motives were willing to pay high fees for this advice! Here are some examples:

- Dr. Dichter studied consumers' views about their cars. Based on his findings, he suggested that a gasoline brand tell consumers to "Put a Tiger in Your Tank!" since in the deep recesses of our minds we actually think of our cars as "power."
- One finding that emerged in many of his studies over the years is that the average American consumer has a streak of "old-fashioned puritanism" that creates a serious barrier to purchasing many products and services. Dr. Dichter's advice: "Every time you sell a self-indulgent product, you have to assuage the buyer's guilt feeling."

The ambivalent reactions many people have to Dr. Dichter's work have been evident for many years. The hidden world of consumer motivations is at once provocative yet disturbing. About 30 years ago, for example, Vance Packard's best-selling book, *The Hidden Persuaders,* made many charges about how Dichter and his fellow motivation researchers were helping marketers to manipulate consumers' minds. As Dr. Dichter relates, "it was a bombshell. And I'm on almost every other page, and I was the big villain. So I got calls from (foreign countries) and all over the United States. And the people said, 'What you're doing is terrible. How much does it cost?' "[9]

(T) Tension Reduction Drives Consumer Behavior

This entry is the most basic of all in our framework. It provides the fundamental reason that *any* behavior is undertaken at *any* point in time. The idea of tension reduction is drawn from studies in biology of the human body's tendency to make adjustments to remain in as steady a condition as possible (equilibrium).[10] For example, we perspire in reaction to a rise in body temperature: it is a natural means of releasing heat and keeping our temperature near normal.

The basic theory is that a nonequilibrium state creates a feeling of tension. When tension gets too high, we experience levels of psychological discomfort, and energy is aroused to reduce this tension. When the body requires nourishment, for example, a tension is created in our systems. We find this mildly uncomfortable, say that we are "hungry," and are motivated to find food to reduce the tension level. Within consumer behavior, tension reduction is inherent in most key concepts. For example, our basic view is that consumers pursue need fulfillment. Need fulfillment, in turn, is based upon desires to reduce tensions brought about by wants that are unsatisfied prior to purchase. In general, then, this entry in our framework stresses that humans are motivated to behave because of tension reduction. We will see many examples of this principle in upcoming chapters.

(I) Internal and External Forces Impact Motivation

The basic point of this framework entry is that motivation is sometimes sparked internally (e.g., hunger) and sometimes sparked externally (e.g., a friend's suggestion). Once sparked, the direction the motivated behavior will take is also determined partially by internal factors and partially by external factors. For example, a food purchase will be directed in part by a person's brand preferences, but also by sale prices or availability of different brands in the store. To understand the foundation for this way of thinking about consumer behavior better, let's consider the nature of Kurt Lewin's **field theory**.

Professor Kurt Lewin (pronounced "Le-veen" or "Lew-in") has been called the most brilliant figure in recent psychological history and has had a profound impact on thinking in the area of motivation.[11] Professor Lewin worked in Germany until the rise of the Nazi movement caused him to emigrate to the United States in the 1930s. The most famous of his contributions is known as *field theory,* which is a system by which we can visualize and quantify how behavior occurs. Its basic premise is captured in Lewin's famous formula:

$$B = f(P, E)$$

This is read, "*Behavior* is a function of both the *person* and the *environment.*"

The person and environment comprise what is called the **life space** or **psychological field**. The life space is the *totality of all forces acting on a person at a point in time.* This includes all internal forces, together with those external aspects of the environment of which the person is aware. In this theory, therefore, the "environment" does not refer to physical reality itself, but to the psychological perception of that reality as each person sees it at that time—as we'll see in our chapters on perception (Chapters 8 and 9), this is an important aspect of consumer behavior.

(V) Consumer Motivation Has Valence

This framework entry provides a good basis for analyzing the direction behavior will take, and which alternatives consumers are likely to choose. The term **valence** is a *measure of the degree of attractiveness* that a particular object, such as a product, holds for us. A valence is either positive (when the product is attractive to us) or negative (when it is unattractive to us). Valence also reflects the strength of the attraction—it can be low or high, depending on how much we are attracted or repelled by the product in question. The concept of valence occupied an important role within Lewin's field theory.

One important application area for the valence concept involves **motivational conflicts**. As we've noted earlier, the typical consumer faces multiple alternatives, has multiple motives, and is limited in both the time and money that he or she can spend. This means that *conflicts* will arise on how to allocate attention and purchases. Lewin identified three types of motivational conflicts, each having two forces acting in opposite directions within a given life space:

- Approach-avoidance
- Approach-approach
- Avoidance-avoidance

Approach-avoidance conflicts are very common in consumer behavior. They occur when a consumer is considering both positive and negative features of a single alternative. In a motivational sense, the consumer wishes to move toward the positive features, but away from the negative ones. This is because most products offer positive benefits to us, engendering approach forces. At the same time, however, there are several types of "perceived risks" that can engender avoidance forces in us. These include performance risks, financial risks, physical

Approach-approach conflict: Which shall it be, a vacation in Acapulco or some new furnishings for the condo?

injury risks, and social risks. The topic of perceived risk has received considerable attention in consumer research.[12]

The consumer behavior likely in an approach-avoidance conflict depends on the relative strength of the opposing forces. However, *the forces themselves are subject to being influenced by marketers.* Advertising can provide information and excitement to enhance the approach force, as can a salesperson. Sale prices can weaken the avoidance force, as can easy credit, product guarantees, and other marketing tools.

Approach-approach conflicts are the most pleasant type and are also quite common in consumer behavior. Here we are attempting to decide between two alternatives and are concentrating only on their attractive features. For example, Joan Cohen wants to celebrate a successful year, and is trying to decide between a trip to Acapulco and refurnishing her condominium. Joan may feel that this is a difficult choice to make and may well think more about each alternative. Since she is moving toward a positive result, though, she will want to make the choice and obtain the benefits from either her trip or her furnishings.

Avoidance-avoidance conflicts are quite the opposite situation. These are the most unpleasant type of motivational conflict, since they involve a choice between two behaviors with negative valences. The person in this situation is motivated to move *away from* both alternatives and is not likely to purchase at all until his or her perceptions of the situation shift. Fortunately, since most consumer purchases are voluntary on our part (that is, we are rarely *forced* to buy or use products that we don't wish to have), this is not a typical conflict found in brand choice. In areas such as health problems and household maintenance, however, we do often see this conflict arising. For example, most of us wish to avoid having a dirty oven, but also wish to avoid the task of having to clean it. In these cases, a product that works well and also simplifies the cleaning task would reduce the size of the conflict we are experiencing and would be seen positively for this contribution to bettering our lives.

(A) Consumers are Motivated to Achieve Goals

This framework entry offers many useful marketing applications. It represents one of the major schools of motivation theory—the expectancy × value (often called *E* times *V*) approach. **Expectancy × value theory** represents an extension of the key concepts of Lewin's work, together with the work of several other scientists on such topics as learning (Tolman), achievement motivation (Atkinson), and economic decisions (Edwards).[13]

The $E \times V$ approach places great emphasis on how *goals lead to specific behaviors.* Its major proposition is

> *The strength of the tendency to act in a certain way depends on the strength of the* expectancy *that the act will be followed by a given consequence (or goal) and the* value *of that consequence to the individual.*[14]

Stainmaster became a major new product success by vividly portraying that the consumer could have a high expectancy (E) of achieving highly valued (V) consequences if accidents should happen with Stainmaster carpets.

Thus we evaluate each possible behavior (such as the purchase of a particular brand) in terms of how desirable we expect its consequences to be for us.

As we might expect, $E \times V$ theory has powerful implications for helping us to understand consumer behavior. It views a consumer as a problem solver, approaching situations as opportunities to gain new information, new product benefits, or other positive goals that he or she may have. Key aspects of $E \times V$ theory are already much used within marketing. We will return to this topic in the next chapter.

(T) Consumers Have a Thirst for Variety

This entry extends the fundamental idea of tension reduction (the earlier "T" in our framework), by stressing that consumers sometimes *seek* tension rather than avoid it. This reminds us that consumers are *active as well as reactive*. We consumers do not only strive to resolve issues in as efficient a way as possible: we also enjoy being stimulated (such as in a movie), even though this increases our bodily tensions during the event. In a sense, we go through our lives as "tension managers." Although this point may appear to undercut tension reduction as the basis for motivation, in fact the general theory of tension reduction can incorporate these exploratory behaviors on our part. This can be done by assuming that the optimal level of tension (or stimulation) for our human systems is not zero, but is instead some slight positive level. If the existing stimulation level is too low, then, we will feel a tension (for example, we "feel bored") and will want to raise the level of stimulation ("do something interesting") to reduce the tension level in our system.[15]

This framework entry has a broad array of interesting implications for consumer behavior, including such issues as why consumers are so curious and interested in variety and adventure. These factors work *against* long-term brand loyalty. They underpin consumers' *willingness to try new products and new stores.* On a pragmatic basis, of course, consumers' trial of new products represents the future of most firms (and their managers) and is extremely important to all of marketing.

Consumers' *curiosity* is a key factor. One area of marketing that relies upon

Big winners, big losers

A dozen magazines reveal the covers of their best and worst selling issues on the newsstands this year. One moral: Sigourney's hot, Jesse's not

Vanity Fair
Tina Brown, editor
"Our cover image can help circulation by an extra 20,000 or so, but it's really the red 'flash' band on the side that sells at the newsstand.

"The August issue had Sigourney Weaver on the cover but she didn't really do it as much as the red flash about the Shah. We sell on coverlines, and the flash is the hot scoop.

"The Jesse Jackson issue was probably the worst. There's a guaranteed risk putting a politician on the cover—I knew all about that. We did it anyway and it did not work. Also, it was January and that's never a good month. We're definitely spoiled because we've had so many gains at the newsstand.

"The perfect *Vanity Fair* cover is glamor and class in the image and a hot flash item. It's tough to find that, and sometimes we go for a funny glitz cover and that works, too."

Esquire
Lee Eisenberg, editor in chief
" 'Dubious Achievements' is a perennial winner for us. Why that is is self-evident, I think. It's a publishing institution that's talked about and debated.

"The worst issue, Prince Charles, didn't go badly—it wasn't a disaster—but it was the weakest of six strong issues.

"The story itself is something we're proud of but the photo was not particularly warm. It was regal, as befits the prince, but we didn't get the chance to shoot it ourselves. Had we shot the photo it may have played better.

"The men we usually put on the cover must stand for some kind of real character that our readers can relate to. The more emulatable they are, the better. The pool is relatively shallow that we fish from to get our cover subjects."

New England Monthly
Daniel Okrent, editor
"I'm not surprised [at which was the worst and best cover in 1988]. We do best when we feature a place and evoke places of the heart that people in New England love.

"The ones that sell the worst are those with harder journalism. The issues with topics fare poorly compared to those on places.

"No matter how important newsstand sales are, we are overwhelmingly a subscription magazine and the topic issues are important to our readers, our subscribers. If you looked at 12 issues on destinations in New England you wouldn't have a good picture of what the magazine is all about.

Texas Monthly
Gregory Curtis, editor
"There's definitely a different look each month. It's very much a seat-of-the-pants decision. There are no constants. But I try to think what is on people's minds and then try to find some way to do a story about it.

"The trouble is, there might not be a single theme in the air or there is and you don't identify it, but there's a certain amount of luck involved.

"A cover that is perceived as ugly will not sell; but a beautiful cover may not sell either. A cover has to attract people's eyes, but what the cover promises must be what readers want."

Harrowsmith
Thomas H. Rawls, editor
"Our name is nothing but a problem for us on the newsstand. What is a *Harrowsmith,* anyway?

"Where are you going to put us? Do you put us in the H's next to *Hustler*? Do you put us with the home and lifestyle books? Do you put us with gardening magazines?

"Part of the reason we put that positioning statement [The Magazine of Country Life] on there was so that some kid in a convenience store somewhere who's stacking magazines will read it and know where to put us.

"We prefer illustrated covers to photographs even though researchers say photos fare better, and we stay away from a lot of cover copy. Because we don't live by the newsstand, we can break some of the rules.

"Historically, January-February is our best issue for a variety of reasons. People like the catalog listing.

"The barn cover will probably sell the least at the newsstand. It's a pleasing piece of art and a good cover but it's less colorful and it's got less pop."

Rolling Stone
Jann S. Wenner, editor & publisher
"What goes into selecting each cover is the newsworthiness of the subject, its appeal to our target audience and the quality of the photograph. A cover story can't be a cover story if there's not a good picture.

"Who's on the cover and how they look is what sells on the newsstand. It's an editorial/circulation decision as to what goes on the cover, what's going to jump off the newsstand."

(Continued on Page S-48)

consumer curiosity and interest in variety is magazine publishing, where newsstand sales depend heavily on the appeal of the covers of each issue. The real covers from a variety of magazines pictured here show which had the higher consumer sales. If you are interested, you may enjoy trying to pick the winning covers!

What Appeals to the "Cosmo Girl"?

Cosmopolitan became a highly successful magazine through its glorification of the "Cosmo Girl." According to Helen Gurley Brown, editor, "I knew what she should look like . . . sexy, gorgeous, friendly. . . . I love lots of hair, cleavage at least every other month. . . . I doubt we will ever do the scrubbed look!" Ms. Brown's husband, David, writes the blurbs for each cover. He explains, "In deciding whether a blurb will attract newsstand buyers, I ask myself whether the subject can involve the reader. . . . I call this the 'you' factor." Among Mr. Brown's tips for top cover blurbs: the use of humor and surprise, recognizing that consumers' desire to learn is one of the most powerful urges (he believes it surpasses sex in the long run); realize that consumers' hope springs eternal; and try to promise something for every problem. Overall, Mr. Brown concludes, ". . . emotional pull is still the big lure . . . newsstand sales prove it."[16]

Entire industries are built on the "thirst for variety" motive on the part of consumers. For example, think about the kind of consumer motivations on which television, nightclubs, sports, and tourism are based. Moreover, these industries promise to expand in the future, particularly in the area of "designed experiences."

What Will the Future Bring?

In recent years the "designed experience" industry has been booming. Middle-aged athletes now pay $3000 per week to adult baseball camps to play against the stars they remember from their childhood. Businesses use designed experiences to reward their sales forces and major clients (recently, for example, a group of American executives flew to England, where a firm had prepared the setting for them to return to the Middle Ages as Robin Hood and his Merry Men in Sherwood Forest!).

Technology continues to expand possibilities. Already "interactive television" has appeared. Here consumers in their homes can play the actual "Wheel of Fortune" game with the lovely Vanna White (and can win the actual prizes on the show), they can play sports games, participate in electronic sweepstakes, and shop and order from department stores and supermarkets (J. C. Penney's test system is called an "electronic shopping mall" since it allows the viewer to shop and order from 40 different retailers, just as in an actual mall). Beyond this, a leading marketing professor has predicted even further developments in "consumer experiences." Which of the following would you personally like to experience?

- *Total television.* Screens curve around entire rooms, accompanied by authentic noises, smells, and costumes.
- *Sensory wiring.* Wired helmets induce specific combinations of sights, sounds, touch, and taste.

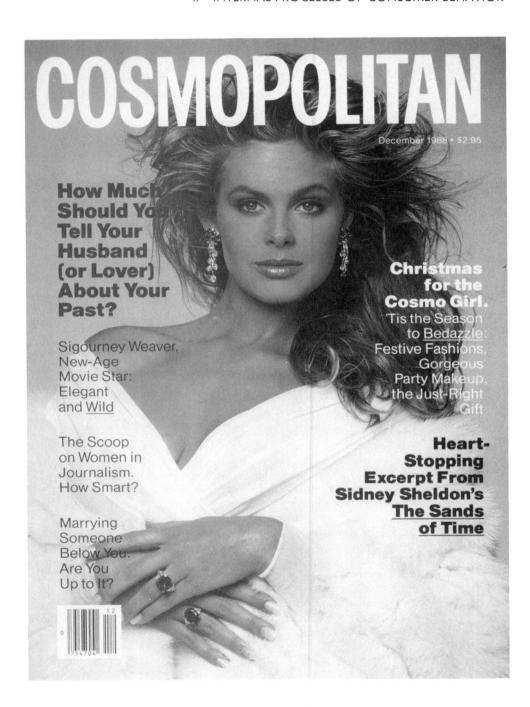

- *"Experience" pills.* Controlled hallucinations could allow a consumer to take a pill, then "dream" his or her way through a desired experience, such as climbing Mount Everest as a member of Hillary's expedition.[17]

Most of us have limits as to how far we'd like our curiosity, novelty, and pleasure-seeking motives to take us. Even if all the foregoing possibilities are not attractive, we should recognize from them the power of our motivations in this area. (In recent years consumer researchers have been especially interested in pursuing research on this area; if you would like to learn more about their views and findings, you may wish to pursue the readings listed in Note 18.)[18]

(I) Consumer Motivation Reflects Individual Differences

This framework entry refers to the fact that consumers differ from each other in what, where, and how they buy. If we are to understand buying behavior, we need to understand why these differences occur.

Some of the individual differences we observe are obviously due to external factors, such as income, age, and social pressures. Nonetheless, it also seems that there is a natural inclination for consumers to have different preferences. For example, let's assume that everyone had the same income and that age differences didn't matter. Would we then expect everyone to buy the same brands and models of products? Obviously not. Theoretically, individual differences have been studied in the field of personality research. Personality research has received considerable attention in consumer behavior and has yielded some surprising findings, which we'll examine in Chapter 7.

(O) Consumers Desire Order in Their World

This framework entry stresses that consumers are motivated to do more than simply acquire products and services—all consumers are also motivated to understand (or see order in) their world. In practice, this means that they are constantly estimating what is responsible for, or causes, various events. This process of estimating causes is called *attribution* and is the focus of the broad psychological field of **attribution theory**.[19]

Attributions occur frequently in consumer behavior, sometimes quite consciously and sometimes not. How many times, for example, have consumers responded "It's only an ad . . ." when they see strong positive claims about a product? What they are really doing is *attributing the claim to one cause* (that advertisers consciously exaggerate) *rather than another cause* (that the product really *is* fantastic). Similarly, if a salesperson tells Jack Evans that the used Camaro is in excellent condition, Jack is likely to ask himself whether he should accept that statement as true or attribute it to the salesperson's desire to sell this car.

Another common example involves purchases of products in which features and quality can be added to each model. In these instances, consumers will often find the salesperson recommending a higher-priced model that offers additional features. In this situation, consumers are confronted with a choice of which attribution to make about the salesperson's recommendations: "Is she trying to sell me the premium model because she believes it is better for me, or because her commission will be higher?" Note that this attribution is not only an academic question—the model that we will end up buying depends on which attribution we make!

Attributions are also important *after* a purchase, in evaluating product performance. If we are dissatisfied, for example, will we attribute the problem to ourselves ("I must not have operated it right" or "I sure made a bad buy here"), the manufacturer ("This is a shoddy product, and should not have been put on the market"), the retailer or salesperson ("I'll never go there again; they obviously don't care what they sell to the customer"), or to some other events ("If the timer had gone off, it wouldn't have been burned"). Successful product performance is important as well, since we can attribute it either to ourselves ("I really know how to make a pizza!") or to the marketing system ("This brand makes a great pizza!").

"Foot in the Door" and "Door in the Face"

In addition to making attributions about why events happened and about other people's behaviors, we also make *attributions about ourselves* and our own behaviors. The area of self-perception stresses how we examine our own behavior *after* we've undertaken it. Psychologists have used this theory to recommend two approaches for gaining compliance with requests: the *foot-in-the-door* (*FITD*) approach and the *door-in-the-face* (*DITF*) approach. Both FITD and DITF are based on the premise that "two requests are better than one," when the goal is to have consumers agree to behave in a certain way (such as subscribe to a newspaper or contribute blood). In essence, the first request is used to "set the stage" for the second, by stimulating certain self-perception processes in the mind of the consumer.

The FITD technique begins by asking consumers to agree to a small request: once they've done this, their chances of agreeing to a larger request (the one actually desired by the seller) are higher than they would be if the large request alone had been made. The DITF technique proceeds in just the opposite fashion. It first asks the consumer to comply with a very large request; after being turned down, it makes a smaller, more reasonable request (the one actually desired by the seller).

The attribution theory explanation for both techniques is that a consumer, after having agreed to or denied the first request, will attempt to explain to himself or herself exactly why he or she took that action. In the FITD case, the initial small request will have led to compliance, so the consumer will be attempting to answer why he had agreed to do this (put a sign in the window supporting safety for children, for example). One likely (and personally acceptable) answer is that he really does support safety for children. This personal stance will then be invoked when the representative returns with the second request—now the consumer is seeing himself as a supporter of the cause and is more willing to do something more to help!

In the DITF case, however, the initially large request was likely refused (say, using his house as a neighborhood playground to keep the children safe.) In this case an acceptable attribution is that the request itself was simply too large—although the cause itself is worthwhile and the consumer does support it. Then, when the second request comes shortly thereafter, the consumer is not able to employ the same attribution again, since this request (volunteer some time to help get a new playground in the neighborhood) is clearly a reasonable one.

In closing, we should note a considerable theoretical debate about exactly when and why either of these techniques work. Not everyone accepts that the "self-perception" process is as powerful as suggested: some persons point to a "bargaining" system at work in these situations. (If you are interested in pursuing the debates or research findings, you may wish to begin with the readings listed in Note 20.) As you may have experienced, marketers are well aware of FITD and DITF. These techniques are widely used in selling and fund-raising activities.

(N) Consumers Are Guided by the Need Hierarchy

This final framework entry shifts our attention to the actual *content* of motivated behavior. Here we will focus on the nature of needs (or motives—we'll use the terms interchangeably in this discussion) and will examine three major points:

- Needs exist in a hierarchy.
- Needs can be identified.
- Consumer behavior derives from needs.

In our next chapter we will return to this topic to examine some techniques marketers use to work with this theory.

Maslow's Need Hierarchy

Abraham Maslow was a founder of the school of **humanistic psychology**, which has gained popularity in recent years. Maslow felt that too much attention had been given to negative views of people's psyches and not enough to their potentials. This spirit of personal growth is embodied in this theory of **need hierarchy**. There are several key propositions in this theory. First, the environment is extremely important in establishing which needs will be active within a person at a particular time. Second, when a need has been satisfied, it is no longer active as a need (though it may return later). Third, there is a systematic *order* within the basic needs; a person will not feel a second-level need until the first-level needs have been sufficiently satisfied, and so forth through the five levels of the

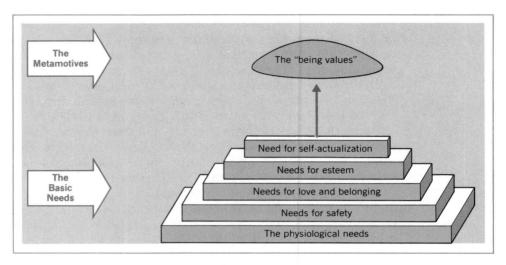

FIGURE 6-1 Maslow's Need Hierarchy

hierarchy. Therefore, Maslow concluded, if people are able to create a positive environment for themselves, they should be able to move up the need hierarchy toward the higher levels of personal growth, as depicted in Figure 6-1.

Level 1: The Physiological Needs These are the demands that our bodies place on us for survival and health. They include air, water, a balance of nutrients, a comfortable temperature, and elimination of bodily waste. These are the *prepotent* needs because they *must* be satisfied before other needs are activated. For example, a starving man needs food. In most modern cultures, these needs are satisfied most of the time. This releases them from active domination of our systems and allows us to proceed to higher-order needs.

Level 2: The Safety Needs This set of needs is actually much broader than its title suggests. In addition to physical safety, Maslow referred to psychological security. Thus stability, familiarity, and predictability are important needs. Since our culture is generally designed to provide physical safety and organized institutions (religions, schools, families, etc.), these safety needs are usually not active for most of us. When they are, however, they can easily dominate our thoughts and behaviors. Consider, for example, people who are afraid to ride in subways or walk the city streets. In the psychological realm, consider friends you might know who are constant "worriers." Note how their concerns with possible disruptions to their lives can preoccupy their thoughts. Within marketing, as the proportion of women business travelers has gone to 40 percent (from 1 percent in 1970), major hotel chains have found that "club floors" offering increased security have been a strong selling point.

Level 3: The Needs for Love and Belonging If both the physiological and safety needs are fairly gratified, the needs for love, affection, and belonging are likely to emerge. If these needs are not satisfied, a person is likely to feel "lonely" and perhaps depressed. Depending on the situation, a special friend or a small group can help toward resolving this set of needs.

Level 4: The Esteem Needs This reflects the general need for an individual to evaluate himself or herself positively. Maslow divided this set into two classes: inward directed and outward directed. The inner-directed needs refer to desires for competence and for confidence as to our own capability. The outward needs refer to the evaluations we receive from others, including recognition and appreciation. If these needs are not satisfied, a person feels inferior, and sometimes helpless. If the needs are satisfied, a person feels self-confident and capable.

Level 5: The Need for Self-actualization A person reaching this level will have already achieved much in life—he or she will have high self-esteem based upon accomplishments, will be valued and recognized by others, will be loved and belong in a social fabric, will feel safe and secure, and will be healthy physically. Not bad! However, since each of these levels has to be maintained, most people are never able to reach the self-actualization phase on a regular basis. Self-actualization means the fulfillment of a person's *unique potential*—the becoming of everything that one is capable of becoming. People in this stage are now motivated by what Maslow calls **metamotives** or ultimate values. These include truth, beauty, "aliveness," goodness, justice, and unity.

Although controversial in some respects, Maslow's hierarchy gives insights into today's consumer culture. For people whose physiological and safety needs are largely satisfied, most focus on social, psychological, and personal growth needs.[21]

Murray's List of Social Needs

Henry Murray was a surgeon, held a Ph.D. in biochemistry, and was the director of the Harvard Psychological Clinic during the decades from the 1920s to the early 1960s.[22] His training in biology and medicine, combined with a deep interest in psychology, allowed Murray to adopt a particularly broad view of motivation. This breadth makes his theory hard to describe in our limited space, but it also allows it to be used in many applications.

The basis of **Murray's inventory of social needs** is that *needs* are the basic motivating forces for people. He defined a **need** as a force in the brain region that influences a person to perceive and act in ways to turn unsatisfying situations into more satisfying ones. He believed that needs could be provoked by either internal or external stimuli and that they could be weak or strong at any particular time. He further believed that, after observing a person under many conditions for extensive time periods, certain systematic needs would appear, thus accounting for that person's "personality." Based upon the thousands of investigations by himself and his staff, Murray suggested that there is a limited number of some 20 needs that all humans seem to have in one degree or another. These are listed in Table 6-2.

The list of needs is called *instrumental* or *social* because they are often aroused in regard to others and they help us to determine how best to act. They are not independent from each other and often combine ("fuse") together to lead to a particular behavior. For example, let's consider n Sentience, which refers to a need to seek and enjoy sensuous impressions and pleasures. In some situations, this need might fuse with n Affiliation and lead to a desire for romantic love. In other situations, it might fuse with n Achievement, leading to a desire to create works of art, or it may fuse with n Exhibition, leading to a desire to purchase and display erotic or aesthetic products. Also, of course, n Sentience can combine with n Sex. Although brief, this should be sufficient to give you an idea of the richness of Murray's theory. It has been extremely influential in both psychology and consumer behavior. Murray, for example, was a codeveloper of the TAT instrument we described in our section on motivation research and "hidden" motives. He also developed evaluation procedures for the OSS—the U.S. spy agency that operated during World War II. Also, his theory is the basis for one of the most used personality tests in recent times, the Edwards Personal Preference Schedule (EPPS), which many readers of this book have likely taken.

TABLE 6-2 AN ILLUSTRATIVE LIST OF MURRAY'S NEEDS

Need	*Brief Definition*
n Abasement	To submit passively to external force. To accept injury, blame, criticism, punishment. To become resigned to fate. To admit inferiority, error, wrongdoing, or defeat. To confess and atone. To seek and enjoy pain, punishment, illness, and misfortune.
n Achievement	To accomplish something difficult. To master, manipulate, or organize physical objects, human beings, or ideas. To do this as rapidly and as independently as possible. To overcome obstacles and attain a high standard. To excel oneself. To rival and surpass others. To increase self-regard by the successful exercise of talent.
n Affiliation	To draw near and enjoyably cooperate or reciprocate with an allied other (an other who resembles the subject or who likes the subject). To please and win affection. To adhere and remain loyal to a friend.
n Aggression	To overcome opposition forcefully. To fight. To revenge an injury. To attack, injure, or kill another. To oppose forcefully or punish another.
n Autonomy	To get free, shake off restraint, break out of confinement. To resist coercion and restriction. To be independent and free to act according to impulse. To be unattached, irresponsible. To defy convention.

TABLE 6-2 AN ILLUSTRATIVE LIST OF MURRAY'S NEEDS *Continued*

Need	Brief Definition
n Counteraction	To master or make up for a failure by restriving. To obliterate a humiliation by resumed action. To overcome weaknesses, to repress fear. To efface a dishonor by action. To search for obstacles and difficulties to overcome. To maintain self-respect and pride on a high level.
n Defendance	To defend the self against assault, criticism, and blame. To conceal or justify a misdeed, failure, or humiliation. To vindicate the ego.
n Deference	To admire and support a superior. To praise, honor, or eulogize. To yield eagerly to the influence of an allied other. To emulate an exemplar. To conform to custom.
n Dominance	To control one's human environment. To direct the behavior of others by suggestion, seduction, persuasion, or command. To prohibit.
n Exhibition	To make an impression. To be seen and heard. To excite, amaze, fascinate, entertain, shock, intrigue, amuse, or entice others.
n Harm avoidance	To avoid pain, physical injury, illness, and death. To escape from a dangerous situation. To take precautionary measures.
n Infavoidance	To avoid humiliation. To quit embarrassing situations or to avoid conditions which may lead to belittlement: the scorn, derision, or indifference of others. To refrain from action because of the fear of failure.
n Nurturance	To give sympathy and gratify the needs of a helpless object: an infant or any object that is weak, inexperienced, lonely, sick. To feed, help, protect, nurse.
n Order	To put things in order. To achieve cleanliness, arrangement, organization, balance, neatness, tidiness, and precision.
n Play	To act for "fun" without further purpose. To like to laugh and make jokes. To seek enjoyable relaxation of stress. To participate in games, sports, dancing, drinking parties, cards.
n Rejection	To separate oneself from a negative object. To exclude, abandon, expel, or remain indifferent to an inferior object. To snub or jilt an object.
n Sentience	To seek and enjoy sensuous impressions.
n Sex	To form and further an erotic relationship. To have sexual intercourse.
n Succorance	To have one's needs gratified by the sympathetic aid of an allied object. To be nursed, supported, protected, loved, advised.
n Understanding	To ask or answer general questions. To be interested in theory. To speculate, formulate, analyze, and generalize.

Source: Calvin S. Hall and Gardner Lindzey, *Theories of Personality,* 2nd ed. (New York: John Wiley, 1970), pp. 176–177.

What do you get after spending 75 years   making America's favorite dress shirt?

"Members of the University Glee Club of New York City."

Bored.

Arrow

Which of Murray's Needs will be sparked here?

198

Recap: The Basics of Motivation Theory

We have discussed the broad, complex field of motivation at some length, and it may be useful to recap briefly the basic points here. Most consumer behavior experts accept the elements of motivational theory that we have been discussing within our framework. As a check on your understanding of this material, see if the following descriptions, which do not use exactly the same language, make sense. In summary, consumer behavior experts believe that

(M) We need to focus on both energy and direction.
(O) It will be hard to identify all motives in a situation.
(T) The underlying process is drive reduction.
(I) Field theory helps us to recognize factors.
(V) Consumers move toward and away from all marketing stimuli.
(A) Basically, consumer behavior is "goal directed."
(T) Consumer behavior brings stimulation to people's lives.
(I) Consumers will behave differently from each other.
(O) Consumers want to understand their environment and behaviors.
(N) Basic motives drive all human behavior.

 SUMMARY

Key Characteristics of Motivation

Motivation refers to the processes that move a person to behave in certain ways. As we'd expect, this is a very broad area. To simplify our task, the chapter was organized around a 10-point MOTIVATION framework:

(M) Motivation contains two major components: *energy* and *direction*. Energy is required for any type of behavior to occur, whereas direction is required to channel the energy into specific activities. *Emotion* is closely related to the energy dimension by virtue of its special power to make us want to act (marketers, realizing this, often strive to evoke emotions). Meanwhile, the direction taken in behavior is largely determined by the purposes one is trying to achieve.

(O) The second statement in our framework recognizes the distinction between *overt* and *hidden motives*. Discerning a consumer's motivation is almost always difficult, partially because we have multiple motives and partially because people are often unable to report their true motives. This notion of hidden or unconscious motivation was first raised by Sigmund Freud and has been used in marketing by motivation researchers. Two of this group's contributions to consumer research are a *stress on the symbolic nature of products* and *refinement of qualitative research methods*.

(T) This entry stresses the role that *tension reduction* plays in motivating behavior. Basically, a disequilibrium state creates a feeling of "tension." Energy is directed into behaviors that will reduce the tension.

(I) Consumers are motivated by both *internal* and *external forces*. Lewin's *field theory* highlighted the view that an individual's behavior at any point in time is a function of both the person and his or her psychological environment.

(V) The direction that behavior will take is reflected by the concept of *valence*, a measure of the degree of attractiveness that a particular object, such as a product, holds for us. We can use this type of model to understand which of two desirable alternatives a consumer will be motivated to choose.

(A) The *expectancy value* (E × V) *theory* of motivation is based on the fact that consumers are motivated to *achieve goals*. Its major proposition is that our behavior depends on what we *expect* will happen, and whether we place a positive or negative *value* on each possible outcome. This theory has a strong cognitive orientation and is related to our study of consumer information processing.

(T) Consumers have a *thirst for variety*. Sometimes consumers will seek to *increase* tension rather than to reduce or avoid it. This tendency explains why we consumers are curious, and like to try out new products.

(I) Consumer motivation also reflects *individual differences*. While some of these differences are due to observable characteristics (age, sex, etc.), consumers' differences in motivation go beyond their demographic makeup. Much of our next chapter is devoted to examining how individual differences affect consumer behavior.

(O) Consumers *seek order* in their world. That is, consumers are constantly attributing causes to the various events that they experience. The attribution the consumer makes regarding the exact reason a salesperson is recommending a high-priced model is very likely to affect the consumer's purchase decision.

(N) Our final framework entry stresses that consumers are guided by a *need hierarchy*. Maslow, for example, believed that physiological and lower-level needs must be satisfied before higher needs (such as esteem or "self-actualization") can be activated. A second influential theory—Murray's inventory of human needs— was also introduced in this section. This major work has provided much of the basis for research in the "consumer personality" area, which is the subject of our next chapter.

KEY TERMS

motivation	motives
consumer inertia	overt motives
purposive behavior	hidden motives
primary motives	unconscious motivation
selective motives	unaware

symbolic nature	valence
qualitative research	motivational conflicts
id	approach-avoidance conflict
libido	approach-approach conflict
pleasure principle	avoidance-avoidance conflict
ego	expectancy x value theory
reality principle	attribution theory
superego	humanistic psychology
focus group	need hierarchy
in-depth personal interviews	metamotives
projective tests	Murray's inventory of social needs
field theory	need
life space/psychological field	

REVIEW QUESTIONS AND EXPERIENTIAL EXERCISES
[E = Application extension or experiential exercise]

1. Explain the relationship between motivation and consumer activities. What implications for marketers are associated with understanding consumer motivation?

2. Purposive behavior is an important concept in consumer motivation for both consumers and marketers. Explain, citing examples.

3. Individual differences are mentioned as one of the major aspects of consumer motivation. What exactly does this term mean? Are consumers really so different? Don't we all really want the same things in life? At which levels of motivation do consumers differ? What implications do your answers have for marketers?

[E] 4. After reading all elements of the MOTIVATION framework, select the three that you believe will be most useful for marketing decisions. Briefly describe your reasoning (together with examples, if possible).

[E] 5. Reflecting our discussions of projective techniques, try a sample application for yourself (you may wish to use a market-research text or library reference source for detailed guidance). For example, select three brands or stores from a competitive product or service category. Have 10 people write (or relate to you) an obituary for each of the brands or stores (e.g., "Let's pretend that the Tide brand has just disappeared from the market . . . what would you write in a brief obituary for Tide?") Do the 10 obituaries show a consistent pattern? What particular implications do these reports have for the competing marketers? Does this seem to be useful technique, and how might it be improved? Write a report on your study.

[E]   6. Interview a market researcher from a company, research firm, or advertising agency. Discuss his or her firm's use of qualitative research. Write a brief report on your findings.

[E]   7. Use the references in Note 9, at the back of the book, or in your library's reference section for further reading on Ernest Dichter's views on hidden motivation (or the views of other researchers). If possible, obtain and read the classic book by Vance Packard, *The Hidden Persuaders*. Write a brief report on your findings.

[E]   8. Using some of the readings in Notes 17 and 18 or the reference section of your library read about recent developments in marketing planned experiences and in other marketing appeals to consumers' thirst for variety. Write a brief report on your findings.

[E]   9. Using some of the readings near the end of Note 20 or the reference section of your library read more about attribution theory and its recent applications to marketing management (for example, you may wish to read more about the FITD or DITF selling techniques). Write a brief report on your findings.

[E] 10. Choose two recent purchases you have made that have required some shopping and deliberation. Think back over the process for each one, including all your interactions with marketing stimuli and salespersons. For each purchase, analyze the three stages (your prepurchase process, purchase process, and postpurchase process) in terms of the attribution processes in which you engaged. Write a brief report of your analysis, including implications for both the successful and unsuccessful marketers involved in your purchases.

[E] 11. What are the levels of Maslow's need hierarchy? For each level, give an example of how consumer behavior relates to it. Overall, what is your estimate of the importance that each level represents in terms of consumers' dollar spending (that is, rank the levels on this measure). Write a brief report summarizing your findings and noting their implications for marketers.

[E] 12. Read carefully through Murray's list of needs and the definitions given in Table 6-2. Select any five of the needs and suggest some ways in which each is reflected in typical forms of consumer behavior. Then consider five possible ways in which pairs of these five needs might fuse together to drive particular forms of consumer behavior.

[E] 13. One of the examples at the start of this chapter described the controversy over a "scare" campaign concerning diabetes. Assume that you were empowered to rule on whether or not this campaign would be allowed to air on television in your area. How would you rule? Why?

[E] **14.** In discussing the two elements of consumer motivation—energy and direction—the chapter raised the example of recalls for the Pinto automobile and for Firestone tires. Using Table 6-2's listing of Murray's needs as a guide, think about why consumer inertia might exist for these recalls (keep in mind, however, that only some consumers are contributing to the problem). Review the list of Murray's needs to select several that you believe may be relevant. Create several appeals to these needs that you believe might work to overcome inertia and spark positive consumer reactions to the recalls. Write a brief report on your suggestions.

[E] **15.** Refer to the best- and worst-selling issues of several magazines shown on page 188. Based on the material in this chapter, why did one do better? What consumer motives were tapped?

CHAPTER 7

Consumer Personality, Values, and Involvement

The Longest Ride

Consumer involvement is a matter of degrees. At one extreme is Mr. Philip Miuccio, a 67-year-old Floridian, who went to a Daytona Beach cemetery and requested the construction of a $30,000 marble mausoleum with bulletproof windows to house his remains inside his DeLorean sports car. At last notice, cemetery officials were trying to talk him out of the idea of the windows! According to Mr. Miuccio, "Who says you can't take it with you?"[1]

■ ■ ■

HOW COMPUTERS LED THE WAY

The marketing and consumer research world discovered the computer about 1960, just about the time that computer technology was developing on a large scale. This discovery opened new vistas for research on consumer markets. For the first time it was possible to analyze data on *large samples* of consumers, using *many questions* and sophisticated statistical analyses. Thus began the **quantitative era** of marketing research, which is still in force today. Three major extensions of our MOTIVATION framework have been stressed during the quantitative era and will be covered in this chapter: consumer personality, consumer values and laddering research, and consumer involvement.

PERSONALITY AND CONSUMER BEHAVIOR

The concept of **personality** is one of the great topics of behavioral science. Thousands of books and articles have been written on this subject over the centuries. The idea in most definitions of personality is to stress a person's *consistency in behaviors and reactions to events* in various phases of their lives. Thus we are interested in classifying individuals into "types" of people.

Theoretical Essentials

Sigmund Freud's psychoanalytic theory provided a starting point for theories of personality, and many prominent theories today represent extensions of Freud's original work. As we noted in Chapter 6, Freud stressed the role of the ego in coming to manage the strong, irrational urges from the id and superego. Freud also believed that each of us develops our personalities while in childhood, as a function of how we are able to resolve crucial periods focusing on sexual regions of our bodies. According to Freud, a child who does not resolve the crisis at any stage will grow into an adult personality in which those crises will still be operating to determine interests and behaviors. This will not be readily apparent to observers, however, since for many years the ego will have been learning how to employ various defense mechanisms against socially unacceptable impulses. **Defense mechanisms** are strategies the ego uses to reduce psychic tensions (see Note 2 if you wish to read more about these).

Freud's theory was viewed as powerful but restrictive, and several of his colleagues broke with him to develop their own broader views of personality theory. Carl Jung, for example, believed that personality continues to develop during the adult years. Jung went on to suggest that people could be classified into eight basic categories depending on which orientations a person tends to exhibit. In brief, a person fits into one of the eight categories as the following three questions are clarified:

- "Is he or she more extroverted or more introverted?"
- "Does he or she tend to be more of a thinker or a 'feeler'?"
- "Does he or she rely more on sensing (the real world) or intuition (focusing on one's inner thoughts)?"

While we are unable to detail the specifics of Jung's theory here, it is extremely interesting. (For a modern, modified test you can take to classify yourself, as well as a source of findings on personality differences based on Jung's theory, you may wish to pursue the reference in Note 3.)

Other personality theorists have stressed somewhat different themes. Alfred Adler, for example, was another Freudian colleague who broke away to stress his own theory. Adler focused much more on the social environment within which each of us lives and stressed that a person would attempt to grow throughout life. An important element of Adler's theory was his invention of the term "inferiority complex," which would normally be encountered as a child recognized his or her innate weaknesses. Throughout later life, then, this feeling could serve strongly to affect many forms of behavior, as a function of the social environment surrounding each person.

Brief though it has been, the foregoing discussion should be helpful in providing a general idea of the nature of personality theories. Each stresses a somewhat different aspect of a person's intrinsic motivations or extrinsic surroundings. There are a number of useful sources available for in-depth reading in the personality field. One excellent source that reviews all the major theories is the classic text by Hall and Lindzey, whose reference is given in Note 4.

Personality Research in Marketing

The burst of published research on consumer personality began in 1959, when Franklin B. Evans asked, "Do Ford owners have different personalities from Chevy owners?"[5] His paper set off a furious debate and began a spurt of research on this topic. Currently, there are over 200 articles on personality in the marketing literature.[6] To appreciate the type of research that's been done, let's briefly examine two classic articles:

What Drives Auto Buys: The "Ford Versus Chevy" Study

Evans surveyed over 1600 adult males in a Chicago suburb, all of whom owned either a Ford or a Chevy. Each respondent filled out a shortened form of the Edwards Personal Preference Schedule (EPPS), a personality test based upon Henry Murray's list of needs we examined in Chapter 6. Ford and Chevy were comparably priced cars, but were generally thought to be portraying different "brand images" in their advertising—Fords (and their owners) were seen as independent, impulsive, masculine, and self-confident, while

Chevrolets (and their owners) were thought to be more conservative, thrifty, and prestige conscious.

When he analyzed his results, Evans found some surprises. First, of the 11 needs he studied, only 4 showed significant differences: Ford owners seemed to have higher needs for exhibition and dominance, whereas Chevy owners had higher needs for autonomy and affiliation (you may wish to refer back to Table 6–2 for explanations of these needs). Even for the four significant needs, however, the amount of difference in scores was small—for example, for affiliation, both groups of car owners scored fairly high, although Chevy owners (with an average score of 11.1) were slightly higher than Ford owners (at 10.1). To see if there was an *overall* difference, Evans had to combine all need scores through the use of a multivariate statistical method called *discriminant analysis*. When he did this, he found that he could correctly predict, 63 percent of the time, whether the car owned was a Ford or a Chevy. Since random guesses would have produced about 50 percent correct predictions, Evans concluded that the personality information—even though significant in a statistical sense—provided only a minor insight into the differences between auto owners.

Evans found these results disappointing. He decided to give the personality tests another chance, just in case the weak results had come from some aspect of the statistical method. He therefore contacted 18 psychologists who specialized in motivation research within marketing. He provided each of these judges with the EPPS scores of 10 consumers in his sample and told them that 5 Ford owners and 5 Chevy owners were in the group. The judges' task was to assign each owner to the correct auto. Again, we should expect to see a 50-50 chance of guessing correctly. The actual results were therefore both surprising and interesting—1 judge got 6 of the 10 right, 15 judges were correct on 4 of the 10, and 2 expert judges assigned only 2 of the 10 consumers correctly! Evans's results came as a shock and a challenge to consumer researchers. Some reacted by pointing out issues his study had not addressed, whereas others performed further analyses on his data to search for stronger results. For example, if we concentrate only on consumers with extreme scores on a need, and ignore those with moderate levels, we may be able to see stronger personality effects. When he subtracted the affiliation scores from the dominance scores, for example, Kuehn found that consumers who had the highest net score toward dominance (comprising one-fourth of the entire sample) were likely to *own Fords 67 percent of the time,* whereas those with the highest net scores toward affiliation (another one-fourth of the entire sample) were likely to *own Chevys 70 percent of the time.*[7] Kuehn, however, was then criticized for "picking and choosing" among the data to search for extreme results. The debate over Evans's findings continued to rage for many more years. (If you are interested in the various issues that arose, Note 8 lists the key readings.)

"C," "A," or "D," Which Is He?

Another classic personality study was reported by Joel B. Cohen in the mid-1960s. Cohen was interested in how people behave toward each other and their environments, reflecting a more social or "interpersonal" orientation toward personality. In this case, Cohen chose to work with the theory of Karen Horney (pronounced "Horn-eye").[9] Horney classified individuals into three groups: those who move *toward* people (**compliant**), those who move *against* people (**aggressive**), and those who move *away from* people (**detached**). A compliant person wants to be loved and appreciated by others. These individuals seek friendship and an accepted place within groups. Aggressive individuals, on the other hand, desire to stand out and excel. They seek power and admiration from others. Detached people desire freedom from obligations. They wish to be independent from others and are little interested in either influencing them or being influenced by them. Horney believed that, although each of us has some of each tendency, usually one of the three comes to predominate in each individual's personality. This occurs primarily during childhood and depends on which strategy seems to work most effectively for the child attempting to deal with his or her family and peers.

Cohen took Horney's theory and developed a new test called the CAD Scale, reflecting the compliant, aggressive, and detached personality types. He believed, for example, that aggressive persons might prefer products that suggest success or strength. In his study, Cohen administered the CAD scale to students at several universities while also obtaining information on the brands they preferred. The results were interesting. In terms of the *strength* of the personality measures these findings were generally similar to those of Evans—of the 15 product categories Cohen chose as most likely to demonstrate personality differences, 7 showed statistically significant differences and 8 did not. The size of the differences was not huge in most of the cases.

Among Cohen's interesting findings: *mouthwash* was used by 74 percent of compliant (C) individuals, but by only 56 percent of detached (D) persons. C's were also found strongly to prefer *Dial soap* (47 percent), compared with only 31 percent of D's (38 percent of the detached sample expressed no particular brand preference for soap, compared with only about 20 percent in the C and A categories). Within *deodorants*, aggressive men's favorite brand was Old Spice, whereas both C and D types preferred the market leader, Right Guard (of the 8 students who reported no use of deodorants, 7 were D's). A's also were more likely to use cologne and after-shave lotion, more strongly preferred manual razors as a shaving method, and were more likely to name Coors as their favorite beer. D's, meanwhile, were more likely to drink tea on a regular basis, but less likely to drink wine than either of the other types. Cohen was concerned with developing a valid personality instrument and did not attempt to decide that the findings were either quite strong or too weak (as had Evans). A number of researchers have examined the CAD scale with this in mind, but without the controversy of the Evans study. As for Cohen, he concluded that his preliminary results were sufficiently strong that the issue of personality's link with consumer behavior deserved much further study in marketing.[10]

Summary of Findings on Personality and Consumer Behavior

The 1960s and 1970s saw the heyday of personality research in marketing. Following the Ford versus Chevy study, over 200 more studies were reported in marketing over the next 20 years. This number does not include, of course, the thousands of studies done privately by companies and advertising agencies. The published studies included issues such as

- Do brand-loyal buyers have different personalities?
- Do "innovators" have different personalities?
- Are certain personality types easier to persuade?

If you have an interest in personality issues in consumer behavior, you may wish to read the splendid reviews developed by two leading thinkers in this area, Harold Kassarjian and William Wells, listed in Note 11.

Overall Findings: "Equivocal"

Overall, what have these studies found? As Kassarjian reports in his review of these research studies,

> *(They) can be summarized in the single word "equivocal." A few studies indicate a strong relationship. . . . A few indicate no relationship. . . . And the great majority indicate that if correlations do exist they are so weak as to be questionable or perhaps meaningless . . .*

In essence, then, most research has found personality results similar to those obtained by both Evans and Cohen. Some personality measures show statistically significant results with consumer behavior, but many do not. Of those that do, the relationships appear to be weak, explaining only about 10% of the variation amongst consumers. Does this mean personality doesn't work, then? First, we need to better understand why the statistical results seem weak.

Why Are Results Weak?

Why would personality results in consumer behavior explain such a low proportion of variation in the data? In concept, this is not difficult to understand if we think about the following cases, using CAD personality types for convenience.

Case 1

Mary Jackson and Kimberly Lane are both aggressive (A) personality types. Mary, however, is 80 years old, and Kimberly is 22. Given such an age difference, we'd well imagine that their tastes in many product classes would be different.

Case 2

Stephen Robbins and Jane Winters both score as compliant (C) personality types. Since Steve is a male, however, he does not even buy many of the products that Jane does, and vice versa. In addition, social factors influence Steve toward certain preferences and Jane toward other preferences.

Case 3

Carter Brown and Ralph Smith are both detached (D) types. Carter, however, comes from an extremely wealthy family, while Ralph's family has faced divorce and welfare conditions for much of his life. Because of their incomes and backgrounds, these two young men shop in entirely different types of stores and search for different quality levels. In total, Carter spends far more money than Ralph does over the course of the year.

These examples could go on and on, of course. The point they are making, however, is that—even if two people share many of the *same personality* traits, they're likely to *differ in many other factors* that are also important in determining actual consumer behavior. Thus, unless these other factors are somehow taken into account, our research on personality wouldn't show terribly strong results.

Unfortunately, this is not the only problem faced by consumer researchers interested in personality's effects. Consider the following examples as well:

Case 4
All the people in Cases 1, 2, and 3, except Carter, believe that "soup is good food," and all of them eat Campbell's soup at least occasionally.

Case 5
Kimberly and Ralph each bought a Chevy recently, but for different reasons. Kimberly was sold on the basis of several of her friends' experiences, together with the clear popularity of the car. Ralph, on the other hand, wasn't sure what he wanted, but was talked (driven?) into buying by a skilled salesperson who appealed to his intelligence and achievements.

Case 6
All the people like soft drinks, except Mary, who prefers tea. As to brands, each person occasionally drinks Coke, Pepsi, 7-Up, and others. Carter and Jane happen to prefer Coke, though, whereas Kimberly and Ralph prefer Pepsi and Steve likes 7-Up the best.

Cases 4, 5, and 6 show us how reasonable it is that people with *different personalities* might prefer the *same product,* particularly if we are talking about a brand that is frequently purchased and/or quite popular. When consumers exhibit these types of preferences, again we would see very weak personality results emerging in research, partially for theoretical reasons and partly for statistical reasons.

Overall, then, it is clear that there are many reasons why past studies in personality have obtained the results they did. As we've noted, this does not mean that personality exerts no influence on consumer behavior. On the other hand, it does indicate that personality's influence is only one of many significant factors and cannot be expected to dominate all the others.

Recent Trends in Personality Research

Recent work on personality and consumer behavior reveals three distinct trends, each stemming from the lessons learned in the past:[12]

Trend 1: Studying Patterns of Behavior Rather Than Single Decisions Because there are so many factors involved in each specific purchase, and since different brands can be chosen from one time to the next, it is wise to examine more general strategies that consumers use over a set of situations and multiple behaviors. Recent work along this line has shown relationships between personality and types of brand choice strategies, between personality and patterns of information search, and between personality and food behaviors. If we were to think even more broadly, examining such issues as preferences for forms of entertainment, colors, spending versus saving decisions, and so forth, we might also uncover some systematic relationships between personality and consumer behavior.

Trend 2: Focusing on Consumption Rather Than General Needs Because personality reflects patterns of needs, it should be helpful to concentrate on products or situations (e.g., innovations) especially geared to satisfying these needs in a consumer setting. Consumers often buy products and services for specific benefits. Therefore, it should be helpful to stress psychological measures that are consumer oriented.

Trend 3: Shifting Attention to Develop Related Areas As we noted at the start of the chapter, personality is an extremely broad topic. Beyond the "mainline" approaches we've examined, let's take a quick look at three interesting examples of developments in personality-related topics:

It's In My Blood!

Medical researchers have long known that *physiological differences* can cause differences in behavior. Some of this research has recently been extended to consumer behavior. For example, in one highly exploratory recent study, blood tests showed that consumers with low levels of the enzyme monoamine oxidase (MAO) are more likely than others to make more risky investment decisions (this extends earlier research that related low levels of MAO to some people's increased desire to climb mountains and jump out of airplanes). The marketing applications of this finding are not yet entirely clear (and this author is not aware that this issue has been rigorously tested). If this *is* valid, however, it appears that brokers would benefit from obtaining blood test results from their prospective clients (sounds vial, doesn't it?).[13]

Have a Fit!

Consumer researchers have long been interested in the area of **self-concept**. The belief is that a consumer will prefer those products that help to express that consumer's image of himself or herself. These images, in turn, can reflect either the **actual self** (the "real me") or the **ideal self** (the "person I'd like to be"). Consumer products are useful for both images: we can use them to reflect who we are, and sometimes use them to become more like who we'd like to be. If we think briefly about it, we can recognize this link to store images, to brand images, and to advertising appeals to sophistication, youth, popularity, fashion, and so forth. There is a strong personal component to the self-concept: this is easy to recognize when the actual self and idealized self don't match too well, as mirrored in the following:

Which piece of clothing do women most hate to buy? The runaway winner: the swimsuit! According to Heidi Goldstein, a 30-year-old advertising coordinator, "I really, really hate buying bathing suits. It's humiliating." Cathy Guisewite, the thirtyish author of the "Cathy" comic strip, says she sometimes breaks down and sobs in the fitting room and is happy to escape with "some shred of dignity." According to a consumer researcher for the swimwear industry, "I didn't find one adult woman in the United States who enjoyed buying swimsuits." Over one-third of consumers described the purchase as "traumatic."

Why is this? According to a fashion sociologist, "it has nothing to do with vanity," but instead reflects consumers' fears about social standards for how they should look in a swimsuit. She points out that European women don't have these same hang-ups, and they buy more than twice as many swimsuits as Americans. The industry is now attempting to increase sales by clever engineering of new suits, installing pink light bulbs in dressing rooms to replace the harsh fluorescent lights that create ghastly skin, playing mellow music, and so on. However, they realize that they are up against a powerful self-concept phenomenon. Even women who sell swimsuits can hate buying them. One young sales

cathy®   by Cathy Guisewite

clerk reported hopefully, "Maybe I'll get sick and lose weight in the next month . . . or maybe something exciting will happen and I'll be too busy to eat."[14] (Not all aspects of the consumer self-concept are negative, of course. If you would like to learn more about developments in this area, you may wish to consult Note 15.)

What Types of Women Buy Premium Cosmetics?

Another major extension of personality research in marketing has been the creation and development of **psychographics**. Since we have already discussed this topic in Chapter 4, we need not go into detail here. We should note, however, that the development of this field reflects trend 2 above—a strong desire to represent personality-type differences in a realistic consumer context.[16] Table 7-1 provides examples of some of the psychographic dimensions used by Grey Advertising, Inc., in a study of female consumers of premium cosmetics. Looking only at the dimensions in the table, which four would you say will

TABLE 7-1 SOME DIMENSIONS USED IN A PSYCHOGRAPHIC STUDY OF PREMIUM COSMETIC BUYERS

Dimension	*Definition*
Narcissism	Preoccupied with one's personal appearance. (H)
Appearance conscious	Emphasis on looking properly groomed. (H)
Exhibitionism	Tendency toward self-display and attention seeking. (NS)
Order	Tendency to be compulsively neat, live by rules. (NS)
Fantasied achievement	Aspiration for distinction and personal recognition. (H)
Capacity for status	Personal qualities that lead to status. (L)
Dominant	Need to be in control and in the forefront. (L)
Sociable	Need for agreeable relationship with others. (H)

Source: Adapted from Shirley Young, "The Dynamics of Measuring Unchange," in Russell I. Haley (ed.), *Attitude Research in Transition* (Chicago: American Marketing Association, 1972), p. 62.

characterize buyers of premium cosmetics? Which two are likely to be irrelevant in distinguishing these people? And on which two dimensions are premium buyers likely to be lower than the average woman? (At the right of each definition, (H) indicates high scores for premium users, (L) indicates low scores, and (NS) indicates no significant difference from other women). Notice how these results can be used in the development of advertising appeals![17]

 ## CONSUMER VALUES AND LADDERING RESEARCH

What Are Consumer Values?

While consumer personality research has stressed why people are *different* from one another, consumer values research stresses the *important goals* most people are seeking. In psychological theory, **values** are closely linked to needs, but exist for us at a more obvious, realistic level. According to Henry Murray (whose list of needs we examined at the end of the last chapter), values are the mental representations of our underlying needs, after they have been transformed to

Percent Surveyed Who Most Wanted To:			% Change (from 1967)	Rank	
				1967	1985
Be very well off financially	1985	70%[a]	+63%	4	1
	1967	43%			
Help others	1985	63%	−9%	2	2
	1967	69%			
Have administrative responsibility	1985	43%	+95%	6	3(T)
	1967	22%			
Develop a meaningful philosophy of life	1985	43%	−46%	1	3(T)
	1967	82%			
Keep up with political affairs	1985	38%	−34%	3	5
	1967	58%			
Become an expert in finance and commerce	1985	26%	+100%	7	6
	1967	13%			
Clean up the environment	1985	20%	−59%	4	7
	1967	49%			

0 10 20 30 40 50 60 70 80 90 100

[a]Numbers show percentage of students who ranked each value as one of the top three in importance to them. *Source*: Adapted from "Data Bank: Youth Marketing," *Advertising Age*, February 1, 1988, p. S–32.

FIGURE 7-1 **Ranking of Priority: College Students' Values (Over Time), 1985 Versus 1967**

take into account the realities of the world in which we live. In other words, values are our ideas about what is desirable. There are two main types of values: (1) terminal and (2) instrumental. **Terminal (or end-state) values** are beliefs we have about the goals or end-states for which we strive (e.g., happiness, wisdom). **Instrumental (or means) values**, on the other hand, refer to beliefs about desirable ways of behaving to help us attain the terminal values (e.g., behaving honestly, accepting responsibility).[18]

Since values are transmitted through cultures and subcultural groups, most people in a society will agree that they are good. What differs, however, is *how important* each value is in each person's daily life and thinking. Some people will stress some values, while other people will stress other values. Also, the prominence of different values can change over time. Figure 7-1 shows how this has happened for college students of the 1960s versus those of the mid-1980s. Notice how strongly the prevailing values shifted during this time! Notice also, however, that for each value listed, how very many college students would *not* place it in their three most pressing goals. We can thus see how individual differences (and market segmentation) are present in the values area as well. Although research on values poses some difficult measurement problems, much progress has been reported recently, as indicated in the following example.

All We Need Is LOV

In recent years researchers have been working to develop short lists of values that can be measured in a reliable manner. One contribution, by Lynn Kahle, is simply termed the "List of Values" (LOV). It contains nine summary terminal values:

- Self-respect
- Self-fulfillment
- Security
- Sense of belonging
- Excitement
- Sense of accomplishment
- Fun and enjoyment in life
- Being well respected
- Warm relationships with others

In one exploratory study, researchers found that LOV related well to various aspects of consumer behavior. For example, people who highly value a "sense of belonging" are more heavily involved in leisure activities, particularly those involving groups. Meanwhile, consumers who highly value "fun and enjoyment" preferred more exciting media (*Playboy, Rolling Stone*) and more exciting sports. Conversely, consumers who highly value "security" engaged in fewer high-energy activities, but watched more television and reported more hobby activities.[19]

The Next Step: Laddering

You may recall that the "A" topic in Chapter 6's MOTIVATION framework stressed the idea of goal-directed behavior, and indicated that we would be returning to a discussion of expectancy-value models. We have now arrived. These models assert that people act to satisfy underlying *needs*. These needs, in turn, are realistically represented by the *values* that we hold. The result is a view of consumer behavior as being a **means to an end**: consumers act in order to achieve the benefits they are seeking. Thus marketers have found it useful to think of products as "bundles of benefits."

In recent years this thinking has been built into an approach called **laddering**, which attempts to trace the linkages between a consumer's values and the par-

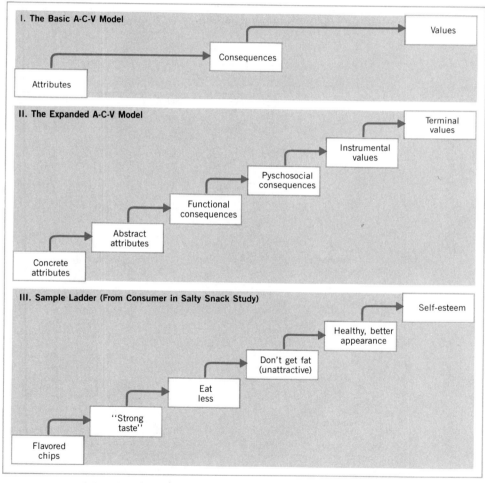

Source: Adapted from discussions in Thomas J. Reynolds and Jonathan Gutman, "Laddering Theory, Method, Analysis, and Interpretation," in T. Reynolds (Ed.), *Understanding Consumer Motivation* (in progress).

FIGURE 7-2 **Means-end Laddering**

gAAA='/>

Z2F2b

YXZha

ticular product attributes managed by marketers. These linkages—sometimes called a **means-end chain**—are shown in Figure 7-2. Notice that the basic **A-C-V model** contains just three steps: (1) products offer *attributes* to consumers, (2) consumers experience *consequences* when they consume the attributes, (3) the consequences help consumers attain particular *values*. The more tightly a marketer can link the attributes to value attainment, the stronger the attraction his or her product or service will have for consumers.

In the middle of Figure 7-2 we see a slightly expanded A-C-V model. Here distinctions are made between concrete and abstract attributes, functional and psychological or social consequences, and instrumental or terminal values. The sample ladder shown at the bottom of Figure 7-2 helps us see how these various

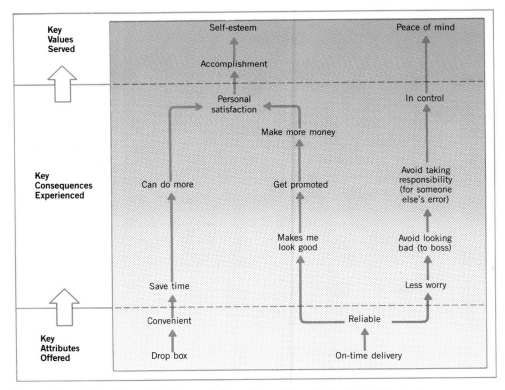

Source: Adapted from Figure 2 in Thomas J. Reynolds and Alyce B. Craddock, "The Application of the MECCAS Model to the Development and Assessment of Advertising Strategy," in Thomas Reynolds (Ed.), *Understanding Consumer Motivation* (in progress).

FIGURE 7-3 **Summary "Hierarchical Value Map" for Federal Express Study (Executive Secretaries' Links for Attributes to Consequences to Values)**

levels interrelate in one consumer's views of the salty snack category. Notice how the concrete attribute of "flavor" in a chip product has meanings and implications that trace back to an important terminal value for that consumer.

Within the real world of marketing, of course, there are many possible concrete attributes for a product or service, and many possible ladders moving back toward consumers' values. The relationships for some will be much stronger than relationships for others; thus laddering research can be quite complex. If valid information can be obtained, however, tremendously valuable insights for product development and advertising strategy can become available, as shown in the following example.

Why Fool Around with Anyone Else?

Federal Express has long been known for humorous advertising that helped to make a giant industry out of overnight delivery services (ODS). A few years ago, when competition increased significantly, Federal Express turned to the laddering techniques developed by Thomas Reynolds and Jonathan Gutman. The company first determined that one of its prime market segments consisted of executive secretaries. Following a large number of in-depth personal interviews with secretaries, advanced statistical methods were used to generate the "summary hierarchical value map," shown in Figure 7-3. Notice how the two concrete attributes at the bottom (availability of convenient "drop boxes" and on-time delivery) are traced through three different laddering routes in the typical customer's

FIGURE 7-4 **The MECCAS Approach for Federal Express Advertising**

I. THE NEW STRATEGY (BASED ON LADDERING RESEARCH):

Target market	Secretaries/"facilitators" of overnight delivery service.
Driving force (value)	Peace of mind.
Leverage point (value)	In control re: company can trust.
Executional framework	Humorous execution with a secretary working hard at finding status information of an ODS. The boss and employee are interruped and taken by guide to view Federal Express satellite communication system used to track exact status of overnight letters and packages. Secretary realizes the benefits available in using Federal Express.
Customer benefit	Reliable/dependability; makes work easier.
Message elements	Superior tracking system; integrated satellite communications network.
Tag line	"Why fool around with anyone else?" *Continued*

FIGURE 7-4 **The MECCAS Approach for Federal Express Advertising** *Continued*

II. ADVERTISING RESEARCH RESULTS: OLD VERSUS NEW CAMPAIGN:

	Percentage Description Endorsement (0–100%)	
Description	*Previous Campaign*	*New Campaign*
Driving Force		
Self-esteem	10	10
*Peace of mind	10	50
Leverage point		
*Trust in company	40	70
*In control	20	50
Executional framework		
*Ad shows reality	40	60
*Can laugh at situation	70	60
Demonstrates personal service	20	50
*Situation hectic	90	70
Customer benefit		
*Dependable service	70	90
*Less worry	40	90
Makes me look good	30	10
Message elements		
Numerous delivery locations	30	0
*Relevant service facts	40	70
*Advanced communications system	Not asked	100

*New ad target.
Source: See Figure 7-3.

mind, having different lengths and serving different values. (Notice also that the number of levels is different for each ladder—applied work often runs into cases in which consumers reveal shorter or longer ladders.)

Based on these results, together with tests of competitors' advertising, the researchers worked to develop a new advertising campaign using the **MECCAS model** (Means-End Conceptualization of the Components of Advertising Strategy). The top section of Figure 7-4 outlines the MECCAS approach and summarizes the resulting ad campaign aimed at the secretarial target segment. Notice how it stresses the rightmost ladder in Figure 7-3, aiming to make a strong connection to the "peace of mind" value. Notice also how the execution blends the concrete attributes with a humorous approach to maintain continuity with the past Federal Express ads that the target customers are likely to remember (perhaps you even recall the tag line). Finally, the bottom half of Figure 7-4 reveals some copy test results of the new campaign versus the previous one (as asterisk indicates a key target of the new campaign). Notice how generally successful the new ads were in improving scores on the desired targets! (If you would like to learn more about recent developments on laddering and the MECCAS model, you may wish to begin with the readings in Note 20).

 ## CONSUMER INVOLVEMENT

The final topic in our coverage of motivational issues concerns **consumer involvement**. As we've noted previously, in recent years this concept has become a major center of interest in consumer behavior. We have already discussed it in several chapters and will again be discussing detailed aspects of its effects in several upcoming chapters. Since involvement is so closely related to individual needs, however, this chapter is an especially appropriate place for us to focus on laying out some of its basic dimensions.

What Is "Consumer Involvement?"

The Reality of Consumer Involvement

The concept of consumer involvement relates to a sense of personal relevance: it can be easily identified if we adopt our consumer perspective toward consumer behavior, as we outlined in Chapter 2. Let's begin by listening in on some typical incidents reported by consumers:

I'm really involved when I'm getting ready for a date. . . . I care a lot about my appearance—my overall look! . . . Sometimes I just sit at my dressing table and lose track of the time . . . to some extent I guess I'm anxious about looking good so my date will be impressed, but it's really more than that usually . . . I think I really am interested in people's appearance, especially my own!

—Debra Brooks, brand manager

I can get into driving powerful machines—feeling them surge over the ground, catching the wind blowing through my hair, and feeling free. . . . Sometimes there's skill involved, too, and I enjoy seeing how far I can go before it gets too dangerous.

—Richard Redmond, zone manager

I enjoy photography and everything about it. . . . I spend hours reading and talking about new developments and testing out new products.

—David Taylor, accountant

I am very involved with my family life. . . . We just built a new home and I spent months making all the detailed decisions about room arrangements, fabrics, colors, and the like. Now I'm on to the furnishings, and having a ball . . . if we can afford everything, it's going to be a great home!

—Martha Hook, salesperson

All these examples show instances of *high* consumer involvement. We see consumers highly involved in enjoying experiences (Debra and Richard), highly involved in thinking and learning about products (David), and highly involved in making purchase decisions (Martha). (Please note, however, that for some consumers *compulsive behaviors* do cause serious problems.)[21]

The Theory of Consumer Involvement

Overall, we can define consumer involvement (or CI) as *a state of energy (arousal) that a person experiences in regard to a consumption-related activity.* CI thus includes both major components of motivation: energy and direction. **High involvement**, therefore, requires that high levels of energy are aroused within the consumer and that this energy is directed toward a particular consumer activity. A person who is *highly involved* is likely to be thinking more, or feeling more strongly. **Low involvement**, on the other hand, occurs when consumers invest less energy into their thoughts or feelings. Theoretically, the CI concept can be traced back to the basic theory of motivation that asserts that a person's ego will take control of the id's psychic energy and direct it primarily toward objects (or people, products, activities, etc.) that are most likely to satisfy basic needs that the person is experiencing.[23] Thus involvement is closely related to personality theory and values theory as well, since the same forces are operating.

Several key points are included in our view of CI:

1. *CI occurs within specific consumer-related episodes.* Every type of consumer activity contains some level of CI. The exact CI will differ by consumer and by occasion, so that each separate episode has its own CI level.

2. *High CI is likely to occur when a person's "self" is closely tied to the consumer activity episode.* A good example of this point is provided by Martha's description in our examples. Notice that she begins by pointing out how important her family is to her. The intensity she is experiencing is closely tied to her "self-concept" as a wife and mother as well as her "self's" desires to be creative, to build, and to exercise power in decision making.

3. *CI includes both feelings and thoughts.* Both cognitions (thoughts) and emotions (feelings) are present in every instance of CI, although their relative importance may differ. David, for example, clearly experiences pleasurable feelings during his studies of photography. His thinking processes, however, are very important in terms of learning about products and deciding which ones merit purchase.

4. *The study of CI requires difficult decisions on how to group episodes together, how to measure energy, and how to specify directional aspects.* This point addresses advanced research issues of characterization, and you may not wish to try to resolve them within an introductory course on consumer behavior. However, it is useful to recognize that these issues pose problems for consumer researchers. In all our quotations, for example, our consumers *already* grouped

When TV talk show host Oprah Winfrey revealed that
she had lost almost 70 pounds on Optifast's liquid diet
program, the firm received 200,000 phone inquiries
from consumers in 48 hours!

together many distinct episodes for us and presented us with an overall description of high CI. Can low-CI episodes so easily be grouped together and
described, however? Also, how can different types of thoughts or feelings be
compared as to energy level—is Debra more involved than is Richard? Further,
should we say that Debra is highly involved with the *products* she uses in her
beauty sessions (lipstick, blush, perfume, etc.), or are these merely accom-
paniments to the *beauty sessions* themselves. Although all these are advanced
questions, to study CI, consumer researchers have to decide how to treat them.

Research Contributions on Consumer Involvement

Recent years have seen a number of contributions from researchers toward better understanding CI. Entire conferences have been held on this topic and there have been numerous speeches and articles. Among the interesting and useful insights are

- *Four facets of CI*. Laurent and Kapferer have suggested that consumers will be more involved in a particular purchase as a result of four elements: (1) the product is *important* to them, (2) there is high *perceived risk* in the purchase, (3) there is a *symbolic* or *"sign"* value to the product, and (4) there is an *emotional* ("hedonic") value to the product. Any combinations are possible. Thus there are identifiable causes of high CI, and we can begin to understand why a consumer will or won't be highly involved in a particular purchase.[24]

- *Different types of involvement*. Researchers have devoted much attention to how best to categorize different types of involvement. For example, one useful distinction is between *product-class involvement* and *brand-choice involvement*. **Product-class involvement** represents the average interest a consumer has in a product category on a day-to-day basis (in our examples, David indicated high product-class involvement for cameras). **Brand-choice involvement** refers to the specific arousal during a purchase process (in our examples, even if Debra had low product-class involvement with cameras, she still might become highly involved during a purchase occasion: a related distinction is between **enduring involvement** and **situational involvement**. Another useful distinction is between the *cognitive* and *affective* dimensions of CI. **Cognitive involvement** refers to the degree of thinking aroused during an episode, while **affective involvement** represents the arousal of feelings and emotions. Another recent distinction of interest points out that *brand commitment* may represent a further type of involvement held by loyal customers. (If you would like to learn more about these and other useful distinctions, Note 25 is a good place to start.)

- *Measurement of CI*. Useful contributions to measurement have recently been offered and are presently under discussion and extensions. Thus marketers will be able to do even more testing and development on CI in the future.[26]

- *Locating products by CI levels*. Foote, Cone, & Belding, a major advertising agency, has taken research advances and used them to create a "grid model" for planning advertising. This grid model was recently judged to be a "classic" deserving of special recognition by the Advertising Research Foundation. Figure 7-5 presents some of the results of a study of almost 1800 consumers, aimed at locating a large number of products and services on the grid (only a few are shown here, for clarity). Notice that the grid consists of four quadrants, depending upon the degree of thinking versus feeling consumers have for the product, and the intensity level of the involvement they have. These locations reflect the average for all consumers: some special segments may exist at other map points. On average for example, insurance and appliances are "high-

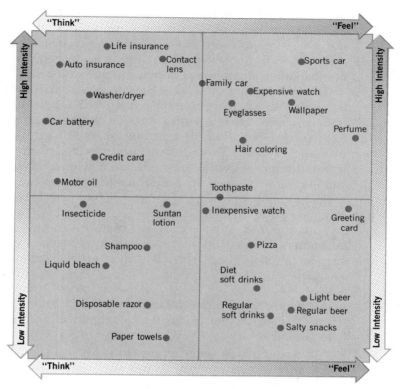

*Note: Only some products are displayed here, and positions are approximate.

Source: Adapted from Brian T. Ratchford, "New Insights About the FCB Grid," *Journal of Advertising Research,* Vol. 27, no. 4 (August–September 1987, p. 31)

FIGURE 7-5 **The Foote, Cone and Belding Involvement Grid***

involvement/thinking" products, while expensive watches and wallpaper are "high-involvement/feeling" products. The family car has almost equal components of both thinking and feeling, while a sports car is much more a "feeling" product. Finally, notice how the more frequently purchased products tend to be lower in involvement intensity, and how food products tend to be higher on the feeling dimension![27]

The Stress on "Low Involvement"

In a significant presidential address to the Association for Consumer Research, Harold Kassarjian discussed how much—perhaps most—of consumer behavior is *low in risk and low in involvement.*[28] For most people, family, social events, love lives, job success, illnesses, births, and so forth are all far more important than is the next purchase of toothpaste, or many other products. While we do care about making "good" purchases, we don't usually approach our shopping as if it were a major event in our lives. On a relative basis, then, most consumer decisions really are low in CI. In turn, this affects the ways consumers deal with the marketing environment and make their decisions.

Thus the level of CI that has most intrigued marketers over the past 20 years has been *low CI*. If we think about it briefly, the reasons behind this interest become clear—marketers may well *not be able to do very much to change the basic levels of involvement* that consumers bring to their encounters with the marketing system. If this is true, astute marketers are better off to *adapt* their marketing mixes to deal most effectively with the actual levels of CI they encounter. As we've seen, traditional models such as the hierarchy of effects have built-in assumptions of high CI. As such, they need to be altered when consumers bring low CI to the marketplace.

Thus the interest in low CI has been driven by a need to understand how consumers do make up their minds about purchases when they just don't care very deeply about them. The following questions typify marketers' concerns with low CI:

- If consumers have low, rather than high, CI with my product class, will it be easier to switch them to my new brand, or will they not even take the trouble to switch?
- Will consumers pay more for my brand because they're not very sensitive about the price of this product, or will they switch away to a lower-priced brand because they're not willing to try to figure out quality differences?
- If I advertise extensively, will consumers with low CI make little or no effort to process my ads, or is constant repetition of my brand name the best strategy, since these consumers won't be thinking much beyond brand names in any event?

These strategic questions relate directly to issues of how consumers process information and the nature of consumer decision processes. Now that we understand the involvement concept itself, we will turn to more detailed discussions of how consumer involvement affects important marketing issues in upcoming chapters.

SUMMARY

Personality and Consumer Behavior

The widespread availability of computers ushered in the *quantitative era* of consumer research. This development spurred a great deal of research on such topics as consumer personality, psychographics, and consumer involvement. The term *personality* refers to a consistency in a person's behaviors and re-actions to events. In the first section of the chapter, we examined further aspects of Freud's *psychoanalytic theory*, which provided the basis for most modern theories of personality. Several colleagues of Freud viewed his theory as powerful but unduly restrictive. Carl Jung, for example, emphasized that personality continues to develop during the adult years. Alfred Adler placed emphasis upon the social environment, introducing the term *inferiority complex* into the literature.

Our section on personality research in marketing examined two classic research studies. Evans's study asked whether the owners of Fords had different personalities from those of owners of Chevy's. He concluded that they basically did not. Eighteen expert motivation researchers also performed poorly when challenged to pick out the owners of each brand. Cohen's study reported a new test called the *CAD scale*. He classified each consumer as being primarily *compliant, aggressive,* or *detached* and then examined brand preferences where these social traits might be important. Over 200 studies of consumer personality have since been reported, and their findings have been summarized by one expert as "equivocal." Thus we should not conclude that personality exerts no influence; rather, the evidence indicates that it does not dominate all other factors that bear on consumer behavior.

Consumer Values and Laddering Research

The second section of the chapter examined consumer *values* and showed how they meld our basic needs with reality. Here we discussed some types of values; then we turned to how marketers are working with them. The new research technique of *laddering* was presented, together with an application for Federal Express.

Consumer Involvement

In the final section of the chapter we moved to examine the roots of *consumer involvement*. CI was defined as a motivational *state of arousal* that a person experiences in regard to a consumption-related activity. A person who is highly involved is thinking and/or feeling more strongly about the consumption activity at hand. Among the key points on CI, (1) it occurs within specific episodes, (2) high CI is likely when the person's "self-concept" is closely involved in the consumer activity, and (3) CI includes both feelings and thoughts. We saw why this topic is challenging for marketing researchers and summarized some recent research contributions. We also noted that many consumer behaviors are actually low in CI. Marketers unable to change the basic level of consumers' involvement must adapt to this lower level. Further discussion of CI's impact on consumer behavior will occur in upcoming chapters.

KEY TERMS

quantitative era
personality
defense mechanisms
compliant
aggressive
detached
CAD scale
self-concept
actual self
ideal self
psychographics
values
terminal values
instrumental values

means to an end
laddering
means-end chain
A-C-V model
MECCAS model
consumer involvement
high involvement
low involvement
product-class involvement
brand-choice involvement
enduring involvement
situational involvement
cognitive involvement
affective involvement

REVIEW QUESTIONS AND EXPERIENTIAL EXERCISES

[E = Application extension or experiential exercise]

1. What is "personality?" Do you believe that personality affects consumer behavior? Do the studies reported in this chapter support your opinion?

2. Compare the Evans and Cohen studies. Were their results roughly equivalent to what you would have predicted? Why are the results called "equivocal?"

3. "Involvement" is an extremely significant concept in the field of consumer behavior. What exactly is it? What implications does low involvement hold for each of the 4 P's?

[E] 4. Assume that you had CAD personality scores available on a large sample of consumers, and were offered the opportunity to ask them four consumer behavior or marketing-related questions. If your goal was to uncover strong relationships between personality and consumer behavior, what four questions would you ask? For each question, briefly indicate the kind of response you expect each personality type would provide.

[E] 5. The text discussion of self-concept indicated that consumer products sometimes serve to express the actual self, and sometimes to help the consumer feel more like his or her ideal self. Search through magazine ads, looking for examples of these applications. Cut out three examples of each type, attaching brief explanations of your reasoning.

[E] 6. Using Note 16 at the back of the book, locate and read William Wells' classic article on psychographics. Write a brief report on your findings.

[E] 7. Table 7-1 presented four psychographic dimensions for which buyers of premium cosmetics gave high scores (narcissism, appearance conscious, fantasied achievement, and sociable). Search through magazine ads for premium cosmetics and perfumes, looking for examples of appeals to each of these dimensions. Cut out at least one example for each dimension, and attach a brief explanation of your reasoning.

[E] 8. Locate—in your library or bookstore—the paperback personality book, *Please Understand Me: Character and Temperament Types,* by David Keirsey and Marilyn Bates (Fifth Edition, 1984, Prometheus Nemesis Book Company). Take the personality test included in this book, and score it to identify your own personality type. Then read the interpretations provided, together with the research findings on managerially-related topics. Write a brief report on your findings.

[E] 9. Use the references in Notes 18 and 19 at the back of this book to find informative discussions on the topic of values. Read through these discussions and prepare a brief report on your findings.

[E] 10. Figure 7-1 reports changes in college students' priority values over time. Develop a brief survey in which you ask a number of friends and acquaintances to choose their three highest priority values from the list provided in the figure. (*Note:* you may wish to reorder this listing). Before doing this survey, think about what kinds of consumer behavior differences you might expect from people who would have different value priorities. Include several questions in your survey asking about these consumer behaviors. Administer the survey to at least 30 persons, then analyze the results to determine:
    (a) which values scored highest over your entire sample
    (b) whether those who had different value priorities revealed consumer behavior differences as well

[E] 11. The chapter's discussion of the MECCAS Laddering System indicated how an advertiser could use consumer research in developing a campaign aimed at consumers' values. As a creative exercise, examine the sample ladder for Salty Snacks shown at the bottom of Figure 7-2. Based on this information, create a proposed magazine ad for a new brand of flavored chips. Accompany your ad with a brief explanation of your reasoning.

[E] 12. Using the references in Notes 24–28 at the back of the book, select and read some of the recent literature on consumer involvement, its measurement, effects, and implications for marketers. Write a brief report on your findings.

[E] 13. Figure 7-5 presented the Foote, Cone & Belding ad agency's consumer involvement grid. Using Note 27 at the back of the book, read the article by Richard Vaughn on how this grid is helpful for planning advertising. Write a brief report on your findings.

[E] 14. Figure 7-5 presents the Foote, Cone & Belding ad agency's consumer involvement grid. Search through magazines for examples of ads for products in each of the four quadrants. Develop a large enough sample that you can begin to generalize about the kinds of appeals being used for each quadrant. Cut out good examples (and examples that don't fit, also) and attach a brief report on your reasoning.

8

Consumer Perception (I):
Selecting Consumer Stimuli

The "Cocktail Party" Problem

A classic example demonstrates the power of selecting stimuli in our perceptual process. See if you've experienced something close to it. Imagine that we're standing in a crowded room while friends and acquaintances are socializing all around us. The sounds of conversations, laughter, glasses clinking, and music are loud and confusing. We are attempting to carry on a reasonable conversation in our little circle but are having trouble hearing the others speak. All of a sudden, from across the room, we hear our name mentioned. Immediately, *selective attention* operators spring into overdrive. We now find it easier to screen out other stimuli, pick out the discussion of interest, and overhear it.

Scientists studying attention pose an interesting question that arises in this setting, however: How were we able to recognize our name, given all the other stimuli so confusing just the moment before? Further, how are we now able to screen them out so effectively?

■ ■ ■

Throughout this book we will recognize that both external and internal factors are important influences on consumer behavior. In Chapter 5 the examination of the consumer information processing (CIP) perspective provided us with a general framework for understanding how consumers combine the external world with the inner world of their minds. In this chapter and the next we'll take a closer look at the "front end" of this process—how we consumers perceive the world in which we live.

DEFINING CONSUMER PERCEPTION

In a broad sense, the topic of **perception** is concerned with the translation from the external, physical world to the internal, mental world that each of us actually experiences. Although we don't often think about it, we are able to experience only a limited degree of the total physical world, and our mental experiences are themselves usually biased to a greater or lesser extent. Since shopping, purchase, and use activities all require interactions with the external world, the topic of perception is crucial to our understanding of consumer behavior. All marketing stimuli exist in the consumer's external world and must be perceived to have any impact at all.

In reading this chapter, it will be helpful to think in terms of our CIP framework from Chapter 5. The basic system is reproduced in Figure 8-1 (you may wish to refresh your understanding of each sector at this point). We will define consumer perception as *the process of sensing, selecting, and interpreting consumer stimuli*

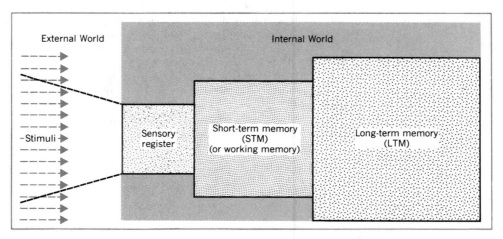

FIGURE 8-1 **The Consumer Information Processing System**

in the external world. Thus all sectors of our CIP system are involved—the sensory register, the short-term memory (STM), and our long-term memory (LTM).

Two Key Factors in Perception

As we saw in the CIP chapter, our human information processing system is capable of dealing with a remarkably wide array of stimulus inputs and works at extremely rapid speeds (in thousandth's of seconds). Thus our perceptual processes are at work continuously, dealing with many stimuli at great speeds. This presents a serious challenge to researchers: a basic framework is quite helpful in appreciating what goes on.

The most basic point of our framework is that there are two key factors that determine what will be perceived and how it will be perceived:

- Stimulus characteristics
- Consumer characteristics

Since consumers are subject to capacity constraints in their CIP systems, we know that they will be incapable of—and uninterested in—fully perceiving and processing all aspects of their environments. **Stimulus characteristics** help us to understand which properties of a stimulus will cause it to receive attention. Since marketers control stimulus characteristics, they are interested in understanding how this factor affects consumer perception.

Consumer characteristics, on the other hand, refer to the influences that our physical and conceptual systems have on what we perceive and how we perceive it. For example, let's consider what really goes on while we are watching TV and an ad comes on. The screen itself will contain many dots emitting light waves of varying magnitudes. Our sensory system picks up those light waves and delivers them to the sensory register, where they are briefly held available for interpretation and any further processing by our CIP system. *Notice, however, that we are unable even to begin to interpret these signals without using our prior knowledge of the world that is stored in LTM.* Without using LTM, we could not know that the dots were portraying a mountain scene, or a laughing surfer, or a miraculous new cleanser for the home.

Scientists who study perception usually make a choice as to which perspective to take on this process. Those who stress the role of the external stimuli emphasize a "bottom-up" or **data-driven view** of the perceptual process. Those who stress the role of personal characteristics employ a "top-down" or **theory-driven approach**. Because of our interest in the applications of perceptual processes within the consumer behavior and marketing environment, we will find both approaches useful in helping us appreciate this topic. Within this chapter, therefore, we'll emphasize both stimulus characteristics and consumer characteristics as they affect consumer perception.

Breaking Down the Process of Perception

Because of the incredible speed of the perception process, it is very difficult to break it down into discrete stages. There are, however, three basic functions that are contained in our definition of perception:

- *Sensing* a stimulus in the external world.
- *Selecting and attending* to certain stimuli and not others.
- *Interpreting* the stimuli and giving them "meaning."

As a set, these functions move from the early stages of a perceptual episode (when it is concentrated on the external environment) to the later stages (when it is concentrated on dealing with the new information in STM). In our discussions we will treat these as isolated stages and examine them separately. In the first half of this chapter, therefore, we concentrate on consumers' sensory processes: how we become aware of consumer stimuli in our environment. In the second half of this chapter, we shift our focus to consumers' selectivity operators, emphasizing the role that attention plays within the perceptual process. Then, in Chapter 9, we'll examine the topic of consumers' interpretive processes. As we discuss each topic we'll see applications that reflect the importance of consumer perception in the real world of marketers, consumers, and public policy.

CONSUMERS' SENSORY SYSTEMS

The Sensory Receptors

Most humans rely on the "five senses" to bridge the gap between the external world and their mental worlds. That is, we see, we hear, we taste, we smell, and we touch the world around us in order to sense it. Our sensory receptors are our organs—eyes, ears, mouth, nose, and skin—that receive inputs from the environment and transmit them to our conceptual system. All five of our sensory receptors are employed in consumer behavior.

Marketing Applications of Sensation

As we noted earlier, all elements of the marketing mix that are presented to consumers must be perceived before they can have any impact at all. Thus an understanding of sensory processes is an important issue for marketers. The following examples indicate some of the many issues that arise within this topic:

Taste, Smell, and the Science of Food

In the English language there are only four words to describe what one tastes. Something will be *sweet, bitter, sour,* or *salty* or some combination of these. Food marketers know that the chemistry of sourness and saltiness is quite simple, while sweetness and bitterness

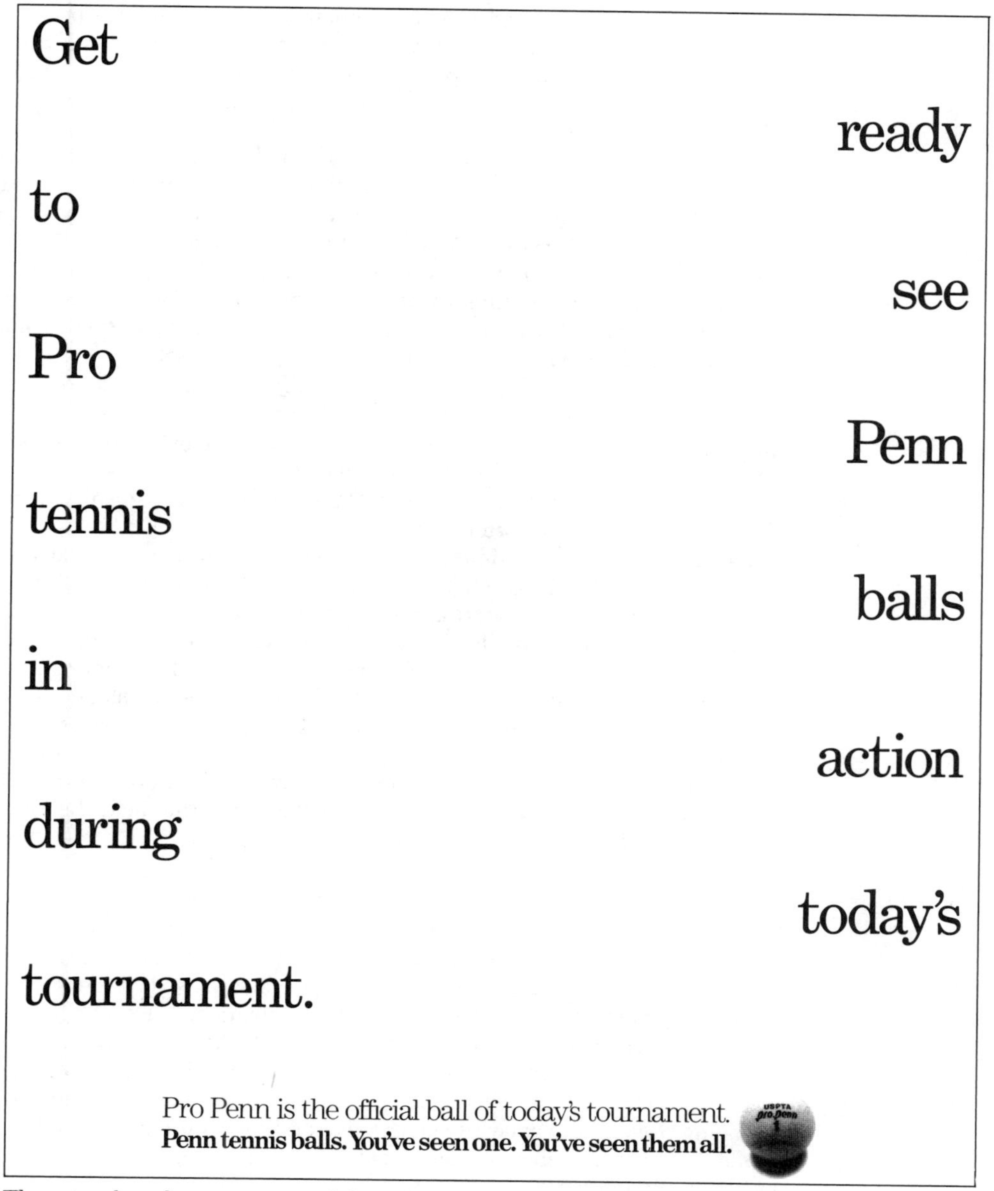

Get

to

Pro

tennis

in

during

tournament.

ready

see

Penn

balls

action

today's

Pro Penn is the official ball of today's tournament.
Penn tennis balls. You've seen one. You've seen them all.

The stimulus characteristics of this ad encourage "data-driven" consumer perception. However, someone who knows tennis can use "top-down" processing to perceive the ad more quickly.

are more complicated. Food producers know that the tastes we perceive are really the result of a complex interaction of two senses—taste and smell. As a simple test to detect this interaction, try taking a sip of liquid (wine, soft drink, liquor, etc.), then hold your nose. The flavor will probably seem to diminish. Then release your nose and the flavor will come up again.

Marketers know that the sense of smell is much more complex than the sense of taste. That is why most of us have a very difficult time using specific terms to describe smells. Instead, we tend to use the names of objects that possess the scent—something "smells like a rose," or pine, or a skunk, and so on. Food producers know that humans have 10 million olfactory receptors for sensations of smell, while the number of taste receptors is only one-tenth to one-hundredth as large. They also know that consumers can indeed smell something inside the mouth, and it is likely that smell contributes more to consumers' perceived taste of food and drink than the taste sense itself![1]

The Strange Case of Tab

Marketers also know that heredity plays a role in a person's sense of taste and that about 7 of every 10 consumers will find a specific chemical (known as PTC) to be bitter, while the other three will not. Those who find PTC bitter are likely to dislike the taste of saccharin, which they also taste as bitter.

The differences in consumers' taste of PTC and bitterness may have accounted for the strange case of Tab's reception by consumers during its first 20 years on the market (when it used a distinctive taste relying on saccharin as a sweetener). According to the senior vice president of marketing for Coca-Cola, Tab "turned off more people than it turned on. A lot of people took a sip, made a face and said, "Yuk!" They never tried it again. It was a brand that polarized people very much." However, there was another market segment in which Tab did very well—the so-called "Tab fanatics." These consumers contributed over $100 million in sales each year that Tab was relying on saccharin as its major sweetening ingredient. It was not until consumer taste tests showed greater preference for Tab containing NutraSweet that the company reformulated the brand away from its historic taste basis.[2]

Vanity, Impaired Sensation, and Package Design

A typical large supermarket now stocks about 20,000 different items, and marketing competition to gain attention from shoppers who pass by in the aisles is fierce. Package design and color are important factors in this competition, as we'll discuss in a further section of the chapter. With respect to the topic of consumers' use of their sensory systems, however, consider what marketers should do with the knowledge that many consumers are shopping with impaired sensory systems. Specifically, package designers know that *one out of every six shoppers* who needs eyeglasses doesn't wear them while shopping. In designing packages to appeal to consumers and to sell the product effectively, therefore, marketers must also allow for less efficient sensory receptors on the part of a significant portion of the market.[3]

I'll Bet You Didn't Know . . .

Retailers and service providers are very sensitive to the stimuli that consumers encounter in their stores and offices. For example, fast-food chains have designed their plastic seating not only to be durable, but also to be somewhat uncomfortable. This is done so that consumers will not linger over their meals, thereby causing seating problems for new arrivals.

Recently, a major hotel-casino in Atlantic City let a $7 million contract to an interior design firm to "create an environment that relaxes the morality of people." The designers hired a psychologist to suggest how this might be done. Among the changes were

1. Lobby windows replaced by sheets of marble, so "people won't relate to time."
2. Materials added to increase casino noise because "noise creates excitement."
3. Lighting for the blackjack tables designed to extend out to envelop the player but not far enough to include spectators, since this may interrupt the player's sense of security.
4. In the free hotel suites used by "high rollers," decor in bold, contrasting colors with very bright lighting and enhanced noise materials. The intent was to have the gamblers wish to spend as little time as possible in their rooms.[4]

Consumer "Sensitivity"

Psychophysics is the science that studies how the actual physical environment gets translated into our personal psychological environments. One basic question involves the limitations that we humans have in our abilities to sense everything that actually exists in the world. In other words, what are humans *not able* to perceive, because their sensory systems are not sensitive enough?

A **threshold** is a level at which an effect begins to occur. Within the field of sensation, the **absolute sensory threshold** is defined as the minimum amount of energy that can be detected by a particular sensory receptor. For example, sounds below the absolute threshold cannot be heard or billboards that are too distant cannot be seen. Most of us are conceited enough simply to assume that our sensory system is providing us with a complete record of the outside world. If we consider all the waves (radiation, television bands, etc.) around us in the atmosphere, however, we can easily begin to recognize limitations to our sensory systems. If we compare our sensory abilities with those of other animals the lesson becomes even more clear.

Dogs have a sense of smell that is as much as 1 million times more sensitive than that of a human, birds can sense magnetism from the earth, dolphins employ sonar, and some moths can smell each other from a mile away. By comparison, then, we humans could easily be described as "somewhat insensitive" creatures. Our strong suits are in sight and touch, our hearing is fair, and our sense of smell and taste are very weak in comparison to those of other living species.[5] At a practical level, of course, we have adapted our world to living within our absolute sensory thresholds.

The **differential sensory threshold** refers to the ability of our sensory systems to detect *changes or differences* in stimuli. Differences that are too small will not be recognized as differences at all. For example, we're all aware that quality control can't be perfect. This means that all packages of a given brand will have minute differences in shapes and colorings, yet these are usually undetectable to us. The very slight variations in taste, smell, and consistency within a package also often go undetected.

"JNDs" and Weber's Law

Another term for differential threshold is the **just noticeable difference**, or **JND**. This is defined as the minimum actual change in a stimulus that can be detected as a change. Well over 100 years ago, the German scientist Ernst Weber discovered a systematic process involving JNDs: *as stimulus intensities get larger, it takes more of a change in the stimulus to be detected as a change*—a 1-pound change in weight will be much easier to detect in a 3-pound bag than in a 75-pound bag, a whisper is easier to hear in a silent room than in a noisy one, and so forth. (Note 6 discusses some technical details of Weber's law, for those readers interested in pursuing it further.)[6]

"Downsizing" and the JND

Despite some limitations, Weber's law remains an important generalization for marketing. There are two basic situations in which the JND concept comes into play—those in which marketers want a difference to be detected and those in which they do not. Consider the case in which a soft drink firm believes that its sales will increase if it can achieve a taste that consumers will perceive as sweeter. Adding sugar will yield a sweeter taste. As sugar costs money, however, the managers realize that this change will increase production costs. Thus they want to add as little additional sugar as possible, consistent with consumers being able to detect a sweeter taste to the drink.

The second example—changes not to be detected—frequently involves lowering costs while maintaining prices at a constant level. This is known as *downsizing*. In recent years, for example, when most gins dropped their alcoholic contents from 90 proof to 80 proof, distillers saved 15 to 21 cents a fifth in federal taxes, as well as saving on ingredient costs. It is not likely that many consumers were able to detect the difference in taste. When gasoline prices went sky-high, United Airlines reduced its seat width by 1.3 inches and the distance between rows by 2 inches. These changes allowed the introduction of more seats, and thus more passengers. Package changes are also frequently made because of squeezes on costs, and sometimes they are done in such a way as to minimize the noticeable differences in quantity. When Procter & Gamble reduced the contents of its Sure spray deodorant from 9 ounces to 8, for example, it did not change the price or size of the cans.[7]

Beyond Sensory Processes

A careful analysis of our examples might well lead to the question,

> *Wait a minute! Are we talking about* capability *of sensing a difference, or are we really asking whether consumers will* actually notice *that a change has occurred? There are probably a lot of cases in which consumers could* detect changes that had been made in a brand, but they just don't try.

Sensory threshold concepts refer to *capability* of sensory detection. These concepts do not say that changes in stimulus intensity *will* be noticed, but only that they *can* be noticed if the consumer chooses to try to do so.

Although sensory thresholds are important, in most practical applications marketers are interested in how likely consumers are actually to perceive changes or differences in stimuli. Lawry's Seasoned Salt, for example, wanted to change its somewhat stodgy package and "L" symbol, but did not want to lose its fine reputation with loyal customers. The firm decided to introduce very minor packaging changes over a series of years. As its president explained,

> *When we started, we were sensitive to the damage that a too radical change in packaging graphics could do to consumer recognition of Lawry's. So we changed all the individual elements, but left the overall look—colors, proportions . . . , positioning of the elements—sufficiently similar to ease the transition in the marketplace . . . in all, it took us 12 years to get where we wanted to go from the beginning.*[8]

In this case consumers could easily see that the new label was different from the old one, if asked to compare them on a side-by-side basis. The question of interest, however, was whether consumers would choose to make this sort of comparison on their own. The more similar the new label was to the old, Lawry's management believed, the less likely consumers would be to notice any difference at all.

The downsizing examples raise this question even more clearly. Although consumers may not have been able to detect a change in the *taste* of the gin, for example, they could easily have used their sight sense to detect the alcoholic content on the label. Similarly, although P&G did not highlight the quantity change in Sure's can, the labels did accurately depict the amount of Sure in the can. Availability of information that may be otherwise difficult or impossible for a consumer to sense is a key basis for most labeling laws.

Sensory Discrimination and "Blind Taste Tests"

To this point in our discussion we've focused on sensory discriminations *within* the same brand. In marketing, however, considerable attention is also paid to *comparisons between brands*. Consumers are encouraged to believe that there are substantial differences between brands, and to become loyal to a certain brand that appeals most to their tastes. Most of us do exhibit such beliefs and loyalties and are confident that we "know what we like and what we don't." In many cases there *are* significant differences between brands, and we are able to perceive them accurately. However, the nature of certain food and drug categories leads to them being known within marketing as "parity products," indicating that the actual differences among brands are very slight. Examples include analgesics (headache remedies and pain killers), soft drinks, cereals, cigarettes, and beer. It is no accident that these product classes have among the highest ratios of dollars spent on advertising to dollars in sales—the cigarette industry, for example, spends over $2 billion per year to differentiate its brands.

As Debbie Strednak illustrates in Exhibit 8-1, many consumers find it difficult to accept that brands are really all that similar in these categories. "Maybe some other people can't tell the difference," they say, "but I certainly can." Most of us are likely to feel, for example, that we prefer our favorite brand of beer or soft drink because it really does taste better to us. The interesting question, however, is whether this better taste arises from our sensory system or from the associations we make from the brand image that we hold in

EXHIBIT 8-1   DEBBIE LOVES PEPSI

Let's listen to Debbie Strednak as she takes a blind taste test for colas. After trying four unidentified cups (nibbling a cracker between each taste), Debbie doesn't even ask about the real brands—they're so *obvious*. She prefers the second cup: "It's Pepsi," she confides. "I guess I'm just used to the taste." She wrinkles her nose with distaste for the first cup, and ranks it last. . . . "I can't drink Coke, it gives me a headache . . . it has an aftertaste. I have Pepsi with everything."

In fact, Ms. Strednak has gotten it all wrong. Her favorite was Coke Classic. She wasn't even given Pepsi in the test. She expressed shock: "No!" she shrieks, slapping her forehead. "Are you sure? Oh, that is horrible!"[9]

LTM. Producers of these products know that sensory reality is subtle and that either factor can be at work. Considerable private testing goes on within the industry. The literature, moreover, presents mixed results.

In one classic study, for example, a beer company teamed up with a professor to conduct an experiment with beer drinkers, who were provided with a six pack of mixed brands, all in identical containers that did not disclose their identities. As the people consumed each bottle (the study was conducted over weeks of time!), they rated the contents on a tag. These ratings were based only on sensory stimuli. During the next period, the firm provided similar six-packs, but this time with the labels present. How did the ratings compare?

Basically, consumers appeared unable to distinguish their favorite brand from the others when no label was provided. When loyal users of each brand rated all five brands without labels, in no case was their favorite brand rated significantly higher than all the other brands. Two of the brands did receive some higher ratings, one brand's users rated all five equal, and two brands were rated significantly lower by their own users! When labels were provided, of course, these ratings changed back to reflect the brand preferences stated at the start of the test. The brewing company concluded that

physical product differences had little to do with the various brands' relative success or failure in the market . . . (instead, success was due to) various firms' marketing efforts, and, more specifically, . . . the resulting brand images.[10]

Further research in this area has shown that the method used in a study can make the discrimination task easier or more difficult for consumers (for example, had the beer company asked consumers to taste small amounts of two or three beers at a time, the consumers likely would have done better in discriminating among them). Also, some consumers are better able to discriminate among brands than others. Expert "tasters," for example, are retained by companies because of their highly developed sensory palates. What about the "average" consumer, though? According to the head of a large consulting firm's flavor science unit, beer drinkers appear to be split into three equal-sized segments:

1. Those who can't tell taste differences well at all.
2. Those who can detect taste differences, but buy beer on a price basis or other reason,
3. Those who can discriminate between brands and buy what tastes best to them.[11]

Summary: Sensory Processes

Our discussion to this point is helpful in indicating the basic role that sensory processes play in the larger process of consumer perception. If there are objective differences in the external world, consumers may or may not actually notice them. A necessary but not sufficient requirement is that they be *capable* of detecting the difference—that the stimulus intensity be above the relevant sensory threshold. Beyond this, consumers need to employ their CIP systems to detect such differences as may exist in the world. Many consumers likely did not take this step in either the gin or Sure examples, cases in which marketers themselves may not have desired to highlight the changes made. Even when marketers do wish to highlight changes, however, consumers often still do not choose to take notice. Thus the issue of which stimuli consumers *choose to perceive* becomes a key question. We'll take this up in our next section, which examines consumer selectivity and attentional processes.

SELECTIVITY AND ATTENTION

Recall the cocktail party example at the start of this chapter? It indicates several important points about consumer attention.[12] For example, it shows how both stimulus and personal factors are important in capturing and guiding attention. A stimulus with particular properties (in this case, our name) is quite capable of interrupting our other CIP processes and capturing attention from our system. At the same time, this attention was selectively focused because our personal factors were geared to that type of stimulus. The example also shows how *attracting* attention and *maintaining* attention are really quite different processes. The maintenance of attention is much more determined by personal factors than by stimulus characteristics. In this case, for example, we might have already heard the story being told about us. If so, we might shift our attention to the listeners, to monitor their reactions, or we may decide to ignore that conversation and again focus our attention on our attractive partner for the evening.

As consumers, consider how many packages we pass on a store shelf without consciously perceiving them, how many ads we fail to process, and so forth. Our sensory system makes a wide range of stimuli from the external environment available to us. To live our lives in a rational manner, however, we must choose to "perceive" some elements and ignore other elements of that world. Thus the issue of *selectivity* is crucial. For marketers, of course, understanding how consumers' selectivity operators work offers guidance for designing ads that "break through the clutter" to gain attention, packages and displays that attract attention in the store, and so forth.

The Selectivity Operators

Consumers use four types of **selectivity operators** in helping to order our lives and the mental world in which we live them. These are

- *Selective exposure.* Consumers use **selective exposure** to decide to which situations and stimuli they'll be exposed at all. In general, we expose ourselves to situations we view as interesting or necessary and avoid others with unpleasant characteristics. Political strategists have long known, for example, that audiences for candidates' speeches are largely comprised of people who have already decided to support that candidate. Marketers must adapt their marketing mixes to fit the selective exposure patterns of their target segments. In practice, selective exposure is extremely important in both the "place" and "promotions" elements of the marketing mix. Store location decisions, for example, are based largely on where consumers are likely to be driving. Similarly, measures of selective exposure such as ratings points for TV and radio determine what shows advertisers will support.
- *Selective attention.* While selective exposure vastly reduces the range of stimuli available to a person, it does not decide which remaining stimuli will be perceived. This is determined by **selective attention**, which we'll analyze in this chapter.
- *Selective interpretation.* Once an external stimulus receives attention from us, the material we bring from long-term memory (LTM) is crucial to determining exactly how that stimulus is categorized and interpreted by us. We'll examine **selective interpretation** in more detail in the next chapter.
- *Selective retention and retrieval.* In many cases we choose to stress some aspects of a person or brand and play down other aspects. We may remember a date as being "wonderful," for example, although the early part of the evening actually dragged a little. We may even have had some dates a few years ago that we actually cannot remember. This element of **selective retention and retrieval** is quite common in consumer behavior as well.

Attention!

The scientific treatment of **attention** is very similar to the way in which most of us normally think of this concept. That is, *attention refers to the momentary focusing of our information processing capacity on a particular stimulus.* It thus involves an allocation of processing capacity to one stimulus and, by implication, away from other possible stimuli to which we might have attended during that brief period of time.

It is useful to distinguish three types of attention in consumer behavior:[13]

- Planned attention
- Spontaneous attention
- Involuntary attention

Planned attention occurs when consumers use their attentional processes to help with their consumption activities. When we set out for the gas station, for example, we use planned attention to locate our car, find the ignition, turn at the right spots, identify the station, and so forth. Notice how important LTM is in this example—for many of us, the entire "picture" of the process already resides there (as we'll discuss later, this is termed a perceptual "script").

At the other extreme, **involuntary attention** occurs when an external stimulus literally forces its way into our consciousness. A loud "BANG!" a flashing light, or a tap on the shoulder are usually sufficient to capture the attention of most of us.

Between these extremes lies **spontaneous attention**, a combination of the other two types. Here we are not concentrating too narrowly and are ready to attend to new stimuli. On the other hand, no particular stimulus is forcing its way into our consciousness. Our attention, therefore, is "spontaneous" in that it simply arises at that point in time. This appears to be the most common case in consumer behavior, as our attention moves from object to object, sometimes sparked by our mental interests and sometimes by features of the stimuli.

Stimulus Factors That Attract Attention

As stressed throughout our discussion, the need to attract and maintain consumers' attention is one of the major problems confronting marketers in today's very competitive marketplace. An interesting episode that occurred prior to the 1984 Olympics provides a humorous "snapshot" of this type of competitive struggle:

Please Don't Look Up There . . .

Every four years marketers bid against each other for the right to be called an "official product" of the Olympic Games. In 1984, when the Olympics were held in Los Angeles, two sets of "official" rights were sold—one for the U.S. trials (held earlier to determine the U.S. team members) and one for the games themselves. In the film product category, the Japanese firm, Fuji, was named the official brand for the games, while the American firm, Kodak, was named the official brand for the trials. Upon arrival in Los Angeles, Fuji sent its blimp up for a test run over the Los Angeles Coliseum. However, it happened that at this time the U.S. trials were in progress. True to the exclusive marketing agreements signed with Kodak, U.S. officials were perturbed at this sight. What should they do to minimize this disruption? An amazing decision was reached—over the loudspeakers boomed the following announcement: "WE WOULD APPRECIATE IT IF YOU WOULD NOT LOOK AT THE BLIMP PASSING OVERHEAD." At this point, of course, *everyone* shifted his or her attention to the sky and watched the Fuji blimp being driven away by a helicopter (whether it was the official helicopter of the trials is unknown).[14]

There appear to be two key dimensions of marketing stimuli that will help marketers to attract attention: *position* and *contrast*.

How "Position" Attracts Attention

Position works because there is a higher probability that a consumer's sensory system will encounter the stimulus. *Size,* for example, is one position characteristic that works this way. Larger ads and larger signs are likely to receive more attention, in part because a consumer is simply more likely to see them.

Placement in the stimulus field is another important position factor. In cultures that read from left to right, for example, consumers' eyes have been trained to proceed in a systematic manner across a page. This training carries over into our casual scanning as well. For example, our eyes are most likely to drift to the top left as we turn a magazine page. It is not surprising, therefore, that an ad placed on the upper half of a page tends to receive greater attention than does one on the lower half or that it is likely to receive greater attention on the left-hand side than on the right. "Readers are ignoring at least 50% of advertising in magazines," reports the president of a research firm. "Without a good position, the odds are that people will turn the page without even seeing your brand name."[15]

Similarly, consumers' eyes travel along certain paths in supermarkets and

discount stores. Brands that sit along those paths are more likely to receive attention from the consumer. Some consumer research firms use sophisticated cameras to track the movements of consumers' eyes as they shop, measuring which products and shelf positions receive the most attention (special cameras are also used to learn the exact patterns used in reading ads and finding which copy elements attract the most attention). Findings from this type of research are interesting; for example, one eye camera research study in stores showed

- Brands on an upper shelf received 35 percent greater attention than did those on a lower shelf.
- Increasing the number of rows of a brand (called "facings") from two to four resulted in a 34 percent increase in attention from consumers.
- An ideal shelf position can result in a 76 percent increase in visibility.[16]

Increased consumer attention can increase a brand's chance of being included in an evoked set, thus leading to increased sales. With these kinds of impacts, it is little wonder that competition is fierce for improved shelf positions in stores!

Retailers are also stressing attention principles in store layout decisions. One former marketing professor, for example, has built a very profitable business helping chains to redesign their stores. Among the strategies he recommends are

- Dropping long aisles in favor of short aisles and arranging them as a honeycomb. This way, shoppers are often encountering aisle ends or "windows" that are eyecatchers and attract increased attention.
- Installing more interior walls to organize products and attract attention to them.
- Eliminating fixtures and signs to emphasize the products themselves.

This perceptually based system seems to work. As a manager of a client store said, "We've had comments from customers who thought we had brought in new merchandise or improved our lines of merchandise. But we haven't." According to an executive of the chain, "If we judge success by the bottom line [profits], we'd have to give [the professor's firm] high marks."[17]

How "Contrast" Attracts Attention

One important insight into attention processes is called **adaptation theory.** This states that consumers tend to adapt to constant levels of stimuli and pay less attention to them over time. When we enter an air-conditioned store on a hot summer day, for example, we're very likely to pay attention to the temperature change. After a few minutes, however, our sensory system has adapted to the new temperature, and we are much less likely to notice it. This reflects the physical characteristic that our sensory receptors fire in response to change rather than to constant conditions. **Contrast,** then, because it represents a change to our sensory systems, will activate our sensory receptors and stimulate our attentional processes.

Intensity of the stimulus is one basic means of creating contrast and drawing attention. Stronger scents, louder noises, and brighter lights are all commonly used by marketers for this purpose. *Movement* is another device that creates contrast for the sensory receptors and sparks them to send impulses. Moving signs and store displays, for example, are employed to help that stimulus stand out, while much of the great success of television is due to its ability to portray movement to our eyes.

Color is another means of creating contrast in our sensory system, since the light waves are recognized as different by our sensory receptors (warm colors such as red have high wavelengths, while cold colors such as blue have shorter wavelengths). Interestingly, there is also evidence that attending to different colors has physiological effects on our bodies. For example, blood pressure increases under red lights and decreases under blue, as does eyeblink frequency, and brain waves are slightly different depending on the color being sensed.

Personal Factors That Direct Attention

Automaticity and Motivational Underpinnings of Attention

Of our three types of attention, both planned and spontaneous attention require inputs from a person. However, as we have seen in our discussion of sensory processes, much of perception is extremely rapid, and we are not entirely conscious of every step that is taking place. The concept of **automaticity** is helpful in our recognizing how attention operates when it is not at a conscious level: This refers to processes that are performed with minimal effort and without conscious control. As an example, let's consider a consumer who has been loyal to Tide for many years. Notice that this consumer would have repeated a specific visual detection task many times—sensing a Tide box and recognizing it. This particular task has now been practiced so often that it is "overlearned," and will continue to occur whether the consumer desires it to or not. When in the grocery store, then, this consumer will automatically detect the Tide box, even without conscious effort or control (*note:* the consumer may not be consciously aware

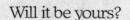

Will it be yours?

Of the 50 million dogs in America, a million will now enjoy a dry dog food never before available.
A dog food for the fortunate one dog in fifty.
Will it be yours?
That depends on the price you place on quality.
Because quality is what our new dog food is all about.

We named our dog food Purina O.N.E.® Short for "Optimum Nutritional Effectiveness." "Optimum" because, ounce for ounce, there is no leading dog food that is more nutritious than Purina O.N.E.
We used a number of expensive ingredients not used in most other dry dog foods.
Our main ingredient is chicken

—a highly digestible source of protein and other nutrients for dogs.
What you won't find in Purina O.N.E. is important, too. It's free of fillers, and artificial colors and flavors. It only has good things for your dog.
But even the best dog food won't do your dog any good if he won't eat it.

Dogs don't always know what's good for them, but they usually know what they like.
So good taste isn't just a nicety. It's a necessity.
Happily, your dog will love the taste of Purina O.N.E. Taste tests prove it's more palatable

than even the leading dry dog food.
Unhappily, not all dogs will get the chance to eat Purina O.N.E.
For one thing, we can't make enough of it to go around.
But the real determining factor is cost.

Not every dog owner is willing to pay the price for a dog food of this quality.
We suggest you pick up a bag of Purina O.N.E., and compare its ingredients to the dog food you're now serving.
Then compare the price.
And decide if your dog is worth the difference.

For dog lovers, the photo of 50 dogs can help attract, then maintain, attention to the ad and its message.

that he or she has attended to the box, but will notice that it is very easy to recognize if he or she desires to do so!). When consumers' automatic attention processes are sparked by the Tide box, the Coca-Cola sign, or the Golden Arches, these marketers benefit strongly from this type of preconscious attention.[18]

The conscious level of attention is much easier to understand, as we are aware of it, and have a considerable degree of control over it. Our discussions of motivation in Chapter 6 covered the primary personal factors that direct attention. Our *needs and goals* cause us to be more sensitive to potential stimuli that might satisfy them. For example, we are more sensitive to food odors when we're hungry. Similarly, consider how many gasoline stations we begin to notice when we're on a trip and our gauge begins to drift toward the "empty" mark!

Novelty and *curiosity* can also cause us to direct our attention toward an interesting stimulus. Marketers have long used such words as "New!" "Improved," and "Free!" to play upon this factor in attracting attention from potential customers. Finally, our *moods* and emotions also influence our attentional processes. When we're tired, for example, we seem generally less alert to external stimuli; when we are rushed, the field of our attention seems to narrow; and so forth.

Maintaining Attention

Because our perceptual systems work at such incredible speeds, the issue of *maintaining attention* is equally as important as, or even more important than, attracting attention. The natural course of attentional processes is to move rapidly from stimulus to stimulus. To maintain our attention on a particular stimulus, then, we must usually concentrate on it and use some degree of will power to keep our attention from drifting elsewhere. Whether or not we will *choose* to concentrate depends primarily on our motivations, interests, and how well the stimulus seems to be satisfying them. This has important implications for marketers. In advertising, for example, the very stimuli that may be highly successful in *attracting* attention to an ad (such as sex or music) might then hinder *maintaining* attention to the brand and its message (since the viewer is now enjoying his or her further thoughts about the sexual or musical stimulus that attracted interest). For this reason many ads are "scripted" to assist the consumer in moving along with the message. To examine more about how this works, we'll need to move into the remaining stage of the perceptual process—how we consumers "interpret" the information we are receiving. We will be dealing with this topic in our next chapter. Before moving to it, however, we'll take a brief look at a topic that has intrigued professors and students of marketing for years—the puzzling phenomenon known as subliminal perception.

The Puzzling Case of Subliminal Perception

During a six-week period in 1956, a New Jersey movie theater was reported to have flashed the subliminal messages "Hungry? Eat Popcorn" and "Drink Coca-Cola" during the popular movie *Picnic*. Over 45,000 people attended the theater during this period and apparently were influenced by the subliminal ads. Compared with previous sales records, the sales of popcorn increased 58 percent and Coca-Cola increased 18 percent during this time. When this story hit the press, a popular uproar arose. Angry charges of "sinister plots," "breaking and entering people's minds," and the like were freely raised. But what exactly is subliminal perception? What was all this furor about?

The Concept of Subliminal Stimulation

Contrary to what some consumers believed, **subliminal perception** does not refer to an "invisible" stimulus. Strictly speaking "sub-liminal" means "below the threshold" (*limen* is the technical term for a threshold). A subliminal stimulus, therefore, is one that cannot be discriminated by our conscious perceptual processes. To "stimulate" us, however, it must be capable of being sensed by our sensory system. The two major types of subliminal stimulation, therefore, are (1) visual stimuli presented so briefly that we cannot consciously detect them (this was the method reportedly used in the movie theater study) and (2) sound messages that are presented very rapidly and at such a low volume that we cannot detect them.

Is subliminal perception possible? The answer seems clearly to be "Yes." A number of well-controlled studies in psychology shows results that would only have occurred if the subjects had been perceiving the subliminal stimuli in the study.[19] This should not be surprising to us, since it is clear that our sensory system has strong powers and can work at extremely high speeds. The truly controversial issues in this area deal with the *effects* that subliminal stimulation might have.

Subliminal Advertising and Persuasion

The 1950s furor really concerned possible abuses of subliminal stimulation for *persuasive purposes*. Brainwashing was feared, in which consumers would be manipulated by forces that they could not consciously perceive or even know about. This raises the question, "how effective is subliminal stimulation in the area of persuasion?" Note that this question introduces a further step in the process—not only must the subliminal stimulus be perceived, but a consumer's behavior must also be affected.

The evidence on this question is mixed. Most studies indicate that such "hidden persuasion" is unlikely to occur. The original results claimed in the movie theater, for example, have been strongly criticized. There were no scientific controls in the theater test, and the results could have been due entirely to other factors, such as consumer reaction to the movie's scenes of eating and drinking, the summer weather, or the types of customers. It is notable that the theater results have not been repeated (replicated) in later studies (and there is some question as to whether the study was even actually performed).[20] Also, a more controlled study on TV ads in Indianapolis was conducted shortly thereafter and showed no evidence of even the slightest effects in persuading the mass audience.[21]

Within marketing, one study did report significant effects, but other studies have provided no significant effects of subliminal ads.[22]

On balance, then, the evidence seems to suggest that subliminal advertising will not be very effective in persuading consumers to buy. Many leaders in the advertising community, moreover, view this as an unethical technique and would likely support legislation to ban it if it were found to be effective.

As to a scientific judgment of its effectiveness, however, the jury is still out. Given our analysis of the CIP system, we must maintain an open mind as to the possibility that subliminal messages could be effective under some conditions. The sparse evidence to date within marketing settings does not suggest that the effects would be powerful, if they were to occur at all. Nonetheless, while we can at this point conclude that persuasion is not likely, this should be accepted as a tentative rather than a firm conclusion.

Persuasion Without Awareness

As we just noted, a subliminal stimulus is one that we cannot consciously perceive. A much broader issue, however, concerns stimuli that we *can* consciously perceive if our attention is directed to them but that *will not be* consciously perceived by most or all consumers in their normal activities. When these stimuli affect our feelings and evaluations without our realizing why, a case of **persuasion without awareness** occurs. Although little formal work has been done on this topic, it would seem possibly to occur frequently in advertising. For example, various cues in the background of a picture might affect our feelings and evaluations, without our realizing that they are doing so. As we've already seen, colors can have this effect as well.

This area has not seen a great deal of published research on consumer behavior, so there are presently many unresolved questions in it. However, you may be interested in briefly reviewing some issues in this area:

Key's Erotic Implants

Although he termed his work *Subliminal Seduction,* persuasion without awareness is in fact the primary basis for the sensationalist writings of Wilson Bryan Key. Key (whose work has found its way into many high school and college courses studying other subjects than marketing and consumer behavior, where it does not receive a professional analysis) claims to have found numerous erotic stimuli and messages in ads. He further asserts that they've been deliberately placed there by malicious advertisers and that they have a significant effects on consumers in the audience.[23] Many leaders in the advertising industry became irate at these charges, viewing them to be irresponsible and without foundation. On the other hand, it certainly is possible that a few isolated advertising people might have done this on a few occasions—this is an issue that's virtually impossible to determine with certainty.

Beyond his chilly reception by ad professionals, Key's arguments have not been met with much acceptance by consumer researchers either. Several recent marketing studies have attempted to test Key's contention that ads that "embed" sexual symbols do create a subconscious receptivity to the suggestions in the ad. These studies compared normal ads against the same ads in which sexually oriented *embeds* (sometimes call *implants*)

Which photo is more appealing?

Which photo is more appealing?

had been added. Although consumers could recognize the embeds after they'd been pointed out to them, they did not report recognizing them when viewing the ads the first time. The question for these studies: "Did ads with the implants affect consumers differently than those without?"

One study analyzed verbal reactions to the ads and did find significantly more consumer comments that suggested that the erotic implants had had an effect on people's feelings. This study did not, however, contain any measures of effects on brand attitudes or purchase behavior and, therefore, gives no evidence on the issue of whether consumers were at all persuaded by the embeds.[24] The other studies did examine persuasion measures, but again the results are mixed. In general, their evidence suggested no systematic persuasion effect. However, some evidence did emerge to suggest that under certain conditions, some form of persuasion *might* occur. This tentative conclusion is consistent with recent research developments in classical conditioning, which will be further examined in Chapter 10.[25]

Pupils and Attraction: The "Eyes" Have It!

Sexual-oriented stimuli are, of course, only a fraction of the potential types that might lead to persuasion without awareness. For example, another paper in marketing has presented two provocative findings on the subtle impacts that a person's eyes can have on the feelings of other people. (Before describing them, we should note that to this author's knowledge, these studies have not been replicated, and their findings should be viewed as tentative).

The first study concerned pupil size and attraction. There is a physiological tendency for our eyes to dilate (that is, the pupils become larger) when we have a special interest in something. In this case the marketing researcher was interested in whether we consumers may have learned this human trait through our years of observation and might apply it to our processing of ads, even though we're not aware of it. Accordingly, he took two identical photos of a young female student, the only difference being that one had been modified to create a dilated pupil size. The 50 participants in this study were simply shown the two photos and asked,

1. "Do you see any differences in these pictures?"
2. "Whether you see differences or not, which would you select as having more appeal?"

None of the participants noticed the manner in which the photos differed. Over half said that they saw *some* difference, but none of these could describe precisely what it was. Which photo did they choose? According to the report, all 50 selected the woman with the enlarged pupils!

What Kind of a "Looker" Are You?

The second study shifted its focus to movement of the eye, but again looked for subtle indications that persuasion might occur. It seems that some of us tend characteristically to look toward the left while we're thinking, while others tend to look toward the right. These differences may be linked to the concept of "brain hemisphere dominance." Scientists know that the functions of the brain are located in specific areas, some in the left side and some in the right side. The left-side functions are related to logical thought processes, while the right side of the brain contains functions dealing with such areas as emotions and music. The relationships with eye movements, however, are reversed: right-brain dominance is associated with "left-lookers" and vice versa.

In this exploratory study, participants were shown two photographs of the same model.

These were identical, the only difference being that in one shot the model was looking to her left and in the other she was looking to her right (the negative was simply switched to produce this effect). Participants were asked to select the photo that had the strongest appeal to them. Later, each participant was given simple math problems during a face-to-face interview, and the direction that he or she tended to look was categorized by the interviewer. The research hypothesis was that people would prefer models to look in the same direction as their personal eye-movement tendency. That is, left-lookers should prefer the model looking to her left, while right-lookers should prefer the model shown looking to her right. The results supported this hypothesis—left-lookers preferred the left-looking model by a 3-to-2 margin, while right-lookers preferred the right-looking model by a 3-to-1 margin. Again, none of the participants could specify the reason they chose one photo rather than the other as being more attractive! Recently, further research has shown similar kinds of results using advertisements as stimuli in a different type of task.[26]

Results such as these are indicative of the fascinating and subtle ways in which our perceptual systems can work. In the next chapter we'll examine further interesting processes within perception, as we turn to how consumers *interpret* the stimuli in our marketing-consumer environment.

SUMMARY

Defining Consumer Perception

Perception is defined as "the process of sensing, selecting, and interpreting consumer stimuli in the external world." This chapter focused on the sensory and selectivity processes of consumer perception (the following chapter concentrates on interpretation.)

Consumers' Sensory Systems

We first examined some instances to illustrate how an understanding of *sensation* can be useful to marketers. We then discussed key terms and concepts. An *absolute threshold* defines the minimum amount of energy that can be detected. *Differential thresholds* refer to a person's ability to detect changes in stimuli: this concept has been generalized into *Weber's law*, which quantifies the notion of the *JND*, or *just noticeable difference*.

Selectivity and Attention

Our discussion of selectivity began by pointing out that attracting attention and maintaining attention are different processes. Consumers must cope with the wide range of stimuli that are in the environment. Thus the *selectivity operators*—exposure, attention, interpretation, and retention/retrieval—are of crucial importance. The concept of *attention* refers to the momentary focusing of our information processing capacity on a particular stimulus. Attention may be planned, spontaneous, or involuntary. With respect to marketing applications, we saw how *stimulus factors* such as position and contrast can be used to attract attention, whereas *personal factors* such as motivation and interest have a stronger impact on maintaining attention.

The further aspects of perceptual processes are the subject of our next chapter. Before leaving this one, however, we briefly examined the controversial topic of *subliminal persuasion*. Available evidence here suggests that its effects would not be powerful, if it occurred at all. Our discussion noted some subtle issues in this area, including persuasion without awareness, which may occur frequently in the consumer's world and is worthy of further investigation.

KEY TERMS

perception	selective interpretation
stimulus characteristics	selective retention and retrieval
consumer characteristics	attention
data-driven view	planned attention
theory-driven approach	involuntary attention
psychophysics	spontaneous attention
threshold	position
absolute sensory threshold	adaptation theory
differential sensory threshold	contrast
just noticeable difference (JND)	automaticity
selectivity operators	subliminal perception
selective exposure	persuasion without awareness
selective attention	

REVIEW QUESTIONS AND EXPERIENTIAL EXERCISES
[E = Application extension or experiential exercise]

1. Discuss the general topic of consumer perception:
   a. Define the process of consumer perception.
   b. Explain the two key factors in consumer perception.
   c. Describe how the sectors of the CIP system are involved.
   d. Indicate why an understanding of consumer perception is important for marketers. Is it important for consumers as well? Why or why not?

2. What is involved in consumers' sensory systems? Which human senses are relatively the strongest and the weakest? Briefly evaluate print versus radio versus television in terms of their impacts on consumers' sensory systems.

3. What is the subject matter of psychophysics? Compare and contrast the concepts of absolute and differential thresholds. Discuss what types of implications these concepts hold for marketers. Provide examples.

4. For each of the five senses, cite an actual marketing example of how to appeal to consumers using this sensory receptor.

5. Why make a distinction between attracting consumer attention and maintaining consumer attention? Which is likely to be more difficult for the marketer? Why?

6. The text describes three types of consumer attention. Define each of these, providing examples. In what ways is this distinction helpful to marketers?

7. Describe the four types of selectivity operators consumers use to help order their lives. Provide illustrations of each as they occur in consumer behavior.

[E] 8. Early in the chapter the text stated that a significant number of consumers shop without wearing their eyeglasses. In exactly what ways would this affect their shopping behaviors? In your opinion, have retailers and manufacturers adjusted for this factor adequately? Go to a supermarket and look for evidence regarding marketers' responses. Write a brief report on your findings.

[E] 9. Conduct a "blind taste test" for various brands and types of soft drinks. Write a brief report summarizing your findings. What implications do they hold for the marketing mix of any particular brand you tested?

[E] 10. Use the *Business Periodicals Index* (or other reference source) to locate articles allowing you to trace the recent history of the Pepsi-Coke marketing war. What role did blind taste tests and other concepts from this chapter play? Write a brief report on your findings.

[E] 11. Assume that you were given the power to rule on the following questions. How would you rule, and what would your explanation be?
   a. Should subliminal message be allowed in broadcast advertising? Should they be allowed on sound systems or point-of-purchase materials in stores?
   b. Should "embeds" be allowed in advertisements? Should they be allowed on sound systems or point-of-purchase materials in stores?

[E] 12. Assume that you were retained as a consultant for a major advertising agency. Would you recommend that they consider using subliminal or related techniques in the campaigns they are developing? If so, what ideas would you advance (draw on actual brands for your example). If not, what exactly would you include in your report and recommendation?

[E] 13. As a consultant for a marketer in each of the categories below, suggest some ways in which each of the major topics in this chapter can improve the marketing mix.
   a. A family restaurant
   b. A new dentist
   c. A candy bar manufacturer
   d. A golf equipment and apparel firm

C H A P T E R

9

Consumer Perception (II): Interpreting Consumer Stimuli

Nothing But the Best . . .

"Is it rich Co-REEN-thee-an leather?" Actor Ricardo Montalban asked this question for years in his commercials for Chrysler's luxury cars. Then he answers, "Of course. We wanted the best." But (1) What *is* Corinthian leather? (2) Is it from the ancient city in Greece? (3) Is it really the best?

Answers: (1) It's a name dreamed up by the marketers at Chrysler to suggest both elegance and the Mediterranean image of its Cordoba model. (2) the leather comes from various U.S. suppliers, including one in Newark, New Jersey. (3) It's good, but since it gets heavy wear on car seats, it can't be the highest grade of leather. "It's just a name, really," reports Mr. Montalban. "That's all."[1] For millions of consumers, though, that isn't all. In this chapter we'll step further into the world of consumer perception, now to concentrate on how consumers interpret what they perceive.

■ ■ ■

Up to this point in our analysis of consumer perception, we have stressed the sensation and attention stages of the perceptual process and have placed emphasis on external stimuli in the consumer's world. In this chapter we move further into the perceptual process and further into the consumer's mind.

THREE ACTIVITIES IN CONSUMER INTERPRETATION

When we "perceive" something, we make efforts to "interpret" it. Interpretation refers to the *meaning* that a consumer will attach to a particular stimulus. Three basic processes—organization, categorization, and inference making—are involved. To appreciate the nature of these processes, let's begin at the sensory stage. Although some of us (the author included!) are always surprised when reminded of the fact, it is the case that *people don't sense the real world directly*. Instead we sense the real world through molecular intermediaries such as light waves, sound waves, scents, and so on. The first stage in interpreting external stimuli, therefore, is to determine which of the huge numbers of molecules in our environment actually *belong together*. This activity is termed **perceptual organization**.

Once a stimulus has been sensed, the problem becomes one of identifying it, so that we "know" what it is. This activity is termed **perceptual categorization**. After a stimulus has been categorized, however, we're often also interested in thinking more about it. This process involves **perceptual inference**. In the sections that follow, we examine each process in greater detail, indicating implications for marketers, consumers, and public policymakers.

PERCEPTUAL ORGANIZATION

The Gestalt School

The basic principles of perceptual organization have been developed by scientists of the **Gestalt school** of psychology, which began about 75 years ago in Germany.[2] The primary principle is that of *organized wholes*—the belief that people perceive entire objects rather than just the separate parts of them (the German term *Gestalt* is roughly translated to mean "whole" or "pattern"). This suggests that the whole has an identity beyond the sum of its parts. When a consumer drives into a parking lot, for example, Gestalt theory suggests that he or she is much more likely to perceive a "store" rather than just glass windows, bricks, and a sign—the total arrangement is more important than the parts individually.

Gestalt psychologists also believe that people strive to have "good Gestalts." That is, people desire to have perceptions that are simple, complete, and meaningful. Most of these processes are carried out at an unconscious level, but they have a strong impact on our perceptions. Based on this desire for a good Gestalt, most of us will perceive our worlds as being consistent with the following principles (illustrated in Exhibit 9-1 and in Figures 9-1 and 9-2):

1. *Figure and ground.* Perception tends to feature one object at a time, and to view the remaining stimuli as background, which is less important and which is assumed to continue on behind the "figure." Perception can be rapidly reorganized, however, so that the part of the ground becomes the new figure, while the old figure moves into the ground. In Exhibit 9-1, for example, can you see both the vase and the people at the same time? Which did you see first? In Figure 9-1, how old would you say the woman is? What if you were told you're way off—what would your next guess be?

EXHIBIT 9-1   *GESTALT PRINCIPLES OF ORGANIZATION*

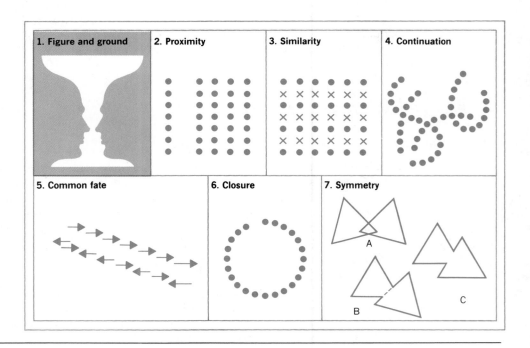

FIGURE 9-1 **An Interesting Woman**

2. *Proximity.* Elements that are close together in space or time are seen as belonging together, to form a unit. In Exhibit 9-1's example of proximity effects, do you see rows across the figure or rows down the figure?

3. *Similarity.* Elements that are similar in appearance seem to form a unit. For example, notice how the substitution of "x" for "o" in some positions of the exhibit's illustration now leads us to see rows across the figure.

4. *Continuation.* Elements that together form a line or a curve seem to form a unit. If we look carefully at the illustration, we're likely to find our eyes "crossing" lines as we follow the curves. This will lead us to see four separate figures.

5. *Common fate.* Moving elements traveling in the same direction seem to form a unit. Notice how much easier it is for us to follow the top figure than it is to follow the bottom arrows.

6. *Closure.* Perception favors a complete or closed figure. For example, as shown in the exhibit, a 320-degree arc is perceived by most people to be a complete circle.

7. *Symmetry.* Perception favors a symmetrical form over an asymmetrical one. In the exhibit's illustrations, for example, many of us will see separate triangles rather than the overall form in A. In B, we may focus more on the triangle than the irregular four-sided shape. In C, however, we'll tend to see the more regular overall outline and may even "shape it" to a more symmetrical form of an arrow.

The Importance of Context and Constancy

This set of principles leads to two further insights into consumer perception: the notions of perceptual context and perceptual constancy. The following sections briefly introduce each of these important concepts.

Do Our Eyes Play Tricks?

The concept of **perceptual context** states that, because we are concerned with perceiving a "well-organized" whole, various stimuli will affect our perceptions, even if subconsciously. Figure 9-2 contains some simple illustrations of how context affects even our simplest perceptions. In panel A, for example, which line is longer? Most of us will miss this question unless we've been warned to expect a trick. Take a ruler and measure them. You'll easily see how objective reality can differ from subjective reality: in this case the flow of the arrows (as we took them into account) actually intruded on our perception of the horizontal lines themselves.

In panel B, to which top line does the arrow belong? Although most of us assume that we're "seeing" the continuation of the line behind the middle bars, in fact we're taking those bars into account, and our eyes are traveling slightly to the left as we do so. Again, if we use a ruler we can easily see objective reality in the absence of the context effect. Such systematic misperceptions, or "illusions," would clearly not occur if we had simply perceived the lines by themselves and not taken the other elements (that is, the "context") into account.

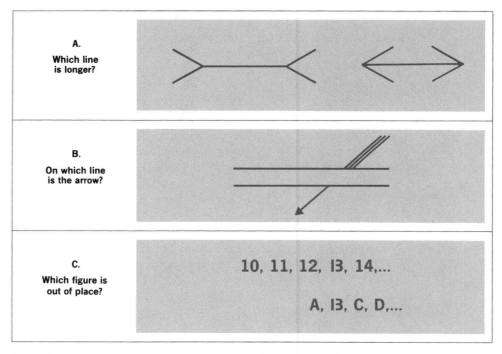

FIGURE 9-2 **Three Instances of Perceptual Context Effects**

Panel C of Figure 9-2 extends the topic of context effects into the area of "meaning." Notice that most of us would say that "13" and "B" both belong where they've been placed. Notice, however, that to make that form into a number we had to subtly interpret distance between the line and the curves. Then, to fit the alphabetic context, we had to subtly ignore the small gaps and employ closure for this context.

How Much Does the World Change?

Perceptual constancy is also a very powerful concept. This concept points out how strongly our past experience influences our perceptions of the present. Perceptual constancy refers to the fact that we strive to perceive our world as a relatively stable environment, even though our sensory receptors are providing us with changing sensory impressions.

Let's consider a simple example—our perceptions of the size and shape of a Tide detergent box. For example, if we know the approximate height and width of a box of Tide, we'll tend to "perceive" that size even as we walk toward the shelf from the other end of the aisle (at the sensory level, however, the box is much larger at 2 feet away than at 30 feet). Similarly, we'll continue to perceive the box as rectangular, even though its retinal image from all but a 90-degree angle is in fact trapezoidal. Finally, we'll see the same orange, yellow, and blue colors on the box, even if they are physiologically closer to brown under poor lighting conditions. Perceptual constancy works on all other products as well, of course. Imagine what it does to our perceptions of the taste of Coke or Pepsi, the feel of a stocking, and the words of a salesperson!

Wonder Builds Strong Bodies

Although our examples of context and constancy were simplistic, we should not miss the larger points that they make. Our perceptions are almost always affected by them! Normally, of course, our perceptions are appropriate to the context (we've been socialized to make them that way),so we are not reminded of how powerful the contextual and constancy effects really are.

Occasionally, however, something happens to bring the point home clearly. This happened during an important FTC hearing against the makers of Wonder Bread. One of the key issues in the trial was whether Wonder Bread had the right to its claim "Builds Strong Bodies Twelve Ways." This claim was based on the nutrients in the flour (the FTC's charge of deception was based on the fact that all other enriched white breads also used this flour, so Wonder Bread's ad could mislead consumers into thinking that it offered something other brands did not).

In examining consumer research, an interesting sidelight emerged: many consumers reported that they especially liked the fact that it built strong bodies *eight* ways. In checking back, it was found that old ads used to make the claim as "eight ways" because that was the number of nutrients that had been discovered as beneficial at that time. When new nutrients were discovered, the claim had been changed to "twelve ways," and had been run for many years. Despite the many years of hearing the 12-way commercials, liking the brand, and using the bread, these older consumers continued to perceive the claim as "building strong bodies eight ways"! As we will discuss shortly, this is an instance in which these consumers' long-term memories (LTM's) were taking over the perceptual process early, and thus processing the actual stimulus from Wonder Bread in a quite incomplete manner.

The Concept of Perceptual Set

In a different sphere of work, Gestalt scientists investigated the role that perception plays in solving problems, and thereby opened a vast new area of study that has significant implications for consumers and marketers. In this area, they discovered the importance of the "perceptual set," which is defined in the following research report:[3]

Monkey See, Monkey Do?

One of the most influential of the Gestaltists, Wolfgang Kohler, conducted studies of perception while trapped on the Canary Islands by a British blockade during World War I. A a typical study would confront an ape named Sultan with a problem, such as how to obtain a basket of fruit hanging from the top of the cage. Various tools would be available, but only one would allow him to be successful. Observation of Sultan's actions clearly showed that *his perception of the situation was a key to his solving the problem or not.* If he were trying unsuccessful methods, he would have to *reorganize* his perceived situation—to shift his figure-ground relations—to see the answer. In one study, after collapsing against the walls of the cage to rest from his energetic failures trying to bash the fruit down with various sticks, Sultan happened to glance at a box on the floor. After a short pause (during which the box moved from background to figure in his perceptions), he jumped up, moved the box under the fruit, and easily reached his goal.

Across the series of studies Kohler discovered that the apes found it difficult to change their perceptions of a problem situation. These "fixed" perceptions hindered problem solving. This led to the concept of **perceptual set**, which is defined as a *readiness to perceive or act in particular ways in a situation.* After Sultan had learned about the boxes, for example, he was able to use this "set" the next time he confronted a problem to structure his figure-ground relations, find the boxes rapidly and solve the problem quickly. When the problem required a different solution from piling the boxes, however, his "set" interfered with a solution, and Sultan had a hard time shifting away from it.

Applications of Gestalt Principles in Marketing

The Gestalt principles of perceptual organization have many implications for marketing practice. Marketers have long been aware of these principles and have used them in many areas of the marketing mix. For example,

Physical Design

Many products are designed with a view toward the perception of their forms. Clothing is often designed to have the wearer be perceived as taller, wider, or slimmer. The chrome and painting of autos and boats often provide perceptions of speed. Signs are created to suggest movement. Displays are designed to direct the consumer's eye to the product.

Problems with Perceptual Sets—Maxim Is "Too Much"

The concept of perceptual set relates to consumers' expectations about where to shop, what to buy, and how to use products. This may have special implications for innovations, when their use may deviate from existing sets consumers hold: General Foods discovered this when it created "freeze-dried" Maxim coffee. In blind taste tests consumers preferred it by 56 percent to 44 percent over Instant Maxwell House, which was very successful in

Notice the Gestalt principles in this award-winning advertising.

the marketplace. The firm's expectations for success were high. When it was introduced, however, Maxim did not live up to the firm's expectations, in large part because of consumers' perceptual sets at the time. Since Maxim was produced in a much stronger "concentrated" form, consumers were informed that they should put less than a teaspoonful into a cup. Because of their perceptual sets for preparing instant coffees, however, many triers of the brand continued to perceive the problem as they always had and put in the amount they normally used. The resulting cup was much too strong for their tastes, and repeat sales suffered. To break this perceptual set, GF had to address it in advertising and through such programs as placing small plastic measuring spoons on the Maxim bottles![4]

PERCEPTUAL CATEGORIZATION

Perceptual categorization is the process we go through to translate sensory inputs into a mental "identification" of a particular stimulus. At a simple level, we might categorize a line or a color. At more complex levels we might categorize stores (Macy's), products (a car), brands (Tylenol), and so on. This process works extremely rapidly, and usually at the unconscious level. When we've encountered the external stimulus previously and have a strong category for it in long-term memory (LTM), the process is similar to "recognizing" the stimulus pattern and calling forth the right node from LTM. When we've not encountered this particular external stimulus before, however, the categorization process must rely on using "cues" from the stimulus to infer or "figure out" which identity seems right for it.

Categorization's Importance in Consumer Behavior

This process is extremely important in consumer behavior. The way in which we initially categorize a stimulus will affect how interested we'll be in it, what we'll expect from it, whether we'll evaluate it positively or negatively, and so forth. Thus there are direct implications for how consumers evaluate products and decide what to buy.

In most cases, a consumer's categorization of a new brand is a private event that goes unnoticed by the rest of the world. Occasionally, however, enough consumers miscategorize a brand to reveal an underlying problem with the marketing mix. The following cases demonstrate instances when consumers are (1) *unable* to categorize a new offering, (2) *unwilling* to change their categorization of a brand offering, and (3) *misled* into miscategorizing the new offer, with negative outcomes as a result.

What You See Is What You Get!

"Generic" food products originated in France in 1976 and became a phenomenal success in the United States, until dropping in popularity in recent years. Retailers who sell them find them to be quite profitable because their costs are lower. Consumers who buy them pay 30 to 40 percent less than for major advertised brands and about 20 percent less than for a supermarket's private labels. Consumer studies showed, however, that the group *most* expected to buy generics—those on low incomes for whom the savings are most substantial—tended not to be purchasing these items. Further investigation revealed one major reason: a significant proportion of low-income persons are "functionally illiterate" and cannot read well enough to perform everyday shopping tasks. Because generic products were wrapped in plain labels, these persons *could not categorize* the product in the can or box. Since they didn't know whether the generic can would contain peas or beets, these shoppers stayed with the brands having pictures on the contents of the package.[5]

"Gerber Is For . . ."

Gerber Products, which claims about 70 percent of the baby food market, was interested in expanding its base into the teenage consumer group as well. "We know there are closet users out there in the 15–22 age bracket," said one Gerber executive. The firm launched a major promotional campaign to teens with the theme: "The secret's out. Gerber isn't just for babies!" Teen consumers thought otherwise, however, and wouldn't bite. Evidently,

Notice the process required to correctly categorize these generic products.

the name "Gerber" was a strong cue to the LTM category "baby food." Millions of teens would not change this perceptual categorization and purchase a product perceived to be in this category.[6]

Sunlight's Not Right

In launching its new Sunlight brand of dishwashing liquid, Lever Bros. designed a major product sampling campaign in large metropolitan areas. Sample plastic bottles were delivered by mail. The brand was attractively packaged in a bright yellow bottle, with a picture of a sun and lemon prominent on the label (highlighting its new feature of lemon juice as an ingredient). When sampling began in Baltimore, however, a totally unexpected development occurred—local medical facilities and the Poison Control Center reported receiving many frantic phone calls from frightened consumers who had drunk the contents of the bottle before realizing that they had miscategorized it as a new lemon drink! Just as this news made its way into the national press, a similar outbreak was reported in Tampa Bay, the second area to receive the mail samples. No deaths or serious injuries were reported, but the phenomenon was widespread. When pressed for a reaction, a company person defended the package, pointing out that it clearly stated that this was a dishwashing liquid. He also indicated that the company did not make a practice of marketing brands through the poison control centers![7]

As the preceding examples show, perceptual categorizations lead to later expectations. However, categorizations are themselves strongly influenced by the prior expectations that a consumer brings from LTM. These can combine into a **schema** that acts to guide the overall perceptual process. There are many theories about schemas, but in general, we can define a schema as *a cognitive structure that represents a person's knowledge about a given object or behavior.*[8] One good way to think of a schema is to recall our network diagram of LTM that we examined in Chapter 5 (Figure 5-4). A schema would consist of those particular beliefs (nodes) that are most likely to be brought into STM when a consumer begins to think about a topic. When a schema is strong—as when we know a lot about a topic, or have engaged in a particular act many times before—it can take over to guide our perceptual processes and physical activities.

One form of schema, for example, is a script, or an organized sequence of

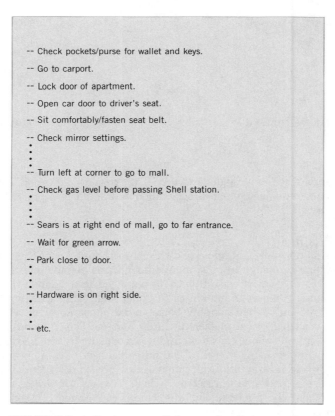

FIGURE 9-3 **A Script-type Schema for Going to the Store**

behavioral events, much like a movie script or cartoon series. Figure 9-3 summarizes some familiar steps in this type of script. To see just how powerful these are, close your eyes and imagine going to your local Sears (or other familiar store) for a particular purchase. Notice how we visualize so easily, and how the process is so strongly structured! This indicates the potential power that LTM has to guide our categorization processes. Of course, not all categorization occurs from LTM: the stimuli being categorized ought to play a strong role as well! Let's look briefly at how the process works.

Understanding the Categorization Process

Perceptual categorization has received a great deal of attention from psychologists. The classic view of the categorization process, developed by Jerome Bruner, consists of four states:

- *Stage 1: Primitive categorization.* This simply reflects that a particular form of stimulus (a sound, an object, etc.) is in the environment.
- *Stage 2: Cue search.* This stage begins a more careful examination of the stimulus for cues that will help to identify what type of sound or object the stimulus is. When we're already quite familiar with it, this stage may lead easily to a correct recognition. When we're not, this stage is open to using any available cues.
- *Stage 3: Confirmation check.* Once we've arrived at a tentative categorization, our cue search changes. Now we use our knowledge from that category's node in LTM to suggest what other cues ought to be present. As we find such cues, our confidence increases.
- *Stage 4: Confirmation completion.* Now that the categorization is almost complete, we are not very open to additional cues that suggest we're wrong. In a sense, a perceptual set has taken over, and a deviant cue must be very strong for us to recognize it as such.[9]

In recent years consumer researchers have also begun to focus on categorization. It is now clear that there are different types of categorization processes and that different consumers will at times use different processes. (For our purposes in this text, Bruner's model is sufficient, but if you would like to read more about this complex but interesting topic, you may wish to begin with the readings in Note 10.) Beyond the process itself, consumer researchers are interested in the effects of categorizations on what consumers think and do. The existence of these effects means that marketers are able to *influence* consumer behavior by influencing how consumers categorize brands and stores, and what further *inferences* they make about them. The following section examines this interesting topic.

Last night, I performed for the Metropolitan Ballet.

"I was just about to lift my prima ballerina up in triumph when I noticed she didn't look so good. The varnish I used wasn't trapping to the photo like it should. It was passable. But it wasn't perfect. And nothing leaves my press until it's absolutely perfect.

I knew what I had to do. And I did it. Lucky for my ballerina I'm quick on my feet."

If you want it perfect, you want W.E. Andrews. We can handle any sheet fed, half web or full web job. 140 South Road, Bedford, MA 01730, (617) 275-0720/ 1-800-343-4061. In Connecticut, 206 Murphy Road, Hartford, CT 06114, (203) 527-5570.

W. E. Andrews Co., Inc.

One ad's clever use of categorization to gain interest and readership.

PERCEPTION AND CONSUMER INFERENCES

The Concept of Perceptual Inference

Once a stimulus has been categorized, the issue turns to further attention we'll give to that stimulus. Most objects we perceive in our environment will not receive much further attention from us, and the perceptual episodes for these uninvolving objects simply end. For example, think of all the occasions we are driving along, sense a new object, categorize it as a car, and then turn our attention back to the highway.

When we're *interested* in an object, however, we're very likely to go on to make further interpretations about it. These interpretations are termed **inferences**. An inference is defined as *a belief that we develop based on other information* (e.g., if a person's name is Sue, the person is likely to be a girl; if a product has a high price, it is likely to be higher quality). Not all inferences will be correct, though we'd like them to be. In a strict sense, all our thought processes require inferences. Here, however, we'll focus on perceptual inferences that stem directly from stimulus cues.

Again, the incredible speed of our CIP system means that many of these inferences will be made at an unconscious level—we can view these as "subtle" inferences, since consumers may not be aware that they've made them. Other perceptual inferences will be at the conscious level, however, and we will know we're making them (we'll term these "conscious inferences").

Illustrating the Concept of Perceptual Inference

Returning to our car example, let's assume that we've taken an interest in a car that's on display as we drive by and decide to pay further attention to it. In this case we're almost certain to begin to make inferences about it. Conscious inferences might include whether it's a new or old model, expensive or not, and a domestic or foreign make. More subtle inferences might include estimates of whether it is prestigious or not, or stylish or not. These inferences might then contribute to a further conscious inference that it is "my kind of car" or not. Perceptual inferences thus play a major role in directing consumer behavior. Because they stem from consumers' processing of cues from the stimulus, inferences can be encouraged or discouraged by marketing mix decisions.

Sensory Cues and Consumer Inferences

In an earlier discussion of sensory cues, we stressed their role in triggering sensory receptors, thus starting the perceptual process. However, sensory cues can also be important in leading to consumer inferences about what characteristics products are likely to have, and how much we'll like them. The following cases illustrate some of the many ways in which sensory cues work on inferences.

Sight: A Cheery Blue

Many years ago, Procter & Gamble introduced Cheer as a new product that was "good for tough-job washing." Consumers apparently perceived it to be just another detergent, however, and it was not particularly successful. Then P&G changed its color, made it into a blue powder, and continued its promotion as a "tough" detergent. This color change altered consumer perceptions of the brand. Apparently, the blue color allowed inferences that this detergent was capable of powerful cleaning. Cheer became a major national success.[11]

Sounds Abound

Consumers often use sound as a cue to make inferences about the quality of particular products. In motorcycles and lawn mowers, for example, a loud engine may be believed to be more powerful than a quiet one. Marketers who try to sell well-muffled models that purr may find their brands spurned by most of the market. On the other hand, for other purposes quiet is perceived as indicating better quality. For example, a quiet car inside is perceived to be better built and more luxurious than a noisier one. Consumer inferences about sound are taken into account within marketing programs. For example, many salespersons in stereo stores set controls heavy on bass, as they believe that consumers infer this to be a higher quality sound.

Touch: Which Tastes Better?

Many consumers use touch to allow inferences about the freshness of foods, including fruits and bakery products. For packaged goods, however, the wrapping can also contribute to the perception of freshness. For example, in one study, identical potato chips—all very fresh—were placed in two types of bags, an easy-to-open wax-coated paper bag and the hard-to-open polyvinyl bag. Supermarket shoppers were asked to take a bag, open it, and taste the product. Most consumers had real difficulty opening the polyvinyl bags—reactions included biting the bags, yanking them apart and spilling the contents on the floor, and giving up in despair. Even though the contents of the bags had identical tastes (this was established in a separate taste study), shoppers overwhelmingly reported that they preferred the chips in the polyvinyl packages. These chips were perceived as being both "crispier" and "tastier." When asked about which package they preferred, 93 percent of the shoppers indicated the polyvinyl bag, despite the difficulty in opening it.

An interesting question emerges from this study: Did consumers perceive a taste difference because (1) they inferred that a difficult-to-open package contains better contents, or (2) they inferred that it protects its contents better, or (3) they knew that polyvinyl bags offer longer shelf life to products and inferred that these bags had been on the shelf a long enough time for their contents to have been affected? In any of these cases, of course, an inference to the current taste and crispiness still had to be made and consumers showed themselves quite willing to make this perceptual inference.[12]

Smell: The Nose Knows Hose

A classic study of how sensory cues can affect inferences of product quality was conducted over 50 years ago by a professor and students at Colgate University. In the study 250 women were asked which of four pairs of hosiery was highest in quality and why they thought so. In reality, the hosiery was from the same manufacturer and was selected to be as identical as possible. The only difference was that a faint scent had been added to three of the four pairs—the intensity of this scent was controlled to be at the same level as the normal scent of the fourth pair, which arose from the manufacturing process. Of the three scents, one was a fruity type, one a sachet, and one a narcissus. In making their judgments, only 6 of the 250 housewives mentioned noticing the scent differences. After making their choice as to the highest quality, they explained that their choices were based on such product attributes as texture, weave, durability, shine, and weight.

But which hose did the women choose? Given the form of this study, if scent did not have an effect, we would expect that each pair should randomly receive 25 percent of the choices. In reality, however, the "natural" hose received only 8 percent of the choices, while the narcissus hose was favored in 50 percent of them. Thus it is clear that the sensory cues did affect quality inferences made by these consumers, even though the consumers were not aware of the correct reason for their judgments. (As a student of consumer behavior, you may find this postscript to the study of personal interest: the study was originally planned for a larger sample, but it had to be suspended when a housewife became suspicious that the interviewer was not trying to sell his product and suspected a potential robbery. She called the police, and their investigative report was featured in the Utica city newspaper. This report explained the nature of the study and the use of the scents.)[13]

THE MARKETING MIX AND CONSUMERS' PERCEPTUAL INFERENCES

Our discussions to this point make it clear that consumers are engaging in inferential processes on a very regular basis. Within this section we'll briefly examine implications for marketing decision makers.

Product Decisions and Consumer Inferences

Because products and packages are complex, tangible stimuli (that is, they can be sensed with our sensory systems), virtually all decisions on a product's physical characteristics can affect consumers' perceptual inferences. We've already noted examples in which a product's color, scent, noise, and feel have impacted. Here we'll examine how brand names and symbols can also stimulate perceptual inferences.

Names Can Be Seductive

In general, a **brand name** offers an opportunity to gain ground in consumers' minds by suggesting special qualities or characteristics of the product or its owner. Consider, for example, what inferences are sparked in your mind by such names as "Senchal" perfume, "Craftsman" tools, "Ultra-Brite" toothpaste, "Sunkist" fruits, and "Whirlpool" washers. As one marketer explained, "Naming is a form of seduction." One paint firm believes this. Its color "Ivory" was in twentieth place in sales when the name was changed to "Oriental Silk"—two years later it had risen to sixth place in sales.[14]

The Outbreak of Ayds

Brand names can also cause problems, however, when consumers draw erroneous or negative inferences from them. Nissan auto sales dropped sharply in the late 1980s, in part due to consumer inferences about certain models. As its marketing vice president explained, research showed "people thought Maxima was a checking account. They thought Pulsar was a watch." For the 1990s, Nissan is hoping that its Infiniti brand name will yield inferences of luxury and quality.

At least consumers weren't laughing at Nissan, as they were in the Georgia test market of LAX beer from Anheuser-Busch. "The company should have known consumers would put an "X" in front of the name!" snickered one stock market analyst.

Then there was the plight of Ayds dietetic candy, which found its sales sinking as the AIDS health epidemic continued to spread. The firm didn't want to lose the long-term benefits from its successful brand name, but knew that consumers' inferences were hurting sales. The solution: try a compromise name, "Diet Ayds," to see if that would be enough different (meanwhile the name "Aydslim" began testing in a foreign market).[15]

It's All in the Family

Family branding is another strategy firms often use to stimulate specific perceptual inferences by consumers. Here a firm such as General Electric or Campbell will give its established name to a new product entry. The expectation is that consumers will use the firm's name in their categorization process, thus inferences such as "tested," "high quality," and "dependable" are more likely to be made.

Family branding is thus a means for capturing further efficiency from a well-developed brand name in the marketplace. This strategy can backfire, however, when the perceptual inferences required of consumers seem to cross natural categories. When this happens, consumers may find the inferences to be *contradictory* and react negatively. Consider, for example, these new products and what perceptual inferences come to mind when you consider them:

- Listerol, a household cleaner from Listerine.
- Sara Lee Chicken & Noodles au Gratin.
- Arm & Hammer Antiperspirant.

All these were new product entries that failed in the consumer marketplace.[16]

Winter Wonders?

The Toro Corporation was very pleased with engineering developments that permitted the production of a new lightweight but efficient snow thrower. To highlight its lightweight feature, Toro named it the Snow Pup. When sales were far below expectations, consumer research was undertaken to discover why. The research indicated that the name Snow Pup had to go—consumers were inferring that the product lacked power and was not durable. When the name was changed, Snowmaster sales increased significantly.[17]

In a similar vein, consider the remarkable success story of the Matex Corp. and its product, Thixo-Tex. Chances are that you can't recall this name, since it was changed to one that's more memorable and easy to categorize, having a symbol with positive perceptual inferences. Thixo-Tex was a superior rustproofing compound that bonded itself to metal and worked very well on automobiles. Prior to its name change, retail sales were about $2 million per year. When the name change was tested in radio ads in Buffalo (supposedly the rusty car capital of the world), sales increased 250 percent. When a trade character was created to go along with the name change, sales took off on a nearly vertical climb.

Four years later sales were at $100 million per year! The name and the symbol (and their accompanying consumer perceptual inferences) were key elements in this success story. (The new name, character, and recent developments are described in Note 18.)

Place Decisions and Consumer Inferences

Consumer inferences in this area pertain primarily to the retail store. Retailers are increasingly sensitive to the various cues that consumers encounter while shopping. This concern extends across store layout, displays, merchandise, salespersons, and service. In general, the physical considerations fall within a topic known as **atmospherics**. Atmospherics leads to the creation of a planned environment in which cues are used by a marketer to stimulate particular perceptions and behaviors on the part of consumers.

Perceptual Inferences of the "Bargain Hunters"

From the consumer's point of view, a retail store presents many individual stimulus cues from which perceptual inferences can be made. Experienced retailers are aware of many of these types of inferences and adjust their environments accordingly. Sometimes, however, the consumer inferences are not immediately obvious. Once, for example, a famous Harvard professor of decision sciences was retained by a retailer to suggest ways to improve sales efficiency in its store. When he arrived, he became especially concerned with the women's blouse subdepartment in the "bargain basement." This area seemed to be extremely inefficient. Blouses were strewn about in a jumble and shoppers wasted many minutes attempting to find their correct size. Upon mentioning this to management, the professor was invited to return the next morning to observe the entire process from scratch. He noted that prior to the store opening hour, employees neatly arranged all the blouses by size. Then, however, they threw them on the counter and thoroughly mixed them up! The first shoppers had to spend more time than usual to locate their correct size. This created a small crowd of women searching for the correct sizes in a style they liked. This small crowd, in turn, seemed to serve as a magnet for other shoppers, who seemed to be inferring that special blouse bargains were available since so many other shoppers had already been attracted to this area.[19]

Advertising Decisions and Consumer Inferences

Because advertising is a communication form, the issue of which perceptual inferences consumers are led to make is crucial to an ad's success or failure. Perceptual inferences have substantial impacts on how much *attention* is paid to an ad, and what types of *thoughts* might be stimulated. We should, however, recognize that advertisements are complex stimuli and that the perceptual process for them can easily extend over a 30- to 60-second time period. During this time the precise stimulus being perceived will shift as the consumer proceeds further into the ad. Perceptual inferences will shift as well, and will continue as long as attention is being paid to the ad.[20]

Size and Subtle Inferences: "The Giant and the Sprout"

Subtle perceptual inferences are often called forth by the detailed stimuli contained within ads. The following case provides a good example. The Jolly Green Giant is one of the most successful characters in advertising history. In his early years his fame led his firm to change its name from the Minnesota Valley Canning & Packing Co. to the Green Giant Company. At his peak, a national poll showed that more people could correctly identify him than they could the president of the United States. After some years, however, consumers began to pay less attention to ads featuring him doing his same "stand up and smile" routine, and the firm began to look for new ad strategies.

Consumer research revealed, as expected, that viewers enjoyed the Giant's "Ho-ho-ho" at the end of each commercial. However, consumers were very sensitive to how the Green Giant acted within the commercial—this sensitivity was due to perceptual inferences they were making beyond the actual scenes. For example, if ads showed the Giant walking around his valley, consumers reacted negatively—it seems that the thought of his walking raised images of happy little helpers and crops being stepped on by giant green feet. When close-up views of the Giant's face were used, consumers also reacted negatively, indicating that he was no longer friendly—it seems that a giant is only jolly if he is far away from us! As a result of these consumer inferences, the ad agency worked to develop a new character who provided most of the benefits of the Giant, but didn't pose these special problems. Finally, the "Little Green Sprout" was born. When he was introduced, special cues were given so that consumers' *categorizations* would be correct but their *inferences* would not be negative. Specifically, the Sprout's name and song clearly indicated a small size ("not very big, about the size of a twig") but a direct relationship to the Jolly Green Giant himself ("that's how Jolly Green Giants start out").[21]

Bush League Brushbacks?

We are all aware that U.S. presidential politics is a high-stakes, "hardball" affair. We may not be aware, however, of some of the tricks that are used to influence voters' perceptual inferences in subtle ways. During the early stages of the 1988 campaign, for example, George Bush had been trounced by Senator Robert Dole in the Iowa primary election and desperately needed to win in New Hampshire if he was to capture the Republican party's nomination. His key TV commercial—one that attacked Senator Dole for "straddling" on the big issues—was credited by both observers and Dole advisors as turning the tide away from Dole and toward Bush. An interview with the video editing artist who "touched up" the commercial gives us some insights:

■ Why did Senator Dole look so strange in this commercial? "I do believe we might have flipped his photo around," laughed the editor, "It's nothing one would notice, but the senator's hair is parted on the wrong side and his face looks awkward."

■ Why did Mr. Bush look so good? One reason was the thin "halo" of light that appeared around his head in each photo of him.

■ In other ads, similar techniques were used. Mr. Bush's photos were always outlined in blue, Mr. Dole's in black. Any people in Mr. Bush's background were colorfully dressed (Mr. Dole's fans were washed out). Enthusiastic cheers from a soundtrack were added to crowd scenes for Mr. Bush (in one slip-up, the camera showed the audience with all mouths closed while the cheers rang on). Finally, each time a Dole position was typed on the screen, it would be underlined in red ("hot-tempered"), while the Bush positions were underlined in a calm, cool blue.

This type of editing wasn't just used for Mr. Bush, of course. According to the editor, "Political commercials are now filled with special effects . . . what we do one night in an editing room in New York can have such a big effect one day later."[22]

Price Decisions and Consumer Inferences

The pricing area presents us with an interesting set of issues. First, as compared to product, place, and promotion cues, price is usually a much simpler stimulus cue. Because of this, researchers have a more manageable task in attempting to study perceptual inferences consumers make in response to price cues. Second, as compared to all the other marketing mix areas, price would seem to represent a cost rather than a benefit to consumers—price measures what we must *give up* in a transaction to receive the benefits we desire. If price is only a cost, though, what kinds of perceptual inferences would it stimulate? The brief discussions that follow explain some of these:

"You Get What You Pay For!"

If we think briefly about this common phrase, we'll see that consumers don't always view price as only a cost. Instead, we also can view price as an "extrinsic" or external cue that helps us judge the quality of the product itself. This **perceived quality inference** may be grounded in reality. It might, for example, stem from a recognition that higher quality often requires higher production costs, which in turn produce higher prices. It might also stem from elements of perceived status or prestige, or even from inferences that the higher prices represent a scarcity of the good.

Considerable consumer research has been conducted on this type of inference. In general, this research has shown that consumers *do* infer product quality from the price charged for the product. They are more likely to rely on the price cue when other information to help with the quality inference is not available and when they have less personal experience with the product itself. While further research remains to be done, we can conclude at this point that the price-quality perceived inference is active in the consumer marketplace.[23]

How Good Is It?

In practice, the perceived quality inference can sometimes lead to unexpected results. A store's prices can be perceived as being "too low," and consumer demand for a product may actually decrease because it is perceived as lacking in desired quality. In one case, for example, a discount chain received a large shipment from the Orient of teen jewelry costing a few cents per unit. It was shipped to its stores and priced at 19 cents per unit, allowing a large percentage profit on each sale. However, the jewelry received little interest from shoppers. At this point an experienced retailing executive proposed that prices be raised dramatically. A few weeks later, the new promotional plan went out from headquarters, repricing these items at 59 cents per unit, and featuring this price with in-store posters. Sales picked up immediately, and the shipment sold out in just a short time!

Reference Pricing and Price Lining

In many cases consumers are not entirely confident about what price to expect and are quite willing to rely on other external cues to help with this judgment.[24] Thus many retailers use **reference prices**. For example, sales are often announced with both a reference price and the special sales price ("Regularly $29.95, now $18.95!"). The reference price provides a "normal" price for consumers and encourages perceptual inferences of special savings. Reference prices are also used by some outlets to project an image of more value for the money, especially when the product is not a well-known brand ("Compare to products costing $50, here priced at only $34.95!"). In many instances reference prices do help consumers accurately perceive special price savings. However, reference prices can be used for unscrupulous purposes as well. In these cases, reference prices are artificially inflated in order to deceive consumers as to the actual value of the offering.

Price lining is a retail practice stemming from consumers' price expectations. Here the seller will stock several grades of a good, then price each at the top of the "line" that different consumers expect (or are willing) to pay for that good. For example, let's assume that Kathryn Alexander comes to a store expecting to pay about $25 for a gift item. How can the retailer increase profits? Perhaps by pricing the item at $28, which Kathryn may still infer is within the grade level she desires and is not so distant from her expected price that she reacts negatively. In this case, the retailer might be better off to establish the price lines at $18 (if Kathryn will see this as being below the grade she desires for her gift) and $28 than at the original $15 and $25. To plan this with precision, of course, consumer research may be necessary.

"Why Do So Many Prices End in '9'?"

This question refers to *odd-even pricing practices* that lead to most prices ending in either a "9" or a "5." No one knows exactly how this custom has arisen. Some speculations are interesting, however:

- *Speculation 1.* It leads to consumer inferences that the product costs less than it actually does. Consumers' perceptions focus on the larger-digit positions, so the ending number (which represents pennies) gets rounded down. Since it is the larger-digit positions that are recalled accurately, a good priced at $28.59 will be recalled as being "about $28" rather than "about $29."
- *Speculation 2.* The circles in double nines ("99") attract attention to the object.
- *Speculation 3.* Odd endings force the store to give the consumer change, and consumers like to receive change when they check out.
- *Speculation 4.* Discount stores use odd pricing because it connotes savings, but prestige or fashion retailers use even pricing because it connotes status.[25]

What do you think?

Summary: The Marketing Mix and Consumers' Inferences

Within this section we have examined many detailed examples of marketing applications within each of the 4 P's. Before closing, however, we should note that an especially powerful treatment occurs when a marketer is able to *coordinate* each of the elements of the marketing mix to work together to influence consumer inferences. For example, Ivory Soap's purity positioning is conveyed by the *product's* color, brand name, the fancy lettering but simple packaging, and the *promotional* slogan of "99 and 44/100% pure" and the use of the Ivory girl in advertising. Notice also that the Ivory girl wears no makeup, stands by a white picket fence in a pastoral setting, rides a 3-speed girls' bicycle, and wears a simple white shirt and jeans. (Readers wishing to pursue this issue of image management for a strategic brand concept should consult Note 26 for this chapter, located at the back of this book.)[26]

In closing this section, we should also note that a considerable amount of advanced consumer research has recently been undertaken to more closely assess the precise nature of how consumers make inferences and how these inferences affect memory, judgments, and purchase decisions (see Note 27 for citations). We will be returning to those topics in upcoming chapters. At this point, however, let us turn to briefly consider how consumers' perceptual inferences can raise public policy difficulties.

PUBLIC POLICY AND CONSUMERS' PERCEPTUAL INFERENCES

In its role as regulator of the setting for transactions between marketers and consumers, public policy frequently must deal with perceptual inferences. Usually these involve sales or advertising stimuli that tend to lead to mistaken inferences on the part of a reasonable number of consumers. In bait and switch advertising (in which the retailer does not intend to sell the advertised item), for example, consumers are likely to infer that the product is available for sale. Because these inferences can be expected, marketers are prohibited from engaging in this practice. Policymakers also believe that consumers infer that a product is safe if no warning to the contrary appears—when a product does have health or safety hazards, then, warnings of these are required. In the area of deceptive advertising, it is again a concern with mistaken inferences by consumers that leads to regulatory actions.

Price-Quality Associations

As we've seen, consumers display a tendency to use price as a cue to infer product quality. If prices are in fact based on quality levels, this inference can be helpful to consumers. If prices are not based on quality levels, however, this inference might not only mislead a consumer on a particular purchase, but send signals to marketers that they should increase prices to raise profits. A key question emerges: *to what extent are prices and quality levels correlated?*

Do We Get What We Pay For?

In a broader sense, consumers' tendency to infer product quality from price reflects an implicit belief that there is a 1:1 relationship between price and quality. That is, that we really do "get what we pay for." Considerable research has been conducted on this objective price-quality relationship, to see how *actual prices* correlate with *actual product quality* within our consumer economy.

With a typical study, a neutral product rating service such as *Consumer Reports* magazine is used to provide both quality ratings and list prices for products. In each product class, the various brands will be ranked by quality level and again by price level. The two rankings will then be correlated. If prices and quality match on a 1:1 basis, a correlation of +1.0 will result. If there is no systematic relationship between quality and price, correlations will be low, around the 0.0 level.

Research to date in this area has been very controversial. To calculate a correlation, for example, we must be able to agree on how to measure "quality." Also, our measure of quality should pertain to everyone, so that different consumer tastes will not be represented in the measure. Pricing is also something of a problem, since these correlations do not take into account special sale prices or bargaining—list prices are typically used in these studies.

The results of the research, however, are quite interesting. One study, for example, covered 135 different product categories, calculating a price-quality correlation in each category. The average correlation for all the products was only +0.26. The researcher also found a wide range of correlations—from +0.90 (10-speed touring bikes) to −0.66 (for antenna rotators). In the antenna class, those models ranked best in product quality averaged about $50 each, while those ranked worst in product quality averaged $70, with a systematically negative relationship across the models!

The overall findings of the study indicated that just over half of all products (51 percent) showed a *positive* price-quality correlation: here consumers can expect to get more for their money as they pay higher prices. Another one-third (35 percent) of the products showed *no particular pattern* of prices and quality levels—some products with higher prices were good, but so were some products with lower prices. Finally, 14 percent of the products—about one of every seven product classes—were found to have a *negative* price-quality pattern: in these cases, as consumers pay more, they're likely to get less.[28]

This study's findings are typical of the results emerging from this type of analysis over recent years. Within any one product category, however, the results are not very stable—prices and quality might be significantly related one year, but not the next. For these reasons, consumer economists have long argued that more objective quality information should be made available to consumers in a timely fashion. As you may know, the government agencies and some marketers have been active in attempting to provide such information. We'll return again to the topic of consumer information provision in Chapter 18.

Marketing and the Law: Imitation Versus Infringement

To this point in our discussion we have tended to ignore the *competitive aspect* of the marketing-consumer environment. In fact, however, competition plays an extremely important role in what consumers perceive about the marketplace and options in it. One interesting public policy problem in this regard concerns the law toward trademark protection. Once a marketer has legally gained the right to use a brand name to consumers, what actions can competitors employ and still be within the boundaries of the law? Within this area, consumers' perceptual processes of categorization and inference often become key issues in disputes:

Trademark Infringement: "Tide" Versus "Tibe"

Consumers' perceptual processes are usually the target of competitors who enter a market with imitations of successful brands. Confused consumer inferences might then shift sales and profits from the established brand to the imitator. In these instances the successful brand has a right to sue for trademark infringement and to try legally to recover monetary damages to its sales and reputation. In recent years many cases have been brought in this

An exhibit used in a recent case to illustrate possible consumer confusion.

area. For example, how would you vote in each of the following trademark infringement cases, in favor of the original brand (listed first) or the new competitor (listed second)?

Case 1: Pampers versus Rumpers diapers?
Case 2: Vantage versus Advance cigarettes?
Case 3: Opici wine versus Amici wine?
Case 4: Duet bottled cocktails versus Duvet brandy?
Case 5: McDonald's hamburgers versus McBagel restaurant?
Case 6: McDonald's hamburgers versus McSleep Inns?
Case 7: Jordache jeans versus Lardashe jeans?

If you're interested in how the cases came out, you may wish to turn to Note 29.

Sometimes these cases result from honest mistakes rather than deliberate infringement, and often there are good arguments on both sides of the issue. In many of these cases, advanced consumer research can be used to study the perceptual inferences made by consumers with respect to these products and can contribute to a wise decision in the case.

In some cases, however, the infringement strategy is obviously deliberate and can cause serious difficulties. Recently, for example, P&G filed suit to seize more than 100 tons of detergent products made in Singapore—the brand names used included Tibe, Tike, Tile, and Tipe. None of the copycat detergents was sold in Singapore or the United States—all were exported to Arab countries. This fact raised further legal problems for P&G and meant that it may not win the case.[30]

 SUMMARY

Three Activities in Consumer Perception

In our framework for perceptual processes, sensation and attention (the topics of our previous chapter) are followed by *perceptual interpretation.* Here the consumer identifies the meaning of a stimulus. Three key activities are involved in perceptual interpretation: (1) organization, (2) categorization, and (3) inference making.

Perceptual Organization

The chapter's first section examined *perceptual organization.* Here we discussed *Gestalt theory,* which holds that people perceive entire objects (not just individual parts)—that we strive for good Gestalts or perceptions that are simple, complete, and meaningful. The major Gestalt principles of organization are figure and ground, proximity, similarity, continuation, common fate, closure, and symmetry. We also discussed how *context* and *perceptual constancy* affect consumers' perceptions.

Perceptual Categorization

The second section turned to *categorization,* which is the process of *identifying* a stimulus. Here we are interested in how a stimulus is recognized and tentatively classified from our LTM. Categorization will strongly influence our further CIP processes (e.g., interest in a stimulus and positive or negative evaluation of it). Expectations (such as in "shopping scripts") also play an important role in categorization. Researchers are now examining several approaches consumers may use.

Perception and Consumer Inferences

Our third section of the chapter discussed *perceptual inferences.* These are beliefs we form based on other information, such as stimulus properties. Since all thinking involves some form of inferences, this topic is crucial. Product, place, promotion, and price-related consumer inferences were all examined.

Public Policy and Consumers' Perceptual Inferences

The final section of the chapter turned to some broader issues such as whether price-quality inferences are warranted in the actual consumer marketplace and what problems can crop up with product imitations.

KEY TERMS

perceptual organization	script
perceptual categorization	inferences
perceptual inference	brand name
Gestalt school	family branding
perceptual context	atmospherics
perceptual constancy	perceived quality inference
perceptual set	reference prices
schema	price lining

REVIEW QUESTIONS AND EXPERIENTIAL EXERCISES

[E = Application extension or experiential exercise]

1. What three factors influence how consumers attach meaning to a particular stimulus? Explain. How can marketers apply these factors to their activities?

2. Describe the principles that determine whether or not a specific perception will qualify as a "good Gestalt."

3. Explain figure and ground. What are the implications for marketers?

4. Provide examples of how a "perceptual set" may work as an advantage and as a disadvantage for marketers.

5. Describe briefly, giving examples:
   a. A schema
   b. A shopping script

6. What is an inference? How are subtle inferences different from conscious ones?

[E] 7. Provide examples (different from those in the text) of how consumers form quality inferences based on
   a. Sound   c. Smell
   b. Touch   d. Color

[E] 8. How can "reference pricing" either help or mislead consumers?

[E] 9. What are some implications for marketers and public policymakers of a study that finds the price-quality relationship in a product class is low or negative?

[E] 10. Give examples of current products using a family branding strategy well. Suggest three further brands you think should try this strategy for a new product (that is, you suggest the product and the name).

[E] 11. Choose a local retailer with which you are familiar. Discuss the implications of consumer perceptions of product quality for this retailer's decisions regarding
   a. Store layout   c. Price
   b. Logos

[E] 12. Go to your local library and consult *Consumer Reports* magazine. For five product categories, examine the price-quality relationships in the ratings. How do the results compare with those in the studies reported in this chapter? For each product, which brands and models are "bad buys"? Which are "good buys"?

[E] 13. Interview an "expert" in a particular product category (product engineer, store manager, experienced salesperson) concerning the price-quality inferences made by most consumers. How do prices and quality actually compare? How do reference prices work? Summarize your findings.

[E] 14. Search magazine ads for examples of the perceptual topics discussed in this chapter. Cut out two or three examples of each of the following and attach a brief explanation of your reasoning.
   a. Gestalt principles in ads
   b. Possible problems with categorization
   c. Possible problems with perceptual inferences

[E] 15. Visit a supermarket with which you are very familiar, on a normal shopping trip. This time, however, be sure to monitor your schemas and scripts from the time you enter the store. If you were a consultant for a minor brand in each of these categories, what would you recommend it consider doing?

a. Pickles

b. Frozen pizza

c. Soup

d. Gravy mix

e. Paper towels

CHAPTER 10

Consumer Learning

Sixty-seven-year-old Reuben Ware, the manufacturer of Aunt Grace's Magic Carpet Shampoo, decided to retire and stop producing his brand. Aunt Grace's (named after the inventor's wife) was a very small regional brand sold only in the Atlanta area through the Rich's Department Store chain. The product was advertised as capable of removing blood, lipstick, doggie stains—almost everything from almost any surface, from your carpet to your hair. When it became unavailable, Rich's received 3500 complaints, protesting letters, and phone calls from customers. A spokesperson reports, *"People went crazy."* One consumer argued to the inventor that he had produced the greatest product to ever hit the carpet profession and that he owed it to the public to put it back on the market. Mr. Ware decided she was right and made a comeback. Rich's welcomed the return with a special "Aunt Grace's Days" promotion in honor of the product. The price: a 48-oz. tube sells for $29.99.[1]

■ ■ ■

WHAT IS CONSUMER LEARNING?

Those 3500 consumers who called for Aunt Grace's return represent a high degree of *brand loyalty,* backed up by considerable consumer learning about this product. In this chapter we'll examine more about how consumer learning occurs. First, though, let's examine carefully what learning really is. It is not just what we normally think it to be. Unless you have already studied psychology, our opening discussion may contain some surprises!

Broadly speaking, **learning** refers to the *effects of information and experience.* The scope of consumer learning is very broad. All of our environment and internal processes (e.g., perception) *contribute* to consumer learning. In addition, however, all consumer behavior *depends on* learning from our prior experience. This topic is so broad, in fact, that experts have long disagreed about the best way to study it.[2] The result is that there are now two different "schools" of learning, each of which has much to offer us.

The Two Schools of Learning

As we noted, learning reflects the effects of experience. When we think further about this point, we can recognize five major factors that are involved:

- (S) Stimuli or conditions
- (M) Memory or knowledge (LTM)
- (I) Internal thought processes
- (T) Time or "experience episodes"
- (R) Responses or behaviors

An overall model of learning would include each of these factors as important. For example, the appearance of a particular stimulus (S) sparks certain internal thought processes (I) on the part of a consumer, who uses her memory (M) to guide these processes and provide relevant information. Then she responds (R) in some fashion, perhaps by a physical action such as talking or buying, or perhaps by mentally updating her information and opinions in memory (M). The next time (T) a similar stimulus (S) appears, she can call on her updated memory (M) to guide new internal processes (I) toward new responses (R).

Although this example seems simple enough, it hides a key fact for researchers who want to study learning: *there are too many variables* to be studied in any one research effort. This crucial point has had an enormous impact on the history of research on learning. It forced experts to face the question: "Since I can't study every aspect of learning, what shall I stress, and what shall I ignore?" Their answers led to two quite different approaches to research on learning, each of which offers useful insights for consumer behavior.

Behavior Versus Knowledge

The two approaches can be termed the **learning as behavior (LAB)** view and the **learning is knowledge (LIK)** view. The LAB approach concentrates on the stimuli (S) and the response behaviors (R) made over time (T). This research stream has thus focused on the *external world of learning*. Because of its stress on behavior as representing learning, this approach is sometimes called **behaviorism**.

In contrast, the LIK approach stresses knowledge rather than behavior as the best measure of learning. This approach emphasizes the *internal world of learning*. In the spirit of the CIP perspective we've stressed, LIK has achieved great popularity recently. However, we should recognize that by concentrating on these internal sectors, the LIK view gives up strength in studying stimuli and conditions (S), behavioral responses (R), and the role of time (T) in learning.

While it is true that either school is capable of introducing some improvements in its weak areas, their differences are quite real. In the remainder of this chapter we'll take a closer look at each of these approaches, and some current applications within the field of consumer behavior. We'll begin our analysis with the LIK view of learning, since this is the basic approach we have been taking in the textbook to this point.

THE LEARNING IS KNOWLEDGE (LIK) VIEW

The LIK perspective on learning focuses on internal characteristics rather than on behavior. Almost all our coverage in the earlier chapters of the text has reflected this LIK view, since LIK learning processes are forms of consumer information processing (CIP). For example, we're quite familiar with the fact that within CIP, long-term memory (LTM) plays an absolutely essential role—it provides the information we use to interpret external stimuli as well as the rules we use to integrate these stimuli with our existing nodes in LTM. This is highly consistent with the LIK view of learning. The LIK school stresses LTM as the storage center for our knowledge and views increases in this knowledge base (LTM) to constitute learning. *Thus, we've already examined a number of significant issues related to the LIK approach.* In this chapter, therefore, we'll restrict our further discussion of LIK learning to three topics that aren't covered elsewhere in the text.

I: Consumer Learning in Children

Children form an especially important group for the study of learning from an LIK perspective, since they are building so much basic knowledge during this time. Childhood is also the period in which we form our individual consumer values and buying styles. Beyond this is the fact that there are systematic barriers in children's learning. In this section we'll briefly examine why this is so.

Childhood Learning Stages

Research on stages of development has been inspired by the work of the Swiss psychologist, Jean Piaget, beginning about 60 years ago.[3] Piaget discovered that children pass through four stages of cognitive growth. Within each stage, the child is limited in what he or she may learn and in the ways that they go about learning and thinking. A brief description of Piaget's stages is provided in Table 10-1. Notice that in the early years up to age 2, a baby's lack of language ability restricts abstract thought. When language has developed, however, young children are still restricted in their learning abilities. In a famous experiment, Piaget demonstrated how "perceptual boundedness" restricts a "preoperational" (ages 3–7) child's reasoning processes: he first showed children two identical glasses, tall and thin, that were filled to the same level. He then poured the contents of one of the glasses into a short broad jar; the children at this stage refused to believe that the two containers had the same amount of liquid, but insisted that the tall glass contained more! By the time they move to the next (concrete operational) stage, at about age 8, the children are easily able to answer this question correctly.

The "KidVid" Issue: Advertising to Children

Piaget's theories hold many significant implications for consumer behavior.[4] For example, because of reading deficiencies, children receive much of their consumer information from television advertising. The average child spends about 25 hours per week watching television and thus is exposed to about 20,000 ads in a year. As we'd expect from Piaget's work, however, younger children lack certain skills necessary to process ads very well. They are likely to focus on only a limited amount of available information and to have difficulty in using reasoning processes. Preschoolers, for example, often believe that advertising is "real" and that there are little people inside the television. Even when outgrowing this perspective, children may think that a person speaking from the set is addressing them personally and may have difficulty in understanding the difference between an ad and the program itself.[5]

Research in consumer behavior has consistently shown age differences in children's ability to process television advertising. These differences stem from developmental differences in children's abilities to (1) *store* information in the proper nodes in LTM and (2) successfully find and *retrieve* the proper information with which to interpret TV messages. (Much research has been done recently on this topic in the consumer behavior field. If you are interested in reading more about it, you may wish to start with the readings listed in Note 6.)

An interesting summary of research findings has been provided by Dr. Charles Atkin, a communications professor who specializes in the study of children:

1. *Types of ads directed to kids.* Food—particularly cereals and snacks—are the most frequently advertised products, followed by toys. Message appeals tend to be emotional and emphasize fun themes. Ads tend to be fast paced and light rather than discuss the product. Premium offers are featured.

2. *Kids' understanding of advertising.* Sophistication regarding advertising increases sharply with age. Children below age 8 display low understanding of selling intent and make little distinction between programming and advertising.

TABLE 10-1 PIAGET'S FOUR STAGES OF CHILD DEVELOPMENT

Stage Name	*Characteristics*
Sensorimotor Stage (from birth to age 2)	The infant is not capable of abstract thought since language ability is only slowly beginning. Behavior is mainly physical (motor), driven by stimuli (sensory inputs).
Preoperational Thought Stage (from ages 3 to 7)	The young child is developing the ability to use symbols (language, mental images). However, most thinking is still driven by stimuli in the outside world. Attention spans are very short, and thinking focuses on only one dimension of a problem at a time.
Concrete Operational Stage (from ages 8 to 11)	The child's internal thought processes are becoming stronger, so he or she is better able to "think about" objects. Such thinking is "concrete," however, in that the objects need to be physically present.
Formal Operational Stage (from age 11 up)	At about this age the child begins to think more like an adult, especially in the sense of being capable of abstract thought. Ideas and logical systems take on more meaning, perception is less crucial for thinking, and the child can consider multiple characteristics of a problem.

Sensorimotor Stage

Preoperational Thought Stage

3. *Belief in TV ads.* Few children below age 8 exhibit any generalized distrust of advertising. Kids are skeptical about claims for toys they already own, but readily accept claims of medical or nutritional nature. Heavy viewers of commercials are more likely to believe ads than are light viewers.

4. *Influence of ads.* Exposure to advertising increases asking for and consumption of advertised products. Children who watch much TV are far more likely to request parents to buy food and toy products for them. Parents reject between one-third and one-half of children's requests for products—this leads to conflicts in about half of all families, although such arguments are reported to be mild.

5. *Parental guidance.* Parents do not play a strong direct role in educating children about advertising. Most do not watch the ads with their children, and less than half of the mothers say they teach their children about advertising.[7]

Given these types of findings about children's learning processes, everyone—marketers, parents, and public policymakers alike—agrees that the children's advertising area deserves special attention. There is disagreement, however, about how this should best be handled.

Self-regulation in Children's Advertising
About 15 years ago advertising trade associations developed guidelines for marketers to follow in creating ads aimed at children. Shortly thereafter, the National Advertising Division (a self-regulatory body) established its Children's Advertising Review Unit (CARU). CARU monitors advertising directed to children under 12 years of age, and within the self-regulatory process, seeks modification or discontinuance of ads it finds to be inaccurate or unfair. CARU has also developed detailed guidelines for advertisers in this area.

Government Regulation: Get Rid of KidVid?
In spite of the careful attention given to children's advertising by the industry's leaders, many consumers remain distrustful of the practice and occasionally proposals arise to

Concrete Operational Stage

Formal Operational Stage

restrict it further. Prior to the deregulatory era of the 1980s, the Federal Trade Commission's staff recommended that the FTC should enact rules that would regulate advertising to children. In brief, the recommendations were

1. *Ban* all TV advertising directed to young children (under 8 years of age).
2. *Ban* TV advertising for sugared food products directed to older children (ages 8 to 12).
3. Require all other TV advertising for sugared food products seen by significant proportions of older children to be balanced by health messages paid for by the advertisers.

Reaction to this proposal was massive and heated. Companies and advertising agencies banded together to fight any regulations resembling those suggested. They charged that the FTC was attempting to become a "National Nanny" and was willing to ride rampant over the right of free speech accorded to businesses in this country. They also charged that the FTC staff's descriptions of children's limitations were overstated and that children could learn more about commercials if appropriate education were provided.

During the hearings extensive lobbying was being undertaken in Congress, against the concept of the FTC issuing rules of any type. Congress reacted against the FTC and the children's rule making was dropped. However, given that this outcome was largely determined by political forces, many persons believe that the area of children's advertising is yet unresolved in the United States. (For example, the Canadian province of Quebec has prohibited all commercial advertising aimed at children under 13 years of age.) Given the research on children's learning, should there be restrictions on kids' advertising, in your opinion?

II: Measuring Consumer Learning

A second topic arising from the LIK approach moves to the question of how to measure consumer learning itself. One of the most interesting aspects of our current marketing-consumer environment is that *no organization is engaged in the overall measurement of what consumers learn.* Put another way, apart from the limited test of consumers' skills used in a few consumer education classes, we simply do not know what consumers do or do not know. As we saw in Chapter 2, part of this problem is due to the wide range of topics about which consumers learn—everything from money management skills to individual brand jingles.

Academic researchers have begun to consider the nature of consumer knowledge, but little descriptive information is presently available in the literature.[8] The primary reason is that marketers specialize in particular product categories. Individual marketers study what consumers have learned and what they are learning from current promotional strategies, but only for the product or service being sold. These firms usually do not release their findings, of course, because of their profit implications. Thus there is no general source available on consumer learning.

Marketing Research Techniques

As noted, however, marketers do carry out many individual studies involving consumer learning. The primary technique for measuring consumer learning is the consumer survey. Consumer surveys allow marketers to discover which products consumers do and do not use, what they know about those products, what they view the strengths and weaknesses of each brand to be, and so forth. These surveys are then useful for designing new marketing programs aimed at particular segments. Surveys of consumer knowledge can yield valuable insights for public policymakers as well. In recent years, for example, such surveys have allowed assessments of consumers' diets, health knowledge, insurance coverage, and so forth.

Cognitive Responses to Advertising

In a related area, marketers also invest considerable money in studying exactly what consumers learn from individual advertisements. This research often takes the form of **copy testing**, to help advertisers choose which ad ideas show promise for being run and how they might be modified. "Day-after" recall tests (as we will discuss in Chapter 17) and ad recognition tests are both efforts to measure some of what consumers have learned. In recent years advertising researchers have given much attention to the area of **cognitive responses** as a method of measuring how consumers are reacting to an ad and what they are learning from it.

Basically, researchers would like to monitor all the thoughts that a consumer has while watching an ad. This is an extreme challenge, given that consumers' CIP systems work at such remarkable speeds. However, considerable work has been done. Among the interesting findings are (1) in general, print ads yield more cognitive responses than broadcast ads, and (2) some cognitive responses stem from the message itself, while others arise from the receiver's own life. To appreciate better what is involved, one basic system of classifying cognitive responses can provide us with useful insights. This system contains three types of cognitive responses that are of most interest to an advertiser. **Support arguments** are cognitive responses in which the consumer is agreeing with the points being made by the ad ("I agree, Tide really does get my clothes white and bright."). **Source derogations** are responses in which the consumer disagrees with the ad, but does so by reacting to its source rather than its message ("What would you expect a salesman like that to say anyway . . . ; I doubt that he really knows much about jewelry in the first place"). **Counterarguments**, on the other hand, are responses in which the consumer disagrees with the message claims themselves ("I tried that cleaner and it just spread the grease around in a larger area . . . it's terrible!"). Not surprisingly, ads that evoke more support arguments have been found to yield positive attitude change by consumers, whereas those that spark more negative responses are less persuasive. Of particular value, however, are the insights into the kinds of reactions consumers are having. If you're interested in reading more about this area of consumer research, you may wish to begin with the readings listed in Note 9. (We will also be examining the closely related issue of attitudes, involvement, and advertising in our next chapter.)

III: "Mis-Learning" Issues in Consumer Behavior

A third interesting topic reflecting the LIK view of learning involves "mis-learning." **Mis-learning** refers to cases in which what consumers learn about their environment is incorrect. Sometimes this is the consumer's own fault, while on other occasions, it may have been aided by certain marketing practices.

Deceptive Advertising

It is often difficult for a consumer to know when he or she has mis-learned something. For this reason each year there are many efforts made to ensure against misleading ads: Most of these are taken by businesses themselves: they occur before the ads are run—within the advertising approval systems of companies, agencies, and the media. Some misleading ads do survive this process, however, and are presented to consumers. In some instances, cases are brought within the self-regulatory system. In other instances, cases are brought within the formal regulatory system, which involves state governments, or especially the Federal Trade Commission (FTC). Traditionally, the FTC has moved against ads that had a "tendency or capacity" to mislead or deceive consumers. Within the law, however, deception has not been specifically defined. This provides regulators with flexibility for their decisions in individual cases. (A recent FTC policy statement on deception pointed to elements that would guide decisions in this area, but even these are subject to interpretation. Interested readers may wish to consult Note 10.)

In recent years many consumer researchers have become interested in measuring deceptive advertising. David M. Gardner, a marketing professor, has described three basic types of deceptive ads.[11] The **unconscionable lie** reflects an ad that contains statements that simply are not true ("Regularly sells for $250," or "Guaranteed to last 10 years" when these are untrue descriptions). In a **claim-fact discrepancy**, the ad's description needs some further information to avoid misleading implications. For example, in one case the FTC ruled that showing various television sets together might well lead consumers to the impression that all the sets were available at the advertised price—to avoid this, the prices of the other sets could have been listed, or they could have been removed from the photo.

The **claim-belief interaction** occurs when all the information in the ad is literally correct but might be expected to be interpreted in a misleading way by consumers because of their existing knowledge and beliefs. In other words, as we discussed in Chapter 9, consumers' inferences may be led to be incorrect. In another FTC case, for example, a carpet retailer had featured very attractive prices in his ad but had expressed these as price *per square foot* rather than price per square yard. Because the commission felt that consumers would expect to see such prices in square yard units, it ruled the ad to be deceptive.[12]

In general, then, ads can be deceptive when they are either literally false or potentially misleading. To gauge falsity, we need only to examine the ad itself, together with background facts. To gauge "misleadingness," however, we need to consider how consumers will interpret the ad and what they will learn from it. Consumer researchers have stressed what consumers learn from ads as the basis for studying deception. (If you would like to read more about advances in this area, you may wish to pursue the readings given in Note 13.)

Consumer Miscomprehension of Ads

Miscomprehension results when the receiver of a message extracts either an incorrect or confused meaning from it. Surprisingly, consumer miscomprehension has simply not been much studied. In this regard, a study of adults and teens has raised striking new questions about what consumers *are* learning in our society.

What's Right and What's Wrong?

Advertisers, concerned that their ads might be charged as being deceptive whenever some consumers misunderstood what was being said, decided to fund a large-scale study to discover what the "normal" rate of miscomprehension might be. Twenty-seven hundred consumers across the United States participated. Three types of communications were used: (1) TV commercials, (2) public service announcements (PSAs), and (3) program excerpts from TV news and entertainment shows. In total, 60 different communications, each 30 seconds long, were studied. Each consumer saw two of the communications. After viewing the first, a six-item true-false quiz was given to the participant. This procedure was repeated after the second viewing as well. Each quiz was designed to have two correct statements and four false answers.

Results were surprising. *The average consumer missed 3.5 of the 12 items, for a miscomprehension rate of 30 percent!* Less than 4 percent of the people were correct on all 12 quiz questions (12 percent missed 1 question). Those with college and graduate degrees still had miscomprehension rates of over 25 percent! Turning to the communications, the researchers found that all three types fared badly. This indicates that miscomprehension seems to be rampant as we watch all forms of TV.[14]

This study proved to be controversial and sparked several comments from critical marketing professors associated with the FTC, together with replies by the study's authors, who stood behind their findings. Then a new analysis of these data appeared (conducted by other researchers), which included statistical corrections for consumers' guessing on the comprehension quizzes. What do you think happened to the estimated rate of consumer miscomprehension? (Note 15 reports these results and provides a list of readings in this controversial research area.)

This completes our discussion of the LIK approach to consumer learning in this chapter. However, many of the topics discussed in later chapters will continue to build on this view, so our learning about LIK is not complete. At this point, though, we will turn to a consideration of the LAB approach for the remainder of this chapter.

THE LEARNING AS BEHAVIOR (LAB) VIEW

This approach defines learning as *a relatively permanent change in behavior that occurs as a result of experience.* "Behaviorism" has a long history in studying learning and applying this knowledge to the real world. In fact, the founder of behaviorism, John B. Watson, moved to the advertising world in 1920, where he applied behaviorist principles for many years.

Perhaps the most distinguishing characteristic of the behaviorist approach is its emphasis on the external world (as opposed to internal mental processes). Behaviorist scientists emphasize objective control of the external environment and objective measurement in the external world—in their research we find that stimuli, responses, and time are rigorously manipulated and monitored. Experimental methods are employed to study how precise changes in stimuli would produce precise changes in response—external facts and evidence are of utmost importance to behaviorists. **Mental concepts** such as attitudes are viewed as unnecessary, and possibly dangerous!

Many of the founders of this field were trained in physiology and were comfortable with measurements of slight body movements and other changes in body measurements. To achieve control in their studies, they often used animals as subjects (this gave rise to the term "rat psychology"). When animals were used, of course, opportunities for verbal reports of reactions to stimuli were lost, so that even more emphasis was placed on overt behaviors as representing learning (in this regard, Watson did suggest that human subjects be placed in the same style "discrimination boxes" that delivered either bread or electric shocks to hungry rats penned within, but was rebuffed on the grounds that this was demeaning to human dignity).[16]

Through its rigorous studies, the LAB approach has developed key basic concepts of learning:

- *Conditioning.* This term refers to the acquisition of new behavior relationships with stimuli and thus represents the learning process.
- *Practice.* This term refers to repeated learning episodes.
- *Contiguity.* Meaning "close together," contiguity refers to having stimuli or responses designed to occur closely together so as to increase certain forms of learning.
- *Reinforcement.* This term refers to the strengthening of learned associations between stimulus and response. A positive reinforcer increases the probability of learning a behavior when it appears, while a negative reinforcer increases the probability of learning a behavior when it is taken away, or does not appear.
- *Extinction.* This term refers to the weakening of a response behavior to the point that it is no longer elicited by the stimulus.

Within the LAB approach there are two primary theories: classical conditioning (CC) and instrumental conditioning (IC). Each has potentially powerful applications in the world of consumer behavior.

Classical Conditioning

The key figure in **classical conditioning** (CC) is Ivan Pavlov. The son of a Russian priest, Pavlov was trained in physiology and pharmacology (his work on the physiology of digestion, in fact, won him a Nobel Prize in 1904).

The Tune and the Fork

Given his background, Pavlov's approach to the study of learning is understandable. His famous experiments used dogs as subjects and showed how new response behaviors could be created simply by manipulating stimuli, contiguity, practice, and reinforcement. In brief, a dog would be harnessed into a still position and a tuning fork rung. The resulting tone (S_1) led to normal auditory responses (R_1) reflecting the dog hearing the sound. Shortly thereafter (with high contiguity), a dry meat powder (S_2) was given to the dog, whose normal physiological reaction to food included salivation (R_2). This procedure was repeated over a number of episodes, representing "practice." As the episodes progressed, the food began to be associated with the tone and served as a **reinforcement**. Finally, the dogs reached the point at which the ringing of the tone alone would bring salivation, whether or not meat powder was provided later. At this point the new stimulus-response behavior (tone causes salivation) had been *conditioned*.

Several points should be noted regarding classical conditioning. First, in this case the learner is relatively passive—the "learning" seems to occur in an almost automatic fashion. Second, the learning is based upon an already existing stimulus-response (S-R) relationship. This potentially places power in the hands of someone who can discover these already existing relationships and mold the stimulus environment to take advantage of them. (For a discussion of modern developments in Pavlovian psychology, the interested reader may wish to consult Note 17.)

Classical Conditioning and Marketing

Curiously, until recently the formal topic of classical conditioning has received little research attention in the marketing and consumer literature. Learning in this fashion tends to occur naturally in consumers' everyday lives, of course. Consider, for example, how certain stimuli often tend to "go together" in contiguous fashions. These pairings, over time, lead to our "learning" new associations and response behaviors. Symbols, visuals, and music come to have meaning for us and seem able to evoke strong emotional reactions at times.

From the marketing side, however, little systematic effort seems to have been given to studying how exactly to manipulate stimuli so as to condition consumers in the Pavlovian style. This may be due to the fact that the individual marketer *lacks significant control* over much of his or her customers' lives and cannot present stimuli to them as they are harnessed into a fixed position. While this does not place a marketer in a powerful position vis-à-vis the consumer (which may be a good thing from an ethical point of view), there are occasions in which marketers do have opportunities to present stimuli in contiguous fashions. Let's look at two examples:

Have a Coke and a Smile . . .

One common advertising strategy is to place a brand close to other stimuli that are known to evoke strong and favorable emotional responses from consumers in the target audience. Recent research is beginning to indicate that classical conditioning can work in advertising, and firms are paying more and more attention to this area. Recently, for example, Coca-Cola acknowledged that it has developed a new ad-testing procedure based on Pavlov's behavioral principles. A high-ranking executive at Coke said, "We nominate Pavlov as the father of modern advertising. Pavlov took a neutral object and by associating it with a meaningful object, made it a symbol of something else . . . that is what we try to do in modern advertising."

While this statement doesn't emphasize the behavioral responses stressed by Pavlov, apparently the company's tests are concerned with this link. The specifics of Coke's test

are secret, but it is known to involve the measurement of how well a positive image can be transferred to the product and then to sales. According to one report, in three years of testing, ads that scored high on this measure almost always resulted in higher sales of a soft drink.[18]

Grease Pens Outdraw Indian Ink

A study by Gerald Gorn has directly raised issues as to how classical conditioning might work. In this research, preference for a pen color was conditioned by music during an advertising exposure. In prior testing, it was discovered that light-blue and beige pens were each evaluated as "neutral" by most students. It was also discovered that music from the movie *Grease* provoked a positive emotional response, whereas classical East Indian music produced a negative emotional response by most of the sample.

Four groups were used. Two of the groups received an ad picturing the pen while the "liked" music was playing (a light-blue pen was used in one group and a beige pen in the other). The other two groups saw the same pen visuals, but paired with the "disliked" music. All groups had been told that an ad agency was trying to select music for use in a commercial for a pen. No attention was drawn to the color of the pen. After viewing the ad, the students provided brief ratings on the music they'd heard. They were then told that the agency wanted to thank them by giving them one of the pens and that two colors were available. The blue pen box was on the left side of the room; the beige pen box was on the right side. According to the classical conditioning hypothesis, if the music were liked, the pen color should also be liked, whereas if the music were disliked, that pen color should likewise become disliked. Thus the experiment was cleverly designed to predict that in *two groups* the blue pen should be chosen (once when advertised with liked music, the other when not advertised but disliked music had been used for the beige pen). In the other two groups, however, the beige pen should be chosen if conditioning had taken hold.

Results supported the hypothesis: when "liked" music was played, the color of the pen in the ad was chosen by a 3.5:1 ratio over the color that had not appeared. When "disliked" music had been played, however, the color that had *not* appeared was chosen 2.5 times more often than the "advertised" color! This effect occurred for both the blue and beige colors, so they were not the cause. Moreover, when asked for the reasons for their choice of a color, only 2 percent of the students mentioned the music. Over half indicated simply that they "liked" the color they'd chosen (if this were the real reason, the experiment would not have worked), while others could give no particular reason for their choice.[19]

Thus Gorn's results suggest that a form of classical conditioning may be capable of working within even a single exposure and that consumers will not necessarily be aware that it is at work. As we have seen before, however, whenever consumer unawareness is at issue (as with hidden motives in Chapter 6 and subliminal perception in Chapter 8), strong disagreements will crop up between researchers. Thus it is not surprising that research following Gorn has pointed to further questions on the nature of these effects, and how they might hold up in the more tumultuous setting of the marketplace. Readers interested in pursuing these developments and debates about classical conditioning in marketing might wish to begin with the readings in Note 20.

Instrumental Conditioning

Instrumental conditioning (IC) is a theory developed to explain learning that is goal directed. The term "instrumental" refers to the fact that the appropriate behavior is viewed as an instrument by which we can attain our goal. It has three distinctive differences from classical conditioning (CC):

- Whereas CC has a *passive* learner, IC has an *active* learner.
- Whereas CC depends primarily on *contiguity* (pairing stimuli and responses), IC depends primarily on *reinforcement.*
- Whereas CC depends primarily on the *stimuli* that comes *before responses,* IC depends primarily on the *reinforcements* that come *after responses.*

In essence, IC shifts the focus from the stimulus side to the behavior side. For example, while the appearance of a can of 7-Up might lead us to pick it up and drink it, we won't do so *every* time we see it, but only those times when we wish to take a drink. This type of voluntary behavior is called an **operant response**, and IC theory is sometimes called **operant conditioning**.

Buying by the Peck

The key figure in instrumental conditioning theory is B. F. Skinner, a famous professor at Harvard. His basic point was that people and animals behave in "purposive" ways all the time—we buy products in order to receive benefits, ask questions in order to receive answers, and so on. Although Skinner accepted that some learning might be of the CC variety, he viewed this as relatively unimportant—most human behavior, Skinner believed, is instrumental and depends upon the reinforcements we've received in the past.

Since reinforcement is the key to this form of learning, it is important that the rat, pigeon, or human figure out which response produced the reinforcement. Once the cause is identified, the actor will be able to reach his goal by producing the proper behavior: He will have *learned* how to get something he wants.

Skinner's major contributions went well beyond this simple point. In particular, he showed how reinforcements could be varied to produce certain forms of behavior. By providing **intermittent reinforcement** (that is, the subject's behavior is not rewarded on every occasion, but only sometimes), Skinner was able to show strong forms of learning that would persist for long periods of time. By varying his reinforcements for different forms of behavior, he was able to produce **shaping** of behavior. For example, a new pigeon might first be rewarded whenever he moved to the right side of the box, then only rewarded when he moved toward the bar, then only when touching the bar, then only when touching the bar three times, and so on. Eventually, the pigeon's behavior can be shaped into a very precise sequence of activities.

The many years of research by Skinner and his followers has had enormous impact. The stress on the importance of manipulating external stimuli has led to many applications of IC. In education, for example, Skinner was primarily responsible for the creation of *programmed learning.* In medicine, *biofeedback* and *behavior modification* programs are both drawn from his principles. Skinner believed that his principles could work to improve society as well: he wrote a novel, *Walden Two,* which takes place in a Utopian community built along Skinnerian principles. This stress on external control made Skinner a major and controversial figure in our society. (If you're interested in reading more about him, you may wish to pursue the readings listed in Note 21.)

Instrumental Conditioning and Marketing

As consumers, the operation of this form of learning in the marketplace is common and is obvious to us. On a daily basis we learn which products and stores bring positive reinforcements to us and which ones do not. We "learn from our experience," avoid repeating purchases that disappoint us, and return for more that have rewarded us.

For marketers, however, the challenge is to control the external environment strongly to create IC learning in their target markets. Three areas of application of IC in marketing include **reinforcement schedules, shaping,** and **discriminative stimuli.**[22] The normal case for marketers is to strive for consumers to receive *continuous reinforcements*—each time they buy and use the brand, they will be satisfied. Trading stamps, rebates, premiums, and in-box coupons can also serve reinforcement functions. In some promotional situations *intermittent reinforcement* can also be used—sweepstakes, games, and lotteries are examples of these strategies.

Shaping involves the reinforcement of a series of behaviors that will gradually bring the consumer to the desired final behavior. For example, positioning of sale items in a particular corner of a store can, over time, shape the path that some consumers will use as they shop there. Finally, *discriminative stimuli* are those that, when present, increase the probability of purchase behavior. Marketers strive mightily to achieve this status with logos, brand names, and in-store signs. The sight of the "golden arches" on a billboard or at roadside has led many a driver to veer off in that direction. Similarly, a "Clearance Sale!" sign on a display can attract special purchase probabilities from many retail shoppers.

Customer, You're a Gem . . .

In one published study, a small jewelry store in Texas experimented with simple forms of reinforcement on its clientele. Names and phone numbers of over 400 customers were divided into three groups. Those in the "control" group received no contact. The other groups were contacted by phone: in one, the caller simply introduced himself (herself) and said, "I would like to thank you for being one of our customers." In the second group, the customer was thanked and also told about an upcoming diamond sale during the next two months. What were the results of this reinforcement? Store salespersons reported an immediate increase in store visits, with many persons from the first contact group stopping in to comment about "that nice person who called." Apparently, the simple "thanks" was seen as being more sincere than the call mentioning the special sale (this topic involves "attribution theory," which we examined in Chapter 6). Although sales for the year to date had been down, sales that month went up 27 percent over the prior year! Purchases by customers in the control group were unchanged—the entire increase came from customers who had received the reinforcing calls. Seventy percent came from customers in the first group, who had received only the simple "Thank you."[23]

Further LAB Approaches to Modifying Consumer Behavior

While CC and IC are basic theoretical approaches to learning, recent extensions in this area have many implications for consumer behavior, marketing, and public policy. In this section we'll take a brief look at three such approaches:

Modeling Effects on Consumer Behavior

Albert Bandura has stressed the importance of **modeling** in modifying behavior. Modeling is achieved by having a person observe the actions of others (the models) and the consequences of the models' behaviors. Three ways that modeling can influence consumers are

- *Educating consumers in new behaviors.* Salespersons, friends, and ads all present models for consumers. Parents serve as models for children. Thus, before ever performing an actual behavior, consumers are able to have mentally practiced it.

- *Increased purchase probabilities.* Modeling can also be used to focus on the consequences of behaviors, thereby representing a form of **vicarious reinforcement**. For example, when we see the pleasure that a model receives from a loved one's telephone call, we can easily feel that pleasure for ourselves. The probability of such a behavior on our part increases.

- *Discouraging negative consumer behaviors.* Modeling is also useful for discouraging consumers from behaviors such as smoking, drinking, and littering.[24] Here consumers will see a model experiencing negative outcomes from his or her actions and may be led to change the behavior rather than encounter the same consequences personally.

Ecological Design

Behavior modification is also apparent in the area called "ecological design," which refers to the deliberate design of environments and stimuli to modify human behavior.[25] For example, some retail stores are using subliminal messages as a means of reducing negative behavior by some customers. Messages such as "Stealing is dishonest . . . ," "I won't steal . . . ," "I am honest . . . ," and so forth are played on the store's sound system, but at a volume below the conscious threshold. According to one unconfirmed report, a large decline in shoplifting occurred during the nine months following the introduction of these stimuli.[26] (Notice that LAB does not claim that thinking does not occur here, but simply is interested in changing the shopper's environment so that desired behavior does occur.) Results from another ecological design study, this time involving music, are also indicative of the potential power of this area in modifying customers' behavior:

Buying Beets by the Beat

Consumers and store managers both like having music in the store—it makes shopping a more pleasing experience and customers may spend more money. In one recent study, this suggestion was tested over a two-month period in a medium-sized supermarket in the southwest United States. Each day, one of three randomly chosen treatments was used in the store: no music (the control condition), "slow" music (averaging 60 beats per minute), or "fast" music (averaging 108 beats per minute), with the volume set to soft background music. Measures were taken of shoppers' awareness of the music, walking

"...looks like a warehouse clearance sale. But we're looking good considering all the miles we've traveled since you waved goodbye. Called AT&T before we moved. You know me...can't be out of touch even for one minute. So now all I have to do is figure how to make three rooms of furniture look great in eight...and how to keep from missing all you guys back at the office."

"Sounds like you already solved that last one."

For more information, call
1 800 222-0300.

Before you move, one call to AT&T helps put everything in place. AT&T. We take you right there and keep you this close.

AT&T
The right choice.

speed, and sales. Results showed that consumers paid little attention to the music itself—when asked if music had been playing in the store they'd just left, customers were equally likely to report "Yes," "No," or "Don't Know." Whatever effects might occur, then, would seem to be happening without conscious control by consumers.

And interesting behavioral effects were found. The average consumer walked 17 percent faster with the fast music than with the slow music (when no music was playing consumers walked at a pace about midway between the two). Most important from the marketers' point of view, the days in which slow music was played had *38 percent higher dollar sales* than when fast music had been playing—this amounted to an almost $5000-per-day

FROM NOW ON, SHOPLIFTING IN THE U.S. IS A VERY, VERY DIRTY BUSINESS.

For the last four years, Colortag has significantly cut losses for European store owners.

The device is a plastic tag that doesn't beep, but sprays permanent ink on the garment when the thief breaks it open. A fifty dollar shirt becomes worthless. The motive to steal it is gone.

No false alarms. No big installations. No guards. No action needed from the store clerks. No expensive prosecutions.

And thefts are down by as much as 90%.

Cut your losses and increase your profits with Colortag. Because it's time shoplifting got even dirtier. Call Don Barnett at our New York office for the full story. (212) 888-1629.

Colortag

Colortag, Inc., 3 West 57th Street, New York, NY. 10019.

An ad aimed at reducing shoplifting. The product is a special tag attached to apparel in retail stores. When a garment is shoplifted, the thief is likely to find it ruined by the burst of dye that emerges when the tag is incorrectly removed. Thefts reportedly dropped from 70 to 90 percent in European stores that used this tag.

increase in sales for that store! (Again, the days without music averaged sales that were midway between the music figures). This would seem to call for marketers to use soft, slow music to retain customers in their stores, where they'll buy more. However, in other situations, such as fast-food outlets at lunch time the management may want to switch on the rock n' roll to move business through the store. As a consumer, moreover, the next time you hear "Muzak" in a store, you may want to step up your pace a bit if you want to save money![27]

Ethical Considerations in Behavioral Modification

Consumers are obviously quite responsive to stimuli in their environments. Marketers control some aspects of these stimuli (especially within a store and within an ad). Since LAB learning theory has stressed how behavior can be shaped and controlled, it is a natural force for marketers to use. In so doing, however, we cannot escape questions of responsible behavior. Nord and Peter, in proposing that attention be given to behavior modification, recognized that "there are major ethical/moral issues involved" in its use in marketing:

We maintain that behavior modification is not, in itself, immoral or unethical, but that valid ethical/moral concerns stem from (1) the ends to which the technology is used and (2) the process by which these needs are determined. The application of these techniques in marketing seems ethically vulnerable on both these counts. Efforts to market products rarely include the subject whose behavior is modified, as a full participant in determining either the use of the technology or the ends to which it is put. There are, of course, examples . . . which many people believe are socially desirable (reduction in littering, pollution, and smoking and consumer education efforts). However, there appear to be many other applications which have few redeeming social benefits. . . . Since it is clear that the type of emotions often labeled "needs" or motives can be developed through conditioning and modeling processes, the defense that marketing satisfies needs is not fully adequate.[28]

There are no easy answers in this area. In the abstract, we need to address complex systems of philosophy and ethics, about which persons of good will can disagree. At a practical level, answers will depend on how effective various techniques actually are. At this stage consumer researchers have few answers to this question. For example, several years ago a chief official of the FTC charged that cigarette companies were running ads showing background scenes whose message was health, freshness, and well-being (for example, scenes of mountain lakes, or young handsome men and women). Is it likely that CC would work to influence consumers' actual views of cigarettes in this way? Should such scenes be banned? (If you are interested in pursuing further thinking in this area, you may wish to begin with the readings listed in Note 29.)

Understanding Consumer Purchase Patterns

As a final topic within the LAB perspective, let's switch our focus to strictly purchase behaviors, and briefly examine consumer purchase patterns. For many frequently purchased items, it is the pattern of consumer's purchases over time that makes the difference between success or failure. Marketers purchase **consumer panel data** from research firms. These firms gather samples of consumers who agree to provide records of all their purchases over a long time. If a panel is representative, its results can be projected to the marketplace as a whole, to provide marketers with insights as to "what's going on out there."

In particular, marketers are interested in how their promotional, product, or price decisions will affect purchase patterns, how brands compete with each other, and how to predict the probabilities that a particular brand will be chosen on the next purchase occasion. The chances that a particular brand will be bought at a particular time are hard to predict with certainty, because considerable brand switching goes on. This means that the topic of probability becomes central to research on purchase patterns. Marketers for some time have been interested in developing quantitative **probability models** (technically termed *stochastic* (stō-kas-tic) models) of purchase behavior.

Once purchase patterns are modeled as probabilities, consumer researchers can investigate a number of strategic issues. For example, we are able to assess which consumers are loyal users, which are "switchers" among brands, and which are not using the product at all. We can also easily see which consumers are "heavy users" and which are "light users." Since the panel data also contains information about each consumer's demographics (age, income, etc.) we are able to evaluate who is in each segment and how easy it may be to reach them.

Beyond segmentation strategy, information on consumer purchase patterns can be used to study the effects of specific marketing mix decisions. In one recent study, for example, researchers discovered that the effects of coupons were different between margarine and flour, with margarine the more sensitive product for coupon use. Distinct effects on consumer purchase patterns were measured—normally about 40 percent of consumers switch their margarine brand purchase, but when a coupon was included, 65 percent of consumers switched brands.[30]

These kinds of analyses can be conducted for many forms of promotion—price deals, displays, coupons, and advertising—simply by tracing their effects on consumers' purchase patterns. With the advent of new technologies, the study of brand loyalty and brand switching is growing even more rapidly. For example, the Universal Product Code scanners at supermarket checkout counters have revolutionized the study of consumer purchase patterns. Consumer panel research firms now use these devices to register every brand and purchase as it occurs at the checkout. The members of these panels use special credit cards to make their purchases, so all information is immediately available in the computer. Also, in some panels, the consumers' television sets at home are arranged (via "split cables") to receive different versions of TV commercials. These consumers' purchases can be analyzed to discover which type of advertising produces more sales. Thus new technology means that very fast feedback on effects of special promotional campaigns is now possible through studying consumer purchase patterns (if you are particularly interested in pursuing these developments, you may wish to begin with the readings in Note 31).

Stability in Purchase Patterns: Brand Loyalty

Our discussion of purchase patterns to this point has stressed the instability brought about through brand switching. Clearly, however, consumer behavior also has a large component of stability to it. This stability reflects consumers having learned specific purchase behaviors and having found these to be rewarding. Our "Aunt Grace" story at the start of this chapter is a striking example. The term we apply to this class of behaviors is **brand loyalty**. Brand loyalty can bring positive benefits to both consumers and marketers.

For a consumer, brand-loyal behavior offers savings in time and decision-making effort and lowers risks of buying an unsatisfactory product. On the other hand, it may mean paying higher prices, and it also carries the risk of missing new improvements available from other brands in the market. For the marketer, brand loyalty is also beneficial, since it provides a solid base of customers into the future. Within the competitive market, of course, this is a double-edged sword, since consumers who are loyal to other brands are difficult to attract away.

In a research vein, we should note that brand loyalty is a more difficult phenomenon to define in detail than we might first expect. For example, one insightful overview reports that over 50 different definitions of brand loyalty have been offered in the consumer literature![32] Whatever the research difficulties in brand loyalty, though, the fact is that marketers are striving to achieve it for their brands, as the following discussion shows.

Rewarding the Loyal: Treat Them Royal!

The airline industry has traditionally faced difficult marketing problems, since prices can easily be met by competitors, as can in-flight services. Time is an important factor for many travelers, and scheduled departures will often override all but the strongest brand preferences in this market. A few years ago, however, the airlines developed a unique program to "create" brand loyalty among their most important class of passengers—the "frequent flyers." Frequent flyers (typically businesspersons, often marketers) are the 20 percent of airline passengers who account for about 80 percent of an airline's revenues because they fly so often. As a frequent flyer flew a particular line more often, he or she would build up more points, which could then be cashed in for such rewards as upgraded seating to first class, free tickets, or, if many miles had been accumulated, free vacations at international resorts.

Consumer response was so positive that the idea spread rapidly, first to all the airlines, then to their travel partners (major hotel chains, car rental firms, etc.), then to a host of other businesses. Food products ("The Kool-Aid Club"), department stores (Dallas-based Neiman-Marcus provides its "In Circle" members deluxe rewards in exchange for minimum purchases of $60,000 per year), restaurants, and dog foods are among those with programs. According to a senior vice president of Hyatt Hotels, "Frequent-user marketing is the way companies will market themselves in the 1990s and for years to come." Might this go too far, though? The continuing decline in hard liquor sales has led several brands—Cutty Sark and Dewar's White Label among them—to create "Frequent-Drinker" programs for their customers![33]

SUMMARY

What is Consumer Learning?

Learning is concerned with the effects of *experience*. There are five key factors involved in consumer learning: (1) stimuli, (2) internal processes, (3) responses, (4) memory, and (5) time. The fact that all these factors cannot be studied at the same time has led to two distinct approaches to research on learning: *learning as behavior (LAB)* and *learning is knowledge (LIK)*. Both views offer useful insights into consumer behavior.

The Learning is Knowledge View

The chapter devoted less space to the learning is knowledge (LIK) view, since this has been the dominant approach taken in earlier chapters in this text. The LIK view is based upon consumer information processing theory. The LIK approach emphasizes the "internal world" of the consumer and has enjoyed great popularity in recent years. It stresses that knowledge, rather than behavior, is the best indicator of learning. Within the LIK view of learning, LTM provides the storage center for our knowledge—increases in this knowledge base constitute learning. Three LIK application areas were examined. First, we examined why cognitive limitations can cause controversy over advertising aimed at children. We then turned to the issue of measuring consumer learning, including the study of cognitive responses to advertising. Our third topic concerned *consumer mis-learning*, including both deceptive advertising issues and some surprising findings about consumers' miscomprehension of broadcast messages.

The Learning As Behavior (LAB) View

The second half of the chapter examined the learning as behavior (LAB) approach. The LAB approach is associated with behaviorism. It views learning to be relatively permanent change in behavior that occurs as a result of experience. *Mental concepts* such as attitudes are seen as superfluous and irrelevant. Within the LAB approach there are two primary theories of learning: *classical conditioning* (CC) and *instrumental conditioning* (IC). We first discussed Pavlov's famous CC experiments, which taught dogs to salivate at the sound of a tuning fork. We noted applications of this conditioning approach in the real world of marketing, including the design of Coke's advertising and an experiment involving pens and music. We then examined the different approach taken by Skinner's famous IC experiments, which were developed around the idea of goal-directed learning. An experiment in a jewelry store indicated the positive effects *reinforcement* can have. Our next section discussed recent developments that spring from CC and IC backgrounds, including modeling effects and ecological design (example: music in the supermarket). Both reflect the emerging practice of *behavior modification*, in which an environment is structured to develop certain types of consumer behaviors. We also noted that this practice has raised some ethical questions for marketers in the future. Our final section then discussed the marketing importance of understanding consumer purchase patterns, including both *brand switching* and *brand loyalty*.

KEY TERMS

learning	support arguments
learning as behavior (LAB)	source derogations
learning is knowledge (LIK)	counterarguments
behaviorism	mis-learning
CARU	unconscionable lie
copy testing	claim-fact discrepancy

miscomprehension	reinforcement schedules
mental concepts	discriminative stimuli
classical conditioning (CC)	continuous reinforcements
reinforcement	modeling
instrumental conditioning (IC)	vicarious reinforcement
operant responses	brand switching
operant conditioning	consumer panel data
intermittent reinforcement	probability models
shaping	brand loyalty

REVIEW QUESTIONS AND EXPERIENTIAL EXERCISES

[E = Application extension or experiential exercise]

1. Compare and contrast the two basic research approaches to learning.

2. The text discussed childhood as the period in which we form our individual structures of consumer values and buying styles. It also stated that children are a "vulnerable segment." What does this mean? What are its implications?

3. Comment on the "miscomprehension" results presented in the text. What do you think are some reasons why consumers miscomprehend TV ads? What if anything can or should be done about this?

4. Explain, providing examples, the differences between classical conditioning and instrumental conditioning.

5. Consumer research concludes that consumers are responsive to environmental stimuli that lead to their behavior being shaped and controlled. What are the ethical implications for marketers? For public policymakers?

6. Assume you were arguing in favor of stronger controls on behavior modification attempts by marketers. What would your key arguments be? If you were opposed to such controls, what would your key arguments be?

7. Explain why marketers should be interested in learning about consumers' purchase patterns for their products.

8. Brand loyal behavior offers advantages and disadvantages for both consumers and marketers. Explain. Is "proportion of purchases" a good measure of brand loyalty? What might a better one include?

[E] 9. Learn more about the issues surrounding the "childrens'" television debates. Choose one of the following options and write a brief report on your findings:

   a. Use the references in Notes 5 to 7 to locate readings on the subject.

b. Use the reference section of your library to locate recent articles on the subject.

c. Arrange to watch several hours of Saturday morning television with children at different age stages of Piaget's system. Observe their reactions and interview them if possible

[E] 10. Create a "Word Game" quiz, listing 15 product categories. Ask a sample of 20 people to list the first and second brands that come to mind. Summarize your findings in a brief report. Some possibilities:

a. tires _____, _____
b. tissues _____, _____
c. pizza (delivery) _____, _____
d. toilet paper _____, _____
e. ketchup _____, _____
f. cameras _____, _____
g. running shoes _____, _____
h. soft drinks _____, _____
i. bacon _____, _____
j. dress shoes _____, _____
k. polo shirts _____, _____
l. business suits _____, _____

[E] 11. Show four ads to at least five different friends. Ask them to write down all thoughts that came to mind while reading each ad. Classify these thoughts as support-arguments, source derogations, and counter-arguments. How do the patterns of these thoughts relate to your friends' preferences for the products advertised?

[E] 12. Use the listings in Notes 9 through 15 to locate readings on recent developments on *one* of the following topics that most interests you. Write a brief report on your findings.

a. cognitive responses to advertising
b. deceptive advertising
c. miscomprehension of advertising

[E] 13. Search through magazines to locate efforts by advertisers to pair positive stimuli with their brands. Provide three generalized statements about what you discovered, and cut out examples of each.

[E] 14. Use the listings in Notes 19 through 29 to locate readings on *one* of the LAB-related topics in marketing. Write a brief report on your findings.

[E] 15. Interview a local store manager concerning LAB-related topics such as music in the store, efforts to combat shoplifting, planned reinforcements, placement of strategic stimuli, and so forth. Are consumers responsive to particular types of stimuli? Write a brief report on your findings.

CHAPTER 11

Consumer Attitudes

Brands Worth Many Grands

As the decade of the 1990s began, powerful forces were changing the face of consumer marketing. *Megamergers*—in which one giant firm would buy another and capture its markets—had begun to sweep the United States. Philip Morris, for example, gobbled up the giant General Foods corporation, then turned and creamed Kraft. RJR, another tobacco giant, crunched Nabisco into its spreading empire. Many other deals were in the works.

According to the new buyers, these firms were giant bargains sitting on the stock market shelf. The vice president of mergers and acquisitions at Kidder, Peabody & Co. explained that a key factor is that the concept of *brand equity* was missing from the accounting assets for these firms: "Brand equity, being an off-balance-sheet item, [underlies] under-valued or bargain companies." The president of Canada Dry stated: "Brand equity is driving all of Wall Street."

What is "brand equity"? Simply, it is the extra value that belongs to a brand name. As one market manager put it, *"A petroleum-jelly factory is much more valuable if its output can be called 'Vaseline.'"* In reality, brand equity is based upon the *attitudes* that consumers hold about a particular brand. In this chapter we'll learn more about what consumer attitudes are, how they can be measured, and what they mean for topics such as "brand equity."[1]

■ ■ ■

WHAT ARE CONSUMER ATTITUDES?

*Of all the concepts in consumer behavior, many experts believe that **attitudes** are the most significant.* Why are attitudes such a key concept? What do they represent? Basically, *attitudes represent our summary evaluations* of various elements in the world around us. "I like Bud" and "I can't stand 'Ring Around the Collar' ads" are the types of attitudinal statements that we make every day.

Because their purpose is to summarize a consumer's evaluation of a particular product, attitudes can offer tremendously important information to marketers. By knowing what consumers' attitudes are, a marketer should be able to (1) *understand* why current sales are strong or not and (2) *improve* the marketing mix to improve consumer's attitudes. For these reasons marketers are continuously monitoring consumers' attitudes. Besides sales themselves, attitudes may well be the most measured aspects of consumer behavior.

Defining the Concept

The term **attitude** is derived from the Latin words for "posture" or "physical position." The general notion was that a body's physical attitudes suggested the type of action in which a person would engage. The famous statue of the Greek discus thrower, for example, presents a striking attitude that leaves little doubt of the movements that are to come. In recent times, the concept of attitude has been broadened to reflect a person's mental position. Gordon Allport's classic definition is

> *Attitudes are learned predispositions to respond to an object or class of objects in a consistently favorable or unfavorable way.*[2]

Several aspects of the definition help us to understand this topic. The fact that attitudes are *mental positions* means that marketers must try to infer them through research measures—they cannot be observed directly. The fact that attitudes are *learned* means that they will be affected by information and experiences. While attitudes are relatively enduring (that is, we tend to hold them for rather long periods of time), *attitude change* is possible. For obvious reasons, great attention is given to the topics of attitude formation and attitude change by marketers. The fact that attitudes are **predispositions to respond** indicates their relationship with consumer's *actual behaviors*. Knowing a consumer's attitudes toward a particular brand should help us to understand how he or she will react to that brand in the future. For example, if Jean does not like Cheer, we would not expect to see her buying it.

The term *object* in our definition has a broad meaning. Consumers have attitudes toward entire product categories ("I never did care for squid"), subcategories (Japanese cars), stores (K-mart), salespersons (the overbearing clerk), brands (Pepsi), styles, and so forth. Beyond this, we can hold attitudes about broad issues

such as consumerism, environmental safety and so on. Thus it's clear that consumers have a vast array of attitudes. These attitudes are important reflectors of what we think and how we behave.

The Components of Attitude

The primary view of human behavior, at least since the time of the early Greek philosophers, has been that all behavior is actually a combination of mental, emotional, and physical dimensions (popularized as the "think-feel-do" perspective we've seen elsewhere in the text). This perspective resulted in the classical "three component" view of attitudes. As depicted in Figure 11-1, the traditional model viewed attitudes as consisting of three components. The **cognitive component** refers to the knowledge and opinions the person has about the attitude object. The **affective component** reflects feelings ("affect" is the technical term for positive or negative feelings) or evaluations regarding the attitude object. The **conative component** reflects behavioral tendencies toward the attitude object.

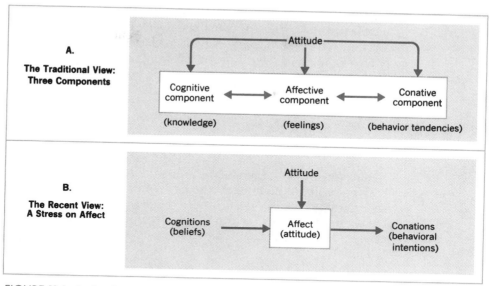

FIGURE 11-1 **Attitude Components: The Two Views**

During the last 20 years, however, consumer researchers have shifted their emphasis away from the three-component view toward a more singular view of *attitude as affect.* This shift does not discount the importance of the other two components: it simply does not define them as attitude. Instead, the recent view—as shown at the bottom of Figure 11-1—proposes an ordered relationship among the three sectors. This is indicated by the flow of the arrows: affect (attitude) is seen as being built upon beliefs, while intentions usually depend on both the beliefs and the attitude. At this stage it is not important that the details of these relations be clarified as within the chapter we will first examine the linkage between cognitions and affect; then we will examine the linkage between affect and conations. It is important to recognize, however, that when modern consumer researchers speak of attitudes, they are referring to the affective component—the liking or disliking of specific products, brands, or stores.

Cognitive consistency—the concept that we consumers strive for harmonious relationships in our thoughts and feelings—is a key concept underlying consumer attitudes. As we saw in our chapter on motivation, a psychic tension is likely to arise when we have inconsistent thoughts. For example, how would you feel if you held the following thoughts: "I really like that Mercedes . . . it is an ugly car." Most consumers would feel slightly uneasy with these thoughts representing their current state of affairs. Thus we expect to see a basic consistency among the components of a consumer's attitude. This point holds several key implications for marketers. Regarding *attitude change,* for example, it indicates that we need to plan for some possible resistance to our persuasive attempts that may arise because of consistency in operation. Regarding *attitude formation,* it suggests that marketers try to use already favorable attitudes to help create a new favorable attitude. Product endorsement ads are a common example of this strategy. Having our favorite celebrity endorse a new product increases our chances of developing a positive attitude toward that product.

CONSUMER ATTITUDES AND MARKETING MANAGEMENT

Brand Management and Consumer Attitudes

Before turning to a detailed examination of consumer attitudes themselves, it may be useful to highlight some key points about why marketing managers are so interested in consumer attitudes. Traditionally, this interest has been centered on **brand attitudes**, or the feelings and evaluations consumers hold about a brand. Measurement of brand attitudes is a truly basic part of the management of a brand.

Figure 11-2 demonstrates this point well. It outlines the program that a major advertising agency, Ogilvy & Mather, recommends to marketers for a brand that is not doing well. According to Ogilvy & Mather's president, "If you're in charge of a brand which is in need of revitalization, then you're in charge of a brand/consumer relationship which is no longer healthy, which is no longer working. You need to find out what's gone wrong with the relationship." Notice the significance of consumer attitudes in this proposal: each tinted step in Figure 11-2 involves decisions based upon the measurement of consumer attitudes.[3] Thus we can see how central they are for brand management in marketing.

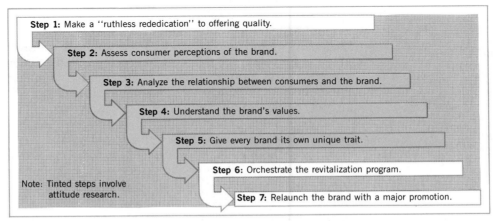

FIGURE 11-2 **A Program for Revitalizing a Lagging Brand**

Source: This figure is based on information in "Revive Sluggish Brand With Seven-Step Plan," *Marketing News,* October 9, 1987, p. 28.

Consumer Attitude and "Brand Equity"

The opening vignette for this chapter indicated how **brand equity** has become a key issue in corporate takeovers. As noted there, brand equity refers to the value of a brand name for the company that owns it. In this section, let's look at the marketing implications of brand equity. Do marketing managers see brand equity as important? When the Marketing Science Institute polled its members—comprised of many of the world's most prominent marketing companies—on priority issues, brand equity was the runaway winner as top research priority. "We buried brand equity in the middle of the deck to see what would happen, and all of the groups pulled it out and put it on top," reports MSI's president. "That says something about it." Recently, Colgate-Palmolive Co. hired a director of equity management to guard the value in Colgate-Palmolive brands. Canada Dry also created a similar position.

Market researchers are now at work to try to measure brand equity. According to Joseph Smith, president of a major research firm, "There are four factors you must measure. First is *prominence,* which is easy. Just ask people what name comes to mind. Second is how favorable the *associations* are—also easy . . . third is the *"portrait"* enlisted by a brand or image . . . fourth is the *flexibility* of the brand—can the brand be generalized or used on other things? [Then] the task of weighting the various factors and pulling the techniques together remains to be done."[4]

Exhibit 11-1 gives us some insight on how consumers view certain brands. You might enjoy seeing how well you can predict the "Top 10" brand names, then see if you can even name the product or service offered by those at the bottom. Beyond these listed, you may have insights into the five competitive battles among the leaders that are listed at the end of the exhibit.[5]

Brands Borrow on Equity

When a brand name has high brand equity, one natural way to capitalize on it is to offer **brand extensions,** to which consumers should respond positively because of their attitude toward existing products from the same marketer. This worked well for Dole, which recently retained a research firm to investigate the nature of brand equity for its name. The firm's president reports: "Dole had a readout that went way beyond pineapple. It was all about health, sunshine . . . and health foods." These results guided Dole to its new logo, a bright yellow sunburst, and to market Dole Fruit Juice Bars, which were highly successful.[6]

Cadillac Loses Equity and Interest

While brand extensions can be extremely lucrative, they are subject to limitations based upon the exact nature of consumers' images of the brand. For example, a Walt Disney Co. study found that consumers would not accept Disney movies for adults—Disney meant children's and family entertainment. Rather than try to fight this consumer image, Disney launched Touchstone Films.

Cadillac wasn't so fortunate in the 1980s when it introduced the Cimarron model, a small car that was a relative of the Pontiac 2000 and Chevrolet Cavalier models. The

EXHIBIT 11-1   AMERICA'S TOP (AND BOTTOM) BRANDS

Listed below are the product categories for the 10 "most powerful" brand names, according to a recent survey of American consumers, who were asked about both their *recognition* of the name and their *opinion* of the brand. This listing is followed by the 10 brand names that finished at the bottom of the 672 name list. See how well you can do in guessing the name of the most powerful brands, then in guessing the product or service of the least powerful brands names. The answers are given in Note 5.

I.

	Product/service	The "Top 10" Brand name	My attitude toward this brand is:
1.	Soft drinks	_____	_____
2.	Soups	_____	_____
3.	Soft drinks	_____	_____
4.	Long distance telephone	_____	_____
5.	Hamburgers	_____	_____
6.	Credit card, traveler's checks	_____	_____
7.	Breakfast cereals	_____	_____
8.	Computers	_____	_____
9.	Jeans	_____	_____
10.	Retailing giant	_____	_____

II.

	Product/service	The "Bottom 10" Brand name	My attitude toward this brand is:
663.	_____	Export "A"	_____
664.	_____	Klipsch	_____
665.	_____	Primerica	_____
666.	_____	Bang & Olufsen	_____
667.	_____	Asahi	_____
668.	_____	Blue Mountain	_____
669.	_____	Daewoo	_____
670.	_____	Gaggenau	_____
671.	_____	Ricola	_____
672.	_____	Exide	_____

III. **Competitive Struggles: Which brand name is more powerful?***

1. Colgate versus Crest? _____
2. Marlboro versus Winston? _____
3. Mobil versus Shell versus Texaco? _____
4. Hershey's versus M&M? _____
5. ABC versus CBS versus NBC? _____

*"Power" reflects a combination of consumers' *recognition* of the brand name and their *opinion* of the brand.

Source: Based on a 1988 survey by Landor Associates, as reported in Edward C. Baig, "Name That Brand," *Fortune,* July 4, 1988, pp. 9ff.

Cimarron was aimed at a less affluent buyer who would not be likely to buy a Cadillac. "The decision was . . . shortsighted," reflects a General Motors executive. "Financial analysts would argue that . . . any sale would be one we wouldn't have gotten otherwise . . . the bean counters said, 'We'll get this many dollars for every model sold,' [but] there was no thinking about brand equity . . . a horrible mistake."

The Cimarron was dropped in 1988. Although there is no precise estimate of its cost to Cadillac's brand equity, the survey reported in Exhibit 11-1 gives us some interesting insights (not shown in the exhibit). Cadillac ranked 16 in *public awareness* of the brand name—a very strong showing. On the other component of the power index, *opinion* or esteem for the brand, however, Cadillac landed in eighty-fourth place. A General Motors analyst muses, "even though brand equity may sometimes be hard to [precisely] define, it's pretty clear when you lost it."[7]

Although a number of new issues have been raised concerning brand management and brand equity, our major point is to appreciate the central role that consumers' attitudes play for marketing decisions. Our next section delves into the nature of these attitudes, and how marketers obtain measures of them.

THE ATTITUDE REVOLUTION: MULTIATTRIBUTE MODELS

A little over 20 years ago, the marketing world discovered the area of multiattribute attitude models and reacted with an explosion of research studies. Within this section we'll briefly examine the nature of these models and how they can help to provide marketing insights into the dynamic consumer marketplace. In terms of the three components we examined in Figure 11-1, our discussion in this section focuses on the relations of cognition and affect, or beliefs and attitudes.

The Basic Multiattribute Model

At this point you may be wondering why marketers don't just ask consumers "How much do you like or dislike Tide?" In other words, if **overall affect** is what we're after, why not just measure it directly? The answer is that marketers do measure it directly and do use the overall measure for certain purposes. Notice, however, that such a simple measure of attitude *doesn't tell us why the consumer feels the way he or she does,* nor does it suggest anything that we might be able to do about changing that attitude. It is precisely in this area that multiattribute attitude models offer their strongest benefits.

Basically, a *multiattribute model* views an attitude object (brand, store, etc.) as possessing *many attributes* (characteristics) that provide the basis on which consumers' attitudes will depend. Thus *the affect a consumer feels toward a brand will depend on the beliefs that consumer holds about what the brand has to offer.* Each belief pertains to one attribute, thus leading to the designation as a multiattribute model. The major advantage of multiattribute models over the simple overall affect measure of attitude is in gaining understanding of attitudinal structure. *Diagnosis* of brand strengths and weaknesses on relevant product attributes can suggest specific changes in a brand and its marketing support.

To gain a clear understanding of the nature of these models, we'll begin by stressing one basic form that has been much used within marketing. (Some researchers in marketing prefer other forms of this model, but this one is especially easy to learn and use.) The basic formula for a multiattribute model is

$$A_{jk} = \sum_{i=1}^{n} B_{ijk} \, I_{ik}$$

where

i = attribute or product characteristic

j = brand

k = consumer

such that

A = consumer k's *attitude* score for brand j
I = the *importance* weight given attribute i by consumer k
B = consumer k's *belief* as to the extent to which a satisfactory level of attribute i is offered by brand j

Although the formula may appear complex, in fact it is not, and with a little practice you'll easily see how this type of model works. Since this model is a *compositional* one, we will begin with the separate attributes and together "compose" them into the larger measure of over-all attitude. Exhibit 11-2's example helps with the discussion. **To learn the model best, enter your personal ratings into Exhibit 11-2 as we go along and then calculate your attitudes toward these outlets.**

Attributes (i)

Attributes provide the basic dimensionality of this model and are of crucial importance. Notice that the left-hand column contains five attributes that consumers might associate with the fast-food product category. To understand the model better, it is a good idea for you to add some further attributes to the listing, in the space below "Price."

Importance (I)

Although all the attributes are relevant, we'd not expect them to be equally important. Thus the "importance weight" element of the model allows us to vary the impact that different attributes will have on consumers' attitudes. Within our example, we've included Andy's ratings for discussion purposes, using a 1 to 7 scale (with 1 = unimportant and 7 = very important). Notice that Andy is quite concerned with "atmosphere" and taste and reports that price is relatively unimportant to him. (We'll expect other consumers to

---

EXHIBIT 11-2   MULTIATTRIBUTE ATTITUDE MODEL CALCULATIONS

Attribute (i)	Importance (I)	Beliefs (B)				
		Watta-Burger	McDonald's	Burger King	Wendy's	(Other)
"Atmosphere"	(6)___	(2)	___	___	___	___
Location	(6)___	(4)	___	___	___	___
Taste	(7)___	(6)	___	___	___	___
Nutrition	(4)___	(3)	___	___	___	___
Price	(2)___	(7)	___	___	___	___
___	___		___	___	___	___
___	___		___	___	___	___
___	___	___	___	___	___	___
Attitude score: (A) =		(104)	___	___	___	___
Overall preference (ranking)		___	___	___	___	___

Scales: Importance: 1 = (unimportant) through 7 (very important)
          Beliefs: 1 = (very poor) through 7 (very good)

have different patterns of importance.) You should enter your own weights at this point on the empty lines, using the additional attributes you've added as well as the ones listed here.

Beliefs (B)

In our form of the model, the belief measure represents the extent to which each fast-food restaurant offers satisfaction on the attribute in question. Andy's ratings of his local Watta-Burger are shown in the exhibit (again on a 1 to 7 scale, with 1 = very poor and 7 = very good). Notice that Andy views Watta-Burger to have good-tasting food at very low prices, but to offer little atmosphere and little nutrition and to be in a somewhat inconvenient location. Continuing with your own example, fill in *your* belief ratings for each attribute for McDonald's, Burger King, Wendy's, and any other fast-food outlets you'd like to assess.

Model Calculations

Model structure refers to the ways in which the ratings are combined and calculated within the model. In our basic model, the multiplicative relations between importance and beliefs, the summation over all attributes, and the nature of the ratings all suggest that this is a *linear compensatory* attitude model. Within an attribute, notice that each rating unit is assumed to provide equal marginal utility to consumers—this allows high scores on one attribute to "compensate" for low ratings on another attribute.

With respect to the modeling of your personal attitudes in Exhibit 11-2, you should at this point move to the bottom of the exhibit and provide a ranking of the fast-food outlets you will be rating. That is, give a "1" to the outlet you most prefer, a "2" to your next favorite, and so forth. In Andy's case we're now ready to calculate his attitude score toward Watta-Burger by simply following the form given in our basic model's formula. That is, we'll take each attribute in turn, multiplying the importance weight that Andy gives it times the belief that Andy has for Watta-Burger on this attribute. Once all the attributes have been multiplied, we'll add up their scores to arrive at a total attitude score that Andy holds toward this fast-food restaurant. In our example, this means that

$$\text{Attitude score} = (6 \times 2) + (6 \times 4) + (7 \times 6) + (4 \times 3) + (2 \times 7)$$
$$= 12 + 24 + 42 + 12 + 14$$
$$= 104$$

This score has little meaning in itself until it is compared either with (1) other consumers' attitudes toward Watta-Burger or (2) with Andy's attitude scores toward other fast-food outlets. Notice, however, how these patterns of scores can give us insight into Andy as a potential Watta-Burger customer. First, it doesn't look as if there's a very good match here. For example, even though Andy's belief rating is "very good" for Watta-Burger's price, this doesn't add very much to his attitude score (only 14 points) because Andy's importance rating for this attribute is quite low—price is just not very important to this consumer. Watta-Burger's lack of atmosphere, on the other hand, hurts it considerably with Andy—although it could have added 42 points to its attitude score with a very good atmosphere rating (that is, if Andy had given a belief rating of 7), the current store draws only 12 position points. Overall, then, we would expect that Andy does not patronize Watta-Burger very often.

Now proceed with your multiplication and summation processes to arrive at your total attitude scores for each outlet. Use your overall scores from the model to rank the outlets and compare this ranking with your simple preference ranking given at the bottom. How do the two rankings match up? That is, does your favorite outlet have the highest attitude score, does the second favorite have the second highest score, and so forth? Finally, go back through the calculations to conduct your *marketing diagnostics* exercise—what attributes is each outlet strong on and in what areas does it need help? What proposals would you suggest to the management of the various fast-food marketers?

Issues in Using the Model

The exercise we've just presented should be helpful in appreciating why the multiattribute model approach is so widely used by marketers. It clearly allows us to see what is important to consumers, how well our brand does in providing the attributes that are important, and how we stack up against our competitors.

Because of these benefits to marketers, you may well find yourself using a multiattribute model to help you with business decisions in the future. You should know that there is a large literature available in the multiattribute area. As you'll discover if you attempt your own study, there are many challenging decisions you'll have to make, but if the stakes are high, you'll want to make sure the model is done right. At this point, you'll be pleased to discover that efforts to create the best models possible have led consumer researchers to examine such key questions as

- How can I develop complete, and meaningful, lists of attributes?
- About how many attributes can I expect to be in a model—3, 5, 10, more?
- Are importance weights really important . . . what if I used only the belief ratings in the model?
- How should I deal with attributes in which different consumers want different levels, such as sweetness in an iced tea? Can I ask consumers what their "ideal point" is for sweetness, then measure beliefs in terms of how far away our brand is from the ideal?
- How likely are "halo effects" in this model? (Halo effects occur when a consumer who likes a brand reports all favorable beliefs on every attribute, thus hindering our attempts to diagnose attribute strengths and weaknesses.)
- Once I have the data from a large sample of consumers, I have many analysis options. What are the proper comparisons to make with these models? Should I concentrate on attributes, importances, beliefs, or over-all attitude scores?

If you find yourself wishing to pursue further details of any or all of these issues, you may want to begin with the readings listed in Note 8.

APPLICATIONS OF MULTIATTRIBUTE CONCEPTS

Now that we've examined the basic form of the multiattribute attitude model, we'll turn to the uses to which these concepts can be put within marketing. In this section we'll examine the amazing potential of this approach for understanding consumer behavior and offering inputs to marketing strategy.

Strategies for Changing Consumer Attitudes

The fundamental purpose of the multiattribute model is to provide an insight into the structure of a consumer's attitude—to tell us why consumers like certain brands, for example, and why they dislike others. But what can we do about what we find out? The answer involves the important topic of **attitude change**. Again, academic researchers have demonstrated that changing the *components* of the attitude (the right side of the formula) does lead to changes in the *overall attitude score* (on the left side of the formula).[9]

In the marketing arena we are interested in *how to improve consumers' attitudes* toward the enterprise we are managing. As Boyd, Ray, and Strong pointed out, the multiattribute approach offers useful guidance to us. Let's return to our basic model to see how

$$A_{jk} = \sum_{i=1}^{n} B_{ijk} \, I_{ik}$$

where

i = attribute   and A = attitude score

j = brand B = belief

k = consumer I = importance weight

If we work logically through the model, we'll locate five prime marketing strategies to raise the attitude scores consumers hold for our brand relative to our competitors.[10]

Strategy 1: Increase Belief Ratings for Our Brand on Key Attributes

This is the most common strategy used by marketers. If it is attainable, it is a surefire way to improve consumer attitudes for us. Unfortunately, almost all our competitors also recognize this strategy. And consumers have seen it so often that they have come to expect it. Thus we're likely to need more than just a promotional program (unless our product or service isn't very well known yet). An actual improvement in the product, an offer of better value (perhaps through special prices), or the use of product demonstrations, are all actions that can yield increases in consumer belief ratings. Sometimes this strategy is clearly called for:

Fire over Six Flags

Several years ago a funhouse fire killed eight people at Six Flags Great Adventure amusement park in New Jersey. Consumers reacted swiftly: attendance that had been running 6 percent ahead of the prior year's suddenly dropped off to 15 percent behind. Consumer research helped to clarify the problem. As the park's marketing director explained, "we found that . . . safety in theme parks in general was a big concern . . . we decided that the best approach was to speak out . . . and tell people we were making our park as secure as possible." To do this, a direct-mail campaign was sent to 650,000 households in the area. The cover letter, written to parents, stressed the safety attribute. It explained how all the park's rides are inspected several times daily and that a new multimillion-dollar fire and safety program had been instituted. Included with the letter was a certificate good for two free admissions to the park, inviting the parents to come for themselves and see how safe it really is. Within the month, 10,000 certificates had been redeemed. Management felt that this strategy had turned around the volume decline.[11]

Strategy 2: Increase the Importance of a Key Attribute

This strategy involves the selection of an attribute in which our brand is stronger than the competition, then stressing to consumers that this attribute deserves higher weighting in their views of the product category. Price and value for the money are related attributes for which this strategy is often used. Purex home care products and low-cholesterol margarines are examples of successful pursuits of this strategy. Health, safety, and risks are attributes that often lend themselves to this strategy. Warranties and money-back guarantees can also be used by retailers and direct marketers to shift consumers' patronage patterns by stressing the reduction of risk.

Strategy 3: Add an Entirely New Attribute to Consumers' Attitudes

This is the most exciting marketing strategy, as it usually involves the creation of a new benefit. When successful, this strategy can lead to major profit increases. About 30 years ago, for example, P&G had added fluoride to its Crest toothpaste and won the only Seal of Approval from the American Dental Association. Almost immediately, its share of the market jumped from 10 percent to over 33 percent! (Again recently, when it introduced the new attribute of tartar control, its share moved from 29 percent to 39 percent of the huge market.)[12] As we discussed in Chapter 3, P&G experienced a similar success with Pampers, when it introduced the new attribute of disposability into the baby diaper market. Recently, the adult cereal market has seen a growth spurt as new types of health-related benefits have been added. A related strategy is introducing new uses for an existing product.[13]

Arm & Hammer's Knockout Punch

One of the classic examples of introducing new uses for an existing brand is the Arm & Hammer baking soda story. Until 1969, Arm & Hammer was a sleepy, one-dimensional brand of sodium bicarbonate. In that year, the company hired a new marketing vice president, who undertook a policy of promoting new uses for this brand name. Based on consumer research, the firm determined that many housewives felt guilty about not cleaning their refrigerators often enough. Since one attribute of baking soda is that it is an excellent deodorizer, the firm ran a West Coast advertising test promoting this attribute as a new use for the product. Faced with phenomenal success (out-of-stock conditions all across the Western states), the company went national with this campaign. Sales increased 72 percent, and research showed that consumer behavior had indeed been changed—the percentage of households that had ever used baking soda as a refrigerator air freshener went from less than 1 percent in 1972 to over 90 percent by the end of the decade!

However, once the box was in the refrigerator consumers showed a tendency to forget about it, thus reducing repeat purchases. How could this be combatted? The answer: suggest yet another usage for Arm & Hammer—once it's done its job in the refrigerator (a box should last about two months) consumers were exhorted to remove it and pour its contents down the kitchen drain to deodorize that also. Within a two-year period, households that had ever performed this chore increased from 40 percent to almost 70 percent! The firm looked for other logical extensions. One easy link was from the refrigerator to the freezer. A campaign suggesting an extra box for the freezer was run in the late 1970s,

What's next?

and was again successful. Research showed that consumer usage for this purpose increased from 12 percent to 28 percent in four years!

What's the current status of this brand? The firm's sales have increased to a level over 10 times greater than in 1969. The brand name is recognized by 97 percent of women, and surveys show that about 95 percent of all U.S. households have one or more packages currently in their homes. The raw material is plentiful and cheap to produce, there are no strong brand competitors, and there are many other possible uses. Each year the firm receives letters from thousands of consumers suggesting new uses that they personally have encountered (recently, for example, the product has been promoted as a carpet deodorizer and as a toothpaste). What happened to the marketing vice president? He became president of the company and is interested in early reports that this product, when added to cow feed, produces more and better milk![14]

Strategy 4: Decrease the Importance of a Weak Attribute

Under this strategy if we find that we have an attribute on which we *do not* rate as highly as our competitors, we might suggest to consumers that this attribute is not as significant as they may otherwise think. Many marketers of high-priced goods face this problem: one way to employ this strategy is to stress a trade-off of a strong attribute for the weak one. L'Oréal hair tints, for example, acknowledge that they "cost a little more" but that their users believe "I'm worth it." The promotional themes for fine jewelry also stress this theme: "Diamonds Are Forever" stresses many years of pleasure, while downplaying initial concern over price. Price is not the only attribute that may have to be downplayed, of course. One of America's classic ad campaigns was for the Volkswagen "Bug"—it humorously acknowledged the car's less than stylish looks and lack of yearly design changes, but stressed that consumers should weight the Bug's quality, dependability, and economy very highly in their own purchase decisions. Similarly, many products and services use appeals to love, status, or health to lower the impact of other attributes on which the brand is not as strong.

Strategy 5: Decrease Belief Ratings for Competitive Brands

This strategy has been used for years by salespersons in retail settings. When a consumer asks for advice, a salesperson will often indicate both positive and negative aspects of different brands and stores. It was not a strategy often used in advertising, however, until the advent of comparative ads about 20 years ago. The strategy is sometimes very successful—Schick, Inc.'s controversial comparative ad campaign for its Fleximatic electric shaver, for example, was credited with a rapid increase from an 8 percent to a 24 percent share of the market, a gain of almost $30 million in sales.[15]

We should note that this strategy is risky, however, and can become unfair to

Dealing effectively with price.

Think small.

Our little car isn't so much of a novelty any more.

A couple of dozen college kids don't try to squeeze inside it.

The guy at the gas station doesn't ask where the gas goes.

Nobody even stares at our shape.

In fact, some people who drive our little flivver don't even think 32 miles to the gallon is going any great guns.

Or using five pints of oil instead of five quarts.

Or never needing anti-freeze.

Or racking up 40,000 miles on a set of tires.

That's because once you get used to some of our economies, you don't even think about them any more.

Except when you squeeze into a small parking spot. Or renew your small insurance. Or pay a small repair bill. Or trade in your old VW for a new one.

Think it over.

An ad in the classic VW campaign.

competing firms. Many persons in the advertising industry dislike the practice of comparison advertising: they stress that the technique lends itself to disparaging competitors. Indeed, much of the caseload of the advertising self-regulatory system is concerned with comparative ad cases, and many lawsuits have been filed in court as well. In one of the earliest, Alberto-Culver won a large settlement from Gillette because Gillette claims about its "Balsam" hair conditioner had driven the brand out of the market. In summary, this strategy is risky and somewhat unpleasant, but it can be quite effective.

Summary Comments: Multiattribute Marketing Strategies

The multiattribute attitude model thus suggests five different strategies that a marketer can pursue to raise consumers' attitudes toward his or her brand. There is also the possibility of staging the strategies in a particular sequence. Mazola's marketing program demonstrated how this can be done. First, the firm pursued strategy 3 by introducing the new attribute (i) of 100 percent corn oil in margarine. Then, once consumers were aware of the attribute, Mazola shifted its stress to strategy 2. To increase the importance (I) of this attribute in consumers' minds, Mazola's advertising extolled the health virtues of corn oil as compared to the other vegetable oils that had been used in margarines. Finally, after having established corn oil as a very desirable attribute, Mazola shifted to strategy 1. Here the stress was on brand beliefs (B)—in this campaign the firm used comparison ads to clarify that, among the three leading brands, only Mazola contained 100 percent corn oil.[16]

Our discussion in this section has thus indicated the basic values the multiattribute approach can offer marketers. There are further developments also of interest, involving *product positioning* decisions. These are briefly described in Appendix 11-A. The discussions there are nontechnical and applications are discussed. Readers who wish to learn about sophisticated applications might enjoy reading the appendix after completing this chapter.

Attitude Research in Public Policy

Thus far our discussion has stressed how marketing managers can use this important information. Before leaving this topic, we should note, however, that consumer attitude concepts are also quite useful for public policy decisions. For example, periodic surveys of beliefs and attitudes toward cigarette smoking have been used to track the remarkable shifts occurring in this area of consumer behavior during the past 25 years. Broader-scale surveys are also run on consumers' attitudes toward their economic well-being (e.g., the Index of Consumer Sentiment) and of consumers' buying intentions for major purchases in the near future. Since consumer purchases are so important to the economic vitality of our system (you may recall that they account for about two-thirds of the U.S. GNP), these surveys provide important information for both government and private business.

Consumer attitude research is also useful in the regulatory area of public policy. The author was involved in one case, for example, in which Hawaiian Punch was required to run a corrective disclosure on its label until consumer surveys would show that high proportions of consumers (67 percent, 80 percent, or 95 percent, depending on which market segment was being surveyed) no longer held a mistaken brand belief about the amount of fruit juice actually in Hawaiian Punch. A number of recent developments, in fact, suggest that the role of consumer attitude research is likely to increase in public policy in the future.[17]

HOW DO CONSUMER ATTITUDES RELATE TO CONSUMER BEHAVIOR?

Up to this point we have examined the link between the cognitive and affective ("thinking" and "feeling") components of Figure 11-1. Now let us turn our attention to the next linkage in the figure—that between affect and conation ("feeling" and "doing"). Typically, we will assume that knowing about a consumer's attitude will allow us to predict that consumer's behavior at a later time. While this is not a bad assumption for us to make, it turns out that this issue is more interesting than it might first appear.

Consumer Attitudes and Brand Purchase Behavior: Empirical Results

One good way to examine the relationship between attitudes and behavior is to take measurements of the same consumers at several points over a time period. Once a brand has been purchased, the researcher can look back to see what types of brand attitudes that consumer held prior to the purchase. In one famous marketing report, Alvin Achenbaum reported that in numerous studies of specific brands his ad agency had found strong relationships between consumer attitudes and brand purchase behaviors.[18] Figure 11-3 shows a typical form of this relationship for one brand of a dental product. Notice that of all those consumers who rated the brand as "Excellent," 78 percent are current users of the brand. At the other extreme, of all those who rated the brand as "Not So Good" or "Poor," only 8 percent were users of the brand during the period measured. If we look toward the attitudes of *former* users of the brand, however, an almost mirror image emerges—of those rating it "Excellent," only 8 percent have stopped using it, while of those consumers rating it to be "Poor," a full 76 percent no longer purchase the brand. In his more detailed analyses of these types of data, Achenbaum also discovered that consumers whose attitudes changed positively toward a brand were more likely to purchase that brand in the future, while those whose attitudes changed negatively were less likely to purchase the brand in the future. Thus this basic evidence tends to support our basic assumption that there is a strong relationship between attitudes and behavior.

So what's all the fuss about? Why are we reading a special section on this topic?

If we look again at Figure 11-3, we can see the answer to this quite reasonable question. Note that while the relationship itself is obviously positive, there are really quite a lot of consumers who don't seem to be behaving in accord with our

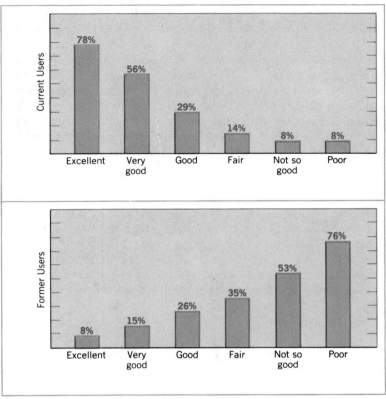

FIGURE 11-3 **Achenbaum's Findings on Attitudes and Behavior for a Representative Product**

From Alvin A. Achenbaum. "Knowledge Is a Thing Called Measurement." in Lee Adler and Irving Crespi. eds.. *Attitude Research at Sea.* Attitude Research Committee. American Marketing Association. Chicago. 1966.

assumption. For example, why would those 22 percent of consumers (i.e., 100%–78%) who rate our brand as "Excellent" not be buying it, and why would 44 percent of those rating it to be "Very Good" not buy it either? At the other extreme, why in the world would any consumer who thinks our brand is "Poor" go out and buy it? Thus the answer to the question, "Why all the fuss?" is that when we actually measure consumers, *we find that the correlations between their attitudes and their behaviors are far from perfect.* This lowers the predictability of our models, increases our uncertainty as marketers, and might lead to reduced profits from our decisions. Thus we're quite interested in finding out why the correlations aren't higher than they are.

As a first step, we can look at other factors that may be at work. For example,

Achenbaum's analyses showed that **product use experience** was a very significant factor in changing people's attitudes toward a brand. This poses another issue: *Which comes first, the attitude or the behavior?* In other words, are we better off to assume that positive attitudes are needed before a product will be purchased or—to the contrary—that product use behavior is needed before any meaningful attitudes can be formed?

The correct answer is "Both statements can be true," which means that we must look further into the conditions under which either is more likely. Many researchers now believe that the key to disentangling these paths lies in understanding the nature of **consumer involvement** with a particular product purchase. When consumers are highly involved with a purchase, marketers can expect attitude change preceding behavior. When consumer involvement is low, attitudes will have a weaker role to play in determining purchase behavior. In this case, if behavior occurs, the product use experience is likely to affect strongly the later attitudes that consumers will hold. Research by Fazio and Zanna indicated that attitude-behavior correlations are higher for those with direct experience than for people who simply read information. Smith and Swinyard have extended this point to address marketing strategy questions such as directly promoting product trial (for example, through free samples) versus using advertising aimed at changing consumers attitudes.[19]

Complexities in the Relationship

But even if we're not sure about the direction of causality between attitudes and behavior, why aren't the correlations higher than they'd seem to be in Figure 11-3?

This is another good question, but fortunately it has received considerable attention already. Among the best explanations are the following:

- *Not all attitudes are tied closely to behavior.* Consumers hold many attitudes toward people we'll never meet, brands we never buy, and so on. For example, many consumers hold positive attitudes toward Rolls-Royce autos and large homes with sweeping lawns. Usually these attitudes are not held with the idea of a purchase in mind, due to other factors such as income limits. If these other factors were favorable, however, such attitudes might become predictors of behavior.
- *Consumers have positive attitudes toward multiple brands.* In most product categories, consumers are favorable to a number of the brand alternatives. If we measure "behavior" by single-time purchases, obviously many of the brands with favorable attitudes will not be purchased at that time.
- *The role of time and change is important.* Attitudes can change after they've been measured in a study, and this might easily affect the correlations we obtain. Achenbaum found, for example, that about 75 percent of the consumers

in his study changed their attitude ratings toward the average brand during a six-month period. (We should note that some of this apparent change might simply reflect unreliability in the attitude ratings, as when a consumer is somewhat uncertain about which ratings (e.g., "good" or "very good") to give the brand and in the second rating provides a different rating from the first rating.) Whether the differences in attitude ratings reflect true change or response reliability, there is a lot of it, which means that correlations with behavior are likely to be depressed. This is due to the fact that behavior change occurs less frequently. In Achenbaum's study only 20 percent of consumers switched brands during the six-month period.

- *Situational effects can alter purchase plans.* Many situational factors can intercede between a person's attitude and his or her actual purchase behavior. Special price deals, out-of-stock conditions, new brands to try, or a usage situation calling for a specific type of brand are all fairly common occurrences.

- *Personal factors can affect purchase behavior.* Numerous factors in our personal lives can have strong impacts. Purchases of expensive products, for example, are strongly affected by the dollars we have available to spend. Similarly, diets can alter our food buying behaviors, although underlying attitudes haven't changed at all. Inputs from salespersons, friends, and advertising can also lead to a purchase that we had not anticipated earlier and that would not be reflected in our earlier attitude ratings. Also, some consumers will have a higher consistency than others: Research has shown that more knowledgeable consumers and those with a higher "need for cognition" are likely to hold attitudes more predictive of their behaviors.[20]

- *CIP factors are important as well.* Recent research has shown that **attitude accessibility** is also a key factor in attitude-behavior relationships. Basically, *accessibility* refers to how likely any single attitude is to "come to mind" (i.e., to move from LTM to STM) when an attitude object is being considered. More accessible attitudes come to mind more quickly, and are likely to play a larger role in consumers' perceptual processes and behaviors. Thus, the attitude-behavior relationship should be higher for consumers whose relevant attitude is more accessible. In one recent study, for example, the consumers with lowest-accessibility attitudes were found to select brands that had been placed in less prominent shelf positions only 40 percent of the time, whereas the consumers with highest-accessibility attitudes picked these brands 50 percent of the time. As both groups' brand attitudes were equally favorable, the difference was due to shelf position playing a stronger role for those with less-accessible attitudes, whereas accessible brand attitudes played a stronger role for those who worked beyond the front shelf positions to find the brand they liked the most.[21]

The Extended Fishbein Model

These types of considerations were sufficient to convince Martin Fishbein (who had developed a slightly different form of the multiattribute model from the one we studied) and a co-worker, Izek Ajzen, to develop their *theory of reasoned action.* While the original multiattribute model was appropriate to describe a person's attitude *toward an object,* Fishbein believed it was not sufficient to describe a person's attitude *toward behaving toward that object.* Fishbein's point makes sense, as the Rolls-Royce and mansion examples indicate. Marketers interested in predicting specific behaviors should consider using Fishbein's extended model in this effort.

The logic behind the **extended Fishbein model** is presented in Figure 11-4. There are two key changes from the multiattribute model that should be noted:

■ *The attitude model itself is different.* Here we are interested in a person's attitude toward a behavior rather than an object. The appropriate attributes thus concern the consequences that may follow from that behavior rather than the attributes of the product itself. One *consequence* of buying a Rolls-Royce, for example, might be bankruptcy: if this were likely, the attitude toward the behavior would be much more negative than the attitude toward the brand itself. (These factors are presented in the top left corner of Figure 11-4.)

■ *A normative component has been added.* The new component is called the **subjective norm**. This represents the consumer's perception of what other

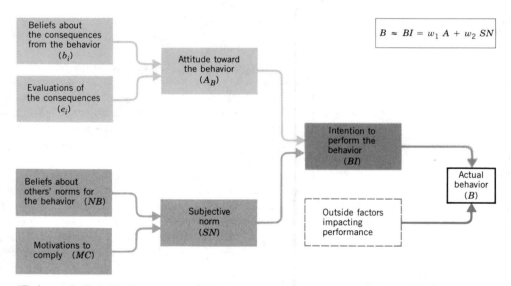

$$B \approx BI = w_1\,A + w_2\,SN$$

*To be read: "Behavioral intention, which is approximately equivalent to behavior, is determined by a person's attitude toward performing the behavior, together with the impacts that social norms will have on performing that behavior. The relative contributions of the attitudinal and normative components are represented by the weighting factors, w_1 and w_2."

FIGURE 11-4 **The Logic of Fishbein's Extended Model**

people believe that he or she should do. (This factor is represented in the bottom center of Figure 11-4.) In some cases this component won't be very relevant (when we don't much consider what other people might think, as in purchases of a brand of chewing gum). In these cases, the consumer's personal attitude toward the behavior (A_B) will have more weight. In other cases, however, the normative component can be *extremely* important. Many students, for example, have felt the weight of the normative component in deciding which college to attend. Fishbein's SN component is intended to model this aspect of their behavioral decisions. To understand these points better, let's consider how the model would work in the example that follows.

Example: Sherry's College Choice

Let's consider Sherry's dilemma as she's deciding on which university will benefit from her presence in the forthcoming year. Because she loves her parents and wants to please them, Sherry has a high motivation to comply (MC) with their positions as to which school she should choose. Let's assume that she believes that her parents' norms are strongly opposed to State U. (perhaps because of its reputation as a wild party school in which she may be led astray by bad influences). In this instance, Sherry's model will show a strong negative NB for State: together with her strong positive MC, this will yield a strongly negative SN for State, reducing the chances that she'll go there. Similarly, let's assume that both parents are fervent alums of Slippery Rock and would like nothing better than for Sherry to carry on the family tradition. This would yield a strong positive NB, which together with the strong positive for MC, produces a strongly positive SN for this alternative, thus increasing the probability of Sherry's becoming a "Rock-ette" ("Rocket," "Rocker," "Pebble," ???) next year.

Sherry's actual model is likely to be much more complex than we've described, of course, since she may have others whose normative views are important. Her boyfriend Matt, for example, may have an impact on this decision, as might her best girlfriends, her guidance counselor, and others. Even so, her decision will not necessarily be guided by the normative component—she may have such a strongly favorable attitude toward Tech that she'll go there despite the fact that others believe that she should go elsewhere! Whatever her final decision, we can see that it is likely to reflect both an attitudinal component and a normative component and that the Fishbein model's approach should allow us to diagnose which factors are most significant.

Further Contributions from Academic Researchers

In recent years there has been considerable consumer research done by marketing professors on the theory of reasoned action. The general conclusions are quite positive—it does seem that this approach offers a considerable potential for understanding consumer behavior. At the same time, there have been some heated debates about the model's form and measures, as well as new extensions that propose potential improvements in the approach. (If you would like to read more about developments in this research area, you may wish to pursue the readings listed in Notes 22 and 23.) At this point we'll turn to a final area that relates to the attitude-behavior relationship—the role of *low involvement* in affecting this linkage.

ATTITUDES, INVOLVEMENT, AND ADVERTISING

In closing this chapter we should note an interesting combination of issues in which attitudes play a key role—the combination of attitudes, involvement, and advertising influences. An increasing number of researchers are asking such questions as "Do consumers with low involvement process *different cues* in an ad from those who are highly involved?"

Two of the most important developments in this regard are the elaboration likelihood model of persuasion and the concept of "attitude toward the ad." Following a brief description of each, we'll turn to a recent study that demonstrated surprising results that indicate why advertisers are taking a close look at this area.

The Elaboration Likelihood Model

The **elaboration likelihood model (ELM)**, recently developed by John Cacioppo and Richard Petty, has had a major impact on recent research on consumer behavior and advertising.[24] This interesting model stresses the view that *the process of persuasion will be fundamentally different when consumers elaborate on an ad than when they do not.* **Elaboration** in this model refers to thinking about the information provided in the advertising message. Greater elaboration is likely when the consumer has the motivation, opportunity, and capability to process the information in the message. When consumers do elaborate, this model predicts that the *central route* to persuasion will be taken. Two examples of models assuming the central route is used are the hierarchy of effects model and our multiattribute model of attitude in this chapter (that is, both of these models assume basically that attitudes toward the product will be formed on the basis of important attributes and relevant brand beliefs).

When elaboration likelihood is low, however, the consumer is *not* likely to engage in much cognitive effort in processing arguments in the ad. Instead, he or she may ignore much of it, attend to the attractive models rather than the product message, and so forth. When this occurs, the ELM model says that the *peripheral route* to persuasion is taken. Within the peripheral route, much less emphasis is given to brand beliefs and product attributes. Instead, other aspects of the ad, such as the credibility of the source, his or her attractiveness, the number (not quality) of the arguments presented, and so forth, are likely to determine how favorable or unfavorable the consumer will be. One of the major determinants of which route—central or peripheral—will be taken is consumer involvement. When involvement is high, the central route is more likely, but when it is low, the peripheral route is more apt to be operating.

Attitude Toward the Ad

A separate but closely related stream of research is geared specifically to the impact that advertising might have on consumers' behavioral intentions. The concept of **attitude toward the ad (A/ad)** was proposed in 1981 by Terence Shimp and, in a separate article, Andrew Mitchell and Jerry Olson.[25] Their major point was that, when watching or reading an ad, consumers have reactions to the ad itself. Thus there are *two attitudes* of interest that are either formed or changed through exposures to advertising: the attitude toward the brand and the attitude toward the ad. For example, it is quite possible for a consumer to enjoy an ad greatly but to have a neutral attitude toward the sponsor's brand.

The concept of creating ads that consumers will enjoy is of course nothing new—ad agencies have been measuring detailed viewer reactions to ads for years. What is new about this approach, however, is that it asks, "What exact role does a consumer's affective reaction to a commercial play in his or her larger intentions to purchase the product or not?" Is it possible that A/ad has no impacts at all on a consumer's attitude toward a brand? Alternatively, does A/ad affect the attitude toward buying the brand (which then affects behavioral intention), or does A/ad affect behavior directly? If the first explanation is true, we're likely to *like* brands more because we like their commercials. If the second explanation is true, we're more likely to *buy* brands because we like their commercials.

In each case there are subexplanations that are also important. For example, if A/ad affects our brand attitude, does it do so in a conscious manner, or through some sort of classical conditioning process? These more detailed questions go on and on. Research in this area will be quite complex and controversial, as it attempts to "tease out" these subtle forms of effects. Early research on A/ad has indicated that its impact is likely to be greatest when consumers are in low-involvement processing modes. In these instances (which reflect ELM's peripheral persuasion route), consumers are likely to process little of the substance of an ad's message about a brand, but are more attuned to other aspects that might capture their casual attention and interest. Does this really happen? Let's look at the interesting results of a study that tried to find out:

Shena: The Shampoo for That Special Woman

Park and Young created several viewing conditions to examine the impact that involvement might have on how consumers formed their brand attitudes and attitudes toward the ad. To ensure that new attitudes were being formed, the researchers created professional-appearing commercials for a fictitious new brand of shampoo, "Shena, from Estee Lauder." In the portions of the study that concern us here, two groups of women were formed—we'll call them the "high-involvement group" and the "low-involvement group."

The *high-involvement group* was told that *Consumer Reports* had found substantial quality differences in shampoo brands, that one key performance characteristic might dominate and that they were to watch the following commercial as if they were trying to learn about the new brand and how effectively it performed. The *low-involvement group,* on the other hand, was told that *Consumer Reports* had found that the leading brands of shampoos didn't differ very much in their performance and that group members should assume that they had just stocked up on shampoo and were not planning to buy any more for quite a long while. This group was also told to assume that they'd just received word that a long-time friend was seriously ill and they were just sitting in front of the TV when this commercial happens to come on. Given these sets of instructions, we'd expect the high-involvement condition to produce the central route to persuasion while the low-involvement condition would produce the peripheral route. Since the Shena commercial contained both product performance claims and attractive scenes, models, and hair, the audience members could devote their processing to either type of ad element, and this should show up in their later ratings.

Park and Young's analysis used correlations with an overall measure of consumers' attitudes toward Shena and is shown in Figure 11-5. The important comparison for us is that between the brand beliefs model and an attitude toward the ad measure. *Which should do better in predicting a consumer's overall brand attitude?* As we might guess, given our discussion in this section, the correct answer is "It depends on the level of involvement!" The actual results showed that the brand beliefs model did significantly better than attitude toward the ad *when involvement was high:* the correlations with overall attitude toward Shena were +0.62 versus +0.26, respectively. *When involvement was low, however, the*

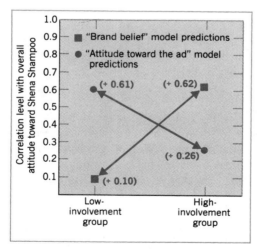

FIGURE 11-5 **Effects of "Low Involvement" Level on Processing an Ad**

Source: Adapted from data presented in C. W. Park and S. M. Young, "Types and Levels of Involvement and Brand Attitude Formation," in R. Bagozzi and A. Tybout, (eds.) *Advances in Consumer Research,* Vol. 10, (Association for Consumer Research, Ann Arbor, Mich., 1983), pp. 320–324.

results were reversed: brand beliefs correlated only +0.10 with overall attitude toward Shena, while attitude toward the ad scored a +0.61 correlation. This dramatic reversal of directions is shown in Figure 11-5.[26]

Thus there appears to be a strong linkage among the concepts of attitude and involvement, and this linkage has special implications for the challenging world of advertising management. If you wish to learn more about developments in this area, you may wish to begin with the readings listed in Notes 24, 25, and 26. In the meantime, however, let's just think briefly about the kinds of implications that these findings might have for advertising practice. It is clear that ads can be successful through both the central and the peripheral routes to persuasion. However, if an advertiser knows that most consumers will be in low-involvement states when they're exposed to ads for his or her brand, wouldn't he or she be better off *to design ads to appeal specifically to this peripheral mode of processing?* If so, what would these ads contain? Perhaps lots of action, color, sound, sex appeal, and fast movement, with rapid cuts from one scene to the next to preserve attention? Music and dancing? Moods and appeals to emotions? As you think about these issues, you may wish to turn on the TV and observe how commercials for low-involvement products are being constructed these days!

SUMMARY

What Are Consumer Attitudes?

In this chapter, the important *role of attitude in consumer behavior* was discussed. The chapter was divided into four major sections. The first began with a *definition of attitudes* as "learned predispositions to respond to an object . . . in a consistently favorable or unfavorable way." Several *key theoretical pespectives on attitude* were discussed, including the traditional model that viewed attitudes as a composite of three elements: *cognitive, affective,* and *conative.* We noted that this conceptualization has recently been downplayed in favor of defining *attitude as affect,* then exploring its links to the cognitive and conative components.

Consumer Attitudes and Marketing Management

The second section of the chapter examined why marketers are so interested in measuring consumer attitudes, particularly in brand management activities and in the emerging area of *brand equity.* Here we saw that consumer attitudes offer useful measures of how a brand or store is regarded by consumers, and thus supply insights about both what the future will bring and also what a manager might do to improve it. We then took a quiz on the strongest (and weakest) brand names in the United States.

The Attitude Revolution: Multiattribute Models

The third section focused on the links between the cognitive and affective components—between beliefs and attitudes. Here we discussed *multiattribute attitude models,* an approach that has achieved great popularity in marketing, and we examined the structure of the *marketing model.* We saw how these models provide insights into the dynamics of consumer behavior and we analyzed five strategies for changing consumer attitudes.

How Do Attitudes Relate to Consumer Behavior?

The chapter's concluding section focused on the *relationship between consumer attitudes and consumer behavior.* A brief review of the research evidence here showed that the attitude-behavior link is often not as strong as one might expect. We noted a number of reasons for this gap and then investigated the *extended Fishbein model* in some detail. This model helps us to note some of the other factors that intercede between attitudes and behavior itself. Following this discussion, we turned to a topic of much current research interest: consumer attitudes, involvement, and advertising. Two new concepts—the *elaboration likelihood model* and *attitude toward the ad*—were introduced. These topics relate to how low involvement can dramatically change the way in which consumers are processing the advertising they receive.

Throughout the chapter we have stressed the key role that consumer attitudes play for marketers. Appendix 11-A expands on this point by summarizing a popular approach to applying attitudes in marketing decisions—*product positioning.*

KEY TERMS

attitudes
predisposition to respond
cognitive component
affective component
conative component
cognitive consistency
brand attitudes
brand equity
brand extensions
overall affect

multiattribute model
attitude change
product use experience
consumer involvement
attitude accessibility
extended Fishbein model
subjective norm
elaboration likelihood model (ELM)
elaboration
attitude toward the ad (A/ad)

APPENDIX 11A TERMS

positioning   preference map
determinant attributes   multidimensional scaling (MDS)
perceptual map

REVIEW QUESTIONS AND EXPERIENTIAL EXERCISES
[E = Application extension or experiential exercise]

1. Why is "attitude" considered a central concept in consumer behavior? Consumer attitudes toward products may be one of the most monitored aspects of consumer behavior by marketers. Why is this so? Provide examples.

2. What is "brand equity," and why has it been important in financial takeovers of consumer marketing firms?

3. What is the basic rationale behind a multiattribute attitude model? Discuss the formula for this model, pointing out each of the key components.

4. Evidence appears to support the basic assumption that there is a relationship between attitudes and behavior, but that it sometimes can be distressingly low. Discuss six basic reasons for this, using an example for each.

5. Describe the extended Fishbein model. Why might it be more useful to marketers in predicting a particular consumer behavior than the basic multiattribute model would be? Explain, using an example.

[E] 6. "Advertisers should look closely at the results of the elaboration likelihood model." Explain what the speaker might mean by this.

[E] 7. In what different ways might attitude toward the ad affect brand purchase? Provide examples for each.

[E] 8. Consider the five prime marketing strategies for changing consumer attitudes. Analyze a number of advertisements, searching for instances of each strategy. Clip out one example of each. Briefly explain your rationale.

[E] 9. Using either the relevant Notes for this chapter, or the reference section of your library, investigate recent developments in one of the following:
   a. brand equity
   b. product positioning
   c. conjoint analysis (a positioning technique)
   d. multidimensional scaling (MDS)

[E] **10.** Using either the relevant Notes for this chapter, or the reference section of your library, investigate one of the following topics in greater depth:

    a. the multiattribute model

    b. attitude accessibility

    c. the elaboration likelihood model (ELM)

    d. attitude toward the ad

[E] **11.** Using Figure 11-A1 in the appendix (a market map for beer in Chicago), identify what positioning strategies you would have recommended for Miller beer based on Aaker and Shansby's product strategies. Write a brief report summarizing your analysis.

[E] **12.** Conduct a multiattribute attitude project for a local retail outlet (e.g., fast-food restaurant, bar, grocery store). The following steps might prove helpful:

    a. Outline the essential elements as shown in Exhibit 11-2.

    b. Create a consumer questionnaire to obtain actual measures for each element (the cited references in the notes may be helpful here).

    c. Pretest your questionnaire and revise it to ensure that consumers can answer it appropriately.

    d. Survey ten consumers (this size will be too small for strategic purposes, but it will provide you with insights into the model).

    e. Perform the essential calculations.

    f. Interpret the results and offer marketing strategy recommendations using the five options from the multiattribute model. Write a report summarizing your project, results, and recommendations.

[E] **13.** Interview members of two local health clubs you believe to be appealing to different consumer segments. Try to identify the relevant product attributes, then try to determine whether the members differ in their importance weights for these attributes, and what their belief ratings are for the two clubs. Are both clubs seemingly competing successfully? Write a brief report on your findings, and any recommendations you have.

[E] **14.** Interview the managers of two or three local bars (or restaurants, or clothing stores) you believe are offering different levels of attributes to consumers, such as sports bars, dance clubs, jazz clubs, neighborhood bars, and so forth. Identify the views each manager holds about his or her consumer market, the key attributes for the bar's customers, and the present strong and weak points of the marketing strategy. How might the concepts from this chapter help to improve the marketing strategy for one of these establishments? Write a brief report on your findings.

[E] **15.** Interview an executive of a market research firm as to the types of consumer attitude studies his or her firm offers to marketing and advertising managers.

Obtain literature if available, and ask about sample sizes (and selection), operational issues, timing, and costs. Learn also about how the results can be used, and any cases in which they were clearly helpful. Write a brief report on your findings.

 APPENDIX 11-A *APPLICATION OF ATTITUDE MODELS FOR PRODUCT POSITIONING*

Multiattribute Concepts in Product Positioning

A number of years ago two marketing men, Ries and Trout, trumpeted the message, "The Positioning Era Cometh."[27] Since that time marketers have had an enormous interest in this area. **Positioning** *refers to a managerial process of deliberately designing a marketing mix that will lead consumers to perceive the brand as having a distinctive image in comparison to brands offered by competitors.* Multiattribute concepts are at the core of this approach, since the key to the approach is to view a product as a "bundle of attributes." The positioning itself will depend on which attributes (i) are most important (I) to the target segment of consumers, at what levels they will be offered, and what brand beliefs (B) consumers will be encouraged to have.

Since multimillion-dollar markets are often at stake in brand positioning, actual marketing programs can be very detailed. Aaker and Shansby,[28] however, have suggested six basic positioning strategies for marketers to consider:

- *Strategy 1. Stress a specific performance attribute:* Volvo offers "durability," Fiat offers "craftsmanship," and so on.
- *Strategy 2. Offer a specific balance of price and quality:* Saks offers high quality at high prices, Sears is moderate on both bases, Zapper Stores is low on both, and so on.
- *Strategy 3. Stress specific use occasions:* Gatorade satisfies an athlete's thirst, Arm & Hammer baking soda should be used as a refrigerator deodorizer, and so on.
- *Strategy 4. Stress the types of product users:* Baby shampoo is directed toward infants and toddlers, *Seventeen* is designed to appeal to teen and preteen girls, Charlie fragrance is marketed to socially active young women and so on.
- *Strategy 5. Positioning as a new product variation:* Imperial margarine features the taste of butter, Caress is "bath oil" soap, and so on.
- *Strategy 6. Associate with or compare against a well-known competitor:* Consider Sabroso versus Kahlúa, Avis versus Hertz, Meisterbrau versus Budweiser, and so on.

Consumer Research for Positioning

Since the stakes are high, several hundred thousand dollars might be spent on advanced consumer research methods within a positioning project. This research will try to determine exactly what our positioning options are and then to estimate quantitatively and model how consumers (and competitors) are likely to react to various options we might choose for our brand.

Shocker and Srinivasan[29] have outlined the process as a sequence of five stages:

- *Stage 1. Determine the relevant product market:* This stage answers the questions, "Which brands compete with each other and which consumer segments are involved."
- *Stage 2. Identify the determinant attributes for each submarket:* This stage isolates **determinant attributes**, namely, those particular product characteristics that are most crucial in determining which exact brand a consumer will choose. Determinant attributes must be *both* important *and* ones in which brands are seen to differ.[30]
- *Stage 3. Create an abstract representation of each submarket:* This stage involves the development of a perceptual map of the relevant market (we'll look at perceptual mapping following this list of research steps).
- *Stage 4. Develop consumer models to predict preference and choice:* These models often take the general form of our basic multiattribute attitude model, but are extended in a different direction. Interest here is in obtaining the best quantitative estimates of parameters within the model (for example, the specific regression coefficient for each brand belief). These models involve advanced statistical methods.[31]
- *Stage 5. Evaluation of product positions to find the best options:* This step involves several quantitative estimates, namely, (1) the consumer sales appeal of each positioning strategy, (2) the profit implications of each strategy (including required investment and cost factors), and (3) possible competitive reactions. Close work with a firm's management is likely to be needed to obtain these judgments. Based on predicted profits from each positioning option, the firm then begins to develop its marketing mix to achieve the desired "niche" in the marketplace.[32]

Even though the heavy mathematical emphasis in the later stages of this process may be beyond the scope of our treatment, our earlier discussions of the multiattribute model should allow us to understand what the researchers are trying to achieve. For the stages to be even more clear, let's take a closer look at how a *market map* can be developed and used.

Mapping Markets and Minds

Perceptual mapping is a particularly interesting approach to studying consumer attitudes and can easily be visualized. For example, Figure 11-A1 displays two

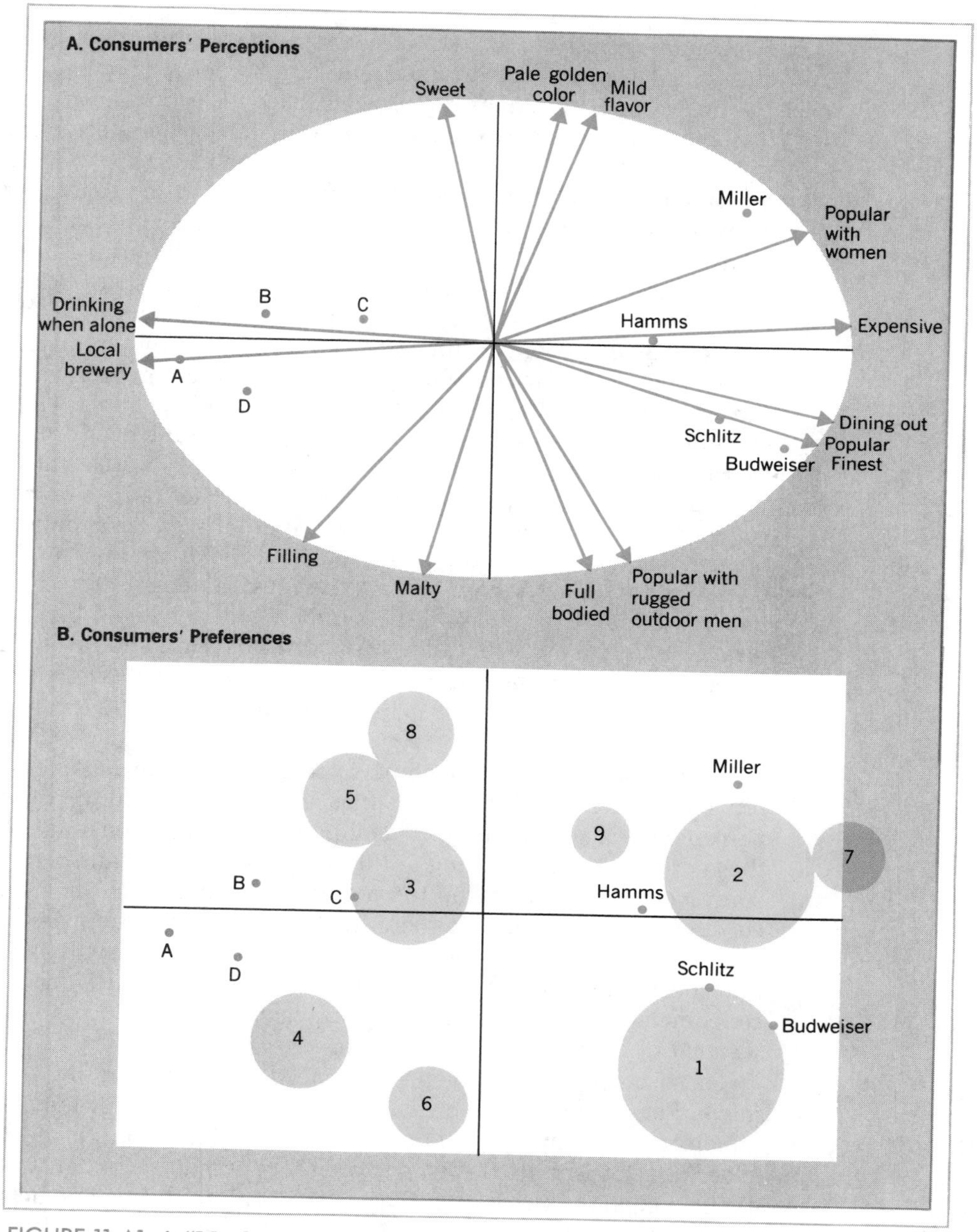

FIGURE 11-A1 A "Market Map" for Beer in Chicago

Source: Richard M. Johnson, "Market Segmentation: A Strategic Management Tool," *Journal of Marketing Research,* February 1971, pp. 13–19.

related maps of the Chicago beer market some years ago. These were produced by Richard Johnson, a market researcher who was working on a project for one of the local brewers (note that the four local brands are not identified by name).[33]

The first map describes the *product space* for beer, as consumers perceive it. It is thus known as a **perceptual map**. It shows where each brand is "located" in consumers' minds (we shall return to this point!). The second map represents the preferences that consumers have for various attributes and is thus known as a **preference map**. (We should note that a product space actually exists in as many dimensions as there are independent key attributes, but is most easily seen when simplified to two-dimensional space and graphed out. If three dimensions were noted, a Tinkertoy model might be built.) The shaded circles represent different segments of consumers, in terms of what they want in a beer.

The general research approach in producing these maps is easy to understand, though the actual mathematical techniques can be complex. Basically, the perceptual map in Figure 11-A1 was produced by asking beer drinkers how similar the eight beer brands were to each other. ("Similarity" can be measured in several ways. In this study, Johnson asked for brand belief ratings on the 35 attributes, some of which are shown in the map. Another popular approach would simply present consumers with the names of three of the brands, say, Miller, Bud, and Coors, and then ask which two are the most similar.) After all different combinations of brands were used, the similarity ratings could be put through some form of a special analysis called **multidimensional scaling (MDS)**. This computer program then produces the perceptual map that best fits the ratings that the consumers have provided. Johnson's approach to this step yielded the first map in Figure 11-A1.

For the second map, consumers are asked now to rank the brands in their order of preference. These rankings are analyzed within the confines of the perceptual map to define the "ideal point" that each consumer would prefer on these dimensions. According to this analysis, each consumer has only one ideal point located somewhere on the preference map. The closer a brand comes to a consumer's ideal point, the more that consumer will like what the brand has to offer. The ideal points from the various beer drinkers were then grouped together into the numbered *preference circles* shown on the map. Since these represent consumers having similar ideal points, each preference circle is akin to a *market segment* of beer drinkers in Chicago.

These points can easily be understood by examining the details of the two maps. For example, notice that the perceptual map indicates that the two key dimensions appear to be (1) a *price-quality* dimension on the horizontal, with lower-priced brands to the left and premium brands to the right and (2) a *mildness* dimension on the vertical, with mild beers toward the top and heavy beers toward the bottom. Each brand's current positioning can easily be located on the perceptual map. Miller High Life, for example, showed up as a relatively mild beer that was seen to be popular with women.

But where are the best places to be? The *preference map* on the bottom of the figure can allow us to answer this important question. Notice that nine consumer segments seem to exist here, representing different ideal points for these dimensions. Segment 1, for example, is a large group that is not very price sensitive and wants a slightly heavier brew. Budweiser and Schlitz were likely to have been appealing to these drinkers. Segment 2 is another large group that is also willing to pay premium prices, but which is looking for a "lighter" beer such as Hamms and Millers were seen to be. Segment 4, on the other hand, is seeking a heavier, "filling" beer at a lower price. No brand was ideally positioned for this segment at the time, though local brand D was closest.

"Welcome to Miller Time"

Assuming that these maps are accurate, what strategies should the different brands follow? To answer this question in reality, we would have to proceed through the types of analyses suggested for stages 4 and 5 of the positioning process, drawing upon much more detailed information from the particular firm for which we're working. To see the potentials for this type of approach, however, we can look back at several actual developments with Miller Beer and note how they relate nicely to the information contained in Johnson's study.

About the time the maps in Figure 11-A1 were developed, the Miller Brewing Company was purchased by the cigarette giant, Philip Morris, Inc. At the time, Miller's prime brand was Miller High Life, which was being promoted as "The Champagne of Bottled Beers." Overall, the firm held only about 3 percent of the national beer market. When Philip Morris took over, it introduced the aggressive promotional techniques of the cigarette industry to the beer market, striving to increase sales sharply and gain market share. As a key part of this strategy, the flagship Miller brand was *repositioned* away from being a "woman's beer." Studies showed that although this segment was potentially large in numbers, its members didn't actually consume very much beer. The heavy beer drinkers instead were blue-collar working men who would not respond well to the female-oriented positioning of the Miller brand. Accordingly, Miller placed huge advertising expenditures behind a repositioning of its flagship brand, now promoting it as a rugged brew for the heavy drinking blue-collar working man. Such themes as "Welcome to Miller Time . . ." were used in this effort to move the beer "from the champagne bucket into the lunch bucket."

In terms of Figure 11-A1's preference map, Miller moved substantially toward the segment 1, thereby challenging Budweiser and Schlitz on a head-to-head basis. Shortly thereafter, in part for other reasons, Schlitz dropped dramatically in sales and popularity, while Miller passed it and moved in on the market leader.

Then, in 1975, Miller successfully introduced its new "Lite" beer. In this effort, the brewer teamed the claims "Tastes Great!" and "Less Filling!" in its famous advertising campaign that featured rugged ex-sports heroes to endorse this new type of beer. The use of these men clearly signaled that this was a macho brew (retired stars were used in part because active athletes don't endorse beers due to their position as role models for children and teenagers). Notice that the "Lite" strategy does not fit as nicely on our map, since it involved at least three distinct sectors on the right side of the chart (light, rugged men, and premium price). It is likely, however, that Miller Lite was able to capture much of segment 2. It is also worthwhile to note that this brand—by making the concept of a "diet beer" acceptable to many drinkers—probably restructured the beer market into at least a three-dimensional map. Overall, how did these programs fare for Miller? Not bad—its new positionings shot its share of the national beer market from 3 percent in 1970 to 25 percent by the end of the decade![34]

PART III

External Influences on Consumer Behavior

In this part of the book—Chapters 12–17—we will examine the key external factors that can act to shape, guide, and influence our behavior as consumers. In Chapter 12, we will begin by examining the subtle but powerful forces of culture, noting how strongly consumer behavior responds to new trends that appear in a culture. In Chapter 13, we'll continue our discussion of cultural influences, but now with an emphasis on international differences and the important role that symbolism plays in consumer behavior. Chapter 14 narrows the field of influences a little, as we focus on social and situational influences and how they operate. Chapter 15 strikes closer to home, as we discuss families and households. Each of these four chapters provides many insights for marketers. In our final two chapters of Part Three, however, we turn specifically to the issue of how marketers influence consumer behavior: Chapter 16 digs into salespersons' influences, whereas Chapter 17 tackles the complex world of advertising's influences on consumer behavior. In the entire Part Three, you'll encounter some influences that are obvious, but many that are not, and you'll see many implications for yourself as both a marketer and a consumer. So turn the page, and let's get started!

CHAPTER 12

Cultural Influences on Consumer Behavior

Two Women

Seeta Singh wiped her brow and sighed softly. It was a hot, humid day in the rural village of Rampur, India, and Seeta was very tired. She was a pretty, 20-year-old brunette and was now in her seventh month of pregnancy with her second child. Her family had arranged her marriage to Deepak some four years earlier, when she had reached the age of 16 and Deepak had been 24. Their son, Ram, was now 3 years old and was a chore for Seeta to handle when she was tired and the days were so hot. Deepak would be home in a few hours, however, and could help out with Ram that evening. Meanwhile, a continent away to the west, Revital Ofir was also wiping her brow and sighing softly. She had just come in from mock combat maneuvers and was very tired. Already it was hot and dusty outside—it looked to be a long day ahead. Revital was a pretty, 20-year-old brunette who was looking forward to the end of her stretch in the Israeli army. She had already been accepted into the university, where she planned to study hard and enjoy an active social life!

What neither woman knew, however, was the fact of their biological similarity—they were identical twins, born to Iranian parents hours before the catastrophic earthquake had destroyed many of the settlements in the eastern foothills. During the ensuing tumult, their mother had perished, and the twins had been inadvertently separated by the workers of the humanitarian agencies who had been flown in to help. Their paths had diverged, one to the east and other to the west, as they had been taken in by new families and raised in new cultures.

■ ■ ■

WHAT IS CULTURE?

The story of the two young women is certainly not typical, but it does serve as dramatic evidence of the powerful forces contained within culture. Imagine how different the twins are from each other—their (1) languages, (2) religions, (3) clothing (4) appearance, (5) housing, (6) family relationships, (7) daily activities, (8) memories, (9) values, (10) views of the world, (11) possessions, (12) and entire futures are all different because they have been determined by different cultures. There are, of course, also some similarities between these women, some of which are due to their common heredity and some because their cultures do have some elements in common.

Slightly over 100 years ago, just after the United States' Civil War, Sir Edward B. Tylor, an Englishman, introduced the scientific concept called *culture*. Tylor was one of the early leaders of the field of anthropology, which was just beginning to formalize its study of human beings and their life-styles.[1]

Tylor's original 1871 definition of culture still stands as a classic statement:

Culture is that complex whole which includes knowledge, belief, art, morals, custom, and any other capabilities and habits acquired by man as a member of society.[2]

This definition presents a *descriptive* view of culture—it concentrates our attention on the way of life of a society. As is true for most really important concepts, there are many different facets that might be recognized in a definition. One of the most basic divisions is between (1) external, material culture and (2) internal, mental culture.

The Components of Culture

External, Material Culture

External, material culture refers to the *tangible* objects of our world—the things that we can see, touch, and use in our day-to-day living. Our material culture allows us to express ourselves aesthetically (as, for example, in art and music), protect ourselves (with clothing, buildings, etc.), and enjoy our leisure (with books, sports equipment, etc.). It includes the means by which we make ourselves more attractive, and it allows us to perform bodily functions (eating, sleeping, shaving) more safely. Material culture also provides a means for division of labor, so that each of us can exchange the products of our work for the output of others and thereby raise the living standards of all parties. Much of the difference we see in the lives of Revital Ofir and Seeta Singh derives from differences in the external, material dimensions of their cultures.

An increasingly important dimension of material culture is *technology* and the change that it brings to our world. To see what this might mean, consider briefly what the culture was like before television. What did children do on Saturday mornings? What did families do each evening? How did people discover what was going on overseas or in Washington? Similar questions can be asked about the great changes in our way of life (and, therefore, in our culture) that have occurred because of the airplane, or the automobile, or movies, or the telephone.

Internal, Mental Culture

Internal, mental culture refers to the ideas and points of view that are shared by most members of a society. The most prominent of these include *knowledge systems* (such as language, sciences, and objective descriptions of the material culture), *belief and value systems* (such as religious, political, or social philosophies), and the *social normative system*. We are quite familiar with the first two categories, but perhaps less so with the third. What are the basic concepts here?

The most basic concept is that of a norm.[3] **Norms** are guides or rules for behaving in certain situations or for adopting a particular role. **Sanctions** are used to enforce norms; these consist of some form of reward for behavior in keeping with the norm and some sort of punishment for behavior in violation of the norm. Norms can be classed into four basic categories: fads and fashions, folkways, mores, and laws. **Fads**, which come and go very quickly, and **fashions**, which have only a little longer existence, are the least significant of the norms because they do not persist for long times in the culture. Both fads and fashions have certain interesting characteristics, however. They are associated with enthusiasm and intensity. The social forces for conforming with a fad or fashion can be quite powerful, and a person who refuses to conform risks being labeled "out-of-date," an "oddball," or worse. We should also recognize that *fashion* does not only apply to the clothing field; politics, entertainment, literature, and management are all subject to "fashionable" views and practices.

Folkways refer to norms for most routine activities in our everyday life; they define what is socially correct and are subject to only informal sanctions. Every culture has thousands of folkways. Examples include how to greet someone you know only slightly ("Is it expected that I kiss him or her?") and how to dress in a business setting ("Can I wear my running shoes?"). An important aspect of folkways is that over time we accept these behavioral rules as the way we personally do act. As they become a part of us, we tend not to question them or even recognize their existence.

Mores (pronounced mor-ays) are more significant behavior norms than are folkways, and are subject to more intense sanctions if violated. Mores tend to be associated with moral and religious values in a culture and are treated as being absolute rules for behavior. Consider how you react to cannibalism, nudity on the street, or killing babies of an undesired sex. Each of these taboos would receive strong negative sanctions in the culture of the United States, but we should realize that all have been accepted at one time or another in some cultures in the world. Finally, **laws** are specific rules of behavior created and enforced by some type of special power in the culture. They allow for the formal imposition of sanctions against prohibited behaviors and, thus, are used to enforce the mores of the dominant sector of the society.

In terms of our personal mental development, we should recognize that cultural influences build up over our lives. They strongly affect what we "know" about our world and thus account for a substantial portion of our beliefs and opinions in long-term memory (LTM). Cultural influences also help us interpret external events. This is why, for example, we'd be surprised to have a 56-year-old show up as our blind date, or to see a store paying its customers to take away the merchandise, or an ad telling consumers to buy a competing brand because it's really better! These events don't occur in our culture, and they are not in accord with the beliefs and expectations we have in our minds.

Because of its powerful presence in every person's mind, cultural influence is also a powerful force in our external social world. Social norms, in fact, are actually beliefs and rules that are held in people's minds in exactly the same ways. Because of this, there is a pervasive force toward *conformity* arising from cultural influences in the external consumer environment, since each of us agrees about these particular aspects of the world. In the main, this is a stabilizing force that helps people to adapt to their world. As noted, over time we *internalize* the prevailing cultural values into our own personal values. This process is termed **enculturation**, or the learning of a person's own culture. The learning of a different culture, as when a person might immigrate or be transferred to work in a different land, is known as **acculturation**. For marketing purposes, the topic of acculturation becomes very important in international markets. (We examine this topic further in the following chapter, where we discuss differences across cultures.)

Cultural Universals

The notion of **cultural universals** springs from an interest in the *similarities* between cultures or the search for "the universal pattern" that all cultures share. The results of this search are very interesting and are worth taking a short time to think about.[4]

For example, according to leading anthropologists, all the cultures ever known have created some type of system to deal with such topics as language, cooking, housing, hygiene, law, medicine, education, and kinship and marriage. "Of course," someone might object, "what's so surprising about that? All those things are related to important needs that we all have." What is really interesting is that the list doesn't stop there. Figure 12-1 lists 21 elements that were found to be present in all known human cultures (and this is only a partial listing). It is interesting to read the entries in a leisurely fashion. Think, for example, what it means that virtually every person in the entire history of the world has been involved in each of these activities.

In summary, when we stress the differences between cultures we are dealing with the content and substance of everyday life. When we stress the similarity

FIGURE 12-1 **A Partial List of Cultural Universals**

All cultures known in history have possessed or engaged in some form of

Athletics	Feasting	Magic tricks
Body decoration	Forbidden foods	Music
Calendar making	Funeral ceremonies	Myths and legends
Courtship	Games	Personal names
Dancing	Giving of gifts	Supernatural beings
Dream interpretation	Hair styling	Religious rituals
Etiquette	Joke making	Status and prestige ranks

Source: Adapted from George P. Murdoch, "The Common Denominator of Cultures," in Ralph Linton (ed.), *The Science of Man in the World Crisis* (New York: Columbia University Press, 1945), pp. 123–142.

of cultures we are dealing with the nature of humans. George Murdock, an anthropologist, summed it up well:

> *This basis (for a universal cultural pattern) cannot be sought in history, or geography, or race, or any other factor limited in time or space, since the universal pattern links all known cultures, simple and complex, ancient and modern. It can only be sought, therefore, in the fundamental biological and psychological nature of man and in the universal conditions of human existence.*[5]

If you would like to read more about these types of cultural characteristics and their implications for marketing, you might wish to pursue the excellent article in Note 6.

THE CHANGING CONSUMER CULTURE

One of the outstanding aspects of cultural effects on consumer behavior in developed countries is the *extremely high rate of change* in the modern consumer environment. This occurs for both the internal, mental component and the external, material component. It is an extremely important issue for most marketers, who must adapt to survive.

All of us have lived during a period of constant flux, so that, without thinking much about it, we tend to accept and expect change in our lives. We *share* these types of changes with huge numbers of people—these are the cultural shifts that have the major impacts on consumer behavior in the marketplace. Changes in the consumer market sometimes occur suddenly, as in the case of fads, but more often they tend to move slowly into the lives of more and more people until they

---

EXHIBIT 12-1   *RECENT CHANGES IN CONSUMER BEHAVIORS AND MARKETS*

Where Do We Shop?

Thirty years ago, there were fewer than 1000 shopping centers in the entire United States. None were enclosed, climate-controlled "malls" as we know them today. Altogether, shopping centers accounted for only 7 percent of retail purchases. Today, there are about 20,000 shopping centers in the United States, *accounting for half of all consumer retail purchases in the nation!* Thus have shopping centers become a key element in the life-styles of millions of American consumers today.[7]

Cosmetics and Style Changes

In 1940, Charles Revson revolutionized the cosmetic field by matching lipstick to his Revlon nailcare line. Stylish lips matched fingertips for the first time, and Revlon's sales increased 50 percent! Vibrant red was the decade's color, and rouge, cake mascara, and leg makeup (nylon was being rationed for the war effort) accompanied the heavy use of lipstick and nail polish. The 1950s saw a shift to the eyes, as eyeliner was introduced and mascara became available in different colors. In the 1960s, hair moved to center stage, first with elaborate beehives and pageboy fluffs, then with wigs, falls, and fake eyelashes. Then flower children and the women's liberation movement moved to the fore. Long hair and natural ingredients dominated the late 1960s and early 1970s, then were replaced by short cuts and natural looks. As the beauty industry moved into the 1990s, the cultural changes that had taken hold over the years were causing harder times for marketers. Total sales are huge (over $10 billion), but are almost flat from year to year. The industry is looking harder at males as their main target for future sales growth. Would men be willing, though, to increase greatly their use of cosmetics and beauty aids?[8]

In Touch with the Media

Consumers' access to media technology stands out as one of the major changes in our history. In 1950, for example, 40 percent of U.S. households did not have their own telephones. Television had just appeared, and less than 10 percent of households owned this new communications marvel, which offered its programs in living black and white! If we consider these figures today, we can quantify the incredible change in consumers' life-styles. Telephones are now in over 96 percent of all homes, radios in 99 percent (with six sets per household), and television in 98 percent (with almost two sets per household). Cable systems are rapidly penetrating our daily lives, as are home computers. The only medium that's declined is newspapers, as consumers have been shifting their allocations of time and activities: as of the early 1990s, one newspaper was being printed for every four American consumers, down from one for every three consumers in 1950. The proportion of adults who read newspapers continues to decline: it has dropped from 72 percent in the mid-1970's to 65 percent today.[9]

EXHIBIT 12-1

RECENT CHANGES IN CONSUMER BEHAVIORS AND MARKETS
CONTINUED

Paying Less in a World of Inflation

During the past 20 years the consumer price index has soared: goods costing $100 in 1967, for example, cost about three times that much today. Did you know, though, that in the 1960s the famous Nieman-Marcus catalog was offering a home video recorder for $34,000? Or that ballpoint pens were introduced after World War II for $12.50 for a utility version. Or that a portable calculator used to weigh 3 pounds, while a portable dictating machine tipped the scales at 8 pounds and cost $650? Many other examples exist, but those given indicate how strongly technological advances and mass production have brought affordable changes to the consumer culture of our modern world.[10]

Fitness as a Consumer Life-style

During the last 25 years the proportion of American adults who report exercising regularly has increased from 24 percent to almost 50 percent. So what, you say? During this same time, there has been a 25 percent decline in deaths from coronary heart disease and a 33 percent drop in the incidence of strokes. There have been booming markets in various food and recreation product categories aimed at fitness, whereas marketers of products associated with health risks have seen declines in their total demand levels. Milk, cream, butter, and egg consumption have all declined. Cigarette and cigar smoking by adults has fallen also. Finally, hard liquor marketers are quite concerned about their declining sales: the average consumption is dropping each year, especially in brown liquors. Scotch sales, for example, have fallen about 35 percent in the past 15 years, a fact that has sharpened the brand competition in this category.[11]

American Consumers' Discovery of Wine

Some years ago, a market research firm asked Americans who they thought drank wine. The three answers were "foreigners," "rich people," and "bums." This attitude had persisted for many years, as few consumers even considered using this product. In 1960, for example, the U.S. market was still small. Red wine was by far the consumers' favorite, accounting for 75 percent of all sales. By the 1980s, however, the situation had changed markedly. Not only were millions of consumers drinking wine, but their tastes had changed as well. White wine was now the favorite, with rose and blush varieties in second place. Red wines were now the least favored, with only 15 percent of sales.

As we move into the 1990s, not only have consumer tastes changed sharply, but wine seems to be slipping slightly from consumers' favor, with U.S. sales beginning a slight decline in volume of sales. Of further importance to marketers, the current market is highly segmented by user groups. For example, a mere 5 percent of the U.S. consumers account for 50 percent of the wine consumed! Women, who drink only 20 percent of the beer in the United States, consume over half of the wine. About one-third of American adults drink wine, while another third refuse to do so for health and religious reasons. The wine industry is viewing the remaining third as its huge potential growth market and would like to know how to convert them to regular usage. Any suggestions?[12]

are recognized as having "arrived." This process of acceptance across a society is known as **diffusion**, and it will be discussed in depth later in this chapter. For the present, however, let's consider some examples of changes that have occurred in some very different areas of consumer behavior in the recent past. These are listed in Exhibit 12-1.

While reviewing the examples in the exhibit, ask yourself which had you already known, and whether consumers generally would be aware of them. Also, notice how each set brings with it new *challenges* for some marketers (as markets move away from their product offerings and profits fall) and new *opportunities* for other marketers alert enough to "be there" with a marketing mix to fit the new consumer behaviors. These are just a few examples of the massive shifts that continually occur in the consumer marketplace. Even though these are just a few examples, we can go through the exhibit to see how a given person's consumer behavior will have shifted over recent years. Consumers have changed where they shop, what they view as being in style, what they watch and read, and what they can afford. Modern consumers have also changed what they eat and what they avoid, what they do for fitness, and how they spend their leisure time.

From a marketer's perspective, if a shift similar to one of these occurs, it can mean either huge rewards or bankruptcy. *It is clearly important to adapt the marketing mix appropriately*. To do this best, we need to understand what forces are behind the changes that are occurring and to identify what trends are likely in the future. Our next section describes some major approaches to the monitoring of cultural change.

Monitoring Cultural Trends

Cultural trends are broad and sweeping: No one of us can possibly be exposed enough in our personal life to discern each trend as it is developing. There are, however, some research-based approaches that can be used in the attempt to discern key trends. One method is to use content analysis, a technique refined during World War II by America's spy agency, the OSS (now the CIA). **Content analysis** is a systematic method of objectively studying what is contained in a given set of communications.[13] The best known user of content analysis to study cultural trends is John Naisbitt, author of the 1980 best-seller *Mega-trends*, which sold over 5 million copies, in 17 languages. Naisbitt's firm monitors each issue of 200 daily newspapers in the United States. Every local news article is coded into a massive databank, which is analyzed to discover the total amount of attention that is being devoted to any particular topic. The results are tabulated in a *Trend Report* sent to subscribing firms and agencies on a regular basis.[14]

Content analysis represents an indirect research approach to assessing cultural trends. A *direct* approach is to use survey research techniques. Here the researcher simply asks people about their current views about the world around them and their places in it. If the sample is selected well, if the questions are

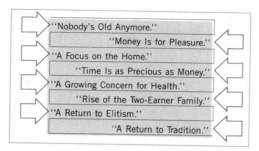

FIGURE 12-2 **Eight Cultural Trends from Market Research**

appropriate and worded well, and if people answer them honestly, this survey-based approach can yield valuable insights into our culture. Such an undertaking is no small matter, however, as it might involve in-depth interviews (1–2 hours long) with a nationally representative sample of over 2000 consumers. Since these measures are relevant to many marketers, however, they can be sold similarly to the content analysis reports, on a subscription basis to marketers who pay from $15,000–$25,000 for the findings.

In terms of current trends, Figure 12-2 lists eight major changes as seen by such leading trend-watchers in the marketing research field as Joseph Smith, Florence Skelley, Judith Langer, Faith Popcorn, and Daniel Yankelovich. Let's take a brief look at each, to clarify the nature of the trend:[15]

- "Nobody's Old Anymore" refers to the fact that more people are living longer and are active during most of this time. Many of these people genuinely don't feel old, and they don't want to be forced to live as if they were.

- "Money Is for Pleasure" refers to a change in consumers' views about the value and purpose for this asset. In past generations, money was seen as a security guarantee, to protect against bad times or an unforeseen event. More recently, people have been shifting their views toward seeing money more as a tool for achieving pleasure and less as a protective device.

- "A Focus on the Home" reports a return to the home as a place to relax, entertain, or be entertained. Driven by the increase in the number of working women (for whom a night out is not always a pleasant prospect), and by new entertainment technologies (VCRs, cable TV, and computer games), this shift, sometimes called *cocooning*, is also reflected in an increase in "do-it-yourself" home projects.

- "Time Is as Precious as Money" is a feeling that results from the expanded number of obligations and options faced by a number of people today. For these persons, there simply doesn't seem to be enough time to do everything they have (want) to do. If they can gain time by sacrificing some money (as by paying more for a convenience product) they are very pleased to do so.

- "A Growing Concern for Health" deals with fitness ("feeling healthy and looking good") as well as avoidance of disease and early demise. This trend should soon clash with the rising costs of the U.S. health system (now over 10 percent of the gross national product) to produce changes in the medical practices of the nation.
- "Rise of the Two-Earner Family" contributes to several of the other trends in terms of changes in time pressures, life-styles, and incomes. For some of these families, the incomes are moderate, but for others—households in which two professionals are bringing home paychecks—this trend is resulting in the creation of a new class of "rich" consumers whose problems lie in finding the time to spend the money they have!
- "A Return to Elitism" seems to be occurring on the part of a growing subgroup of the population that has achieved higher levels of education, income, and status. Increasingly, this group is beginning to flaunt their achievements through increasingly elegant living and "high-end" products and services.
- "A Return to Tradition" may be related to the middle-life stage of the baby-boom generation. Proms are back, as are ceremonial, social-event weddings. Organized religion is increasing again. Nostalgia is rising on the radio, and the sexual revolution is moving back toward more monogamous relationships.

INTRODUCING CHANGE TO A CULTURE: THE "DIFFUSION OF INNOVATIONS"

Thus far in the chapter we have seen that both the external and internal components of culture will change over time, and that some of these changes will have *massive* effects on consumer behavior and on marketers. In this section we'll shift our attention to examine exactly *how* such changes occur, and how this analysis is relevant to marketing managers. The key concept in this area is called **Diffusion of Innovations**.

What is Diffusion?

An **innovation** is something that is new. It can include new ideas, new inventions, new ways of doing things, and so on. The term **diffusion**, meanwhile, comes from the Latin word meaning "to spread out." Diffusion is exemplified by the way that gases or vapors slowly expand and spread out through available space. Thus the general topic of diffusion of innovation refers to *the manner in which new ideas, products, or practices spread through a culture*. It represents the fundamental manner in which entire societies change and grow.

Diffusion Is Not Automatic

This topic is challenging because experience has shown that the diffusion process is not an automatic one—most new ideas (and new products) do *not* diffuse through the population. Instead they are rejected and disappear from view. This often happens even when a new idea or product is clearly an improvement over current practices (recall the many times you've heard a "build a better mousetrap" analogy). Thus, in addition to humans' willingness to change, the *reluctance* of human beings to change their views and behaviors is also an important facet of diffusion theory.

The "Black Holes of Marketing"

Recalling the black holes in outer space, into which matter disappears, marketers sometimes call new product development "The Black Hole" into which their dollars disappear. While exact numbers vary, most marketers accept that 80 to 90 percent of new products fail, at enormous costs to the firms that launched them. In the food industry, for example, it is estimated that the costs of launching a new product run $15–20 million, and that over *$300 billion* has been lost in new product failures over the past seven years. The launching of thousands of new food products each year "is sheer lunacy!" exclaimed the executive vice president of Nabisco Brands, Inc. "[Food marketers] would have done much better had we just taken our new product dollars . . . and put them in an ordinary passbook savings account." His basic message: Marketers *must* introduce new products, but must manage this process better than in the past.[16]

Diffusion Is of Interest in Many Fields of Study

Marketers have an obvious and keen interest in diffusion research because it deals so closely with the topic of new products and their success or failure in the marketplace. Marketing was not the first discipline to study diffusion of innovation, however.

Rural sociology, for example, is a field that has long dealt with this area. Such serious problems as how to persuade farmers to adopt new strains of crops or new methods of cultivation have been studied here. (When we recall that in many areas of the world the failure of a year's crop means literal starvation for a farm family, we can appreciate better why they are reluctant to switch from time-proven methods.) Other fields also have strong interests in diffusion, including medicine (how do doctors come to adopt or reject new medicines and treatment methods, given the demands on their time?), education (how do teachers learn themselves, and how do they adopt new teaching methods?), and a large number of subject areas associated with modernization in developing countries (why are new methods of family planning or sanitation practices, for example, so hard to infuse into these societies?). Finally, in the realm of ideas, the field of communication research has long been interested in how people come to change their views of what is correct, what is popular, what is "out," and so forth (many nations have followed on the Nazi example of World War II, in stressing centralized communications agencies to work on achieving agreement among citizens on key social questions).

Social Marketing's Special Interest in Diffusion

Marketing is a key discipline for the diffusion of innovation, even for the other fields just mentioned. For example, marketers sell the new seeds, farm equipment, pharmaceuticals, and so on that are purchased in developing countries. Marketers also possess the expertise to research and reach the consumers targeted for the innovations. In our modern world, therefore, private marketers are a major force for change and progress. In addition, the subfield of **social marketing** employs advanced techniques to market new ideas and innovative social practices. Sometimes this work is done on behalf of governmental agencies, sometimes for charitable organizations (for example, encouraging people to have their blood pressure checked) and sometimes for educational, religious, or civic organizations.

The Role of Persuasion

Social marketing often stresses *persuasion*, attempting to have people change their present beliefs and behaviors. In this sense social marketing tends to be *pro innovation:* it assumes that the change involved is good and that people *should* adopt it. In many cases, of course, almost everyone would agree that this is true— blood pressure checks are good things to do, and so is improving the nutritional level of poor children, be they in the United States or in some other country.

In other cases, however, there is a clash between the innovation's meaning and one or more cultural values within a society. Recently, for example, young mothers in Indonesia were targeted for nutritional education: it was believed that many babies in Indonesia were not receiving enough nourishment because of a custom of mothers breastfeeding only with the left breast. This was based on Islamic religious beliefs relating to use of the hands: "the right hand is for food and the left hand is for toilet." A busy mother whose right hand was involved with cooking, therefore, would be unable to feed the infant according to the baby's needs. According to the marketing consultant involved in this project, "[t]hese resistance points were obstacles to effective education, and the messages had to concentrate on effectively challenging them."[17]

Marketers as Advocates of Change

Thus both private marketers and social marketers find themselves in the position of generally advocating changes in peoples' behaviors and views of the world. Sometimes there are strong forces *against* such change, and marketers are viewed with suspicion and even disfavor. Those Indonesians who believe deeply in the customs would not like to think of them as "obstacles to effective education," for example. On the other hand, marketers are also responsible for successfully bringing many positive and generally noncontroversial innovations to the consumers of the world. In entering our analysis of the diffusion literature, then, we should be aware that the theory tends to assume that the innovations are valuable and should be adopted. It does not ask the hard questions posed by the attempts to break down and replace long-standing cultural values, beliefs, and customs.[18]

THE ADOPTION OF INNOVATIONS

Types of Innovations

When marketers begin to dig into this area, one of the first questions to arise is, "What exactly do we mean by 'an innovation'?" This is important, since the speed and pattern of diffusion will depend on the type of innovation itself. There are three major types of innovations:

A discontinuous innovation changed communication patterns.

- A **discontinuous innovation** is the most significant type. This is a new product or service that represents a *major change* in the benefits offered to consumers and in the behaviors necessary for them to use the product (i.e., consumers must in some way "discontinue" their past patterns to fit the new product into their lives). Examples include the automobile, airplane, radio, telephone, television, and personal computer. Major technological changes create these types of innovations.
- A **dynamically continuous innovation** is a moderate-level category, in that consumers have to alter their behaviors somewhat for this type of product, but not too greatly. Examples of this type of innovation include electric toothbrushes, electric blankets, and self-correcting typewriters.
- A **continuous innovation** represents the least degree of change from current consumer practices (that is, consumers can "continue" their present behaviors, with only minor changes in product benefits). Examples here include new models of automobiles, new flavors of soft drinks, most of those new product failures in foods, and so on. This category contains by far the most new products brought to the consumer market.[19]

The Adoption Process

Across a society, the diffusion of an innovation develops from a series of adoption decisions made by individuals, families, or company managers. In attempting to understand these adoption decisions, marketers have relied on a hierarchy of effects type of decision model. Figure 12-3 depicts our modification of the hierarchy of effects model to reflect adoption decisions in the **adoption-process model**. Notice that the flow of the model is from left to right, across time. **Awareness** of the innovation is the first step toward eventual adoption. Once awareness is achieved, if there is no strong external influence at work; the route goes to **knowledge**. Here the consumer is beginning to learn about the new idea or product and gradually comes to understand its characteristics, and strong and weak points. As knowledge increases, **liking** (or **disliking**) begins to develop as well. The nature of the like/dislike attitude will in part depend on how well our consumer feels the innovation will meet his or her needs.

Up to this point, the model is identical to the basic hierarchy of effects we discussed in Chapter 5. However, in the special case of an innovation, a consumer is likely to perceive uncertainty and risk. Our model thus suggests that some form of a **trial** will occur next. Here our consumer will attempt to "try out" the product, but without making a long-term commitment in case it doesn't work out too well. Since the purpose of the trial is to provide the consumer with more information, the **use evaluation** stage is crucial. If this result is positive, **adoption** of the innovation is likely. If not, the liking level will be revised downward, and future adoption is not likely, at least until some aspects of the situation have changed.

The figure also makes it clear that *time* is a variable factor in the process. For

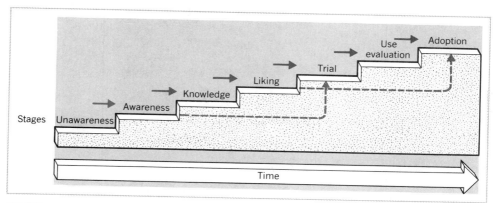

FIGURE 12-3 **A Modified Hierarchy for the Adoption Process**

example, some people might move through the entire process very rapidly, within a day or two. Other persons may take months to complete the same process. Others, of course, will stop at various points and may never adopt the particular innovation.

Finally, the dashed arrows in Figure 12-3 address the question of whether a consumer would have to experience the series of steps in exactly the order shown in the figure. Under some conditions we might find slightly different processes. If friends apply social pressures to try a new food product, for example, we might be willing to go right from awareness to trial without knowing very much about the new product (on the other hand, notice that our chances of trial do go up if our friends tell us about it and reassure us that "You'll like it!"). Marketers also attempt to stimulate this awareness-to-trial linkage by providing free trials (e.g., test drives of cars), free samples, and valuable coupons. Sometimes a true trial might be unreasonable, such as with a new surgical procedure or a custom-built home. In these instances the link must go from liking to adoption, as indicated by the second dashed arrow. As we'll discuss later, this situation is likely to slow down the adoption process, extending it over a longer time period.

The Five Categories of Adopters

Different people proceed through the adoption process at very different rates. This means that some consumers are—psychologically speaking—"in the market" for a new product at a given time, while other consumers are not, though they may be later. Managers therefore are interested in finding "who" each of these types of people is, so that the group can be targeted with the appropriate marketing mixes at the appropriate times.

If we take an individual-level perspective on the adoption process, it is useful to classify consumers in terms of how soon they are likely to adopt a particular innovation. Figure 12-4 shows the classification, developed by Everett Rogers, a

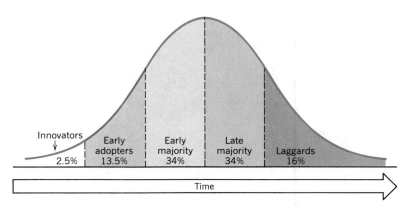

FIGURE 12-4 **Adopter Categories**

leading figure in diffusion theory. After reviewing over 500 research studies, Rogers proposed a simple but powerful scheme that divides the market into five "types" of consumers, ranked from those who first adopt the innovation to those who come last to the adoption phase.[20]

His fundamental assumption is that the numbers of people falling into each category will approximate a *normal distribution*. This means that, starting from the time that the innovation is first introduced, most people will adopt at some "average" length of time (the mean of this distribution). A few people will adopt very early—these are the **innovators**. Rogers assigned the first 2.5 percent of adopters to this category, representing those who are more than two standard deviations away from the mean time taken for all adopters. Notice that this is a very small portion of the market and that it consists only of those persons who are very early purchasers of the new product. The innovators are soon followed by a somewhat larger group of **early adopters**, who comprise 13.5 percent of the adopting population. This group is followed by the **early majority**, a sizable group comprising just over one-third of all those who will end up adopting the innovation. At this point we have reached the average time for all consumers who will eventually adopt this innovation. Another large group—the **late majority**—now enters the market. Finally, about one-sixth of the target population is seen as trailing in at later points in time (beyond one standard deviation past the mean time for adoption). These are the **laggards**.

The S-Shaped Diffusion Curve

Roger's specification of adopter categories relates directly to the pattern we are likely to see in the process of diffusion of an innovation across a marketplace. This relationship is shown in Figure 12-5, which graphs the *cumulative* number of adopters over the same time period as that shown for our adopters figure. That is, the **S-shaped diffusion curve** reflects what proportion of people at any given

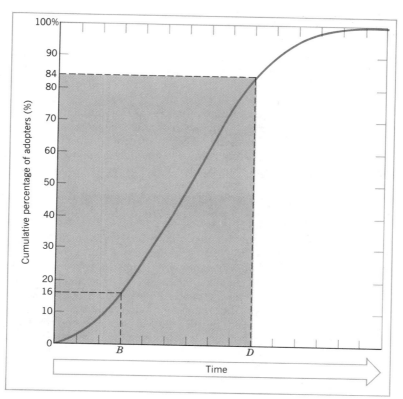

FIGURE 12-5 **The S-Shaped Diffusion Curve**

time have *already* adopted the innovation in question. Notice, for example, that if we choose an early time when only the innovators and early adopters have yet entered (time B in the figure), only about 16 percent of the potential adopters will have entered the market. At time D, however, 84 percent will have entered, with only the laggards still to come in.

The resulting curve is in the shape of an "S," which carries important implications for a marketing strategist. The essential message is that we can expect a successful innovation to start out rather slowly in terms of its market acceptance, then begin to grow at a more rapid pace as the early adopters and then early majority enter the market in increasing numbers. After this point, we can still expect the market to continue its growth, but the *rate* of the growth will begin to slow as we work through the late majority and then the laggards.

The S-shaped diffusion curve is important for *market forecasting and corporate planning purposes.* When we are talking about a discontinuous innovation, marketers face a situation in which entirely new plants need to be built, new employees hired, and many other business investments made, all before a single item of the new product is even produced. These decisions can involve spending millions of dollars. Since we are talking about a discontinuous innovation, however, there is bound to be considerable uncertainty about how consumers are going to respond to it. This makes the role of consumer research and marketing models especially important.[21]

Dial "D" for Diffusion

During the 1980s, the Federal Communications Commission began to issue a restricted number of licenses for firms to offer cellular radio telephone service in many urban areas of the United States. Advances in technology made it possible to offer a completely mobile telephone service having as high a quality as the best service found in homes and businesses. The user could travel anywhere (within the service area, typically an entire urban area) and could call or receive calls from anywhere in the world. All that they needed was a small unit either mounted in a car or carried around in a pocket like a package of cigarettes. Many prominent business analysts expected this to be the major consumer innovation of the 1980s and 1990s.

To decide which few firms would be granted a license, the FCC decided to require very detailed plans for engineering, financing, operations, and marketing strategy. *Before any of these detailed plans could be set, however, a detailed consumer research project had to be constructed,* assessing the potential market's size, locational needs, product preferences, and likely response to different pricing schedules. Competition was intense among the applicants. A key input to all the engineering and financial plans was, of course, a detailed forecast of expected sales, both in the beginning and over the course of the next 5 to 10 years. The diffusion curve provided the framework that the applicant companies used, as they developed highly mathematical models based on the S-shaped diffusion curve to arrive at their forecasts and then to design and finance their technical systems.

Estimating the Diffusion Rate

The potential success and speed of diffusion will depend on the innovation itself, and on the culture or market into which it is being introduced. Three characteristics of cultures that are more receptive to innovations are (1) a positive view of change as a good aspect of life, (2) members who interact frequently with other social systems, and (3) a positive view of science and education.[22] With respect to innovations themselves, six characteristics have been found to affect speed and success rates:

- **Relative advantage:** the degree of improvement that the new innovation represents over existing alternatives. In general, the greater the relative advantage possessed by an innovation, the faster it will be accepted. Classic marketing examples include the first fluoridated toothpaste (Crest shot to the market leadership position when it was endorsed by the American Dental Association for its decay preventive benefits for children), the first "thirst quencher" designed to scientifically replace important fluids in athletes while exercising (Gatorade), and the first disposable diapers (the incredible success of Pampers). More recent examples include fax machines and 35mm self-focusing cameras.

NYNEX has a special offer for the mobile phone haves and have-nots.

1 **For those who have a mobile phone, we'll make you a two car-phone family.**

If you're already enjoying the convenience of a mobile phone, now you can double it. Because for a limited time, you can move up to a sophisticated NYNEX 832 channel mobile phone at a very special price, and get your calls through even faster. Then, you can pass along the convenience of your original phone to your spouse, or a business associate.

And we've added NYNEX Sales and Installation Centers throughout the New York, New Jersey area, so you'll have no problem buying or servicing your 832.

NYNEX will help you select the model you want, install it expertly, and perform all your follow-up maintenance promptly and professionally.

You've never had an opportunity like this to step up to NYNEX's most advanced mobile phone. But this offer won't last long. So find out more today. Call 1-800-443-BELL.

1-800-443-BELL

"NYNEX is a registered mark of NYNEX Corporation."
© Copyright 1989 NYNEX Mobile Communications

2 **For those who don't have a mobile phone, NYNEX makes it easy.**

If you've been waiting for the right time, the right phone, the right offer – it's right here. But it won't last long.

Now, for a limited time, you can get a sophisticated NYNEX 832 channel mobile phone at a very special price.

And it couldn't be easier to buy and service. You have a choice of NYNEX Sales and Installation Centers throughout the New York, New Jersey area.

NYNEX can help you select the model you want, give you expert installation and perform all follow-up maintenance promptly and professionally.

A NYNEX mobile phone and cellular service makes your life easier by keeping you in touch with friends, family and business associates. And if you ever have any questions, just dial 611 toll free from your NYNEX mobile phone. Our Customer Service Consultants are ready to help.

There's never been an opportunity like this to enjoy the convenience of a NYNEX mobile phone. Don't miss this chance to join the mobile phone "haves." Call today for our special offer: 1-800-443-BELL.

For mobile communications, the answer is NYNEX.

NYNEX
Mobile Communications

Will cellular become the major innovation of the 1990s?

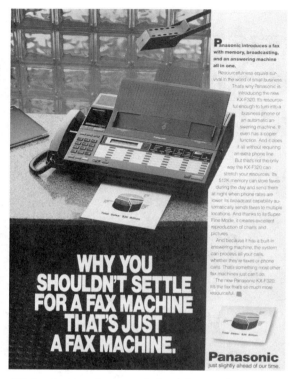

High relative advantage helped fax machines to diffuse more quickly.

How do cordless telephones/answering machines rate on the six diffusion characteristics?

- **Complexity:** the inherent difficulty associated with the new idea or product. High levels of complexity can make it more "expensive" for a consumer to try to learn about the innovation, and increases the chances that misunderstandings will occur. The converse of complexity is simplicity: simple innovations will, all other things being equal, be diffused faster through a population. Many potential consumers, for example, had a hard time imagining how a personal computer works. If computers were inherently simpler machines, they would have diffused more rapidly through the consumer market.

- **Communicability:** the ease with which the essence of the innovation can be conveyed to potential adopters. New products that lend themselves to usage demonstrations, as automobiles, telephones, and television did, are highly communicable, even though complex. In these cases many consumers were willing to adopt the innovation because they could easily perceive its benefits for them. Innovations, particularly those with long-term benefits that are difficult for consumers to detect (nutritional practices, health maintenance practices, and energy-saving appliances, for example), are apt to diffuse more slowly.

- **Compatibility:** how well the innovation fits with the existing beliefs and practices of potential adopters. Sometimes compatibility refers to beliefs or values. In Moslem or Hindu nations, for example, many new products from the West will diffuse slowly (if at all) because their implicit message is incompatible with the cultural beliefs or customs. At other times compatibility refers to consumers' existing ways of using the products themselves. Crest, Gatorade, and Pampers were all compatible with prior consumer use patterns, as are cellular telephones. Automobiles and home computer systems, on the other hand, are examples of successful innovations that had to overcome problems of incompatibility, as consumers needed to invest considerable time and effort to learn how to use these products.

- **Divisibility:** an innovation's capability of being "tried out" in smaller doses by potential adopters. Within the product realm, some innovations lend themselves easily to consumer trial (again, the famous examples of Crest, Gatorade, and Pampers are relevant), while others offer some problems on this (in general, durable goods such as solar energy systems, microwaves, and sonar pest machines can be demonstrated, but their full use cannot easily be experienced by a consumer prior to purchase). The result is that an initial purchase can be a major event, and the diffusion process overall is slowed.

- **Perceived risk:** consumers' judgments about the adoption of the innovation, especially in terms of possible negative social, economic, or physical consequences. In social settings, for example, ownership of certain innovations (birth control pills or minidresses in conservative cultures, for example) may carry considerable social risks to the potential adopter. Economic and physical perceived risks tend to increase as the cost of an innovation rises, if breakdowns can be a problem, or if repair service may be hard to obtain. Similarly, the pace of innovation itself can be a problem: many consumers perceived that immediate purchases of personal computers were risky in that more options would soon appear and prices would fall as well. Thus there are many reasons that perceived risks can arise to slow the diffusion of an innovation.[23]

IMPROVING PROSPECTS FOR DIFFUSION SUCCESS

Once marketers are able to discern which of the six key characteristics may hinder the diffusion of a particular innovation, a host of strategies are available to enhance the prospects of success. Some of these are summarized in Figure 12-6. If we examine each problem in turn, we can see how particular weaknesses can be addressed. If we look across the categories, moreover, several interesting issues arise. First, notice that product redesign pops up several times: many innovations have been *technology driven,* and careful attention to *consumer-driven* design issues can pay large dividends. Second, product trials or demonstrations are also frequently mentioned: because innovations are by definition

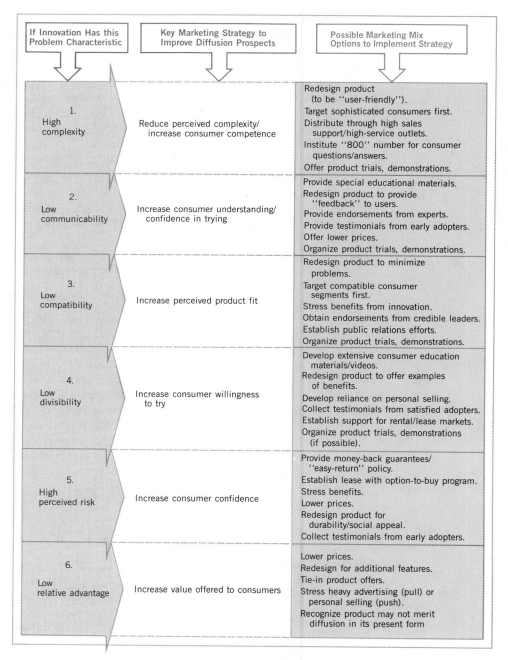

If Innovation Has this Problem Characteristic	Key Marketing Strategy to Improve Diffusion Prospects	Possible Marketing Mix Options to Implement Strategy
1. High complexity	Reduce perceived complexity/increase consumer competence	Redesign product (to be "user-friendly"). Target sophisticated consumers first. Distribute through high sales support/high-service outlets. Institute "800" number for consumer questions/answers. Offer product trials, demonstrations.
2. Low communicability	Increase consumer understanding/confidence in trying	Provide special educational materials. Redesign product to provide "feedback" to users. Provide endorsements from experts. Provide testimonials from early adopters. Offer lower prices. Organize product trials, demonstrations.
3. Low compatibility	Increase perceived product fit	Redesign product to minimize problems. Target compatible consumer segments first. Stress benefits from innovation. Obtain endorsements from credible leaders. Establish public relations efforts. Organize product trials, demonstrations.
4. Low divisibility	Increase consumer willingness to try	Develop extensive consumer education materials/videos. Redesign product to offer examples of benefits. Develop reliance on personal selling. Collect testimonials from satisfied adopters. Establish support for rental/lease markets. Organize product trials, demonstrations (if possible).
5. High perceived risk	Increase consumer confidence	Provide money-back guarantees/"easy-return" policy. Establish lease with option-to-buy program. Stress benefits. Lower prices. Redesign product for durability/social appeal. Collect testimonials from early adopters.
6. Low relative advantage	Increase value offered to consumers	Lower prices. Redesign for additional features. Tie-in product offers. Stress heavy advertising (pull) or personal selling (push). Recognize product may not merit diffusion in its present form

FIGURE 12-6 **Marketing Strategies to Improve Diffusion**

new to consumers, these marketing tools help to familiarize potential adopters. Third, notice that the options use all "4 P's" of the marketing mix: marketers control many means of attracting consumer adoption behaviors. Fourth, the final entry under "low relative advantage" recognizes that many new products—while new for the firms offering them—really do not offer significant new benefits to customers. As the Nabisco executive pointed out, most of these "me-too" products are not really "innovations" and have no real basis for market success. Fifth, two of the entries mention targeting consumer segments. For our closing section to this chapter, we'll examine such segmentation possibilities, paying special attention to those consumers who come early to the market.

Locating the Consumer Innovators

A substantial number of studies have been done on identifying the kinds of consumers who are the *very first* people to try and buy new products and services.[24] What, in general, has been learned?

We're All Innovators at Heart . . .

We should begin by reminding ourselves that almost everyone is interested in novelty—in new ideas, new stores, and new products. Indeed, the word "new" has long been recognized by experts as one of the most *arresting* terms that can be placed in a headline! (The fact that it may be often misused by marketers searching for something to say about a slight modification to a brand, thus making consumers dubious when they see this claim, does not detract from its inherent attraction to us.) What would our lives be like if nothing new ever entered?

Each of us, therefore, is a potential innovator in the sense that we are likely to be interested in trying something that is new to us.[25] To qualify for this title within the consumer marketplace, however, we have to be among the *first* consumers to adopt a particular innovation. Thus the issue is not simply the adoption of something that's new *to us,* but something that's new to the entire market. Also, early consideration of an innovation is not enough to be considered an innovator either: In the research literature those people who were interested and looked into it, but then decided not to adopt, are termed **rejectors**. Rejectors have been little studied at all.[26] Should rejectors be viewed as innovators also? Whichever direction we might advocate, we need to keep this issue in mind as we review the findings from past research.

Continuous Innovations Bring Out Product-Specific Innovators

With this brief background, we can easily appreciate why, for *continuous* types of innovations, there does *not* seem to be a general pattern to describe who is likely to be the innovative consumer. Recall that continuous innovations are those that follow along existing product lines, usually representing new features, styles, and so forth. Purchases of these types of innovations are thus driven by a person's specific interest in a product category. For example, all of us know some people who are very interested in cars, and these are precisely the people we would expect to be first in trying new automotive tools or new accessories. At the same time, we may know others who are caught up with personal computers (though we may not see them often!), others who love music, or fashionable clothes. As long as the new products for these categories represent relatively minor modifications, our friends who specialize in each category will likely be the first to learn of the innovations, as well as having the most interest in trying them.

More generally, this product-specific nature of innovativeness can be traced to constraints we all face in our lives as consumers. Since none of us has unlimited time or unlimited funds, we simply *cannot* innovate across very many categories. In fact, we often are not even aware of the continuous-type innovations until after they have already been adopted by the very first set of consumers! Across all products and services, therefore, *different people tend to act as innovators in different product classes*, very much in keeping with their personal interests and daily life-styles.

Innovators Exist for Discontinuous Innovations, Though

In contrast, when a major new innovation arrives, anyone adopting will have to change drastically some elements of his or her consumer life-style. Are there some people who seem to do this systematically more than others? What are their characteristics?

Within consumer behavior, some of the most prominent findings relate to the *ability to afford* the high prices associated with the initial appearance of prototypes in the market. Innovators have been found to be persons with higher income levels, higher occupational status, and higher levels of education (whether education plays an independent role in creating an innovator, or whether its presence is due to its role in providing the higher income level, is not clear).

Another set of characteristics relates to interests in learning about new products and their opportunities to do so at an early stage. Innovators have been found to be more cosmopolitan and to travel and read magazines extensively. Thus they are more *socially mobile*, come into contact with many groups, and are exposed to a high level of communications about the world around them. A third set of characteristics reflects *psychological traits*. As we might expect, innovators are less rigid than the average person in dealing with change, and they are *risk takers* in their approach to living. In general, these persons are more *venturesome* than most of the rest of us.

Interestingly, though, the true innovator tends *not* to be very well integrated into his or her social groups. Instead, these are *inner-directed individuals* who do not wish to rely on others' judgments of which products are good ones to own and use. Somewhat surprising, therefore, is the conclusion that marketers and public policymakers are not wise to rely *too* heavily on innovators as targets for their marketing efforts. This segment is by definition small—only the very first adopters of the innovation—which can make it somewhat inefficient to reach through mass promotional techniques (since the true innovator actually *wants* to buy new ideas and products, however, he or she doesn't require much promotion to create a purchase). The more significant characteristic is the lack of close relationships with social groups. Since innovators tend not to be guided by the norms of their groups, the other members of the groups tend not to be very influenced by the innovators either! Although it is important to have the innovators buy so as to get the process started, they should not be counted on to be the influential "opinion leaders" who will *really* create the burst of adoption interest across the broad consumer market.

The Remaining Adopter Categories, in Brief

Early adopters represent the next 13.5 percent of consumers and, together with the early majority, constitute the key targets for marketing and public policy strategists. Early adopters bear some similarities to innovators, in that they are interested in change and willing to take risks. These people have been found to be very different from innovators in some other significant respects, however. Early adopters tend to be much more integrated with their social groups—they believe in the group norms and are guided by them in their lives. As such, they are less cosmopolitan than innovators, preferring to center their attention within the local community in which they reside. Because they are so well tied to their groups, other consumers are well aware of their purchases, and become more likely to view purchase as an acceptable step to take. Thus the early adopter serves as an **opinion leader**: an example for the other consumers in their social systems.

Members of the *early majority* enter the market next, often after having been influenced by an early adopter that they know and respect. These people, who constitute a large and important market segment, tend to be less willing to take risks, although they are interested in acquiring new products. Their shopping may take longer, therefore, as they search for the best alternative available at the time.

As time goes on, and more and more consumers adopt the innovation, its "newness" declines, as do the risks associated with owning it. The *late majority*, therefore, is not really buying a new product on the market. In part, this may be due to their financial circumstances: these consumers have somewhat lower incomes than average and tend to be older. They may also be less directly influenced by others in their social group and tend to be more influenced by advertising and other mass media information about the product and its benefits.

Finally, the *laggards* enter the market after the innovation has been well accepted in general and when few risks are present. At times, in fact, these people are buying the original innovation while early adopters are moving on to a new innovation that offers further improvements, but at higher prices and with greater risks. When it appears that a product's future prospects are not bright, an alert marketer may choose to target this market segment for special promotional efforts, since the laggards may still be good candidates for an initial purchase if the price is right. Laggards have generally not been studied within the field of marketing, so our information about them is sketchy. In other fields, however, a fairly clear picture emerges: laggards are relatively isolated from their community social groups (preferring to communicate within their families) and are not very influenced by others' views (in this sense they are similar to innovators). They tend also to be older, to have lower incomes, and to be traditionalists in their outlook on life.[27]

SUMMARY

What Is Culture?

This chapter begins Part Three's study of external influences on consumer behavior. We began with the broadest of all of these influences—The impact of culture. *Culture* refers to the way of life of a society. It is a very powerful force in shaping people's lives. Two major components of culture are *external, material culture* and *internal, mental culture. Cultural norms* range from fads and fashions (that may come and go very quickly), to folkways (everyday practices), to mores (moral or religious values), to laws (strict codes of behavior). *Cultural universals* refer to the patterns of similarities that cultures share.

The Changing Consumer Culture

One key attribute shared by developed countries in the modern world is a rapid rate of *change in the consumer marketplace.* The second section of the chapter examined a number of markets that have seen great changes in recent years. These included shopping centers, cosmetics and styles, health and fitness, and technological advances and falling prices. We noted how dramatically each of these changes has affected millions of consumers and marketers! We then examined how marketers and policymakers attempt to anticipate cultural change and its implications, and briefly reviewed eight current trends as diagnosed by leading market researchers.

Introducing Change to a Culture

In the third section of the chapter, we moved to the topic of *diffusion of innovations,* or the spread of new ideas or products through a culture. A number of fields have an interest in this topic, since it bears so directly on making the world a better place in which to live. Marketers play a key role in advocating and introducing innovations, which at times makes them unpopular and at other times quite popular.

Innovations are of three main forms. Those that cause major shifts in accompanying consumer behaviors are labeled *discontinuous innovations. Dynamically continuous innovations* are more moderate in the changes that they bring, and *continuous innovations* bring little changes in the way that consumers use them.

The adoption of innovations tends to follow specific patterns. Consumers can be divided into five categories—*innovators, early adopters, early majority, late majority,* and *laggards*—based on the time they take to adopt an innovation. Mathematical models, used to forecast the pattern of new product sales, usually rely on the general S-shaped nature of the cumulative adoption curve. This pattern of adoption is very important to marketing strategists. In this regard, *relative advantage, complexity, communicability, compatibility, divisibility,* and *perceived risk* are all important determinants of the speed with which a particular innovation will diffuse through a consumer market.

Improving Prospects for Diffusion Success

Our coverage concluded with a discussion of how marketers can influence the speed and success of diffusion, and how each type of adopter category can be identified and understood.

KEY TERMS

culture
external, material culture
internal, mental culture
norms
sanctions
fads and fashions
folkways
mores
laws
enculturation
acculturation
cultural universals
content analysis
"nobody's old anymore"
"money is for pleasure"
"a focus on the home"
"time is as precious as money"
"a growing concern for health"
"rise of the two-earner family"
"a return to elitism"
"a return to tradition"

innovation
diffusion
the "black hole of marketing"
social marketing
discontinuous innovation
dynamically continuous innovation
continuous innovation
adoption-process model
innovators
early adopters
early majority
late majority
laggards
S-shaped diffusion curve
relative advantage
complexity
communicability
compatibility
divisibility
perceived risk
opinion leader

REVIEW QUESTIONS AND EXPERIENTIAL EXERCISES

[E = Application extension or experiential exercise]

1. Exhibit 12-1 summarizes six examples of recent shifts in consumer behaviors and markets. Which of these would you say is the *most important* for consumers? Which would you say is the *least important*? Rank the examples in their order of importance. Explain your ranking.

2. What is a cultural trend? How do the methods to measure these trends differ? As a marketing manager, why is it important to be aware of new trends as they arise?

3. The text briefly described eight trends as seen by leading market researchers. Which of the trends are most significant for each of these marketers:

   a. Singer sewing machine   e. United Way
   b. Chevrolet   f. United Distillers
   c. AT&T   g. Democratic party
   d. Sears, Roebuck   h. Heinz ketchup

4. Reviewing the eight trends as seen by leading marketing researchers, evaluate same in terms of their compatibility with one another. Which trends seem to be related to each other? Which, if any, seem to be conflicting?

5. How would the model depicting the hierarchical adoption decision process vary according to the three major types of innovations?

6. What are the six basic dimensions associated with the speed and success rates for diffusion of an innovation? Are they of equal importance? Comment, using examples.

7. "An individual's adopter category remains unchanged across products." Do you agree with this statement? Why or why not? Provide examples.

[E] 8. How does a marketer's strategy change to reflect the various adopter categories? Substantiate with clippings of ads that seem to be aimed at each of the categories.

[E] 9. Interview a friend or relative from an older generation about the changes he or she has seen in the consumer culture (you may wish to use the examples in Exhibit 12-1 as a starting point). Write a brief report on what you learned from this interview.

[E] 10. Use the business reference section of the library to locate recent articles on cultural trends and changes in the consumer marketplace. Write a brief report on your findings.

[E] 11. Interview a department or specialty store manager about his or her experience with innovative new products. What types of consumers are interested in them? What are the typical problems with them? Select two or three current examples and have the manager classify them according to the six characteristics affecting diffusion rate (Figure 12-6). What, if anything, are the marketers doing about the problem areas? Write a brief report on your findings.

[E] 12. Interview a supermarket manager about his or her experience with new product entries. How do they get on the shelf? How well do they sell? What are two or three examples of success? Of failure? What recommendations would the manager offer to a marketer with a new food product to introduce?

[E] 13. Use the business reference section of your library to locate detailed analyses, reports, or overview articles about specific innovations (e.g., cellular telephones, fax machines, health maintenance organizations, new music technologies). Select one of these innovations as the basis for a report.

CHAPTER 13

Cross-Cultural and Symbolic Dimensions of Consumer Behavior

Cross-cultural Customs Quiz

The rapid growth of international business means that many readers will be dealing across cultures in the future. When they do, they will discover many interesting points of similarity and of difference. The following quiz raises just a few of these:

1. True or false: Direct eye contact is considered rude in Europe.
2. True or false: In China, it is a good idea to present a clock to a business associate.
3. True or false: In Hungary, be careful about asking about buses.
4. Which brand of Australian beer probably won't be imported to the United States?
5. Which Anheuser-Busch subsidiary in Europe probably won't export its brand name for bread to the United States?

Answers: (1) False, it is a sign of sincerity; in the Far East, however, it does border on rude behavior. (2) False, since a clock symbolizes death. (3) True, the English pronunciation means fornication. (4) Fourex (a name already used in the United States by a condom brand). (5) Bimbo, a market leader of premium baked goods!

In this chapter we will examine much more about consumer behavior across cultures, and the key role that symbolism plays in this process.

In Chapter 12 we focused on the topic of change, and saw how cultural trends and innovations come to influence consumer behavior. In this chapter we'll shift our emphasis slightly. Here we focus on more stable types of influences that a culture has on the consumer behaviors of its people, and particularly on the crucial role that symbols play. We also broaden our attention to include many cultures beyond that of the United States.

In the first half of the chapter, we examine some of the primary ways in which cultures differ from each other. We will look at some of the problems that language differences can cause and—since multinational marketing is increasingly important in today's world—we ask a key question: "Are consumers around the world *really* very different?" In the second half of the chapter we examine the role of symbolism in consumer behavior. Here we look at how consumers use symbols to communicate with other consumers as well as how marketers employ symbols as strategic tools. Let's begin our analysis, though, with a look at consumer behavior in different cultures.

CONSUMER BEHAVIOR ACROSS CULTURES

It is interesting to realize that many of the recent changes we've seen in our lives are specific to our own country. People living in other cultures have experienced other kinds of trends, based on differing life-styles and events in their cultures. There are, of course, an increasing number of forces that cut across cultures to create similarities. Over time, with international trade, travel, satellite communication, and immigration, cultures have come to have increasing effects on one another. Even so, the fact remains that cultural *differences* provide a key set of considerations within the field of consumer behavior. What are some primary dimensions of these differences?

Economic, Technological, and Political Dimensions

Why does consumer behavior differ in different countries? Some of the answers are obvious, while others are less clear on the surface. Let's consider some of the most obvious dimensions leading to differences in consumer behavior:

- Consumer incomes.
- Economic infrastructures.
- Government policies.

In most instances within the U.S. culture, a consumer exchanges money for products or services. In some other cultures of the world, though, money is a less used medium for exchange simply because a large number of consumers do not possess enough of it to be able to acquire their basic needs for living. Of all the countries of the world, therefore, only a relatively few would qualify as consumer economies that are basically similar to that of the United States.

Another factor related to the consumer behavior observed in various cultures is that many products considered a necessity in the United States may not be very functional in large sections of other cultures. Electricity, for example, is not readily available in many rural areas of the world: this presents an obvious barrier to use of household appliances. Supplies of gasoline, refrigerant, and other specialty commodities may not readily available, or the routine supply of repair parts and trained repairpersons may be a problem. All the foregoing points relate to the larger **economic infrastructure** of a culture.

Finally, governments in all nations have adopted policies that have the effect of encouraging different forms of consumption in their countries, while discouraging other forms. For example, most (if not all) nations have traditionally erected trade barriers against certain imported products to protect their home-based industries against possibly ruinous competition. (This practice usually has the effect of raising consumer prices for the products in question, but protects the jobs of domestic workers in the affected industries, thus shielding their personal incomes and consumer spending.)

At the extreme, some governments have for many years controlled the production of consumer products to be able to allocate national resources to particular economic sectors (for example, power plants, steel mills, railroads, and armaments). And in many countries, certain goods are singled out for "luxury taxes" (for example, cigarettes, liquor, and jewelry) to raise their actual prices to consumers and perhaps to discourage their use. In many U.S. states and cities, for example, these "sin taxes" are popular alternatives to increasing existing property or income levies.

An important point for us is that the greater the degree of government controls—whether or not they are desirable on other grounds—the less we are able to use marketplace behavior as a guide to the true desires of consumers. When different countries build in different kinds of government controls, this has the effect of enlarging the differences we see in consumer behavior across cultures. All the foregoing types of differences—standard of living, economic infrastructure, and government regulations—act to change the *material elements of culture.* That is, each person living in another culture in fact lives within a *different consumer and marketing environment* and therefore faces a different set of forces on his or her behaviors than you do.

Life-style, Language, and Belief Dimensions

Beyond the economic and material realm, many of the cultural differences in consumer behavior occur because of the ways that different people have learned to want to live their lives. Consumer behavior springs from the value systems and daily life-styles of a people and generally serves to support their preferred ways of living and of viewing the world. Before turning to comparisons across cultures, let's briefly examine some dominant cultural values of the U.S. culture.

Traditional American Values

At a cultural level, values are reflected by widely held beliefs about what is desirable. However, the attempt to identify the major values of the American culture is extremely difficult. Most of us do not talk about our values—indeed, they do not even seem to enter our consciousness in any neat and clean form (also, not every American subscribes to the dominant values of the culture, and some values are becoming less strong in the current generation, while other values are becoming stronger today). Recognizing these difficulties, one of the most impressive attempts to isolate key American values was made by Robin Williams, a sociologist who proposed *six summary propositions* for American values.[1] Let's look at each of these:

1. **Attempts at active mastery.** Americans stress power, approve of assertiveness, encourage expressions of desire, and refuse to accept temporary setbacks. Active mastery falls at the other extreme from passive acceptance of what the world may bring.

2. **Focus on the external world.** American culture is interested in tangible things and current events more than it is geared to inner experiences involving meaning and feeling. The American genius is in manipulation rather than contemplation.

3. **An open view of the world.** Americans accept and even welcome an open system—one that provides for growth, change, and movement. The American personality is outgoing and adaptive and expects things to be different tomorrow from what they were yesterday.

4. **A rationalist faith.** In keeping with their openness to the future and their willingness to entertain change, Americans stress scientific approaches to the daily world. Tradition is not as important as in some other cultures, but orderly planning for the future is quite important.

5. **Belief in egalitarian ethics.** American culture shows a strong position toward equality of opportunity for all; this also translates into a universalist ethic, in which laws are meant to apply to everyone equally. In interpersonal relations, there is relatively more stress on peer relations than on superior-subordinate relationships.

6. **Respect for the Lone Ranger.** Americans retain an underlying respect for the individual pursuing his or her own vision in the world and have somewhat less regard than other cultures for group identity and responsibility to a group.

Although it may be difficult for Americans to recognize, each of these characteristics differs from the traditional values of many other cultures of the world. As they experience other cultures through travel, discussions, or postings in international business, they will increasingly encounter contrasts with these traditional beliefs. (In addition, Appendix 13-A provides a summary discussion of social stratification in cultures, which will further address some of the bases for differences both among and within cultures of the world.)

Life-style and Belief Differences

Figure 13-1 summarizes a number of the key life-style and belief bases that underpin differences in consumer behavior across cultures. First, **differences in cultural values** can be a key factor in cross-cultural consumer behavior. For example, according to some American marketers, a good way to sell to consumers in Southeast Asia is to stress the previous success of the product being offered. The reason: Asian people prefer to be harmonious with their social group rather than stand out through individual choice. As an illustration, Phillip Morris has been very successful with its Marlboro brand in Hong Kong by citing the brand's dominant market share in the United States. Each time a new report on cigarette brand market shares is issued, the results are beamed by satellite to Hong Kong consumers and announced on TV.[2]

Cultural conventions are a second important factor, as these reflect the normal ("conventional") ways that consumers of a given culture have learned to think and act in a wide variety of ways. For example, a well-known story concerns the large detergent manufacturer that shipped a new set of ads to its Middle East subsidiary. The ads showed pictures of a laundry sequence: a picture of soiled clothes, followed by a picture of the soap box, followed by a picture of clean clothes. The firm's headquarters forgot, however, that consumers in these countries read from the right to the left! A logical interpretation of the package, therefore, was that this product soils clothes.[3]

Climate and geography raise a third set of important considerations for consumer behavior. Many vehicles are simply not engineered for operation in very cold climates, for example, or in rugged terrain. **Physiological differences** also exist between cultures and can sometimes be very significant factors to consider. In one case, overlooking this factor led to consumers using a product in a way that the marketers never intended or expected. This happened when a

FIGURE 13-1 **Dimensions of Differences in Cross-cultural**
                Life-styles and Beliefs

Basis of Difference	Example
Cultural values	Marlboro in Hong Kong
Cultural conventions	Detergent Box in Middle East
Climate and geography	Vehicles in rough terrain
Physiological characteristics	Powdered milk in South America
Needs and use environment	Toothbrushes in Vietnam
Perceptions of product need	Deodorant usage
Past product experience	Cambell's soup in England
Product usage customs	Detergent in Peru
Existing product preferences	Cornflakes in Japan

foreign aid program sent huge quantities of powdered milk to natives in South America. Claiming that it made them ill, the natives instead used it to whitewash their houses! It later turned out they were right: an enzyme needed to break down the product is present in the digestive systems of North Americans and Europeans, but not in most South American adults, who were unable to digest this product. Novel product uses can also occur when the **cultural need and use environment** is quite different. About 20 years ago, for example, a U.S. firm was very pleased with its high rate of toothbrush sales in South Vietnam. It later found out that the sales spurt had been due to the Vietcong soldiers using the product to clean their weapons as they fought the American and government forces!

Perceptions of product need also differ across cultural boundaries. For example, should everyone use a deodorant? Almost all American consumers agree with this premise (89 percent), but only half of Australians do (53 percent), and only three of five French consumers agree (59 percent), according to surveys conducted by a major advertising agency. In addition to differing need perceptions across cultures, **past product experience** also is likely to be different across cultures. Campbell's soup initially failed, because of this factor, when it first tried to enter the British market for soup. It turned out that English consumers had never seen "condensed" soup before and interpreted the size of the can as providing them with far too little soup for the money. In this case, Campbell's chose to modify its product by adding water rather than attempting to teach the public the difference in soup styles.

Product use customs, when unnoticed by marketers, can sometimes cause real problems for a firm. A foreign detergent maker, for example, once encountered troubles in Peru when it introduced its new stain-removing enzyme product. After a good trial rate was achieved, sales dropped off quickly. The reason: the local Peruvian consumers had always believed that they must boil their wash to kill germs. Such boiling, however, happened to destroy the enzymes in this product. When this happened, the detergent became useless and did not perform as advertised!

Existing product preferences is the final factor in our list, and it reminds us that the consumers of another culture were managing to get along for many years before our product became available to them. During this time, they have undoubtedly developed sets of preferences for products that we are hoping to supplant with our new entry. Sometimes, however, these existing preferences can be hard to overcome. Food is often a problem in this regard, especially when the product type has not previously appeared in the local culture. An American cornflake manufacturer, for example, failed miserably in introducing its product to the Japanese market. The Japanese were not used to breakfast cereals and were simply not interested in them. Similarly, a large U.S.-based ketchup maker also failed in its attempt to enter the Japanese market: it forgot that soy sauce was a dominant feature of the Japanese culture! Rather than quit, however, the firm was flexible: it began to import the Japanese soy sauce to the American market!

Thus there are many aspects to the life-style and belief system differences underlying differences in consumer behavior across cultures. Unfortunately, even these are not all the factors that need to be considered. In particular, a host of additional problems stem from language barriers across cultures.

Language Differences and the Troubles They Cause

Written and spoken language serves the fundamental purpose of allowing humans to *communicate* with each other. Within a given culture, language serves to provide continuity and an opportunity for consensus to emerge. Based on our language, we share many concepts in our minds with others in our culture. Across different cultures, however, language differences can set up distinct barriers and sometimes can create aggravating problems. This property of language has affected marketers in particular ways, as they have attempted to cross cultural boundaries. Sometimes the results have been amusing: Exhibit 13-1 lists some of the language-based marketing social blunders that have become famous in the field.

EXHIBIT 13-1   *MARKETING MISTAKES WITH LANGUAGE*

- The same word often has different meanings in different languages. One major detergent manufacturer decided to check on this before marketing a new brand name. It found that the brand's name, which meant "dainty" in English, meant "song" in Gaelic, "horse" in an African language, "dimwitted" in the Mideast, and "out of one's mind" in Korea. In the Slavic languages, moreover, the name was obscene and offensive.

- Automakers, for some reason, seem to have had more than their share of these problems. For example, Ford's problems with the Spanish language are widely discussed. It introduced a low-cost truck, the "ugly old woman" (Fiera), into some less developed countries. Its Caliente model did not do well in Mexico, perhaps because this is a slang term for a streetwalker there. Finally, in Brazil, the Pinto was changed to the Corcel after its initial introduction: this meant that the "small male appendage" became a "horse" in Portuguese.

- In similar fashion, the foreign firm selling Evitol shampoo in Brazil was embarrassed to discover it was claiming to be a "dandruff contraceptive."

- Pet Milk has problems with French-speaking consumers, since this word can be translated as "to break wind." Similarly, Fresca soft drinks appeared to be aiming at a specialized market segment in Mexico: the word there is slang for lesbian. And a new airline trying to enter the Australian market chose EMU as its symbol: unfortunately, the emu is an Australian bird that cannot fly.

EXHIBIT 13-1 — *MARKETING MISTAKES WITH LANGUAGE* CONTINUED

- Other types of problems can occur when there is no similar collection of letters in another language, so that some translation must occur into different words. When Coca-Cola was attempting to enter China in the 1920s, it developed a group of Chinese characters that sounded like Coca-Cola. Unfortunately, when these characters were placed on the bottles, they translated as "bite the wax tadpole."
- When Hunt-Wesson attempted to introduce its Big John brand into French-speaking Canada, the translation Gros Jos turned out to be slang for a woman with large breasts. The brand did sell well, however.
- General Motors, touting its "body by Fisher" to Belgian consumers, found that the phrase was interpreted there as "corpse by Fisher."
- The famous Pepsi-Cola slogan "Come alive with Pepsi!" was translated in Germany as "Come out of the grave!" and in Taiwan as "Bring your ancestors back from the dead."
- Recently, Oregon-based Taco Time fast food restaurants decided to expand into Japan, when management learned that "tako" can mean either "octopus" or "idiot" in the Japanese language. The company's president commented, "Well, we'll have to do a bit of marketing."[4]
- Sometimes there are problems because of high illiteracy rates, so that written language cannot be used. One large food company maintained its normal practices in selling baby food in Africa. The local population, most of whom could not read, looked at the labels with pictures of infants and interpreted them to mean that the jars contained ground up babies!
- American marketers are not the only ones to encounter language problems. A popular chocolate candy in Europe, for example, did not sell well in the United States. Its name: Zit.
- Similarly, a large Japanese industrial firm entered the United States market with ads promoting its new specialty steel named Sumitomo High Toughness steel. Rather than writing this out each time in the ads, the firm used the acronym in bold capitals throughout the advertising, which closed with a claim that this product "was made to match its name."
- Finally, to attract American tourists, a dress shop in Paris featured the sign: "Come in and Have a Fit!"

Source: These examples are given in an interesting book by David A. Ricks, *Big Business Blunders: Mistakes in Multinational Marketing* (Homewood, Ill.: Dow Jones-Irwin, 1983).

Cross-cultural Hidden Languages

In addition to the overt use of language, people use a variety of other means with which to communicate with each other. Edward T. Hall, the noted anthropologist, has termed these **hidden languages**. Since most of us learn to communicate almost entirely within our own cultures, we share an implicit understanding of what these hidden languages mean. We are comfortable with them and know how to use them, even if we are not always conscious of doing so. This point is especially apparent when we encounter someone who does not apparently understand the hidden language the way we do. In these instances both of us can easily be frustrated.

The *use of space* is one of the hidden dimensions of culture, and very strict (albeit unspoken) rules develop as to how space is to be handled in personal interactions. As a simple example, consider how you feel when someone you don't know well stands very close to you while talking and breathes directly into your face. In some cultures this is the accepted mode of communication: to do otherwise is to insult the person with whom you are trying to talk.

Some of the other significant hidden dimensions of culture are

- Body movement.
- Eye contact and avoidance.
- Type of clothing.
- Body posture.
- Voice tone and pace.
- Use of touch.

Note that the same action (for example, staring into another's eyes) can mean very different things depending on the other person's relationship to you, his or her status or role, and the general situation. Within consumer behavior, these topics have particular importance for communication situations such as salesperson-customer interactions and in reaching business sales agreements. (If you are interested in finding out more about these dimensions, and how a businessperson might adapt to them, you might wish to pursue the references listed in Note 5.)

Cross-cultural Developments in Consumer Policy

The development of specific government policies toward consumers and marketers provides one of the clearest areas for cultural differences to emerge. In almost all public policy instances of cultural impacts, the primary focus is within a single country, reflecting the question of which policies are most appropriate for that culture. As we'd expect, different countries have arrived at different answers, with religious forces and political philosophies playing an important role in these decisions. Several years ago in Indonesia, for example, the president abruptly announced a ban on all television advertising. He explained that he did so because advertising stirs materialist wants and acts to retard development of the nation.[6] In Norway, a Singapore Airlines ad to business travelers was banned by the consumer ombudsman. The ad, which stressed an attractive Oriental

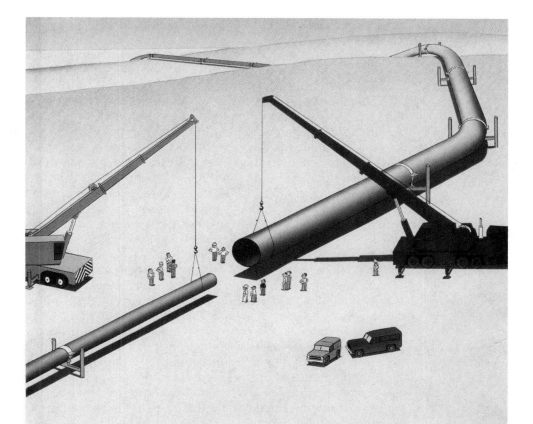

The need for a common language is something anyone can understand.

Marketing research is supposed to be a conduit for information that can make your job easier.

You gather the facts, process them and then sit down to talk turkey. Unfortunately, to the people you're talking to, sometimes it sounds more like Turkish.

So how do you translate research into action? You work with Nielsen.

We've been refining scanning data longer than anyone else around. And we don't just pump out numbers. We put them in a language that manufacturers and retailers can both understand.

So things match up better on both ends. For more information, talk to the infor-

mation people at Nielsen Marketing Research, Nielsen Plaza, Northbrook, IL 60062, or call 312/498-6300. And learn marketing's common language. It's the talk of the industry.

Nielsen Marketing Research

a company of
The Dun & Bradstreet Corporation

stewardess bringing a pillow and serving brandy to a tired male passenger, was intended to focus attention on the gracious service offered by this airline. The ombudsman, however, said that women are not pleasant, smiling servants and cannot be used to sell airline flights.[7]

The development of consumer policy is often difficult when there are strong differences in subcultures within a country. Here we find pressures arising from different groups of consumers (and from the marketing community) who are attempting to operate according to their views of what is best. In the United States, for example, a key issue involves the balance of marketer freedoms against consumer protection. In many other cultures, however, religious values are placed on a much higher level than are individual freedoms. For example, one-fourth of the world's consumers are Moslems. Some countries with Moslem majorities have at various times simply banned products or marketing practices that conflicted with tenets of the religion. Even when this was done, however, the policymakers had to deal with the forces for economic growth and consumer subcultures that wanted to see Westernized practices in the country.

Pakistan, for example, is an Islamic country that had been a rather freewheeling consumer nation under both democratically elected governments and military dictatorships since its formation by the partition of a British India in 1947. Then, about 15 years ago, a strongly religious military dictatorship took over the country. The new government instituted traditional Moslem punishments for serious violations of social laws—a thief's right arm is severed and an adulteress is sentenced to death by stoning, for example. Within the consumer sphere, while dancing, lingerie, and alcohol were banned as representing decadent behavior, television advertising was allowed to continue for other products. However, an influential national commentator then took to the air to complain that Pakistani women were being exploited and commercialized and that these practices were in clear violation of God's will that women have a position of sanctity in the society. His solution: the government should ban all women from appearing in advertising. This sentiment received strong support from the dominant subculture in the nation. Another subculture, however—represented by the All-Pakistan Women's Association—immediately staged an angry demonstration against both the premises and proposal of the commentator. What should the public policymakers do in this instance?[8]

Thus the making of consumer policy is a controversial and complex process in most cultures. Those of us who live within only a single culture cannot easily see just how very differently cultures deal with the same types of issues. For marketers engaged in international business, however, such differences are crucial. Let's briefly examine a few facets of this issue.

The "Global Village": Implications for Marketers

Our discussion to this point has indicated how significant economic, political, and life-style dimensions are in determining consumer behavior across cultures. Each of these also impacts marketing managers in many specific ways, depending

FIGURE 13-2 Cross-cultural Laws Regarding Sales Promotions

Regulatory Pattern	Type of Promotion			Number of Countries[d,e]
	Premiums[a]	Gifts[b]	Competitions[c]	
A	Allowed	Allowed	Allowed	15
B	Allowed	Allowed	Restricted	8
C	Allowed	Allowed	Mostly banned	1
D	Restricted	Allowed	Allowed	1
E	Restricted	Allowed	Restricted	1
F	Restricted	Restricted	Restricted	6
G	Restricted	Restricted	Banned	1
H	Mostly banned	Restricted	Restricted	1
I	Mostly banned	Restricted	Mostly banned	2
J	Mostly banned	Mostly banned	Mostly banned	2
K	Banned	Allowed	Banned	1
L	Banned	Restricted	Restricted	2
M	Banned	Banned	Restricted	1
13				42

[a]An extra value offer, or special price coupon.

[b]Anything free with purchase.

[c]Games, sweepstakes, contests.

[d]Countries surveyed exclude communist nations and represent the free market economies of Europe, Asia, Africa, and the Americas.

[e]Laws and regulations are changing in various directions, so count is approximate.

Source: Based on discussions in J. J. Boddewyn, *Premiums, Gifts, Competitions, and other Sales Promotions: Regulation and Self-Regulation in 42 Countries* (New York: International Advertising Association, 1988).

on the product and country in question. Therefore, it is virtually impossible to generalize about "the international picture" for most marketing situations. For example, Figure 13-2 summarizes the confusing picture that confronts a marketer considering an international promotional campaign for a consumer product. While the United States, reflecting pattern A in the figure, will allow considerable flexibility for all three popular techniques, the other 41 nations in this study treat each technique in a variety of different ways (ranging from allowing it, allowing it with significant restrictions, almost banning it with few exceptions, to banning the approach entirely: the exact restrictions and exceptions, moreover, are different from country to country). The result is that *marketers must approach each country individually* to ensure the program will be in compliance.

Despite these types of barriers, the rapidly increasing importance of international business is introducing significant changes into the courses offered by business schools and executive training institutes. Thus a number of managerial tips and techniques are available in current courses, books, and articles in this area. Beyond the managerial specifics, however, there are several broader issues that deserve our attention.

Population Trends Across Cultures

The Ties That Bind

As the world's largest market, the People's Republic of China attracts considerable attention in the marketing world. One manager from the Nike shoe company was reported recently as saying, *"When I hear about one billion Chinese, I see two billion feet!"*[9] Hearing this callous description, one philosophical comic responded, *"When I hear about one billion Chinese, I see two billion souls (soles?)!"*

Consumer markets fundamentally depend upon population. The cross-cultural picture of population is interesting: a glimpse at trends indicates a global future quite different from our recent past. As you may know, growth has virtually stopped in the most affluent countries of the world, but is continuing rapidly elsewhere. For example, at current rates, Canada's population will not double for 90 years, the United States's for 100 years, Japan's and France's for 150 years, Britain's for 300 years, and Italy's for 2300 years! In contrast, at current rates India—which already has the world's second largest population—will double its population in just over *30 years*, as will Pakistan, Bangladesh, Nigeria, and many smaller countries. In 30 years, then (about the time when many of this book's readers should be enjoying successful senior executive positions), the entire population of the affluent markets of the world today will have a combined population under 700 million, or about half that of either China or India alone![10]

This simple analysis does not account for many other important factors such as infrastructures, politics, competition, buying power of the consumer population, and so forth. It does, however, indicate where the massive future growth in the world will be occurring, and it has clearly captured the attention of business and government planners around the globe!

Toward the Year 2000: Fundamental Changes in Economic and Political Systems

It is difficult to express the incredible degree to which our futures are likely to have been altered by the events across cultures in just the past few years. Although we may not recognize it on a day-to-day basis, we are living in a remarkable period: it now appears that the decade of the 1990s (together with the 1980s) will prove to be one of the most important periods of fundamental restructuring in our world's history! Let's briefly consider some examples, noting the key, related roles of the economic system and political systems in each case:

Major Changes in the People's Republic of China

Beginning in 1979, under Deng Xiaoping, China undertook a series of economic reforms (meant to revitalize a lagging economy), while the political system (a strong form of communism) was left unchanged.[11] During the 1980s, international businesses moved into numerous joint ventures and trading agreements with emerging businesses in China, and vast changes began in the life-styles of some Chinese citizens (one study, for example, reported that 61 percent of a set of urban households owned washing machines by the late 1980s, up from only 6 percent in 1981).[12] Within the huge country, some regions—

Change in China: Consumers clamor for TV sets in Shanghai.

especially those near the seacoast—moved strongly toward an international, entrepreneurial business approach (price freedom, import/export, private ownership, private lending, etc.), while other regions—especially those in the interior—remained with their traditional approach to enterprise (prices set by Beijing, managers appointed by the communist party, state-owned and financed, sales within the country).

During the 1980s, tensions rose, as did economic growth. International marketers encountered cultural differences in ways of approaching business transactions, and began to complain increasingly of self-serving, corrupt practices on the part of some government officials.[13] Within China, tensions between the new businesses and the state enterprises rose, as they seemed to be serving different goals. Finally, increasing marketplace freedoms brought increasing demands from citizens for political freedoms as well. The 1989 government-student confrontations in Tiananmen Square (Beijing) and other cities brought this poignant struggle to the world's attention. As we move into the 1990s, therefore, the economic/political situation of China is still in the process of working toward some form of economic and political equilibria, with complex pressures at work, and much uncertainty facing the participants.

Major Changes in the USSR and Eastern Europe

Beginning in 1985, under Mikhail Gorbachev, the USSR undertook major reforms to improve some nagging problems within the nation. In some ways these were the mirror image of the Chinese efforts, since the initial efforts were *political reforms* known as **glasnost** (openness). The *glasnost* movement was broadly based, including a rollback of the centralized power of the communist party (through elections), lessened control over the nations of Eastern Europe, withdrawal from Afghanistan, willingness to discuss arms race reductions with the western alliance, popular visits to China, Japan, Western Europe, and so forth. At the dawn of the 1990s, the "cold war" political tensions that had plagued the globe since World War II had been considerably eased under *glasnost*.

During this same period Gorbachev was also attempting—with considerably less success—to institute economic reforms. **Perestroika**, the restructuring and rebuilding of the Soviet economic system, was an effort to make the Soviet system more responsive to market demands, yet retaining the top-down economic planning that was the hallmark of the system. As one Soviet official explained: "For you in the West, marketing is one of the means of making profits. But for us, marketing is a means of satisfying the needs of society. . . ."[14]

However, for the early years at least, centralized planning and market sensitivity did not seem to go together. Huge shortages of key consumer goods persisted: as another Soviet official explained, "It's the opposite of America . . . we have the money to buy things, but not enough things to spend it on!"[15] For example, those citizens with the cash to buy a new car still needed to wait five years for delivery! Since the Soviets were unwilling to

Consumers stand in line at GUM Department store in Moscow.

allow prices to change in response to demand (instead, prices were set centrally and used in all official transactions), there was little mechanism for change within the bureaucracies, and the Soviet economy continued to flounder. The economic situation then actually worsened as political freedoms increased. Since wages were increased, product shortages became more severe, and a vast black market thrived as products not available through official channels could be obtained (for much higher prices) through unofficial channels. This in turn spurred a soaring crime rate within the country.

In an effort to obtain better allocations and higher productivity, Gorbachev attempted further economic reforms. These moved toward decentralized decision powers, smaller cooperative ventures, and so forth, but entrenched bureaucrats worked to undermine these, and workers' attitudes toward increasing productivity were sometimes problems. A third Soviet official commented, "Our economy was functioning within its own closed circuit as it were. Over the past three years, we have achieved some progress in changing the rules of the game. We are also attempting to change the mentality of our people."

Meanwhile, the nations of Eastern Europe were undergoing related changes as their political bounds loosened. Initially, Hungary and Poland moved most strongly toward economic and political reforms, but in all cases the future was difficult to forecast. Ending centralized control in one giant step, for example, would risk chaos because of the consumer goods shortages: one representative of Solidarity, the Polish trade union movement, estimated that food prices would immediately soar, which would almost certainly "mean riots." As the 1990s began, each nation was moving toward further international trade and investment options, but at different rates, with different sets of concerns, and without a firm guarantee that the political freedoms under *glasnost* would continue into the indefinite future.[16]

Western Europe: 1992 and Beyond

Massive changes have not been restricted to the communist world in recent years. The year 1992 is when the European Economic Community (EEC) plan to eliminate trade, technical, and monetary barriers between nations begins to take effect.[17] Under this plan, many forms of barriers—technical standards, business regulations, tariffs, and so forth—would be removed to facilitate trade. The effect would be similar to trade in the United States, in which commerce across states has been deliberately simplified to allow free trade. The impetus behind the change in Europe? Serious concern with the growing gap between the trade successes of Japan and the United States and the lagging growth of European countries (one French Government ad touting the change, for example, featured a thin French boxer squared off to battle a giant American football player and huge Japanese sumo wrestler . . . suddenly 11 friends—the other EEC members—rush to his aid!).

Economically, the united states of Europe would comprise a huge consumer market of some 320 million people, larger than either the United States or Japan. It will unquestionably offer opportunities for long-term economic growth, but also number of uncertainties. Just as in our discussions of China and the USSR, the interplay of economic and political systems is at work. The 12 EEC countries have strong national and local political identities, as well as local vested interests that will want to benefit in final decisions. Thus it is possible that some internal aspects of the agreement will not be smoothed out by 1992, or even in this century! Externally, it is also possible that the EEC will decide to protect its now large market, and will erect trade barriers to lower competition from Japan, Korea, the United States and others. (In fact, some observers believe that the globe is slowly forming into four giant trading blocs based in (1) North America (with Canada, the

Toward 1992 and beyond, major changes ahead in European consumer marketing.

United States, and Mexico also recently agreeing to remove barriers for freer trading), (2) Japan and the market nations of Asia, (3) the communist nations of Eastern Europe and the USSR, and (4) the united states of Europe.) Not only would this restrict the overall level of free trade, but might also increase difficulties for growth in those developing nations not in one of the four blocs, which could also lead to further political unrest.

At the managerial level, marketers have been planning and reorganizing for some time now, getting ready for the opening of the European marketplace. However, many managerial questions remain. For example, under the European plan, unified regulatory standards will do away with the kinds of differences we saw in Figure 13-2. This would allow marketers to use a single ("standardized") marketing mix in all the EEC countries, which would lower production and marketing costs. However, marketers do not know whether the standardized approach is likely to be effective! As we read, marketers are still wrestling with this basic issue. Two key considerations: (1) competition will be very heavy, as local firms fight to maintain their clients while newcomers battle to gain market share, and (2) national and local identities will continue. As one marketer comments, "The thing to remember [is] . . . consumer traits aren't going to change overnight . . . culture and language differences will still mean a lot."

The Key for Marketers: Subcultures and Segments

As a final point in our consideration of marketing across cultures, it is important to note that *each marketer will only be concerned with a portion of each relevant market.* This will usually be sufficient for profitability and can make matters easier when natural segments exist. One maker of dishwasher detergent, for example, decided to use a direct-mail campaign in France, where some 15 percent of the population owns the machines. Across countries, moreover, similar segments will likely exist for similar reasons: wealthier, educated dishwasher owners will also be found in other EEC countries, so the detergent manufacturer is able to transfer at least some of the successful campaign elements to other countries as well. According to one executive in Europe, "What you have to do is determine what appeal will travel well. For example, recent college graduates entering the work force in New York, London, or Barcelona may all be looking for the same thing."[18] According to another European executive, as a consumer a Paris business executive will likely have more in common with business executives from Oslo or Rome than with a small-town French cafe-owner: "Once you have identified the same group in different markets, you can develop a strategy that appeals cross-culturally." Benetton, for example, has done this by appealing to young people in different countries who all want stylish, affordable clothes. Even so, the local campaigns are likely to be modified somewhat to work more smoothly within each culture.[19]

The fact that there are similar segments across different cultures reflects the presence of strong *subcultures* within each society. The basic underpinning of subculture theory lies in the ways in which societies are organized internally. This in turn leads to *social classes*, an interesting and important topic in understanding cultural influences. If you have lived all your life in the United States, you may not be aware of just how significant this topic is in most other cultures, where social classes are more sharply divided. If you would like to read more about this area, Appendix 13-A provides an overview and discussion. At this point, however, we will turn our attention to a different important issue—the important role that symbols play in cultural influence on consumer behavior.

CULTURE, SYMBOLISM, AND CONSUMER BEHAVIOR

Symbolism provides a significant basis for a culture's influences on its members.

Each of us lives in a symbolic world. All humans use a process of symbolizing to think about and elaborate upon the physical world around us. Understanding symbols provides real insights into the field of consumer behavior.

What do these statements mean? Basically, a **symbol** is anything that stands for or represents something else. Words are one common form of symbol: "Tree," for example, represents a certain type of object to us. Numbers and mathematical signs are also symbols. Symbols are more than words and numbers, however. For example, a particular arrangement of musical notes can become a fight song and symbolize a university. A national flag is much more than a scrap of colored cloth. And a uniform is more than just a piece of clothing.

Symbols Are Helpful

Within consumer behavior, symbols perform two important functions: (1) they improve our *efficiency* as consumers, and (2) they add to the *enjoyment* of our activities as consumers. Product names and store names serve as symbols that improve our efficiency as consumers. These symbols allow us to "learn" about the marketplace and to plan our future behaviors better. For example, store names allow us to consider where we might shop and what we might experience when we get there. Prices are also expressed symbolically (that is, through numbers and monetary units). When prices are communicated in ads or on the packages, they help us to evaluate a possible purchase much more quickly than if we had to negotiate with each seller on each item. Symbols also enliven and *enrich* our experience as consumers. For example, the products we place on our bodies gain symbolic meaning in our minds; that is, consumers are very interested in how clothing and cosmetics can be used to create a certain image, to create beauty, to commemorate particular events, and so on.

These deeper symbolic dimensions of consumption have recently become the subject of "postmodernism" in consumer research, which has been the subject of considerable controversy involving scientific methods and philosophy of science. Postmodern writers have generally stressed a much broader view of consumption than has been typical within marketing. For example, focus has been given to what we are consuming when we listen to music or attend a play and to describing the importance of our feelings and attachments to the money we save, the pets we own, family heirlooms, and so forth. Thus there is concern with a more "holistic" view of consumers than marketing's typical focus on what consumers are buying, and many of these articles are written without attempting to draw marketing conclusions about the subject. (If you would like to read more about these approaches and controversies, you may wish to consult Note 20.)

As we might expect, symbolism plays a prominent role in much of the work in this area. An increasing number of marketers are applying **semiotics** (the study of signs or things with meaning), others are examining *rituals* associated with consumer behavior (for example, think about the various settings in which eating and drinking serve symbolic functions), while other work is stressing the symbolic nature of social interactions. In our discussions concluding this chapter, we will delve more deeply into the roles that symbols play in consumer behavior.

Symbols Have Different Levels of Elaboration

Basically, something becomes a symbol to us because of how we react mentally to it. Obviously, then, almost everything can be a symbol. An important issue, therefore, is the *level of elaboration* that is stimulated by a particular symbol. It is useful for us to make a major distinction between two extreme levels of elaboration—very low and very high. At very low levels we find **objective symbols**, while at very high levels we find **evocative symbols**.

Objective symbols are commonly used simply to describe or identify something, and thereby to transfer information. Each of the letters on this page, for example, is serving as an objective symbol for you as you read the page. Its function is straightforward: to allow the reader to deal with larger forms of symbols (words, then sentences). In contrast, a symbol is evocative when it leads a person to expand upon the narrow meaning of the symbol itself and somehow to bring to mind ("evoke") further interpretations or feelings during the symbolizing process. Words and sentences can be used for this process (consider, for example, how easy it is to unleash our imaginations upon such words as "furry," "passionate," "evil," and so on). In general, though, the evocative purpose of symbols seems to be expressed better through artistic means that often avoid the use of language. We've all experienced emotions (love, tenderness, anger), tastes (biting into a sweet, ripe cherry, the first taste of a dill pickle, etc.), or sensations of touch that have meaning far beyond the realm of language. In fact, these types of experiences are so subjective that they seem to require the artists of the world—the poets, musicians, sculptors, and painters—to symbolize them for us.

What Does a Prune Symbolize?

Since both thinking and feeling are involved when we are engaged in symbolic elaboration, it can be difficult for us to assess the total amount of elaboration we are experiencing. From a marketer's perspective, moreover, this problem is even more severe, since consumers' elaborations are private to them and unobservable to us. This means that we need to undertake consumer research to try to find out what's really going on in consumers' minds when they symbolize. One classic marketing case that tried to do this occurred about 30 years ago.[21]

The California Sunsweet Growers Association was attempting to figure out why the per capita sales of prunes had been declining for some time. The association hired a famous "motivation researcher," Dr. Ernest Dichter, to suggest what might be done. After studying consumers using his motivation research methods (we discuss these in Chapter 6), Dr. Dichter reported that *a large segment of American consumers did not dislike the taste of prunes but seemed bothered by what this fruit symbolized to them.* In particular, six major symbols were causing consumers to shy away from eating this food that they liked on other grounds:

■ *Prunes are seen as symbols of old age and sterility.* Many consumers associated prunes with cafeterias, older people, and an older life-style.

■ *Prunes are seen as symbols of loss of vitality and natural powers.* Many consumers did not like the look of stewed prunes, lying in their juice, and this vision conjured up further elaborations in their minds.

■ *Prunes are symbols of digestive problems.* Prunes were seen as laxatives or medicines. While they were good for this purpose, many consumers evoked images of a person who needed to eat prunes probably also having other health problems.

■ *Prunes are symbols of parental authority.* Some consumers had been forced to eat prunes by their parents. These consumers now viewed this product as a symbol of enforced discipline. Now that they are adults, and had a choice, they would not choose this product.

■ *Prunes are symbols of plebeian tastes and lack of prestige.* Some consumers saw prunes as good basic foods, but not something to serve to others. If they are to be eaten, this should be done in the privacy of one's own kitchen.

Now on Network TV!

FEATURING: Emmy Award Winning Actress Erika Slezak of "One Life To Live."

"Fresh Picked" :15

ERIKA: What's the best kind of fruit?

The kind that's fresh, moist, and plump.

That's why Sunsweet are my favorite kind of pitted prunes. Moist, plump and fresh.

Sunsweet. Because the best prunes . . . are fresh prunes.

A recent ad for prunes: Notice the appeals being used here.

■ *Prunes are symbols of food for peculiar people.* Many consumers saw prunes as a favored food by "health nuts" and older people with health problems. These consumers did not wish to imitate their behaviors and perhaps become more like these prune users.

The marketing strategists noticed that each of these symbols seemed to have started from accurate observations about the appearance of the fruit, the benefits it offered, and the kinds of persons who consumed it. In each case, however, consumers had apparently gone much farther in their own minds (this is the elaboration process), until they reached the point of having unpleasant feelings about the prune itself. The marketing team was quite unsure about what do do next—should it strive to overcome this negative symbolism by attacking it head on or should it ignore the negative connotations and try to provide the prune with positive symbolic qualities for consumers to seize upon? After 30 years of trying various approaches, this problem still exists: What would you recommend if you were consulting for the California Prune Board?

Symbols Don't Always Mean the Same Thing

The levels of elaboration concept also raises another important aspect of symbols—consumers can differ in how they'll react to various symbols. Loyal users of prunes, for example, might be shocked to learn what others think about it! For the "objective" level of symbolizing, with very little elaboration, most consumers within the same culture are likely to agree upon the meaning. This is true because we have usually learned the same language, rules, and customs. As a symbol becomes more evocative, the chances for different consumers to attach different meanings to it begin to increase. Partially, this is due to subcultural differences, reflecting differences in our backgrounds and current experiences. Partially, it is due to our personalities and interests: some people are more "imaginative" than others, some people are more "observant," "religious," and so on.

CONSUMPTION AS A SYMBOLIC PROCESS

In this section, we will examine three key ways in which we, as consumers, use symbolism in our everyday consumer behaviors: (1) symbolic expression within ourselves, (2) interpreting symbols used by others, and (3) sending symbolic messages to others.

Private Symbolic Expressions

Very often, a consumer behavior activity serves a private symbolic purpose for us. For example, let's look at some reports by graduates in which they've recognized symbolic dimensions within their consumption acts:

When I put on my very best jewelry and my very best clothes . . . I think they symbolize my worth as a person, and they make me feel good about myself, even if I don't go anywhere or see anyone.

Sometimes when I have to go somewhere important, and to look good and speak well, I spend an extra long time shaving. Even though no one else could possibly notice the difference, it makes me feel like I'm taking good care of myself, and it builds my confidence before I leave.

I sometimes really love the feeling I get when I step into my new car, slam the heavy door, start it up with a roar, and begin to move . . . especially the smooth and powerful acceleration. It symbolizes my power and control over my life and the world around me, even for a short time.

Listening to tapes and records provides me with many moments of symbolic expression. Some music leads me to feel love, some makes me feel free and sexy, some to feel lonely, some to feel physical, some to feel rebellious, and on and on. Usually it's better when no one's around, so I can relax and not be embarrassed.

I'm not sure whether this is consumer behavior or not, but I feel that dropping a dollar into the Salvation Army's bucket is a symbolic act on my part. I don't try to be noticed when I do it, I just feel that it expresses my goodwill toward man.

In all these cases, notice how the primary symbolic expression was directed inward and was personal in nature. One stream of research relevant to this form of symbolizing involves the *self concept*, discussed in Chapter 7, which suggests that consumers buy products to help to express the "inner self." Within the postmodern literature, Belk argues that consumers use possessions to create, maintain, and extend meaning in their lives through different life stages.[22]

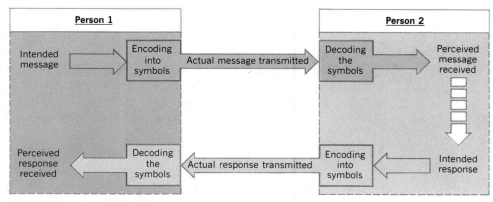

FIGURE 13-3 **Outline of a Communication Process**

Communicating with Others Through Consumer Behavior

In keeping with our discussions elsewhere in the book, Figure 13-3 shows a basic framework for understanding the communication process between two people. Notice that much of this process occurs within the inner worlds of our minds and cannot be observed. Three processes are involved: encoding, transmission, and decoding. **Encoding** refers to the choice and arrangement of symbols to represent the intended meanings of person 1. **Transmission** refers to the actual movement (through light waves, sound waves, TV systems, etc.) of the message from the sender to the receiver. **Decoding** then requires the receiver to take the message and interpret the symbols so as to take away meaning from it. When person 2 responds, the process works in the opposite direction.

Not everyone sees a symbol the same way: A group of American Indian parents in Minnesota used this poster to sway high schools to change their nicknames.

Decoding Symbols from Others

A number of research studies have found that consumers definitely make inferences about others based on their use of products and services. These include clothing, eyeglasses, cosmetics, grooming services and styles, restaurants, automobiles, housing, furnishings, and so on. But how does this really happen? To begin to analyze this process, try jotting down the first brief impressions you have about each of the following people:

- Ted Marston drives a red Firebird and smokes Marlboros. _____
- Mark Abelson drinks Tab. _____
- Ann Fleming bought her new dress from Sears. _____
- Jennifer Dawson wears her Tri-Delt pin frequently. _____

If you had no particular impression based on any of these short descriptions, it is likely that the product involved does not have a strong symbolic meaning for you even though it may for others. Try giving this exercise to a few of your friends and see what their impressions are. Do they seem to agree? In either event, are the inferences that we're making fair to the consumers involved? Are they fair to the brands? If you were a marketing manager for each, would you be pleased with these results? What, if anything, would you recommend doing?

A Marketing Classic: Symbolism and Nescafé

The marketing field contains its share of "war stories" that are useful to demonstrate certain fundamental points about consumer behavior. One of the best known has been passed along in classrooms for years and demonstrates how consumers use products as symbols that they decode to make judgments about other consumers. In this case, the product was a negative symbol, and its sales were suffering.

Shortly after World War II, the Nestlé Company, headquartered in Switzerland, attempted to introduce the new form of soluble (instant) coffee into the huge U.S. market. No longer would a consumer have to fuss with the problems of cleaning old grinds or waiting for the coffee to perk. No more would consumers have to make an entire pot of coffee when all they needed was a single cup. No more would they be tempted to drink a stale cup because it was "left over" from the morning's brew. Although the new instant coffee would surely not replace drip grind entirely, it was likely to be a smashing success, especially since it tasted good in addition to being convenient. Thus was Nescafé launched to the American public.

But something went wrong. After achieving a strong rate of trial purchases, consumers seemed to stop buying the brand. When asked why, they responded that they didn't really like its flavor. The brand's managers knew, however, that this couldn't be the real reason, based on the company's own consumer taste tests, taken when consumers didn't know what kind of coffee they were drinking. Instead, there appeared to be something about this product itself, perhaps its name, that symbolized something negative to potential purchasers. A professor, Mason Haire, began some research to discover the real problem.

Haire conducted a test to see what the use of Nescafé seemed to be symbolizing in the minds of consumers. He presented a shopping list to participants in the study and asked them to write a brief description of what they thought the woman would be like (her personality and character) who had brought home these groceries. The twist was that there were actually two shopping lists used, and half of the participants got one list while the other half responded to the other list. The lists included seven typical items, ranging from meat and bread to canned peaches, with brand names included. The lists were identical except for a single change in one entry—one list had Nescafé Instant Coffee listed in the fifth position while the other listed Maxwell House Coffee (Drip Grind) in that position.

The results were surprising, as it was clear that the single little change in type of coffee had led the participants to *infer two very different types of women shoppers*. Those receiving the Maxwell House list, with its common coffee form, did not have any particular image in mind of the shopper, though the adjectives they used were generally positive. The two most common descriptions were "Good Wife," and "Thrifty."

The consumers who had received the Nescafé list, however, showed strong agreement about their shopper: the most common descriptions were "Lazy" and "A Poor Planner," with each coming from half of all the participants who saw this list. From these results, the firm decided to alter its advertising approach to show consumers that using Nescafé was something good to do, since it gave a busy and active woman more time to devote to her real chores as a wife, mother, and guardian of the household. Following this shift in emphasis, and as more brands entered the market, instant coffee became increasingly popular in the U.S. market, and Nescafé became a major brand.

A follow-up study conducted in 1968 found no differences in participants' responses to the two shopping lists, indicating that the negative symbols that had been so strong for instant coffee in 1950 had disappeared from consumers' minds a few years later.[23]

Sending Messages to Others

It stands to reason that the same consumers who are decoding symbols from others will begin to wonder about possible messages *they* may be sending—inadvertently or not—to others who may be decoding them. As a person begins to think about the signals that he or she may be sending out, it is just a short step to then realize that it is possible to "manage" these signals to create symbolic messages about oneself (the theoretical term for this process is **impression management**, or *self-presentation*). Notice, however, that our culture has already taught us the "proper" ways to appear neat and clean, or alert, or confident, or attractive. For consumer behavior purposes, this reasoning is simply extended to how products act to enhance the impression management process, serving as "props" of a sort.

For example, assume that each person in the list that follows is an acquaintance who has asked you for some good advice. In each case, what would you advise?

- Bob Johnston wants a good social life . . . what kind of car should be think about driving? What kinds should he avoid? _____

- Todd McNeill wants to be seen as sophisticated . . . what should he order at the bar? _____

- Diana Carry has taken a new position in which she will manage a bank branch with 25 employees . . . What colors and styles of clothing should she buy? What colors and styles should she avoid? _____

Again, the extent to which it was easy or difficult to answer each question is an indication of how closely you associate symbolism with each of the product areas. Notice, however, that this time the process was slightly different: we *first* had to take the perspective of the encoder of the message, *then* look out to possible decoders to anticipate their reactions and find the product that brings out the best anticipated reaction, and *then* pass this information along to the encoder. In this regard, notice how very important the particular social group is that will be decoding the symbolic messages (that is, the answers for Todd McNeill might differ for executives and college students, and even within each population the answers might differ for certain subgroups). This reflects the concept of reference groups, which will be examined in the next chapter.

Status Symbols and Conspicuous Consumption

Before leaving the topic of how consumers use products to send symbolic messages, a brief mention of status symbols is appropriate. **Status symbols** are products that often combine the characteristics of private and public symbolic expressions. They not only serve to send others a message about the elevated status of a person, but also serve to tell the person internally that he or she "has arrived" or has personal value.

Status symbols are no recent phenomenon in the consumer marketplace. In 1899, for example, Thorstein Veblen published his famous book, *The Theory of the Leisure Class*, in which he strongly questioned the "conspicuous consumption" and "conspicuous waste" that he saw all around him.[24] Veblen's ire was directed to a narrow band of upper-class society: his examples of status symbols included mansions, yachts, private railroad cars (an interesting thought for today!), and parties of a special sort (one social couple spent $370,000 to convert the interior of the Waldorf-Astoria Hotel in New York City to a replica of the palace at Versailles—for one evening's party).[25]

The world has changed in many ways since Veblen wrote, but the essential nature of status symbols has remained much the same. A long list of social critics have observed the stress on status symbols throughout this century. Some have been favorable, but most have not.[26] Today, given the much higher standard of living, and the marketing of credit to the general consuming public, most consumers are able occasionally to engage in status seeking through consumption. What are some products or services that serve as status symbols for you?

MARKETING'S USE OF SYMBOLS

Our stress in the last section was on the consumer's behavior with respect to symbols. In this section, we'll shift our focus to the marketer, and indicate some of the ways in which symbols are important in marketing strategy. Because symbols can be powerful, we might expect controversies over how and when marketers should use them.

Selling Through Symbols

When we stop to think about it, it is clear that evocative symbols are used by marketers in all aspects of the marketing mix they present to consumers. Within the *product* sector of the marketing mix, for example, many elements can be extremely important symbols, including the brand name (for confirmation, think of a few bad names for perfumes), the colors available, the packaging sizes and shapes, and so on. Within the *price* sector, consumers frequently assume that higher prices are good signs (symbols) of higher-quality products. Within the *place* sector, the atmosphere and image of the retail store is frequently a very significant factor in consumer purchase decisions. All this also holds for consumer services: many physicians, for example, employ professional designers to create an office atmosphere that inspires confidence and trust and creates tranquility. (Even the framed diplomas on the walls are strategically placed to send a symbolic message to the patients waiting for a consultation in the office.)

Symbols in Advertising

The most obvious symbolic system in marketing occurs, however, within the *promotion* sector of the marketing mix. If we briefly recall the basic model of communication in Figure 13-3, we can see that *all promotion is symbolic communication.* The only questions that remain are (1) to what extent should evocative symbols be used, as opposed to the more objective types of symbolization, and (2) exactly how should the symbols be put together to accomplish best the kind of communication desired by the marketer, given his or her particular situation. (Chapter 17 is devoted entirely to the topic of advertising; here we will focus only on the issue of how widespread symbolism in advertising is. If we begin to evaluate ads with this in mind, we can easily detect the use of symbols by marketers.)

In so doing, we need to be careful to keep the marketers's objectives clearly in mind. An ad need not be beautiful to be effective, for example, nor does it have to evoke powerful emotions within its audience (at times, in fact, evoking strong emotions can lead consumers to ignore the rest of the ad while they emote within themselves and miss the brand's name entirely!). Also, a product or store will often be aiming at the mass market, so that its symbols have to be meaningful to all members of its target group and to evoke positive reactions from all of them.

Another Marketing Classic: The Symbol of the "Marlboro Man"

When it was first introduced, the Marlboro brand was advertised as a sleek, sophisticated cigarette for women.[27] Its name seemed derived from English royalty (though its spelling had been changed to reflect the modern times of America), the package was feminine, and the cigarette itself was lipstick red and ivory tipped. After years of this positioning, but without great marketplace success, management decided to change the image of Marlboro and try to sell it to men.

Realizing that this could backfire if the brand's personality wasn't changed to be clearly a "man's" product, the strategists decided to try to place Marlboro as the most masculine brand on the market, even more macho than Camel was at that time. Advertising was the obvious candidate to effect most of this change (the package was changed as well), but the symbolism used in the ads would have to be carefully constructed. Ultimately, several rules were set:

1. No women would ever be shown in the ads.
2. Only very virile men would appear (an early ad had employed an average male model with a manicure, and many consumers wrote in to point out the discrepancy).
3. The men had to appear as forceful as possible and as successful as they wished to be, to inspire admiration from men in the audience.
4. Each man would reveal a tattoo to the audience. This would be seen not only as a symbol of virility, but also hint of a romantic past when he was traveling the world with the U.S. Navy.

Although it wasn't planned this way, the combination of these symbols also evoked strong emotional reactions from many female consumers. Also, the campaign symbols seemed to be tapping some very basic human emotions, as Marlboro was able to move quite successfully into many countries and cultures of the world. The only culture in which it clearly failed was Hong Kong, which is so crowded that the inhabitants couldn't even imagine the open country settings, horses, and so forth. For Hong Kong, then, Marlboro had to create a new campaign featuring a city man with a motorcycle!

With television available for cigarette advertising at that time (cigarette ads were banned from broadcast media in 1971, by the U.S. Congress), Marlboro was able also to use powerful music and sweeping images of cowboys in rugged terrain as further symbols in its repositioning move.

The result? Marlboro moved successfully into its new positioning and found increasing popularity as it moved up in the share of market rankings. About 15 years ago, it closed in on, then passed, Winston, the previous market leader, and has been the number one brand since that time. It now holds about 25 percent share of market—one of every four cigarettes sold in the United States—and earns about $3 billion profit each year for Philip Morris. Advertising remains faithful to the Marlboro code: Talent scouts still search in cowboy country for ranch hands with Marlboro Man potential, since models aren't used. As one female executive explains: "It's how he gets on the horse, how he sits . . . absolutely and exactly macho. There is never a limp wrist in Marlboro country."

The profile of U.S. Marlboro smokers seems to fit these sentiments: 65 percent male, 70 percent between the ages of 18 and 34, 70 percent high school or less education, 92 percent white. Among Marlboro's key sales promotions are sports events and country music events. Thus this classic use of symbols has created a truly powerful brand name. When asked whether we might someday see it used on other products as well, such as Marlboro Beer, an executive replied, "You might."[28]

In addition to the highly evocative nature of the symbols used by Marlboro, it was also necessary that the advertising contain a proper blend of symbols that did not contradict each other (the manicure was perhaps the last contradiction allowed in this campaign!). Across the field of marketing, however, there are many examples of ads that *do* contain conflicting symbols, and it should be easy for you to find some cases if you look for them. Why does this happen so often? Primarily, because evocative symbols do result in many consumer reactions, and these can differ among segments of the audience. If the advertising copywriter doesn't happen to have the right target segment in mind, or doesn't know this segment very well, ineffective symbols can easily creep into the ads. We will be

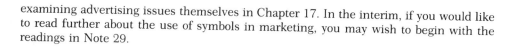

examining advertising issues themselves in Chapter 17. In the interim, if you would like to read further about the use of symbols in marketing, you may wish to begin with the readings in Note 29.

SUMMARY

Consumer Behavior Across Cultures

In this chapter two interrelated aspects of cultural influences on consumer behavior were discussed: *cross-cultural issues* and the *role of symbolism*. In our discussion of cross-cultural comparisons, we noted that consumer behavior is different in different cultures for many reasons. *Economic conditions* have major impacts, since these determine both the income and goods that are available. *Technology* and the *infrastructure* help to determine what products are viable within a culture. *Government policies* also have major impacts through such instruments as trade barriers, tax policies, and plans for production. Another major set of differences stems from *cultural values, beliefs,* and *life-styles.* We examined many examples of these impacts. *Language* provides another barrier, as do the *hidden dimensions* of culture such as the use of space, time, and color. Our closing discussion of cross-cultural topics dealt with current events and their implications for marketers. Here we noted differences in population trends of affluent versus developing societies, and the major changes that are occurring in China, the USSR and Eastern Europe, and in Western Europe as it moves toward a single trading community in 1992. We also noted the importance of subcultures for marketing success, and that similar consumer subcultures are likely to exist in different countries. (Appendix 13-A provides a more theoretical discussion of social class across cultures.)

Culture, Symbolism, and Consumer Behavior

In our discussion of symbolism, we noted that a "symbol" is basically something that stands for something else. In this regard, we recognized that there is a huge number of symbolic elements in consumer behavior. We then made a distinction between two extreme types of symbols—*objective* and *evocative*. Objective symbols are commonly used to identify something: most members of a culture have learned what these mean and easily "decode" them. Evocative symbols, however, lead the receiver of the symbol to elaborate upon it mentally, adding further thoughts and feelings. Therefore, the same symbol may have different meanings for different consumers.

Consumption as a Symbolic Process

The importance of symbolism derives from the fact that much of consumer behavior is symbolic. Prunes provided an interesting illustration of this point. Consumers use products to express their own private concepts of themselves as well as to communicate with others through consumption behaviors. Thus, on the one hand, we express ourselves through the use of particular products and brands and, on the other, use the consumption behavior of others to form judgments about them (the Nescafé case illustrated how significant this process can be).

Marketing Use of Symbols

Symbolism also serves as a powerful tool for marketers. Both objective and evocative symbols are used by marketers in all aspects of the marketing mix. The price of the product, its packaging, the location of its sales can all serve important symbolic functions. The fourth element of the marketing mix—promotion—relies almost entirely on symbolic communications. The major decisions here involve the relative reliance on objective versus elaborative symbols. The case of the "Marlboro man" showed how powerful symbols can be when they are well chosen for a promotional campaign.

KEY TERMS

economic infrastructure	product usage customs
attempts at active mastery	existing product preferences
focus on the external world	hidden languages
an open view of the world	glasnost
a rationalist faith	perestroika
belief in egalitarian ethics	symbol
respect for the lone ranger	semiotics
differences in cultural values	objective symbols
cultural conventions	evocative symbols
climate and geography	encoding
physiological characteristics	transmission
needs and use environment	decoding
perceptions of product need	impression management
past product experience	status symbols

APPENDIX 13-A TERMS

social stratification	power
property	life-styles
prestige	life chances

social change
inherited status
earned status
closed system
open system
social mobility
caste systems
class systems
estate systems
functionalist theory

marketplace theory
privilege level
upper-upper class
lower-upper class
American mainstream
upper-middle class
middle class
working class
lower Americans

REVIEW QUESTIONS AND EXPERIENTIAL EXERCISES
[E = Application extension or experiential exercise]

1. The cross-cultural differences *between* versus *within* countries have different implications for marketers than public policymakers. Comment.

2. "Marketing's use of symbols is primarily restricted to a firm's advertising efforts." Comment.

3. Review the research findings on behalf of the California Sunsweet Growers Association. What marketing recommendations would you make to the association at this point in time? What is your actual estimation of the chances for success?

4. Discuss the concept of "levels of elaboration." What is the essential distinction between *objective* and *evocative* symbols? Can a symbol be both objective and evocative?

5. Define the three bases of social inequality described in the Appendix. Which of the three seems to be most easily acquired? Which seems most important in the culture of the United States?

6. What are some of the practical problems and ethical issues marketers face when selling to the lower-lower class?

[E] 7. Select one of the following areas as a topic for a "current developments in marketing" research project. Use the reference section of your library to locate recent articles. Prepare a short summary of your findings.

a. China
  Soviet Union

c. Western Europe
  Eastern Europe

e. Japan or South Korea
  Other nations

[E] 8. Use the reference section of your library to discover recent articles reporting developments and issues in international marketing. Write a brief report on your findings.

[E] 9. Use the Note listings for Chapter 13 at the back of the book to locate good references for learning about "hidden languages" across cultures. Write a brief report summarizing good lessons for international marketers to learn.

[E] 10. Arrange for an informal interview with one or two people (including fellow students) who have been raised in other cultures than your own. Ask about contrasts and similarities across the cultures (a good ice-breaker is, "What things did you find most surprising or different when you moved into my culture?"). During the interview try to cover such topics as family, education, economic system, politics, social classes, economic infrastructure, values, media, shopping, marketplaces, and so forth. Write a brief report summarizing your findings.

[E] 11. Using either the Chapter 13 Note listings or the reference section of your library, read further about one of the following topics.
   a. Semiotics/symbolism in marketing
   b. Interpretivism in consumer research
   c. "Post-modern" consumer behavior research

[E] 12. Look through a number of magazine ads, noting how symbols are used in each. Clip out one example of each of the following:
   a. An ad that has, in your opinion, a use of symbolism that led to *positive* emotions or reactions on your part.
   b. An ad that has a *negative* use of symbolism in your opinion (i.e., it led to negative reaction on your part).
   c. An ad that seems to have *conflicting* symbols within the ad itself.
   d. An ad that uses symbols in a way likely to be *controversial*.

   Briefly explain your reasoning related to each example.

[E] 13. Interview the creative director of an advertising agency concerning his or her views of symbolism in advertising. Try to gain several specific examples. Write a brief report on your findings.

[E] 14. List five current consumer status symbols in your subculture. For each, briefly describe the symbolic meaning being communicated to others and the types of consumers possessing the status symbol.

[E] 15. As a creative exercise in symbolic management, select three of the entries listed below. For each, propose (1) a bad symbolic *name* for a client firm to use in this product or service category; (2) a bad symbolic *color* to adopt; (3) a bad symbolic *package design or logo*; (4) bad symbolic *theme music*; and (5) a bad *advertising theme*.

a. a new perfume
b. a new bank
c. a new automobile model
d. a new fast-food restaurant

e. a new womens' basketball team
f. a new housing development
g. a new clothing shop
h. a new stomach remedy.

APPENDIX 13A   SOCIAL CLASSES ACROSS CULTURES

The Concept of Social Stratification

How Are Societies Structured?

Just as culture is the key concept for describing an entire society, social stratification is the key concept for analyzing the structure or internal organization of that society. The term **social stratification** refers to groups (or strata) of people who are arranged in some sort of ranked order, much like different layers of a pyramid. People who are ranked within the same stratum or level will tend to view each other as social equals. They will tend to feel comfortable with each other, spend time together, and share interests and activities.

When we begin to look at *different* strata, however, we come up against the root characteristic of social stratification—*inequality.* People within any one stratum will tend to view those in other classes as being either socially superior or socially inferior to themselves.

Stratification is found in some form or other in every society in the world. Stratification is in essence a social agreement about what should be looked up to versus what should be looked down upon. It derives its support from a culture's values and social institutions. Whatever its details, however, *stratification has important implications for the lives of every group and individual in a society.*

The Bases of Inequality

One of the great sociological thinkers, Max Weber, developed an extremely influential theory of social stratification.[30] Weber, a German writing at the turn of the century, was particularly interested in the performance of capitalism as an economic system. This led him to ask why inequality seemed always to spring up within societies. In his theory, Weber first recognized that *social inequality is not a simple concept.* It exists in many forms, each with a different basis. Weber isolated three bases as being most important: property, prestige, and power.

Property differences, according to Weber, are the key basis for the creation of *classes* in a society, whereas **prestige** differences generate *status levels,* and **power** differences create *parties* or political interest groups. The importance of the three separate bases lies in the fact that they each constitute a distinct form of social stratification. Some people, for example, are *respected* because of their property holdings (land, wealth, products owned, etc.). Other people are *obeyed* because of the power that they command (such power might flow from an organizational position, personal strength, leadership abilities, etc.) Still other people are *admired* because of their abilities or accomplishments, reflecting the prestige of the roles that they can play within the society.

Also, however, the three bases tend to correlate with each other. Whichever resource (property, prestige, or power) a person acquires first, it can help to achieve the other two. Wealth, for example, can allow access to prestige—a wealthy person can buy "the right" products and services, join "the right" clubs and churches, and so on. Wealth can also provide an entry to the *corridors of power,* through heavy financial support of political parties, or control of such corporate decisions as where to locate a new plant, from whom to purchase equipment, services, and so on. In like manners, prestige can open doors to gains in property and power, whereas power can be effectively used to improve an individual's property and prestige.

Life-styles and Life Chances

Max Weber also made a second important contribution when he pointed out that social stratification has two significant types of *consequences* for the lives of members of a society: different life-styles and different life chances. **Life-styles** refers to overall patterns of living. This term is meant to include almost every aspect of our daily lives—where we live, what we do with our time, what we eat, how we talk, and so forth. Weber pointed out that people within each social stratum tended to associate more with each other (and less with those from other strata). In this process of daily associations, each stratum develops different life-styles. In contrast to life-styles, **life chances** stresses the inequality that is present in social stratification. People are provided with differential advantages and disadvantages in their lives. Those born into upper strata receive greater material rewards within the system and find good prospects for their futures. In contrast, children born into lower social strata begin from a lower starting point and face more barriers in their futures. These generalizations tend to hold true across societies and across history.

Consumer Behavior Reflects Life-styles One contribution in isolating these two types of consequences lies in the fact that each one provides substantial ground for study. Marketers and consumer behavior professionals have concentrated almost entirely on the life-style dimension, as this reflects most directly the purchasing patterns of different social classes. We have continued this stress within this text, particularly with our analysis of market segments in Chapter 4. However, it is important that we also briefly consider the types of attention that other fields give to the life chances dimension of social stratification.

Other Fields Stress Life Chances There are several subtle aspects of the life chance dimension that lead to different kinds of analyses from those used for life-styles. First, life chances differ by social strata because of various *inequalities* in a social system. Inequalities can be (though they are not necessarily) the result of the exploitation of some groups at the hands of other groups. Issues of "fairness" and "unfairness" thus can arise in this area, and these can sometimes flare into intense emotional reactions.

Second, life chances deal with the *realities* of life, not simply with abstract or academic concepts. Disparities in property, power, and prestige can mean drastic differences in some peoples' abilities to live at all, especially in less developed societies. Consider, for example, that people in the lowest stratum of *property* (wealth) may confront filth, disease, malnutrition, and early death as routine elements of life in their class. People in the lowest stratum of *power* may be born into lives of servitude or slavery, always at the beck and call of those who hold power in the society. People in the lowest levels of *prestige* may be incapable of respecting themselves and unable even to win the admiration of their young children.* Third, since each society's stratification system is socially decided, it *is* possible for at least part of the system to be modified if enough members desire such a change and are able to push for it. The issue of **social change** thus becomes an important topic as well.

Life Chances and Marketers The topic of life chances is extremely complex. Its importance bears notice if you are planning a career in business. This is the topic that feeds the fires of social critics and political activists. The business community is often a target of criticisms. Easy answers to its questions are not to be found. Good people disagree about such issues as why some people are at the top while others are at the bottom, whether or not inequality is a necessary social condition, and what, if anything, should be done.

Several fields of study have long been involved in this topic, including sociology, philosophy, economics, and political science. A vast literature on life chances exists. We should realize, however, that this literature is often *not* neutral in its approach (a national survey of sociology professors, for example, showed that 5 percent rated themselves as "Conservative," 12 percent as "Middle-of-the-Road," 63 percent as "Liberal," and 20 percent as "Leftist").[31] While these figures may no longer be quite accurate, they do indicate the prevailing orientation of persons writing in this area. Business people are often viewed as supporting the current stratification system, since they hold wealth and wield power in it. They are also seen as being generally insensitive to the plight of

---

*The realities of life chance differences are numerous. For example, babies born into lower strata are more likely to die in their first year, to live shorter lives, sustain more injuries, have more illness, to have more children, undergo more divorces. They are less likely to be educated, more likely to be criminals, and also more likely to be victims of crimes. Thus, in a number of interrelated ways, a person's *chances in life* will depend on his or her parents' position in the social stratification system.

people in the lower social strata. There is a particular mistrust of marketers and advertisers. Questions are raised, for example, about pricing in poor neighborhoods, credit restrictions, and many other marketing practices that affect the poor.[32] Much of this literature calls for more government regulation of business and much more government involvement in redistributing property and power in society.

Different Cultures, Different Systems

Inherited Versus Earned Status Across international cultures, a key distinguishing factor in stratification systems is the extent to which they rely on inherited versus earned status.[33] **Inherited status** is automatically assigned to individuals without any control on their part or any possibility of their influencing the process. This happens at birth, and high or low status is immediately assigned to the infant. The parents' and family's position, the sex of the child, the nationality, and the religion are extremely important factors in the assignment of inherited status. **Earned status**, on the other hand, is based on a person's actions and performance. It is typically assigned, of course, in late childhood and in adult life stages.

Some amount of inherited status is present in every stratification system. The *degree* to which it dominates earned status, however, can differ dramatically and provides a good clue to the overall social structure of a culture. Cultures in which inherited status dominates tend to be **closed systems**; those in which earned status is dominant tend to be **open systems**. Open systems allow for high degrees of **social mobility**. People are able, through their own effort, to move up/or down within the system. In closed societies, people born into one stratum can virtually never leave it.

Since a person in a closed system must be assigned to his or her level at birth, the basis for assignment must be *very* clear. Closed systems thus have sharp boundaries between their social classes. Tradition is very important. Socializing between classes is always discouraged and is sometimes prohibited. Social distance is considered proper. In open systems, on the other hand, the greater social mobility means that the initial assignment to a social class is less important, class distinctions are less important, and class boundaries are blurred. This occurs because some people are moving up in class, while others are moving down; each type of person is bringing some characteristics from his or her original class into the other class.

Caste Systems and Class Systems Caste and class systems are the two basic models for social stratification in our present world. **Caste systems** are very rigid structures, with social inequality as the core value in the society. Their social classes are called *castes*. Caste systems rely on inherited status, have no social mobility, and reflect very sharp boundaries between the castes. The best example of a true caste system can still be found in parts of the rural society of India, where it has served for several thousand years. There are many fascinating differences between the Indian caste system and the set of cultural values we saw for the United States at the start of the chapter. You might enjoy reading the summary of such characteristics provided in Exhibit 13A-1.

Class systems conform in most respects to open systems. They rely on a mixture of inherited and earned status, have moderate opportunities for social mobility and are found in the United States, Russia, and other industrialized societies. Class systems arose with the Industrial Revolution about 200 years ago. They replaced the **estate systems** in which a few nobles (kings, dukes, barons) held high status and almost everyone else (peasants, serfs, etc.) held low status.[35] The estate systems were based on land holdings. The Industrial Revolution, with its development of transportation and factories, shifted the center of society from rural estates to new large cities. Lower-class citizens found that they could earn money and live better by working in production rather than agriculture. New classes of merchants, bankers, and traders emerged and began to grow wealthy. New forms of governments were needed, and bureaucrats began to gain power. Political thinking began to change also. By the late 1700s, the French and American revolutions represented the shift of social ideals toward personal freedom for all citizens.

One result of these changes was a dramatic increase in a person's social mobility. New people could gain property and power (especially industrialists), while others could gain prestige by developing specialized knowledge and skills. Over time, emphasis shifted more and more toward economic success as a means for improving one's status. During the 1900s, the class system has evolved in new directions as well. Workers formed unions to improve their power standing and raise their incomes and working conditions. Education was made compulsory in many countries: this allowed millions of people to prepare for new occupations (another route toward social mobility). Finally, the entire standard of living has risen dramatically. Almost everyone is living better than their ancestors did, whether or not their relative social standing is higher.

A class system, however, can still reflect substantial inequality. As we all know, different countries have chosen to handle this situation in quite different ways. Karl Marx had a major influence in the course of history with his writings in *The Communist Manifesto*.[36] In terms of social stratification, Marx believed that social inequality was *not* necessary and should not exist in any society. He argued that a society could be arranged to have everyone at the same level. At the opposite extreme from Marx stands the **functionalist theory** of social stratification. In brief, the functionalists argue that at least two of the three bases—prestige and property—*must* be handed out unequally for a society to function well. Their position is that human nature requires extra incentives for someone who must work especially hard or receive special training to do his or her job well. If society does *not* allow extra wealth or prestige, these jobs won't be done well. Thus the functionalist position supports the **marketplace theory** of capitalist systems.

The Nature of the Caste System

Every Hindu in India belongs to one and only one caste or *jat*.[34] Membership is hereditary and is permanent. At one time, the caste system provided a basis for the division of labor in an area. All men in the same caste had to pursue the same occupation, with defined duties to perform and other duties to avoid. Within a living area such as a village, therefore, all tasks were assigned by birth. In total there were over 3000 subcaste groupings in this very complex, highly structured society. These subcastes were derived, however, from four major castes:

- Priests and scholars   *Brahmins* (pronounced 'brahm-en)[a]
- Warriors and princes   *Kshatriyas* (pronounced 'cha-trē)[a]
- Merchants and artisans   *Vaisayas* (pronounced 'vish-uh)[a]
- Laborers and servants   *Sudras* (pronounced 'soo-draah)[a]

Beneath the four castes there was another group of persons, estimated at 20 percent of the population, who were known as *Outcasts* or *Untouchables* because they were considered to be outside the spiritual community.

In terms of Weber's three bases, the caste system was designed to provide high status to one caste on each basis. Brahmins were very high on prestige; they were viewed as almost godlike and deserving of all respect. Kshatriyas were very high on power, as befitted their occupational roles as warriors and princes. Vaisayas were very high on property, as they specialized in business and economic matters. Over time, however, each of the high castes was able to use its strong base to raise its levels on the other bases—Brahmins gained power and wealth, Kshatriyas gained prestige and wealth, and Vaisayas gained power and prestige.

The Importance of the Hindu Religion

The caste system was so powerful that it dominated almost every aspect of people's lives in India. How could such a strong system be accepted, especially by those assigned to low status for all of their lives? One key factor was the power of the Hindu religion and its teachings. Basically, in Hinduism, unlike many Western religions, a person's soul lives an endless existence on earth. When someone dies, his or her soul is reborn (reincarnated) into a new and different body. Any one person's lifetime is thus just a short time in the soul's existence. For that short time, the soul is assigned its duties on earth (*dharma*) by being born into a particular caste. If the soul performs its duties faithfully, it will be rewarded by being assigned to a higher caste in its next life. There is *no social mobility* possible in the present life, however, since the soul's duties have been assigned at birth.

This strong religious backing resulted in Hindus accepting that some people were spiritually "better" than other people, since their souls were being highly rewarded while

[a]Because the language sounds are different, these terms are difficult for many non-Indians to pronounce correctly. For example *Webster's Dictionary* indicates a pronunciation of "(kə)'sha-trē-l(y)ə" for the warrior caste.

414

the souls of others were being punished for their performance in earlier lives. Over time, though not a part of the religion itself, a complex set of social codes arose for each caste to follow. For example, if a Brahmin were to be touched by (even by the shadow of) an Untouchable, he or she must go immediately to wash off. If requested to provide a drink of water by a member of a lower caste, a Brahmin felt compelled to provide it (as a holy act), but could not allow the cup to touch the other person. The Brahmin therefore had to pour the water into the other person's cupped hands. If by chance the person touched the cup, the Brahmin would have to throw it away as forever unclean.

Impacts of the Industrial Revolution

In modern India the caste system is less powerful, due to such forces as industrialization, radio and television, education, the growth of a national government, and other modernizing influences in the society. It still is, however, a basic framework for many members of the society and is ingrained in their lives. As an example, you might be interested in some recent advertisements appearing in a U.S. newspaper that serves Indians now living in America. These ads were run for the purpose of arranging suitable marriages. Note the presence of status appeals in the descriptions given.

Matrimonial, Female

Parents invite suitable medico or well-settled professional match, under 29, for tall, slim, beautiful, 23, immigrant Punjabi Hindu Kshatri women, from a status family with exceptional merit. Convent school education in India and college in U.S.A. from a known university. Reply (box number).

Brother invites matrimonial correspondence for his sister, Gujarati Brahmin, 35, . . . nice personality. Caste no barrier.

Correspondence invited from immigrant Punjabi Agarwals for beautiful, homely, 22, 5′3″, sister in India. Write with returnable photographs.

Kerala Iyer, Vadama family seeks match for very beautiful daughter, 28, 5′4″, fair, slim, convent educated, B.Sc., L.L.B. (Bombay), from handsome, non-Kaushika Tamil Iyer professionals under 34.

Matrimonial, Male

Medico, 27, 5′7″, handsome, fair, Green Card holder, seeks exceptionally beautiful and fair women. No dowry. No caste barrier. Preferably Kashmiri, Himachili Brahmin, B.Sc. medical or nursing.

U.S.A. settled professional, 34, 5′11″, slim, handsome, youthful, Kerala Iyer, Vadama invites matrimonal correspondence from non-Kaushika Tamil families. Women should be a graduate, beautiful, slim, under 26.

Physician, American citizen, invites correspondence from tall, attractive, educated Telugu Brahmin women, early 20s, for his tall, handsome brothers, engineer (28), physician (26), both immigrating to U.S. shortly. Respond with recent photograph and horoscope.

Correspondence invited from parents of extremely beautiful, cultured, well-educated young ladies, 20–23, preferably settled in North America, for very handsome, 25, successful MBA, Hindu young man.

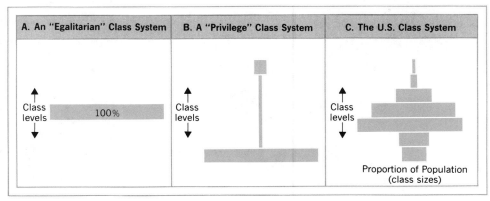

FIGURE 13A-1 **Patterns of Social Stratification**

(Our brief summary here obviously does not cover many key issues. If you wish to read more about functionalist theory, the reading in Note 37 is a good place to begin.)[37]

The result of different cultural decisions about stratification is that our modern world has a wide range of stratification systems. As shown in Figure 13A-1, the type of egalitarian system desired by Marx would have a long, narrow shape (Modern Russia has somewhat this form for property, but clear differences on power and prestige: as *perestroika* progresses, moreover, we may see increasing class differences on property). At the other extreme, Part B of the figure shows a variant of the *privilege* society found in many developing nations of the world. Here we see a small number of extremely powerful and wealthy families at the top, virtually no middle class at all, and then a huge class of peasants and poor who spend their lives supporting the rich and powerful. Finally Part C of the figure shows that the U.S. system is roughly in the form of a *diamond* (in which the middle classes are by far the largest). In the closing section of this appendix, let's turn to consider the social classes of the United States.

Social Classes in the United States

The Social Class Structure

Because it is a young society that has emphasized earned status, immigration, and growth, describing social class in America is a complex, judgmental activity. There is no single answer for the number of social classes or their exact nature. Some people may see 20 social classes while others see 6. Here we will choose to discuss a 7-level structure that is generally accepted in marketing circles. Figure 13A-2 presents the conclusions of one expert in this area, Richard Coleman, as to the current makeup of American society. (If you would like to see a

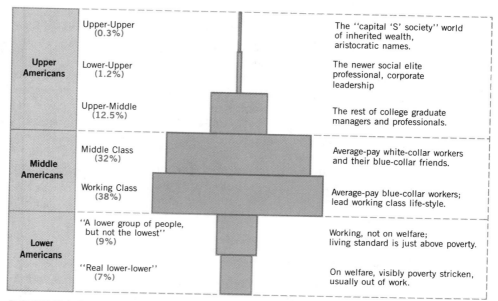

Upper Americans	Upper-Upper (0.3%)	The "capital 'S' society" world of inherited wealth, aristocratic names.
	Lower-Upper (1.2%)	The newer social elite professional, corporate leadership
	Upper-Middle (12.5%)	The rest of college graduate managers and professionals.
Middle Americans	Middle Class (32%)	Average-pay white-collar workers and their blue-collar friends.
	Working Class (38%)	Average-pay blue-collar workers; lead working class life-style.
Lower Americans	"A lower group of people, but not the lowest" (9%)	Working, not on welfare; living standard is just above poverty.
	"Real lower-lower" (7%)	On welfare, visibly poverty stricken, usually out of work.

FIGURE 13A-2 **Social Classes of the United States**

Source: Adapted from Richard P. Coleman, "The Continuing Significance of Social Class to Marketing," *Journal of Consumer Research,* December 1983, pp. 265–280.

guide that measures consumers' social classes, Coleman's article presents an actual questionnaire: see Note 38).

Notice that seven social classes are present, ranging from the "Lower-lower" class to the "Upper-upper" class. Notice also that the two uppermost classes are tiny in terms of population: it is the fact that they are so high on power, property, and prestige that makes them so important. Finally, we can see that it is the three classes in the center (the upper-middle class, middle class, and working class) who really define the mainstream, where five out of six people live.

As a final point about class structure, Coleman has contributed the concept of **privilege level** within each class into the marketing field.[39] This concept recognizes that within each social class, income levels can vary widely. For example, some middle-class households earn $42,000 per year, whereas others are at $18,000. Coleman would label the first household as an *overprivileged family* and the second as an *underprivileged family*. A *class average family* here would have an income at about the average for the class, say, $30,000 in this case.

Since income provides a basis for consumer spending, there are some behavioral differences between privilege levels. In cars, for example, it is the overprivileged in each class who tend to buy expensive autos (in the working-class or lower-class levels, the choice is often a used model of one of the expensive lines). In leisure spending, we can expect to see an underprivileged upper-middle (UM) family making very different purchases from our earlier overprivileged middle class (MC) family, even though both may have incomes of $42,000. The over-privileged MCs are much more likely to own motor boats, campers, and backyard pools. The underprivileged UMs, on the other hand, are much more likely to spend their money on club memberships and private school tuitions.

Thus income and social class are actually different concepts. While there is a general increase in average income as we move from lower to upper levels, the statistical correlation between social class and income is only modest, at about +0.40. Thus marketers can choose both measures to use in predicting consumer spending for various products.[40]

Our closing discussion of this chapter summarizes aspects of each of the primary social classes outlined in Figure 13A-2. We'll do so in two parts: first we'll concentrate on the American mainstream; then we'll move to the extreme social classes.[41]

The Classes of the American Mainstream

The **American mainstream** consists of three social classes: the upper-middle (UM) class, the middle class, and the working class. Taken together, these three classes account for five of every six citizens, about 83 percent of the population. Because some households will shift class levels over time, because the sons and daughters of one class can move into another (especially through education and occupational choices), and because there is some overlap in incomes, it is some-times difficult to distinguish these three groups clearly. On the other hand, each class has some distinguishing characteristics, as summarized next.

The Working Class (38 percent of the population) This is the single largest social class, accounting for two of every five citizens. People here typically occupy blue-collar or manual jobs, perceiving themselves as hard working and honest. Job security is a threat, however. Income is about at the same level as spending (so that savings are hard to accumulate). Perhaps because of the nature of the work, many members sharply separate their workplace from the social sphere of their lives. When off the job, they do not think much about it, and the spouse is unlikely to know the co-workers very well.

WC Americans are "family folk." One study found, for example, that about half of WC people live within a mile of a relative, against only one of five MCs and only one in eight UMs. In television news, WCs prefer local segments rather than national or world news, and WC vacations are often spent either at home or within a two-hour drive. WC persons are also highly patriotic and supportive of American industry. For example, WCs' ownership of foreign cars is only one-third to one-fifth the rate found in the MC and UM classes. In summary, the WC world is closer to traditions. Family, neighborhood, long-time friends, struc-tured sex roles for man and woman, and a stress on "enjoying today" are all important elements of this life-style.

The Middle Class (32 percent of the population) MCs constitute the other very large segments of the American population. These are white-collar workers in average pay brackets and skilled blue-collar craftsmen. Many MCs have college backgrounds. Unlike most WCs, who are living their lives on an immediate day-to-day basis, many MCs are interested in "investing" time and effort today so they can improve their lives in the future. In this regard there is some attention paid to what those in the UM class are doing and some effort to engage in similar behaviors. Money and high morals are important to MC Americans. Among important purchases are nice homes in nice neighborhoods, college educations for the children, and good brand names. There is a strong interest in being seen as "respectable" by others: the appearance of the "public areas" in a home—those that are seen by visitors—is quite important, for example.

The Upper-Middle Class (13 percent of the population) UMs are characterized primarily by high levels of education and the expert knowledge associated with it. Many lawyers, accountants, engineers, and managers fit into this class. Not only are incomes higher here, but UMs are usually more secure economically because they can transfer their knowledge from one setting to another. In contrast to most WCs and to many MCs, the work center and co-workers are likely to play a major role in a UM's life while on the job and off it.

The UM class is usually visible and respected in a community. They value money for both the status it brings and the comfortable life-style it can buy. UM children tend to be enrolled in the public schools and are pointed toward gaining higher education from an early age. UM parents are likely to be involved in self-interest and voluntary "cause" associations such as the school PTA and Chamber of Commerce. UMs often belong to country clubs. They watch less TV than WCs or MCs, but read more books and newspapers. In general, UMs are interested in prestige brands and stores, and spending "with good taste." As their incomes increase, many UMs seek to travel more, to add more "help in the house," and to gain prestigious educations for their children.

The Extreme Social Classes in America

Most Americans can easily relate to the life-styles of the WC, MC, and UM social classes. There are, however, three social classes that occupy the extreme positions of social status in America—the upper-upper, lower-upper, and lower-class Americans—with whose lives we may be less familiar. Because of either small size or low incomes, these three classes are often not considered to be key sectors of the mass market to which many large marketers cater. Because they are extreme, however, they are useful in highlighting some subtle aspects of social class and are quite interesting in themselves. Thus we will devote slightly more attention to them in our coverage here.

The Upper-Upper Class (less than one-half of 1 percent of the population) These are the "aristocrats" of the society. Family background and "breeding" is very important. *Inherited, old wealth* is the key to membership in the Blue Blood society. In America, this wealth came from land holdings and corporate fortunes, most of which were amassed about a century ago, during the "robber baron" business era (you may be familiar, for example, with names such as Rockefeller, Mellon, Vanderbilt, Carnegie, Whitney, and so on). Thus the upper-upper (UU) class of America is different from that of most other countries—it is not based on royalty bloodlines (from the Estate class). Its business heritage instead represents both the relative youth of the United States as a nation as well as the national stress on business success. As we would expect, the UU class holds tremendous power behind the scenes of business and government in the United States.

The UU class is a closed society unto itself. It has erected many barriers to entry for persons not born into this select grouping. Members of this class are well buffered from the mainstream of society. Their privacy is guarded by social secretaries, security personnel, and exclusive clubs. The UU class in America is largely Protestant, especially belonging to the Episcopalian and Presbyterian denominations. There is pressure to marry within the class; a wedding here represents the joining of one family with another much more so than in other classes. UU children are educated at private, elite preparatory schools, followed by attendance at the best colleges and universities. (Dick Cavett, the television personality, was a non-UU scholarship student at Yale. One day, when asked where he had "prepped," Cavett supposedly replied, "I didn't 'prep,' I 'highed' out in Nebraska.")

With respect to their life-styles, the UU class is an interacting group. Its members tend to know each other either personally or by reputation. They engage in elite leisure pursuits, including fox hunts, polo matches, and tennis. They are active in charity balls and social visits. In addition, they belong to the best clubs and actively support major charitable foundations and arts activities. Most members of this group do not need to work, but many choose to do so; they occupy important positions in business, the professions, and philanthropic organizations. In this regard, it is fairly common that the family name be memorialized through charitable foundations.

In terms of overall consumption in the United States, the UU class is not a significant factor due to its very small size. With respect to wealth and power, however, there is quite another story—it is estimated that the top 200,000 households in the United States (less than one-half of 1 percent of the population) control about 22 percent of the personal wealth of the country! The UU class's consumption expenditures per person are quite large, and it can be a significant market for a few specialty marketers of products and services.

Because its members are comfortable and feel well-established in their social positions, this class tends not to engage in "conspicuous consumption" to the extent that some other classes do. Their life-style tends to be mannered and genteel; their purchases tend to be conservative and tasteful. UU women, for example, appear to be relatively independent of the changing fashion in clothing; they avoid the "daring styling" of Paris fashions, instead staying with the woolens and tweeds that distinguish the well-bred British woman. They also tend to shop in different ways from other classes; there are retailers who cater exclusively to this class and to whom an introduction is needed before a new customer can attempt to undertake a purchase. Finally, UUs serve as an "aspirational reference group" for some members of less prestigious classes who wish to strive for social acceptance. These people are watching carefully to see what the UUs are purchasing; when possible, they attempt to undertake similar consumer behaviors.

The Lower-Upper Class (1 percent of the population) These are the very high achievers in the American society—those with extremely successful careers in business, the professions, and entertainment. These people can be *extremely* wealthy; it is not uncommon for LU families to be more wealthy than many members of the UU class. The distinction, however, is that the LU family wealth was not passed down through family generations but has been amassed recently. In social terms, this represents "new" money—these people are the *nouveau riche*.

This class is characterized by high ambition and excellent performance. Many of its members, however, have to confront a conflict after their success has been achieved. At that point, they *must seek a new balance* between the genteel, cultured life-style to which they aspire and their strong personal drives for more achievement, power, and success. Since many of these persons have just entered the LU class during their own lifetimes, they lack the established family traditions and support that is available in the UU class. Even as adults, for example, many LU persons are having to learn new values and behavior norms.

Unlike the UUs, LUs often feel that they have less impressive family pasts to look back on. They are more geared to the present and future. LUs are *not* accepted into the UU social elite, but their children and grandchildren *may* be, if they are sent to the "right" schools, develop the correct social graces and viewpoints, and are able to marry wisely. This, of course, places even more pressure on an LU family's behavior patterns. Many LUs are *very* active in civic, charitable, and philanthropic causes. As there is usually no shortage of money, consumption can become an important outlet for LUs. They can use consumption to reward themselves, to reinforce the idea that they have arrived at success, and to show others that they have both succeeded and know what to do with their success. At times they will be addressing those in the UU class; at other times, they will be aiming at those in less prestigious classes.

Accordingly, many LUs spend freely on products that are visible to others and that can serve as status symbols of success and power. Success and high-style living is represented by purchases of larger, plush homes, second and third residences and retreats, luxury automobiles, expensive forms of adornment (fine furs, jewelry, and clothing), custom services (tutors, interior designers), large boats, and so on. This is the class that supports high fashion from Paris; a designer name serves a very important communication function so that the purchaser of the clothing can ensure that other people see just what a fine purchase it is.

Because power is so often important to their success, many LUs strive to acquire and employ power symbols in just the right way. This can reach an art form in itself. For example, consider the following power symbols that were recently in vogue in business:

- *Highly polished shoes.* Many power people have their shoeshine person visit their offices twice a day, once early in the morning and again after lunch.
- *The right type of shoe.* These come from the right shoemakers and should usually be very simply styled. At times there are fashion trends for power people, however. Recently, for example, Gucci loafers were acceptable, but the terms under which they could be acquired were demanding. Reportedly, one man was overheard to tell another (who had just asked him to visit Gucci with him to help him buy the right loafer), "I will, but if you need help, maybe you're not ready for Guccis. You can't put Guccis on Florsheim feet, you know."
- *Limousines.* Even better than a Rolls-Royce was a Mercedes 600 with chrome painted black and tinted windows so that no one could see the occupants inside.
- *Telephone styles and usage.* Having ornate telephones instantly available to you (for example, in your limo and airplane, plugged in at your table at lunch, built into trees around your estate) is a good sign of your vital importance to others.
- *Briefcases.* The slimmer and more elegant, the better. Best of all, of course, is being able to walk around empty-handed; this demonstrates that you are able to command others to do all the work![42]

Similarly, furniture, decorations (original works of fine art), watches, and other objects are commonly used to advantage by accomplished LUs, as well as by striving members of the UM class. Overall, the lower-upper class is too small to be an important target for mass marketers. It can, however, be a significant market for specialized, high-quality goods and services.

The Lower-American Class (16 percent of the population) At the other extreme of the U.S. class structure are the two groups of **lower Americans**. Also termed the *poverty class*, this is a very diverse set of people whose major common characteristic is the fact of their very low incomes. Included here are those subject to continuing unemployment, plus low-paid service workers, the elderly poor, illegal immigrants, abandoned families, and some people with deviant life-styles. There are many minorities in this class, although the majority of its members are white persons born in the United States. As a group, these people could be viewed as the "outcasts" of society rather than being an integrated class within the social structure. Their lives do not come close to reflecting the ideals of the

American society, and many mainstream members of the other classes have a tendency to regard all L-As as disreputable persons, and worse.

Other attributes of life in the L-A class are closely tied to the low income levels. Members of this class represent unskilled labor and the lowest educational levels and are more likely than those in other classes to have physical or mental handicaps. Many are recipients of government welfare and subsidy programs. If they live in urban areas, they reside in slums or poor neighborhoods; very few own their own homes, and most live in substandard housing conditions. Average family sizes are larger than in the other social classes, and there are many more single-parent households; these factors combine to limit the per capita income and to stretch its use over more children.

These factors contribute to a highly *insecure* existence, especially for lower-lower class members. With respect to the three bases of stratification, these people have no prestige, wield little or no power, and possess almost no property. Several social and psychological reactions typify their adjustments to this sort of insecurity. They are more likely than other classes to rely on relatives for social and financial support; they are less likely to participate in community functions. Over time, many L-As exhibit a distrust of others, a pessimism about the future, and a feeling that they themselves have virtually no control over what their lives will bring (this is termed *fatalism*, suggesting that fate and luck are extremely important forces in a person's life). In turn, these beliefs can lead to low expectations, reduced feelings of personal responsibility, little ambition for the future, and a short time horizon, so that the person tends to "live for today" and "enjoy what's available." These mental outlooks not only contribute to antisocial behaviors in the short run (for example, juvenile delinquency, crime, alcoholism, drug dependency) but almost guarantee a continuation of the poverty cycle in the long run. These descriptions represent generalizations and surely do not typify every L-A. However, these issues are at the heart of the heated debates over government social policy in the United States, and the lower-American class is the target for most government social assistance programs.

There are several interesting aspects of the consumption practices of the L-A class that bear mention. First, it is a large group of people, accounting for about one out of every six persons in the United States. Given its low average income, however, its overall importance for consumer spending is much less—perhaps representing only $1 of every $12 to $15 spent. For this reason, many marketers do not stress this class in their planning. If, however, a product tends to be a necessity, and doesn't easily fit into the resale (used) market, the L-A class can emerge as a significant factor in the overall consumer market. Groceries, for example, fit these criteria, and government food stamp programs assist in making this a large market for retail foodstuffs.

Consumer research has also indicated that the L-A class behaves in some ways that we might not expect from a strictly economic point of view. For example, L-As often engage in what Rotzell has termed *compensatory consumption*[43]— they purchase appliances at a fairly high rate and were among the early adopters of color television sets. They tend not to buy the cheapest items available, but instead rely on name brands more than do some other classes. L-As also spend higher proportions of their incomes on personal appearance items and on personal gifts. Finally, and in part related to their unemployed status, L-As on average watch much more television than any other social class. They must surely gain ideas about consumption from the ads there, and some frustration must result from the realization that they are unable to afford many of the products advertised or the life-styles glamorized on the air.

A final topic that bears mention has to do with pricing and selling practices, credit policies, and consumer protection. Many L-As are *vulnerable consumers*. Some are functionally illiterate, others do not speak the English language. Many are unable to perform simple arithmetic. The availability of credit is important in allowing them to obtain expensive merchandise, but these are exactly the people who are more likely to be poor credit risks. Transportation is a problem for many people in this class, so they tend to shop close to their homes. They are also often poorly informed about what alternatives they have in terms of products, prices, and retail outlets.

The net result is that a subset of marketers has come to serve these clients. While most of the marketing mainstream is available to them, it is not patronized as often. If a retailer chooses to cater to this market, he or she can expect to incur higher costs through shoplifting and vandalism and to work in less pleasant surroundings. Often this means that retail prices will be higher, that bad debts will raise interest rates for credit, and that an attitude of mistrust between retailers and customers may develop. Unfortunately, this negative outlook can cause some honest businesspeople to decide not to serve the lower-class communities. While many honest retailers choose to remain, there is also an opportunity for the unscrupulous operator. Thus we find many of marketing's "shameful practices" (perpetuated by only a small percentage of all marketers) occurring here. These include misrepresenting merchandise, overpricing, deliberately inflating the totals obtained by addition, selling shoddy and defective goods, high-pressure selling, hiding exorbitant interest rates by misleading pricing schemes, and so on. Overall, the marketing and consumer behavior issues in the lower-American social class are not pleasant to think about, but they are a real part of life in the United States and cannot simply be ignored in our coverage of this society. (If you would like to read more in this area, the references in Note 32 for this chapter provide a good starting point.)

CHAPTER 14

Social and Situational Influences on Consumer Behavior

Ray Bans Are Exposed, Take Off

The Bausch & Lomb company developed Ray-Ban (antiglare) sunglasses during the 1930s, with some considerable success. During the 1950s it created its "Wayfarer" model of Ray-Bans, also with considerable success. By 1981, however, the Wayfarer line was viewed as old and tired and was scheduled to be killed at the end of the year. Suddenly, however, sales began to spurt on the West Coast, and Wayfarers sold out the entire inventory in a short period of time. The company, shocked by this reversal of trend and the almost 600 percent increase in sales, checked into what had happened. It turned out that . . . [discussion continues later in this chapter].

■ ■ ■

425

SOCIAL INFLUENCES BEGIN EARLY

Social influences are at work in all phases of consumer behavior—they affect which products we aspire to own, which styles we prefer, at which stores we'll shop, and so forth. Social influences can be at work when other people are present or even when they're absent (if we think about their reactions). This is a broad and powerful force in the consumer world.

Because this topic is so broad, it is helpful for us to have a strong base for analyzing it. Therefore, in the first sections of this chapter we will review some key concepts such as socialization and social influence processes. We then discuss how these concepts appear in the real world of consumer behavior and note many marketing application possibilities. Then, in the final section, we turn to the interesting topic of situational influences on consumer behavior, noting both concepts and marketing applications here.

The Socialization of Children

Social influences go to work very early in our lives, through **socialization**, the process by which each individual learns to live and behave effectively as a person among other people.[1] Socialization is the principal means by which we learn and are affected by our larger society. Socialization occurs throughout our lives, but is most crucial during childhood.[2] Here the baby makes the basic discovery that people and objects are separate from himself or herself and that he or she must learn to *interact* with them. As time goes on, the young child learns that there are *rules* for such social interactions, and that the world of social *roles* is important. They learn that certain behaviors are expected when they have a certain role (e.g., a baseball outfielder should not laugh and point when the ball is hit to him, nor should she throw it over the fence!). Children also learn that the rules of organized social structures apply to everyone, not just them, and that they need to be accepted to participate. Finally, the thousands of social interactions during childhood also help each child to find what works well and provides personal enjoyment, and what does not. Through this social process each of us begins to develop our unique identity without our world.

Socialization in Adolescence and Adulthood

Changes over Time

Socialization continues, but its nature changes as we move through our lives. Adolescence is a difficult bridging time as a child becomes an adult. Part of the difficulty stems from physical changes, but part also stems from three difficult social **role transitions**: (1) a shift from being submissive to being independent, (2) a shift from nonresponsible to responsibility roles, and (3) a move from in-hibited sexuality to acceptable sexual roles.[3] For many teenagers the major so-cializing institutions, including the family, do not provide clear guidance on how to make these difficult changes, and the teenage subculture and friendship groups emerge to help with them.

In adulthood, because people have more freedom than during their school years, they tend to pursue their personal preferences to a greater extent and experience widely differing socialization experiences. Much adult socialization involves the learning of new roles and appropriate behaviors for them. For example, many readers can still look forward to learning the roles of a parent, spouse, in-law, rising executive or entrepreneur, manager of others, community leader, appliance buyer, and so forth.

Five Sources of Adult Socialization

There are five primary sources leading to most adult socialization.[4] First, **residential moves** require a person to break from past routines and integrate into the new community. In the consumer realm, this brings many new product purchases (housing, appliances, supplies), new service purchases (utilities, banks, medical), and the need to develop new patronage patterns for stores and suppliers. A second source, **social mobility**, refers to movements up or down the social ladder. Because certain values and behaviors are expected in different social classes, people moving to a new class often devote significant effort to learning and adopting new life-styles for themselves. (Some readers may be participating in a form of this already—**anticipatory socialization** refers to preparing yourself for future roles by learning about and rehearsing appropriate behaviors.) A third, more extreme, source for some adults is **institutionalization**. This occurs for varying periods of time when one is immersed in a tightly controlled institutional environment, such as the military, prison, hospital, or even some universities! **Resocialization** is the key concept here, as the person is required to adopt a new set of behaviors required by the institution (there are of course degrees of difference here, particularly when the person is voluntarily within the institution: fraternities and sororities are likely to require more resocialization of their members than are dorms).[5]

The two final sources of adult socialization are broadly shared by everyone. The fourth source, **social change**, is occurring on a continuous basis and demands adaptation from almost all adults. Consider that within our lifetimes we have seem dramatic changes occur in recreational drug use, women's roles, sexual practices, health threats, and government's role, to name just a few examples. Now consider those adults who were living before these changes became powerful, and how they had to in some manner react and adapt to each of them (sometimes by fighting the change, sometimes by accepting it). In the consumer realm, social change brings new products and services, new fashions, new stores, and so forth.

Our final source, the **adult life cycle**, refers to systematic changes in our lives as we grow older. There has recently been great interest in "adult growth stages" in which every American adult is seen as passing through a sequence of psychosocial periods, each of which is 5 to 10 years long. During each period some "predictable crises" are likely to occur, and the person needs to develop ways to cope with them. The period from ages 23 to 28 (the *entering adult world* stage), for example, is viewed as a stressful time, as men and women search for goals to which they can commit themselves. (If you would like to read more about this area, you may wish to refer to Note 6). Much of the consumer research in this area has concentrated on the consumer life cycle, which we'll examine in the next chapter.

Key Socializing Institutions

As a final point in understanding socialization, we should note that these processes are heavily controlled by a few powerful agents or institutions in our society.[7] For many people, the **family** is the first, and most powerful, socializing institution. The values and life-style of the other family members is internalized by the child as he or she forms a personal identity: although these may change through the years, a basic part of ourselves is formed here. The onset of **schooling** introduces much formal socialization of the child into the culture of the society, including learning the bases for written communication, calculation, history, societal governance, and so forth. Increasingly, **mass media** has become a potent socializing force in society. Messages from television, radio, newspapers and magazines convey much information about the world beyond our doorsteps: these messages can challenge or reinforce our current values and teach us about new forms of behaviors.

The three remaining socializing institutions have more diverse impacts across the society. People who are active in **organized religions** can experience strong socializing influences on their lives, but many persons are not active in a religion and are not subject to these direct influences. The same comments hold for **work centers**, since many persons are not exposed to daily socializing influences from this source. Those who are exposed, however, can be strongly affected in dress, speech, and leisure activities and life-styles. **Social groups**, meanwhile, are so diverse that it is impossible to generalize about exact socialization impacts. They are so important, however, that we shall shortly return to consider their impacts on consumer behavior. At this point let us shift our attention from the broad topic of socialization to the more pointed issue of social influence, and how it works.

HOW DOES SOCIAL INFLUENCE OPERATE?

"How important are other people to me?"
"How important am I to others?"
"How much influence goes on between other people and myself?"

This section deals with the effects that other persons have on us and on our behaviors and, on the flip side, our influences on other people: these are interesting questions, and their answers can give each of us insights about the nature of social and group influences in our lives.

Within consumer behavior, social influences occur before, during, and after transactions. Interactions with salespersons often reflect social influence processes, for example. So do many discussions with family or friends. Social influences are also important even when others are not present, as when we "think ahead" to anticipate how others might react if we buy a certain item or wear a particular outfit. Within the professional world of business, social influence processes are constantly at work as well. We will frequently need to work effectively with others. We'll be interested in our boss having a favorable impression of us. And, of course, we'll be engaged in social influence processes with our customers. Thus this topic is professionally relevant in many ways. Let's now examine it in more detail.

Theories of Social Interactions

Social interaction has been studied by philosophers, sociologists, and psychologists throughout history. There are many ways to analyze social interactions. For example, social interactions can be analyzed by the dominant elements that each one contains.[8] Four important elements that are often found in social interactions are

- Power.
- Conflict.
- Social exchange.
- Cooperation.

Any particular interaction will contain some combination of these elements. **Power** reflects a difference in the authority levels (or other power sources) between the participants. A salesperson who knows a great deal about stereo systems, for example, possesses certain power in an in-store discussion. If the customer also knows a great deal, the seller's power is reduced, while if the consumer feels inadequate, the seller's power is increased. **Conflict** interactions are those of the "I win, you lose" variety: competition, either overtly or hidden, is active here. Within consumer behavior these issues often arise when we are forced to allocate resources (money, time, effort) in a joint decision situation. Which vacation should the family choose, which car to buy, and which movie to see are just a few examples.

Social exchange is also a basic element in many interactions. It occurs when one person provides benefits of some sort to the other, usually with the expectation of some reciprocal benefits that will be returned. In purely economic exchanges, the obligations of the seller and buyer are likely to be quite formalized. In social interactions, however, the "obligations" are often less clear. This leads to such dimensions as personal liking, trust, gratitude, and so on being extremely important in social exchanges. **Cooperation** is another element often found in social interactions. It refers to two participants joining together to accomplish a common goal. There are many forms that this can take: it can be set in the terms of a contract, it can be directed (as by higher management in an organization or parents in a family), or it can be spontaneous. Within consumer behavior, a salesperson and customer often work together to find the most suitable purchase, and a husband and wife will strive to cooperate in reaching their important purchases. Even friendly word-of-mouth advice often reflects this element.

The Situation as an Element in Social Interaction

Consider how differently most of us act when we are at a formal dinner versus a wild party. Some of our behavioral difference is due to the other people with whom we are interacting. Most of the variation, though, is due to *the overall situational context*. Within each specific situation, we turn to our expectations of what "is supposed to happen," and how the other people present will act themselves and will expect us to act. This is one major reason that new environments are often difficult for us to adjust to: we are simply not very certain about what to expect or how to behave. Situational influence is closely related to the subject of social roles, the topic of our next section. In addition, situational influence plays a major role in consumer behavior, which we'll examine at the end of this chapter.

The Importance of Social Roles

Imagine the following scene as it might unfold:

> *Pat and Lee strolled casually through the entrance of the exclusive shop in the mall. Chris, turning around, saw them coming and . . .*

How did you cast this scene? What was Chris going to do? In general, how important are the roles that we assign to people?

For example, would it have made much difference if Pat were a father, Lee were his son, and Chris were Lee's mother? What if Chris was a salesperson, and Pat and Lee were teenage girl shoppers? Or if Pat and Lee were police officers and Chris were a criminal? Notice that all three names could denote a male or female. Did your view of the scene depend on this at all? The essential point of the example is that, just as in a play, *the role that one occupies really helps to define the actions we expect*. More formally, a **role** can be defined as a set of accepted rules for appropriate behaviors in a particular situation.[9] Social interaction is greatly assisted by the presence of roles, since they help us to predict something about the behavior of others with whom we will interact. However, roles do not specify everything; this allows for some individual freedom, as long as the behavior is within the accepted boundaries of the role. For example, Chris, as a salesperson, can rush over to wait on Pat and Lee, or can simply look over at them with a friendly, inquiring appearance. If the behavior is outside the boundaries of the role, however, the social interaction is likely to suffer, since the expectations of the other person are not being met. For example, Chris cannot refuse to look at Pat and Lee, or order them to leave the store, and still expect a smooth sales interaction.

We all adopt many roles during our daily lives. A **role repertoire** refers to the set of all roles that an individual possesses. A young woman, for example, might have such roles as rising young executive, wife, mother, daughter, sister, jogger, shopper, club member, and friend to various others. As we move through our lives, we are likely to add new roles and give up some past roles. Most of the roles that we add are our choice, and we enjoy carrying them out.

The impact of roles has received some degree of attention in consumer research, and more is likely in the future. We'll see more about this topic in Chapter 15 (when we examine household decision making) and Chapter 16 (when we focus on salesperson influences on consumer behavior).

"Impression Management"

Approximately 30 years ago, the sociologist Erving Goffman developed an approach—**impression management**—that captured the interest of many college students and their teachers.[10] Goffman focused on the concepts of people playing roles and communicating with each other through symbols. He reasoned that people *manage* the symbols they use during social interactions to create certain impressions in the minds of others. These impression management (or "self-presentation") strategies reflect how we want to be viewed and treated by others. Since everyone is simultaneously giving off impressions to others while searching for impressions from them, everyone finds impression management to be useful.

Goffman's approach is called a **dramaturgical perspective** because he comes to view life as a theater, with people being social performers. He stresses, for example, how sensitive we sometimes are to the symbols that other people present to us, both directly (what they say, for example) and indirectly (by their gestures, facial expressions, and body language). In turn, we are sometimes very aware of others watching us. This awareness causes us to act deliberately in certain ways (smiling eyes, stomach in, proud appearance, etc.) to project a certain image to them. He then goes much farther, suggesting that everyone is always playing a social role, that people wear different "masks" as appropriate to the occasion. As applied to consumer behavior, then, we can think of consumers as actors and actresses, giving *performances* to their *audience*.

Goffman's approach has been criticized for being unduly cynical in portraying people as manipulators and for leaving little or no room for relaxed personal interchange.[11] Goffman's primary emphasis, however, was on the *stylized nature* of most social interactions and how they seem to require people's constant attention to roles and impressions. There is little doubt that much of this does go on in our lives and that it influences our behaviors.

Influence from Social Groups

Each of us belongs to many groups during our lives. Groups can give us friendship, security, and opportunities to express ourselves. Groups are important in marketing and consumer behavior. A company, a sales department, a civic organization, a church committee, a family, and a friendly club all represent groups to which we might belong. Understanding group processes is important for marketers who sell to company buying committees, to institutions, or to households. Beyond this, the social processes that go on within a social group can be fascinating in themselves.

The term **group** refers to two or more individuals who share a set of norms, values, or beliefs; have certain role relationships; and experience interdependent behavior.[12] A group is thus more than simply a collection of individuals who happen to be in the same place at the same time. It usually has a continuing life, and its members share a sense of belonging to it. There are many types of groups, each with some different characteristics. A *primary group* is a small, intimate group of people who relate to each other in direct, personal ways. Examples include a family, or close friends. *Secondary groups,* in contrast, are those in which we are less closely involved in a personal sense. They are often more organized and focus on skills or interests rather than on our personality. Examples might include our school, our company, or our professional associations (such as the American Marketing Association). With respect to our own situations, several distinctions are useful. *Ingroups* are those to which we belong and which we identify ourselves ("we" is used when we think about fellow members). *Outgroups* are those to which we do not belong (outgroup members are "they"). *Closed groups* are difficult to join (and for this reason can be viewed as having a certain degree of desirability to them). *Open groups* have few barriers to entry and can be joined by almost anyone who wishes to.

Why a Group Has Social Power

Social power is defined as the potential influence that an individual or group can have over a person.[13] Each of us is subject to social power and also possesses it over others. Five types of social power were identified by French and Raven:

- Legitimated power.
- Expert power.
- Referent power.
- Coercive power.
- Reward power.

Each type reflects a different reason for an individual to "go along with" someone else's recommended behavior.

In brief, **legitimated power** stems from a person's belief that another person has the right to suggest (or even order) a particular behavior. For example, a junior executive might carry out the assignment from her boss. In general, this type of power reflects group organizations, when a member accepts his or her role within the group. **Expert power**, on the other hand, reflects the belief that another person "knows what she's talking about," perhaps through long experience or intensive studies of a particular issue. Here a recommendation is seen as good because of the expert background involved. **Referent power**, meanwhile, reflects a person's desire to feel that he or she "belongs" with another individual or group and wants to act so as to express this identity (this is a key topic for consumer behavior, which we'll examine again shortly).

The final two types of social power represent more activity on the part of the other person or group. **Coercive power** rests on the threat, real or imagined, that the group can punish the member if he or she does not comply with the recommended behavior. For example, a group might ridicule the member, remove some privileges, or even expel the person from membership. **Reward power**, conversely, is the other side of the coin: in this instance a person will comply because he or she expects to receive material benefits, praise, or other positive recognition if the group members like what he or she has done.

Group Influence Processes: Kelman's View

Social power theory helps us see why groups are influential, but not exactly how the process might work. Herbert Kelman has helped us with this question by identifying three types of **group influence processes** that focus on the individual being influenced:[14]

- Compliance.
- Identification.
- Internalization.

The first case, **compliance**, represents a response to the group's power to reward or punish a person (either physically or socially). In this case, a person is likely to go along with the group whether or not he or she believes in the norm, because of the external power the group has to reward or punish.

The other two cases are different in that the person is more internally motivated. **Identification** represents a social response: the individual desires to create a close relationship with the group. To attain this closer relationship, he will adopt the behavioral norms of the group, even though the norms themselves may be of little importance to him. **Internalization**, on the other hand, is directly related to the group norms being accepted by the individual. In this case the individual discovers what the group believes and personally agrees that this is appropriate for him as well.

Reference Groups and Referent Others

As a final topic in groups, it is appropriate that we raise the subject of reference groups. The term **reference group** was coined in 1942 by a psychologist, Herbert Hyman, who was studying social status.[15] According to Hyman, a reference group was the group against which a person would compare himself or herself (that is, "refer to") to determine his or her own social standing in the community. Since that time, however, the concept has broadened considerably in the field of consumer behavior. Today, the term has come to mean a group to whom we look for guidance for our own behavior.

Reference groups can be large or small, formal or informal. We do not even need to be a member of the group or to be in physical contact with it. When an individual is very important to us and serves this function, he or she is called a **referent other**. Reference groups are especially important because we identify with at least some aspects of that group. *Normative reference groups* provide us with values and standards for our behavior. Our family is our first normative reference group. Some groups serve as *negative reference groups*: these represent norms or behaviors that we do not admire or seek for ourselves. On the other hand, some groups serve as *aspirational reference groups*, positive groups that we hope to join in the future. Many readers, for example, might view successful business executives in this light.

A major contribution of the reference group/referent other concept is that it extends the social influence far beyond the membership groups with whom we physically interact. Fantasies, heroes, stars, and other models can enter the analysis. As you might expect, this has important applications for marketing. We will return to this topic later in this chapter.

Psychological Reactance

All the preceding discussion has assumed that the social influence attempts are accepted. This clearly doesn't happen much of the time. In some cases, consumers don't mind the influence efforts, but occasionally they do become upset by them. Why is this the case? Jack Brehm developed a theory called **reactance** to explain why this sometimes happens.[16]

The basic premise is each of us is accustomed to having freedom of choice most of the time. Social influence attempts can represent threats to this freedom, when they attempt to direct how a person should behave. From the recipient's point of view, then, there is a *felt pressure* to behave in a certain way. This felt pressure can bring about reactance on our part. Reactance arousal, in turn, can lead to a person becoming more involved in the issue. As involvement increases, anger is possible, and the person becomes more likely to *move against* the desires of the influencer. In this case, the potential influencer—either person or group—will see a "boomerang effect," as people resist the influence more than they would have had they not felt their freedom to be threatened. Given that marketing is so clearly geared to influencing consumers, this theory has strong implications for managers. Consider, for example, various techniques that salespersons can use. Which is better, a *hard sell* or a *soft sell*? While this depends on a number of circumstances, reactance theory provides a basis for examining how consumers might react against a hard sell.

CONSUMER "WORD OF MOUTH" BEHAVIORS

At this point we will turn to a direct focus on social influences in the consumer marketplace, drawing on our earlier concepts as needed. We know, of course, that marketers are actively trying to influence consumers, but we sometimes overlook the fact that consumers are in frequent communication with each other and that much influence occurs here as well. Let's begin with a closer look at some key dimensions here.

The "Web of Word of Mouth"

The phrase "web of word of mouth" comes from a classic marketing study by William H. Whyte, published in *Fortune* magazine about 35 years ago.[17] Room air conditioners had recently been introduced to the consumer market, and Whyte had noticed that this had led to an interesting phenomenon. In urban neighborhoods, the conditioners were often used in front window, and an interesting pattern was apparent. Even within the same neighborhood, air conditioners appeared in clusters rather than in random fashion. For example, six houses in a row might each have an air conditioner, while the three houses on either side

Swimming pools and the 'web of word of mouth'.

would not. From this simple observation, Whyte expanded on his notion that the purchase of these goods reflected *patterns of social communication* within the neighborhood: the people who talked together about the products were the people who bought them. (Television was becoming very popular at that time as well, and similar patterns could be observed with TV antennas. Also, you can still see these patterns when flying over urban areas in an airplane and noting how home swimming pools are clustered, even in the same neighborhoods.)

This basic observation leads to the consideration of just how powerful an influence consumer **word-of-mouth communication** can be. Most consumer word of mouth seems to be of an *approach* nature. That is, we enter freely into these discussions and enjoy them for their sake, whether or not they influence our behaviors. Through consumer discussions, we learn about product and service options. We also have the chance to tell others about our opinions and experiences.

Analyzing Consumer Networks

Although the study of social networks has long been of interest in sociology, there has recently been some very interesting work done in consumer research.[18] Figure 14-1 provides a portion of a certain type of consumer word-of-mouth network called a **referral network**, in this case reflecting the recommendations for a physician in a university town. Notice that this research begins with the choice of that physician (G) by a new professor (A) at the university. To create the network shown, it basically works backward in time, discovering who had issued each recommendation, and to which other persons referrals had also been offered.

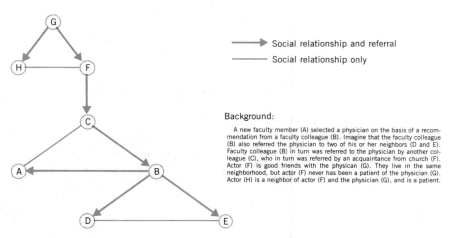

FIGURE 14-1 **Portion of a Referral Network for a Physician**

Source: Adapted from Peter H. Reingen and Jerome B. Kernan, "Analysis of Referral Networks in Marketing: Methods and Illustration," *Journal of Marketing Research*, Vol. 23, no. 4, November 1986, p. 371.

In reality, the physician's entire word-of-mouth referral network would of course include many other people who use her, and would be very much more complex to create and to analyze. Even in Figure 14-1, though, we can identify some typical characteristics of consumer word-of-mouth networks. For example, (1) the consumer referral network (arrows) is a subset of a larger social network (both arrows and thin lines) and largely depends on it in order to function; (2) neighborhoods, work centers, and social organizations are all important sources for consumer word-of-mouth activity; (3) these networks tend to operate as almost independent smaller clusters (for example, notice that if it hadn't been for the single discussion at church, the entire professor cluster might well be seeing a different physician); and (4) some consumers play the role of opinion leaders within a social network, as indicated by B's importance in influencing the decisions of others in the group.

The Power of Consumer Recommendations

We all know how powerful consumer word-of-mouth discussions can be in influencing our consumer behaviors, but why is this so? The power of consumer recommendations appears to stem from three key factors: First, consumer communications usually have **high source credibility**. Most of our discussions are with either friends or family. We enter them with a feeling of trust and openness. Also, the discussions tend to be friendly and can offer us support for trying certain behaviors. (If we are providing information to others, we can also receive some support for our own views or behaviors when they accept our advice.)

Second, unlike the one-way flow of communication from television advertising or consumer reporters, consumer word-of-mouth employs a two-way flow. The power of the **two-way flow of communication** stems from the fact that we can ask questions, obtain clarifications, follow-up on issues that interest us and also spend as much time as we desire on the communication. Thus the word-of-mouth process itself is conducive to a successful learning situation.

The third strength of consumer word of mouth comes from its **vicarious trial** attributes. (The word *vicarious*, from Latin, means an "imagined" experience or substitute for an actual experience.) We can gain some of the experience of having tried a movie, for example, and have a better idea of how much we might like it, simply by asking a friend who has seen it already. If his or her recommendation is negative, our chances of actual product trial can go down dramatically, whereas a strong positive recommendation might well create a new customer for that movie. Similarly, we can gain some idea of how a hair style holds up, how a suit "wears," and so forth, without actually having personally to buy and use it.

Consumers' Social Integration

We all know that some people are "more sociable" than others. Some of us are extroverts, some are introverts. Some of us have many friends, some of us have few close friends. Do these factors influence our word-of-mouth communications?

Yes, they do. The concept of **consumer social integration** is a useful framework for understanding word-of-mouth behavior.[19] The basic nature of consumer social integration is depicted in Figure 14-2. Note that there are four "types" of consumers in this framework:

- Socially integrated.   ■ Socially dependent.
- Socially independent.   ■ Socially isolated.

These categories take into account the two-way flow of word-of-mouth communication, and thus represent an improvement over earlier stress on "opinion leadership" alone, which took a one-way flow look at word-of-mouth influence. To use the two-way flow, consumers need to be classified in terms of both opinion giving (to other consumers) and information seeking (from other consumers).

Consumers who score high on both opinion leadership and information seeking are classed as **social integrateds**. Those who score high on influencing others, but low on being influenced themselves, are classed as **social independents**. These two groups comprise the **opinion leader** segment of the market. Social dependents, on the other hand, are those who score low on influencing others, but high on being influenced by others. **Opinion follower** might be a good term for these consumers. Finally, **social isolates** score low on both types of influence: they are simply less involved in the web of word of mouth for a given product or service.

It is important to recognize that these assignments are *product class specific.* Every consumer is interested in some products but not in others. Being classed as a social isolate for personal computers, for example, does not mean that a consumer is a hermit, but only that he or she is not very involved in consumer word of mouth for this product category. Most college students, for example, would probably be classed as social isolates for baby furniture, yachts, or retire-

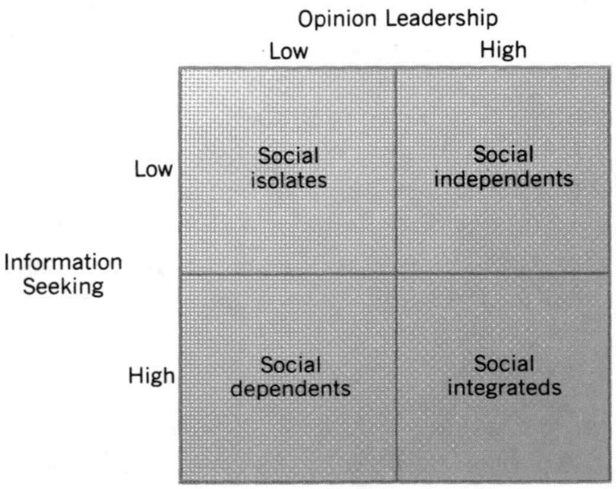

FIGURE 14-2 **The Basics of Consumer Social Integration**

ment homes, but be placed in one of the other three categories for music or restaurants.

Interesting recent research has continued to shed light on consumer word-of-mouth. For example, it appears that most word-of-mouth comments about automobiles fall into four categories: (1) **advice-giving** about which cars to buy or where to shop, (2) **product news** about cars' characteristics and new features available, (3) **positive personal experiences** about one's own car or how it was purchased, and (4) **negative comments** about either cars or a consumer's experiences. In terms of what leads to each type of comment, the same study found that the higher a consumer's basic interest (enduring involvement) in automobiles, the more likely he or she is to provide product news to others and to serve as an opinion leader. Opinion leaders for autos, in turn, are more likely than other consumers to give advice, provide product news, and tell other consumers about their positive automotive experiences. Meanwhile, those consumers who have bought a car recently (high situational involvement) were not found to be more likely to serve as opinion leaders, but they did share their positive experiences at a higher than average rate. Finally, an interesting result appeared for negative comments in this study—*none* of the foregoing factors (enduring involvement, opinion leadership, or situational involvement) correlated significantly with it![20] It thus appears that negative word-of-mouth is a different type of phenomenon: it may be that consumers only relate negative comments when they've had negative experiences, and that the timing of the negative experience doesn't matter too much—consumers have long memories for bad experiences!

Consumer Folklore Is All Around Us

Across our society there are millions of general consumer beliefs, opinions and stories. The total set of these beliefs, opinions, and stories has been termed **consumer folklore**.[21] Consumer folklore ranges from accurate beliefs to wildly inaccurate—and even bizarre—myths and rumors. It includes old kernels of wisdom passed down through families for generations ("Feed a fever, starve a cold," "Chicken soup and bed rest is the best cure for almost any ailment," "The whiter the bread, the quicker you're dead," and so on). It also includes the latest in important and interesting information.

New rumors about popular stores and products are especially favored in some consumer circles, and are passed along with enthusiasm. Exhibit 14-1 summarizes a few recent rumors that were reported by consumers in a recent study, as well as some reported by marketers. You may have heard them yourself.

Marketing Implications from Word-of-Mouth

What Can Marketers Do About Rumors?

Informal consumer communications present many problems and opportunities for marketers. One of the most serious class of problems arises for firms that are hit with negative rumors. The McDonald's worm rumor (see Exhibit 14-1), for

EXHIBIT 14-1   RUMORS BY CONSUMERS

Recent Rumors as Reported by Consumers

- "I remember hearing about McDonald's supposedly putting worm meat in their hamburgers . . . Burger King may have started that."
- "I heard that a guy bought a bucket of Kentucky Fried Chicken, . . . he and his girlfriend were eating it in the dark at the drive-in. She noticed it tasted funny, so they turned on the light, and she saw she had been eating a rat. She . . . supposedly died right after that."
- "A certain baby formula was deemed unsafe by the USDA for consumption in the United states . . . caused cancer or something . . . they just kept manufacturing it and sold it overseas, mainly in the Third World countries."
- "Procter & Gamble's corporate symbol looks like a half moon, with an old man's face, and thirteen stars. Supposedly the reason that Procter & Gamble's so successful is that it's in with devil worshippers and all that. If you . . . connect the thirteen stars in a certain way, it would come out to 6-6-6—that's a symbol for the devil. The half moon looks like the devil."
- "This . . . candy called Space Dust, or Pop Rocks . . . you put it in your mouth and it starts crackling . . . that kid 'Mikey' on the commercial for Life cereal . . . put some of the candy in his mouth and had a lot of Coca-Cola, and he died from that!"
- "This 17-year-old girl won a trip to Hawaii and wanted a nice tan for the trip. She went to a tanning parlor, and they would only allow her to stay in for a half hour. Well, she wanted a great tan fast, so she went to seven places for a half hour each. Now she's in the regional hospital, she's totally blind, and she has cooked herself from the inside out, like a microwave. There's nothing they can do for her, she only has 26 days to live."

Recent Rumors Reported by Marketers

- Corona Extra became the second most popular beer in the United States during the late 1980s, based largely on extremely favorable consumer word-of-mouth. Then a false rumor began, that the Mexican beer was contaminated with urine. Sales, which had been up over 80 percent just before the rumor, began to drop sharply in many key markets.
- A restaurant in a midsized Illinois town became the subject of a false rumor that one of its employees was suffering from AIDS. According to one businessperson who dined there, "Leo's was virtually empty at lunch."
- Rumors have international appeal as well, with similar dangers for marketers. Recently an anonymous list of 60 products said to contain pork fat appeared in Indonesia. Word began to spread rapidly among the country's 160 million Moslems, since this would mean that such brands are not *halal*, the Moslem equivalent of Kosher. The rumor wasn't true for many leading brands on the list, but sales dropped sharply anyway (e.g., Indomie Noodles sales were off over 30 percent, while Bango, the nation's leading ketchup, had to close its plant for one week after the rumor began).

Sources: See Note 22.

example, reportedly caused sales drops of up to 30 percent in areas where the rumor circulated. General Foods was hit hard by the Pop Rocks rumor, as were Procter & Gamble with the Satanic story, Corona beer, Leo's restaurant, and a number of brands in Indonesia.

The key question confronting a marketer when a negative rumor begins is, "How do I combat it?" In McDonald's case, management took a *refutational approach* and tried to mount arguments to refute, or overcome, consumers' beliefs that the rumor may be true. For example, the company posted a letter from the Secretary of Agriculture that stated that McDonald's products met all government standards. It also modified its TV and magazine ads to emphasize the phrase "100 Percent Pure Beef" and issued information pointing out that worm meat was so much more expensive than hamburger meat that substitution would not be a cost-effective approach in any event. Very little guidance was available to McDonald's as to what strategy might work best. What do you think might have been better? (If you are interested in reading more about this, see Note 23.)

What the Devil

In another recent case, Procter & Gamble—widely considered to be the best consumer marketing firm in the world—confronted a similar dilemma with the rumor about its Satanic corporate symbol (this rumor was also reported in the folklore study in Exhibit 14-1). Were this rumor to mushroom, the impact could be huge, since P&G markets so many brands with strong leadership positions in many product categories. At first, the company attempted to keep a low profile regarding this rumor, not wanting to give it any extra public attention. The rumor, however, continued to spread rapidly throughout conservative sections of the country. As it became clear that its strategy of benign neglect was not working well, P&G managers tried another approach: it requested, and received, highly credible testimonials from conservative religious leaders, including Billy Graham and Jerry Falwell. When even this strategy did not kill off the rumor, the company resorted to filing well-publicized lawsuits against several persons who had publicly been spreading the rumor. This did smooth matters for several years, but in 1985 the rumor began to strongly surface again in several mid-Atlantic states. At this point P&G threw in the towel. Its consumer research showed that the symbol was offering the firm no apparent benefits and was providing some costs because of the persistent rumor. It then decided to phase out the symbol from all P&G packages. As of the mid-1980s, the company's symbol was to be seen no more, a victim of consumer word-of-mouth.

Advertising Appeals Using Word-of-Mouth

In a more positive vein, marketers can use consumer word of mouth in various ways to promote brand sales. The *slice-of-life approach* in advertising, for example, often depicts two or more normal-appearing consumers conversing about a typical consumer problem (this varies by the product and target audience, of course). After the nature of the problem is made clear, one of the consumers will pass on the key information as to how successful he or she was when using the sponsoring brand to solve the problem.

If the ad is successful in getting the audience to relate to the actors as normal consumers, the effect is to obtain something similar to a *consumer testimonial* in a word-of-mouth context. In terms of our dimensions of word-of-mouth for automobiles, a slice-of-life commercial can show any or all of the four types: advice-giving, product news, and/or positive personal experiences are typical, while even negative comments (about competitors) are possible if done in a tasteful and legal manner.

Creating Consumer Word-of-Mouth

An even more direct marketing approach involves *influentials' stimulation* to try to create consumer word-of-mouth. This strategy requires locating the socially integrated and socially independent consumers for a particular product category and then promoting the product especially to them, even giving it to them free.

The Rock Music Experiment

An interesting test of this approach has been reported in the rock music category. There are hundreds of new records released each week, and the marketing challenge—to create a hit using unknown artists—is severe. The typical promotional program employs a *push strategy*, attempting to sell radio and TV stations, disk jockeys, and record outlets, hoping that they will in turn influence consumers to buy the records.

In this marketing test, however, no push strategy was used. Instead, a *pull strategy* was employed in a special way. The high school population in a number of trial cities was targeted as the key consumer market due to their heavy purchase rate for rock records. The researchers then obtained the names of various types of student leaders in each school in each city. Each of these students was sent a letter inviting him or her to join a "select panel" of leaders that was being formed to evaluate rock records. Each week for a period of several months, the students received packets of free records. For each record, they were asked to return their evaluations, plus the opinions of any friends and acquaintances who might care to give them.

The results? Several of the records hit the "Top Ten" in the cities with the panels. In all other cities in the nation, where normal promotions had been used, not a single one of these records ever reached the hit lists! This effect was achieved without any contacts with either radio stations or record stores in the trial cities: the new hits had been "pulled" through the channels by the power of consumer word-of-mouth![24]

This rock music application represents a case in which marketers could rely on the strong interests of opinion leaders to help create word-of-mouth, once the opinion leaders knew about a particular product's benefits. A variation of this approach is to contact trusted opinion leaders, but *not* in their roles as consumers. For example, food manufacturers have begun to provide physicians with detailed information regarding the nutritional benefits of foods sold to consumers in supermarkets. According to one industry executive, "Patients are now asking doctors about diet and nutrition, and doctors are now contacting companies to get more information. A company can run all the ads it wants, but if a consumer doesn't understand what saturated fats are, or why they're important, the message is wasted. Doctors can explain that, and suggest ways for their patients to cut down. . . ."[25]

Consumer word-of-mouth operates perhaps most frequently in terms of local market retailing and services. So far, we have discussed this as an entirely voluntary activity on the part of consumers, operating independently of any marketer involvement. Word-of-mouth can be *so valuable* to manufacturers, stores, and salespersons, however, that sometimes they become more active in attempting to stimulate this activity directly. Various approaches are possible, ranging from a salesperson simply asking a customer to "Spread the word if you're satisfied with the service you've gotten from me" to providing payments for successfully directing new purchasers to the marketer. In many cases the term *referral fee* is used, in which the person providing advice about where to seek service will receive a payment from the marketer (lawyer, doctor, stockbroker, contractor) who has received the new client or customer. While many word-of-mouth referrals do not have payment involved (Figure 14-1's referral network, for example, did not), within business and the professions this practice is fairly common. In this regard, a recent creative variation merits our brief attention:

Brown Bag Feasts as Pyramid Builds

The Brown Bag Software Company was in serious financial trouble a few years ago, because it couldn't provide software dealers with sufficient incentives to learn its systems and sell them against industry giants such as Lotus or Microsoft. Out of desperation, Sandy Schupper, chairman of the firm, decided to employ some consumer research that had shown that 95 percent of working professionals were willing to pay a reasonable price (about $100) for software they had been given free, but liked well enough to continue using. "What made that 95 percent figure so hard to swallow is the fact that our biggest problem in this industry is consumer theft," Schupper explains. "We're not talking about sampling here either, because once they've got it, they've *got* it. They don't have to come back to you and buy it again."

As a hedge against total trust in a computer honor system, Brown Bag decided to reduce its cost of goods to a minimum and to introduce incentives for users to pay up. Rather than using diskettes, it eliminated cost of goods sold by placing the software on over 1000 local on-line "bulletin boards," so that computer enthusiasts could simply download the program to their personal machines and use the self-contained, working Brown Bag program. The firm then offered two different incentives for the consumer to then send in a payment. One was a product improvement (upon payment, the consumer would be sent a diskette with additional features and a more complete manual).

The other incentive was the prospect of future financial rewards if the consumer was willing to engage in favorable (and successful) word-of-mouth for Brown Bag's programs. This worked as follows: each diskette sent out had a personal serial number enclosed. The buyer was encouraged to make as many copies as he or she desired and give them to friends to try. If any friends liked the program and wanted to buy a diskette for themselves, they had to send in that serial number, and the original buyer would receive a 10% commission. The friend's new diskette, however, would have a new serial number for him or her, and she could begin to copy it for other friends and begin to earn commissions as well. How has this approach worked? Brown Bag now has a commission-only sales force that numbers in the thousands, it has expanded into international markets, and it is planning the introduction of six new software products each year, which will allow its past customers to continue with their referral activities. In contrast to the bleak times, Mr. Schupper now reports, *"I make millions giving software away free!"*[26]

Focus Groups in Marketing Research

Before turning to a discussion of social influence issues in marketing, we should briefly address one remaining issue about word-of-mouth. Consumer word-of-mouth represents such a powerful force in the consumer marketplace that—if they could—marketers would listen in on every consumer conversation about their particular product or service category. After hearing them, the marketer would try to adjust the marketing mix accordingly. In reality, "listening in" would, of course, represent invasion of consumers' privacy in addition to being a very inefficient process. The point is, though, that the information contained in these discussions is extremely valuable to marketers.

In place of the real discussions, therefore, marketing researchers have developed several research forms to try to capture consumer word-of-mouth characteristics in a research setting. One extremely popular research technique, for example, is called the *focus group study*. A typical **focus group** brings 8 to 12 consumers from the target market together, seats them in a manner conducive to easy discussion, and asks them to talk freely about their opinions. A trained moderator keeps the discussion flowing and ensures that the key topics for the marketer are covered within the session, which lasts from one to two hours.

One purpose of this research method is to try to obtain exactly the sort of information that consumers pass along to each other freely in their daily discussions, but to do so on behalf of a sponsoring marketer (often, these studies are held in special rooms with two-way mirrors, so that researchers and sponsors can sit in the next room and monitor the session). The groups are tape recorded and then interpreted by researchers to pull out significant themes and results from the sessions in formal reports to the sponsors of the research.

Because of its low cost, fast turnaround, and insights into actual consumer opinions and language, focus group research is extremely popular across all facets of the marketing field. If you are interested in learning more about this technique, as well as some drawbacks of it, you may wish to begin with the sources listed in Note 27.

 CONSUMERS AND CONFORMITY

Why Such Similarity?

Consumer conformity has long been a subject of intense debate among marketers and social critics. Many critics believe that consumer conformity is bad. They point to consumers "acting like sheep" and striving to be accepted by buying only socially approved brands and styles. For us to appreciate these issues better, however, we first need to consider the concept of a conforming behavior. A **conforming behavior** is that which follows and is similar to the behavior of others. If we think briefly about it, we can see thousands of examples of conforming behaviors in the everyday world around us. Almost all of us drive cars, watch TV, and wear clothes that fall into a relatively few categories. Our hair styles are similar to those of our peers, we wear similar-looking watches and rings, and eat similar kinds of foods. An outsider looking at our society thus could easily decide that consumer conformity is indeed very high here.

This may not be true, however. There are in fact a number of reasons for such similarity in our consumer behaviors. For example,

- Consumers face a *restricted range* of product and style alternatives. The products available for purchase tend to reflect the preferences of large numbers of consumers, as mass marketers seek to maximize profits.
- The marketing system's stress on a restricted range of alternatives is also associated with *economic incentives for consumer conformity*. Mass production offers dramatically lower costs, thereby bringing many products into affordable price ranges.
- In addition, many products *are popular for functional reasons*—they simply serve our needs very well. For example, consumers enjoy watching TV, walking in well-cushioned soft shoes, and keeping cool with shorts or warm with sweaters.

Thus we can see that there are many conforming behaviors that the critics would not complain about. Their concern is thus not with similarity itself, but with the **social pressures** that are sometimes placed on consumers' shoulders, and with the fact that marketers sometimes try to use social influences in various ways, so as to obtain desired behaviors from consumers. Let's now look at some of the ways this can be done.

Marketing Applications of Consumer Conformity

Using Two Types of Social Influences

There are two basic forms of consumer social influence: normative and informational.[28] Essentially, **normative social influence** occurs when there is a heavy weighting of social factors in the decisions that consumers make. For example, if Stacy Phillips buys Reebok shoes only because she is interested in gaining approval (reward) from others or avoiding disapproval (punishment), we are seeing normative social influence at work on her decision. There is also, however, another common way in which social influence can occur in consumer behavior. Consumers often learn relevant information about products, movies, restaurants, and so on from other people and from groups. When they are influenced by the *contents* of this new knowledge (but do not feel pressured to behave one way or another), **informational social influence** is at work. *The key difference is thus whether we are primarily influenced by the pressure we perceive (normative) or by the contents of the new knowledge (informational).* While some decisions will reflect both types of influence, one type will usually dominate.

Certain characteristics of effective influencers for each type have been identified. Normative influences are stronger when the influencing person or group is important to the consumer, when they are able to deliver clear rewards or punishments (including social disapproval) to the consumer, when their desires are clear, and when the consumer's behavior is public.

The dimensions that best explain whether a person or group will exert strong informational influence are quite different. Three key dimensions of a highly influential person or group are expertise, trustworthiness, and empathy. **Expertise** refers to the quality of the information offered to a consumer by someone else. The person need not be an expert in a technical sense, but the more that we believe his or her information is important and true, the more likely we are to be influenced by it. **Trustworthiness** relates to the presence or absence of a manipulative intent on the part of the influencer. Can we trust what we are hearing, or is the information likely to be biased toward the benefit of the information source? **Empathy**, on the other hand, refers to how similar the other person's value judgements are to our own. The more similar these are, the more relevant the information is likely to be for our personal needs.

Marketers wishing to employ either of these types of social influences can benefit from a careful understanding of these source characteristics. We will return to this topic in two chapters to come (on salespersons and on advertising). The application below gives an interesting indication of the power in this area.

Life's Precious Gift

There are certain products and services in which consumers are "squeamish" and influence is particularly difficult. Blood donation is an example. Even though most people say they support the idea of donating blood, the turnouts for most blood drives are quite low, and blood banks must rely heavily on "regular" donors. Organizational drives (which involve heavy doses of normative influence) are also effective.

Recently, LaTour and Manrai conducted an interesting experience with a Chicago-area blood center to see if they could directly employ the concepts of normative and social influence to increase donations of blood during a drive. In the first of several experiments, they divided area citizens into four groups: (1) the *control group* received no special influence attempts; (2) the *information group* received a direct-mail piece explaining that blood donations help other people, and that the blood donation process is short, painless, and not likely to result in tiredness. Examples of blood needs in the area, and a picture of a child whose life was saved by blood donations were included in an enclosed brochure. The letter then requested that the person come and donate blood; (3) the *normative group* received a telephone request from another community member, and was asked personally to agree the come and donate blood; and (4) the *combined group* received first the direct mailer and then the telephone call.

The results were very interesting. The control group turned out 2 percent of its members for the blood drive (representing what was expected if no special influence attempts were made). The information group, having received the direct mailing, turned out over 4 percent of its members. The normative group responded even better to its phone requests and turned out over 7 percent of its members. However, the combined group's response was overwhelming—about 22 percent of its members poured out to fill the blood center's vessels! In accord with the predictions of the researchers, the staged application of an informative strategy followed by a normative social influence attempt was much more effective than was a single application of either approach by itself.[29]

Direct Manipulations of Social Pressure

Opportunities for strong manipulations of this strategy are rare, but they do exist. For example, the employment of typical consumers as sales agents—selling to their friends—has been quite successful. The fabled Tupperware party (at its peak, one of these parties began every 10 seconds somewhere in the world) is one instance of this technique. Let's look at what's involved here in terms of pressure on consumers:

Social Pressure: I Really Ought To. . .

A typical Tupperware party involves a relatively small group (of 10 to 20 people, usually women) invited as guests to a friend's house for a party of games and refreshments. Near the end of the party, the dealer demonstrates each of the Tupperware items and passes out order forms. While doing so, however, the dealer informs the guests that their friend, the hostess, will only win a big prize if two of the guests agree to hold future parties in their homes. Also, a strong flow of orders from the guests will be needed for their hostess to be rewarded. The social pressure and sense of obligation of each of the guests is quite strong in this environment! Over the years, millions of lettuce crispers and other household items have found their ways home with the departing customers. In recent years, with women moving increasingly to the workplace, Tupperware office parties have been designed for lunch hours: these now account for over $60 million in sales each year![30]

The personal presence of other consumers within the sales context obviously contributes much of the power to the Tupperware case. Even when other consumers are not present, however, marketers can try to *simulate their social pressures*. This approach involves an indirect manipulation of social pressure.

A tupperware party at a Dallas law office.

Indirect Manipulations of Social Pressure

Consumer conformity can be indirectly stimulated by attempting to raise anticipations of how other consumers will react if a certain product is or is not purchased. Usually, the approach is a "positive" one, stressing how purchase of a particular brand will impress others (that is, act as a status symbol) or in some way will lead to acceptance by them because of the superior—sometimes even magical—qualities of the brand. We are all familiar with the man who dabs on the aftershave and fights off the females, the man who drives home his new car and watches the neighborhood gather round in admiration, the woman who wins admiring glances as she strolls down the sidewalk in her custom-look business suit, and so forth.

The Special Case of Social Fear

Sometimes a conformity-based theme is a negative one—stressing that embarrassing social consequences lie ahead if a certain product is not used. This is termed *social fear advertising*.[31] Social fear is a theme that is used frequently in certain product categories, particularly those that involve the body's functions. To gain a general appreciation of this point, watch for television and magazine ads for such products as deodorants, feminine hygiene sprays, dandruff shampoos, and mouthwash. Notice how one of the main selling themes often involves the product's ability to protect its user from embarrassing himself or herself in the presence of others. The prime reason that these claims are so effective, of course, is that we really *do* expect that others would react the way they are portrayed in the ads and that our reputation would actually suffer. In this sense, then, the ads are realistic, even though they are playing upon areas sensitive to us. One of advertising's "classics" is built on this theme:

"Ring Around the Collar!"—An Advertising Classic

"That's a really obnoxious ad" is a description marketing professors heard for years, as their students have reacted to various television commercials. One ad campaign probably earned this description more than any other, however—the "Ring Around the Collar!" commercials for Wisk, a liquid detergent marketed by Lever Brothers.

Wisk was introduced about 30 years ago as the first liquid detergent. It initially experienced success in the intensely competitive detergent market, but by the mid-1960s its share had fallen to less than 3 percent. Lever's focus group was used to search for possible new ad themes. Within the studies, dirty shirt collars were frequently mentioned by housewives who were heavy users of detergents. Based on the focus group research, the new ad campaign was built around the schoolyard "Ring Around the Rosie" chant, an evocative symbol of other peers chanting in unison around the person in the middle.

The commercials used adult settings, of course, but relied heavily on social embarrassments as their theme. The early commercials placed the blame clearly on the housewife, who had apparently been responsible for laundering her husband's shirts. One ad showed the happy couple arriving in Hawaii, bending down to receive their honorary lei's, when the beautiful native girl shrinks back in disgust at what she discovers, and loudly points it out to everyone in the vicinity. The wife is mortified with embarrassment. However, the commercial ends with the couples reunited in bliss: the woman has obviously followed the announcer's advice and used Wisk to remove the ring.

In the late 1970s and through the 1980s, the campaign was toned down somewhat: the blame for the rings was taken off the wife's shoulders and placed more squarely on competitive brands that had not done the job they should. After 20 years of "Ring Around the Collar," Wisk was in a pitched battle with Liquid Tide for second place in the huge detergent market. As the 1990's dawned, however, Lever brothers announced that it was moving the account from the ad agency that had created this classic campaign. All of advertising watched with bated breath: Was it time for the "Ring" to finally disappear?[32]

The Special Case of Consumer Identification

Consumer identification is one of the primary processes by which social influences work. Basically, *identification* reflects a positive orientation of the consumer, who wishes to identify himself or herself with a desirable reference person or group. Consumer products can often serve as external symbols (emblems) of this association, so they are especially susceptible to the identification process. Thus an ordinary pair of basketball shoes can convert the wearer to a vicarious

An effective testimonial campaign featuring actress Lynn Redgrave.

Reebok and McDonalds each paid golfer Greg
Norman $500,000 per year to wear their logos on
televised golf tournaments.

life as "Magic" Johnson, Larry Bird, or "Air Jordan." A few lines sewn on the back
pocket of a pair of jeans—when coupled with the right advertising and right
name—can allow a tripling of the retail price compared to a similar product
without these identifying symbols. The mechanism behind this behavior on consumers' part is related to identification, in this case with glamour and chic.
Interestingly, this phenomenon seems to be worldwide—many youths in Russia
display an avid desire for Western jeans, whether or not they have design affil-
iations! In this case, the identification seems to be with freedom and another
culture rather than with the fashion figures.

Marketers are able to employ identification rather easily in their marketing
mixes, either by showing the product being used by the relevant reference group

or person or even more directly by having it endorsed by them. In advertising there are two types of endorsements: appearance-only endorsements and testimonials. **Appearance-only endorsements** are those in which a celebrity acts as a spokesperson for the brand, but does not pretend to offer any special expertise with the product. In this case, the ads are likely using the celebrity for attention getting and pleasant advertising overtones. The **testimonial** is the more powerful form of endorsement. Here the celebrity has personally used the product in his or her field of expertise and is attesting to its quality and usefulness. In 1984, Lean Cuisine was outselling Weight Watchers frozen entrees by a 3-to-1 margin. After four years of a campaign featuring actress Lynn Redgrave (who had long had weight problems), Weight Watchers was in a virtual tie for the first place position.[33] Testimonials are so effective for sports equipment, in fact, that stars are "signed" to endorsement contracts just as they are to playing contracts. The battle for visibility of sport shoes, for example, has been escalating yearly, with some makers driven into bankruptcy.

Usually, the exact value of an endorsement for a marketer is hard to calculate. Occasionally however, the value of stimulating consumer conformity behaviors through specific exposures with desirable people or settings becomes apparent, as in the following example.

Ray Bans Are Exposed, Take Off

The Bausch & Lomb company developed Ray-Ban (antiglare) sunglasses during the 1930s, with some considerable success. During the 1950s it created its "Wayfarer" model of Ray-Bans, also with considerable success. By 1981, however, the Wayfarer line was viewed as old and tired and was scheduled to be killed at the end of the year. Suddenly, however, sales began to spurt on the West Coast, and Wayfarers sold out the entire inventory in a short period of time. The company, shocked by this reversal of trend and the almost 600 percent increase in sales, checked into what had happened. It turned out that *Gentlemen's Quarterly* magazine had used the sunglasses in a feature on a male supermodel and that several other fashion magazines had then also used the line in their spreads.

Seeing the light, the firm began a deliberate strategy of "planting" the sunglasses in visible, positive settings. The next year Tom Cruise wore them in the movie *Risky Business*, and sales increased another 300 percent. During the next five years Ray-Ban models were deliberately placed in scores of television shows (e.g., *Miami Vice*) and movies, including the megahit *Top Gun*, which featured numerous close-ups of Tom Cruise and the other pilots wearing their Ray-Ban "Classic Metal" aviator glasses as they dispensed their cool into the world. Demand continued to soar, with worldwide sales of Ray-Bans at the 8 million unit level in only seven years, up from only 18,000 in 1981.

The movie appearance emphasis continues today (Ray-Bans appeared in 160 films in a recent year), but further public exposure is now also a key part of the Ray-Ban promotional program. Last year another 10,000 pairs were given away to leading rock stars, movie stars, and athletes, with the hope that they would wear them in MTV videos and during other appearances. When Billy Joel left for his tour of the Soviet Union, for example, he took 500 pairs along, courtesy of the firm. Obviously this is not a tightly controlled promotional activity, but just how valuable is this type of public exposure for the Ray-Ban line? According to one executive, "As far as we're concerned, if we give away 1000 sunglasses and 1 gets into a movie, it's worth the other 999."[34]

Reference Groups and Product Differences

Our final topic of this section concerns how products and services are likely to differ in their susceptibility to reference group influences. Marketers of some products need not concern themselves very much with this area, since consumers are not likely to respond to reference group influences when buying their products. Marketers of other products, however, would be very wise to pay careful attention to developments in this field of study, since reference group effects should be strong.

After examining a number of studies, Francis Bourne concluded that the best way to understand how reference groups impact on product choice was to examine the degree of *conspicuousness* related to ownership of the product.[35] Conspicuousness contains two significant elements. First, it reflects *visibility* to other persons. Second, it reflects some degree of *exclusivity;* if everyone already owns a product, it is less conspicuous than if only a few persons own it. Bourne then went on to study how products "fit" into different categories of conspicuousness. His assignments are now out of date, but an interesting study by William Bearden and Michael Etzel provides us with some recent results and extensions. Their framework is depicted in Figure 14-3.[36]

Combining Public-Private and Luxury-Necessity Dimensions with Product and Brand Purchase Decisions

		Product	
		Weak reference group influence (−) on product purchase	Strong reference group influence (+) on product purchase
Brand	Strong reference group influence (+) on brand selected	**Public necessities** Influence: Weak for product and strong for brand Examples: Wristwatch, automobile, man's suit	**Public luxuries** Influence: Strong for product and for brand Examples: Golf clubs, snow skis, sailboat
	Weak reference group influence (−) on brand selected	**Private necessities** Influence: Weak for product and weak for brand Examples: Mattress, floor lamp, refrigerator	**Private luxuries** Influence: Strong for product and weak for brand Examples: TV game, trash compactor, icemaker

FIGURE 14-3 **How Reference Group Influence Differs by Product**

Source: Adapted from William O. Bearden and Michael J. Etzel, "Reference Group Influence on Product and Brand Purchase Decisions," *Journal of Consumer Research,* September 1982, p. 185. Reprinted with permission.

Notice that Bearden and Etzel represent exclusivity in terms of necessity goods (at the left) versus luxury goods (at the right). Thus necessities will be owned by most consumers and will not be very conspicuous, whereas products that are luxuries will be owned by fewer consumers and will be more conspicuous. Notice also that the figure has a public-private dimension. This means that products consumed in public (at the top) are more conspicuous, whereas products consumed in private are less so.

Another important aspect of the framework is its statements about whether the social influence will be directed toward the *product class overall* or toward *particular brands or styles* within a product class. These impacts will differ depending on the cell of the table into which a product falls. For example,

- For *public luxuries,* reference groups should be strong influences on both (1) obtaining the product at all and (2) which style or brand will be obtained. Since fewer people own these, having the product itself will bring an exclusivity benefit. Also, since the product is visible, the brand or model will be noticed. Thus the potential for reference group influence is very high.

- For *private luxuries,* fewer people own these, so having the product will provide an exclusivity benefit. However, since it will not be easily seen by others, the brand or style chosen should be less influenced by reference groups.

- For *public necessities,* reference group influences will not be very strong for product class purchase, since almost everyone already believes that they need this product. Because the product is visible, however, reference group influences on the brand or style chosen will be strong.

- For *private necessities,* reference group influences are expected to be weak. These products are required by almost everyone and are not easily visible to others.

SITUATIONAL INFLUENCES ON CONSUMER BEHAVIOR

Within the final section of this chapter we'll examine the impacts of situations on consumer behavior. **Situational influences** are immediate forces that do not come from within the person, or from the product or brand being marketed. Instead, these temporary forces stem from particular settings or conditions in which consumers find themselves, usually for short periods of time. Situational influences often involve social influences but, as we'll see shortly, they *need* not involve them. (See Note 37 if you are interested in pursuing further details about the definitional question.)

Situational influences pose an interesting question for consumer research. If we focus only on consumers and the products they buy, we implicitly are assuming that situations do not influence consumer behavior. On the other hand, we know that situational influences *do* affect consumer behavior. The problem is that *all* consumer behavior might be affected by situational influences. The challenge for consumer researchers, then, is to figure out which situations are *most likely* to affect consumer behavior on a regular basis. As a marketer, your problem will be somewhat simplified, since you can focus only on those situations most likely to affect your product.

How Do Situations Affect Consumer Behavior?

As an indication of the wide range of possible situational influences, let's consider the following quotations (we'll be referring back to these as we discuss various concepts):

I have a big date coming up Saturday night with Mike, and I need to start planning now. Should I get my hair done, or can I make it with the way it is? Which outfit shall I wear? Does the pink dress need to be cleaned? What color fingernail polish should I use?

—Jennifer Holmes, student

Procter & Gamble just called and asked if I would interview with them next week. Wait 'til I call my folks! I'd better learn what's expected of me. Maybe there's a book that lays all this out. . . . I think I'll look at a new suit and maybe a good pair of dress shoes. . . .

—Steve Smith, student

Oh no! Jim, come here! . . . The refrigerator isn't working, and the freezer section is dripping all over the floor! Do you think we should call the repairman now, or just go and look for a new one? . . . No it can't wait!

—Janet Meyer, realtor

The baking business runs on a daily basis—consumers demand fresh baked goods. Demand fluctuates daily. For example, if it's raining or snowing, bread sales drop off immediately. The days of the week are important too, depending on when the food ads are published. Thursday, Friday, and Saturday are usually the big days. Many chains run special promotions for the slow days to even out demand patterns, though, so we have to stay on top of this too.

Then there are seasonal changes—people's diets change in the summer and bread sales are down generally. On really hot days, bread sales just die! . . . Holidays are big sale times, except in ethnic areas where people bake for themselves at these times. Specialty products increase a lot because of holiday parties, and sandwich bread is big after the holidays since it is used with the leftover turkey or ham.

Finally, time of the month is important. . . . The first week of the month usually has much higher sales because the welfare checks, Social Security checks, and pay-checks are all available at this time. . . . Yes, based on my experience I'd say that situational influences play a major role in my marketing planning!

—John Meehan, plant manager

These quotations provide many useful insights on situational influences. In each case, notice how consumers are adapting their behavior to their situation (this means that these can be considered *contingent behaviors,* since they depend in part on external situations). For example, consumers' *personal economic* situations, if temporary, can be considered situational influences. These can vastly restrict consumption or stimulate purchases at particular times (as John Meehan reports). Our *physical environment* (weather, season, geographic location) can also affect what we consume, and when. And *product failures* can literally force unanticipated purchases to occur, as Janet and Jim Meyer just discovered with their refrigerator! In addition, *social factors* also play strong roles with many situations. Specific situations often lead us to want to play a certain role or to make a particular kind of impression on others, and consumer purchases help our impression making. Steve Smith, for example, feels that he needs a specific appearance to do well in his interview.

Marketing Applications of Situational Influences

As consumers, we have all felt some of the pressures described in our quotes, and can easily recognize that situations affect our behaviors. Surprisingly, however, there is little formal research available on situational influences in consumer behavior. In fact, much *less* research has been done on situational influences than on person or product variables. The research that has been done, however, shows a *very significant impact* of situational influences. The following sections briefly summarize how significant four types of situations are:

- Temporary economic situations.
- Product depletion and failure.
- Usage situations.
- The special case of gift-giving.

Impacts of Temporary Economic Situations

Consumers can find themselves in **temporary economic situations** that can dramatically affect consumption. In economic terms, the presence of funds does not *cause* purchases, but the absence of funds can prevent or postpone them. Thus we say that economic situations *enable* consumer purchases to occur.[38]

In Figure 14-4, notice how consumer purchases can vary from one year to the next. The purchase variations shown did not arise because consumers or products were very different from year to year—instead they arose largely from the temporary economic situations in which millions of consumers found themselves at particular times (since this figure reports yearly data, timing of purchases within a year are not reflected here, thus understating actual situational effects). We should also note that the figure reports percentage changes in consumer purchases from one year to the next (adjusted for price changes). Consumer purchases in the durable goods, nondurables, and service categories range from $250 billion to $1 trillion per year. These markets are huge—a change of only a few percentage points in sales thus translates to several billion dollars per year!

Marketers are very interested in the actual percentage changes shown in Figure 14-4. On the left side, we can see that *nondurables* (food, household products,

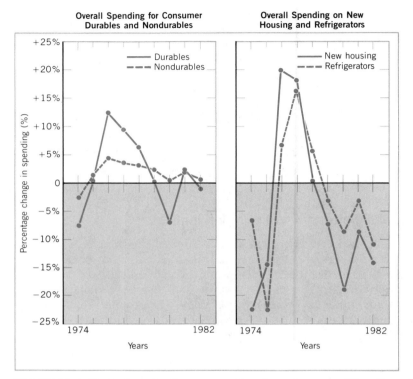

FIGURE 14-4 **Variations in Consumer Purchases, over a Nine-Year Period**

Source: National Income and Product Accounts of the United States, Government Printing Office, Washington, D.C., July 1983.)

etc.) have a general consistency in purchases—changes from one year to the next were always below 5 percent. This suggests that, as a group, nondurables are not very sensitive to economic situations, probably because many purchases are treated by consumers as necessities.

Durable goods (automobiles, houses, appliances, etc.), on the other hand, show high volatility from year to year. Within durable goods, moreover, there are certain product categories for which consumers are especially sensitive to temporary economic situations. The right side of Figure 14-4 graphs consumer purchases of both new housing and refrigerators. Notice that, not only did purchases *decline* often, but by very large amounts—down as much as 23 percent in each category. When times were good, however, consumers could and did respond, with purchase *increases* by as much as 20 percent in one year. These drastic swings in consumer behavior were caused by temporary changes in such economic situations as money available (employment, personal income), and interest charges (mortgage costs). Having now seen how strongly consumers respond to economic factors, we can better appreciate the special challenges marketing managers face in the "boom or bust" industries of consumer durable goods.

Product Depletion and Product Failures

As we've noted, a person's temporary economic situation does not *force* purchases to occur, even when it is positive. There are some situations that do precipitate (stimulate or cause) consumer purchases directly, however. Two of the prime categories of **purchase precipitators** are *product depletion* and *product failure*.

Product depletion refers to the using up of a product during consumption. Food, for example, is depleted through eating and gasoline is depleted through driving. The situational influence stemming from product depletion, then, occurs at the point in which we realize that we are "out of stock" and need to repurchase the particular item. Viewed in this manner, it is obvious that product depletion situations precipitate a *massive amount of consumer spending* in our society.

The second category—**product failure**—constitutes a special form of depletion. Product failures occur most often in durable goods and are also extremely important in stimulating consumer spending. Each failure forces a consumer to choose from among losing the product's service, making a repair purchase to restore service, or making a replacement purchase of a new or used product.

How important are product failures in precipitating consumer purchases? In one national study, Wilkie and Dickson found that 60 percent of buyers of major home appliances (refrigerators, freezers, clothes washers, and dryers) had been stimulated by a breakdown or a need for repair of the existing appliance in the home. This translates to about 10,000 new refrigerators being sold each day to U.S. consumers who are shopping directly because they have had a breakdown or repair need at home! Over a year's period, some 3.5 million units, worth $3 billion, are sold because of this situational influence. (This figure does not, moreover, include the additional money spent by consumers who choose to repair their refrigerators, nor purchases of used units.) When we recall that product breakdowns also occur for automobiles, TVs, washers, dryers, ovens, and many other products, we can see the huge importance of this situational factor in consumer behavior.[39]

The Importance of Usage Situations

In a sense, economic situations, product depletion, and product failures have relatively straightforward effects on consumer behavior. Each of these operates to precipitate, prevent, or postpone new purchases. None of them operates, however, to direct the specific *type* of purchase that might be made within a given product category.

The situational category that has drawn the most attention from the consumer behavior experts is the **usage situation**.[40] This refers to the exact purposes, settings, and conditions under which a consumer expects to be consuming the product. For example, our choice of clothing is often strongly affected by usage situations, as evidenced in the quotations from Jennifer Holmes and Stephen Smith earlier in the chapter. In general, for some usage situations, consumers see different product subtypes as being appropriate for different situations. When this effect is strong—as for beverages—we see consumers choosing orange juice for certain situations (e.g., breakfast), but not others (e.g., weddings), beer for certain situations (e.g., parties), but not others (e.g., breakfast), and so forth. One strategy for marketers, then, is to position a brand as being just right for a particular usage occasion. When Lunch Bucket microwaveable meals were introduced with taste sampling at 135 Jewel supermarkets, for example, the stores sold over 400,000 containers in two days: there was obviously a situational need in the marketplace that this new product could meet![41]

Thus consumers who are likely to be in a particular situation will be especially interested in products geared especially for that situation: the majority of Lunch Bucket meals, for example, are eaten in work centers that have microwave ovens available. Lunch Bucket's marketing strategy is an example of a more general approach advanced by Peter Dickson, who calls it **person-situation segmentation**. Dickson points out that when conditions are right, marketers can benefit from the approach in designing their marketing mixes. For example, heavy users of shotgun shells tend to have the personal characteristics of being young males from the rural South, having lower educational levels and blue-collar jobs. Situationally, of course, the shells are used in hunting. Beyond this, we can identify *related activities* in which people engage within hunting situations, such as camping, playing cards, drinking, and cooking out. These related activities can suggest both product development opportunities and advertising themes that are likely to appeal to this person-situation market segment.[42]

The Special Case of Gift-Giving

Our final situational type returns to a heavy weighting of social influences. **Gift-giving** is a special type of situation, and is a very important activity in our economy—gifts are estimated to account for about 10 percent of all retail sales. Many retailers experience one-third to one-half of their total yearly sales volume during the months of November and December alone. Given retailers' fixed costs of operations, the fourth quarter (October, November, and December) often contributes 60 percent of their profits for the entire year! These astounding figures are due primarily to heavy gift-buying during the holidays, of course.[43]

In addition to economic significance for marketers, gifts also present us with interesting insights into consumer behavior. For example, Russell Belk has noted that gifts perform four important functions.[44]

1. *Gifts serve as forms of symbolic communication.* When we give a gift, we are conveying symbolic messages as well as the physical product. Much of the time and energy we spend in searching for a gift in fact, is usually devoted to our concern with delivering the correct message. This is sometimes difficult to achieve, since we run the risk that the message we intend to send may not be properly represented by the product we choose and may be misinterpreted

by the receiver of the gift. This may be the primary reason that traditional products are used so often as gifts—they are safe to give because the people receiving them understand their messages already.

2. *Gifts help to establish and maintain social relationships.* There is a curious characteristic inherent in much of gift-giving—it helps to define a relationship between one person and another. Gifts can reflect intimacy of relationships (lingerie), respect for superiors (presents for presidents, English royalty, etc.), compassion (charitable presents), gratitude for services (tips to waiters, hairdressers, etc.), congratulations (baby showers, weddings, etc.), friendship, and so forth. Underlying much of the ritual of gift-giving, moreover, is the notion of **reciprocity**, or "I'll scratch your back if you'll scratch mine." As many astute consumers know, giving a gift can place the receiver in a position of owing the giver either a gift in return or some other future consideration.

3. *Gift-giving provides economic value.* In addition to symbolic messages and social dimensions, many gifts also satisfy functional needs of the receiver. For example, candy provides pleasant taste experiences, and flowers provide beauty.

4. *Gift-giving provides a socializing function.* This occurs primarily in the case of children. Consider, for example, how the gifts they receive (e.g., dolls, guns) might impact a child's development of his or her identity (female versus male) and how gifts are used as a means for encouraging good behavior (millions of children have believed that Santa Claus was endowed with magical powers to monitor good and bad behavior just before Christmas Day!).

Gift-giving is also interesting because the giver must often consider what the receiver already expects. Sometimes a buyer's concern about these anticipated judgments becomes more important than the gift itself, the thought behind it, or the occasion that produced it! Thus, *product cues* acquire a special significance in gift-giving. Product quality, appearance, brand name, and the store from which the gift is purchased can all be important considerations to the prospective buyer. In addition, *price* assumes special importance within a gift purchase. Consumers frequently search for the "right" price to spend rather than a "best value for the money" purchase. If the correct messages are to be sent, the gift-giver should spend an appropriate amount—neither "too much" nor "too little." Spending too little might connote, for example, that the giver does not value the person receiving the gift, or that he or she is having financial difficulties or is just cheap. Spending too much, on the other hand, could be seen as reflecting that the giver is insecure. When the gift is purchased in a reciprocal exchange situation (as during holidays), the search for appropriate price is often even more serious, since usually neither party wishes the other to feel awkward after the exchange.

Because gift-giving has been a ceremonial aspect of human existence since prehistoric times, many interesting analyses of this practice are available in a variety of fields, including anthropology, sociology, psychology, and marketing. (If you are interested in reading more about the hidden dimensions of gift-giving behavior, you may wish to refer to Note 45.)[45] Gift-giving situations also pose interesting issues for marketers of gift products. For example,

Flower Power and Wilting Demand

In recent years, the cut flower industry has faced a demand level that has remained about constant. While costs and prices have risen, the industry has also seen a decline in the number of consumers who purchase cut flowers. Although gift-giving accounts for a high proportion of flower sales, flower sales in turn account for only a small percentage of the total gift market. Thus there would seem to be a lucrative opportunity for growth in gift sales, but the decline in number of consumers seems to run counter to this point. Managers in this industry face the question, "Should we encourage the purchase of flowers for personal use (nongifts), or should we try to increase the purchase of flowers as gifts?" The answer is not obvious: recent consumer research shows that heavy buyers of flowers buy for both personal use and for gifts, while light buyers buy flowers only for gifts. Given these findings, what would you recommend? Should the industry target on heavy users, or on light users? What should it recommend that these consumers do? What kinds of appeals do you think might be successful?[46]

SUMMARY

Social Influences Begin Early

This chapter presented an overview of the broad and important topics of social and situational influences on consumer behavior. *Socialization* was defined as the process by which individuals learn to live and behave effectively in the larger society. Socialization occurs throughout our lives, but is most crucial during childhood, where the child is introduced to the world of social roles, organizations, and other social concepts. Adolescence bridges childhood and adulthood. It is a trying period because many role transitions occur at this time. During adulthood, socialization experiences continue, but differ greatly among people. Five sources of adult socialization experiences were outlined: social mobility, social change, geographic mobility, institutionalization, and progress through the life cycle. This was followed by a discussion of the impact of the key *socializing institutions:* the family, the educational system, religious institutions, mass media, work centers, and social groups.

How Does Social Influence Operate?

Our discussion of *social influence* began by making the point that we both influence others and are influenced by them. *Social interactions* provide a basis for social influence. Power, conflict, social exchange, and cooperation are elements often found in social interactions to different degrees. *Social roles* are extremely important in understanding social interactions. *Impression management* studies how an individual will manage symbols to create certain impressions in the minds of others.

   Social groups were then considered. These may be distinguished on many dimensions, such as primary versus secondary groups. The *power* that a group may have over a person can arise from different bases—legitimate, expert, reference, coercive, and reward power. Three types of *group influence processes*—compliance, identification, and internalization—were then explained. We then briefly examined the theory of *reference groups and referent others*, which act to extend social influences for beyond our daily social interactions. Our final topic in this section was *psychological reactance theory*, which helps explain why consumers often resist social influence attempts.

Consumer Word-of-Mouth Behaviors

The second section of the chapter examined consumer *word-of-mouth*. An early study of the *web of word-of-mouth* was first reviewed together with the idea of consumer referral networks. We then noted the power of consumer recommendations. Three elements behind this power are *high credibility*, a *two-way communication flow*, and the *chances for vicarious learning*. The pattern of consumer word-of-mouth is related to the concept of *social integration*, which reflects the extent to which a consumer both gives influence to others and is influenced by them. Marketers can have a difficult time dealing with consumer word-of-mouth, as we saw in our discussion of consumer folklore and rumors. We also saw, however, how marketers can try to stimulate word-of-mouth and how focus groups offer a way for marketers to tap into the contents of consumer discussions.

Consumers and Conformity

The next section of the chapter examined the broad topic of *consumer conformity*, which sometimes serves as a focal point for social critics. Here we saw that there are many factors contributing to *conforming behavior*, including economic incentives and functional reasons, in addition to social influences. We then examined two types of social influences, *normative* and *informational*. Marketing applications of these concepts include neighborhood selling parties, ads that stress how others will react in a positive manner, ads that play on social fears, and ads that stress consumer identification with famous persons through endorsements and testimonials.

We then turned our attention to the fact that some products are highly susceptible to social influences, while others are not. A key here is the *conspicuousness* of the product, which can relate to both the visibility of the product and its exclusivity. Reference group influence should be greatest when both factors are present and lowest when neither is present. When visibility is high but exclusivity is low, reference group influence should focus on the *brand* or style of the product. When exclusivity is high but visibility is low, reference group influence will pertain more to purchase of the *product* itself and less to the particular brand or style.

Situational Influences on Consumer Behavior

In our final section we turned to *situational influences*, which represent immediate forces that do not come from within the consumer, or from the product or brand being marketed. Thus this is a broad, important topic, but has not been heavily researched in consumer behavior. Our discussions here focused on four types of important situational influences: (1) *temporary economic situations*, which especially impact on durable goods sales; (2) *product depletion and product failures*, which fuel many replacement purchases; (3) *usage situations*, which offer key possibilities for segmentation strategies; and (4) *gift-giving*, which has a heavy social influence component and which accounts for 10 percent of all retail sales.

KEY TERMS

socialization

role transitions

sources of adult socialization

social mobility

anticipatory socialization

institutionalization

resocialization

adult life cycle

key socializing institutions

power

conflict

social exchange

cooperation

role

role repertoire

impression management

legitimated power

expert power

referent power

coercive power

reward power

compliance

identification

internalization

reference group

referent other

reactance

word-of-mouth

referral network

two-way flow of communication

vicarious trial

social integrateds

social independents

opinion leader

social dependents

opinion follower

social isolates

consumer folklore

focus group

conforming behavior

normative social influence

informational social influence

expertise

trustworthiness

empathy

consumer identification

appearance-only endorsement

testimonial

situational influences

product depletion

product failure

usage situation

person-situation segmentation

gift-giving

reciprocity

REVIEW QUESTIONS AND EXPERIENTIAL EXERCISES
[E = Application extension or experiential exercise]

1. Consider how adolescent and adult socialization can impact on how consumers buy, and what they buy. List three impacts you recall from your adolescence. Also discuss three impacts you currently are experiencing.

2. Discuss examples of how each of the four dominant elements of social interactions (power, conflict, social exchange, and cooperation) occur in
   a. Household consumer discussions
   b. Consumer word-of-mouth discussions
   c. Salesperson-consumer discussions in an appliance store, stereo shop, or other major purchase setting

3. Do you believe that Goffman's "impression management" view accurately reflects typical consumer behavior? Discuss three ways in which it does, and three ways in which it does not.

4. Consider the following consumer purchases. Indicate what types of social influences (i.e., normative, informational, or both) are likely to be operating and in which ways they would operate.
   a. A new automobile
   b. An air conditioner
   c. A candy bar
   d. A pair of designer jeans
   e. A vacation
   f. A pair of theater tickets
   g. A tube of toothpaste
   h. A case of beer

5. Employing the Bearden and Etzel matrix (Figure 14-3) provide two additional product examples per quadrant. Include reasons why. For those products satisfying the "visibility" dimension of conspicuousness, identify particular brands, that is, give brand names.

6. Consider how situational influences can affect the purchase of the following goods and services. In thinking about these, be sure to consider each of the four types of situations identified in the text.
   a. Life insurance
   b. Stereo systems
   c. New car
   d. Beer
   e. Perfume or cologne

7. Gift-giving offers a unique situation that is specific to consumer behavior. Explain the four functions of gift-giving, using examples from your personal experience. Finally, briefly discuss the best gift you've ever given and why.

[E] 8. Interview an official of your local blood bank concerning its sources of supply and the psychological barriers it faces in stimulating donations. Discuss topics of normative and informational social influence with the official. Write a brief report summarizing what you've learned.

[E]   9. Consider carefully the consumer behaviors of one relative and one friend. For each person, choose a product example for which he or she is in each one of the four categories of social integration. That is, for what product or service is your friend a "social independent?" For what product is he or she a "social isolate," and so forth. Finally, classify yourself for each category.

[E]   10. Analyze a number of advertisements for, (a) the use of "social fear" appeals, and (b) the use of endorsements and testimonials. Clip out two ads of each type. Write a brief report analyzing why each ad is or is not likely to be effective.

[E]   11. Using some references in Note 27 (located at the back of the book, under Chapter 14's listings) read several reports on the advantages and problems with focus group research. Write a brief report on your findings.

[E]   12. Conduct an interview with a focus group researcher and, if possible, sit in and watch a focus group study (names of researchers might well be available from a local advertising agency or market research firm). Write a brief report on your findings.

[E]   13. Conduct an interview with a manager or experienced salespersons in a clothing shop (womens', mens', or childrens') concerning the social influence topics covered in this chapter. Write a brief report on your findings.

[E]   14. Conduct an interview with a manager or experienced salesperson in a gift shop, concerning Belk's dimensions of gift-giving. Write a brief report on your findings.

[E]   15. Select a recent consumer recommendation you have received. Trace back and diagram the referral network behind this.

CHAPTER 15

Household Influences on Consumer Behavior

Did you know that . . .

. . . The number of single-person households in the United States has doubled in the last 20 years?

. . . About one in four children in the United States lives with just one parent, and one in two kids will do so at some time while growing up?

. . . Over one-fourth of today's male and female executives with children turn down job promotions or transfers because it would mean sacrificing family time?

. . . Over 90 percent of American adults marry at least once?

. . . Over 40 percent of families have three or more TVs?

. . . Women now buy more subcompact cars than do men?

. . . There is a systematic pattern of spending related to the "consumer life cycle"?

. . . There are key strategies households use to reduce conflicts over purchases?

. . . "DWM, 28, is ISO S/DWF, 22–32"?

All of this, and more, lies ahead in this chapter!

■ ■ ■

Although we've tended to emphasize either the consumer market or consumers as individuals in our discussions to this point, in reality many consumption decisions—especially the "big money" ones— are *made within a household context.* Many changes have been occurring in household structures recently—divorce and remarriage, living together or waiting longer before marriage, having fewer or no children, establishing single-parent families, and women pursuing careers are just some of these (the aggregate statistics for these changes were discussed in Chapter 3).

Within this chapter we will discuss four key topics in helping us understand household influences on consumer behavior:

1. *Household types.* The market data on household purchases are based on a strict set of definitions by the Census Bureau. It is important that we understand these to understand best the overall picture of our modern society.

2. *Consumer socialization.* The family household unit is one of the most important socializing institutions in our culture. Lessons learned here are likely to influence a person's consumer behavior for the rest of his or her life.

3. *Household decision making.* Within a household, many products and services are consumed by more than one person. The exact decisions on what to buy, therefore, are subject to intimate influences from various members. These reflect *joint decision making* which is far more complex than the decisions made personally by individuals. For marketers selling products that tend to be bought on a joint basis, therefore, an understanding of the flows of influences is essential.

4. *The consumer life cycle.* Much consumer spending is *systematic*—it stems from natural needs that change as a consumer goes through typical stages of life. Understanding these life stages adds insights about consumer markets.

 WHAT ARE HOUSEHOLDS?

Household Types

We should begin our discussion by understanding that the U.S. Census Bureau bases its household data on *residential units* rather than on love, affection, or any other dimension we might find important. According to the Census, therefore, every occupied housing unit in the nation comprises one **household.** Thus an apartment with three roommates, a single person living alone, and a large family is each one household. As we noted in Chapter 3, every American except those living with institutional quarters (prisons, dormitories, etc.) is viewed as living within one household. There are now about 95 million households, containing 98 percent of the total population.[1]

Figure 15-1 displays the relative proportion of various types of households in

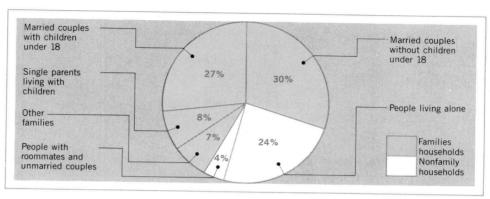

Married couples with children under 18

Single parents living with children

Other families

People with roommates and unmarried couples

27%

30%

8%

7%

4%

24%

Married couples without children under 18

People living alone

Families households

Nonfamily households

FIGURE 15-1 **Proportions of Census-defined Household Types**

our society. Notice that the three largest categories are "Married couples without children present," "Married couples with children present," and "People living alone." "Single parents with children present" and "other family units" comprise reasonably large segments, with "people with roommates and unmarried couples" constituting the smallest major grouping.

Statistically, one major division used by the Census concerns "family" and "nonfamily" households. A **family household** is defined as having at least two people—related by blood or marriage—living together. As we can see in Figure 15-1, 72 percent of all households are defined as family hosueholds.

Household Shifts and Formations

Further examination of Figure 15-1 can help us see how natural it is for people to shift from one household category to another. "People with roommates," for example, often shift to either living alone, or into a married couple unit. Similarly, "people living alone" may shift into the "roommate" category, or into a married couple state, while divorce moves people from the married couple category into one or two of the other categories (and in the process creates an extra household).

"DWM, 28, ISO S/DWF, 22–32"

As many readers recognize, these abbreviations ("divorced white male, 28, in search of single or divorced white female, between the ages of 22 and 32") reflect the mate-matching efforts found in many magazines and newspapers. While other motives are strong, to be sure, many of these ads represent new households formed through divorces, and the potential for further new households with remarriages (46 percent of marriages are remarriages for one or both partners). In either event, most Americans want to marry, and over 90 percent will at some point in their lives. However, more young Americans are putting off this step, as the average age for first marriage is now the highest in our history: Almost 24 years old for women and 25 for men.[2]

Career, Family, and the Future

National surveys have consistently documented that, while some values change, others remain the same. For example, famous pollster Lou Harris reports that 63 percent of adult women said they want to "Combine marriage, a career, and children," whereas 26 percent prefer "marrying, having children, and no career," (as a measure of continuing change, these numbers were 52 percent and 38 percent just ten years earlier). Similarly, in a poll conducted for the Conde Nast publishing group (Vogue, Glamour, Self, etc.), 82 percent of adult women said that they felt that "all women have a part of them that wants to stay home with their family," but 92 percent say a woman can have a job and still be a good mother. In an interesting split, 59 percent say marriage has always been their primary goal, whereas 21 percent opt for their career as the primary goal. Finally, in a poll of 18 to 34-year-old women, the Census Bureau asked how many children each woman expected to have. The winning numbers? Two (48 percent) and three (20 percent), 14 percent expect one child, 9 percent expect none, and 9 percent expect four or more.[3]

CONSUMER SOCIALIZATION IN THE HOUSEHOLD

Consumer socialization is defined as "the process by which young people acquire skills, knowledge and attitudes relevant to their functioning as consumers in the marketplace."[4] Several aspects of the family's role are of interest. Basically, *consumer socialization seems to occur in subtle ways*—families usually do not "teach" a child how to be a consumer. They do not prepare lectures to be memorized. Instead,

- *The parents act as models* for the child on numerous occasions. Here, the child learns through observation, usually silently, and without the parents' conscious awareness or intention to teach.
- *Parent-child discussions* also occur about consumer activities. These often involve either requests from children or explanations from parents about particular products (why they are good for you, why they are not, of what they're made, etc.). Other socializing influences such as TV ads and friends often stimulate these family discussions.
- *Child-child interactions* can also be important socializing influences within a family. These influences can be especially important for younger children as they learn from and emulate their older siblings.
- *The child begins to handle money* as he or she becomes older. Thus, through gifts and "allowances," the family provides opportunities for a child to become more experienced as a consumer.[5]

What Is Learned in Consumer Socialization?

Children live with their families for a period of about 18 years—*imagine the enormous amount of consumer learning that occurs* during this time! This learning falls into one of two basic categories:[6]

1. *Directly relevant consumer skills.* These are basic skills necessary to carry out actual consumer behaviors. The ability to count, to budget money, and to understand prices or contracts are all examples of direct consumer skills required in today's world. Families do not transmit *all* this information to their children, but do account for much of it. A child raised in a family with good consumer budgeting and buying skills is much more likely to possess those same strengths than is a child from a family having consumer skill deficiencies.

2. *Second-order consumer knowledge.* These are not direct skills in actually performing shopping functions, but are indirect skills related to the social sphere. For example, what types of clothes are appropriate for which occasions? Which stores are to be patronized and which types should be avoided. During childhood, consumers develop awareness of these social dimensions and begin to learn how to cope with them. The family starts out to be very important. As the child begins to interact more outside the home, at school, and with friends and media, the family gradually loses its significance in this area.

Intergenerational Consumer Influences

Intergenerational means "between the generations" and refers to what is passed along from parents to their children.[7] Figure 15-2 outlines the sense of this passage of influences over time, from grandparents to parents, from parents to children, and from the children to their children in the future. . . . Many forms of influences are passed along, including religious values, voting preferences, and attitudes toward education, sports, and social life. Our interest here is in the role that intergenerational influences play in forming product and brand preferences.

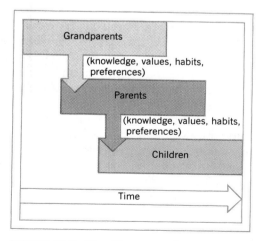

FIGURE 15-2 **The Concept of Intergenerational Carryover**

How strong are intergenerational influences? This is an interesting question that has not yet received a great deal of attention within consumer research. Its potential effects, however, are very powerful, as was found in a study in the insurance industry:

The Case of Auto Insurance
There are over 600 firms offering auto coverage in the United States, and the 20 largest firms account for only 60 percent of the market. Despite this basic fact, a study conducted by the State Farm Insurance Company found that *almost 40 percent of families held auto policies with the same company as the husband's parents did!* Statistically, it is obvious that consumer choice here is not random and that family intergenerational influences are very strong in this product class. But how long do these influences last? We would expect the effects to decline over time, since each family has more opportunities to change its buying behavior. In the State Farm study, when the 40 percent overall figure was broken out by age, it was found that almost 65 *percent of the husbands in their twenties held the same auto policy as their parents.* This number fell to 55 percent for husbands in their thirties, and on down to only 25 percent for those over 50 years old.[8]

Intergenerational influences can be extremely important to marketers, since they mean that every year a new generation of consumers goes out on their own, to continue using products they had been socialized to use while living at home. *Seventeen* magazine stresses this point strongly in selling advertising space to the marketing community. According to research commissioned by *Seventeen,* for typical cosmetic products, almost half the women ages 20 to 24 are still using the same brand they decided upon when they were teenagers. Although this percentage drops to 25 percent when the women reach the 30 to 34 age group, this is still a major advantage for the marketers capitalizing on such loyalty. (In case you're interested, the women in this study were most loyal to their original brands of mascara and mouthwash and least loyal to their first brands of bras, panty-hose, and bath soap.)[9]

Recent research suggests that intergenerational carryover effects are stronger for convenience goods than for products that involve much shopping, that they are equally strong for men and women, and that they decline with age and time away from home.[10] It is also possible that we might add some *reverse* arrows to Figure 15-2: In many families children influence some of the parents' consumer behaviors, interests, and preferences over time!

Before leaving the topic of consumer socialization, we should be clear that this process does continue into adulthood and through the rest of our lives. Figure 15-3, for example, summarizes some interesting results from a survey by *Rolling Stone* magazine.[11] "Here the "postwar generation" of younger adults (18–44) were asked what they were like as adults—and how this compared to what they thought they'd be like! We'll return to this topic in our closing section on the "Consumer Life Cycle." For now, however, let's turn to the key topic of how households make consumer decisions.

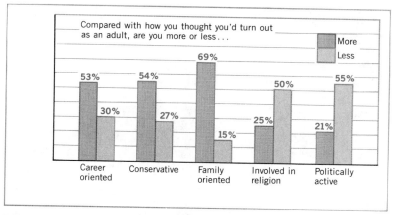

FIGURE 15-3 **Changes in the Adult Years**

Source: From "Portrait of a Generation," *Rolling Stone,* April 7 and May 5, 1988.

HOUSEHOLD DECISION MAKING

The topic of how households reach their purchase decisions is among the most important of all areas for marketers to understand in planning their strategies. At the same time, it is among the most challenging of all consumer behavior topics on which to do research. (Almost all the research in this area has been done with families, so we will focus on this form of household in this section. Many of the points made can pertain to other household types as well, however.)

The Family Purse String Study

"The woman of the house controls 80 percent of the money that's spent, so go after her hard!" This marketing adage controlled the marketing planning of many firms for years. It led to many products being developed for and advertised exclusively to housewives. It caused sales managers at men's magazines of that time (*True* and *Field and Stream* were examples) and at general interest magazines read by both men and women (*Look, Life, Time,* etc.) to tear their hair out trying to entice advertisers to aim at husbands as well as their wives.

These publications commissioned many studies aimed at understanding who was involved in family purchase decisions. Their results showed, again and again, that the actual picture of family decisions was much more complex than marketing managers of that time thought that it was. Wives did in fact make most purchases in most categories, but the involvement level of husbands and other family members often turned out to be very high as well. These magazines' message to advertisers: don't overlook either husbands or wives—advertise to them both! (More recently, *Seventeen* magazine has taken a similar approach, offering advertisers consumer research showing products for which teenage girls exert considerable purchase influence within families.)

Seventeen magazine and its competitors study the roles their prime audiences play in household purchasing.

Finally, the source of the original "80 percent finding" was tracked down. It turned out that this "marketing truth" had been based on a "study" that had counted the number of shoppers in a department store one day and had found that 80 percent were women![12]

Thus, for at least 40 years marketers have been studying the issue of how family households make their purchasing decisions. How many members are involved in each decision? How are they involved? What is the best way to reach each of them? Despite all the research efforts over the years, the topic of household decision making remains elusive—there are real challenges facing the person who tries to master this area.

Six Challenges to Consumer Research

One of the most puzzling aspects of the topic of household decision making is that, although it is clearly important, and although most of us easily relate to the issues that are involved here, this remains one of the most formidible research areas in the entire field of consumer research! Why is this the case? Let's think about the following characteristics of families, the most common form of households:

1. *Families make and spend money continuously*, day after day, for many years. The sheer number of decisions is so large that it is almost impossible to measure them all or to generalize about them accurately.

2. *Family decisions are made within a private, intimate, social group.* They are therefore not easy to observe, and may depend upon past personal histories within the family of which the researcher is unaware.

3. *Family consumption decisions are often not independent from one another—* thus they are difficult to study in isolation. In most families, limited income is exceeded by members' needs and desires for purchases. Allocation of resources is thus necessary, and trade-offs among alternative products and services occur. College for Sue, for example, might compete with a new Pontiac for the family, or with that long-awaited trip to Europe for the parents' twenty-fifth anniversary. The possible combinations are enormous, and they continue to be handled by families on a continuing basis over the years.

4. *Families have multiple decision makers.* Decisions range from individual choices made by members within the home, to truly joint decisions that may involve any combination of members. The husband and wife might be deciding about a bed, for example, while the wife and daughter are thinking about a dress, and so on. Capturing what actually goes on when multiple decision makers are involved, of course, adds a special research challenge to this area of study.

5. *Family decision making differs by the type of product or service being studied.* Most marketers are interested in family decision processes for "their" particular product or service. Unfortunately, what is true for one marketer may not be true for another. Family decisions on a new TV receiver would likely differ

from those for which restaurant to use for a special celebration or which toothpaste to pick up. Specific studies thus need to be done for each type of product.

6. *Families differ significantly from each other.* In addition to individual personalities, families differ in wealth, age, social standing, life-styles, goods already owned, and so forth. In addition, decision styles vary: some families are patriarchies, in which the father exercises influence over major consumer decisions. Other families are matriarchies, in which the mother rules supreme. Still others are more egalitarian: here the power is more equally shared, with the children perhaps weighing in with considerable influence of their own.

Overall, then, it is difficult to generalize about how families make decisions. This does not mean, however, that the topic should be overlooked. The marketing community, then, must strive to understand as much as possible about this area.

Household Roles and Buying Behavior

Much of the consumer behavior exhibited by families and many group households results from a well-developed **role structure**. For example, two basic functions needed by all families are instrumental leadership and expressive leadership.[13] **Instrumental behaviors** are aimed at successfully completing the basic tasks of the group, whereas **expressive behaviors** stress instead family affection, pleasure, and lower levels of tension. Families also require **external leadership** and **internal leadership**. In traditional families, the father played most of the instrumental and external roles, while the mother performed most of the internal, expressive roles.

These distinctions can easily be recognized in the marketplace. For example, men have traditionally been important consumers for automobiles, repair services, tools, and mechanical products. Women, on the other hand, have constituted the dominant market segment for expressive and nurturance products. This has been true even for products worn exclusively by husbands, such as men's colognes (women buy 70 percent of this product category)[14] and men's underwear and shirts. In recent years, of course, these distinctions have become more cloudy as both men's and women's roles have shifted toward external careers in the workplace and as households have shifted in their makeup. Even so, role structure theory requires that someone in the household adopt each role or that several persons share these responsibilities.

Consumer Roles Within the Household

There are multiple roles enacted within a household's buying process. Depending on the product and situation, some roles will be more important than others. Also, it is possible for the same person to play all the roles (in which case, it is really an individual decision within a household context) or for many members to be involved at various stages. Seven of the most important buying roles are

- *Stimulator.* This person first brings up the idea of the purchase.
- *Influentials.* These are the members whose opinions have either direct or indirect influences on the final purchase decision.
- *Experts.* These members contribute information about the product, the options possible, where it can be bought, and so on. Often, this person or persons will shop around, talk to friends or consult *Consumer Reports* to obtain the information that will be passed on to other members.
- *Decision maker.* In a joint decision, several persons will perform in this role, which decides exactly what to buy (or not buy). In other purchases only one of the members will actually make the final decision, often while in the store.
- *Buyer.* This person actually purchases the product, pays for it, and either takes it home or arranges for delivery. At times, this person is acting as a purchasing agent for another member, as when a roommate wants a particular cereal or the father needs a pack of razor blades. At other times, of course, the buyer is the decision maker.
- *Consumer.* This is the person or persons who actually use the product or service. Since many products are jointly consumed within the household setting, the set of persons likely to consume is a good indicator of who may be involved in the other roles as well.
- *Caretaker.* This is the person or persons who undertake various tasks to store the product, prepare it for use, and maintain it in operating condition.

These roles can be enacted either openly or through nonverbal means. Several lend themselves to a **gatekeeper** activity. This means that a person can decide either to "let in" certain information or products if he or she is in control of the "gate" through which it would enter. A father, for example, could decide not to act as a stimulator and not mention a party dress he saw on sale at the department store. Or he might ask Aunt Carolyn to bring up the subject of a vacation when she comes for dinner. Similarly, a mother acting as an expert for furniture might easily decide not to mention that the Scandinavian Shop is having a sale if she's already decided that she'd like to buy a colonial style for the living room.

Because many households are so close, moreover, members can play roles even when they are not aware of the fact. Marketers' private studies of women food shoppers, for example, have shown that traditional homemakers are very sensitive to each family member's preferences. Women from small families, for example, tend to think about each member's food preferences while shopping at a supermarket. They try to give everyone (except themselves!) a turn at having their favorite foods at mealtimes, and this goal is extremely important in their shopping decisions. They are also willing to allow any family member to veto foods they dislike, especially the fathers at dinner (in general, then, once the spouses are aware of the mate's preferences, the mates can often indirectly influence the family's consumption). Related to this stream of in-store thinking the wives preferred to go shopping alone: their children, on the other hand, liked to go along and use the opportunity to act as purchase stimulators and influencers![15]

The general role structure just presented pertains to all households. Differences between households occur in terms of how much attention is given to various roles and who actually performs them. For example, recent social changes in women's roles, dual-earner families, one-parent families, "latch-key" children (children whose parents are at work when they arrive home from school, so that they have to carry their own keys to gain admission into the home), house husbands, and so on have all had dramatic effects on exactly who performs each of the roles.[16] In general, children, teens, and husbands have become more active as buyers and consumers.

Purchase Influences and Role Specialization

Most household research in marketing has focused on an overall measure of purchase influence and has usually restricted attention to the husband and wife part of a family. Within this framework, surveys of family purchase influence have been completed and have often classified purchases as being *husband dominant, wife dominant,* or *joint.* When either partner is dominant for a particular product, that product decision is said to be attributed to **role specialization**.[17]

As we would expect, family members tend to specialize in products for which

TABLE 15-1 MARITAL ROLES IN SEVERAL PRODUCT DECISIONS

	Laundry (Washer)			*Carpeting*			*Television*		
	Husband	*H/W*	*Wife*	*Husband*	*H/W*	*Wife*	*Husband*	*H/W*	*Wife*
Brought up idea	10%	20%	70%	10%	30%	60%	55%	30%	15%
Decided on style or type	20	30	50	5	40	55	45	45	15[b]
Decided on size	20	30	50	15	45	40	45	45	15[b]
Decided on brand	20	40	40	15	45	40	45	45	10[b]
Decided how much to pay	30	45	25	20	55	25	45	45	10[b]
Visited stores or showroom	15	65	20	5	65	30	30	60	10
Decided on specific store	30	45	25	15	55	30	45	45	10[b]
Actually made purchase	40	40	20	20	50	30	50	40	10
Average	23	41	36	13	49	38	45	44	11[b]

Source: Arch Woodside and William Motes, "Husband and Wife Perceptions of Marital Roles in Consumer Decision Processes for Six Products," in N. Beckwith et al. (eds.), *1979 Educators' Conference Proceedings* (Chicago: American Marketing Association, 1979).

[a]To be read: "In the instance of a clothes washer, when asked who brought up the idea of purchasing, 10% of families responded that it was primarily the husband, 20% that the husband and wife had approximately equal influence, and 70% that the wife primarily brought up the idea."

[b]In the case of television sets: These items received somewhat different response patterns from husbands than from wives. Numbers here represent approximations.

they have particular interest. Also, however, the influence of various members differs depending on the stage of the decision-making process.

Roles on the Stage

In one representative study, Woodside and Motes asked 200 couples to describe their purchase processes for three different products.[18] The results, summarized in Table 15-1, allow us to reach several general conclusions:

- *Product differences* are evident, with the wife's influence stronger for carpeting and clothes washers, while the husband's influence is stronger for television sets.

- For each of these products, however, the "average" score (listed in the bottom row) is highest for joint decisions in which the husband and wife bring approximately equal influence. Thus *joint decision making* is common even for products that appear to be sex-role defined.

- For each of the products, and for every subdecision listed, there is at least one substantial subgroup of families reporting a different influence pattern from the norm. This indicates that *market segmentation* is likely to exist in many situations.

- Finally, note that an *interesting pattern* emerges as the decision moves from initial consideration stages toward final purchasing. In general, one or the other spouse will tend to dominate the early stages, then the process will shift toward joint decision making.

What Happens in Joint Decision Making?

Among his significant contributions to the literature on household decisions, Harry Davis has discussed the two basic conditions that a household can face when making a syncratic (joint) decision—either everyone agrees about the *goals* (desired outcomes) of the decision, or they do not.[19] This leads to two types of joint decisons: consensual and accommodative. For example, if everyone feels that "getting away and relaxing" would be fine use of vacation time, the family would be undertaking a **consensual decision**: the goals are agreed upon, but the exact destination still remains to be decided. If, on the other hand, Suzanne wants an exciting visit to a large city, Bob wants to relax, Mark wants to surf, and Donna wants to stay home to be near her new boyfriend, this family is headed for an **accommodative decision** in which *conflict resolution* has to occur: the goal differences have to be resolved in some manner. How, then, do these decisions actually occur? Table 15-2 outlines the major strategies.

Decision Strategies Under Consensus

When household members agree about goals, the burden on the decision is considerably lightened. As shown in Table 15-2, several useful strategies are available. Within a given area of decisions, such as food shopping, a **role structure strategy** is feasible: here one member can simply assume the role of a *specialist* and handle most decisions on a routine basis. Alternatively, budgets, or a **rule strategy** can be set up by members, and someone can act as a *controller*

Joint decision making characterizes important household purchases.

to see that the rules are followed. For example, a child can be told, "We only buy
one bag of candy per week in this home." Notice that the rule can be applied on
an impersonal basis, thus avoiding hard feelings directed at any one person.

In other cases, a **problem-solving strategy** can also be used for particular
decisions. Many tactics are possible here. For example, *experts* can be relied on
for good advice, or family discussions can be held to discover a *better solution.*
Also, *multiple product purchases* sometimes solve particular issues—second cars,
several TV sets, and additions to the house are all common means of lessening
tensions and better achieving goals that all members agree are good ones.

Decision Strategies Under Accommodation (Conflict)

When household members *disagree* about goals, decisions are much more difficult
to reach without bringing out the inherent conflict in the situation. The two basic
ways to deal with accommodation situations are a *persuasion strategy* and a
bargaining strategy. The basic distinction between these two related processes is
that, under persuasion, a member is led to make a decision that he'd rather not
make, while bargaining tries to create conditions under which the member will
want to make the decision.

TABLE 15-2 ALTERNATIVE DECISION-MAKING STRATEGIES

Goals	Strategy	Ways of Implementing
Consensus (family members agree about goals)	Role structure Budgets Problem solving	The specialist The controller The expert The better solution The multiple purchase
Accommodation (family members disagree about goals)	Persuasion	The irresponsible critic Feminine intuition Shopping together Coercion Coalitions
	Bargaining	The next purchase The impulse purchase The procrastinator

Source: Harry L. Davis, "Decision Making Within the Household," in R. Ferber (ed.), *Selected Aspects of Consumer Behavior* (Washington, D.C.: U.S. Government Printing Office, 1977), p. 89.

- **Persuasive strategies.** Since there is conflict inherent in these situations, strategies range from openly recognizing the conflict, to trying to minimize and avert it. The *irresponsible critic,* for example, already knows that he or she will not be making the final decision (and perhaps doesn't even want to) and so feels free to "snipe" at the person(s) who will be responsible for it. If the decision turns out well, the critic will benefit along with everyone else; if not, he or she can always say, "I told you so. . . ." *Feminine intuition,* on the other hand, reflects an ability to sense exactly when other members are susceptible to being persuaded and employs well-designed persuasion only at those times. This strategy, of course, is in no way limited to women: some men have developed this to a high art form, as have many children!

  Shopping together is done in the hope that additional influences from a salesperson and/or actual experience with the product itself can sway the reluctant member into a positive purchase decision. *Coercion,* on the other hand, is the use of power or authority simply to announce that a decision will be made (this is not "persuasion" in the normal sense of the term!). Finally, *coalitions* are often formed when some members agree on the decision and put pressure on other members by banding together to present their viewpoint.

- **Bargaining strategies**. These involve more "give and take" within the household than do the persuasion strategies. A *next purchase* strategy allows one member to have his or her way in a decision, with the understanding that another member will have the choice next time. An *impulse purchase* strategy isn't as friendly—it involves one member racing out to buy the product. A husband, for example, might buy a new remote-control wall system with the hope that his wife will be less likely to argue that he should take it back. Finally, *procrastination* represents delaying a purchase in the hope that either something better will come along that everyone favors, or that some members will change their minds. Given, in our society, that many purchases represent desires rather than immediate needs, this strategy is frequently employed as a means of reducing conflict.

Consumer Research Findings

In general, research has found that underlying decision conflict is common but that most households work hard to minimize its appearance and effects. This is a natural outgrowth of the family's strong thrust toward intimacy and maintenance of pleasant relations.

How Partners Handle Disagreements

When Spiro asked a sample of husband-wife pairs about a recent household durable purchase decision, 88 percent of the couples reported that they had encountered disagreements and had had to undertake accommodative strategies. The husbands and wives completed separate questionnaires. Among the questions asked were items involving the "strategies" that each partner used on the other when the disagreement occurred. Results were interesting. Most of the sample reported only low or moderate attempts to influence their partners. Those who reported high use of influence attempts, moreover, seemed to try "every trick in the book" rather than rely on only one or two techniques. When the partners were asked about what their spouses had tried on them, their answers did not come close to matching what their spouses reported they were trying![20]

To learn more about the types of strategies used, Nelson surveyed 284 households (only one consumer per household responded in this study) about a recent purchase conflict. Four general types of strategies emerged:

1. *Use of negative emotion, punishments, and so on.* (e.g., "I refused to do something expected of me, e.g., chores").
2. *Use of positive emotion and subtle manipulation* (e.g., "I was especially pleasant, helpful, or charming before bringing up the subject").
3. *Use of withdrawal and egocentrism* (e.g., "I clammed up and refused to discuss the issue").
4. *Use of persuasion and reason* (e.g., "I tried to convince or persuade the other person that my way was best").

If you are interested in moving further into this research area, you may wish to begin with the readings in Note 21.

The "Muddling Through" Study

Another interesting study was recently reported by C. W. Park, who analyzed how couples went about buying a house. He found that avoiding conflicts was an extremely important part of the overall process. In fact, rather than a highly rational, well-planned procedure (called *synoptic decision making*), Park found a process he described as *muddling through*.

House buying is often a "muddling-through" process.

Here, each spouse is not quite sure of his or her own preferences in a house (since it is such a complex decision). Beyond this, they have little or no idea of what their partner prefers until they are actually going through the process. Park describes the resulting experience as "groping" while striving to avoid conflict. In his terms, the family "believes that it 'makes' a decision jointly, when in fact it 'reaches' a decision through a disjointed, unstructured, . . . strategy."

How did couples avoid conflict? First, for objective house characteristics (price, number of bedrooms, etc.), the partners tried to find out which ones they agreed upon early in the process, and these were set as goals. Second, for characteristics in which one partner had expertise (kitchen, plumbing, etc.), he or she was assigned the major decision responsibility. Third, when differences arose on other characteristics, the spouse who felt less strongly about that characteristic made a concession to the other about it ("Well, I don't really care for the idea of a fenced yard, but if you really want it. . . .")

In terms of the partners' decision plans themselves, both the husband and wife thought they had approached the decision in a similar way, when in fact their approaches had been quite different! As was found in Spiro's study, the family members were not very successful in identifying relative influence by their spouse, nor did they seem to know about the other's actual decision strategy. To improve performance in the actual decision, therefore, Park recommends that spouses sit down beforehand, have each lay out his and her plan for making the decision, and then discuss them together.[22]

Thus we have seen two important lessons in the consumer research conducted in this area: families encounter *considerable conflict* in their joint decisions, and the partners seem to have *much less insight* into their mates' goals and strategies than they think they have. In another study, over 200 married couples were asked to respond to a number of concepts for new products and services. The results were only slightly greater than if husbands and wives had been randomly thrown together! Not only did their reactions to the concepts not match very well, but they again showed very little ability to predict how their spouse was reacting to the same concept.[23] These kinds of results present a major challenge to consumer research in the future, particularly the most efficient types of studies in which one of the members of a household is surveyed, and provides answers for the household as a whole. Given its importance, this is one research field that bears watching for the future.

THE CONSUMER LIFE CYCLE

The passage of time has interesting effects on our lives as consumers. Some of these effects come simply from *age*—as we grow older, our activities and preferences change and evolve. Some of the effects come from *income*—as we grow older, our incomes tend to rise until retirement, when they fall again. Some of the effect also comes from *stock of goods*—once we own durable goods, we are not in the market again until it is time for replacements. A major portion of the effects, however, comes from *changes in our social circumstances*—with whom we spend our free time, what responsibilities we have to others, and so forth. Within the area of social circumstances, the *family situation* is often the strongest factor affecting consumer behavior. For this reason the early work on this topic was termed the "family life cycle." With the recent changes in households and life-styles, however, it is now appropriate to think of this as a more general "consumer life cycle."

The concept of **consumer life cycle (CLC)** represents a belief that there is a systematic basis for much of consumer behavior. The earliest work on life cycles occurred in the field of sociology, with emphasis on such issues as life stages of poverty, and the impact of children on a nuclear family. Within consumer behavior, interest in the CLC concept began when economists began carefully to analyze the patterns of income and expenditures by age groups.[24] Then, in 1966, a very influential paper was published by Wells and Gubar. Based on some new analyses of consumer spending data, the authors proposed an eight-stage framework for a consumer-oriented family life cycle. The following section outlines some of the major characteristics of each of their stages.[25]

The Stages of the Consumer Life Cycle

The Young Single Stage

About 10 percent of the adult population falls into the **young single stage**, which consists of single people under the age of 35. Although their incomes are relatively lower since they are starting out in their careers, young singles have fewer financial burdens than do most other adults, and thus have considerable discretionary funds to spend on consumption. On average, this group spends less money on products that might restrict their mobility and more money on cars, convenience products, entertainment, and other "mating game" products and services.

The Newly Married Stage

People in the **newly married stage** are young and married but do not yet have children in the family. In total, this group is small, accounting for only 3 percent of the U.S. population. However, marriage requires substantial adjustments, and there is an *incredible burst of spending activity*. In a recent year, for example, about 2 percent of the U.S. population got married for the first time: this group, however, accounted for a total of 13 percent of all service and retail sales! In one recent year, they spent over $6 billion on home furnishings.[26] In terms of their importance in specific product categories, another study showed that consumers in the act of forming families (three months before and after the wedding) accounted for

- 58 percent of all sterling flatware sales.
- 41 percent of stereo sales.
- 25 percent of bedroom furniture sales.[27]

Newlyweds represent 2 percent of the population, but 13 percent of all retail and service sales.

During this time, both partners are likely to keep working, so that the overall financial situation of the family is quite good. Many of the purchases made during this time are symbolic, as the couple attempts to shift into a new family situation. Housing and its adornments can be important as are leisure activities and vacations that the couple can take together.

The Full Nest I Stage

When children arrive, the couple moves to the **full nest I stage**, which is characterized by having the youngest child under 6 years of age. This stage has a much larger number of consumers in it, accounting for about 25 percent of the population. Beyond the thrill of parenthood and the internal bonding within the home, powerful new pressures arise on the family. Increased expenses put a squeeze on the incomes of many families. (For example, a recent study estimates it costs over $30,000 to raise a child to age 5!)[28] Also, young mothers lose much of their former freedom, and the husband-wife pair loses some of its former social companionship. With respect to consumption, this stage has the highest level of debt associated with it, as housing, appliances, and insurance are purchased at high rates. In addition, the baby brings with it a host of required purchases, ranging from medical expenses through toys, cribs, and baby foods.

The Full Nest II Stage

In the **full nest II stage**, the house still has children, but the youngest is now over 6 years old. As a group, this stage accounts for about 13 percent of the population. The family's financial position is better, since the spouses' careers are improving with more experience and some of the wives have returned to their careers as the children are in school. Within the consumption area, these families begin buying larger-sized packages and multiple-unit deals. The children are heavy influences in certain categories, such as bicycles, pianos, dental care, music lessons, and baseball equipment.

The Full Nest III Stage

The **full nest III stage** is characterized by children still at home, but in their midteen years. This group accounts for about 15 percent of the population. Here, the family's financial position is continuing to improve, with the children beginning to earn money outside the home as well. These families have higher purchase rates for durables, due to a combination of necessary replacement purchases, multiple purchases for spouse and teen use (cars, stereos, etc.), and higher discretionary income.

The Empty Nest I Stage

In the **empty nest I stage** the children have left the home and are not usually dependent on the parents for support anymore. The parents are still working, with career earnings at a high level, however. This group accounts for only 6 percent of the population, but it is a very lucrative consumer market because of the combination of higher income and lower expenses for required purchases. As a result, this group engages in travel and recreation, gifts, and luxuries.

The Empty Nest II Stage

In the **empty nest II stage**, the couple has retired from active participation in the labor force and experiences a sharp drop in income. This group accounts for about 5 percent of the population. It is a strong market for such types of goods as medical products and services. Many consumers in this stage will also move from their former homes to a smaller home, perhaps in a retirement community.

The Solitary Survivor Stage

On a proportional basis, the **solitary survivor group** is the smallest, accounting for only about 2 percent of the population. These persons are likely have even lower incomes and increasing medical needs. In addition, they have special needs for attention, affection, and security.

Issues and Uses of the CLC Concept

Current Issues with the CLC

Most researchers agree that there is a large systematic component to consumer behavior and that the CLC is a useful concept for capturing this. At the same time, however, researchers disagree as to exactly how the CLC should best be defined. The eight-stage framework is probably still the most commonly used in marketing.

At the same time, however, the dramatic social changes of recent years suggest that some improvements may be needed in that framework. This framework was developed before most of these changes had occurred and may need some alteration to reflect current spending patterns. For example, note that the proportions of the population given for each of the stages do not total 100 percent. This is because some people simply cannot be classified in the current CLC framework. This has always been true, of course, but in recent years the proportion has been increasing, due to

- *Fewer children per family.* Couples have been waiting longer to have their first child and have been having fewer children. In total, then, this means that the newly married stage is stretched longer than in the past and that the full nest I stage is shorter. Also, more families are choosing not to have children at all; and there is no stage to handle these persons once they pass the age of 35.
- *Divorce.* The divorce rate has risen sharply but there is no provision in the current framework for single parents with children. Since these families often have lower incomes due to only a single paycheck, we would expect their consumption behaviors to differ in some important respects.

■ *Unmarrieds.* More people are choosing to remain single for longer periods of time. This group includes both persons who have never married and persons who have divorced, but are without children. The current CLC handles these persons well while they are young but makes no provision for them once they reach middle age.

The result of these changes has been a movement toward modifying the current structure. Patrick Murphy and William Staples, for example, have proposed a "modernized family life cycle" that adds stages to account for divorce and the absence of children in a marriage: their framework contains 13 stages and is able to assign 6 percent more of the population than our basic framework.[29] Another recent proposal, by Mary Gilly and Ben Enis, removes marriage as a requirement for assignment to life-cycle stages, in recognition of increasing proportions of children born out of wedlock and couples living together without marriage. Their framework is able to assign all but 3 percent of the U.S. population.[30]

Which framework is the best? This is a considerably more complex issue than it first sounds. First, the exact purpose for which we're using the CLC needs to be taken into account. Assigning larger proportions of the population is one indicator, to be sure, but we must also be concerned with the ability of the categories to distinguish meaningfully among the consumption behaviors of American consumers. These obviously differ for different products and services: it is possible, therefore, that different CLC schemes might perform better in different categories. In a recent test of clothing expenditures, for example, Wagner and Hanna found that the Wells-Gubar and Murphy-Staples frameworks performed at about comparable levels. They also discovered that income effects were quite significant across all stages (that is, as we'd expect, consumers who have more money are likely to spend more money on clothing, regardless of the CLC stage) and that the CLC's effects, while significant, were smaller.[31] Whether this finding holds across other measures for other consumer goods categories remains to be seen, however.

Marketing Applications of the CLC

Since government statistics are easily available for each of the measures used in defining CLC stages, marketers can use this concept to estimate segment sizes and forecast demand. In addition, the consumer media—magazines, newspapers, TV, and radio—usually make these data easily available to marketers as a promotional tool to sell more advertising space or time. Finally, marketers have available to them syndicated research services that measure exactly which products are purchased by which types of consumers. These figures can be translated into CLC terms and bridged—usually through computerized analysis—into media buying schedules.

Beyond the area of advertising scheduling, the CLC has applications in all portions of marketing mix development. Often, for example, it is combined with studies of family decision making to understand better particular aspects of a consumer category. For example, several studies have found that joint decision making *decreases* as families move through the life cycle. That is, young married couples tend to engage in high levels of joint decision making, but as time goes on one or the other begins to take over particular decision areas—an instance of increasing role specialization.[32] Research in specific product areas, then, can yield useful marketing strategies. For example, one study found that a mother yields to a child's cereal request almost 90 percent of the time, but for snack foods and clothing, whether or not the mother yields depends on the child's age (clothing agreements go from 20 percent when children are ages 5 to 7, to almost 60 percent when they are 11 to 12 years old).[33] Kelloggs, General Mills, and other makers of cereals, then, can confidently direct much of their promotion for kids' cereals directly to the children themselves. Sears, on the other hand, would need to take life cycle stages into account and direct promotion at both mothers and children.

SUMMARY

What are Households?

This chapter began with an examination of the nature of *households*. We saw that this is actually a technical term of the Census Bureau, and refers to residential units. We noted that there are now about 95 million households in the United States, about 70 million of which are *families*. We also saw how typical it is for people to shift types of households, and how new households are formed through both divorce and marriage.

Consumer Socialization in the Household

Consumer socialization refers to the process by which we "learn" to become consumers, from the time we are young children. This occurs in subtle ways, being affected by parental models and discussions between family members. Children learn *directly relevant consumer skills* like budgeting and buying, but also *second-order skills* that involve an awareness of the social dimensions of consumption. Researchers are beginning to examine how product and brand preferences are transmitted from one generation to the next. We saw, for example, how auto insurance coverage shows marked brand preferences within families.

Household Decision Making

The area of *decision making* is very important, but it poses strong challenges for consumer researchers. Within a household, there are different roles that have to be filled by members. These include consumer roles, in which specialization can occur by product as well as stage of decision making. The chapter discussed different modes of decision making. At times family members agree in their goals and can use *decision strategies of the consensus type*. At other times the goals differ, and *strategies of accommodation* are called for to reach decisions. Consumer research for very important decisions (such as houses) has shown that most couples seem to muddle through to reach their decisions. They work hard to avoid conflicts but they do not seem to know very much about what their partners really desire in the purchase. As pointed out in the chapter, this poses a serious barrier to efficient consumer research studies.

The Consumer Life Cycle

In the last section of the chapter we turned to the topic of the *consumer life cycle (CLC)*. This concept has been of interest within consumer behavior for many years, since it represents a series of typical stages of life that a person will experience. As these stages change, so do the demands for certain types of goods and services, and the income available to buy them. We examined a *CLC framework* consisting of eight stages: (1) *young single*, (2) *newly married*, (3) *full nest I*, (4) *full nest II*, (5) *full nest III*, (6) *empty nest I*, (7) *empty nest II*, and (8) *solitary survivor*. Recently shifts in family structure and life-styles have raised the issue of whether this framework is still sufficient in today's marketplace. We reviewed some of the evidence on this issue, which is still a question. In the final section we saw how the CLC concept is employed by marketers.

KEY TERMS

household	purchase influence	shopping together
family household	role specialization	coercion
consumer socialization	consensual decision	coalitions
role structure	accommodative decision	the next purchase
instrumental behaviors	role structure strategy	the impulse purchase
expressive behaviors	rule strategy	the procrastinator
external leadership	problem-solving strategy	consumer life cycle (CLC)
internal leadership	persuasive strategies	young single stage
stimulator	bargaining strategies	newly married stage
influentials	the specialist	full nest I stage
experts	the controller	full nest II stage
decision maker	the expert	full nest III stage
buyer	the better solution	empty nest I stage
consumer	the multiple purchase	empty nest II stage
caretaker	the irresponsible critic	solitary survivor group
gatekeeper	feminine intuition	

REVIEW QUESTIONS AND EXPERIENTIAL EXERCISES

[E = Application extension or experiential exercise]

1. Despite major shifts in sex roles and life-styles in recent years, polls concluded that these changes have not had a major impact on women's desires to be part of a family. How would you account for these seemingly inconsistent phenomena?

2. Consider the four primary ways in which family influences are transmitted. What is the relative impact of each on the consumer socialization process?

3. The text lists six challenges to consumer researchers who are trying to understand consumption decisions in households. Relate these characteristics to reference group influences on consumer behavior (Chapter 14). Are these challenges limited to the family influence, or can some/all apply to reference groups as well? Comment.

4. Consider the family buying process for the following goods or services. Indicate, providing rationale, who "normally" would play the most important buying roles:
   a. A summer vacation
   b. Breakfast foods
   c. A wedding present
   d. An automobile

5. Describe the primary distinctions among the three decision strategies in which consensus exists as to the goals (role structure, budgets, and problem solving). Provide an example of each of the five ways of implementing these strategies as you've experienced them in your own family.

6. Describe the primary distinctions between the two decision strategies that have accommodation as the goal (persuasion and bargaining). Provide an example of each of the eight ways of implementing these strategies as you've experienced them in your own family.

7. Describe the consumer behavior-related effects of age, marriage, and the presence of children as one goes through life.

[E] 8. Marketers of what kinds of goods or services would be most uncomfortable with the traditional eight-stage FLC framework? Why?

[E] 9. Identify two products whose marketing strategy would be heavily influenced by the FLC. Identify two products whose marketing strategy might be almost independent of any stage in the FLC.

[E] 10. Interview a person with experience in selling to couples or families making joint decisions (e.g., a salesperson in real estate, appliances, automobiles). Focus on the pertinent issues as raised in the text, such as conflict, disagreement as to goals, use of influence strategies, insights into the partner's preferences, the role that children play, and so on. Write a brief report summarizing your findings.

[E] 11. Reflect on the question "How has my family influenced my consumer behavior?" Write a brief report summarizing your thoughts on this, providing specific examples.

[E] 12. Using the reference sources in your library, locate discussions of how marketers are using data on households and families for marketing mix decisions. Write a brief report summarizing your findings.

[E] 13. Using either reference sources or the Notes for Chapter 15 at the back of this book, read more about the consumer life cycle (family life cycle). Write a brief report on your findings.

C H A P T E R 16

Salespersons' Influences on Consumer Behavior

**A Candid Interview with an Appliance Salesperson**

Q. Can you recall any particular advice or "rules" that your sales manager would stress during your early time as a salesman?

A.   He tried hard to teach me how to sell in that setting and gave me a lot of "advice." My first few weeks, I tried to sell the product on benefits alone. I spent hours and hours reading the brochures from the manufacturers and really stressed the product benefits when I talked to a customer. People walked out on me, however; I wasn't doing well. If they did buy, they tended to buy the low-margin items that I wasn't supposed to sell . . . when you get paid on the quantity you sell, and the margin you sell it at, the old sayings about the "customer always being right" and "fitting product benefits to customer wants" soon go by the wayside. So I started to listen to my boss and brought his "laws" into my sales presentations. As a result, sales doubled over what they were at the start.

Q. What were some of his laws?

A.   He had a bunch of them . . . the one I'll never forget, though, was about "Be-Backs." . . . (Interview continues in Exhibit 16-2.)

■ ■ ■

"What was your most useful source of information for a major purchase recently?" A national sample of consumers answered: "My salesperson," by a 3-to-1 margin over the next closest source, friends and relatives![1]

In this chapter we focus on another important source of influence on consumers—the role and impacts of the salesperson. Although not all aspects of consumer behavior are affected by salespersons (vending machines and self-service stores, for example), many types of purchases—especially the major ones—are conducted through sales representatives. In total, there are over 11 million consumer salespersons in the United States, with another 9 million salespersons in the industrial marketing area.

How important are salespersons? The quotation gives some indication of how consumers rate salespersons' significance when product purchase stakes are high. Marketers also rate this function as extremely important, especially in industrial marketing, where businesses deal with businesses. One study, for example, found that executives of industrial firms rated the sales function as 5 *times more important than advertising* in their marketing mixes; for consumer durables marketers, sales was rated 1.8 times as important as advertising, while for consumer nondurables, advertising and personal selling were rated as about equally important.[2] Our primary interest in this chapter is in the nature of the external social influences that salespersons have on consumer behavior. We thus begin by focusing on the nature of a sales transaction itself.

 WHAT GOES ON DURING A SALES TRANSACTION?

The Nature of Sales Influences

Sales influences are quite different from the others we've examined so far, primarily because they are *marketer controlled and they occur close to the point of transaction*. Salespersons are thus the closest representatives of marketers to consumers. In addition, salespersons perform the *transaction*, or **exchange function** between marketers and consumers—they provide the means by which actual purchases are made. The transaction then allows marketers to be paid for their efforts and for consumers to receive the benefits from the goods. Most salespersons do more than ring up transactions, of course. Particularly with important consumer purchases, they play key roles in informing consumers about the options available and helping consumers decide which option best fits their needs, desires, and ability to pay.

Within this process, both objective and subjective information is used. Personal selling frequently involves *influence* and *persuasion* along these subjective lines. As we shall see within this chapter, consumers usually know that these elements are present and often welcome them as an aid to making purchase decisions. At other times, of course, some salespersons engage in inappropriate selling techniques, resulting in dissatisfied consumers and a need for better control by companies and policymakers. In the main, however, personal selling serves as a basic means by which consumers are able to serve their wants and needs through purchases of goods and services in our society.

Analyzing the Interaction Dyad

A marketing professor, Franklin B. Evans, had a strong impact on the field when he proposed that to understand the nature of personal selling, it is necessary to focus on the **interaction dyad**. A dyad is a pair of individuals engaged in a common activity. Within the selling situation, this perspective helps us to see that *both* the salesperson and consumer are involved and that the result of the contact depends on how the two parties view and react to each other. It is not enough that we concentrate on either the salesperson or consumer alone.[3]

Surprisingly, there are relatively few studies that have focused on the salesperson-customer interaction process itself. In one famous study, Willett and Pennington monitored over 200 different consumer transactions for large-ticket home appliances. Each interaction was recorded by a hidden microphone placed in the salesperson's clothing. The tape recording of the entire sequence was then analyzed using a technique known as *interaction process analysis*.[4]

Their results are interesting. The average transaction lasted 23 minutes, and within that time almost 200 separate transaction "acts" were performed by either the salesperson or the consumer. This averaged about 10 acts per minute. Most of these involved trading opinions and explanations. As we would expect, the customer asked more questions (four times as many as the salesperson) and provided fewer answers (only one-third as many as the salesperson). The study also showed, interestingly, that the *customer* contributed more of the *positive* statements made in a sales interaction (by a 3-to-2 ratio). Relatively few *negative* statements were made, but of these, *salespersons* contributed eight times more than customers! Overall, the authors noted that it appeared that salespersons held considerable power (control) as to the direction that the sales process would take.[5]

Salesperson Power in the Interaction

The issue of **salesperson power** was further investigated by Richard Olshavsky, who reanalyzed the original tapes of these transactions. He characterized the sales interaction process as a three-stage sequence:

1. **Orientation phase.** Here the salesperson is learning about the consumer's interests and the consumer is learning about the store's offerings.

2. **Evaluation phase.** Here the alternative products are examined and discussed.

3. **Consummation phase.** Here the consumer decides either to buy or not. If a positive decision is reached, issues such as payment, credit, and delivery are discussed.

In his analysis of the tapes, Olshavsky arrived at several interesting conclusions. First, he found that the *orientation phase was usually very brief:* over half of the appliance salespeople did not ask any questions of the customer, and no salesperson asked more than two (these findings appear to contradict most marketing textbooks on selling, which emphasize the need for the salesperson to learn about customer wants and needs before offering choice alternatives). Most customers, moreover, volunteered very little information: they mentioned only one or two product characteristics in which they were particularly interested.

As a result, the process moved into the evaluation phase very quickly, and on the basis of little information having been shared. The evaluation phase accounted for most of the time spent in the transaction. Here, *the salespeople were found to dominate the evaluation process:* they selected the order and the number of product alternatives that would be evaluated and used their semiprepared presentations to guide the customers' attention to each model. In many cases, in fact, the customer simply gave up his or her power in the interaction and asked the salesperson for a recommendation, which was then followed.

The key result of this study is that the salesperson often plays an extremely powerful role in influencing the customer's actual choice and purchase.[6] Rather than assuming that salespersons strive to first learn about, and then cater to, customers' wants and needs, it would seem that salespersons are much more active in guiding customer choices toward the brands and models favored by the salesperson. This is, of course, only one study concerning a limited sample of salespersons, customers, and products. If its findings hold up across the marketing-consumer environment, the way such sales power is used by marketers becomes an important and interesting issue.

 ## THE MARKETING PERSPECTIVE ON PERSONAL SELLING

Multiple Views on Selling

The personal selling situation is one that calls for extra care in our analysis of the marketing perspective. In a channel of distribution, each level—manufacturer, wholesaler, and retailer—is an independent business. The channel itself thus represents a *cooperative arrangement* for the purpose of transferring goods from factories to consumers' homes.

Retail salespersons work at the end point of the entire channel and represent actual contact points with consumers. *In practice, however, salespersons usually represent themselves and their stores rather than the larger channel.* To do well, the retail salesperson often needs to earn commissions on purchases made by his or her customers. Commissions usually increase either by selling more products or selling products with higher prices and profit margins. At one extreme of the channel, then, a brand manufacturer may have one set of goals, such as serving the needs of target consumers. At the other extreme, however, this firm will be represented by thousands of salespersons. These sales personnel have their own personal needs to be met by the sales interaction—needs that can be somewhat different from those of the sales manager, store owner, product supplier, product manufacturer, or the customer. The salesperson's view of the situation will be affected by these needs, a key one of which is to earn income through successful sales to consumers.

Exhibit 16-1 provides examples of these different perspectives. It contains quotations from college students who were asked the question, "How does the marketer view the consumer?" The first set of quotations comes from students who have never worked as salespersons and who answered this question from the viewpoint of the initial marketing course. The second group of quotes is from students who have worked as salespersons and who reported from their personal experiences. Notice how strongly the quotes differ in how they view the consumer! While certainly not a representative sampling of marketer views, these statements do indicate the different perspectives that are found in the real world of selling.

Exhibit 16-1   *HOW DO MARKETERS VIEW THE CONSUMER?*

Students Who Have Not Yet Worked in Marketing

Jim L. "Consumers are the lifeline to profits and the sole route to success. Therefore, everything we do in business is related to consumer satisfaction. . . . The customer has the right to be sold a quality product. . . . Personal attention and friendliness are qualities that have immeasurable value. Gearing to their customer's needs is what sets most successful businesses apart from their competitors."

Lisa S. ". . . today, the marketer views the consumer in a totally different light. He realizes that the consumer knows what kind of product he wants. The consumer demands good quality and will accept nothing less."

Marie K. "As a beginner, without having any marketing experience in working with the so-called consumer, it seems obvious enough. . . . The consumer will vote with his or her money and the marketer must listen and care about the product's users in order for any system to work. Through this two-way communication . . . the marketer must always listen and react according to the needs of the consumer."

All these comments are true and offer useful insights about marketing and consumer behavior. Because these students had not experienced work as a salesperson, however, their reports were necessarily more abstract, reflecting the exposure they had received in their marketing courses to this point. For some students who had worked as salespersons, however, the responses to this question were quite different:

Students Who Have Worked as Retail Salespersons

Dawn F. "In my personal experience as a retailer, I merely viewed the consumer as the object of my salesmanship technique. It did not matter what I sold . . . each person was a potential buyer and would be instrumental in boosting my sales record or quota for the day. . . . It is the marketer's duty to sell anyone his product. It is of no importance whether he is interested in the product at that time, or merely browsing. A good marketer can often arouse a need for that particular good.

"My memories of retail clothing . . . my sole intent was a quick, expensive sale . . . the store I worked at was a high-pressure fashion boutique complete with swirling lights and disco music. Employees had only one thing on their minds, and that was to sell, sell, sell! We had hourly sales quotas, and sometimes fought over who would wait on a customer . . . if you were low on your hourly quota, you would tell a customer anything. . . . Marketing is a strange business, but it is an art in and of itself. I feel marketers view customers as merely a means to an end, with that end being a sale of the product and another chalk-up on your sales record."

J.R. "I have done some buying, selling, and advertising for about six years. My general opinion of a consumer is that he is out there waiting to be taken advantage of . . . there just is not enough time in the day to research each item, and he must trust the promises

EXHIBIT 16-1   *HOW DO MARKETERS VIEW THE CONSUMER?* CONTINUED

of the seller when he goes to market. He does not want the seller to think he is ignorant, so often he will not ask the questions necessary to protect himself from a bad deal . . . he will also tend to pay a higher price for an item due to either his lack of knowledge or his demand for a status symbol . . . the consumer wants to be one of the crowd . . . a good marketer will convince the consumer to buy his product by exploiting the buyer's short-comings. To paraphrase an old saying, 'Never give a consumer an even break!' "

Wendy O.   "Working as a salesperson in a retail clothing store provided an excellent opportunity to interact with consumers, and to be on the other side of the fence as a seller—a marketer. When business was slow, the owner of the store would complain about profits being too low. Then we would see customers as prey, or targets. Our goal was to sell to anyone and everyone, the idea being to move the merchandise! The customers lost their individuality in the eyes of the salespeople, and were simply means to increase sales, and please the owner. When sales were good, though, the tension lightened . . . customers were seen as family, friends, and new faces to meet. Selling was not only to generate dollars, but was fun and sociable."

Tracing the Flow of a Sales Interaction

As noted earlier, both the salesperson and the customer are acting in specific roles within a sales transaction. Of the two, the salesperson's role is generally more structured, which should give him or her an advantage in most interactions. For example, a salesperson generally has commanding knowledge of the brands in his or her domain and also has a well-thought-out, heavily practiced set of approaches to guide him or her through each customer interaction. The customer, on the other hand, generally has much less detailed product knowledge, less sales interaction experience, and a less developed interaction strategy than the salesperson. Even so, there is a considerable degree of flexibility needed by a good salesperson. Think how ineffective a salesperson would be if he or she presented exactly the same "canned" (memorized) sales presentation to every consumer, despite what the consumer was interested in, or had to say during the interaction!

The Flow in Life Insurance Selling

An interesting study by Taylor and Woodside reports on the structure of life and health insurance sales interactions between agents (all men, in this study) and prospects. They found a six-stage process of selling effort, as follows:

1. Contact initiation/"prospecting" ....   5 percent of all acts
2. Building rapport/"common ground" ....   5 percent of all acts
3. Information swaps/"clarify needs" .... 40 percent of all acts
4. Persuasive attempts/"selling" .... 30 percent of all acts
5. Attempts to "close" the sale .... 15 percent of all acts
6. Ending discussion/"follow-up" ....   5 percent of all acts

Since this product category is one in which the salesperson must work hard to create consumer motivation to buy, the analysis of the kinds of acts that occur within each stage are especially interesting. Most of the salesperson's references to mutual acquaintances, his similarity to the customer's situation, and his expertise with insurance occurred during the rapport building stage. Most of the questions occurred during the information exchange stage, which is also when most of the price limits were discussed.

During the persuasion stage, attention was focused on the alternative policies themselves, and almost all the mention of potential catastrophes occurred here. The average sales presentation then contained *three* attempts to get the prospect to say "yes" during the closing attempt stage. The salesman also made all efforts to have the customer increase the amount spent at this stage. Then, during the last stage, conversation returned to a social level, with the salesperson attempting to lay the groundwork for a long-term relationship with this customer.[7]

The ISTEA Model of Effective Sales Interactions

Our analysis to this point has concentrated on describing the sequence of events during a sales interaction. This sequence is primarily the result of a preplanned strategy on the part of the well-trained salesperson. What does this strategy look like, however?

To understand how a salesperson can best blend preplanning with necessary flexibility during a sales interaction, let's briefly examine Figure 16-1. This displays a model developed by Barton Weitz.[8] Weitz calls his model **ISTEA** (pronounced "iced tea"), an acronym for the five stages the salesperson experiences in a customer-sales interaction. In the first stage, the salesperson develops an **impression** of the consumer: this results from combining past information, stereotypes about similar consumers, and whatever information is available at the time of the interaction. The second activity—**strategy formulation**—depends on the customer impression that was formed. Here, the salesperson decides on his or her basic plan for persuading the customer to buy, and which exact messages would be best. The third stage—**transmission**—then involves the actual delivery of these messages to the customer. The fourth stage—**evaluation**—is very closely related to the transmission activity. As the salesperson delivers each message, he or she watches and listens carefully for even minor reactions from the customer, to see how the message is working. Customer re-

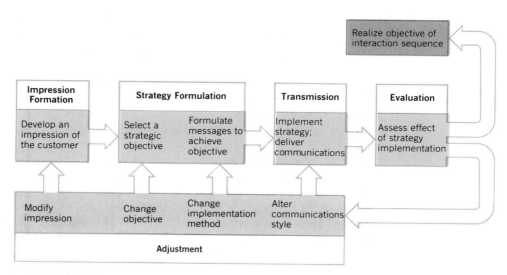

FIGURE 16-1 **The Sales Interaction as Seen by the Salesperson**

Source: Barton A. Weitz, "The Relationship Between Salesperson Performance and Understanding of Consumer Decision Making," *Journal of Marketing Research,* November 1978, p. 502.

actions can range from clear statements down to flickers of the eyes, shifts of body posture, or other signs of heightened interest, displeasure, or other emotions.

Referring to Figure 16-1, we can see that after the evaluation stage, the flow of the model diverges. If the customer agrees to purchase the product, for example, the upper branch is taken and the sales interaction draws toward an end. If, on the other hand, the interaction is still in its early stages, we move along the bottom arrow to stage 5—**adjustment**. Adjustment is a key factor in Weitz's model. It suggests that the salesperson should continually "customize" his or her presentation during the sales interaction. Notice that there are many types of adjustments possible. You can modify your impression of the customer, change your strategic objective, change your types of selling messages and/or the way in which they are delivered.

Practical Tips for Selling Strategies

If you have never worked as a salesperson, you may be especially interested in Table 16-1. Although not as detailed as the ISTEA model, it does capture some of the impressions that salespersons might reach about a customer who begins a sales interaction. For each consumer type, the table presents some time-tested tips to complete a successful sale.

The Marketing Literature on Sales Effectiveness

Given the clear significance of personal selling in the field of marketing, it is no surprise that there is a huge literature on this topic. Part of this literature focuses on personal sales techniques, and part on how to manage a sales force. These issues are the subject of entire marketing courses and numerous company training efforts. Our interest here, however, is in the nature of the influence process as it affects consumer behavior. For example, we noted earlier that the salesperson often seems to have considerable power over the flow of the consumer interaction. How does this power arise? How can a salesperson effectively control a transaction?

Two predominant sources of power are expert power and reference power. **Expert power** arises when the consumer believes that the salesperson has superior knowledge or skills in regards to the product or service. **Referent power**, on the other hand, comes from a consumer's feelings of identification with the salesperson. In general, it is believed that the more a consumer *likes* a salesperson, the more positive he or she is likely to be toward following the recommendations. Characteristics related to *similarity* are important here: these include race, age, sex, and interests. An interesting study on these factors was reported by Woodside and Davenport.[9] They were interested in finding out whether it was more important for a salesperson to be similar to his or her customer (that is, to serve as a "referent other") or for the salesperson to possess knowledge and expertise about the product class.

TABLE 16-1 TEN "TYPES" OF CUSTOMERS AND HOW TO HANDLE THEM

Type	Sales Tips
The "Silent Prospect"	Get a response, ask questions. Be more personal.
The "Procrastinator"	Summarize benefits customer will lose by failing to act. Be positive, self-assured. Suggest that the customer has the ability to make decisions. Use showmanship.
The "Talker"	Keep leading this prospect back into the sale. This person sells you, but doesn't seem to buy. Say, "By the way, that reminds me, ..." Keep on the track—be brief.
The "Slow and Methodical" Type	He appears to weigh every word, so slow down and amplify on details. Adjust your tempo to his.
The "Chip-on-the Shoulder" Type	Usually insincere and tries salesperson's patience. This customer type is a difficult type to deal with but sincerity and respect on the salesperson's part create respect.
The "Timid" Type	Take it slow and easy. Reassure on every point. Use logic, but make it simple.
The "Suspicious Customer"	Acknowledge the customer's background, stay with facts, be conservative in statements.
The "Grouch"	Ask questions to ascertain real problem. Listen and let the customer tell his or her story.
The "Flighty Buyer"	Be rapid, speed up, concentrate only on important points, omit details when possible.
"Mr. or Ms. Opinionated"	Give them rope. Flatter them. Cater to their whims. Listen attentively. Take the cash and let the credit go.

Source: Adapted from Joseph W. Thompson, "A Strategy of Selling," in Steven J. Shaw and Joseph W. Thompson (eds.), *Salesmanship* (New York: Holt, Rinehart and Winston, 1966), pp. 13–25.

The Stereo Kit Experiment

This study dealt with the purchase a new type of cleaning kit for stereo tape players. Customers who came to the checkout counter of a music store with tapes were presented with one of five conditions: some received no sales presentation about the new product, but could purchase it from a display set up next to the cash register. This was the "control" condition, and it resulted in 13 percent of the consumers buying the product.

The other four conditions were combinations of the saleswoman appearing to be "high" or "low" on the expertise and similarity dimensions. High expertise meant that her brief sales talk indicated that she knew what she was selling ("Here is a device . . . will clean the dirt and tape oxide from the guides . . ."), while the lower expertise talk admitted that she did not (". . . they tell me it will keep your tape player clean. I don't really know how it works, but you can read the directions right here . . . this thing is supposed to help the tape player a lot. It's only $1.98. Would you like one?). In the high similarity condition, she noted the kind of tapes being purchased, and praised them, and indicated that she owned the same songs and enjoyed them very much: in the low similarity condition she indicated personal preference for an opposite kind of music, but wished the buyer enjoyment with the tapes. The results of the experiment:

- When the saleswoman was low on both dimensions, only 13 percent of the customers purchased the new kit (the same rate as in the control condition).
- When high on similarity but low on expertise, 30 percent purchased.
- When low on similarity but high on expertise, 53 percent purchased.
- When the saleswoman was high on both, 80 percent purchased.

Of course, this was one study with specific kinds of treatments, and for a specific kind of product, so we must be careful of generalizing too far from its results. If you are interested in pursuing other literature in this area, you may wish to begin with the suggested readings listed in Note 10.

What Goes on Behind the Scene?

As a final element of salesperson-customer interactions, you may be interested in reading Exhibit 16-2, which presents the candid observations and explanations of one former salesperson, identified here as Bill B. There are many kinds of marketers, salespersons, and selling situations, and we do not present Bill's experiences as being representative of most of them. If you have experience as a salesperson, you may find yourself agreeing with some of his observations and disagreeing with others. If you do not have experience as a salesperson, you may wish to show the exhibit to friends with experience, to see their reactions. In either event, the practices that Bill reports *are* relatively common in retail selling, and some of them may be new to you.

EXHIBIT 16-2   A SALESPERSON'S VIEW OF CONSUMER BEHAVIOR

The following is a candid discussion with Bill B., a former salesman in a medium-sized appliance store. While his experiences will not be true for all selling situations, neither are they atypical. To begin, we asked Bill about his training period:

Q. *Can you recall any particular advice or "rules" that your sales manager would stress during your early time as a salesman?*

A. He tried hard to teach me how to sell in that setting and gave me a lot of "advice." My first few weeks, I tried to sell the product on benefits alone. I spent hours and hours reading the brochures from the manufacturers and really stressed the product benefits when I talked to a customer. People walked out on me, however; I wasn't doing well. If they did buy, they tended to buy the low-margin items that I wasn't supposed to sell . . . when

EXHIBIT 16-2   A SALESPERSON'S VIEW OF CONSUMER BEHAVIOR CONTINUED

you get paid on the quantity you sell, and the margin you sell at, the old sayings about the "customer always being right" and "fitting product benefits to customer wants" soon go by the wayside. So I started to listen to my boss and brought his "laws" into my sales presentations. As a result, sales doubled over what they were at the start.

Q. What were some of his laws?

A. He had a bunch of them . . . the one I'll never forget, though, was about "Be-Backs." He'd tell me about three times a day for the first few months on the job, "Bill, Be-Backs don't exist! Before a customer leaves this store, I want a yes or no from them. Before you let someone hit the door, I want you to have every salesperson in this store talk to the guy, including myself! That's because when they say they'll be back, they won't. Be-Backs don't exist!"

He also had a lot of other strong beliefs . . . he used to say, "I'll take one salesman who knows people over five who know products."

Q. Did he give you tips on how to sell?

A. Definitely. For example, "Don't ask customers 'Can I help you?' Ask "What do you need to buy today?' " He also said: "Act like your customer. If he works with his hands, you work with your hands; if he's a bank executive, act like a bank executive!" He also gave me some good advice about selling to couples . . . "If you're selling to a group, pick the person most supportive and let them sell the product. . . . Reinforce *any* positive comment he or she makes."

Q. What about your own views of consumers . . . did you see many differences?

A. That's the point, after a while you can really tell . . . the type of customer that you can dictate what they were going to buy. And those would be the most desirable customers because you can take them to the most expensive pieces of merchandise, or if they can't afford the expensive piece of merchandise, you can at least steer them to a piece of merchandise that has the highest margin. They just have a look about them, it's hard to explain, probably not as self-assertive, the type of people that need to be told what to buy.

Q. Did you have a fairly fixed process you went through in selling a customer?

A. For every line of merchandise we had in a store, whether it was refrigerators or TVs, there was a set procedure. We'd go to the same TV first, or the same refrigerator, and the refrigerator we would go to first would be stripped, the lowest-selling model. It would be the one that would go in the newspaper at $398. It wouldn't have crispers and it wouldn't have dividers in the freezer; it wouldn't have things that people look for. We'd do our best to show them it didn't have those things most wanted.

Q. Why did you go to it first?

A. Because it was a tool to make them feel we were trying to get them the best deal possible. They'd walk in and we'd say, "Oh, would you like to see our sale model first?" and I'd open up the door and say, " . . . it's on sale for $398 this week. Do you like crispers

Continued

EXHIBIT 16-2   A SALESPERSON'S VIEW OF CONSUMER BEHAVIOR CONTINUED

in your refrigerator? Oh, you do, well this one doesn't have that . . . maybe you'd like to see something else?"

Q. *Were there any consumers that seemed to give you more trouble than others?*

A. Definitely! Landlords and apartment owners were the worst . . . apartment building owners would come in not caring what they got as long as they got something for their tenants and then we would be in a mess because we would actually lose commission by selling the leader items. Their margin was so low; they bring down our average margin for the week.

Q. *Were you allowed to give price concessions to customers?*

A. The first two or three months I had to get the sales manager's approval on everything: any time I lowered it below the retail price. . . . By the time the manager got to know me, and I had a good sales record, I could lower it on my own accord, but I would tell the customer that I had to ask the sales manager. What I would do is walk into the other room and get a Coke or something and sit down by myself for two minutes and then come back out and say that I talked to the sales manager and he'll give you this price, a special deal for you today only.

Q. *You said earlier that your store did not do bait-and-switch selling, is that right?*

A. Legally, we didn't. In a true bait-and-switch operation, the sales merchandise is never sold. We'd avoid selling to the point of lying about the durability of the refrigerator to get a point across, saying "Well you might spend $300 for this sale model, but it's only going to last you 2 years. You're going to come back in 2 years from now and spend another $300, when you could spend $500 on this refrigerator here, and it will last 10 years."

Q. *What about "spiffing," did you ever get involved with that?*

A. Yes, definitely! The best way to get a salesman's attention is to offer a **spiff**. When a spiff is offered that product will suddenly become what every consumer needs . . . Generally, it would be the sales representative from a manufacture who would come in and announce that a spiff was on for a certain product. And every month we would get a spiff check from the company, based on how many spiff items we had sold that month.

Q. *As I understand it, a spiff is an added bonus on certain items, is that right?*

A. Yes, it comes directly from the sales rep, and it supplements your commission.

Q. *How much is an average spiff worth?*

A. That depended on the price of the item. For economy models, the spiffs were usually low, or they didn't have them. . . . For a midrange model that would sell for maybe $400, the spiff might be $15, and for the expensive model, the spiff might be $25, to give you incentive.

Q. *How common were the spiffs, would you say?*

A. There were some periods when no spiffs were on, but usually one out of every three

EXHIBIT 16-2   A SALESPERSON'S VIEW OF CONSUMER BEHAVIOR CONTINUED

or four lines would be offering spiffs to us . . . some companies didn't offer them very much, but others seemed to have it as part of their marketing strategy.

Q. How sensitive would you say sales were to these spiffs?

A. I'd say 35 percent of the customers that came in didn't have a clear idea of what they wanted and they didn't have a clear knowledge of the product. They are very malleable people and I could steer them to any spiff item I wanted. I would only highlight the great parts of the product and the true advantages it had over other products. I wouldn't lie about it, but the next day if that line lost its spiff, and the other line that I was saying wasn't so great offered a spiff, I could change the story making the new spiff line appear superior. Again, this was not lying, but it would be a distortion of the picture and I would certainly be creating the want.

Q. How valuable was a spiff to you as a salesman, in terms of your commission on each sale?

A. Hard to say, since our commissions depended on how well we did over a time period. I guess . . . the spiff would about double the amount we got from a particular sale. . . .

Q. And the store didn't seem to take a position about the spiff, is that right?

A. Not unless things really got out of line, and we were only selling the spiff items. Sometimes, then, the reps from the other lines would complain, but this didn't happen very often.

Q. Wasn't there a temptation for you to cut the price on the spiff items to up your income?

A. Certainly. But that's something the sales manager can control. We were never supposed to lower a price until the customer was ready to walk. We would only cut price if we had to—if the customer knew what she was doing in negotiating with us. I never, ever, would lower the price unless it was clear that I had to, to make the sale. It's a timing thing, if you wait too long they might walk on you, and you lose the sale, but if you don't wait long enough, you may be selling . . . at a price below what you could have gotten . . . there's also a matter of credibility involved—if you offer a discount right off, they may think that the product is low quality.

Q. One last thing about spiffs . . . were they usually for lower-quality products?

A. (Pause) It's hard to generalize, but I wouldn't say so. They were used by most of our lines, and certainly for the higher-priced, good models that needed a strong selling pitch.

Q. What about pricing, did your store have a policy of meeting competitors' lowest prices?

A. Yes, but it wasn't a major marketing element. We'd run it in ads every once in a while, and that would stimulate some more consumers coming in with competitive offers.

Q. About what percentage of your consumers would you say would bring competitive prices to their negotiations with you?

A. Surprisingly, only about 30 to 40 percent, when we ran an ad, would come in with a competitor's quote.

Continued

Exhibit 16-2   *A SALESPERSON'S VIEW OF CONSUMER BEHAVIOR* CONTINUED

A. What about Sears?

A. Sears did a lot of damage, especially its washers and dryers, because its prices were quite a bit lower than any of the independent brand names. We would have to be good at overcoming the higher price objection because Kenmore was also real big at putting a lot of gadgets on its washers and driers.

Q. So if a customer came in and said that, "I can get a Kenmore for $150 less than what you're trying to sell me . . . "

A. It wouldn't matter; we'd say, "Well sure, and you can buy a Volkswagen cheaper than a Mercedes . . . you are comparing apples and oranges here."

Q. But what if the customer was ready to walk out and buy that Kenmore?

A. That's when you would definitely go into price cutting: "Let me talk to the sales manager." You have to. In that case it was necessary to convince the person that quality-price trade-offs exist between a Kenmore and GE or Amana, because there is no way you are going to get the price down to be compatible. You have to take an argument, "Look, I'll cut the price 15 percent; dollar for dollar you're getting a much better deal with this Amana. . . . Plus, we have our own service department and plus, plus . . . ". If he's still going to walk, you usually try to bring the sales manager out in person to talk to the guy, you might try to bring other sales people in . . . get as many guns as possible.

Q. What about browsers?

A. We had a store policy not to allow browsers to roam the store unattended. If they said "just browsing," we would let them be for a couple minutes, then ease our way into a conversation. This was in response to another of our laws: "Browsers Don't Buy!"

Q. Was there anything else you sold that was different from what we've already talked about?

A. Yes, extended warranty plans, and that was a big money maker for salesmen. First we would sell somebody, whether it was a TV, a refrigerator, washer, dryer, it didn't matter, then we would start offering extended service plans: You get a one-year warranty on this Mrs. Jones, but if you pay a little more we'll give you five years' parts and labor, everything. You'll never have to worry about this again. I'm selling you a good piece of equipment, but you never know, even the best manufacturers occasionally make a lemon, so you can protect yourself." A big pitch, and they're great because we would get about 25 percent commission on those deals.

Q. How much do they cost?

A. Washer and dryer might cost $150, a TV might cost a little more than that, and refrigerator might be $175 for the full five years. But they had the option to buy one extra year, two extra years, three extra years, or four extra years also. We had a contest because nobody was ever selling these things and the sales manager finally got down and arranged an incentive, whoever could sell $2000 in warranties first would get another $150 bonus."

Exhibit 16-2   A SALESPERSON'S VIEW OF CONSUMER BEHAVIOR CONTINUED

Q. $2000 of these warranties?

A. Yes. And the first one to get there would get a $150 bonus, plus all the commissions on the warranties themselves. I really blew everybody away on that one! (laughter). I got to $2000 before anyone else was at $400 . . . because I was practicing and practicing. . . . At home I made little charts, trying to figure out how to approach every possible contingency.

Q. What proportion of consumers bought the service warranty, would you say?

A. Before the contest maybe 1 out of 20: it was something the salespeople just didn't like to bring up, because when you work real hard, oftentimes, by the time the sale has been made, both parties are tired, and the buyer is a little intimidated by the amount of money he or she is about to pay. At this point we found it difficult to say, "Well, for $150 more you get this . . . "—especially when you've been haggling over $20 for the last 15 minutes. It's just hard to approach the person on that, so we did really poorly. But during the contest, I'd say maybe 1 out every 3 bought it. It was just breaking through the barrier of being hesitant and cautious.

Q. What about consumers, is there any way you can characterize the classic "sucker"?

A. Yeah, I'm ashamed to say it, but I would say the poor working-class people. And they would come in and they would buy on credit and they would buy just about what you told them to buy. Now none of the salesmen got to the point of really exploiting them and making them buy something that was really not what they came in for, but they were always easy sales, because they had very little product knowledge and I don't think they understood a lot of the pitch if you went down to product features a lot. I think they just pretty much wanted to be reassured what they were buying was good.

Q. Could you characterize what type of consumer seemed to be at the other extreme and get the best deal possible from you?

A. A middle-aged professional . . . they would come in and they would know everything. . . . At least they thought they knew everything. . . . Many times they had misinformation, but they would hardly allow me to go through a pitch; that would be a very rational sale.

Q. What about family decision making . . . did this present any special challenges for you?

A. I was extremely worried selling to a young couple if only the wife or husband was present. Sometimes they would come back and sometimes they wouldn't. There was nothing I could do to close the sale. I think either the husband or the wife would go out on a fact-finding mission and go to maybe five or six stores, and then they would make a narrowing-down process at home. Then both would go to perhaps the final two or three alternatives and make the decision together. With older couples, on the other hand, I got the distinct impression that one person had the authority to make the decision and that when they did leave, using the reason, "I need to talk it over with my husband/wife," it was an excuse. They generally didn't come back. Older couples also engaged in joint decision making, but to a lesser degree.

Continued

| EXHIBIT 16-2 | A SALESPERSON'S VIEW OF CONSUMER BEHAVIOR CONTINUED |

Q. What percentage of your sales, would you say, were to joint purchasers?

A. There were a lot of young couples moving into that area, and it was almost always a joint decision because they were buying a household of appliances.

Q. Did they know coming in that they could get 35 percent off?

A. That was one of the first things we told them. If I ever see a couple coming in I would ask if they were building a house, and if so, I would offer them contract pricing. If you didn't, you usually ended up dead, because anybody that is going to be buying six or seven appliances will shop in more than one place, and the other place will offer contract prices.

Q. And with the younger couples, did there seem to be specific roles for the man or woman?

A. It seemed that it was a true joint decision in most of the cases, and it was definitely the case if both had a job, and there wasn't anything like clear role definitions.

Q. Did you see more of that with the older consumers?

A. With the older people, the refrigerator, washer/dryer decisions would tend to be made by the women, TVs were joint, and air conditioners were usually handled by the men.

THE CONSUMER'S PERSPECTIVE OF A SALES INTERACTION

In contrast to the large literature on the marketing perspective of sales interactions, there is almost no literature on the consumer perspective on this same topic. As we discussed in Chapter 2, there are many books dealing with "how to be a better consumer" in such fields as consumer economics. Unfortunately, the specific topic of dealing with sales interactions is not much discussed in these books either. In general, however, experts agree strongly on certain *principles* for wise consumers to follow. Here are a few of the most important (as you read them, think back to the points made by Bill B. in his interview):

Principle I: Knowledge Is Power

There is usually an imbalance between the knowledge of the salesperson and the knowledge of the consumer. The salesperson works daily with the products or services offered, knows the terms at which they might be offered, understands principles of influence and persuasion, and has been trained to use effective techniques to work with his or her customers. However, most consumers know little about many of the larger products and services they buy, little about the range of offers that the store might make to them, and little about persuasive techniques and bargaining methods.

According to experts in consumer economics, the more that a consumer can do to learn something about each of these topics, the better off he or she will be when venturing out for a major purchase. As one old saying goes, *"If you're in the market for a car, the best place to start shopping is your local library."* Here you can learn, not only about product qualities and alternatives, but also the prices that dealers are paying for the models, their common forms of price mark-ups, and the type of deal you can probably get if you bargain well. There are other good sources of information as well, an issue we'll discuss in Chapter 18, when we take up consumer information search. However, the key point is that a consumer who wants to buy the best product at the best terms needs to be willing to make an effort to learn important facts about the product, its prices, and how it is sold.

Principle II: Understand the Marketing Theory of Price Discrimination

To serve consumers over the long term, marketers have to attain profits from their operations. In theory, marketers can maximize revenues by selling to each customer at the highest price he or she is willing to pay, assuming that the sale is profitable to the marketer. This approach to selling is known as **price discrimination**, and is not intended to be a negative term. Usually, a price discrimination strategy involves personal selling, to obtain the best price offer possible from each consumer. Recall, for example, that Bill B.'s store would cut prices, but only at the last moment, and only when the salesperson recognized that a sale depended on doing so. In addition to those retailers who practice price discrimination as a strategy with their sales force, there are also many retailers who choose *not* to practice price discrimination. Their reasons usually involve the store's overall marketing strategy (high-volume outlets, for example, may wish to have people spend as little time on any one item as possible, so as to shop for a large variety of products) and sometimes legal restrictions.

When Consumers Should Negotiate

When a price negotiation approach is taken by a retailer, a consumer who doesn't understand that this is happening will almost always end up paying more for the product than he or she would have had to. According to Scott Maynes, a leading consumer economist, consumers can expect to find negotiable prices *most of the time* for

- Used items.
- Purchases involving trade-ins.
- Automobiles.
- Appliances.
- Houses.
- Home repairs and improvements.

Fees for professional services (doctors, lawyers, decorators, brokers, etc.) are sometimes negotiable, while mail-order goods are almost never negotiable.[11]

Principle III: Have a Strategy for the Transaction

To make the most advantageous sales arrangement, a consumer should know how to adopt a negotiating approach and have a **transaction strategy**. By understanding the role and needs of the salesperson—just as the salesperson attempts to do with customers—the consumer will carry more "clout" into the sales interaction. Research has shown that the major reasons that some consumers pay less than others for the same brands and models are (1) they know more and (2) they use greater bargaining strength.[12] Personal characteristics can help or hinder a customer within the interaction. Who are the most successful "bargainers" in sales transactions? In one of the rare studies in this area, it was discovered that the most successful people in bargaining within a sales interaction were those with dominant personalities—who were highly efficient, and not very tolerant of others. Other descriptions of successful bargainers include people who have "high levels of aspiration" and those who "are more flexible," "look out for themselves," and "are psychologically assertive."[13]

If a consumer has these tendencies, he or she will certainly want to use them in a purchasing situation. If a consumer does not have these traits, however, it may be overly dramatic to try to change his or her entire personality just to save a few dollars! They can, however, work to develop purchasing strategies that will improve their performance and with which they do feel comfortable. For example, *comparison shopping* is a useful way to learn about alternatives and gain price concessions. In this case, "walking out" on the salesperson does not represent rejection, but part of a planned shopping experience. Some consumers, however, do not wish to shop around, either because they don't enjoy it or because it is costly in terms of time and effort. In these cases, some consumers use a variant of the *Dutch auction technique* (this differs from the normal auction in which prices go up by consecutive bidders—in a Dutch auction, the auctioneer begins at a high price and reduces it slowly; the first person who accepts the current price wins the bidding!). These consumers simply inform the salesperson that they do not wish to haggle, but want his or her best price and terms so that they can either accept them or go elsewhere to buy. In another simple strategy, the consumer decides beforehand what he or she is willing to pay, then goes to the store and proposes exactly those terms. If they are accepted, the sale is made; if not, the consumer leaves and tries elsewhere.

As we have noted several times already, consumers typically do not enter sales interactions with clear strategies aimed at minimizing the prices they will pay. Scholars in the fields of marketing, economics, and psychology have long had strong disagreements about why this seems to be the case. Would you say that this description applies to your behavior? If so, why? Would you shift your sales interaction strategies if you were in a position to easily do so? To gain further realistic appreciation for these issues, consider how each of the three principles in this section applies to the following report.

Pleas for Fees . . . Omissions on Commissions

When the stock market drops, small investors usually cut their transactions sharply. In a recent period, industry volume was down over 20 percent, and pressures increased on retail brokers to sell harder. But which financial products would they choose to push to their clients?

Although many investors do not realize it, commissions and other sales charges are generally unregulated in the investment world, and are used as incentives for brokers to sell particular products. This can pose problems. According to one former broker, "the broker's incentive to sell lies with the varied products that may provide the least investment benefit to clients . . ." and making recommendations based on a commission rate "isn't . . . occurring only at second-rate firms . . . it provides a temptation so great it represents a whole new level of investment risk."

Commissions can vary widely depending upon the type of investment—for a client investing $10,000, for example, a financial advisor could earn $0 (if a no-load mutual fund is purchased), $50 (if a Treasury bond is bought) $200 (if it is common stock), $600 (if it is a new mutual fund with load), or $1000 or more (if it is limited partnership or similar venture). Often, the riskiest, most complicated financial investments offer salespeople the greatest compensation, because these are the hardest products to sell. According to officials of the Security and Exchange Commission, clients—whether out of embarrassment, ignorance, or misplaced courtesy—almost *never* inquire about the compensation brokers receive from investment recommendations. Explains one broker, "If people really understood what they were paying sometimes, they wouldn't pay it." Of course, many good brokers rely on long-term relationships with their valued clients and base their recommendations on the investment strategy worked out with the client. Even so, many clients are not aware that commissions on many transactions are in fact highly negotiable. As a rule, more attention by clients to the issue of commissions is clearly appropriate. As an SEC official comments, "We could use a little paranoia in this area," on the part of consumers.[14]

THE PUBLIC POLICY PERSPECTIVE

Our discussion to this point contains several significant messages. First, it is clear that personal selling is a very important function for both marketers and consumers. The personal selling function helps to deliver many of our most prized possessions as consumers—homes, automobiles, and products with which we live our daily lives and entertain ourselves. Further, salespersons and customers usually have goals in common. Usually, the customer *wants* to make a purchase, and the salesperson *wants* him or her to make that purchase. The conflicts that arise concern exactly *which* purchase should be made, under *what terms*, and *from which source.*

The Challenges to Public Policy

The key role for public policy is to act to protect consumers' rights while preserving the benefits and freedoms that are associated with personal selling in our society.

From the public policy perspective, the staggering size of the economy presents a real problem. As we noted, there are over 11 million salespersons working with consumers every day (with *several billion dollars* in customer purchases daily). Most of these individuals do not cross the line from legal to illegal sales activity, or from scrupulous to unscrupulous sales behavior. However, if only 1 percent of these individuals, for whatever reason, acts to mislead or pressure consumers to act against their best interest, a problem of staggering proportions would exist. According to a former prominent U.S. senator, Warren Magnuson (D., Wash.),

> *Deceptive selling by the unscrupulous few in the business underworld is, in fact, our most serious form of theft. It cheats Americans of . . . more than is lost through robbery, burglary, larceny, auto theft, embezzlement, and forgery combined. . . . Today's modern bandits of the marketplace are the masters of the light touch . . . these men can reach even deeper into our pockets without producing a rustle to disturb the law, or often the victim himself.*[15]

High-Pressure Sales Techniques

Our discussion to this point has concentrated on salesperson-consumer interactions in a retail setting. In most of these cases, the customer has *chosen* to come to the store and is likely to have some advanced interest in making a purchase. There are, however, other instances in which the sales interaction begins with *no* purchase interest on the part of the customer. Door-to-door selling and telephone soliciting are the best examples of this. When a consumer has not even thought about purchasing a particular product or service, two characteristics are likely to govern aspects of the encounter. First, the consumer's knowledge— which we noted in Chapter 2 is often low in general—is likely to be especially low with no prior planning or development of a shopping strategy for the sales interaction. Second, the consumer has a low motivation to buy, at least in the sense of having planned to purchase. Thus, the salesperson's major task is creating a purchase motivation. In these instances, "high-pressure" selling is often used. Various tactics are brought into play, including both product promises and plays upon the customer's emotions. High-pressure selling is not in itself deceptive, of course, but the opportunities and temptations are much heightened in this setting.

Frauds by Clods

Consumer activists have a long list of tales concerning fraudulent practices in high-pressure selling. "Creating a consumer want" has a much more cynical meaning here. It includes such actions as altering the customer's product in a hidden manner and then pointing out the problem. Gas stations on interstate highways, for example, have been caught plunging ice picks into tires and placing foreign chemicals into batteries to cause adverse reactions. "Termite inspectors" have been caught placing the bugs in houses and then informing the frightened residents of the imminent collapse of their structure. Traveling "tree surgeons" have thrived by pointing out undetectable diseases in large trees overhanging a house, and then removing them at high prices. The classic case in using

Probably *not* a case of a gas station altering this car!

this type of fear sell, though, is that involving the Holland Furnace Company, which employed 5,000 persons in its 500 offices around the United States. Its primary sales method was for the employees to introduce themselves to housewives as "safety inspectors," go to the furnace and dismantle it, and then condemn it as "so hazardous that I must refuse to put it back together—I can't let myself be an accessory to murder!" According to Senator Magnuson, the salesmen were merciless. One elderly woman was sold *nine new Holland furnaces in six years, costing over $18,000!*[16]

Misrepresentations of Selling Intent

Other situations involve lowering the consumer's defenses against a sales pitch. A consumer might be told that he or she has "just won a valuable prize in our contest" or that the caller is "taking a survey and would appreciate your answers to a few brief questions." Once the ice is broken, and the discussion becomes more relaxed, the salesperson's prepared script calls for a gradual shift into the sales presentation. At this point, the consumer may feel some social obligation to consider the discussion, and in fact may be enjoying it.

Selling Knowledge, by the Book?

An important Federal Trade Commission (FTC) case against the Encyclopaedia Britannica Company included a number of charges concerning this initial description by the firm's sales representatives. According to sworn testimony during the trial, the sales representatives were provided with a memorized introductory speech and a letter from a senior company official stating that the person is an "interviewer" who is studying the effectiveness of the company's advertising. According to one salesman who testified,

> The two most common objections were, "Are you selling anything?" We were specifically told to say, "No, I am not selling anything, but may I come in?" Then were were supposed to start to go in. The other one was, "Well, how long will it take?" And we were supposed to say, "Only a couple of minutes. May I come in?"[17]

In fact, a full sales presentation would take at least an hour and sometimes over two hours. The FTC then went on to find a number of further deceptive and misleading selling practices throughout each stage of the sales presentation, contract signing, and debt collection activities of the firm. After four years of investigation and trial, the FTC issued a lengthy order aimed at fixing these practices in the future. Among the terms of the order were:

- In advertising used to gain the names of sales prospects, offers of contests or free gifts must include a clear statement that Britannica's salespersons may call.
- In door-to-door sales, the Britannica salesperson must, at the start, hand the consumer a 3- by 5-inch card stating that the purpose of this call is to sell encyclopaedias.

The company sharply criticized this order and appealed it to the federal court system. After considerable controversy, the FTC announced that it had modified its order to allow the salesperson to present a business card rather than the larger card. The business card had to have the term "sales representative" on it, but did not require a statement concerning the purpose of the call, nor was the salesperson required to tell the consumer to read the card. The two major reasons behind these modifications were (1) the First Amendment's freedom of speech for marketers and (2) the fact that the FTC had not done consumer research on its earlier required statement!

Bait and Switch and Other Deceptive Practices

You may recall that Bill B. mentioned that his firm did not engage in true bait and switch, although it did come close. Bait-and-switch practices stem from the retailer's need to get customers into the store where they can be persuaded by salespersons to make purchases. One good way to do this, of course, is to use advertising that is effective in bringing "traffic" to the store. **Bait and switch**, then, is a clever combination of advertising and personal selling. The advertising sets the "bait," and the consumer takes the bait and comes to the store, where the salesperson "switches" the consumer from the advertised item to a more expensive, more profitable model.

It is important to recognize that there is a distinction between the salesperson's natural desire to "trade up" a customer (thereby obtaining a higher price and higher profit contribution) and the practice of bait and switch. Trading-up is legal and can be seen as a natural part of the retail selling process. In a trading-up situation, the customer is free to purchase whichever item he or she desires. In bait and switch, however, the store has never intended to sell the advertised item! The salesperson is typically under orders *not* to sell that item and is often fined if he or she does sell the item. In salesroom parlance, the bait model is "nailed to the floor." A variety of tricks are used: from not having the item on the floor at all ("Our latest shipment hasn't come in yet . . .") to the use of a truly unattractive model that the customer is almost certain to find unappealing when he or she inspects it ("Isn't that ugly! I don't know why they would make something like that, but that is the one we have on sale today. . . . Maybe you'd like to see this one over here . . .").

There are, of course, many variations on this theme, some of which are legal and some of which are not. Even such large and reputable retailers as Sears, Roebuck have been charged with instances of this practice. In the Sears case, the FTC charge concerned sewing machines, and the company *did* have a policy of selling the advertised machines at the low price. The FTC, however, was moving against the in-store sales practices of some of Sears' salespersons: they would routinely advise customers that the advertised model was noisy, came without a standard guarantee, and might take a long time to deliver. According to Sears' chairman,

> *The incidents which came to light in recent FTC hearings were violations of Sears' policy as well as FTC standards. We regret that even one such case occurred in our annual transactions of some 9.5 million major home appliances.*[18]

In many other cases of bait and switch, however, the retailers involved have been more clearly guilty of illegal and fraudulent practices. Since the appeal is primarily geared to low price, this technique hits hardest at low and moderate-income consumers. The practices also tend to occur with smaller retail operations in local markets. Monitoring and enforcement by local officials is therefore extremely important.

Despite the fact that the FTC stresses national cases in its regulatory activities, its files are packed with fraudulent personal sales examples. In three related cases in the Washington, D.C., area, for example, the FTC moved against carpet retailers who were advertising incredible bargains, plus free gifts, in their local advertising. As a remedy for the bait and switch practices of these retailers, the FTC ordered them to include, in each ad, the following statement:

> The Federal Trade Commission has found that we engage in bait and switch advertising; that is, the salesman makes it difficult to buy the advertised product and he attempts to switch you to a higher priced item.

This notice had to be ringed with a black border and set off in a conspicuous place in the ad. The firms were ordered to run it for a period of at least one year. If they had changed their selling practices by that time, the remedy was open for revision.[19]

Industry and Government Responses to Personal Selling Abuses

Even though the kinds of abuses we have been discussing are not typical of most marketers, they do cause severe problems for both the marketing community and for consumers in our society. For public policymakers, a great deal of the difficulty arises from special characteristics of the salesperson-customer interaction itself. Consider, for example, how this differs from either print or broadcast advertising: (1) Much advertising occurs on a national or regional level: personal selling always occurs on a local level; (2) the number of instances that need to be monitored is much higher with personal selling than with advertising; (3) advertising leaves a record of what was said, whereas personal selling almost never leaves a record; (4) advertising is typically brief, with only a few basic points being made, while personal selling usually includes many more points, within an interactive discussion framework; and (5) if an advertising order is issued, future advertising can easily be checked to see whether or not it has complied with the terms of the order. If a personal selling order is issued, however, future sales interactions are still extremely difficult to monitor for compliance.

For these reasons, regulation of deceptive selling practices is extremely difficult. As noted earlier, state and local agencies are heavily involved in this process. In addition, the creation of laws that specify consumers' rights become especially important. **Cooling-off laws**, for example, allow consumers three business days in which to obtain a full refund if they decide they do not wish to carry through a purchase (greater than $25) they had agreed to with a door-to-door salesperson. The intention here is to protect consumers against caving in to slick, high-pressure selling techniques: the regulation requires the salesperson to provide a consumer with a "notice of cancellation" that can be returned within the three-day period to void the sale. Notice that this regulation makes door-to-door selling less efficient. It is designed, however, to overcome the regulatory limitations brought about by the nature of personal selling itself. The presence of these types of laws is intended to help consumers to protect themselves. We will return to this topic in Chapter 20, when discussing postpurchase consumer behavior.

Businesses' Reactions to Selling Abuses

It is particularly important that we recognize that fraudulent and deceptive practices by some sellers are also injurious to the marketing community of reputable businesspersons. Not only does the credibility of marketing suffer in general, but honest retailers in the community lose business each time that a customer is misled by a deceptive operation. And retailers are not the only persons to suffer: the manufacturers of lines sold in the reputable stores also suffer losses of sales and profits. For this reason, many businesspersons support codes of conduct for their industries and such local organizations as the Better Business Bureau.

Marketers Are Angry

Another interesting—and damaging—effect of unscrupulous sellers has been felt by the marketing research community. Because so many firms have used "Hello, I'm taking a market survey . . ." as their openers for sales solicitations (either by telephone or in person), consumers have naturally reacted with suspicion and anger. This has made the legitimate consumer research task considerably more difficult (and more expensive), as "refusals" to participate in legitimate surveys have risen. The American Marketing Association, a professional group with over 30,000 members, has developed a Research Code of Ethics that addresses this practice directly:

> No individual or organization will undertake any activity which is directly or indirectly represented to be marketing research, but which has as its real purpose the attempted sale of merchandise or services. . . .

Beyond the issue of selling abuses there are other interesting questions involved in the ethics of conducting marketing and consumer research. If you are interested in these questions, you may wish to pursue the references listed in Note 20.

SUMMARY

What Goes on During a Sales Transaction?

Unlike other social influences we've encountered, *salesperson influences* are marketer controlled and occur close to the point of transaction. Both these factors render the salesperson of utmost importance to the marketer. Moreover, a plurality of a national sample of consumers who had recently purchased a consumer durable named the salesperson as their most useful source of information. With over 11 million consumer salespersons in the United States, it is evident that salespersons exert a pervasive and important influence upon consumer behavior. The first section of the chapter was devoted to the *sales transaction* itself. We saw here how research focuses on the *consumer-salesperson interaction dyad.* In the few studies that have been done, one of the surprising results is how powerful a position the salesperson is often in during these interactions.

The Marketing Perspective on Personal Selling

In our next section we examined salesperson influences from the marketing perspective. The *ISTEA model* of effective sales interactions was introduced. This model describes how a salesperson can blend preplanning with the flexibility necessary to achieve his or her objectives. We then examined some key dimensions of salesperson effectiveness. *Expert power* and *referent power* are two key factors: a record shop study demonstrated how they can vary. This section closed with a candid interview with Bill B., a former appliance salesman.

The Consumer's Perspective of a Sales Interaction

The third section examined the *consumer's perspective on salesperson influences.* Here we saw how a general lack of knowledge concerning products, persuasive techniques, and bargaining methods hinders many consumers. In this light, *three principles* were reviewed: (1) knowledge is power, (2) understand the theory of price discrimination, and (3) have a strategy for the transaction. Even the consumer who may not be psychologically assertive will benefit from adopting a reasonable prepurchase strategy.

The Public Policy Perspective

In our final section we examined some of the *public policy issues* in this area. The basic issue involves how to protect consumers' and competitors' rights while preserving the benefits and freedoms associated with personal selling in our society. Given the hundreds of millions of sales transactions each day, if only a tiny percentage of sales behaviors are illegal or unscrupulous, the magnitude of the resulting loss to consumers is staggering. In this regard we reviewed some examples of fraudulent high-pressure selling, misrepresentation of selling intent, and bait-and-switch advertising. We also examined the difficulty involved in regulating personal selling, since it occurs at a local (versus national) level, it seldom leaves a record of what was said, and it is hard to monitor compliance with orders when they are issued. Thus preventive actions such as consumer protections (e.g., cooling-off laws), industry codes of conduct and self-policing, and consumer vigilance are all important.

KEY TERMS

exchange function	evaluation
interaction dyad	adjustment
salesperson power	expert power
orientation phase	referent power
evaluation phase	spiff
consummation phase	knowledge is power
ISTEA	price discrimination
impression	transaction strategy
strategy formulation	bait and switch
transmission	cooling-off laws

REVIEW QUESTIONS AND EXPERIENTIAL EXERCISES

[E = Application extension or experiential exercise]

1. Compare and contrast salespersons' influences on consumer behavior with reference group and family influences. Be specific.

2. Compare the salesperson's view and customer's view of the sales transaction.

3. Relate the six-stage processes of selling developed by Taylor and Woodside to the ISTEA model developed by Weitz.

4. Consider the results of the stereo kit experiment. Identify two other products that might generate comparable effects of the expertise and similarity dimensions of the salesperson. Identify two products you believe would have opposite effects: high similarity more significant than high expertise.

5. Summarize the key points concerning salespersons' influence that you learned from the Bill B. interview. Which of these had you already known? Did he make any statements with which you disagree?

6. Describe exactly how a wise consumer should follow the text's three principles for dealing with sales interactions in this situation: "Your broker, whom you've recently met, calls and offers you 1000 shares of a secondary stock issue of Marsea Corp., a small company with which you are not familiar. The stock is offered at $10 per share. He says it will sell fast, and he needs to know your decision."

7. Why might a public policymaker prefer to regulate advertising as opposed to personal selling?

8. Evaluate the various unfair or deceptive selling methods noted in the text in terms of the severity and prevalence of these practices in today's economy. Be specific and cite examples from your personal experience.

[E] 9. Conduct a brief interview with an experienced salesperson to learn about consumer behavior in a sales interaction (you may wish to use the Bill B. interview as a guide). Write a brief report summarizing your findings.

[E] 10. Accompany a friend or relative on a shopping trip in which an interaction with a salesperson will occur (do not inform your partner of your purpose before the trip). Listen and watch the interaction closely, relating it to the concepts in this chapter. Did the stages proceed similarly? Where did most of the acts occur? Write a brief report summarizing your findings.

[E] 11. Based on the notes listed for Chapter 16 at the back of the book, select several research studies likely to be of interest to you. Write a brief report on your findings.

[E] 12. Locate the book, *Influence: The New Psychology of Modern Persuasion*, by the psychologist Robert B. Cialdini (New York: William Morrow and Co. (Quill), 1984). Read the portions pertaining to salesperson activities. Do you agree with his assertions? Write a brief report summarizing your reactions.

[E] 13. Locate two books aimed at salespersons, to assist them in selling more effectively. As you review their contents, select several insights concerning (a) consumer behavior, and (b) effective selling techniques. Write a brief report summarizing your findings.

CHAPTER 17

Advertising's Influences on Consumer Behavior

"Does She or Doesn't She?"

". . . Only her hairdresser knows for sure," was a daring headline for Clairol hair colorings during the conservative 1950s. It connected with consumers' hopes: Sales increased 400 percent in the next six years, and almost half of U.S. women tried tinting their hair. This campaign created an industry and became an advertising classic.[1]

"Herb Definitely Doesn't"

The mid-1980s saw another classic ad campaign, but this time in the other direction. Burger King, which had been extremely successful until then, was searching for a campaign that would capture the public's fancy. It chose to feature "Herb the nerd" and spent $40 million pointing out that he'd never been to Burger King. The advertising trade press still loves to discuss this campaign: marketing blunders are called "Herb-Marketing," while failure to understand consumers is evidence of a "Herb Gap." Even the folks at Burger King admit the fiasco. One executive reports that history there is marked "B.H." and "A.H."—Before Herb and after Herb: It's "When Kennedy was shot and when Herb was launched, where were you?"[2]

■ ■ ■

Every year an incredible amount of money is spent on advertising and sales promotion. As of the early 1990s over $130 billion is being spent on advertising each year in the United States alone, with many billions more being spent for other types of sales promotion (sweepstakes, displays, coupons, etc.). Advertising is a major industry in our nation: about 3 percent of our GNP. Almost every business firm advertises, as do many nonprofit institutions (churches and hospitals, for example). Although it sounds obvious, we should remember that everyone who advertises does so in the belief that he or she will benefit more by putting these dollars into advertising than by putting them to other uses or not spending them at all. Thus it appears that advertising must be highly influential in terms of impacts on consumer behavior. In this chapter we'll delve more deeply into this very interesting issue.

The two primary actors bring quite different perspectives to the topic. **Marketing managers** create and distribute advertising: each firm makes its decisions in its own best interests. Conversely, **consumers** primarily *react* to advertising, usually on a personal, individual level. As consumers, however, our reactions are highly affected by the fact that we are exposed to *so many ads* for so many competing products and brands. Most consumers ignore most ads most of the time, either because they're for products of little or no interest or because the consumer is busy with other matters. On the other hand, sometimes a certain ad captures our attention and evokes strong responses. Of most significance for our text is the fact that consumers are both informed and influenced by advertising. In fact, over the course of the average advertising campaign, enough consumers are informed and influenced that managers continue to invest in advertising during future periods.

Advertising is so visible and so interesting that all of us are already "experts," in the sense that we've talked about this phenomenon for years. Thousands of articles about advertising appear each year. Many books are available, and many universities offer courses (and even majors) in advertising. Given the scope of the subject, we must limit our goals and coverage in this chapter. We'll do this by presenting useful basic frameworks about the nature of the advertising-consumer interface. We'll begin with an overview of advertising decisions, then turn to examine advertising as communication. Our third section focuses on the persuasive element of advertising (as you may know, the origin of the word *advertise* meant "to turn someone . . ."). Our final section briefly highlights some approaches used in controlling this sprawling, brawling, exciting field. In addition, two appendices are available for interested readers. Appendix 17-A summarizes the major social and economic debates about this field and Appendix 17-B summarizes some managerial factors involved in successful ads.

AN OVERVIEW OF ADVERTISING DECISIONS

This section provides a brief overview of advertising decision areas in order to broaden our appreciation of the marketing perspective on advertising. As we'll see later in this chapter, it is clear that *the average ad, by itself, is not likely to have a major impact on consumer behavior.* This means that, from the marketer's perspective, it is the overall program that is most important. If the product is not very appealing, or is not received well by consumers when they use it, it is doubtful that even the best advertising campaign can influence consumers to purchase this brand over any extended period of time.

At the same time, *most marketers and consumers would agree that advertising does have an impact on consumer behavior* and that for most brands it returns a profit on the money invested. As we saw in our opening quotes, provided the remainder of the marketing mix is of reasonable quality, advertising holds the potential to tip the "bottom line" toward great success, moderate profitability, or even failure. In assessing advertising's influences, then, we need to keep the paradoxical question, "Is advertising's impact really strong or really weak?" in mind. Although it is a frustrating issue, this is the question with which advertising experts have been wrestling for years.

Ads Are Inherently Complex

At the very start, we should recognize that there are many factors within any single ad campaign that will determine its impacts on consumers. Consider, for a moment, the almost infinite number of detailed decisions that are made in creating any ad. Most of these are very subtle. For example, we need to decide whether the model should be sitting or standing, wearing red pants or blue, facing to the right or the left; whether the music should be soft or loud; and on and on (notice, by the way, that our example assumed that we had already decided to have a model and music and had already chosen which person and which tune). An enormous number of detailed decisions need to be made in developing even a single advertisement.

The 7 M's of Advertising

When we think of entire advertising *campaigns,* the scope of the decisions widens even farther. One thought-provoking framework for advertising decisions, for example, is known as the **7 M's of advertising** management.[3]

- **Merchandise:** What is it that we have to promote?
- **Markets:** To whom are we advertising?
- **Motives:** Why do these consumers buy?
- **Messages:** What appeals will work best?
- **Money:** How much should we spend, and when?
- **Media:** Where and when should we reach our audience?
- **Measurement:** How can we learn to do this better?

Notice the first six factors contribute to the impact of every ad campaign, and since each of the six has many subfactors within it, we can see how difficult it is to single out any one variable and generalize about its true impact on advertising effectiveness. The seventh factor, measurement, refers to the use of consumer research within advertising. Because of the large gains possible from a significant improvement in an advertising campaign, consumer research is commonly used to provide insights and help with advertising decisions in the first six areas.

ADVERTISING AS COMMUNICATION

A General Model of Communication

It is important at the start for us to appreciate how complex the process of communications can be. As we'll see, this complexity poses real challenges for advertising (and adds significantly to the interest in this topic). Let's begin by examining Figure 17-1, which diagrams a very general model of communication. Here the **source** of the communication develops a message, then delivers it to the **receiver** through a **channel** (personal contact, letter, television). The flow of the system is from left to right, and the communication ends when the message has been received.

Advertising Is a One-Way Communication Flow

Unfortunately, while our basic model is easy enough to understand, it doesn't really capture how most communications seem to work. In most cases (for example, social or salesperson influences), communication flows are two way; that is, the source is not only sending messages to the receiver, but the receiver is sending messages back to the source. Often the two persons quickly alternate in the source and receiver roles as the discussion goes on. Advertising, then, is *not* a typical type of communication situation. As a one-way communication form, advertising holds both advantages and disadvantages. Let's consider a few of these.

Disadvantages of a One-Way Communication Flow

Two-way communications between persons offer some distinct advantages that advertising cannot offer to us. As consumers, for example, when we discuss a

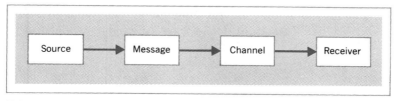

FIGURE 17-1 **A General Model of Communication**

product with a friend, we can ask for *clarification* of the message points that may be not clear. Also, we can *tailor* the discussion to matters of specific interest. Finally, we are not required to communicate within a tight *time* limit—the discussion can extend out until one or both parties wish it to end.

Two-way communications also afford significant advantages to marketers. First, unlike advertising and other one-way modes (such as class lectures!), two-way communication situations are much more likely to command *attention* from customers (since they bear some responsibility within the communication itself). Second, within a two-way communication situation, the message sender is able to obtain immediate *feedback* easily on how well the message is being received. If the receiver is not understanding or is receiving a meaning different from that which we intend (this is technically termed "distortion"), there is an opportunity for us to try to *clarify* our message. Finally, if we see that the customer is not reacting positively to the persuasive aspects of our message, we are able to *alter the message* (or our presentation style) to try to improve our effectiveness. As we saw in the ISTEA model (Chapter 16), an astute salesperson is constantly interpreting verbal and body signals from customers and adjusting accordingly.

Advantages of a One-Way Communication Flow

The situation is not entirely bleak for advertising, however. Since advertising is a one-way mode, the source can concentrate on a single message that can be sent to any number of receivers if the channels are available. *Cost per thousand customers*, for example, is a common term that captures the efficiency with which advertising can contact the mass consumer market. In comparison, a salesperson-customer interaction only involves one or two consumers at a time.

A one-way flow is sometimes described as the *hypodermic needle approach* to communication, bringing to mind a picture of a needle through which the source injects the audience with his or her message. This model is most appropriate for those situations for which the audience is "captive" and *must* receive the message (e.g., prisoner-of-war camps, schools, consumer behavior classes). In the real world of advertising, on the other hand, few consumers feel that they must sit still for such injections. The hypodermic analogy does, however, help us to see how an advertiser controls all aspects of the message's contents and timing in a one-way communication. It indicates the potential to create highly efficient messages and helps us recognize why consumer research on messages can be very helpful to advertisers.

THE PERSUASIVE ASPECT OF ADVERTISING

"I know that half of the money I spend on advertising is wasted, but I can never figure out exactly which half it is!"

Spuds Sells Suds as Night Falls

A national poll of consumers showed that the "Spuds MacKenzie" ad campaign was one of the most popular of recent years. It worked on purchases, too, as Bud Light sales increased 20 percent in one year with the English bull terrier. His bosses at Anheuser-Busch were pleased with this success, but puzzled with the performance of their "The Night Belongs to Michelob" campaign featuring Phil Collins's catchy rock music. It also scored as one of the country's most popular campaigns in the consumer poll, but Michelob's sales dropped 5 percent.[4]

Why Is Advertising Complex?

What do these reports tell us about advertising? The experiences of Bud Light and Michelob (and Clairol and Herb at the chapter opening) are examples of the successes and failures with which advertising is associated on a regular basis. It can succeed, sometimes strikingly, but it can also fail, sometimes spectacularly! And, because advertising is but one of the elements of the overall marketing mix, its actual contributions to a product's success or failure are often difficult to isolate.

The quotation, on the other hand, is an advertising "classic" repeated frequently around the field. It is attributed to John Wanamaker, a Philadelphia merchant who built his department stores to be one of the most successful businesses in America at the turn of the twentieth century. It remains a classic even today because it captures two of the essential characteristics of advertising: (1) businesses use advertising because it *does* work but (2) no one is yet quite sure *how* it works.

Because advertising costs money, and because that money could be pocketed as profits if not spent in this way, the concept of "wasted dollars" is important. For example, if Procter & Gamble were able to discover a way to achieve equal sales while spending only 10 percent less on advertising, the firm would add over $100 million to its profits before taxes! The issue of *how advertising works* is thus a major question for marketers in the quest for efficiency and profit.

An Ideal Persuasive Communication System

Although we've seen that advertising is supposed to be complex, we've yet to see why this might be the case, or what might be done about it. Let's start with Figure 17-2 which portrays a slightly expanded version of our general communication model geared especially to advertising. Notice that the figure shows six stages in the system, arrayed three on the advertiser's side and three on the consumer's side.

Stage I, **advertising goals**, represents management's aims for the upcoming advertising campaign. These goals depend on many factors, including current share of market, profit status, competition, and nature of the *target audience*. Four common types of advertising goals are (1) **persuasion** (for example, convincing consumers of a brand superiority claim), (2) **reinforcement** (e.g., assisting favorable consumer evaluation following a purchase), (3) **reminder** (e.g.,

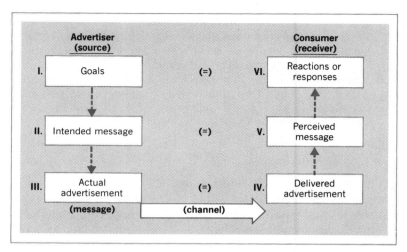

FIGURE 17-2 **Advertising as a Communication System**

for consumers favorable to the brand, to "keep it alive" in their evoked sets), (4) **purchase precipitation** (e.g., encouraging consumers to "buy now").[5] Notice that all these ad goals depend on consumer responses to be effective. In Figure 17-2, the equal sign between "Goals" and "Reactions or responses" indicates that a perfect operating system (from the advertiser's viewpoint) would result in consumers behaving exactly in accord with the goals of the advertising campaign.

Stage II, **intended message**, begins campaign planning. After settling on specific goals for the campaign, brand managers and the advertising agency must decide on their strategy by which these goals are to be attained. In essence, they must decide on their intended message to be sent to their consumer audience. In making this decision, they will be guided in part by research findings about consumers' interests and present behaviors, as well as by their past experience about what types of advertising messages seem to work well.

Stage III, **actual advertisement**, involves the "encoding" of the message. This stage reflects the "art" of advertising, as the ad agency converts the mental strategy for the campaign into the physical reality of an actual ad. As we noted earlier, literally thousands of interacting decisions need to be made in this stage, including the exact words, models, colors, actions, music, timing, and so forth. (If you've never had to analyze advertisements from this perspective, you might find it interesting and worthwhile to do so. The next time you're reading a magazine or watching TV, analyze the likely strategy the firm had in mind for the ad, and speculate what each ad might have been like had different decisions been made when converting the strategy into the ad itself.) In conjunction with all these decisions about the actual ads managers need to select and purchase time or space in specific **channels** (media) to deliver the ads to the target consumer market.

Stage IV, **delivered ads**, turns our attention to the other side of the figure—to consumer reception processes. The first stage here concerns delivery of the ad from the channel to the consumer, including the conditions under which it is received—or whether it is even received—by the target consumer.

Stage V, **perceived message**, concerns the fact that physical delivery of an ad is either accompanied by (in the case of radio or TV) or followed by (in the case of print) the consumer's mental processing of the ad to yield a perceived message. As we've already discussed in earlier chapters, the mental processes involved in the "decoding" (perception) of an external communication can be quite complex. The *equal sign* between "Intended message" and "Perceived message" indicates that the advertiser wishes consumers to take away exactly the same message as was originally intended to be sent.

Stage VI, **reactions or responses**, involves any later thoughts or behaviors that consumers might undertake because of the ad. As we noted earlier, this is an ideal communication system from a brand manager's viewpoint when a consumer's responses and reactions match perfectly with the goals that the managers had at the first stage of the system.

The System in Reality—Potential Gaps and Pitfalls

In reality, of course, advertisers face communication situations that fall far short of the ideal system we just examined. One problem is that it is too inefficient to try to communicate only with even a small number of consumers. Instead, the advertiser must strive to communicate effectively with a very large audience comprised of different types of people with different levels and types of interests. Thus an ad that is perfect for Jim Hunt might be neutral for his sister, and even disliked by his parents. Paying to send that ad to Jim's parents and sister is an inefficient step—and one to be avoided if possible.

When we think about the vast differences that exist between consumers, we can see that communication efficiency is a very significant issue for advertisers. It is for this reason that the concept of **market segmentation** is so significant. If the market can be segmented into large subgroups that are appropriate for the product in question, the marketer can create special product versions and advertising campaigns aimed especially at each subgroup and can more directly tailor messages to that group's key interests. Even though segmented advertising can offer major efficiencies, there are still significant challenges that confront our ideal system. In particular, there are five **potential gaps** that can occur: these are depicted in Figure 17-3.

Potential Gap 1

The first potential pitfall represents an instance in which *the advertising strategy is not capable of achieving the goals that have been set for the campaign*. This could occur because the goals have been set at an unrealistically high level, because the goals have not been set clearly, or because the strategy chosen (in

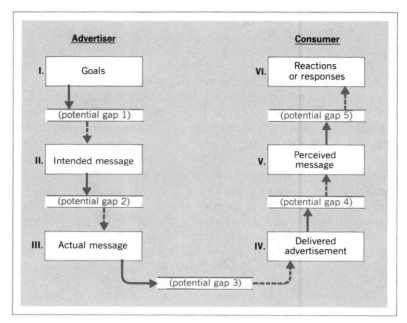

FIGURE 17-3 **Potential Gaps in the System**

other words, the intended message) just isn't effective enough to achieve the goals. A top official of Burger King, for example, commented that his company's advertising strategy of several years earlier had probably been misdirected:

> We had a very experiential positioning, that Burger King was the superior place . . . but when we found out that we couldn't out-McDonald McDonald's, we decided to compete in a different arena—the product.[5]

Potential Gap 2

The second potential gap recognizes *the thousands of tactical decisions that go together to make up the actual advertising campaign.* This potential gap will occur in those cases in which the actual advertising does not capture the intended strategy for the campaign, or where there is some type of mistake made in the ad itself. The Burger King executive commented on this strategy gap in discussing a later campaign:

> Frankly, I think those commercials may have gotten a bit off track. . . . Our overall strategy was based on food quality, but you didn't see a lot of food presence in those last commercials. . . . It's very easy to get off track . . . but rest assured, (our) future . . . ads are going to be based on the positioning—quality food.[7]

Exhibit 17-1 presents several bizarre, but real, examples of further mishaps that demonstrate this gap in reality.

EXHIBIT 17-1	SOME ADVERTISING "HERB-BLUNDERS"

As we have noted, ads have thousands of details involved in their creation. Sometimes some details don't quite work out. Here are four of those times:

Truth in Lending? Hackers Whack Back

Wells Fargo Bank recently sent some strange ad messages with its monthly statements to customers. Down at the bottom, Wells Fargo wrote, "*You owe your soul to the company store. Why not owe your home to Wells Fargo? An equity advantage loan can help you spend what would have been your children's inheritance.*" It turned out to be the work of some of the bank's computer programmers. A bank executive attempted to explain: "Someone with a misplaced sense of humor used this for a test . . . obviously it does not convey the opinions of the bank and its employees . . ."[9]

A Week for the Weak

The Wall Street Journal commented: "This commercial [for Continental Airlines MaxSaver fares] goes right for the heart. And it doesn't let the facts get in the way." The ad featured a telephone call, in which a mother learns that her daughter in another city is ill. Happily recalling Continental's low fares, she bubbles: "Don't worry . . . I can fly in . . . you get into bed . . . I'll fix some soup and get the kids off to school." However, someone listening to the ad's background voice would learn that there is a big problem facing Mom. These low fares require a minimum of seven days advance purchase for the ticket. If her daughter does get into bed, that household will have some problems![10]

Coin Strikes Mint

"A gross artistic miscarriage," thundered *Coin World* magazine. "I almost died when I saw it! If I weren't with the government, I would sue them," said the U.S. Mint's chief sculptor-engraver. At issue were ads for commemorative coins for the 1988 Olympic Games. The coin in question was a $5 gold piece featuring the face of Nike (the Greek goddess of victory). Because a photo of the coin wasn't yet available, the advertising agency had used a computer-enhanced rendition in its ads. The computer, however, made several changes in the face of the goddess—she had a wave of hair hung over her forehead, a crooked mouth, a turned-up nose, and her right cheek had been sliced off. All in all, stated a lawyer, "The ads do an abominable job . . . presenting what a really exquisite coin looks like."

Since by law a coin can't be photographed until it's officially struck, the agency didn't see what its options could be. In response to the charges, a senior executive said, "I don't know what her problem is with the artwork. It was an incredible time crunch."[11]

Continued

EXHIBIT 17-1   *SOME ADVERTISING "HERB-BLUNDERS"* CONTINUED

If This Is Their Best . . . !

Sometimes advertising deadlines cause problems in local media as well. This happened in one ad run by a car dealership that had the bold headline "Here's Our Best to You!" Obviously an untrained assistant had handled the art, which showed no wheels on the right side of the luxury auto (a different brand than in our mock-up shown here!), and some tires on the left that give a new meaning to the term "flat tire!" How many autos do you think that ad might have sold?

Potential Gap 3

The third potential gap reflects *any problems that may occur in the physical transmission or delivery of an ad to the consumer for whom it's intended.* One type of problem is whether the physical ad is transmitted in its original form. Static, interruptions, or audio or video problems for example, sometimes occur for television ads. Print smears or faulty color reproduction sometimes occur in print ads. In any of these cases (or other, such as newspapers left out in the morning rain, dogs honing their incisors on magazines in the mail delivery, or children changing channels as they discover they can now reach the TV knobs), the ad that is "delivered" is something less than the ad that was sent. A general term for this phenomenon is **noise**, indicating that the system is not operating in a trouble-free manner.

The other major problem in this sector is whether the ad is actually delivered at all—that is, is there a consumer at the other end who actually receives it?

We're all familiar with the times that we leave the room while the TV or radio is on, the days that we're too busy to read some sections of the newspaper, the times our attention is diverted and we miss a highway billboard, and so forth. Most recently, remote controls have aided consumer **zapping**, the practice of flipping channels to check on other programs when a commercial break begins. Research estimates indicate that zapping might be costing a 10–15 percent loss in viewership between programs and commercials, and is especialy heavy in wealthier households, those with cable, and during sports-event time periods.[8] **Zipping**, or running the VCR on fast forward through commercials, is a less serious problem at present. Overall, we can see that delivery of an ad is not the automatic process that it at first might appear to be. Part of the reason that ads are repeated with such frequency is to overcome the problem with delivery.

Potential Gap 4

The fourth potential gap refers to *any problem that may occur during consumers' perceptions of each ad as it is delivered to them.* Recall that the advertiser's objective here is that the consumer's perceived message be equivalent to the advertiser's intended message. In reality this potential gap stands as a major stumbling block to advertising effectiveness. To decode and interpret a message correctly, for example, consumers must be able to understand its language and symbols as they've been used by the sender. (In this regard, you may have heard advertising criticized as being "written for 12-year-olds!"; this simplicity of thought, language, and symbolism is largely due to advertisers' wishing to ensure that almost all the mass audience is able to perceive the intended messages correctly.) In addition to *capability* of understanding the message, *motivation* to process it is also important (as we've discussed, consumer low involvement is a common problem). Finally, of course, each consumer's interpretation of the message will depend on exactly which nodes in LTM are triggered by the ad and are brought into STM (short-term memory) for processing. *Perceptual processes* are thus also central to this area.

Within the working world of advertising, there is daily evidence of this gap. The "miscomprehenion" results we explored at the end of Chapter 8 indicate that a shocking 30 percent of points are being misunderstood regularly! Thus it may not be surprising that Wendy's has encountered some difficulties with its popular tongue-in-cheek campaign in which comsumers would choose the pathetic "Hamburger B" over the clearly superior "Hamburger A" from Wendy's. A company executive reported: "A small group of people can't understand why the consumers . . . don't pick 'A'."[12] Thus an astute marketer must be aware that there often will be a serious gap between the "ad that's delivered" and the "ad that's perceived" by a consumer.

Potential Gap 5

The final potential gap refers to *the advertiser's goal that the perceived message lead to particular responses or reactions on the consumer's part.* This gap involves two distinct and important processes. First, consumers need to in some manner *retain* the message after the ad exposure is over. This can be done either by recalling the message itself (that is, by having it stored in LTM) or by having formed a more favorable impression of the brand itself and maintaining this favorable impression in LTM. Second, consumers need to be *influenced* or *persuaded* by the advertising. As we noted in our discussion of ad goals, there are some occasions in which consumers have already been persuaded, and the ads are geared to reminders or purchase precipitation goals. In most cases, however, strong competitive brands are a fact of life facing the advertiser, and consumer persuasion toward your brand is a necessary component of advertising.

All advertisers know that effective consumer persuasion is very difficult to achieve. We can recall (from Chapter 2) that much of this difficulty stems from the nature of our marketing system, which delivers numerous ad appeals for competing offerings. The *total set of ads* proposes that a consumer buy *all* products and services: we realize that we cannot allow ourselves to be persuaded to buy most of the goods being advertised to us. Also, if an ad attempts to shift us toward a brand or store we dislike, we're likely to be "hard to sell" on the notion that we should change our behaviors to those recommended by the ad.

Across the field of advertising, then, advertisers must expect to encounter *consumer defensiveness* at this stage as a normal course of affairs. The key for a marketer is to restrict these problems to the minimum possible and strive for effective communication with specific target segments.

The Hierarchy of Advertising Effects

A useful perspective on how advertising works was developed by William McGuire, an eminent social psychologist with considerable experience in advising advertisers. It is depicted in Figure 17-4. This system is similar to the general hierarchy of effects model we discussed in Chapter 5. The steps are assumed to occur in a specified sequence: failure to achieve any step means that the next step cannot be reached. In brief, McGuire's hierarchy of advertising effects requires that (1) a consumer first be *exposed* to a message, (2) he or she then *pay attention* to it, (3) it be *understood*, (4) it lead to the consumer being *persuaded* as to the ad's conclusions and recommendations, (5) the persuasion or influence be *retained* over some time span, and finally (6) the overt *purchase behavior* the ad desires to be taken by the consumer.[13]

As we noted in Chapter 5, marketers can design an ad to appeal to a particular stage in the hierarchy. Some ads are aimed at gaining attention, others at persuading, while others attempt to directly stimulate purchase, for example. We should also understand the notion of a **probabilistic linkage** between the stages of the system. This means that, from the advertiser's point of view, each stage will only occur for some fraction of consumers in the market, and for any given consumer, it may occur at some times but not at others. There is, therefore, some probability of success at each stage (for example, 40 percent of consumers may be exposed to the message).

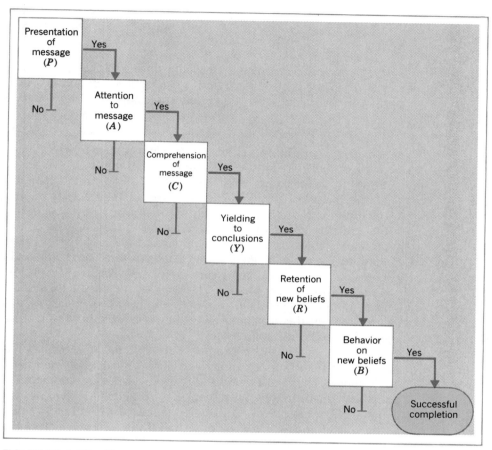

FIGURE 17-4 **The Hierarchy of Advertising Effects**

Source: William J. McGuire, "An Information Processing Model of Advertising Effectiveness,"
in H. Davis and A. Silk (eds.), *Behavioral and Management Sciences in Marketing* (New York:
Ronald Press/John Wiley, 1978), p. 161.

Calculating the Level of Ad Impact

Since this is an hierarchical model, we should multiply the probabilities for each
stage if we want to calculate the overall impact of a single showing of the ad on
consumers' purchase behavior. To see how this model works, let's begin by simply
assuming that each stage's probability is 0.5 (that is, that each stage has a 50–
50 probability of success with each consumer). What is the overall impact of this
advertisement? The formula to calculate this is

$$P\text{ (purchase)} = P(P) \times P(A) \times P(C) \times P(Y) \times P(R) \times P(B)$$

$$= 0.5 \times 0.5 \times 0.5 \times 0.5 \times 0.5 \times 0.5$$
$$= 0.0156$$

In this example, then, the ad would have a probability of only 1.6 percent of leading to the desired behavior! As several commentators have remarked, this view of advertising leads one to question how it has any effect at all!

Analyzing the Level of Effect

Is a 1.6 percent impact at all reasonable as a measure of advertising's influence on consumers? Before we can answer this question, we need to consider five other important points. First, the *probabilities for the system will clearly depend on the product class.* For example, we all realize that it's much easier for a consumer to buy a beer or soft drink than it is to buy a car, but we may not have thought through what this difference means for the role of advertising in each product category (and its probabilities of leading directly to purchase behavior). Ford, for example, is likely to use its ads to stimulate potential buyers to look for Fords on the road and appreciate their better points and to want to visit the Ford dealer to investigate further. The dealers, meanwhile, use local newspaper ads and limited-time offers to stimulate immediate shopping visits. Few sales occur directly from the ads themselves, however, since the role of the salesperson is crucial to "closing" many sales.

Second, *our initial assumption of a 0.5 probability for each consumer who reaches a stage is quite unrealistic*—it is probably *too high* for most if not all of the stages. The realistic probability for the overall system in most product classes is thus much, much lower than the 1.6 percent we've just calculated. (If you find this hard to accept, try calculating the sales that Ford would get from a single showing of an ad for a $15,000 model if the ad reached 10 million adults. Then extend your analysis by multiplying your results for only 10 showings of this ad, and then extend them to all ads for all models of all brands of automobiles.)

Third, the *probabilities for the system's stages are almost certainly not equal.* It is much easier for an advertiser to obtain consumer exposure than consumer attention, for example, and either of these stages is much easier to obtain than consumer purchase behavior. Also the probability for a stage's success depends on the ad itself. Fourth, *repetition's effects will change some of the probabilities within the system.* The second, third, and subsequent times we are exposed to the same commercial, for example, we will be able to draw upon our LTM to help recall parts of it and to anticipate what will be coming. In this way a consumer might move through the hierarchy's stages over time, as probabilities for later stages slowly increase. (Of course, repetition won't continue to work positively forever.)

Our fifth and final point is an important reminder that these *probabilities need to be applied to the huge consumer market* toward which the advertising is directed. Depending on the product, we may be talking about millions of consumers, which means that even a small probability can lead to a large sales volume and high profits. Thus, if we are able to improve the probabilities by even a few percentage points, this can mean very large increases in sales and profits!

How Strong Are Advertising's Impacts?

Our dual coverage of the advertising communications system and the hierarchy of advertising suggests that ads may not actually be nearly as powerful on one exposure as we may have thought. In this section we'll briefly examine two important studies on what actually happens with consumer ads.

The Starch Study of TV Commercials

A number of years ago a leading advertising research firm, Daniel Starch, Inc., made waves through the advertising community when it publicized the results of a special research study it had run on what consumers take away from commercials. Within this study, consumers were first "qualified" as having watched particular programs within two hours before being questioned in the study. All consumers had thus had their ads "delivered" in the terms of our ideal system and were "exposed" according to McGuire's framework. Out of every 100 audience members, how many would you think remembered having seen the average commercial?_____ With respect to the intended message, what percentage could correctly answer "What brand was advertised?"_____ How frequently did a consumer come up with an incorrect brand name to this question? _____ After providing your estimates, you may wish to check the brief description of the study's findings in Note 14, contained in the listings for Chapter 17 at the back of the book.

The Gallup & Robinson Study of Ad Effectiveness

Gallup & Robinson (G&R), another leading advertising research firm, examined its research findings for several years on all ads in five different product categories (autos, tires, men's colognes, television sets, and insurance). For each ad, consumers were again qualified as having either read the magazine or viewed the TV program within which the test ad was contained. Rather than two hours after exposure, however, G&R conducted its interviews the day following ad exposure (this technique is often termed 24-hour recall).

Results varied widely based on which ad was studied. One key measure, for example, is *registration of the featured idea* in an ad. This measure ranged from 0 percent for several ads (that is, not one consumer could remember any point from a particular ad to which they'd been exposed a day earlier) to a high of 39 percent registration for one auto ad that had appeared in a magazine. The highest average rate was 10 percent for television ads in the cologne product class, while the lowest rate was for insurance ads appearing in magazines, which averaged only 3 percent registration. In numbers, these findings indicated, for example, that of 5462 viewers of a TV commercial for tires, an average of only 300 (5.5 percent) would recall the key point of the commercial by the next day.[15]

Controversy: Is the Hierarchy the Only Way?

Before leaving the topic of advertising's persuasive aspects we should note that controversies exist in this area. As we discussed, no one entirely understands how advertising works its influences on consumer behavior. It is not surprising, therefore, that the hierarchy will have some limitations in its explanations.

One area in which this point is particularly raised is in respect to low involvement, which we've discussed earlier in the book. Michael Ray, a recognized expert on marketing communication, has suggested that low-involvement situations change the order of the hierarchy's stages from a "think-feel-do" order into a "think-do-feel" ordering.[16] In terms of Figure 17-4, this would mean that consumers won't pay enough attention to ads to *yield* to their conclusions. Instead, ads in low-involvement situations work by skipping the yielding stage and focusing their low-intensity effects on the retention and behavior stage probabilities. Rather than having an immediate impact within a single exposure, moreover, these effects build up slowly over a long time period and many repetitions of the ad. Toward the end of this longer time frame, the consumer knows the brand name and knows it's heavily advertised, but doesn't feel strongly one way or another about the brand itself.

How would the alternative think-do-feel hierarchy work in the real consumer setting? Let's assume that Donna Smith, as she stands in a drug store, sees a display for Creemo face cream, recalls that she's seen this brand advertised a lot, and decides to "try it" and see how it works. Only after she brings it home and uses it will she commit herself to a positive or negative feeling about the brand and either "yield" or "not yield" to the Creemo ad's statements about the brand.

When the low-involvement situation is operating, implications for advertising strategy will be different from those when the traditional hierarchy is at work. According to Ray, some conditions leading to the low-involvement situation are (1) little differences in the brands of the product class (a so-called "parity product" situation), (2) a mature stage of a product life cycle (that is, most brands have been in the market for quite a while, and consumers are aware of this fact), and (3) heavy use of advertising in the mass media.

Recent research has investigated several interesting aspects of the low-involvement hierarchy approach. According to Andrew Ehrenberg of England, advertising is usually "a weak, reinforcing influence on consumers rather than a strong persuasive influence." It increases awareness and interest, suggests trial, and reinforces the feelings of satisfaction after purchase.[17] William Wells, a senior advertising research executive, points out that advertising can also have a special type of **transformational effect** on consumers: it can help them to look for certain effects from a brand and can thereby change (transform) the experiences they have following purchase and use.[18] For example, this is often the case with a status symbol, or with a performance automobile.

Beyond these particular points, there is a large literature on advertising decisions and advertising effectiveness. If you wish to read more on these topics, you may want to consult Appendix 17-B, which offers a summary of findings and a guide to locating useful sources for further reading.

The Growing Role of Promotions

One key message from our discussion of advertising's influence is that a single ad exposure is apt to have only a low-level impact on the audience. Over time and repetitions, however, advertising does seem to "cumulate" its effect. Thus there appears to be a *long-term impact from advertising* to consumers. In recent years, however, U.S. business has faced increased pressures for *short-term impact*. Stock investors want increased profits. New brand managers want to make their mark quickly. How do we attain short-term impact on consumers? "*Use sales promotions!*" is the increasing answer.

Coupons, refunds, premiums or gifts, samples, cents-off specials, and sweepstakes are all popular forms of consumer promotion. Because they are aimed directly at short-term impacts on consumers' buying behavior, sales promotions offer advantages in measuring effectiveness and in creating a quick jump in business for the successful firm. Also, of course, they are popular with consumers:

Raisin' Their Sales at Hardee's

"It was beyond our wildest dreams," reports the executive in charge of the California raisin figurine promotion run by Hardee's hamburger chain. Each of four Claymation® "grapevine" dancers was sold for 99 cents to customers at Hardee's. The tie-in was with the firm's cinnamon and raisin biscuits for breakfast, an area in which Hardee's wanted higher sales. The campaign's goal was for a 5 percent sales increase for the promotional month. The results: sales increased by 18 percent, with some outlets reporting 30 percent jumps. The figurines have become collectibles and are now commanding hefty prices on resale![19]

The Hardee's Raisin promotion: a grape success!

Coupons help create consumer purchases.

While many promotions work well with consumers, some marketers are concerned about putting too heavy reliance on them. When auto brands offer rebates, sales go up, but when the rebate ends, sales drop as consumers wait for the next round. Similarly, sweepstakes may make an impact, but do not build consumer loyalty. Also, couponing—which actually represents price competition—may threaten to lower average prices for branded products. In the longer run, "brand equity" might be threatened. In general, then, marketers are seeking a proper balance between the short run and the long run: it appears that both promotions and advertising have important roles to play. The availability of detailed data from computerized supermarket checkout scanning systems has begun to allow specific tests of how well both advertising and sales promotions work. To learn more about developments in this area, you may wish to begin with Note 20.[20]

CONTROLLING THE INSTITUTION OF ADVERTISING

As we noted at the very start of this chapter, advertising is a huge and important institution in our society. At the same time, since millions of private businesses are active in placing their ads into the larger environment, *advertising in our society is ultimately an uncontrollable activity*. This will continue to be the case unless government would begin to engage in the types of widespread censorship and restrictions that are viewed as unacceptable in a market-based economic system that prizes freedom of speech. Appendix 17-A details many of the key issues and debates concerning the social and economic roles of advertising. In this section we will concentrate on how the institution itself is monitored.

Government Regulation of Advertising

In Chapter 21, we discuss in some detail the nature of government regulation of marketing, especially that by the Federal Trade Commission (FTC). As noted there, the FTC has long been criticized for being either too harsh or too soft in its regulatory activities, and has shifted directions several times. Recently, for example, we saw an era of deregulation in which the FTC and other agencies cut back significantly on their regulatory efforts. Marketers realize, however, that if advertising abuses become too widespread, or if opponents of advertising become sufficiently powerful, the government is likely to turn around and move against the advertising industry with restrictions and regulations.

The threat of governmental interference provides one reason for leaders in advertising to seek ways to control the quality of advertising. Beyond this, advertising leaders realize that negative practices breed consumer cynicism and lead to lower effectiveness of all advertising. Finally, many people in the industry are personally angered by ad practices that they believe are at or beyond the edge of ethics, fairness, or taste (for example, an industry trade publication, *Advertising Age*, frequently includes an "Ads We Can Do Without" feature in its "Letters to the Editor" column). For all these reasons, the advertising industry has sought to supplement government regulation with its own programs of self-regulation.

Self-regulation in Advertising

Advertising industry codes represent a common basis for industry self-regulation. It is helpful to have guidelines for developing advertising campaigns. Industry trade associations representing advertisers, agencies, media, and research firms all regularly publish codes of ethics and guidelines for their members to follow voluntarily. Many firms also publish their own policies for advertising.

Advertising approval processes often also exist for each advertising campaign. Most large advertisers and ad agencies, for example, follow a formal "approval" process for ads after the storylines have been developed by the marketing department and ad agency (but before expensive production has taken place). This process usually includes approval, in writing, by the public relations department, technical departments, and top management. In addition, the legal department will typically go over the ads carefully and ask for revisions when they feel they may be needed.

Media clearance procedures follow the internal reviews at the agency and firm. Advertising must be submitted to the media for "clearance" before it will be accepted. Television networks are probably the most severe in attempting to adhere to high standards in clearing their commercials. The broadcast standards department at CBS, for example, reviewed over 30,000 commercials in a recent year and raised objections to over 11,000 of them, primarily on the basis of poor taste or lack of substantiation. When this occurs, the advertiser must reach agreement with the network on changes to be made before the ad will be cleared

Merry Christmas to all, and to all a good night.

We probably nestled your grandmother all snug in her bed. And probably her mother, too.

For over 125 years, we've spent every waking moment caring about the way young America sleeps.

Of course, we've made some changes along the way.

Zippers that won't stick. Soft fabrics protected by Scotchgard™ Stain Release for easy care, for fabrics that stay new-looking longer.

And for little feet that wander, there are special skid-resistant soles that help protect your child from slips and falls. But through the years we've never tampered with the essential things that Dr. Dentons are made of— warmth, comfort, caring and love. For those are the things that dreams–and holidays–are made of.

Dr. Denton
We've Tucked In
Six Generations Of America.

Scotchgard
FORTREL

Dr. Denton® is a DIVISION OF SALANT CHILDREN'S APPAREL GROUP

The Good Housekeeping seal helps in consumer trust—an important dimension of this ad.

to be run. Some magazines also take pride in their standards and clearance procedures (*Good Housekeeping* employs a seal of approval for products advertised in its pages, for example), while others are more lax. Newspapers, on the other hand, often face short lead times because the specific dates for retail sale ads and must employ clearance processes that are less comprehensive.[21]

The **advertising self-regulatory system** was created as a further check by the business community since the three prior stages are not sufficient to remove all potential difficulties from a huge market-based activity with competitive and persuasive aims. If problems arise after an ad has appeared, the logical alternatives are that it be handled either through public means (either the courts or the government's regulatory system) or private means (an agreement is reached between a consumer and a firm, or between two competitors, or the firm decides to modify its advertising with the help of a neutral third party). When an industry sets up a continuing arrangement to encourage such private means of dispute settlement, it is said to be engaging in self-regulation. Self-regulation must be voluntary and, therefore, depends on the cooperation of the firms in the industry.

The NAD/NARB System

Since 1971, the advertising industry has had its own **NAD/NARB system**—a very successful program of self-regulation. The system consists of two agencies—the National Advertising Division (NAD) and the National Advertising Review Board (NARB). NAD is the first stage of the system and acts as its investigatory arm. The NAD collects and evaluates data concerning the ad, and arrives at an initial decision as to whether the claims in the ad have been substantiated or not. If the NAD feels the ad is not satisfactory, it negotiates with the advertiser to have the campaign modified or discontinued. Cases that cannot be resolved at the NAD are appealed to the NARB and are heard by a panel of five "judges" from firms, ad agencies, and the public sector.

Advertising cases arise from several sources. The NAD has its own monitoring program, which initiates many inquiries to firms about their advertising claims. Local Better Business Bureaus also forward complaints to the NAD: these account for about one in every six cases. Individual consumers may, and do, institute complaints to the NAD: these account for about one in eight cases. Finally, competitors may complain about advertising they perceive to be harmful to their interests. In recent years this has increased dramatically, to about 40 percent of the cases. Several thousand cases have now been heard by the self-regulatory system. In about half of these cases the NAD determined that the ad claims are reasonable and had been substantiated. In almost all remaining cases the advertiser voluntarily agreed to either modify or discontinue the campaign. Only 2 percent of the cases were appealed to the NARB, sometimes by the NAD (because it could not reach agreement with the advertiser) and sometimes by the original complainant, who was displeased with the NAD's decision in the matter.[22]

According to industry observers and government regulators alike, the advertising self-regulation program has been extremely successful. It has shifted many cases from the antagonistic setting of government proceedings and has speeded up the processing of these cases (the average case concludes in six months, as opposed to several years in government proceedings). While not solving all the problems that advertising faces on its social dimensions, this system should be credited with helping to improve the character of consumer advertising in our society.

SUMMARY

An Overview of Advertising Decisions

This chapter has dealt with the influences of advertising on consumer behavior. Advertising is a major industry in our nation, comprising about 3 percent of GNP. The two chief actors in the advertising sphere—marketers and consumers—are here arrayed as *senders and receivers of messages*. Marketers control the basic decisions about the advertising that is distributed, while consumers control their reactions to it.

In the first section of the chapter we briefly examined the complex nature of advertising decisions. The 7 M's *framework* is useful in this regard. The first six factors—*merchandise, markets, motives, messages, money, and media*—all contribute to the overall impact of an ad, while the seventh factor—*measurement*—attempts to monitor and refine this impact through research.

Advertising as Communication

The second section began with a basic model of advertising as communication. Four elements are present in the simple model: the *source* of the communication develops a *message* and then delivers it through a *channel* to the *receiver*. We noted that, unlike most other communications, advertising is a one-way communication flow. This poses certain disadvantages and advantages.

The Persuasive Aspect of Advertising

The third section focused on the *persuasive nature of advertising impacts*. Here we examined a staged framework. First, marketers need to set advertising goals. Possible goals could be to persuade, to reinforce, to remind, or to stimulate an immediate purchase. Next, the advertising goals must be translated into an intended message, or a strategy for the ad campaign. Third, the intended message must be developed into an actual advertisement. Designing the actual ad entails going through thousands of interacting decisions on art and execution. Fourth, the ad must be delivered to the consumer, via planned channels. Fifth, the consumer takes away a perceived message from the communication. In the final stage, the consumer's reactions or responses to the perceived message occur. We noted, however, that in reality the system does not work so smoothly and discussed the gaps that appear between each of the stages.

The chapter next presented a *hierarchy of advertising effects model*. A consumer must first be *exposed* to an ad, must *pay attention* to it, and must *understand* it. The ad must lead to the consumer being *persuaded*, and such persuasion must be *retained* over time and should lead to *purchase behavior* as advocated by the ad. According to this model, an effective ad must take the consumer through all these stages. Our analysis showed that the probability of success with a single advertisement is indeed very small. However, we need to remember that these probabilities depend on the type of product and amount of repetition and may differ for each stage of the model. Further, in a mass consumer market, even a minute probability translates into a large volume of sales dollars. Also, we noted why the "low involvement" (think-do-feel) hierarchy may be a better model for some product classes. Next, we discussed how the stress of short-term influences on consumer behavior has increased sales promotions by marketers.

Controlling the Institution of Advertising

The chapter concluded with a discussion of the various organizations and codes that have been created to control the institution of advertising. Some are governmental, but most have arisen within the industry itself. We saw how these programs have helped to improve the character of advertising directed to consumers in our society.

Appendix 17-A moves beyond this coverage to present a broader look at the subject of advertising's influence on consumers. The economic and social roles for advertising are topics of heated debates. The basic positions are summarized in this interesting and thought-provoking appendix. Meanwhile, Appendix 17-B should be consulted by readers interested in learning more about advertising decision-making, as it summarizes some findings and provides useful guides for further reading.

KEY TERMS

marketing managers
consumers
merchandise
markets
motives
messages
money
media
measurement
source
receiver
channel
advertising goals
target audience
persuasion
reinforcement
reminder
purchase precipitation
intended message
actual advertisement
delivered ads
consumer reception processes
perceived message
reactions or responses
market segmentation
potential gap 1
potential gap 2

potential gap 3
potential gap 4
potential gap 5
noise
zapping
probabilistic linkage
transformational effect
advertising industry codes
advertising approval processes
media clearance procedures
advertising self-regulatory system
NAD/NARB system

APPENDIX 17-A TERMS

barrier to entry
market power school
information school

APPENDIX 17-B TERMS

source credibility
trustworthiness
expertise
attractiveness
comparison advertising

REVIEW QUESTIONS AND EXPERIENTIAL EXERCISES

[E = Application extension or experiential exercise]

1. Compare/contrast how the general model of communication (Figure 17-1), if applied to family or salesperson influences on consumer behavior, would differ from its application to advertising influences on consumer behavior. Which is a more effective marketing tool, advertising or salespersons?

2. Consider the four basic types of advertising goals described in the text. Analyze a number of ads, searching for two examples of each type of goal.

3. Consider the "potential gaps" in the advertising communication system (Figure 17-3). Which would you say is the most frequent? Which is most serious?

4. One advertising approach to persuade consumers to buy a particular product is to use a fear message. How frequently are these used? Do you believe they are generally effective? Why or why not?

5. Humor is another approach used in advertising. How frequently is this employed? Do you believe it is effective? Why or why not?

6. Indicate at what stage of the "hierarchy of advertising effects" model (Figure 17-4) you are currently located for the following products or services. Provide rationale.

   a. Charmin   d. Gerber pudding
   b. Rolling Rock   e. Subaru
   c. Butter Buds   f. American Express

7. One of the basic propositions in Appendix 17-B states that advertising effects depend on source, message, and media fctors, as well as on the receiver. Of the first three, which would you judge is usually the most significant? Why? Provide examples.

8. How do the two major schools of economics (discussed in Appendix 17-A) differ in their answers to the questions of advertising's effects on prices and on competition (as an entry barrier)? Which side do you tend to favor?

9. Many social criticisms of advertising are listed in Appendix 17-A. Which, if any, do you find to be either completely in error or lacking justification? Which, if any, do you find you agree with?

[E] 10. During recent years movements arose to ban advertising for certain products. Develop a brief, well-designed set of arguments either for or against the following proposal: "Broadcast advertising for beer and wine should be banned."

[E] 11. Use your library to locate back issues of the *Journal of Advertising Research* and the *Journal of Advertising*. Write a brief report summarizing the topics discussed and a few of your best findings from the articles.

[E] 12. Select one of the four factors—source, message, media, and receiver—discussed in Appendix 17-B. Using the relevant Note listings at the back of this book, or the reference section of your library, read several key articles on the subject. Write a brief report on your findings.

[E] 13. Review a series of magazine ads, analyzing each in terms of the advertising system shown in Figures 17-2 and 17-3. Cut out several examples of what you believe are especially good or bad ads. For each, present a brief analysis of your position, pointing out any "gaps" that you may have found.

[E] 14. Interview a manager or copywriter for an ad agency. Discuss, in detail, the process of creating and placing an ad. Write a brief report on your findings.

APPENDIX 17-A ECONOMIC AND SOCIAL ISSUES IN ADVERTISING

As we've stressed throughout the chapter, advertising is essentially a business function. It is planned and run as an integral part of the marketing mix. The benefits that flow from advertising are typically economic and are planned to go to the sponsor of the ads. When we move beyond the single firm to consider advertising from a broader viewpoint, we find debates about its social and economic character in our society. Within this appendix we'll begin with the economic dimensions, then turn to social criticisms.

Economic Debates on Advertising

Prominent economists, advertising leaders, and public policymakers are divided on how well advertising performs its economic roles. Among the questions that are debated are:

- Is advertising a barrier to entry?
- Does advertising raise or lower prices?

Advertising and Barriers to Entry

A **barrier to entry** is something that hinders a potential competitor from entering a product class and competing for sales in it. Large plant investments, lack of access to raw materials, or inability to gain retail shelf space are examples of entry barriers. With respect to advertising, the barriers to entry debate concerns the effects that advertising has on competition with a product class. The data are clear that (1) firms with higher shares of market tend also have higher shares of advertising expenditures and (2) firms with higher profits also tend to advertise more. The question is "Why?" Does advertising by large firms act to keep out other, smaller firms who may have superior products? If so, advertising would be acting in an anticompetitive manner.

It is important to note that this need not be a result of a conscious effort by a large company to act in an anticompetitive manner. For example, the economics of advertising tend to work in favor of size, as fixed costs of production can be spread over more exposures and volume discounts are typically available from the media. Also, for some media (especially national television), the lowest levels of money necessary to gain exposure can be quite high (e.g., $300,000 for a 30-second spot on a popular show in prime time). These amounts are well within the ability of large firms to afford but may be risky for the financial health of a smaller firm.

The actions of channel members and consumers might also serve to make advertising a barrier to entry by new firms. For example, since retailers are interested in giving their valuable shelf space only to brands they are confident will be quickly purchased, a smaller firm may be less able to convince whole-salers and retailers that the new product will be in demand. Consumers, of course, lie at the heart of this issue, as a function of how receptive they are to trying new entries to the market. If consumers are only willing to buy heavily advertised brands whose names are familiar to them through advertising, for example, new firms will have a more difficult time in successfully offering their products.

Economists who believe that advertising has these types of effects often belong to the **market power school** of thought. They stress advertising's *persuasive aspects* and believe that successful advertising often contributes to increasing industry concentration in which a few firms come to form an oligopoly to dominate production and sales. In the brewing industry, for example, hundreds of local and regional beer brands have gone out of business as Budweiser, Miller, and a few other major brands have come to dominate the market.

Economists who reject these effects from advertising often belong to the **information school** of thought. They argue that the situation is just the opposite—that advertising actually acts to ease the path of a new competitor's entry into the market. They stress that advertising offers *information* to consumers, who are free to choose whether to buy or not. If the product or service is worthwhile, consumers will try it and will return for more in the future. Advertising is an efficient way of informing consumers about such new offerings and can offer handsome returns to firms that are willing to invest in it, even if they have to borrow to do so. The fact that firms with higher share of market advertise more, then, indicates to this school that these firms are offering a product that the public values.

As you may know from a course in economics, detailed answers to the questions raised in these debates require advanced quantitative analyses of the special conditions of each case. Even then, the opposing sides are likely to continue to disagree. (If you are not familiar with these types of arguments, or would like to read more about them, Note 23 provides a good place to begin).

Advertising's Effects on Prices

"Does advertising raise or lower prices to consumers?" This interesting question again raises arguments among the experts. Here the data are clear that consumers pay higher prices for advertised brands than for those not advertised, that retailers also pay higher prices for these brands (a store's markup is usually higher for its private-label brand than for the national brands on the shelves), and that advertisers have to pay to create and place their ads. For all these reasons, it would appear that advertising would act to *raise* consumer prices, since "Someone Has to Pay for It!"

Members of the market power school support this concern about higher prices coming from heavy advertising in an industry. Because they stress advertising's persuasive aspects, they see advertising as creating an inelastic demand curve for a brand (through consumers' building a preference and loyalty for that brand, and being willing to pay higher prices for it). If this is based on "image" rather than performance factors—as it may be in the case of some beer brands, for example—then consumers would be paying more than they otherwise would have to if advertising were less significant in the industry.

Also, when primary demand (total unit sales for the entire product class) is dropping, logic indicates that high advertising expenditures cannot be returning increased unit sales to all advertisers. The cigarette industry, for example, spends over $2 billion per year in promotional activities, even though its sales are falling as more people quit smoking for health reasons. For at least some of the brands, then, advertising represents an added cost in the losing fight for increased sales and helps to keep prices higher than they otherwise would be.

Members of the information school again hold just the opposite views. They point out that advertising is often a very efficient means of creating a mass market for a product, by communicating with large numbers of consumers at a low cost per person. When successful, this affords a much larger sales base for the firm. This larger base usually lowers per unit costs for materials, production, distribution, and overhead because of efficiencies associated with higher volumes. In turn, these lower costs allow the firm to *lower* the price for the product, even though the advertising's cost is included in the selling price. Also, since this school believes that advertising helps new competitors to enter the market, it sees markets with heavy advertising to be quite competitive, with constant competitive pressures to either lower prices or improve products to gain market share and increase profits.

Implications for Public Policy

Thus each side has strong grounds for holding its positions, and the debates continue. These are not just irrelevant debates, however. Depending on the answers, public policymakers should take different positions on how advertising should be treated. For example, should there be certain conditions under which advertising should not be tax deductible as a business expense? Are there market conditions under which a cap should be placed on the amount of advertising that an industry is allowed? Should utilities be allowed to charge customers for the advertising they do? These debates occur at both the federal and state government levels and are often very heated. Since millions of dollars are typically involved in these decisions, the stakes are high, and economic debates on advertising are sure to continue far into the future.

Social Dimensions of Advertising

Almost everyone has opinions about advertising, ranging from aspects that we like to those that we dislike most intensely. Some of the most important opinions relate to broader social and economic concerns about advertising. Within this section we'll briefly examine some of the questions and controversies involving advertising's role in our society.

What Do Consumers Like and Dislike About Advertising?

In a famous study of advertising in America, two leading experts, Raymond Bauer and Stephen Greyser, asked consumers about their views of this institution, including what they liked and disliked. When asked why they like advertising, many points emerged:

The Consumers' View: Pros and Cons

1. A majority of consumers mentioned first the *information* that advertising provides. Consumers reported that ads help them to understand products better, learn about new products and services, and help them to stay current about prices and specials.
2. *Economic* reasons were also mentioned by about one in five persons—these reflect appreciation of the roles that advertising plays in providing employment to many workers and in contributing to lowering prices for mass-market products.
3. *Entertainment* was also recognized, in two ways. First, some consumers mentioned that they liked some of the humorous, warm, and exciting ads themselves. Second, some consumers expressed appreciation for advertising subsidizing television, radio, newspapers, and magazines and lowering the costs of these entertainment and information sources.

When asked what they disliked about advertising, consumers in the Bauer and Greyser study also raised a number of criticisms:

1. The most frequently mentioned objection was the *intrusiveness*—advertising was seen as "intruding" on our lives too often and too strongly. People mentioned that they felt there are simply too many ads and that some ads are repeated far too often. Concern was also expressed that TV ads are recorded at higher volumes and are too loud.
2. *Falsity* and *exaggeration* were also frequently raised points, with consumers registering a belief that some ads don't present quite a true picture of the product or service and might be misleading.

3. Among the list of other dislikes mentioned was *silliness*, reflecting a belief that ads talk down to people and are sometimes irritating.[24]

Broader Social Criticisms: The Seven Sins of Advertising

A brief consideration of the issues just raised shows that (1) advertising has both positive and negative aspects and (2) neither the positives nor the negatives apply to all ads. We should recognize, therefore, that attempts to characterize *all of advertising* mean that a person has to generalize. This process brings difficulties. Nonetheless, a series of broad criticisms of advertising in modern society have been raised by serious observers, primarily persons outside of the business community (these were also raised by small numbers of consumers in the Bauer and Greyser study). If you are not already familiar with these charges, you may wish to stop and think about how you feel about them. How generalizable is each, and how accurately does it reflect legitimate concerns? What—if anything—do you feel should be done about each of the "seven sins" charged by advertising's critics?[25]

Charge 1: Advertising Persuades People to Do Things They Otherwise Wouldn't
This is the broadest attack on advertising. It raises fundamental questions about the nature of commercial persuasion, the use of sophisticated theories, research, and technologies to make this persuasion as effective as possible, and the ends toward which the persuasion is directed. Among the specific questions that arise in this area are

1. Under what conditions, if any, is it appropriate to *try to create new desires* in consumers for no reason other than profits to the advertiser? Does advertising actually arouse desires?
2. Under what conditions, if any, is it appropriate to *play on people's emotions* for no reason other than increasing profits for the advertiser? Why not simply deliver only factual product information that accurately portrays functional properties and benefits of products and services, including any dangers, or drawbacks?
3. What are consumers' *true needs*? Are there such things as "bad" wants or needs? Does advertising either create or encourage them? What would people desire to buy if there were no advertising?

Charge 2: Advertising Propagandizes in Favor of a Materialistic Life
This charge shifts focus to the fact that advertising is used by each firm to increase its sales. In the aggregate, therefore, advertising is used to encourage people to consume more and more. Several key questions arise in this area, such as

1. Does advertising cause people to *judge themselves and others* on the basis of their possessions rather than their personal qualities?
2. Does advertising *stress conformity* with others as a goal to be sought by consumers?
3. Does advertising encourage consumers to *use, then throw away*, rather than care for and maintain products?

4. Does advertising advocate that people obtain more and more possessions even if they can't *afford* them?

Charge 3: Advertising Lowers the Values and Ethical Standards of Society

This charge continues the issues raised in charge 2, but now concentrates on what may be lost if a person or society pursues a materialistic life-style. Some questions here include

1. Does advertising encourage people to feel that they badly need more money, so that they come to *change what they think about, feel, and do* on a daily basis? For example, does advertising lead people to take on more work (e.g., a part-time job) or neglect their families as they strive to increase their material possessions?
2. Does advertising glorify possessions to such an extent that some persons even *engage in crime* (e.g., shoplifting or writing bad checks) to obtain more material possessions?
3. Does advertising *discourage people from noneconomic activities* such as volunteer work, religious devotion, or appreciating the arts, because of its emphasis on buying more?
4. Does advertising *encourage a desire for instant gratification*?

Charge 4: Advertising Employs Bad Taste and Questionable Morals

This charge moves attention to what is included in ads rather than their function of selling products. Among the issues arising here are

1. Does advertising *embarrass* sectors of the audience by discussing and protraying products, such as those used for feminine hygiene? What, if anything, should advertisers do about this, or do they have an absolute right to act as they see fit?
2. Does advertising use social fear techniques to *make people feel inferior or inadequate* for no reason other than to increase the profits of the advertiser? Should this type of advertising be allowed?
3. Does advertising *use sexual themes and innuendoes* to make products seem desirable? What effects might this have on various members of the audience?
4. Does advertising *stress youth and beauty* in selling its products? Everyone is getting older, and most audience members are much less physically attractive than the models used in ads. Does this constant stress on youth and beauty have the effect of making people uneasy and dissatisfied with themselves? For example, is advertising a major factor behind so many young women having anorexia nervosa and bulimia? What should advertisers and media do about this, or is this actually a positive element of advertising in representing ideals?

Charge 5: Advertising Employs Negative Stereotypes

This charge stresses the ways in which particular types of people are represented in ads and what effects this might have on the views of those in the audience. Some key questions in this area include

1. Does advertising portray *blacks* or *Hispanics* in roles as members of lower classes in society, but not as doctors, professors, or successful businesspersons? If so, what effects does this have on whites' views of minority persons' competencies and roles in society? What, if anything, should advertisers and the media do about this?

2. How should advertising portray *women* in modern society? Is it demeaning to use the "housewife slice-of-life" ad to sell detergents, waxes, and household cleaning products? Is it demeaning to portray women in slinky gowns to sell perfume and other cosmetics? What about using women in slinky gowns to sell cars or industrial machinery?

3. How should advertising portray *older citizens*? Should they only appear in ads for denture products and medical supplies? Why aren't they portrayed as having the wisdom of experience and as having much to offer society in general and younger persons in particular? Why isn't this stage of life portrayed in a positive light in advertising, or is it actually portrayed with accuracy?

4. Overall, should advertising attempt to portray life as an *ideal or as reality*? Should advertising try to help *lead* societal trends or *reflect life* as it still is in the mainstream of society?

Charge 6: Advertising Has Strong Adverse Effects on Society's "Underdogs"

This charge continues the thrust of charge 5 but now focuses on possible effects of advertising on certain groups and persons who are less able to participate fully in the consuming society. The basic question in this area is as follows:

1. Over a period of years, what effect does advertising have on *poor persons* in our society? Do they consciously realize that they'll probably never possess the glamorous houses, clothes, or trips offered in some ads? Do the ads inspire them to achieve more or serve to remind them of their prospects and thereby act as a depressant? Does constant exposure to ads make these persons feel less worthwhile?

Charge 7: Advertising Exploits the Innocence and Immaturity of Our Children

This charge has led to years of controversy and regulatory battles in Washington, D.C., as consumer groups have fought for further restrictions on advertising aimed at children. We examine these issues in Chapter 10, but the general nature of the questions is:

1. Do advertisers *take advantage of limitations in children's abilities* to know that they are being persuaded to buy products for no other reason than to increase profits of the advertiser?

2. Does advertising *stress impulsive purchases* of toys at inflated prices, without regard to their durability or likelihood of delivering enjoyment over a period of time? Why is plastic stressed so much and why does it crack so easily—is this a case of planned obsolescence to increase industry sales?

3. Does advertising *push sugared products and junk foods* on children and thereby contribute to lifelong problems with dental caries, obesity, and unbalanced diets? Why don't fresh fruits and vegetables get advertised as much as candy, cookies, and chips?

4. Does advertising try to *create materialistic values* in children, thereby capturing them as consumers for life? Does it play on their most basic qualities of curiosity, and desire to learn and experience what the world has to offer?

5. Does advertising *contribute to family problems* by encouraging kids to want too many products and in particular certain brands that are overpriced because of the advertising?

Given the subjective nature of all of these charges, it seems apparent that most of the issues will never be fully resolved. As citizens, consumers, and professionals in marketing, however, they pose significant questions for us to consider and debate.

APPENDIX 17-B   KEY FACTORS IN ADVERTISING'S IMPACTS

In this appendix we will combine the concepts from our chapter frameworks to investigate key factors in advertising's impacts on consumers. Within this section we briefly examine two key advertising propositions and then illustrate them using the case of comparison advertising. Our first proposition reflects the essentials for Figure 17-1 at the start of the chapter.

Proposition 1: Effects Depend on Source, Medium, Message, and Receiver

Source Factors Persuasive communications are affected by who presents them—some sources are better at communicating than are others. As a source, advertisers face a special problem, since consumers know their purpose to be self-serving. At the same time, of course, consumers are interested in making good purchases, so there is a potential for successful communication to occur.

One special characteristic of advertising is the flexibility as to who should be identified as the source. The next time you see an ad, for example, notice that the ad agency's name is probably not presented. Often, in fact, the name of the manufacturer is not even provided—only the brand name is given (particularly in broadcast commercials, where time is at a premium). There is no single "rule" for how to best handle the question of identifying the ad source. Since most consumers will provide their own inferences about the source, however, advertisers want to provide sufficient clues that the inferences made will be positive ones.

Conceptually, the answer lies in achieving **source credibility**. Source credibility refers to believability, the extent to which consumers feel that they can believe and act upon what the source is telling them. Low source credibility evokes feelings of distrust and suspicion, thus hindering prospects for persuasion to occur. Studies have shown that two key dimensions of source credibility are trustworthiness and expertise. **Trustworthiness** means that the source can be relied upon—that he or she is basically honest and is not trying to manipulate the audience. **Expertise,** on the other hand, refers to the qualifications of the source to make knowledgeable recommendations about the product or service being advertised.[26] Another important source factor is **attractiveness,** namely the consumer's perceptions of how prestigious the source is, how empathic (similar to the consumer) the source is, and how physically attractive he or she may be. In all these instances, the more attractive source is likely to bring forth more positive reactions from the audience, assuming that the attractiveness does not detract from the message itself.[27]

Advertisers have several options in creating source identifications. One is to use the company or brand name prominently, especially if it holds a strong reputation. A related technique is to identify the company with an attractive slogan, such as "Panasonic—We're Just Slightly Ahead of Our Time." A third option is to use a seal of approval, such as *Good Housekeeping's* or *Parent's Magazine*, or test results from independent research organizations. Finally, an advertiser can employ a special "spokesperson" in the ads, to benefit from the goodwill or trust that the public has for the speaker.

Media Factors Beyond delivering messages, media can also enhance or hinder special characteristics of those messages. For example, television allows the advertiser to use demonstrations of a product that may be otherwise difficult to describe in use. Television also allows excitement to be created, through its combination of sight and sound. Print, on the other hand, allows the consumer to spend a longer time with an ad, thus allowing the advertiser to explain more concepts, in more detail. Print also offers a longer time frame within which the advertising may be read, since a particular ad may be seen a week after the magazine arrives at a home. Several media offer immediacy: ads can be quickly inserted in local newspapers or on local radio stations. Finally, an advertiser using specialized media can obtain an extra "tone" for his or her ads. *Cosmopolitan*, for example, adds the sense of the product being modern and popular, while *The New Yorker* lends sophistication, and *Road & Track* lends an air of expertise to its advertisements.

Message Factors The message comprises the heart of most ads. There are two general considerations in this area: (1)*what is said* in the message and (2) *how it is said.* The first depends on the consumer's interests, the properties of the seller's brand, and the ads being run by competitors. The second, however, is much more open to various decisions. For example, should an ad use one-sided appeals only (that is, say only positive things about the brand), or should it try a two-sided appeal (which might recognize some areas in which a brand isn't so strong)? Should emotional appeals, such as fear or humor, be used? Unfortunately, there is no simple answer to these kinds of questions, because of the many variables that interact within the ad itself. In the real world of advertising, creators of messages usually do not rely on generalized rules and research findings. Instead, each ad is developed as a whole, and research (if undertaken) will be directed to that specific message, to see whether or not it is working well. As a result, the theories that appear in the literature are only used as general guides, and not as "the final word." Unfortunately, because advertisers want to protect their insight into what works and what doesn't, most advertising research is treated as proprietary in nature, and is kept secret. If you have a special interest in learning more about message factors, however, you will find some useful articles appearing in the advertising trade publications, as well as the sources indicated in Note 28. In this regard, you may also wish to pay special attention to the rapid developments in computerized "expert systems" that rely on knowledge about what works well in advertising.[29]

Receiver Factors The **receivers** of an ad actually determine whether or not it will succeed in its mission. The most significant receiver factors involve needs for the product, interest in the product and messages about it, and the prior attitudes and brand loyalties that consumers bring to the advertising exposure.

All these factors are usually available to advertisers through marketing research and are taken into account in designing messages and choosing media schedules. Beyond this, there has been some general research on receiver's personal characteristics and how they relate to *persuasibility*. For example, an ad using high fear appeals will work best for receivers who have high self-esteem, who try to "cope" with their problems, who are not normally "anxious" individuals, and who presently see the product as low in relevance for them. Persons who do not hold these characteristics are more likely to resist ads with high fear appeals: for these people, either low-fear or no-fear appeals would be a better advertising approach. Thus, insurance companies might find that fear appeals are appropriate for groups who see themselves as not needing insurance at this time. Thus fear appeals may be particularly appropriate for advertisers attempting to break into new market segments. A number of recent studies have examined additional receiver factors such as consumers mood states, and commitment to particular brands (see Note 30 for a guide to readings in this area).

Proposition 2: Ads Affect Different Stages Differently

This point refers to the different levels in the hierarchy, and points out that different types of ads are aimed at different levels of effects. The point is quite straightforward, but very significant in helping us to analyze how an ad is likely to work at the consumer level. Assume, for example, that you were asked for *three ideas* for an ad that would *capture attention*. What might you suggest? _____, _____, _____. What might you suggest for an ad that would maximize the probability of having its message be *comprehended*? _____. What about "*yielding*"?_____. Notice that these techniques might well work *against* each other—a very simple message might be more easily comprehended, for example, but consumers might be less likely to be persuaded by it, and may even find it less interesting. As a general rule, then, an advertiser needs to decide which level of effect he or she wishes to most achieve, and design the message accordingly.

Example: Comparison Advertising

As just one example of how our frameworks can be applied, let's briefly consider the case of comparison advertising. **Comparison advertising** is defined as advertising that (1) compares two or more specifically named (or recognizably presented) brands of the same product class and (2) makes such a comparison in terms of one or more specific product attributes.

Until the early 1970s, almost no comparison ads had ever been run in the United States. The advertising industry's codes prohibited this practice, and most media refused to accept ads in which competitive brand names appeared. Then the Federal Trade Commission (FTC) pushed for the removal of these bans, so that advertisers could use this method if they so desired. Many advertisers did desire to use it, and the practice spread rapidly. Estimates of its use range from 7 to 25 percent of all ads in recent years. As you may know, many of these ads have proven to be controversial. A number of lawsuits have been filed, as competitors named in ads have claimed that their brands have been misrepresented.

Our interest in this section, however, lies with *comparison advertising as a message strategy* and how it might work at the consumer level. One analysis of this issue was conducted by William Wilkie and Paul Farris and is summarized in Table 17B-1. Notice that part A of the table reflects source and message factors, whereas part B stresses receiver factors and effects. In part A we see some of the message strategy questions that an advertiser needs to decide in creating a com-

TABLE 17B-1 APPLYING THE FRAMEWORKS TO COMPARISON ADVERTISING

A *Message Strategy* **Questions**	B *Possible Consumer* **Effects**
1. **Brand comparisons and positioning** *How many and which brands* should be used for comparisons? What role should brand positioning play? Would, for instance, a desired economy car image be best achieved by a sharp contrast with a luxury car or less stark comparisons with compacts? 2. **Product dimensions for comparison** *Which product attributes* should be used? Might use of a "trivial" attribute be considered deceptive? *How many* attributes should be used? Should the advertiser's brand "win" on *every* attribute? 3. **Use of tests** Should tests be *stressed or avoided*? How *conclusive* should tests be before including the results? How restrictive should conditions be?	1. **Attention** The novelty of a comparison ad will cause it to receive more attention than will a standard ad. Comparison ads will receive more attention from users of competing brands mentioned than from users of brands not mentioned. Increasing the prominence of competing brands will increase attention from their users, but will also increase misidentifications of the sponsoring brand. Aggregate recall levels of comparison ads will be higher than those for standard appeals. 2. **Comprehension** Exposure to a comparison ad will lead to a "clearer brand image" than will exposure to a standard ad. Consumers will rate comparison ads as more "informative" and more

Continued

TABLE 17B-1 APPLYING THE FRAMEWORKS TO COMPARISON ADVERTISING
CONTINUED

A *Message Strategy Questions*	B *Possible Consumer Effects*

3. **Use of tests** *Continued*
  Should competitors receive the results before or after campaign launch, or not at all?
4. **Brand identification**
  How should a comparison ad be *constructed* to reduce audience misidentification of the sponsoring brand?
  Will some media be better than others for this problem?
5. **Product/market factors**
  Which product/market factors are important?
  Is a highly segmented market most appropriate for this tool?
  Are shopping goods special candidates because consumers often compare two or more brands before purchasing—or, for the same reasons, are these poorer prospects for comparison advertising?
  Will, as some fear, minor brands use comparison advertising to trade on the images of the market leaders?
	2. **Comprehension** *Continued*
	  "interesting" than most standard ads.
	  Users of a named competing brand are more likely to admit the sponsor brand into their evoked set than are users of brands not mentioned.
	  Users of the sponsored brand are more likely to *reduce* the size of their evoked set when exposed to a comparison ad than when exposed to a standard ad.
	3. **Message acceptance**
	  Claims made in a comparison ad are more likely to be accepted as "correct" than are those in a standard ad.
	  Naming a competing brand will tend to increase support arguments by users of the sponsoring brand and counterarguments by users of the competing brand.
	  The level and duration of counterarguing will be negatively related to changes in brand preference.
	  Comparison ads will yield higher variance (i.e., increased polarity) in postexposure brand preferences than will standard advertisements.
	  On the average, comparison ads are *more effective* in improving consumer preference for the sponsored brand than are standard advertisements.

Source: William L. Wilkie and Paul W. Farris, "Comparison Advertising: Problems and Potential," *Journal of Marketing,* Vol. 39 (October 1975), pp 7–15, Table I, p. 11, and Table 2, p. 14.

parison ad. To gain a better appreciation for these issues, take two recent comparison ads from a magazine (one that you feel is good and one that is not) and see how each one handled this list of issues in part A. For the ad you liked less, does the list suggest some ways it might have been improved?

Part B lists some of the effects Wilkie and Farris expected the typical comparison ad to have on consumers. Notice how these effects are divided into three categories that correspond to sections of our hierarchy framework: attention to the ad, understanding the message, and yielding to its conclusions. As you read through part B, see whether you agree with each of the hypotheses listed (research on comparison ads has offered mixed results as to whether or not it is more effective that other types of ads). Be aware that these statements pertain to the "average" case, and not to every ad. If you are interested in reading more about comparison advertising, you will find the references listed in Note 31 to be a good starting point.

Consumer Decision Processes

Part Four of this book consists of three chapters, and focuses on the *consumer decision process*. Consumer decisions can range widely in time (from split-second choices to deliberations taking months or even years) and in the amount of effort given to the choice. Nonetheless, we can learn a great deal by examining the basic stages that distinguish most consumer decisions. In Chapter 18, we will look at the starting stages of consumer decisions—problem recognition and information search. These are known as *prepurchase processes* and are very significant in determining *which* product and services consumers will buy at all, and *when* they will do so. In Chapter 19, *purchase processes,* we focus on the final decision and actual purchase. Finally, in Chapter 20, we turn our attention to *postpurchase processes.* Here our interest is in what happens after a purchase is made, both for consumers and for marketers.

Since much of this book is written from a decision-process perspective, the topics in Part Four mesh well with topics in other chapters. If you are reading this part at the end of your course, it can serve as a useful synthesis and extension of many familiar issues. If you are reading it early in the course, it can serve as a framework into which other topics will fit. In either event, there is some very interesting material in the chapters ahead, so let's move forward!

18

Consumer Decision Processes (I): Prepurchase Issues

▰ **Searchers Report on Prepurchase Processes**

In-depth interviews with consumers provide helpful insights for marketers. Let's listen in on different consumers talking about their prepurchase activities when buying a car in Chicago (key prepurchase dimensions are noted in parenthesis):

(*Time and effort*) "Every spare minute that we had we were at a car lot. We went to at least 12 to 15 dealerships . . ."

(*Social influences*) "It seems whenever I've got a decision I talk to friends and people and just get their general opinion . . . to me if you talk to enough people eventually you can find the right key . . ."

(*Sources of information*) "I went to one of the bookstores. They have books there that tell you how much the dealers pay for them, how much they're marked up."

(*Safety*) "But I think the baby was the biggest concern. He kept talking about a smaller car and I don't want to drive the baby around in a little car. If we were hit, I want . . . a car that would back us up."

(*Learning*) ". . . the more I looked into it the more I wanted to keep investigating, trying to know as much as possible (so I would be) able to go from one dealer to the next and basically say, listen, this is the kind of deal I can get, what can you do for me?"

(*Source*) "I was trying very hard to buy an American-made car . . . I had real difficulty feeling that I was slightly undermining the economy by buying a Japanese car . . . in a way I resent it because I want the best for my money and I don't like to feel that I am buying something to save America and screwing myself at the same time! And that's what I felt I did to a certain extent. I really did! When I saw what the Toyota Camry had to offer, it killed me! I love my Buick Somerset, but for the little bit of price difference—and there's not much—it was very hard to do . . ."

(*Price*) "I would have went to Indianapolis if I could get a better deal. If I would have broke $1000 I would have went to Indianapolis!"[1]

▪ ▪ ▪

SHOCKING NEWS AND CONSUMER REACTIONS

Do you remember reading any headlines like these?

"Sales of tampons dip 20%."
"Suzuki Samurai's sales have plunged."
"Sales of aspirin soar."

Occasionally a major breakthrough occurs, or something serious goes wrong with a consumer product. When either happens, we see almost instantaneous consumer reactions in the marketplace. The three headlines, for example, all appeared in recent years. Let's examine what happened to consumers' decision processes in each case.

TSS and P&G

The tampon headline arose from a medical connection with toxic shock syndrome (TSS), a virulent blood-related disease that began striking females about 10 years ago. As experts began tracking down the cases a pattern began to appear. The pattern related to extended use of superabsorbent tampons, a new entry into the market. Procter & Gamble had built a very strong brand—Rely tampons—that had been reportedly used by many of the victims. When the news broke, Rely, which held a 20 percent share of the market, was simply withdrawn from distribution at a cost of millions to P&G. Tampon sales of all types dropped 20 percent immediately thereafter, with gains going to sanitary napkin brands. Analysts expected that over time, assuming that the remaining products were shown to be safe, consumer sales patterns would return to precrisis levels. P&G planners studied the pattern of earlier product crises such as the botulism found in canned tuna and the cancer announcement associated with cyclamates in soft drinks. In each case, it took about one year for consumers to return fully to earlier behavior patterns.[2]

Samurai's Sayonara?

Several years ago, *Consumer Reports* magazine published an article announcing that its tests for auto safety showed that the Suzuki Samurai had a "dangerous propensity" to roll over in sharp turns. The company, which had been doing very well with its four-wheel-drive sport-utility vehicle, vehemently denied the accusation. It increased its advertising, and changed the theme to safety from fun. This damage-repair effort did not work in the short-run, however. Sales plunged 70 percent in the following month, and dealers were very worried. One dealer was even considering giving buyers free life insurance policies to entice their interest![3]

Heart Report Pumps Profits
Several years ago the prestigious *New England Journal of Medicine* reported a study showing that daily aspirin use by healthy men may lower the risk of heart attacks. Aspirin sales, which had been on a downward trend (down 7 percent) shot up between 35–50 percent in the next month. According to a researcher, "There's no doubt . . . that study had a big impact on consumers!"[4]

In Chapter 1, the concept of a *consumer decision process* was stressed as one of the major perspectives in our field. Since that chapter we've repeatedly discussed how difficult consumer decisions are for marketers to influence. The shocking news examples, however, demonstrate that consumer decisions can change rapidly. In each case, however, a single new input into the decision process had a startling impact on consumer behavior—millions of consumers changed their prior purchase and use patterns almost instantaneously. Although these examples are certainly not typical, they do graphically demonstrate the inherent flexibility of consumer decision processes and further suggest that these processes are worth understanding.

 TYPES OF CONSUMER DECISIONS

Consumers make many types of decisions in their day-to-day lives. In analyzing them, we can stress two dimensions: the **substance of the decision** (that is, what is decided) and the **complexity of the decision process** (that is, how important or complicated is the decision process).

Substance Variations in Decisions

There are four primary types of decisions that we consumers must make:

- Budget allocations.
- Product purchase (or not).
- Store patronage.
- Brand and style choice.

Budget allocation involves our choices of how to spend (or save) our available funds, how to time our spending, and whether to borrow in order to buy. Rather than one giant overall budget allocation decision, we make many "yes-no" purchase choices continuously. In this manner each household allocates spending into many product and service categories. Consumers differ in how much consideration they give to the budget constraints. A few consumers are highly deliberative, using much preplanning. For some other consumers, budget constraints rarely enter their decision processes. Most consumers, however, are ever, are somewhere in between. In these cases, some budget will be given to necessities, with the remainder of funds (viewed as **discretionary**) available for spending or saving as occasions arise.

The second category of decisions—**product purchase or not**—reflects choices made with respect to each product or service category itself. In some cases, such as household appliances, purchases are often ordered into *priority acquisition patterns*. The Ronsell family, for example, might have started with a TV set and a vacuum in their rented apartment, then added a washer/dryer, then a microwave. When moving to their home, they needed to buy a refrigerator and range, and they are now saving for a dishwasher. These decisions have a great impact on the *size of consumer markets*. From a consumer research viewpoint, we are also interested in how these decisions get made—how are they influenced, how consciously are nonpurchase decisions made—(that is, how many consumers decide not to buy a given product or service versus never even considering the purchase in the first place?), and related issues.

Once a consumer has decided to purchase something in a product or service class, the remaining two types of decisions come into play. Both introduce direct competition into our consideration. **Store patronage** refers to the decision of which source to use to obtain the product. Usually this is a retail store, although in recent years direct response and catalog shopping have become significant.

Brand and style decisions refer to the details of exactly which item is purchased. This choice acts to reward marketers for strong performance by stimulating a larger dollar flow back to those firms creating better products and marketing mixes. Not surprisingly, given marketers' interest in maximizing profits, this decision has received by far the most attention in consumer research.

Complexity Variations in Decisions

Some decisions are rather simple and easy to make, whereas others are difficult and involved. This means that the nature of the decision process is different in these cases. Two very useful perspectives are available to help us better appreciate the processes that occur at different levels.

Involvement, Order, and Effort

As we've already discussed at several points in the text, the **level of involvement** is a crucial determinant of the type of decision process a consumer will undertake. High involvement suggests that the order of decision making will follow our hierarchy of effects model in the think-feel-do sequence—beliefs will be formed, attitudes will develop, and purchase behaviors will follow. Consumers will put effort into the decision, will treat it as important, and will likely compare brands, stores, styles, and prices. With low involvement, on the other hand, the consumer decision process will be quite different. Much less effort will be given prior to a purchase. Consumers may be less attentive to marketing stimuli and the arguments they present. Less effort will be given to the overall decision, with perhaps less concern about which brand is purchased. Even the order of the decision process may change—we may see decisions being made impulsively or for trial purposes, with little in the way of beliefs or attitudes having been formed before the purchase itself has been made.

Time, Learning, and Complexity

Another important perspective stresses the fact that some products are purchased time and time again, whereas others are purchased only infrequently. Repeat purchasing allows consumers to *learn* what is available and what they like. Consumers are thus able to make choices from a position of considerable strength. John Howard has captured this phenomenon in his definition of three types of processes:

1. **Extensive problem solving.** Many consumers face this process when making their first purchase in an important product category. Here they must learn about important attributes, which brands offer which benefits and at what costs, and must develop their own criteria to evaluate which option is best for them. This mode of decision making requires much effort, can take a long time, and is complex. House buying, choice of a university, and purchase of a car are three cases where this form might be adopted.

2. **Limited problem solving.** This is an intermediate type of decision making in which the consumer knows about the product category, but is unfamiliar with the exact brand, style and price options that are currently available. For example, if a consumer had already purchased one or more suits, but was now in the market again, this might well be the mode of decision making. Emphasis will be primarily on search for a suitable alternative, with less concern given to learning about the product itself (since this is a broad category that lies between the extremes of extensive problem solving and routinized response behavior, it is the most difficult to characterize). Most consumer decisions are probably of this type.

3. **Routinized response behavior.** In this least complex mode of decisions, the consumer has purchased the product frequently in the past, knows what it can do, and has clear likes and dislikes among the brands available. Thus there is no perceived need for external search, and decisions can be made quickly and easily. Many purchases in supermarkets and drugstores are of this variety.[5]

Subtleties in the Perspectives

We should note several subtleties that are important in understanding these perspectives on the complexity of consumer decision processes. Don't miss, for example, the *importance of long-term memory* (LTM). As our LTM develops (that is, learning occurs) with respect to a product category, we are able to move toward less demanding forms of decision making. For example, there is often a marked shift from relying on external sources of information to a stress on our own internal knowledge, experience, and brand preferences.

Another subtlety concerns *how good a decision needs to be*. As we've noted before, consumer behavior theory has increasingly had to recognize that consumers do not seek to "optimize" the purchase itself—this would require that too much effort be devoted to search and evaluation each time a purchase is made. Instead **satisficing** appears to describe the goal for most consumer purchases— we wish to obtain a product with which we will be pleased—which is "good enough"—even if it does not represent the absolutely best buy that might be available if we work hard enough to find it.

Given this background, we can now see that Howard's framework of the three decision types is actually quite complex in reality. Some decisions are made very quickly—in flashes of a second—while others extend over months or even years. Some decisions are backed up by much thought, careful analysis, and even great worry, while others are made in the most flippant and casual of manners. The underlying order in which cognitive, affective, and behavioral aspects occur is not always the same. In some consumer decisions, external influences are extremely important, while in others they are not. Marketing programs are successful in changing the course of some decisions, while others remain immune to even the most expensive and sophisticated advertising and selling efforts. Because the real world is complex and has many factors at work, the decision process perspective can offer many useful insights for us.

THE CONSUMER DECISION PROCESS

Figure 18-1 depicts the four essential stages of the consumer decision process.[6]

1. **Problem recognition** represents the start of a decision process. This stage occurs when we first begin our move toward a purchase decision. As we'll see, this step is extremely important to marketers and consumers alike.
2. **Information search and alternative evaluation** represents the second stage of the process. Here the necessary information is gathered and used to evaluate mentally the options that are open to us.
3. **Purchase processes**, the third stage, represents the activities that occur during the final decision making and actual purchase of the product or service. The shaded overlap in the figure indicates that often this stage is hard to disentangle from the second stage (as when a salesperson helps us to decide which tape player to buy, then writes out the order and arranges the payment). In other decisions, however, the prior stage may be carried out over an earlier period, with the purchase stage occurring at a later point (for example, when we decide to order from a catalog after searching many stores).

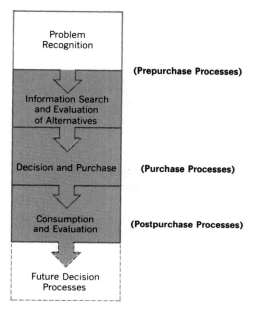

FIGURE 18-1 **Major Stages in a Consumer Decision Process**

4. **Postpurchase processes** represents the final stage of the decision process. Here our interest is in what happens *after* a purchase is made. This stage can be of critical importance to future marketing sales potentials, since a consumer's usage experience with a product leads to new attitudes that will come into play during the next consumer decision process for a similar product. Thus—in an important way—postpurchase processes cycle into future decision processes and strongly influence them.

Within the remaining sections of this chapter, we'll examine the first two stages of the consumer decision process, problem recognition and information search.

THE PROBLEM RECOGNITION STAGE

In Plain Sight, But Out of Contact

A national survey recently showed that 65 percent of American adults wear eyeglasses. Age is a factor, with this figure ranging from 30 percent of those 18 to 24 years old to 93 percent of those over age 50. But only 9 percent of all consumers wear contact lenses (although 30 percent have considered doing so, and young consumers are much more likely to wear them than are their parents). Makers and marketers of contact lenses realize that there is a huge market potential if only consumers can be persuaded to begin purchase decision processes. These marketers are wondering how best to go about stimulating increased problem recognition.[7]

P-O-P Contests Spark Sales Gains

As a means of increasing the "push" from retailers to consumers, manufacturers frequently run promotional campaigns and contests. Recently, for example, the American Dairy Association offered $100,000 in prizes for the best point-of-purchase ("P-O-P") displays created by retail store employees. The theme for the displays was "Cheese Adds a Slice of Life." ADA officials estimated that employees of over 4000 stores built displays. The effect was quite noticeable—during the three-month promotion, 90 million pounds more cheese was sold (an increase of 16 percent in sales)! Some of the winners did much better: a Dutch windmill display, for example, led to a 100 percent sales increase for a California market.[8] Successful displays are not limited to cheese, of course. In an Arm & Hammer promotional contest, a P-O-P display suggesting "1001 Uses" increased a store's sales from the normal level of 3 cases a week to over 70 cases a week![9]

The Concept of Problem Recognition

The foregoing examples show what marketers and retailers have known for years— that the consumer decision process can be triggered into action by the right forms of external stimuli and that large sales increases can result. On the other hand, this process does not always occur, as the makers of contact lenses have discovered. Within this section we'll take a structured look at the many factors relevant to this question.

Problem recognition represents the beginning of a consumer decision process. It is here that the consumer *perceives a need and becomes motivated* to solve the

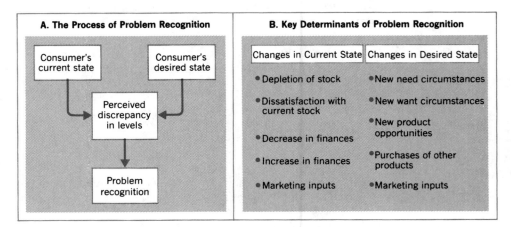

FIGURE 18-2 **Determinants of Problem Recognition**

"problem" that he or she has just recognized. Once the problem is recognized, the remainder of the consumer decision process is invoked to determine exactly how the consumer will go about satisfying the need. Figure 18-2 diagrams the process of problem recognition and summarizes some of its key determinants. Conceptually, *problem recognition occurs when the consumer perceives a gap or discrepancy* between his or her **current state** and **desired state**. Notice that the term "problem" is not intended to be negative in this definition—it actually represents the recognition of a goal that the consumer wishes to achieve. While a "problem" could be somewhat unpleasant, it might also represent an opportunity, such as the chance to obtain heart protection with aspirin, good savings on a product, and so on.

Causes of Problem Recognition

As noted, the dynamics of problem recognition occur when a large enough discrepancy is recognized. Basically, a discrepancy can arise from one of two sources: a change in the consumer's current state or a change in the desired state.

Changes in the Current State: Major Causes

- *Depletion of stock.* This refers to running down the available supply of products or services, usually through consumption. When gasoline is used to power a car, for example, its current state becomes depleted as the needle moves toward "E." At some point, the discrepancy between the current amount of gasoline and the desired amount of gasoline becomes sufficiently large that we recognize there is a problem. Depletion occurs with all frequently used food and household products and is probably the most frequent single cause of consumer problem recognition.

- *Dissatisfaction with current stock.* This change occurs when we perceive that the products that we currently own are insufficient to continue to serve their purpose (even though they may not have been depleted). Clothing and fashion is a common example, with both males and females perceiving that their older-style clothing is no longer suitable for current social demands and triggering search for new clothing.

- *Decrease in finances.* When funds run low (whether due to unemployment or other uses of the money), consumers will recognize problems that require a *reduction* in spending. Discretionary purchases are usually the ones to go, such as cutting down on movies or concerts or repairing durable goods rather than replacing them.

- *Increase in finances.* An unexpected increase in finances, through a new job, bonus, or gift, can lead the consumer to rethink the desired state to spend the money. Investments and luxury items are among the uses that may arise from this type of problem recognition.

Changes in the Desired State: Major Causes

■ *New "need" circumstances.* As we encounter changes in our daily lives, we often find that entirely new categories of consumer needs arise. The consumer life cycle captures many such events. A young single, for example, is unlikely to even imagine problem recognition for diapers, baby furniture, or pediatricians, but in several years may well be in the midst of these decision processes.

■ *New "want" circumstances.* Noting some distinction between wants and needs, new circumstances can create problem recognition of a "want" variety. For many students, for example, the move away to college opens new possibilities: travel to other countries, classical books, music, or art might appear on one's horizon, as might attendance at new types of functions.

■ *New product opportunities.* The marketing world is constantly providing consumers with new options for purchases. Prior to our becoming aware of a new product, we're unlikely to experience problem recognition for it. Once the product has been explained to us—perhaps through advertising or by friends—we can experience a substantial increase in our "desired state" for it.

■ *Purchases of other products.* Sometimes problem recognition is sparked by having purchased a different product. Once having bought a computer, for example, consumers are likely to recognize opportunities for using certain software packages and other accessories. A VCR purchase similarly affords prospects for problem recognition for tapes, movie rentals, and cameras.

The Role of Marketing

Without considerable activity by marketers to stimulate and direct problem recognition, they would face possibly lower sales and certainly great uncertainty about sales patterns.[10] Analysis of Figure 18-2 shows that marketers can influence consumer problem recognition through either side of the equation. Relatively less marketing attention seems directed to the current state, however (perhaps because this will vary so much among consumers). The most likely form of marketing strategy here seems to be to try to induce some dissatisfaction with the current stock of goods. Examples include asking whether a husband is underinsured or stressing the social punishments that await someone who is out of step with the current styles. While these types of *fear appeal strategies* can sometimes be effective, notice that they do carry a negative tinge to them, which might lead to negative reaction by the consumer against the marketer who is attempting this strategy.

Most marketing inputs seem to be aimed at affecting the levels of the desired state. Presentation of products as problem solutions can thus lead to consumers recognizing the problems in the first place! Thus we see new products marketed as ways to achieve more convenient, safer, or more exciting experiences for consumers. We see *bundling strategies:* secondary products (e.g., VCR supplies) marketed in terms of added benefits from the primary product. Finally, we see

They're here! The first walking heels!

You put these pumps on and you feel like walking everywhere. Because these slender, streamlined, buttery little numbers are real anti-shock walking pumps— engineered inside with the very same patented Shockproof Suspension System you'll find in the famous Easy Spirit sneaks. Come try them on. The minute you do, you'll feel...the sneakers! The bounce. The lift. The uplift! The energy from the ground up. Now, even in slender, whistlebait pumps, you can walk for miles—and your feet won't feel a thing. No shocks. No pavement. No pain. In 2 heel heights. A rainbow of colors. And the right fit! Sizes 4 to 12. 7 widths AAAA to EE! WHEEE! For the store nearest you, call 1-800-EASY-244 (1-800-327-9244).

EASY SPIRIT DRESS

New Easy Spirit Dress

LOOKS LIKE A PUMP, FEELS LIKE A SNEAKER.

This ad stimulates problem recognition by reminding women of a possible gap between current state and desired state for shoe comfort (and proposing a solution!).

many products marketed essentially through reminding consumers of their basic desires for satisfying wants and needs.

INFORMATION SEARCH AND ALTERNATIVE EVALUATION

Coupon Fanatics Hit Supermarkets

David Carlisle's wife was hospitalized and he was unemployed when, in desperation, a partial solution to his problems came to him in a dream—to use cents-off coupons to reduce his food spending. After great preparation, he called his local IGA store to explain his plan and ask for their cooperation. He arrived on a Friday morning at 9:30 with coupons and list. After nine hours in the store, he checked out at 6:30 with 15 grocery carts packed with food and household goods. The total value was over $1800, but with his coupons Mr.

Carlisle paid only $125! Since then he has continued this practice—his wife, now home, spends six hours per day cutting coupons from home publications, while he sorts and organizes them. Similar results were reported by an Indiana woman who won a national "Longest Tape" contest. Cindy Dorgan's cash register tape measured nearly 37 feet! She purchased $1287 worth of goods, but with 18 feet, 3 inches of coupon deductions, paid only the sales tax of $25.30. "When that first $1.00 refund check arrived in the mail, I was hooked!" she said.[11]

In the decision process framework the problem recognition stage activates a goal and motivates the consumer to act. In our next stage—information search and alternative evaluation—the consumer moves toward achievement of the goal. To reach the goal of matching the levels of actual and desired states, consumers need to discover what their options are, process information about them, and decide which alternative to choose. There are many interesting issues hidden within this simple stage structure, however. For example, let's consider Mr. Carlisle's story as an instance of prepurchase processes. Mr. Carlisle's story received special treatment in news reports *not* because he behaved as an irrational consumer, but because most of the rest of us don't behave this way. Given the huge potential savings, however, why don't more of us follow Mr. Carlisle's and Ms. Dorgan's leads? How much information search do we undertake?

The Nature of Search and Evaluation

The classic discussions of "information" refer to its ability to *reduce uncertainty* about the state of nature. That is, as we gain information, we learn more about a particular issue. The phrase **consumer information search**, therefore, refers to a deliberate attempt to gain knowledge about a product, store, or purchase. The decision process perspective is interested in how information search impacts on the decision. This raises several subtle but important implications:

- First, information search can lead to *increases* in uncertainty as we learn more. This is because our relevant "uncertainty" is often about which purchase we should make rather than only about understanding more about the alternatives available.[12] Because of this, consumer information search can become "*psychologically costly*," which might mean that we'll do less of it than otherwise expected.
- Second, the information relevant for a consumer purchase decision might come either from inside our LTM or from the external world.

Types of Information Search

There are two primary modes of consumer information search. The first mode, **incidental learning**, refers to gaining information when we're not actually making a consumer decision. Each of us, for example, engages in considerable information search each time we browse through shops at the mall.[13] This form of

Window-shopping at Bloomingdales (New York City): Much incidental learning occurs this way.

information acquisition leads to increases in long-term memory (LTM) for use later when an appropriate purchase occasion might arise.

A second primary mode—**directed search and evaluation**—refers to conscious search for information to help us make a particular purchase decision. Within this area there are three basic types of purchases:

1. *Internal search only purchases.* These decisions employ the simplest form of "search"—here we recognize a problem, invoke our LTM to help consider it, and end by making the purchase. There are, however, two different varieties of internal search decisions: loyalty decisions and impulse decisions. **Loyalty decisions** occur when our LTM has strong experience and brand preference to guide it. The decision is made in a well-practiced manner and is quite deliberate. **Impulse decisions**, in contrast, represent very little impact from LTM. In these instances, an external stimulus display stimulates problem recognition, but no external search is undertaken. The remaining search is internal and brief; then the purchase is made.[14]

2. *Purchases employing both internal and external search.* In these cases a consumer first engages in an internal search of LTM. If she finds LTM's current information to be insufficient, she turns to the external world to gain assistance. Her purchase-directed external search can involve stores, friends, and

other appropriate information sources. As new alternatives arise, they are evaluated using both internal and external information.

3. *"No purchase" decisions.* These are decision processes that lead to nonpurchase outcomes—the products we don't buy and that never appear in any formal records of consumer behavior. All of us have frequently experienced these episodes. Sometimes purchase is postponed, and we vow to make it later, while other times we simply decide not to buy. In either instance, of course, we have engaged in information search. "No purchase" decisions represent lost opportunities for marketers.

Challenges to Consumer Research

The range of types of search processes poses several challenges for consumer researchers. First, since most directed search is conducted with a purchase in mind, it often turns out to be difficult for us to separate where search stops and evaluation begins. Second, as noted, the distinction between "internal" search and "external" search is important. Internal search of LTM is always conducted to some extent, while the degree of external search can vary widely. Internal search is hard for a researcher to measure, however. Third, incidental learning is also important: it adds significantly to the contents of LTM and, thus, plays a

A comparison ad aimed at travelers' prepurchase planning.

key indirect role in guiding our consumer purchase behaviors. Finally, researchers need to consider both purchase and nonpurchase outcomes, since it is important to understand why purchases are *not* made as well as why they are.

Key Factors in External Information Search

The overall theory of information search is based on *costs versus benefits*. A consumer will search more when he or she perceives either high benefits from the search or sees the costs of search to be low. When opposite conditions exist, consumers should undertake less external information search. There are, however, many factors that combine to affect costs and benefits. Table 18-1 summarizes a number of these.[15] Within the table, note the three general types of

TABLE 18-1 FACTORS LIKELY TO AFFECT EXTERNAL INFORMATION SEARCH

	Factors Associated With	
	Lower Search Levels	*High Search Levels*
Overall	High perceived costs of search, with low perceived benefits	High perceived benefits from search, low perceived costs
Psychological factors	Low involvement Much past experience Current satisfaction Dislike of shopping Brand loyalty	High involvement Little relevant experience Enjoyment of shopping Curiosity Favorable attitudes toward several stores/brands
Situational factors	Social pressures for a particular choice High time pressure Physical constraints Special price offer Easy return guarantees Low cost/low risk Effective selling	Social pressures to search (e.g., husband and wife "team") Easy to shop Many sources Long time horizon for purchase Long product life High price/high risk Significant differences exist in prices and/or quality levels Technological improvements in the product
Information processing factors	Inability to understand information Lack of confidence with salespersons	Desire to learn more Confidence in ability to use information Higher number of evaluative criteria (key attributes)

influences—psychological, situational, and information processing factors. Note also that the entries are often not identical on the left and right sides: the table reports influences that tend to either encourage or discourage further searching by consumers. Thus there are a number of factors relevant to this area of consumer behavior. A few minutes spent looking through Table 18-1 will help us to appreciate better what these are.

Type of Good Affects Search

The distinctions among types of goods and types of characteristics are helpful for understanding consumer search behavior. One useful distinction in economics, for example, is among search characteristics, experience characteristics, and credence characteristics. **Search characteristics** are those which consumers can evaluate through search and shopping (such as the style of a dress). **Experience characteristics** are those for which the consumer must purchase the good and try it out before the consumer is able to evaluate its quality (e.g., the taste of a food product). **Credence characteristics**, meanwhile, are those which typical consumers will never be able to precisely evaluate, even after purchase and use (e.g., the quality of internal stitches during an operation). For credence characteristics, consumers must rely on marketers' assurances and reputations.[16]

One common division in marketing separates the categories of nondurables, durables, and consumer services. **Nondurables** are products that are consumed quickly and are often repurchased on a frequent basis. They usually do not inspire high levels of external search by consumers. Their prices are often low, and the consumer's risks from a bad purchase are low as well. The frequent repurchases provide an LTM base of experiences with various brands and types. This allows us to often use *internal information search* as a replacement for external information search in nondurable product categories.

The information search picture for **services** is less clear. Services are often intangible in nature, and are often "customized" for each consumer. In addition, many services are infrequently purchased and are often high in price. Thus they would seem to be natural candidates for high levels of external information search. However, because services *are* customized and intangible, it can be difficult for a consumer to assess the information he or she gains during external search. (How does Jim Parks really know, for example, whether one dentist will be better than another for him?) Such characteristics of services often lead consumers to rely heavily on either the reputation of the service provider or word-of-mouth recommendations from friends. Other forms of external information search for services are often low.[17]

Consumers' Information Search and Shopping for Durable Goods

Most research on consumer information seeking has studied **durable goods**— products that provide benefits over long time periods, such as houses, autos, and appliances. In glancing through Table 18-1 we can see many reasons why higher levels of information search should occur in durables purchases. For example, there is often very high consumer involvement with durables purchases. Since durables are not purchased often, little recent information may be available in LTM, for internal search to rely upon, and new product features are likely to be available that had not been encountered before. Also, since a consumer will have to live with the product for a long time, the benefits from a good durable purchase are higher, and risks of buying a "lemon" are also higher. Finally, the marketing system for durables tends to encourage shopping. Different brands are often sold through different stores. For all these reasons we would expect to see high levels of information search for durable goods. What do we actually find however? To appreciate this area more fully, let's examine highlights from a recent research study of a national sample of consumers:

The Wilkie and Dickson Report on Search and Shopping
Peter Dickson and William Wilkie have reported the results of a national survey on consumer information search and shopping behavior.[18] This research focused on recent purchasers of refrigerators, freezers, and clothes washers and dryers. Their study was conducted under the auspices of the Marketing Science Institute and was financially sponsored by four major corporations—Sears, General Electric, Whirlpool, and Frigidaire— whose managements were interested in using the findings to improve their marketing mix decisions. Table 18-2 presents a subset of the results. In examining them, you might usefully consider two questions:

1. Why would the results have come out this way—what explanations are appropriate?
2. What implications do the findings have for a marketing strategist?

The first results reported in the table reflect *purchase circumstances*. In part A of the table, note how significant the situations of "failure," "repair problems," and "household moves" are in stimulating the purchases of these particular appliances. Parts B, C, and D then report further background descriptions of the purchasers. Note that women comprise the major portion of the market for these products, although about half the purchases are made as a joint effort with husbands. There is an interesting range of experience available from past purchases, and most consumers are familiar with some local stores from which they might buy.

Parts E, F, G, and H of the table report typical measures of consumers' information seeking behavior before buying their appliances. "Total time," for example, reflects the total elapsed time between *first thinking about making the purchase* until the actual purchase itself. Notice how wide the range is here—some consumers purchase the same day the thought arises, while others wait over three months before the actual buy! The other statistics here provide measures of the shopping activity itself. In reviewing them, you may find yourself to be somewhat surprised—notice that the largest groups of consumers report that they considered only one brand, visited only one store, and spent less than two hours in total time (including traveling) shopping for their purchase!

Parts I, J, and K move us further into the details of store search and information source usage. Of particular note here are (1) the *dominant position occupied by Sears* as a seller of appliances—it appears that over half of all consumers in the United States shop at Sears when in the market for one of these products, (2) the low number of information sources

A. Purchase Circumstances

Applicance failure	36%
Replacement of working unit	
Needs some repair	24
Working well	14
Residential move	18
Other	8

B. Who Participated in the Decision?

Homemaker solely	29%
Homemaker primarily	11
Joint effort w/spouse	52
Spouse primarily/solely	8

C. Previous Purchase Experience

None	35%
One prior purchase	33
Two or more purchases	32

D. Familiarity with Local Stores

None	4%
One to three stores	24
Four or more stores	72

E. Total Time Spend Considering the Purchase

Same-day purchase	9%
Within first week	24
1–4 weeks	33
1–3 months	11
3–6 months	11
Over 6 months	13

F. Total Number of Stores Visited

One	37%
Two	19
Three	19
Four or more	25

G. Total Number of Brands Considered

One	32%
Two	26
Three	26
Four or more	16

H. Total Time Spent Shopping

Less than two hours	45%
Two to four hours	28
Five to eight hours	14
More than eight hours	14

I. Types of Stores Shopped

1. Appliance store[a]	59%
2. Sears	57
3. Department store	27
4. Discount store	25
5. Wards	18
6. Furniture store	15
7. Penney	12
8. K-mart	9
9. Other type	13

[a]To be read, "Fifty-nine percent of the purchasers shopped in at least one specialty appliance store during their decision process, while 57 percent shopped at Sears, et cetera."

J. Number of Information Sources Used

1. Number of "independent" source types (friends and relatives, *Consumer Reports*):

Zero,	52%	Range = 0 to 2 sources used
One,	37%	Mode = 0 sources used
Two,	11%	Mean = 0.58 sources used

2. Number of marketer source types (of the seven listed in part K, following):

Zero,	15%	Four,	6%	Range = 0 to 7 sources used
One,	27%	Five,	5%	Mode = 1 source used
Two,	25%	Six,	2%	Mean = 2 sources used
Three,	19%	Seven,	—	

K. Ratings of Source Usefulness

Information Source	Buyers Who Consulted	Buyers Who Found Source Useful	Buyer's "Most Used" Info Source
1. Appliance salesperson[b]	59%	49%	41%
2. Newspaper ad	39	28	13
3. Friend or relative	38	31	13
4. Catalog	35	28	9
5. Brochures/labels	28	25	9

K. Ratings of Source Usefulness *Continued*

Information Source	Buyers Who Consulted	Buyers Who Found Source Useful	Buyer's "Most Used" Info Source
6. *Consumer Reports*	20	18	9
7. Appliance repairperson	14	10	5
8. Magazine ad	12	7	1
9. TV ad	10	5	1

[b]To be read, "Fifty-nine percent of the buyers reported having consulted a salesperson as an information source. Almost all these people (49 percent of the total sample) reported finding the salesperson to be a 'useful' source of information. When asked which source had been the 'most useful,' 41 percent of consumers reported that the salesperson had been."

L. Consumers' Search Interests

(Forced choice: pick one or the other)   "I was most interested in learning:

{ "As much as possible about the appliance."   69%
vs.
"Just enough to make a choice."   31% }

(Forced choice)   "I was most interested in:

{ "Enjoying the search . . . because it was interesting."   32%
vs.
"Spending as little time as possible."   68% }

M. Consumers' Search Strategies

(Forced choice)   "During my decision process I primarily relied on:

{ "Past experience and knowledge."   69%
vs.
"New information from search."   31% }

(Forced choice)   "During my decision process I primarily relied on:

{ "Past experience and knowledge."   68%
vs.
"Knowledgeable others' advice."   32% }

N. Where Purchased

Store Type	Share of Market	Bought on Sale	Negotiated Lower Price	Bought at First Store
Specialty Appliance	37%	51%	28%	34%
Sears	30	89	4	46
Wards	9	92	8	22
Furniture	6	41	22	48
Discount	5	80	20	30
Department	4	69	13	38

O. Purchase Behavior

Bought at special low price		76%
a. On sale	70%	
b. Negotiated with salesperson	17%[c]	
Brand loyalty		31%

[c]Some consumers both bought on sale and negotiated a special low price; thus, the total exceeds 76 percent.

P. Postpurchase Satisfaction with New Appliance

Very satisfied	71%
Satisfied	24
Neutral	3
Dissatisfied	2
Very dissatisfied	—

Source: William L. Wilkie and Peter R. Dickson, "Consumer Information Search and Shopping Behavior," working paper, University of Florida, Gainesville, 1985. Reprinted with permission.

used, and (3) the surprisingly dominant position of the *salesperson* as the "most useful" information source encountered by the largest group of consumers. Parts L and M report findings on the primary forces within consumers' search interests and strategies. Again, the results may be somewhat different from what we might predict. Notice, for example, the potential conflict between "Learning as much as possible" and "Spending as little time as possible." In the area of search itself, it is clear that "past experience and knowledge" (which probably represents internal search) clearly dominates both measures of external search during shopping.

Part N of the table provides insights into the nature of retail competition. Again the performance of Sears is noteworthy—it appears to sell about one of every three machines in the nation. Its policy against its salespersons negotiating against posted prices comes through clearly in the data (along with Ward's). Finally, the statistic "bought at first store" suggests that Sears's marketing mix is inordinately successful in converting consumers from "searchers" to "buyers" during their store visit; its rate on this measure is approached only by the furniture stores, which account for a much smaller market.

Parts O and P of the table report key measures of the purchase itself. Most of these appliances are purchased at a sale price, but negotiation is not used often (some consumers both negotiated and bought on sale, which accounts for the fact that the numbers do not add to 76 percent). Brand loyalty—the purchase of the same brand as that owned previously—was surprisingly low in these product categories. Finally, part P reveals consumers' reports of how satisfied they were with their purchases after having owned them for up to a year. Notice the extremely strong results—95 percent of the participants in this survey reported that they were "Satisfied" or "Very satisfied" with their appliance. This level is so high that it is obvious that the wide range of consumer differences in information search and shopping behaviors does not lead to systematic differences in early consumer satisfaction, since virtually everyone is satisfied.

The results reported by Wilkie and Dickson are quite consistent with findings of earlier major studies in this area. (If you are interested in reading more of the findings, you may wish to consult the discussion in Note 19.)

Consumer Search Segments

The findings by Wilkie and Dickson are useful in describing overall information search behavior. In reviewing the results, however, we can see that there is high variation for almost every measure taken—some consumers seem to search very little before they buy, while others search a great deal. Notice, however, that Table 18-2 did not tell us whether one type of search might be substituting for another type. To discover whether this is the case, we need to examine the "patterns" of a consumer's search behaviors. Also, Table 18-2 did not tell us *who* the various consumers were who were searching a little or a lot. Fortunately, research on consumer search segments has addressed each of these areas:

Patterns of Search
Several interesting studies have investigated patterns of information search for durable goods.[20] In one study, for example, Westbrook and Fornell used advanced statistical analysis and discovered four primary search segments for major household appliances.[21]

- *Personal advice seekers.* This segment comprised about 20 percent of all consumers. They relied heavily on the advice and opinion of friends and family members, did not use much other information, and visited an average of only two stores.
- *Store intense shoppers.* Representing about 30 percent of consumers, this segment primarily relied on store visits to learn about and evaluate their alternatives. On average, this segment visited four to five stores before buying.
- *Objective shoppers.* This segment made up about 20 percent of consumers. These persons did not use personal sources at all, but made heavy use of objective sources such as *Consumer Reports*, brochures, magazine articles, and so on. This group also shopped extensively, visiting between three and four stores on average.
- *Moderate shoppers.* Comprising 30 percent of the sample, this segment visited only one store, tended not to rely on friends or relatives, and used only a moderate amount of other forms of information before making their purchases.

Who Are the "Information Seekers"?

In an interesting set of studies, Hans Thorelli and associates examined persons who subscribe to reports of product testing agencies (e.g., *Consumer Reports*) in the United States, Norway, and West Germany.[22] They found the same type of people in all three cultures—information seekers have high income, high education, own more consumer durables, and read more magazines and newspapers than does the average consumer. Their beliefs are also different—they have high expectations for product performance, are less favorable toward advertising, and are not likely to be innovators (though they are opinion leaders).

Recent research by Duncan and Olshavsky and by Muncy has examined consumers' "beliefs about the marketplace." Consumers who held the following beliefs were found to *search less* for information before buying their products:

- "Most store salespersons are well informed about the products they sell."
- "The best brands are usually the ones that sell the most."
- "I am a poor judge when it comes to evaluating products that are mechanical . . ."
- "Competition . . . tends to keep the prices of different brands about the same."[23]

APPLICATION AREAS: CONSUMER INFORMATION PROVISION

Marketing Applications

When we think of the marketing mix, we can see what a large portion of the mix is devoted to appealing to customers at the prepurchase stage. The *product* must be designed, packaged, and named so as to attract the interest of the potential buyer. *Place* decisions are crucial in bringing the product and the buyer together so that a transaction may actually occur—if Kathy Fitzgerald is shopping at the Northway Mall while our product is being offered elsewhere, we run the risk of losing a sale. *Price* decisions are also important, since these might define our product out of further consideration if we're seen as being "too high" or "too low."

And *promotion* decisions are aimed right at buyers in the prepurchase stage. One of the key options that marketers have, of course, involves *providing consumers with useful information*. The field of consumer information has many issues that have been recently addressed. Let's take a look at three interesting reports.

Home Shopping? Head for the Library!

Consumer Housing Libraries, Inc. (CHL), is changing the way many consumers buy homes in the Washington, D.C., area. House-hunters are free to browse through the housing information displays: included is a wealth of information on residential developments, home builders and lenders, facts on schools, zoning, transportation, and so on. The CHL charges businesses $1000 a month for the right to set up promotional displays. According to the founder of CHL, the appeal to advertisers is the high-quality prospect who visits the library: "A developer can buy a quarter page ad in the Saturday *Washington Post* for $3000," he explains. "That same amount will get them 3 months with us . . . and our ratio of buyers to visitors is much better." The average visitor spends about 1 hour looking at the various exhibits and takes away as much print information as he or she desires. Once the visitor leaves, however, CHL faces a problem—how to track the later purchase behavior of its visitors (this information is obviously of great interest to prospective exhibitors at CHL). As one effort, CHL's managers asked visitors to return an information postcard after they buy, and promised a CHL house-warming gift in return for this feedback![24]

How Nice Is the Price?

One area in which consumer research can contribute involves the form ("format") in which information is provided to consumers. Improved formats can attract attention, assist comparisons, decrease the chances of miscomprehension, and aid in retention of the information. As an example, J. Russo and his associates have reported several studies involving the provision of unit pricing information by supermarkets.

Unit pricing refers to a store providing shelf tags in which all its prices in a product category are presented on a common "per unit" weight or volume basis, such as cents per ounce for ketchup, cents per pound for sugar, and so forth. Unit pricing was originally proposed to help shoppers who might want to compare prices of different sized packages. This can be a very difficult task—several studies challenged consumers to select the most economical buys in various categories and found error rates of about 50 percent.[25] Many grocery chains introduced unit pricing as a convenience for their patrons. Following introduction, there was great interest in how many consumers were using this new tool, and how they were reacting to it.

The initial consumer research reports were surprisingly mixed. The studies that asked consumers "What do you think of unit pricing?" showed that consumers were very favorable and reported using it often to help them buy better. Those studies that examined consumers' actual purchase behavior, however, revealed very little evidence that consumers were buying any differently then they had before. Russo, speaking from a CIP perspective, suggested that this disparity might be because it was still difficult for a consumer to compare unit prices of different brands and sizes: since the tags were up and down along the shelves, a consumer would be placing some strains on short-term memory (STM) to keep the other prices in mind while searching out new ones to compare. His solution: reduce the strain by placing *all the unit prices* for a product class in the same spot for easy reference. This could be done by posting a product list, ranking the brands from lowest to highest unit prices, in a prominent location amidst the shelf display.

One retail chain tested this idea for several product categories over a five-week period (typically, private labels offer higher profit margins to the retailer—thus if a unit pricing program were to shift sales toward private labels, the store's overall profits should increase). The results of the trial showed a significant shift in sales toward the lower-priced brands, averaging a 2 percent decrease in the average prices paid for purchases for the test product categories while the posted lists were in operation.[26]

More Is Better, or Is It?

Every marketer faces the decision of the amount of information to attempt to convey. The space available on package labels and in ads is limited. Normally, however, we would expect that more information is desirable, since it can cover more aspects of the product and can present different elements of appeal to consumers. Before leaving the topic of marketing applications, we should mention that one of the most interesting debates in the consumer behavior field concerns the topic of **consumer information overload**. This issue was originally raised by Jacob Jacoby and his co-workers. They were concerned that some people were making the assumption that "if some information is good, then more information must be better." For example, at that time there was a movement to place nutritional information on package labels. But how much of this information should be provided? Is there any danger from providing higher amounts of information?

Jacoby proposed that such a danger might well exist. As you'll recall from our discussions of the CIP system, STM (the work center of the system) is subject to severe capacity constraints. If too much information is forced upon STM, it is possible that it will become "overloaded." If overload occurs, one possible result is that the consumer will become confused and could make worse decisions than would have been made without the extra information. Alternatively, many consumers might simply ignore some information they would have used if so much hadn't been provided. However, supporters of more information argue that if information isn't made available, it *can't* be used. Also, they point out that some consumer segments will wish to use different information than other segments, so having more available is positive.

A number of interesting empirical studies have been undertaken to try to clarify these issues, with further debates on how the findings should be interpreted. If you would like to learn more about this interesting area, you may wish to consult Note 27.

Public Policy Applications

In addition to marketing's interest in consumer information, this topic is also a primary center of interest for public policy's regulatory activities. Three key characteristics to keep in mind when we consider public policy's interests in this area are:

1. *Fully informed consumers.* Our market-based economic system rests on a theoretical assumption that consumers are fully informed about the alternatives they have when making their purchases. Being fully informed (according to the theory), consumers are able to allocate their resources in the most efficient manner. Although we know that consumers are not *actually* fully informed, policymakers have an obligation to work toward having all important information as available to consumers as possible.

2. *Choice-neutral information.* Unlike a marketer's stress on providing information to *influence* the consumer's choice of a brand, public policy is interested in providing information to allow a consumer to make the best choice for him or her, which might be any brand available. Thus the emphasis is on knowledge rather than choice, and the information should be objective rather than subjective.

3. *Cost and freedom trade-offs.* When regulators consider which forms of information should be made available, they need to consider the costs involved, the benefits likely to accrue to consumers, and the extent to which the provision of the information might restrict legitimate freedoms of marketers. The last several U.S. presidential administrations have differed significantly on these issues, so we have not seen a consistent information policy in the U.S. government.

Key Questions About Consumer Information Programs

In all, over 30 federal agencies and many state and local offices are currently engaged in disseminating information to consumers. You may have seen, for example, ads for the Consumer Product Information Center in Pueblo, Colorado, which serves as a distribution center for many government publications. Many citizens do not expect the government to carry the burden (and costs) of developing all consumer informational and educational materials. Since marketers are reaching consumers directly every day, and are engaging in information programs themselves, these citizens suggest that marketers should be either asked or required to provide certain types of information as a necessary part of their programs.

While most experts would agree that consumers should be as fully informed as possible, they disagree—sometimes heatedly—over how this best should be accomplished. Four key questions that arise again and again are:

1. *What* information should be provided?
2. *How much* information should be provided?
3. *In what form* should the information be provided?
4. Will consumers *use* the information?

We already have a good basis for appreciating the types of issues raised by these questions. The rights of consumers have to be balanced off against the rights of marketers; unwise government regulations can work against a fair and efficient market system. Also, our previous coverage of such topics as "low involvement," social influences, and impulse purchasing has warned us that consumers may not always use information when it is made available. For these reasons the debates in this area are especially sharp, since no one is really certain of the answers to the four questions just posed. Also, since all information programs present some costs, questions of which exact information to provide are often controversial. Information programs can have several types of goals. These range from helping consumers to compare brands and prices, to informing consumers about contents and possible hazards, to clarifying terms of sale and contracts. To gain a better feel for some issues that can crop up, let's take a look at a program involving energy efficiency.

Energy Tags Lack Power, but LCC Adds Punch

In response to the energy crisis some years ago, the U.S. government decided to encourage consumers to demand more energy-efficient products. Here special tags would be placed on each machine for sale in a store. These tags would inform consumers of the costs to operate that appliance for one year, with the hope that consumers would shift their purchases toward the machines that cost less to run. In the government's plan, a bright yellow and black label would be prominently posted on each new appliance. This label would provide (1) the estimated annual electricity cost to run the appliance and (2) the range of costs offered for similar-sized machines on the market, thus offering a baseline for comparing that model with the other options a consumer would find if he or she shopped around. A consumer research study conducted by Dennis McNeill and William Wilkie indicated, however, that the government's plan—although likely to be successful in informing consumers of actual costs—wasn't likely to affect consumers' appliance purchasing behavior.[28] As a policy aimed at reducing energy consumption, therefore, it seemed likely to fail.

R. Bruce Hutton and William Wilkie then suggested that a *large part of the problem was the type of information the government was trying to convey.* Instead of telling consumers about yearly operating costs, they argued that a new form of information—**life-cycle cost (LCC)**—be used instead. LCC has been routinely used for years by financial analysts and engineers in business when planning large projects. Rather than equating "cost" with selling price, as many consumers are used to doing, LCC considers all the costs we can expect to encounter. With most appliances, these consist of purchase price, service, and energy costs. Refrigerators, for example, typically require more spending for electricity during their 10 to 15 years of life than they do for the original purchase price.

When Hutton and Wilkie studied the impact of giving LCC information to consumers, they found that appliance buyers did change their behavior in a significant manner. The LCC labels (although presenting the same basic type of information as the government energy labels) highlighted the fact that energy savings occur for many years (not just one) and should be added together (and discounted to a present value) to compare best the options available. When consumers saw this, they shifted their purchases toward their own financial interests and rewarded manufacturers of the more energy-efficient machines with increased purchases. The shift in purchases in this study was so strong, in fact, that when the authors extrapolated their results to the entire nation, they calculated that, for refrigerators alone, LCC tags would save the nation's consumers over $4 billion every year in energy costs. If you were a judge with responsibility for consumer energy information, would you order a move toward LCC labels? (If you'd like to read more about this possibility, you may wish to pursue the readings in Note 29.)

Applications for Consumers

In closing our discussion of prepurchase processes we should return briefly to the topics of Chapter 2, in which we recognized that much of the material in a consumer behavior book has important implications for individual consumers. In this regard, you may wish to review briefly the contents of this chapter from your own personal perspective as a consumer. In so doing, consider how an understanding of problem recognition processes might be helpful, for example, or how you might benefit from a fuller appreciation of the nature of information search. In the next chapter we will focus on what research has found about consumer purchase processes.

SUMMARY

Types of Consumer Decisions

In this chapter we began our examination of *consumer decision processes* by concentrating on *prepurchase processes*. Our introductory vignettes stressed the importance of understanding consumer decision processes and showed how flexible they can be—just a single new input can have a profound effect on how consumers will make their decisions, what they will buy, and even whether they'll buy at all.

Four basic types of consumer decisions were identified in the chapter's first section: budget allocation, product purchase, store patronage, and brand choice. *Complexity variations in these decisions* was also examined—we discussed how consumer involvement affects the effort and order of a decision process and how time, learning, and complexity differ among such decision processes as *extensive problem solving, limited problem solving*, and *routinized response behavior*.

The Consumer Decision Process

A *model of consumer decision processes* was presented in the chapter's second section. This model consists of four stages: (1) problem recognition, which leads to (2) information search and alternative evaluation, which is followed by (3) the purchase itself, which is followed by (4) postpurchase processes. In this chapter, the first two stages—problem recognition and information search—were discussed, with the remaining stages examined in the two following chapters.

The Problem Recognition Stage

The *problem recognition* stage begins a decision process. Problem recognition results from a discrepancy between a consumer's "current state" and "desired state." Several key causes for such a discrepancy were described and the role that marketing plays in this process was analyzed.

Information Search and Alternative Evaluation

Our discussion of the *information search and alternative evaluation* stage pointed out the two major types of search that consumers employ: incidental learning and purchase-directed search. We then focused on the many factors that combine to affect the amount and nature of search. These can be classified into three general categories: psychological, situational, and information processing factors.

Finally, we discussed detailed findings from a recent national study of how consumers shop for major appliances.

Application Areas: Consumer Information Provision

In our final section, we examined several applied issues of consumer information provision. These addressed such questions as "Will consumers use unit price information?" "What is information overload and is it a problem for marketers?" and "What information can move consumers to conserve energy?" In each area we saw that consumer research provides useful marketing insights.

KEY TERMS

substance of the decision
complexity of the decision process
budget allocation
discretionary funds
product purchase or not
store patronage
brand and style decisions
level of involvement
extensive problem solving
limited problem solving
routinized response behavior
satisficing
consumer decision process
problem recognition
information search and
   alternative evaluation
purchase processes
postpurchase processes

current state
desired state
consumer information search
incidental learning
directed search and evaluation
loyalty decisions
impulse decisions
search characteristics
experience characteristics
credence characteristics
nondurable goods
services
durable goods
search segments
information overload
life-cycle costs (LCC)

REVIEW QUESTIONS AND EXPERIENTIAL EXERCISES

[E = Application extension or experiential exercise]

1. Consider the four primary types of substance variations in decisions.
   a. Indicate the nature and extent of the relationship(s) to one another.
   b. Address the issue of ordering of these decisions. Is it fixed or variable?

2. Identify three recent purchases classified as "low-involvement" goods or services.

   a. Indicate the rationale for the "low-involvement" classification.

   b. Note any changes in the order of the decisions from that presented in the hierarchy of effects model.

   c. Comment on the type and level of effort expended in the overall decision.

3. Based on John Howard's definition of the three different types of behavior processes, identify two additional examples of each. What are the marketing implications associated with these behavior processes?

[E] 4. Figure 18-2 lists the key determinants of problem recognition.

   a. Consider three of your recent durable goods purchases and five recent nondurable purchases. Identify the key determinant(s) of your problem recognition.

   b. For each purchase, analyze the nature and extent of marketing's influence on the problem recognition stage for you.

[E] 5. Interview a recent purchaser of a durable good (as a guide, you may wish to use the items contained in Table 18-2). Try to probe for further explanations of the nature and reasons for the particular search pattern. Write a brief report to summarize your findings.

[E] 6. Answer for the following products: shampoo, video disc, VCR, bank.

   a. What primary sources of information are consumers likely to consult/rely on?

   b. How are the sources and types of information utilized likely to vary by individual based on experience, for example? Importance of the decision?

   c. For any one of the above, detail three marketing implications.

[E] 7. Why do some marketers supply limited, if any, information regarding their brands in advertising? For example, consider the typical ad for soft drinks or pain remedies. If you were a brand manager in one of these product categories, how would you regard an alternative approach that supplied more information?

[E] 8. What are the characteristics of the four primary segments in the Westbrook and Fornell analysis? As a consumer, where would you place yourself? Why?

[E] 9. Choose any four products or services. For each, give two actual examples of how marketers attempt to:

   a. Minimize the cost of information.

   b. Enlarge the consequences of nonsearch.

   c. Alter the weight attached to different information sources.

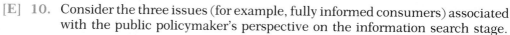

[E] 10. Consider the three issues (for example, fully informed consumers) associated with the public policymaker's perspective on the information search stage.
   a. Are these issues independent?
   b. In an effort to ensure that consumers are fully informed, is it possible for such information to remain choice-neutral and not restrict the freedom of marketers? Comment, using examples.

[E] 11. Consider two major household purchases in which you have been involved. Address the question, "How does information search vary in a multiperson unit, such as a family?" (You may need to conduct interviews to answer this.) Write a brief report on your findings.

[E] 12. To gain some insight into the nature of browsing as a form of incidental learning, conduct two interviews with consumers just as they return from a shopping trip. Ask them what they learned during the trip, then probe for new thoughts/information they had while browsing (*tip:* you may want to have them "replay" the trip slowly to capture more of these). If time is available, monitor your own or a friend's reactions *during* a trip. Write a brief report on your findings.

[E] 13. Interview an experienced automobile salesperson concerning consumers' prepurchase processes (*tip:* you may want to begin by asking about the quotes opening this chapter). Also ask about marketing and sales techniques he or she and their agency use to influence consumers at this stage. Write a brief report on your findings.

[E] 14. Interview an experienced manager or salesperson in a stereo, appliance, or up-scale clothing store concerning how consumers shop, the role of consumer information, and what techniques he or she finds useful for the problem recognition/information search stages of the decision process. Write a brief report on your findings.

[E] 15. Use Notes 19–29, or the reference section of your library, to locate recent readings on a prepurchase topic of personal interest to you. Write a brief report on your findings.

C H A P T E R

19

Consumer Decision Processes (II): Purchase Decisions

■ **Buyers Report on Auto Choices**

Let's listen in again on the in-depth interviews with Chicago auto buyers. This time, we'll cover some aspects of their purchase decision processes:

(*Purchase timing*) "Then when the $2000 rebate came up . . . I said if we're ever going to do this, this would be the time."

(*Evaluation*) "And we test drove the same car—two Corsica's—one was a four-cylinder, one with a six-cylinder just to see the difference . . . and the six-cylinder just won! . . . She didn't care . . . I liked the performance."

(*Time pressure*) "We couldn't wait [because of the wife's new job] for a car coming in on order, that was out of the question. So we had to buy."

(*Desire for benefits*) "No, I could have taken three months . . . I wanted what I wanted and would do whatever I had to do."

(*Negotiation*) "The thing that gets me is, when you go in . . . they'll say, what are you looking to pay. So you tell them. . . . He goes in and he talks to the manager and you sit there. And then he comes back and says, 'This is the best I can do.' You say, 'No, I know you can do better than that.' So he goes back in, and watch, the manager is going to come. Sure enough, the manager comes and says, 'Listen, this is the best we can do.' Usually Dick is the one who says no . . . and they keep playing this game back and forth. I think you're just wasting your time, but they're not going to come down to what you want right then and there. Just say, 'If this is just not feasible, fine, let's go!'"

(*Choice*) "It was 2.6 percent financing, four years, $500 down. Actually, to be perfectly honest between you and me, it wasn't the car I wanted. I wanted the other one. But because the financing was so good, we thought OK, for four years we'll take this one and then maybe in four years we'll get the other one."

(*Choice*) "Part of that probably was the $2000 rebate. . . . In the paper it said that for a Cadillac it was just a terrific deal. We bought a couple of cars over the years and I'm thinking my Dad spent $8000 for a car and if he knew I was spending $22,000 he'd roll over in his grave. I said, "What the hell, we got a nice car.""[1]

■ ■ ■

From the marketer's perspective, the purchase stage is particularly crucial, since it is here that the money flow back to the business is generated and long-term marketing success achieved. Consumer purchases serve as a ratification of a brand's marketing mix, whereas purchases of other brands may signal a need for change in the mix. From the consumer's perspective the purchase phase is also very important. Not only is this the point at which we give up money in return for a product, but the choice of only one brand means that we must depend on it to deliver the benefits we're seeking.

In our first chapter on consumer decisions we focused on the early stages of the process: problem recognition and information search. As we saw, these two stages provide much motivation and learning for consumers and pose a number of significant issues. Within the overall decision process, however, they merely "set the stage" for purchase processes. In this chapter we'll discover some frameworks that help us to understand consumer decision processes. We'll see how researchers go about studying these processes and what challenges they face in this task. Then we'll analyze the basic "decision strategies" that we consumers use, and how the selection of a particular strategy can change the brand we end up buying. Finally, we'll examine some interesting recent studies of consumer's purchasing behaviors within retail stores.

MONITORING CONSUMER DECISION MAKING

Since a consumer's decision making is a personal mental process, it can be difficult or even impossible for a marketing researcher to measure directly. Also, the fact that decision making can operate at extremely high CIP speeds only makes matters worse. How, then, *do* researchers study the consumer decision-making process? Two basic approaches are generally used: input-output and process monitoring research.

Input-Output Research

The **input-output approach** usually employs some form of experimentation. Here the researcher provides a certain stimulus *input* to consumers' decisions (e.g., a special price) and then observes how consumers' behaviors—the *outputs*—change from what they were before. Often several types of inputs are pitted against each other to discover which works best. Input-output research does not, however, measure the decision process itself.

Marketers frequently use input-output methods before committing themselves to large expenditures in their marketing mixes. Sometimes these are conducted on small samples of consumers in "laboratory" conditions that are carefully controlled. Advertising is frequently studied this way, through special forms of "copy tests." In this form of test, for example, alternative Jell-O ads would be used to see which themes work best with the target audience for these commercials.

The "real world" can also be used for input-output research, in a *field experiment*. While the conditions cannot be as carefully controlled, field experiments have the advantage of providing results under realistic conditions. For example, Pepsico might conduct field pricing experiments for its Frito-Lay products. Using combinations of test cities, the firm can use different price levels in different cities and then monitor shifts in sales and profits. These kinds of tests are also run on other aspects of the marketing mix, of course. For example, you may have noticed publishers testing different covers for the same book or magazine to see which ones "draw" best at the newsstand. Also, as we have discussed at several points in the book, supermarket scanners now allow for considerably more testing—coupons, displays, ads, price changes, shelf spacing, and so forth can now be tested using computerized sales figures.

Input-output designs are also crucial in academic research that studies the nature of consumer decision making. Here we find lab experiments developed to test theories of how consumers make decisions. These studies challenge the researcher's ingenuity, since the researcher must develop a set of stimuli and conditions that will allow the consumer's decision outputs to identify which process the consumer had followed. The theory testing work of academics is very likely to be carried out in lab experiments, often using college students as consumer subjects in the studies. Although a quite technical area, this approach has received considerable attention in the field and has contributed much to our understanding, as we'll see shortly.[2]

Process Monitoring Research

The second approach to studying consumer decision making places less emphasis on stimuli and decision outcomes themselves. Instead, **process monitoring** focuses on *trying to capture the reality of the decision process itself, as it occurs* (thus the spirit of this approach is quite similar to that of the direct monitoring of advertising that we saw in Chapter 10). Three types of process monitoring methods have been popular: verbal (Exhibit 19-1), physical, and observational.

Verbal monitoring methods simply ask the consumer to verbalize his or her thinking about the decision as it occurs (or sometimes to "play it back" to the researcher after the decision has been made). For example, a researcher may accompany a consumer while shopping in a supermarket. Observations the con-

EXHIBIT 19-1   A "VERBAL PROTOCOL" FROM A DECISION STUDY

Mike, a consumer, is choosing a hand-held calculator based upon product information presented to him in the form of a multiattribute matrix of brands and their characteristics. The information display is similar to that shown in Figure 19-1, except that the brand names have been disguised and the attributes are those for calculators.

Mike's Discussion as He Makes His Choice

"The first thing I'm going to do is look for size," he said. "I like smaller ones better than a real big one. And I've got a large one and it's a hassle carrying it to class. So let's check, let's check out the compacts first. . . . OK, versatility would be the first thing. Medium, very high, and uh . . .

(Pause) "Ok, so far Brand F has got compact size, and very high versatility, easy to use, very convenient. Brand F's looking pretty good. And battery life really doesn't matter, it's 6 hours and the warranty's 9 months. . . . The highest warranty is 12, this one's 9. It's got . . . not a bad battery.

"Brand F looks to be the best, I'm going to check out brand E 'cause that's still in a compact size. It's got medium versatility, it's fairly convenient, 3 hours, 3 months, and it's standard size, so forget that one.

"Brand C, very high versatility, fairly convenient, 6 hours, 12 months, credit card size . . . hmm . . .

"Ok, Brand D, another credit card size, it's got high versatility, it's fairly convenient, 6 hours, 3 months.

"I, I'm going to go with Brand F. . . . Yes, Brand F, definitely!"

Source: Courtesy of Dipankar Chakravarti.

---

sumer is making are taped by the researcher, who may also ask occasional clarifying questions. When the recording is analyzed, a *verbal protocol* of the purchase decision process is available and several types of analyses can be run to compare the strategies used by different consumers. Sometimes, a *decision net* is also developed. This is a formal map that traces the process from the beginning to the end and notes all steps along the way. Exhibit 19-1 demonstrates a verbal protocol recording the thoughts of one student in a recent decision-making study.[3]

Information display boards (IDB's) are a popular representative of **physical monitoring methods**.[4] A sample IDB is shown in Figure 19-1, as it would appear to a consumer participating in an IDB study. Note how this array of information is similar to the multiattribute matrix of brands and attribute ratings we examined in Chapter 11's discussion of consumer attitudes. In the usual IDB study, how-

FIGURE 19-1 **A Sample Information Display Board**

Attributes	Martin Gardens	Parker Place	Whispering Willows	Tiki Village	Tanland Park
Rental prices					
Location					
Age					
Style					
Tenant types					
Children play					
Pet policy					
Leisure facilities					
Lease terms					
Safety record					
Etc.					

ever, the specific cells' ratings are not yet visible to the consumer at the start of the study. Instead, the consumer is informed that he or she should make a purchase decision in the product category and can obtain any information desired simply by physically acquiring it from the appropriate cell in the matrix.

How Does an IDB Work?

To see more clearly how an IDB can work, let's assume that Marilyn Hart is a new transfer student entering her junior year at the university. She needs to find an apartment as soon as possible and has Figure 19-1's IDB available to her. Let's also assume that she decides to start her decision process by finding out the prices for rentals at the Whispering Willows complex, since she's intrigued by the name. Her exact instructions for using the IDB would depend on the nature of the IDB's design, but if the IDB were in the form of a honeycomb of boxes (similar to the rental boxes at a post office), Marilyn would

1. Reach in to the third box in the top row.
2. Remove one of the cards having Whispering Willow's rates on it.
3. Examine the information and use it for her decision making.
4. Place the card face down in another container that holds the physical record of the information she is acquiring.
5. Decide which piece of information she'd like next and repeat the process of acquisition.

If the IDB is on a computer terminal, Marilyn needs only to push the appropriate button representing that position in the array. In any of the methods, if she wants to look at the information again later, she can do so by repeating the process.

Why go through all this? Researchers are interested in how many tabs Marilyn will turn, and in what order, before she makes her decision. From this, they are able to infer the types of decision processes that are being used. For example, Marilyn might pursue either a **processing by attributes (PBA)** strategy or a **processing by brands (PBB)** strategy. As an example of the PBA case, she might start by pulling information all across the price attribute row to find out which apartments are most expensive and which are cheapest. She might then eliminate a few (because they're too high priced or seem too low priced) and move to the location attribute row, to compare the remaining apartments on how convenient they'll be. In general, then, a BPA strategy will have Marilyn moving across the rows of the table.

The PBB process is quite different. What if Marilyn has heard that Whispering Willows is "the place to be" and that she should try to get in there if at all possible? Here it would be natural for her to find out more about this particular complex before she looks at the competition, and we might expect her to begin by pulling information down the Whispering Willows column of Figure 19-1. In general, then, a PBB strategy will have Marilyn moving down the columns of the table as she learns more about each apartment's features.[5]

Observational monitoring methods have also been used in consumer research. *Eye cameras,* for example, detail exactly where consumers' eyes travel as they are confronted with product labels or IDB displays. Based on this information, researchers can infer what information is being considered and what is being ignored, as well as the timing of information usage.[6] In general, however, observational methods are used less frequently than are the other process monitoring approaches. This is due in part to cost considerations (it is hard to observe more than one consumer at a time, and specialized equipment is sometimes required). Also, however, if we merely observe physical movements, we are not learning very much about the thinking processes that are occurring during the same time.

In recent years there has been an increasing tendency for consumer researchers to combine both the input-output and process monitoring methods into even more complex studies. With careful designs of this type, consumer researchers have recently been able to investigate how long-term memory (LTM) affects consumers' internal search for information and how internal search affects external search.[7] We'll examine these developments in more detail following our coverage of the topic of consumer decision rules.

 CONSUMER DECISION RULES

What Are They?

Experts have defined a number of basic strategies consumers can use in arriving at their decisions. These are known as **decision heuristics** or the "rules of thumb" that help us make up our minds. "I always buy the best" or "I only buy

---

EXHIBIT 19-2

LUGGAGE RATINGS[a] FOR DECISION RULES[b]

Attribute	Importance	Brands[c]			
		A	B	C	D
Style	40	6	8	8	3
Price	30	7	7	8	7
Covering	20	7	4	1	8
Durability	10	6	7	3	9

[a]Belief rating scale = 1 to 10, with 10 most favorable.
[b]Assume Ed's conjunctive cutoff = 5.0.
[c]Brands are A = Air Attache, B = Beauty Brief, C = Comfort Case, D = Downtowner.

---

on sale" are two common heuristics. For our purpose, we'll simply refer to these as **decision rules**. Decision rules are important because they provide *guidance* while making decisions. Usually, in fact, they offer a shortcut to a decision: they allow use of only part of the available information. Of course, using less information makes it more likely that a consumer won't make the optimal purchase, but most people are willing to settle for a "satisficing" purchase when the mental or physical costs of evaluation are high. Consumer researchers have identified three basic types of decision rules. Using Exhibit 19-2 will help us appreciate how they operate.[8] Let's assume that three people close to graduation are interested in buying new sets of luggage. We'll also assume that they'll be using the exhibit's multiattribute ratings for their decision making, and that each person will use a different decision rule. Then we'll see how this leads each to buy a different product.

The Compensatory Rule

The **compensatory rule** requires the most effort of all the decision rules, since it is aimed at discovering the best overall brand of luggage. The rule itself is identical to the calculations we undertook within the multiattribute attitude models. That is, the consumer must use a PBB strategy and work down the columns in turn. For each brand, the consumer must calculate the product of the importance weight and the attribute rating for each attribute, and then sum these over all the attributes to arrive at a total brand score. Paul, who prides himself on his analytical bent, adopts this rule. After working through to his decision, he is pleased with the outcome. However, in analyzing his decision rule, he notices that it didn't matter in what order he took things: as long as he used every piece of information in the table (in the correct manner!), he would arrive at the same decision every time. In reviewing his calculations, he's also struck by the way in which a high rating on one attribute had the effect of compensating for a low rating on another attribute and can understand how his decision rule got its name! What brand did Paul buy?

The Lexicographic Rule

The importance weights play an even more significant role in this decision rule than they did in the compensatory model. This is fine with Sandy, since she knows what she wants and is willing to work to ensure that she gets it! In effect, the **lexicographic rule** says, "I want to ensure that I buy the brand that is best on the attributes that are the most important to me, even if I have to give up something on some of the lesser attributes." To use this rule, Sandy must first rank the important attributes in order, from most to least important. Then she must evaluate all the brands on the most important attribute. If one stands out, this is chosen. If two or more tie, they remain as candidates for purchase while all the other brands are dropped from further consideration. The consumer then takes the remaining candidates on to the second most important attribute, where they are again compared to find the best performer. If two or more remain tied, they remain as candidates as the consumer moves to the next most important attribute. The process continues until a single brand survives and is chosen. Sandy is very pleased with her purchase and notices that it didn't take her nearly as long to make it as it took Paul. Unlike Paul, however (who understands why his rule is compensatory), Sandy still has no idea why her rule is called lexicographic. (If you'd like to know, see Note 9.) What brand did Sandy buy?

The Conjunctive Rule

Conjunctive decision rules are quite commonly used by consumers as a means of eliminating a number of alternatives in a fast and simple manner.[10] In our earlier example of Marilyn's use of the IDB for apartments, she employed a conjunctive type of rule when she dropped some apartments from further consideration because they were priced too high for her budget or located too far from the university. In a formal sense, a consumer using the conjunctive rule must create a minimum level of performance that is acceptable on each important attribute. Each brand is evaluated only in terms of whether or not the minimal levels are reached. If a brand falls short on *any* attribute, it is rejected. If a brand passes all the standards, it remains a candidate for purchase.

Thus, it is possible either for multiple brands to remain after the rule has been invoked or for no brand to survive all the levels. In either case, the consumer is likely to go on to use another decision rule to make the final choice or to reset the minimum levels so that a choice can be made.

For our luggage example in Exhibit 19-2, let's consider Ed's case. Ed is a conservative shopper who knows little about luggage. His major concern is avoidance of a bad mistake. Therefore he decided to use the conjunctive rule, which he'd heard tends to weight negative information about a brand more heavily and helps the consumer avoid a brand that has any glaring weaknesses. To be reasonable, Ed decided to require a minimum level of 5.0 for each attribute. When his decision was over, he was surprised at how easy it had been and was pleased that only one brand had remained, so the final choice had been easy. What brand did Ed buy? (If you're interested in checking your answers for these consumers' choices, they're in Note 10.)

 ## BEYOND THE BASIC DECISION RULES

The Concept of "Mixed Strategies"

It is obvious that consumers rarely use one of the basic decision rules in its pure form to make a decision. They often, however, use **mixed strategies**—or combinations of the rules in a sequence. Conjunctive rules, for example, are often used first, since these are good ways to eliminate options quickly and reach a manageable number of brands (all of which possess desired attributes to some extent). At this point the consumer can move to another decision rule to use on the remaining brands. In recent years much research on consumer decision making has moved to consider the nature of mixed strategies. Among the findings are that **task factors** have strong effects on the decision strategies consumers use: that is, that consumers adapt their decision-making to fit the situations they are in at the time. For example, time pressure can be an important task factor, as can be the amount of information (number of attributes) available to the consumer. The number of alternatives he or she has to choose from is also a key task factor—as we've already noted, when the number of alternatives gets high, a consumer is likely to use a screening rule (such as conjunctives or lexicographic) first, then use a compensatory strategy for the remaining few brands.[11]

Memory's Impact on Decision Strategies

Sometimes consumers rely on specific decision strategies they've used many times before and have stored in memory (e.g., "I always buy whichever paper towels are on sale"). More often consumers need to think somewhat about how they will make their choice at the time they are deciding: they need to "construct" a decision strategy for that purchase. Whether the strategy is already stored or needs to be constructed, though, memory (LTM) will play a very important role.[12]

Peter Wright, for example, highlighted this point when he proposed a special decision rule—called **affect referral**—that consumers may use when purchasing a product they know very well.[13] In these cases, rather than evaluating much external information at all, the consumers may simply call back (refer to) their "affect" (attitude) for one of the brands (e.g., "I always buy Tide . . . it's the best."). Much of the recent research in this area has focused on the role that a consumer's *prior knowledge* plays during a decision. What does a well-developed LTM do for us while we're buying?

Study 1: "Prior Knowledge—Sew What?"

In an award-winning study, Merrie Brucks examined the effect of knowledge on how consumers search for information. A notable aspect of her study featured a new computerized information method designed to overcome some drawbacks in the traditional IDB study. Glancing back at Figure 19-1, we can see that an IDB presents a consumer with an *already selected* set of attributes and brands set into a *tabular (matrix) format*. These factors can affect the way a participant in a study will begin the decision process.

Brucks changed this procedure by having each participant type in a request for the information she desired, using a computer terminal (the participant's task was to "shop" for a sewing machine). The researcher sat in another room, received and interpreted the questions, and then sent back prespecified messages with the proper information via the computer terminal. Through this means the participants were able to "phone" stores with simple questions, "visit" stores for detailed shopping, and ask for a salesperson's advice. Among the findings:

- When the decision task was a difficult one, consumers who had more knowledge about sewing machines searched for more information than did less knowledgeable consumers (who likely expected that they might not be able to understand some of the information). When the decision task was easy, however, both groups searched at the same level.
- When the decision task was difficult, more knowledgeable consumers searched more efficiently (that is, they screened out bad models more quickly).
- Consumers who had more confidence in their own knowledge about sewing machines asked for fewer salesperson evaluations and relied more on their own judgments.[14]

Study 2: "Expertise Comes into Focus"

In another award-winning study, Mita Sujan used verbal protocol methods to analyze how memory affects consumers' processing of messages. She was interested in how "expertise" affects the categorization consumers make while receiving messages (you may recall that we discussed categorization as being one of the key processes within perceptual interpretation, in Chapter 9). Since "expertise" refers to higher levels of knowledge about a given topic, consumers with more expertise should also have better developed categories in LTM and should use these when making evaluations and decisions.

To examine the impacts of expertise, Sujan took consumers who knew a great deal about photography ("experts") and compared their responses to consumers who knew very little ("novices"). Ads for two types of cameras—35mm single lens reflex and simple 110 cameras—were created. A total of four ads were used: two of the ads described a typical camera of the type being promoted, while two of the ads used descriptions that were inconsistent with the type of camera in the headline (e.g., the 110 camera was described as having interchangeable lenses). Each participant received one of the ads and was asked to form an impression of the camera being advertised. The time they took to do so was recorded; then they were asked to think back and verbalize all their thoughts while they had been reading the camera description. Some findings of the study:

- Experts had more thoughts than novices.
- "Mismatch" ads (those in which a nontypical description was used) generated more thoughts than normal ads did. This was true only for the experts, however, who recognized that the descriptions of the camera did not match the attributes their LTM categories were telling them that this type of camera actually offers. Novices did not generate any more thoughts when there were mismatches than when there were not.
- Experts preferred 35mm camera when it was correctly labeled and also preferred it when it was mislabeled as a 110 model—they used the *attribute* information to evaluate the quality of the camera. Novices, on the other hand, preferred the 35mm camera when it was correctly labeled and the 110 camera when it was called a 35mm type: they used the *label* rather than the attribute information in evaluating the product.[15]

Thus we can see how the CIP orientation can address a number of issues to help us understand better the nature of consumer decision making as well as various subtle influences on it. In this section, we've concentrated on LTM's effects. In the next section we'll look at some other factors.

Other Key Factors Affecting Decision Making

Other important factors have also been found to influence consumer decision processes. For example, *joint decisions,* such as those made in households or in social contexts, can profoundly affect consumer decision processes. The *format* in which information is provided to consumers can also have significant effects. We've just reviewed some of these effects in our last chapter, in the unit price posting study and in the life-cycle costs study. In addition, the many examples of perceptual processes (Chapters 8 and 9) attest to the impacts that information format can have on consumer behavior. In addition, however, there are newer concepts, problem framing, and starting point. We'll briefly review these in the following sections.

Problem Framing Changes the Picture

Recent studies indicate the subtle power that our mental **frame of reference** has in even simple choices that we make. For example, what would most consumers do if, after prepurchasing a play ticket for $10, they discover that they've lost the ticket as they enter the theater? If they are unable to prove they had bought it earlier, would they pay another $10 for another ticket? Most consumers say *they would not*—the idea of paying a double price for the same performance is quite negative.

What if their frame of reference changes slightly, however? Another group was asked what they would do if they were going to a theater to see a play, and upon arrival discovered that they'd lost a $10 bill. Would they go ahead and buy a $10 ticket to the play? Almost all consumers said *they would*. This research, one of a stream of studies by Amos Tversky and Daniel Kahneman on **prospect theory,** indicates how sensitive consumers can be to the way in which they *perceive* a problem, and in the connections they make.[16] Even slightly different framings of problems can change choices quite substantially.

Recent work by consumer researchers is now investigating such issues as whether the problem is framed in positive (gain) or negative (loss) terms. In one study, for example, consumers expressed higher satisfaction with ground beef when it was described as "percent lean" rather than "percent fat" (actual price and actual quality were equal). The key role of "reference point" is also being examined. According to Thaler, for example, this explains why a man lying on the beach would be willing to give his friend more money for a can of beer if the friend is going to buy it from a resort hotel bar rather than the grocery store (although the exact reason is subtle, we all see that this does occur).[17]

These issues have major implications for marketers. In pricing, for example, a "SALE!" or "CLEARANCE" sign helps to create certain frames for consumers. Reference prices ("An $89.95 value, now only $49.95"), coupons, rebates, are other popular forms. Although marketers obviously already recognize the value of these approaches, this work provides a strong framework by which their effects can be better understood (if you are interested in learning more about this area, you may wish to begin with the readings in Notes 16 and 17). As consumers, how can we protect ourselves against inconsistent reasoning and outside manipulation? The researchers suggest stepping back, trying to "reframe" the decision in other ways, and testing whether or not our preferences remain the same.

Pathways to Purchase

As a final point in our coverage of consumer decision rules, we should reiterate the importance of the concept of **start point** in the direction and outcome of a decision process. Earlier in the book, for example, we examined the concept of **evoked set,** or those few brands that come to mind when a consumer considers his or her purchase decision. If decision time is short and no other factors intervene into the process, the chances that a purchase will be made from the evoked set are very high.

For any particular brand, then, gaining entry to consumers' evoked sets means higher probabilities of purchase. In a recent award-winning study, for example, Nedungadi showed how (1) asking consumers to answer several background questions about a brand at the start of the session (simply to make that brand name more "accessible" or likely to be retrieved from LTM) could (2) make these brands more likely to be in the evoked set in a later choice task and (3) raise the probabilities they would be chosen. Grey's Poupon mustard, for example, increased its choice probability from 3 percent to 22 percent with those early questions, Vlasic pickles increased theirs from 0 percent to 22 percent, whereas Tropicana orange juice moved from 22 percent to 47 percent in this laboratory study.[8]

Of course, brands are not the only elements that might be evoked in a consumer decision process. *Stores* are also likely candidates for evoked set contents, as are sources of information. In the Wilkie and Dickson report we examined in Chapter 18, for example, appliance buyers were questioned about the first information source they consulted in their decision process. From this information the pathways to purchase were calculated, and some very interesting results emerged. Considering only buyers at Sears and specialty appliance stores, how much impact did their source first consulted have on the final purchase decision? A great deal, as shown by the following findings. Of those who began their search by consulting

■ *Consumer Reports*	81% purchased at specialty stores
■ Repairpersons	73% purchased at specialty stores
■ Salespersons	63% purchased at specialty stores
■ Friends/relatives	about 50% purchased at each type
■ Newspaper ads	61% purchased at Sears
■ Catalogs	72% purchased at Sears

In some respects, these results reflect the marketing mixes of these types of stores.[19] The fact remains, however: *What you do first will have a strong impact on the remainder of your consumer decision process!*

CONSUMERS' IN-STORE PURCHASING BEHAVIOR

Up until this point in the chapter we have focused our attention on the mental operations that underpin decision making. However, as we've seen earlier in this book—and have surely experienced in our own lives as consumers—there are many influences at work in the real world of consumer behavior. How do these translate into actual decision processes when we're at the point of sale? Let's first look at several studies that examined how much time consumers spend in making their supermarket purchases:

Study 1: Search in the Supermarket
One interesting consumer research study, by Kendall and Fenwick, timed over 200 supermarket shoppers as they chose specific items. Some interesting findings emerged. Over all consumers and products, the decision times obtained ranged from almost instantaneous (less than 1 second) to 5.5 minutes (yes, one consumer did stand in front of the display this long, trying to make up her mind!). Almost all purchases were at the low end of the time range, of course.

It turned out, however, that consumers spent much longer in choosing some products than others. This would indicate either that the decisions were more difficult or that less LTM was available for the choice, requiring some reading of the product labels while standing in the aisle. For products such as canned meat, tuna, and powdered soup, the typical consumer spent about half a minute on the purchase (within the study this was classed as a "label reader"). For products such as rice and spaghetti, on the other hand, the most common consumer was classed as a "grabber" who spent *less than 1 second* standing in front of the shelf—many buyers didn't even stop but simply reached out and "grabbed" the package they desired as they swung on by![20]

Study 2: Clearing Out the Stock

A related study, by Wayne Hoyer, focused only on detergents. In brief, an observer recorded the total time spent from entering the detergent display (a large section of an aisle) until the chosen package was dropped into the shopping cart. Then the buyer was briefly interviewed. Some of the results:

- Most detergent buyers (72 percent) examined only one package (another 18 percent examined two packages).
- Most consumers (74 percent) made no comparisons across different brands.
- Very few consumers (11 percent) examined any shelf tags (which might provide unit price information, for example).
- The average consumer spent just over 8 seconds from entering the aisle until making the purchase. Recalling the length of the detergent displays, we can see that much of this time is spent simply in traveling along the display.
- When asked why they had bought the brand they did, about 20 percent of consumers reported "price" reasons (low price, on sale, or coupon), 30 percent gave "performance" reasons (this brand cleans well), 20 percent reported general "affect" reasons (like the brand), and 10 percent gave "social norm" reasons (my wife wants this brand).

Other research along these lines has given similar findings.[22] Thus we can see why consumer researchers have been concentrating on CIP-oriented studies of decisions. It is clear that internal search of LTM plays an extremely important role in many consumer purchases and that for some consumers there is very little else that goes on for many of the purchases they make in the supermarket.

This does not tell the entire story, however, since we have thus far looked at only a small sampling of all the purchases that consumers make. Let's next look at the findings of a famous study that, while still on supermarkets, has a much broader base of products.

The POPAI/DuPont Study

A classic set of studies undertaken by the Point-of-Purchase Advertising Institute (POPAI) and the E. I. duPont company has alerted marketers to the consumer dynamics of decisions within the supermarket. A recent study surveyed the buying practices of over 4000 consumers across the United States. In brief, the researchers found that *most purchases consumers make are not planned in advance—that in-store decision making is the norm, rather than the exception.* To examine this issue, the researchers categorized each purchase into one of four classes:

1. *Specifically planned.* Here the consumer had plans to buy the item before entering the store. This category accounted for 34 percent, or one out of every three purchases made in this study.
2. *Planned in general.* Here the consumer had the general intention to buy something in the product class but did not have a specific brand in mind when entering the store. This category, which we might expect would be the most frequent of the types, accounted for 11 percent, or about one out of every nine purchases.

3. *Substitute purchases.* Here the consumer changed his or her mind while in the store and substituted a related product or different brand. Only 3 percent of the purchases were of this type.

4. *Unplanned purchases.* These items reflect "impulse" decisions: here the consumer did not report a plan to buy the item at the time he or she entered the supermarket. Instead, the entire decision process—from problem recognition to actual purchase—occurred while in the store. Over half of all the purchases recorded in the study (53 percent) were of this type.

Thus (adding together the three last categories), 67 percent of purchase decisions were found to be made in the store. As we would expect, however, there were distinct *product differences* in terms of the way they fit into the categories just listed. (This information is particularly important to marketing managers, who are most concerned with the consumer decision process for their particular product categories). Product-specific analysis showed that products likely to be subject to a "depletion" type of problem recognition were least likely to have unplanned purchases made: examples here included coffee, milk, and baby foods. At the other extreme, almost all "general merchandise" (nongrocery) products provided high levels of unplanned purchases. As you may know, these products often carry high profit margins for the stores, and it is not hard to imagine why they've been receiving more space in the latest supermarket designs! Many of us can also easily relate to some of the other "high-flier" products in impulsive purchasing by considering our taste buds: these included baking mixes, relishes and mustards, almost all frozen foods, fresh cakes, pies, and doughnuts, and all categories of candies, crackers, cookies, and snacks![23]

Marketing Implications

What implications do the POPAI findings hold for marketing managers? They indicate that, for certain products especially, *consumer demand is not fixed but is likely to be quite responsive to various forms of promotional efforts.* At the start of the last chapter, for example, we saw how point-of-purchase displays for cheese were able to boost sales substantially. Studies over broader ranges of products have shown similarly strong results:

- One study of in-store displays in supermarkets showed an average increase of 570 percent in unit sales.[24]
- Another study, this time focusing on newspaper ads for groceries, also reported finding very substantial effects. If the item was advertised in small type in a list, sales were 80 percent higher than when not advertised, while if the item was advertised in a separate section (i.e., not in a list), the increase was 800 percent. For items advertised in large type, the sales changes were even more dramatic—ad weeks' sales for items in a large print list were over 1000 percent higher, while a large type, separate section led to average sales almost 1700 percent higher than in nonadvertised weeks![25] (However, we should recall the nature of newspaper advertising for foods and be careful not to attribute all these effects to the promotions themselves—advertised items are often priced

at special low levels.) Thus it seems reasonable that advertising, displays, and prices work in an interactive fashion: the ad or display helps bring a brand into the evoked set, then the price appeal helps to "close the sale."

In terms of our current interest in purchasing processes, these numbers are significant in helping us recognize just how flexible consumer decision processes can be. Thus there *are* significant opportunities for marketers to appeal successfully to consumers both prior to the shopping experience (with advertising, direct mail, and coupons) and during shopping itself (with point-of-purchase displays, shelf placement, packaging appeal, and personal salespersons). Exhibit 19-3 describes some high-tech possibilities we can expect to see in the near future. (If you are interested in learning more about these options, you may wish to consult the sources listed in those Notes).

The relationship between promotions and consumer response is not a simple one, however.[32] As the "search in the supermarket" studies showed, most consumers make most of their purchases in a very rapid manner and do not seem to be very sensitive to point-of-purchase materials. In another recent study, in fact, Peter Dickson and Alan Sawyer found that only slightly over half the buyers of four common purchases (margarine, coffee, toothpaste, and cold cereal) *even checked the price* in the store before they bought the item. As we might expect, less than 50 percent of buyers were then able to give the correct price of their choice right after putting it in their shopping cart (most of those who hadn't checked indicated that the price just wasn't important to them). Even so, almost 30 percent of the brands purchased in this study had been bought at a special low price (of these buyers, however, only about half—15 percent of the total sample—knew that this was a price special, while another 7 percent had bought an item they thought was on special when it was not!)[33]

Thus it is apparent that considerable slippage occurs in the real in-store purchasing environment. At the same time, impressive sales gains can be chalked up by marketers who are successful in shifting only a relatively small proportion of the (huge) total consumer market. Again we see why "market segmentation" is such a key topic in the marketing field.

OTHER ASPECTS OF THE PURCHASE TRANSACTION

As the decision process moves through information search, alternate evaluation, and decision making, *we finally reach the point at which the actual purchase is made.* Since we've all made thousands of purchases in our lives, the mechanics of this process are quite clear. In simple store purchases, there is a direct transfer of money for product, with the consumer departing in physical possession of his or her new property. Notice that money, ownership, and physical possession are all exchanged during this basic form of transaction. None of these elements *has* to be exchanged at this time, however. In some purchases consumers pay in

EXHIBIT 19-3   *WHAT WILL THE FUTURE HOLD IN-STORE?*

In recent years evidence has continued to accumulate as to just how flexible consumer purchase decisions really are, and how effective in-store-promotions can be. This trend is probably accelerating, moreover, as dual-career households struggle to find free time in their lives. For example, the recent POPAI study also discovered these significant changes: 70 percent of grocery consumers did not prepare a shopping list (up to 9 points from 1977); 75 percent ignored newspaper ads before shopping (up 13 percent), 90 percent of shoppers did not look at store circulars, and 80 percent did not redeem coupons.[26] While each of these measures relate only to one shopping trip, the message is nonetheless clear: *Consumers are waiting until they are in the store before they make many final decisions!*

These kinds of results have begun a revolution in marketing—the future will see even more promotional effort directed at consumers in the stores. Retailers will begin to charge directly for store space, and high-tech methods of influencing consumers will appear. For example, here are a few interesting developments we can expect to see in the near future (perhaps you've already experienced some of them!):

"Sniff-Teaser" Spends Scents

As we've seen earlier in the book, consumers can be highly responsive to subtle stimuli (colors, music, etc). A **Sniff-Teaser device** is now available that emits a product's smell into the store aisle near its display, and is expected to raise sales of detergents, coffee, baked goods, and so on. Sound devices are now available that will broadcast a brief message when a consumer passes by ("Psst . . . over here" supposedly generated a 300 percent increase in sales for a TV set, and other sound messages have been reported to show sales increases over 100 percent.) Also, holograms are likely in special settings: Don't be surprised if the 3-D image of George Washington or another famous figure beams into an aisle to talk to you about a purchase![27]

Radio Wendy's Is On the Air!

Drive-through customers at certain Wendy's stores see signs telling them to tune their radios to a particular FM frequency to hear "Radio Wendy's." This station, with a broadcast range of only a few blocks, discusses the menu, special deals, and new products. The idea, according to a Wendy's spokesperson, is to increase the use of drive-throughs and to get customers thinking about the menu before they order, thus speeding up the flow and perhaps increasing sales as well. Thus the radio message delivers a "secret word." If the customer uses the secret word while ordering, he or she receives a special discount.[28]

POP Rocks While the Smart Cart Rolls

A company called POP Radio markets its in-store broadcasts to retailers as a "sales-driving tool." In its recent agreement with the Muzak Corp., POP adds DJ discussions and commercials to the musical programming provided by Muzak. These tapes are provided to retailers at very low to no cost because of the advertising contained on them. Thus, beyond music, customers hear commercial announcements as they shop. Several firms are so excited by the prospects that they have signed on for exclusive rights in their product

EXHIBIT 19-3   WHAT WILL THE FUTURE HOLD IN-STORE? CONTINUED

POP sales assistance for Clarion Cosmetics.

categories. For example, at Maybelline, the product manager for Shine Free cosmetics said she was "amazed" at the difference that POP radio made: *"We were seeing double-digit increases on every single Shine Free product in stores that had the ads,"* she reports. According to the vice-president of A&P, one participating retailer, POP's management "has done excellent research" and the consumer response has been "tremendous."[29]

And while hearing POP ads, we will also be seeing computers at work around the store. For example, the new **Coupon Solution computer system,** hooked to a supermarket's scanner display, analyzes a customer's purchases as they are being made, and spits out coupons tailored to that buyer. For example, if a shopper buys diapers, the machine may issue a coupon for those diapers, or perhaps for a competing brand, attempting to induce a trial purchase. (In early tests of this system, 8 percent of these competitor coupons have been redeemed). In another system, backed by Procter & Gamble, discounts are shown on the screen at the checkouts. In one test, for example, shoppers who bought four of six designated P & G products received a 10 percent discount ($3 maximum) on their grocery bill. Another test created a "frequent shopper program" that adds up a member's purchases from particular brands and stores to give special prizes at different levels.[30]

Finally, we'll soon be piloting special **VideOcarts** through the aisles if Information Resources Inc. has its way. IRI is the nation's fifth largest market research company, based on its specialty work in gathering and analyzing supermarket scanner data. Its plans are to put the equivalent of laptop computer displays in shopping carts. Triggered by sensing devices, *these displays will show commercials as consumers reach the brand's shelf space in the store* (but only two commercials per aisle will be allowed). An advertiser is thus able to gain the customer's attention at exactly the point of purchase and to offer any special promotions at that time. Further, the cart computer will record the exact path of each shopper through the store, the time spent in each aisle, sound an alarm if the cart leaves the parking lot, play trivia games while waiting in the checkout line, and so forth. Thus, for IRI (which is betting a bundle on this new technology), the cart combines the best of consumer research and consumer selling in the same package![31]

Continued

EXHIBIT 19-3   *WHAT WILL THE FUTURE HOLD IN-STORE?* CONTINUED

VideOcart puts a six-by-eight inch computer display in each shopping cart.

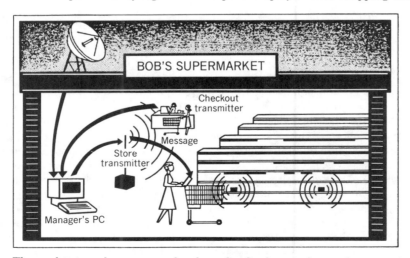

The sophisticated system sends ads to the display, so that each sponsor's ad will come up on the screen as the shopper nears that shelf space! Price specials, coupons, or other information can also be supplied.

advance (e.g., some direct-mail, telephone, or catalog orders), while in others credit or financing arrangements allow for payment at later times. Similarly, physical possession can be moved forward (e.g., by shipping a product and enclosing a bill to be paid later) or backward (e.g., by paying for an item and arranging for delivery at a later time). Legal ownership, on the other hand, tends to be tied to payment of the full purchase price.

As we've noted since the early stages of this book, *the purchase transaction is the key point at which marketers and consumers come together in our economic system.* Its fundamental purpose is positive for both parties—marketers gain the revenues they need to continue profitable operations in the future, while consumers gain the product or service they seek to gain the benefits offered from its consumption. One outstanding attribute of modern marketing-consumer environments is the emphasis given to *easing the act of purchase.* Salespersons are trained to move the consumer into the purchase stage and "close" a sale. If self-service is involved, arrangements aimed at speedy and smooth checkout are commonplace, with items likely to be impulsively purchased strategically placed near the purchasing area. The rise of bank credit cards (Visa, Mastercard) has also eased the act of purchase for consumers, by making an independent form of credit available for the store to accept. The fact the stores are willing to pay significant fees (of about 3 percent) for card charges is a good indication of the extent to which they wish to ease the purchase transaction for the consumer.

Within the decision process perspective, the act of purchase serves as a culmination of sorts, since all the search, evaluation, and choice activities now reach a single resolution for the consumer. In another sense, however, *the act of purchase serves as a bridge* for the consumer, who can now shift his or her attention to postpurchase activities, which include consuming the product and enjoying the benefits that have been sought all along. Accordingly, we too will now turn to examine the postpurchase phase in our next chapter.

SUMMARY

Monitoring Consumer Decision Making

In this chapter we focused on the middle stages of the consumer decision process—consumer decisions and in-store purchasing behavior. Given that much material relevant to these topics has already been covered in earlier chapters, here we concentrated on research approaches, decision strategies, and in-store purchasing behavior. The first section of the chapter covered methods to monitor consumer decision making. Because this is a personal mental process, it can be difficult for marketing researchers to measure. Two basic approaches are generally used: *input-output research* and *process monitoring research.* Input-output research usually employs some form of an experiment in which the researcher provides a special stimulus to consumers (special price, new advertising theme), then observes how consumers react to it (the outputs of the process). Advertising copy tests are a common form of this approach. Process monitoring, on the other hand, places less emphasis on the stimuli and the outcomes but more emphasis on trying to capture the reality of the decision process itself, as it occurs. Three methods used here are verbal protocols, physical monitoring methods (such as an information display board (IDB)), and observational monitoring methods (such as eye cameras). In recent years, researchers have begun to combine several of these methods in the same study.

Consumer Decision Rules

Decision rules are the strategies consumers use to help make up their minds when choosing from a set of alternatives. We examined three basic decision rules in this chapter, using luggage information from an IDB as the basic for our example. The *compensatory rule* requires the most effort and is aimed at discovering the best overall brand. It is similar to the multiattribute model we discussed in Chapter 11. The *lexicographic rule* relies on attribute importance as its key; the brand that stands out on the most important attribute will be chosen here. The *conjunctive rule*, on the other hand, is frequently used to eliminate many alternatives in a fast manner. A minimum level of performance is set for each important attribute, and each alternative is judged by whether or not it meets this minimum level. If it falls short on any attribute, it is rejected; if it passes all the standards, it remains a candidate for purchase.

Beyond the Basic Decision Rules

In extending our discussion on the decision rules, we noted that *mixed strategies* are likely to be found in the actual consumer world. Sometimes consumers construct decision rules as they go along; other times they rely on their LTM to supply stored rules. *Affect referral*, for example, is one such stored decision rule. We also noted that the degree of expertise or prior knowledge will affect decision strategies, as will joint decisions, information format, *problem framing,* and the *starting point* at which consumers begin their search and shopping activities.

Consumers' In-Store Purchasing Behavior

The final section of the chapter examined several studies of in-store purchasing behavior. Here we noted that most consumers in supermarkets seem to shop very quickly. We also reviewed the POPAI/DuPont study, which concluded that in supermarkets in-store decision making is the norm, rather than the exception. In accord with this finding, we saw that in-store displays can increase sales dramatically, and that many consumers are not aware of the exact price they are paying. Thus in-store behavior and stimuli are extremely significant factors in consumer behavior. Our review of how marketers are using new technology indicates what we can expect to see in future years.

KEY TERMS

input-output approach
process monitoring
verbal monitoring methods
physical monitoring methods
processing by attributes (PBA)
processing by brands (PBB)
observational monitoring methods
decision heuristics
decision rules
compensatory rule
lexicographic rule

conjunctive decision rules
mixed strategies
task factors
affect referral
frame of reference
start point
evoked set
sniff-teaser device
coupon solution computer system
VideOcarts

REVIEW QUESTIONS AND EXPERIENTIAL EXERCISES

[E = Application extension or experiential exercise]

1. Briefly explain the input-output method in consumer decision research, citing specific examples to illustrate.

2. What significance do flexibility and affect referral have for the decision making process? Cite examples of each from your experience as a consumer. What implications do they hold for marketers?

3. What generalization was drawn from the Wilkie and Dickson study concerning the start point of a decision? Do their data support this?

4. What generalizations are suggested about P-O-P behavior in the supermarket studies summarized in this chapter? Why does the author maintain that "market segmentation" is a key topic in marketing decision making?

5. Some of the studies in the chapter suggest that consumers make their supermarket purchases very quickly, with many people not looking at either prices or alternatives. Other studies suggest that most decisions are made in the store. Still others show that ads and displays can have large impacts. How can all of this be true? Prepare a logical series of points that explain all of this.

[E] 6. As an interesting project to link the prepurchase and purchase chapters together, select a recent decision you (or a friend or relative) have made.

Think back (or interview) through the stages of the decision process as shown in Chapter 18. Create the brands/attributes matrix (similar to Figure 19-1 or Exhibit 19-2) as it was *at the problem recognition* stage of your purchase. Then, as you replay the decision process, *modify* the matrix by adding alternatives, dropping alternatives, adding attributes, adding information, and so forth, as you did when you went through the search, evaluation, and final decision stages. Write a brief report on your findings.

[E]   7. a. Accompany a friend to the supermarket and observe his or her behavior there: the time it takes to shop, the time spent pondering alternatives, and the number of products purchased. Summarize your findings.

b. At the conclusion of the shopping trip (back at home or apartment) determine the extent to which the purchase of each item was planned or unplanned. Compare your results with the findings of the PO-PAI/DuPont study.

[E]   8. Stroll through a supermarket or discount store, noting the placement, design, and appeals of the special displays. Predict which three you believe will be most effective and three that might be ineffective. Then interview a store manager about the displays, their effectiveness, and the marketing process involving point-of-purchase. Write a brief report summarizing your findings.

[E]   9. Conduct an observational study of shoppers in a supermarket, similar to those reported in the chapter. Compare your findings with those reported in the chapter, in a brief report. (*Hint:* you may wish to use the Note references to locate details of how a study was done).

[E] 10. Refer to Note 17 for some interesting readings concerning the impacts and applications of "problem framing." Write a brief report on your findings.

[E] 11. If you are interested in learning more about the study of decision rules and decision making processes, excellent (but technical) references are available in the Notes listed for each specific decision topic in the chapter. Write a brief report on what you have found.

[E] 12. To help gain a manufacturer's view of in-store behavior and the revolution in supermarket retailing, arrange to interview a sales representative for a major grocery manufacturer (your local supermarket manager should be able to provide names of possible people). Based on the material in this chapter, ask about how shelf space is gained, how new products are introduced, promotions are run, and so forth. Probe for insights on consumers' responsiveness to marketing programs, and for which types of marketing techniques seem to work best. Write a brief report on your findings.

CHAPTER  20

Consumer Decision Processes (III): Postpurchase Decisions

The Owners Speak

Let's listen again to the Chicago-area car buyers, now as they describe some aspects of their postpurchase experiences:

"... two years ago I wouldn't be caught dead in a four-door ... the statement it kind of makes. [Now] even when ... I don't have the little guy in the car, it's like I'm a family man now."

"People ... do not admit they made a bad decision unless it's fairly obvious ... the minute you buy something you start an internal process of convincing yourself that this was the right thing ... "

"I've had a tremendous number of compliments on its appearance, which makes me feel so good ... I know in GM ... it's one of the top-level cars, which made me feel better ... it was a Buick, and hopefully it was a better car."

(Wife): "I'm a Cadillac person."

(Husband): "... When Karen gets on her nice diamonds and puts on her big fur, and she gets in her Cadillac, and goes to the women's club ... she looks as good as anyone."

(Wife): "It's real special. When I get in the car and turn the stereo on where I have the tape in there, you feel good. And I didn't realize you got a gold key ... there's a special gold one. I thought, 'A gold key!' it's just kind of those little touches."

"I won't be comfortable that we got our value until maybe a year from now ... to see how it performs ... I'm a little insecure. But any decision where you're spending that amount of money, you're going to be a little insecure ... so far we're happy with it."[1]

■ ■ ■

WHY ARE POSTPURCHASE PROCESSES IMPORTANT?

In this chapter we'll explore the interesting world of postpurchase processes, or what goes on after the consumer makes a purchase. If we think briefly about the *consumer's perspective,* we can see that *the goal of the consumer's decision lies in consumption and consumption occurs during the postpurchase phase.* Purchases are only "means to an end," with the end being the attainment of benefits from consuming the product or service. We benefit from our purchases of Tide and Chrysler not when we purchase them, but during the postpurchase phase, when our clothes become fresh and clean and we're traveling in comfort and style. The postpurchase phase is extremely important for the *marketing perspective* as well, since *it is here that long-term profits are built.* During the postpurchase phase, consumers evaluate the brand they've purchased. Marketers who stress favorable *post*-purchase evaluations are the ones like to receive favorable *pre*purchase evaluations in future consumer decisions.

A FRAMEWORK FOR POSTPURCHASE

While we're all familiar with the general form of activities following purchase, most of us haven't given a great deal of structured thought to them as we've gone about our normal lives. To help us begin our analysis, let's consider a few subtle points contained in the framework in Figure 20-1. Notice that the postpurchase phase accounts for two of the three major activities in an overall consumption

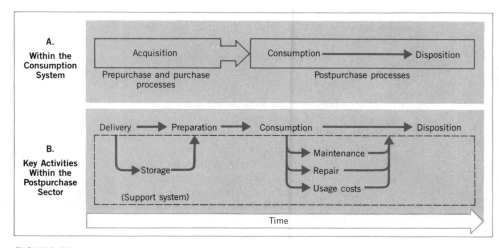

FIGURE 20-1 **The Postpurchase Phase**

system. This is in contrast to the overwhelming emphasis that the field of consumer behavior research has given to the "Acquisition" stage. In the bottom of Figure 20-1 note the role that *time* plays. The total time for the postpurchase phase can vary widely, ranging from only a few seconds (as in consuming a piece of candy) through several hours (attending a movie) to a number of years (as with a piano). Figure 20-1 also shows a *support system: storage* is often required to cushion the period between purchase and use; *service* (maintenance and repair) and *energy* (e.g., gas for an auto) are often needed as well. Thus *further expenditures* are also involved in a postpurchase system. Finally, some means for *disposing* of the product is usually needed when consumption is complete.

The Consumption of Products and Services

The analysis of how consumers consume products and services can provide marketers with useful insights. The following dimensions of consumption were suggested by Philip Hendrix: notice the many marketing implications that emerge.[2]

Consumption Frequency

A focus on **consumption frequency**—how often a product is used—can offer useful insights about the market for our product or service. Consumption of a few products and services is essentially *continuous*, as with housing, electricity, and insurance. For most products, however, consumption is *discontinuous*—it occurs on discrete occasions. One way to increase demand, therefore, is to increase consumers' frequency of **perceived use occasions** for your product. Sometimes this option can be handled through the concept of product storage. For example, millions of American consumers enjoy the taste and wiggle of Jell-O and are happy to buy it in the supermarket. Recently, however, the company discovered that sales levels were falling short of potential for the simple reason that consumers tended to "forget" about the product once it was put away in the cupboard. A new promotion strategy was thus born—ads reminded consumers how good Jell-O is and suggested that it was probably already "right there in the cupboard."

Consumption Amount

A product's total demand is comprised of the frequency of use times the **average amount consumed**. Strategies to *increase the average amount consumed* thus translate directly into higher sales. Marketers recognize this when they use special pricing plans that reduce the marginal cost of additional units' consumption. Many home carpet cleaning firms, for example, price their offerings so that each additional room costs less to have cleaned, thus encouraging more carpet cleaning during a home visit.

Consumption Intervals

New opportunities can arise by examining the nature of the **intervals between consumption occasions**. In some categories there may be an option to replace storage with a new product form that will offer *continuous service*. This was the case in the recent introductions of "stick-up" room deodorizers, continuous-release toilet bowl cleaners, and time-release capsules for medicines. The *pattern* of consumption intervals can also be a key factor in restricting demand. For example, many products face time-dependent use patterns. Orange juice manufacturers elected to fight their restrictive image with the

Storyboard for a campaign to change consumers' patterns of consumption intervals.

". . . isn't just for breakfast anymore!" campaign, while Stove Top stuffing mix decided to position this product against potatoes to expand the types of meals at which consumers would see the product as appropriate.

Finally, the *regularity* of use can also be a significant factor. Consumption of electricity, for example, has a large irregular component determined by the temperature each day. Utilities would very much like to smooth out this pattern, and they are experimenting with "time-of-day" pricing, in which consumers are charged less for electricity if they use it during the less busy times of day and are charged premium rates for use during busy times (this is similar to the pricing for long-distance telephone service, which was adopted for much the same reason). Other marketers have also designed successful strategies along this line. Prince Spaghetti, for example, has long promoted Wednesday in the Northeast as Prince Spaghetti Day.

Consumption Purposes

A final key consumption dimension for marketing concerns the exact **consumption purposes** that consumers perceive as appropriate for the brand. Some brands have been notably successful with narrow and precise positionings. Woolite, for example, has carved out a unique niche for itself by restricting its consumption purposes. On the other hand, Coke, Pepsi, and most other soft drinks suggest that they are appropriate for many occasions and settings. The classic example of extending consumption purposes, of course, remains Arm & Hammer baking soda, which was able to raise its sales dramatically by extending perceived consumption purposes, first to the refrigerator and then to the freezer and on to further new uses over the years.

Product Disposition

Following consumption, the final stage in a product's life occurs when the consumer *disposes* of it. There are three major options in **product disposition**:

- Trash it!
- Save it (either store it or repair it).
- Sell or give it away.

There are substantial product differences in disposition modes. At one extreme, some products (especially foods) are disposed of during consumption itself. At the other extreme, products that are used over periods of time usually do face disposition decisions. It is likely that almost all product packaging, and most products themselves, ultimately find their ways to the trash bins of the nation. This can differ by product type, however. In one study, for example, consumers reported throwing away used toothbrushes but storing high proportions of wristwatches and phonograph records. Used stereos and bicycles, on the other hand, were most likely to be given away, traded, or sold to others.[3]

In the Aggregate, a National Concern

Because everyone disposes of products and packages as a matter of daily living, at the aggregate level several national problems arise. The sheer volume of garbage in our country, for example, presents problems of safe disposal. For example, when Oakland, California, decided that it would no longer serve as the garbage repository for San Francisco, matters got so severe that the daily trash from the "City by the Bay" was mounted on huge barges and carted far out to sea to be dumped. Product disposition decisions also pose special problems with respect to hazardous materials and threats to ecology. For example, the volume of our national laundry became evident to consumers a few years ago, when several rivers began to "suds up" due to heavy concentrations of detergent that wasn't

You may recall the famous Islip (Long Island) garbage barge that kept getting turned away from other locations. Here it is arriving, at last, in Brooklyn.

breaking down in the sewer systems! Marketers reacted by changing the nature of the product ingredients to lessen such problems. More recently, disposable diapers were found to pose a long-term disposal threat, since they did not biologically degrade in the trash disposal system. Major manufacturers went to work to try to remedy this problem.

Many other issues begin to emerge when we think about the ramifications of product disposition. For example, the state of Florida is seriously concerned about its future:

Floridians Bash Trash

Because of its high water table, much of the state of Florida could not bury trash, and the exploding state faced a crisis as it neared the 1990s. In response, it passed a 185-page law aimed at changing consumers' disposal behaviors. Among its provisions: unauthorized dumping becomes a felony crime, detachable metal pop-tops are banned, plastic shopping bags have to degrade within four months, newsprint is taxed if not recycled, and so forth. Further, beginning in 1992, each container sold in a retail store will cost an extra penny (rising to 2 cents in 1995) if its container type is not recycled at a 50 percent rate statewide. Local governments are given strong incentives also: they must cut their trash dumping by 30 percent, or funds may be cut off. Thus local governments are expected to encourage consumers to recycle in order to achieve their targets. One business expert forecast: "I envisage a five-garbage-can backyard . . . one can each for aluminum, glass, paper, and plastics, and one for everything else."[4]

Product Disposition, Time, and Market Potentials

As a final topic in our coverage of product disposition, let's again think briefly about the concept of time. *When* do people decide to dispose of their products? As we saw in the shopping study conducted by Wilkie and Dickson, most large appliance purchases were sparked by breakdowns or operating problems with the existing machine. This suggests that consumers wait until their present product breaks before moving to dispose of it and undertake a new purchase. In this sense, an existing product, late in its life, presents a *barrier* to a new purchase the consumer might otherwise be willing to make. Alert marketers may be able to overcome this barrier and increase overall product demand by attempting to move the disposition decision to an earlier point in time. This would seem especially likely for products that can be "traded up" for better features or new advances, such as computers and stereos. IBM, in fact, recently announced such a plan when it introduced its PS/2 line of personal computers.

Second, you may also recall that Wilkie and Dickson found that brand loyalty seemed quite low for these products. Could this be due to the fact that consumers are displeased with their product after it has broken down? That is, Sears might have a much higher chance of selling another refrigerator to Rachel Smith if she disposes of it in the twelfth year (while it's still working well) as opposed to the thirteenth year, after it has broken down. This does not mean, of course, that a consumer is necessarily better off to dispose of old products earlier. On some occasions, however, this could well be the case. New energy developments, for example, can offer increased operating efficiencies in newer models of appliances, new tires can offer increased safety in a person's automobile, special price deals at slow periods can offer substantial dollar savings, and so forth. Thus, for both marketers and consumers, the issue of changing the timing of product disposition bears increasing attention.

PSYCHOLOGICAL PROCESSES DURING POSTPURCHASE

One of the most interesting aspects of the postpurchase phase involves the several forms of psychological processes consumers can experience following a purchase. One key psychological process is **postpurchase learning**. Here the consumer discovers something of objective reality about a product or service, stores this new knowledge in LTM, modifies relevant attitudes, and is ready for the next decision process with an improved base of knowledge. Since we've already discussed this, we need not delve into it further here. There are, however, two other psychological topics relevant to postpurchase that we've not discussed earlier, *cognitive dissonance* and *consumer satisfaction/dissatisfaction*.

Cognitive Dissonance

About 30 years ago Leon Festinger, a Stanford psychology professor, propounded what was to become one of the most popular and controversial theories in all of psychology: cognitive dissonance.[5] Cognitive dissonance belongs to the family of cognitive consistency theories we've already discussed in our chapter on consumer motivation. Let's first examine the theory, then its implications.

Basics of the Theory

Each person has many cognitions (beliefs or opinions) about himself or herself, other people, and the decisions he or she makes. Any two cognitions can be *unrelated* (e.g., "I like fresh green peas," and "Ward sells Buicks") or *related*. If they are related, their relationship can be described as either *consonant* ("I like Ward" and "Ward sells good cars") or *dissonant* ("I don't like Dan" and "I'd like to buy a Buick from Dan."). That is, elements are **consonant cognitions** if one follows logically from the other, whereas they are **dissonant cognitions** if there is a logical inconsistency between them. For any consumer decision we're likely to have many cognitions (e.g., our Buick purchase would produce many elements involving ourselves, the car, the dealer, and the decision itself). The thrust of **cognitive dissonance theory** is that (1) dissonance is likely to occur *after* a choice has been made, and (2) will reflect a natural occurrence *because* the choice has been made.

In terms of postpurchase processes, it is the *total amount of dissonance* that we experience that is important. The more dissonant cognitions we have about the decision, and the more important these are to us, the higher our dissonance will be. And, since dissonance produces unpleasant feelings, we'll be motivated to act to *reduce* the amount of dissonance we are experiencing.

We should recognize that cognitive dissonance is not a significant factor in all situations. Basically, dissonance should be higher (1) when a choice was a close decision and (2) when the purchase was important to us. But why is this? Let's examine a typical case.

Carrie's College Choice

Carrie Parker is due finally to make up her mind as to which school she'll attend next year. Her decision is down to two universities (we'll call them X and Y so as not to offend anyone). Each school has a number of points in its favor. University X is closer to home, is a little less expensive, has many course options, and a number of Carrie's friends are already there and urging her to join them. University Y, on the other hand, is slightly more prestigious, has a strong marketing department, has a pretty campus with ivy-covered walls, and Carrie's mother is an alum who loves the school.

Let's consider *what happens if Carrie chooses University X*. All the positive aspects of Y will now become dissonant elements in her decision—Carrie has given up some prestige, a beautiful campus, and a top-flight major in marketing, and she has a slightly disappointed Mom. Of course she's also gained the positive elements of X, and these produce consonant cognitions for her. Unless X is perfect, though, there will also be a few drawbacks to it (parking problems, several bad teachers, etc.) that will add some further dissonant elements to her total consideration. Overall, since the decision is important to her, and since University Y did offer a number of attractive attributes, Carrier will experience at least a moderate amount of dissonance after making her decision.

What will Carrie do to handle this dissonance? In theory, she'll be attempting to reduce her total dissonance score by (1) reducing the number of dissonant elements, (2) reducing the importance weights she attaches to the dissonant elements, and/or (3) raising the number of consonant elements. For example, she may decide that ivy-covered walls are actually irrelevant to the quality of a college experience and that the school her mother knew 25 years earlier isn't the same place today. She might also be pleased to hear that the star professor at University Y has left the school for greener pastures at A&M. Finally, she may not seek out too many supporters of University Y over the next week or so, not wanting to hear any new points that could create new dissonant elements for her.

With respect to University X, Carrie will strive to increase the number and importance of the consonant elements. She may reread the promotional materials from the school, stopping to linger over the attractive photographs of student life, buildings, and campus landscapes. She'll notice the story in the paper about the rising academic prestige of the university and may well point this out to her parents after dinner. And she'll seek out her friends from the university to let them know of her decision, and receive their congratulations and assurances. Over time, Carrie will feel somewhat more favorably toward her chosen school and will be somewhat less favorable toward the school she almost chose. This "spread of attitude" between Universities X and Y will help to ease the dissonance Carrie has experienced and will allow her to set off with enthusiasm for her college experience.

Marketing Implications of Dissonance

The special contribution of cognitive dissonance theory rests in its explicit stress on the consumer's motivation to reduce tension following an important purchase decision. From this basis, a number of predictions emerge:

1. *Attitude spread.* As in Carrie's case, one likely outcome is that consumers will strive to see their chosen brand as significantly better than the rejected ones.
2. *Selective information seeking.* Promotional materials and ads provide very favorable information about a brand, as do satisfied owners of the product. For this reason we'd expect consumers to seek out such information as a means of reducing their dissonance. Some marketers believe that consumers read more ads (for the brand they've chosen) *after* they purchase than they had before they bought!
3. *Motivated opinion giving.* More acceptance by others can also serve to reduce dissonance. Thus—especially for innovations, which most consumers haven't yet accepted—we'd expect to see early adopters wanting to bring about further acceptance. One way to do this is to engage in favorable influence attempts on their friends.

These predictions suggest some useful strategies for marketers. For example, some marketers *provide reassurance* through congratulating recent buyers and reviewing strong product attributes in the manuals provided to new purchasers.

Several auto makers publish special editions of magazines geared to recent purchasers, provided free of charge to them. In addition, some advertising appeals can be geared to recent purchasers as well as potential buyers—the auto ads featuring recent buyers leaping in the air beside their new Toyotas are incorporating this feature. Also, salespersons of "big-ticket" items are often instructed to call their recent buyers within a day or so after purchase, to offer further information and assurances.

These are examples of the many interesting speculations that the theory of cognitive dissonance offers us. Before leaving the topic, however, we should note that scientists have been debating for years over the precise nature of dissonance theory and its explanations. These debates do not mean that dissonance does not occur or that it cannot lead to significant impacts on consumer behavior. The debates do, however, suggest caution in accepting dissonance explanations too easily or expecting that the results will always occur. (For our purposes we need not delve into the detailed arguments here: if you are interested in pursuing this further, Note 6 provides a summary of issues, and a good set of readings.)

Consumer Satisfaction/Dissatisfaction ("CS/D")

Consumer satisfaction *is a topic in which marketers and consumers have common interests.* Marketers strive to have satisfied customers—this makes the daily business more pleasant, provides a good base for repeat purchases, and sets the stage for favorable word of mouth to potential customers. On the other side of the transaction, consumers enjoy being satisfied. Not only does this indicate that they are obtaining the benefits they seek, but satisfaction also provides a pleasant feeling in itself.

Consumer dissatisfaction *brings quite different reactions, and often serves to set marketers' interests in opposition to those of consumers.* Dissatisfaction is unpleasant for consumers and indicates problems with a product, store, or service provider. It is also bad for the marketer, who risks the loss of future business, negative word of mouth, and the prospect of some unpleasant encounters with dissatisfied patrons.

The topic of CS/D has recently become one of the most studied issues in the field of consumer behavior (the acronym "CS/D" was devised by Keith Hunt). There have been some 700 papers written on this topic in the last 15 years. Special CS/D conferences are held so that researchers can report their latest findings and stay current on the work of others and a new journal has now been started on this topic. (If you are interested in reading collections of papers on CS/D, Note 7 explains how to locate them.)

The Concept of Satisfaction

Satisfaction/dissatisfaction refers to an emotional response to an evaluation of a product or service consumption experience.[8] In Figure 20-2, notice that a time dimension underlies this process, which has five key elements:

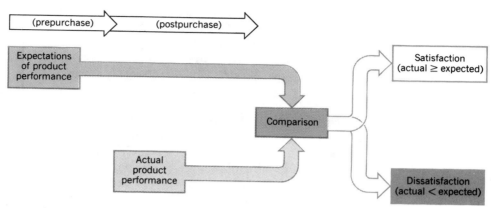

FIGURE 20-2 CS/D as a Comparison Process

1. **Expectations.** The seeds of consumer satisfaction are planted during the *prepurchase* phase, when consumers develop "expectations" or beliefs about what they expect to receive from the product. These expectations are carried forward into the postpurchase phase, when they are again activated at the time of consumption.

2. **Performance.** During consumption we experience the actual product in use and perceive its performance on the dimensions that are important to us.

3. **Comparison.** After use, the availability of both the prepurchase expectations and actual performance perceptions allow us to conduct a comparison between them.

4. **Confirmation/disconfirmation.** The comparison results in either a "confirmation" of the consumer's expectations (when the two performance levels are equal) or a "disconfirmation" of expectations (when actual performance is *either* greater than or less than the expected level).

5. **Discrepancy.** If the performance levels are not equal, a discrepancy measure indicates how different one is from the other. For negative disconfirmations—those in which actual performance falls below expected levels—larger discrepancies should produce higher levels of dissatisfaction.

Thus the basic process of CS/D is reasonably straightforward: consumer satisfaction is likely to result when actual performance levels either meet or exceed expected levels (notice that satisfaction thus occurs with both confirmation and positive disconfirmation outcomes). Dissatisfaction occurs when a *negative disconfirmation* is present—when actual outcomes fall below the expected levels of performance.

In reality, of course, matters can be more complicated. For example, if a consumer is quite *inexperienced* with a product, his or her expectations of performance are likely to be uncertain. In this case, using the product for the first time provides information for the consumer. One outcome can be to revise the earlier expected levels (during the comparison process) up or down toward the actual performance level. Thus a dissatisfaction outcome is less likely to occur in this instance, as compared to a case in which a consumer has had more experience on which to base his or her initial expectations. Similar revisions of judgments can occur on the actual performance side. This usually happens when a consumer has a hard time in judging actual performance. For example, consider how well most of are able to judge the actual performance of such products as vitamins, modern art exhibits, and new roofing. Thus, when we know we aren't too accurate in our appraisal of performance, our judgments might be selectively nudged toward our earlier expectation levels. As we pay the roofer for our new roof, for instance, we notice that it looks all right, and we're happy to believe it's fine, in part because we expected (and desired) that it would be fine.

How Satisfied Are Consumers?

The Overall Level is High   In general, the results of many CS/D surveys—by academics, government agencies, and businesses—show that the overall level of consumer satisfaction is high. For example, a mail survey of Sears, Roebuck customers found that four out of five customers (81 percent) reported that they were "completely satisfied" with their most recent Sears' purchase, whereas only 3 percent were "not too satisfied" (the remainder was "fairly satisfied").[8]

We've Got the Power!

"There isn't a car manufacturer around that can ignore a J. V. Power report," says one auto news chief. "It is an extremely credible source and its data carries quite a bit of weight." The report in question is the automobile Consumer Satisfaction Index issued annually by the Power firm. Power waits a year, then sends out over 100,000 questionnaires to owners of new cars and trucks. Questions focus on the quality of the car and the service received. Over 130 different models are rated in the survey. Power charges clients an average of $35,000 to examine the CSI report and also uses its expertise to conduct private surveys for interested clients. As you scan auto ads, you will probably notice some (high-ranking!) cars featuring the Power rating results. According to Mr. Power, "By measuring consumer satisfaction . . . auto makers now see how they fare against the competition. That always wakes a business up . . . and we all benefit from their awareness."[9]

But Problem Areas Do Exist   Although the overall level of consumer satisfaction is high, this doesn't mean that all products and services are trouble free. Are there certain sectors in which consumer *dissatisfaction* is a particular problem? To see if this was the case, the White House Office of Consumer Affairs sponsored a major investigation a few years ago:

The White House/TARP Study of Consumer Problems
A Washington-based consulting firm, TARP, conducted the research for the White House office.[10] Over 2500 consumers across the United States were interviewed. Each respondent was shown a list of possible consumer problems and asked if any had been experienced in the past year. For each problem mentioned, follow-up questions were asked to learn details of the problem, how consumers reacted, and the ultimate outcome. We should note that the TARP study concentrated only on dissatisfaction and is therefore unable to address the overall question of how satisfied consumers are. It is significant, however, that *two-thirds of the consumers reported that they had not experienced any consumer problems during the past year.* While this does not strictly mean that these consumers had no dissatisfaction at all, it does suggest that they would have experienced only mild forms at most.

The other *one-third of the TARP sample did report experiencing consumer problems* (at a rate of almost two problems per household over the year). Table 20-1 lists the types of problems they most frequently reported. In examining this list, it is interesting to see that product performance, while sometimes a difficulty, doesn't account for most consumer problems. Instead, the *service elements* of the marketing mix (availability, repair, delivery, etc.) more frequently cause problems for consumers. When TARP analyzed the problems

TABLE 20-1 CONSUMER RATINGS OF CS/D

Type of Consumer Problem	Households Having This Type Problem
1. Store did not have product advertised for sale	25%
2. Unsatisfactory performance/quality of product	22
3. Unsatisfactory repair	20
4. Unsatisfactory service (unrelated to repair)	16
5. Long wait for delivery	10
6. Failure to receive delivery	10
7. Overcharge or excessive price	10
8. Distasteful or offensive advertising	9
9. Product/service not as ordered/agreed on	9
10. Incorrect/deceptive or fraudulent billing	9
11. Deceptive advertising/packaging/pricing	8
12. Goods received in damaged condition	8
13. Manufacturer/dealer didn't live up to guarantee/warranty	7
14. Dealer/salesperson misrepresented product/service	7
15. Failure to receive refund	5
Others (all less than 5%)	

[a]N = 814 households in the survey experienced consumer problem(s); there were 1582 incidences of problems.

Source: Marc A. Grainer, Cathleen A. McEvoy, and Donald King, "Consumer Problems and Complaints: A National View," In William L. Wilkie (ed.), *Advances in Consumer Research*, Vol. 6 (Ann Arbor, Mich.: Association for Consumer Research, 1979), p. 496.

in terms of the products/services involved, this point became even more clear—*automobile repair and appliance repair are the two major individual sources of consumer problems.*

How Do Consumers Respond to Dissatisfaction?

What can a consumer do when dissatisfied? Figure 20-3 displays five options in this regard. Notice that they are roughly arrayed in order of increasing severity and that a consumer might decide to undertake several of the options. How many of these have you employed? In examining the figure, note that those listed are only some of the options a consumer might choose. How often do consumers undertake each response shown? No data can answer this question entirely, but some findings are suggestive. *First, most consumers do not move into the right side of Figure 20-3 in most instances of dissatisfaction.* One major survey, conducted by Alan Andreasen and Arthur Best, covered many product categories, and found that 70 percent of dissatisfied consumers did not voice a complaint into the marketing system.[11] The TARP study did, in contrast, find more than a majority of consumers report having either sought "redress" (that is, a product exchange, money return, repair, etc.) or complained to an outside agency. TARP, however, had asked only about the *most serious* problem that the consumer had experienced and found that almost 70 percent of consumers had sought redress for these (even here, however, 30 percent of consumers did not complain).

What influences a consumer's decision to complain or not?[12]

■ *Level of dissatisfaction.* For a mild form of dissatisfaction, it may not be worthwhile. The world is not perfect. When a high level of dissatisfaction occurs, however, the likelihood of consumer responses increases.

■ *Importance.* Products or services that are more important to us are more likely to generate complaints when unsatisfactory experiences occur. A face lift that goes bad or a new car that won't run is likely to generate redress actions.

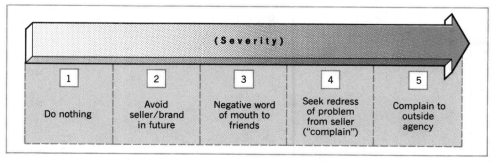

FIGURE 20-3 **Alternative Actions in Response to Consumer Dissatisfaction**

- *Costs/benefits of actions.* We are more likely to complain when our expected benefits are high and our expected costs of complaining our low. A defective purchase made on vacation 2000 miles away may not yield a return to that store, while that same purchase around the corner is likely to be returned.
- *Personal characteristics.* Studies have shown that some people are more likely to complain than others. Highly educated persons are more likely to seek redress, as are people with more time available. Personality characteristics such as aggressiveness also determine whether a person complains or not.
- *Attribution of blame.* If Dee Sequin has a problem, but believes that she could possibly be at fault, she's less likely to complain than if she attributes the cause of the problem to the manufacturer. One common source of difficulty for marketers occurs because of this attribution process, when the seller and the buyer each attribute the problem to be the other party's fault! This situation is made even more difficult because emotions are involved and the persons may not communicate clearly.

In regard to consumer attributions—and as a reward for reading this far into the chapter—you may enjoy reading the quotes in Exhibit 20-1. These are actual statements from insurance policyholders reporting how the auto accident had occurred. While not exactly complaint reports, they do demonstrate forms of blame attributions and give a sense for what it's like in the real world!

What Happens When Consumers Complain?

When consumers do seek redress (complain), most go directly to the store. This means that *retailers* receive most complaints about a given product, while the manufacturer receives relatively little direct feedback from consumers. This can be undesirable, since considerable information can be lost if not fully passed along. What about consumers contacting outside agencies, such as the Better Business Bureau, Federal Trade Commission, local agencies, or newspapers? Outside agencies are the *least* likely to be contacted: they accounted for less than 10 percent of the complaints in the TARP study and only 1 percent in the Best and Andreasen research.

How successful are consumers in having their dissatisfaction handled well? The TARP research found that 40 percent of the complaining households obtained either "completely satisfying" or "acceptable solution" responses from the business. Another 13 percent got "something" but were not completely satisfied, while another 40 percent were "not at all satisfied" with the way in which their complaints were resolved. The TARP research team concluded that serious difficulties exist with actions to resolve consumer problems. They pointed out that, adding the 30 percent of consumers who did not complain at all to the 40 percent who were displeased with the resolution of their complaints, suggests that about 70 percent of serious consumer problems are not being satisfactorily remedied. As we'll see in the next section, this poses some serious problems (and opportunities) for marketers.

EXHIBIT 20–1   CONSUMER ATTRIBUTIONS OF ACCIDENT CAUSES:
A BIASED SAMPLE

"Not My Fault!"

- "No one was to blame for the accident but it never would have happened if the other driver had been alert."
- "A pedestrian hit me and went under my car."
- "I had been shopping for plants all day. . . . As I reached an intersection a hedge sprang up obscuring my vision. I did not see the other car."
- "I was on my way to the doctors with rear end trouble when my universal joint gave way causing me to have an accident."
- "As I approached the intersection, a stop sign suddenly appeared where no stop sign had ever appeared before. I was unable to stop in time. . . ."
- "My car was legally parked as it backed into the other vehicle."
- "The indirect cause of this accident was a little guy in a small car with a big mouth."
- "The telephone pole was approaching fast. I was attempting to swerve out of its path when it struck my front end."
- "An invisible car came out of nowhere, struck my vehicle, and vanished."

"It Was My Fault, But . . ."

- "I pulled away from the side of the road, glanced at my mother-in-law, and headed over the embankment."
- "In my attempt to kill a fly I drove into a telephone pole."
- "The accident occurred when I was attempting to bring my car out of a skid by steering it into the other vehicle."
- "I had been learning power steering. I turned the wheel . . . and found myself in a different direction going the opposite way."
- "I was taking my canary to the hospital. It got loose and flew out the window. The next thing I saw was his rear end and there was a crash."
- "When I saw I could not avoid a collision, I stepped on the gas and crashed into the other car."
- "The pedestrian had no idea which way to go, so I ran over him."

"I'm Still Dazed by It All . . ."

- "I collided with a stationary truck coming the other way."
- "I told the police that I was not injured but on removing my hat, I found that I had a fractured skull."
- "I saw her look at me twice, she appeared to be making slow progress, then we met on impact."
- "A guy was all over the road, I had to swerve a number of times before I hit him."
- "I was thrown from my car as it left the road. I was later found in a ditch by some stray cows."

Source: These quotes were abstracted from information submitted to the FTC project on consumer life insurance information disclosure and reflect actual policyholder reports.

MARKETING APPLICATIONS OF POSTPURCHASE CONCEPTS

John Czepiel succinctly described the tasks of marketing as follows:

> In any organization, marketing bears the responsibility for three key tasks: (1) *design* of an offering to meet consumer needs, (2) *attraction* of clients to that offering, and (3) *monitoring and control* of results to ensure the continued meeting of customer needs in a changing environment.[13]

This perspective reminds us that marketers should consider *all* aspects of the consumer's decision process—activities at the prepurchase stage, during purchase, and during postpurchase—when designing their management system. Alert marketers have already recognized some useful guidelines from the consumption and satisfaction dimensions of consumer behavior. Let's briefly examine five examples of these insights.

Insight 1: Consumer Use Can Guide New Product Positioning

Alert marketers monitor how consumers are using various products. Procter & Gamble, for example, in monitoring consumers' laundry behaviors, discovered that households were washing more frequently and using cooler water to wash new artificial fabrics. Based on this information, the firm developed Cheer detergent to wash effectively in all water temperatures. P&G takes consumer use problems seriously: when it learned that people in high-altitude regions were having difficulty preparing baked goods, the firm added special "high-altitude baking" directions to its Duncan Hines packages. The product disposition stage also offers opportunities for enterprising marketers. For example, a new machine that accepts empty soda and beer cans, crushes them, and returns a nickel to the consumer is now on the market. These machines are rented to retailers in states with "bottle laws."[14]

Insight 2: Don't Overpromise—Consumer Dissatisfaction Can Be Costly

As Czepiel's quote reminded us, marketing involves the distinct processes of both *attracting consumers and satisfying* them. Glowing promises are useful ways to attract purchasers, but marketers should bear in mind that these promises may form the basis for consumer expectations. Since consumer dissatisfaction springs from negative disconfirmations of these expectations, some instances of dissatisfaction could be avoided if consumers simply expected less in the first place. Thus marketers are wise to strike a reasonable balance between performance promised and that consumers are likely to experience.

How costly can dissatisfaction be? According to a TARP study on automobiles, *disgruntled auto owners are likely to vent their frustration to 16 additional people!* On the other hand, a satisfied owner provides positive word of mouth to 8 other people, plus being likely to buy four more cars of the same make over the next 12 years![15] Similar results were also uncovered in a TARP study conducted for Coca-Cola. In this research, consumers who complained and were not satisfied typically told 9 or 10 friends about their experience, and 30 percent of these persons said they stopped buying Coke products altogether (another 45 percent said they'd buy less in the future). However, when the complaint was resolved satisfactorily, the average consumer told 4 or 5 people about the positive experience.[16]

Insight 3: See If a Guarantee of Postpurchase Satisfaction Is Possible

It would be naive to assume that a firm should always strive to obtain the highest possible level of consumer satisfaction. Many factors need to be considered. For example, *some consumers may be wrong* when they complain (repairpersons report that one of their most common experiences is the discovery that the appliance the consumer believes to be defective has in fact become unplugged from the wall socket!). Also, increasing the probability of consumer satisfaction is likely to bring *higher costs* into the system, and in some cases there is an *inherent uncertainty* in the product. This uncertainty means the costs of guaranteeing consumer satisfaction may be too high and the consumer is better off to assume some risk of being dissatisfied. *Used cars* provide a classic case of this point. Most of us recognize that used car dealers hold one of the lowest reputations for consumer satisfaction guarantees in all of marketing, but we may not have thought why this would tend to occur. Note that part of the used car dissatisfaction syndrome is due to inherent uncertainties about the product itself. What is the history of the car, how much abuse has it already suffered? What will happen in the car's future—how will it be driven, and what will break down? Thus, if it were possible to guarantee complete satisfaction, the costs of doing so would raise the prices of used cars for all buyers, and some consumers might find this undesirable. In a sense, then, the consumer is choosing either to pay for "satisfaction insurance" when buying a used car (by buying from a reputable dealer who offers warranty protection) or to bear the risks personally and buy from a dealer who offers "as is" cars at lower prices.

There are, of course, many situations in which strong guarantees can work to a marketer's advantage. The famous Zippo lighter, for example, was marketed with an ironclad guarantee that any consumer problem would be promptly corrected, free of charge, at the factory. Similarly, many finer retailers offer "Free Return If Not Completely Satisfied" policies to guarantee their customers' postpurchase satisfaction.

In their recent quest to regain quality parity with Japanese autos, U.S. makers have been moving toward "risk-free car buying." According to Lee Iacocca' pledge to Chrysler buyers: "You have a right to get your money back." Plans tested included money back (if car returned within 30 days or 1,000 miles) or a replacement Chrysler (when Pontiac tried a replacement pledge in a California test, only 14 of 3000 cars were exchanged). In addition, U.S. makers have been extending their warranty coverage and length.[17] And Domino's has shot to its powerful position in pizza by guaranteeing delivery within 30 minutes, or a $3 refund. Nationally, Domino's hits this time on 92 percent of its pizzas (in order for this to work, an efficiency system was developed that prepares a pizza from phone order to delivery truck in 7 minutes!).[18]

Insight 4: Stay in Contact with Consumers During Postpurchase

The prevailing attitude at the best consumer marketing companies is to encourage consumer complaints and questions after purchase—to view these as an opportunity rather than a problem. Tom Peters, author of the best-selling book *In Search of Excellence*, quotes Joe Gerard (the highest-volume auto salesman in the country) as saying that he "likes to sell a lemon . . . then he can show the customer how well he'll perform on after-sales service." Similar reactions were voiced by representatives of IBM and other major firms: "this gives us a chance to convert a dissatisfied customer into a positive supporter of our firm and our products. Also, the word of mouth is terrific."[19] As the head of P&G's Consumer Services Department put it, "if people have a problem with one of our products, we'd rather they tell us about it than switch to a competitor's product or say bad things about ours over the backyard fence."[20]

With this in mind, many firms have introduced toll-free "800" telephone lines for consumers to use in contacting the firm. Surprisingly, most of the calls *don't* reflect complaints. General Electric's "GE Answer Center," for example, receives 60,000 calls per week! About 25 percent are asking for information about a GE product they are considering, 35 percent are seeking help in caring for their appliances, and the remaining 40 percent have a problem with the appliance and want diagnostic help. Only 15 percent of all calls are actual complaints. Internal studies indicate that an average call costs $2–$5, but that service is highly profitable: 700,000 callers are referred to dealers, 95 percent of callers are satisfied with the outcome of their call, and many of these become more loyal to GE. According to the center's manager, "Most businesses don't understand that customer service is really selling."[21]

Finally, in an extreme application of this point, Oldsmobile recently began mailing consumer satisfaction surveys to people who had bought its three best-selling models three years earlier. Why these people? Because most consumers start to think about a new car after three years. What's done with the results? Those owners who are dissatisfied receive a range of offers, from free service or repairs on their current cars to $1500 rebates on a new Oldsmobile (of the first 150,000 people surveyed, rebates were offered to 5000). Reports the program's manager: "We're trying to make Oldsmobile ownership a good experience."[22]

Insight 5: Manage the Consumer Satisfaction System Well

Consumer postpurchase satisfaction involves more than abstract systems, information, and technical product quality. *People* are involved, on both the business and consumer sides. Recognizing this fact, many marketers have found that paying closer attention to their own internal management systems can pay handsome dividends. The Bell Telephone System, for example, has taken pride in maintaining high customer service levels for over 30 years. When it examined its program carefully, however, the firm discovered that it was using internal operating criteria (the number of seconds required to locate a customer's record) rather than consumer-based criteria to guide the program. As a spokesperson explained, "it became apparent that customers don't particularly care whether it takes 15 seconds or 45 seconds, or even longer, to find customer records. *What they do care about is courteous, accurate service.*"[23]

Many postpurchase problems are unique, and both the business representative and the consumer are operating in an uncertain situation. How can a marketer know whether the firm's representatives are making the best decisions? One approach (used recently in a study conducted for a home products manufacturer) asked a sample of consumers and managers from the company to judge five consumer complaint letters. The consumer respondents were asked to take the role of the letter writer, while the managers were to indicate how they would normally respond to that letter. Results were surprising. *In general the managers gave more to consumers than the consumers themselves expected to receive!* The average cost of consumers' expectations in this study was $135, whereas the average cost for the managers' responses was $167. Managers with over 10 years of experience were much more liberal in their complaint resolutions, while less experienced managers tended to be more inflexible and less likely to please the customer. Are these results good or bad? A more liberal complaint resolution is more likely to please the customer, but also represents a higher commitment of corporate resources. It thus appears that the firm would benefit from developing a more streamlined system[24]

As a final point, we should again note that many instances of consumer dissatisfaction arise from the nature of the interaction with the firm or store's representatives. To handle this problem, most firms have developed systems and procedures to aid their employees in dealing with customers. This can be challenging, however, especially for firms whose employees are either low paid or who work under stressful conditions.

Notice, for example, the extreme emphasis that many well-run organizations (retailers such as McDonald's, service providers such as the police force, and highly automated, time-dependent operations such as United Airlines) place on operating procedures for their employees to follow when interacting with consumers. In all these cases, the operation is geared to providing a maximum service for the customer or citizen, but with minimal extra social interactions. Those interactions that must occur, moreover, are highly programmed, even to the point of requiring memorized statements and smiles on cue. While these procedures may at first appear "cold" it is interesting to understand why they are deemed necessary by managers charged with achieving both work efficiency and customer satisfaction.[25]

POSTPURCHASE ISSUES IN PUBLIC POLICY

Marketers are not the only parties with a keen interest in the postpurchase phase. Public policy is also highly involved, since *it is usually at this stage of the process when problems arise between consumers and marketers*. There are two basic issues we'll briefly examine in this section: *postpurchase remedies* and *product liability*.

Postpurchase Remedies

Postpurchase remedies, or **PPRs**, is an area of regulation that poses many difficult issues: product safety can provide us with just one brief illustration.

What to Do About Product Safety?

One question in this area is how to minimize problems consumers will face when they use various products. Let's consider insecticides—most of these chemicals are toxic (poisonous) and can cause serious health problems or even death. Why is this issue difficult? First, insecticides perform a function that millions of consumers seek. In this sense there are *clear benefits from these products*. Unfortunately, there are also *clear risks* associated with using insecticides. It is these risks that bring public policy into the picture. In considering regulatory options, several key characteristics complicate matters. For example, not all insecticides are equally toxic: some have much more severe effects than others. Also, some are more effective than others, and there is likely to be a *correlation* between toxicity and effectiveness—insecticides that are more effective are also likely to be more toxic.

The problem is further complicated when we consider the consumers who are involved. Most consumers *don't know* very much about chemicals and poisons and can't be counted on to use them as experts would. Also, many potential users are *not able to read* very well (this group includes those with vision difficulties, the estimated 25 million persons who are functionally illiterate, and any young children who may come into contact with the insecticides at home). In addition, some insecticides have *long-lasting traces* on the surfaces of carpeting, walls, or furniture—many households have young children and pets who roam through the house with curious hands and tongues. Even though they may not be the purchasers or even the users of the product, there is a danger that they'll be "consumers" of it! Finally, we know that many consumers are "low involved" and don't make much effort to listen carefully to ads or read package labels and use instructions. And the *conditions of use* don't encourage careful thought and reading, as when consumers use the product on an intruder such as a mosquito.

What should public policy be toward the packaging, labeling, and advertising of various insecticides? Notice that our options range from doing nothing, to requiring only minimal information (warnings, detailed instructions for safe use, etc.), to outright product bans (for example, if a new insecticide is found to kill people, the best remedy may be to ensure that it's not available for use by the general public). As we move toward stronger remedies, however, note that we are restricting marketing freedoms and depriving consumers of effective products that some might possibly desire.

In the area of postpurchase remedies, the role of public policy is to provide a system that (1) minimizes postpurchase problems and (2) provides for corrective actions when serious problems do occur. In creating this system, it is important that public policymakers clearly recognize both the *rights of the consumer* and the *freedoms of the marketer*. The system should be fair to both parties, and it should support other desirable goals, such as economic growth, innovation, and efficiency.

Types of Postpurchase Remedies

There are three basic approaches that public policymakers can employ in the PPR area: (1) informational remedies, (2) enforcement remedies, and (3) mandatory PPRs.[26] **Informational remedies** aim at having consumers know about products and how to use them. The care labels we find in clothing, for example, are aimed at reducing unsatisfactory postpurchase experiences by informing consumers of the proper cleaning procedures for that particular garment. In another sector, *vocational schools* are now required to inform prospective students of the job placement rates of recent graduates. Also, considerable attention has also been given to the informational aspects of *warranties*. Historically, many firms had their warranties drawn up by attorneys who used the instrument as a means of limiting the responsibilities of the firm. Millions of consumers thus grew up with little hope of even *attempting* to read a product warranty—they knew that it would only befuddle them. Because consumers were not attempting to read the warranties, firms that sold more durable products were finding it difficult to compete effectively on this basis. Thus the U.S. Congress led a movement to improve warranties, and relied mostly on informational remedies. Clear and simple disclosure of warranty conditions was required, and the act also required that consumers be informed of the step-by-step procedures to follow to obtain redress of a postpurchase problem.

Enforcement remedies ensure that the rights of consumers are protected if they encounter postpurchase problems. One option is for private mechanisms to resolve disputes, such as *arbitration boards* consisting of independent persons.

Such boards are low in cost, provide speedy decisions, and are designed for easy consumer access. Other enforcement remedies have involved regulations for the timely *delivery* of mail-order merchandise (some sellers were not sending out the goods for long periods after receiving payment) *refunds* for defective products and *repairs* for defective automobiles. Of course, each case has its own set of facts. In the auto case, for example, Ford had found that in some small cars the pistons were scuffing cylinder walls, necessitating major engine repairs. Even though the warranties on some cars had expired, the firm was opting to make free repairs for those customers who came in to complain. The FTC, however, argued that these adjustments were actually "secret warranties" that the firm should make known to all buyers, not just to those who complained about it. The firm then notified about 2 million owners about the program.[27]

Mandatory PPRs constitute the strongest form of postpurchase remedy; here the government steps directly into the terms and conditions for contracts. This step is usually taken reluctantly. *Product bans,* such as those we discussed with insecticides, are one form of mandatory PPR. *Cooling-off laws* reflect another form of mandatory remedy, giving the buyer a right to cancel the sale within a certain time, usually three days to two weeks. These laws were passed in response to the complaints of thousands of consumers that they had been "pressured" into buying magazines, land, and other products. When they thought it over or discussed it with their spouses, they found that they were bound by the contract they had signed and now owed hundreds or even thousands of dollars for something they no longer wished to own. Since in most cases the goods have not yet been delivered, the intention of these laws is clear: to give the buyer enough time to reconsider the purchase in the absence of high-pressure selling.

Required trial periods are another, stronger form of mandatory remedy. In one case the FTC required a reducing salon to offer consumers the option to cancel a long-term contract after their first visit. In another case a land sales company was required to offer its customers the option of canceling the purchase after they had a chance to visit the land they were contracting to buy. This is not the general rule, however: the FTC created these orders in response to the high-pressure sales tactics used by the firms in the cases. Since all mandatory remedies restrict freedoms and are likely to raise the costs of selling, they are the most controversial form of postpurchase remedy.

The Puzzling Case of Product Liability

Before leaving public policy applications, we should briefly examine a puzzling problem area that crops up primarily in the state court systems—the issue of **tort liability** for injuries caused by products. Tort law is concerned with what *compensation* is due one party for the wrongs committed by another party. For example, how would you rule in these three cases?

Torts in the Courts
Case 1. A teenager attempted to scent a candle by pouring perfume (made by Fabergé) over it. The candle, however, was already lit, and the perfume ignited. A friend nearby

was burned in the neck region. The friend sued Fabergé, claiming that no warning had been given that the perfume was flammable. Should the consumer win? If so, how much compensation should be awarded?

Case 2.   A Florida high school student was paralyzed due to a head injury suffered while playing football with the school team. He sued the maker of the helmet, Riddell, Inc., claiming that the helmet did not adequately protect him from severe physical injury and that this was intended to be its major function. Should the student win? If so, how much compensation should be awarded?

Case 3.   The classified ad in *Soldier of Fortune* magazine read: "Ex-marines—'67–69 'Nam vets. Ex-DI, weapons specialist, jungle warfare, pilot, M.E., high-risk assignments, U.S. or overseas (phone #)." Mr. Black saw the ad, contacted the man who placed it, and four months later hired him to kill Mrs. Black. Mrs. Black's family sued the magazine for negligence in running the ad. Should the family win? If so, how much compensation should be awarded?

While there is not enough detailed information on the cases to allow firm conclusions as to the proper verdict, thinking about them allows us to recognize some of the basic principles involved in this area of public policy and the law. (If you're interested in the outcomes, they are briefly described in Note 28.)

Types of Product Defects

As noted, product liability law is concerned with compensating consumers who have been wrongfully injured. Judges and juries are called upon first to decide whether the manufacturer is *liable* for the injury and then to decide on the appropriate amount of *damages* to award. There are three basic ways in which a product can be judged to be defective:[29]

1. *A Quality-Control Problem.* This occurs when the item in question does not meet the manufacturer's own standards for quality or safety. The famous "mouse in the soft drink bottle" is an example, and injured consumers are likely to win.

2. *Inadequate Warnings or Instructions.* This concerns the seller's responsibility to provide buyers with information that allows them to use products properly and warns them of special risks. (The Fabergé case reflects this category.)

3. *Product Design Defects.* In these instances the firm is charged with having built a problem into the product. When the design has been repeated on a mass-production basis, this category lends itself to "class action" suits that represent large numbers of consumers and can run into multimillion-dollar damage levels. In the *Grimshaw v. Ford Motor Company* case, the company was charged with having designed a defect into the gas tanks of its Pinto line of cars, causing the tanks to explode when the car was hit in the rear.

The "Strict Liability" Controversy

In recent years marketers have been bemoaning the development of the **doctrine of strict liability**. To appreciate exactly what this is and why marketers are so concerned, let's go back to see how it came about.

How "Strict Liability" Developed

For years the traditional rule in liability law was the **negligence doctrine**. Under this doctrine, injured consumers could only recover for product-related injuries when the seller failed to exercise reasonable and prudent care in design, quality control, and informational decisions affecting the consumer. However, while the *principle* of negligence may have been appropriate, its *practice* raised serious problems for consumer rights. To understand why, let's briefly consider the fundamental nature of our court system.

Essentially, our courts are ruled by *the principle of evidence*. As we all know, a person (or firm) is "innocent until proven guilty." This means that factual evidence establishing guilt is necessary. Under the negligence doctrine, "guilt" meant negligence, and it was necessary for a court to have solid proof that the firm had acted in a negligent manner before it would rule in behalf of an injured consumer. This meant that the entire burden of proof fell on the injured consumer. He or she not only had to show that an unreasonable injury had occurred, but also to prove that the seller had been negligent (and that this negligence had led to the injury).

The result of this doctrine was that in many cases consumers who had been severely injured were unable to recover, while many others were advised not to even bring a case. In both instances the injured party either didn't have access to the materials needed to prove negligence or the records simply didn't exist. The courts recognized that this situation was unfair, and ways were sought to provide consumers with more of an equal footing.

In recent years courts have experimented with other types of doctrines and now seem to have settled on strict liability. This doctrine does require proof that the product was in a "defective condition" (or was "unreasonably dangerous") when sold, but does not require that the consumer prove that the marketer was negligent in any way. This would appear to be reasonable from the perspective of what might be reasonable for the injured party to prove.

When we consider the marketer's viewpoint, however, the strict liability doctrine becomes a real threat. In brief, it means that a seller can be held liable for damages even when he or she has exercised all due care in manufacturing, designing, and packaging of a product. Many marketers are outraged, since this seems to say that they can be sued even when they've done nothing wrong that they can control.

The Current Controversy The result of the changing doctrines has been a dramatic increase in the number of consumer product injury lawsuits and in the size of damage awards as well. Critics claim that consumer prices have to increase to cover the risks of the new system and that product innovation is stifled, since firms fear possible suits arising from new, less tested products. As we'd expect, insurance costs for product liability suits have skyrocketed in recent years. Riddell, the helmet maker that lost the football case, now spends 14 percent of the cost of its helmet on insurance and litigation costs (compared to only 1 percent prior to the suit). Many firms cannot even obtain insurance coverage and are searching for ways to band together to insure themselves.

Consumer Research May Provide Answers It does seem obvious that modifications in the strict liability doctrine will have to be made in future years. Several are essentially legal in nature (e.g., a firm's compliance with appropriate industry standards might be used as a defense against liability judgments). Our interest, however, lies in modifications that involve increasing attention to the consumer behaviors in these cases. If consumers have altered the product (as in gas emission devices for autos), have not read warnings or instructions, or have misused the product (as in underinflating tires, then suing when they blow out), they might well not deserve to collect huge damage awards. Some states have begun to recognize this stance, and are moving toward a **"comparative fault" doctrine** in which damages would depend upon the extent to which the injured party contributed to the creation to the problem. To resolve these issues, further participation by consumer behavior experts will be needed to establish reasonable baselines for consumer information processing and use behaviors. As a marketer, you may be called upon to defend your practices in this arena. As a consumer and a citizen, your inputs into the system can be significant. The legal system does face frustrating problems in trying these cases, and in turn poses frustrating problems for marketers and consumers who must deal with it.

The fact remains, however, that dangerous and defective products are sold on a regular basis in our economy, some quite innocently and some with a negligent disregard for potential users. Some consumers do misuse these products, while some do not. Tragic injuries do occur, and some people are forced to live with the aftermath of those accidents. And, although infrequent at the individual level, in the aggregate this is a *huge* problem area. As an indicator of its magnitude, the Consumer Product Safety Commission was involved in recalling over 1200 products during its first six years of existence, with millions of individual items being recalled because of product hazards.[30] (If you would like to read further about product liability, you may wish to pursue the readings in Note 31.)

CONSUMER APPLICATIONS OF POSTPURCHASE CONCEPTS

Our previous sections have covered many topics pertinent to the consumer's perspective of the postpurchase phase. Two of the important points are (1) *Many marketers have a primary interest in long-term consumer satisfaction.* They wish to have loyal patrons and will work to achieve consumer satisfaction within the bounds of reasonable decisions. While they don't like to have problems arise, they'd rather hear about them and have a chance to resolve them than lose the goodwill and future purchases of dissatisfied customers and their friends. And (2) *many public policymakers have an interest in seeing that consumers are able to exercise their rights* within our system. They focus primarily on minimizing dissatisfaction in the system. There are several types of remedies available to consumers experiencing postpurchase dissatisfaction.

How to Avoid Consumer Problems

Although consumer problems can't be avoided entirely, there are several clear steps that consumers can take to minimize the probability that they'll crop up. The best place to start is during the prepurchase stage. Consumers have the right to be informed, but this right brings with it a responsibility to inform themselves. They should seek information. They should shop comparatively. The more capable consumers recognize that sellers are motivated to make sales and that often negotiation is possible. Also, a little effort at the library can yield substantial benefits from a better purchase.

The choice of a seller *does* make a difference. It is primarily important to avoid disreputable or fraudulent sellers. A simple telephone call to the local Better Business Bureau is one way to screen for this possibility. This agency is supported by local merchants; it maintains complaint records from consumers and will indicate the status of a seller's complaint record to consumers who call to inquire. Also, we know that retailers pursue different strategies. Some offer higher prices but high levels of postpurchase services and guarantees. These sellers may not seem as attractive when only initial selling prices are considered, but if postpurchase aggravation is factored in, they may actually be quite competitive. Moreover, a number of these high-service retailers are willing to "meet competitive prices." If so, our willingness to ask about this policy can result in both buying at a lower price *and* obtaining better guarantees of postpurchase satisfaction.

Finally, experts know that a buyer's leverage is much higher *before* the purchase is made than it is right afterward. It is at this time that many potential postpurchase problems can be minimized. Speedy deliveries can often be arranged, trial periods can often be arranged, and, for large purchases, inspections are an intelligent option. We've all experienced postpurchase problems that are our own fault. Reading and following instructions, taking reasonable precautions, and otherwise avoiding foreseeable problems are responsibilities for consumers that mirror the product liability responsibilities of marketers.

Handling Postpurchase Problems

The options that consumers have for redress have been noted at various points in the chapter. The most typical first step is to return to the seller to explain the difficulty and try to arrange for a satisfactory resolution. In many cases of defective products, the fault lies with the manufacturer rather than the retailer, and the retailer deserves the right to resolve the problem rather than lose the customer's future business. A consumer who approaches this step with a strategy in mind (e.g., asking for certain actions that are easy for the seller to take) is more likely to achieve a reasonable resolution at this stage.

When the problem cannot be resolved directly, several options exist. If a defective product is involved, direct contact with the manufacturer is a good option. If the firm has a toll-free consumer number (a consumer can inquire by calling 1-800-555-1212 and asking whether a toll-free number is listed), there is likely to be a well-developed system available to handle consumer problems. Also, letters to high-level company executives can sometimes bring speedy results. The names and addresses of executives are listed in Standard & Poor's *Register of Corporations,* available in most libraries.

If problems exist with local retailers or service providers, complaints to the local Better Business Bureau can be worthwhile. Another option in many localities is a local media-sponsored "consumer action line" that specializes in resolving such problems. There may be local consumer groups available, and many universities have legal service offices. Finally, a good source to contact is often the city, county, or state office of consumer protection (these operate under a variety of names, so consumers are advised to call the information office of the government unit to locate the appropriate office). Since these officials deal with consumer problems daily, they often have excellent contacts by which to satisfy disputes on a voluntary basis.

Sometimes, when all voluntary avenues have been exhausted, the only remaining recourse is to enter into some form of system that will enforce compliance with the law (consumers can, of course, lose their cases as well as win them). As discussed earlier in the chapter, consumer arbitration is emerging as a reasonable option for dispute resolution, since the system is being designed precisely to offer easy-access, low-cost routes for consumers to follow. For other circumstance, such as when dollar amounts at issue are less than $1000–$2000, small claims courts are a good option to investigate, since these are designed for consumers to represent themselves, without attorneys, to hold down costs ("The People's Court" television series, featuring the famous Judge Wapner, depicts a small claims court). When dollar amounts are larger, the advice of an attorney is likely to be the best alternative for the consumer to pursue.

A Closing Note

It is unsatisfying to close this chapter with a discussion of contacting an attorney, going to small claims court, or otherwise engaging in disputes with marketers. As we all know, these occurrences are not typical, and while we consumers should be aware of our options, we should also not be planning to have to exercise them very often. As we noted at the start, it is in the postpurchase phase of consumer behavior that we experience the benefits offered by our highly developed, sophisticated consumer marketing system. All parties involved in this system— marketers, public policymakers, and consumers alike—face complicated decisions that need to be made in the face of uncertainties about the future. As we've seen, all three parties make some mistakes and could improve. At the same time, it seems appropriate to close by noting that the overall marketing-consumer system is working rather well!

SUMMARY

Why Are Postpurchase Processes Important?

The *postpurchase phase* can actually be the most important stage in a decision system. From the consumer's perspective, this stage represents the point at which consumption actually occurs and when benefits are received. From a marketer's perspective, long-term success flows from having consumers experience satisfaction during the postpurchase phase. Finally, postpurchase processes account for two of the three major activities within the overall consumption system: consumption and disposition.

A Framework for Postpurchase

The chapter began by noting *four key dimensions of consumption:* (1) frequency, (2) amount, (3) consumption intervals, and (4) consumption purposes. Each presents implications and opportunities for marketing managers. We next discussed the *process of disposition* and saw that it is more complex than we may first imagine. Product disposition, in the aggregate, raises serious ecological questions. The question of when people decide to dispose of their products also raises important issues for marketers.

Psychological Processes During Postpurchase

In the next section of the chapter we examined *two key psychological processes* that operate during the postpurchase stage. *Cognitive dissonance theory* suggests that consumers experience tension following a difficult decision and may behave in some "strange ways" in an effort to reduce the dissonance. *Consumer satisfaction/dissatisfaction* (CS/D) is determined by five elements: (1) consumer expectations, (2) actual performance, (3) the comparison between expectations and performance, (4) confirmation or disconfirmation of expectations, and (5) the size and direction of the discrepancy score. The chapter then presented data on actual levels of CS/D. Although problem areas exist (notably in automobile repair and appliance repair), overall levels of consumer satisfaction are quite high. Next we examined the *alternative actions available to a dissatisfied consumer.* The range was from doing nothing to actively complaining. Consumers usually do not take action when dissatisfied: very few voice complaints back into the marketing system. Marketers, however, generally *do* want to receive complaints.

Marketing Applications

The final section of this chapter discussed *application issues.* Among the implications for marketers are (1) study of consumer-use patterns can guide positioning, (2) overpromising performance may lead to dissatisfaction, (3) marketers should explore means to guarantee satisfaction after purchase, (4) consumer complaints can be viewed as an opportunity, and (5) it is important to manage the consumer satisfaction system well.

Postpurchase Issues in Public Policy

Problems between marketers and consumers introduce a role for public policy. Three basic approaches are employed: (1) informational remedies, (2) enforcement remedies, and (3) mandatory remedies. Another public policy issue—"product liability"—concerns the compensation due to a consumer for wrongful damage caused by product defects. Our final section of the chapter discussed why consumers should take an active interest in resolving their postpurchase problems and examined a number of pointers for how to do this successfully.

KEY TERMS

consumption frequency
perceived use occasions
average amount consumed
intervals between consumption occasions
consumption purposes
product disposition
postpurchase learning
consonant cognitions
dissonant cognitions
cognitive dissonance theory
consumer satisfaction
consumer dissatisfaction
expectations

performance
comparison
confirmation/disconfirmation
discrepancy
postpurchase remedies (PPRs)
informational remedies
enforcement remedies
mandatory PPRs
tort liability
doctrine of strict liability
negligence doctrine
"comparative fault" doctrine

REVIEW QUESTIONS AND EXPERIENTIAL EXERCISES

[E = Application extension or experiential exercise]

1. What are the roles of time, support system, and disposal in postpurchase?

2. Explain the five key elements in the consumer satisfaction/dissatisfaction process depicted in Figure 20-2. Which is probably the most important?

3. Consider how each of the following aspects may influence the nature of postpurchase evaluation (whether or not evaluation occurs and if so, how). For each, give an example in which the aspect has influenced the postpurchase evaluation of products or services you have consumed.
    a. Importance of benefits sought from consumption.
    b. Strength of beliefs/expectations prior to purchase.
    c. Complexity of product.
    d. Nature of consuming unit—whether an individual or group.
    e. Product consumed alone, or with complementary products.

     f. The degree to which desired benefits are social in nature.

     g. The (in)tangibility of the good—(professional services, dry-cleaning).

     h. Time span of use.

4. What are the five factors influencing a consumer's decision to complain or not? Provide examples from your own experience.

5. Discuss the concepts of informational remedies, enforcement remedies, and mandatory PPRs, including examples of each.

6. Why are marketers so opposed to the concept of strict liability? Why does this concept exist? Can you suggest a better option?

[E] 7. Four dimensions of consumption proposed by Hendrix were reviewed. Explain each one, in each case providing an example of a new strategy you would propose to Procter & Gamble as a consultant for their consumer product groups.

[E] 8. Explain the distinction between consonant and dissonant cognitions. Using "Carrie's College Choice" from the chapter as a guide, analyze your own decision to join your present university (the harder that decision was, the more interesting this will be). List the primary alternatives, the major positive aspects and drawbacks of each, and the manner in which you handled your choice. Would you say you experienced (any, some, large) cognitive dissonance? Did you engage in any symptomatic post-choice behaviors? Write a brief report on your analysis.

[E] 9. Consider a product or service with which you were dissatisfied. How was your dissatisfaction manifested? To what extent was the marketer responsible for your dissatisfaction? What steps would you recommend this marketer take to avoid creating dissatisfied consumers in the future?

[E] 10. Interview five friends or relatives about memorable cases of consumer dissatisfaction. Try to learn exactly what they did or did not do about it. As part of the interview, learn exactly how many others they told about it, and what they had to say. Write a brief report on your findings.

[E] 11. Conduct an interview about CS/D, consumer complaining, and marketers' responses with a representative of your local newspaper's "Action Line" or with a local government consumer representative.

[E] 12. Use the reference section of your library to locate readings on recent developments in product liability. Write a brief report on your findings.

[E] 13. Use the reference section of your library to locate recent articles on how marketers are handling customer service, consumer affairs, and so forth. Write a brief report on your findings.

[E] 14. Interview the manager of a local retail store, auto repair shop, hospital, or other interesting enterprise concerning their typical experiences with the topics in this chapter. What are the major problems they face? What policies do they follow? Are the laws very important? Write a brief report on your findings.

15. (Bonus Question)   Choose your favorite report from Exhibit 20-1. Explain what, if anything, this has to do with attribution theory and the topic of this chapter.

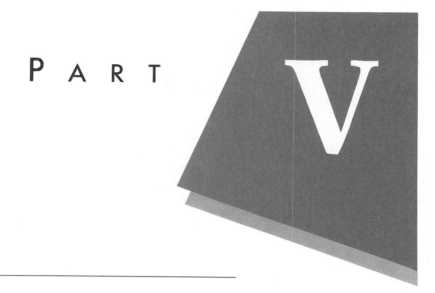

PART V

Special Topics in Consumer Behavior

This very short part of the book consists of two chapters that deal with topics that are out of the "main stream" of consumer behavior, but are quite important in our daily world. Chapter 21, "Public Policy Perspectives on Consumer Behavior," introduces the areas of government regulation and industry self-regulation as they affect the way marketers actually deal with consumers in a marketplace system. As both a marketer and a consumer, you will likely find it interesting to consider how the rights and responsibilities of both parties interact. Chapter 22, "Organizational Buying Behavior," then shifts emphasis to consider how buying behavior occurs within organizations, and what implications this has for marketers who are attempting to sell to these buyers. As we'll see, most of the concepts we've examined for consumer behavior are also useful in this context, but there are some new considerations as well. Because most readers of this book are likely to be involved in this area at some point in their careers, the contents of this chapter should have professional value in the future.

Thus these two chapters introduce us to two different and important contexts. They contain many interesting facts and insights, so let's begin!

C H A P T E R

21

Public Policy Perspectives on Consumer Behavior

▰ **Business Hates Government Regulation, or Does it?**

A former editor of *The Wall Street Journal*, Vermont Royster, once said:

> *The cry of our time is for "deregulation." Deregulate everything. The airlines. The banks. Stockbrokers. The drug companies. The theory behind this is that the marketplace will do the regulating. . . . Much of this cry for deregulation is justified . . .*
>
> *[But] I shudder at the thought of a wholly deregulated society. I prefer knowing my pharmacist has to be licensed and that someone checks on him. . . . We shouldn't forget that a great deal of the regulation we encounter today in business . . . arose from a recognized need in the past. . . . As society (our way of life) gets more complicated there will be newer areas calling for some kind of regulation . . . genetic manipulation . . . surrogate motherhood . . . organ transplants . . . trade in human tissue. . . .*
>
> *We the people must collectively decide not only what should be regulated but how. . . . But . . . we should never make the mistake of thinking that "regulation" is a dirty word.*[1]

■ ■ ■

647

ESSENTIALS OF THE PUBLIC POLICY PERSPECTIVE

In spirit, this chapter is most similar to Chapter 2, where we examined the marketing perspective and the consumer perspective on consumer behavior. However, since most students of consumer behavior have less background in the public policy area, in this chapter we'll stress an introductory look at the public policy perspective.

The public policy sector is the center of heated debates and controversial decisions. Unlike the consumer and marketing perspectives, the public policy perspective does not focus on transactions themselves. Instead, the public policy perspective stresses the setting within which consumer transactions occur. This setting is termed the **marketing-consumer environment**. The basic question confronting public policy is *"What exactly should the marketing-consumer environment look like in our society?"* Given the massive scope of the economy, there are many issues related to this question. There is, however, a basic guide available for us, the primary goal of public policy. This goal is to have a marketing-consumer environment that is *efficient but fair for marketers and consumers alike*.

You may recall that our early discussions in Chapter 2 indicated that consumers, marketers, and public policymakers were the three primary groups involved in the marketing/consumer environment. Table 21-1 reintroduces Table 2-1 in which the consumer's perspective was contrasted with the marketer's perspective. Our table now adds a third column to represent the public policymaker's perspective. Notice that the **public policy view** reflects an interesting

TABLE 21-1 COMPARING THE THREE PERSPECTIVES

Characteristic	Marketer's Perspective		Consumer's Perspective		Public Policymaker's Perspective
A. Point of view	External ("buyers")	vs.	Internal ("me")	vs.	External ("buyers and sellers")
B. Level of interest	Aggregate ("market")	vs.	Individual ("myself")	vs.	Aggregate ("affected groups")
C. Scope of Interest	Product specific ("what I make")	vs.	Across products ("what I buy")	vs.	Across products ("all products and services")
D. "Correct" choice	Brand specific ("my brand")	vs.	Best alternative ("best brand for me")	vs.	Neutral ("maximize utility")
E. Role of Influence	Influence behavior ("please buy this")	vs.	Handle behavioral influence ("what should I really buy?")	vs.	Neutral ("must be fair and not deceptive")

combination of the marketer and consumer viewpoints. Similar to the marketer, the public policymaker takes an *external* view (but applies it to both marketers and consumers), which is primarily *aggregate* in nature. Similar to the consumer, the public policymaker adopts an *across-products* scope of interest (but this extends to all products and services).

In the last two dimensions public policy must depart from both of the other parties. While interested in seeing that consumers be able to buy "the best brand for them," the public policymaker is usually unable to determine what that brand is—a **neutral view of actual choice** must be adopted in our free society. Instead, the policymaker places stress on the *setting* within which those choices are made, assuming that if buyers are fully informed and free to act in their own best interests, they will in fact do so. This applies to marketers as well: those sellers offering the best alternatives are assumed to prosper when the marketplace is working freely. Thus, with respect to the role of influence, the public policymaker is again *neutral,* stressing that the setting must be open and the information presented be fair and not misleading.

Marketing Freedoms

All societies face the questions of how their economic systems will be formed and allowed to function in the best interests of the citizens of that society. As we discuss in Chapter 13, some nations, such as those of the communist world, have chosen to stress centralized planning and control for the economy. One result of this type of system is that consumers may not be able to purchase as much as they wish of any type of good, since the production of that good may have been restricted in the economic plan.

Western nations have generally opted for more of a **market system**, in which the desires of consumers play a much more important role in determining what is produced in the economy. For this type of system to work, marketers must have considerable freedom to anticipate and react quickly to consumer desires.

In fact, when we stop to think about it, we can see that *the basic freedoms granted to marketers are quite remarkable!* In the United States, for example, a person can choose to go into virtually any type of business (with the exception of those few that have been deemed illegal or that require licenses) at any time and in any location. He or she can produce any kind of product or service, in any quantity, and can offer it for sale under almost any conditions the seller desires. Prices, product characteristics, locations, and promotional devices are all up to the individual marketer.

Consumer Rights

On the other side of the transaction, the society of the United States has also agreed that consumers have certain rights that must be respected by the economic system. In 1962 President John F. Kennedy sent the U.S. Congress a now-famous message concerning the **Consumer Bill of Rights** in our society. In that message, the president summarized consumer rights as shown in Figure 21-1.

Several important points are implicit in the Consumer Bill of Rights. First, these are closely related to the fundamental basis for our economic system. As you may recall from introductory economics, *our society is assumed to prosper when consumers are able to make good purchase decisions*—decisions that reward marketers of good products and do not reward marketers of inferior or defective goods. Thus the **right to be informed** and the **right to choose freely** are key underpinnings of our system.

The **right to safety**, meanwhile, is geared more toward the use of products. It asserts that consumers should not be exposed to some undue hazards at all (such as cancer-causing additives in foods) and, for other potential hazards, should be sufficiently warned and instructed prior to purchase (many household chemicals fall into this category). The consumer right to safety has become increasingly important as technology has made new substances available.

The **right to be heard** raises a third implicit message: that the government should play a major role in interpreting consumer rights and in ensuring that they are protected in the marketplace. This was the most controversial of President Kennedy's statements, since in practice, this means more regulation of marketers. Not surprisingly, marketers tended to view such moves as governmental interference in the marketplace. On the other hand, many consumer advocates, led

---

FIGURE 21-1 **The Consumer Bill of Rights**

I. The Right to Safety
Consumers have the right to be protected against products and services that are hazardous to health and life.

II. The Right to Be Informed
Consumers have the right to be protected against fraudulent, deceitful, or misleading advertising or other practices and to be given the facts they need to make an informed choice.

III. The Right to Choose
Consumers have the right to be assured, wherever possible, access to a variety of products and services at competitive prices. In those industries in which competition is not workable, government regulation is substituted to assure satisfactory quality and service at fair prices.

IV. The Right to Be Heard
Consumers have the right to be assured that consumer interests will receive full and sympathetic consideration in the formulation of government policy and fair and expeditious treatment in its administrative tribunals.

Source: Executive Office of the President, *Consumer Advisory Council, First Report* (Washington, D.C.: U.S. Government Printing Office, October 1963).

by Ralph Nader, viewed such programs as ways to create a proper balance in the marketplace that would allow consumers to buy wisely. Thus came controversy.

Our society did see dramatically increased governmental programs during the 1960s and 1970s, reflecting strong increases in the regulation of marketing practices. *For example, in just 10 years, between 1970 and 1980, spending for federal regulatory activities in consumer health and safety increased over 500 percent!* During the 1980s, under President Reagan, the pendulum swung back toward deregulation, with government showing less desire to restrict marketer freedoms. The Bush Administration prefers deregulation in general, but pressure has been building among marketers and consumers alike for more regulation in a number of areas (including stock and bond markets, savings and loans, marketing solicitations by telephone, and so forth). Thus the 1990s are likely to see some swing back toward more government involvement.

In addition to President Kennedy's list of four basic rights, several others have been proposed more recently. President Richard Nixon, for example, proposed that citizens have a **right to consumer education**. Esther Peterson, who ran the White House Office for Consumer Affairs, suggested that the path of much legislation reflected a **right to consumer recourse and redress**, that is, a right to have a fair settlement of problems that consumers encounter. Finally, another, broader, consumer right also emerged during the 1970s: the consumer's **right to an environment that enhances the quality of life**, reflecting increased concern for ecology, pollution and hazardous waste issues.[2]

Consumer research has come to play an increasingly important role in public policy matters. Notice how the right to be informed, for example, raises issues of consumer knowledge, learning, shopping, processing of advertising, and so forth, whereas the right to be heard raises issues of how, and when, consumers complain.

Inherent Responsibilities for All Sectors

There is another side to rights and freedoms—the **inherent responsibilities** that are associated with them. For marketers, there are responsibilities to conduct business in accord with the spirit and laws of our system. Consumers have responsibilities as well; these include informing themselves about products, purchasing within the bounds of their finances, and abiding by the terms of the contracts they sign.[3] For government, meanwhile, there is the major responsibility to strive to preserve freedoms while protecting rights and to be fair and judicious in the exercise of its power.

Slippage in the Marketing Sector

Most marketers, of course, have chosen to abide by the rules and meet their responsibilities to consumers by offering good products at fair prices. Over the long run, these businesspersons feel that ethical behavior is in their own best interest as well as that of their customers. Unfortunately, however, a small percentage of marketers have opted to engage in illegal and/or unethical practices as a way of business. Even though these cases don't characterize most of marketing, we should realize that this type of behavior has generated citizen support for more government regulation of marketing. It has also had the unfortunate consequence of lowering the credibility of all marketers in the eyes of many consumers. In this regard, you may wish to read the "Code of Ethics for Marketers," in Appendix 21-B.

High-Pressure Selling to Vulnerable Groups

Some sellers focus on elderly, or poor, or lonely consumers because they can be talked into deals that most consumers would turn down. Among the many examples are the firm in Chicago that convinced a widow to pay thousands of dollars to replace "cancerous bricks" on her house, the "dance studios" that extract thousands of dollars from lonely oldsters for dance lessons, and the "home repair" representatives who deliberately create a problem while "inspecting it" (for example, dumping some termites under the carpet), then pointing out the problems in anguished tones to the fearful homeowner. In the classic case of the Holland Furnace Company, for example, inspectors would dismantle the homeowner's furnace, condemn it as hazardous, and then refuse to reassemble it because they "wouldn't be an accessory to murder." This firm, which had 50 offices around the country, operated for 30 years, with many of its salesmen practicing this technique. One elderly New England woman, in fact, was sold nine new furnaces over a six-year period![4]

Mail Frauds

The *sting artists* in this area cause problems for honest direct-response marketers as well as for the consumers they "hook" with their schemes. Some play with language, such as when Solardry, Inc., offered a solar clothes dryer, a "new innovation developed by space-age technology," guaranteed to work, to lower utility bills, to make clothes brighter." The price was only $36.99, and a special aid kit of "solar stabilizers" was available (at $9.99, down from $25). Or when the Mar-Dee Corporation offered its "scientifically tested" miracle liquid, W-L-40, that would attack body fat and expel it through the pores of the skin. As proof, an unnamed client attested to having lost 61 pounds in only five 15-minute baths in the miracle product, which was offered for $9.98. What were these products? A clothesline kit and a bottle of bubblebath![5]

Sometimes several marketers link up in questionable activities. Dream-Away diet pills, for example, were advertised on 160 TV stations for over a year, offering 42 tablets for $19.95. The claim: consumers would lose weight while they slept. In a California court case, the company was ordered to stop selling the product and to pay $162,000 in penalties. It was also revealed that some of the TV stations carrying the ads had been receiving commissions on each bottle they helped to sell.[6]

Slippage in the Consumer Sector

Almost all consumers also abide by the rules and generally meet their responsibilities. There are, however, enough examples of bad consumership all around us to lend support to critics who question whether consumers really deserve increased protection by government programs and/or whether such programs can really work. As we've discussed in Chapter 2, there are good reasons why consumers don't make perfect decisions all the time. Further, this is a free society, and we citizens are free to spend our money as we desire.

Nonetheless, the theory of our economic system is important. Our system does require that consumers try to choose wisely if the system is to work and marketers are to be given correct signals as to what to offer in the marketplace. Some serious commentators, for example, view many consumers to be not as price conscious as would be desirable for the economy as a whole. They suggest, for example, that this characteristic was a major factor in fueling the inflationary pressures of recent times, which then led to recession and enormous deficits in the 1980s. Their reasoning: if the vast majority of consumers don't stop buying when prices are increased on a given item, there is no pressure on suppliers to reduce costs or price levels. Instead, alert retailers should raise prices even more! Also, consumers who don't pay their bills, who abuse physical property, switch price tags, or file false insurance claims cause problems for marketers and undermine the marketing-consumer environment.

Cheats with Cleats

One hallmark of the marketing concept in retailing is to provide consumers with satisfaction after the sale. Some consumers abuse this practice, however, as the following report attests: "Mark is a soccer player who needs new shoes frequently, and has developed a system to get them from a local store that will take back 'defective' shoes. Once or twice a season, Mark will remove the sole on a shoe, slice off a cleat or two, or place a rip in the tongue, in each case in a way that is hard to detect. He then brings the shoes to the store in exchange for a new pair. At last count he had received eight pairs this way! Mark is sure to go to a different clerk on each visit, and unless someone carefully checks records for returned items, Mark probably won't get caught in the near future."

Coupon Misredemptions Increase to Epidemic Proportions

Most coupons promise the retailer the face value plus a small handling charge as reimbursement. Note that this policy provides no incentive for retail stores to monitor closely the coupons they accept. In fact, the more coupons accepted, the higher the payment a store will receive from the manufacturer. Many consumers, aware of this fact, have recently been redeeming coupons for either the wrong brand or for products they didn't buy at all. How widespread is this practice? A recent study using the new "scanners" at checkout counters showed that some brands—Diet Pepsi, Keebler cookies, Cheezits among them—had misredemption rates higher than 40 percent! (This means that these marketers were paying bonuses for consumers to buy competing brands or nothing at all, almost half the time!) In total, coupon fraud—partially from dishonest consumers and partially from dishonest retailers and "clipping gangs"—is costing manufacturers over half a billion dollars per year, or about one-quarter of the total worth of consumer coupons redeemed.[7]

Slippage in the Government Sector

Public policy problems almost always involve disputes regarding the balance of competing interests and points of view. It is difficult, therefore, to find areas in which everyone would agree that a particular step was entirely good or entirely bad. This does not mean, however, that the issue of slippage in public policy decisions is not a very serious one. In particular, policymakers can make two types of errors: errors of commission and errors of omission. **Errors of omission** refer to a lack of activity when activity is warranted. Examples include a failure to act quickly against problems such as a nuclear plant leaking radioactive dust or a deceptive ad campaign luring customers to a useless purchase. Given the nature of bureaucratic organizations, lengthy delays and periods of inactivity are relatively common. Since salaries are being paid during the time, and since attorneys are likely to be involved on both sides of the issue, dollar costs from time delays can be very large. Beyond this, civil service is often a "safe" job in which there is little reward or incentive to act quickly or to take risks. The more this is the case, the more likely that errors of omission will occur.

Errors of commission, on the other hand, occur when policymakers commit unwise or bad actions. Much of the public policy decision-making system is geared to the reduction of errors of commission by offering various levels of appeals to regulatory rulings. It is not atypical, for example, to find an appeals court modifying some aspects of regulatory rulings that were appealed. To appeal, however, a citizen or company needs to be able to afford high-priced legal talent.

In general, then, public policy faces situations in which **cost-benefit analysis** is needed—the benefits of a particular action must be compared against the costs involved in the action, including indirect costs to marketers and consumers. Given the size of our economy, the aggregate benefits from government actions can be large. According to the Consumer Product Safety Commission (CPSC), for example, its product recalls have prevented over 1 million consumer injuries. Similarly, the CPSC worked out some voluntary product standards with industry in some dangerous areas: it estimates that these prevent 200 deaths and 200,000 injuries each year.[8]

Cost-benefit analysis is frequently complex and highly subjective. Consider, for example, how often benefits will not be easy to measure in dollar terms. What, for example, is the value of a person's life? If a product recall would be likely to save three people's lives in the next year, but would cost $6 million, should that recall be ordered? These are some of the types of decisions that confront agencies such as the Food and Drug Administration (FDA):

The Thalidomide Tragedy

One long-debated topic concerns the FDA and its role as the government watchdog for pharmaceutical products in the United States. Before a product can be sold on a prescription basis, the FDA must examine tests for its effectiveness and safety. These tests are arranged and conducted by the sponsoring firms. Many times it is not possible for the tests to be absolutely foolproof, especially if harmful side effects might take years to develop. Further, the new drug might offer significant relief to U.S. citizens suffering from a particular ailment.

One such drug emerged in the early 1960s, and provided a serious disagreement in the United States, between persons who wanted it approved as soon as possible and those who wanted to wait for further tests. The drug was known as thalidomide. It was designed as a sedative, to be used in sleeping tablets. After testing on animals it had been routinely approved for use in some European countries and became a popular sleeping pill. Encouraged by this success, marketers began to combine thalidomide with other medicines to treat coughs, colds, headaches, and asthma. A liquid form was made for West German children. Pregnant women found one version useful for combatting the nausea of early pregnancy and another version helpful for a good night's sleep. Soon, thalidomide was being sold at the rate of 20 million tablets per month in Germany alone, and many other countries approved the drug for sale. In the United States, the Merrell Company applied to the FDA for a license to market it under the brand name Kevadon. Included with the firm's application were reports on animal tests and the several years of human use in Europe. All indications were that the drug had no side effects. The firm pressed the FDA's project officer for a speedy approval to sell it in the United States.

The FDA's project officer was Dr. Frances Kelsey, who had only recently joined the agency. In reading the testing reports, she was puzzled to discover that the drug had not been effective as a sedative for the animals. With humans, however, it worked well as a sedative. She decided to ask Merrell for more test evidence to discover why thalidomide seemed to affect humans differently from animals. This FDA request would mean a lengthy delay, which not only would reduce profits for Merrell, but would also mean that American consumers would not benefit from the superior performance of the drug. Dr. Kelsey's insistence on further test evidence resulted in thalidomide being kept off the U.S. market for almost two years. During this time the company increased its pressure on her—Dr. Kelsey was contacted over 50 times and her senior FDA officials were also approached in efforts to obtain approval.

Then, in early 1962, Merrell suddenly withdrew its application. At this point it had become clear that thalidomide had been responsible for over 10,000 deformed babies born in West Germany. The type of deformity was striking and sad—babies were born without arms and legs or with short, flipperlike hands or fingers attached to the shoulders. Many died at birth. Several mothers committed suicide, and one was charged with a mercy-killing of her child. Hundreds of others required psychiatric help to overcome their feelings of guilt.

Upon publication of these facts—together with pictures—in national magazines, it became clear to millions of U.S. citizens that the doctor at the FDA had almost single-handedly prevented a national disaster. (If you'd be interested in reading more about this case, you may wish to pursue the readings listed in Note 9.)

The thalidomide case is a striking, but not typical, illustration of the stakes that are involved when dealing with health and safety of consumers. This tragedy did not come about because marketers were negligent; it took scientists a long time to link the deformities to the drug, even after the epidemic appeared. Nor is delay or refusal to license a new drug a good rule to follow for every case; new drugs can save lives and relieve human suffering when they are available for use. Recent and current issues concerning new drugs for cancer, AIDS, and other diseases reflect the same kinds of tradeoffs today. Thus there is a great need for public policymakers to strike a sound balance between risk and innovation. Slippage in public policy occurs when government employees lose sight of this goal.

THE INSTITUTIONS OF PUBLIC POLICY

Government Involvement

Within the federal government, the executive, legislative, and judicial branches are all active in consumer behavior issues. In the executive branch, most recent presidents have made public statements similar to President Kennedy's. They have arranged for the government departments to carry out consumer programs consistent with the current administration's beliefs about the best forms of government presence. In the legislative branch, the U.S. Congress has traditionally been very active with respect to consumer matters, although the directions taken have again differed as a function of the prevailing political climate. The Congress has passed consumer laws, has over the years created our structure of regulatory agencies, and each year appropriates increases or decreases in support for consumer-related programs.

The judicial branch of government is also active in consumer policy matters, primarily through decisions as to the legal powers of government agencies. A major means for the judicial branch to become involved is to have significant cases appealed into the court system. In recent cases, for example, actions by the U.S. Supreme Court have given doctors and lawyers the right to advertise and supported the government's authority to order marketers to run "corrective advertising" (Appendix 21-A contains a review of this interesting program).

State and local governments are also active in consumer matters. Many cities have personnel available to help with consumer disputes, and a *small claims court system* is available when negotiation fails. Similarly, local agencies work to control fraudulent business operators, monitor the accuracy of scales used in stores and gasoline stations, and enforce sanitation codes in restaurants.

Marketer and Consumer Involvement

Not all of the activity in public policy is conducted by government. Marketers have chosen to undertake **industry self-regulation** in a number of areas. An extensive advertising self-regulatory system has heard several thousand cases. It has been successful in having many ad campaigns modified and others voluntarily stopped and has taken the place of much government regulation. (Chapter 17 examines this system in more detail.) In addition, individual marketers sometimes encounter other situations that call for public policy perspectives. Sometimes these involve lobbying, and sometimes use of the court system.

"Miami Vice" Isn't Nice

Product counterfeiters pirate an estimated $20 billion a year from marketers of strong brand names such as Gucci, Microsoft software, and General Motors auto parts. In a typical case, bogus goods are imported from unauthorized plants overseas and are sold to businesses and consumers as the genuine articles. Sometimes the customers are aware of the "scam" and sometimes not. Sometimes the products are of adequate quality, but sometimes not (auto brakes and birth control pills are among the long list of defective items sold). In every case, the original marketer is losing rightful sales, since the counterfeit name and package is instrumental to the sale.

However, branders are now fighting back. Under the Trademark Counterfeiting Act of 1984, companies get search warrants and hire groups of private detectives for raids on pirate firms. "We're the *Miami Vice* of civil law!" brags one raider. Merchandise and business records are seized in these raids, and the business pirates can be turned over to criminal authorities for indictment and sentencing.[10]

Two Firms in a Lather

Recently, the Gillette Company and its advertising agency agreed to pay the Alberto-Culver Company over $4 million to settle a court case. The case involved a Gillette ad comparing its brand of hair conditioner (Tame) against the Alberto Balsam brand. According to Alberto-Culver, the ads had "disparaged" its brand by inaccurately showing that it left a greasy, oily residue on the hair. At the time the campaign had begun, Alberto Balsam was a highly successful entry in the market, holding a 12 percent share (Tame had 17 percent). In only five months, Alberto Balsam's share had dropped to 6 percent and was continuing to shrink. After it fell to under 3 percent, the company removed its brand from the market.[11]

Consumers and consumer groups are also active in this arena, though not nearly so well organized. In addition to dealing with government agencies and businesses, consumers have also employed the court system, sometimes as individuals and sometimes in class action lawsuits. In summary, there are a number of institutions involved in various aspects of the marketing-consumer environment. The backbone of the public policy perspective is our system of laws—both in the courts and in the adminstrative agencies.

REGULATING THE MARKETING-CONSUMER ENVIRONMENT

The period from 1968 to the present has been a turbulent time in marketing regulation. *Activism* and *deregulation* have each held center stage during the period. The question "What is the proper way to regulate marketing?" has been continually addressed. The answers to this question have reflected different weightings of how to balance marketer freedoms against consumer rights. The Federal Trade Commission is our nation's key regulatory agency for most of the marketing-consumer environment. In this section, therefore, we'll focus on the FTC and take a look at some of its consumer protection programs.

The FTC's Vague Mandate

The Federal Trade Commission was established in 1914 as the government's chief economic regulatory agency. As such, it is broadly charged with the responsibility for providing a **fair competitive environment** for the nation's economic system. Its actual responsibility (or mandate) is, however, surprisingly vague. Section 5 of the FTC act originally declared "unfair methods of competition in commerce" to be unlawful. In 1938, this was amended to add "unfair or deceptive acts or practices" to this category.

Thus are two basic types of issues. One type involves one firm's dealing with other firms; these issues fall in the area of competition and reflect **antitrust regulation**. The other category involves a firm's interactions with its consumers: the regulatory area of **consumer protection**.

One effect of the FTC's vague mandate is uncertainty as to its authority to undertake various programs. This uncertainty must usually be resolved by either the Congress or the courts. Thus it is normal for the FTC to propose new programs, without having a complete assurance that it has the legal authority to carry them out. Throughout its history, in fact, the FTC has been roundly criticized by both liberals and conservatives, sometimes because it has not advocated enough new regulatory efforts and sometimes because it has advocated too many!

The Political Setting

Any overview of public policy would be incomplete if it did not note that politics and political philosophies play an extremely important role. Political power is important, as are the desires of important **constituents**.

The stage was set for 20 years of FTC controversy by Ralph Nader and followers, known as Nader's Raiders. Following a critical report of the FTC by this group in 1969, the president of the United States requested the American Bar Association (ABA), a prestigious professional organization of attorneys, to investigate the FTC's activities. The ABA's committee returned with a conclusion similar to the Nader group's report. Both reports urged the FTC to increase its efforts to protect consumers and regulate marketers. President Nixon and the Congress appeared to support such changes during the early 1970s. The FTC received larger budgets each year, as it became more activist in its regulations. (If you are interested in reading more about these programs, you may wish to pursue the reading in Note 12.)

Following a brief respite in the mid-1970s, liberal Democrats gained control of the FTC when President Jimmy Carter was elected. The FTC's activism was renewed. By 1980, this had sparked a major backlash from the business community, which went to its legislative representatives. The Congress began to subject the FTC to harsh scrutiny, and in 1980 it cut the budget and programs of the agency, after threatening to disband it entirely. These congressional actions were in part the result of a massive lobbying effort by businesses across the country. Funeral directors, for example, were incensed at FTC proposals for requiring changes in funeral marketing practices. Insurance companies and agents were upset over FTC-proposed rules that would have required each insurance salesperson to give a consumer information as to whether or not there were better prices available than the agent was offering them! Auto dealers were also angry at the FTC: the agency wanted stronger regulations regarding guarantees for used cars. In terms of the political setting, notice that all three of these businesses are well represented in thousands of communities across the land. Their members are usually involved in civic affairs and are respected town citizens. When these people (and their local Chambers of Commerce) contact their legislative representatives to complain, they receive serious consideration.

Beyond lobbying in Congress, the political nature of consumer policy is particularly evident with the election of a new president. When this happens every four (or eight) years, the top officials of many of the regulatory agencies are replaced, some programs are dropped, while others are expanded. Priorities change drastically, as do spending levels for specific programs. When a Republican administration came into office in 1981, for example, it undertook **deregulation**. Deregulation is the deliberate reduction of government control of business activities, based on the belief that the marketplace works best when individuals are most free to operate in their own self-interests. Most policymakers accept that this theory is strong in the abstract, but there is much disagreement about where to draw the line in the real world (especially over possibilities that some powerful persons will take advantage of smaller businesses and consumers). Recall, for example, our discussions in Chapter 2, concerning the low levels of knowledge many consumers have. How well would they fare in a totally unregulated marketplace? Recent deregulatory efforts, such as in the airline industry, have brought controversy in both the areas of antitrust (mergers) and consumer protection.

Who's Trusting Now?

The area of antitrust has few direct effects on consumer behavior, but important long-term effects in the form of which firms supply the consumer market, what products they can offer, and what prices they charge (Philip Morris, for example, used to produce a number of the top brands of cigarettes. Now, through buying other large firms, it also controls all brands of the Miller Brewing Company, General Foods Corporation, and Kraft Foods Corporation).

The recent deregulatory U.S. policy has allowed virtually all kinds of mergers, including the largest "megamergers" of huge corporations in the nation's history. In the eight years of the Reagan administration, there were no government challenges to mergers of companies in different industries, or to any "vertical" mergers (between suppliers and customer firms in the same industry). "Horizontal mergers" (between competing firms in the same industry, such as airlines) went largely unchallenged also. Overall, less than 1 percent of mergers large enough to have been challenged by the government were challenged during this period![13]

Opponents of this policy argue that these mergers pose huge costs and risks, primarily so that a few "power brokers" can reap huge personal rewards. They argue that these mergers have already cost many employees their jobs and, in the process, have destroyed the notion that a manager or worker should feel loyal to his or her company. Also, they warn that the new firms have gained market power that they might use to restrict competition. Finally, they warn that, because many such mergers were financed by "junk bonds" (new debt issued to pay the previous owners and bearing very high interest rates), the future burden of interest payments might drag these firms under and plunge the American economy into a financial crisis. The supporters of the mergers are equally strong in their defense—they argue that such mergers have benefitted the shareholders by gaining them much higher prices than before the merger, and that this represents the benefits of marketplace operation. They also argue that the mergers will bring efficiencies to the firms that remain after the process, and that this will make the new firms more competitive in world markets. As we move into the 1990s, the Bush administration must somehow seek to handle the strong positions held by both sides, and the increasing congressional pressure for more government oversight of the financial markets.

Are the States Fed Up?

Recent U.S. deregulatory policy has also hit hard at consumer protection agencies, especially at the Consumer Product Safety Commission (CPSC) and the Federal Trade Commission (FTC). The staff at each agency was cut almost in half (to 500 and 900 persons, respectively), while dollar budgets were slashed also. Similar to the antitrust situation, these efforts have won both supporters and critics, but with pressure building for the Bush administration to move back toward more regulation in the 1990s. For example, one Republican at the CPSC predicts that "... *conservatives will now live to see the day [of] doubling budgets and bringing things back . . . they were overzealous, and now we're going to get in trouble for that.*"[14] Meanwhile, an FTC commissioner warns that by the end of the 1980s the FTC had been cut back to its size in 1961, and was in danger of becoming a "stealth agency—one whose presence would elude detection" by anyone looking for it! *"If there is no change,"* he warns, *"the states will continue to take on more responsibility."*[15]

Indeed, this has been happening in recent years. As federal regulation has decreased, the state attorneys general (each U.S. state elects its own) have become much more active. In recent years they banded together to force $16 million in payments from Chrysler to certain purchasers of its cars (odometer tampering), $4 million in payments from Minolta for camera pricing manipulation, forced the divestiture of Filene's Department Stores in one merger case in New England, and challenged several advertising practices, including those featuring airline fare specials but without indicating the restrictions. Since the prospect of having different states creating different sets of requirements is such a major threat to managers trying to plan national programs, the marketing community is also interested in seeing the federal government be more effective in setting national regulations.[16]

No Easy Answers

Thus the early 1990s face an especially challenging time in marketing regulation in the United States. President Bush, the Congress, the regulatory agencies, and the independent state attorneys general all must deal with the conflicting forces toward regulation and deregulation. As shown in Table 21-2, the American public supports government efforts to find a proper balance.[17]

It is fair to summarize by saying that public policy issues are almost always interesting, are often important, and are invariably controversial. The people involved in a particular matter are usually highly committed to one side or the other, and personal interests and philosophies are usually involved as well. For those of us who are not personally caught up in the public policy battle, however, it is easy to see that there are two sides to most questions and that both sides can raise good arguments. In our dual roles as consumers and as marketers, we

TABLE 21-2 WHAT DO THE PEOPLE THINK?

Issue	% of Public Who Respond That		
	"Business Will Do"	versus	"Government Must Watch"
Invest in new products/services	65		31
Advertise honestly	29		65
Make safe products/services	25		71
Not engage in price fixing	15		79
Clean up air and water pollution	11		85

Source: Adapted from "Need for Government Oversight," Adweek, October 12, 1987, p. 78.

have a stake in seeing regulation handled in the best possible manner. Toward that end, we'll now examine a basic framework that captures many dimensions of the regulatory settings.

A BASIC FRAMEWORK FOR REGULATION

Consumer information, because of its significance in the Consumer Bill of Rights and its relatively nonrestrictive nature (that is, consumers can still buy freely when an information program is in effect), has long been a favorite option for marketing regulation. To learn more, let's look at an interesting framework by a team working with the Federal Trade Commission.[18] The essentials of the framework are outlined in Figure 21-2. Note that there are three stages for analyzing a possible consumer information program.

Stage 1: Is the Remedy Worthwhile?

The first stage asks whether any program at all seems to be needed. This involves a comparison of costs and benefits. In the consumer information area, there are three types of costs that can be significant to consider:

1. *Compliance costs.* These are the additional costs to the marketers for supplying the information, including testing, space, and personnel costs.
2. *Enforcement costs.* These are the costs to the government for enforcing the information remedy. They can include personnel, travel costs, and court costs.
3. *Unintended side effects.* These are additional costs to either marketers or consumers that crop up as an unforeseen by-product of the remedy. For example,

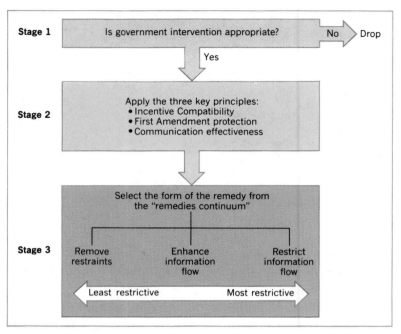

FIGURE 21-2 **A Framework for Consumer Information Regulation**

Source: Michael B. Mazis, Richard Staelin, Howard Beales, and Steven Salop, "A Framework for Evaluating Consumer Information Regulation," *Journal of Marketing,* Vol. 49, Winter 1981, p. 12.

forcing TV commercials to include too much detailed information might lead consumers to ignore them entirely, or might lead marketers to shift to less efficient forms of promotion to get their messages across.

There are also three classes of benefits that could flow from increased consumer information:

1. *Improved consumer decisions.* These would flow from consumers being better informed about the strengths and weaknesses of each alternative.
2. *Enhanced product quality.* In some cases, increased consumer information can cause marketers to upgrade the performance of their brand, if they believe that consumers will now recognize quality better and reward it with purchases.
3. *Lower prices.* In some cases, increased advertising can use lower price to attract new customers. A high-quality new brand, for example, can advertise a low price to gain trial. Its larger competitors might then match these prices to retain sales.

In deciding on a potential public program, the likelihood and size of each type of cost and benefit needs to be estimated. If the costs are likely to exceed the benefits, the program will be dropped. If not, consideration will move to stage 2.

Stage 2: The Three Principles

There are, of course, many ways in which a program can be designed. Stage 2 suggests that three "principles" be followed. **Incentive compatibility** refers to an attempt to create regulations that marketers would *like* to comply with rather than those they will fight against. For example, the FTC used to prohibit cigarette manufacturers from making claims about low tar and nicotine content in their brands. When it lifted its ban, the marketing landscape immediately lit up with "tar derby" advertising. Competing brands outdid themselves to suggest how low they were on this measure, while many new brands were created to take advantage of a low-tar positioning. Consumers in turn became more sensitive to tar and nicotine content and rewarded low-tar brands by purchasing them. Overall, the average level of these ingredients dropped dramatically within a few years.

The second principle, **communication effectiveness**, reflects that consumer information be designed to communicate effectively to the target market for whom it is intended (this point seems natural to marketers, but is a good reminder for many attorneys and economists who are often involved in creating these programs). At a minimum, consumers should be able to understand what is being said. Beyond this, the disclosure should also be interesting, noticeable, and so forth. The third principle, **first amendment protection**, reminds regulators to strive to maintain freedom and not simply order marketers around by whim. This principle reflects a belief that consumers will benefit most when the marketing-consumer environment has a free flow of marketing information in it.

Stage 3: Selecting from the "Remedies Continuum"

Public policymakers can take quite different approaches toward handling consumer problems. The arrows at the bottom of Figure 21-2 suggest that the regulator should consider different levels of "restrictions" with these remedies. Let's look at three representative levels.

Little or No Restrictions

At the left side of the figure, notice that some policy alternatives are *not very restricted at all* and could even remove restraints rather than impose them.

I Can See Clearly Now . . .

The case of eyeglasses and contact lenses provides a good example. Until about 15 years ago, most states banned eyeglass advertising on grounds of health, safety, and quality assurance. This meant that doctors were the source for most eyeglasses, acting as intermediaries for the labs where they were made to order. A few states did allow eyeglass

Removal of advertising bans spurred the growth of this type of optical outlet.

advertising, however, and retail eyeglass shops were operating in these states. Several consumer research studies showed that consumers were paying substantially higher prices (by 25 to 40 percent) in the states that restricted the advertising.[19] Policymakers decided that the states' ad bans were keeping marketers from informing consumers about prices and thus not allowing price to be used as a competitive tool. The FTC moved *against the bans*, freeing marketers to advertise and compete on price bases in all states. Prices dropped substantially as the competitive market began to work more freely.

Following the eyeglass rule, regulators moved into cases in the *professions*. Societies of doctors, dentists, attorneys, and accountants had created codes that banned most forms of marketing to potential clients. Since the professions deal largely in intangible *services* rather than more standardized *products* such as eyeglasses, the issues are more debatable, and this area has experienced much controversy. Quality, for example, is a key issue; price advertising might be used to sell lower-quality legal, dental, surgical, or other services. On the other hand, these services *are* expensive, and it would seem that prices would decrease if price competition were fostered. At present, the competitive information flow view seems to have won the battles. Most professional societies have changed their codes to allow advertising, at least in certain forms. However, many professionals have staunchly refused to engage in active marketing to consumers, and they continue to view (and treat) those who do as outcasts. (If you know one of these professionals well, you may find a discussion of this topic most interesting.)

Moderate Restrictions

Moving toward the center of the remedies continuum in Figure 21-2, there are a range of possible ways to enhance the flow of consumer information. One option is to give the consumer *more time* to make a decision. **Cooling-off laws**, for example, often allow three days for a consumer to cancel sales agreements that they may have made under high-pressure selling conditions (as in door-to-door sales or telephone solicitations). Another option involves the *separation of "diagnosis" from "treatment."* As part of the eyeglass regulations, for instance, the eye examiner was required to inform a consumer, in writing, of his or her exact prescription (diagnosis). Now that the consumer has this information, he or she would have the option to shop elsewhere for their lenses and frames (the "treatment," in this case). Notice that similar possibilities exist in such areas as automobile repairs, medical records, and so on. Two other forms of enhancing consumer information flow include (1) *setting information standards* and (2) *requiring certain disclosures* by the marketer. Since both forms are frequently used, let's look briefly at each:

Standards Are All Around Us Standard setting allows all marketers to communicate using a similar basis, and affords consumers the chance to compare different brands on a comparable basis as well. Although we don't often think about it, **product standards** are a necessary part of the marketing-consumer environment. In the area of food, for example, the calorie, pound, U.S. RDA (recommended daily allowance), and grades of meat (Prime, Choice, etc.) are all standards that have been decided in public policy. There are tens of thousands of standards currently in use. Current public policy questions involve what *new* standards should be set (if any) and at what levels. For example, should there be specific requirements that have to be met before a food can be sold as a "natural food" or "low-calorie" food or "hypoallergenic" cosmetic?

Requiring Marketers to Disclose As another way to enhance information flow, albeit a more restrictive one, policymakers can consider **affirmative disclosures**, which *require* marketers to disclose certain information to consumers. Familiar examples include cigarette warnings, food ingredient listings, warranty descriptions, and mileage ratings for cars. Notice that these affirmative disclosures are required by *all marketers* in a product class. Other affirmative disclosure orders pertain only to a *particular marketer* and usually occur as a result of consumers having been misled because certain important facts about the product had not been provided to them. The FTC has used this type of remedy quite often Wilkie reports over 200 such orders in a seven-year period.[20]

Heavy Restrictions

The final zone of the remedies continuum moves toward the strongest form of government regulation—*restricting information flow*. **Free speech** is a right

Notice how much information is included on these required labels . . . is it too much or not enough?

guaranteed for both consumers and marketers by the First Amendment, so any restrictions of free speech must be approached with great care. Most public policy experts agree that these remedies should probably be reserved for only those cases that cannot be sufficiently handled by any of the less restrictive options we have been discussing.

There are, however, some situations in which restrictions might receive wide

Products headed for further restrictions?

support. The U.S. ban of cigarette advertising on TV and radio, for example, was enacted in 1970 and seemed to enjoy majority support from consumers.[21] Many European countries also ban TV advertising for cigarettes; in addition, France and Britain prohibit the remaining cigarette ads from praising the product or linking it with fast cars or sexual allure. Recently, the Canadian Parliament has gone even further—it banned all tobacco ads, free samples, and sponsorship of events.[22]

A variety of other options are possible, depending on the situation. Sometimes the *type and style* of information might be restricted in preference to banning it entirely (this has happened with advertising to children, for example, and with advertising prescription drugs to consumers). Sometimes consumer policy restricts the *timing* of information. For example, increasing pressures to restrict telephone marketers from "cold-calling" homes at dinner time or late in the evening make these restrictions likely in the near future. Similarly, the discovery that credit-checking firms are selling mailing lists to direct marketers will also likely bring restrictions on the *distribution* of such information as personal finances, medical histories, and group memberships. When one woman was told, "I see you have been making a lot of phone calls to Newark and Wilmington . . ." in a phone solicitation, she joined the movement to change the laws that allow this (if you are keenly interested in politics, you may be interested to know that the proposed "Bork Bill," restricting such direct marketing list sales without signed

What public policy actions, if any, do you believe are appropriate to protect the teenagers of our society?

consent, arose because the U.S. Senate's review of Judge Robert Bork's nomination to the Supreme Court included the public release of a list of videos he had rented for private viewing).[23]

Finally, we should be aware that restrictions are sometimes *lifted* as well. This has recently happened in the cases of TV advertising for feminine hygiene products and for condoms.

Concluding Note on the Framework

There are many ways in which public policy can tend to its mandate of encouraging and ensuring a fair competitive and consumer environment. Each option will probably have strong points and drawbacks, and most are quite controversial.

It is difficult to apply a simple rule to cover every case. You will encounter more issues of this type in our other chapters. If you are interested in learning a little more about some of the issues that arise in the world of public policy at this point, however, you may wish to read the material in Appendix 21-A, which describes the FTC's program of corrective advertising.

SUMMARY

Essentials of the Public Policy Perspective

This chapter is an optional companion to Chapter 2 (marketing and consumer perspectives). Here we introduced the public policy perspective on consumer behavior. The first section focused on how the overall character of a society and its economic system broadly determines the environment for consumers and marketers. In the *market system* of the Western nations, for example, marketers and consumers are awarded significant freedoms to act in their own self-interest. As a part of these freedoms, consumers hold certain rights. The *Consumer Bill of Rights* asserts consumers' rights to be informed, to choose freely, to be heard, and to safety. In addition to rights and freedoms, however, marketers and consumers also have *responsibilities*. For marketers there are responsibilities to conduct business in accord with the spirit and laws of the system. Consumers are responsible for informing themselves, purchasing wisely, and abiding by contracts. The government is granted certain powers, but also has the responsibility of preserving freedoms and acting fairly in the exercise of its power. We saw how these aspects of the system are often quite controversial and are heavily influenced by the political climate.

The Institutions of Public Policy

In our next section we examined the various institutions of public policy—the involvement of the executive, legislative, and judicial branches of government, as well as industry self-regulatory boards and consumer groups.

Regulating the Marketing-Consumer Environment

The following section centered on consumer protection regulation itself, with special emphasis on the Federal Trade Commission (FTC). Here we examined its history, its vague mandate, and its controversial political setting.

A Basic Framework for Regulation

As one guide for regulatory options, we then examined a framework for consumer information regulation. This included three stages. In the first stage, the potential value of a remedy is considered using a cost-benefit analysis. Stage 2 involves three principles: *incentive compatibility, communication effectiveness,* and *First Amendment protection.* At stage 3, different potential remedies are considered along a dimension of relative restrictiveness. The least restrictive forms of remedies involve the removal of present restraints on information flow. At a moderately restrictive level we find remedies such as "affirmative disclosures," in which marketers may be required to disclose facts about the product or service. At the most restrictive level we see government banning certain advertising. Thus there are many options available in attempting to achieve a "fair and efficient environment" for marketers and consumers alike. In Appendix 21-A we look more closely into the FTC regulatory program of corrective advertising. In Appendix 21-B we present the "Code of Ethics for Marketers," as drafted by the American Marketing Association.

KEY TERMS

marketing-consumer environment

public policy view

neutral view of choice

market system

Consumer Bill of Rights

right to be informed

right to choose freely

right to safety

right to be heard

right to consumer education

right to consumer recourse and redress

right to an environment that
   enhances the quality of life

errors of omission

errors of commission

cost-benefit analysis

industry self-regulation

fair competitive environment

antitrust regulation

consumer protection

constituents

deregulation

consumer information

incentive compatibility

communication effectiveness

first amendment protection

cooling-off laws

product standards

affirmative disclosures

free speech

REVIEW QUESTIONS AND EXPERIENTIAL EXERCISES
[E = Application extension or experiential exercise]

1. Contrast the viewpoints of marketers, consumers, and public policymakers.

2. What prompted the Consumer Bill of Rights? What prompted the additional rights to be added later? Indicate the general effects of each of the rights on marketers, consumers, and government agencies.

3. Discuss, with examples, how slippages in marketer, consumer, and government responsibilities affect a market-based economic system.

4. "One cannot separate politics and political philosophies from public policy issues." Is this true? Is this desirable? Comment.

5. Describe briefly the shift in perspective that occurred at the FTC between the 1960s and the 1990s. What are its implications for marketing practices? What is your regulatory prediction for the climate of the 1990s?

6. Briefly describe the concept and history of corrective advertising (see Appendix 21-A). Do you believe this type of remedy should be used?

[E] 7. Use the reference section of the library to learn more about the differences between public policy toward marketing in socialist systems versus market systems. Write a brief report summarizing your findings.

[E] 8. Recent years have seen dramatic changes occurring in the public policy perspectives taken in China and in Russia. Use the library reference facilities to learn more about these events. Summarize your findings.

[E] 9. Many interesting books have been written about problems with marketing practices, government regulation, and consumer protection. Locate this section in your library and review the materials there. Summarize your findings.

[E] 10. Detailed coverage of public policy topics can be found in such publications as *Regulation* magazine and the *Antitrust Bulletin*. Articles on specific topics can also be found in the *Journal of Public Policy & Marketing, Journal of Consumer Affairs, Journal of Marketing,* and *Journal of Advertising* (see the "Notes" for this chapter for examples). Locate one or more of these sources in the library and review its contents. Summarize your findings.

[E] 11. How do state and local governments involve themselves in consumer matters? Call or visit a local government agency dealing with these matters. Interview an official regarding the agency's activities and priorities. Write a brief report summarizing your findings.

[E] 12. How does public policy impact day-to-day marketing practice? Arrange to interview a marketing, advertising, or retailing executive on this question. Summarize your findings.

[E] 13. Monitor your local advertising media to locate advertising by local professionals (doctors, dentists, lawyers, accountants, etc.). Arrange a brief interview to examine their experiences with this practice, and how consumers and other professionals have responded.

[E] 14. Read carefully "The Code of Ethics for Marketers" in Appendix 21-B. Do you see any problems with it? Discuss this code with friends or acquaintances who work in retailing, purchasing, advertising, sales, research, or industrial marketing jobs. What realistic reactions do they have?

APPENDIX 21-A CORRECTIVE ADVERTISING

Corrective advertising is a regulatory program that can force a marketer, who had run deceptive advertising in the past, to run new advertising to correct any deceptions still existing in consumers' minds. This remedy is a special form of the FTC's affirmative disclosure program. It has always been very controversial, since it represents a clear government intrusion into a marketer's control of its own promotional strategies. On the other hand, it may bring real benefits to consumers and competitors. There is much complexity in this area. Our coverage will focus on some of the highlights.[24]

A "Brief" History

The Soup Case

The seeds for corrective advertising were planted by a small group of law students from George Washington University. As part of a course project, these students banded together under the acronym SOUP (Students Opposed to Unfair Practices) and tried to intervene in a case against Campbell Soup Company. That case involved ads that showed bowls of vegetable soup with the vegetables piled above the liquid level, suggesting quite ample portions. A complaint had been lodged with the commission (rumored to have come from the H. J. Heinz Company, which manufactures most stores' private-label soups, but which has for years had trouble gaining a strong position for its own soup brands). After an investigation, the FTC found that the ad agency had achieved the vegetable-piling effect by placing clear glass marbles in the bottoms of the soup bowls before filling them with the soup and forcing the solid ingredients to the top. As a remedy in the case, the FTC intended to issue a cease-and-desist order against Campbell. This order would require the company to stop showing these types of ads and never to engage in such a practice again in the future.

The law students, however, did not believe that this was the best remedy for FTC to use. Instead, they proposed that a *corrective* message be ordered, to inform consumers who may have been misled by the false ads. Otherwise, SOUP argued, a deceived consumer might never become aware that he or she had been misled!

FTC did not accept SOUP's argument in this case, since it is obvious that a person who buys the soup would soon see the actual ingredient quantities. Thus, the chances of a continuing deception were low in this case. The commission also noted, however, that the *concept* of a correction was interesting, and perhaps would be appropriate in more serious cases. Thus was corrective advertising born.

A Spurt of Activity

Over the next few years, the FTC announced many corrective advertising investigations that it intended to consider. These received great attention in the press, and in business circles. Supporters of corrective advertising saw it as a

EXHIBIT 21-A1   TEXTS OF FOUR EARLY CORRECTIVE ADS

I. Profile Bread

"Hi (celebrity's name), for Profile Bread. Like all mothers, I'm concerned about nutrition and balanced meals. So, I'd like to clear up any misunderstanding you may have about Profile Bread from its advertising or even its name.

"Does Profile Bread have fewer calories than any other breads? No. Profile has about the same per ounce as other breads. To be exact, Profile has 7 fewer calories per slice. That's because Profile is sliced thinner. But eating Profile will not cause you to lose weight. A reduction of 7 calories is insignificant. It's total calories and balanced nutrition that count. And Profile can help you achieve a balanced meal because it provides protein and B vitamins as well as other nutrients.

"How does my family feel about Profile? Well, my husband likes Profile toast, the children love Profile sandwiches, and I prefer Profile to any other bread. So you see, at our house, delicious taste makes Profile a family affair."

(To be run in 25 percent of brand's advertising, for one year)

II. Ocean Spray

"If you've wondered what some of our earlier advertising meant when we said Ocean Spray Cranberry Juice Cocktail has more food energy than orange juice or tomato juice, let us make it clear: we didn't mean vitamins and minerals. Food energy means calories. Nothing more.

"Food energy is important at breakfast since many of us may not get enough calories, or food energy, to get off to a good start. Ocean Spray Cranberry Juice Cocktail helps because it contains more food energy than most other breakfast drinks.

"And Ocean Spray Cranberry Juice Cocktail gives you and your family Vitamin C plus a great wake-up taste. It's . . . the other breakfast drink."

(To be run in one of every four ads for one year)

III. Amstar

"Do you recall some of our past messages saying that Domino Sugar gives you strength, energy and stamina? Actually, Domino is not a special or unique source of strength, energy and stamina. No sugar is, because what you need is a balanced diet and plenty of rest and exercise."

(To be run in one of every four ads for one year)

IV. Sugar Information, Inc.

"Do you recall the messages we brought you in the past about sugar? How something with sugar in it before meals could help you curb your appetite? We hope you didn't get the idea that our little diet tip was any magic formula for losing weight. Because there are no tricks, or shortcuts, the whole diet subject is very complicated. Research hasn't established that consuming sugar before meals will contribute to weight reduction or even keep you from gaining weight."

(To be run for one insertion in each of seven magazines)

boon to consumers and to competitors, in which a wrongdoer would be rightly "denied the fruits of a violation." Also, of course, there was a feeling that this stronger remedy would cause other advertisers to think twice before engaging in deceptive ads—thus the potential *deterrence* effect might also be large. Opponents of corrective advertising raised a series of objections. They argued that the remedy was beyond the FTC's powers and represented further intrusion by government bureaucrats into the market system and a further attack on marketing freedoms.

Interestingly, most of the early corrective ad *complaints* issued by the FTC did *not* lead to actual corrective advertising orders. Most of the orders that *were* issued, moreover, seemed to be weak. Exhibit 21A-1 shows the text of four of the earliest corrective ads. What do you think about each of them?

Beyond the corrective ads themselves, however, most of the marketing community's anxiety dealt with the threat of further government intrusion into marketers' freedoms. For this reason, a legal test of the FTC's powers was important.

The Listerine Case: A Legal Test

The first case to test FTC's legal power to order corrective advertising involved the Warner-Lambert Company's Listerine brand of mouthwash. Warner-Lambert had advertised—for over 50 years—that gargling with Listerine helped prevent colds and sore throats because Listerine killed the germs that caused these illnesses. This marketing program had been extremely successful—Listerine was by far the dominant brand of mouthwash (at one time holding over a 60 percent share of market) and was believed by many consumers to be an excellent safeguard for their families' health.

The FTC's staff believed that the advertising was erroneous and that corrective advertising was needed to rectify the mistaken beliefs held by so many consumers. Warner-Lambert, on the other hand, argued that the advertising was *not* erroneous and, further, that FTC did not have the power to order corrective advertising in any event. After four months of hearings, covering 4000 pages of testimony, the commission *did* order corrective advertising. The company then took the FTC to court, appealing its decision. The circuit court of appeals upheld the FTC in general (it did, however, remove part of the required corrective phrase).

Listerine's corrective campaign was run for a period of 16 months, stretching from late 1978 until early 1980. As ordered, just over $10 million was spent on these ads, almost all of it on television. The required disclosure was placed midway in the commercial, taking up about 5 seconds of the 30-second spot. Consumer research (based on our multiattribute attitude model discussed in Chapter 11) showed an interesting pattern of results from this corrective campaign. A study by the FTC showed that many consumers did change their beliefs about Listerine and cold prevention. Also, however, many consumers did *not* get the message or else did not believe it. Over 40 percent of Listerine users, for example, still believed (at the end of the campaign) that Listerine was still being promoted as effective for colds and sore throats. Almost 60 percent of Listerine users continued to say that cold and sore throat effectiveness was a key for their purchasing.

Given these results, would you say that the Listerine corrective ad campaign was a success (from a public policy perspective), or not? If not, what should the FTC or Warner-Lambert do now?

Lessons Learned

Since the Listerine campaign, there was little activity on corrective advertising through the 1980s. The political backlash from Congress and the administration's deregulation program reduced the chances of further use of this remedy at the time. At present, however, the FTC retains the power to order corrective adver-

---

EXHIBIT 21-A2   *SUMMARY CONCLUSIONS ON CORRECTIVE ADVERTISING*

---

1. The FTC is empowered to order corrective advertising as a remedy against deceptive advertising campaigns.
2. There are important legal constraints as to when and in what manner the FTC can employ this remedy form.
3. Corrective advertising holds the potential to yield beneficial effects for consumers.
4. Corrective advertising appears to hold the potential to affect the sales and/or image of the advertised brand.
5. There is little evidence of a systematic FTC program for corrective advertising:
   a. Bursts of case activity have been followed by long periods of inactivity.
   b. Philosophical and personnel changes occurred throughout the 1970s and early 1980s, at both the staff and commissioner levels.
   c. Past orders have used a wide range of requirements for corrective advertising.
6. Consent negotiations between FTC staff members and company representatives have play a key role in the exact requirements in almost every case to date.
7. Consumer effectiveness of corrective advertising has not been the primary concern of the orders issued to date.
8. In communication terms, past corrective advertising orders against major advertisers appear to have been weak.
9. In terms of consumer impacts, the major corrective advertising orders appear *not* to have been successful in remedying consumer misimpressions across the marketplace.
10. If corrective advertising is to continue as an FTC remedy, some changes in the form of the orders will be required.

Source: William L. Wilkie, Dennis L. McNeill, and Michael B. Mazis, "Marketing's Scarlet Letter: The Theory and Practice of Corrective Advertising," *Journal of Marketing,* Spring 1984, p. 26. Reprinted with permission.

tising. It may well be, therefore, that we will see it return in the future. Exhibit 21-A2 reports 10 conclusions about corrective advertising, as reported by three marketing professors who conducted an in-depth analysis of the program. What is *your* general position regarding corrective advertising? Would you like to see it return as a remedy that the FTC is using, or would you prefer to have it never arise again?

APPENDIX 21-B   THE ETHICS CODE FOR MARKETERS*

Members of the American Marketing Association (AMA) are committed to ethical professional conduct. They have joined together in subscribing to this Code of Ethics[25] embracing the following topics:

Responsibilities of the Marketer

Marketers must accept responsibility for the consequences of their activities and make every effort to ensure that their decisions, recommendations, and actions function to identify, serve, and satisfy all relevant publics: customers, organizations, and society.

Marketers' professional conduct must be guided by

1. The basic rule of professional ethics: not knowingly to do harm.
2. The adherence to all applicable laws and regulations.
3. The accurate representation of their education, training, and experience.
4. The active support, practice, and promotion of this Code of Ethics.

Honesty and Fairness

Marketers shall uphold and advance the integrity, honor, and dignity of the marketing profession by

1. Being honest in serving consumers, clients, employees, suppliers, distributors, and the public.
2. Not knowingly participating in conflict of interest without prior notice to all parties involved.
3. Establishing equitable fee schedules including the payment or receipt of usual, customary, and/or legal compensation for marketing exchanges.

Source: "AMA Adopts New Code of Ethics," *Marketing Educator,* Fall 1987, pp. 3ff.

Rights and Duties of Parties in the Marketing Exchange Process

Participants in the marketing exchange process should be able to expect that

1. Products and services offered are safe and fit for their intended uses.
2. Communications about offered products and services are not deceptive.
3. All parties intend to discharge their obligations, financial and otherwise, in good faith.
4. Appropriate internal methods exist for equitable adjustment and/or redress of grievances concerning purchases.

It is understood that the above would include, *but it is not limited to,* the following responsibilities of the marketers:

In the area of product development and management,

- Disclosure of all substantial risks associated with product or service usage.
- Identification of any product component substitution that might materially change the product or impact on the buyer's purchase decision.
- Identification of extra-cost added features.

In the area of promotions,

- Avoidance of false and misleading advertising.
- Rejection of high-pressure manipulations or misleading sales tactics.
- Avoidance of sales promotions that use deception or manipulation.

In the area of distribution,

- Not manipulating the availability of a product for purpose of exploitation.
- Not using coercion in the marketing channel.
- Not exerting undue influence over the reseller's choice to handle a product.

In the area of pricing,

- Not engaging in price fixing.
- Not practicing predatory pricing.
- Disclosing the full price associated with any purchase.

In the area of marketing research,

- Prohibiting selling or fundraising under the guise of conducting research.
- Maintaining research integrity by avoiding misrepresentation and omission of pertinent research data.
- Treating outside clients and suppliers fairly.

Organizational Relationships

Marketers should be aware of how their behavior may influence or impact on the behavior of others in organizational relationships. They should not demand, encourage, or apply coercion to obtain unethical behavior in their relationships with others, such as employees, suppliers, or customers. Marketers should

1. Apply confidentiality and anonymity in professional relationships with regard to privileged information.
2. Meet their obligations and responsibilities in contracts and mutual agreements in a timely manner.
3. Avoid taking the work of others, in whole, or in part, and represent this work as their own or directly benefit from it without compensation or consent of the originator or owner.
4. Avoid manipulation to take advantage of situations to maximize personal welfare in a way that unfairly deprives or damages their organization or others.

Any AMA member found to be in violation of any provision of this Code of Ethics may have his or her Association membership suspended or revoked.

CHAPTER  22

Organizational Buying Behavior

(Because this is a specialized field of study, this chapter was prepared by Dr. Darrel Miller, University of South Florida, in conjunction with the text's author, so that it fits well with the spirit and content of our other chapters.)

The Secrets of Linda H.

Note: Linda H. is a buyer of women's ready-to-wear clothing for a major chain. Let's listen in to portions of an interview with her . . .

Q. *Is buying different with other product lines like hardware, domestics, or electronics?*

A. I think so; they have different situations. Their business is so planned out, they almost have to *marry* their resource. Also, I don't think that every buyer approaches things in the same way, even in ready-to-wear. I'm just giving you my approach to business.

Q. *Your job is one link in providing products to your firm—how do you see yourself in this chain?*

A. Middle portion of the chain. I look to give directions below. I look for certain types of direction from above. Not so much for the details of my assortment, but . . . [interview continues in chapter].

■ ■ ■

This chapter focuses on a special context for buyer behavior—purchasing done by organizations rather than by individual consumers. In actual dollars, organizational buyers spend substantially more money than do the individual consumers in our economy. Not only are purchases typically for larger amounts of money, the total is much greater as well. Many readers of this book are likely to work in organizational buying or selling sometime during their careers. It is thus important for us to look more closely at how "organizational" consumers make purchases. We will examine three primary topics in this chapter: (1) the organizational context, (2) the process of organizational buying, and (3) relationships between buyers and sellers.

THE CONTEXT OF ORGANIZATIONAL BUYING

Organizational buying refers to the purchasing processes and decisions within organizations. Organizations can be industrial firms, government agencies, retail businesses, service establishments, and so forth. Organizational purchases are made by a **decision-making unit** (**DMU**), which can consist of a single individual or any number of individuals in a variety of subunits within the organization. In some ways organizational buying is similar to consumer buying, but in other respects it is different.

Similarities to Consumer Buying

Leading the list of similarities is that *organizations and consumers use the same basic decision processes* we discuss throughout this text. Organizations also have needs. Their purchase processes also involve search for information about alternative products and sellers. A number of external factors also influence their choice, including social influences, salespersons, and advertising. Once a purchase decision is reached, it is also later evaluated to see if the purchase performs to expectations.

Some consumer behavior experts believe that the models marketers use for understanding individual consumer behavior are also useful for organizational buyer behavior. One recent study, for example, focused on the effects of an organizational buyer's previous purchasing experience. The researchers found that the more experienced the buyer, the broader the set of alternatives he or she would consider. More experienced buyers also needed less *external* information, because they were able to draw upon their prior experiences with the product category. These types of findings allowed the researchers to conclude that organizational buyers use the same basic cognitive purchasing strategies as individual consumers.[1]

Further evidence of similarities involves the *increasing use of advertising and promotional techniques* by organizational sellers. Some of this may be due to the increasing number of consumer products marketing managers taking jobs in industrial products firms,[2] but increased competition is the chief reason organizational marketers are finding consumer-selling techniques so useful.

Using Toys to Sell Chemicals

Industrial companies are discovering the power of advertising, but it is sometimes difficult to convince some experienced managers that innovative ads work. For example, a new campaign for Ethyl Chemicals Group used toys to drive home attributes for such complex products as alpha olefins and alcohol ethyoxylates. One manager said, "Isn't that kind of childish?" on first seeing an ad with a toy fire engine. The headline read, "When you need help with alpha olefins, you get it fast from the world's largest supplier." However, this ad campaign helped the company differentiate itself from competitors and cost half as much as previous ad campaigns, thus giving the company more money for broader promotional coverage. A company executive noted, "Ads are tools. They don't get orders as such; they get leads, inquiries over a period of time."[3]

Psychedelic Machines Speed Sales

Rather than focusing on product specifications, some mature products are advertised with an extra twist. Sumitomo Machinery Corporation advertises its variable-speed drives [small machines] painted in psychedelic colors, candy stripes, and other styles. The copy gives product specifications and offers to paint any machine to the customer's desires for an extra charge. An executive with the company attributed a 20 percent sales increase to this campaign.[4]

A third similarity between consumer and organizational buying involves the *number of people who participate* in the decision process. The purchase in either the consumer household or the organization can be made by one individual or by multiple persons. For example, just as family members and friends may influence the purchase decision of an individual consumer, the organizational buyer may consult with colleagues who will either use the product or who may have some expertise about it.

Differences from Consumer Buying

There are, however, some significant differences to consider. One major difference between an individual consumer purchase and an organizational purchase is that *the organizational buyer is usually not the end user* of the product. When an individual consumer makes a purchase, the end result is that the product is taken home and used or consumed in some fashion. The organizational buyer, however, is buying the product either for use in the manufacturing process or for reselling to other customers. Thus, the role of the organizational buyer is different from that of the individual consumer. (It is somewhat similar to the role played by the person in a household who is charged with doing all the shopping. The "buying agent" for the household makes some purchases on behalf of the household as a whole, and others according to the needs and wants of individual household members.)

A "DMU" in action.

A second major difference involves the *roles of people who participate* in the decision process. An organizational purchase is entrusted to a **decision-making unit** (**DMU**). Depending on the structure and internal dynamics of the organization, the decision-making unit's makeup is flexible. For example, a manufacturing firm purchasing prefabricated parts might employ a DMU with representatives from the engineering and production departments. Each department, again depending on the organization, may have a greater or lesser degree of participation. The possibilities are limitless and can change with personnel changes within the organization.

A third difference is that the *quantities involved in organizational purchases can be enormous.* For example, an individual shopper seldom purchases more than one or two dresses on a shopping trip. A department store buyer, on the other hand, often purchases hundreds of dresses (and mistakes may be very costly). A fourth difference is that *organizational decisions are sometimes more structured processes,* in which bids from competing suppliers are invited, and are to be based on a complex set of **specifications**. Such "specs" detail the exact product to be purchased and are designed by the buyer's DMU to reflect precisely the role the new machinery, for example, will perform in the production process. When complex purchases are being made, other provisions may also be built into the organization's purchase process. If a business purchases a new computer system, for example, employee training and service contracts are just two of the special postpurchase specifics likely to be agreed upon formally.

Exhibit 22-1 provides excerpts from an interview with Linda H., a buyer for a major discount department store chain. Her experiences are not meant to be representative of all buyers, but they do offer some interesting illustrations of overall purchasing experiences. As you read it, think about what is similar and what is different from consumer buying behavior.

EXHIBIT 22-1   **AN ORGANIZATIONAL BUYER REVEALS HER SECRETS**

The following is an excerpted interview with Linda H., a buyer of women's clothing for a major discount department store chain. Linda earned her undergraduate degree in education, then took her first job as a secretary in a prestigious department store. As she "became interested in the business," she took further college courses and store training programs. She now has 13 years of experience as a buyer, in three department store chains.

Q. *What were your impressions the first time you went out as a buyer?*

A. The first time I went as an associate buyer in infants' wear. The children's market is very conservative. People are nice, there's not a lot of pressure. Then I moved to ready-to-wear dresses. In ready-to-wear, the competition is much greater. People are a lot more aggressive . . . a lot more pressure filled, a lot crazier, a lot funnier, a lot more exciting. There's nobody like the dressmaker! You can have one dress resource or you can have five dress resources making the same dress—all within the same price range. And who you buy from is really the person with whom you develop a relationship.

Q. *Did you frequently have "straight rebuys"?*

A. Yes, in children's I'd say probably 70 percent was on straight rebuys. But not in ready-to-wear. Here, by and large, it's a new buy. You could buy 10 items and maybe 2 are reorder and you buy 8 new things. This means in ready-to-wear, you travel to market every month; in children's you travel only four times a year.

Q. *Where's the market?*

A. New York and California.

Q. *What types of dress marketers do you deal with?*

A. With the brand-name labels, the people are corporate types. It's when you're dealing with people that aren't labeled where you get the characters. And they can be wackos!

Q. *How do you deal with the wackos?*

A. Most of the wackos are probably very good. They're out to make money and that's what we're all in business for. But generally, they're willing to do anything you need to get business. And I'd say that 90 percent of them, as wacko as they are, are reliable and trustworthy. And 10 percent are not reliable—not somebody you would trust.

Continued

EXHIBIT 22-1   AN ORGANIZATIONAL BUYER REVEALS HER SECRETS CONTINUED

Q. *Is change in the retail structure creating a disruption?*

A. Oh yes! For instance, when you have mergers, like when Jordan Marsh and Maas Brothers merged, vendors say they don't make a buck. Say you were a manufacturer selling to both companies involved in the merger, your business will drop off afterward because the dress buyer isn't going to be accustomed—she used to buy for 20, now she's buying for 60 stores—she's not going to buy three times more than she bought before. It's frightening to a buyer. If you were only selling to one of the stores, it could go either way. If a vendor was doing business with Maas Brothers, and Maas will now be buying for Jordan Marsh and Maas, he'll benefit from it. If he was doing business with Jordan and the person at Maas is the person now buying for Jordan, he's gonna lose.

Q. *What is a "garmento"?*

A. I define the garmento as a sleaze who will do anything to get a sale. Will promise you anything.

Q. *Have you had experience with one?*

A. I've not done business with them, but I've met a couple. I wouldn't trust them. I have a very difficult time dealing with somebody I feel that way about. And sometimes you have to. Sometimes they have something that you need, so you have to interact with them.

Q. *How do they talk? Is it a line they have?*

A. Yes. "I've got the hottest thing," "It's on fire around the country," "You gotta get into it," "Maybe I can steal you some so you can get into it immediately." You know the type.

Q. *Does this immediately clue you?*

A. Yeah. If it's so hot, they're not going to steal me any. And they're not going to be able to get it to me immediately. Like the phone call I just received. He had something real hot that he could ship right now, would I be interested?

Q. *I take it there are buyers out there, or these guys wouldn't continue this approach?*

A. I don't know who would. I can't see very many buyers doing this. But I'll tell you what *does* happen in retail organizations. A lot of these garmentos become friendly with merchandise managers and vice presidents and presidents, so they don't have to deal with the buyers. They can dial up a merchandise manager and say, "My merchandise is really hot, can I ship some?" Some divisionals will say yes, and write up the order. So they get accustomed to succeeding in certain ways if they have a friend in the organization. It doesn't happen here, but it does happen in a lot of department stores.

Q. *As we've been talking I get a sense that dealing with sellers can be exciting . . .*

A. I really feel that you learn from everybody. You can get a lot of good ideas from these people. They deal with your business everyday, thousands of retailers they deal with. They get ideas, merchandising ideas, advertising ideas, so it's not only just shopping their line but listening to what they have to say. For example, when I bought sportswear, an old friend told me of a successful advertising event his firm did. I applied it to sportswear, and it was like record sales for our firm! It came from this angle I received from a vendor that I don't even do business with because he's not in my line. But he came up with a good idea.

EXHIBIT 22-1   AN ORGANIZATIONAL BUYER REVEALS HER SECRETS CONTINUED

Q. *If you had to deal with only the corporate people . . .*

A. That would not be real swift. Not that you can't learn from the corporate people, but it's a different type of learning. When I started I knew very little about buying dresses. I dealt with a substantial dress company, and the president of that company—a corporate-type person, a "don't buy if you don't want to"–type—he sat me down and I learned dresses from him. Every month I would visit and learn something from him and I was a success. He actually taught me how to buy dresses. So I've had to rely on different resources, corporate, wacko, whatever, to learn and to grow.

Q. *Is buying different with other product lines like hardware, domestics, or electronics?*

A. I think so; they have different situations. Their business is so planned out, they almost have to *marry* their resource. Also, I don't think that every buyer approaches things in the same way, even in ready-to-wear. I'm just giving you my approach to business.

Q. *Your job is one link in providing products to your firm—how do you see yourself in this chain?*

A. Middle portion of the chain. I look to give directions below. I look for certain types of direction from above. Not so much for the details of my assortment, but direction about how are we going to sell what I buy—the advertising, pricing strategy, what kind of fixtures I am going to have for my merchandise. All that will affect how I approach the market and what I buy. And then it's also my job to inform my divisional manager of what I see is important to market and what I think we could sell. And then it's actually his job to make sure the people under and over are aware of it.

Q. *So there's a smooth flow from top to bottom . . .*

A. No, it's not. There are many advantages working in our chain, but the flow is smoother in the major department stores. We run into a product presentation difference. In a department store atmosphere, the people working in the store—the link under me—it's their job to merchandise the product and to sell it. In a department store, those store people are striving to get to a higher position in the company. They're generally the best that college had to offer, and they want to become a buyer and to go up the corporate ladder. They take a little bit of training and they know what they're doing. They know stock turnover, they know on-order, they know markdown, markups, all this. Those people do a better job. When you go into our stores, there's not as much help as in the major department stores. They don't know what to do when the goods come in. And a lot of what I perceive it looking like when it hits the floor . . .

Q. *Is fiction?*

A. Right, it's definitely in my head. I can't go into a store and see that. So, going into a store in my organization is not the bright spot in my day . . . and it really whips me for a couple of days. . . . We spend a lot of time tracing my sell, going over assortments, what's it gonna look like in a C store, B store, and A store and you're all excited about it when you buy it and then all of a sudden, when I see it, any similarity is purely coincidental!

Continued

685

EXHIBIT 22-1   AN ORGANIZATIONAL BUYER REVEALS HER SECRETS CONTINUED

Store layouts do differ.

| EXHIBIT 22-1 | AN ORGANIZATIONAL BUYER REVEALS HER SECRETS CONTINUED |

Q. *What about price?*

A. Price is the bottom line in all negotiations. But there's something more important than price, and that is *value*. If that $70 item in our store is similar to what's carried in another store for $140, that's value. As far as negotiating for the lowest price, yes. I will fight and negotiate. And to do that intelligently, you have to know the market and what it's actually worth.

Q. *How do you judge quality? Higher price, higher quality?*

A. Not necessarily. That's how it should be, but not necessarily. You can go into a Fifth-Avenue store and spend $1000 on an outfit and get it home and see how it's made. I have merchandise at $24 that's made better than the $1000 outfit. The price should dictate the quality of the garment, but it's not what's happening in ready-to-wear. In fact, there's been many articles in magazines about that right now.

Q. *So how do you judge a product?*

A. On a new buy, it's almost a stab in the dark. I go out and shop better stores every week. I read fashion magazines and as many women's wear publications as I can get. I look and see what I could utilize from this information, then I go to market and look for it. I might not be able to do it in silk, but I may be able to do it in crepe-de-chine, and give the customer the same look. So, there's a lot of things that go into it. It's not just off-the-wall stab in the dark. Price is very important, quality is important, value is important.

The Nature of Organizations

The term **organization** refers to a group interacting together on the basis of shared identity and goals. In this regard, you may have heard the term "industrial buying" used synonymously with organizational buying. For our purposes, there is no major difference in terms, except that we must be clear that we are referring to many types of organizations, including (1) industrial firms; (2) governmental agencies; (3) nonprofit organizations, such as hospitals; (4) the service sector—banks, restaurants, and so on; and (5) retail stores. All have DMUs or centers that make purchasing decisions for their organizations. They often purchase in large quantities and fulfill other definitional characteristics of organizational buying outlined earlier.

There are, of course, differences in how different organizations do buy. However, in effect, the various entities that are grouped under organizational buying can be viewed as different market segments. Although any individual supplier may sell to several of these "segments," some products are so specialized as to be appropriate only for one.

Types of Buy Situations

One important distinction in organizational buying relates to the amount of past experience available for a purchase. Robinson, Faris, and Wind have categorized purchases into three types—straight rebuy, modified rebuy, and new buy.[5]

- The **straight rebuy** is a largely routine purchase. It involves frequently purchased items that have been purchased before by the organization. Information search and concern with specifications is minimal.
- The **modified rebuy** is also a routinized purchase; however, product specifications may have been changed or the organization has decided to change suppliers.
- The **new buy** is not a routine purchase. Since the item has never been purchased before by the organization, information search is high. Specifications must be researched and developed, and vendors must be evaluated.

After the new buy, if the vendor performs well and the product continues to meet needs, rebuys require very little further input by either the buyer or supplier. *Thus, in the rebuy stages it is difficult for competitors to dislodge an established vendor.* For this reason a new buy usually becomes the focal point for salespeople as they analyze the organizational buying process.

THE PROCESS OF ORGANIZATIONAL BUYING

Roles in the Buying Center

The process of organizational buying encompasses a number of actors on both the buying and selling side. On the buyer's side, the decision-making unit is often referred to as the **buying center**.[6] Webster and Wind have identified a number of functional roles associated with the buying center:

1. *Initiators*—those within the organization who first identify the need for a service or product.
2. *Influencers*—those who affect a purchase decision either indirectly or directly.
3. *Gatekeepers*—anyone who controls the flow of information into the buying center.
4. *Users*—those within the organization who will use the produce or service.
5. *Buyers*—those who will actually make the purchase.
6. *Deciders*—those who have the authority to decide on which supplier will provide the product or service.

This large number of roles within an organization can be a serious complicating factor for a new supplier or vendor. For example, notice that the buyers and deciders are at the bottom of the list. This suggests that they may enter the process at a later stage. When a supplier's salesperson contacts a purchasing agent (buyer), therefore, it is even possible that the supplier may have already been eliminated as a possible vendor because of decisions or preconditions set by other executives or scientists in the earlier stages of the purchasing decision process. Coupled with these various roles, the supplier must also deal with a formal organizational structure as exemplified by the traditional corporate organizational chart. In fact, this formal organizational chart may be all the supplier has when first contacting an organization in a new buy situation!

Tech Reps: An Innovative Sales Approach

According to one sales research firm, salespeople often reach only 3 out of 10 "influentials" involved in the average purchasing process. In addition, often purchasing agents themselves are not aware of some purchases by departments (especially in the case of research and development departments, where this information might lag for more than a year!).[7] To overcome these constraints, AmCast Industrial Corporation recently replaced its traditional sales force with college-educated technical representatives. The job of the new "tech reps" is to get involved in the decision-making process of their potential customers as early as possible. They are to contact engineering and design personnel at the target companies and find out what assistance they can give in designing new products. They are to try to get to know *everyone* within the organization and try to become "quasi-members" of the customer's team.[8] This is one step toward **relationship marketing**, in which suppliers and customers cooperate for long-term advantages for each. This approach recently led to the design of a new disk brake for General Motors and a substantial contract for AmCast.[9]

The "Buygrid/Buyphase" Model

Because of the complexity of organizational purchasing, marketers have relied on models for helping to identify roles, stages, and influences within the organizational purchasing process. One of the most widely used models is the Buygrid framework.[10] It relates the three types of buy situations discussed earlier—new buy, straight rebuy, and modified rebuy—to eight key "Buyphases." These are shown in Figure 22-1. Let's examine the framework briefly.

The process begins with the identification of the need for an item. This usually occurs in the using department, which provides a statement of the problem and a general description of the need to the buying center. Marketing research indicates that the sooner a supplier can get involved in the process, the more likely he or she will be selected to supply the needed item. For a new buy situation, it is difficult for the supplier to become involved at this stage unless one is already an "in" supplier. In that case, previous contacts and sales calls within the organization may help. The "in" supplier usually has an even greater advantage in the rebuy situations.

In stage 2, the using department puts together a description of the item and defines parameters. In stage 3, the buying center seeks information from outside sources, including suppliers. In these two stages, the "out" supplier (one currently

FIGURE 22-1 **Buygrid Framework for Organizational Buying**

	BUYCLASSES[a]		
BUYPHASES[b]	*New Task*	*Modified Rebuy*	*Straight Rebuy*
1. Recognition of a problem (need) 2. Determination of characteristics and quantity of needed item (internal) 3. Description of needed item to potential suppliers 4. Qualification of potential sources 5. Acquisition of proposals 6. Evaluation of proposals and selection of supplier(s) 7. Selection of an order routine 8. Performance feedback and evaluation			

[a]The most complex buying situations occur in the upper left portion of the BUYGRID matrix. Thus, a New Task in its initial phase of problem recognition generally represents the greatest difficulty for management.

[b]As Buyphases are completed, moving from phase 1 through phase 8, the process of "creeping commitment" occurs, and there is diminishing likelihood of new vendors gaining access to the buying situation.

Source: Adapted from Patrick J. Robinson, Charles Faris, and Yoram Wind, *Industrial Buying and Creative Marketing* (Boston: Allyn & Bacon, 1967), p. 14.

not selling to the organization) has greater opportunities to affect the decision process in all three buy situations. In stage 4, the search for potential sources, the buying organization decides which suppliers can meet the needs set forth in the previous stages. A marketer's reputation and any previous contact that the buying organization might have had with them are important.

Once the possible suppliers are identified, specific proposals and price quotations are sought in stage 5. In stage 6 the proposals are evaluated and a final decision is made. In stage 7, selection of an order routine, the buyer monitors the sending of the purchase order, the vendor's progress in filling the order, and internal reporting to the using department of progress by the vendor. Finally, in stage 8, the buying organization evaluates the performance of the purchased item. Service and other follow-up activities by the supplier are also evaluated. Satisfaction at this stage determines a supplier's future opportunities with the purchasing organization.

An Expanded Model

The Buygrid model is helpful in laying out basic stages, but does not detail some realistic influences and considerations. When we add these, the model appears

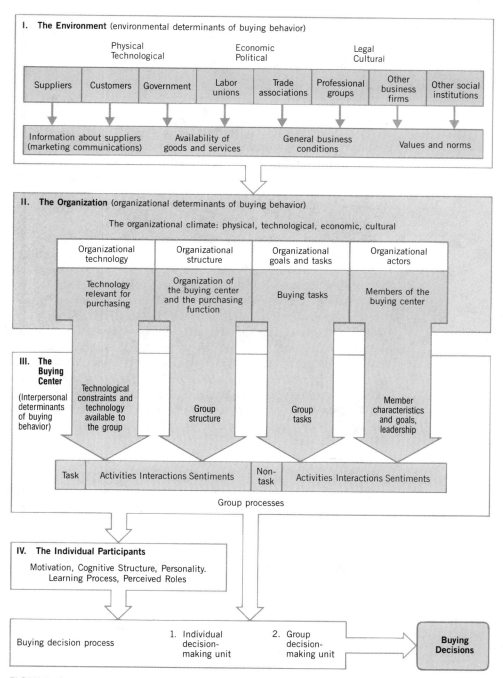

FIGURE 22-2 **A Model of Organizational Buying Behavior**

Source: From Frederick E. Webster and Yoram Wind, "A General Model for Understanding Organizational Buying Behavior," *Journal of Marketing,* Vol. 36, no. 2, 1972, p. 15.

to be more complex, but is actually much more realistic. Let's consider Figure 22-2, which presents a more general model developed by Webster and Wind. Notice that its major components (reading down) include the *environment*, the *organization*, the *buying center*, the *individuals*, and then the *decision process* itself.

As shown, there are many types of possible **environmental factors** that might impact organizational buying. Environmental determinants are external to the organization yet impact the purchase decision process, such as labor unions, governmental regulations, or the number of business competitors. In many respects, **organizational determinants** are the internal equivalents of environmental determinants. As those with business experience can testify, "organizational cultures" do exist: managers must make specific adaptations to work effectively within any given organization. These are unique to each organization and consist of relevant technology, structure, goals, and actors.

Within the buying center, **interpersonal determinants** are at work. These reflect social influences on the buying center's group activities, interactions, and feelings (sentiments) as members undertake buying tasks and other actions. Notice that the social influences do not just involve the entire group, but that subgroups (e.g., engineers versus accountants or friends versus a new manager) can also be extremely important. As shown in component IV, exactly who the **individual participants** are can also be extremely important. For example, Sherry Oliver might react positively to the technical presentation by Ajax Engineering, whereas George Wratney might push for a different supplier.

In sum, the process of organizational buying is complex. It includes individuals and small groups of people. Knowing how these people interact and what external and organizational constraints are affecting a decision is important. (If you would like to learn more about recent research in this area, please see Note 11.)

ORGANIZATIONAL BUYER AND SELLER BEHAVIOR

The Organizational Buyer

What about the person who is designated as a "buyer" for an organization? Our models to this point have stressed the overall buying center's decision-making process. There are, however, also *models that center on the behavior of the individual organizational buyer*. Perhaps the most widely used is that of Jagdish Sheth, shown in Figure 22-3. Although it does appear complex, it is helpful if we concentrate on the basic process. Note that the basic process consists of the central stages numbered: (1) Expectations, (2) Industrial Buying Process, and (3) Conflict Resolution. Significant substeps and influences are designated at each stage as (1a), (1b), (1c), and so forth. The strength of Sheth's model is that he focuses on the variables or stimuli that affect the behavior of individuals involved in the decision-making process.

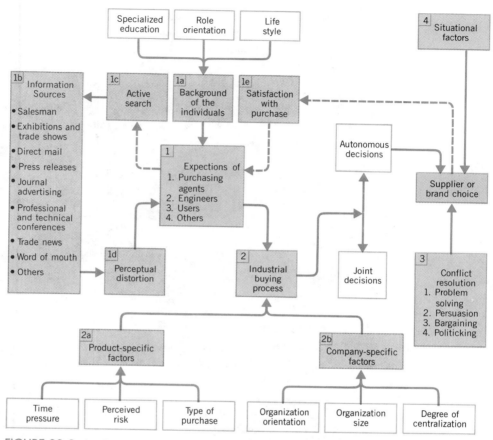

FIGURE 22-3 **An Integrative Model of Organizational Buying Behavior**

Source: From Jagdish N. Sheth, "A Model of Industrial Buyer Behavior," *Journal of Marketing*, Vol. 37, no. 4, 1973, p. 52.

Individual Differences in the Buying Center

Research has shown that individuals within any buying center are looking for different things when they are deciding about a purchase. For example, for a particular piece of machinery, the firm's purchasing agent's most important product attributes might be low price and economical delivery, while the engineer might seek high quality and standardized design, and the plant's operating department may be stressing durability, energy efficiency, and ease of servicing. This is the reason that stage (3), conflict resolution, occupies such a key role in Sheth's model (Figure 22-3).

Notice, however, that the seller isn't shown as having a very prominent role in Sheth's model, appearing only as one player in (1b). To focus more on the seller's role, let's examine the **"exchange model,"** developed by Thomas Bonoma, Gerald Zaltman, and Wesley Johnston, shown in Figure 22-4.[12] This model

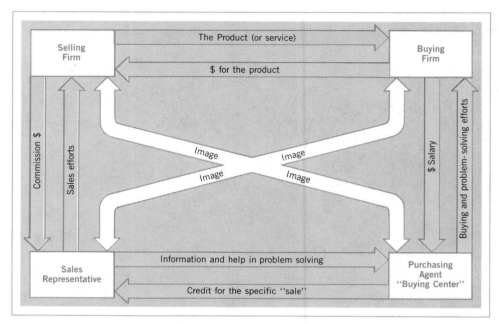

FIGURE 22-4 **The Industrial Buying Process as an Exchange**

Source: Adapted from Thomas Bonoma, Gerald Zaltman, and Wesley Johnston, *Industrial Buying Behavior,* Marketing Science Institute, Cambridge, Mass., 1977, p. 27.

focuses on the *exchanges* taking place between the buying organization and the selling organization. Exchange takes place at the primary level of the **buyer/seller dyad**.

Focus on the dyad rather than the individual demonstrates the interrelationships that are an integral part of the purchase process. As Figure 22-4 illustrates, the purchasing agent and sales representative are (1) each part of their respective organizations (exchanging work for money) as well as (2) separate entities who negotiate help and credit among themselves. In addition, they arrange for the top flows in Figure 22-4, in which different departments of the organizations actually deliver goods and services, and payments for them. Notice how this look at the process allows us to appreciate how the details of transactions (e.g., price) are influenced by other factors at work within the dyad.

The Seller

What are the key issues that affect the salesperson in the organizational buying context? Many of the points presented in Chapter 16, "Salespersons' Influences on Consumer Behavior," are also appropriate for the organizational context. The major difference is that in this case the *customer's perspective* is that of an organizational buying center, and the salesperson needs to adapt to this.

TABLE 22-1 HOW PRIORITY SALES SKILLS DIFFER BY CUSTOMERS

Priority Skills for Distributors' Salespersons	Priority Skills for Manufacturers' Salespersons
1. Time management habits.	1. Skill in listening
2. Tempering optimism with reality.	2. Ability to establish goals.
3(T). Skill in solving customer problems.	3. Effective communication.
3(T). Ability to field questions.	4. Develop continuing rapport.
3(T). Develop continuing rapport.	5. Time management habits.
3(T). Effective communication.	6. Apply judicious judgment.
3(T). Courteous communication.	7. High ethical standards.
3(T). Skill in listening.	8. Ability to field questions.

Source: Adapted from results reported in James R. Moore, Donald Eckrich, and Lorry T. Carlson, "A Hierarchy of Industrial Selling Competencies," *Journal of Marketing Education,* Spring 1986, pp. 79–88.

The importance of the types of customers on the selling task is nicely illustrated in Table 22-1.[13] This summarizes a study of which sales skills are most important, according to industrial salespersons themselves. Notice that the priorities given by salespersons who work for manufacturers are different from those who work for industrial distributors. This is due to the differences in the sales tasks that each type of salesperson performs, and the customers on whom he or she calls. The manufacturer's salesperson will typically be selling to either larger businesses or distributors, sometimes with customized products. Order quantities can be high, and time may stretch out before a decision is made by the buyer. A distributor's salesperson, on the other hand, is likely to represent many more products (maybe in the thousands), produced by many manufacturers. He or she contacts many more customers, perhaps every factory in a given geographical area. Customers may order from catalog books, especially for smaller items of a standardized nature. For many distributor salespersons, then, the emphasis is more on "servicing" accounts than on "selling" to them.

The Value of Trust

Swan and Trawick have examined how industrial salespeople gain the trust of their customers.[14] As indicated by the high ranking of "develop continuing rapport" in Table 22-1, the issue of trust is a key determinant of success in establishing long-term relationships between buyers and suppliers. **Customer trust** develops from five attributes of a salesperson: *dependability, honesty, competence, customer orientation,* and *likability.* The more a salesperson exhibits these five characteristics, the more he or she is perceived as trustworthy. Salespeople report that when they are perceived as trustworthy, the relationship with customers is more open and less strained. This is especially helpful for "accessibility," as in making appointments or making product suggestions to the purchasing agent.

Establishing trustworthiness takes time, and occurs place over a series of sales calls. Also, after an initial sale, the postsale follow-up allows the salesperson to prove his or her trustworthiness by ensuring timely delivery of an order or by making sure that the customer's order is not "short-shipped" (shipping a lesser quantity than ordered). These kinds of concrete demonstrations of trust can be beneficial to both buyer and seller by turning a new buy situation into a less time-consuming (and less competitive!) rebuy situation.

Since many organizational purchases turn into rebuy or repeat purchases, the establishment of a trusting relationship can save time and money for both the buying and selling organizations.[15] For the buyer, for example, it can reduce the risk of purchasing a large quantity of a product which is inferior or not delivered on time. *Risk reduction* on large purchases can be a significant factor in the decision process.

Let's listen in again on the retail clothes buyer, Linda H., and see what she reports about trust in buyer/supplier relationships:

Q. *What are the characteristics of a trustworthy supplier?*

A. *Honesty.* He's up-front. *Follow-through.* He takes an interest in the account and how it's performing. He's interested in us because we're partners and it's profitable for both companies. He *services the account.* He makes sure that reorders are available if the item sells well. He fights for deliveries on time and for me to get the lowest possible price.

Q. *What do you do to encourage "trust" from a supplier?*

A. I lay my cards on the table. Since I'm not locked into a resource [supplier] structure, I have a free hand with resources. When you're talking to a resource, you sense that honesty is present in the relationship. Trust is a growing process and through experience you learn who you can't trust.

Ethics: A Serious Concern

Related to the issue of trust is concern for **ethical behavior** among organizational buyers. Ethical behavior refers to actions that are carried out in accordance with a personal code of justice and morality—a code that also does not violate acceptable standards of society as a whole.

In any exchange relationship, we should recognize that both the buyer and the seller hold certain *expectations.* Basically, the buyer trusts the seller to deliver a product or service in a timely fashion and to bill at the price agreed upon. The seller also trusts the buyer to honor negotiated prices and to keep confidences about the purchase negotiations.

Because of severe competition, however, many questionable practices can arise on the part of both sellers *and* buyers. In one survey, for example, an overriding concern about problems was discovered.[16] Purchasing managers and sales managers alike expressed an interest in ethical practices. Padding expense accounts and giving gifts to make a sale were two issues of concern to both sides.

Trust and ethical issues thus are critical to the purchase process; however, in the actual course of conducting business, there are often no clear and easy solutions to the problems that arise concerning these issues. Awareness of the possibility of problems and practice in resolving hypothetical situations is perhaps all that can be suggested for business professionals. (If you would like to read more about these issues, you may wish to begin with Note 17.)

 ## SUMMARY

The Context of Organizational Buying

Although organizational buying behavior displays both similarities and differences when compared to individual consumer buying behavior, it has been treated in this chapter as primarily a separate activity. A key characteristic of this topic is that the organizational buyer acts within the context of a larger group—the organization—that affects how and why decisions are made. The primary objective of this chapter was to understand and characterize organizational buying, both as a process and as buyer behavior.

The first section of the chapter defined organizational buying in terms of similarities and differences with consumer behavior as represented in the rest of this text. Similarities included the meeting of needs through the purchase process and the search for information about products that would satisfy that need. The key differences noted were that the organizational buyer is not usually the end user of the product and that the purchase decision within an organization is often made by a group of people. This section also reviewed the types of organizations that make purchases and, in effect, provided a possible segmentation scheme for the market. We then examined the three types of buy situations: (1) new buy, (2) straight rebuy, and (3) modified rebuy.

The Process of Organizational Buying

In the next section, we discussed the various models that are used to describe what goes on within the decision-making unit in a buying center. They ranged from a description of the roles and stages in the process and how they are affected by the buying situation, Buygrid/Buyphase, to a more complex model by Webster and Wind that included variables both internal and external to the organization. Other more recent models were also discussed to focus on the personal social networks within the organization that may affect the buying process.

Organizational Buyer and Seller Behavior

The organizational buyer and seller were highlighted in a separate section. The psychology of the decision maker was cited as a fundamental factor in an organizational purchase decision, much as it is in an individual consumer purchase decision. Again, however, the joint nature of decision process causes a variety of other influences to come into play. A model was presented to illustrate the process from the individual perspective. A second model included the seller as a part of the purchase or buying dyad and focused on the nature of the exchanges that are taking place. In the final section of the chapter, we examined the role of the seller. Here we noted some of the priority skills needed for selling to organizations, and then discussed the need for trust in the relationship between the members of the dyad, and ethical behavior in organizational buying.

KEY TERMS

organizational buying

decision-making unit (DMU)

specifications

organization

straight rebuy

modified rebuy

new buy

buying center

relationship marketing

environmental factors

organizational determinants

interpersonal determinants

individual participants

"exchange model"

buyer/seller dyad

customer trust

ethical behavior

REVIEW QUESTIONS AND EXPERIENTIAL EXERCISES

[E = Application extension or experiential exercise]

1. Summarize the major similarities and differences between consumer buying and organizational buying.

2. Suggest examples of the three types of organizational purchases—straight rebuy, modified rebuy, and new buy. Indicate the product, the purchasing agency, and any situational circumstances that might cause the purchase to be classed in one category and not in another.

3. Discuss how environmental factors—those outside of the organization—can affect an organizational purchase.

4. Why is the behavior of individuals such an important part of understanding what goes on within the buying center? Discuss in terms of both individuals and dyads.

5. How does trust enter into a typical organizational buying situation?

6. Can you identify organizational buying situations in which ethical issues might arise? Such situations often appear in the media; can you think of a recent prominent case?

[E] 7. In your library find the *Standard Industrial Classification Manual* and list the major divisions. Then locate the *Census of Manufacturers* and choose five products that might be sold in an organizational buying situation. List the value of product shipped and other geographic (for your region) information about those products.

[E] 8. Consult the following articles about DMUs and prepare a brief report about the main points of each article:
   a. Anita M. Kennedy, "The Complex Decision to Select a Supplier: A Case Study," *Industrial Marketing Management*, Volume 12, 1983, pp. 45–56.
   b. Jim Holden, "Selling to Buying Committees: Separating the Rubber Stamps in a Politically Charged Environment," *Business Marketing*, December 1983, pp. 30–36.

[E] 9. In your library's periodicals section, consult several different magazines. Find examples of ads that are innovative and others that are more traditional. How do the appeals of the two types of ads differ? Which ads might be most successful? Why?

[E] 10. Interview a purchasing agent or organizational buyer in your community. They can be employed by manufacturing, service, or retail entities, but don't forget governmental organizations such as schools, county/city agencies, or hospitals. Concentrate your questions on who they consult when making buying decisions, what kind of information they collect and from where, and how a final decision is made.

[E] 11. Locate a formal organizational chart for a business or agency. Your own college or university might be an interesting example. Select a particular purchase situation and try to decide where you might find initiators, influencers, gatekeepers, users, buyers, and deciders within the organization. Imagine that you are a salesperson for that product, what would your plan of action be?

[E] 12. Use your library's reference section to locate articles on business ethics written within the past few years. Read several that are likely to deal with issues that arise between organizational purchasers and salespersons (alternatively, you may wish to consult the Laczniak and Murphy book referenced in Note 17, as a source for this reading). Prepare a brief report on your findings.

Notes

Here it is—the section you have all been waiting for! Welcome to the fascinating world of *Notes!* Here you will find the references from which the findings and reports in the book have been drawn. Beyond this, however, you will also find pathways for further reading in areas that may be particularly interesting to you. At some points we offer brief extensions of text discussions, at some points we offer specific answers to questions raised in the text, and at some points we provide extensive reading lists that trace the developments of thoughts and findings on key topics in consumer behavior. Therefore, if you are able to spend some time looking through the relevant notes for each chapter, you will see numerous opportunities for customizing your learning experience, and reading further about both concepts and marketing applications.

Please be aware that this "Notes" section is organized by chapters, so be sure that you have the correct chapter heading when searching for a particular note number! Finally, the references have been listed with the assumption that you will have access to a college library that possesses the source materials. As you will see, two of the most commonly cited sources are the publications *Advances in Consumer Research* and *AMA Educators' Proceedings,* which are published on a yearly basis. In the event your library wishes to order any volumes, the former is published by the Association for Consumer Research, with offices in Provo, Utah (telephone 801/378-2080); the latter is published by the American Marketing Association, with offices in Chicago (telephone 312/648-0536).

As you will find if you search, this section holds the keys to hours of (thrills?) (fun?) (mild pleasure?) productive reading and engaging thought. Enjoy!

Chapter 1:   Consumer Behavior as a Body of Knowledge

1. GNP and consumer spending are estimated from figures provided by the U.S. Department of Commerce. Calculations were performed by this author. Readers should note that these numbers do not include spending for purchases of used goods.
2. Stephen Barlas, "Researchers Rally 'Round Customer Focus," *Marketing News,* January 2, 1989, pp. 46–47.

Chapter 2:   Marketers' and Consumers' Views of Consumer Behavior

1. "The Gravyest?" *Sales & Marketing Management,* February 6, 1979, p. 19; Nancy Giges, "Smooth & Easy Brand's Short Life Was Anything But . . . ," *Advertising Age,* September 10, 1979, pp. 3ff.
2. Adam Smith, *The Wealth of Nations,* 1776 (quoted in 1937 reprinting), as cited in Dick Berry, "The Marketing Concept Revisited." *Marketing News,* July 18, 1988, p. 26.
3. The concept of the marketing mix was originally proposed by James Culliton of the Harvard Business School and then developed and presented to the field in a classic article by Neil H. Borden, "The Concept of the Marketing Mix," *Journal of Advertising Research,* June 1964, pp. 2–7.
4. The "4 P's" framework is another classic presentation in the field. Developed by E. Jerome McCarthy, it appeared in the first edition of his best-selling text, *Basic Marketing: A Managerial Approach* (Homewood, Ill.: Richard D. Irwin, 1960), pp. 45–48.
5. Kim Foltz, "Marketer of the Year: Ford's Donald Petersen," *Adweek,* August 3, 1987, pp. 12–13.
6. William F. Gloede, "Here to Stay," *Advertising Age,* August 24, 1987, p. 1; and William Gloede, "Today's Price Hike Cuts Sales," *Advertising Age,* October 8, 1984, p. 102.
7. David Arnold, "Video Puts Muscle into Sales Efforts," *Advertising Age,* October 11, 1984, pp. 48–49; and Cara S. Trager, "Video Catalogs a Moving Experience," *Advertising Age,* October 26, 1987, p. s-3.
8. Alice Z. Cuneo, "FCB Creativity Bears Fruit," *Advertising Age,* July 6, 1987, p. 25.
9. William L. Wilkie, "A New Framework for Assessing the Context of Marketing Decisions—The '5 C's'," working paper, Graduate School of Business, University of Florida, Gainesville, Fla., 1985.
10. Ralph Gray, "Future Shock: Too Many Autos, Not Enough Buyers," *Marketing Week,* June 22, 1987, p. 17; and Cleveland Horton and Raymond Serafin, "Automotive Doomsday?" *Advertising Age,* February 22, 1988, p. 36.
11. Jolie Solomon and Carol Hymowitz, "P&G Makes Changes . . . ," *The Wall Street Journal,* August 11, 1987, pp. 14.
12. Arthur Buckler, "Holly Farms' Marketing Error . . . ," *The Wall Street Journal,* February 9, 1988, p. 36.
13. Susan Harrigan, "How One Motor-Home Dealer Accelerates in Midst of Slump," *The Wall Street Journal,* June 8, 1981, p. 23.
14. "Marketing-Oriented Lever Uses Research to Capture Bigger Dentifrice Market Shares," *Marketing News,* February 10, 1978, p. 9.
15. David Kiley, "Small Firms Grow Strong on Steady Diet of Data," *Marketing Week,* May 16, 1988, pp. 17ff.
16. T. O. Stanley, E. T. Garman, and R. D. Brown, "Test of Consumer Competencies," in *Manual of Directions* (Bensenville, Ill.: Scholastic Testing Service, 1976).

Chapter 3:   Aggregate Perspectives of Consumer Behavior

1. The story of the development of Pampers is told in "Consumer Choice, the Driving Force of a Market Economy," published by Procter & Gamble, Inc., Cincinnati, Ohio, 1977. The company's estimate of the size of the market was that there were more than 15 billion diaper changes per year in the United States! How successful was the new product? Within six years after its national introduction, Pampers was being worn by half the babies in the United States!
2. For an interesting discussion of fertility and issues in forecasting it, see Jane Newitt, "How to Forecast Births (and Be Right)," *American Demographics* (January 1985), pp. 30 ff; the data presented in Table 3-2 represent calculations by the author from data appearing in the *Statistical Abstract of the United States,* 1988 (Washington, D.C.: U.S. Government Printing Office 1988), and "Projections of the Population of the United States, by Age, Sex, and Race, 1983–2080," *Current Population Reports,* Series P-25, #952.
3. Randolph E. Schmid, "Statistics: National Death Rate Drops to Record Low," *Associated Press* Wire Service, February 8, 1985.

4. *Statistical Abstract of the United States, 1988* (Washington, D.C.: U.S. Government Printing Office, 1988), p. 10.

5. Table 3-3 contains author's calculations based upon data presented in Fabian Linden, "Who Will Buy? A Preview of Tomorrow's Customers," *Progressive Grocer*, August 1979, pp. 85–89; and the *Statistical Abstract of the United States, 1988*, p. 15.

6. Points in the table are based on discussions in a variety of sources, most prominently, Landon Y. Jones, *Great Expectations: America and the Baby Boom Generation* (New York: Coward, McCann & Geoghegan, 1980).

7. Richard L. Strout, "Old Soon to Outnumber Young," *Christian Science Monitor* Service, August 10, 1982.

8. The following discussion is based on a number of sources discussing population and aging statistics. See Louise B. Russell, *The Baby Boom Generation and the Economy* (Washington, D.C.: The Brookings Institution, 1983); Conrad Taeuber, "A Changing America," *American Demographics*, January 1979, pp. 9–15; and Landon Jones, *Great Expectations*.

9. Bryant Robey, "Busters Will Be Wealthier and Wiser Than Boomers," *Marketing Week*, October 3, 1988, p. 16.

10. Figure 3-1 is adapted from Taeuber, "A Changing America," p. 11.

11. "Fewer Apply to Top Colleges in 1989," *Associated Press*, February 9, 1989; Brad Edmondson, "Colleges Conquer the Baby Bust," *American Demographics* (September 1987), pp. 27ff; Ian R. Stewart and Donald G. Dickason, "Hard Times Ahead," *American Demographics* (June 1979), pp. 12–24; William Bulkeley, "Baby Bust Enrollment Drop Seen Having an Uneven Effect," *The Wall Street Journal*, December 14, 1982, p. 33.

12. Diane Chun, "Can You Read This?" *Gainesville Sun*, August 1, 1982, p. H-1.

13. The answers to the mobility questions are (1) 45 million, (2) the average mobility rate has been roughly constant for the past 35 years, (3) about 1 in 6 American consumers will move in any one year, (4) 1 out of every 2 consumers will move at least once in any five-year period, (5) the average person will move about 12 times in his or her lifetime! For further reading, see John Gottko and Paul Sauer, "Toward Development of a Model of the Mediating Effects of Household Geographic Mobility on Consumption, Patronage, and Social Status Mobility," *Advances in Consumer Research*, Vol. 16 (1989), pp. 81–84; John Gottko and Paul Sauer, "Household Geographic Mobility and the Impact on Macro Market Segments," *Advances in Consumer Research*, Vol. 16 (1989), pp. 85–92; and James N. Morgan, "A Conditional Analysis of Movers' Housing Responses," *Advances in Consumer Research*, Vol. 16 (1989), pp. 93–104.

14. Ben Simon, "Success Comes in Numbers," *Advertising Age*, July 20, 1981, pp. S–18 ff.

15. *Statistical Abstract of the United States, 1988*, p. 20; see also Bryant Robey, "Smaller Populations Expected for Industrial States," *Marketing Week*, February 13, 1989, p. 48.

16. Data in this section are based on *Statistical Abstract of the United States, 1988*, p. 43; "One Family in Four Has a Single Parent," *Associated Press Wire Service*, May 15, 1985; "Households Change in New Census Data," *Advertising Age* (April 1982, p. 64; Cheryl Russell, "Inside the Shrinking Household," *American Demographics*, October 1981, pp. 28–29; and Arthur J. Norton and Paul C. Glick, "What's Happening to Households?" *American Demographics* (March 1979), pp. 19–23.

17. *Statistical Abstract of the United States, 1988*, p. 40.

18. *Statistical Abstract of the United States, 1988*, p. 84; James A. Weed, "Divorce: Americans' Style," *American Demographics*, pp. 36–37; "Openers," *American Demographics*, October 1981, pp. 11–12.

19. *Statistical Abstract*, pp. 48–50; Peter Francese, "One-Parent Families Joining a Crowd," *Advertising Age*, August 2, 1984, p. 36.

20. "Bargain-Priced Census Data a Boon to Consumer, Market Researchers," *Marketing News*, May 1981, p. 14. Also "Inside the Board," *American Demographics*, September 1981, pp. 38–39. For detailed marketing discussions, see John W. McCann and David J. Reibstein, "Forecasting the Impact of Socioeconomic and Demographic Change on Product Demand," *Journal of Marketing Research*, Vol. 22 (November 1985), pp. 415 ff; and Louis G. Pol, "Marketing and the Demographic Perspective," *Journal of Consumer Marketing*, Vol. 3 (Winter 1986), pp. 57–66.

21. "The Changing American Family and Its Effect on Real Estate," *Real Estate Today*, June 1981, pp. 52–55.

22. Richard Dearworth, "Setting Your Sites," *American Demographics*, February 1979, pp. 21–23; Martin L. Cohen, "Getting to Know You," *American Demographics* (January 1979), pp. 17–21.

23. Christy Marshall, "PRIZM Adds Zip to Consumer Research," *Advertising Age*, November 1980, p. 22.

24. Daniel Finlay, "Demographic Editions," *American Demographics* (November 1980), pp. 46–47.

Chapter 4:   Market Segmentation

1. Raymond Serafin, "How GM Is Shifting Gears," *Advertising Age,* January 4, 1988, pp. 1 ff.

2. Much of the material in this chapter is based on longer discussions in other works by the author and his colleagues. See especially William L. Wilkie and Joel B. Cohen, "An Overview of Market Segmentation: Behavioral Concepts and Research Approaches" (Cambridge, Mass.: Marketing Science Institute Report 77-105, June 1977); and Dipankar Chakravarti, Philip E. Hendrix, and William L. Wilkie, *Market Segmentation Research,* Volumes I and II (Palo Alto, CA: EPRI, 1987).

3. Wendell R. Smith, "Product Differentiation and Market Segmentation as Alternative Marketing Strategies," *Journal of Marketing,* July 1956, pp. 3–8. For an interesting further discussion, see also Peter R. Dickson and James L. Ginter, "Market Segmentation, Product Differentiation, and Market Strategy," *Journal of Marketing,* Vol. 51 (April 1987), pp. 1–10.

4. George S. Day, "Strategic Market Analysis and Definition: An Integrated Approach," *Strategic Management Journal,* Vol. 2, (July–September 1981), pp. 281–299. See also Richard D. Czerniawski, "Cluster Marketing: An Alternative Approach to Marketing Planning and Implementation," *Journal of Consumer Marketing,* Vol. 3 (Spring 1986), pp. 81–86.

5. Nelson Foote, "Market Segmentation as a Competitive Strategy," in Leo Bogart (ed.), *Current Controversies in Marketing Research* (Chicago: Markham, 1969), pp. 129–139. Segmentation is also an important issue in public policy. See, for example, Christine Moorman and Linda Price, "Consumer Policy Remedies and Consumer Segment Interactions," Working Paper, University of Pittsburgh, 1989.

6. John Koten, "Upheaval in Middle-Class Market Forces Changes in Selling Strategies," *The Wall Street Journal,* March 13, 1987, p. 21. See also Kenneth D. Bahn and Kent Granzin, "Alternative Means of Market Segmentation in the Restaurant Industry," *AMA Educators' Proceedings,* (1986), pp. 321–326.

7. Alvin Achenbaum, "Round Research Pegs in Square Marketing Holes," *Marketing Week,* May 16, 1988, p. 12. See also Peter J. Danaher, "A Log-Linear Model for Predicting Magazine Audiences," *Journal of Marketing Research,* Vol. 25 (November 1988), pp. 356–362.

8. James Cox, "Automakers Now Turn to Women," *USA Today,* June 17, 1988, p. B-1; Janet Neiman, "Infiltrating the Women's Market," *Adweek,* July 6, 1987, pp. 18–22. Age is another demographic measure frequently used for segmentation. For recent research findings on older consumers, for example, see Warren A. French and Richard Fox, "Segmenting the Senior Citizen Market," *Journal of Consumer Marketing,* Vol. 2 (Winter 1985), pp. 61–74; Alan J. Greco, "The Fashion-Conscious Elderly: A Viable, But Neglected Market Segment," *Journal of Consumer Marketing,* Vol. 3 (Fall 1986), pp. 71–76; James R. Lumpkin, "Shopping Orientation Segmentation of the Elderly Consumer," *Journal of the Academy of Marketing Science,* Vol. 13 (Spring 1985), pp. 272–289; Don R. Rahtz, M. Joseph Sirgy, and H. Lee Meadow, "Elderly Life Satisfaction and Television Viewership: An Exploratory Study," *Advances in Consumer Research,* Vol. 15 (1988), pp. 141–145; Benny Barak, Barbara B. Stern, and Stephen J. Gould, "Ideal Age Concepts: An Exploration," *Advances in Consumer Research,* Vol. 15 (1988), pp. 146–152; William Lazer, "Dimensions of the Mature Market," *Journal of Consumer Marketing,* Vol. 3 (Summer 1986), pp. 23–34; Ganesan Visvabharathy and David R. Rink, "The Elderly: Still the 'Invisible and Forgotten' Market Segment," *Journal of the Academy of Marketing Science,* Vol. 13 (Fall 1985), pp. 71–100; Ruth B. Smith, George P. Moschis, and Roy Moore, "Effects of Advertising on the Elderly Consumer: An Investigation of Social Breakdown Theory," *AMA Educators' Proceedings* (1984), pp. 1–5; Louise A. Heslop, "Cohort Analysis of the Expenditure Patterns of the Elderly," *Advances in Consumer Research,* Vol. 14 (1987), pp. 553–557; and Mariea Grubbs Hoy and Raymond P. Fisk, "Older Consumers and Services; Implications for Marketers," *Educators' Proceedings* (1985), pp. 50–55.

9. Laurie P. Cohen, "Slowdown in Advertising to Blacks Strains Black Ad Firms and Media," *The Wall Street Journal,* March 23, 1988, p. 27.

10. "Monitoring Hispanic Minds," *Marketing Week,* March 14, 1988, p. 29.

11. Bryant Robey, "California's Growth Now Comes from Abroad," *Marketing Week,* May 22, 1989, p. 44.

12. Jack Fuerer, "To Segment or Not to Segment?" *Marketing Week,* April 11, 1988, p. 17; Jose deCorboa, "More Firms Court Hispanic Consumers—But Find Them a Tough Market to Target," *The Wall Street Journal,* February 18, 1988, p. 25.

13. Michel J. Bergier, "Predictive Validity of Ethnic Identification Measures: An Illustration of the English/French Classification Dilemma in Canada," *Journal of the Academy of Marketing Science,* Vol. 14, no. 2 (Summer 1986), pp. 37–42. See also Chankon Kim, Michel Laroche, and Brenda Lee, "An Empirical Study of the Relationship Between Ethnicity and Leisure Participation,"

Working Paper, Concordia University, Montreal, February 1988; Jean M. Lefebvre, "Preferences of Nationalists and Assimilationists For Ethnic Goods: An Experiment with French-Canadians," *Advances on Consumer Research,* Vol. 14 (1985), pp. 497–501; Michel Laroche, "Consumer Research on French-Canadians: Historical Perspectives and Methodological Issues," in Chin Tiong Tan and Jagdish Sheth (eds.), *Historical Perspectives in Consumer Research: National and International Perspectives,* National University of Singapore (1985), pp. 37–41; and Charles Schaninger, Jacques Bourgeois, and W. Christian Buss, "French-English Canadian Subcultural Consumption Differences," *Journal of Marketing,* Vol. 49 (Spring 1985), pp. 82–92.

14. For general background research on race and ethnic groups, see Milton J. Yinger, "Ethnicity," *Annual Review of Psychology,* Vol. 11, pp. 151–180. For historical background in marketing, see Frederick D. Sturdivant, "Subculture Theory: Poverty, Minorities and Marketing," in S. Ward and T. Robertson (eds.), *Consumer Behavior: Theoretical Sources* (Englewood Cliffs, NJ: Prentice Hall, 1973), pp. 469–520. See also Melanie Wallendorf and Michael Reilly, "Ethnic Migration, Assimilation and Consumption," *Journal of Consumer Research,* Vol. 10 (December 1983), pp. 293–302; Elizabeth C. Hirschman, "American Jewish Ethnicity: Its Relationship to Some Selective Aspects of Consumer Behavior," *Journal of Marketing,* Vol. 45 (Summer 1981), pp. 102–110; Thomas Ness and Melvin Stith, "Middle-Class Values in Blacks and Whites," in R. Pitts and A. Woodside (eds.), *Personal Values and Consumer Psychology* (Lexington, Mass.: D. C. Heath, 1984), pp. 231–237; Ronald E. Goldsmith, J. Dennis White and Melvin T. Stith, "Values of Middle-Class Blacks and Whites: A Replication and Extension," *Psychology & Marketing,* Vol. 4 (Summer 1987), pp. 135–144; Humberto Valencia, "Developing an Index to Measure Hispanicness," *Advances in Consumer Research,* Vol. 12 (1985), pp. 118–121; Joel Saegert, Robert Hoover, and Marye T. Hilger, "Characteristics of Mexican-American Consumers," *Journal of Consumer Research,* Vol. 12 (June 1985), pp. 104–109; Rohit Deshpande, Wayne Hoyer, and Naveen Donthu, "The Intensity of Ethic Affiliation: A Study of the Sociology of Hispanic Consumption," *Journal of Consumer Research,* Vol. 13 (September 1986), pp. 214–220; Ronald J. Faber, Thomas C. O'Guinn, and John McCarty, "Ethnicity, Acculturation, and the Importance of Product Attributes," *Psychology & Marketing,* Vol. 4 (Summer 1987), pp. 121–134; Robert E. Wilkes and Humberto Valencia, "Shopping-Related Characteristics of Mexican-Americans and Blacks," *Psychology & Marketing,* Vol. 3 (Winter 1986), pp. 247–260; Thaddeus H. Spratlen and Pravat K. Choudhury, "Political/Ethnic Issues in Marketing Cosmetics to Black Consumers," *AMA Educators' Proceedings* (1987), pp. 177–182; and Sigfredo A. Hernandez and Carol J. Kaufman, "Coupon Use Differences Between Hispanics and Anglos: Barrio and Anglo Neighborhood Samples," *AMA Educators' Proceedings* (1989), pp. 233–238.

15. For excellent overviews of this approach, see Joseph T. Plummer, "The Concept and Application of Life Style Segmentation," *Journal of Marketing,* Vol. 38 (1974), pp. 33–37; and William D. Wells and Stephen C. Cosmas, "Life Styles," in R. Ferber (ed.), *Selected Aspects of Consumer Behavior* (Washington, D.C.: U.S. Government Printing Office, 1977), pp. 299–316. For more recent discussions, debates, and findings, see John L. Lastovicka and E. H. Bonfield, "Exploring the Nomological Validity of Life Style Types," *Advances in Consumer Research,* Vol. 7 (1980) pp. 466–472; John L. Lastovicka, "On the Validation of Lifestyle Traits: A Review and Illustration," *Journal of Marketing Research,* Vol. 19 (February 1982), pp. 126–138; Stephen C. Cosmas, "Life Styles and Consumption Patterns," *Journal of Consumer Research,* Vol. 8 (March 1982), pp. 453–455; W. Thomas Anderson, Jr., and Linda L. Golden, "Lifestyle and Psychographics: A Critical Review and Recommendation," *Advances in Consumer Research,* Vol. 11 (1984), pp. 405–411; William D. Wells, "Attitudes and Behavior: Lessons from the Needham Life Style Study," *Journal of Advertising Research,* Vol. 25 (February–March 1985), pp. 40–44; and Ernest Dichter, "Whose Lifestyle Is It Anyway?" *Psychology & Marketing,* Vol. 3 (Fall 1986), pp. 151–164.

16. A detailed description of these findings is provided in Sunil Mehrotra and William D. Wells, "Psychographics and Buyer Behavior: Theory and Recent Empirical Findings," in A. Woodside, J. Sheth and P. Bennett (eds.), *Consumer and Industrial Buying Behavior* (New York: Elsevier/North Holland, 1977), pp. 54–55.

17. William D. Wells "Psychographics: A Critical Review," *Journal of Marketing Research,* Vol. 12 (May 1975), pp. 196–213. See also John J. Burnett, "Psychographic and Demographic Characteristics of Blood Donors," *Journal of Consumer Research,* Vol. 8 (June 1981), pp. 62–67; Marvin E. Goldberg, "Identifying Relevant Psychographic Segments: How Specifying Product Functions Can Help," *Journal of Consumer Research,* Vol. 3 (December 1977), pp. 163–169; Alfred S. Boote, "Interactions in Psychographics Segmentation: Implications for Advertising," *Journal of Advertising,* Vol. 13, no. 2 (1984); Ralph W. Jackson, Stephen W. McDaniel, and C. P. Rao, "Food Shopping and Preparation: Psychographic Differences of Working Wives and Housewives," *Jour-*

nal of Consumer Research, Vol. 12, no. 1 (June 1985), pp. 110–113; and Jack A. Lesser and Marie Adele Hughes, "The Generalizability of Psychographic Market Segments Across Geographic Locations," *Journal of Marketing,* Vol. 50 (January 1986), pp. 18–27.

18. Two early papers credited with laying the foundations for psychographics research were written in 1966, one by Edgar Pessemier and Douglas Tigert and the other by Clark Wilson, a research director at a major advertising agency. See Sunil Mehrotra and William D. Wells, "Psychographics and Buyer Behavior: Theory and Recent Empirical Findings," in Arch G. Woodside, Jagdish N. Sheth, and Peter D. Bennett (eds.), *Consumer and Industrial Buying Behavior* (New York, North-Holland, 1977), pp. 49–65.

19. Joseph Pernica, "The Second Generation of Market Segmentation Studies: An Audit of Buying Motivations," in W. Wells (ed.), *Life Style and Psychographics* (Chicago: American Marketing Association, 1973), pp. 277–313.

20. See especially the fine discussion in William D. Wells, "Psychographics: A Critical Review," *Journal of Marketing Research,* Vol. 12 (May 1975), pp. 196–213.

21. James Atlas, "Beyond Demographics," *Atlantic Monthly,* October 1984, pp. 49–58.

22. These findings are reported in Marion Long, "Food for Thought," *Family Weekly,* June 10, 1984, p. 22. For recent research findings on geographic segmentation, see, for example, Lynn R. Kahle, "The Nine Nations of North America and the Value Basis of Geographic Segmentation," *Journal of Marketing,* Vol. 50 (April 1986), pp. 37–47; Frederick W. Langrehr and Virginia B. Langrehr, "A Geographic Comparison of Food Shoppers: The Foundry Versus the Empty Quarter Regions," *AMA Educators' Proceedings* (1986), pp. 19–21; U. N. Umesh, "Transferability of Preference Models Across Segments and Geographic Areas," *Journal of Marketing,* Vol. 51 (January 1987), pp. 59–70; and James W. Gentry, Patriya Tansuhaj, L. Lee Manzer, and Joby John, "Do Geographic Subcultures Vary Culturally?" *Advances in Consumer Research,* Vol. 15 (1988), pp. 411–417.

23. Calculated by the author from "TV Ratings Vary by Region . . . ," *The Wall Street Journal,* October 26, 1982, p. 35.

24. Alan B. Miller, Jr., "L.A. Consumer Thinks Rice Is Nice but Nixes Bacon Mixes," *Advertising Age,* March 22, 1982, pp. M-22–25; and Alan B. Miller, Jr., "They Like Their Tea Iced, Their Waffles Frozen," *Advertising Age,* May 31, 1982, pp. M-6–27.

25. The examples provided here are given in Stuart Elliott, "Marketers Say Clusters Are Us," *USA Today,* March 16, 1989, pp. B-1 ff.

26. Russell I. Haley, "Benefit Segmentation: A Decision-Oriented Research Tool," *Journal of Marketing,* July 1968, pp. 30–35.

27. Some good articles in this area include ibid.; Russell I. Haley, "Beyond Benefit Segmentation," *Journal of Advertising Research,* Vol. 11 (August 1971), pp. 3–8; Russell I. Haley, "Benefit Segments: Backwards and Forwards," *Journal of Advertising Research,* Vol. 24 (February–March 1984), pp. 19–25; Richard M. Johnson, "Market Segmentation: A Strategic Management Tool," *Journal of Marketing Research,* Vol. 8 (February 1971), pp. 13–18; Paul E. Green, Yoram Wind, and Arun K. Jain, "Benefit Bundle Analysis," *Journal of Advertising Research,* April 1972, pp. 31–36; William L. Wilkie and Joel B. Cohen, "An Overview of Market Segmentation: Behavioral Concepts and Research Approaches," Working Paper Series, Marketing Science Institute, Cambridge, Mass., 1977; Roger J. Calantone and Alan G. Sawyer, "The Stability of Benefit Segments," *Journal of Marketing Research* (August 1978), pp. 395 ff. Girish Punj and David W. Stewart, "Cluster Analysis in Marketing Research: Review and Suggestions for Applications," *Journal of Marketing Research,* Vol. 20 (1982), pp. 134 ff. Russell I. Haley, "Benefit Segmentation—20 Years Later," *Journal of Consumer Marketing,* Vol. 1, no. 2 (1984), pp. 5–13. For recent findings and methodological advances, see also Kenneth D. Bahn and Nimish Gandhi, "Benefit Segmentation in the Generics Food Product Market," *AMA Educators' Proceedings* (1987), pp. 88–92; Ronald Hoverstad, Charles W. Lamb, Jr., and Patrick Miller, "College Benefit Segmentation Analysis: Approach and Results," *Advances in Consumer Research,* Vol. 16 (1989), pp. 332–338; Wagner A. Kamakura, "A Least Squares Procedure for Benefit Segmentation with Conjoint Experiments," *Journal of Marketing Research,* Vol. 24 (May 1988), pp. 157–167; and Paul E. Green and Abba Krieger, "Recent Contributions to Optimal Positioning and Buyer Segmentation, "Working Paper, University of Pennsylvania, 1989.

28. Peter R. Dickson, "Person-Situation: Segmentation's Missing Link," *Journal of Marketing* (Fall 1982), pp. 52–64; see also John M. Browning and Noel B. Zabriskie, "Do-It-Yourself Consumers: Segmentation Insights for Retailers," *Journal of Consumer Marketing,* Vol. 2 (Summer 1985), pp. 5–16.

29. William L. Wilkie and Peter R. Dickson, *Consumer Information Search and Shopping Behavior* (Cambridge, Mass.: Marketing Science Institute, 1985)

30. "A Pilot Study of Brand Differentiation" (Mamaroneck, N.Y.: Starch INRA Hooper, 1988). For a detailed review of related managerial options and developments in the retail sector, see David J. Curry, "Single-Source Systems: Retail Management Present and Future," *Journal of Retailing*, Vol. 65 (Spring 1989), pp. 1–20. See also Pradeep Korgaonkar and George P. Moschis, "The Effects of Perceived Risk and Social Class on Consumer Preferences for Distribution Outlets," *AMA Educators' Proceedings* (1989), pp. 39–44; Michelle A. Morganosky, "Cost-Versus Convenience-Oriented Consumers: Demographic, Lifestyle, and Value Perspectives," *Psychology & Marketing*, Vol. 3 (Spring 1986), pp. 35–46; Arch G. Woodside, Robert L. Nielsen, Fred Walters, and Gale D. Miller, "Preference Segmentation of Health Care Services: The Old-Fashioned, Value Conscious, Affluents and Professional Want-It-Alls," *AMA Educators' Proceedings* (1987), p. 244; James B. Hunt and Mark G. Dunn, "The Impact of Demographics and Usage Variables on Perceptions Toward Emergency Care Clinics," *AMA Educators' Proceedings* (1987), pp. 76–81; and Rajiv Grover and V. Srinivasan, "An Approach for Tracking Within-Segment Shifts in Market Shares," *Journal of Marketing Research*, Vol. 26 (May 1989), pp. 230–236.

31. "A Savings & Loan Hits Home," *Marketing Week*, June 6, 1988, pp. 50–51. For related topics of studies in the academic literature, see Ken Kono, "Are Generics Buyers Deal-Prone? On a Relationship Between Generics Purchase and Deal-Proneness," *Journal of the Academy of Marketing Science*, Vol. 13 (Winter 1985), pp. 62–74; Kapil Bawa and Robert W. Shoemaker, "The Coupon-Prone Consumer: Some Findings Based on Purchase Behavior Across Product Classes," *Journal of Marketing*, Vol. 51 (October 1987), pp. 99–110; David M. Szymanski and Paul S. Busch, "Identifying the Generics-Prone Consumer: A Meta-Analysis," *Journal of Marketing Research*, Vol. 24 (November 1987), pp. 425–431; and E. W. Boatwright, J. Steven Kelly, and William Haueisen, "Off-Price and Outlet Malls: A Profile of 'Heavy' Shoppers," *AMA Educators' Proceedings* (1988), pp. 237–241.

32. Benjamin Seto, "Who Buys Imported Vehicles?" San Francisco Examiner Service, February 27, 1988.

33. Nancy Youman, "Getting to Know You: Data-Base Age Dawns," *Marketing Week*, February 8, 1988, p. 1 ff. See also Teresa J. Domzal and Jerome B. Kernan, "Television's New Technology: Hardware Plus Software Equal Segmentation Research," *Journal of Consumer Marketing*, Vol. 2 (Summer 1985), pp. 17–26.

34. Stan Rapp, "Cigaret Giants Pioneer Data-Base Marketing in Package Goods," *Marketing News*, December 5, 1988, p. 17.

35. The descriptions and statistics presented in Appendix 4-A's discussion of VALS2 were provided by SRI International, Menlo Park, California, to the author.

36. See, for example, Sonia Yuspeh, "Syndicated Values/Lifestyles Segmentation Schemes: Use Them as Descriptive Tools, Not to Select Targets," and the response from Brooke Warrick, "SRI's Response to Yuspeh: Demographics Aren't Enough," both in *Marketing News*, May 25, 1984, p. 1; see also Aimee Stern, "Tired of Playing Mind Games," *Marketing Week*, July 13, 1987, pp. 1 ff; Marcia Harlik, "A Standing Ovation for VALS," *Marketing Week*, October 12, 1987, p. 12; Lynn R. Kahle, Sharon E. Beatty, and Pamela Homer, "Alternative Measurement Approaches to Consumer Values: The List of Values (LOV) and Values and Life Styles (VALS)," *Journal of Consumer Research*, Vol. 13 (December 1986), pp. 405–409; and Sharon E. Beatty, Pamela M. Homer, and Lynn R. Kahle, "Problems with VALS in International Marketing Research: An Example from an Application of the Empirical Mirror Technique," *Advances in Consumer Research*, Vol. 15 (1988), pp. 375–380.

Chapter 5: Consumers as Individuals

1. Al Ries and Jack Trout, *Bottom-Up Marketing* (New York: McGraw-Hill, 1989), as excerpted in "Turning Marketing Upside-Down," *Advertising Age*, November 28, 1988, p. 36.

2. The discussion in this section is based upon Philip Kotler, "Behavioral Models for Analyzing Buyers," *Journal of Marketing*, October 1965, pp. 37–54.

3. Robert J. Lavidge and Gary A. Steiner, "A Model for Predictive Measurements of Advertising Effectiveness," *Journal of Marketing*, Vol. 25 (October 1961), pp. 59–62. See also Lawrence F. Feick, "Latent Class Models for the Analysis of Behavioral Hierarchies," *Journal of Marketing Research*, Vol. 24 (May 1987), pp. 174–186.

4. Michael L. Ray, *Advertising and Communication Management* (Englewood Cliffs, N.J.: Prentice Hall, 1982).

5. See, for example, Glen L. Urban and John R. Hauser, *Design and Marketing of New Products* (Englewood Cliffs, N.J.: Prentice Hall, 1980).

6. See, for example, Herbert A. Simon and Allan Newell, "Information Processing in Computer and

Man," *American Scientist,* Vol. 53 (1964), pp. 281–300; and Allan Newell and Herbert A. Simon, *Human Problem Solving* (Englewood Cliffs, N.J.: Prentice Hall, 1972).

7. Each of the four CIP generalizations has recently received considerable research attention by consumer researchers. Citations for many of these studies are included in conjunction with our discussions of the detailed topics to which they are most pertinent in Parts Two, Three, and Four of this book. For a further overview and more extended discussion of the generalizations and their consumer behavior contexts, see William L. Wilkie, *How Consumers Use Product Information: An Assessment of Research in Relation to Public Policy Needs* (Washington, D.C.: National Science Foundation, 1974). See also James R. Bettman, *An Information Processing Theory of Consumer Choice* (Reading, Mass.: Addison-Wesley, 1979); and John G. Lynch and Thomas K. Srull, "Memory and Attentional Factors in Consumer Choice: Concepts and Research Methods," *Journal of Consumer Research,* Vol. 9 (June 1982), pp. 18–37.

8. The essentials of this system are presented in R. M. Shiffrin and R. C. Atkinson "Storage and Retrieval Processes in Long-Term Memory," *Psychological Review,* Vol. 76 (1969), pp. 179–193; see also R. C. Atkinson and R. M. Shiffrin, "Human Memory: A Proposed System and Its Control Processes," in K. W. Spence and J. T. Spence (eds.), *Advances in the Psychology of Learning and Motivation Research and Theory,* Volume 2 (New York: Academic Press, 1968).

9. George Sperling, "The Information Available in Brief Visual Presentations," Psychological Monographs, Vol. 74, no. 11 (1960); C. J. Darwin, M. T. Turvey, and R. G. Crowder, "An Auditory Analogue of the Sperling Partial Report Procedure," *Cognitive Psychology,* Vol. 3 (1973), pp. 255–267.

10. See, for example, Elizabeth Loftus and Geoffrey R. Loftus, "On the Permanence of Stored Information in the Human Brain," *American Psychologist,* Vol. 35 (May 1980), pp. 409–420. For a closely related "workbench" analog to the work center/warehouse sectors description, see Roberta Klatzky, *Human Memory: Structures and Processes* (San Francisco: W. H. Freeman, 1975).

11. For an appreciation of these issues, see L. R. Peterson and S. T. Johnson, "Short-Term Retention of Individual Verbal Items," *Journal of Experimental Psychology,* Vol. 58 (1959), pp. 193–198. See also B. B. Murdock, Jr., "The Retention of Individual Items," *Journal of Experimental Psychology,* Vol. 62 (1961), pp. 618–625.

12. George A. Miller, "The Magical Number Seven, Plus or Minus Two: Some Limits on Our Capacity for Processing Information," *Psychological Review,* Vol. 63 (1956), pp. 81–97.

13. See, for example, Herbert A. Simon, "How Big Is a Chunk?" *Science,* Vol. 183 (February 1974), pp. 482–488.

14. E. Tulving, "Episodic and Semantic Memory," in E. Tulving and W. Donaldson (eds.), *Organization of Memory* (New York: Academic Press, 1972). For related discussions, see Eleanor Rosch, "Cognitive Representations of Semantic Categories," *Cognitive Psychology,* Vol. 104 pp. 192–233; and Edward J. Shoben, "Semantic and Episodic Memory," in Robert S. Wyer and Thomas K. Srull (eds.), *Handbook of Social Cognition* (Hillsdale, N.J.: Erlbaum, 1984), pp. 213–231. Recent research in consumer behavior has also given considerable attention to "imagery" and related topics. See, for example, Terry L. Childers, Michael J. Houston, and Susan E. Heckler, "Measurement of Individual Differences in Visual Versus Verbal Information Processing," *Journal of Consumer Research,* Vol. 12 (September 1985), pp. 125–134; Jolita Kisielius and Brian Sternthal, "Examining the Vividness Controversy: An Availability-Valence Interpretation," *Journal of Consumer Research,* Vol. 12 (March 1986), pp. 418–431; Deborah J. MacInnis and Linda L. Price, "The Role of Imagery in Information Processing: Review and Extensions," *Journal of Consumer Research,* Vol. 13 (March 1987), pp. 473–491; Joan Meyers-Levy, "The Effect of Gender Differences in Hemispheric Asymmetry on Judgment," *Advances in Consumer Research,* Vol. 14 (1987), pp. 51–53; Michael L. Rothschild, "Hemispheric Lateralization: A Complex and Subtle New Field for Consumer Research," *Advances in Consumer Research,* Vol. 14 (1987), pp. 54–56; Joan Meyers-Levy, "Factors Affecting the Use of Conceptually Driven and Data Driven Processing," *Advances in Consumer Research,* Vol. 15 (1988), pp. 169–173; Keren Johnson, Mary Zimmer, and Linda Golden, "Object Relations Theory: Male and Female Differences in Visual Information Processing," *Advances in Consumer Research,* Vol. 14 (1987), pp. 83–87; and Debbie MacInnis, "Constructs and Measures of Individual Differences in Imagery Processing: A Review," *Advances in Consumer Research,* Vol. 14 (1987), pp. 88–92.

15. As we can appreciate, the distinction we make in this chapter among the three "stores" (sensory register, STM, and LTM) is a functional one; we are attempting to stress three different and important functions that are carried out during information processing. Experts in this area have also developed alternative ways of dealing with these functions. Some more advanced models of information processing do not use an STM sector, but instead view LTM to be the center for

both storage and processing activity; one popular model, for example, relies on the concept of "spreading activation" as processing energy moves through the network system of LTM nodes to move from one thought to the next. For the purposes of this text; we will not need to move into this level of model. If you are particularly interested in more advanced work in information processing, however, you should read more about these alternative models. See, for example, A. M. Collins and E. F. Loftus, "A Spreading Activation Theory of Semantic Processing," *Psychological Review,* Vol. 82 (1975), pp. 407–428; and John R. Anderson, *The Architecture of Cognition* (Cambridge, Mass.: Harvard University Press, 1983).

For discussions of some of the many implications of these and related issues for consumer behavior, see, for example, Thomas K. Srull, "A Model of Consumer Memory and Judgment," *Advances in Consumer Research,* Vol. 13 (1986); Joseph W. Alba and J. Wesley Hutchinson, "Dimensions of Consumer Expertise," *Journal of Consumer Research,* Vol. 13 (March 1987), pp. 411–454; George M. Zinkhan and Abhijit Biswas, "Using the Repertory Grid to Assess the Complexity of Consumers' Cognitive Structures," *Advances in Consumer Research,* Vol. 15 (1988), pp. 493–497; J. Craig Andrews, "Motivation, Ability and Opportunity to Process Information: Conceptual and Experimental Manipulation Issues," *Advances in Consumer Research,* Vol. 15 (1988), pp. 219–225; Adam Finn, "Print Ad Recognition Readership Scores: An Information Processing Perspective," *Journal of Marketing Research,* Vol. 25 (May 1988), pp. 168–177; Naresh K. Malhotra, "Use of Mnemonics in Teaching Marketing Research," Working Paper, Georgia Institute of Technology, Atlanta, November 1988; Clark K. Leavitt, "The Structure and Maintenance of Well-Established Brand Images," Working Paper 89-7, Ohio State University, Columbus, 1989; Joan Meyers-Levy, "The Influence of a Brand Name's Association Set Size and Work Frequency on Brand Memory," *Journal of Consumer Research,* Vol. 16 (September 1989), pp. 197–207; and C. Whan Park, Robert Lawson, and Sandra Milberg, "Memory Structure for Brand Names," *Advances in Consumer Research,* Vol. 16 (1989), pp. 726–731.

16. The answers to the jingles are as follows: (1) Chevrolet; (2) Green Giant; (3) Charmin, Whipple; (4) Armour; (5) Oldsmobile; (6) Bud Light; (7) Wendy's; (8) McDonald's; (9) Sara Lee; (10) Dial. ** Bonus: Oscar Meyer.

17. John G. Lynch and Thomas K. Srull, "Memory and Attentional Factors in Consumer Choice: Concepts and Research Methods," *Journal of Consumer Research,* Vol. 9 (June 1982), pp. 18–37.

18. Raymond R. Burke and Thomas K. Srull, "Competitive Interference and Consumer Memory for Advertising," *Journal of Consumer Research,* Vol. 15 (June 1988), pp. 55–68.

19. Kevin Lane Keller, "Memory Factors in Advertising: The Effect of Advertising Retrieval Cues on Brand Evaluations," *Journal of Consumer Research,* Vol. 14 (December 1987), pp. 316–333. See also Julie A. Edell and Kevin Lane Keller, "The Information Processing of Coordinated Media Campaigns," *Journal of Marketing Research,* Vol. 26 (May 1989), pp. 149–163; Stephen J. Hoch and John Deighton, "Managing What Consumers Learn from Experience," *Journal of Marketing,* Vol. 53 (April 1989), pp. 1–20.

20. Roy Furchgott, "You'll Never Get Bored Driving to South of the Border," *Marketing Week,* April 11, 1988, pp. 20–22.

21. Prakash Nedungadi, "Retrieval Cues at Choice: An Additional Role for Product Attributes," Working Paper, University of Toronto, 1989. The concept of evoked set is one of the most interesting ideas that link CIP to applied marketing issues in consumer behavior. For interesting readings in this area, see John A. Howard and Jagdish N. Sheth, *The Theory of Buyer Behavior* (New York: John Wiley, 1969); Lance P. Jarvis and James B. Wilcox, "Evoked-Set Size—Some Theoretical Findings and Empirical Evidence," *Combined Proceedings* American Marketing Association (1973) pp. 236–260; C. L. Narayana and Rom T. Markin, "Consumer Behavior and Product Performance: An Alternative Conceptualization," *Journal of Marketing,* Vol. 39 (October 1975), pp. 1–6. See also the following articles in *Advances in Consumer Research,* Vol. 6 (1979): Frederick E. May, "Evoked Set Formation and Composition: The Learning and Information Processing Hypotheses," pp. 222–226; Joseph J. Belonax, Jr., "Decision Rule Uncertainty, Evoked Set Size and Task Difficulty as a Function of Number of Choice Criteria and Information Variability," pp. 232–235; Thomas L. Parkinson and Michael Reilly "An Information Processing Approach to Evoked Set Formation," pp. 227–231; and James H. Myers, "Methodological Issues in Evoked Set Formation and Composition," pp. 236–237. Also see Jacques F. Brisoux and Michel Laroche, "Evoked Set Formation and Composition: An Empirical Investigation Under a Routinized Response Behavior Situation," *Advances in Consumer Research,* Vol. 8 (1981), pp. 357–361; Sigurd Villads Troye, "Evoked Set Formation as a Categorization Process," *Advances in Consumer Research,* Vol. 11 (1984), pp. 180–186; Rajendra K. Srivastava, Mark I. Alpert, and Allan D. Shocker,

"A Consumer-Oriented Approach for Determining Market Structures," *Journal of Marketing,* Vol. 68 (Spring 1984), pp. 32–45; Michael Reilly and Thomas L. Parkinson, "Individual and Product Correlates of Evoked Set Size for Consumer Package Goods," *Advances in Consumer Research,* Vol. 12 (1985), pp. 492–497; Joseph W. Alba and Amitava Chattopadhyay, "The Effects of Context and Part-Category Cues on the Recall of Competing Brands," *Journal of Marketing Research,* Vol. 22 (August 1985), pp. 340–349; Juanita J. Brown and Albert R. Wildt, "Factors Influencing Evoked Set Size," *AMA Educators' Proceedings,* 1987, p. 221; Susan Spiggle and Murphy A. Sewall, "A Choice Sets Model of Retail Selection," *Journal of Marketing,* Vol. 51 (April 1987), pp. 97–111; Michel Laroche, Jerry Rosenblatt, Alan Hockstein, and James Convery, "Consumer Selection of a Service Outlet: An Empirical Study of Fast Food Establishments," Working Paper, Concordia University, Montreal, February 1988; and David B. Klenosky and Arno J. Rethans, "The Formation of Consumer Choice Sets: A Longitudinal Investigation at the Product Class Level," *Advances in Consumer Research,* Vol. 15 (1988), pp. 13–18.

22. Scott Hume, "An Un-Happy Seven-Up Returns to Old Theme," *Advertising Age,* March 11, 1985, p. 10.

23. This classification was developed by G. David Hughes and Michael L. Ray, *Buyer/Consumer Information Processing* (Chapel Hill: University of North Carolina Press, 1974).

24. Gordon H. Bower, "Mood and Memory," *American Psychologist,* Vol. 36 (February 1981), pp. 129–148.

25. See, for example, Harold H. Kassarjian, "Consumer Research: Some Recollections and a Commentary," *Advances in Consumer Research,* Vol. 13 (1986), pp. 6–8; Robert B. Zajonc and Hazel Markus, "Affective and Cognitive Factors in Preference," *Journal of Consumer Research,* Vol. 9 (September 1982), pp. 123–131; Joel B. Cohen, "Attitude, Affect and Consumer Behavior," in A. Isen and B. Moore, *Affect and Social Behavior* Cambridge University Press, 1990; James A. Muncy, "Physiological Responses of Consumer Emotions: Theory, Methods, and Implications for Consumer Research," *AMA Educators' Proceedings* (1987), pp. 127–132; Robert A. Westbrook, "Product/Consumption-Based Affective Responses and Postpurchase Processes," *Journal of Marketing Research,* Vol. 24 (August 1987), pp. 258–270; David M. Sanbonmatsu and Frank R. Kardes, "The Effects of Physiological Arousal on Information Processing and Persuasion," *Journal of Consumer Research,* Vol. 15 (December 1988), pp. 379–385; and Punam Anand, Morris B. Holbrook, and Debra Stephens, "The Formation of Affective Judgments: The Cognitive-Affective Model Versus the Independence Hypothesis," *Journal of Consumer Research,* Vol. 15 (December 1988), pp. 386–391.

26. Elizabeth C. Hirschman and Morris B. Holbrook, "Hedonic Consumption: Emerging Concepts, Methods and Propositions," *Journal of Marketing,* Vol. 46 (1982), pp. 92–101. For other interesting examples of these issues, see William J. Havlena and Morris B. Holbrook, "The Varieties of Consumption Experience: Comparing Two Typologies of Emotion in Consumer Behavior," *Journal of Consumer Research,* Vol. 13 (December 1986), pp. 394–404; Roberto Friedmann, "Psychological Meaning of Products: Identification and Marketing Applications," *Psychology & Marketing,* Vol. 3 (Spring 1986), pp. 1–15; and Kathleen T. Lacher, "Hedonic Consumption: Music as a Product," *Advances in Consumer Research,* Vol. 16 (1989), pp. 367–373.

27. James A. Muncy, "Psychophysiological Principles in Consumer Research: An Overview," Working Paper, Clemson University, Clemson, South Carolina, 1989. See also John T. Cacioppo and Richard E. Petty, "Physiological Responses and Advertising Effects: Is the Cup Half Full or Half Empty," *Psychology & Marketing,* Vol. 2 (Summer 1985), pp. 115–126.

28. Robert B. Zajonc and Hazel Markus, "Affective and Cognitive Factors in Preference," *Journal of Consumer Research,* Vol. 9 (September 1982), pp. 123–131. See also Carl Obermiller, "Varieties of Mere Exposure: The Effects of Processing Style and Repetition on Affective Response," *Journal of Consumer Research,* Vol. 12 (June 1985), pp. 17–30; Y. Tsal, "On the Relationship Between Cognitive and Affective Processes: A Critique on Zajonc and Markus," *Journal of Consumer Research,* Vol. 12 (December 1985), pp. 358–362; and R. Zajonc and H. Markus, "Must All Affect Be Mediated by Cognition?" *Journal of Consumer Research,* Vol. 12 (December 1985), pp. 363–364.

29. Meryl Paula Gardner, "Mood States and Consumer Behavior: A Critical Review," *Journal of Consumer Research,* Vol. 12 (December 1985), pp. 281–300. See also Thom Srull, "Memory, Mood and Consumer Judgment," in *Advances in Consumer Research,* Vol. 14 (1987), pp. 404–407; Ronald P. Hill and Meryl P. Gardner, "Product Evaluation: Effects of and on Consumer Mood States," *Advances in Consumer Research,* Vol. 14 (1987), pp. 408–410; Ronald Paul Hill, "The Effects of Advertisements on Consumer's Mood States: An Interactive Perspective," *Advances in Consumer Research,* Vol. 15 (1988), pp. 131–134; James C. Ward, Ronald P. Hill, and

Meryl P. Gardner, "Promotional Games: The Effects of Participation on Mood, Attitude, and Information Processing," *Advances in Consumer Research*, Vol. 15 (1988), pp. 135–140; Meryl Paula Gardner and Dennis W. Rook, "Effects of Impulse Purchases on Consumers' Affective States," *Advances in Consumer Research*, Vol. 15 (1988), pp. 127–130; Ronald Paul Hill and James C. Ward, "Mood Manipulation in Marketing Research: An Examination of Potential Confounding Effects," *Journal of Marketing Research*, Vol. 26 (February 1989), pp. 97–104; David W. Schumann, Esther Thorson, and Deborah Rosen, "Testing the Selection-Processing Model: The Influence of Program Related Needs on Mood-Induced Context Effects," *Advances in Consumer Research*, Vol. 16 (1989), pp. 495–501; and Meryl P. Gardner and Ronald P. Hill, "Context-Induced Mood and Brand Selection Strategy: The Mediating Role of Attention," *Advances in Consumer Research*, Vol. 16 (1989), pp. 492–494.

30. This topic has received a considerable degree of recent attention in the field. For an interesting overview of this topic, see Rajeev Batra and Michael L. Ray, "Affective Responses Mediating Acceptance of Advertising," *Journal of Consumer Research*, Vol. 13 (September 1986), pp. 234–249. For an interesting, recent overview that ties CIP and affective responses, see also Deborah J. MacInnis and Bernard J. Jaworski, "Information Processing from Advertisements: Toward an Integrative Framework," *Journal of Marketing*, Vol. 53 (October 1989), pp. 1–23. For a variety of further insights and findings, see, for example, W. Fred van Raaij, "Affective and Cognitive Reactions to Advertising," Working Paper #84-111, Marketing Science Institute, 1984; David A. Aaker, Douglas M. Stayman, and Michael R. Hagerty, "Warmth in Advertising: Measurement, Impact, and Sequence Effects," *Journal of Consumer Research*, Vol. 12 (March 1986), pp. 365–381; Richard W. Mizerski and J. Dennis White, "Understanding and Using Emotions in Advertising," *Journal of Consumer Marketing*, Vol. 3 (Fall 1986), pp. 57–70; Jacqueline C. Hitchon, "The Schachter Theory of Emotion: Its Relevance to Television Advertising Context Effects," *AMA Winter Educators' Proceedings* (1987), pp. 221–224. Deborah J. MacInnis and Robert A. Westbrook, "The Relationship Between Executional Ques and Emotional Response to Advertising," Working Paper, University of Arizona, Tucson, October 1988; Marvin E. Goldberg and Gerald J. Gorn, "Happy and Sad TV Programs: How They Affect Reactions to Commercials," *Journal of Consumer Research*, Vol. 14 (December 1987), pp. 387–403; Morris B. Holbrook and Rajeev Batra, "Assessing the Role of Emotions as Mediators of Consumer Responses to Advertising," *Journal of Consumer Research*, Vol. 14 (December 1987), pp. 404–420; Julie A. Edell and Marian Chapman Burke, "The Power of Feelings in Understanding Advertising Effects," *Journal of Consumer Research*, Vol. 14 (December 1987), pp. 421–433; Chris T. Allen, Karen A. Machleit, and Susan S. Marine, "On Assessing the Emotionality of Advertising via Izard's Differential Emotions Scale," *Advances in Consumer Research*, Vol. 15 (1988), pp. 226–231; David A. Aaker, Douglas M. Stayman, and Richard Vezina, "Identifying Feelings Elicited by Advertising," *Psychology & Marketing*, Vol. 5 (Spring 1988), pp. 1–16; Thomas J. Page, Jr., Patricia J. Daugherty, Dogan Eroglu, David E. Hartman, Scott D. Johnson, and Doo-Hee Lee, "Measuring Emotional Response to Advertising: A Comment on Stout and Leckenby," *Journal of Advertising*, Vol. 17 (November 1988), pp. 49–52; Patricia A. Stout and John D. Leckenby, "The Nature of Emotional Response to Advertising: A Further Examination," *Journal of Advertising*, Vol. 17 (November 1988), pp. 53–57; Mark A. Pavelchak, John H. Antil, and James M. Munch, "The Super Bowl: An Investigation into the Relationship Among Program Context, Emotional Experience, and Ad Recall," *Journal of Consumer Research*, Vol. 15 (December 1988), pp. 360–367; Judy I. Alpert and Mark I. Alpert, "Background Music as an Influence in Consumer Mood and Advertising Response," *Advances in Consumer Research*, Vol. 16 (1989), pp. 485–491; Ellen Day, "Share of Heart: What Is It and How Can It Be Measured?" *The Journal of Consumer Marketing*, Vol. 6 (Winter 1989), pp. 5–12; and Marian Chapman Burke and Julie A. Edell, "The Impact of Feelings on Ad-Based Affect and Cognition," *Journal of Marketing Research*, Vol. 26 (February 1989), pp. 69–83.

31. For basic discussions of media differences and "low involvement," see Herbert E. Krugman, "The Impact of Television Advertising: Learning Without Involvement," *Public Opinion Quarterly*, Vol. 29 (Fall 1965), pp. 349–356; Herbert E. Krugman, "The Measurement of Advertising Involvement," *Public Opinion Quarterly*, Vol. 32 (1968), pp. 583–596; Herbert E. Krugman, "Brain Wave Measures of Media Involvement," *Journal of Advertising Research*, Vol. 11 (February 1971), pp. 3–9; and Peter L. Wright, "Analyzing Media Effects on Advertising Responses," *Public Opinion Quarterly*, Vol. 38 (1974), pp. 192–205. For recent developments, see Herbert E. Krugman, "Point of View: Limits of Attention to Advertising," *Journal of Advertising Research*, Vol. 28 (October–November 1988), pp. 47–50, and our extensive notes on related topics in Chapters 7, 9, 10, 11, and 17.

32. For basic discussions of a CIP view of advertising wearout, see Bobby J. Calder and Brian Sternthal, "Television Commercial Wearout: An Information Processing View," *Journal of Marketing Research*, Vol. 17 (May 1980), pp. 173–186; Samuel C. Craig, Brian Sternthal, and Clark Leavitt, "Advertising Wearout: An Experimental Analysis," *Journal of Marketing Research*, Vol. 13 (November 1976), pp. 365–372; and R. C. Grass and Wallace H. Wallace, "Satiation Effects of T.V. Commercials," *Journal of Advertising Research*, Vol. 19 (1969), pp. 47–57.

Chapter 6: Understanding Consumer Motivation

1. Al Ries and Jack Trout, *Bottom-Up Marketing* (New York: McGraw-Hill, 1989), as quoted in "Turning Marketing Upside-Down," *Advertising Age*, November 28, 1988, p. 36.
2. Burleigh B. Gardner, "The Consumer Mind," *Advertising Age*, July 27, 1981, p. 42.
3. M. R. Jones, *Nebraska Symposium on Motivation* (Lincoln: University of Nebraska Press, 1955).
4. "Recalls: Why So Many Are Flops," *Changing Times*, October 1980, pp. 29 ff.
5. Lori Kesler, "Diabetes Ads Aim to Shock," *Advertising Age*, October 29, 1984, p. 66S. For a related discussion, see Ronald Paul Hill, "An Exploration of the Relationship Between AIDS-Related Anxiety and the Evaluation of Condom Advertisements," *Journal of Advertising*, Vol. 17 (November 1988), pp. 35–42.
6. J. Jung, *Understanding Human Motivation: A Cognitive Approach* (New York: Macmillan, 1978); and M. H. Marx and T. Tombaugh, *Motivation* (San Francisco: Chandler, 1967). See also Michael E. Hyland, "Motivational Control Theory: An Integrative Framework," *Journal of Personality and Social Psychology*, Vol. 55, no. 4 pp. 642–551.
7. Edward M. Tauber, "Why Do People Shop?" *Journal of Marketing*, Vol. 36 (October 1972), pp. 46–59. For further readings on related topics, see also Jack Lesser and Susan Marine, "An Exploratory Investigation of the Relationship Between Consumer Arousal and Shopping Behavior," *AMA Educators' Proceedings*, 1984, pp. 17–21; Dennis W. Rook, "The Buying Impulse," *Journal of Consumer Research*, Vol. 14 (September 1987), pp. 189–199; Emin Babakus, Peter Tat, and William Cunningham, "Coupon Redemption: A Motivational Perspective," *Journal of Consumer Marketing*, Vol. 5 (Spring 1988), pp. 37–44; Lew G. Brown, "The Strategic and Tactical Implications of Convenience in Consumer Product Marketing," *The Journal of Consumer Marketing*, Vol. 6 (Summer 1989), pp. 13–20; William M. Strahle and E. H. Bonfield, "Understanding Consumer Panic: A Sociological Perspective," *Advances in Consumer Research*, Vol. 16 (1989), pp. 567–573; Pat McIntyre, Mark A. Barnett, Richard Harris, James Shanteau, John Skowronski, and Michael Klassen, "Psychological Factors Influencing Decisions to Donate Organs," *Advances in Consumer Research*, Vol. 14 (1987), pp. 331–334; and Susan Spiggle, "Cigarette Consumption Behavior: Smoking Experiences and Marketing Stimuli," *AMA Winter Educators' Proceedings* (1987), pp. 229–233.
8. Ronald Alsop, "Advertisers Put Consumers on the Couch," *The Wall Street Journal*, May 13, 1988, p. 17. For a related discussion, see Alf H. Walle, "Archetypes, Athletes, and Advertising: A Jungian Approach to Promotion," *Journal of Consumer Marketing*, Vol. 3 (Fall 1986), pp. 21–30.
9. For an entire book describing Dichter's views of the hidden meanings in common consumer products, see Ernest Dichter, *Handbook of Consumer Motivation* (New York: McGraw-Hill, 1964). For shorter descriptions, see Rena Bartos, "Ernest Dichter: Motive Interpreter," *Journal of Advertising Research*, Vol. 17 (June 1977), p. 8; and Katherine Barrett and Richard Greene, "Work Motivates Psychoanalyst," *Advertising Age*, November 1, 1984, pp. 43–45. For a classical critical view, see Vance Packard, *The Hidden Persuaders* (New York: Pocket Books, 1957). For interesting reading to delve further into Freud's theories, see textbooks on personality theory. Some original works have been reprinted and are interesting reading: Sigmund Freud (1900), *The Interpretation of Dreams* (London: Hogarth Press, 1953); Sigmund Freud (1915), *A General Introduction to Psychoanalysis* (New York: Washington Square Press, 1934); and Sigmund Freud (1933), *New Introductory Lectures on Psycho-analysis* (New York: W. W. Norton, 1961).
10. W. B. Cannon, *The Wisdom of the Body* (New York: W. W. Norton, 1932). See also Werner Kroeber-Riel, "Activation Research: Psychobiological Approaches in Consumer Research," *Journal of Consumer Research* (March 1979), pp. 240–250; Michael J. Ryan, "Psychobiology and Consumer Research: A Problem of Construct Validity," *Journal of Consumer Research* (June 1980), pp. 92–96; and W. Kroeber-Riel, "Rejoinder," *Journal of Consumer Research* (June 1980), pp. 96–98. For a recent overview, see James A. Muncy, "Physiological Responses of Consumer Emotions: Theory, Methods, and Implications for Consumer Research," *AMA Educators' Proceedings* (1987), pp. 127–132.
11. This section is based on discussions in Harold H. Kassarjian, "Field Theory in Consumer Be-

havior," in S. Ward and T. Robertson (eds.), *Consumer Behavior: Theoretical Sources* (Englewood Cliffs, N.J.: Prentice Hall, 1973), pp. 118–140); and Bernard Weiner, *Human Motivation* (New York: Holt, Rinehart and Winston, 1980), pp. 141–177.

12. Ivan Ross, "Perceived Risk and Consumer Behavior: A Critical Review," *Advances in Consumer Research*, Vol. 2 (1975), pp. 1–19; Mark G. Dunn, Patrick Murphy, and Gerald Skelly, "The Influence of Perceived Risk on Brand Preference for Supermarket Products," *Journal of Retailing*, Vol. 62 (Summer 1986), pp. 204–216; John Vann, "The Managerial Implications of a Consequence-Chaining, Conditional Probability View of Perceived Risk," *AMA Educators' Proceedings* (1984), pp. 72–75; Bruce K. Blaylock, "Risk Perception: Evidence of an Interactive Process," *Journal of Business Research*, Vol. 13 (June 1985), pp. 207–222; Linda L. Price, Sridhar N. Ramaswami, and Rajendra K. Srivastava, "Are People Always Risk Averse? Contextual Effects of Choice Under Uncertainty," *AMA Educators' Proceedings* (1985), pp. 93–97; G. R. Dowling, "Perceived Risk: The Concept and Its Measurements," *Psychology & Marketing*, Vol. 3 (Fall 1986), pp. 193–210; Janet E. Oglethorpe and Kent B. Monroe, "Risk Perception and Risk Acceptability in Consumer Behavior: Conceptual Issues and an Agenda for Future Research," *AMA Winter Educators' Proceedings* (1987), pp. 255–260; and Robert N. Stone and Frederick W. Winter, "Risk: Is It Still Uncertainty Times Consequences" pp. 261–265.

13. For good basic reading in this topic, see John W. Atkinson, *An Introduction to Motivation* (Princeton, N.J.: D. Van Nostrand, 1964); and Joel B. Cohen (ed.), *Behavioral Science Foundations of Consumer Behavior* (New York: Free Press, 1972), pp. 52–58. For discussions closer to the consumer behavior context, see William J. McGuire, "Psychological Motives and Communication Gratification," in J. Blumer and C. Katz (eds.), *The Uses of Mass Communications* (Beverly Hills, Calif.: Sage, 1974), pp. 167–196; and James R. Bettman, *An Information Processing Theory of Consumer Behavior* (Reading, Mass.: Addison-Wesley, 1979), pp. 43–72.

14. Atkinson, *An Introduction to Motivation*, p. 274.

15. See, for example, Daniel E. Berlyne, *Conflict, Arousal, and Curiosity* (New York: McGraw-Hill, 1960); M. Venkatesan, "Cognitive Consistency and Novelty Seeking," in S. Ward and T. Robertson (eds.), *Consumer Behavior: Theoretical Sources* (Englewood Cliffs, N.J.: Prentice Hall, 1973), pp. 354–384; L. McAlister and E. A. Pessemier, "Variety Seeking Behavior: An Interdisciplinary Review, *Journal of Consumer Research*, Vol. 9 (December 1982), pp. 311–322; R. A. Mittelstaedt, S. Grossbart, W. Curtis, and S. Devere, " Optimal Stimulation Level and the Adoption Decision Process," *Journal of Consumer Research*, Vol. 3 (September 1976), pp. 84–94; P. S. Raju, "Optimum Stimulation Level: Its Relationship to Personality, Demographics, and Exploratory Behavior," *Journal of Consumer Research*, Vol. 7 (December 1980), pp. 272–282; E. Hirschman and M. Wallendorf, "Some Implications of Variety Seeking for Advertising and Advertisers," *Journal of Advertising*, Vol. 9, (1980), pp. 17–25; W. D. Hoyer and N. M. Ridgway, "Variety Seeking as an Explanation for Exploratory Purchase Behavior: A Theoretical Model," *Advances in Consumer Research*, Vol. 11 (1984), pp. 114–119; R. G. Wahlers, M. G. Dunn, and M. J. Etzel, "The Congruence of Alternative OSL measures with Consumer Exploratory Behavior Tendencies," *Advances in Consumer Research*, Vol. 13 (1986); Russell G. Wahlers and Mark G. Dunn, "Optimal Stimulation Level Measurement and Exploratory Behavior: Review and Analysis," *AMA Winter Educators' Proceedings* (1987), pp. 249–254; and William J. Havlena and Susan L. Holak, "The Influence of Variety on the Demand for Bundles of Musical Performances," *Advances in Consumer Research*, Vol. 15 (1988), pp. 22–26.

16. "Creators Keep Cosmo Cookin'," *Advertising Age*, October 24, 1988, pp. S-36–38.

17. Philip Kotler, "The Marketing of Designed Experiences," Working Paper, Northwestern University, Evanston, Ill., April 1984; Blayne Cutler, "Anything for a Thrill," *American Demographics*, August 1988, pp. 38 ff.; Lenore Skenazy, "Interacting with Your TV," *Advertising Age*, August 29, 1988, p. 52.

18. See, for example, E. C. Hirschman, "Innovativeness, Novelty Seeking, and Consumer Creativity," *Journal of Consumer Research*, Vol. 7 (December 1980), pp. 283–295; M. B. Holbrook and E. C. Hirschman, "The Experiential Aspects of Consumption: Consumer Fantasies, Feelings, and Fun," *Journal of Consumer Research*, Vol. 9 (September 1982), pp. 132–140; E. Hirschman and M. Holbrook, "Hedonic Consumption: Emerging Concepts, Methods and Propositions," *Journal of Marketing*, Summer 1982, pp. 92–101; S. C. Cosmas, A. C. Samli, and H. L. Meadow, "Toward an Interdisciplinary Framework for Examining Quality of Life," *Advances in Consumer Research*, Vol. 7 (1980), pp. 582–587; L. S. Unger and J. B. Kernan, "On the Meaning of Leisure: An Investigation of Some Determinants of The Subjective Experience," *Journal of Consumer Research*, Vol. 9 (March 1983), pp. 381–392; O. T. Ahtola, "Hedonic and Utilitarian Aspects of Consumption Behaviors: An Attitudinal Perspective," *Advances in Consumer Research*, Vol. 12

(1985), pp. 7–10; D. W. Rook and S. J. Hoch, "Consuming Impulses," *Advances in Consumer Research*, Vol. 12 (1985), pp. 23–27; L. A. Hudson and J. B. Murray, "Methodological Limitations of the Hedonic Consumption Paradigm and a Possible Alternative: A Subjective Approach," *Advances in Consumer Research*, Vol. 13 (1986).

19. Useful overviews of attribution theory as applied to consumer behavior are available in Richard W. Mizerski, Linda L. Golden, and Jerome B. Kernan, "The Attribution Process in Consumer Decision Making," *Journal of Consumer Research*, Vol. 6 (September 1979), pp. 123–140; and see Harold Kelley, "The Processes of Casual Attribution," *American Psychologist*, Vol. 28 (1973), pp. 107–128. See also R. B. Settle and L. Golden, "Attribution Theory and Advertiser Credibility," *Journal of Marketing Research*, Vol. 11 (1974), pp. 181–185; R. A. Hansen and C. A. Scott, "On Using Attribution Theory to Understand Advertising Effects," *Advances in Consumer Research*, Vol. 9 (1982), pp. 293–295; B. J. Calder and R. E. Burnkrant, "Interpersonal Influence on Consumer Behavior: An Attribution Theory Approach," *Journal of Consumer Research*, Vol. 4 (1977), pp. 29–38; R. R. Dholakia and B. Sternthal, "Highly Credible Sources: Persuasive Facilitators or Persuasive Liabilities?" *Journal of Consumer Research*, Vol. 3 (1977), pp. 223–232; R. W. Mizerski, "Causal Complexity: A Measure of Consumer Causal Attribution," *Journal of Marketing Research*, Vol. 15 (1978), pp. 220–228; T. Robertson and J. R. Rossiter, "Children and Commercial Persuasion: An Attribution Theory Analysis," *Journal of Consumer Research*, Vol. 1 (1974), pp. 13–20; R. E. Smith and S. D. Hunt, "Attribution Processes and Effects in Promotional Situations," *Journal of Consumer Research*, Vol. 5 (December 1978), pp. 149–158; W. R. Swinyard and M. L. Ray, "Advertising-Selling Interactions: An Attribution Theory Experiment," *Journal of Marketing Research*, Vol. 14 (1977), p. 509–516; V. A. Valle and M. Wallendorf, "Consumer Attribution of the Cause of Their Product Satisfaction and Dissatisfaction," in R. Day (ed.), *Consumer Satisfaction, Dissatisfaction and Complaining Behavior* (Bloomington: Indiana University Press, 1977), pp. 26–30; R. M. Sparkman and W. B. Locander, "Attribution Theory and Advertising Effectiveness," *Journal of Consumer Research*, Vol. 7 (December 1980), pp. 219–224; T. Kehret-Ward and R. Yalch, "To Take or Not To Take the Only One: Effects of Changing the Meaning of a Product Attribute on Choice Behavior," *Journal of Consumer Research*, Vol. 10 (March 1984); pp. 410–416; J. M. Hunt, T. J. Domzal, and J. B. Kernan, "Causal Attributions and Persuasions: The Case of Disconfirmed Expectancies," *Advances in Consumer Research*, Vol 9 (1982), pp. 287–292; Donald R. Lichtenstein and Scot Burton, "The Measurement and Moderating Role of Confidence in Attributions," *Advances in Consumer Research*, Vol. 15 (1988), pp. 468–47; Valerie S. Folkes and Barbara Kotsos, "Buyers' and Sellers' Explanation for Product Failure: Who Done It?" *Journal of Marketing*, Vol. 50 (April 1986), pp. 74–80; Mary T. Curren and Valerie S. Folkes, "Attributional Influences on Consumers' Desires to Communicate About Products," *Psychology & Marketing*, Vol. 4 (Spring 1987), pp. 31–46; and Valerie S. Folkes, "Recent Attribution Research in Consumer Behavior: A Review and New Directions," *Journal of Consumer Research*, Vol. 14 (March 1988), pp. 548–565.

20. For a basic discussion of self-perception theory, see D. Bem, "Self Perception Theory," in L. Berkowtiz (ed.), *Advances in Experimental Social Psychology*, Vol. 6 (New York: Academic Press, 1972), pp. 1–62. FITD and DITF studies are described in J. L. Freedman and S. Fraser, "Compliance Without Pressure: The Foot-in-the-Door Technique," *Journal of Personality and Social Psychology*, Vol. 4 (1966), pp. 195–202; P. Pliner, H. Hart, J. Kohl, and D. Saari, "Compliance Without Pressure: Some Further Data on the Foot-in-the-Door Technique," *Journal of Experimental Social Psychology*, Vol. 10 (1974), pp. 17–22; P. H. Reingen and J. B. Kernan, "Compliance with an Interview Request: A Foot-in-the-Door, Self-Perception Interpretation," *Journal of Marketing Research*, Vol. 14 (1977), pp. 365–369; C. A. Scott, "The Effects of Trial and Incentives on Repeat Purchase Behavior," *Journal of Marketing Research*, Vol. 13 (1976), pp. 263–269; C. A. Scott, "Modifying Socially-Conscious Behavior: The Foot-in-the-Door Technique," *Journal of Consumer Research*, Vol. 4 (1977), pp. 156–164; A. M. Tybout, "Relative Effectiveness and Three Behavioral Influence Strategies as Supplements to Persuasion in a Marketing Context," *Journal of Marketing Research*, Vol. 15 (1978), pp. 229–242; C. T. Allen, C. D. Schewe, and G. Wijk, "More on Self-Perception Theory's Foot Technique in the Pre-Call/Mail Survey Setting," *Journal of Marketing Research*, Vol. 17 (1980), pp. 498–502; R. A. Hansen and L. M. Robinson, "Testing the Effectiveness of Alternative Foot-in-the-Door Manipulations," *Journal of Marketing Research*, Vol. 17 (August 1980), pp. 359–364; J. C. Mowen and R. B. Cialdini, "On Implementing the Door-in-the-Face Compliance Technique in a Business Context," *Journal of Marketing Research*, Vol. 17 (May 1980), pp. 253–258; D. H. Furse, D. W. Stewart, and D. L. Rados, "Effects of Foot-in-the-Door, Cash Incentives, and Followups on Survey Response," *Journal of Marketing Research*, Vol. 18 (November 1981), pp. 474–478; P. H. Reingen, "On Inducing Compliance with Requests,"

Journal of Consumer Research, Vol. 5 (September 1978), pp. 96–102; P. Reingen and J. B. Kernan, "More Evidence on Interpersonal Yielding," *Journal of Marketing Research,* Vol. 16 (November 1979), pp. 588–593; A. Tybout and R. Yalch, "The Effect of Experience: A Matter of Salience?" *Journal of Consumer Research,* Vol. 6 (1980), pp. 406–413; C. T. Allen, "Self-Perception Based Strategies for Stimulating Energy Conservation," *Journal of Consumer Research,* Vol. 8 (March 1982), pp. 381–390; P. H. Reingen and W. O. Bearden, "The Salience of Behavior and the Effects of Labeling," *Advances in Consumer Research,* Vol. 10 (1983), pp. 51–55; C. T. Allen and W. R. Dillon, "Self Perception Development and Consumer Choice Criteria: Is There a Linkage?" *Advances in Consumer Research,* Vol. 10 (1983), pp. 45–50; Edward F. Fern, Kent B. Monroe, and Ramon A. Avila, "Effectiveness of Multiple Request Strategies: A Synthesis of Research Results," *Journal of Marketing Research,* Vol. 23 (May 1986), pp. 144–152; Cynthia Fraser, Robert E. Hite, and Paul L. Sauer, "Increasing Contributions in Solicitation Campaigns: The Use of Large and Small Anchorpoints," *Journal of Consumer Research,* Vol. 15 (September 1988), pp. 284–287; Kathleen Debevec, Harlan E. Spotts, and Jerome B. Kernan, "The Self-Reference Effect in Persuasion: Implications for Marketing Strategy," *Advances in Consumer Research,* Vol. 14 (1987), pp. 417–420; and Kathleen Debevec and Easwar Iyer, "Self-Referencing as a Mediator of the Effectiveness of Sex-Role Portrayals in Advertising," *Psychology & Marketing,* Vol. 5 (Spring 1988), pp. 71–84.

21. Abraham H. Maslow, *Motivation and Personality,* 2nd ed. (New York: Harper & Row, 1970). For consumer-oriented applications see George Brooker, "The Self-Actualizing Socially Conscious Consumer," *Journal of Consumer Research,* Vol. 5 (September 1976), pp. 107–112; and William E. Kilbourne, "The Self-Actualizing Consumer vs. the Class Cage," *AMA Winter Educators' Proceedings* (1987), pp. 312–315.

22. This section is based upon discussions in Desmond S. Cartwright, *Theories and Models of Personality* (Dubuque, Iowa: William C. Brown, 1979), pp. 2–25; and Calvin S. Hall, Gardner Lindzey, John Loehlin, and Martin Manosevitz, *Introduction to Theories of Personality* (New York: John Wiley, 1985), pp. 309–339. For recent advances in working with this listing, see Paul T. Costa and Robert R. McCrae, "From Catalog to Classification: Murray's Needs and the Five-Factor Model," *Journal of Personality and Social Psychology,* Vol. 55, no. 2 (1988), pp. 258–265. For related application discussions, see, for example, James U. McNeal and Stephen W. McDaniel, "An Analysis of Need-Appeals in Television Advertising," *Journal of the Academy of Marketing Science,* Vol. 12 (Spring 1984), pp. 176–190; Robert E. Wilkes, John J. Burnett, and Roy D. Howell, "On the Meaning and Measurement of Religiosity in Consumer Research," *Journal of the Academy of Marketing Science,* Vol. 14 (Spring 1986), pp. 47–56; and Winston H. Mahatoo, "A Case for Differentiating Motives from Needs, Drives, Wants," *AMA Winter Educators' Proceedings* (1987), pp. 217–220.

Chapter 7:   Consumer Personality, Values, and Involvement

1. "He'll Die with His Driving Gloves on," *Marketing Week,* November 23, 1987, p. 62.
2. According to Freud's theory, some common defense mechanisms that people use are *repression* (the ego moves certain memories into the unconscious and does not allow us to deal with them at the conscious level), *identification* (unconscious imitation of another person who has apparently resolved the very anxieties that we feel at a particular time), *displacement* (a shift of focus of energy from an unacceptable behavior to an acceptable behavior which substitutes for it), *projection* (a process in which we may unconsciously shift our own unacceptable feelings to another person or group, and believe that they are the people with those negative beliefs or motivations), and *reaction formation* (an unconscious process in which we actually reverse our true feelings and behaviors). For fuller explanations, see the text reference in note 4.
3. David Keirsey and Marilyn Bates, *Please Understand Me: Character and Temperment Types,* 3rd ed. (Del Mar, Calif: Prometheus Nemesis, 1978).
4. Calvin S. Hall and Gardner Lindzey, *Theories of Personality* (New York: John Wiley, 1987).
5. This description is based upon Franklin B. Evans, "Psychological and Objective Factors in the Prediction of Brand Choice," *Journal of Business,* Vol. 32 (October 1959), pp. 340–369.
6. Harold H. Kassarjian and Mary Jane Sheffet, "Personality and Consumer Behavior: An Update," in H. H. Kassarjian and T. S. Robertson (eds.), *Perspectives in Consumer Behavior,* 3rd ed. (Glenview, Ill.: Scott, Foresman, 1981), pp. 160–180.
7. A. A. Kuehn, "Demonstration of a Relationship Between Psychological Factors and Brand Choice," *Journal of Business,* Vol. 36 (April 1963), pp. 237–241.
8. The issues and perspectives raised in this debate are most interesting. In addition to the original Evans article and the Kuehn comment, see also the comments and rejoinders by Pierre Martineau,

"Letters to the Editor," *Advertising Age,* Vol. 30, December 21, 1959, p. 76; Gary Steiner, "Notes on Franklin B. Evans' 'Psychological and Objective Factors in the Prediction of Brand Choice,'" *Journal of Business,* Vol. 34 (January 1961), pp. 57–60; Charles Winick, "The Relationships Among Personality Needs, Objective Factors, and Brand Choice: A Re-examination," *Journal of Business,* Vol. 34 (January 1961), pp. 61–66; Joseph Murphy, "Questionable Correlates of Automobile Shopping Behavior," *Journal of Marketing,* Vol. 27 October 1963), pp. 71–72; Alan Marcus, "Obtaining Group Measures from Personality Test Scores: Auto Brand Choice Predicted from the Edwards Personal Preference Schedule," *Psychological Reports,* Vol. 17 (October 1965), pp. 523–531; and Jacob Jacoby, "Personality and Consumer Behavior: How Not to Find Relationships," *Purdue Papers in Consumer Psychology,* No. 102, Purdue University, Lafayette, Ind., 1969. Rejoinders to these comments were written by Evans: Franklin Evans, "Reply: You Still Can't Tell a Ford Owner from a Chevrolet Owner," *Journal of Business,* Vol. 34 (January 1961), pp. 67–73; "True Correlates of Automobile Shopping Behavior," *Journal of Marketing,* Vol. 26 (October 1962), pp. 74–77; and Evans and Harry Roberts, "Fords, Chevrolets, and the Problem of Discrimination," *Journal of Business,* Vol. 36 (April 1963), pp. 242–249; Evans also replicated his study in Evans, "Ford vs. Chevrolet: Park Forest Revisited," *Journal of Business,* Vol. 41 (October 1968), pp. 445–459.

9. See, for example, Karen Horney, *New Ways in Psychoanalysis* (New York: W. W. Norton, 1939); and Karen Horney, *Our Inner Conflicts* (New York: W. W. Norton, 1945).

10. This description is based upon Joel B. Cohen, "Toward an Interpersonal Theory of Consumer Behavior," *California Management Review,* Vol. 10 (Spring 1968), pp. 73–80; and Joel B. Cohen, "An Interpersonal Orientation to the Study of Consumer Behavior," *Journal of Marketing Research,* Vol. 4 (August 1967), pp. 270–278. Since the time of the original studies, Cohen's CAD instrument has received further testing and use within the marketing field. See, for example, Jerome Kernan, "Choice Criteria, Decision Behavior, and Personality," *Journal of Marketing Research,* Vol. 5 (May 1968), pp. 155–164; Joel B. Cohen and Ellen Golden, "Informational Social Influence and Product Evaluation," *Journal of Applied Psychology,* Vol. 50 (February 1972), pp. 54–59; Jon P. Noerager, "An Assessment of CAD—A Personality Instrument Developed Specifically for Marketing Research," *Journal of Marketing Research,* Vol. 16 (February 1979), pp. 53–59; Arch Woodside and Ruth Andress, "CAD Eight Years Later," *Journal of the Academy of Marketing Science,* Vol. 3 (Summer–Fall 1975), pp. 309–313; Michael Ryan and Richard Becherer, "A Multivariate Test of CAD Instrument Construct Validity," *Advances in Consumer Research,* Vol. 3 (1976), pp. 149–154; Pradeep K. Tyagi, "Validation of the CAD Instrument: A Replication," *Advances in Consumer Research,* Vol. 10 (1983), pp. 112–118; and Mark E. Slama, Terrell G. Williams, and Armen Tashchian, "Compliant, Aggressive and Detached Types Differ in Generalized Purchasing Involvement," *Advances in Consumer Research,* Vol. 15 (1988), pp. 158–162.

11. See, the overviews in William D. Wells and Arthur Beard, "Personality in Consumer Behavior," in Scott Ward and Thomas Robertson (eds.), *Consumer Behavior: Theoretical Sources* (Englewood Cliffs, N.J.: Prentice Hall, 1973), pp. 141–199; and Harold Kassarjian, "Personality and Consumer Behavior: A Review," in H. Kassarjian and T. Robertson, (eds.), *Perspectives in Consumer Behavior,* rev. ed. (Glenview Ill.: Scott, Foresman, 1973), pp. 129–148. See also Harold Kassarjian and Mary Jane Sheffet, "Personality and Consumer Behavior: An Update," in ibid., 3rd ed. (Glenview, Ill.: Scott, Foresman, 1981), pp. 160–180; Joseph T. Plummer, "How Personality Makes a Difference," *Journal of Advertising Research,* Vol. 24, no. 6 (December 1984–January 1985), pp. 27–31; and Paul J. Albanese, "A Paradox of Personality in Marketing: A New Approach to the Problem," *AMA Educators' Proceedings* (1989), pp. 245–249.

12. See, for example, Richard Becherer and Lawrence Richard, "Self-Monitoring as a Moderating Variable in Consumer Behavior," *Journal of Consumer Research,* Vol. 5 (December 1978), pp. 159–162; Raymond Horton, "Some Relationships Between Personality and Consumer Decision Making," *Journal of Marketing Research,* Vol. 16 (May 1979), pp. 233–246; Charles Schaninger and Donald Sciglimpaglia, "The Influences of Cognitive Personality Traits and Demographics on Consumer Information Acquisition," *Journal of Consumer Research,* Vol. 8 (September 1981), pp. 208–216; Chin Tiong Tan and Ira J. Dolich, "Cognitive Structure in Personality: An Investigation of Its Generality in Buying Behavior," *Advances in Consumer Research,* Vol. 7 (1980), pp. 547–551; Lawrence A. Crosby and Sanford L. Grossbart, "A Blueprint for Consumer Behavior Research on Personality," *Advances in Consumer Research,* Vol. 11 (1984), pp. 447–452; Benoy Joseph and Shailesh J. Vyas, "Concurrent Validity of a Measure of Innovative Cognitive Style," *Journal of the Academy of Marketing Science,* Vol. 12 (Spring 1984), pp. 159–175; Robert C. Lewis and David M. Klein, "Personal Constructs: Their Use in the Marketing of Intangible Services," *Psychology & Marketing,* Vol. 2 (Fall 1985), pp. 201–216; Ram Kesavan and Oswald Mascarenhas,

"An Alternate Measure of Cognitive Complexity and Its Comparison with the Bieri Measure," *AMA Educators' Proceedings* (1986), pp. 46–49; Hank Cetola and Kathleen Prinkey, "Intraversion-Extraversion and Loud Commercials," *Psychology & Marketing,* Vol. 3 (Summer 1986), pp. 123 ff; Scott Dawson and Nancy Ridgway, "The Relationship Between Need for Uniqueness and Fashion Opinion Leadership: A Motivational Approach," *AMA Winter Educators' Proceedings* (1987), pp. 225–228; Gordon R. Foxall and Ronald E. Goldsmith, "Personality and Consumer Research: Another Look," *Journal of the Marketing Research Society,* Vol. 30, no. 2 (1988), pp. 111–125; John L. Lastovicka and Erich A. Joachimsthaler, "Improving the Detection of Personality-Behavior Relationships in Consumer Research," *Journal of Consumer Research,* Vol. 14 (March 1988), pp. 583–587; Curtis P. Haugtvedt and Richard E. Petty, "Need for Cognition and Attitude Persistence," *Advances in Consumer Research,* Vol. 16 (1989), pp. 33–36; and Ayn E. Crowley and Wayne D. Hoyer, "The Relationship Between Need for Cognition and Other Individual Difference Variables: A Two-Dimensional Framework," *Advances in Consumer Research,* Vol. 167 (1989), pp. 37–43.

13. "A Blood Sample for Your Broker," *Fortune,* August 15, 1988, p. 12.

14. This is an intersecting area that poses some challenging problems for consumer researchers. For an overview of research in this area, see M. Joseph Sirgy, "Self-Concept in Consumer Behavior: A Critical Review," *Journal of Consumer Research* (December 1982), pp. 287–300. Among the interesting papers in this area are the following: Edward L. Grubb and Harrison L. Grathwohl, "Consumer Self-Concept, Symbolism, and Market Behavior: A Theoretical Approach," *Journal of Marketing,* Vol. 31 (October 1967), pp. 22–27; Ira J. Dolich, "Congruence Relationship Between Self-Image and Product Brands," *Journal of Marketing Research,* Vol. 6 (February 1969), pp. 80–84; Ivan Ross, "Self-Concept and Brand Preference," *Journal of Business,* Vol. 44 (1971), pp. 38–50; Laird Landon, "Self-Concept, Ideal Self-Concept and Consumer Purchase Intentions," *Journal of Consumer Research,* Vol. 1 (September 1974), pp. 44–51; Danny N. Bellenger, W. W. Stanton, and F. Steinberg, "The Congruence of Store Image and Self-Image as It Relates to Store Loyalty," *Journal of Retailing,* Vol. 52 (Spring 1976), pp. 17–32; Terrence V. O'Brien and Humberto T. Sanchez, "Consumer Motivation: A Developmental Self-Concept Approach," *Journal of the Academy of Marketing Science,* Vol. 4, no. 3 (1976), pp. 608–616; Bruce L. Stern, Ronald F. Bush, and Joseph F. Hair, Jr., "The Self-Image/Store Image Matching Process: An Empirical Test," *Journal of Business,* Vol. 50 (January 1977), pp. 63–69; George F. Belch, "Belief Systems and the Differential Role of the Self-Concept," *Advances in Consumer Research,* Vol. 5 (1978), pp. 320–325; James W. Gentry, Mildred Doering, and Terrence V. O'Brien, "Masculinity and Femininity Factors in Product Perception and Self-Image," *Advances in Consumer Research,* Vol. 5 (1978), pp. 326–332; Linda L. Golden, Neil Allison, and Mona Clee, "The Role of Sex-Role Self-Concept in Masculine and Feminine Product Perception," *Advances in Consumer Research,* Vol. 6 (1979) pp. 595–605; Neil K. Allison, Linda L. Golden, Gary M. Mullet, and Donna Coogan, "Sex, Sex-Role Self Concept and Measurement Implications," *Advances in Consumer Research,* Vol. 7 (1980), pp. 604–609; J. Michael Munson and W. Austin Spivey, "Assessing Self-Concept," *Advances in Consumer Research,* Vol. 7 (1980), pp. 598–603; Joseph M. Sirgy and Jeffrey Danes, "Self-Image/Product-Image Congruence Models: Testing Selected Mathematical Models," *Advances in Consumer Research,* Vol. 9; (1981) pp. 556–561; Warren S. Martin and Joseph Bellizzi, "An Analysis of Congruous Relationships Between Self-Images and Product Images," *Journal of the Academy of Marketing Science* (December 1982), pp. 473–488; M. Joseph Sirgy, "Using Self-Congruity and Ideal Congruity to Predict Purchase Motivation," *Journal of Business Research,* Vol. 13 (June 1985), pp. 195–206; M. Joseph Sirgy, "The Moderating Role of Response Mode in Consumer Self-Esteem/Self-Consistency Effects," *AMA Winter Educators' Proceedings* (1987), pp. 50–55; Bernd H. Schmitt, France Leclerc, and Laurette Dubé-Riox, "Sex Typing and Consumer Behavior: A Test of Gender Schema Theory," *Journal of Consumer Research,* Vol. 15 (June 1988), pp. 122–128; and Barbara B. Stern, "Sex-Role Self-Concept Measures and Marketing: A Research Note," *Psychology & Marketing,* Vol. 5 (Spring 1988), pp. 85 ff.

15. Francine Schwadel, "The Bare Facts Show a Suitable Swimsuit Is Difficult to Find," *The Wall Street Journal,* July 6, 1988, pp. 1 ff.

16. For an excellent analysis of the beginnings of psychographics, and its strengths and weaknesses, see William D. Wells, "Psychographics: A Critical Review," *Journal of Marketing Research,* Vol. 12 (May 1975), pp. 196–213.

17. Shirley Young, "The Dynamics of Measuring Unchange," in Russell L. Haley (ed.), *Attitude Research in Transition* (Chicago: American Marketing Association, 1972), pp. 49–82.

18. Milton Rokeach, *Understanding Human Values: Individual and Societal* (New York: Free Press, 1979); see also Milton Rokeach, *The Nature of Human Values* (New York: Free Press, 1973);

Ronald E. Goldsmith, J. Dennis White, and Melvin T. Stith, "Yeasaying and the Rokeach Value Survey: Interactions with Age and Race," *AMA Educators' Proceedings* (1987), p. 238; and J. Michael Munson and Edward F. McQuarrie, "Shortening the Rokeach Value Survey for Use in Consumer Research," *Advances in Consumer Research,* Vol. 15 (1988), pp. 381–386.

19. Sharon Beatty, Lynn R. Kahle, Pamela Homer, and Shekhar Misra, "Alternative Measurement Approaches to Consumer Values: The List of Values and the Rokeach Value Survey," *Psychology & Marketing,* Vol. 2 (Fall 1985), pp. 181–200. The Winter 1985 issue of *Psychology & Marketing* is devoted to this topic, including Lynn R. Kahle "Social Values in the Eighties: A Special Issue," pp. 231–238; Edward McQuarrie and Daniel Langmeyer, "Using Values to Measure Attitudes Toward Discontinuous Innovations," pp. 239–252; Kathy L. Pettit, Sonja Sawa, and Ghazi Sawa, "Frugality: A Cross-National Moderator of the Price-Quality Relationship," pp. 253–266; Robert E. Pitts, Anne Canty, and John Tsalikis, "Exploring the Impact of Personal Values on Socially Oriented Communications," pp. 267–278; and Ved Prakash and J. Michael Munson, "Values, Expectations from the Marketing System and Product Expectations," pp. 279–296. For additional recent findings, see also Lynne R. Kahle and Patricia Kennedy, "Using the List of Values (LOV) to Understand Consumers," *The Journal of Consumer Marketing,* Vol. 6 (Summer 1989), pp. 5–12; Lynn R. Kahle, Sharon E. Beatty, and Pamela Homer, "Alternative Measurement Approaches to Consumer Values: The List of Values (LOV) and Values and Life Style (VALS)," *Journal of Consumer Research,* Vol. 13 (December 1986), pp. 405–409; and Lynn R. Kahle, Basil Poulos, and Ajay Sukhdial, "Changes in Social Values in the United States During the Past Decade," *Journal of Advertising Research,* Vol. 28 (February–March 1988), pp. 35–41.

20. For a summary discussion of the basic laddering approach, see Thomas J. Reynolds and Jonathan Gutman, "Laddering Theory, Method, Analysis, and Interpretation," *Journal of Advertising Research,* Vol. 28, no. 1 (1988), pp. 11–31. For further discussion of the MECCAS model and the Federal Express case, see Thomas J. Reynolds and Alyce Craddock, "The Application of the MECCAS Model to the Development and Assessment of Advertising Strategy: A Case Study," *Journal of Advertising Research,* Vol. 28 (April–May 1988), pp. 43–54.

21. See, for example, Alain d'Astous and Sylvie Tremblay, "The Compulsive Side of 'Normal' Consumers: An Empirical Study," Working Paper, University of Sherbrooke, Quebec, 1989; Gilles Valence, Alain d'Astous, and Louis Fortier, "Compulsive Buying: Concept and Measurement," in K. Blois and S. Parkinson (eds.), *Proceedings of the 17th Annual Conference of the European Marketing Academy* (Bradford, England: University Management Centre, 1988), pp. 601–624; Stephen J. Hoch and George Loewenstein, "Impulse Buying and Consumer Self-Control," Working Paper, University of Chicago Business School, 1988; Ronald J. Faber and Thomas C. O'Guinn, "Compulsive Consumption and Credit Abuse," *Journal of Consumer Policy,* Vol. 11 (1988), pp. 97–109; Thomas C. O'Guinn and Ronald J. Faber, "Compulsive Buying: A Phenomenological Exploration," *Journal of Consumer Research,* Vol. 16 (September 1989), pp. 147–157; George P. Moschis and Dena Cox, "Deviant Consumer Behavior," *Advances in Consumer Research,* Vol. 16 (1989), pp. 732–737; Ronald J. Faber and Thomas C. O'Guinn, "Classifying Compulsive Consumers: Advances in the Development of a Diagnostic Tool," *Advances in Consumer Research,* Vol. 16 (1989), pp. 738–744. Also, an interesting set of articles by consumer researchers who discuss their own "compulsive" behaviors appears in *Advances in Consumer Research,* Vol. 14 (1987), pp. 125–153.

22. David Kiley, "Cutting the Fat," *Marketing Week,* March 13, 1989, pp. 20 ff.

23. The definition is adapted from that given by Joel B. Cohen, "Involvement: Separating the State from Its Causes and Effects," paper delivered to the Conference on Involvement in Marketing, New York University, June 1982. The theoretical basis for CI stems from the concept of **object cathexis** in Freudian theory. This concept later evolved into the concept of ego involvement, reflecting the fact that individuals would perceive some objects and issues as more personally involving with "self." One subset of this concept concerns commitment to a position, as reflected in the oft-cited work by Sherif and others. See, for example, M. Sherif and M. Cantril, *The Psychology of Ego Involvement* (New York: John Wiley, 1947).

24. Gilles Laurent and Jean-Noel Kapferer, "Measuring Consumer Involvement Profiles," *Journal of Marketing Research,* Vol. 22 (1985), pp. 41–53.

25. For example, Michael J. Houston and Michael L. Rothschild, "Conceptual and Methodological Perspectives on Involvement," *AMA Educators Proceedings* (1978), pp. 184–187; and Peter Bloch and Marsha Richins, "A Theoretical Model for the Study of Product Importance Perception," *Journal of Marketing,* Vol. 47 (Summer, 1983), pp. 69–81; for an overview of this research, see Carolyn L. Costley, "Meta Analysis of Involvement Research," *Advances in Consumer Research,* Vol. 15 (1988), pp. 554–562. For conceptual discussions, see also Marsha L. Richins and Peter

H. Bloch, "After the New Wears Off: The Temporal Context of Product Involvement," *Journal of Consumer Research*, Vol. 13 (September 1986), pp. 280–285; Meera Venkatraman, "Involvement and Risk: An Empirical Investigation," *AMA Educators' Proceedings* (1987), p. 126; Banwari Mittal, "A Framework for Relating Consumer Involvement to Lateral Brain Functioning," *Advances in Consumer Research*, Vol. 14 (1987), pp. 41–45; Banwari Mittal and Myung-Soo Lee, "Separating Brand-Choice Involvement from Product Involvement Via Consumer Involvement Profiles," *Advances in Consumer Research*, Vol. 15 (1987), pp. 43–49; Sharon E. Beatty, Lynn R. Kahle, and Pamela Homer, "The Involvement-Commitment Model: Theory and Implications," *Journal of Business Research*, Vol. 16 (March 1988), pp. 149–168; and Richard L. Celsi and Jerry C. Olson, "The Role of Involvement in Attention and Comprehension Processes," *Journal of Consumer Research*, Vol. 15 (September 1988), pp. 210–224.

26. Gilles Laurent and Jean-Noel Kapferer, "Measuring Consumer Involvement Profiles," *Journal of Marketing Research*, Vol. 22 (1985), pp. 41–53; Judith Lynne Zaichkowsky, "Measuring the Involvement Construct," *Journal of Consumer Research*, Vol. 12 (December 1985), pp. 341–352; Edward F. McQuarrie and J. Michael Munson, "The Zaichkowsky Personal Involvement Inventory: Modification & Extension," *Advances in Consumer Research*, Vol. 14 (1987), pp. 36–40; Raj Arora, "Involvement: Its Measurement for Retail Store Research," *Journal of the Academy of Marketing Science*, Vol. 13 (Spring 1985), pp. 229–241; Raj Arora and Robert Baer, "Measuring Consumer Involvement in Products: Comment on Traylor and Joseph," *Psychology & Marketing*, Vol. 2 (Spring 1985), pp. 59 ff; Mark B. Traylor and W. Benoy Joseph, "Reply to Arora and Baer's Comment on Measuring Consumer Involvement in Products," *Psychology & Marketing*, Vol. 2 (Summer 1985), p. 127 ff; Marya J. Pucely, Richard Mizerski, and Pamela Perrewe, "A Comparison of Involvement Measures for the Purchase and Consumption of Pre-Recorded Music," *Advances in Consumer Research*, Vol. 15 (1988), pp. 37–42; and three papers in *Advances in Consumer Research*, Vol. 16 (1989): Thomas D. Jensen, Les Carlson, and Carolyn Tripp, "The Dimensionality of Involvement: An Empirical Test," pp. 680–689; Robin A. Higie and Lawrence F. Feick, "Enduring Involvement: Conceptual and Measurement Issues," pp. 690–696; and Banwari Mittal, "A Theoretical Analysis of Two Recent Measures of Involvement," pp. 697–702.

27. Brian T. Ratchford, "New Insights About the FCB Grid," *Journal of Advertising Research*, Vol. 27, no. 4 (August–September 1987), pp. 24–37 For applications of the grid model, see Richard Vaughn, "How Advertising Works: A Planning Model," *Journal of Advertising Research*, Vol. 20, no. 5 (1980), pp. 27–33; and Richard Vaughn, "How Advertising Works: A Planning Model Revisited," *Journal of Advertising Research*, Vol. 26, no. 1 (1986), pp. 57–66. For further interesting proposals, debates, and findings on CI, see Peter H. Bloch, "Involvement Beyond the Purchase Process: Conceptual Issues and Empirical Investigation," *Advances in Consumer Research*, Vol. 9 (1983), pp. 413–417; Joel B. Cohen, "Involvement and You: 1000 Great Ideas," *Advances in Consumer Research*, Vol. 10 (1983), pp. 324–327; David W. Finn, "Low-Involvement Isn't Low-Involving," *Advances in Consumer Research*, Vol. 10 (1983) pp. 419–424; James A. Muncy and Shelby D. Hunt, "Consumer Involvement: Definitional Issues and Research Directions," *Advances in Consumer Research*, Vol. 11 (1984), pp. 193–196; Robert N. Stone, "The Marketing Characteristics of Involvement," *Advances in Consumer Research*, Vol. 11 (1984), pp. 210–215; Michael L. Ray, "Involvement and Other Variables Mediating Communication Effects as Opposed to Explaining All Consumer Behavior," *Advances in Consumer Research*, Vol. 6 (1979) pp. 197–199; Mark E. Slama and Armen Tashchian, "Selected Socioeconomic and Demographic Characteristics Associated with Purchasing Involvement," *Journal of Marketing* (Winter 1985), pp. 72–82; Richard E. Petty, John T. Cacioppo, and David Schumann, "Central and Peripheral Routes to Advertising Effectiveness: The Moderating Role of Involvement," *Journal of Consumer Research*, Vol. 10 (September 1983), pp. 135–146; Anthony G. Greenwald and Clark Leavitt, "Audience Involvement in Advertising: Four Levels," *Journal of Consumer Research*, Vol. 11 (June 1984), pp. 581–592. See also three further papers in *Advances in Consumer Research*, Vol. 6, 1979: A. A. Mitchell, "Involvement: A Potentially Important Mediator of Consumer Behavior," pp. 191–195; J. L. Lastovicka, "Questioning the Concept of Involvement Defined Product Classes," pp. 174–179; and Larry M. Newman and Ira J. Dolich, "An Examination of Ego-Involvement as a Modifier of Attitude Changes Caused from Product Testing," pp. 180–183. Also see Mark B. Traylor, "Product Involvement and Brand Commitment," *Journal of Advertising Research*, Vol. 21, no. 6 (December 1981), pp. 51–56; John H. Antil, "Conceptualization and Operationalization of Involvement," *Advances in Consumer Research* (1984), pp. 203–209; R. Arora, "Validation of S-O-R Model for Situation, Enduring, and Response Components of Involvement," *Journal of Marketing Research*, Vol. 19 (November 1982), pp. 505–516; T. T. Tyebjee, "Response Time, Conflict, and Involvement in Brand Choices," *Journal of Consumer Research*, Vol. 6 (December

1979), pp. 295–304; and J. L. Lastovicka and D. M. Gardner, "Components of Involvement," in J. C. Maloney and B. Silverman (eds.), *Attitude Research Plays for High Stakes* (Chicago: American Marketing Association, 1979), pp. 53–73. Also see the following articles in *Advances in Consumer Research*, Vol. 12 (1985); Debra Stephens, "Hemispheric Function and Involvement," pp. 285–289; Judith Lynne Zaichkowsky, "Familiarity: Product Use, Involvement or Expertise?" pp. 296–299; Gordon W. McClung, C. Whan Park, and William J. Sauer, "Viewer Processing of Commercial Messages: Context and Involvement," pp. 351–355; Rajeev Batra, "Understanding the Likability/Involvement Interaction: The 'Override' Model," pp. 362–367; George M. Zinkhan and Aydin Muderrisoglu, "Involvement, Familiarity", pp. 356–361; Michael L. Rothschild, "Perspectives on Involvement: Current Problems and Future Directions," pp. 216–217; and Sarah Fisher Gardial and Gabriel J. Biehal, "Memory Accessibility and Task Involvement as Factors in Choice," pp. 414–419. For more recent findings, see, for example, Terence A. Shimp and Thomas J. Madden, "Consumer-Object Relations: A Conceptual Framework Based Analogously on Sternberg's Triangular Theory of Love," *Advances in Consumer Research*, Vol. 15 (1988), pp. 163–168; Judy L. Zaichkowsky, "The Emotional Aspect of Product Involvement," *Advances in Consumer Research*, Vol. 14 (1987), pp. 32–35; Dennis H. Gensch and Rajshekhar G. Javalgi, "The Influence of Involvement on Disaggregate Attribute Choice Models," *Journal of Consumer Research*, Vol. 14 (June 1987), pp. 71–82; Richard L. Celsi, Simeon Chow, Jerry Olson, and Beth A. Walker, "The Trait Validity of Intrinsic Sources of Personal Relevance: An Intra-Individual Source of Involvement," *AMA Educators' Proceedings* (1988), pp. 134–135; Scot Burton and Donald R. Lichtenstein, "Measurement of the Latitude of Price Acceptance," *AMA Educators' Proceedings* 1988, pp. 320–324; James D. Gill, Sanford Grossbart, and Russell N. Laczniak, "Influence of Involvement, Commitment and Familiarity on Brand Beliefs and Attitudes of Viewers Exposed to Alternative Ad Claim Strategies," *Journal of Advertising*, Vol. 17 (November 1988), pp. 33–43; Herbert E. Krugman, "Point of View: Limits of Attention to Advertising," *Journal of Advertising Research*, Vol. 28 (October–November 1988), pp. 47 ff; Russell N. Laczniak, Darrel D. Muehling, and Sanford Grossbart, "Manipulating Message Involvement in Advertising Research," *Journal of Advertising*, Vol. 18 (November 1989), pp. 28–38; Claire P. Bolfing, "Integrating Consumer Involvement and Product Perceptions with Market Segmentation and Positioning Strategies," *Journal of Consumer Marketing*, Vol. 5 (Spring 1988), pp. 49–58; S. Ram and Hyung-Shik Jung, "The Link Between Involvement, Use Innovativeness and Product Usage," *Advances in Consumer Research*, Vol. 16 (1989), pp. 160–166; Susan Schultz, Robert E. Kleine, and Jerome B. Kernan, "These Are a Few of My Favorite Things: Toward an Explication of Attachment as a Consumer Behavior Construct," *Advances in Consumer Research*, Vol 16, (1989), pp. 359–366; and Brian T. Ratchford and Richard Vaughn, "On the Relationship Between Motives and Purchase Decisions: Some Empirical Approaches," *Advances in Consumer Research*, Vol. 16 (1989), pp. 293–299.

28. Harold H. Kassarjian, "Presidential Address, 1977: Anthropomorphism and Parsimony," *Advances in Consumer Research*, Vol. 5 (1978), pp. 13–14; see also H. H. Kassarjian, "Low Involvement—A Second Look," *Advances in Consumer Research*, Vol. 8 (1981). pp. 31–34; and George M. Zinkhan and Claes Fornell, "A Test of the Learning Hierarchy in High- and Low-Involvement Situations," *Advances in Consumer Research*, Vol. 16 (1989), pp. 152–159.

Chapter 8: Consumer Perception (I): Selecting Consumer Stimuli

1. Harold M. Schmeck, "To Appreciate Flavor, Taste with Your Nose," *The New York Times* News Service, June 24, 1982.
2. Nancy Giges, "Why Coke Delayed on Reformulating Tab," *Advertising Age*, May 21, pp. 2 ff.
3. Bill Abrams and David Garino, "Package Design Gains Stature as Visual Competition Grows," *The Wall Street Journal*, August 6, 1981, p. 25.
4. Stephen Morin, "Interior Designer Sets out to Make Casino That Relaxes Your Morality," *The Wall Street Journal*, January 10, 1983, p. 31.
5. Anthony Smith, *The Mind* (New York: Viking Press, 1984), pp. 175–201.
6. The formula for Weber's Law is:

$$JND = K \times I$$

which reads, "The just noticeable difference in a given stimulus is equal to a constant (K) proportion times the original intensity (I) of the stimulus." Subsequent scientific research has established that the value of the constant proportion, K, differs for each type of sensory receptor, that it can differ slightly for each person, that it holds better for normal circumstances than for those cases in which intensities are very high or very low to begin with, and that the relationships are slightly more complicated than the simple multiplication shown in our formula. See Bernard Berelson and Gary A. Steiner, *Human Behavior—An Inventory of Scientific Findings* (New York: Harcourt, Brace & World, 1964). For controversial extensions of this sensory principle to broader perceptual areas in marketing, see Steuart Henderson Britt, "How Weber's Law Can Be Applied to Marketing," *Business Horizons*, February 1975, pp. 21–29. See also Elizabeth J. Wilson, "Using the Dollarmetric Scale to Estimate the Just Meaningful Difference in Price," *AMA Educators' Proceedings* (1987), p. 107.

7. A. Kent MacDougall, "The World Is Becoming a Much Smaller Place in More Ways than One," *New York Post*, June 17, 1978.

8. "Packaging Design Seen as Cost-Effective Marketing Strategy," *Marketing News*, February 20, 1981, pp. 1 ff.

9. Betsy Morris, "In this Taste Test, the Loser is the Taste Test," *The Wall Street Journal*, June 3, 1987, p. 33. See also Bruce Buchanan, Moshe Givon, and Arieh Goldman, "Measurement of Discrimination Ability in Taste Tests: An Empirical Investigation," *Journal of Marketing Research*, Vol. 24 (May 1987), pp. 154–163.

10. Ralph I. Allison and Kenneth P. Uhl, "Influences of Beer Brand Identification on Taste Perception," *Journal of Marketing Research* (August 1964), pp. 36–39. See also Gary A. Mauser, "Allison and Uhl Revisited: The Effects of Taste and Brand Name on Perceptions and Preferences," *Advances in Consumer Research*, Vol. 6 (1979), pp. 161–165; John G. Lynch, Jr., and Thomas K. Srull, "Memory and Attentional Factors in Consumer Choice: Concepts and Research Methods," *Journal of Consumer Research*, Vol. 9, no. 1 (1982), pp. 18–37.

11. William Copulsky and Catherine Marton, "Sensory Cues: You've Got to Put Them Together," *Product Marketing* (January 1977), pp. 31–34. See also Stephen A. Goodwin, "Impacts of Stimulus Variables on Exploratory Behavior," *Advances in Consumer Research*, Vol. 7 (1980) pp. 264–269; and Meera P. Venkatraman and Deborah J. MacInnis, "The Epistemic and Sensory Exploratory Behaviors of Hedonic and Cognitive Consumers," *Advances in Consumer Research*, Vol. 12 (1985), pp. 102–107.

12. E. Colin Cherry, "Some Experiments on the Recognition of Speech, with One and Two Ears," *Journal of the Acoustical Society of America*, Vol. 25 (1953), pp. 975–979. For related discussion, see Armen Tashchian, J. Dennis White, and Sukgoo Pak, "Signal Detection Analysis and Advertising Recognition: An Introduction to Measurement and Interpretation Issues," *Journal of Marketing Research*, Vol. 25 (November 1988), pp. 397–404.

13. These terms are adapted from the original tripartite classification presented by Magdalen D. Vernon, "Perception, Attention, and Consciousness," in K. K. Soreno and C. D. Mortensen (eds.), *Foundations of Communication Theory* (New York: Harper & Row, 1970, p. 138). For marketing applications, see, for example, Scott B. MacKenzie, "The Role of Attention in Mediating the Effect of Advertising on Attribute Importance," *Journal of Consumer Research*, Vol. 13 (September 1986), pp. 174–195; R. L. Celsi and J. C. Olson, "The Role of Involvement in Attention and Comprehension Processes," *Journal of Consumer Research*, Vol. 15 (September 1988), pp. 210–224; and Gary L. Sullivan and Kenneth J. Burger, "An Investigation of the Determinants of Cue Utilization," *Psychology & Marketing*, Vol. 4 (Spring 1987), pp. 63–74.

14. Jack Hairston, "Don't Look Up, Please," *Gainesville (Florida) Sun*, June 26, 1984, p. B-1.

15. Ronald Alsop, "Advertisers See Big Gains in Odd Layouts," *The Wall Street Journal*, June 29, 1988, p. 25. See also Robert M. Schindler, Michael Berbaum, and Donna R. Weinzimer, "How an Attention Getting Device Can Affect Choice Among Similar Alternatives," *Advances in Consumer Research*, Vol. 14 (1987), pp. 505–509; Ronald Hoverstad, "Vividness as a Means of Attracting Attention: A Revised Concept of Vividness," *AMA Winter Educators' Proceedings* (1987), pp. 245–248.

16. "Packaging Research Probes Stopping Power, Label Reading, and Consumer Attitudes Among the Targeted Audience," *Marketing News*, July 22, 1983, p. 8.

17. Dean Rotbart, "Store Designer Raises Profits for Retailers," *The Wall Street Journal*, December 5, 1980, p. 29.

18. For recent discussions of how consumer knowledge affects perceptual automaticity, see, for example, J. W. Alba and J. W. Hutchinson, "Dimensions of Consumer Expertise," *Journal of Consumer Research*, Vol. 13, no. 4 (1987), pp. 411–454; S. Ratneswar, David Mick, and Gail Reitinger, "Selective Attention in Consumer Information Processing: The Role of Chronically Accessible Attributes," in *Advances in Consumer Research*, Vol. 17 (1990); and a series of studies by John A. Bargh and colleagues, for example, J. A. Bargh, Wendy Lombardi, and E. Troy Higgins, "Automaticity of Chronically Accessible Constructs . . . ," *Journal of Personality and Social Psychology*, Vol. 55, no. 4 (1988), pp. 599–605.

19. See, for example, Norman Cousins, "Smudging the Subconscious," *Saturday Review,* October 5, 1957; also H. Brean, "What the Hidden Sell Is All About," *Life,* March 31, 1958, pp. 104–114. For a summary of this work, see Timothy E. Moore, "Subliminal Advertising: What You See Is What You Get," *Journal of Marketing,* Vol. 46 Spring 1982), pp. 38–47; for further details and findings, see Norman F. Dixon, *Subliminal Perception: The Nature of a Controversy* (London: McGraw-Hill, 1971); Norman F. Dixon, *Preconscious Processing* (London: John Wiley, 1981); Ulric Neisser, *Cognitive Psychology* (New York: Appleton-Century-Croft, 1977); Anthony J. Marcel, "Conscious and Unconscious Perception: Experiments on Visual Masking and Word Recognition," *Cognitive Psychology,* Vol. 15, pp. 197–237; Anthony J. Marcel, "Conscious and Unconscious Perception: An Approach to the Relations Between Phenomenal Experience and Perceptual Processes," *Cognitive Psychology,* Vol. 15, pp. 238–301; Daniel Holender, "Semantic Activation Without Conscious Activation in Dichotic Listening, Parafovial Vision and Pattern Masking: A Survey and Appraisal," *The Behavioral and Brain Sciences,* 9 (1986), pp. 1–66; John F. Kihlstrom, "The Cognitive Unconscious," *Science,* Vol. 237 (1987), pp. 1445–1452; and Philip M. Merikle and Jim Chesman, "Current Status of Research on Subliminal Perception," *Advances in Consumer Research,* Vol. 14 (1987), pp. 298–302.

    For a recent indepth marketing look at this topic, see the Winter 1988 special issue of *Psychology & Marketing,* Vol. 5 (1988), which includes Timothy E. Moore, "Guest Editorial," pp. 291–296; Timothy E. Moore, "The Case Against Subliminal Manipulation," pp. 297–316; Nicolaos E. Synodinos, "Review and Appraisal of Subliminal Perception Within the Context of Signal Detection Theory," pp. 317–336; Anthony Pratkanis and Anthony Greenwald, "Recent Perspectives on Unconscious Processing: Still No Marketing Applications," pp. 337–354; and Philip Merikle, "Subliminal Auditory Messages: An Evaluation," pp. 355–372.

20. For an accusation that the movie theater study reported results were fabricated, see Walter Weir, "Another Look at Subliminal Facts," *Advertising Age,* October 15, 1984.

21. M. L. DeFleur and R. M. Petranoff, "A Television Test of Subliminal Persuasion," *Public Opinion Quarterly,* Summer 1959, pp. 170–180.

22. See, for example, D. Hawkins, "The Effects of Subliminal Stimulation on Drive Level and Brand Preference," *Journal of Marketing Research,* Vol. 8 (August 1970), pp. 322–326; the discussions in Moore, "Subliminal Advertising" (note 19); Joel Saegert, "Another Look at Subliminal Perception," *Journal of Advertising Research,* Vol. 19, no. 1 (1979), pp. 55–57; and Joel Saegert, "Why Marketing Should Quit Giving Subliminal Advertising the Benefit of the Doubt," *Psychology & Marketing,* Vol. 4 (Summer 1987), pp. 107–120.

23. W. B. Key, *Subliminal Seduction* (Englewood Cliffs, N.J.: Signet, 1973), W. B. Key, *Media Sexploitation* (Englewood Cliffs, N.J.; Prentice Hall, 1976); and W. B. Key, *The Clamplate Orgy* (Englewood Cliffs, N.J.; Prentice Hall, 1980).

24. G. S. Bagley and B. J. Dunlap, "Subliminally Embedded Ads: A 'Turn On'?" *Proceedings of the Southern Marketing Association* (1980), pp. 296–298.

25. J. S. Kelly, "Subliminal Embeds in Print Advertising: A Challenge to Advertising Ethics," *Journal of Advertising,* Vol. 8, no. 3 (1979), pp. 20–24; and J. G. Caccavale, T. C. Wanty, and J. A. Edell, "Subliminal Implants in Advertisements: An Experiment," *Advances in Consumer Research,* Vol. 9 (1982), pp. 418–423; and Rajeev Kohli and Deborah MacInnis, "Subliminal Advertising: An Empirical Investigation of its Effects in Print Media," Working Paper, University of Arizona, Tucson, 1989. For basic discussion of how persuasion might occur in this area, see R. B. Zajonc, "Feeling and Thinking: Preferences Need No Inferences," *American Psychologist,* Vol. 35 (February 1980), pp. 151–175; Stephan C. George and Luther B. Jennings, "Effect of Subliminal Stimuli on Consumer Behavior: Negative Evidence," *Perceptual and Motor Skills,* Vol. 41 (1975). pp. 847–854; and Ronnie Cuperfain and T. K. Clarke, "A New Perspective on Subliminal Perception," *Journal of Advertising,* Vol. 14, no. 1 (1985), p. 36–41. See also William E. Kilbourne, Scott Painton, and Danny Ridley, "The Effect of Sexual Embedding on Responses to Magazine Advertisements," *Journal of Advertising,* Vol. 14, no. 2 (1985), pp. 48–56; Yehoshua Tsal, "On the Relationship Between Cognitive and Affective Processes: A Critique of Zajonc and Markus," *Journal of Consumer Research,* Vol. 12 (December 1985), pp. 358–362; and R. B. Zajonc and Hazel Markus, "Must All Affect Be Mediated by Cognition?" *Journal of Consumer Research,* Vol. 12 (December 1985), pp. 363 ff.

26. Albert S. King, "Pupil Size, Eye Direction, and Message Appeal: Some Preliminary Findings," *Journal of Marketing* (July 1972), pp. 55–58. For recent research on preconscious processing, see Chris Janiszewski, "Preconscious Processing Effects: The Independence of Attitude Formation and Conscious Thought," *Journal of Consumer Research,* Vol. 15 (September 1988), pp. 199–209.

Chapter 9: Consumer Perception (II): Interpreting Consumer Stimuli

1. Gregory Witcher, "Department of Shattered Illusions: Coreenthian Leather Is Made in . . . ," *The Wall Street Journal*, April 11, 1988, p. 21.
2. This section is based on discussions in J. R. Hayes, *Cognitive Psychology: Thinking and Creating* (Homewood, Ill.: Dorsey, 1978, pp. 52–73); H. R. Schiffman, *Sensation and Perception: An Integrated Approach* (New York: John Wiley, 1976); D. A. Aaker and J. G. Myers, *Advertising Management*, 2nd ed. (Englewood Cliffs, N.J.: Prentice Hall, 1982); and Carolyn Simmons, "Perceptual Issues in Consumer Behavior," Working Paper, University of Florida, Gainesville, 1981.
3. Wolfgang Kohler, *The Mentality of Apes* (London: Routledge and Kegan Paul, 1925); and Wolfgang Kohler, *Dynamics of Psychology* (New York: Liveright, 1940), as reported in Hayes, *Cognitive Psychology*.
4. George S. Day, "General Foods Corporation: Maxim," in G. S. Day et al. (eds.), *Cases in Computer Model Assisted Marketing* (Cupertino, Calif.: Hewlett-Packard, 1973), pp. 65–92.
5. Charles G. Burck, "Plain Labels Challenge the Supermarket Establishment," *Fortune*, March 26, 1979, pp. 70–75.
6. Gail Bronson, "Baby-Food It Is, but Gerber Wants Teen-Agers to Think of It as Dessert," *The Wall Street Journal*, July 17, 1981, p. 29.
7. "Safety First in Sampling," *Advertising Age*, July 26, 1981.
8. The concept of "schema" was developed over 50 years ago, by F. C. Bartlett, *Remembering* (Cambridge, Mass.: Harvard University Press, 1932). For a comprehensive background on schema theories, see Joseph W. Alba and Lynn Hasher, "Is Memory Schematic?" *Psychological Bulletin*, Vol. 93 (1983), pp. 203–231; and W. F. Brewer and G. V. Nakamura, "The Nature and Functions of Schemas," in R. S. Wyer and T. K. Srull (eds.), *Handbook of Social Cognition* (Hillsdale, N.J.: Erlbaum, 1984). For applications to consumer behavior, see the following articles in *Advances in Consumer Research*, Vol. 11 (1984): Jennifer Crocker, "A Schematic Approach to Changing Consumers' Beliefs," pp. 472–477; Meera Venkatraman and Angelina Villarreal, "Schematic Processing of Information: An Exploratory Investigation," pp. 355–360; and Joel B. Cohen, "Does the Emperor Ride Again?" pp. 367–368. See also Ruth Ann Smith, Michael J. Houston, and Terry L. Childers, "The Effects of Schematic Memory on Imaginal Information Processing: An Empirical Assessment," *Psychology & Marketing*, Vol. 2 (Spring 1985), pp. 13–30; and Lawrence W. Barsalou and J. Wesley Hutchinson, "Schema-Based Planning of Events in Consumer Contexts, *Advances in Consumer Research*, Vol. 14 (1987), pp. 114–118.

   The basis of script theory is well described in Robert P. Abelson, "Script Processing in Attitude Formation and Decision-Making," in J. S. Carroll and J. W. Payne (eds.), *Cognition and Social Behavior* (Hillsdale, N.J.: Erlbaum, 1976). Applications within consumer behavior are provided in Ruth Ann Smith and Michael J. Houston, "A Psychometric Assessment of Measures of Scripts in Consumer Memory," *Journal of Consumer Research*, Vol. 12 (September 1985), pp. 214–224.
9. Jerome S. Bruner, "On Perceptual Readiness," *Psychological Review*, Vol. 64 (1957), pp. 123–152.
10. See Joel B. Cohen and Kunal Basu, "Alternative Models of Categorization: Toward a Contingent Processing Framework," *Journal of Consumer Research*, Vol. 13 (March 1987), pp. 455–472; Joseph W. Alba and J. Wesley Hutchinson, "Dimensions of Consumer Expertise," *Journal of Consumer Research*, Vol. 13 (March 1987), pp. 411–454. See also Michel Laroche, Jerry Rosenblatt, Jacques B. Brisoux, and Robert Shmotakagara, "Brand Categorization Strategies in RRB Situations: Some Empirical Results," *Advances in Consumer Research*, Vol. 10 (1983), pp. 549–554; James Ward and Barbara Loken, "The Quintessential Snack Food: Measurement of Product Prototypes," *Advances in Consumer Research*, Vol. 13 (1986); and the more general discussion by Alain D'Astous and Marc Dubuc, "Retrieval Processes in Consumer Evaluative Judgment Making: The Role of Elaborative Processing, Context, and Retrieval Goals," *ibid, Advances in Consumer Research*, Vol. 13 (1986).

    See also E. Troy Higgins, John A. Bargh, and Wendy Lombardi, "Nature of Priming Effects on Categorization," *Journal of Experimental Psychology: Learning, Memory and Cognition*, Vol. 11, no. 1 (1985), pp. 59–69; James Ward, Barbara Loken, Ivan Ross, and Tedi Hasapopoulos, "The Influence of Physical Similarity on Generalization of Affect and Attribute Perception from National Brands to Private Label Brands," *AMA Educator's Proceedings*, 1986, pp. 51–56; Mita Sujan and Christina Dekleva, "Product Categorization and Inference Making: Some Implications for Comparative Advertising," *Journal of Consumer Research*, Vol. 14 (December 1987), pp. 372–378; four articles that appear in *Advances in Consumer Research*, Vol. 15 (1988): Mita Sujan and Alice M. Tybout, "Applications and Extensions of Categorization Research in Consumer Behavior," pp. 50–54, James Ward and Barbara Loken, "The Generality of Typicality Effects on Preference and Comparison: An Exploratory Test," pp. 55–61, Eloise Coupey and Kent Nakamoto, "Learning Context and the Development of Product Category Perceptions," pp. 77–82; S. Ratneshwar and Allan D. Shocker, "The Application of Prototypes and Categorization Theory in Marketing: Some Problems and Alternative Perspectives," pp. 280–285, and Craig Thompson, "The Role of Context in Consumers' Category Judgments: A Preliminary Investigation," *Advances in Consumer Research*. Vol. 16, (1989), pp. 514–547.

11. Pierre Martineau, *Motivation in Advertising* (New York: McGraw-Hill, 1957), p. 114.

12. Carl McDaniel and R. C. Baker, "Convenience Food Packaging and the Perception of Product Quality," *Journal of Marketing*, October 1977, pp. 57–58. For broader discussions, see Ernest Dichter, "What's in an Image," *Journal of Consumer Marketing*, Vol. 2 (Winter 1985), pp. 75–91; Roberto Friedmann, "Psychological Meaning of Products: Identification and Marketing Applications," *Psychology & Marketing*, Vol. 3 (Spring 1986), pp. 1–16; Robert E. Kleine and Jerome B. Kernan, "Measuring the Meaning of Consumption Objects: An Empirical Investigation," *Advances in Consumer Research*, Vol. 15 (1988), pp. 498–504; Johny K. Johansson, Susan P. Douglas, and Ikujiro Nonaka, "Assessing the Impact of Country of Origin on Product Evaluations: A New Methodological Perspective" *Journal of Marketing Research*, Vol. 22 (November 1985), pp. 388 ff; three articles in *Advances in Consumer Research*, Vol. 16 (1989); France LeClerc, Brend H. Schmitt, and Laurette Dube-Rioux, "Brand Name a la Francaise? Oui, But for the Right Product!" pp. 253–257, Joan Meyers-Levy, "Investigating Dimensions of Brand Names That Influence the Perceived Familiarity of Brands," pp. 258–263, and Brian C. Wansink, "The Impact of Source Reputation on Inferences About Unadvertised Attributes," pp. 399–406; and Sung-Tai Hong and Robert S. Wyer, Jr., "Effects of Country-of-Origin and Product-Attribute Information on Product Evaluation: An Information Processing Perspective," *Journal of Consumer Research*, Vol. 16 (September 1989), pp. 175–187.

13. Donald A. Laird, "How the Consumer Estimates Quality by Subconscious Sensory Impressions—with Special Reference to the Role of Smell," *Journal of Applied Psychology*, Vol. 16 (June 1932), pp. 241–246.

14. William Safire, "On Language," *The New York Times* News Service, June 10, 1984.

15. John Bussey and Joseph White, "Nissan Cuts U.S. Exports as Marketing Effort Lags," *The Wall Street Journal*, April 13, 1988, p. 27; Sheryl Harris, "Infiniti Eyes Young, Affluent Crowd," *Advertising Age*, February 29, 1988, p. 5–16; "Beer Bash," *Marketing Week*, December 14, 1987, p. 62; Alice Cuneo, "AIDS Prompts Ayds Move," *Advertising Age*, May 30, 1988, p. 66; Edwin F. Lefkowith and Charles A. Moldenhauer, "Recent Cross-Currents in Brand Name Development—and How to Cope with Them," *Journal of Consumer Marketing*, Vol. 2 (Spring 1985), pp. 73–78; Consumer Behavior Seminar, "Affect Generalization to Similar and Dissimilar Brand Extensions," *Psychology & Marketing*, Vol. 4 (Fall 1987), pp. 225–238; and George M. Zinkhan and Claude R. Martin, Jr., "New Brand Names and Inferential Beliefs: Some Insights on Naming New Products," *Journal of Business Research*, Vol. 15 (April 1987), pp. 157–172.

16. Bill Abrams, "Exploiting Proven Brand Names Can Cut Risk of New Products," *The Wall Street Journal*, January 22, 1981. See also Kenneth N. Thompson, James E. Nelson, and Calvin P. Duncan, "A Moderator Variables Model of Brand Extension Behavior," *AMA Winter Educators' Proceedings* (1987), pp. 45–49.

17. J. Neher, "Toro Cutting a Wider Swath in Outdoor Appliance Market," *Advertising Age*, February 25, 1978, p. 21.

18. The new name was "Rusty Jones." The new character was created to suggest a very strong, hard-working, but friendly individual. The result was an animated man with rust-colored hair, dressed in working clothes, and wearing a friendly smile. In the ads, which placed the animated character in the midst of real scenes and people, "Rusty" just happened to be a foot taller than anyone else. Hooper White, "Name Change to Rusty Jones Helps Polish Product's Identity," *Advertising Age*, February 18, 1980, pp. 47–50. The new service was extremely successful until the latter years of the 1980s, when auto manufacturers began to provide their own rust protections under factory warranty.

19. Philip Kotler, "Atmospherics as a Marketing Tool," *Journal of Retailing*, Vol. 49 (Winter 1973–74), pp. 48–64.

20. For discussions on perceptual inferences drawn from advertising, see, for example, Larry Percy, "The Often Subtle Linguistic Cues in Advertising," *Advances in Consumer Research*, Vol. 15 (1988), pp. 269–274; Pamela S. Schindler, "Color and Contrast in Magazine Advertising," *Psychology & Marketing*, Vol. 3 (Summer 1986), pp. 69–78; Danny L. Moore, Douglas Hausknecht, and Kanchana Thamodaran, "Time Compression, Response Opportunity, and Persuasion," *Jour-*

nal of Consumer Research, Vol. 13, no. 1 (1986), pp. 85–99; Barbara B. Stern, "How Does an Ad Mean? Language in Services Advertising," *Journal of Advertising,* Vol. 17 (November 1988), pp. 3–14; Roberto Friedmann and Mary R. Zimmer, "The Role of Psychological Meaning in Advertising," *Journal of Advertising,* Vol. 17 (November 1988), pp. 31–40; Robert G. Wyckham, "Implied Superiority Claims," *Journal of Advertising Research,* Vol. 27 (February–March 1987), pp. 54–63; and Alan J. Bush and Robert P. Bush, "Should Advertisers Use Number-Based Copy in Print Advertisements? *Journal of Consumer Marketing,* Vol. 3 (Summer 1986), pp. 71–80.

This topic also relates closely to consumer research on imagery and its effects. See for example, Jolita Kisielius, "The Role of Memory in Understanding Advertising Media Effectiveness: The Effect of Imagery on Consumer Decision Making," *Advances in Consumer Research,* Vol 9, (1982) pp. 183–186; Teresa J. Domzal and Lynette S. Unger, "Judgments of Verbal Versus Pictorial Presentations of Products with Functional and Aesthetic Features," *Advances in Consumer Research,* Vol. 12 (1985) pp. 268–272; Julie A. Edell and Richard Staelin, "The Information Processing of Pictures in Print Advertisements," *Journal of Consumer Research,* Vol. 10 (June 1983), pp. 45–61; Ruth Ann Smith, Michael J. Houston, and Terry I. Childers, "Verbal Versus Visual Processing Modes: An Empirical Test of the Cyclical Processing Hypothesis," *Advances in Consumer Research,* Vol. 11 (1984) pp. 75–80; Jolita Kisielius and Brian Sternthal, "Examining the Vividness Controversy: An Availability-Valence Interpretation," *Journal of Consumer Research,* Vol. 12 (March 1986), pp. 418–431; Terry L. Childers, Susan E. Heckler, and Michael J. Houston, "Memory for the Visual and Verbal Components of Print Advertisements," *Psychology & Marketing,* Vol. 3 (Fall 1986), pp. 137–150; Michael J. Houston, Terry L. Childers, and Susan E. Heckler, "Picture-Word Consistency and the Elaborative Processing of Advertisements," *Journal of Marketing Research,* Vol. 24 (November 1987), pp. 359–369; and Ann L. McGill and Punam Anand, "The Effect of Vivid Attributes on the Evaluation of Alternatives: The Role of Differential Attention and Cognitive Elaboration," *Journal of Consumer Research,* Vol. 16 (September 1989), pp. 188–196.

21. "The Birth of a Sprout," *Advertising Age,* October 25, 1982, p. M-5.

22. Lenore Skenazy, "Political Touch-Ups: Special Effects Benefit Bush," *Advertising Age,* April 18, 1988, p. 3.

23. Researchers in the field have studied the topic of price quality inferences in considerable detail. For overview of this research, see Akshay R. Rao and Kent B. Monroe, "The Effect of Price, Brand Name, and Store Name on Buyers' Perceptions of Product Quality: An Integrative Review," *Journal of Marketing Research,* Vol. 26 (August 1989), pp. 351–357; and Valarie A. Zeithaml, "Consumer Perceptions of Price, Quality, and Value: A Means-End Model and Synthesis of Evidence," *Journal of Marketing,* Vol. 52 (July 1988), pp. 2–22. For further recent findings, see, for example, Dena Cox, Anthony Cox, and Rose L. Johnson, "How Do Advertised Price Specials Affect Perceptions of a Store's Overall Price Level?" *AMA Educators' Proceedings* (1988), p. 242; Albert R. Wildt and Tung-Zong Chang, "The Number and Importance of Information Cues and the Price-Perceived Quality Relationship," *AMA Educators' Proceedings* (1989), p. 209; and three papers in *Advances in Consumer Research,* Vol. 15: (1988) Carl Obermiller, "When Do Consumers Infer Quality from Price?" pp. 304–310, Michelle A. Morganosky, "The 'Value for Price' Concept: Relationships to Consumer Satisfaction," pp. 311–315, and Rose L. Johnson and James J. Kellaris, "An Exploratory Study of Price/Perceived-Quality Relationships Among Consumer Services," pp. 316–322.

24. This area has also received considerable research attention. For useful insights and findings see, for example, Robert M. Schindler and Diana M. Bauer, "The Uses of Price Information: Implications for Marketers," *AMA Educators' Proceedings* (1988), pp. 68–73; Susan M. Petroshius and Kent B. Monroe, "Effect of Product-Line Pricing Characteristics on Product Evaluations," *Journal of Consumer Research,* Vol. 13 (March 1987), pp. 511–519; Judith Lynne Zaichkowsky, "Involvement and the Price Cue," *Advances in Consumer Research,* Vol. 15 (1988), pp. 323–327; Donald R. Lichenstein, Peter H. Bloch, and William C. Black, "Correlates of Price Acceptability," *Journal of Consumer Research,* Vol. 15 (September 1988), pp. 243–252; Srinivasan Ratneshwar, Allan D. Shocker, and David W. Stewart, "Toward Understanding the Attraction Effect: The Implications of Product Stimulus Meaningfulness and Familiarity," *Journal of Consumer Research,* Vol. 13 (March 1987), pp. 520–533; Tridib Mazumdar and Kent B. Monroe, "Using Leverage for Developing Pricing Strategies," *AMA Educators' Proceedings,* (1986), pp. 303–308; Rustan Kosenko and Don Rahtz, "Buyer Market Price Knowledge Influence on Acceptable Price Range and Price Limits," *Advances in Consumer Research,* Vol. 15 (1988), pp. 328–333; and Joel E. Urbany and Peter R. Dickson, "Consumer Information, Competitive Rivalry, and Price Setting: When Ignorance Isn't Bliss," *Advances in Consumer Research,* Vol. 15 (1988), pp. 341–347.

For specific findings in this area of reference pricing, see, for example, James M. Lattin and Randolph E. Bucklin, "Reference Effects of Price and Promotion on Brand Choice Behavior," *Journal of Marketing Research*, Vol. 26 (August 1989), pp. 299–310; William O. Bearden and Joel E. Urbany, "Reference Price Effects on Perceptions of Perceived Offer Value, Normal Prices, and Transportation Utility," *AMA Educators' Proceedings* (1989), pp. 45–49; Robert Jacobson and Carl Obermiller, "The Formation of Reference Price," *Advances in Consumer Research*, Vol. 16 (1989), pp. 234–240; William D. Diamond and Leland Campbell, "The Framing of Sales Promotions: Effects on Reference Price Change," *Advances in Consumer Research*. Vol. 16 (1989), pp. 241–247; Joel E. Urbany, William O. Bearden, and Dan C. Weilbaker, "The Effect of Plausible and Exaggerated Reference Prices on Consumer Perceptions and Price Search," *Journal of Consumer Research*, Vol. 15 (June 1988), pp. 95–110; Mary F. Mobley, William O. Bearden, and Jesse E. Teel, "An Investigation of Individual Responses to Tensile Price Claims," *Journal of Consumer Research*, Vol. 15 (September 1988), pp. 273–279; David J. Moore and Richard W. Olshavsky, "The Informative Role of Price Discounts in Brand Choice," *AMA Educators' Proceedings* (1987), pp. 55; and Donald R. Lichtenstein and William O. Bearden, "Contextual Influences on Perceptions of Merchant-Supplied Reference Prices," *Journal of Consumer Research*, Vol. 15 (March 1989), pp. 55–66.

25. Bernard F. Whalen, "Strategic Mix of Odd, Even Prices Can Lead to Retail Profits," *Marketing News*, March 7, 1980, p. 24; see also Robert M. Schindler, "Consumer Recognition of Increases in Odd and Even Prices," *Advances in Consumer Research*, Vol. 11 (1984), pp. 459–462; Anthony D. Cox, "New Evidence Concerning Consumer Price Limits," *Advances in Consumer Research*, Vol. 13 (1986); and Robert M. Schindler and Lori S. Warren, "Effect of Odd Pricing on Choice of Items from a Menu," *Advances in Consumer Research*, Vol. 15 (1988), pp. 348–353.

26. Thanks to Deborah MacInnis for this illustration. For interesting reading on this topic, see C. Whan Park, Bernard J. Jaworski, and Deborah J. MacInnis, "Strategic Brand Concept—Image Management," *Journal of Marketing*, Vol. 50 (October 1986), pp. 135–145.

27. Inference-making is a broad topic that has received much attention in recent consumer research. For theoretical and empirical background, see E. T. Higgins and J. A. Bargh, "Social Cognition and Social Perception," *Annual Review of Psychology*, Vol. 38 (1987), pp. 369–425; and Joseph W. Alba and J. Wesley Hutchinson, "Dimensions of Consumer Expertise," *Journal of Consumer Research*, Vol. 13 (March 1987), pp. 411–454. For interesting applications and findings, see, for example, Raymond R. Burke, Wayne S. DeSarbo, Richard L. Oliver, and Thomas S. Robertson, "Deception by Implication: An Experimental Investigation," *Journal of Consumer Research*, Vol. 14 (March 1988), pp. 483–494; Frank R. Kardes, "Spontaneous Inference Processes in Advertising: The Effects of Conclusion Omission and Involvement on Persuasion," *Journal of Consumer Research*, Vol. 15 (September 1988), pp. 225–233; Gary J. Gaeth and Timothy E. Heath, "The Cognitive Processing of Advertising in Young and Old Adults: Assessment and Training," *Journal of Consumer Research*, (June 1987), pp. 43–54; Gary T. Ford and Ruth Ann Smith, "Inferential Beliefs in Consumer Evaluations: An Assessment of Alternative Processing Strategies," *Journal of Consumer Research*, Vol. 14 (December 1987), pp. 363–371; Paul M. Herr, "Priming Price: Prior Knowledge and Context Effects," *Journal of Consumer Research*, Vol. 15 (March 1989), pp. 67–75; Joan Meyers-Levy, "Priming Effects on Product Judgments: A Hemispheric Interpretation," *Journal of Consumer Research*, Vol. 15 (March 1989), pp. 76–86; Jeen-Su Lim, Richard W. Olshavsky, and John Kim, "The Impact of Inferences on Product Evaluations: Replication and Extension," *Journal of Marketing Research*, Vol. 25 (August 1988), pp. 308–316; Amitava Chattopadhyay and Joseph W. Alba, "The Situational Importance of Recall and Inference in Consumer Decision Making," *Journal of Consumer Research*, Vol. 15 (June 1988), pp. 1–12; Paula Fitzgerald Bone, "An Examination of the Assimilation Effect," *AMA Educators' Proceedings* (1988), pp. 124–127; Valerie S. Folkes, "The Availability Heuristic and Perceived Risk," *Journal of Consumer Research*, Vol. 15 (June 1988), pp. 13–23; Frank R. Kardes, "Basic Rate Information, Casual Inference, and Preference," *Advances in Consumer Research*, Vol. 15, 1988, pp. 96–100; Valerie S. Folkes, Susan Koletsky, and John L. Graham, "A Field Study of Causal Inferences and Consumer Reaction: The View from the Airport," *Journal of Consumer Research*, Vol. 13 (March 1987), pp. 534–539; Joseph W. Alba and Amitava Chattopadhyay, "Salience Effects in Brand Recall," *Journal of Marketing Research*, Vol. 23 (November 1986), pp. 363–369; Paul W. Miniard, H. Rao Unnava, and Sunil Bhatla, "Inhibiting Brand Name Recall: A Test of the Salience Hypothesis," *Advances in Consumer Research*, Vol. 16 (1989), pp. 264–270; Kim R. Robertson, "Recall and Recognition Effects of Brand Name Imagery," *Psychology & Marketing*, Vol. 4 (Spring 1987), pp. 3–16; Claudia Dolinsky and Richard A. Feinberg, "Linguistic Barriers to Consumer Information Processing: Information Overload in the Hispanic Population," *Psychology & Marketing*,

Vol. 3 (Winter 1986), pp. 261–272; Joseph Alba and Amitava Chattopadhyay, "Effects of Context and Part-Category Cues on Recall of Competing Brands," *Journal of Marketing Research,* Vol. 22 (August 1985), pp. 340 ff; and David Mazursky and Yaacov Schul, "The Effects of Advertisement Encoding and the Failure to Discount Information: Implications for the Sleeper Effect," *Journal of Consumer Research,* Vol. 15 (June 1988), pp. 24–36.

28. The study reported is by George B. Sproles, "New Evidence on Price and Product Quality," *Journal of Consumer Affairs,* Vol. 11 (Summer 1977), pp. 63–77. For further discussion and findings, see E. Scott Maynes, *Decision-Making for Consumers: An Introduction to Consumer Economics* (New York: Macmillan, 1976), pp. 84–89. See also R. T. Morris and C. S. Bronson, "The Chaos in Competition Indicated by *Consumer Reports,*" *Journal of Marketing,* July 1969, pp. 26–34; Ellen Day and Stephen B. Castleberry, "Defining and Evaluating Quality: The Consumer's View," *Advances in Consumer Research,* Vol. 13 (1986); Eitan Gerstner, "Do Higher Prices Signal Higher Quality?" *Journal of Marketing Research,* Vol. 22 (May 1985), pp. 209 ff; David J. Curry and David J. Faulds, "Indexing Product Quality: Issues, Theory, and Results," *Journal of Consumer Research,* Vol. 13 (June 1986), pp. 134–145; George B. Sproles, "The Concept of Quality and the Efficiency of Markets: Issues and Comments," *Journal of Consumer Research,* Vol. 13 (June 1986) pp. 146–148; Chr. Hjorth-Andersen, "More on Multidimensional Quality: A Reply," *Journal of Consumer Research,* Vol. 13 (June 1986) pp. 149–154; and David J. Curry and Peter C. Riesz, "Prices and Price/Quality Relationships: A Longitudinal Analysis," *Journal of Marketing,* Vol. 52 (January 1988), pp. 35–51.

29. If you decided in favor of the new competitor in the first four cases, you agreed with the court, which felt that consumer confusion was not likely in any of these instances. For further discussion, see Sidney A. Diamond, "Marked for Dispute," *Advertising Age,* July 5, 1982, p. M-26.

   The two McDonald's cases were decided in favor of McDonald's. Even though the owner of McBagel's name was Ken McShea, the judge ruled that products such as McNuggets, McMuffin, and McD.L.T. had created a "family" of trademarks for food products. In the McSleep Inn case, the head of the chain had been quoted in early news stories as saying, "Obviously, the name is a takeoff on McDonald's and quality at a consistent price." (For further details, see "Judge's McPinion . . . ," *Marketing News,* October 10, 1988, p. 5; and David Kiley, "McDonald's Bares Teeth over Prefix," *Marketing Week,* October 26, 1987, p. 2.)

   The Jordache case was decided in favor of Lardashe Jeans, on the grounds that although it was a parody of the Jordache name, it would not confuse consumers and tarnish the Jordache trademark. The producers of Lardashe, Oink, Inc., indicated they would resume production of the "resigner" jeans after the verdict. (See "Lardashe Jeans Wins Big Court Fight . . . ," *Marketing News,* September 25, 1987, p. 24.)

30. "P & G will Fight Court Order on Tide Copycats," *Advertising Age,* July 9, 1984, p. 40. For related readings, see Ronald F. Bush, Peter H. Bloch, and Claude F. Reynaud, "The Brand Trademark: A Valuable and Vulnerable Resource," *AMA Educators' Proceedings* (1984), pp. 276–279; and Barbara Loken, Ivan Ross, and Ronald L. Hinkle, "Consumer "Confusion" of Origin and Brand Similarity Perceptions," *Journal of Public Policy & Marketing,* Vol. 5 (1986), pp. 195–211.

Chapter 10: Consumer Learning

1. Susan Harrigan, "Loyal Consumers of Magic Cleaner Won't Let Inventor Quit Working," *The Wall Street Journal,* September 17, 1980, p. 33.
2. An excellent overview of the major learning theories and their points of agreement and dispute can be found in Ernest R. Hilgard and Gordon H. Bower, *Theories of Learning* (New York: Appleton-Century-Crofts, 1966), See also Winfred F. Hill, *Learning: A Survey of Psychological Interpretations,* 3rd ed. (New York: Thomas Crowell, 1977).
3. Jean Piaget, *The Child's Conception of the World* (New York: Harcourt Brace, 1928); and Jean Piaget, *The Construction of Reality in the Child* (New York: Basic Books, 1954).
4. Much of the work on children with marketing and consumer behavior has been inspired by Scott Ward. See, for example, Scott Ward, "Consumer Socialization," *Journal of Consumer Research,* Vol. 1 (September 1974), pp. 1–14.
5. Much of this work is summarized in Scott Ward, Daniel B. Wackman, and Ellen Wartella, *How Children Learn to Buy* (Beverly Hills, Calif.: Sage, 1977). See also Marvin E. Goldberg, Gerald J. Gorn, and Wendy Gibson, "TV Messages for Snack and Breakfast Foods: Do They Influence Children's Preferences?" *Journal of Consumer Research,* Vol. 5 (September 1978), pp. 73–81.
6. Recent research, in fact, has identified three levels of CIP skills in children: strategic, cued, and limited. **Strategic processors** (children ages 10 to 11 and older) *are able* to store and retrieve information from LTM to process ads well. **Cued processors** (age 6 to 9) are *sometimes able* to

use appropriate storage and retrieval strategies, but only when reminded to do so. **Limited processors** (children below 6 years old) are *unable* to use these strategies effectively. See Deborah L. Roedder, "Age Differences in Children's Responses to Television Advertising: An Information-Processing approach," *Journal of Consumer Research,* Vol. 8 (September 1981), pp. 144–153. In addition, consumer researchers have addressed a number of further topics in this area. See, for example, Deborah Roedder John. "The Development of Knowledge Structures in Children," in *Advances in Consumer Research,* Vol. 12 (1985), pp. 329–333; M. Carole Macklin, "Classical Conditioning Effects in Product/Character Pairings Presented to Children," *Advances in Consumer Research,* Vol. 13 (1986); Deborah Roedder John and John C. Whitney, Jr. "The Development of Consumer Knowledge in Children: A Cognitive Structure Approach," *Journal of Consumer Research,* Vol. 13 (March 1986), pp. 406–417; Deborah Roedder John and Catherine A. Cole, "Age Differences in Information Processing: Understanding Deficits in Young and Elderly Consumers," *Journal of Consumer Research,* Vol. 13 (December 1986), pp. 297–315; Mariea Grubbs Hoy, Clifford E. Young, and John C. Mowen, "Animated Host-Selling Advertisements: Their Impact on Young Children's Recognition, Attitudes, and Behavior," *Journal of Public Policy & Marketing,* Vol. 5 (1986), pp. 171–184; Carolyn Costley and Merrie Brucks, "Product Knowledge as an Explanation for Age-Related Differences in Children's Cognitive Responses to Advertising," *Advances in Consumer Research,* Vol. 14 (1987), pp. 288–292; Matt J. Rossano and Eliot J. Butter, "Television Advertising and Children's Attitudes Toward Proprietary Medicine," *Psychology & Marketing,* Vol. 4 (Fall 1987), pp. 213–224; M. Carole Macklin, "Preschoolers' Understanding of the Informational Function of Television Advertising," *Journal of Consumer Research,* Vol. 14 (September 1987), pp. 229–239; Donna M. Klees, Jerry Olson, and R. Dale Wilson, "An Analysis of the Content and Organization of Children's Knowledge Structures," *Advances in Consumer Research,* Vol. 15 (1988), pp. 153–157; Merrie Brucks, Gary M. Armstrong, and Marvin E. Goldberg, "Children's Use of Cognitive Defenses Against Television Advertising: A Cognitive Response Approach," *Journal of Consumer Research,* Vol. 14 (March 1988), pp. 471–482; Laura A. Peracchio and Charise Mita, "How Do Young Children Learn to Be Consumers? A Script Processing Perspective," *Advances in Consumer Research.* Vol. 16 (1989), p. 791; and Carole Macklin and Karen Machleit, "The Development of an Attitude Scale Appropriate for Use with Preschoolers," *Advances in Consumer Research,* Vol. 16, (1989), p. 792.
7. Scott Ward, "Researchers Look at the 'KidVid' Rule: Overview of Session," *Advances in Consumer Research,* Vol. 6 (1979), pp. 7–8. For more recent policy discussions, see also Bonnie B. Reece, "Children and Shopping: Some Public Policy Questions," *Journal of Public Policy & Marketing,* Vol. 5 (1986), pp. 185–194; Gary M. Armstrong & Merrie Brucks, "Dealing with Children's Advertising: Public Policy Issues and Alternatives," *Journal of Public Policy & Marketing,* Vol. 7 (1988), pp. 98–113; and Marvin Goldberg, "The Elimination of Advertising Directed to Children in Quebec: A Quasi-Experiment," *Advances in Consumer Research,* Vol. 16 (1989), p. 790.
8. See, for example, *Advances in Consumer Research,* Vol. 13 (1986); Merrie Brucks, "A Typology of Consumer Knowledge Content," Catherine Cole, Gary J. Gaeth, and Surendra N. Singh, "Measuring Prior Knowledge," Fred Selnes and Kjell Gronhaug, "Subjective and Objective Measures of Product Knowledge Contrasted." Four articles on this topic in *Advances in Consumer Research,* Vol. 14 (1987): John Deighton, "A Simple Representation of the Contingent Structure of Knowledge," pp. 12–16, Beth Walker, Richard Celsi, and Jerry Olson, "Exploring the Structural Characteristics of Consumers' Knowledge," pp. 17–21, Barbara Loken and James Ward, "Measures of the Attribute Structure Underlying Product Typicality, pp. 22–26, and Thomas J. Page, Jr., "Comments on Consumer Knowledge and Attribute Structures," pp. 27–28; John Kim and Jeen-Su Lim, "The Dimensionality and Measurement of Familiarity Construct," *AMA Educators' Proceedings* (1989), p. 195; Bonnie S. Guy and William W. Curtis, "In Search of Conceptual and Operational Consistency in the Study and Measurement of Product Class Familiarity," *AMA Educators' Proceedings* (1989), p. 225; Fred Selnes, "The Effect of Experience on Product Knowledge Acquisition," *AMA Educators' Proceedings* (1987), pp. 223 ff. and Stephen H. Hoch and Young-Won Ha, "Consumer Learning: Advertising and the Ambiguity of Product Experience," *Journal of Consumer Research,* Vol. 13 (September 1986), pp. 221–233.
9. Given our topic of learning, we should note that cognitive response research reflects what consumers are "thinking" rather than exactly what they may be "learning" from an ad. However, this research is quite useful for studying advertising effects. A thorough review of work on "direct monitoring" is provided in Peter Wright, "Message-Evoked Thoughts: Persuasion Research Using Thought Verbalizations," *Journal of Consumer Research,* Vol. 7 (September 1980), pp. 151–175. See also George E. Belch, "The Effects of Television Commercial Repetition on Cognitive Responses and Message Acceptance," *Journal of Consumer Research,* Vol. 9 (June 1982), pp. 56–

65; Daniel R. Toy, "Monitoring Communication Effects: A Cognitive Structure/Cognitive Response Approach," *Journal of Consumer Research*, Vol. 9 (June 1982), pp. 66–76; Jerry C. Olson, Daniel R. Toy, and Philip A. Dover, "Do Cognitive Responses Mediate the Effects of Advertising Content on Cognitive Structure? *Journal of Consumer Research*, Vol. 9 (December 1982), pp. 245–262; and Rajeev Batra and Michael L. Ray, "Operationalizing Involvement as Depth and Quality of Cognitive Response," *Advances in Consumer Research*, Vol. 10, (1983), pp. 309–313. For recent developments, see George R. Franke and Nicholas M. Didow, Jr., "Self-Rating Versus Independent-Judge Rating of Cognitive Response Measures," *AMA Educators' Proceedings* (1987), p. 237; Amitava Chattopadhyay and Joseph W. Alba, "The Relationship Between Recall, Cognitive Responses, and Advertising Effectiveness: Effects of Delay and Context, "Working Paper 89-103, Marketing Science Institute, 1989; and Manoj Hastak and Jerry C. Olson, "Assessing the Role of Brand-Related Cognitive Responses as Mediators of Communication Effects on Cognitive Structure," *Journal of Consumer Research*, Vol. 15 (March 1989), pp. 444–456.

10. An excellent analysis of the FTC's policy statement on deception is available in Gary T. Ford and John E. Calfee, "Recent Developments in FTC Policy on Deception," *Journal of Marketing*, Vol. 50 (July 1986), pp. 82–103.

11. David M. Gardner, "Deception in Advertising: A Conceptual Approach," *Journal of Marketing*, Vol. 39 (January 1975), pp. 40–46.

12. Fredric L. Barbour and David M. Gardner, "Deceptive Advertising: A Practical Approach to Measurement," *Journal of Advertising*, Vol. 11, no. 1 (1982), pp. 21–30.

13. See the references in notes 10, 11 and 12, plus Jacob Jacoby and Constance Small, "The FDA Approach to Defining Misleading Advertising," *Journal of Marketing*, Vol. 39 (October 1975), pp. 65–68; Michael T. Brandt and Ivan L. Preston, "The Federal Trade Commission's Use of Evidence to Determine Deception," *Journal of Marketing*, Vol. 41 (January 1977), pp. 54–62; Terence A. Shimp, "Social Psychological (Mis)-representations in Advertising," *Journal of Consumer Research*, Vol. 13 (1979), pp. 28–40; Edward J. Russo, Barbara L. Metcalf, and Debra Stephens, "Identifying Misleading Advertising," *Journal of Consumer Research*, Vol. 8 (September 1981), pp. 119–131; Richard L. Oliver, R. Hoyt Walbridge, and Peter H. Rheinstein, "A Study of Physicians' Perception of Advertising Judged Deceptive by the FDA." *Advances in Consumer Research*, Vol. 11 (1984), pp. 224–228; Joshua Honigwachs, "Is It Safe to Call Something Safe? The Law of Puffing in Advertising," *Journal of Public Policy & Marketing*, 6, (1987) pp. 157–170; Gary J. Gaeth and Timothy B. Heath, "The Cognitive Processing of Misleading Advertising in Young and Old Adults," *Journal of Consumer Research*, Vol. 14, (June 1987), pp. 43–54; and Raymond R. Burke, Wayne S. DeSarbo, Richard L. Oliver, and Thomas S. Robertson, "Deception by Implication: An Experimental Investigation," *Journal of Consumer Research*, Vol. 14 (March 1988), pp. 483–494.

14. Jacob Jacoby and Wayne D. Hoyer, "Viewer Miscomprehension of Televised Communication: Selected Findings," *Journal of Marketing*, Fall 1982, pp. 12–26. For results of a similar study on print media, see Jacob Jacoby and Wayne D. Hoyer, "The Comprehension/Miscomprehension of Print Communication: Selected Findings, *Journal of Consumer Research*, Vol. 15 (March 1989), pp. 434–443.

15. The estimated degree of consumer miscomprehension increased substantially when the guessing factor was applied—to 54 percent! This indicates that for over half of the material about which consumers were asked, they did not know the correct answer (even though they were sometimes able to guess it correctly). See David C. Schmittlein and Donald G. Morrison, "Measuring Miscomprehension for Televised Communications Using True-False Questions," *Journal of Consumer Research*, Vol. 10 (September 1983), p. 147–156.

  For an interesting set of readings in this area, you might begin with the Jacoby and Hoyer article listed in note 14 and then proceed to critical comments and replies from the study's authors. Critical comments were offered by Richard W. Mizerski, "Major Problems in 4As Pioneering Study of TV Miscomprehension," *Marketing News*, Vol. 14 (June 12, 1981), pp. 7–8; Gary T. Ford and Richard Yalch, "Viewer Miscomprehension of Televised Communication—A Comment," *Journal of Marketing*, Fall 1982, pp. 27–31; and Richard Mizerski, "Viewer Miscomprehension Findings Are Measurement Bound," *Journal of Marketing*, Fall 1982, pp. 32–34. Responses to these criticisms are available in Jacob Jacoby and W. D. Hoyer, "Reply to Mizerski's Criticisms: Some Mislead, Others Misrepresent Facts," *Marketing News*, Vol. 15 (July 24, 1981), pp. 35–36; and Jacob Jacoby and Wayne D. Hoyer, "On Miscomprehending Televised Communication: A Rejoinder," *Journal of Marketing*, Fall 1982, pp. 35–43. See also Mark I. Alpert, Linda L. Golden, and Wayne D. Hoyer, "The Impact of Repetition on Advertising Miscomprehension and Effectiveness," *Advances in Consumer Research*, Vol. 10 (1983), pp. 130–135; and two articles in *Advances in Consumer Research,* Vol. 13 (1986): Fliece R. Gates and Wayne D. Hoyer, "Measuring Miscomprehension: A Comparison of Alternative Formats," and Ivan L. Preston and Jeff I. Richards, "The Relationship of Miscomprehension to Deceptiveness in FTC Cases."

16. John B. Watson, "The Place of the Conditioned Reflex in Psychology," *Psychological Review,* Vol. 23 (1916), pp. 89–116.

17. The description provided in the chapter is a "traditional" one, which stresses particular aspects of the approach. In fact, it appears that Pavlovian conditioning can also be represented within a modern framework of thinking, in which it would not appear so distinct. See Robert A. Rescorla, "Pavlovian Conditioning: It's Not What You Think It Is," *American Psychologist,* March 1988, pp. 151–160. See also an interesting consumer-oriented description: Richard A. Feinberg, "Credit Cards as Spending Facilitating Stimuli: A Conditioning Interpretation," *Journal of Consumer Research,* Vol. 13 (December 1986), pp. 348–356.

18. "Coca-Cola Turns to Pavlov . . . ," *The Wall Street Journal,* January 19, 1984.

19. Gerald J. Gorn, "The Effects of Music in Advertising on Choice Behavior: A Classical Conditioning Approach," *Journal of Marketing,* Winter 1982, pp. 94–101.

20. Gorn's results sparked a number of new issues and criticisms as to the exact nature of the effect. See, for example, Chris T. Allen and Thomas J. Madden, "A Closer Look at Classical Conditioning," *Journal of Consumer Research,* Vol. 12 (December 1985), pp. 301–315; Elnora W. Stuart, Terence A. Shimp, and Randall W. Engle, "Classical Conditioning of Consumer Attitudes: Four Experiments in an Advertising Context," *Journal of Consumer Research,* Vol. 14 (December 1987), pp. 334–349; two articles in *Advances in Consumer Research,* Vol. 14 (1987): L. R. Kahle, Sharon E. Beatty, and Pat Kennedy, "Comment on Clasically Conditioning Human Consumers," pp. 411–414, and Gerald J. Gorn, W. J. Jacobs, and Michael J. Mana, "Observations on Awareness and Conditioning," pp. 415–416; Judy I. Alpert and Mark I. Alpert, "Background Music as an Influence in Consumer Mood and Advertising Responses," *Advances in Consumer Research,* Vol. 16 (1989), pp. 485–491; James J. Kellaris and Anthony D. Cox, "The Effects of Background Music in Advertising: A Reassessment," *Journal of Consumer Research,* Vol. 15 (March 1989), pp. 113–118; Chris T. Allen and Chris A. Janiszewski, "Assessing the Role of Contingency Awareness in Attitudinal Conditioning with Implications for Advertising Research," *Journal of Marketing Research,* Vol. 26 (February 1989), pp. 30–43; and Deborah J. MacInnis and C. Whan Park, "The Differential Role of Music on Consumers' Processing of and Reactions to Ads," Working Paper, University of Arizona, Tucson, 1989.

For earlier discussions, together with some speculations on how marketers might use it, see also Frances K. McSweeney and Calvin Bierley, "Recent Developments in Classical Conditioning," *Journal of Consumer Research,* Vol. 11 (September 1984), pp. 619–631; Walter R. Nord and J. Paul Peter, "A Behavior Modification Perspective on Marketing," *Journal of Marketing,* Spring 1980, pp. 36–47; and Werner Kroeber-Riel, "Emotional Product Differentiation by Classical Conditioning," *Advances in Consumer Research,* Vol. 11 (1984), pp. 538–543.

21. Skinner wrote a number of articles and books. Some of these are written in nontechnical language and are interesting to read. See, for example, B. F. Skinner, *Walden Two* (New York: Macmillian, 1948); B. F. Skinner, "How to Teach Animals," *Scientific American,* Vol. 185 (December 1951); pp. 26–29; B. F. Skinner, "Teaching Machines," *Science,* Vol. 128 (1958), pp. 969–977; and Carl R. Rogers and B. F. Skinner, "Some Issues Concerning the Control of Human Behavior," *Science,* Vol. 124 (1956), pp. 1057–1066. See also two of his famous books: B. F. Skinner, *Science and Human Behavior* (New York: The Free Press, 1953); and B. F. Skinner, *Beyond Freedom and Dignity.* (New York: Alfred A. Knopf, 1972).

22. This section is based upon the discussion by Walter R. Nord and J. Paul Peter, "A Behavior Modification Perspective." For further suggestions and clarification of issues, see also Michael L. Rothschild and William C. Gaidis, "Behavioral Learning Theory: Its Relevance to Marketing and Promotions," *Journal of Marketing,* Spring 1981, pp. 70–78; and J. Paul Peter and Walter R. Nord, "A Clarification and Extension of Operant Conditioning Principles in Marketing," *Journal of Marketing,* summer 1982, pp. 102–107. See also Gordon Robert Foxall, "The Role of Radical Behaviorism in the Explanation of Consumer Choice," *Advances in Consumer Research,* Vol. 13 (1986); Blaise J. Bergiel and Christine Trosclair, "Instrumental Learning: Its Application to Consumer Satisfaction," *Journal of Consumer Marketing,* Vol. 2 (Fall 1985), pp. 23–28; and William Gaidis and James Cross, "Issues in Sales Promotion Research: An Applied Behavior Analysis Perspective," *AMA Educators' Proceedings* (1985), pp. 187–191.

23. J. R. Carey, S. H. Clique, B. A. Leighton, and F. Milton, "A Test of Positive Reinforcement of Customers," *Journal of Marketing,* October 1976, pp. 98–100.

24. This section is based upon the discussion in Nord and Peter, "A Behavior Modification Perspective." See also Albert Bandura, *Principles of Behavior Modification* (New York: Holt, Rinehart and Winston, 1969).
25. Nord and Peter, "A Behavior Modification Perspective,"
26. "Mindbenders," *Money Magazine,* September 1978, p. 24.
27. Ronald E. Milliman, "Using Background Music to Affect to Behavior of Supermarket Shoppers," *Journal of Marketing,* Summer 1982, p. 86–91. See also Richard F. Yalch and Eric Spangenberg, "An Environmental Psychological Study of Foreground and Background Music as Retail Atmospheric Factors," *AMA Educators' Proceedings* (1988), pp. 106–110.
28. Nord and Peter, "A Behavior Modification Perspective," p. 45.
29. There is little literature pointed to the specific issues raised in this section. However, a useful overview of thinking in the area of marketing ethics is provided in Patrick E. Murphy and Gene R. Laczniak, "Framework for Analyzing Marketing Ethics," *Journal of Macromarketing,* Spring 1983, pp. 7–18. In addition, a thoughtful discussion of IC in marketing is provided by Rom J. Markin and Chem L. Narayana, "Behavior Control: Are Consumers Beyond Freedom and Dignity?" *Advances in Consumer Research,* Vol. 3 (1976), pp. 222–228.
30. Joe A. Dodson, Alice M. Tybout, and Brian Sternthal, "Impact on Deals and Deal Retraction on Brand Switching," *Journal of Marketing Research,* February 1978, pp. 72–81. See also Barbara E. Kahn, Manohar U. Kalwani, and Donald G. Morrison, "Niching Versus Change-of-Pace Brands: Using Purchase Frequencies and Penetration Rates to Infer Brand Positionings," *Journal of Marketing Research,* Vol. 25 (November 1988), pp. 384–390; and Scott A. Neslin and Robert W. Shoemaker, "An Alternative Explanation for Lower Repeat Rates After Promotion Purchase," *Journal of Marketing Research,* Vol. 26 (May 1989), pp. 205–213.
31. Technological developments are revolutionizing research in this area. See, for example, Lisa Petrison, "Retailers Scan Data Horizon," *Promote,* November 16, 1987, pp. 16–17. For a technical discussion, see Robert C. Blattberg and Kenneth J. Wisniewski, "Issues in Modeling Store-Level Scanner Data," Working Paper 43, Graduate School of Business, University of Chicago, March 1988. For an overview of some available systems, see David J. Curry, "Single-Source Systems: Retail Management Present and Future," *Journal of Retailing,* Vol. 65 (Spring 1989), pp. 1–20.
32. Readers interested in pursuing this area are encouraged to begin with Jacob Jacoby and Robert Chestnut, *Brand Loyalty Measurement and Management* (New York: Ronald/John Wiley, 1978). This volume contains numerous citations of further work on brand loyalty. See also Stephen B. Knouse, "Brand Loyalty and Sequential Learning Theory," *Psychology & Marketing,* Vol. 3 (Summer 1986), pp. 87–98; David Mazursky, Priscilla LaBarbera, and Al Aiello, "When Consumers Switch Brands," *Psychology & Marketing,* Vol. 4 (Spring 1987), pp. 17–30; and Terry Elrod, "A Management Science Assessment of a Behavioral Measure of Brand Loyalty," *Advances in Consumer Research,* Vol. 15 (1988), pp. 481–486.
33. Laurie Petersen, "Marketers Dig Deep for Loyalty," *Marketing Week,* June 29, 1987, pp. 1 ff; Nancy Youman, "Trying Frequent-Drinker Programs," *Adweek,* September 12, 1988, p. 60.

Chapter 11   Consumer Attitudes

1. B. G. Yovovich, "What is Your Brand Really Worth?" *Marketing Week,* August 8, 1988, pp. 18–24.
2. Gordon W. Allport, "Attitudes," in C. A. Murchinson (ed.), *A Handbook of Social Psychology* (Worcester, Mass.: Clark University Press, 1935), pp. 798–844.
3. "Revive Sluggish Brand with Seven-Step Plan," *Marketing News,* October 9, 1987, p. 28. The figure is adapted from discussion in this article.
4. Discussion of the brand equity concept and examples are drawn from B. G. Yovovich, "What Is Your Brand Really Worth?"; and Lance Leuthesser, "Defining, Measuring, and Managing Brand Equity," Report 88-104, Marketing Science Institute, May 1988. See also two papers in *AMA Educators' Proceedings* (1989): pp. 79–83, Michael H. Morris, Ramone Avila, and Alvin C. Burns, "Measuring Source Loyalty: Buyer and Seller Perspectives," and Sallie Hook, "The Development of the Store Image Construct: A Review of Literature from 1958 to the Present," p. 99.
5. Exhibit 11-1 answers are (top 10, in order: Coca-Cola, Campbell's, Pepsi-Cola, AT&T, McDonald's American Express, Kelloggs' IBM, Levi's, Sears); (bottom 10, in order; Canadian cigarettes, loudspeakers, diversified financial services, Danish consumer electronics, Japanese beer, pet food, Korean electronics, German cooking equipment, Swiss coughdrops, batteries); competitive rankings: Colgate (no. 35) nips Crest (no. 39), Mobil (82) outpowers Texaco (126) and Shell (150), Hershey's (12) licks M&M's (42), NBC (13) outrates CBS (32) and ABC (47), and oh yes,

Marlboro burns Winston by 92 places. The original survey was conducted in 1988 by Landor Associates, a San Francisco research firm. This report is based on Edward C. Baig, "Name That Brand" *Fortune,* July 4, 1988, pp. 9 ff.

6. B. G. Yovovich, "What Is Your Brand Really Worth?"

7. Ibid.

8. For detailed reviews of these issues and results on them, see William L. Wilkie and Edgar A. Pessemier, "Issues in Marketing's Use of Multi-Attribute Attitude Models," *Journal of Marketing Research,* November 1973, pp. 428–441; and Richard J. Lutz and James R. Bettman, "Multi-Attribute Models in Marketing: A Bicentennial Review," in A. Woodside, J. Sheth, and B. Bennett (eds.), *Consumer and Industrial Buying Behavior* (New York: North-Holland, 1977), pp. 137–150. For theoretical background and applications of related models in psychology, see Martin Fishbein and Icek Ajzen, *Attitude, Intention and Behavior: An Introduction to Theory and Research* (Reading, Mass.: Addison-Wesley, 1975); Icek Ajzen and Martin Fishbein, *Understanding Attitudes and Predicting Social Behavior* (Englewood Cliffs, N.J.: Prentice Hall, 1980); and Milton J. Rosenberg, "Cognitive Structure and Attitudinal Affect," *Journal of Abnormal and Social Psychology,* November 1956, pp. 367–372. Other significant alterations in the Fishbein model have also been proposed. See, for example, Olli T. Ahtola, "The Vector Model of Preferences: An Alternative to the Fishbein Model," *Journal of Marketing Research,* February 1975, pp. 52–59.

For more detailed discussions of specific issues, see Peter Sampson and Paul Harris, "A User's Guide to Fishbein," *Journal of the Market Research Society,* July 1970, pp. 145–166; Peter Sampson, "Using the Repertory Grid Test," *Journal of Marketing Research,* February 1972, pp. 78–81; William L. Wilkie and Rolf P. Weinreich, "Effects of the Number and Type of Attributes Included in an Attitude Model: More Is *not* Better," *Proceedings of the Third Annual Conference,* Association for Consumer Research, Chicago, 1972, pp. 325–340; Joel B. Cohen, "Toward an Integrated Use of Expectancy-Value Attitude Models," in G. D. Hughes and M. L. Ray (eds.), *Buyer/Consumer Information Processing* (Chapel Hill: University of North Carolina Press, 1974), pp. 331–346; Albert V. Bruno and Albert R. Wildt, "Toward Understanding Attitude Structure: A Study of the Complementarity of Multi-Attribute Attitude Models," *Journal of Consumer Research,* Vol. 2 (September 1975), pp. 137–145; Michael B. Mazis, Olli T. Ahtola, and R. Eugene Klippel, "A Comparison of Four Multi-Attribute Models in the Prediction of Consumer Attitudes," *Journal of Consumer Research,* Vol. 2 (June 1975), pp. 38–52; Douglas J. Lincoln and A. Coskun Samli, "Assessing the Usefulness of Attribute Advertising for Store Image Enhancement: An Experimental Approach," *Journal of Advertising,* Vol. 10, no. 3 (1981), pp. 25–34; Richard J. Lutz, "Changing Brand Attitudes Through Modification of Cognitive Structure," *Journal of Consumer Research,* Vol. 1 (March 1975), pp. 49–59; Punam Anand, Morris B. Holbrook, and Debra Stephens, "The Formation of Affective Judgments: The Cognitive-Affective Model Versus the Independence Hypothesis," *Journal of Consumer Research,* Vol. 15 (December 1988), pp. 386–391; Michael J. Stankey, "The Strategic Dilemma Of Alternate Structures in Expectancy-Value Attitude Models," *Psychology & Marketing,* Vol. 2 (Summer 1985), pp. 105–114; James Jaccard, David Brinberg and Lee J. Ackerman, "Assessing Attribute Importance: A Comparison of Six Methods," *Journal of Consumer Research,* Vol. 12 (March 1986), pp. 463–468; Gene W. Murdock and Robert G. Roe, "Consumer Bank Selection: Attributes of Choice," *AMA Educators' Proceedings* (1986), pp. 12–17; Charles M. Schaninger and W. Christian Buss, "Removing Response-Style Effects in Attribute-Determinance Ratings to Identify Market Segments," *Journal of Business Research,* Vol. 14 (June 1986), pp. 237–252; Donald R. Lichtenstein and William O. Bearden, "Measurement and Structure of Kelley's Covariance Theory," *Journal of Consumer Research,* Vol. 13 (September 1986), pp. 290–296; Naresh K. Malhotra, "An Approach to the Measurement of Consumer Preferences Using Limited Information," *Journal of Marketing Research,* Vol. 23 (February 1986), pp. 33–40; Michael D. Johnson and Claes Fornell, "The Nature and Methodological Implications of the Cognitive Representation of Products," *Journal of Consumer Research,* Vol. 14 (September 1987), pp. 214–228; Douglas M. Stayman, Wayne D. Hoyer and Robert P. Leone, "Attribute Importance in Discounting Product Features in Advertising," *AMA Educators' Proceedings* (1987), pp. 56–60; Richard M. Durand and Zarrel V. Lambert, "Don't Know Responses in Surveys: Analyses and Interpretational Consequences," *Journal of Business Research,* Vol. 16 (March 1988), pp. 169 ff; Morris B. Holbrook and William J. Havlena, "Assessing the Real-to-Artificial Generalizability of Multiattribute Attitude Models in Tests of New Product Designs," *Journal of Marketing Research,* Vol. 24 (February1988), pp. 25–35; two articles in: *Advances in Consumer Research,* Vol. 15 (1988): James H. Myers, "Attribute Deficiency Segmentation: Measuring Unmet Wants," pp. 108–113, and Lawrence J. Marks, Susan Higgins, and Michael A. Kamins, "Investigating the Experiential Dimensions of Product Evaluation," pp. 114–121; Michael D. Johnson,

"Comparability and Hierarchical Processing in Multialternative Choice," *Journal of Consumer Research*, Vol. 15 (December 1988), pp. 303–314; Don L. Coursey, "Preference Trees, Preference Hierarchies, and Consumer Behavior," *Journal of Consumer Research*, Vol. 15 (December 1988), pp. 407–409; and three papers in *Advances in Consumer Research*, Vol. 16 (1989): Mark Snyder, "Selling Images Versus Selling Products: Motivational Foundations of Consumer Attitudes and Behavior," pp. 306–311, Shuzo Abe and Masao Tanaka, "Is Brand Evaluation Independent from Other Brands?" pp. 439–442, and Michael D. Johnson, "On the Nature of Product Attributes and Attribute Relationships," pp. 598–604.

9. Richard J. Lutz, "Changing Brand Attitudes," See also G. R. Dowling and D. F. Midgley, "Product Evaluation in a Dynamic Market," *Psychology & Marketing*, Vol. 3 (Summer 1986), pp. 99–112.

10. For further discussion of these strategy approaches, see Harper W. Boyd, Michael L. Ray, and Edward C. Strong, "An Attitudinal Framework for Advertising Strategy," *Journal of Marketing*, April 1972, pp. 27–33. See also C. Whan Park, Bernard J. Jaworski, and Deborah J. MacInnis, "Strategic Brand Concept-Image Management," *Journal of Marketing*, Vol. 50 (October 1986), pp. 135–145; Robert Jacobson and David Aaker, "The Strategic Role of Product Quality," *Journal of Marketing*, Vol. 51 (October 1987), pp. 31–44; and Sharon Shavitt, "Products, Personalities and Situations in Attitude Functions: Implications for Consumer Behavior," *Advances in Consumer Research*, Vol. 16 (1989), pp. 300–305.

11. Paul L. Edwards, "Mailing by Six Flags Seeks to Reinforce Park's Safety," *Advertising Age*, August 23, 1984, p. 8.

12. "P&G Rides Crest with Leverage," *Marketing Week*, October 5, 1987, p. 58.

13. "How Four Companies Used Strategic Promotion Planning," *Marketing News*, October 30, 1981, p. 13.

14. Jack J. Honomichl, "The Ongoing Sage of 'Mother Baking Soda,'" *Advertising Age*, September 20, 1982, pp. M-2 ff.

15. William L. Wilkie and Paul W. Farris, *Consumer Information Processing: Perspectives and Implications for Advertising* (Cambridge, Mass.: Marketing Science Institute, 1976).

16. Ibid.

17. See, for example, William L. Wilkie, Dennis L. McNeill, and Michael B. Mazis, "Marketing's 'Scarlet Letter': The Theory and Practice of Corrective Advertising," *Journal of Marketing*, Spring 1984, pp. 11–31.

18. Alvin Achenbaum, "Knowledge Is a Thing Called Measurement," in L. Adler and I. Crespi (eds.), *Attitude Research at Sea* (Chicago: American Marketing Association, 1966), pp. 111–126; and Alvin Achenbaum, "Advertising Doesn't Manipulate Consumers," *Journal of Advertising Research*, April 2, 1972, pp. 3–13. See also William D. Wells, "Attitude and Behavior: Lessons from the Needham Life Style Study," *Journal of Advertising Research*, February–March 1985, pp. 40–44.

19. R. H. Fazio and M. P. Zanna, "Attitudinal Qualities Relating to the Strength of the Attitude-Behavior Relationship," *Journal of Experimental Social Psychology*, Vol. 14 (1978), pp. 398–408. See also R. H. Fazio and M. P. Zanna, "Direct Experience and Attitude-Behavior Consistency," in L. Berkowitz (ed.), *Advances in Experimental Social Psychology*, Vol. 14 (New York: Academic Press, 1981), pp. 162–202. For results in marketing, see Michael A. Kamins and Larry J. Marks, "The Effects of Framing and Advertising Sequencing on Attitude Consistency and Behavioral Intentions," *Advances in Consumer Research*, Vol. 14 (1987), pp. 168–172; Mark P. Zanna, "Attitude-Behavior Consistency: Fulfilling the Need for Cognitive Structure," *Advances in Consumer Research*, Vol. 16, (1989), pp. 318–320; and Robert E. Smith and William R. Swinyard, "Attitude-Behavior Consistencies: The Impact of Product Trial Versus Advertising," *Journal of Marketing Research*, August 1983, pp. 257–267.

20. See, for example, work by Richard E. Petty and John T. Cacioppo and their colleagues. A useful review and perspective appears in their chapter in Harold H. Hassarjian and Thomas Robertson, *Handbook of Consumer Behavior* (Englewood Cliffs, N.J. Prentice Hall, 1990). See also Jack M. Feldman and John G. Lynch, "Self-Generated Validity and Other Effects of Measurement on Belief, Attitude Intention, and Behavior," *Journal of Applied Psychology*, Vol. 73, no. 3, (1988), pp. 421–435; and Sadrudin A. Ahmed, "Attitude-Behavior Consistency: The Moderating Effect of Cognitive Style," *AMA Educators' Proceedings* (1985), pp. 7–10.

21. Russell H. Fazio, Martha C. Powell, and Carol J. Williams, "The Role of Attitude Accessibility in the Attitude-to-Behavior Process," *Journal of Consumer Research*, 1990 (in press). For a broader review of this approach, see R. H. Fazio, "On the Power and Functionality of Attitudes: The Role of Attitude Accessibility," in A Pratkanis, S. Breckler, and A. Greenwald (eds.), *Attitude Structure and Function*. Hillsdale, NJ: Erlbaum, 1989, pp. 153–179.

22. For further description of the extended Fishbein model and applications, see Icek Ajzen and

Martin Fishbein *Understanding Attitudes and Predicting Social Behavior* (Englewood Cliffs, N.J.: Prentice Hall, 1980). Within marketing an especially useful basic discussion is provided in Michael J. Ryan and E. H. Bonfield, "The Fishbein Extended Model and Consumer Behavior," *Journal of Consumer Research,* Vol. 2 (August 1975), pp. 118–136.

For empirical findings and extensions in consumer behavior, see David T. Wilson, H. Lee Matthews, and James W. Harvey, "An Empirical Test of the Fishbein Behavioral Intention Model," *Journal of Consumer Research,* Vol. 1 (March 1975), pp. 39–48; Michael J. Ryan and E. H. Bonfield, "Fishbein's Intentions Model: A Test of External and Pragmatic Validity," *Journal of Marketing,* Vol. 44 (Spring 1980), pp. 82–95; Paul R. Warshaw, "A New Model for Predicting Behavioral Intentions: An Alternative to Fishbein," *Journal of Marketing Research,* Vol. 17 (May 1980), pp. 153–172; Three articles in *Advances in Consumer Research,* Vol. 8 (1981): David Brinberg, "A Comparison of Two Behavioral Intention Models," pp. 48–52, Paul R. Warshaw, "A Discussion of Attitude Research and Behavioral Intentions," pp. 53–56, Robert Burnkrant and Thomas J. Page, Jr., "An Examination of the Convergent, Discriminant, and Predictive Validity of Fishbein's Behavioral Intention Model," *Journal of Marketing Research,* November 1982, pp. 550–561; Jeffrey E. Danes, "Attitude Research and Behavioral Intentions: A Critical Review," pp. 57–60. E. H. Bonfield, "Involvement, Attitude, and Behavior: On the Nature of the Relationships," *Advances in Consumer Research,* Vol. 10 (1983), pp. 425–426; J. Bradley Barbeau and William J. Qualls, "Consumers' Perceptions of Attributes and Behavior Intentions: An Extended Comparison-Level Model," *Advances in Consumer Research,* Vol. 11 (1984), pp. 143–147; Terence A. Shimp and Alican Kavas, "The Theory of Reasoned Action Applied to Coupon Usage," *Journal of Consumer Research,* Vol. 11 (December 1984), pp. 795–809; and Banwari Mittal, "Achieving Higher Seat Belt Usage: The Role of Habit in Bridging the Attitude-Behavior Gap," *Journal of Applied Social Psychology,* Vol. 18, no. 12 1988, pp. 993–1016.

The annual conference of the Association for Consumer Research is likely to contain several papers on this topic each year. These can be found in the conference proceedings.

Recent American Marketing Association conferences have also had sessions devoted to this topic. See also Richard L. Oliver and William O. Bearden, "Crossover Effects in the Theory of Reasoned Action: A Moderating Influence Attempt," *Journal of Consumer Research,* Vol. 12 (December 1985), pp. 324–340; Linda F. Jamieson and Frank M. Bass, "Adjusting Stated Intention Measures to Predict Trial Purchase of New Products: A Comparison of Models and Methods," *Journal of Marketing Research,* Vol. 26 (August 1989), pp. 336–345; Thomas J. Madden and Pamela S. Ellen, "A Comparison of the Theory of Planned Behavior to the Theory of Reasoned Action," *AMA Educators' Proceedings* (1989), p. 250; and Blair H. Sheppard, John Hartwick, and Paul R. Warshaw, "The Theory of Reasoned Action: A Meta-analysis of Past Research with Recommendations for Modifications and Future Research," *Journal of Consumer Research,* Vol. 15 (December 1988), pp. 325–343.

23. The heated debates have involved basic aspects of the extended model's concepts, definitions, and measures. For example, one key issue is how to discern the nature of differences between normative beliefs and attitudinal consequences when both might relate to the same outside persons. If this happens, we're not sure which component of the extended model, *A* or *SN*, should reflect this force on the behavior. This point can easily be seen in our college example—Sherry might not only wish to comply with her parents' preferences because she wants to (*SN*), but also because she believes that favorable consequences will ensue if she complies and that unfavorable consequences might result if she does not (*A*).

These issues are important to theorists and to those concerned with obtaining precise and valid measures with which to diagnose specific causes of consumer intentions and behaviors. If you would like to pursue these more abstract issues to understand better the nuances of this model, see the following articles in *Advances in Consumer Research,* Vol. 4, (1976): Olli T. Ahtola, "Toward a Vector Model of Intentions," pp. 481–484, Richard J. Lutz, "Conceptual and Operational Issues in the Extended Fishbein Model," pp. 469–476, and Martin Fishbein, "Extending the Extended Model: Some Comments," pp. 491–497.

Also, for a heated debate featuring strong disagreements about the model, see Paul W. Miniard and Joel B. Cohen, "An Examination of the Fishbein-Ajzen Behavioral Intentions Model's Concepts and Measures," *Journal of Experimental Social Psychology,* Vol. 17 (July 1981), pp. 309–339; Martin Fishbein and Icek Ajzen, "On Construct Validity: A Critique of Miniard and Cohen's Paper," *Journal of Experimental Social Psychology,* Vol. 17 (July 1981), pp. 340–350; and Paul W. Miniard and Joel B. Cohen, "Modeling Personal and Normative Influences on Behavior," *Journal of Consumer Research,* Vol. 10 (September 1983), pp. 169–180.

24. Richard E. Petty and John T. Cacioppo, "Attitudes and Persuasion: Classic and Contemporary

Approaches (Dubuque, Iowa: Wm. C. Brown, 1981); R. Petty, J. Cacioppo, and D. Schumann, "Central and Peripheral Routes to Advertising Effectiveness: The Moderating Role of Involvement," *Journal of Consumer Research*, Vol. 10 (September 1983), pp. 135–146; and J. Cacioppo and R. Petty, "The Elaboration Likelihood Model of Persuasion," *Advances in Consumer Research*, Vol. 11, (1984), pp. 673–675. For insights and extensions, see Thomas K. Srull, "Affect and Memory: The Impact of Affective Reactions in Advertising on the Representation of Product Information in Memory," *Advances in Consumer Research*, Vol. 10, (1983), pp. 520–525; Mary J. Bitner and Carl Obermiller, "The Elaboration Likelihood Model: Limitations and Extensions in Marketing," and Yehoshua Tsal, "Effects of Verbal and Visual Information on Brand Attitudes," both in *Advances in Consumer Research*, Vol. 12, (1985), pp. 265–267; and John L. Swasy and James M. Munch, "Examining the Target of Receiver Elaborations: Rhetorical Question Effects on Source Processing and Persuasion," *Journal of Consumer Research*, Vol. 11 (March 1985), pp. 877–886. See also Anthony G. Greenwald and Clark Leavitt, " Audience Involvement in Advertising: Four Levels," *Journal of Consumer Research*, Vol. 11 (June 1984), pp. 581–592; two articles in *Advances in Consumer Research*, Vol. 15 (1988): Charles S. Areni and Richard J. Lutz, "The Role of Argument Quality in the Elaboration Likelihood Model," pp. 197–203, and Paul W. Miniard, Peter R. Dickson, and Kenneth R. Lord, "Some Central and Peripheral Thoughts on the Routes to Persuasion," pp. 204–208; and Cornelia Dröge, "Shaping the Route to Attitude Change: Central Versus Peripheral Processing Through Comparative Versus Noncomparative Advertising," *Journal of Marketing Research*, Vol. 26 (May 1989), pp. 193–204.

25. For early discussions of the "Attitude Toward the Ad" concept, see Terence A. Shimp, "Attitude Toward the Ad as a Mediator of Consumer Brand Choice," *Journal of Advertising*, Vol. 10, no. 2 (1981), pp. 9–15 ff.; and Andrew A. Mitchell and Jerry C. Olson, "Are Product Attribute Beliefs the Only Mediator of Advertising Effects on Brand Attitude?" *Journal of Marketing Research*, August 1981, pp. 318–332. For related discussions, empirical tests, and extensions of this concept, see Julie A. Edell and Marian C. Burke, "The Moderating Effect of Attitude Toward an Ad on Ad Effectiveness Under Different Processing Conditions," *Advances in Consumer Research*, Vol. 11 (1984), pp. 644–649; R. J. Lutz, "Affective and Cognitive Antecedents of Attitude Toward the Ad: A Conceptual Framework," in Linda F. Alwitt and Andrew A. Mitchell (eds.), *Psychological Processes and Advertising Effects: Theory, Research, and Application* (Lawrenceville, N.J.: Erlbaum, 1984); Betsy D. Gelb and Charles M. Pickett, "Attitude-Toward-the-Ad: Links to Humor and to Advertising Effectiveness," *Journal of Advertising*, Vol. 12, no. 3 (1983), pp. 34–42; Larry G. Gresham and T. A. Shimp, "Attitude Toward the Advertisement and Brand Attitudes: A Classical Conditioning Perspective," *Journal of Advertising*, Vol. 14, no. 1 (1985), pp. 10–17; Meryl Paula Gardner, "Does Attitude Toward the Ad Affect Brand Attitude Under a Brand Evaluation Set?" *Journal of Marketing Research*, May 1985, pp. 192–198; Scott B. MacKenzie, Richard J. Lutz, and George E. Belch, "The Role of Attitude Toward the Ad as a Mediator of Advertising Effectiveness: A Test of Competing Explanations," *Journal of Marketing Research*, Vol. 23 (May 1986), pp. 130–143; Darrel D. Muehling, "The Influence of Attitude-Toward-Advertising-in-General on Attitude-Toward-An-Ad," *AMA Educators' Proceedings* (1986), pp. 29–34; Thomas J. Madden, Chris T. Allen, and Jacquelyn L. Twible, "Attitude Toward the Ad: An Assessment of Diverse Measurement Indices Under Different Processing 'Sets'," *Journal of Marketing Research*, Vol. 25 (August 1988), pp. 242–252. Scot Burton and Donald R. Lichtenstein, "The Effect of Ad Claims and Ad Context on Attitude Toward the Advertisement," *Journal of Advertising*, Vol. 17 (November 1988), pp. 3–11; Douglas M. Stayman and David A. Aaker, "Are All the Effects of Ad-Induced Feelings Mediated by A_{ad}?"*Journal of Consumer Research*, Vol. 15 (December 1988), pp. 368–373; Karen A. Machleit and Robert J. Kent, "What Is the Effect of Attitude Toward the Ad When the Consumer Is Familiar with the Brand?" *AMA Educator's Proceedings* (1989), pp. 215–219; and Scott B. MacKenzie and Richard J. Lutz, "An Empirical Examination of the Structural Antecedents of Attitude Toward the Ad in an Advertising Pretesting Context," *Journal of Marketing*, Vol. 53 (April 1989), pp. 48–65.

26. C. Whan Park and S. Mark Young, "Types and Levels of Involvement and Brand Attitude Formation," *Advances in Consumer Research*, Vol. 10 (1983), pp. 320–324. See also Darrel D. Muehling and Russell N. Laczniak, "Advertising's Immediate and Delayed Influence on Brand Attitudes: Considerations Across Message-Involvement Levels," *Journal of Advertising*, Vol. 17 (November 1988), pp. 23–34.

27. Jack Trout and Al Ries, "Positioning Cuts Through Chaos in Marketplace," *Advertising Age*, May 1, 1972; for a more recent description, see Al Ries and Jack Trout, *Positioning: The Battle for Your Mind* (New York: McGraw-Hill, 1981). See also Frederick W. Langrehr, "Consumer Images of Two Types of Competing Financial Service Retailers," *Journal of the Academy of Marketing*

Science, Vol. 13 (Summer 1985), pp. 248–264. Michael K. Mills, "Strategic Retail Fashion Market Positioning: A Comparative Analysis," *Journal of the Academy of Marketing Science,* Vol. 13 (Summer 1985), pp. 212–225; M. Joseph Sirgy and J. S. Johar, "Self-Image Congruence Models Versus Multiattribute Attitude Models: When to Use What Model for Product Positioning," *AMA Educators' Proceedings* (1985), pp. 1–5; Frank Alpert, "Product Categories, Product Hierarchy, and Pioneerships: A Consumer Behavior Explanation for Pioneer Brand Advantage," *AMA Educators' Proceedings* (1987), pp. 133–138; and D. Sudharshan, Thomas Gruca, and K. Ravi Kumar, "Product Positioning Strategies for Segment Pre-Emption," *AMA Educators' Proceedings* (1988), pp. 47–52.

28. David A. Aaker and J. Gary Shansby, "Positioning Your Product," *Business Horizons,* May–June 1982, pp. 56–62.

29. Allan D. Shocker and V. Srinivasan, "Multiattribute Approaches for Product Concept Evaluation and Generation: A Critical Review," *Journal of Marketing Research,* May 1979, pp. 159–180. For an excellent recent overview of research advances in this area, see Paul E. Green and Abba M. Krieger, "Recent Contributions to Optimal Product Positioning and Buyer Segmentation," Working Paper, University of Pennsylvania (Wharton School), 1989.

30. For discussions of "determinant" attributes, see Mark I. Alpert, "Definition of Determinant Attributes: A Comparison of Methods," *Journal of Marketing Research,* May 1971, pp. 184–191; James H. Myers, "Benefit Structure Analysis: A New Tool for Product Planning," *Journal of Marketing,* October 1976, pp. 23–32; and Mark I. Alpert, "Unresolved Issues in Identification of Determinant Attributes," *Advances in Consumer Research,* Vol. 7 (1980), pp. 83–88.

31. This is an important sector of work that stresses how consumers' subjective ratings can be transformed into objective dimensions that marketing managers can control in their marketing mixes. It has therefore attracted the interest of quantitatively oriented marketers. For some readings presenting various viewpoints and alternative methodologies, see Paul E. Green and Yoram Wind, *Multi-Attribute Decisions in Marketing* (Hinsdale, Ill.: Dryden Press, 1973); Paul E. Green and V. Srinivasan, "Conjoint Analysis in Consumer Research: Issues and Outlook," *Journal of Consumer Research,* Vol. 5 (September 1978), pp. 103–123; Naresh K. Malhotra, "Structural Reliability and Stability of Nonmetric Conjoint Analysis," *Journal of Marketing Research,* Vol. 19 (May 1982), pp. 199–207; Rashi Glazer, "Multiattribute Perceptual Bias as Revealing of Preference Structure," *Journal of Consumer Research,* Vol. 11 (June 1984), pp. 510–521; Rajendra K. Srivastava, Mark I. Alpert, and Allan D. Shocker, "A Customer-Oriented Approach for Determining Market Structures," *Journal of Marketing,* Spring 1984, pp. 32–45.

For recent developments, see, for example, Dick R. Wittink and Philippe Cattin, "Commercial Use of Conjoint Analysis: An Update," *Journal of Marketing,* Vol. 53 (July 1989), pp. 91–96; two articles in *Advances in Consumer Research,* Vol. 15 (1988): Elizabeth Creyer and William T. Ross, "The Effects of Range-Frequency Manipulations on Conjoint Importance Weight Stability," pp. 505–509, and Jordan J. Louviere and George G. Woodworth, "On the Design and Analysis of Correlated Conjoint Experiments Using Difference Designs," pp. 510–517; William L. Moore and Richard J. Semenik, "Measuring Preferences with Hybrid Conjoint Analysis: The Impact of a Different Number of Attributes in the Master Design," *Journal of Business Research,* Vol. 16 (May 1988), pp. 261–274; Rajeev Kohli, "Assessing Attribute Significance in Conjoint Analysis: Nonparametric Tests and Empirical Validation," *Journal of Marketing Research,* Vol. 24 (May 1988), pp. 123–133; two articles in *Advances in Consumer Research,* Vol. 16 (1989); Sanjay Mishra, U. N. Umesh, and Donald E. Stem, Jr., "Attribute Importance Weights in Conjoint Analysis: Bias and Precision," pp. 605–611, and Jordan J. Louviere and Eugene Kaciak, "A Comparison of Several Approaches for Inferring Individual and Aggregate Attribute Effects in Pairwise Comparison Conjoint Choice Tasks," pp. 612–618; and Paul E. Green and Kristiaan Helsen, "Cross-Validation Assessment of Alternatives to Individual-Level Conjoint Analysis: A Case Study," *Journal of Marketing Research,* Vol. 26 (August 1989), pp. 346–350.

32. See, for example, Glen L. Urban, "PERCEPTOR: A Model for Product Positioning," *Management Science,* Vol. 21 (April 1975), pp. 858–871; and Paul E. Green, J. Douglas Carroll, and Stephen M. Goldberg, "A General Approach to Product Design Optimization via Conjoint Analysis," *Journal of Marketing,* Vol. 45 (Summer 1981), pp. 17–37.

33. Richard Johnson, "Market Segmentation: A Strategic Management Tool," *Journal of Marketing Research,* February 1971, pp. 13–19. For recent discussions of related issues and possibilities, see John G. Lynch, Jr., "Uniqueness Issues in the Decompositional Modeling of Multiattribute Overall Evaluations: An Information Integration Perspective," *Journal of Marketing Research,* Vol. 22 (February 1985), pp. 1 ff; Michael D. Johnson, "Consumer Similarity Judgments: A Test of the Contrast Model," *Psychology & Marketing,* Vol. 3 (Spring 1986), pp. 47–60; Donna L. Hoffman

and George R. Franke, "Correspondence Analysis Graphical Representation of Categorical Data in Marketing Research," *Journal of Marketing Research*, Vol. 23 (August 1986), pp. 213–227; Steven M. Shugan, "Estimating Brand Positioning Maps Using Supermarket Scanning Data," *Journal of Marketing Research*, Vol. 24 (February 1987), pp. 1–18; Naresh K. Malhotra, "Validity and Structural Reliability of Multidimensional Scaling," *Journal of Marketing Research*, Vol. 24 (May 1987), pp. 164–173; and Wayne S. DeSarbo and Richard R. Batsell, "A New Multidimensional Scaling Methodology for the Representation of Inter-Product Substitutability," *Advances in Consumer Research*, Vol. 15 (1988), pp. 518–527.

34. Aaker and Shansby, "Multiattribute Approaches for Product Concept Evaluation and Generation"; see also "A-B Miller Brews Continue to Barrel Ahead," *Advertising Age*, August 4, 1980, p. 4; and "These Days It's Miller Time Less Often, Worrying Brewer," *The Wall Street Journal*, February 10, 1983, p. 33.

Chapter 12　Cultural Influences on Consumer Behavior

1. Ernest L. Schusky and T. Patrick Culbert, *Introducing Culture*, 3rd ed. (Englewood Cliffs, N.J.: Prentice Hall 1978).

2. A. L. Kroeber and Clyde Kluckhohn, *Culture: A Critical Review of Concepts and Definitions* (New York: Random House, 1963).

3. Mavis H. Biesanz and John Biesanz, *Introduction to Sociology*, 3rd ed. (Englewood Cliffs, N.J.: Prentice Hall, 1978), pp. 34–53. See also Thomas C. O'Guinn, Ronald J. Faber, Nadine J.J.Curias, and Kay Schmitt, "The Cultivation of Consumer Norms," *Advances in Consumer Research*, Vol. 16, (1989), pp. 779–785.

4. The following discussion is based upon George P. Murdoch, "The Common Denominator of Cultures," in Ralph Linton (Ed.), *The Science of Man in the World Crisis* (New York; Columbia University Press, 1945), pp. 123–142.

5. Ibid., p. 125.

6. For an excellent discussion of further aspects of culture as they apply to marketing, see Frederick D. Sturdivant, "Subculture Theory: Poverty, Minorities, and Marketing," in Scott Ward and Thomas Robertson (eds.), *Consumer Behavior: Theoretical Sources.* (Englewood Cliffs, N.J.: Prentice Hall, 1973), pp. 470-520. For recent discussions, see Grant McCracken, "Culture and Consumption: A Theoretical Account of the Structure and Movement of the Cultural Meaning of Consumer Goods," *Journal of Consumer Research*, Vol. 13 (June 1986), pp. 71–84; John Mager and James G. Helgeson, "The Development of Marketing Thought: Cultural Changes and Marketing Evolution," *AMA Winter Educators' Proceedings* (1987), pp. 326–331; Ronald J. Faber, Thomas C. O'Guinn, and John A. McCarty, "Ethnicity, Acculturation, and the Importance of Product Attributes," *Psychology & Marketing*, Vol. 4 (Summer 1987), pp. 121–134; Martin S. Roth and Christine Moorman, "The Cultural Content of Cognition and the Cognitive Content of Culture: Implications for Consumer Research," *Advances in Consumer Research*, Vol. 15, (1988), pp. 403–410; Janeen Arnold Costa, "Social Processes in the Spread of Consumer Culture: An Anthropological Case Study," *AMA Educators' Proceedings* (1989), pp. 239–244; and Wei-Na Lee, "The Mass-Mediated Consumption Realities for Three Cultural Groups," *Advances in Consumer Research*, Vol. 16 (1989), pp. 771–778.

7. "Shopping Centers Will Be America's Towns of Tomorrow," *Marketing News*, November 28, 1980, pp. 1+.

8. Terry Anderson, "Men's Cosmetic Industry is Groomed for Success," *USA Today*, March 30, 1989, p. 6D; and Mary McCabe English, "The Face of the '80's: What's Ahead?" *Advertising Age*, March 1, 1982, pp. M-9-M-11.

9. "Sights and Sounds," *The Wall Street Journal*, July 6, 1987, p. 13; *The Statistical Abstract of the United States,* 1981 (Washington D.C.: U.S. Government Printing Office, 1982), p. 559; and William F. Gloede, "Industry Delivers Solution to Bad News," *Advertising Age*, July 25, 1985, pp. 15–16.

10. Ralph Blumenthal, "Despite Soaring Inflation, Some Things Are Cheaper," *The New York Times* News Service, March 8, 1981.

11. "Cutty's Image Riding on New Club," *Marketing Week*, March 14, 1988, p. 5; George Lazarus, "Cigar Biz Gasps in New Climate," *Marketing Week*, November 16, 1987, p. 34; George Allen, "Investing in Fitness," *Advertising Age*, February 8, 1982, p. M-12; and Ed Fitch, "Distillers Try Tactics to Brake Sales Slide," *Advertising Age*, July 18, 1985, pp. 13, 14.

12. Ed Zotti, "Consumers Toast to a Vintage Future," *Advertising Age*, March 29, 1982, pp. M-13-M-14, and John Maxwell, "U.S. Wine Industry Uncorks Sales Hike," *Advertising Age*, June 4, 1984, p. 50.

13. Harold H. Kassarjian "Content Analysis in Consumer Research, *Journal of Consumer Research,* June 1977, pp. 8–18.

14. B. G. Yovovich, "His Crystal Ball: The Daily Newspaper," *Advertising Age,* October 11, 1982, pp. M-4 ff; Randall Poe, "Who Will Make the 'Fortunate' 500?" *Consumers Digest,* March–April 1985, pp. 55, 73; and Emily Yoffe, "Naisbitt's Clip Joint: The Selling of Content Analysis and *Megatrends,*" *Marketing News,* March 16, 1984, pp. 2–1 ff; John Naisbitt, *Megatrends* (New York: Warner Books, 1982); Alladi Venkatesh, "A Macroanalytical Study of the Post-Industrial Society," Working Paper, University of California, Irvine, 1989; and Ronald D. Michman, "Why Forecast for the Long Term?" *Journal of Business Strategy,* September/October, 1989, pp. 36–40.

15. This listing is based on discussions in "31 Major Trends Shaping Future of American Business," *Roper's Public Pulse,* 1988; "Popcorn: Trends Last, But Fads Fade Fast," *Marketing News,* March 14, 1988, p. 29; "Scan Social Trends to Develop Effective Marketing Communications," *Marketing News,* November 13, 1981, p. 12.: "Smith Outlines Eight Trends to Watch," *Advertising Age,* August 24, 1981, pp. 22 ff; and "Rules a Glimpse into the New World," *Advertising Age,* July 20, 1981, p. 44. See also Robert Friedmann and Warren French, "Beyond Social Trend Data," *Journal of Consumer Marketing,* Vol. 2 (Fall 1985), pp. 17–22.

16. "Food Marketer: Slow the Frenetic Pace of New Product Introductions," *Marketing News,* March 28, 1988, p. 17; George Lazarus, "Microwaves Heat Up Lunch Biz," *Marketing Week,* November 2, 1987, p. 30. For broader discussions, see William D. Smithburg, "The Development and Marketing of New Consumer Products: Some Successes and Failures," *Journal of Consumer Marketing,* Vol. 2 (Summer 1985), pp. 55–60; and William Copulsky, "Ready, Fire, Aim: Explaining an Entrepreneurial Strategy for New Products," *The Journal of Consumer Marketing,* Vol. 6 (Spring 1989), pp. 45–50.

17. Richard K. Manoff, "When the 'Client' Is Human Life Itself," *Advertising Age,* August 22, 1983, pp. M-4--M-5. For related topics, see P. Rajan Varadarajan & Anil Menon, "Cause-Related Marketing: A Coalignment of Marketing Strategy and Corporate Philanthropy," *Journal of Marketing,* Vol. 52 (July 1988), pp. 58–74; and Bonnie S. Guy and Wesley E. Patton, "The Marketing of Altruistic Causes: Understanding Why People Help," *The Journal of Consumer Marketing,* Vol. 6 (Winter 1989), pp. 19–30.

18. Everett M. Rogers, "New Product Adoption and Diffusion," *Journal of Consumer Research,* March 1976, pp. 290–301.

19. Thomas S. Robertson, "The Process of Innovation and the Diffusion of Innovation," *Journal of Marketing,* Vol. 31 (January1967), pp. 14–19. See also Edward F. McQuarrie and Daniel Langmeyer, "Using Values to Measure Attitudes Toward Discontinuous Innovations," *Psychology & Marketing,* Vol. 2 (Winter 1985), pp. 239–252; and Hubert Gatignon and Thomas S. Robertson, "Technology Diffusion: An Empirical Test of Competitive Effects," *Journal of Marketing,* Vol. 53 (January 1989), pp. 35–49.

20. Everett M. Rogers and Floyd Shoemaker, *Communication of Innovations* (New York: Free Press, 1971.

21. There is a large, but technical, literature of new product models and market forecasting. You may wish to begin by consulting an interesting report by Glen L. Urban, John R. Hauser, and John H. Roberts, "Prelaunch Forecasting of New Automobiles: Models and Implementation," Report 89-104; Marketing Science Institute, 1989; see also Yoram Wind and Vijay Mahajan, *Innovation Diffusion Models of New Product Acceptance* (Cambridge, Mass.: Ballinger Press, 1986). Additional perspectives and applications are available in Ed Russell, Jr., Anthony J. Adams, and Bill Boundy, "High-Tech Test Marketing at Campbell Soup Company," *Journal of Consumer Marketing,* Vol. 3 (Winter 1986), pp. 71–80; Noel Capon and Rashi Glazer, "Marketing and Technology: A Strategic Coalignment," *Journal of Marketing,* Vol. 51 (July 1987),pp. 1–14; Stephen J. Hoch, "Who Do We Know: Predicting the Interests and Opinions of the American Consumer," *Journal of Consumer Research,* Vol. 15 (December 1988), pp. 315 ff; and four papers in *Advances in Consumer Research,* Vol. 16 (1989): Arch G. Woodside, Elizabeth J. Wilson, Nicholas T. van der Walt, and Roderick J. Brodie, "Forecasting Consumer Acceptance of New Products for Multiple Market Segments Using Multiple Methods," pp. 326–331; John R. Rossiter, "Consumer Research and Marketing Science," pp. 407–413; Murlidhar Gao and Gregory E. Wester, "Consumer Research and Demand Forecasting for Wideband Telecommunications Services: Some Perspectives," pp. 619–628; and Robert N. Mayer, "Against All Odds: The State of Videotex in France," pp. 629–633.

22. Rogers and Shoemaker, *Communication of Innovations.* For recent findings, see *Advances in Consumer Research,* Vol. 14 (1987): David Midgley, "A Meta-Analysis of the Diffusion of Innovations Literature", pp. 204–207, and S. Ram, "A Model of Innovation Resistance," pp. 208–212;

and S. Ram and Jagdish N. Sheth, "Consumer Resistance to Innovations: The Marketing Problem and Its Solutions," *The Journal of Consumer Marketing*, Vol. 6 (Spring 1989), pp. 5–14.

23. Rogers and Shoemaker, *Communication of Innovations;* and John A. Howard and Lyman E. Ostlund, *Buyer Behavior: Theoretical and Empirical Foundations* (New York: Alfred A. Knopf, 1973).

24. There is an interesting literature on issues involving the characteristics and actions of the various adopter types. Our discussion in the remainder of this chapter draws upon these sources. See, for example, J. Arndt, "Profiling Consumer Innovations," in J. Arndt (ed.), *Insights into Consumer Behavior* (Boston: Allyn & Bacon, 1968), pp. 71–83; T. S. Robertson, *Innovative Behavior and Communication* (New York: Holt, Rinehart and Winston, 1971), pp. 75–77; D. G. LaBay and T. C. Kinnear, "Exploring the Consumer Decision Process in the Adoption of Solar Energy Systems," *Journal of Consumer Research*, Vol. 8 (December 1981), pp. 271–278; W. Black, "Discontinuance and Diffusion: Examination of the Post Adoption Decision Process," *Advances in Consumer Research*, Vol. 10, (1983), pp. 356–361; M. Dickerson and J. W. Gentry, "Characteristics of Adopters and Non-Adopters of Home Computers," *Journal of Consumer Research*, Vol. 10 (September 1983), pp. 225–235; the following papers in *Advances in Consumer Research*, Vol. 13, (1986): W. O. Bearden, S. E. Calcich, R. G. Netemeyer, and J. E. Teel, "An Exploratory Investigation of Consumer Innovativeness and Interpersonal Influences"; L. L. Price, and L. F. Feick, and D. C. Smith, "A Re-Examination of Communication Channel Usage by Adopter Categories"; J. W. Harvey, "Correlates of Search Patterns for an Innovation"; and T. Hill, N. D. Smith, and M. F. Mann, "Communicating Innovations: Convincing Computer Phobics to Adopt Innovative Technologies"; and Mary C. Gilly and Valarie A. Zeithaml, "The Elderly Consumer and Adoption of Technologies," *Journal of Consumer Research*, Vol. 12 (December 1985) pp. 353–357.

    For recent findings and discussions, see Lawrence F. Feick and Linda L. Price, "The Market Maven: A Diffuser of Marketplace Information," *Journal of Marketing*, Vol. 51 (January 1987), pp. 83–97; Gary J. Bamossy, "Measures of Innovative Behavior in Business Markets: Diffusion of High-Tech in the Lowlands," *AMA Educators' Proceedings* (1988), pp. 95–100; John H. Antil, "New Product or Service Adoption: When Does It Happen?," *Journal of Consumer Marketing*, Vol. 5 (Spring 1988), pp. 5–16; three papers in *Advances in Consumer Research*, Vol. 15 (1988): Gordon R. Foxall, "The Industrial User as Product Innovator: Markets, Hierarchies and Patterns of User-Initiated Innovation" pp. 286–291, William E. Warren, C. L. Abercrombie, and Robert L. Berl, "Characteristics of Adopters and Nonadopters of Alternative Residential Long-Distance Telephone Services," pp. 292–298, and Meera P. Venkatraman, "Investigating Differences in the Roles of Enduring and Instrumentally Involved Consumers in the Diffusion Process," pp. 299–303; two papers in *AMA Educators' Proceedings* (1989): David J. Burns, "Innovative Behavior: Toward a Comprehensive Model," p. 267; and S. Ram and Hyung-Shik Jung, "Does Innovativeness in Purchase Extend to Consumption? A Comparison of the Early Adopters and Early Majority," p. 268; and Robert J. Fisher, "The Socio-Cultural Context of Early Adoption Behavior," in P. Bloom et al. (eds.), *1989 AMA Educators' Proceedings* (Chicago: American Marketing Association, 1989), pp. 269–273.

25. Elizabeth C. Hirschman, "Innovativeness, Novelty Seeking, and Consumer Creativity," *Journal of Consumer Research*, December 1980, pp. 283–295; and Les Carlson and Sanford Grossbart, "Toward a Better Understanding of Inherent Innovativeness," *AMA Educators' Proceedings* (1984), pp. 88–91.

26. David F. Midgley and Grahame R. Dowling, "Innovativeness: The Concept and Its Measurement," *Journal of Consumer Research*, Vol. 4 (March 1978), pp. 229–242.

27. Kenneth Uhl, Roman Andrus, and Lance Poulson, "How Are Laggards Different? An Empirical Inquiry," *Journal of Marketing Research*, February 1970, pp. 51–54.

Chapter 13   Cross-Cultural and Symbolic Dimensions of Consumer Behavior

1. Robin M. Williams, *American Society: A Sociological Interpretation*, 3rd ed. (New York: Alfred A. Knopf, 1970), pp. 438–639.

2. Josh Levine, "Hard Sell Falls Flat for S.E. Asians," *Advertising Age*, June 21, 1981, p. 35.

3. The examples in this section are derived from several sources, most prominently an interesting book by David A. Ricks, *Big Business Blunders: Mistakes in Multinational Marketing* (Homewood, Ill.: Dow Jones–Irwin, 1983).

4. Doreen Lee, "Are Tokyo Tastes Ready for Tacos and Tostadas?" *Marketing Week*, September 14, 1987, p. 32.

5. The noted anthropologist Edward T. Hall has made numerous contributions to the study of issues

related to "hidden languages." His books have been widely read by marketers. You might enjoy reading E. T. Hall, *Beyond Culture* (Garden City, N.Y.: Anchor/Doubleday, 1976); E. T. Hall, *The Silent Language* (Garden City, N.Y.: Doubleday, 1973); and E. T. Hall, *The Hidden Dimension* (Garden City, N.Y.: Doubleday, 1969).

6. Wasief Djajanto, "Indonesia Government Expands Ad Ban," *Advertising Age,* March 16, 1981, p. 22.

7. John Karevoll, "Singapore Girl Nixed in Norway," *Advertising Age,* March 23, 1981, p. 48.

8. David Kline, "How Islam Collides with Advertising," *Advertising Age,* August 2, 1982, pp. M-2–M-3. For related discussions, see also Jen-Hung Huang and Juei-Fu Hou, "The Effects of Regulations on the Level of Information Content of Television Advertising—A Comparison of Three Nations," *AMA Educators Proceedings* (1987), pp. 93–96; Janeen Olsen and Kent L. Granzin, "Economic Development and Marketing Structure: A Conceptual and Empirical Investigation"; two papers in *AMA Educators Proceedings* (1988): pp. 254–259, and Arvind Parkhe and Michael E. Smith, "A General Systems Perspective on the Performance of Marketing in Society," pp. 281–284; and two papers in *Advances in Consumer Research, Vol. 16* Lisa N. Penaloza, "Immigrant Consumer Acculturation," (1989): pp. 110–118, and Dana L. Alden, Wayne D. Hoyer, and Guntalee Wechasura, "Choice Strategies and Involvement: A Cross-Cultural Analysis," pp. 119–126.

9. "Studying Global Trends Leads to Global Marketing Success in 2000," *Marketing News,* July 31, 1987, p. 27.

10. Bryant Robey, "The Year 2020: Populations Double Abroad," *Marketing Week,* June 19, 1989, p. 57.

11. "China Begins a New Long March," *Business Week,* June 5, 1989, pp. 38 ff. See also Joseph O. Eastlack, Jr., and Roberta Lucker, "Is China Moving from Marx to Mastercard?" *Journal of Consumer Marketing,* Vol. 3 (Summer 1986), pp. 5–22; and David Tse, Russell W. Belk, and Nan Zhou, "Becoming a Consumer Society: A Longitudinal and Cross-Cultural Content Analysis of Print Ads from Hong Kong, the People's Republic of China, and Taiwan," *Journal of Consumer Research,* Vol. 15 (March 1989), pp. 457–472.

12. "Studying Global Trends Leads to Global Marketing Success in 2000," *Marketing News,* July 13, 1987, p. 27.

13. See, for example, Louis Kraar, "The China Bubble Bursts," *Fortune,* July 6, 1987, pp. 86–89; Maggie Fox, "In China, 'Guanxi Is Everything,'" *Advertising Age,* November 2, 1987, p. S-12; Lynne Curry, "China Fights Wild Ad Claims," *Advertising Age,* December 21, 1987, p. 15.

14. Wolfgang Koschnick, "Russian Bear Bullish on Marketing," *Marketing News,* November 21, 1988, pp. 1 ff.

15. William Smith, "In USSR, Perestroika Portends Revival of Reklamy," *Marketing Week,* December 7, 1987, p. 34.

16. See "Gorbachev's Reforms: Will They Work?" *Business Week,* June 5, 1989, p. 63, and Gail E. Schares, "Glasnost's Twin Crucibles," *Business Week,* June 5, 1989, pp. 72–80. See also Jacob Naor, "Towards a Socialist Marketing Concept—The Case of Romania," *Journal of Marketing,* Vol. 50 (January 1986), pp. 28–39; and Iacob Catoiu, Constantin Florescu, and Jacob Naor, "Some Socialist Perspectives on Issues of Marketing Theory and Practice—A Romanian Viewpoint," *AMA Winter Educators Proceedings* (1987), pp. 320–325.

17. Discussion is based on Gail Belsky and Noreen O'Leary, "How 1992 Will Change Things," *Adweek,* June 6, 1988, pp. 8 ff; Richard I. Kirkland, "Outsider's Guide to Europe in 1992," *Fortune,* October 24, 1988, pp. 121 ff.; Kevin Cote, "1992: Europe Becomes One," *Advertising Age,* July 11, 1988, pp. 55 ff; Ron Gales, "Looking Toward a North American Market," *Adweek,* June 6, 1988, pp. 32 ff; Laurel Wentz, "1992 to Breed Global Brands," and "Pan-European Ad Faces Regulatory Gymnastics," *Advertising Age,* April 24, 1989; and Edwin A. Finn, "Sons of Smoot-Hawley," *Forbes,* February 6, 1989, pp. 38–40.

18. Linda Keslar, "Getting Post Position in Europe," *Adweek,* June 6, 1988, pp. 24 ff.

19. Madlyn Resener, "Europe's New Mass-Market Appeal," *Adweek,* June 1, 1987, pp. 6 ff; see also Martin van Mesdag, "Winging It in Foreign Markets," *Harvard Business Review* (January–February 1987), pp. 71–74. Considerable attention has been given to those issues in recent years. See, for example, Subhash C. Jain, "Standardization of International Marketing Strategy: Some Research Hypotheses," *Journal of Marketing,* Vol. 53 (January 1989), pp. 70–79; David K. Tse, Kam-hon Lee, Ilan Vertinsky, and Donald A. Wehrung, "Does Culture Matter? A Cross-Cultural Study of Executives' Choice, Decisiveness and Risk Adjustment in International Marketing," *Journal of Marketing,* Vol. 52 (October 1988), pp. 81–95; David K. Tse, John K. Wong, and Chin Tiong Tan, "Towards Some Standardized Cross-Cultural Consumption Values," *Advances in Consumer Research,* Vol. 15, (1988), pp. 387–395; Mary K. Ericksen and Karen Kaigler-Walker,

"Standard Measurement Criteria: Methodology for Cross-Cultural Research on Appearance," *AMA Educators Proceedings* (1987), pp. 11–14; John L. Graham, Dong Ki Kim, Chi-Yuan Lin, and Michael Robinson, "Buyer-Seller Negotiations Around the Pacific Rim: Differences in Fundamental Exchange Processes," *Journal of Consumer Research,* Vol. 15 (June 1988), pp. 48–54; V. H. Kirpalani and Xu Kuan, "Effective Market Potential Assessment—China and the Pacific Rim," *Advances in Consumer Research,* Vol. 14 (1987), pp. 398–402; Ken Kono, "Consumer Perceptions of U.S.-Built Foreign Cars: Quality Assessment," *AMA Educators' Proceedings* (1984), pp. 52–56; Robert O. Jordan, "Going Global: How to Join the Second Major Revolution in Advertising," *Journal of Consumer Marketing,* Vol. 5 (Winter 1988), pp. 39–44; Gordon L. Link, "Global Advertising: An Update," *The Journal of Consumer Marketing,* Vol. 5 (Spring 1988), pp. 69–74; Elana Hudak, "Global Branding and Segmentation: Are They Interdependent?" *The Journal of Consumer Marketing,* Vol. 5 (Summer 1988), pp. 27–34; Barbara Mueller, "Reflections of Culture: An Analysis of Japanese and American Advertising Appeals," *Journal of Advertising Research,* Vol. 27 (June–July 1987), pp. 51–59; Ah Keng Kau, Boon Chye Lim, and Chow Hou Wee, "Choice of Store Types—A Study of Japanese Consumers," *AMA Educators Proceedings* (1987), pp. 245–249; Guarav Bhalla and Lynn Y. S. Lin, "Cross-Cultural Marketing Research: A Discussion of Equivalence Issues and Measurement Strategies," *Psychology & Marketing,* Vol. 4 (Winter 1987), pp. 275–286; Judith Lynne Zaichkowsky and James H. Sood, "A Global Look at Consumers' Involvement and Use of Products," *International Marketing Review* (Winter 1988); Mary C. Gilly, "Sex Roles in Advertising: A Comparison of Television Advertisements in Australia, Mexico, and the United States," *Journal of Marketing,* Vol. 52 (April 1988), pp. 75–85; Susan B. Hester and Mary Yuen, "The Influence of Country of Origin on Consumer Attitude and Buying Behavior in the United States and Canada," *Advances in Consumer Research* Vol. 14, (1987), pp. 538–542; A. N. M. Waheeduzzaman and Lawrence J. Marks, "Halo Effects, Consumer Ethno-National Affinity, and Behavioral Intentions: An Extension of the Multi-Attribute Model of Country of Origin Effects," *AMA Educators' Proceedings* (1989), pp. 252–257; three papers in *Advances in Consumer Research,* Vol. 16 (1989): Carl Obermiller and Eric R. Spangenberg, "Exploring the Effects of Country of Origin Labels: An Information Processing Framework," pp. 454–459, Arthur E. Heimbach, Johny K. Johansson, and Douglas L. MacLachan, "Product Familiarity, Information Processing, and Country-of-Origin Cues," pp. 460–467, and Sung-Tai Hong and Julie F. Toner, "Are There Gender Differences in the Use of Country-of-Origin Information in the Evaluation of Products?" pp. 468–472; and C. Min Han, "Country Image: Halo or Summary Construct?" *Journal of Marketing Research,* Vol. 26 (May 1989), pp. 222–229.

20. The rise of postmodern consumer research has raised many new issues and many new possibilities for the field of consumer behavior. The proceedings of the annual conference of the Association for Consumer Research (*Advances in Consumer Research*) and the *Journal of Consumer Research* have had a large number of postmodern articles recently, together with debates. One recent source containing a range of these viewpoints is Elizabeth C. Hirschman (ed.), *Interpretive Consumer Research* (Provo, Utah: Association for Consumer Research, 1989). An excellent overview is also available in John F. Sherry, Jr., "Postmodern Alternatives: The Interpretive Turn in Consumer Research," in Harold Kassarjian and Thomas Robertson (eds.), *Handbook of Consumer Theory and Research* (Englewood Cliffs, N.J.: Prentice Hall, 1990).

For some interesting examples of these approaches, see also Grant McCracken, "Culture and Consumption: A Theoretical Account of the Structure and Movement of the Cultural Meaning of Consumer Goods," *Journal of Consumer Research,* Vol. 13 (June 1986), pp. 71–84; two articles in *Advances in Consumer Research,* Vol. 14 (1987): Russell W. Belk, "The Role of the Odyssey in Consumer Behavior and in Consumer Research," pp. 357–361, and Fuat A. Firat, "Towards a Deeper Understanding of Consumption Experiences: The Underlying Dimensions," pp. 342–346; Russell W. Belk, John F. Sherry, Jr., and Melanie Wallendorf, "A Naturalistic Inquiry into Buyer and Seller Behavior at a Swap Meet," *Journal of Consumer Research,* Vol. 14 (March 1988), pp. 449–470; Susan Spiggle, "Measuring Social Values: A Content Analysis of Sunday Comics and Underground Comix," *Journal of Consumer Research,* Vol. 13 (June 1986), pp. 100–113; Barbara B. Stern, "Medieval Allegory: Roots of Advertising Strategy for the Mass Market," *Journal of Marketing,* Vol. 52 (July 1988), pp. 84–90; two articles in *Advances in Consumer Research,* Vol. 16 (1989), Morris B. Holbrook, "Seven Routes to Facilitating the Semiological Interpretation of Consumption Symbolism and Marketing Imagery in Works of Art: Some Tips for Wildcats," pp. 420–425, and John F. Sherry, Jr., "Observations on Marketing and Consumption: An Anthropological Note," pp. 515–516; Russell W. Belk, Melanie Wallendorf, and John F. Sherry, Jr., "The Sacred and the Profane in Consumer Behavior: Theodicy on the Odyssey," *Journal of Consumer Research,* Vol. 15 (March 1989), pp. 1–38; Craig J. Thompson, William B. Locander, and Howard R. Pollio, "Putting Consumer Experience Back into Consumer Research: The Philosophy and Method of Existential-Phenomenology," *Journal of Consumer Research*, Vol. 16 (September 1989), pp. 133–146; Terrence W. Witkowski, "Colonial Consumers in Revolt: Buyer Values and Behavior During the Nonimportation Movement, 1764–1776," *Journal of Consumer Research*, Vol. 16 (September 1989), pp. 216–226; and Thomas C. O'Guinn and Russell W. Belk, "Heaven on Earth: Consumption at Heritage Village, USA," *Journal of Consumer Research*, Vol. 16 (September 1989), pp. 227–238.

The postmodern approach has also sparked serious debates about the basic nature of consumer research. See, for example, Morris B. Holbrook, "What Is Consumer Research?" *Journal of Consumer Research*, Vol. 14 (June 1987), pp. 128–132; Jerome B. Kernan, "Chasing the Holy Grail," *Journal of Consumer Research*, Vol. 14 (June 1987), pp. 133–135; Bobby J. Calder and Alice M. Tybout, "What Consumer Research Is . . . ," *Journal of Consumer Research*, Vol. 14 (June 1987), pp. 136–140; Joseph A. Cote and Ellen R. Foxman, "A Positivist's Reactions to a Naturalistic Inquiry Experience," *Advances in Consumer Research*, Vol. 14 (1987), pp. 362–364; Laurel A. Hudson and Julie L. Ozanne, "Alternative Ways of Seeking Knowledge in Consumer Research," *Journal of Consumer Research*, Vol. 14 (March 1988), pp. 508–521; Joseph A. Cote and M. Ronald Buckley, "Measurement Error and Theory Testing in Consumer Research: An Illustration of the Importance of Construct Validation," *Journal of Consumer Research*, Vol. 14 (March 1988), pp. 579–582; Harvey Siegel, "Relativism for Consumer Research? (Comments on Anderson)," *Journal of Consumer Research*, Vol. 15 (June 1988), pp. 129–132; Paul F. Anderson, "Relative to What— That Is the Question: A Reply to Siegel," *Journal of Consumer Research*, Vol. 15 (June 1988), pp. 133–137; Morris B. Holbrook and John O'Shaughnessy, "On the Scientific Status of Consumer Research and the Need for an Interpretive Approach to Studying Consumption Behavior," *Journal of Consumer Research*, Vol. 15 (December 1988), pp. 398–402; Paul F. Anderson, "Relativism Revidivus: In Defense of Critical Relativism," *Journal of Consumer Research*, Vol. 15 (December 1988), pp. 403–406; and Shelby D. Hunt, "Naturalistic, Humanistic, and Interpretive Inquiry: Challenges and Ultimate Potential," in Elizabeth C. Hirschman (ed.), *Interpretive Consumer Research* (Provo, Utah: Association for Consumer Research, 1989).

21. This report is based upon discussions in Ernest Dichter, *Handbook of Consumer Motivations* (New York: McGraw-Hill, 1964); "Algonquin Advertising Agency," in Edward C. Bursk and Stephen A. Greyser (eds.), *Advanced Cases in Marketing Management* (Englewood Cliffs, N.J.; Prentice Hall, 1968), pp. 1–18; and Erik Larson," Admen Try to Make Juice-Loving World Swoon for a Prune," *The Wall Street Journal*, February 15, 1983, pp. 1 ff.

22. See, for example, Russell W. Belk, Kenneth D. Bahn, and Robert N. Mayer, "Developmental Recognition of Consumption Symbols," *Journal of Consumer Research*, June 1982, pp. 4–17. Interested readers may wish to pursue the numerous references there for specific findings in specific product categories. See also Michael R. Solomon, "The Role of Products as Social Stimuli: A Symbolic Interactionism Perspective," *Journal of Consumer Research*, December 1983, pp. 319–329, for another useful overview of this area. For a recent discussion and debate over the role of possessions, see Russell W. Belk, "Possessions and the Extended Self," *Journal of Consumer Research*, Vol. 15 (September 1988), pp. 139–168; Joel B. Cohen, "An Over-Extended Self?" *Journal of Consumer Research*, Vol. 15 (March 1989), pp. 125–128; and Russell W. Belk, "Extended Self and Extending Paradigmatic Perspective," *Journal of Consumer Research*, Vol. 15 (March 1989), pp. 129–132.

23. Mason Haire, "Projective Techniques in Marketing Research," *Journal of Marketing*, April 1950, pp. 649–652, and Frederick E. Webster and Frederick von Pechmann, "A Replication of the 'Shopping List' Study," *Journal of Marketing*, Vol. 34 (April 1970), pp. 61–63.

24. See Thorstein Veblen, "The Theory of the Leisure Class (New York: New American Library, Mentor Books, 1980), originally published in 1899.

25. John Brooks, *Showing Off in America* (Boston: Little, Brown, 1981).

26. The interested reader might wish to consult Brooks for a recent critique and Vance Packard, *The Status Seekers* (New York: David McKay, 1959), for an interesting, popularized account of the midcentury situation.

27. This report is based primarily upon information contained in Pierre Martineau, *Motivation in Advertising* (New York: McGraw-Hill, 1971).

28. Christine Donahue, "The World's Most Powerful Brand," *Marketing Week*, May 9, 1988, pp. 32 ff.

29. Among the classic articles are Burleigh B. Gardner and Sidney J. Levy, "The Product and the Brand," *Harvard Business Review*, Vol. 33 (March–April 1955), pp. 33–39; Sidney J. Levy, "Symbols for Sale," *Harvard Business Review*, Vol. 37 (July–August 1959), pp. 117–124; and Harper

W. Boyd, Jr. and Sidney J. Levy, "A New Dimension in Consumer Analysis," *Harvard Business Review,* Vol. 41 (November–December 1963), pp. 129–140. Among more recent articles, see Sidney J. Levy, "Dreams, Fairy Tales, Animals, and Cars," *Psychology & Marketing,* Vol. 2 (Summer 1985), pp. 67–82; Dennis W. Rook, "The Ritual Dimension of Consumer Behavior," *Journal of Consumer Research,* Vol. 13 (December 1985), pp. 251–264; David Glen Mick, "Consumer Research and Semiotics: Exploring the Morphology of Signs, Symbols, and Significance," *Journal of Consumer Research,* Vol. 13 (September 1986), pp. 196–213; Michael R. Solomon and Susan P. Douglas, "Diversity in Product Symbolism: The Case of Female Executive Clothing," *Psychology & Marketing,* Vol. 4 (Fall 1987), pp. 189–212; John F. Sherry, Jr., and Eduardo G. Camargo, "May Your Life Be Marvelous: English Language Labelling and the Semiotics of Japanese Promotion," *Journal of Consumer Research,* Vol. 14 (September 1987), pp. 174–188; Sayeste Daser and Havva J. Meric, "Does Patriotism Have Any Marketing Value—Exploratory Findings for "Crafted with Pride in USA," *Advances in Consumer Research,* Vol. 14 (1987), pp. 536–537; and Robert E. Kleine and Jerome B. Kernan, "Measuring the Meaning of Consumption Objects: An Empirical Investigation," *Advances in Consumer Research,* Vol. 15 (1988), pp. 498–504.

30. Max Weber, "Class, Status, Party," in H. Gerth and C. W. Mills (eds.), *From Max Weber: Essays in Sociology* (New York: Oxford University Press, 1946), Chap. 7. See also Max Weber, *General Economic History,* trans. by F. H. Knight (New York: Greenberg, 1927).

31. Survey conducted by the Carnegie Commission on the Future of Higher Education. These results were reported in John Helmer, *The Daily Simple Mechanics of Society* (New York: Seabury Press, 1974), pp. 66.

32. See, for example, Alan R. Andreasen, *The Disadvantaged Consumer* (New York: Free Press, 1975); David Caplovitz, *The Poor Pay More* (New York: Free Press, 1967); Leonard L. Berry, "The Low-Income Marketing System: An Overview," *Journal of Retailing,* Vol. 48 (Summer 1972), pp. 44–61; George S. Day and William K. Brandt, "Consumer Research and the Evaluation of Public Policy: The Case of Truth in Lending," *Journal of Consumer Research,* Vol. 1 (June 1974), pp. 21–32; Alan R. Andreasen and Gregory D. Upah, "Regulation and the Disadvantaged: The Case of the Creditors' Remedies Rule," *Journal of Marketing,* Vol. 43 (Spring 1979), pp. 75–83; and Frederick D. Sturdivant, "Subculture Theory: Poverty, Minorities, and Marketing," in S. Ward and T. Robertson (eds.), *Consumer Behavior: Theoretical Sources* (Englewood Cliffs, N.J.; Prentice Hall, 1973), pp. 469–520.

33. This distinction was originally made by Ralph Linton, "*The Study of Man* (New York: Appleton-Century-Crofts, 1936), Chap. 8. His terms for the two status types were "ascribed status" and "achieved status."

34. See, for example, J. H. Hutton, *Caste in India: Its Nature, Function, and Origins,* 4th ed. (London: Oxford University Press, 1962); James Silverberg (ed.), *Social Mobility in the Caste System in India* (The Hague: Mouton Press, 1968); and Gerald D. Berreman, *Caste in the Modern World* (Morristown, N.J.: General Learning Press, 1973). The author also wishes to acknowledge the suggestions of his Indian colleagues.

35. This section is based upon Norman Goodman and Gary Marx, *Society Today,* 3rd ed. (New York: CRM/Random House, 1978), pp. 246–251. See also Gerhard Lenski, *Power and Privilege: The Theory of Social Stratification* (New York: McGraw-Hill, 1966); Reinhard Bendix and Seymour M. Lipset (eds.), *Class, Status, and Power* (New York: Free Press, 1966); Thomas B. Bottomore, *Classes in Modern Society* (New York: Vantage, 1966); Robin M. Williams, Jr., *American Society: A Sociological Interpretation,* 3rd ed.; Samuel N. Eisenstadt, *Social Differentiation and Stratification* (Glenview, Ill.: Scott, Foresman, 1971); Lewis A. Coser, *Masters of Sociological Thought,* 2nd ed. (New York: Harcourt Brace Jovanovich, 1977); and Metta Spencer, *Foundations of Modern Sociology* (Englewood Cliffs, N.J.: Prentice Hall, 1976).

36. Karl Marx and Fredrich Engels, *The Communist Manifesto* (1848) (Chicago: Regnery, 1960).

37. See Kingsley Davis and Wilbert E. Moore, "Some Principles of Stratification," *American Sociological Review,* Vol. 10 (April 1945), pp. 242–249.

38. Richard P. Coleman, "The Continuing Significance of Social Class to Marketing," *Journal of Consumer Research,* Vol. 10 (December 1983), pp. 265–280. See also James E. Fisher, "Social Class and Consumer Behavior: The Relevance of Class and Status," *Advances in Consumer Research,* Vol. 14 (1987), pp. 492–496; Kjell Gronhaug and Paul S. Trapp, "Perceived Social Class Appeals of Branded Goods," *The Journal of Consumer Marketing,* Vol. 4 (Fall 1988), pp. 25–30; and Kjell Gronhaug and Paul S. Trapp, "Perceived Social Class Appeals of Branded Goods and Services," *The Journal of Consumer Marketing,* Vol. 6 (Winter 1989), pp. 13–18.

39. Richard P. Coleman, "The Significance of Social Stratification in Selling," in M. L. Bell (ed.), *Marketing: A Maturing Discipline* (Chicago: American Marketing Association, 1960), pp. 171–

184, and Richard P. Coleman, "The Continuing Significance of Social Class to Marketing," p. 274. For further applications, see W. H. Peters, "Relative Occupational Class Income: A Significant Variable in the Marketing of Automobiles," *Journal of Marketing* (April 1970), pp. 74–82; and R. E. Klippel and J. F. Monoky, "A Potential Segmentation Variable for Marketers: Relative Occupational Class Income," *Journal of the Academy of Marketing Science* (Spring 1974), pp. 351–356.

40. For discussions of the forecasting potentials of income versus social class measures, see, for example, Stuart U. Rich and Subhash C. Jain, "Social Class and Life Cycle as Predictors of Shopping Behavior," *Journal of Marketing Research,* Vol. 5 (February 1968), pp. 41–49; James H. Myers, Roger R. Stanton, and Arne F. Haug, "Correlates of Buying Behavior: Social Class vs. Income," *Journal of Marketing,* Vol. 35 (October 1971); Frederick E. May, "The Effect of Social Class on Brand Loyalty," *California Management Review,* Vol. 14 (Fall 1971), pp. 81–87; John W. Slocum and H. Lee Matthews, "Social Class and Income as Indicator of Consumer Credit Behavior," *Journal of Marketing,* Vol. 34 (April 1970), pp. 69–73; William W. Curtis, "Social Class or Income?" *Journal of Marketing,* Vol. 36 (January 1972), pp. 67–68; H. Lee Matthews and John W. Slocum, Jr., "A Rejoinder to 'Social Class or Income?' " *Journal of Marketing,* Vol. 36 (January 1972), pp. 69–70; James H. Myers and John F. Mount, "More on Social Class vs. Income as Correlates of Buying Behavior," *Journal of Marketing,* Vol. 37 (April 1973), pp. 71–73; and Robert D. Hisrich and Michael P. Peters, "Selecting the Superior Segmentation Correlate," *Journal of Marketing,* Vol. 38 (July 1974), pp. 60–63.

41. The description of the social classes is based on a number of sources. See Richard Coleman, "The Continuing Significance of Social Class to Marketing"; and Burleigh Gardner, "Social Status and Consumer Behavior," in Lincoln H. Clark (ed.), *The Life Cycle and Consumer Behavior* (New York: New York University Press, 1955); Pierre Martineau, "Social Class and Spending Behavior," *Journal of Marketing,* Vol. 23 (October 1958), pp. 121–130; Joseph N. Fry and Frederick H. Siller, "A Comparison of Housewife Decision Making in Two Social Classes," *Journal of Marketing Research,* Vol. 7 (August 1970), pp. 333–337; Sidney J. Levy, "Social Class and Consumer Behavior," in John A. Howard and Lyman E. Ostlund (eds.), *Buyer Behavior* (New York: Alfred A. Knopf, 1973); Gordon R. Foxall, "Social Factors in Consumer Choice: Replication and Extension," *Journal of Consumer Research,* Vol. 2 (June 1975), pp. 60–64; Walter A. Henry, "Cultural Values Do Correlate with Consumer Behavior," *Journal of Marketing Research,* Vol. 13 (May 1976), pp. 121–127; J. Michael Munson and W. Austin Spivey, "Product and Brand-User Stereotypes Among Social Classes: Implications for Advertising Strategy," *Journal of Advertising Research,* Vol. 21, no. 4 (August 1981), pp. 37–45. See also Terence A. Shimp and J. Thomas Yokum, "Extensions of the Basic Social Class Model Employed in Consumer Behavior," in K. Monroe (ed.), *Advances in Consumer Research,* Vol. 8 (Ann Arbor, Mich.: Association for Consumer Research, 1981), pp. 702–707, and Luis V. Dominguez and Albert L. Page, "Stratification in Consumer Behavior Research: A Re-Examination," *Journal of the Academy of Marketing Science,* Vol. 9 (Summer 1981), pp. 250–273.

42. These examples are given in Michael Korda, *Power! How to Get It, How to Use It* (New York: Random House, 1975), Chap. 7.

43. Kim B. Rotzoll, "The Effect of Social Stratification on Market Behavior," *Journal of Advertising Research,* Vol. 7 (March 1967), pp. 22–27.

Chapter 14   Social and Situational Influences on Consumer Behavior

1. For more specific definitions, see Orville G. Brim, "Adult Socialization," in J. Clausen (ed.), *Socialization and Society* (Boston: Little, Brown, 1968), or Edward Zigler and Irwin L. Child, "Socialization," in Gardner Lindzey and Elliott Aronson (eds.), the *Handbook of Social Psychology: The Individual in a Social Context,* Vol. 3 (Reading, Mass.: Addison-Wesley, 1969), pp. 450–589.

2. George Herbert Mead, *Mind, Self, and Society* (Chicago: University of Chicago Press, 1934).

3. Ruth Benedict, "Continuities and Discontinuities in Cultural Conditioning," *Psychiatry,* Vol. 1 (1938), pp. 161–167.

4. Orville G. Brim, "Socialization Through the Life Cycle," in O. Brim and S. Wheeler (eds.), *Socialization After Childhood* (New York: John Wiley, 1966). For consumer applications, see, for example, William R. Darden, Donna K. Darden, Roy Howell, and Shirley J. Miller, "Consumer Socialization Factors in a Patronage Model of Consumer Behavior," *Advances in Consumer Research,* Vol. 8 (1981), pp. 655–661; Karen F. A. Fox and Trudy Kehret-Ward, "Theories of Value and Understanding of Price: A Development Perspective," *Advances in Consumer Research,* Vol. 12 (1985), pp. 79–83; George P. Moschis and Roy L. Moore, "Anticipatory Consumer Sociali-

zation," *Journal of the Academy of Marketing Science,* Vol. 12 (Fall 1984), pp. 109–123; and Scott Ward, Donna M. Klees, and Thomas S. Robertson, "Consumer Socialization in Different Settings: An International Perspective," *Advances in Consumer Research,* Vol. 14 (1987), pp. 468–472. See also our discussion of the life cycle in Chapter 15.

5. Erving Goffman, *Asylums* (Chicago, Aldine, 1962).

6. You many enjoy reading, for example, Gail Sheehy, *Passages: Predictable Crises of Adult Life* (New York: E. P. Dutton, 1976). See also Lawrence R. Lepisto, "A Life Span Perspective of Consumer Behavior," *Advances in Consumer Research,* Vol. 12 (1985), pp. 47–52.

7. Talcott Parsons, *The Social System* (Glencoe, Ill.: Free Press, 1951). See also David A. Goslin, *The School in Contemporary Societies* (Glenview, Ill.: Scott, Foresman, 1965).

8. See, for example, George Homans, *Social Behavior: Its Elementary Forms* (New York: Harcourt Brace and World, 1961); P. Blau, *Exchange and Power in Social Life* (New York: John Wiley, 1964); and R. Nisbet, C. Caputo, C. Legany, and J. Maracek, "Behavior as Seen by the Actor and as Seen by the Observer," *Journal of Personality and Social Psychology,* Vol. 27 (1973), pp. 154–164.

9. Theodore R. Sarbin and Vernon L. Allen, "Role Theory," in G. Lindzey and E. Aronson (eds.), *The Handbook of Social Psychology* (Reading, Mass.: Addison-Wesley, 1968). For applications to consumer behavior and marketing, see David T. Wilson and Lorne Bozinoff, "Role Theory and Buying-Selling Negotiations: A Critical Overview," *Marketing in the 80's* (Chicago: American Marketing Association, 1980), pp. 118–121; Michael R. Solomon, Carol Suprenant, John A. Czepiel, and Evelyn A. Antman, "A Role Theory Perspective on Dyadic Interactions: The Service Encounter," *Journal of Marketing,* Vol. 49 (Winter 1985), pp. 99–111; Elaine Sherman and Ruth B. Smith, "Promising Interactions and Possible Behavioral Effects," *Advances in Consumer Research,* Vol. 14 (1987), pp. 251–254. Robert Prus, "Generic Social Processes: Implications of a Processual Theory of Action for Research on Marketplace Exchange," *Advances in Consumer Research,* Vol. 14 (1987), pp. 66–70; Ronald Paul Hill, "The Impact of Interpersonal Anxiety on Consumer Information Processing," *Psychology & Marketing,* Vol. 4 (Summer 1987), pp. 93–106; and Ronald E. Michaels, Ralph L. Day, and Erich A. Joachimsthaler, "Role Stress Among Industrial Buyers: An Integrative Model," *Journal of Marketing,* Vol. 51 (April 1987), pp. 28–45.

10. Erving Goffman, *The Presentation of Self in Everyday Life* (Garden City, N.Y.: Doubleday/Anchor Books, 1959). For related discussions and overviews within consumer behavior, see Francesco M. Nicosia and Robert N. Mayer, "Toward a Sociology of Consumption," *Journal of Consumer Research,* Vol. 3 (September 1976), pp. 65–75; Dennis W. Rook and Sidney J. Levy, "Psychosocial Themes in Consumer Grooming Rituals," *Advances in Consumer Research,* Vol. 10 (1983), pp. 329–333; Michael R. Solomon, "The Role of Products as Social Stimuli: A Symbolic Interactionism Perspective," *Journal of Consumer Research,* Vol. 10 (December 1983), pp. 319–329; and Robert Prus and Wendy Frisby, "Marketplace Dynamics: The P's of People and Process," *Advances in Consumer Research,* Vol. 14 (1987), pp. 61–65.

11. See, for example, E. Jones and C. Wortman, *Ingratiation: An Attributional Approach.* (Morristown, N.J.: General Learning Press, 1973). For discussions of related issues within consumer behavior, see, for example, M. Joseph Sirgy, "Self-Concept in Consumer Behavior: A Critical Review," *Journal of Consumer Research,* Vol. 9 (December 1982), pp. 287–300; Robert E. Burnkrant and Thomas J. Page, Jr., "On the Management of Self Images in Social Situations: The Role of Public Self Consciousness," *Advances in Consumer Research,* Vol. 9 (1982), pp. 452–455; Ellen E. Moore, William O. Bearden, and Jesse E. Teel, "Use of Labeling and Assertions of Dependency in Appeals for Consumer Support," *Journal of Consumer Research,* Vol. 12 (June 1985), pp. 90–96; and Barbara B. Stern, "Sex-Role Self-Concept Measures and Marketing: A Research Note," *Psychology & Marketing,* Vol. 5 (Spring 1988), pp. 85 ff.

12. Dorwin Cartwright and Alvin Zander, *Group Dynamics* (New York: Harper & Row, 1968).

13. John French and Bertram Raven, "The Bases of Social Power," in D. Cartwright (ed.), *Studies in Social Power* (Ann Arbor, Mich.: Institute for Social Research, 1959), pp. 150–167. Within consumer behavior, applications are provided in Wesley J. Johnston and Thomas V. Bonona, "The Effect of Power Differences on the Outcome of Consumer Bargaining Situations," *Advances in Consumer Research,* Vol. 11 (1984), pp. 170–174, and Gary L. Sullivan and P. J. O'Connor, "Social Power-Based Print Advertising: Theoretical and Practical Considerations," *Psychology & Marketing,* Vol. 2 (Fall 1985), p. 217 ff.

14. Herbert C. Kelman, "Compliance, Identification, and Internalization: Three Processes of Attitude Change," *Journal of Conflict Resolution,* Vol. 2 (1958), pp. 51–60. See also Cathy Goodwin, "A Social Influence Theory of Consumer Cooperation," *Advances in Consumer Research,* Vol. 14 (1987), pp. 378–381.

15. Herbert Hyman, "The Psychology of Status," *Archives of Psychology,* Vol. 38, no. 269 (1942). See also Scott Dawson and Jill Cavell, "Status Recognition in the 1980's: Invidious Distinction Revisited," *Advances in Consumer Research,* Vol. 14 (1987), pp. 487–491.

16. Jack W. Brehm, "Psychological Reactance: Theory and Applications," *Advances in Consumer Research,* Vol. 16 (1989), pp. 72–75; Greg Lessne and M. Venkatesan, "Reactance Theory in Consumer Research: The Past, Present, and Future," *Advances in Consumer Research,* Vol. 16 (1989), pp. 76–78; and Greg Lessne and Elaine M. Notarantonio, "The Effect of Limits in Retail Advertisements: A Reactance Theory Perspective," *Psychology & Marketing,* Vol. 5 (Spring 1988), pp. 33–44. See also Michael B. Mazis, Robert B. Settle, and Dennis C. Leslie, "Elimination of Phosphate Detergents and Psychological Reactance," *Journal of Marketing Research* (November 1973), pp. 390–395; and Mona A. Clee and Robert A. Wicklund, "Consumer Behavior and Psychological Reactance," *Journal of Consumer Research* (March 1980), pp. 389–405.

17. William H. Whyte, Jr., "The Web of Word of Mouth," *Fortune,* November 1954, pp. 140–143. For further concepts and findings of this general topic, see, for example, C. Whan Park and V. Parker Lessig, "Students and Housewives: Differences in Susceptibility to Reference Group Influence," *Journal of Consumer Research,* Vol. 4 (September 1977), pp. 102–110; Scott B. MacKenzie and Judy L. Zaichkowsky, "An Analysis of Alcohol Advertising Using French and Raven's Theory of Social Influence," *Advances in Consumer Research,* Vol. 8 (1981), pp. 708–712; Marsha L. Richins, "Word of Mouth Communication as Negative Information," *Advances in Consumer Research,* Vol. (1981), pp. 697–702; Robert J. Thomas, "Correlates of Interpersonal Purchase Influence in Organization," *Journal of Consumer Research,* Vol. 9 (September 1982), pp. 171–182; Dorothy Leonard-Barton, "Experts as Negative Opinion Leaders in the Diffusion of a Technological Innovation," *Journal of Consumer Research,* Vol. 11 (March 1985), pp. 914–926; David Brinberg and Linda Plimpton, "Self-Monitoring and Product Conspicuousness on Reference Group Influence," *Advances in Consumer Research,* Vol. 13 (1986); Linda L. Price and Lawrence F. Feick, "The Role of Interpersonal Sources in External Search: An Informational Perspective," *Advances in Consumer Research,* Vol. 11 (1984), pp. 250–255; and Peter H. Reingen, Brian L. Foster, Jacqueline J. Brown, and Stephen B. Seidman, "Brand Congruence in Interpersonal Relations: A Social Network Analysis," *Journal of Consumer Research,* Vol. 11 (December 1984), pp. 711–783.

18. Peter H. Reingen and Jerome B. Kernan, "Analysis of Referral Networks in Marketing: Methods and Illustration," *Journal of Marketing Research,* Vol. 23 (November 1986), pp. 370–378. For further insights, see also Peter H. Reingen, "A Word-of-Mouth Network," *Advances in Consumer Research,* Vol. 14 (1987), pp. 213–217; Jacqueline Johnson Brown and Peter H. Reingen, "Social Ties and World-of-Mouth Referral Behavior," *Journal of Consumer Research,* Vol. 14 (December 1987), pp. 350–362; Dennis L. Rosen and Richard W. Olshavsky, "A Protocol Analysis of Brand Choice Strategies Involving Recommendations," *Journal of Consumer Research,* Vol. 14 (December 1987), pp. 440–444; Marsha L. Richins and Teri Root-Shaffer, "The Role of Involvement and Opinion Leadership in Consumer Word-of-Mouth: An Implicit Model Made Explicit," *Advances in Consumer Research,* Vol. 15 (1988), pp. 32–36; Carl S. Bozman, Kathy L. Petit, and James Miner, "The Referral Method: An Inexpensive Means of Increasing Fund-Raising Efficiency by a Non-Profit Organization," *AMA Educators Proceedings* (1989), p. 50; and William R. Wilson and Robert A. Peterson, "Some Limits on the Potency of Word-of-Mouth Information," *Advances in Consumer Research,* Vol. 16 (1989), pp. 23–29.

19. Fred D. Reynolds and William R. Darden, "Mutually Adaptive Effects of Interpersonal Communication," *Journal of Marketing Research,* Vol. 8 (November 1971), pp. 449–454. See also Lawrence F. Feick, Linda L. Price, and Robin A. Higie, "People Who Use People: The Other Side of Opinion Leadership," *Advances in Consumer Research,* Vol. 13 (1986).

20. Marsha L. Richins and Teri Root-Shaffer, "The Role of Involvement and Opinion Leadership in Consumer Word-of-Mouth . . . ," in M. Houston (ed.), *Advances in Consumer Research,* Vol. 15, (Provo, Utah: Association for Consumer Research, 1988), pp. 32–36.

21. This discussion is based upon the work of John Sherry, "Some Implications of Consumer Oral Tradition for Reactive Marketing," Working Paper, Center for Consumer Research, University of Florida, Gainesville, 1983. See also Jeffrey F. Durgee, "Interpreting Consumer Mythology: A Literary Criticism Approach to Odyssey Informant Stories," *Advances in Consumer Research,* Vol. 15 (1988), pp. 531–536.

22. The first five quotes appeared in Sherry, "Some Implications of Consumer Oral Tradition for Reactive Marketing"; the sixth quote is adapted from a report in a "Dear Abby" column, April 2, 1989; and the marketing examples are drawn from Alix M. Freedman, "Corona Beer Sales Are Down Sharply . . . ," *The Wall Street Journal,* August 17, 1988, p. 23, "Eatery Ad Hits Gossip,"

Advertising Age, August 3, 1987, p. 6, and Sid Astbury, "Pork Rumors Vex Indonesia," *Advertising Age,* February 6, 1989, p. 36.

23. For alternative strategies that McDonald's might have used, see Alice Tybout, Bobby Calder, and Brian Sternthal, "Using Information Processing Theory to Design Effective Marketing Strategies," *Journal of Marketing Research* (February 1981), pp. 73–79.

24. Joseph R. Mancuso, "Why Not Create Opinion Leaders for New Product Introductions?" *Journal of Marketing* (July 1969), pp. 20–25.

25. Laurie Freeman and Julie Erickson, "Doctored Strategy: Food Marketers Push Products Through Physicians," *Advertising Age,* March 28, 1988, p. 12.

26. James Watson, "Brown Bag's Giveaway Works," *Advertising Age,* July 11, 1988, p. 39.

27. If you are interested in reading more about focus group research, see, for example, Edward F. Fern, "Focus Groups: A Review of Some Contradictory Evidence, Implications, and Suggestions for Future Research," *Advances in Consumer Research,* Vol. 10 (1983), pp. 121–126. See also Sarah Stiansen, "How Focus Groups Can Go Astray," *Adweek,* December 5, 1988, pp. f4–6; D. N. Bellenger, K. L. Bernhardt, and Jac I. Goldstucker, *Qualitative Research in Marketing* (Chicago: American Marketing Association, 1976); B. J. Calder, "Focus Groups and the Nature of Qualitative Marketing Research," *Journal of Marketing Research* (August 1977), pp. 360 ff.; and Edward F. McQuarrie and Shelby H. McIntyre, "Conceptual Underpinnings for the Use of Group Interviews in Consumer Research," *Advances in Consumer Research,* Vol. 15 (1988), pp. 580–586.

28. M. Deutsch and H. Gerard, "A Study of Normative and Informational Social Influences Upon Individual Judgment," *Journal of Abnormal and Social Psychology,* Vol. 51 (1955), pp. 624–636. For applications in consumer behavior, see also Joel B. Cohen and Ellen Golden, "Informational Social Influence and Product Evaluation," *Journal of Marketing Research,* Vol. 8 (February 1972), pp. 54–59; Robert E. Burnkrant and Alain Cousineau, "Informational and Normative Social Influence in Buyer Behavior," *Journal of Consumer Research,* Vol. 2 (December 1975), pp. 206–215; Dennis L. Rosen and Richard W. Olshavsky, "The Dual Role of Informational Social Influence: Implications for Marketing Management," *Journal of Business Research,* Vol. 15 (1987), pp. 123–144.

29. This report uses our terms and group names and is based upon Stephen A. LaTour and Ajay K. Manrai, "Applying Attitude Theory to Donor Marketing Strategies: Interactive Effects of Informational and Normative Influence," Working Paper, Kellogg Graduate School, Northwestern University, Evanston, Ill., 1985. For further discussions, see Stephen A. LaTour and Ajay K. Manrai, "Interactive Impact of Informational and Normative Influence on Donations," *Journal of Marketing Research,* Vol. 26 (August 1989), pp. 327–335; Robert E. Pitts, Ann L. Canty, and John Tsalikis, "Exploring the Impact of Personal Values on Socially Oriented Communications," *Psychology & Marketing,* Vol. 2 (Winter 1985), pp. 267–278; Michael Klassen, Mark A. Barnett, Vera McMinimy, and Laurel Schwarz, "The Role of Self- and Other-Oriented Motivation in the Organ Donation Decision," *Advances in Consumer Research,* Vol. 14 (1987), pp. 335–337; David J. Moore and Richard Reardon, "Source Magnification: The Role of Multiple Sources in the Processing of Advertising Appeals," *Journal of Marketing Research,* Vol. 24 (November 1987), pp. 412–417; and William O. Bearden, Richard G Netemeyer, and Jesse E. Teel, "Measurement of Consumer Susceptibility to Interpersonal Influence," *Journal of Consumer Research,* Vol. 15 (March 1989), pp. 473–481.

30. Ellen Graham, "Tupperware Parties Create a New Breed of Super Saleswoman," *The Wall Street Journal,* May 21, 1971, p. 1; and John Birmingham, "The New American Office Party . . . ," *Marketing Week,* June 13, 1988, pp. 28–30.

31. See, for example, Michael L. Ray and William L. Wilkie, "Fear: The Potential of an Appeal Neglected by Marketing," *Journal of Marketing* (January 1970), pp. 54–62; Brian Sternthal and C. Samuel Craig, "Fear Appeals: Revisited and Revised," *Journal of Consumer Research,* Vol. 1 (December 1974), pp. 23–34; and John J. Burnett and Richard L. Oliver, "Fear Effects in the Field: A Segmentation Approach," *Journal of Marketing Research,* Vol. 16 (May 1979), pp. 181–190.

32. Bill Abrams, "Ring Around the Collar Ads Irritate Many, Yet Get Results," *The Wall Street Journal,* November 4, 1982, p. 33; "Lever Assigns Wisk to JWT," *Marketing Week,* August 14, 1989, p. 5; and Laurie Freeman, "Wisk Rings in New Ad Generation," *Advertising Age,* September 1989, pp. 1 ff.

33. Judann Dagnoli, "Weight Watchers Gaining . . . ," *Advertising Age,* July 13, 1987, p. 4. See also Robert A. Swerdlow, "Star Studded Advertising: Is It Worth the Effort?" *Journal of the Academy of Marketing Science,* Vol. 12 (Summer 1984), pp. 89–102; Ruby Roy Dholakia, "Source Credibility Effects: A Test of Behavioral Persistence," *Advances in Consumer Research,* Vol. 14 (1987), pp.

426–430; and two articles in *Advances in Consumer Research*, Vol. 15 (1988), Paul Surgi Speck, David W. Schumann, and Craig Thompson, "Celebrity Endorsements-Scripts, Schema and Roles: Theoretical Framework and Preliminary Tests," pp. 69–76, and Tina Kiesler, "The Flip Side of the Persuasion Equation: Does a Product Influence a Spokesperson's Public Image?" pp. 62–68.

34. John Birmingham, "How Bausch & Lomb Keeps Ray-Bay in the Limelight," *Marketing Week*, July 4, 1988, pp. 27–28.

35. Francis S. Bourne, "Group Influences in Marketing and Public Relations," in R. Likert and S. P. Hayes (eds.), *Some Applications of Behavioral Research* (Basel, Switzerland: UNESCO, 1957).

36. William O. Bearden and Michael J. Etzel, "Reference Group Influence on Product and Brand Purchase Decisions," *Journal of Consumer Research*, Vol. 9 (September 1982), pp. 183–194.

37. It is generally agreed that a situation comprises a point in time and space is a more narrow concept than either a "behavior setting" or an "environment." Roger G. Barker, *Ecological Psychology: Concepts and Methods for Studying the Environment of Human Behavior* (Stanford, Calif.: Stanford University Press, 1968). There is, however, some disagreement about whether to define a situation in *objective* terms (e.g., physical or social surroundings that affect consumer behavior) *subjective* terms (i.e., focusing on a consumer's internal interpretations and responses). For our purposes, we need not resolve this question, though it does remain an issue in this field. For a presentation of the "objective" position, see Russell W. Belk, "Situational Variables and Consumer Behavior," *Journal of Consumer Research*, Vol. 2 (December 1975), pp. 157–164, and comments by Roger Barker and Allan Wicker on pp. 165–167 of the same *JCR* issue and by James. A. Russell and Albert Mehrabian, "Environmental Variables in Consumer Research," *Journal of Consumer Research*, Vol. 3 (June 1976), pp. 62–63, with a reply by Belk, "Situational Mediation and Consumer Behavior: A Reply to Russell and Mehrabian," *Journal of Consumer Research*, Vol. 3 (December 1976), pp. 175–177. For a presentation of the "subjective" position, see Richard J. Lutz and Pradeep Kakkar, "The Psychological Situation as a Determinant of Consumer Behavior," *Advances in Consumer Research*, Vol. 2 (1975), pp. 439–454.

38. George Katona, "Psychology and Consumer Economics," *Journal of Consumer Research*, Vol. 1 (June 1974), pp. 1–8; "Appliance Shipments Set Records," *USA Today*, March 14, 1984, p. 1; see also Richard T. Curtin and Christopher J. Gordon, "Coping with Economic Adversity," *Advances in Consumer Research*, Vol. 10 (1983), pp. 175–181; Robert E. Pitts, John F. Willenborg, and Daniel L. Sherrell, "Consumer Adaptation to Gasoline Price Increases," *Journal of Consumer Research*, Vol. 8 (December 1981), pp. 322–330; Peter Doyle and John Saunders, "Economic Expectations and Strategies," *AMA Educators Proceedings* (1985), pp. 183–186; Stephen W. McDaniel, C. P. Rao, and Ralph W. Jackson, "Inflation-Induced Adaptive Behavior," *Psychology & Marketing*, Vol. 3 (Summer 1986), pp. 113–122; William L. James, James P. Keeler, and Mohamed Abdel-Ghany, "Demographic Variations in Consumption of Windfall Income," *AMA Educators Proceedings* (1986), p. 22; Joseph A. Bellizzi and Robert E. Hite, "Convenience Consumption and Role Overload," *Journal of the Academy of Marketing Science*, Vol. 14 (Winter 1986), pp. 1–9; two articles in *Advances in Consumer Research*, Vol. 16 (1989), Sigmund Gronmo, "Concepts of Time: Some Implications for Consumer Research," pp. 339–345, and Jonathan E. Schroeder, "What Time Means to Others: Expectations of Behavior Based on Time Use Information," pp. 354–358; and Marcia Flicker, "Methods of Handling Highly Seasonal Data in Model-Building," *AMA Educators Proceedings* (1989), pp. 165–169.

39. William L. Wilkie and Peter R. Dickson, "Patterns of Consumer Information Search and Shopping Behavior for Household Durables," Working Paper Series, Marketing Science Institute, Cambridge, Mass., 1985.

40. There are a number of interesting points and findings on usage situation's impact on consumer behavior. For further reading of an overview of the issues, you may wish to pursue Pradeep Kakkar and Richard J. Lutz, "Situational Influence on Consumer Behavior: A Review," in H. H. Kassarjian and T. S. Robertson (eds.), *Perspectives in Consumer Behavior*, 3rd ed. (Glenview, Ill.: Scott Foresman, 1981), pp. 204–214; and P. Greg Bonner, "Considerations for Situational Research," *Advances in Consumer Research*, Vol. 12 (1985), pp. 368–373. For further concepts and findings, see William O. Bearden and Arch G. Woodside, "Interactions of Consumption Situations and Brand Attitudes," *Journal of Applied Psychology*, Vol. 61 (1976), pp. 764–769, Richard J. Lutz, "On Getting Situated: The Role of Situation Factors in Consumer Research," *Advances in Consumer Research*, Vol. 7 (1980), Kenneth E. Miller and James L. Ginter, "An Investigation of Situational Variation on Brand Choice Behavior and Attitude," *Journal of Marketing Research* (February 1979), pp. 111–123; Charles H. Ptacek and James Shanteau, "Situation determinants of Consumer Decision Making," Working Paper, Department of Psychology, Kansas State University, March 1979; Kent L. Granzin and Kathryn H. Schjelderup, "Situation as an Influence

of Anticipated Satisfaction," *Advances in Consumer Research,* Vol. 9 (1982), pp. 234–238; Jacob Hornik, "Subjective vs. Objective Time Measures: A Note on the Perception of Time in Consumer Behavior," *Journal of Consumer Research,* Vol. 11 (June 1984), pp. 615–619; Meryl P. Gardner and Marion Vandersteel, "The Consumer's Mood: An Important Situational Variable," *Advances in Consumer Research,* Vol. 11 (1984), pp. 525–529; Joseph A. Cote, Jr., and John K. Wong, "The Effect of Time and Situational Variables on Intention-Behavior Consistency," *Advances in Consumer Research,* Vol. 12 (1985), pp. 374–375; Raymond L. Horton, "Consumer Decision Making: A Situational Analysis," *AMA Winter Educators Proceedings* (1987), pp. 61–65; and U. N. Umesh and Joseph A. Cote, "Influence of Situational Variables on Brand-Choice Models," *Journal of Business Research,* Vol. 16 (March 1988), pp. 91–100.

41. John Birmingham, "Dial's Hearty Office Meal," *Marketing Week,* June 27, 1988, pp. 20–23.

42. Peter R. Dickson, "Person-Situation: Segmentation's Missing Link," *Journal of Marketing,* Vol. 46 (Fall 1982), pp. 56–64; for further discussion of this issue, see Thomas P. Hustad, Charles S. Mayer, and Thomas W. Whipple, "Consideration of Context Difference in Product Evaluation and Market Segmentation," *Journal of the Academy of Marketing Science* (Winter 1975), pp. 34–47; Roger J. Calantone and Alan G. Sawyer, "The Stability of Benefit Segments," *Journal of Marketing Research,* Vol. 15 (August 1978), pp. 395–404.

43. Sharon K. Banks, "Gift-Giving: A Review and an Interactive Paradigm," *Advances in Consumer Research,* Vol. 6 (1979), pp. 319–324, and Jeffrey H. Birnbaum, "Christmas Sales Get Off to a Slow Start, But Stores Hope for the Usual Late Surge," *The Wall Street Journal,* November 20, 1981, p. 56.

44. Russell Belk, "Gift-Giving Behavior," in J. Sheth (ed.), *Research in Marketing,* Vol. 2 (Greenwich, Conn.: JAI Press, 1979), pp. 95–126.

45. An interesting overview of this area is presented in John F. Sherry "Gift Giving in Anthropological Perspective," *Journal of Consumer Research* (September 1983), pp. 157–168. See also the following papers in *Advances in Consumer Research,* Vol. 6 (1979), Sharon K. Banks, "Gift-Giving: A Review and an Interactive Paradigm," pp. 319–324; Roger Heeler, June Francis, Chike Okechuku, and Stanley Reid, "Gift Versus Personal Use Brand Selection," pp. 325–328; Richard J. Lutz, "Consumer Gift-Giving: Opening the Black Box," pp. 329–331; and Douglas J. Tigert, "Three Papers on Gift-Giving: A Comment," pp. 332–334. For further insights and discussions, see *Advances in Consumer Research,* Vol. 10 (1983): Alain J. P. Jolibert and Carlos Fernandez-Moreno, "A Comparison of French and Mexican Gift Giving Practices," pp. 191–196, and Stephen P. DeVere, Clifford D. Scott, and William L. Shulby, "Consumer Perceptions of Gift-Giving Occasions: Attribute Saliency and Structure," pp. 185–190; Alice James and William L. James, "Gift Giving in Rural Ireland: An Analysis," *AMA Educators Proceedings* (1985), pp. 26–29; David M. Andrus, Edward Silver, and Dallas E. Johnson, "Status Brand Management and Gift Purchase: A Discriminant Analysis," *Journal of Consumer Marketing,* Vol. 3 (Winter 1986), pp. 5–14; and Christian Dussart, "Pre-Christmas Toy Guides: A Cross-Sectional Research Study," *Advances in Consumer Research,* Vol. 16 (1989), pp. 374–383.

46. Debra Scammon, Roy T. Shaw, and Gary Bamossy, "Is a Gift Always a Gift? An Investigation of Flower Purchasing Behavior Across Situations," *Advances in Consumer Research,* Vol. 9 (1981), pp. 531–536.

Chapter 15   Household Influences on Consumer Behavior

1. Based upon data in "Households Up," *American Demographics,* August 1988, p. 14 (calculations by author).

2. Kathryn A. London and Barbara F. Wilson, "Divorce," *American Demographics,* October 1988, pp. 23–26, and "Marital Status and Living Arrangements: March 1987" U.S. Census Bureau, 1988.

3. Glenn Collins, "Family Attitudes Show Marked Changes," *The New York Times* New Service, June 17, 1987; Nanci Hellmich, "Marriage Outranks a Career," *USA Today,* October 5, 1988, p. D-1; "Birth Expectations" report, U.S. Census Bureau, January 1988.

4. Scott Ward, "Consumer Socialization," *Journal of Consumer Research,* Vol. 1 (September 1974), p. 2.

5. Scott Ward, Daniel Wackman, and Ellen Wartella, *How Children Learn to Buy* (Beverly Hills, Calif.: Sage, 1977), pp. 175–197.

6. Ward, "Consumer Socialization"; see also George P. Moschis, Roy L. Moore, and Ruth B. Smith, "The Impact of Family Communication on Adolescent Consumer Socialization," *Advances in Consumer Research,* Vol. 11 (1984), pp. 314–319; and the following papers in *Advances in Con-*

sumer Research, Vol. 13 (1986): Sanford Grossbart, Lawrence Crosby, and Laurie Smith, "Parental Diffusion Roles and Effects of Nutrition Education on Parents and Children," and George P. Moschis, Andjali E. Prahasto, and Linda G. Mitchell, "Family Communication Influences on the Development of Consumer Behavior: Some Additional Findings"; see also Kenneth D. Bahn, "How and When Do Brand Perceptions and Preferences First Form? A Cognitive Developmental Investigation," *Journal of Consumer Research,* Vol. 13 (December 1986), pp. 382–393; Karin M. Ekstrom, Patriya S. Tansuhaj, and Ellen R. Foxman, "Children's Influence in Family Decisions and Consumer Socialization: A Reciprocal View," *Advances in Consumer Research,* Vol. 14 (1987), pp. 283–287; two articles in *AMA Educators Proceedings* (1987): Alvin C. Burns and Peter L. Gillett, "Antecedents and Outcomes of the Family Purchase Socialization Process for a Child's Toys and Games," pp. 15–20, and Sanford Grossbart, Les Carlson, and Ann Walsh, "Mothers' Communication Orientations and Related Consumer Socialization Tendencies," p. 21; two articles in *AMA Educators' Proceedings* (1988): Sanford Grossbart, Les Carlson, and Ann Walsh, "Consumer Socialization Motives for Shopping with Children," and Bonnie B. Reece, Sevgin Eroglu and Nora J. Rifon, "Parents Teaching Children to Shop: How, What, and Who?", pp. 274–278; and Les Carlson and Sanford Grossbart, "Parental Style and Consumer Socialization of Children," *Journal of Consumer Research,* Vol. 15 (June 1988), pp. 77–94.

7. Reuben Hill, *Family Development in Three Generations* (Cambridge, Mass.: Schenkman, 1970).

8. The 40 percent figure is based on those who answered the question: 18 percent of the sample did not know which policy their parents held. See Larry G. Woodson, Terry L. Childers, and Paul R. Winn, "Intergenerational Influences in the Purchase of Auto Insurance," in W. Locander (ed.), *Marketing Look Outward: 1976 Business Proceedings* (Chicago: American Marketing Association, 1976), pp. 43–49.

9. "Brand Formations of the Average Product," study conducted for *Seventeen* magazine by Yankelovich, Skelly, and White, March 1980.

10. Susan E. Heckler, Terry L. Childers, and Ramesh Arunachalam, "Intergenerational Influence in Adult Buying Behaviors: An Examination of Moderating Factors," *Advances in Consumer Research,* Vol. 16 (1989), pp. 276–284; Ruby Roy Dholakia, "Intergeneration Differences in Consumer Behavior: Some Evidence from a Developing Country," *Journal of Business Research,* Vol. 12, no. 1 (1984), pp. 19–34; two articles in *Advances in Consumer Research,* Vol. 15 (1988); Elizabeth S. Moore-Shay and Richard J. Lutz, "Intergenerational Influences in the Formation of Consumer Attitudes and Beliefs About the Marketplace: Mothers and Daughters," pp. 461–467, and George P. Mochis, "Methodological Issues in Studying Intergenerational Influences on Consumer Behavior," pp. 569–573; and Patricia Sorce, Philip R. Tyler, and Lynette Loomis, "Intergenerational Influence on Consumer Decision Making," *Advances in Consumer Research,* Vol. 16 (1989), pp. 271–275.

11. See *Rolling Stone,* April 7, and May 5, 1988, Issues for description of results from this survey entitled "Portrait of a Generation."

12. Much of the framework for this section is based upon the seminal article by Harry L. Davis, "Decision Making Within the Household," in R. Ferber (ed.), *Selected Aspects of Consumer Behavior* (Washington, D.C.: U.S. Government Printing Office, National Science Foundation, 1977), pp. 73–97. For perspectives on the broader issues of family financial management allocation of purchases, see Dennis L. Rosen and Donald H. Granbois, "Determinants of Role Structure in Family Financial Management," *Journal of Consumer Research,* Vol. 10 (September 1983), pp. 253–258; Donald H. Granbois, Dennis L. Rosen, and Franklin Acito, "A Developmental Study of Family Financial Management Practices," *Advances in Consumer Research,* Vol. 13 (1986); Marilyn Kourilsky and Trudy Murray, "The Use of Economic Reasoning to Increase Satisfaction with Family Decision Making," *Journal of Consumer Research,* Vol. 8 (September 1981), pp. 183–188; and Sharon Y. Nickols and Karen D. Fox, "Buying Time and Saving Time: Strategies for Managing Household Production," *Journal of Consumer Research,* Vol. 10 (September 1983), pp. 197–208. For discussions of research problems and potentials, see Sunil Gupta, Michael R. Hagerty, and John G. Myers, "New Directions in Family Decision Making Research," *Advances in Consumer Research,* Vol. 10 (1983), pp. 445–450.

13. Bernard Berelson and Gary Steiner, *Human Behavior: An Inventory of Scientific Findings* (New York: Harcourt, Brace & World, 1964).

14. P. Sloan, "Matchabelli Name Readied for Men's Fragrance Line," *Advertising Age,* April 21, 1980, p. 69.

15. Fred D. Reynolds and William D. Wells, *Consumer Behavior* (New York: McGraw-Hill, 1977), pp. 282–283.

16. See Also Mary Lou Roberts and Lawrence H. Wortzel, "Role Transferral in the Household: A

Conceptual Model and Partial Test," *Advances in Consumer Research,* Vol. 9 (1982), pp. 261–266; Charles M. Schaninger and W. Christian Buss, "The Relationship of Sex-Role Norms to Household Task Allocation," *Psychology & Marketing,* Vol. 2 (Summer 1985), pp. 93–104; William J. Qualls, "Household Decision Behavior: The Impacts of Husbands' and Wives' Sex Role Orientation," *Journal of Consumer Research,* Vol. 14 (September 1987), pp. 264–279; Ellen Foxman and Alvin C. Burns, "Role Load in the Household," *Advances in Consumer Research,* Vol. 14 (1987), pp. 458–462; Joan Meyers-Levy, "The Influence of Sex Roles on Judgment," *Journal of Consumer Research,* Vol. 14 (March 1988), pp. 522–530; John J. Burnett, "The Roberts-Wortzel Hierarchical Model: An Extension Through Methodological and Variable Delineation Considerations," *AMA Educators Proceedings* (1989), p. 265; and three papers in *Advances in Consumer Research,* Vol. 16, (1989): W. Thomas Anderson, Jr., Linda L. Golden, William A. Weeks, and U. M. Umesh, "The Five Faces of Eve: Women's Timestyle Typologies," pp. 346–353, Irene Raj Foster and Richard W. Olshavsky, "An Exploratory Study of Family Decision Making Using a New Taxonomy of Family Role Structure," pp. 665–670, and Chankon Kim and Hanjoon Lee, "Sex Role Attitudes of Spouses and Task Sharing Behavior," pp. 671–679.

17. Harry L. Davis and Benny P. Rigaux, "Perception of Marital Roles in Decision Processes," *Journal of Consumer Research,* Vol 1 (June 1974), pp. 51–62. See also E. H. Bonfield, "Perception of Marital Roles in Decision Processes: Replication and Extension," *Advances in Consumer Research,* Vol. 5 (1978), pp. 300–307; A. Burns and S. DeVere, "Four Situations and Their Perceived Effects on Husband and Wife Purchase Decision Making," *Advances in Consumer Research,* Vol. 8 (1981), pp. 736–741; Pierre Filiatrault and J. R. Brent Ritchie, "Joint Purchasing Decisions: A Comparison of Influence Structure in Family and Couple Decision-Making Units," *Journal of Consumer Research,* Vol. 7 (September 1980), pp. 131–140; Charles B. Weinberg and Russell S. Winer, "Working Wives and Major Family Expenditures: Replication and Extension," *Journal of Consumer Research,* Vol. 10 (September 1983), pp. 259–263; Giovana Imperiale, Thomas C. O'Guinn, and Elizabeth A. MacAdams, "Family Decision Making Role Perceptions Among Mexican-American and Anglo Wives: A Cross-Cultural Comparison," *Advances in Consumer Research,* Vol. 12 (1985), pp. 71–74; three papers in *Advances in Consumer Research,* Vol. 14 (1987): Joel Rudd, "The Household as a Consuming Unit," pp. 451–452, Deb Heisley and Paula S. Holmes, "A Review of Family Consumption Research: The Need for a More Anthropological Perspective," pp. 453–457; and Michael C. Mayo and William J. Qualls, "Household Durable Goods Acquisition Behavior: A Longitudinal Study," pp. 463–467; John L. Haverty, "A Model of Household Behavior," *AMA Winter Educators Proceedings* (1987), pp. 284–289; and W. Keith Bryant, "Durables and Wives' Employment Yet Again," *Journal of Consumer Research,* Vol. 15 (June 1988), pp. 37–47.

18. Arch Woodside and William Motes, "Husband and Wife Perceptions of Marital Roles in Consumer Decision Processes for Six Products," *Educators Conference Proceedings* (1979).

19. This discussion is based upon the framework provided in Harry L. Davis, "Decision Making Within the Household." For other useful frameworks and findings, see also Jagdish N. Sheth, "A Theory of Family Buying Decisions," in J. N. Sheth (ed.), *Models of Buyer Behavior* (New York: Harper & Row, 1974), pp. 17–33; Alvin C. Burns and Donald H. Granbois, "Factors Moderating the Resolution of Preference Conflict in Family Automobile Purchasing," *Journal of Marketing Research,* Vol. 14 (February 1977), pp. 77–86; David Brinberg and Nancy Schwenk, "Husband-Wife Decision Making: An Exploratory Study of the Interaction Process," *Advances in Consumer Research,* Vol. 12 (1985), pp. 487–491; Alvin C. Burns and Jo Anne Hopper, "An Analysis of the Presence, Stability, and Antecedents of Husband and Wife Purchase Decision Making Influence Assessment: Agreement and Disagreement," *Advances in Consumer Research,* Vol. 13 (1986), and Kim P. Corfman and Donald R. Lehmann, "Models of Cooperative Group Decision-Making and Relative Influence," *Journal of Consumer Research,* Vol. 14 (June 1987), pp. 1–13.

For related discussions and findings, see Elizabeth S. Moore-Shay and William L. Wilkie, "Recent Developments in Research on Family Decisions," *Advances in Consumer Research,* Vol. 15 (1988), pp. 454–460; Jack J. Kasulis and Marie Adele Hughes, "Husband-Wife Influence in Selecting a Family Professional," *Journal of the Academy of Marketing Science,* Vol. 12 (Spring 1984), pp. 115–127; Robert M. Cosenza, "Family Decision Making: Decision Dominance Structure Analysis—An Extension," *Journal of the Academy of Marketing Science,* Vol. 13 (Winter 1985), pp. 91–103; Marilyn Lavin, "Husband-Wife Decision Making: A Theory-Based, Process Model," *AMA Educators Proceedings* (1985), pp. 21–25; Hazel F. Ezell and Giselle D. Russell, "Single and Multiple Person Household Shoppers: A Focus on Grocery Store Selection," *Journal of the Academy of Marketing Science,* Vol. 13 (Winter 1985), pp. 171–178; Thomas C. O'Guinn,

Ronald J. Faber and Giovanna Imperiale, "Subcultural Influences on Family Decision Making," *Psychology & Marketing,* Vol. 3 (Winter 1986), pp. 305 ff.; Lisa Penaloza Alaniz and Mary C. Gilly, "The Hispanic Family—Consumer Research Issues," *Psychology & Marketing,* Vol. 3 (Winter 1986), pp. 291–304; Kjell Gronhaug, Ingeborg Astrid Kleppe, and Willy Haukedal, "Observation of a Strategic Household Purchase Decision," *Psychology & Marketing,* Vol. 4 (Fall 1987), pp. 239–254; Sidney C. Bennett and Elnora W. Stuart, "In Search of Association Between Personal Values and Household Decision Processes: An Exploratory Analysis," *AMA Educators Proceedings* (1989), pp. 259–264; Michael B. Menasco and David J. Curry, "Utility and Choice: An Empirical Study of Wife/Husband Decision Making," *Journal of Consumer Research,* Vol. 15 (March 1989), pp. 87–97; and Ellen R. Foxman, Patriya S. Tansuhaj, and Karin M. Ekstrom, "Family Members' Perceptions of Adolescents' Influence in Family Decision Making," *Journal of Consumer Research,* Vol. 15 (March 1989), pp. 482–491.

20. Rosann L. Spiro, "Persuasion in Family Decisionmaking," *Journal of Consumer Research,* Vol. 10 (March 1983), pp. 393–402. See also Michael A. Belch, George E. Belch, and Donald Sciglimpaglia, "Conflict in Family Decision Making: An Exploratory Investigation," *Advances in Consumer Research,* Vol. 7 (1980), pp. 475–479; Daniel Seymour and Greg Lessne, "Spousal Conflict Arousal: Scale Development," *Journal of Consumer Research,* Vol. 11 (December 1984), pp. 810–821; Daniel T. Seymour, "Forced Compliance in Family Decision-Making," *Psychology & Marketing,* Vol. 3 (Fall 1986), pp. 223 ff.; and William J. Qualls, "Toward Understanding the Dynamics of Household Decision Conflict Behavior," *Advances in Consumer Research,* Vol. 15 (1988), pp. 442–448.

21. Margaret C. Nelson, "The Resolution of Conflict in Joint Purchase Decisions . . . ," *Advances in Consumer Research,* Vol. 15 (1988), pp. 436–441.

22. C. Whan Park, "Joint Decisions in Home Purchasing: A Muddling-Through Process," *Journal of Consumer Research,* Vol. 9 (September 1982), pp. 151–162. See also C. Whan Park, "A Conflict Resolution Choice Model," *Journal of Consumer Research,* Vol. 5 (September 1978), pp. 124–135.

23. Harry L. Davis, Stephen J. Hoch, and E. K. Easton Ragsdale, "An Anchoring and Adjustment Model of Spousal Predictions," *Journal of Consumer Research,* Vol. 13 (June 1986), pp. 25–37, and Kim P. Corfman, "Meaures of Relative Influence in Couples: A Typology and Predictions for Accuracy," *Advances in Consumer Research,* Vol. 16 (1989.

24. Lincoln H. Clark (ed.), *The Life Cycle and Consumer Behavior* (New York: New York University Press, 1955).

25. The following discussion is based upon the FLC framework presented in William D. Wells and George Gubar, "Life Cycle Concept in Marketing Research," *Journal of Marketing Research,* Vol. 3 (November 1966), pp. 355–363. See also Ronald W. Stampfl, "The Consumer Life Cycle," *Journal of Consumer Affairs,* Vol. 12 (Winter 1978), pp. 209–219.

26. Sarah Stiansen, "A Marriage Made in Heaven," *Advertising Age,* October 25, 1982, p. M-56.

27. Ben J. Wattenberg, "The Forming-Families: The Spark in the Tinder," *Combined Proceedings of the American Marketing Association* (Chicago: American Marketing Association, 1975), p. 52.

28. "America Gives Birth to a 'New Baby Boom," Find/SVP News Release, May 12, 1988.

29. Patrick E. Murphy and William A. Staples, "A Modernized Family Life Cycle," *Journal of Consumer Research,* Vol. 6 (June 1979), pp. 12–22.

30. Mary C. Gilly and Ben J. Enis, "Recycling the Family Life Cycle: A Proposal for Redefinition," *Advances in Consumer Research,* Vol. 9 (1982), pp. 271–276. See also Frederick W. Derrick and Alane K. Lehfeld, "The Family Life Cycle: An Alternative Approach," *Journal of Consumer Research,* Vol. 7 (September 1980), pp. 214–217; and Karen S. Reilly, Sevgin A. Eroglu, Karen A. Machleit, and Glenn S. Omura, "Consumer Decision Making Across Family Life Cycle Stages," *Advances in Consumer Research,* Vol. 11 (1984), pp. 400–404; Alan R. Andreasen "Life Status Changes and Changes in Consumer Preferences and Satisfaction," *Journal of Consumer Research,* Vol. 11 (December 1984), pp. 784–794; and Lawrence R. Lepisto, "A Life-Span Perspective of Consumer Behavior," *Advances in Consumer Research,* Vol. 12 (1985), pp. 47–52.

31. Janet Wagner and Sherman Hanna, "The Effectiveness of Family Life Cycle Variables in Consumer Expenditure Research," *Journal of Consumer Research,* Vol. 10 (December 1983), pp. 281–291.

32. See, for example, Donald H. Granbois, "The Role of Communication in the Family Decision-Making Process" in S. Greyser (ed.), *Proceedings* (Chicago: American Marketing Association, 1963), pp. 44–57; and Harry L. Davis, "Decision Making Within the Household," *Journal of Consumer Research,* March 1976, pp. 241–260.

33. Scott Ward and Daniel Wackman, "Children's Purchase Influence Attempts and Parental Yielding," *Journal of Marketing Research,* Vol. 9 (August 1972), pp. 316–319. For related results, see

also William K. Darley and Jeen Su Lim, "Family Decision Making in Leisure-Time Activities: An Exploratory Investigation of the Impact of Locus of Control and Parental Type on Perceived Child Influence," *Advances in Consumer Research*, Vol. 13 (1986); Kenneth Bahn, "Do Mothers and Children Share Cereal and Beverage Preference and Evaluative Criteria?" *Advances in Consumer Research*, Vol. 14 (1987), pp. 279–282; and Joseph R. Murphy, "Parent-Adult-Child Segments in Marketing," *Journal of Advertising Research*, Vol. 27 (April/May 1987), pp. 38–42.

Chapter 16   Salespersons' Influences on Consumer Behavior

1. William L. Wilkie and Peter R. Dickson, "Consumer Information Search and Shopping Behavior," *Marketing Science Institute* paper series, Cambridge, Mass., 1985.
2. Jon G. Udell, *Successful Marketing Strategies in American Industry* (Madison, Wisc.: Mimir, 1972).
3. Franklin B. Evans, "Selling as a Dyadic Relationship," *American Behavioral Scientist*, May 1963, pp. 76–79.
4. Robert F. Bales, "A Set of Categories for the Analysis of Small Group Interaction," *American Sociological Review*, April 1950.
5. Ronald P. Willett and Allan L. Pennington, "Customer and Salesman: The Anatomy of Choice and Influence in a Retail Setting," in Raymond M. Haas (ed.), *Science, Technology, & Marketing*. (Chicago: American Marketing Association, 1966), pp. 598–616.
6. Richard W. Olshavsky, "Customer-Salesman Interaction in Appliance Retailing," *Journal of Marketing Research*, Vol. 10 (May 1973), pp. 208–212.
7. James L. Taylor and Arch G. Woodside, "An Examination of the Structure of Buying-Selling Interactions Among Insurance Agents and Prospective Customers," *Advances in Consumer Research*, 7 (1980), pp. 387–392. See also Arch G. Woodside and James L. Taylor, "Identity Negotiations in Buyer-Seller Interactions," *Advances in Consumer Research*, Vol. 12 (1985), pp. 443–449.
8. This section is based upon the model described in Barton A. Weitz, "The Relationship Between Salesperson Performance and Understanding of Customer Decision Making," *Journal of Marketing Research*, Vol. 15 (November 1978), pp. 501–516. See also Barton A. Weitz, "Effectiveness in Sales Interactions: A Contingency Framework," *Journal of Marketing* (Winter 1981), pp. 85–103; Robert Saxe and Barton Weitz, "The SOCO Scale: A Measure of the Customer Orientation of Salespeople," *Journal of Marketing Research*, Vol. 19 (August 1982), pp. 343–351; Ronald E. Michaels and Ralph L. Day, "Measuring Customer Orientation of Salespeople: A Replication with Industrial Buyers," *Journal of Marketing Research*, Vol. 22 (November 1985), pp. 443 ff.; Harish Sujan, "Communicating Effectively to Consumers Through Salespeople: A Look at Competent Salespeople: An Overview of This Special Session," *Advances in Consumer Research*, Vol. 15 (1988), pp. 372–374; and Alain D'Astous and Helene Kettler, "Perceptions of an Ongoing Sales Interaction by Expert and Novice Salespersons," *Proceedings of the Annual Conference of the Administrative Sciences Association of Canada*, St. Mary's University, 1988. For an interesting recent book on the nature of selling as seen by an anthropologist, see Robert C. Prus, *Making Sales* (Newbury Park, CA: Sage, 1989).
9. Arch G. Woodside and William J. Davenport, "The Effect of Salesman Similarity and Expertise on Consumer Purchasing Behavior," *Journal of Marketing Research*, Vol. 11 (May 1974), pp. 198–202. See also Gilbert A. Churchill, Jr., Robert H. Collins, and William A. Strang, "Should Retail Salespersons Be Similar to Their Customers?" *Journal of Retailing*, Fall 1975, pp. 29–42; Paul Busch and David T. Wilson, "An Experimental Analysis of a Salesman's Expert and Referent Bases of Social Power in the Buyer-Seller Dyad," *Journal of Marketing Research*, Vol. 13 (February 1976), pp. 3–11; Marjorie Caballero and Alan J. Resnik, "The Attraction Paradigm in Dyadic Exchange," *Psychology & Marketing*, Vol. 3 (Spring 1986), pp. 17–34; Peter J. DePaulo and Bella M. DePaulo, "Nonverbal Communication of Affect and Attempted Deception Among Retail Salespersons and Automobile Customers," *AMA Educators Proceedings* (1986), p. 50; Jon W. Hawes, C. P. Rao, and Kenneth Mast, "Consumer Perceptions of the Importance of Salesperson Attributes," *AMA Educators Proceedings* (1987), pp. 113–118; Carol F. Suprenant and Michael R. Solomon, "Predictability and Personalization in the Service Encounter," *Journal of Marketing*, Vol. 51 (April 1987), pp. 86–96; and Cathy Goodwin and Rose Johnson, "Consumer Preference for Formality and Familiarity in the Service Encounter: Two Pilot Studies," *AMA Educators Proceedings* 1988, pp. 101–105.
10. Peter H. Reingen and Arch G. Woodside (eds.), *Buyer-Seller Interactions: Empirical Research and Normative Issues* (Chicago: American Marketing Association, 1981), contains a number of interesting papers that are relevant to this topic in consumer behavior. See also Marvin A. Jolson, "The Underestimated Potential of the Canned Sales Presentation," *Journal of Marketing*, Vol. 39

(January 1975), pp. 67–68; Richard F. Yalch, "Closing Sales: Compliance-Gaining Strategies for Personal Selling," in R. Bagozzi (ed.), *Sales Management: New Developments from Behavioral and Decision Model Research* (Cambridge, Mass.: Marketing Science Institute, 1979); and Gilbert A. Churchill, Jr., Neil M. Ford, Steven W. Hartley, and Orville C. Walker, "The Determinants of Salesperson Performance; A Meta-Analysis," *Journal of Marketing Research*, Vol. 22 (May 1985), pp. 103–118; Kaylene C. Williams and Rosann L. Spiro, "Communication Style in the Salesperson-Customer Dyad," *Journal of Marketing Research*, Vol. 22 (November 1985), pp. 434 ff.; Terri L. Rittenburg and Robert A. Mittelstaedt, "Validation of the Serial Ordering of a Sales Encounter Script," *AMA Educators Proceedings* (1985), pp. 16–20; Kenneth Anglin, Jeffrey Stoltman, and James Gentry, "Cognitive Scripts and Personal Selling: An Exploratory Investigation," *AMA Educators Proceedings* (1988), pp. 214–219; Robin Peterson, "Sales Representative Perceptions on Various Widely Used Closing Tactics," *AMA Educators Proceedings* (1988), pp. 220–225; Harish Sujan, Mita Sujan, and James R. Bettman, "Knowledge Structure Differences Between More Effective and Less Effective Salespeople," *Journal of Marketing Research*, Vol. 24 (February 1988), pp. 81–86; Jacqueta J. McClung, Stephen J. Grove, and Marie Adele Hughes, "The Importance of Customer Approach Skills on the Customer's Evaluation of Retail Sales Personnel," *AMA Educators Proceedings* (1989), p. 92; Karl B. Boedecker and Fred W. Morgan, "Managing the Salesperson–Prospect/Customer Interaction: Potential Legal Consequences of Salespersons' Statements," *AMA Educators Proceedings* (1989); p. 307; Richard A. Feinberg and Peter Smith, "Misperceptions of Time in the Sales Transaction," *Advances in Consumer Research*, Vol. 16 (1989), pp. 56–58; Abraham D. Horowitz, "Modeling New Car Customer-Salesperson Interaction for a Knowledge-Based System," *Advances in Consumer Research*, Vol. 16 (1989), pp. 392–398; and Siew Meng Leong, Paul S. Busch, and Deborah Roedder John, "Knowledge Bases and Sales-person Effectiveness: A Script-Theoretic Analysis," *Journal of Marketing Research*, Vol. 26 (May 1989), pp. 164–178.

　　For an interesting book that examines the psychology of persuasion, see Robert B. Cialdini, *Influence* (New York: Quill, 1984).

11. E. Scott Maynes, *Decision-Making for Consumers* (New York: Macmillan, 1976).

12. Walter J. Primeaux, "The Effect of Consumer Knowledge and Bargaining Strength on Final Selling Price," *Journal of Business*, October 1970. See also James M. Hunt and Jerome B. Kernan, "The Effects of Expectancy Disconfirmation and Argument Strength on Message Processing Level: An Application to Personal Selling," and Wesley J. Johnston and Thomas V. Bonoma, "The Effect of Power Differences on the Outcome of Consumer Bargaining Situations," *Advances in Consumer Research*, Vol. 11 (1984), pp. 450–454 and 170–174; Mita Sujan, James R. Bettman, and Harish Sujan, "Effects of Consumer Expectations on Information Processing in Selling Encounters," *Journal of Marketing Research*, Vol. 23 (November 1986), pp. 346–353; Randall L. Rose and Peter R. Dickson, "He Says No, But Does He Really Mean It? Bargaining Behavior, Cue Consistency and Attribution," *Advances in Consumer Research*, Vol. 14 (1987), pp. 382–386; and Gloria P. Thomas and Gary F. Soldow, "A Rules-Based Approach to Competitive Interaction," *Journal of Marketing*, Vol. 52 (April 1988), pp. 63–74.

13. G. David Hughes, Joseph B. Juhasz, and Bruno Contini, "The Influence of Personality on the Bargaining Process," *Journal of Business*, October 1973, pp. 593–603. See also Marsha L. Richins, "An Analysis of Consumer Interaction Styles in the Marketplace," *Journal of Consumer Research*, Vol. 10 (June 1983), pp. 73–82; George Coan, Jr., "Rapport: Definition and Dimensions," *Advances in Consumer Research*, Vol. 11 (1984), pp. 333–336; Gary F. Soldow and Gloria P. Thomas "Relational Communication: Form vs. Content in the Sales Interaction," *Journal of Marketing*, (Winter 1984), pp. 84–93; and Paul H. Schurr and Julie L. Ozanne, "Influences on Exchange Processes: Buyers' Preconceptions of a Seller's Trustiworthiness and Bargaining Toughness," *Journal of Consumer Research*, Vol. 11 (March 1985), pp. 939–953.

14. Alexandra Peers, "Commissions on Financial Products Are Often High—and Confusing," *The Wall Street Journal*, January 21, 1988, p. 33.

15. Warren G. Magnuson and Jean Carper, "Caveat Emptor," in D. A. Aaker and G. S. Day, *Consumerism: Search for the Consumer Interest*, 4th ed. (New York: Free Press, 1982), pp. 267–278. See also Joseph A. Bellizzi and Ronald W. Hasty, "Student Perceptions of Questionable Personal Selling Practices," *Journal of the Academy of Marketing Science*, Vol. 12 (Spring 1984), pp. 218 ff.; Alan J. Resnik and Marjorie J. Caballero, "Exploring the Unthinkable: Do Marketers Manipulate?" *AMA Educators Proceedings* (1984), pp. 332–336; Alan J. Dubinsky and Michael Levy, "Ethics in Retailing: Perceptions of Retail Salespeople," *Journal of the Academy of Marketing*

Science, Vol. 13 (Winter 1985), pp. 1–16; and Joseph A. Bellizzi and Robert E. Hite, "Supervising Unethical Salesforce Behavior," *Journal of Marketing,* Vol. 53 (April 1989), pp. 36–47.

16. Magnuson and Carper, "Caveat Emptor."
17. *In the matter of Encyclopaedia Britannica, Inc., et al.* (Docket 8908, 87 F.T.C. 453).
18. Diane Henry, "FTC Tells Sears to Change Practice in Appliance Sales," *The New York Times,* October 22, 1976, p. A-12.
19. See, for example, *In the matter cf William D. Campbell et al. t/a Rhode Island Carpets* (84 F.T.C. 567). For an interesting discussion of the related technique of "low balling," see William Motes, Reginald Brown, Hazel Ezell, and Gail Hudson, "The Influence of Low-Balling on Buyers' Compliance: Revisited," *Psychology & Marketing* (Summer 1986), pp. 79–86.
20. An excellent article in this regard is Cynthia J. Frey and Thomas C. Kinnear, "Legal Constraints and Marketing Research: Review and Call to Action," *Journal of Marketing Research,* Vol. 16 (August 1979), pp. 295–302. For broader issues on the responsibilities of researchers, see Alice M. Tybout and Gerald Zaltman, "Ethics in Marketing Research: Their Practical Relevance," *Journal of Marketing Research,* Vol. 11 (November 1974), pp. 357–368; Robert L. Day, "A Comment on Ethics in Marketing Research," *Journal of Marketing Research,* Vol. 12 (May 1975), pp. 232–233; and Alice M. Tybout and Gerald Zaltman, "A Reply to Comments on Ethics in Marketing Research," *Journal of Marketing Research,* Vol. 12 (May 1975), pp. 234–237.

Chapter 17　Advertising's Influences on Consumer Behavior

1. Fred Danzig, "The Big Idea," *Advertising Age,* November 9, 1988, p. 16.
2. "Oops! Marketers Blunder Their Way Through the 'Herb Decade,' " *Advertising Age,* February 13, 1989, p. 3, and James Cox, "New Ads Aim to Whop McDonald's," *USA Today,* February 17, 1988, p. B-1.
3. This framework is an extension of that provided in Russell H. Colley, *Defining Advertising Goals for Measured Advertising Results* (New York: Association of National Advertisers, 1961), pp. 61–68. For related discussions, see also Richard Vaughn, "How Advertising Works: A Planning Model," *Journal of Advertising Research,* Vol. 20 (October 1980) pp. 27–33; Richard Vaughn, "How Advertising Works: A Planning Model Revisited," *Journal of Advertising Research,* Vol. 15 (February–March 1986), pp. 57–63; Rita Denny, "Pragmatic Dimensions of Advertising," *Advances in Consumer Research,* Vol. 15 (1988), pp. 260–261; and Gerald Zaltman and Christine Moorman, "The Management and Use of Advertising Research," *Journal of Advertising Research,* Vol. 18 (December 1988–January 1989), pp. 11–18.
4. Ronald Alsop, "In TV Viewers' Favorite Ads, Offbeat Characters Were the Stars," *The Wall Street Journal,* March 3, 1988, p. 17.
5. Jagdish Sheth, "The Measurement of Advertising Effectiveness: Some Theoretical Considerations," *Journal of Advertising,* Vol. 3 (1974), pp. 6–11.
6. "Comparative Ads Paying Off for Burger King," *Marketing News,* April 27, 1984, p. 18.
7. Ibid.
8. Dennis Kneale, "Zapping of TV Ads Appears Pervasive," *The Wall Street Journal,* April 25, 1988, p. 21. See also Cathy J. Cobb, "Television Clutter and Advertising Effectiveness," *AMA Educators Proceedings* (1985), pp. 41–47, and William Kilbourne and Steven Hartley, "Medium and Climate Effects on the Evaluation of Image Ads: An Exploratory Study," *AMA Educators Proceedings* (1988), pp. 201–204.
9. Dennis Cauchon, "Bank Tells All—By Mistake," *USA Today,* February 18, 1988, p. B-1.
10. "What's Seven Days When You're Sick," *The Wall Street Journal,* June 5, 1987, p. 31, and John Deighton and Robert M. Schindler, "Can Advertising Influence Experience," *Psychology & Marketing.* Vol. 5, no. 2 (Summer 1988), pp. 103–115.
11. William Power, "At Least They Didn't Add a Logo . . ." *The Wall Street Journal,* June 20, 1988, p. 15.
12. Ronald Alsop, "Ads That Make Fun of Ads Are In . . . ," *The Wall Street Journal,* February 22, 1988, p. 21. As we would expect, considerable consumer research has been devoted to issues concerning the perception process for advertising. For some interesting findings and insights, see, for example, Danny L. Moore, Douglas Hausknecht, and Kanchana Thamodaran, "Time Compression, Response Opportunity, and Persuasion," *Journal of Consumer Research,* Vol. 13 (June 1986), pp. 85–99; Raymond R. Burke and Thomas K. Srull, "Competitive Interference and Consumer Memory for Advertising," *Journal of Consumer Research,* Vol. 15 (June 1988), pp. 55–

68; Herbert E. Krugman, "Point of View: Limits to Attention to Advertising," *Journal of Advertising Research*, Vol. 28 (October–November 1988), pp. 47–50; and David W. Schumann and Esther Thorson, "The Influence of Viewing Context on Commercial Effectiveness: A Selection—Processing Model," Working Paper 238, University of Tennessee, 1989.

13. William J. McGuire, "An Information Processing Model of Advertising Effectiveness," in H. Davis and A. Silk (eds.), *Behavioral and Management Sciences in Marketing* (New York: Ronald Press/John Wiley, 1978), p. 161. See also John A. Howard, Robert P. Shay, and Christopher A. Green, "Measuring the Effect of Marketing Information on Buying Intentions," *The Journal of Consumer Marketing*, Vol. 5 (Summer 1988), pp. 5–14.

14. The Starch study was reported in sworn testimony in a Federal Trade Commission advertising case against Firestone Tires. The study found that, of persons who had been watching during the time that a commercial had been broadcast two hours before the interview, *only 32 percent* remembered having seen the average ad. When asked to identify the brand, only half of this group—or *only 16 percent* of the entire consumer sample—was able to identify the sponsoring brand correctly. One-fourth of this group believed that they knew the sponsor, then gave the wrong brand name! The other one-fourth remembered the contents, but didn't venture a guess as to which brand sponsored it. Commentators pointed out that this meant that the average advertiser was spending only one-sixth of his or her budget to communicate effectively even the most basic information about the brand, and was spending half of this amount to advance the cause of competing brands! [Testimony delivered in the *Firestone Tire and Rubber Company* case (81 F.T.C. 398)]. More recent research using a slightly different "day after recall" identification method by Sami/Burke Research shows similar results (the numbers are not directly comparable due to different methods than Starch used: Burke scores show average recall in 1988 to be 21 percent). See Jeffrey A. Trachtenberg, "Viewer Fatigue?" *Forbes*, December 26, 1988, pp. 120–122. For further reading about advertising research and these types of issues, an extensive literature is available. See, for example, Stephen S. Bell, "Evaluating the Effects of Consumer Advertising on Market Position over Time—How to Tell Whether Advertising Ever Works," Working Paper, *Marketing Science Institute*, July 1988; Kevin Celuch, "A Conceptual Model for Examining the Effects of Advertising Communications," *AMA Educators Proceedings*, (1986), pp. 81–85; Raymond R. Burke and Wayne S. DeSarbo, "Computer-Assisted Print Ad Evaluation," *Advances in Consumer Research*, Vol. 14 (1987), pp. 93–95; Peter R. Dickson and Paul L. Sauer, "Copy Testing, Thought Elicitation and Attitude Theory: Two's Company, Three's a Crowd?" *Advances in Consumer Research*, Vol. 14 (1987), pp. 177–181; Susan E. Heckler, "Bridging the Gap: The Challenge of Integrating Consumer Behavior Research with the Practice of Advertising," *Advances in Consumer Research*, Vol. 15 (1988), pp. 265–268; Laura Yale and Mary C. Gilly, "Trends in Advertising Research: A Look at the Content of Marketing-Oriented Journals from 1976 to 1985," *Journal of Advertising*, Vol. 17 (November 1988), pp. 12–22; Dave Kruegel, "Television Advertising Effectiveness and Research Innovation," *The Journal of Consumer Marketing*, Vol. 5 (Summer 1988), pp. 43–52; Surendra N. Singh, Michael L. Rothschild, and Gilbert A. Churchill, Jr., "Recognition Versus Recall as Measures of Television Commercial Forgetting," *Journal of Marketing Research*, Vol. 24 (February 1988), pp. 72–80; Adam Finn, "Print Ad Recognition Readership Scores: An Information Processing Perspective," *Journal of Marketing Research*, Vol. 24 (May 1988), pp. 168–177; Michael L. Rothschild, Yong J. Hyun, Byron Reeves, Esther Thorson, and Robert Goldstein, "Hemispherically Lateralized EEG as a Response to Television Commercials," *Journal of Consumer Research*, Vol. 15 (September 1988), pp. 185–198; David Walker and Michael F. von Gonten," Explaining Related Recall Outcomes: New Answers from a Better Model," *Journal of Advertising Research*, Vol. 29 (June–July 1989), pp. 11–21; Charles E. Young and Michael Robinson, "Video Rhythms and Recall," *Journal of Advertising Research*, Vol. 29 (June–July 1989), pp. 22–25; Seymour Sudman and Norbert Schwartz, "Contributions of Cognitive Psychology to Advertising Research," *Journal of Advertising Research*, Vol. 29 (June–July 1989), pp. 43–53; David W. Stewart, "Measures, Methods, and Models in Advertising Research," *Journal of Advertising Research*, Vol. 29 (June–July 1989), pp. 54–60; Daniel Seymour, "Soft Data-Hard Data: The Painful Art of Fence-Sitting," *The Journal of Consumer Marketing*, Vol. 6 (Spring 1989), pp. 25–32; Lauranne Buchanan and Amiya Basu, "The Impact of Advertising Copy Testing: Is the Advertiser Getting More than He Bargained For?" *Advances in Consumer Research*, Vol. 16 (1989), pp. 479–484; George M. Zinkhan and Scot Burton, "Refining a Multidimensional Profile for Television Commercials: An Application of Target Analysis," *Advances in Consumer Research*, Vol. 16 (1989), pp. 711–718; and David W. Stewart, "Maintaining the Delicate Balance: Industry and Academic Approaches to Advertising Research," *Advances in Consumer Research*, Vol. 16 (1989), pp. 595–597.

15. Testimony delivered in the *Firestone Tire and Rubber Company* case (81 F.T.C. 398).

16. Michael L. Ray, *Advertising and Communication Management* (Englewood Cliffs, N.J.; Prentice Hall, 1982), pp. 182–188. The original conceptualization of advertising's impact in low-involvement situations was developed by Herbert E. Krugman, "The Impact of Television Advertising: Learning Without Involvement," *Public Opinion Quarterly*, Vol. 29 (1965), pp. 349–356. For more recent discussions, see also Rajeev Batra and Michael L. Ray, "Affective Responses Mediating Acceptance of Advertising," *Journal of Consumer Research*, Vol. 13 (September 1986), pp. 234–249; Herbert E. Krugman, "Points of View: Limits of Attention to Advertising," *Journal of Advertising Research*, Vol. 28 (October–November 1988), pp. 47–49; and George M. Zinkhan and Claes Fornell, "A Testing of the Learning Hierarchy in High- and Low-Involvement Situations," *Advances in Consumer Research*, Vol. 16 (1989), pp. 152–159.

17. Adapted from Stephen S. Bell, "Evaluating the Effects of Consumer Advertising on Market Position Over Time . . . ," Marketing Science Institute Report 88-107, July 1988, pp. 18–19.

18. Adapted from ibid., pp. 12–13. For further reading on this interesting topic, see Stephen H. Hoch and Young-Won Ha, "Consumer Learning: Advertising and the Ambiguity of Product Experience," *Journal of Consumer Research*, Vol. 13 (September 1986), pp. 221–233; John Deighton, "Two Meanings for Transformation," *Advances in Consumer Research*, Vol. 15 (1988), pp. 262–264; Robert E. Smith and William R. Swinyard, "Cognitive Response to Advertising and Trial: Belief Strength, Belief Confidence and Product Curiosity," *Journal of Advertising*, Vol. 17 (November 1988), pp. 3–14; and Stephen J. Hoch and John Deighton, "Managing What Consumers Learn from Experience," *Journal of Marketing*, Vol. 53 (April 1989), pp. 1–20.

19. "Raisin Expectations," *Promote*, April 11, 1988, p. 7.

20. Aimee L. Stern, "The Promo Wars," *Business Month*, July 1987, pp. 44–46. Considerable recent research has also been reported. See, for example, Joseph P. Flanagan, "Sales Promotion: The Emerging Alternative to Brand-Building Advertising," *The Journal of Consumer Marketing*, Vol. 5 (Spring 1988), pp. 45–48; Steven W. Hartley and James Cross, "How Sales Promotion Can Work for and Against You," *The Journal of Consumer Marketing*, Vol. 5 (Summer 1988), pp. 35–42; V. Kumar and Robert P. Leone, "Measuring the Effect of Retail Store Promotions on Brand and Store Substitution," *Journal of Marketing Research*, Vol. 24 (May 1988), pp. 178–185; Thomas E. Buzas and Howard Marmorstein, "Consumers' Knowledge of Supermarket Prices: The Effects of Manufacturer and Retailer Promotions," *Advances in Consumer Research*, Vol. 15 (1988), pp. 360–363; Caroline M. Henderson, "The Interaction of Coupons with Price and Store Promotions," *Advances in Consumer Research*, Vol. 15 (1988), pp. 364–371; Kapil Bawa and Robert W. Shoemaker, "The Effects of a Direct Mail Coupon on Brand Choice Behavior," *Journal of Marketing Research*, Vol. 24 (November 1987), pp. 370–376; Rockney G. Walters and Scott B. MacKenzie, "A Structural Equations Analysis of the Impact of Price Promotions on Store Performance," *Journal of Marketing Research*, Vol. 24 (February 1988), pp. 51–63; Sunil Gupta, "Impact of Sales Promotions on When, What, and How Much to Buy," *Journal of Marketing Research*, Vol. 25 (November 1988), p. 342–355; and Ajay Bhasin, Roger Dickinson, Christine G. Hauri, and William A. Robinson, "Promotion Investments That Keep Paying Off," *The Journal of Consumer Marketing*, Vol. 6 (Winter 1989), pp. 31–36.

21. William M. Weilbacher, *Advertising* (New York: Macmillan, 1979), pp. 264–265, 610–611.

22. National Advertising Division, "Case Report" (New York: Council of Better Business Bureaus, July 15, 1983), pp. 20–23. See also Priscilla A. LaBarbera, "The Diffusion of Trade Association Advertising Self-regulation," *Journal of Marketing*, Vol. 47 (Winter 1983), pp. 58–67; Gary M. Armstrong and Julie L. Ozanne, "An Evaluation of NAD/NARB Purpose and Performance," *Journal of Advertising*, Vol. 12, no. 3 (1983), pp. 15–26; Robert G. Wyckham, "Self-Regulation of Sex-Role Stereotyping in Advertising: The Canadian Experience," *Journal of Public Policy & Marketing*, Vol. 6 (1987), pp. 76–92; Gordon E. Miracle and Terence R. Nevett, "Improving NAD/NARB Self-Regulation of Advertising," *Journal of Public Policy & Marketing*, Vol. 7 (1988), pp. 114–126; and Jean J. Boddewyn, "Advertising Self-Regulation: True Purpose and Limits," *Journal of Advertising*, Vol. 18 (November 1989), pp. 19–27.

23. The debates on each of these issues often involve advanced quantitative analyses that are beyond the scope of this text. If you are interested in learning more about how each issue is treated, excellent discussions are provided in Mark S. Albion and Paul W. Farris, *The Advertising Controversy: Evidence on the Economic Effects of Advertising* (Boston: Auburn House, 1981). See also Gert Assmus, John U. Farley, and Donald R. Lehmann, "How Advertising Affects Sales: Meta-Analysis of Econometric Results," *Journal of Marketing Research*, Vol. 20 (February 1984), pp. 65–74; and Robert L. Steiner, "Point of View: The Paradox of Increasing Returns of Advertising," *Journal of Advertising Research*, Vol. 27 (February–March 1987), pp. 45–53.

24. Raymond A. Bauer and Stephen A. Greyser, *Advertising in America: The Consumer View* (Boston: Research Division, Harvard Business School, 1968). For recent findings on related issues, see

also Robert E. Hite and Cynthia Fraser, "Meta-Analyses of Attitudes Toward Advertising by Professionals," *Journal of Marketing*, Vol. 52 (July 1988), pp. 95–105; John E. Calfee and Debra Jones Ringold, "Consumer Skepticism and Advertising Regulation: What Do the Polls Show?" *Advances in Consumer Research*, Vol. 15 (1988), pp. 244–248; Silva K. Balasubramanian and Wagner A. Kamakura, "Measuring Consumer Attitudes Toward the Marketplace with Tailored Interviews," *Journal of Marketing Research*, Vol. 26 (August 1989), pp. 311–326; and J. Craig Andrews, "The Dimensionality of Beliefs Toward Advertising in General," *Journal of Advertising*, Vol. 18 (November 1989), pp. 26–35.

25. Several of these categories were developed from the discussion in *Appraising the Economic and Social Effects of Advertising: Staff Report of the Marketing Science Institute* (Cambridge, Mass.: Marketing Science Institute, 1971). For further reading on this topic, see David A. Aaker, "The Social and Economic Effects of Advertising," in D. A. Aaker and G. S. Day (eds.), *Consumerism: Search for the Public Interest*, 4th ed. (New York: Free Press, 1982), pp. 190–209; and Leonard N. Reid and Lawrence C. Soley, "Generalized and Personalized Attitudes Toward Advertising's Social and Economic Effects," *Journal of Advertising*, Vol. 11, no. 3 (1982), pp. 3–7. For recent discussions, Richard W. Pollay, "The Distorted Mirror: Reflections on the Unintended Consequences of Advertising," *Journal of Marketing*, Vol. 50 (April 1986), pp. 18–36; Grant McCracken, "Advertising: Meaning or Information?" *Advances in Consumer Research*, Vol. 14 (1987), pp. 121–124; Geoffrey P. Lantos, "Advertising: Looking Glass or Molder of the Masses?" *Journal of Public Policy & Marketing*, Vol. 6 (1987), pp. 104–128; Darrel D. Muehling and Jeffrey J. Stoltman, "Advertising's Influence: Do Perceptions Match Reality?" *AMA Educators Proceedings* (1987), pp. 239–242; Oswald A. J. Mascarenhas, "Toward a Theology of Consumption," *AMA Winter Educators Proceedings* (1987), pp. 71–76; Oliver F. Williams and Patrick E. Murphy, "The Challenge to Marketing Ethics: Can Virtue Be Sold as Easily as Vice?" *AMA Winter Educators Proceedings* (1987), pp. 77; Chaim M. Ehrman, "Can Advertising Be Justified from a Talmudist's Point of View?" *AMA Winter Educators' Proceedings* (1987), pp. 78–80; Donald P. Robin and R. Eric Reidenbach, "Social Responsibility, Ethics and Marketing Strategy: Closing the Gap Between Concept and Application," *Journal of Marketing*, Vol. 51 (January 1987), pp. 44–58; and Marc G. Weinberger and Harlan E. Spotts, "A Situational View of Information Content in TV Advertising in the U.S. and U.K.," *Journal of Marketing*, Vol. 53 (January 1989), pp. 89–94.

For findings and perspectives on advertising to children, see Debra L. Scammon and Carole L. Christopher, "Nutritional Education with Children via Television: A Review," *Journal of Advertising*, Vol. 10, no. 2 (1981), pp. 26–36; Nancy Stephens and Mary Ann Stutts, "Preschoolers' Ability to Distinguish Between Television Programming and Commercials," *Journal of Advertising*, Vol. 11, no. 2 (1982), pp. 16–26; M. Carole Macklin and Richard H. Kolbe, "Sex Role Stereotyping in Children's Advertising," *Journal of Advertising*, Vol. 13, no. 2 (1984), pp. 34–42; Sanford L. Grossbart and Lawrence A. Crosby, "Understanding the Bases of Parental Concern and Reaction to Children's Food Advertising," *Journal of Marketing*, Vol. 48 (Summer 1984), pp. 79–83; and Gerald J. Gorn and Renee Florsheim, "The Effects of Commercials for Adult Products on Children," *Journal of Consumer Research*, Vol. 12 (March 1985), pp. 962–967. (Further discussions and many further references on issues involving the consumer behavior of children are given in Chapters 10 and 15.)

For discussions on other issues related to controversies on the social effects of advertising, see, for example, Terence A. Shimp and Robert F. Dyer, "The Pain-Pill-Pleasure Model and Illicit Drug Consumption," *Journal of Consumer Research*, Vol. 6 (June 1979), pp. 36–46; Eric J. Zanot, J. David Pincus, and E. Joseph Lamp, "Public Perceptions of Subliminal Advertising," *Journal of Advertising*, Vol. 12, no. 1 (1983), pp. 39–45; Daniel C. Bello, Robert W. Pitts, and Michael J. Etzel, "Communication Effects of Controversial Sexual Content in Television Programs and Commercials," *Journal of Advertising*, Vol. 12, no. 3 (1983), pp. 32–42; Peter J. DePaulo, Mary Rubin, and Brenton Milner, "Stages of Involvement with Alcohol and Heroin: Analysis of the Effects of Marketing on Addiction," *Advances in Consumer Research*, Vol. 14 (1987), pp. 521–525; John Petrof and Pandelis Vlahopoulos, "Advertising and the Stereotyping of Women," *AMA Educators' Proceedings*, 1984, pp. 6–10; Marjorie Caballero and Paul J. Solomon, "A Longitudinal View of Women's Role Portrayal in Television Advertising," *Journal of the Academy of Marketing Science*, Vol. 12 (Fall 1984), pp. 93–108; Pat McIntyre, Harmon Hosch, Richard Jackson Harris, and D. Wayne Norvell, "Effects of Sex and Attitudes Toward Women on the Processing of Television Commercials," *Psychology & Marketing*, Vol. 3 (Fall 1986), pp. 181–192; Thomas W. Leigh, Arno J. Rethans, and Tamatha Reichenbach Whitney, "Role Portrayals of Women in Advertising: Cognitive Responses and Advertising Effectiveness," *Journal of Advertising Research*,

Vol. 27 (November 1987), pp. 54–63. P. J. O'Connor, Aylin Baher, Bosco Gong, and Elyse Kane, "Recall Levels of Sexuality in Advertising," *AMA Educators Proceedings* (1986), pp. 2–5; Leonard N. Reid, Charles T. Salmon, and Lawrence C. Soley, "The Nature of Sexual Content in Television Advertising: A Cross-Cultural Comparison of Award-Winning Commercials," *AMA Educators Proceedings* (1984), pp. 214–216; Anthony C. Ursic, Michael L. Ursic, and Virginia L. Ursic, "A Longitudinal Study of the Use of the Elderly in Magazine Advertising," *Journal of Consumer Research*, Vol. 13 (June 1986) pp. 131–133; Alan J. Greco, "Representation of the Elderly in Advertising: Crisis or Inconsequence?" *The Journal of Consumer Marketing*, Vol. 6 (Winter 1989), pp. 37–44; James M. Stearns, Lynette Unger and Steven G. Luebkman, "The Portrayal of Blacks in Magazine and Television Advertising," *AMA Educators Proceedings* (1987), pp. 198–203; and Robert E. Wilkes and Humberto Valencia, "Hispanics and Blacks in Television Commercials," *Journal of Advertising*, Vol. 18 (November 1989), pp. 19–25.

26. The classic paper on this topic is Carl Hovland and Walter Weiss, "The Influence of Source Credibility on Communication Effectiveness," *Public Opinion Quarterly*, Vol. 15 (1951), pp. 635–650. For insights and debate on experimental methods and results, see R. Dholakia and B. Sternthal, "Highly Credible Sources: Persuasive Facilitators or Persuasive Liabilities?" *Journal of Consumer Research*, Vol. 3 (1977), pp. 223–232; Thomas J. Stanley, "Are Highly Credible Sources Persuasive?" *Journal of Consumer Research*, Vol. 5 (1978), pp. 66–67; and B. Sternthal and R. Dholakia, "Rejoinder," *Journal of Consumer Research*, Vol. 5 (1978); pp. 67–69. For more developments, see David W. Finn, "The Validity of Using Consumer Input to Choose Advertising Spokesmen," *Advances in Consumer Research*, Vol. 7 (1980), pp. 776–779; Joanne M. Klebba and Lynette S. Unger, "The Impact of Negative and Positive Information on Source Credibility in a Field Setting," *Advances in Consumer Research*, Vol. 10 (1983), pp. 11–16; Charles Atkin and Martin Block, "Effectiveness of Celebrity Endorsers," *Journal of Advertising Research*, Vol. 23, no. 1 (1983), pp. 57–61; Teresa A. Swartz, "Source Expertise and Source Similarity in an Advertising Context," *Journal of Advertising*, Vol. 13, no. 2 (1984), pp. 49–56; and Joshua L. Wiener and John C. Mowen, "Source Credibility: On the Independent Effects of Trust and Expertise When Attractiveness is Held Constant," *Advances in Consumer Research*, Vol. 13 (1986); David J. Moore and Richard Reardon, "Source Magnification in Advertising," *AMA Educators Proceedings* (1986), p. 80; S. Ratneshwar and S. Chaiken, "When Is the Expert Source More Persuasive?" *AMA Educators Proceedings* (1986), p. 86; Ruby Roy Dholakia, "Source Credibility Effects: A Test of Behavioral Persistence," *Advances in Consumer Research*, Vol. 14 (1987), pp. 426–430; W. Jeffrey Burroughs and Richard A. Feinberg, "Using Response Latency to Assess Spokesperson Effectiveness," *Journal of Consumer Research*, Vol. 14 (September 1987), pp. 295–299; David J. Moore, Richard Reardon, and John Mowen, "Source Independence in Multiple Source Advertising Appeals: The Confederate Effect," *Advances in Consumer Research*, Vol. 16 (1989), pp. 719–722; David J. Moore, Richard Reardon, and John C. Mowen, "Information Utility and the Effects of Multiple Sources in Print Advertising Appeals," *AMA Educators Proceedings* (1989), p. 251; and Michael A. Kamins, Meribeth J. Brand, Stuart A. Hoeke, and John C. Mowen, "Two-Sided Versus One-Sided Celebrity Endorsements: The Impact on Advertising Effectiveness and Credibility," *Journal of Advertising*, Vol. 18 (November 1989), pp. 4–10.

27. See, for example, Michael J. Baker and Gilbert A. Churchill, "The Impact of Physically Attractive Models on Advertising Evaluations," *Journal of Marketing Research*, Vol. 14 (November 1977), pp. 538–555; W. Benoy Joseph, "The Credibility of Physically Attractive Communicators: A Review," *Journal of Advertising*, Vol. 11, no. 3 (1982), pp. 15–23; Leonard N. Reid and Lawrence C. Soley, "Decorative Models and the Readership of Magazine Ads," *Journal of Advertising Research*, Vol. 23, no. 2 (1983), pp. 27–32; Marjorie J. Caballero and Paul J. Solomon, "Effects of Model Attractiveness on Sales Response," *Journal of Advertising*, Vol. 13, no. 1 (1984), pp. 17–23; and Steven W. Hartley and R. Bruce Hutton, "The Impact of Presenter Characteristics on Advertising Evaluation," *AMA Educators Proceedings* (1989), pp. 27–31.

28. The classic overviews of research in this area are C. I. Hovland, I. L. Janis, and H. H. Kelley, *Communication and Persuasion* (New Haven, Conn.: Yale University Press, 1953), and Dorwin Cartwright, "Some Principles of Mass Persuasion: Selected Findings of Research on the Sale of United States War Bonds," *Human Relations*, Vol. 1 (1949), pp. 253–267.

   For more recent comprehensive overviews of findings and approaches, see M. Wayne DeLozier, *The Marketing Communications Process* (New York: McGraw-Hill, 1976), and Jeffery E. Danes and John E. Hunter, "Designing Persuasive Communication Campaigns: A Multimessage Communication Model," *Journal of Consumer Research*, Vol. 7 (June 1980), pp. 67–77. For discussion of an applied perspective, see K. Roman and J. Maas, *How to Advertise* (New York: St. Martin's

Press, 1976). For a discussion of priority research questions, see Diane H. Schmalensee, "Today's Top Priority Advertising Research Questions," *Journal of Advertising Research,* Vol. 23, no. 2 (1983), pp. 46–60.

For recent developments in specific topics, see also Richard W. Mizerski, J. Dennis White, and James B. Hunt, "The Use of Emotion in Advertising," *AMA Educators Proceedings* (1984), pp. 244–248; David W. Stewart and David H. Furse, "The Effects of Television Advertising Execution on Recall, Comprehension, and Persuasion," *Psychology & Marketing,* Vol. 2 (Fall 1985), pp. 135–160; Andrew A. Mitchell, "The Effect of Verbal and Visual Components of Advertisements on Brand Attitudes and Attitude Toward the Advertisement," *Journal of Consumer Research,* Vol. 13 (June 1986), pp. 12–24; Michael A. Kamins and Henry Assael, "Two-Sided Versus One-Sided Appeals: A Cognitive Perspective on Argumentation, Source Derogation, and the Effect of Disconfirming Trial on Belief Change," *Journal of Marketing Research,* Vol. 24 (February 1987), pp. 29–30; Deborah J. MacInnis and Linda L. Price, "The Role of Imagery in Information Processing: Review and Extensions," *Journal of Consumer Research,* Vol. 13 (March 1987), pp. 473–491; Scott S. Liu and Patricia A. Stout, "Effects of Message Modality and Appeal on Advertising Acceptance," *Psychology & Marketing,* Vol. 4 (Fall 1987), pp. 167–188; Robert E. Burnkrant and Hunumantha R. Unnava, "Effects of Variation in Message Execution on the Learning of Repeated Brand Information," *Advances in Consumer Research,* Vol. 14 (1987), pp. 173–176; Murphy A. Sewall and Dan Sarel, "Characteristics of Radio Commercials and Their Recall Effectiveness," *Journal of Marketing,* Vol. 50 (January 1986), pp. 52–60; Arno J. Rethans, John L. Swasy, and Lawrence J. Marks, "Effects of Television Commercial Repetition, Receiver Knowledge, and Commercial Length: A Test of the Two-Factor Model," *Journal of Marketing Research,* Vol. 23 (February 1986), pp. 50–61; Pamela Kiecker, "Use of Distraction to Increase Advertising Effectiveness," *AMA Educators Proceedings* (1987), pp. 190–195; four articles in *Advances in Consumer Research,* Vol. 15 (1988): Wendy Bryce and Thomas J. Olney, "Modality Effects in Television Advertising: A Methodology for Isolating Message Structure from Message Content Effects," pp. 174–177, Karen Ann Hunold, "Verbal Strategies for Product Presentation in Television Commercials," pp. 256–259, Chris T. Allen, Karen A. Machleit, and Susan S. Marine, "On Accessing the Emotionality of Advertising via Izard's Differential Emotions Scale," pp. 226–231, and Arthur E. Heimbach and Richard F. Yalch, "The Affective and Cognitive Dimensions of Pictures in Advertising: An Extension of Mitchell & Olson," pp. 178–183; James M. Munch and John L. Swasy, "Rhetorical Question, Summarization Frequency, and Argument Strength Effects on Recall," *Journal of Consumer Research,* Vol. 15 (June 1988), pp. 69–76; Dena S. Cox and Anthony D. Cox, "What Does Familiarity Breed? Complexity as a Moderator of Repetition Effects in Advertisement Evaluation," *Journal of Consumer Research,* Vol 15 (June 1988), pp. 111–116; Terence A. Shimp, Joel E. Urbany, and Sarah E. Camlin, "The Use of Framing and Characterization for Magazine Advertising of Mass Marketed Products," *Journal of Advertising,* Vol. 17 (November 1988), pp. 23–30; Daniel J. Howard and Thomas E. Barry, "The Prevalence of Question Use in Print Advertising: Headlines Strategies," *Journal of Advertising Research,* Vol. 28 (August–September 1988), pp. 18–25; three articles in *Advances in Consumer Research,* Vol. 16 (1989): Craig A. Kelley, "A Study of Selected Issues in Vividness Research: The Role of Attention and Elaboration Enhancing Cues," pp. 574–580, April Atwood, "Extending Imagery Research to Sounds: Is A Sound Also Worth a Thousand Words?" pp. 587–594, and Scott Ward, David Reibstein, Terence A. Oliva, and Victoria Taylor, "Commercial Clutter: Effects of 15-Second Television Ads on Consumer Recall," pp. 437–478; Douglas R. Hausknecht, J. B. Wilkinson and George E. Prough, "Advertorials: Do Consumers See the Wolf in Sheep's Clothing," *AMA Educators Proceedings* (1989), pp. 308–312; and Henry A. Laskey, Ellen Day, and Melvin R. Crask, "Typology of Main Message Strategies for Television Commercials," *Journal of Advertising,* Vol. 18 (November 1989), pp. 36–41.

29. Raymond R. Burke, Arvind Rangaswamy, Jerry Wind, and Jehoshua Eliashberg, "ADCAD: A Knowledge-Based System for Advertising Design," Working Paper, University of Pennsylvania, 1988.

30. Fear appeals are discussed and reviewed in Michael L. Ray and William Wilkie, "Fear: The Potential of an Appeal Neglected by Marketing," *Journal of Marketing,* Vol. 34 (January 1970), pp. 54–62; and Brian Sternthal and C. Samuel Craig, "Fear Appeals: Revisited and Revised," *Journal of Consumer Research,* Vol. 1 (December 1974), pp. 22–34. For further insights and results, see also John R. Stuteville, "Psychic Defenses Against High Fear Appeals: A Key Marketing Variable," *Journal of Marketing,* Vol. 34 (April 1970), pp. 39–45; John J. Burnett and Richard L. Oliver, "Fear Appeal Effects in the Field: A Segmentation Approach," *Journal of Marketing Research,* Vol. 16 (May 1979), pp. 190–191; John J. Burnett and Robert E. Wilkes,

"Fear Appeals to Segments Only," *Journal of Advertising Research,* Vol. 20 (October 1980), pp. 21–24; and Michael S. LaTour and Shaker A. Zahra, "Fear Appeals as Advertising Strategy: Should They Be Used?" *Journal of Consumer Marketing,* Vol. 6 (Spring 1989), pp. 61–70. The use of humorous appeals is discussed and reviewed in Brian Sternthal and C. Samuel Craig, "Humor in Advertising," *Journal of Marketing,* Vol. 37 (October 1973), pp. 12–18; P. Kelly and P. J. Solomon, "Humor in Television Advertising," *Journal of Advertising,* Vol. 4 (1975), pp. 33–35; John H. Murphy, Isabella C. M. Cunningham, and Gary B. Wilcox, "The Impact of Program Environment on Recall of Humorous Television Commercials," *Journal of Advertising,* Vol. 8 (Summer 1979), pp. 17–21; Avraham Shama and Maureen Coughlin, "An Experimental Study of the Effectiveness of Humor in Advertising," in *Educators Conference Proceedings* (Chicago: American Marketing Association, 1979), pp. 249–252; Thomas W. Whipple and Alice E. Courtney, "How Men and Women Judge Humor: Advertising Guidelines for Action and Research," in J. Leigh and C. Martin (eds.), *Current Issues and Research in Advertising* (Ann Arbor: University of Michigan Press, 1981); George W. Brooker, "A Comparison of the Persuasive Effects of Mild Humor and Mild Fear Appeals," *Journal of Advertising,* Vol. 10, no. 4 (1981), pp. 29–40; Thomas J. Madden and Marc G. Weinberger, "The Effects of Humor on Attention in Magazine Advertising," *Journal of Advertising,* Vol. 11, no. 3 (1982), pp. 8–14; Calvin P. Duncan, James E. Nelson, and Nancy T. Frontczak, "The Effect of Humor on Advertising Comprehension," *Advances in Consumer Research,* Vol. 11 (1984), pp. 432–437; Melissa Burnett, Raymond Fisk, and Dale Lunsford, "Humorous Appeals in Television Advertising: A Content Analysis," *AMA Educators Proceedings* (1987), p. 183; and Marc C. Weinberger and Harlan E. Spotts, "Humor in U.S. Versus U.K. TV Commercials: A Comparison," *Journal of Advertising,* Vol. 18 (November 1989), pp. 39–44.

Much research has focused on receiver factors as well. See, for example, Rajeev Batra and Michael L. Ray, "Situational Effects of Advertising Repetition: The Moderating Influence of Motivation, Ability, and Opportunity to Respond," *Journal of Consumer Research,* Vol. 12 (March 1986), pp. 432–445; Marian C. Burke, "Ad Reactions over Time: Capturing Changes in the Real World," *Journal of Consumer Research,* Vol. 13 (June 1986), pp. 114–118; Richard Weijo and Leigh Lawton, "Message Repetition, Experience and Motivation," *Psychology & Marketing,* Vol. 3 (Fall 1986), pp. 165–180; Richard Mizerski, Marya J. Pucely, and Charles Patti, "The Influence of Consumer Confidence in the Truthfulness and Accuracy of Advertising on Their Subsequent Processing of Ad Messages," *AMA Educators Proceedings* (1986), pp. 28; Greg J. Lessne and Nicholas M. Didow, Jr., "Inoculation Theory and Resistance to Persuasion in Marketing," *Psychology & Marketing,* Vol. 4 (Summer 1987), pp. 157 ff.; Sanford Grossbart, Jim Gill, and Russ Laczniak, "Influence on Brand Commitment and Claim Strategy on Consumer Attitudes," *Advances in Consumer Research,* Vol. 14 (1987), pp. 510–513; James E. Nelson, Calvin P. Duncan, and Pamela L. Kiecker, "Some Psychometric Properties of a Self-Report Measure of Distraction Beliefs," *AMA Educators Proceedings* (1987), pp. 285; Karen A. Machleit and R. Dale Wilson, "Emotional Feelings and Attitude Toward the Advertisement: The Role of Brand Familiarity and Repetition," *Journal of Advertising,* Vol. 17 (November 1988), pp. 27–35; Ronald Paul Hill, "The Effects of Advertisements on Consumers' Mood States: An Interactive Perspective," *Advances in Consumer Research,* Vol. 15 (1988), pp. 131–134; Kevin Lane Keller, "Memory Factors in Advertising: The Effect of Advertising Retrieval Cues on Brand Evaluations," *Journal of Consumer Research,* Vol. 14 (December 1987), pp. 316–333; Frank R. Kardes, "Spontaneous Inference Processes in Advertising: The Effects of Conclusion Omission and Involvement on Persuasion," *Journal of Consumer Research,* Vol. 15 (September 1988), pp. 225–233; Lorne Bozinoff, Victor Roth, Colin May, and Rachel Ladouceur, "States of Involvement with Drugs and Alcohol: Analysis of Effects of Drug and Alcohol Abuse Advertising," *Advances in Consumer Research,* Vol. 16 (1989), pp. 215–220; William O. Bearden, F. Kelly Shuptrine, and Jesse E. Teel, "Self-Monitoring and Reactions to Image Appeals and Claims About Product Quality," *Advances in Consumer Research,* Vol. 16 (1989), pp. 703–710; and Brian Davis and Warren A. French, "Exploring Advertising Usage Segments among the Ages," *Journal of Advertising Research,* Vol. 29 (February–March 1989), pp. 22–29.

31. The topic of comparison (comparative) advertising is interesting in a number of respects. The articles cited here constitute much of what is available on this topic. To trace the development of work in this area, see, for example, William L. Wilkie and Paul W. Farris, "Comparison Advertising: Problems and Potential," *Journal of Marketing,* Vol. 39 (November 1975), pp. 7–15; Kanti V. Prasad, "Communications Effectiveness of Comparative Advertising: A Laboratory Analysis," *Journal of Marketing Research,* Vol. 13 (May 1976), pp. 128–137; Subhash C. Jain and Edwin C. Hackleman, "How Effective Is Comparative Advertising for Stimulating Brand Recall?"

Journal of Advertising, Vol. 7 (Summer 1978), pp. 24–30; William Pride, Charles W. Lamb, and Barbara A. Pletcher, "The Informativeness of Comparative Advertisements: An Empirical Investigation," *Journal of Advertising,* Vol. 8 (Spring 1979), pp. 29–35; Terence A. Shimp and Robert C. Dyer, "The Effects of Comparative Advertising Mediated by Market Position of Sponsoring Brand," *Journal of Advertising,* Vol. 7 (Summer 1979), pp. 13–19; Linda L. Golden, "Consumer Reactions to Explicit Brand Comparisons in Advertisements," *Journal of Marketing Research,* Vol. 16 (November 1979), pp. 21–26; R. Dale Wilson and Aydin Muderrisoglu, "An Analysis of Cognitive Responses to Comparative Advertising," *Advances in Consumer Research,* Vol. 7 (1980), pp. 566–571; George E. Belch, "An Examination of Comparative and Noncomparative Television Commercials: The Effects of Claim Variations and Repetition on Cognitive Response and Message Acceptance," *Journal of Marketing Research,* Vol. 18 (August 1981), pp. 333–349; John H. Murphy and Mary S. Amundsen, "The Communications-Effectiveness of Comparative Advertising for a New Brand on Users of the Dominant Brand," *Journal of Advertising,* Vol. 10, no. 1 (1981), pp. 14–21; William R. Swinyard, "The Interaction Between Comparative Advertising and Copy Claim Variation," *Journal of Marketing Research,* Vol. 18 (May 1981), pp. 175–186; Michael Etgar and Stephen A. Goodwin, "One-Sided Versus Two-Sided Comparative Message Appeals for New Brand Introductions," *Journal of Consumer Research,* Vol. 8 (March 1982), pp. 460–464; Robert R. Harmon, Nabil Y. Razzouk, and Bruce L. Stern, "Information Content of Comparative Magazine Advertisements," *Journal of Advertising,* Vol. 12, no. 4 (1983), pp. 10–19; Z. S. Demirdjian, "Sales Effectiveness of Comparative Advertising: An Experimental Field Investigation," *Journal of Consumer Research,* Vol. 10 (December 1983), pp. 362–364; Stephen B. Ash and Chou-Hou Wee, "Comparative Advertising: A Review with Implications for Further Research," *Advances in Consumer Research,* Vol. 10 (1983), pp. 370–376; Gerald J. Gorn and Charles B. Weinberg, "The Impact of Comparative Advertising on Perception and Attitude: Some Positive Findings," *Journal of Consumer Research,* Vol. 11 (September 1984), pp. 719–727; Angelina Villareal-Camacho, "Effects of Product Class Knowledge on the Evaluation of Comparative Advertising," *Advances in Consumer Research,* Vol. 12 (1985), pp. 504–509; Beth A. Walker, John L. Swasy, and Arno J. Rethans, "The Impact of Comparative Advertising on Perception Formation in New Product Introductions," *Advances in Consumer Research,* Vol. 13 (1986), Norman Kangun, Darrel D. Muehling, and Sanford L. Grossbart, "An Empirical Investigation of the Cognitive Effects of Alternative References to Competition in Comparative Advertising: Implications for the FTC," *AMA Educators Proceedings* (1984), pp. 314–318; David Boush and Ivan Ross, "The Influence of Substantiation Details on Perceptions of Comparative Advertising Claims: An Exploratory Investigation," *AMA Educators Proceedings* (1986), pp. 340–344; Michael D. Johnson and David A. Horne, "Subject/Referent Position in Comparative Advertising: A Pilot Study," *Advances in Consumer Research,* Vol. 14 (1987), pp. 164–167; Cornelia Dröge and Rene Y. Darmon, "Associative Positioning Strategies Through Comparative Advertising: Attribute Versus Overall Similarity Approaches," *Journal of Marketing Research,* Vol. 24 (November 1987), pp. 377–388; and Easwar S. Iyer, "The Influence of Verbal Content and Relative Newness on the Effectiveness of Comparative Advertising," *Journal of Advertising,* Vol. 17 (November 1988), pp. 15–21.

Chapter 18   Consumer Decision Processes (I): Prepurchase Issues

1. These quotes are reported in Patrick E. Murphy, "Measuring Consumer Perceptions of the Dimensions of Price," Working Paper, University of Notre Dame, Notre Dame, Ind., 1989.
2. Jennifer Alter, "Sales of Tampons Dip 20%," *Advertising Age,* December 22, 1980, pp. 2 ff.
3. Bradley Stertz, "Suzuki Samurai's Sales Have Plunged Since Consumers Union Called It Unsafe," *The Wall Street Journal,* July 7, 1988.
4. Laurie Freeman, "Sales of Aspirin Soar After Study," *Advertising Age,* March 28, 1988, p. 3.
5. John A. Howard, *Consumer Behavior: Application of Theory* (New York: McGraw-Hill, 1977), and John A. Howard and Jagdish N. Sheth, *The Theory of Buyer Behavior* (New York: John Wiley, 1969).
6. As noted in earlier chapters, the decision process perspective has had an enormous impact on consumer behavior thought and research. Among the most influential proponents of this approach were James Engel, David Kollatt, and Roger Blackwell. Other influential early models incorporating a decision process perspective included those by Franco Nicosia, by John Howard and Jagdish Sheth, and by Flemming Hansen. See, for example, James F. Engel, David T. Kollat, and Roger D. Blackwell, *Consumer Behavior,* 2nd ed. (New York: Holt, Rinehart and Winston, 1973); Francesco M. Nicosia, *Consumer Decision Processes: Marketing and Advertising Implications* (Englewood Cliffs, N.J.: Prentice Hall, 1966); Howard and Sheth, *The Theory of Buyer*

Behavior; and Flemming Hansen, *Consumer Choice Behavior: A Cognitive Theory* (New York: Free Press, 1972).

See, however, Richard W. Olshavsky and Donald H. Granbois, "Consumer Decision Making—Fact or Fiction?" *Journal of Consumer Research,* Vol. 6 (September 1979), pp. 93–100; a comment on this article by Michael Ursic, "Consumer Decision Making—Fact or Fiction?" *Journal of Consumer Research,* Vol. 7 (December 1980), pp. 331–333; and the rejoinder by the authors on page 33 of the same volume; Richard W. Olshavsky, "Toward a More Comprehensive Theory of Choice," *Advances in Consumer Research,* Vol. 12, (1985), pp. 465–470; and Franco M. Nicosia, "Consumer Decision Processes: A Futuristic View," *Advances in Consumer Research,* Vol. 9, (1982), pp. 17–19.

7. "Marketing Briefs," *Marketing News,* August 31, 1984, p. 27. See also Gordon C. Bruner II and Richard J. Pomazal, "Problem Recognition: The Crucial First Stage of the Consumer Decision Process," *Journal of Consumer Marketing,* Vol. 5 (Winter 1988), 53–64.

8. Lee W. Dyer, "Display Contest Adds Big Slice to Cheese Sales," *Progressive Grocer,* Vol. 60, no. 6 (June 1981), pp. 89–94.

9. Lee W. Dyer, "How to Win Display Contests . . . and Win Extra Sales Too!" *Progressive Grocer,* Vol. 60, no. 9 (September 1981), pp. 130–132.

10. See Lauranne Buchanan and Wanru Su, "Coping With the Uncertainty of Consumer Markets," *Advances in Consumer Research,* Vol. 15 (1988), pp. 396–402.

11. Martin Sloane, "Hoosier Wins Longest Tape Contest," United Features, April 13, 1987; "Coupon Fanatic spends $125 for over $1800 in Groceries," Associated Press, New York, December 28, 1982; Caroline M. Henderson, "Modeling the Coupon Redemption Decision," *Advances in Consumer Research,* Vol. 12 (1985), pp. 138–143; and Linda L. Price, Lawrence F. Feick, and Audrey Guskey-Federouch, "Couponing Behaviors of the Market Maven: Profile of a Super Couponer," *Advances in Consumer Research,* Vol. 15 (1988), pp. 354–359.

12. William L. Wilkie, *How Consumers Use Product Information: A Report Prepared for the National Science Foundation* (Washington, D.C.: U.S. Government Printing Office, 1975).

13. See, for example, Peter H. Bloch and Marsha L. Richins, "Shopping Without Purchase: An Investigation of Consumer Browsing Behavior," *Advances in Consumer Research,* Vol. 10 (1983), pp. 389–393; Jack A. Lesser and Sanjay Jain, "A Preliminary Investigation of the Relationship Between Exploratory and Epistemic Shopping Behavior," *AMA Educators Proceedings* (1985), pp. 75–81; and Peter H. Bloch, Daniel L. Sherrell, and Nancy M. Ridgway, "Consumer Search: An Extended Framework," *Journal of Consumer Research,* Vol. 13 (June 1986), pp. 119–126.

14. See also Stephen J. Hoch and George F. Loewenstein, "A Theory of Impulse Buying," Working Paper 40, University of Chicago, 1987.

15. The entries in this table were developed from a number of sources, including especially Donald H. Granbois, "Shopping behavior and Preferences," in R. Ferber (ed.), *Selected Aspects of Consumer Behavior* (Washington, D.C.: U.S. Government Printing Office, 1977), pp. 259–298; Joseph W. Newman, "Consumer External Search: Amount and Determinants" in A. Woodside, J. Sheth, and P. Bennett (eds.), *Consumer and Industrial Buying Behavior* (New York: North-Holland, 1977), pp. 79–94; and William L. Wilkie, *How Consumers Use Product Information: A Report Prepared for the National Science Foundation* (Washington, D.C.: U.S. Government Printing Office, 1975). See also Banwari Mittal, "Must Consumer Involvement Always Imply More Information Search?" *Advances in Consumer Research,* Vol. 16 (1989), pp. 167–172.

16. See, for example, E. Scott Maynes, "Towards Market Transparency," Working Paper, Cornell University, Ithaca, N.Y., 1985; Joel E. Urbany, "An Experimental Examination of the Economics of Information," *Journal of Consumer Research,* Vol. 13 (September 1986), pp. 257–271; Brian T. Ratchford and Pola B. Gupta, "On Measuring the Informational Efficiency of Consumer Markets," *Advances in Consumer Research,* Vol. 14 (1987), pp. 309–313; Paul N. Bloom, "Behavioral Perspectives on the Economics of Information: An Overview," *Advances in Consumer Research,* Vol. 15 (1988), pp. 232–233; John E. Calfee and Gary T. Ford, "Economics, Information and Consumer Behavior," *Advances in Consumer Research,* Vol. 15 (1988), pp. 234–238; Gary T. Ford, Darlene B. Smith, and John L. Swasy, "An Empirical Test of the Search, Experience and Credence Attributes Framework," *Advances in Consumer Research,* Vol. 15 (1988), pp. 239–243; and Joel E. Urbany, Peter R. Dickson, and William L. Wilkie, "Buyer Uncertainty and Information Search," *Journal of Consumer Research,* Vol. 16 (September 1989), pp. 208–215.

17. See Duane Davis, "Alternate Predictors of Consumer Search Propensities in the Service Sector," in *Proceedings,* American Marketing Association, Chicago, 1980, pp. 160–163; Teresa A. Swartz and Nancy Stephens, "Information Search for Services: The Maturity Segment," *Advances in*

Consumer Research, Vol. 11 (1984), pp. 244–249; Minette E. Drumwright and Nancy M. Kane, "Failures of Information in Health Care Marketing," *Advances in Consumer Research*, Vol. 15 (1988), pp. 249–255; and Jon B. Freiden and Ronald E. Goldsmith, "Prepurchase Information Seeking for Professional Services," *Journal of Services Marketing*, Vol. 3 (Winter 1989), pp. 45–55.

18. William L. Wilkie and Peter R. Dickson, "Consumer Information Search and Shopping Behavior," Working Paper, University of Florida, Gainesville, 1985.

19. Since these results are based upon consumers' recollections of their past behavior, they may be prone to understate somewhat the actual amount of information search (since some elements may have been forgotten). One study provided evidence on this possibility by first *observing* consumers while they were purchasing shoes and then later *asking* them about their search and decision processes. See Joseph W. Newman and Bradley D. Lockeman, "Measuring Prepurchase Information Seeking," *Journal of Consumer Research*, Vol. 2 (December 1975), pp. 216–222. Results showed that the survey method led to less reported search than the researchers had actually observed. See also George Katona and Eva Mueller, "A Study of Purchasing Decisions," in Lincoln Clark (Ed.), *The Dynamics of Consumer Reaction*. Vol. 1, *Consumer Behavior* (New York: New York University Press, 1955); Joseph W. Newman and Richard Staelin, "Prepurchase Information Seeking for New Cars and Major Household Appliances," *Journal of Marketing Research*, Vol. 9 (August 1971), pp. 249–257; Girish N. Punj and Richard Staelin, "A Model of Consumer Information Search Behavior for New Automobiles," *Journal of Consumer Research*, Vol. 9 (March 1983), pp. 366–380; Girish N. Punj and David W. Stewart, "An Interaction Framework of Consumer Decision Making," *Journal of Consumer Research*, Vol. 10 (September 1983), pp. 181–196; Anthony Cox, Donald Granbois, and John Summers, "Planning, Search, Certainty and Satisfaction Among Durables Buyers: A Longitudinal Study," *Advances in Consumer Research*, Vol. 10 (1983), pp. 394–399; Joseph P. Guiltinan and Kent M. Monroe, "Identifying and Analyzing Consumer Shopping Strategies," *Advances in Consumer Research*, Vol. 7 (1980), pp. 745–748; James H. Leigh, "Reliability and Validity Assessment of Patterns of Information Source Usage," *Advances in Consumer Research*, Vol. 10 (1983), pp. 673–678; Scott A. Neslin and Gert Assmus, "Consumer Response to Information That Presents a Range of Possible Performance Levels for a New Product," *Journal of Consumer Affairs* (Summer 1983), pp. 81–106; Narasimhan Srinivasan, "A Path Analytic Model of External Search for Information for New Automobiles," *Advances in Consumer Research*, Vol. 14 (1987), pp. 319–322; Sharon E. Beatty and Scott M. Smith, "External Search Effort: An Investigation Across Several Product Categories," *Journal of Consumer Research*, Vol. 14 (June 1987), pp. 83–95; and Barry L. Bayus and Su Leep Halder, "A Longitudinal Analysis of the Purchase Order of Consumer Durables," *AMA Educators Proceedings* (1989), pp. 280–284.

The field of economics has long held consumer information search as one of its central concepts. For related discussions see, for example, Brian T. Ratchford, "Consumer Search Among Stores and Brands," *Advances in Consumer Research*, Vol. 13 (1986); two articles in *Advances in Consumer Research*, Vol. 7 (1980): Loren V. Geistfeld, E. Scott Maynes, and Greg Duncan, "Informational Imperfections in Local Consumer Markets: A Preliminary Analysis," pp. 180–185, and John J. Wheatley, Richard F. Yalch, and John S. Y. Chiu, "In Search of the Economists' Consumer: The Effects of Product Information, Money, and Prices on Choice Behavior," pp. 533–537; and Linda K. Zimmerman and Loren V. Geistfeld, "Economic Factors Which Influence Consumer Search for Price Information," *Journal of Consumer Affairs* (Summer 1984), pp. 119–130.

Recent studies of search from a CIP perspective include Srikumar Rao and John U. Farley, "Effects of Environmental Perceptions and Cognitive Complexity on Search and Information Processing," *Psychology & Marketing*, Vol. 4 (Winter 1987), pp. 287–302; two articles in *Advances in Consumer Research*, Vol. 15 (1988): Julie L. Ozanne, "Keyword Recognition: A New Methodology for the Study of Information Seeking Behavior," pp. 574–579, and Narasimhan Srinivasan and Jagdish Agrawal, "The Relationship Between Prior Knowledge and External Search," pp. 27–31, Richard Spreng and Richard Olshavsky, "Exploring the Headwaters of the Prior Knowledge-Search Relationship," *AMA Educators Proceedings* (1989), pp. 220–224; and Jeffrey J. Stoltman, Shelley R. Tapp, and Richard S. Lapidus, "An Examination of Shopping Scripts," *Advances in Consumer Research*, Vol. 16 (1989), pp. 384–391.

20. See, for example, John D. Claxton, Joseph N. Fry, and Bernard Portis, "A Taxonomy of Prepurchase Information Gathering Patterns," *Journal of Consumer Research*, Vol. 1 (December 1974), pp. 35–42; and David H. Furse, Girish N. Punj, and David W. Stewart, "A Typology of Individual Search Strategies Among Purchasers of New Automobiles," *Journal of Consumer Research* (March 1984), pp. 417–431. See also Geoffrey Kiel and Roger Layton, "Dimensions of Consumer Information Seeking Behavior," *Journal of Marketing Research*, Vol. 18 (May 1981), pp. 233–239; and

David F. Midgley, Grahame R. Dowling, and Pamela D. Morrison, "Consumer Types, Social Influence, Information Search and Choice," *Advances in Consumer Research,* Vol. 16 (1989), pp. 137–143.

21. Robert A. Westbrook and Claes Fornell, "Patterns of Information Source Usage Among Durable Goods Buyers," *Journal of Marketing Research,* Vol. 16 (August 1970), pp. 303–312.

22. See, for example, Hans G. Thorelli and Jack L. Engledow "Information Seekers and Information Systems: A Policy Perspective," *Journal of Marketing,* Vol. 44 (Spring 1980), pp. 9–27; and Ronald D. Anderson and Jack Engledow, "A Factor Analytic Comparison of U.S. and German Information Seekers," *Journal of Consumer Research,* Vol. 3 (March 1977), pp. 185–196.

23. Calvin P. Duncan and Richard W. Olshavsky, "External Search: The Role of Consumer Beliefs," *Journal of Marketing Research,* Vol. 19 (February 1982), pp. 32–43; James A. Muncy, "Beliefs and External Information Search: A Replication," *AMA Educators Proceedings* (1986), pp. 62–67; Deborah Roedder John, Carol A. Scott, and James R. Bettman, "Sampling Data for Covariation Assessment: The Effect of Prior Beliefs on Search Patterns," *Journal of Consumer Research,* Vol. 13 (June 1986), pp. 38–47; and James R. Bettman, Deborah Roedder John, and Carol A. Scott, "Covariation Assessment by Consumers," *Journal of Consumer Research,* Vol. 13 (December 1986), pp. 315–326.

24. Randall Bloomquist, "Consumer Libraries: New Way to Advertise Real Estate," *Marketing Week,* October 5, 1987, p. 25.

25. See, for example, Monroe P. Friedman, "Consumer Confusion in the Selection of Supermarket Products," *Journal of Applied Psychology,* Vol. 50 (December 1966), pp. 529–534; and Michael J. Houston, "The Effect of Unit Pricing on Choices of Brand and Size in Economic Shopping," *Journal of Marketing,* Vol. 36 (July 1972), pp. 51–54. For more recent reports on the same phenomenon, see Noel Capon and Deanna Kuhn, "Can Consumers Calculate Best Buys?" *Journal of Consumer Research,* Vol. 8 (March 1982), pp. 449–452; and Valarie Ziethaml, "Consumer Response to In-Store Price Information Environments," *Journal of Consumer Research,* March 1982, pp. 357–369. For related discussions, see especially Joseph W. Alba and J. Wesley Hutchinson, "Dimensions of Consumer Expertise," *Journal of Consumer Research,* Vol. 13 (March 1987), pp. 411–454, and Joseph W. Alba and Howard Marmorstein, "The Effects of Frequency Knowledge on Consumer Decision Making," *Journal of Consumer Research,* Vol. 14 (June 1987), pp. 14–25.

26. J. Edward Russo, Gene Krieser, and Sally Miyashita, "An Effective Display of Unit Price Information," *Journal of Marketing,* Vol. 39 (April 1975), pp. 11–19. For a review of the experience with unit pricing programs, see David A. Aaker and Gary T. Ford, "Unit Pricing Ten Years Later: A Replication," *Journal of Marketing* Vol. 47 (Winter 1983), pp. 118–122.

See also Thomas E. Muller, "Structural Information Factors Which Stimulate the Use of Nutrition Information: A Field Experiment," *Journal of Marketing Research,* Vol. 22 (May 1985), pp. 143 ff.; J. Edward Russo, Richard Staelin, Catherine A. Nolan, Gary J. Russell, and Barbara L. Metcalf, "Nutrition Information in the Supermarket," *Journal of Consumer Research,* Vol. 13 (June 1986), pp. 48–70; Catherine A. Cole and Gary J. Gaeth, "Cognitive and Age-Related Differences in the Ability to Use Nutritional Information in a Complex Environment," *AMA Educators Proceedings* (1988), p. 123; and Donna J. Hill and Maryon F. King, "Preserving Consumer Autonomy in an Integrative Informational Environment: Toward Development of a Consumer Aid Model," *Advances in Consumer Research,* Vol. 16 (1989), pp. 144–151.

27. For a comprehensive coverage of this topic, see Jacob Jacoby, Donald E. Speller, and Carol A. Kohn, "Brand Choice Behavior as a Function of Information Load," *Journal of Marketing Research,* Vol. 11 (February 1974), pp. 63–69; William L. Wilkie, "Analysis of Effects of Information Load," *Journal of Marketing Research,* Vol. 11 (November 1974), pp. 462–466; John O. Summers, "Less Information Is Better?" *Journal of Marketing Research,* Vol. 11 (November 1974), pp. 467–468; Jacob Jacoby, Donald E. Speller, and Carol A. Kohn, "Brand Choice Behavior as a Function of Information Load: Replication and Extension," *Journal of Consumer Research,* Vol. 3 (March 1974), pp. 33–42; J. Edward Russo, "More Information Is Better: A Reevaluation of Jacoby, Speller, and Kohn," *Journal of Consumer Research,* Vol. 1 (December 1974) pp. 68–72; Jacob Jacoby, "Information Load and Decision Quality: Some Contested Issues," *Journal of Marketing Research,* Vol. 14 (November 1977), pp. 569–577; Richard Staelin and John W. Payne, "Studies of the Information-Seeking Behavior of Consumers," in John S. Carroll and John W. Payne (eds.), *Cognition and Social Behavior* (Hillsdale, N.J. Erlbaum, 1976), pp. 185–201; Debra L. Scammon, " 'Information Load' and Consumers," *Journal of Consumer Research,* Vol. 4 (December 1977), pp. 148–155; Naresh K. Malhotra, "Information Load and Consumer Decision Making," *Journal of Consumer Research,* Vol. 9 (March 1982), pp. 419–430; Naresh K. Malhotra, Arun K. Jain, and Stephen Lagakos, "The Information Overload Controversy: An Alternative Viewpoint," *Journal of Marketing,* Vol. 46 (Spring 1982), pp. 27–37; Jacob Jacoby, "Perspectives on Information

Overload," *Journal of Consumer Research,* Vol. 10 (March 1984), pp. 432–435; Naresh K. Malhotra, "Reflections on the Information Overload Paradigm in Consumer Decision Making," *Journal of Consumer Research,* Vol. 10 (March 1984), pp. 436–440; Roger J. Best and Michael Ursic, "The Impact of Information Load and Variability on Choice Accuracy," *Advances in Consumer Research,* Vol. 14 (1987), pp. 106–108; Kevin Lane Keller and Richard Staelin, "Effects of Quality and Quantity of Information on Decision Effectiveness," *Journal of Consumer Research,* Vol. 14 (September 1987), pp. 200–213; Robert J. Meyer and Eric J. Johnson, "Information Overload and the Nonrobustness of Linear Models: A Comment on Keller and Staelin," *Journal of Consumer Research,* Vol. 15 (March 1989), pp. 498–503; and Kevin Lane Keller and Richard Staelin, "Assessing Biases in Measuring Decision Effectiveness and Information Overload," *Journal of Consumer Research,* Vol. 15 (March 1989), pp. 504–508.

28. Dennis L. McNeill and William L. Wilkie, "Public Policy and Consumer Information: Impacts of the New Energy Labels," *Journal of Consumer Research,* Vol. 6 (June 1979), pp. 1–11. For related discussions, see also Craig A. Kelley and Teresa A. Swartz, "An Empirical Test of Warranty Label and Duration Effects on Consumer Decision Making: An Information Processing Perspective," *AMA Educators Proceedings* (1984), pp. 309–313; R. Bruce Hutton, Gary A. Mauser, Pierre Filiatrault, and Olli T. Ahtola, "Effects of Cost-Related Feedback on Consumer Knowledge and Consumption Behavior: A Field Experimental Approach," *Journal of Consumer Research,* Vol. 13 (December 1986), pp. 327–336; Monroe Friedman, "Survey Data on Owner-Reported Car Problems: How Useful to Prospective Purchasers of Used Cars?" *Journal of Consumer Research,* Vol. 14 (December 1987), pp. 434–439; James W. Harvey and Kevin F. McCrohan, "Is There a Better Way of Improving Compliance with the Tax Laws? Insights from the Philanthropic Literature," *Journal of Public Policy & Marketing,* Vol. 7 (1988), pp. 138–151; Robert F. Dyer and Thomas J. Maronick, "An Evaluation of Consumer Awareness and Use of Energy Labels in the Purchase of Major Appliances—A Longitudinal Analysis," *Journal of Public Policy & Marketing,* Vol. 7 (1988), pp. 83–97; and Jeannet H. van Houwelingen and W. Fred van Raaij, "The Effects of Goal-Setting and Daily Electronic Feedback on In-Home Energy Use," *Journal of Consumer Research,* Vol. 15 (March 1989), pp. 98–105.

29. R. Bruce Hutton and William L. Wilkie, "Life Cycle Cost: A New Form of Consumer Information," *Journal of Consumer Research,* Vol. 6 (March 1980), pp. 349–360.

Chapter 19 Consumer Decision Processes (II): Purchase Decisions

1. From Patrick E. Murphy, "Measuring Consumer Perceptions of the Dimensions of Price," Working Paper, University of Notre Dame, Notre Dame, Ind., 1989.

2. See, for example, John G. Lynch, "Adventures in Paramorphic Modeling: Models of Consumers' Processing of Negative Information," Working Paper, Center for Consumer Research, University of Florida, Gainesville, 1984; For general considerations, see Alan G. Sawyer, "Demand Artifacts in Laboratory Experiments in Consumer Research," *Journal of Consumer Research,* Vol. 1 (March 1975), pp. 20–30; and Jordan J. Louviere, "Hierarchical Information Integration: A New Method for the Design and Analysis of Complex Multiattribute Judgment Problems," *Advances in Consumer Research,* Vol. 11 (1984), pp. 148–155; Sarah Gardial and Gabriel Biehal, "Measuring Consumers' Inferential Processing in Choice," *Advances in Consumer Research,* Vol. 14 (1987), pp. 101–105; and Eva Hyatt, David Snyder, and Terence A. Shimp, "Demand Artifact: Which Is Worse, the Problem or the Solution," *AMA Educators' Proceedings,* 1989, p. 226.

3. See James R. Bettman, *An Information Processing Theory of Consumer Choice* (Reading, Mass.: Addison-Wesley, 1979); James R. Bettman and C. Whan Park, "Effects of Prior Knowledge and Experience and Phase of the Choice Process on Consumer Decision Processes: A Protocol Analysis," *Journal of Consumer Research,* Vol. 7 (1980), pp. 234–248; Gabriel Biehal and Dipankar Chakravarti, "Experiences with the Bettman-Park Verbal Protocol Coding Scheme," *Journal of Consumer Research,* Vol. 8 (1982), pp. 442–448; Gabriel Biehal and Dipankar Chakravarti, "Reactivity and Reliability of Concurrent Verbal Protocols," Working Paper, Center for Consumer Research, University of Florida, Gainesville, 1984; two articles in *Advances in Consumer Research,* Vol. 10 (1983): Thomas W. Leigh and Arno J. Rethans, "Experiences with Script Elicitation Within Consumer Decision Making Contexts," pp. 667–672, Banwari Mittal, "Consumers' Cognitive Journey Through the Product Forest," pp. 464–469; Joel Rudd, "A Consideration of Verbal and Interactive Protocol Methodologies in Consumer Information Processing Research," *Advances*

in Consumer Research, Vol. 11 (1984), pp. 363–366; and Gabriel Biehal and Dipankar Chakravarti, "The Effects of Concurrent Verbalization on Choice Processing," *Journal of Marketing Research,* Vol. 26 (February 1989), pp. 84–96.

4. Jacob Jacoby, "Perspectives on a Consumer Information Processing Research Program," *Communication Research,* Vol. 2 (July 1975), pp. 203–215; W. E. Patton III, "Quantity of Information and Information Display Type as Predictors of Consumer Choice of Product Brands," *Journal of Consumer Affairs,* Vol. 15 (Summer 1981), pp. 92–105; Russell G. Wahlers, "Number of Choice Alternatives and Number of Product Characteristics as Determinants of the Consumer's Choice of an Evaluation Process Strategy," *Advances in Consumer Research,* Vol. 9 (1982), pp. 544–549; Joel Rudd and Frank J. Kohout, "Individual and Group Consumer Information Acquisition in Brand Choice Situations," *Journal of Consumer Research,* Vol. 10 (December 1983), pp. 303–309; and Douglas M. Stayman and Michael R. Hagerty, "Methodological Issues in Simulated Shopping Experiments," *Advances in Consumer Research,* Vol. 12 (1985), pp. 173–176.

5. James R. Bettman and Jacob Jacoby, "Patterns of Processing in Consumer Information Acquisition," *Advances in Consumer Research,* Vol. 3 (1976), pp. 315–320; James R. Bettman and Pradeep Kakkar, "Effects of Information Presentation Format on Consumer Information Acquisition Strategies," *Journal of Consumer Research,* Vol. 3 (March 1977), pp. 233–240; Robert J. Meyer, "The Learning of Multiattribute Judgment Policies," *Journal of Consumer Research,* Vol. 14 (September 1987), pp. 155–173; Noreen M. Klein and Stewart W. Bither, "An Investigation of Utility-Directed Cutoff Selection," *Journal of Consumer Research,* Vol. 14 (September 1987), pp. 240–256; and Ann McGill and Punam Anand, "Processing by Attribute Versus Brand: The Mediating Role of Imagery," *Advances in Consumer Research,* Vol. 15 (1988), p. 184 ff.

6. J. E. Russo, "Eye Fixations Can Save the World: A Critical Evaluation and a Comparison Between Eye Fixations and Other Information," *Advances in Consumer Research,* Vol. 5 (1978), pp. 561–570; Raymond J. Smead, James B. Wilcox, and Robert E. Wilkes, "An Illustration and Evaluation of a Joint Process Tracing Methodology: Eye Movement and Protocols," *Advances in Consumer Research,* Vol. 7 (1980), pp. 507–512.

7. Gabriel Biehal and Dipankar Chakravarti, "Consumers' Use of Memory and External Information in Choice: Macro and Micro Perspectives," *Journal of Consumer Research,* Vol. 13 (March 1986), pp. 382–405. Several other papers in a series by the same authors are also of interest, see "Information Presentation Format and Learning Goals as Determinants of Consumers' Memory Retrieval and Choice Processes," *Journal of Consumer Research,* Vol. 9 (March 1982), pp. 431–441; and "Information Accessibility as a Moderator of Consumer Choice," *Journal of Consumer Research,* Vol. 10 (June 1983), pp. 1–14. See also John G. Lynch, Jr., and Thomas K. Srull, "Memory and Attentional Factors in Consumer Choice: Concepts and Research Methods," *Journal of Consumer Research,* Vol. 9 (June 1982), pp. 18–37.

8. We should note that consumers may well employ different rules when *evaluating* products and brands (that is, making judgments about them) than when *deciding* which particular brands to buy. For example, it is easy to like several brands, but it is difficult to buy all the brands we like at one time. The rules we use to judge liking can thus easily be different from the rules we might use when faced with an actual decision. For further discussion of these rules and their settings, see Peter L. Wright, "Consumer Judgment Strategies: Beyond the Compensatory Assumption," in M. Venkatesan (ed.), *Proceedings of the Third Annual Conference* (Chicago: Association for Consumer Research, 1972), pp. 316–324; and Hillel J. Einhorn, "Use of Nonlinear, Noncompensatory Models in Decision Making," *Psychological Bulletin,* Vol. 73 (1970), pp. 221–230. For related discussions, see also David E. Kanouse, "Explaining Negativity Biases in Evaluation and Choice Behavior: Theory and Research," *Advances in Consumer Research,* Vol. 11 (1984), pp. 703–708; Michael D. Johnson "Consumer Choice Strategies for Comparing Noncomparable Alternatives," *Journal of Consumer Research,* Vol. 11 (December 1984), pp. 741–753; Chezy Ofir and John G. Lynch, Jr., "Context Effects on Judgment Under Uncertainty," *Journal of Consumer Research,* Vol. 11 (September 1984), pp. 668–679; Eric J. Johnson and Robert J. Meyer, "Compensatory Choice Models of Noncompensatory Processes: The Effect of Varying Context," *Journal of Consumer Research,* Vol. 11 (June 1984), pp. 528–541. For recent insights and findings, see also Jordan J. Louviere, Herb Schroeder, Cathy H. Louviere, and George G. Woodworth, "Do the Parameters of Choice Models Depend on Differences in Stimulus Presentation: Visual Versus Verbal Presentation," *Advances in Consumer Research,* Vol. 14 (1987), pp. 79–82; T. C. Srinivasan, "An Integrative Approach to Consumer Choice," *Advances in Consumer Research,* Vol. 14 (1987), pp. 96–100; Barbara Kahn, William L. Moore, and Rashi Glazer, "Experiments in Constrained

Choice," *Journal of Consumer Research*, Vol. 14 (June 1987), pp. 96–113; John C. Mowen, "Beyond Consumer Decision Making," *The Journal of Consumer Marketing*, Vol. 5 (Winter 1988), pp. 15–26; Wayne D. Hoyer and Cathy J. Cobb-Walgren, "Consumer Decision Making Across Product Categories: The Influence of Task Environment," *Psychology & Marketing*, Vol. 5 (Spring 1988), pp. 45–70; Steven P. Brown, "Moderators and Mediators: A Review of Concepts and Usage in Marketing Research," *AMA Educators Proceedings* (1989), pp. 170–175; and Elizabeth Cooper-Martin, "The Effect of Three Contingency Factors on Consumer Choice Strategies: A Test of Awareness of Cost and Benefit," *Advances in Consumer Research*, (1989), pp. 130–136.

9. If Sandy turns to her dictionary she'll easily be able to see the answer, since the term *lexicography* refers to the principles used in making a dictionary. If we consider these principles briefly, we can recognize the basic rule used to "order" the alternative words in the dictionary—the first letter is most important, followed by the second, the third, and so forth. Thus, in making a dictionary, Sandy would first consider all possible words on the "most important attribute" (i.e., that the starting letter is an "A"). All words with other starting letters are dropped from consideration at this point. All those that have a starting "A" remain in the set. Sandy will then turn to her second most important attribute and continue with her choice process to pick the word that will have the honor of starting out her dictionary of the English language! After choosing this word, she'll then begin a new choice process to discover the second word in her listing, and will again employ the "lexicographic" choice rule. By the way, what's your guess on the first and second words she'll discover? (As an aside, Sandy bought a Comfort Case.)

10. John G. Lynch, Jr., "Adventures in Paramorphic Modeling: Models of Consumers' Processing of Negative Information," Working Paper, Center for Consumer Research, University of Florida, Gainesville, 1984. (The other consumers' purchases: Paul bought a Beauty Brief, Ed bought an Air Attache.)

11. These are also termed "phased strategies." See Amos Tversky, "Elimination by Aspects: A Theory of Choice," *Psychological Review*, Vol. 79 (1972), pp. 281–299; Peter Wright and Fredric Barbour, "The Relevance of Decision Process Models in Structuring Persuasive Messages," *Communication Research*, Vol. 2 (July 1975), pp. 246–259; Denis A. Lussier and Richard W. Olshavsky, "Task Complexity and Contingent Processing in Brand Choice," *Journal of Consumer Research*, Vol. 6 (1979), pp. 154–165; and Eric J. Johnson, Robert J. Meyer, and Sanjoy Ghose, "When Choice Models Fail: Compensatory Models in Negatively Correlated Environments," *Journal of Marketing Research*, Vol. 26 (August 1989), pp. 255–270.

12. Alain d'Astous and Dominique Rouzies, "Selection and Implementation of Processing Strategies . . . ," *International Journal of Marketing*, Vol. 4 (1987), pp. 99–110; Biehal and Chakravarti, "Consumers' Use of Memory . . . " (note 7); James R. Bettman and Michael A. Zins, "Constructive Processes in Consumer Choice," *Journal of Consumer Research*, Vol. 4 (1977), pp. 75–85; David M. Sanbonmatsu, Frank R. Kardes, and Bryan D. Gibson, "The Impact of Initial Processing Goals on Memory-Based Brand Comparisons," *Advances in Consumer Research*, Vol. 16 (1989), pp. 429–432; and Noreen M. Klein and Manjit S. Yadiv, "Context Effects on Effort and Accuracy in Choice: An Inquiry into Adaptive Decision Making," *Journal of Consumer Research*, Vol. 15 (March 1989), pp. 411–421.

13. Peter L. Wright, "Consumer Choice Strategies: Simplifying Versus Optimizing," *Journal of Marketing Research*, Vol. 11 (1975), pp. 60–67. See also John G. Lynch, Jr., Howard Marmorstein, and Michael F. Weigold, "Choices from Sets Including Remembered Brands: Use of Recalled Attributes and Prior Overall Evaluations," *Journal of Consumer Research*, Vol. 15 (September 1988), pp. 169–184, and Joan Meyers-Levy and Alice M. Tybout, "Schema Congruity as a Basis for Product Evaluation," *Journal of Consumer Research*, Vol. 15 (March 1989), pp. 39–54.

14. Merrie Brucks, "The Effects of Product Class Knowledge on Information Search Behavior," *Journal of Consumer Research*, Vol. 12 (June 1985), pp. 1–16. For related issues, see also Richard W. Olshavsky and Franklin Acito, "The Impact of Data Collection Procedure on Choice Rule," *Advances in Consumer Research*, Vol. 7 (1980), pp. 729–732; Amardeep Assar and Dipankar Chakravarti, "Attribute Range Knowledge: Effects on Consumers' Evaluation of Brand-Attribute Information and Search Patterns in Choice," *AMA Educators' Proceedings*, 1984, pp. 62–67; Itamar Simonson, Joel Huber, and John Payne, "The Relationship Between Prior Brand Knowledge and Information Acquisition Order," *Journal of Consumer Research*, Vol. 14 (March 1988), pp. 566–578; and Merrie Brucks, "Search Monitor: An Approach for Computer-Controlled Experiments Involving Consumer Information Search," *Journal of Consumer Research*, Vol. 15 (June 1988), pp. 117–121.

15. Mita Sujan, "Consumer Knowledge: Effects on Evaluation Strategies Mediating Consumer Judgments," *Journal of Consumer Research*, Vol. 12 (June 1985), pp. 31–46. For related discussions,

see also Lawrence J. Marks, Michael A. Kamins, and Donna Murphy, "The Effects of Level of Expertise on the Processing of Framed and Unframed Pictorial Print Advertisements," *AMA Educators Proceedings* (1986), pp. 57–61; Frank R. Kardes, "Effects of Initial Product Judgments on Subsequent Memory-Based Judgments," *Journal of Consumer Research*, Vol. 13 (June 1986), pp. 1–11; and James R. Bettman and Mita Sujan, "Effects of Framing on Evaluation of Comparable and Noncomparable Alternatives by Expert and Novice Consumers," *Journal of Consumer Research*, Vol. 14 (September 1987), pp. 141–154.

16. Philip M. Boffey, "Subtle Factors Influence Simplest Choices of Our Lives," *The New York Times* News Service, December 20, 1983, and Amos Tversky and Daniel Kahneman, "The Framing of Decisions and the Psychology of Choice," *Science* (1981), pp. 453–458. For further in-depth discussions, see Daniel Kahneman and Amos Tversky, "Prospect Theory: An Analysis of Decision Under Risk," *Econometrica*, Vol. 47 (March 1979), pp. 263–291; and Daniel Kahneman and Amos Tversky, "Choices, Values, and Frames," *American Psychologist*, Vol. 39 (April 1984), pp. 341–350.

17. Readings might best begin with the *Science* article in note 16. For extensions, see Richard Thaler, "Mental Accounting and Consumer Choice," *Marketing Science*, Vol. 4 (Summer 1985), pp. 199–214; Irwin P. Levin, Richard D. Johnson, Craig P. Russo, and Patricia J. Deldin, "Framing Effects in Judgment Tasks with Varying Amount of Information," *Organizational Behavior and Human Decision Processes*, Vol. 36 (December 1985), pp. 366–377; the following articles in *Advances in Consumer Research*, Vol. 14 (1987): Kent B. Monroe, "The Framing of Consumer Choices," p. 182, Noreen M. Klein and Janet E. Oglethorpe, "Cognitive Reference Points in Consumer Decision Making," pp. 183–187, Debra Rowe and Christopher P. Puto, "Do Consumers' Reference Points Affect Their Buying Decisions," pp. 188–192, Kent B. Monroe and Joseph D. Chapman, "Framing Effects on Buyers' Subjective Product Evaluations," pp. 193–197, and James W. Gentry, Joshua L. Wiener and Melissa Burnett, "The Story, the Frame, and the Choice," pp. 198–202. See also Christopher P. Puto, "The Framing of Buying Decisions," *Journal of Consumer Research*, Vol. 14 (December 1987), pp. 301–315; William D. Diamond, "The Effect of Probability and Consequence Levels on the Focus of Consumer Judgments in Risky Situations," *Journal of Consumer Research*, Vol. 15 (September 1988), pp. 280–283; Irwin P. Levin and Gary J. Gaeth, "How Consumers Are Affected by the Framing of Attribute Information Before and After Consuming the Product," *Journal of Consumer Research*, Vol. 15 (December 1988), pp. 374–378; articles in *Advances in Consumer Research*, Vol. 16 (1989): Joel E. Urbany, Joan T. Schmit, and Danny D. Butler, "Insurance Decisions (or the Lack Thereof) for Low Probability Events," pp. 535–541, and Amna Kirmani and Peter Wright, "Message and Cuing Effects on Decision Framing," pp. 173–175; Scot Burton and Laure A. Babin, "Decision-Framing Helps Make the Sale," *The Journal of Consumer Marketing*, Vol. 6 (Spring 1989), pp. 15–24; Stephen J. Hoch and John Deighton, "Managing What Consumers Learn from Experience," *Journal of Marketing*, Vol. 53 (April 1989), pp. 1–20; and Itamar Simonson, "Choice Based on Reasons: The Case of Attraction and Compromise Effects," *Journal of Consumer Research*, Vol. 16 (September 1989), pp. 158–174.

18. Prakash Nedungadi, "Recall and Consumer Consideration Sets: Influencing Choice Without Altering Brand Preference," Working Paper, University of Toronto, 1989. See also articles in *Advances in Consumer Research*, Vol. 16 (1989): John Roberts, "A Grounded Model of Consideration Set Size and Composition," pp. 749–757, Girish Punj and Narasimhan Srinivasan, "Influence of Expertise and Purchase Experience on the Formation of Evoked Sets," pp. 507–514, Thomas S. Gruca, "Determinants of Choice Set Size: An Alternative Method for Measuring Evoked Sets," pp. 515–521, Frank R. Kardes, Paul M. Herr, and Deborah Marlino, "Some Light on Substitution and Attraction Effects," pp. 203–208, and C. Whan Park, Robert Lawson, and Sandra Milberg, "Memory Structure for Brand Names," pp. 726–731.

19. Wilkie and Dickson, "Consumer Information Search and Shopping Behavior," Working Paper, University of Florida, Gainesville, 1985.

20. K. W. Kendall and Ian Fenwick, "What Do You Learn Standing in a Supermarket Aisle?" *Advances in Consumer Research*, Vol. 6 (1979), pp. 153–160.

21. Wayne D. Hoyer, "An Examination of Consumer Decision Making for a Common Repeat Purchase Product," *Journal of Consumer Research*, Vol. 11 (December 1984), pp. 822–829.

22. See, for example, Alain D'Astous, Idriss Bensouda, and Jean Guindon, "A Re-Examination of Consumer Decision Making for a Repeat Purchase Product: Variations in Product Importance and Purchase Frequency," *Advances in Consumer Research*, Vol. 16 (1989), pp. 433–438; Cathy J. Cobb and Wayne D. Hoyer, "Direct Observation of Search Behavior . . . ," *Psychology & Marketing*, Vol. 2 (Fall 1985), pp. 161–179; Patricia M. Anderson, "Personality, Perception, and Emotional-State Factors in Approach-Avoidance Behavior in the Store Environment," *AMA Ed-*

ucators Proceedings (1986), pp. 35–39; Adam Finn, "A Consumer Acceptance of Unobstrusive Observation in a Shopping Center," *AMA Educators Proceedings* (1989), pp. 176–181; Laurette Dube-Rioux, Bernd H. Schmitt, and France Leclerc, "Consumers' Reactions to Waiting: When Delays Affect the Perception of Service Quality," *Advances in Consumer Research*, Vol. 16 (1989), pp. 59–63; Cathy Goodwin and Charles D. Frame, "Social Distance Within the Service Encounter: Does the Consumer Want to Be Your Friend?" *Advances in Consumer Research*, Vol. 16 (1989), pp. 64–71; and C. Whan Park, Easwar S. Iyer, and Daniel C. Smith, "The Effects of Situational Factors on In-Store Grocery Shopping Behavior: The Role of Store Environment and Time Available for Shopping," *Journal of Consumer Research*, Vol. 15 (March 1989), pp. 422–433.

23. Laurie Petersen, "Study Confirms Impulse Buying on Rise," *Promote*, October 12, 1987, pp. 6–10.

24. Michel Chevalier, "Increase in Sales due to In-Store Display," *Journal of Marketing Research*, Vol. 12 (November 1975), pp. 426–431.

25. "Is Type Size Key Factor in Ads?" *Chain Store Age Executive*, February 1977, p. 12. For further review of this area, together with more sophisticated analyses, see J. B. Wilkinson, J. Barry Mason, and Christie H. Paksoy, "Assessing the Impact of Short-Term Supermarket Strategy Variables," *Journal of Marketing Research*, Vol. 9 (February 1982), pp. 72–86. See also P. S. Raju and Manoj Hastak, "Consumer Response to Deals: A Discussion of Theoretical Perspectives," *Advances in Consumer Research*, Vol. 7 (1980), pp. 296–301; Meryl P. Gardner and Roger A. Strang, "Consumer Response to Promotions: Some New Perspectives," *Advances in Consumer Research*, Vol. 11 (1984), pp. 420–425; Moshe Handelsman and J. Michael Munson, "On Integrating Consumer Needs for Variety with Retailer Assortment Decisions," in E. C. Hirschman and M. B. Holbrook (eds.), *Advances in Consumer Research*, Vol. 12 (1985), pp. 108–112; Bruce E. Mattson and Alan J. Dubinsky, "Shopping Patterns: An Exploration of Some Situational Determinants," *Psychology & Marketing*, Vol. 4 (Spring 1987), pp. 47–62; Catherine Cole and Goutam Chakraborty, "Laboratory Studies of Coupon Redemption Rates and Repeat Purchase Rates," *AMA Educators Proceedings* (1987), pp. 51–54; Timothy W. Sweeney and William J. Sauer, "Patronage Behavior: An Empirical Study of the Shopping Preference Subsystem," *AMA Educators Proceedings* (1988), p. 75; Robert Mittelstaedt and Robert Stassen, "The Role of Retail Assortments in Shopping Effectiveness and Efficiency," *AMA Educators Proceedings* (1988), p. 76; Sunil Gupta, "Impact of Sales Promotions on When, What, and How Much to Buy," *Journal of Marketing Research*, Vol. 25 (November 1988), pp. 342–355; Dhruv Grewal, "The Effects of Contextual Information Cues on Buyers' Product Evaluations and Behavioral Intentions," *AMA Educators Proceedings* (1989), p. 274; Jerry N. Conover, "The Influence of Cents-Off Coupons on Brand Choice Decisions at the Point of Purchase," *Advances in Consumer Research*, Vol. 16 (1989), pp. 443–446; and Kapil Bawa and Robert W. Shoemaker, "Analyzing Incremental Sales from a Direct Mail Coupon Promotion," *Journal of Marketing*, Vol. 53 (July 1989), pp. 66–78.

26. Judann Dagnoli, "Impulse Governs Shoppers," *Advertising Age*, October 5, 1987, p. 93.

27. "Ideas From POPAI's Marketplace '87," *Promote*, December 14, 1987, p. 12.

28. Laurie Freeman and Judann Dagnoli, "Point-of-Purchase Rush Is On," *Advertising Age*, February 8, 1988, p. 47.

29. Jim Connolly, "POP Radio: It's Music to the Ears . . . ," *Marketing Week*, May 2, 1988, p. 17.

30. Lori Kesler, "Catalina Cuts Couponing Clutter," *Advertising Age*, May 9, 1988, p. 5–30, and David Kiley, "Sales Promotion in a Flash," *Marketing Week*, December 21, 1987, p. 1.

31. "VideOCart Shopping Cart with Computer Screen Creates New Ad Medium . . . ," *Marketing News*, May 9, 1988, p. 1.

32. See Dudley M. Ruch, "Effective Sales Promotion Lessons for Today . . ." Marketing Science Institute Report 87-108, 1987; Robert C. Blattberg and Kenneth J. Wisniewski, "How Retail Price Promotions Work," Working Paper, University of Chicago, December 1987.

33. Peter R. Dickson and Alan C. Sawyer, "The Point of Purchase Behavior and Price Perceptions of Supermarket Shoppers," Working Paper, Ohio State University, Columbus, 1985. See also Valarie A. Zeithaml, "Consumer Response to In-Store Price Information Environments," *Journal of Consumer Research*, Vol. 8 (March 1982), pp. 357–369; Rosemary Walker and Brenda Cude, "In-Store Shopping Strategies: Time and Money Costs in the Supermarket," *Journal of Consumer Affairs*, Vol. 17 (Winter 1983), pp. 356–369; Olli T. Ahtola, "Price as a 'Give' Component in an Exchange Theoretic Multicomponent Model," *Advances in Consumer Research*, Vol. 11 (1984), pp. 623–626; Peter R. Dickson and Alan G. Sawyer, "Entry/Exit Demand Analysis," *Advances in Consumer Research*, Vol. 11 (1984), pp. 617–622; Easwar S. Iyer and Sucheta S. Ahlawat, "Deviations from a Shopping Plan: When and Why Do Consumers Not Buy Items as Planned,"

Advances in Consumer Research, Vol. 14 (1987), pp. 246–250; and Jerry N. Conover, "Shoppers Recall of Grocery Product Prices," *AMA Educators' Proceedings* (1988), pp. 62–67.

Chapter 20 Consumer Decision Processes (III): Postpurchase Decisions

1. Patrick E. Murphy, "Measuring Consumer Perceptions of the Dimensions of Price," Working Paper, University of Notre Dame, Notre Dame, Ind., 1989.

2. This section is adapted from material presented in Philip E. Hendrix, "Product/Service Consumption: Key Dimensions and Implications for Marketing," Working Paper, Emory University, Atlanta, Ga., August 1984.

3. Jacob Jacoby, Carol Berning, and Thomas Dietvorst, "What About Disposition?" *Journal of Marketing,* Vol. 41 (April 1977), pp. 22–28. For other readings in this area, see also James W. Hanson, "A Proposed Paradigm for Consumer Product Disposition Processes," *Journal of Consumer Affairs* (Summer 1980), pp. 49–67.

4. Eugene Carlson, "Florida Readies Broad Assault on Garbage," *The Wall Street Journal,* July 20, 1988, p. 23.

   Consumer researchers have been interested in issues of "socially conscious consumption" for many years. See, for example, M. Joseph Sirgy, A. C. Samli, and H. Lee Meadow, "The Interface Between Quality of Life and Marketing: A Theoretical Framework," *Journal of Public Policy & Marketing,* Vol. 1, no. 1 (1982), pp. 69–84.

5. Leon Festinger, *A Theory of Cognitive Dissonance* (Stanford, Calif.: Stanford University Press, 1957). See also A. G. Greenwald and D. L. Ronis, "Twenty Years of Cognitive Dissonance: Case Study of the Evolution of a Theory," *Psychological Review,* Vol. 85 (1978), pp. 53–57, and J. Beauvois and R. Joule, "Dissonance Versus Self-Perception Theories: A Radical Conception of Festingers's Theory," *Journal of Social Psychology,* Vol. 117 (1982), pp. 99–113.

6. Readers interested in the controversies should be aware of three key points: (1) In technical terms, dissonance theory is not highly specific. (2) It is difficult to create research conditions to allow clear tests of whether or not dissonance is the only concept that is operating in a study. (3) Finally, everyone recognizes that many factors beyond dissonance will affect a consumer's behavior in the real world. For example, if Kevin Baker's new Camaro won't start easily, the fact that he's motivated to want to like the car probably won't stand up against his knowledge that he's being stranded on a regular basis! In addition to the readings in note 5, there is an interesting literature in marketing. See Joel B. Cohen and Danny L. Moore, "Postdecision Consistency Enhancing Processes," University of Florida, Gainesville, Center for Consumer Research Paper, 1988, for an overview. See also William H. Cummings and M. Venkatesan, "Cognitive Dissonance and Consumer Behavior: A Review of the Evidence," *Journal of Marketing Research,* Vol. 13 (August 1976), pp. 303–308; and Valerie S. Folkes and Barbara Kotsos, "Buyers' and Sellers' Explanation for Product Failure: Who Done It?" *Journal of Marketing,* Vol. 50 (April 1986), pp. 74–80.

7. A useful overview of this field is available in E. Scott Maynes et al. (eds.), *Research in the Consumer Interest: The Frontier* (Columbia, Mo.: American Council on Consumer Interests, 1988). In this volume see especially H. Keith Hunt, "Consumer Satisfaction/Dissatisfaction and the Consumer Interest," Robert A. Westbrook, "Consumer Satisfaction: An Affirmation of Possibilities," and Folke Olander, "Consumer Satisfaction/Dissatisfaction and the Consumer Interest."

   This area has received so much attention recently that a new journal has been started: the *Journal of Consumer Satisfaction, Dissatisfaction, and Complaining Behavior.* If you or your librarian wishes to subscribe to this journal, contact H. Keith Hunt, Graduate School of Management, 632 TNRB, Brigham Young University, Provo, Utah 84602 (telephone 801/378-2080).

8. This section is based on discussions by Richard L. Oliver, "A Cognitive Model of the Antecedents and Consequences of Satisfaction Decisions," *Journal of Marketing Research,* Vol. 17 (November 1980), pp. 460–469, H. Keith Hunt, "CS/D: Overview and Future Research Directions," in H. K. Hunt (ed.), *Conceptualization and Measurement of Consumer Satisfaction and Dissatisfaction* (Cambridge, Mass.: Marketing Science Institute, 1977); and the following articles in Ralph L. Day and H. Keith Hunt (eds.), *International Fair in Consumer Satisfaction and Complaining Behavior* (Bloomington: Indiana University Division of Research, 1983): Robert A. Westbrook, "Consumer Satisfaction and the Phenomenology of Emotions During Automobile Ownership Experiences," pp. 2–9, Ralph L. Day, "The Next Step: Commonly Accepted Constructions for Satisfaction Research, pp. 113–117, Robert B. Woodruff, Ernest R. Cadotte, and Roger L. Jenkins, "Charting a Path for CS/D Research," pp. 118–123, John E. Swan, "Consumer Satisfaction Re-

search and Theory: Current Status and Future Directions," pp. 124–129, and H. Keith Hunt, "A '10' Based on Expectations, but Normatively a '3,6371'," pp. 130–131.

For additional recent perspectives on the nature of CS/D, see, for example, *Advances in Consumer Research,* Vol. 11 (1984): Ellen M. Moore and F. Kelley Shuptrine, "Disconfirmation Effects on Consumer Satisfaction and Decision Making Processes," pp. 299–304; and Ivan Ross and Richard L. Oliver, "The Accuracy of Unsolicited Consumer Communications as Indicators of 'True' Consumer Satisfaction/Dissatisfaction," pp. 504–508; Ved Prakash and John W. Lounsbury, "The Role of Expectations in the Determination of Consumer Satisfaction," *Journal of the Academy of Marketing Science,* Vol. 12 (Summer 1984), p. 1–17; Ved Prakash, "Validity and Reliability of the Confirmation of Expectations Paradigm as a Determinant of Consumer Satisfaction," *Journal of the Academy of Marketing Science,* Vol. 12 (Fall 1984), pp. 63–67; Richard L. Oliver and William O. Bearden, "Disconfirmation Processes and Consumer Evaluations in Product Usage," *Journal of Business Research,* Vol. 13 (June 1985), pp. 235–246; James H. Leigh, "An Examination of the Dimensionality of Satisfaction with Housing," *Psychology & Marketing,* Vol. 4 (Winter 1987), pp. 399 ff.; Robert A. Westbrook, "Product/Consumption-Based Affective Responses and Postpurchase Processes," *Journal of Marketing Research,* Vol. 24 (August 1987), pp. 258–270; Ernest R. Cadotte, Robert B. Woodruff and Roger L. Jenkins, "Expectations and Norms in Models of Consumer Satisfaction," *Journal of Marketing Research,* Vol. 24 (August 1987), pp. 305–314; Richard L. Oliver and Wayne S. DeSarbo, "Response Determinants in Satisfaction Judgments," *Journal of Consumer Research,* Vol. 14 (March 1988), pp. 495–507; David K. Tse and Peter C. Wilton, "Models of Consumer Satisfaction Formation: An Extension," *Journal of Marketing Research,* Vol. 24 (May 1988), p. 204–212; Claire P. Bolfing and Robert B. Woodruff, "An Examination of Involvement Effects on the Disconfirmation Paradigm," *AMA Educators Proceedings* (1988), pp. 128–133; Joseph A. Cote, Ellen R. Foxman, and Bob D. Cutler, "Selecting an Appropriate Standard of Comparison for Post-Purchase Evaluation Process," *Advances in Consumer Research,* Vol. 16 (1989), pp. 502–506; Diane M. Halstead, "Cognitive and Affective Determinants of Consumer Satisfaction for a Durable Good," *AMA Educators Proceedings* (1989), pp. 285–289; and Richard L. Oliver and John E. Swan, "Consumer Perceptions of Interpersonal Equity and Satisfaction in Transactions: A Field of Survey Approach," *Journal of Marketing,* Vol. 53 (April 1989), pp. 21–35.

For an interesting related perspective on the personal characteristics dimension, see Alan R. Andreasen, "Life Status Changes and Changes in Consumer Preferences and Satisfaction," *Journal of Consumer Research,* Vol. 11 (December 1984), pp. 784–794.

For the Sears results, see Donald A. Hughes, "Considerations in the Measurement and Use of Consumer Satisfaction Ratings," in William Locander (ed.), *Marketing Looks Outward* (Chicago: American Marketing Association, 1977).

9. Joel Newman, "J.D. Power Play: It's the Auto-Marketing Authority," *Marketing Week,* February 8, 1988, p. 21.

10. Marc A. Grainer, Kathleen A. McEvoy, and Donald King, "Consumer Problems and Complaints: A National View," *Advances in Consumer Research,* Vol. 6 (1979), p. 496.

11. Alan R. Andreasen and Arthur Best, "Consumers Complain—Does Business Respond?" *Harvard Business Review* (July–August 1977), pp. 94–104.

12. E. Laird Landon, "A Model for Consumer Complaint Behavior," in R. Day (ed.), *Consumer Satisfaction, Dissatisfaction, and Complaining Behavior* (Bloomington: School of Business, Indiana University, 1977). For an excellent recent discussion on consumer complaining, see Alan R. Andreasen, "Consumer Complaints and Redress: What We Know and What We Don't Know," in E. Scott Maynes (ed.), *The Frontier of Research in the Consumer Interest.* (Columbia, Mo.: American Council on Consumer Interests, 1988), pp. 675–722. In this same volume see also W. Keith Bryant, "Consumer Complaints and Redress: Some Directions for Future Research," pp. 723–726, and Robert O. Herrmann, "Consumer Complaints and Redress . . . ," pp. 727–730. See also Claes Fornell and Robert A. Westbrook, "The Vicious Circle of Consumer Complaints," *Journal of Marketing,* Vol. 48 (Summer 1984), pp. 68–78; Richard L. Oliver, "An Investigation of the Interrelationship Between Consumer (Dis)Satisfaction and Complaint Reports," *Advances in Consumer Research,* Vol. 14 (1987), pp. 218–222; Jagdip Singh, "Consumer Complaint Intentions and Behavior: Definitional and Taxonomical Issues," *Journal of Marketing,* Vol. 52 (January 1988), pp. 93–107; and Cathy Goodwin and Susan Spiggle, "Consumer Complaining: Attributions and Identities," *Advances in Consumer Research,* Vol. 16 (1989), pp. 17–22.

13. John A. Czepiel, "Managing Customer Satisfaction in Consumer Service Businesses," Working Paper, Marketing Science Institute, September 1980.

14. J. A. Presbo, "At Procter & Gamble, Success Is Largely due to Heeding the Consumer," *The Wall Street Journal*, April 29, 1980, p. 23, and P. A. Engelmayer, "Before You Discard That Soda Can, You Might Look for This Machine," *The Wall Street Journal*, September 7, 1983, p. 33.

15. "Detroit's Tonic for Lemon Buyers," *Business Week*, April 4, 1983, pp. 54–55.

16. "Coke Drinkers Talk a Lot . . . ," *The Wall Street Journal*, October 22, 1981, p. 29. See also Steven P. Brown and Richard F. Beltramini, "Consumer Complaining and Word of Mouth Activities: Field Evidence," *Advances in Consumer Research*, Vol. 16 (1989), pp. 9–16.

17. "Carmakers Are Driving the Risk Out of Buying," *Business Week*, October 24, 1988, p. 31.

18. "Domino's Great Delivery Deal . . . ," *Adweek*, August 3, 1987, p. 35.

19. Interview with Tom Peters on "Business Times Management Report," November 1984.

20. Prestbo, "At Procter & Gamble."

21. Patricia Sellers, "How to Handle Customers' Gripes," *Fortune*, October 24, 1988, pp. 89 ff.; and Eileen Norris, "Applying Know-How to Appliances," *Advertising Age*, August 30, 1984, p. 19.

22. Doug Carroll, "Gripe with Oldsmobile Could Lead to Rebate," *USA Today,* July 12, 1988, p. 28.

23. Czepiel, "Managing Customer Satisfaction."

24. Alan J. Resnik and Robert R. Harmon, "Consumer Complaints and Managerial Response: A Holistic Approach," *Journal of Marketing*, Vol. 47 (Winter 1983), pp. 86–97. For further discussion of useful actions in this area, see also F. Robert Dwyer and Ronald J. Dornoff, "The Congruency of Manufacturer Redress Actions and Consumer Redress Norms and Expectations," in K. Bernhardt et al. (eds.), *The Changing Marketing Environment: New Theories and Applications* (Chicago: American Marketing Association, 1981), pp. 162–165; Joseph G. Smith, "Consumer Affairs: Opportunity Unexploited," *Journal of Consumer Marketing*, Vol. 2 (Spring 1985), pp. 67–72; Mary C. Gilly and Richard W. Hansen, "Consumer Complaint Handling as a Strategic Marketing Tool," *Journal of Consumer Marketing*, Vol. 2 (Fall 1985), pp. 5–16; Harrie Vredenburg and Chow-Hou Wee, "The Role of Consumer Service in Determining Customer Satisfaction," *Journal of the Academy of Marketing Science*, Vol. 14 (Summer 1986), pp. 17–26; Michelle Morganosky and Hilda M. Buckley, "Complaint Behavior: Analysis by Demographic Lifestyle and Consumer Values," *Advances in Consumer Research*, Vol. 14 (1987), pp. 223–226; Cathy J. Cobb, Gary C. Walgren, and Mary Hollowed, "Differences in Organizational Responses to Consumer Letters of Satisfaction and Dissatisfaction," *Advances in Consumer Research*, Vol. 14 (1987), pp. 227–231; Claes Fornell and Birger Wernerfelt, "Defensive Marketing Strategy by Customer Complaint Management: A Theoretical Analysis," *Journal of Marketing Research*, Vol. 24 (August 1987), pp. 337–346; Denise Smart and Charles Martin, "Consumer Correspondence: Are Companies Responding Like They Say They Are?" *AMA Educators Proceedings* (1988), pp. 206–212; Nessim Hanna and John S. Wagle, "Who Is Your Satisfied Customer?" *The Journal of Consumer Marketing*, Vol. 6 (Winter 1989), pp. 53–62; Gary Clarke and Peter F. Kaminski, "Consumer Complaints: Advice on How Companies Should Respond Based on an Empirical Study," *1989 AMA Educators Proceedings* (1989), p. 159; and Cathy Goodwin, Kelly Smith, and Ivan Ross, "Responses to Consumer Service Complaints: A Procedural Fairness Approach," *AMA Educators Proceedings* (1989), pp. 313–319.

For discussions of the related topic of warranties, see, for example, Joshua Lyle Wiener, "Are Warranties Accurate Signals of Product Reliability?" *Journal of Consumer Research*, Vol. 12 (September 1985), pp. 245 ff.; Ellen Day and Richard J. Fox, "Extended Warranties, Service Contracts, and Maintenance Agreements—A Marketing Opportunity?" *Journal of Consumer Marketing*, Vol. 2 (Fall 1985), pp. 77–90; John W. Vann, "A Conditional Probability View of the Role of Product Warranties in Reducing Perceived Financial Risk," *Advances in Consumer Research*, Vol. 14 (1987), pp. 421–425; and Craig A. Kelley, Jeffrey S. Conant, and Jacqueline J. Brown, "Extended Warranties: Retail Management and Public Policy Implications," *AMA Educators Proceedings* (1988), pp. 261–265.

25. Czepiel, "Managing Customer Satisfaction." For additional perspectives and findings in the area of consumer services, see, for example, Alan R. Andreasen, "Consumer Satisfaction in Loose Monopolies: The Case of Medical Care," *Journal of Public Policy & Marketing*, Vol. 2, no. 1 (1983), pp. 122–135; William O. Bearden, "Profiling Consumers Who Register Complaints Against Auto Repair Services," *Journal of Consumer Affairs*, Vol. 17, no. 2 (Winter 1983), pp. 315–335; Stephen W. Brown and Teresa A. Swartz, "Consumer Medical Complaint Behavior: Determinants of and Alternatives to Malpractice Litigation," *Journal of Public Policy & Marketing*, Vol. 3, no. 1 (1984), pp. 85–98; and Valarie A. Zeithaml, Leonard L. Berry, and A. Parasuraman, "Communication and Control Processes in the Delivery of Service Quality," Working Paper, Marketing Science Institute, Cambridge, Mass., 1987. See also Betsy Gelb, "How Marketers of Intangibles Can Raise

the Odds for Consumer Satisfaction," *Journal of Consumer Marketing,* Vol. 2 (Spring 1985), pp. 55–62; three papers in *Advances in Consumer Research,* Vol. 16 (1989): Jagdip Singh, "The Patient Satisfaction Concept: A Review and Reconceptualization," pp. 176–179, Aida N. Rizkalla, "Sense of Time Urgency and Consumer Well-being: Testing Alternative Causal Models," pp. 180–188, and Keith Neergaard and Alladi Venkatesh, "An Holistic Approach to Household Management of Well-being: A Thick Description," pp. 189–194; and Stephen W. Brown and Teresa A. Swartz, "A Gap Analysis of Professional Service Quality," *Journal of Marketing,* Vol. 53 (April 1989), pp. 92–98.

26. Lawrence Kanter et al., *Briefing Book for Policy Review Session* (Washington, D.C.: Federal Trade Commission, April 1980). Examples that extend beyond the Federal Trade Commission were not drawn from this source.

27. Walter Guzzardi, "The Mindless Pursuit of Safety," *Fortune,* April 9, 1979, pp. 54–64.

28. The first two cases were decided in favor of the injured consumers. (1) In the candle case Fabergé argued that it should not be expected to "foresee" that someone might attempt to pour perfume into a flame and thus should not be liable. On the other hand, the court ruled that the flammability was a significant concern for this type of product and that consumers should be warned about this potential hazard. The injured student was awarded $27,000. (2) In the football case the jury agreed with the player and awarded a $5 million judgment against the helmet maker. (3) In the killing case, the jury ordered the magazine to pay Mrs. Black's family $9.4 million because it neglected to check on the meaning of the ad! See "An Impossible Liability Standard," *Advertising Age,* March 14, 1988; and "The Devils in the Product Liability Laws," *Business Week,* February 12, 1979, pp. 72–79.

29. This typology and the ensuing discussion on strict liability follows that given by Louis W. Stern and Thomas L. Eovaldi, *Legal Aspects of Marketing Strategy* (Englewood Cliffs, N.J.: Prentice Hall, 1984), pp. 89–99.

30 "The Mindless Pursuit of Safety."

31. The legal issues in product liability are continuing to evolve as further court decisions are made. See, for example, Phillip E. Downs and Douglas N. Behrman, "The Products Liability Coordinator: A Partial Solution," *Journal of the Academy of Marketing Science,* Vol. 14 (Fall 1986), pp. 58 ff., and Fred W. Morgan, "Strict Liability and the Marketing of Services vs. Goods: A Judicial Review," in *Journal of Public Policy & Marketing,* Vol. 6 (1987), pp. 43–57.

Chapter 21 Public Policy Perspectives on Consumer Behavior

1. Vermont Royster, "Regulation Isn't A Dirty Word," *The Wall Street Journal,* September 9, 1987, p. 30.

2. This section's discussion of consumer rights is based upon David A. Aaker and George S. Day, "A Guide to Consumerism," in D. Aaker and G. Day (eds.), *Consumerism: Search for the Public Interest,* 4th ed. (New York: Free Press, 1982), pp. 2–20.

3. Hans B. Thorelli, "Consumer Information as Consumer Protection," in J. Cady (ed.), *Marketing and the Public Interest* (Cambridge, Mass.: Marketing Science Institute, 1978), pp. 269–290.

4. Warren G. Magnuson and Jean Carper, "Caveat Emptor," in Aaker and Day (eds.), *Consumerism: Search for the Consumer Interest,* pp. 267–278.

5. Doris Chandler, "Fraud by Mail Still Is Bilking Consumers," *Gainesville* (Florida) *Sun,* July 8, 1985, p. 1-c.

6. David Horowitz, "Dream-Away Diet Pills Banned," *Gainesville* (Florida) *Sun,* May 23, 1985, p. 10-c.

7. Nancy Giges, "Coupon Loss Put at $500,000,000," *Advertising Age,* February 13, 1984, p. 75. For additional discussions of consumer slippage topics, see Noel B. Zabriskie, "Fraud by Consumers," *Journal of Retailing,* Vol. 48 (Winter 1972–72), pp. 22–27; Marvin A. Jolson, "Consumers as Offenders," *Journal of Business Research,* Vol. 2 (January 1974), pp. 89–98; Robert E. Wilkes, "Fraudulent Consumer Behavior," *Journal of Marketing,* Vol. 42 (October 1978), pp. 67–75; Ronald W. Stampfl, "Multi-Disciplinary Foundations for a Consumer Code of Ethics," in Norleen M. Ackerman (ed.), *Proceedings, 25th Annual Conference of the American Council on Consumer Interests* (1979), pp. 12–20; John H. Antil, "Socially Responsible Consumers: Profile and Implications for Public Policy, *Journal of Macromarketing,* Vol. 4 (Fall 1984), pp. 18–39; Joseph H. Miller, Jr., and Michael C. Budden, "Biorhythm and Shoplifting: An Empirical Investigation," *AMA Educators Proceedings* (1985) pp. 56–58; M. Jeffrey Kallis, Kathleen A. Krentler, and Dinoo J. Vanier, "The Value of User Image in Quelling Aberrant Consumer Behavior," *Journal of the Academy of Marketing Science,* Vol. 14 (Spring 1986), pp. 29–35; George P. Moschis, Dena Saliagas Cox, and James J. Kellaris, "An Exploratory Study of Adolescent Shoplifting Behavior,"

Advances in Consumer Research, Vol. 14 (1987), pp. 526–530; and James A. Muncy and Scott Vitell, "Consumer Ethics: An Empirical Investigation," Working Paper, Clemson University, Clemson, S.C., 1989.

8. Consumer Product Safety Commission, *Annual Report* (Washington, D.C.: U.S. Government Printing Office, 1981), pp. 223–226.

9. See Helen B. Taussig, "The Thalidomide Syndrome," *Scientific American,* August 1962, pp. 29–35; "The Thalidomide Disaster," *Time,* August 10, 1962, p. 32; "Thalidomide Homocide," *Time,* November 16, 1962, p. 67; and Steven M. Spencer, "The Untold Story of the Thalidomide Babies," *Saturday Evening Post,* October 20, 1962, pp. 19–27.

10. Pete Engardio, "Companies Are Knocking Off the Knockoff Outfits," *Business Week,* September 26, 1988, pp. 86–88. For recent developments in related topics, see also Dorothy Cohen, "Trademark Strategy," *Journal of Marketing,* Vol. 50 (January 1986), pp. 61–74; James M. Maskulka and Melissa O'Neal, "Gray Market Consumers: New Channel Captains?" *AMA Educators Proceedings* (1987), pp. 1–4; Kevin F. McCrohan, James D. Smith, and James W. Harvey, "Informal Markets: An Examination of Attitudes, Expectations, and Behavior," *AMA Educators Proceedings* (1987), pp. 5–8; Larry S. Lowe and Kevin McCrohan, "Gray markets in the United States," *The Journal of Consumer Marketing,* Vol. 5 (Winter 1988), pp. 45–52; Fred W. Morgan, "Tampered Goods: Legal Developments and Marketing Guidelines," *Journal of Marketing,* Vol. 52 (April 1988), pp. 86–96; and Dale F. Duhan and Mary Jane Sheffet, "Gray Markets and the Legal Status of Parallel Importation," *Journal of Marketing,* Vol. 52 (July 1988), pp. 75–83.

11. Edwin McDowell, "Oh, For the Good Old Days of Brand X," in Roy Adler, Larry Robinson, and Jan Carlson (eds.), *Marketing and Society: Cases and Commentaries* (Englewood Cliffs, N.J.: Prentice Hall, 1981), pp. 200–204.

12. William L. Wilkie and David M. Gardner "The Role of Marketing Research in Public Policy Decision Making," *Journal of Marketing,* Vol. 38 (January 1974), pp. 38–47. For informed discussions of the past and future Federal Trade Commission, see Patrick E. Murphy and William L. Wilkie (eds.), *The FTC in the 1990's.* Notre Dame, Ind.: University of Notre Dame Press, 1990.

13. Mariann Caprino, "World of Mergers Awaits Bush's Influence," Associated Press Wire Service, November 13, 1988.

14. Margaret E. Kriz, "Leashed Watchdog," *National Journal,* October 24, 1987, pp. 2663–2665. See also Robert D. Miller and Debra Jones Ringold, "The Economic Theory of Information and Public Policy: Reregulation of the Air Transportation Market," *AMA Educators' Proceedings* (1989), pp. 293–298.

15. "FTC Member Hints of Attack on Food Ads," *Advertising Age,* November 21, 1988, p. 60.

16. Paul M. Barrett, "Attorneys General Flex Their Muscles," *The Wall Street Journal,* July 13, 1988, p. 22.

17. For an excellent source of current research on public policy matters in marketing, see the *Journal of Public Policy and Marketing,* published by the University of Michigan and edited by Patrick Murphy, University of Notre Dame. For an excellent source of invited papers by experts in consumer policy, see E. Scott Maynes et al. (eds.), *The Frontier of Research in the Consumer Interest* (Columbia, Mo.: American Council on Consumer Interests, 1988). For further discussion of these issues, see John F. Gaski and Michael J. Etzel, "The Index of Consumer Sentiment Toward Marketing," *Journal of Marketing,* Vol. 50 (July 1986), pp. 71–80, and Linda B. Samuels, Richard L. Coffinberger, and Kevin F. McCrohan, "Legislative Responses to the Plight of New Car Purchasers: A Missed Marketing Opportunity," *Journal of Public Policy & Marketing,* Vol. 5 (1986) pp. 61–71.

18. The discussion is based upon Michael B. Mazis, Richard Staelin, Howard Beales, and Steven Salop, "A Framework for Evaluating Consumer Information Regulation," *Journal of Marketing,* Vol. 44 (Winter 1981), pp. 11–21. For related discussions, see Gerhard Scherhorn, "Implications of the Theory of Consumer Behavior for Consumer Policy Research," *Advances in Consumer Research,* Vol. 7 (1980), pp. 52–55; Terence A. Shimp and Ivan L. Preston, "Deceptive and Nondeceptive Consequences of Evaluative Advertising," *Journal of Marketing,* Vol. 45, no. 1 (Winter 1981), pp. 22–32; Michael B. Mazis and Richard Staelin, "Using Information-Processing Principles in Public Policymaking," *Journal of Marketing and Public Policy,* Vol. 1, no. 1 (1982), pp. 3–14; Herbert J. Rotfeld, "The Compatibility of Advertising Regulation and the First Amendment—Another View," *Journal of Marketing and Public Policy,* Vol. 1, no. 1 (1982), pp. 139–146; Donald J. Hempel, Michael V. Laric, and Lewis R. Tucker, Jr., "Developing an Information-Based Marketing Strategy for a Consumer Protection Agency: A Case Study," *Journal of Consumer Affairs,* Vol. 16 (Winter 1982), pp. 347–361; Donald P. Robin, "The Need for a New Class of Information

to Aid Public Policy Decision-Makers," *Journal of Public Policy & Marketing,* Vol. 6 (1987), pp. 58–75; Craig A. Kelley, "Consumer Product Warranties Under the Magnuson-Moss Warranty Act: A Review of the Literature," *AMA Educators Proceedings* (1986), pp. 369–374; Joshua Lyle Wiener, "An Evaluation of the Magnuson-Moss Warranty and Federal Trade Commission Improvement Act of 1975," *Journal of Public Policy & Marketing,* Vol. 7 (1988), pp. 65–82; and Christine Moorman and Linda Price, "Consumer Policy Remedies and Consumer Segment Interactions," Working Paper, University of Pittsburgh, 1989.

This topic of information is a key issue with economists as well as marketing-oriented consumer researchers. Useful discussions from this perspective include E. Scott Maynes and Terje Assum, "Informationally Imperfect Consumer Markets: Empirical Findings and Policy Implications," *Journal of Consumer Affairs,* Vol. 16 (Summer 1982), pp. 62–87; Loren V. Geistfeld, E. Scott Maynes, and Greg Duncan, "Informational Imperfections in Local Consumer Markets: A Preliminary Analysis," *Advances in Consumer Research,* Vol. 7 (1980), pp. 180–185; Melissa S. Burnett, Raymond P. Fisk, and Roxanne Stell, "Free Ridership: Concept Development and Research Propositions," *AMA Educators Proceedings* (1987), pp. 14–19; and Wagner A. Kamakura, Brian T. Ratchford, and Jagdish Agrawal, "Measuring Market Efficiency and Welfare Loss," *Journal of Consumer Research,* Vol. 15 (December 1988), pp. 289–302.

For recent findings on energy information alternatives, see, for example, R. Bruce Hutton, Gary A. Mauser, Pierre Filiatrault, and Olli T. Ahtola, "Effects of Cost-Related Feedback on Consumer Knowledge and Consumption Behavior: A Field Experimental Approach," *Journal of Consumer Research,* Vol. 13 (December 1986), pp. 327–336; Richard J. Sexton, Nancy Brown Johnson, and Akira Konakayama, "Consumer Response to Continuous-Display Electricity-Use Monitors in a Time-of-Use Pricing Experiment," *Journal of Consumer Research,* Vol. 14 (June 1987), pp. 55–62; and Jeannet H. van Houwelingen and W. Fred van Raaij, "The Effect of Goal-Setting and Daily Electronic Feedback on In-Home Energy Use," *Journal of Consumer Research,* Vol. 15 (March 1989), pp. 98–105.

For recent discussions on deceptive advertising, see, for example, Gary T. Ford and John E. Calfee, "Recent Developments in FTC Policy on Deception," *Journal of Marketing,* Vol. 50 (July 1986), pp. 82–104; Gary J. Gaeth and Timothy B. Heath, "The Cognitive Processing of Misleading Advertising in Young and Old Adults," *Journal of Consumer Research,* Vol. 14 (June 1987), pp. 43–54; Raymond R. Burke, Wayne S. DeSarbo, Richard L. Oliver, and Thomas S. Robertson, "Deception by Implication: An Experimental Investigation," *Journal of Consumer Research,* Vol. 14 (March 1988), pp. 483–494; and Ivan L. Preston and Jef I. Richards, "The Costs of Prohibiting Deceptive Advertising: Are They as Substantial as Economic Analysis Implies?" *Advances in Consumer Research,* Vol. 16 (1989), pp. 209–214.

19. See, for example, Lee Benham and Alexandra Benham, "Regulating Through the Professions: A Perspective on Information Control," *Journal of Law and Economics,* Vol. 18 (October 1975), pp. 421–447, and Alex R. Maurizi, Ruth L. Moore, and Lawrence Shepard, "The Impact of Price Advertising: The California Eyewear Market After One Year," *Journal of Consumer Affairs,* Vol. 15 (Winter 1981), pp. 290–300. For recent findings in related topics, see Robert E. Hite and Edward Kiser, "Consumer's Attitudes Toward Lawyers with Regard to Advertising Professional Services," *Journal of the Academy of Marketing Science,* Vol. 13 (Spring 1985), pp. 321–339; Ronald B. Marks, "Consumer Response to Physicians' Advertisements," *Journal of the Academy of Marketing Science,* Vol. 12 (Summer 1984), pp. 35–52; Lyndon E. Dawson, Morris L. Mayer, and Janet E. Keith, "Resale Price Maintenance: Changing Perspectives and Future Directions," *Journal of Consumer Marketing,* Vol. 3 (Fall 1986), pp. 83–90; and Sandra E. Gleason and Ronald Stiff, "The Federal Trade Commission's Contact Lens Study: Implications for Public Policy," *Journal of Public Policy & Marketing,* Vol. 5 (1986), pp. 163–170.

20. William L. Wilkie, "Affirmative Disclosure: Perspectives on FTC Orders," *Journal of Marketing and Public Policy,* Vol. 1 (Winter 1982), pp. 95–110. For further discussions related to this area, see, for example, Charles F. Keown, "Risk Judgments and Intention Measures After Reading About Prescription Drug Side Effects in the Format of a Patient Package Insert," *Journal of Consumer Affairs,* Vol. 17 (Winter 1983), pp. 277–289; Gaurav Bhalla and John L. Lastovicka, "The Impact of Changing Cigarette Warning Message Content and Format," *Advances in Consumer Research,* Vol. 11 (1984), pp. 305–310; G. Ray Funkhouser, "An Empirical Study of Consumers' Sensitivity to the Wording of Affirmative Disclosure Messages," *Journal of Public Policy and Marketing,* Vol. 3, no. 1 (1984), pp. 26–37; James R. Bettman, John W. Payne, and Richard Staelin, "Cognitive Considerations in Designing Effective Labels for Presenting Risk Information," *Journal of Public Policy & Marketing,* Vol. 5 (1986), pp. 1–28; M. Venkatesan, Wade Lancaster, and Kenneth K. Kendall, "An Empirical Study of Alternative Formats for Nu-

tritional Information Disclosure in Advertising," in *Journal of Public Policy & Marketing*, Vol. 5 (1986), pp. 29–43; William L. Wilkie, "Affirmative Disclosure at the FTC: Strategic Dimensions," *Journal of Public Policy & Marketing*, Vol. 5 (1986), pp. 123–145; William L. Wilkie, "Affirmative Disclosure at the FTC: Communication Decisions," in *Journal of Public Policy & Marketing*, Vol. 6 (1987) pp. 33–42; Richard F. Beltramini, "Perceived Believability of Warning Label Information Presented in Cigarette Advertising," *Journal of Advertising*, Vol. 17 (November 1988), pp. 26–32; Edward T. Popper and Keith B. Murray, "Format Effects on an In-Ad Disclosure, *Advances in Consumer Research*, Vol. 16 (1989), pp. 221–230; James H. McAlexander and Debra L. Scammon, "Are Disclosures Sufficient? A Micro Analysis of Impact in Financial Services Market," *Journal of Public Policy & Marketing*, Vol. 7 (1988), p. 185–202; and Ellen R. Foxman, Darrel D. Muehling, and Patrick A. Moore, "Disclaimer Footnotes in Ads: Discrepancies Between Purpose and Performance," *Journal of Public Policy & Marketing*, Vol. 7 (1988), pp. 127–137.

21. William L. Wilkie, "Applying Attitude Research in Public Policy," in W. Wells (ed.), *Attitude Research at Bay* (Chicago: American Marketing Association, 1976). For recent analyses, see Stanley I. Ornstein and Dominique M. Hanssens, "Alcohol Control Laws and the Consumption of Distilled Spirits and Beer," *Journal of Consumer Research*, Vol. 12 (September 1985), pp. 200–213; Susan L. Holak and Srinivas K. Reddy, "Effects of a Television and Radio Advertising Ban: A Study of the Cigarette Industry," *Journal of Marketing*, Vol. 50 (October 1986), pp. 219–227; John E. Calfee, "Cigarette Advertising Regulation Today: Unintended Consequences and Missed Opportunities?" *Advances in Consumer Research*, Vol. 14 (1987), pp. 264–268; Debra Jones Ringold, "A Preliminary Investigation of the Information Content of Cigarette Advertising: A Longitudinal Analysis," *Advances in Consumer Research*, Vol. 14 (1987), pp. 269–273; Gary T. Ford and John E. Calfee, "Market Forces, Information and Reduced Flammability Cigarettes," *Advances in Consumer Research*, Vol. 14 (1987), pp. 274–278; and George P. Moschis, "Point of View: Cigarette Advertising and Young Smokers," *Journal of Advertising Research*, Vol. 29 (April–May 1989), pp. 51–60.

22. Peggy Berkowitz, "Canadian House Approves Curbs on Tobacco Ads," *The Wall Street Journal*, June 1, 1988, p. 39, and "Anti-Smoking Lobbyists, Laws Gaining Influence in Europe," Associated Press Wire Service, November 29, 1987. See also Marvin Goldberg, "The Elimination of Advertising Directed at Children in Quebec: A Quasi-Experiment," *Advances in Consumer Research*, Vol. 16 (1989), p. 790.

23. Richard Edel, "The Privacy Debate," *Advertising Age*, October 17, 1988, p. S–12.

24. This section is based upon William L. Wilkie, Dennis L. McNeill, and Michael B. Mazis, "Marketing's 'Scarlet Letter': The Theory & Practice of Corrective Advertising," *Journal of Marketing*, Vol. 48 (Spring 1984), pp. 11–31. For an excellent review see also Debra L. Scammon and Richard J. Semenik, "Corrective Advertising: Evolution of the Legal Theory and Application of the Remedy," *Journal of Advertising*, Vol. 11, no. 1 (1982), pp. 10–20. For additional findings in this most interesting area, see H. Keith Hunt, "Effects of Corrective Advertising," *Journal of Advertising Research*, October 1973, pp. 15–24; Robert F. Dyer and Philip G. Kuehl, "The Corrective Advertising Remedy of the FTC: An Experimental Evaluation," *Journal of Marketing*, Vol. 38 (January 1974), pp. 48–54; Harold H. Kassarjian, Cynthia Carlson, and Paula Rosin, "A Corrective Advertising Study," *Advances in Consumer Research*, Vol. 2 (1974), pp. 631–642; Gary M. Armstrong, Metin N. Gurol, and Frederick A. Russ, "Detecting and Correcting Deceptive Advertising," *Journal of Consumer Research*, Vol. 6 (December 1979), pp. 237–246; Neil K. Allison and Richard W. Mizerski, "The Effects of Recall on Belief Change: The Corrective Advertising Case," *Advances in Consumer Research*, Vol. 8 (1981), pp. 419–422; Tyzoon T. Tyebjee, "The Role of Publicity in FTC Corrective Advertising Remedies," *Journal of Marketing & Public Policy*, Vol. 1, no. 1 (1982), pp. 111–122; George F. Belch, Michael A. Belch, Robert B. Settle, and Lisa M. De Lucchi, "An Examination of Consumers' Perceptions of Purpose and Content of Corrective Advertising," *Advances in Consumer Research*, Vol. 9 (1982), pp. 327–332; Kenneth L. Bernhardt, Thomas C. Kinnear, Michael B. Mazis, and Bonnie B. Reece, "Impact of Publicity on Corrective Advertising Effects," *Advances in Consumer Research*, Vol. 8 (1981), pp. 414–415.; Jacob Jacoby; Margaret C. Nelson, and Wayne D. Hoyer, "Correcting Corrective Advertising," *Advances in Consumer Research*, Vol. 8 (1981), pp. 416–418; Gary M. Armstrong, Metin N. Gurol, and Frederick A. Russ, "A Longitudinal Evaluation of the Listerine Corrective Advertising Campaign," *Journal of Marketing & Public Policy*, Vol. 2, no. 1 (1983), pp. 16–28; Michael B. Mazis, Dennis L. McNeill, and Kenneth L. Bernhardt, "Day-After Recall of Listerine Corrective Commercials," *Journal of Marketing & Public Policy*, Vol. 2, no. 1 (1983), pp. 29–37; Thomas C. Kinnear, James R. Taylor, and Oded Gur-Arie, "Affirmative Disclosure: Long-Term Marketing Monitoring of Residual Effects," *Journal of Marketing & Public Policy*, Vol. 2, no. 1 (1983), pp. 38–45; and

Kenneth L. Bernhardt, Thomas C. Kinnear, and Michael B. Mazis, "A Field Study of Corrective Advertising Effectiveness," *Journal of Public Policy & Marketing,* Vol. 5 (1986), pp. 146–162.

25. "AMA Adopts New Code of Ethics," *Marketing Educator* (Fall 1987), pp. 3 ff.

Chapter 22 Organizational Buying Behavior

1. Vicky Crittendon, Carol A. Scott, and Rowland T. Moriarity, "The Role of Prior Product Experience in Organizational Buying Behavior," *Advances in Consumer Research,* Vol. 14 (1986), pp. 387–391. See also Edward Fern and James Brown, "The Industrial/Consumer Marketing Dichotomy: A Case of Insufficient Justification," *Journal of Marketing,* Vol. 48 (Spring 1984), pp. 68–77.

2. Bill Abrams, "Consumer-Product Techniques Help Loctite Sell to Industry," *The Wall Street Journal,* April 2, 1981.

3. Bill Kelley, "Business-to-Business Gets Better and Better," *Sales and Marketing Management,* April 28, 1986, p. 30.

4. Larry Riggs, "A Must for Today's Marketers," *Sales and Marketing Management,* April 22, 1985, p. 36. See also Jakki Mohr and J. Paul Peter, "Organizational Buyer-Seller Communications: A Review of Recent Literature," *AMA Educators Proceedings* (1988), pp. 84–89; Kaylene Williams and Rosann Spiro, "Communication Style in the Salesperson-Customer Dyad," *Journal of Marketing Research,* Vol. 22 (November 1985), pp. 434–442; and R. Dale Wilson, "Segmentation and Communication in the Industrial Marketplace," *Journal of Business Research,* Vol. 14 (December 1986), pp. 487–500.

5. Patrick J. Robinson, Charles Faris, and Yoram Wind, *Industrial Buying and Creative Marketing* (Boston: Allyn & Bacon, 1967). See also Daniel F. Muzyka, Vicky L. Crittenden, and William F. Crittenden, "Market Segmentation in Industrial Marketing Strategy," *AMA Educators Proceedings* (1986), pp. 315–320; and Rowland T. Moriarty and David J. Reibstein, "Benefit Segmentation in Industrial Markets," *Journal of Business Research,* Vol. 14 (December 1986), pp. 463–486.

6. Frederick E. Webster and Yoram Wind, "A General Model for Understanding Organizational Buying Behavior," *Journal of Marketing,* Vol. 36, no. 2 (1973), pp. 12–19. For recent research results, see, for example, Michele Bunn, "Structure in the Buying Center: The Case of the Adhocracy," *AMA Educators Proceedings* (1984), pp. 32–36; Michael Morris, "A Model of Coalition Formation in the Industrial Buying Center," *AMA Educators Proceedings* (1984), pp. 40–44; Paul D. Boughton, Guy R. Banville, and David R. Lambert, "Conflict in the Buying Center: A Study of Organizational Buying Behavior," *AMA Educators' Proceedings* (1986), pp. 87–92; two articles in *Advances in Consumer Research,* Vol. 14 (1987): Julia M. Bristor and Michael J. Ryan, "The Buying Center Is Dead: Long Live the Buying Center," pp. 255–258, and Michael D. Hutt and Peter H. Reingen, "Social Network Analysis: Emergent Versus Prescribed Patterns in Organizational Buying Behavior," pp. 259–263; Joseph A. Bellizzi, Robert E. Hite, and Jane C. Engele, "Role Ambiguity and Product Management: Comparisons Between Industrial and Consumer Goods Product Managers," *AMA Educators Proceedings* (1986), pp. 230; Julia M. Bristor, "Coalitions in Organizational Purchasing: An Application of Network Analysis," *Advances in Consumer Research,* Vol. 15 (1988), pp. 563–568; and Ajay Kohli, "Determinants of Influence in Organizational Buying: A Contingency Approach," *Journal of Marketing,* Vol. 53 (July 1989), pp. 50–65.

7. "The 'Short Reach' of Salespeople," *Sales and Marketing Management,* July 2, 1984, p. 24.

8. "Positioning Reigns for Consumer or Industrial Products," *Marketing News,* May 9, 1986, p. 14. See also Barbara Jackson, "Build Customer Relationships That Last," *Harvard Business Review,* 63 (November–December 1985), pp. 120–128; S. T. Parkinson, "Factors Influencing Buyer-Seller Relationships in the Market for High-Technology Products," *Journal of Business Research,* Vol. 13 (February 1985), pp. 49–60; Gary Soldow and Gloria Penn Thomas, "Relational Communication: Form Versus Content in the Sales Interaction," *Journal of Marketing,* 48 (Winter 1984), pp. 84–93; Robert E. Spekman and Wesley J. Johnston, "Relationship Management: Managing the Selling and the Buying Interface," *Journal of Business Research,* Vol. 14 (December 1986), pp. 519–532; Roger A. More, "Developer/Adopter Relationships in New Industrial Product Situations," *Journal of Business Research,* Vol. 14 (December 1986), pp. 501–518; F. Robert Dwyer, Paul Schurr, and Sejo Oh, "Developing Buyer-Seller Relationships," *Journal of Marketing,* 51 (April 1987), pp. 11–27; and Gary L. Frazier, Robert E. Spekman, and Charles R. O'Neal, "Just-in-Time Exchange Relationships in Industrial Markets," *Journal of Marketing,* Vol. 52 (October 1988), pp. 52–67.

9. Gregory Stricharchuk, "Smokestack Industries Adopt Sophisticated Sales Approach," *The Wall Street Journal,* May 12, 1984.

10. Robinson, Faris, and Wind, *Industrial Buying and Creative Marketing.*

11. For overviews of findings in this area, see, for example, K. E. Kristian Moller, "Special Section on Organizational Buying Behavior: An Introduction," *Journal of Business Research,* Vol. 13 (February 1985), pp. 1–2 (and papers following); Wesley J. Johnston and Robert E. Spekman, "Special Section on Industrial Marketing and Purchasing Strategies: Introduction," *Journal of Business Research,* Vol. 14 (December 1986), pp. 461–462 (and papers following); and Deborah Salmond, *Business Buying Behavior: A Conference Summary,* (Cambridge, Mass.: Marketing Science Institute, 1988).

    For cross-cultural comparisons, see Wesley J. Johnston, "Industrial Buying Behavior: Japan versus the U.S.," *Advances in Consumer Research,* Vol. 14 (1987), pp. 326–330; A. Coskin Samli, Dhruv Grewal, and Sanjeen Mathur, "International Industrial Buyer Behavior . . . ," *Journal of the Academy of Marketing Science,* Vol. 16 (Summer 1988), pp. 19–29; and Jerzy Dietl, "Industrial Product-Buyer Behavior in a Centrally Planned Economy," *Journal of Business Research,* Vol. 14 (August 1986), pp. 285–294.

    For recent research proposals and findings, see, for example, Erin Anderson, Wujin Chu, and Barton Weitz, "Industrial Purchasing: An Empirical Exploration of the Buyclass Framework," *Journal of Marketing* Vol. 51 (July 1987), pp. 71–86; Niran Vyas and Arch Woodside, "An Inductive Model of Industrial Buyer Choice Processes," *Journal of Marketing* Vol. 48 (Winter 1984), pp. 30–45; Dawne Martin and Kenneth A. Hunt, "Toward an Integrative Model of Organizational Buying Behavior," *AMA Educators Proceedings* (1987), pp. 290–294; David T. Wilson, "Merging Adoption Process and Organizational Buying Models," *Advances in Consumer Research,* Vol. 14 (1987), pp. 323–325; Kjell Gronhaug and Alladi Venkatesh, "A Theoretical Assessment of Needs in Organizational Buying," *AMA Educators Proceedings* (1987), p. 243; Donald Jackson, Janet Keith, and Bruce Pilling, "Examining the Relative Importance of Industrial Pricing Components Across Different Buying Situations," *AMA Educators' Proceedings* (1987), pp. 41–45; and William J. Qualls and Christopher P. Puto, "Organizational Climate and Decision Framing: An Integrated Approach to Analyzing Industrial Buying Decisions," *Journal of Marketing Research,* Vol. 26 (May 1989), pp. 179–192.

12. Thomas Bonoma, Richard Bagozzi, and Gerald Zaltman, "The Dyadic Paradigm with Specific Application Toward Industrial Marketing," in Thomas Bonoma and Gerald Zaltman (eds.), *Organizational Buying Behavior* (Chicago: American Marketing Association, 1978). For related findings, see Lowell Crow, Richard Olshavsky, and John Summers, "Industrial Buyers' Choice Strategies: A Protocol Analysis," *Journal of Marketing Research,* Vol. 17 (February 1980), pp. 34–44; and Klaus Backhaus, Margit Meyer, and Andreas Stockert, "Using Voice Analysis for Analyzing Bargaining Processes in Industrial Marketing," *Journal of Business Research,* Vol. 13 (1985), pp. 435–446;

13. This table reports partial results from the study in James R. Moore, Donald Eckrich, and Lorry T. Carlson, "A Hierarchy of Industrial Selling Competencies," *Journal of Marketing Education* (Spring 1986), pp. 79–88. For related findings, see "PA's Examine the People Who Sell to Them," *Sales and Marketing Management,* Vol. 135 (November 11, 1985), pp. 38–41; Paul A. Dion and Peter M. Banting, "The Purchasing Agent: Friend or Foe to the Salesperson?" *Journal of the Academy of Marketing Science,* Vol. 16 (Fall 1988), pp. 16–22; Thomas W. Leigh and Patrick F. McGraw, "Mapping the Procedural Knowledge of Industrial Sales Personnel: A Script-Theoretic Investigation," *Journal of Marketing,* Vol. 53 (January 1989), pp. 16–34; and Siew Meng Leong, Paul S. Busch, and Deborah Roedder John, "Knowledge Bases and Salesperson Effectiveness: A Script-Theoretic Analysis," *Journal of Marketing Research,* Vol. 26 (May 1989), pp. 164–178.

14. John Swan and Fredrick Trawick, Jr., "Building Industrial Trust in the Industrial Salesperson," in Arch Woodside (ed.), *Advances in Business Marketing* (Greenwich, Conn.: JAI Press, 1987). See also Paul H. Schurr and Julie Ozanne, "Influences on Exchange Processes: Buyers' Preconceptions of a Seller's Trustworthiness and Bargaining Toughness," *Journal of Consumer Research,* Vol. 11 (March 1985), pp. 939–953.

15. Darrel Miller, "Long-Term Trusting Relationships in Channels of Distribution: A Proposed Model," unpublished manuscript, University of Florida, Gainesville, 1988.

16. John Browning and Noel Zabriskie, "How Ethical Are Industrial Buyers?" *Industrial Marketing Management,* Vol. 12 (1983), pp. 219–224.

17. For an introduction and overview of many of the ethical issues confronted by marketing managers, see the various topic chapters in Gene R. Laczniak and Patrick E. Murphy (eds.), *Marketing Ethics: Guidelines for Managers* (Lexington, Mass.: Lexington Books, 1985). For further discussions, see Lawrence D. Chonko, James R. Lumpkin, and Marjorie J. Caballero, "Perceptions of Ethical Situations by Purchasing Managers: A Preliminary Explanation of Differences," *AMA Educators Proceedings* (1986), pp. 93–98; Joseph A. Bellizzi and Robert E. Hite, "Supervising

Unethical Salesforce Behavior," *Journal of Marketing,* Vol. 53 (April 1989), pp. 36–47; Ronald E. Michaels, William L. Cron, Alan J. Dubinsky, and Erich A. Joachimsthaler, "The Influence of Formalization on the Organizational Commitment and Work Alienation of Salespeople and Industrial Buyers," *Journal of Marketing Research,* Vol. 25 (November 1988), pp. 376–383; Shelby D. Hunt, Van R. Wood, and Lawrence B. Chonko, "Corporate Ethical Values and Organizational Commitment in Marketing," *Journal of Marketing,* Vol. 53 (July 1989), pp. 79–90; and Ismael P. Akaah and Edward A. Riordan, "Judgments of Marketing Professionals About Ethical Issues in Marketing Research: A Replication and Extension," *Journal of Marketing Research,* Vol. 26 (February 1989), pp. 112–120.

Photo Credits

CHAPTER 1 Page 10: (top left) Emilio Mercado/Jeroboam, Inc.; (top right) Ellen P. Scheffield/ Woodfin Camp & Associates; (bottom left) Mike Mazzaschi/Stock, Boston; (bottom right) Hazel Hankin.

CHAPTER 2 Page 33: Courtesy of Ford Taurus. Page 35: Courtesy of Soloflex, Inc. Page 36: Courtesy of The California Raisin Advisory Board.

CHAPTER 3 Page 62: Courtesy of the Proctor & Gamble Company. Page 65: (top) Jim Mahoney/ The Image Works; (bottom left) Baron Wolman/Woodfin Camp & Associates; (bottom right) Ulrike Welsch. Page 73: Courtesy of The Chronicle of Higher Education. Page 75: Jean-Claude Lejeune/ Stock, Boston. Page 78: Courtesy of Allied Van Line, Inc. Page 83: (top left) UPI/Bettmann Newsphotos; (top right) Hanzel Hankin; (bottom) UPI/Bettmann Newsphotos. Page 84: Judy S. Gelles/ Stock, Boston. Page 90: Courtesy of Philadelphia City Planning Commission.

CHAPTER 4 Page 106: Ray Solomon/Monkemeyer Press Photo Service. Page 109: Courtesy of John Hancock Mutual Life Insurance Co., Boston, MA and subsidiaries. Page 110: (bottom) The Seven-Up Company, 1989. The "Spot" character is a trademark identifying products of the Seven-Up Company, Dallas, Texas; (top) Courtesy of Cadbury Schweppes, Inc. Canada Dry and The Shield are registered trademarks of the Canada Dry Corporation. Page 111: Courtesy of MTV.

CHAPTER 5 Page 160: Courtesy of South of the Border, Dillon, South Carolina. Page 161: Courtesy of The Seven-Up Company, 1989.

CHAPTER 6 Page 182: Guy Gillette/Photo Researchers, Inc. Page 185: (top) Courtesy of Mexicana Airlines; (bottom) Peter Southwick/Stock, Boston. Page 187: Courtesy of DuPont Stainmaster. Page

188: Courtesy of *Advertising Age*. Page 190: Courtesy of *Cosmopolitan*. Page 198: (top) Courtesy of Arrow Shirts; (bottom) Courtesy of Arrow Shirts.

CHAPTER 7 Page 212: Cathy, Copyright 1989, Universal Press Syndicate, reprinted with permission, all rights reserved.

CHAPTER 8 Page 233: Courtesy of Penn Racket Sports and McCool & Company. Page 242: Courtesy of Fuji Photo Film U.S.A., Inc. Page 244: Courtesy Ralston Purina Company, Copyright 1987. Page 245: Ralston Purina Company, Copyright 1987. Page 249: (top left) John Lei Photography; (top right) John Lei Photography. Page 249: (bottom left) Simplicity Pattern Co., Inc.; (bottom right) Simplicity Pattern Co., Inc.

CHAPTER 9 Page 261: Photograph courtesy of Steuban Agency: Doyle Graf Mabley. Page 263: Courtesy of Pathmark Supermarkets—Supermarkets General Corp. Page 266: Courtesy of W.E. Andrews, Inc.

CHAPTER 10 Page 286: (left) Suzanne Szasz/Photo Researchers, Inc.; (right) Jenny Howard/Stock, Boston. Page 287: (left) Elizabeth Hamlin/Stock, Boston; (right) Michal Heron/Woodfin Camp & Associates. Page 294: Courtesy of the Coca Cola Company. Page 298: (top) Courtesy of McDonald's Corporation; (bottom) John Maher/Stock, Boston. Page 300: Courtesy of AT&T and N.W. Ayer, Inc. Page 301: Courtesy of Colortag, Inc.

CHAPTER 11 Page 310: Alinari/Art Resource. Page 322: Courtesy of Arm & Hammer. Page 323: Courtesy of Cosmair, Inc. Page 324: Courtesy of Volkswagon of America, Inc. and DDB Needham Worldwide, Inc.

CHAPTER 12 Page 359: The Bettmann Archive. Page 365: Courtesy of NYNEX and Lohmeyer Simpson Communications, Inc. Page 366: (left) Courtesy of Panasonic; (right) Courtesy of Panasonic.

CHAPTER 13 Page 385: Courtesy of Neilson Marketing Research and Frankenberry, Laughlin & Constable, Inc. Page 389: J-P Laffont/Sygma. Page 390: Stuart Cohen/Stock, Boston. Page 392: Courtesy Commission of European Communities. Page 396: Courtesy of California Sunsweet Growers Association. Page 399: Created by Markin/Williams Advertising, Inc.

CHAPTER 14 Page 435: George Hall/Woodfin Camp & Associates. Page 447: Tim·Bode Photography, Dallas, TX. Page 449: DDB Needham for Weight Watchers International, Inc. 1989. Page 450: Copyright Rich Pilling, *The Sporting News*.

CHAPTER 15 Page 472: Courtesy of *Seventeen* Magazine. Page 478: Joel Gordon Photography. Page 481: Fredrik D. Bodin/Stock, Boston. Page 483: David Strickler/The Image Works.

CHAPTER 16 Page 494: Andy Mercado/Jeroboam, Inc. Page 498: Michael Weisbrot & Family/Stock, Boston. Page 513: Joel Gordon Photography.

CHAPTER 17 Page 537: Courtesy of Hardee's Food Systems, Inc. and The California Raisins™ Claymation® design and creation by Applause Licensing.

CHAPTER 18 Page 571: Courtesy of Easy Spirit Shoes, U.S. Shoe Corp. Page 573: Bernard Pierre Wolff/Photo Researchers, Inc. Page 574: Courtesy of Embassy Suites, Inc. of Irving, Texas.

CHAPTER 19 Page 607: Courtesy Noxell Corp., Hunt Valley, Md. Page 608: Courtesy of Information Resources, Inc.

CHAPTER 20 Page 616: Courtesy State of Florida, Dept. of Citrus. Page 618: Maiman/Sygma.

CHAPTER 21 Page 664: Courtesy of Precision LensCrafters. Page 667: Herman LeRoy Emmet/ Photo Researchers, Inc. Page 668: (left) Elizabeth Crews/Stock, Boston; (right) Elizabeth Crews/ Stock, Boston.

CHAPTER 22 Page 682: Copyright Jeffrey Dunn Studio/The Picture Cube. Page 686: (top) Barbara Rios/Photo Researchers, Inc.; (bottom) Richard Pasley/Stock, Boston.

NAME INDEX

Numbers without prefix indicate text pages; numbers with N prefix indicate Notes pages

110

SUBJECT INDEX